ADVANCED PEDIATRIC ASSESSMENT

Ellen M. Chiocca, MSN, CPNP, APN, RNC-NIC, is a clinical assistant professor in the School of Nursing at DePaul University. She received a master of science degree in nursing and a postmaster nurse practitioner certificate from Loyola University, Chicago, and a bachelor of science degree in nursing from St. Xavier University. Prior to joining the faculty at DePaul University, she taught at Loyola University, Chicago, from 1991 to 2013. Ms. Chiocca's clinical specialty is the nursing of children. Her research focuses on how various forms of violence affect children's health. She is certified in neonatal intensive care nursing and as a pediatric nurse practitioner. In addition to teaching at DePaul, Ms. Chiocca also continues clinical practice as a pediatric nurse practitioner at a community clinic in Chicago. Ms. Chiocca has published more than 25 journal articles and book chapters, and is also a peer reviewer for the journal *Neonatal Network*. She is currently pursuing a PhD in nursing.

ADVANCED PEDIATRIC ASSESSMENT

SECOND EDITION

Ellen M. Chiocca, MSN, CPNP, APN, RNC-NIC

SPRINGER PUBLISHING COMPANY
NEW YORK

Springer Publishing Company, LLC
11 West 42nd Street
New York, NY 10036
www.springerpub.com

Acquisitions Editor: Elizabeth Nieginski
Composition: diacriTech

ISBN: 978-0-8261-6175-8
e-book ISBN: 978-0-8261-6176-5
ISBN (Study Guide): 978-0-8261-6177-2
e-book ISBN (Study Guide): 978-0-8261-6178-9
Set ISBN: 978-0-8261-2862-1
Set e-book ISBN: 978-0-8261-2868-3

15 16 17 18 / 5 4 3 2

The author and the publisher of this Work have made every effort to use sources believed to be reliable to provide information that is accurate and compatible with the standards generally accepted at the time of publication. Because medical science is continually advancing, our knowledge base continues to expand. Therefore, as new information becomes available, changes in procedures become necessary. We recommend that the reader always consult current research and specific institutional policies before performing any clinical procedure. The author and publisher shall not be liable for any special, consequential, or exemplary damages resulting, in whole or in part, from the readers' use of, or reliance on, the information contained in this book. The publisher has no responsibility for the persistence or accuracy of URLs for external or third-party Internet websites referred to in this publication and does not guarantee that any content on such websites is, or will remain, accurate or appropriate.

Library of Congress Cataloging-in-Publication Data
Chiocca, Ellen M., author.
  Advanced pediatric assessment / Ellen M. Chiocca. — Second edition.
    p.; cm.
  Includes bibliographical references and index.
  ISBN 978-0-8261-6175-8 — ISBN 978-0-8261-6176-5 (e-book)
  I. Title.
  [DNLM: 1. Child. 2. Medical History Taking—methods. 3. Physical Examination—methods. 4. Adolescent. 5. Age Factors. 6. Infant. 7. Pediatrics—methods. WS 141]
  RJ50
  618.92—dc23
                          2014035040

Special discounts on bulk quantities of our books are available to corporations, professional associations, pharmaceutical companies, health care organizations, and other qualifying groups. If you are interested in a custom book, including chapters from more than one of our titles, we can provide that service as well.

For details, please contact:
Special Sales Department, Springer Publishing Company, LLC
11 West 42nd Street, 15th Floor, New York, NY 10036-8002
Phone: 877-687-7476 or 212-431-4370; Fax: 212-941-7842
E-mail: sales@springerpub.com

Printed in the United States of America by McNaughton & Gunn.

To the two great loves of my life—

My daughter, Isabella Grace Pan Di Chiocca, for bringing me such great joy,
and for being the brilliant, beautiful, wonderful person that you are.

My husband,
Ralph Zarumba, the great love of my life,
whose intelligence, unlimited kindness, generosity,
and patience never cease to amaze me.

And to my father—
Frank Joseph Chiocca, Jr.
(1939–1987)
RIP

Contents

Preface

Pediatric health care experts agree that the health care needs of children are vastly different from those of adults. From infancy through adolescence, a child experiences many dramatic physiologic, psychosocial, developmental, and cognitive changes. Thus, it is critical for the pediatric health care provider to possess specialized knowledge and skills to accurately assess children during health and illness. Concepts related to the health assessment and physical examination of adults cannot be universally applied to the care of children; children are not simply little adults.

The goal of the second edition of *Advanced Pediatric Assessment* mirrors that of the first: to emphasize the uniqueness of children when conducting a health assessment and to show that, depending on the child's age and developmental stage, the approach to obtaining the history and physical assessment can vary dramatically. Because this book focuses only on infants, children, and adolescents, the physical, psychosocial, developmental, and cultural aspects of child assessment can be addressed in greater detail than is possible in across-the-life-span textbooks. Consequently, this book has a dual focus: to serve not only as a course textbook in advanced practice nursing programs, but also as a reference for practicing pediatric health care providers.

The second edition of *Advanced Pediatric Assessment* is divided into four units. Unit I, "The Foundations of Child Health Assessment," comprises five chapters that provide readers with the foundational approach to health assessment of the pediatric patient. Chapter 1 begins with a general overview of the anatomic and physiologic differences among infants, children, and adolescents, and continues with a brief survey of growth and development, a discussion of the communication skills required to work with children, a focus on the parent–child relationship, and general strategies for obtaining the child health history and performing the physical examination. Chapter 2 provides a detailed overview of the general principles of growth and development, including a discussion of selected developmental theorists. Both physical and psychosocial growth and development are discussed, including gross and fine motor, language, psychosocial, and cognitive development. Detailed tables list normal growth and developmental milestones from birth through adolescence, as well as developmental red flags and selected developmental screening tools. Chapters 3, 4, and 5, which are devoted to communication with children, family assessment, and cultural assessment of children and families, complete the unit.

Unit II, "The Pediatric History and Physical Examination," focuses on obtaining subjective and objective data specific to the child health examination. Chapter 6 is devoted to the pediatric health history and Chapter 7 to assessing the safety of the child's environment. Chapter 8 details the specifics of the pediatric physical examination, including assessment techniques; developmental approaches to examining infants, children, and adolescents; and sequencing of the physical examination according to age and developmental level. Chapter 9 focuses on the well-child examination and Chapter 10 on assessment of nutritional status in the pediatric patient. Chapter 11 is devoted to an in-depth discussion of assessment of the neonate.

The remaining 11 chapters in the unit focus on physical assessment by body system. Each chapter is organized as follows:

- Anatomy and Physiology
- Developmental Considerations
- Cultural, Ethnic, and Racial Considerations
- Health History
- Physical Examination
- Common Diagnostic Studies
- Documentation of Findings

It is hoped that this uniform presentation of content will help the reader to think in a systematic and organized manner.

Unit III, "Assessment of Child Mental Health and Welfare," includes two chapters focusing on psychosocial issues. Chapter 23 surveys mental disorders in children, including screening for addiction, depression, and suicidal ideation. Chapter 24 specifically addresses various types of child abuse and neglect, and peer victimization.

Unit IV, "Synthesizing the Components of the Pediatric Health Assessment," is a new addition to the second edition of *Advanced Pediatric Assessment*. Its sole chapter is devoted to integrating the knowledge gained from all previous chapters in the text, and using this knowledge in an organized manner to conduct a full, age-appropriate, head-to-toe pediatric health examination.

Other noteworthy features of the second edition include all-new illustrations and photos; summary boxes listing notable clinical findings, which conclude chapters in Units II and III; and updated clinical practice guidelines reflecting the most recent recommendations. An added feature with this edition is a separate *Study Guide to Accompany Advanced Pediatric Assessment, Second Edition: A Case Study and Critical Thinking Review,* which can be purchased separately or with this textbook as a two-book set.

Child health care is both complicated and challenging, but every child deserves the safest, most comprehensive, culturally sensitive health care possible. It is my sincere hope that *Advanced Pediatric Assessment, Second Edition,* will assist both students and practicing pediatric health care providers to achieve this goal.

Ellen M. Chiocca

Acknowledgments

It was both an honor and privilege to write the second edition of my book for Springer Publishing Company. I am especially grateful to the wonderful Elizabeth Nieginski, Executive Editor, who never ceases to amaze me with her kindness, patience, supportiveness, and diplomacy. I am especially thankful for her never-ending encouragement, and for working so hard to keep me moving across the finish line.

An enormous thanks goes to my brilliant photographer, Aris Michaels, who is endlessly calm and tolerant, kind, talented, and creative. A very special thank you is due to Christine Michaels, Paul Chiocca, Elizabeth Gariti, and Claudia Brown for their hard work and patience during the photo shoot. And a special thank you to Lucas Michaels, who was especially patient, accommodating, and such a good sport.

Thank you to Claire Sorenson for her help with Chapter 7.

I sincerely appreciate the work of my chapter contributors for the first edition, and I thank them for sharing their knowledge and expertise. Thank you Diane Boyer, Patricia Sullivan, Shirley Butler, Pat Hummel, Gloria Jacobson, Lisa Kohr, and Joanne Kouba.

Thank you so much to my intensely adored, beloved, and precious daughter Isabella, whom I love more each day. Thank you, Bella, for being so understanding, yet again, while I worked on this project.

And last, but not least, I want to thank my wonderful husband Ralph Zarumba, whom I love so dearly, resolutely, and infinitely. Thank you from the bottom of my heart for providing me with continuous encouragement, support, and love throughout this process, as well as doing far beyond your fair share around the house while I wrote into the wee hours. I am eternally grateful to you not just for this, but for all that you are.

THE FOUNDATIONS OF CHILD HEALTH ASSESSMENT

CHAPTER

Child Health Assessment: An Overview

Children experience dramatic changes in their bodies and minds, beginning at birth and continuing through adolescence. Because of these anatomic, physiologic, and developmental changes, it is crucial for the pediatric health care provider to possess specialized knowledge and skills to accurately assess infants, children, and adolescents during health and illness. Concepts related to health assessment and physical examination of the adult patient cannot be applied to children; they are *not* simply little adults. In order for the health care of children to be safe, thorough, and developmentally appropriate, the pediatric health care provider must ensure that child health assessment is based on a thorough knowledge of pediatric anatomy and physiology, pathophysiology, pharmacology, and child development. The child's social situation, the community in which he or she lives, and the family's culture are other important components that should be included. In addition, when working with children of different ages and developmental levels, effective, developmentally appropriate communication skills are essential. These skills are used to build rapport with children, their families, or caregivers, as well as to provide clear and objective documentation of assessment findings.

ANATOMIC AND PHYSIOLOGIC DIFFERENCES IN INFANTS AND CHILDREN

In order to recognize abnormalities found during the physical examination, the pediatric health care provider must have strong knowledge of the anatomic and physiologic differences between infants, children, and adults. Because each body system is immature until at least age 2 years, the provider must adjust his or her expectations for physical findings according to the child's age. In addition, an infant or young child's physical condition can go from stable to life-threatening very quickly because of immature body systems that lack fully developed feedback

mechanisms. This helps to explain both the varied physiologic responses seen in infants and children, and why infants and young children absorb, distribute, metabolize, and excrete drugs very differently than adults. These factors affect the frequency, timing, and length of pediatric health care visits. Table 1.1 presents an overview of the major anatomic, physiologic, metabolic, and immunologic differences among infants, children, and adults, and the corresponding clinical implications of these differences.

GROWTH AND DEVELOPMENT

The physical, psychosocial, and cognitive aspects of child development are interrelated key indicators of the child's overall health and must be assessed at every health care visit. The assessment of a child's growth and development helps to evaluate the child's physical growth and progress toward maturity, can provide clues to health conditions that impeded physical growth, shows cognitive delays, and may point to abuse or neglect. Normal growth and development occurs in a *predictable* sequence but at a *variable* rate and pace. Deviations from this pattern may signify an abnormality, making it essential for the provider to be familiar with normal developmental milestones and children's growth patterns, and to monitor these trends over time.

In this text, infants, children, and adolescents are arranged into six age groups: neonates, infants, toddlers, preschoolers, school-aged children, and adolescents. The corresponding ages are:

- Neonates: birth to 28 days
- Infants: 1 month to 1 year
- Toddlers: 1 to 3 years
- Preschoolers: 3 to 6 years
- School-aged children: 6 to 12 years
- Adolescents: 12 to 21 years

TABLE 1.1	Anatomic and Physiologic Differences in Infants, Children, and Adolescents		
BODY STRUCTURE/ FUNCTION	**ANATOMIC/PHYSIOLOGIC DIFFERENCES**	**AGE GROUP AFFECTED**	**CLINICAL IMPLICATIONS**
Skin	Thin stratum corneum	Infants; toddlers until approximately age 2–3 years, when skin becomes thicker because of daily friction and pressure	Blood vessels are visible through newborn's skin, causing ruddy appearance; increased absorption of topical drugs; skin burns easily; prone to hypothermia and dehydration
	Thin layer of subcutaneous fat	Neonates	Affects temperature control
	Epidermis is more loosely bound to dermis (Ball, Bindler, & Cowen, 2012)	Infants; children through early school age	Skin layers separate readily, causing easy blistering (e.g., adhesive tape removal); susceptible to superficial bacterial skin infections and more likely to have associated systemic symptoms with some skin infections; skin is a poor barrier, contributing to fluid loss
	Sebaceous glands are active in neonate because of maternal androgen levels (Hockenberry & Wilson, 2011) and again at puberty because of hormonal changes (Ball et al., 2012)	Neonates; adolescents	Milia develop in neonates; acne develops in adolescents
	Eccrine glands are functional at birth; full function does not occur until age 2–3 years (Vernon, Brady, Barber Starr, & Petersen-Smith, 2013)	Infants; toddlers until preschool age	Palmar sweating occurs; helps to assess pain in neonate
	Apocrine glands are nonfunctional until puberty (Vernon et al., 2013)	Adolescents	Function of apocrine glands at puberty causes body odor
	Production of melanin reaches adult levels by adolescence (Ball et al., 2012)	Infants; children until adolescence	Affects assessment of skin color as child ages
	Greater body surface area	Infants; toddlers until age 2 years	Increases exposure to topically applied drugs; may result in toxicity in some instances
Head and neck	Head is proportionately larger than other body structures because of cephalocaudal development. Head circumference exceeds chest circumference from birth to age 2 years	Infants; toddlers until age 2 years	Larger, heavier head increases potential for injury during falls or collisions when body is thrown forward, resulting in a high incidence of head trauma in this age group
	Cranial sutures are not fully fused at birth to accommodate brain growth	Infants: Posterior fontanelle should be closed by 2 months; anterior fontanelle should be closed by 12–18 months	Full anterior fontanelle can indicate increased intracranial pressure; sunken anterior fontanelle can indicate dehydration

TABLE 1.1   Anatomic and Physiologic Differences in Infants, Children, and Adolescents (continued)

BODY STRUCTURE/ FUNCTION	ANATOMIC/PHYSIOLOGIC DIFFERENCES	AGE GROUP AFFECTED	CLINICAL IMPLICATIONS
	Short neck and prominent occiput (Bissonnette et al., 2011). Neck lengthens at age 3–4 years (Hockenberry & Wilson, 2011)	Infants; children until age 3–4 years	Increased potential for injury in infants and toddlers; airway structures are closer together; affects intubation technique in children younger than preschool age
Eyes	Eye structure and function are immature at birth; pupils are small with poor reflexes until about 5 months of age; transient nystagmus and esotropia are common in neonates younger than 6 months of age (Ball et al., 2012); irises have little pigment until 6–12 months of age (Hockenberry & Wilson, 2011)	Neonates; infants	Affects expected findings in physical examination
	Vision is undeveloped at birth; by age 4 months, infants can fixate on an image with both eyes simultaneously; ability to distinguish color begins by age 8 months; children are farsighted until about age 6–7 years (Ball et al., 2012)	Infants; children until school age	Affects expected findings in and approach to physical examination and vision screening
Ears	Newborns can hear loud sounds at 90 decibels (Hockenberry & Wilson, 2011)	Neonates	Newborns react to loud sounds with startle reflex; they react to low-frequency sounds by quieting; differences affect techniques for hearing assessment
	Short, wide eustachian tube, lying in horizontal plane	Infants; toddlers until approximately age 2 years	Fluid in middle ear cannot easily drain into pharynx; prone to middle ear infections and effusions
	External auditory canal is short and straight with upward curve	Infants; toddlers until age 3 years	Pinna should be pulled down and back to perform otoscopic examination
	External auditory canal shortens and straightens as child grows	Preschoolers aged 3 years and older	Pinna should be pulled up and back to perform otoscopic examination
Mouth, nose, throat, and sinuses	Saliva is minimal at birth; increases by age 3 months; salivary secretions increase after age 3 months (Hockenberry & Wilson, 2011)	Infants	Increased aspiration risk; presence of drooling does not signify teething
	Deciduous teeth should erupt between ages 6 and 24 months	Infants; toddlers	Delay may signify hypothyroidism or poor nutrition
	Obligate nose breathers	Neonates; infants until age 4–5 months	Nasal passages are easily obstructed by secretions; affects airway patency and ability to feed

(continued)

TABLE 1.1	Anatomic and Physiologic Differences in Infants, Children, and Adolescents (*continued*)		
BODY STRUCTURE/ FUNCTION	**ANATOMIC/PHYSIOLOGIC DIFFERENCES**	**AGE GROUP AFFECTED**	**CLINICAL IMPLICATIONS**
	Airway and nasal passages are small and narrow; larynx is narrowest at level of cricoid cartilage (subglottis) (Bissonnette et al., 2011); 1 mm of edema can narrow an infant's airway by 60% (Bissonnette et al., 2011)	Infants; children through age 5 years (Bissonnette et al., 2011)	Increased potential for airway obstruction and infection; endotracheal intubation difficult, and accidental extubation more likely with movement (Bissonnette et al., 2011)
	Large tongue in proportion to mouth size (Bissonnette et al., 2011)	Infants; children until age 8–12 years when mandible has a growth peak	Potential for airway obstruction is greater
	Proportionately large soft palate and large amount of soft tissue in the airway	Infants; children until approximately age 11–12 years (Bissonnette et al., 2011)	Any soft tissue swelling increases the risk for airway obstruction
	Ability to coordinate swallowing and breathing is immature (Bissonnette et al., 2011)	Neonates; infants until age 4–5 months	Increased risk of aspiration and gastroesophageal reflux (GER) (Bissonnette et al., 2011)
	Proportionately large, floppy, and long epiglottis (Bissonnette et al., 2011)	Infants; children through school age	Increased potential for airway obstruction with swelling; endotracheal intubation difficult
	Maxillary and ethmoid sinuses are small and undeveloped (Hockenberry & Wilson, 2011)	Infants; toddlers until age 3 years	Often early sites of infection; can be visualized on radiograph by age 1–2 years (John & Brady, 2013)
	Sphenoid and frontal sinuses become visible on radiograph at 5–6 years of age (John & Brady, 2013)	School-aged children; adolescents	Sphenoid sinuses become sites of infection by age 3–4 years; frontal sinuses by age 6–10 years (John & Brady, 2013)
Thorax and lungs	Hypoxic and hypercapnic drives are not fully developed (Bissonnette et al., 2011)	Neonates; infants until age 3 months	Periodic breathing (i.e., apnea ≤ 10 seconds) without cyanosis or bradycardia is within normal limits because of neurologic immaturity of respiratory drive. Central apnea lasts longer than 20 seconds and is outside normal limits
	Chest circumference should closely match head circumference from age 6 months to 2 years; chest circumference should exceed head circumference at age 2 years (Hockenberry & Wilson, 2011)	Infants; toddlers	Assists provider in assessing normal growth
	Easily compressible cartilage of chest wall (Bissonnette et al., 2011) with very little musculature	Infants; toddlers until age 2 years	Limits tidal volume; lowers functional residual capacity; rib cage is flexible and provides little support for lungs; negative intrathoracic pressure is poorly maintained, causing increased work of breathing (Bissonnette et al., 2011); soft thoracic cage collapses more easily during labored breathing

TABLE 1.1	Anatomic and Physiologic Differences in Infants, Children, and Adolescents (*continued*)		
BODY STRUCTURE/ FUNCTION	**ANATOMIC/PHYSIOLOGIC DIFFERENCES**	**AGE GROUP AFFECTED**	**CLINICAL IMPLICATIONS**
	Rounded thorax in infancy; ribs lie in horizontal plane; xiphoid process is moveable (Bissonnette et al., 2011)	Infants; toddlers until age 3 years	Limits tidal volume (Bissonnette et al., 2011); ribs are flexible and provide very little support for lungs; negative intrathoracic pressure is poorly maintained, causing increased work of breathing
	Alveoli are thick walled at birth; infants have only 10% of the total number of alveoli found in the adult lung; over the child's first 8 years of life, alveoli increase in number and size (Bissonnette et al., 2011)	Infants; children through age 8 years	Affects gas exchange; oxygen consumption in neonates is almost twice that in adults (Bissonnette et al., 2011); accounts for increased respiratory rate; children with pulmonary damage or disease at birth can regenerate new pulmonary tissue and may have normal pulmonary function; contributes to high number of respiratory diagnoses when infant or child is acutely ill; respiratory failure is common in premature infants because of surfactant deficiency, causing alveolar collapse (Bissonnette et al., 2011)
	Smaller lung volume; tidal volume is proportional to child's weight (7–10 mL/kg) (Ball et al., 2012)	Infants; children until age 10 years	High respiratory rate, which decreases to adult value by adolescence
	Newborns produce little respiratory mucus (Bissonnette et al., 2011)	Neonates	Increased susceptibility to respiratory infections
	Mucous membranes lining the respiratory tract are loosely attached and very vascular	Infants; toddlers	Potential for airway edema is greater, causing potential airway obstruction; more respiratory secretions are produced, increasing the potential for obstruction or aspiration
	Larynx is located 2–3 cervical vertebrae higher than in adults at level of C3–C4 (Bissonnette et al., 2011)	Infants; children until approximately age 8–10 years	Child is vulnerable to aspiration
	Proportionately small and narrow oropharynx; trachea is proportionately shorter and has a small diameter (Ball et al., 2012); tracheal cartilage is elastic and collapses easily; the trachea continues to grow in diameter until age 5 years (Ball et al., 2012) and triples in size between birth and puberty	Infants; children until adolescence	Great potential for airway obstruction, mucus, and foreign body; resistance to airflow; air is warmed and humidified much less effectively
	Right bronchus is significantly shorter, wider, and more vertical than left (John & Brady, 2013); child's trachea bifurcates at higher level than adult's (Ball et al., 2012)	Children beginning at age 2 years	Breath sounds are loud and high in pitch; easily heard through thin chest wall; inhaled foreign bodies are easily aspirated into right bronchus

(continued)

TABLE 1.1	Anatomic and Physiologic Differences in Infants, Children, and Adolescents (*continued*)		
BODY STRUCTURE/ FUNCTION	**ANATOMIC/PHYSIOLOGIC DIFFERENCES**	**AGE GROUP AFFECTED**	**CLINICAL IMPLICATIONS**
	Tracheobronchial tree has large amount of anatomic dead space where gas exchange does not take place (Bissonnette et al., 2011)	Infants; children through school age	Fast respiratory rate is needed to meet oxygen requirements; child is at risk for respiratory acidosis if lungs cannot remove carbon dioxide (CO_2) quickly enough
	Infants and children breathe using diaphragm and abdominal muscles	Infants; children until age 6 years (Ball et al., 2012)	Respirations may be inefficient when crying or with anything that restricts breathing, such as abdominal distention; child may retain CO_2 as a result, causing acidosis
	Breathing becomes thoracic as in the adult	Children aged 8–10 years	Respiratory rate decreases to near adult levels
	Intercostal, scalene, sternocleidomastoid, and diaphragmatic muscles have few type I muscle fibers, which are used in sustained respiratory activity (Bissonnette et al., 2011)	Infants; toddlers until approximately age 2 years (Bissonnette et al., 2011)	Immature respiratory muscles must work hard to assist in respiratory effort; nasal flaring may occur; poorly developed respiratory muscles hinder expulsion of thick respiratory secretions; muscles are easily fatigued, which can lead to CO_2 retention, apnea, and respiratory failure
Heart and vasculature	With first breath at birth, pulmonary vascular resistance falls	Neonates	Increased pulmonary blood flow; low systemic blood pressure (BP)
	Left atrial pressure is greater than right atrial pressure	Neonates	Foramen ovale closes within first hour of life
	Increased arterial oxygen tension	Neonates	Ductus arteriosus closes about 10–15 hours after birth; fibroses develop within 2–4 weeks of age; systolic murmurs may be audible in the first 24–48 hours of life because of transition from fetal circulation
	Relatively horizontal position of heart at birth becomes more vertical as child grows	Infants; children until age 7 years	Heart sounds are easily audible because of thin chest wall; apical pulse is heard at fourth intercostal space to left of the midclavicular line; apex reaches fifth intercostal space at the midclavicular line by age 7 years; heart may seem enlarged when percussed; displacement of the apical pulse may indicate pneumothorax, dextrocardia, or diaphragmatic hernia
	Stroke volume is somewhat fixed because of less muscular and poorly developed left ventricle (Bissonnette et al., 2011)	Neonates; infants	Poor compliance and reduced contractility (Bissonnette et al., 2011)
	Resting cardiac output is high: 300–400 mL/kg/min at birth and 200 mL/kg/min within a few months (Bissonnette et al., 2011), decreasing to 100 mL/kg/min by adolescence (Bissonnette et al., 2011)	Neonates; infants through adolescents	Cardiac output must be high in neonate and infant to meet tissue oxygen demands; this is attained by increasing heart rate

TABLE 1.1	Anatomic and Physiologic Differences in Infants, Children, and Adolescents (*continued*)		
BODY STRUCTURE/ FUNCTION	**ANATOMIC/PHYSIOLOGIC DIFFERENCES**	**AGE GROUP AFFECTED**	**CLINICAL IMPLICATIONS**
	Cardiac output is heart-rate dependent, not stroke-volume dependent (Bissonnette et al., 2011)	Neonates; children until late school age; adolescents (Ball et al., 2012)	Heart rate is rapid in children; the younger the child, the more rapid the heart rate because of increased oxygen and energy needs for growth and higher metabolism. The provider should be familiar with age-specific norms for heart rate; the pulse rises with fever and hypoxia; tachycardia during sleep is abnormal
	Vagal parasympathetic tone dominant (Bissonnette et al., 2011)	Neonates; young infants	Prone to episodes of bradycardia
	EKG readings differ from adult's; heart rhythm varies more in children than adults (Bissonnette et al., 2011)	Infants; young children	EKG changes reflect ongoing development of myocardium (Bissonnette et al., 2011); sinus arrhythmia is within normal limits in children and common in adolescence
	Left ventricular muscle is undeveloped until age 6 years	Infants; children until school age	Radial pulse may not be palpable until age 6 years; apical pulse should be taken until then; the younger the child, the lower the BP; BP rises as child matures in correlation with increased blood volume and body weight, reaching adult levels by adolescence
	Reduced catecholamine stores; poor response to exogenously administered catecholamine (Bissonnette et al., 2011); baroreceptor reflexes are immature	Neonates; infants	Poor response to hypotension via vasoconstriction; hypotension without tachycardia is seen with hypovolemia in neonates and infants (Bissonnette et al., 2011)
	Innocent murmurs are common in children; may be present in up to 80% of children (Bissonnette et al., 2011)	Infants; preschool-aged children through adolescents	Innocent murmurs are heard during systole; they do not cause cyanosis, fatigue, shortness of breath, or failure to thrive
Abdomen	Weak abdominal musculature; abdomen is protuberant in neonates and is prominent in toddlers while standing but flat when supine	Infants; toddlers	Liver and spleen are not well protected; contributes to "pot-bellied" appearance in infants and toddlers
	Abdomen is larger than chest in young children	Infants; children until age 4 years	Distended or scaphoid abdomen is indicative a pathologic finding
	Abdomen is cylindrical in shape	Infants	Peristalsis may be visible and may indicate a pathologic finding such as pyloric stenosis
	Abdominal contour changes to adult shape by adolescence	Preschool-aged children to adolescents	Affects provider expectations during physical examination
	Stomach lies in a transverse plane	Infants; toddlers until age 2 years	Affects normal area for auscultation and palpation during physical examination
	Gastric pH is alkalotic at birth; gastric acid production slowly increases to adult levels by age 2 years (Bissonnette et al., 2011)	Infants; toddlers until age 2 years	Affects oral medication absorption; increases incidence of GER

(continued)

TABLE 1.1   Anatomic and Physiologic Differences in Infants, Children, and Adolescents (*continued*)

BODY STRUCTURE/ FUNCTION	ANATOMIC/PHYSIOLOGIC DIFFERENCES	AGE GROUP AFFECTED	CLINICAL IMPLICATIONS
	Neonate has small stomach capacity (approximately 60 mL); stomach capacity reaches approximately 500 mL by toddler age (Ball et al., 2012)	Neonates; infants; toddlers	Need for small feeding amounts at birth; increases incidence of GER
	Stomach capacity reaches 1,000–1,500 mL by adolescence	Adolescents	Correlates with increased appetite
	Lower esophageal sphincter tone (Ball et al., 2012)	Neonates	Increases incidence of GER
	Prolonged gastric emptying time (6–8 hours) and transit time through the small intestine (Guthrie, 2005)	Neonates; infant: reaches adult levels by approximately age 6–8 months (Guthrie, 2005)	Affects absorption of nutrients and medications, increasing the chance of adverse side effects and toxicities
	Length of small intestine is proportionately greater, with greater surface area for absorption relative to body size (Hockenberry & Wilson, 2011)	Infants; toddlers	Child loses proportionately more water and electrolytes in stool with diarrhea
	Large intestine proportionately shorter with less epithelial lining (Ma & Dowell, 2012)	Infants	Less water absorbed, explaining soft stools of infancy
	Pancreatic enzyme (e.g., amylase, lipase, trypsin) activity decreased at birth (Ball et al., 2012)	Neonates; infants until age 4–6 months (Ball et al., 2012)	Varied bioavailability of drugs that may depend on specific enzymes to aid in drug absorption; enzymes not present in sufficient quantities to digest food fully
Liver and biliary glands	Liver functionally immature at birth (Bissonnette et al., 2011)	Neonates; infants (Ball et al., 2012)	Bilirubin is excreted in low concentrations in newborns; prothrombin levels in neonate are only 20%–40% of adult levels, which affects clotting; vitamin storage is inadequate, which contributes to young children's frequent infectious illnesses; process of gluconeogenesis is immature
	Liver occupies more of abdominal cavity than in adults; palpable at 0.5–2.5 cm below the right costal margin in infants, 1–2 cm below the right costal margin in toddlers (Hockenberry & Wilson, 2011). Liver reaches adult size and function by adolescence	Infants; children until adolescence	Affects normal area for palpation and percussion; organs are typically nonpalpable by school age; enlarged liver can indicate right-sided heart failure
	Decreased hepatic enzyme function in young children (Bissonnette et al., 2011); drug enzyme systems mature at different rates	Infants; children until age 3–4 years	Enzyme systems for biotransformation of drugs are not fully developed, which affects drug dosing; infants and children metabolize drugs more slowly than adults; can easily build up toxic levels of drugs
	Liver conjugation reactions are impaired (Bissonnette et al., 2011)	Neonates	Jaundice; long drug half-lives (infants and children have short drug half-life) (Bissonnette et al., 2011)

TABLE 1.1	Anatomic and Physiologic Differences in Infants, Children, and Adolescents (*continued*)		
BODY STRUCTURE/ FUNCTION	**ANATOMIC/PHYSIOLOGIC DIFFERENCES**	**AGE GROUP AFFECTED**	**CLINICAL IMPLICATIONS**
	Liver synthesizes and stores glycogen less effectively (Bissonnette et al., 2011)	Neonates; infants until 1 year	May become hypoglycemic easily; hypoglycemia in neonate can cause permanent neurologic damage; young children need to eat more frequently during childhood (e.g., a.m. and p.m. snacks)
	Maternal iron stores in liver are depleted by age 6 months	Neonates; infants until age 6 months	Infant requires outside source of iron (e.g., iron drops, fortified cereal) beginning at age 6 months
	Lower level of plasma albumin and globulin (Bissonnette et al., 2011); endogenous compounds such as bilirubin and free fatty acids are already bound to albumin	Neonates; infants until age 1 year	Protein binding of drugs is decreased in newborns; high levels of free drug remain in bloodstream, which can lead to toxic level of drug or neonatal coagulopathy; endogenous compounds (e.g., bilirubin) can also displace a weakly bound drug; high loading doses of protein-bound drugs may be needed in neonate. Certain drugs (e.g., sulfonamides) can displace bilirubin from albumin-binding sites, causing kernicterus in the neonate
Lymphatics	Lymph tissue is well-developed at birth and reaches adult size by age 6 years; it continues to grow until age 10–12 years, when a maximum size of approximately twice the normal adult size is reached; lymph tissue then rapidly declines to normal adult size by end of adolescence (Ball et al., 2012)	Infants; children through adolescence	Potential for airway obstruction with upper respiratory infections, chronic tonsillar or adenoidal swelling, or both; large tonsils and adenoids can make intubation difficult
	Spleen may be palpable 1–2 cm below the left costal margin (Hockenberry & Wilson, 2011)	Infants; toddlers	Affects approach to physical examination; spleen should be nonpalpable by preschool age
Blood	Vitamin K–dependent clotting factors and platelet function are inefficient	Neonates through early infancy	Vitamin K is administered at birth to prevent bleeding disorders in newborns
	Blood volume is weight dependent. Total circulating blood volume (mL of blood per kg of body weight) is greater than adult by 25%. Blood volume is highest in neonate (80–90 mL/kg); in premature infants approximately 105 mL/kg; normal adult values are 70–80 mL/kg (Bissonnette et al., 2011)	Neonates	Overhydration and dehydration occur more quickly than in an adult; blood loss can cause hypovolemic shock and anemia in infant or young child more quickly than in an adult
	At birth, 70%–90% of hemoglobin is fetal hemoglobin (HbF) (Bissonnette et al., 2011, 2005)	Neonates; infants until age 4 months	HbF has higher affinity for oxygen than adult hemoglobin (HbA); protects red blood cells from sickling in those with sickle cell disease; oxygen saturation curve is left-shifted for HbF; oxygen is not delivered as readily to tissues; HbF is replaced by HbA by age 4 months

(*continued*)

TABLE 1.1	Anatomic and Physiologic Differences in Infants, Children, and Adolescents (*continued*)		
BODY STRUCTURE/ FUNCTION	**ANATOMIC/PHYSIOLOGIC DIFFERENCES**	**AGE GROUP AFFECTED**	**CLINICAL IMPLICATIONS**
Immunity	Infants fight infection primarily by passive immunity acquired transplacentally (Ball et al., 2012) and by breastfeeding (Hockenberry & Wilson, 2011)	Neonates; infants until age 6–8 months (Ball et al., 2012) or until breastfeeding is discontinued	After age 6 months, infants are prone to infection and build immunity to common illnesses as they are exposed to them
	Humoral and cell-mediated immunity is not fully developed	Neonates; children until age 6 years (Ball et al., 2012)	Frequent infectious illnesses occur in children younger than approximately 6 years
	Reticuloendothelial system is active in childhood	Infants; children until approximately age 10 years	Lymphatic tissue, tonsils, and adenoids swell rapidly in response to mild infections; swollen tissues can cause airway obstruction
Kidneys and urinary tract	Kidneys are proportionately larger than in adults, and are surrounded by less fat (Ball et al., 2012)	Infants; toddlers; preschoolers	Tip of right kidney may be palpated because of thin abdominal wall, especially during inspiration; child's kidneys are susceptible to trauma
	Ureters are relatively short; urinary bladder lies between symphysis and umbilicus (Hockenberry & Wilson, 2011)	Infants; toddlers	Bladder descends into pelvis by age 3 years; until then location affects provider's approach to physical examination
	Kidneys are immature at birth; increased renal vascular resistance; incomplete glomerular and tubular development causes decreased renal blood flow, glomerular filtration rate, and tubular function (Bissonnette et al., 2011)	Neonates; toddlers until age 2 years (Bissonnette et al., 2011)	Kidneys cannot concentrate and dilute urine effectively (most pronounced in first year of life); young infants cannot handle large amounts of solute-free water or concentrated infant formulas; prone to dehydration with fluid losses (e.g., diarrhea, vomiting) or decreased oral intake; prone to fluid overload; electrolyte secretion and absorption are suboptimal: infants' kidneys cannot conserve or excrete sodium; kidneys play a role in excreting metabolized drugs, determining half-life of drugs excreted through glomerular filtration; prolonged dosage adjustments may be needed; minimum urine output is 1–2 mL/kg/hr
	Renal system is not mature at birth	Premature neonates	Decreased creatinine clearance; poor sodium retention, glucose excretion, and bicarbonate reabsorption; ineffective ability to concentrate and dilute urine; great potential for fluid overload, insensible losses, and dehydration; consequent potential cardiac complications, and electrolyte imbalances
	Testicles enlarge between 9.5 and 13.5 years	School-aged children; adolescents	Early puberty is present if testicles enlarge before 9.5 years

TABLE 1.1	Anatomic and Physiologic Differences in Infants, Children, and Adolescents (*continued*)		
BODY STRUCTURE/ FUNCTION	**ANATOMIC/PHYSIOLOGIC DIFFERENCES**	**AGE GROUP AFFECTED**	**CLINICAL IMPLICATIONS**
Fluid balance	Proportion of fluid to body weight is larger than in adults; total body water is 80%–85% of body weight in infants (90% in premature infants); total body water reaches adult values (65%) by approximately age 3 years (Bissonnette et al., 2011); this change is caused by decrease in extracellular fluid, which is approximately 45% in a term infant and reaches adult levels (25%) by age 3 years (Bissonnette et al., 2011)	Infants; toddlers until age 2 years	Poor adjustment to fluid deficit or overload; increased potential for dehydration or hypovolemia in children younger than 2 years; response to fluid loss is tachycardia and vasoconstriction, causing increased capillary refill time and mottling; greater fluid volume for distribution or dilution of a drug in young children may require dose adjustment
	Large body surface area	Infants; toddlers until age 2 years	Increased potential for insensible water loss (e.g., perspiration, tachypnea, fever); increased risk for dehydration; metabolism and heat production influence fluid loss; allows large amounts of fluid to be lost via insensible water loss through perspiration
Bones and muscles	Spine is C-shaped at birth (Hockenberry & Wilson, 2011)	Infants until age 3–4 months	Affects infant's head control
	Bones are not fully ossified until adulthood; bones are soft and easily bent (Ball et al., 2012)	Infants; children through adolescence	Types and locations of fractures in very young children must be fully evaluated to distinguish between intentional and unintentional injuries
	Percentage of cartilage in ribs is high; ribs are flexible and compliant (Ball et al., 2012)	Infants; children through adolescence	Rib fractures are uncommon in young children; ribs provide minimal protection to underlying organs and blood vessels
	Lordosis is a normal variation in infants and toddlers (Hockenberry & Wilson, 2011)	Infants; toddlers	Causes appearance of abdominal distention in this age group
	Skeleton grows continuously (at varying rate and pace among children) over a period of 19–20 years (Ball et al., 2012)	Infants; children through adolescence	Normal growth pattern
	Skeleton grows faster than muscles	Adolescents	Hands and feet grow faster than body
	Body growth spurts occur during puberty	Adolescents: peaks at age 12 years for females and 14 years for males	Provider should expect considerable growth during this time
	Bow-leggedness because of leg muscles bearing weight of relatively large trunk	Infants; toddlers	Normal growth pattern

(continued)

TABLE 1.1	Anatomic and Physiologic Differences in Infants, Children, and Adolescents (*continued*)		
BODY STRUCTURE/ FUNCTION	**ANATOMIC/PHYSIOLOGIC DIFFERENCES**	**AGE GROUP AFFECTED**	**CLINICAL IMPLICATIONS**
	Lower muscle mass (Bissonnette et al., 2011)	Neonates	Use of intramuscular route for medication administration limited
	Muscles have less tone and coordination during infancy; muscles comprise 25% of weight in infants compared with 40% in adults (Ball et al., 2012)	Neonates; infants	Increased risk for injury; muscle growth contributes greatly to weight gain during childhood; walking and weight bearing stimulate growth of bone and muscle
Brain and nerves	The neurologic system is anatomically complete at birth; however, since it is not fully myelinated, it is functionally immature; myelination is rapid in the first 2 years of life and is completed by approximately age 7 years (Bissonnette et al., 2011)	Infants; children through school age	Nerve impulses do not travel as quickly down unmyelinated nerves; these impulses are slower and less predictable. Myelination occurs cephalocaudally and proximodistally and corresponding advances in gross and fine motor function are seen, as evidenced by more localized stimulus response, increasing sphincter control, and better balance, memory, and comprehension; most actions in newborns are primitive reflexes
	Blood–brain barrier (BBB) underdeveloped at birth but develops quickly postnatally (Bissonnette et al., 2011)	Neonates	More permeable BBB allows passage of large, lipid-soluble molecules (e.g., bilirubin) and some drugs (e.g., some antibiotics, barbiturates, opioids) (Bissonnette et al., 2011), causing some drugs to have an increased and variable central nervous system effect or unpredictable duration of action
	Brain growth is very rapid; half of postnatal brain growth is completed by age 1 year; brain reaches 75% of adult size by age 3 years (Hockenberry & Wilson, 2011)	Infants; toddlers until age 2 years	Head circumference should increase as a reflection of brain growth
	Brain reaches 90% of adult size by age 6 years (Hockenberry & Wilson, 2011); brain reaches adult size by age 12 years	School-aged children; adolescents	Reflection of brain growth
	Spinal cord ends at intervertebral level L3, reaching adult level of L1–L2 by age 8 years (Bissonnette et al., 2011)	Infants; children until age 8 years	Necessitates altered approach for lumbar puncture and epidural anesthesia in children younger than 8 years
	Cerebral vessels are thin-walled and fragile (Bissonnette et al., 2011)	Premature infants	Increased risk for intraventricular hemorrhage
	Immature parasympathetic and sympathetic function (Bissonnette et al., 2011)	Neonates; infants	Neonates have less ability to control BP; they may respond to pain with tachycardia, increased BP

TABLE 1.1	Anatomic and Physiologic Differences in Infants, Children, and Adolescents (*continued*)		
BODY STRUCTURE/ FUNCTION	**ANATOMIC/PHYSIOLOGIC DIFFERENCES**	**AGE GROUP AFFECTED**	**CLINICAL IMPLICATIONS**
Thermoregulation	Body surface area is three times that of an adult; head is proportionately larger until age 2 years, creating a greater surface area for heat loss in infants, especially when the head is exposed	Neonates; infants	Heat loss is greater in children than in adults; susceptible to hypothermia and hyperthermia; thermoregulation is difficult because of thin epidermis, little subcutaneous fat, and poorly developed sweating and vasoconstriction mechanisms (Bissonnette et al., 2011); the premature infant is even more prone to hypothermia because of thin skin and minimal fat stores; low body temperature can cause respiratory depression, acidosis, and decreased cardiac output (Bissonnette et al., 2011)
	Body heat is lost by radiation, conduction, convection, and evaporation	Neonates	Lower body temperature increases risk for respiratory depression, acidosis, and infection; when neonate loses body heat, body attempts to conserve heat through acrocyanosis (i.e., hands and feet turn blue); if infant's hands or feet do not become pink when warmed, provider should consider congenital heart disease
	Thermogenesis by shivering is undeveloped (Bissonnette et al., 2011)	Infants; children until age 6 years	Requires body heat to be produced in other ways (e.g., brown fat thermogenesis), which causes metabolic acidosis; oxygen consumption also increases in cold-stressed neonates because it is needed to metabolize brown fat
	Sweating and vasodilation mechanisms not fully developed; peripheral vasodilation is inefficient because of incomplete myelination	Infants; toddlers until age 2 years	Infants do not flush to release body heat with increased body temperature or fever; body does not cool as fast, making child prone to febrile seizures
Metabolism	Metabolic rate is higher than in adults	Infants; children through adolescence	Need more oxygen than adult to support rapid body growth, work of breathing; metabolic rate increases during fever or illness; children have difficulty maintaining homeostasis during illness; young children are prone to hypoxia and dehydration, have high heart rates, and have high caloric and fluid requirements to support active metabolism; certain drugs are metabolized faster in children than adults
	Proportion of fat to lean body mass increases with age (Bissonnette et al., 2011)	Infants; children until age 12 years	Distribution of fat-soluble drugs is limited in children; a drug's lipid or water solubility affects the dose for the infant or child
Endocrine glands	Not fully mature until adolescence with hormonal and physical changes that occur in puberty	Infants; children until adolescence	Affects bone growth, thyroid function, adrenal cortex, and secretion of sex hormones
	Thelarche normally takes place between 8 and 13 years; pubarche between 8 and 14 years; menarche about 2 years after thelarche	School-aged children; adolescents	Affects physical examination; provider should be aware of precocious or delayed puberty; gynecomastia in adolescent boys may be caused by pubertal changes, obesity, or use of marijuana or anabolic steroids; pubic hair heralds the onset of puberty in boys; thelarche signifies puberty in girls

BP, blood pressure, GER, gastroesophageal reflux.

For each age group, the pediatric provider must be knowledgeable about age-appropriate developmental abilities:

- *Gross and fine motor abilities*, particularly until age 6 years.
- *Language and communication abilities.* Assessment of language milestones is very important; delays can signal hearing loss, learning problems, even neglect. Depending on the child's age, temperament, and developmental level, the child may not be able to verbalize anxiety, fear, or pain, making it necessary for the provider to make these assessments independently or to rely on the parent.
- *Cognitive abilities* depend on interplay of genetics as well as family, educational, and social environment. These abilities change and develop as the child grows.
- *Psychosocial and behavioral stages.* Knowledge of normal psychosocial developmental stages can be used to make an accurate developmental assessment of a child and to engage the child in the health care encounter in an age-appropriate manner. (See Chapter 2 for a discussion of developmental assessment.)

COMMUNICATION SKILLS REQUIRED TO WORK WITH CHILDREN

The pediatric health care provider must be able to communicate with children of all ages and at all developmental levels. This is quite challenging because each developmental stage requires vastly different approaches specific to the age, developmental stage, and temperament of the child. The provider must also know when the child is developmentally, cognitively, and temperamentally able to provide his or her own answers during the medical history. In addition, each child must be viewed within the context of his or her family, culture, and social situation. (See Chapter 3 for a discussion of the communication skills needed to work with children and families.)

OBTAINING THE PEDIATRIC HEALTH HISTORY

The reason for the child's visit dictates the type of history that the health care provider obtains (see Chapter 6). For example, interval histories involve a specific complaint and require only injury- or illness-specific data. During health maintenance visits, the provider obtains a very complete history. Data that provide information about the child's growth and development, nutrition, daily life, health and safety, environment, parental knowledge base, and teaching needs are especially important. The complexity of life in the 21st century presents new risks to children that also require assessment such as obesity; exposure to violent and sexually explicit media; exposure to community and domestic violence; assessment of television, computer, and video time; family structure, including an assessment of all persons living in the home and their relationship to the child; parenting style and disciplinary methods; as well as assessment of depression, eating disorders, and sexual activity. (See Chapter 6 for a detailed discussion of the pediatric health history.)

THE PEDIATRIC PHYSICAL EXAMINATION

A child's age and developmental level determine the provider's approach to the physical examination. The approach also depends on the severity of illness or injury and whether the child's primary caregiver is present. It is usually recommended that a complete physical examination be done in an organized, head-to-toe fashion to minimize any omissions of body system assessments. However, this sequence should be adjusted to the child's age, temperament, and developmental level. For example, infants and toddlers dislike intrusive procedures such as inspection of the throat and ears, and these examinations often elicit crying. For this reason, it is wise to first auscultate the young child's heart, lungs, and abdomen when the child is quiet, and inspect the ears and mouth last. Children who are preschool age and older are typically able to cooperate with a physical examination that proceeds in a head-to-toe direction. (See Chapter 8 for an in-depth discussion of physical assessment.)

UNDERSTANDING THE CAREGIVER–CHILD RELATIONSHIP

In all pediatric health encounters, whether the child is well or ill, the provider should appraise the child's social situation and home environment, paying particular attention to the parent–child interaction during the health care encounter. The caregiver's responses to and interactions with the child can provide a wealth of information regarding the child's emotional health and the parent–child relationship. Children are also highly influenced by the emotional state of their caregiver. This can be reflected in the child's overall behavior, sleep patterns, appetite, school performance, and peer relationships. The provider must also be sure to assess these relationships within the context of the family's culture. (See Chapter 4 for further discussion of family assessment and Chapter 5 for a discussion of cultural assessment.)

ROLE OF THE PEDIATRIC HEALTH CARE PROVIDER

The role of the pediatric health care provider is to collaborate and cooperate with the child's parent or primary caregiver and to advocate for and protect the child's best interests. Children are dependent on the adults in their lives for many years, and the health care provider can greatly influence the quality of care that they receive from their family. If parents feel supported and validated by the health care provider, they are more likely to feel comfortable asking questions that will enhance their child's emotional and physical health. This can be achieved by creating a partnership with the child and family in promoting health and preventing illness. Bright Futures, a developmentally based approach to child health assessment, health promotion and illness prevention, has delineated six steps for building the provider–child–family partnership (Hagan, Shaw, & Duncan, 2008):

1. Model and encourage open, respectful, non-judgmental communication, building trust and empathy.
2. Identify health issues through effective listening and by asking open-ended questions.
3. Affirm strengths of the child and family, praising the achievements of the child and family.
4. Identify mutual and shared goals, reinforcing the notion of a partnership between provider, child, and family. Refer the child and family to appropriate community resources as needed.
5. Develop a plan of action based on shared goals. Goals should be simple, achievable, measurable, and time-specific.
6. Evaluate the effectiveness of the partnership on an ongoing basis.

The pediatric health care provider cares for the entire family when assessing and treating a child. During the health care encounter, the provider can have a significant impact on the parent's and child's confidence, competence, and health behaviors through teaching, role modeling, positive reinforcement, and reassurance. Fostering a trusting, caring, provider–family relationship leads to healthful behaviors and healthy psychosocial development of the child. Having well-developed pediatric assessment skills is the first step in delivering excellent care to the child and family.

References

Ball, J. W., Bindler, R. C., & Cowen, K. J. (2012). *Principles of pediatric nursing: Caring for children* (5th ed.). Upper Saddle River, NJ: Pearson Education.

Bissonnette, B., Anderson, B. J., Bosenberg, A., Engelhardt, T., Mason, L. J., & Tobias, J. D. (2011). *Pediatric anesthesia: Basic principles—state-of-the-art future.* Shelton, CT: People's Medical Publishing House.

Guthrie, E. W. (2005). Pediatric dosing considerations. *U.S. Pharmacist, 30*(12), 5–10.

Hagan, J. F., Shaw, J. S., & Duncan, P. M. (Eds.). (2008). *Bright futures: Guidelines for health supervision of infants, children and adolescents* (3rd ed.). Elk Grove Village, IL: American Academy of Pediatrics.

Hockenberry, M. J., & Wilson, D. (2011). *Wong's nursing care of infants and children* (9th ed.). St. Louis, MO: Mosby.

John, R. M., & Brady, M. A. (2013). Respiratory disorders. In C. E. Burns, A. M. Dunn, M. A. Brady, N. B. Starr, & C. G. Blosser (Eds.), *Pediatric primary care* (5th ed., pp. 708–738). St. Louis, MO: W. B. Saunders.

Ma, A., & Dowell, M. (2012). Gastrointestinal alterations. In N. L. Potts & B. L. Mandelco (Eds.), *Pediatric nursing: Caring for children and their families.* New York, NY: Delmar.

Vernon, P., Brady, M. A., Barber Starr, N., & Petersen-Smith, A. (2013). Dermatologic disorders. In C. Burns, A. M. Dunn, M. A. Brady, N. B. Starr, & C. Blosser (Eds.), *Pediatric primary care* (5th ed., pp. 877–927). St. Louis, MO: W. B. Saunders.

Assessment of Child Development and Behavior

The developmental assessment is a significant and essential part of the health care of a child, as normal growth and development is a key indicator of the child's health and well-being. The pediatric health care provider must possess a thorough understanding of human growth and development to conduct an accurate, age-appropriate, developmental assessment. The developmental assessment includes an evaluation of physical growth; neurodevelopmental maturation; and cognitive, language, and psychosocial development. Early identification of developmental delays is essential so that appropriate referrals may be made; if untreated, the child with such delays is at risk for physical injury, poor academic performance, and social difficulties.

INFLUENCES ON CHILD DEVELOPMENT

Both modifiable and nonmodifiable influences on a child's growth and development must be considered. *Modifiable influences* include nutrition, illness, caregiver quality, provision of developmentally appropriate toys and activities, opportunities to develop motor abilities, caregiver discipline style, timing, and quality of education, and the physical and psychosocial environment. *Nonmodifiable influences* include culture, temperament of the child and caregiver, genetics, and the basic principles of human growth and development.

Principles of Human Growth and Development

To accurately assess growth and development in children, the pediatric health care provider must understand basic principles of human growth and development. These principles follow well-defined and consistent patterns, regardless of child, environment, or culture.

Cephalocaudal Development

Cephalocaudal development refers to physical development that occurs in a *head-to-toe* direction

(Figure 2.1). This progression is dramatically illustrated when the infant is in utero; the head is much larger with more complex functions than the lower part of the body, which remains smaller and underdeveloped until later in fetal life. This disproportion in size persists until the child is 2 years of age, when the chest circumference finally equals the head circumference. Cephalocaudal development occurs concurrently with neuronal myelination and is exemplified in the achievement of gross motor milestones: head control, shoulder and trunk control, sitting, standing, crawling, cruising, and walking (Figures 2.2 and 2.3); these are followed by complex gross motor abilities, including running, jumping, balance, coordination, hopping, and skipping.

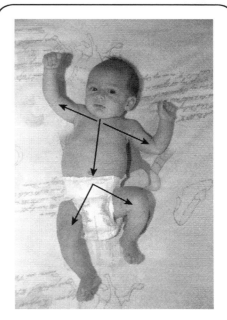

FIGURE 2.1 Cephalocaudal development in the infant.

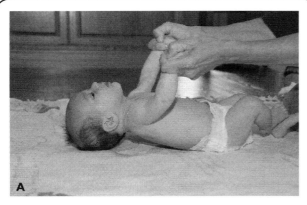

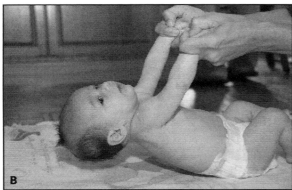

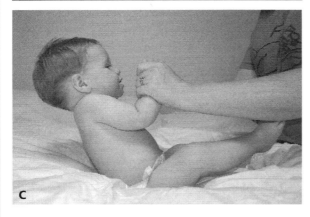

FIGURE 2.2 Progression of head control from birth to 4 months of age.

Proximal to Distal Development

Proximal to distal development occurs in a *near-to-far* manner. In utero, for example, this is seen in the embryonic stage as limb formation proceeds from buds to paddles to plates, progressing finally to digits. Proximal to distal development also corresponds to neuronal myelination and is seen when a child first demonstrates shoulder control, then upper extremity control, and finally fine motor control of the hands, which refines from a palmar grasp to a fine pincer grasp (Figure 2.4).

Simple to Complex Development

Simple to complex development involves the progression of cognitive abilities and motor skills that evolve from uncomplicated to more sophisticated tasks. Neuronal myelination plays a role in this development. The gross motor developmental sequence beyond walking (including stooping, hopping, jumping, skipping, and riding a bicycle) and the progressive development of fine motor skills (progressing from "raking" to writing and drawing) exemplify this process.

Predictable Sequence of Development

The attainment of developmental milestones (i.e., gross and fine motor skills, cognitive abilities, acquisition of language, social interaction) occurs in an *orderly, anticipated* sequence, following predictable brain growth and myelination patterns, for *all* children, regardless of culture, socioeconomic background, or environment. For example, all children develop head control before they stand, grasp objects before they have fine motor control of their hands, possess receptive language abilities before they can speak, and play alone ("parallel play") before they socialize in groups.

Variable Rate of Growth and Development

While development occurs in a predictable sequence, it occurs at a variable rate among children of the same age and in the individual child. For example, in the individual child, physical growth slows dramatically after the first birthday, but language development blossoms. Two children of the same age with similar medical histories may walk at different ages (e.g., 11 months and 15 months): both are within normal limits.

Critical Sensitive Periods

Critical sensitive periods are developmental periods in which a child is especially susceptible to particular influences. *Critical periods* begin and end quickly and are considered to be a time after which a particular phenomenon will not appear. *Sensitive periods* begin and end gradually and involve a time of maximum sensitivity to a specific stimulus. For example, the first year of life is a critical sensitive period for infant–caregiver attachment. Consistent, predictable care is needed from one person (primarily) for the infant to develop trust and to feel secure. If this does not occur, the infant will likely find it difficult to develop healthy, loving attachments later in life. This condition is known as inhibited reactive attachment disorder and is often seen in children with an early experience in foster care or orphanages where they may have had inconsistent caregiving or multiple caregivers (Zeanah & Smyke, 2008).

FIGURE 2.3 Development of locomotion. **A.** Infant pushes up from the prone position **B.** Crawling with abdomen off floor. **C.** Infant pulls to stand. **D.** Infant cruises along by holding on to furniture. **E.** Infant walks with assistance. **F.** Infant walks without assistance.

Language development is another example of a critical, sensitive period. Language is normally acquired in children in the following order: phonology (the sound of words), semantics (the meaning of words), and finally syntax (the rules of grammar). This acquisition sequence is shaped by factors within the central nervous system (CNS), and the different stages have different time frames for optimal shaping, making language acquisition a time-dependent process (Ruben, 2005).

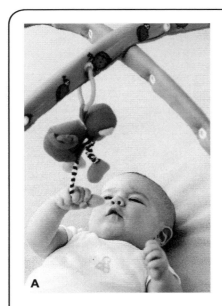
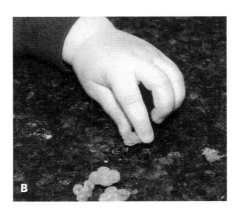

FIGURE 2.4 Progression of fine motor control from **A.** palmar grasp to **B.** fine pincer grasp.

Culture

It is essential for the health care provider to be culturally sensitive when evaluating a child's growth and development. In some cultures, for example, direct eye contact is considered disrespectful; this is important to know when assessing behavior in the child. In other cultures, children never speak directly to an adult, which may make expressive language assessment difficult.

Differences have been measured in the attainment of developmental milestones among cultural groups, but some of these differences disappear when socioeconomic status is controlled (Kelly, Sacker, Schoon, & Nazroo, 2006). Other differences remain, depending on cultural values such as independence, autonomy, and provision of learning opportunities. Children from cultures that value independence and autonomy achieve feeding, sleeping, and toilet-training milestones early (Schulze, Harwood, Schoelmerich, & Leyendecker, 2002).

Culture is also important to consider when assessing behavior. For example, the concept of time for Hispanics is *polychronic* insofar as several activities may be accomplished simultaneously and in an unstructured manner. In contrast, European Americans are largely *monochronic*, accomplishing tasks in a linear, orderly fashion, one at a time. Because of this cultural difference, Hispanic children may be at greater risk for being identified as inattentive or impulsive and may be incorrectly diagnosed with attention deficit hyperactivity disorder (ADHD) (Starr, 2007). Health care providers must be certain to use behavioral or developmental assessment tools that have been adapted for use for specific cultural groups; if one is not available, say if the provider has a tool written only in English, a trained medical interpreter must be sought. (See Chapter 5 for a discussion of cultural assessment.)

Developmental Theories

Knowledge of developmental theories can help the pediatric health care provider integrate information about physical, psychosocial, cognitive, and psychosexual growth and development in children into the developmental assessment. For example, Freud (1938) focused on the psychosexual development of children and adolescents, as well as self-esteem, temperament, and personal motivation. Erikson (1950) expanded on Freud's work and emphasized an individual's psychosocial development throughout the life stages, which he delineated. Piaget (1969) focused on a child's cognitive development and the way in which the child learns about the world as his or her abilities to reason correspond to cognitive growth.

Kohlberg (1969) expanded on Piaget's work, focusing on moral development in children. Because Kohlberg's research involved only boys, Gilligan (1982) postulated that Kohlberg's theory would not hold true for girls. This led to her development of a theory of moral development in girls. Table 2.1 summarizes these developmental theories.

In 1995, Chess and Thomas published their work regarding the effect of *temperament*, in which they explain how children as young as infants have innate tendencies to react to their environment in certain ways. The temperamental characteristics and accompanying behaviors, presented in Table 2.2, underlie what Chess and Thomas (1995) term the "goodness of fit" between the child and parent; that is, the degree to which the

TABLE 2.1	Developmental Theories				
AGE AND DEVELOPMENTAL STAGE	**ERIKSON (PSYCHOSOCIAL DEVELOPMENT)**	**PIAGET (COGNITIVE DEVELOPMENT)**	**FREUD (PSYCHOSEXUAL DEVELOPMENT)**	**KOHLBERG (MORAL DEVELOPMENT)**	**GILLIGAN (MORAL DEVELOPMENT)**
Infant (birth–1 year)	**Trust versus mistrust** Infant must know he or she will receive needed physical care; care should be largely rendered by one person to allow infant to develop trust; quality of caregiver and environment are critical to infant developing trust	**Sensorimotor (birth–2 years)** Infant learns about environment through five senses; object permanence develops; primitive and postural reflexes are first steps in cognitive development	**Oral stage** Source of pleasure is primarily oral	**Preconventional (birth–9 years)** "Amoral" stage 1 Punishment and obedience	**Preconventional** Goal is individual survival
Toddler (1–3 years)	**Autonomy versus shame and doubt** Toddlers are more in control of their bodies and environment; they want to do things for themselves and be more independent	**Preoperational (2–7 years)** Children in this stage are egocentric and see only their own perspective; they have a limited concept of time	**Anal stage** Child's interest in anal region predominates; child learns that he or she can withhold or give; power struggles may arise with toilet training	**Preconventional (birth–9 years)** *Stages 1–2* **Stage 1 Punishment and obedience** Children obey rules to avoid punishment and to obtain reward; they have no understanding of reasons behind why they must obey rules **Stage 2 Instrumental relativist orientation** Behavior fits child's own needs; sharing, loyalty, and gratitude are not yet seen	**Preconventional** Goal is individual survival
Preschooler (3–6 years)	**Initiative versus guilt** Child wants to explore; creativity is enhanced when given freedom; child develops a conscience and morals; magical thinking begins	**Preoperational (2–7 years)** Child is still egocentric but beginning to see another's point of view; demonstrates concrete, tangible thinking and begins to use memory	**Phallic** Child recognizes differences between two sexes and is interested in genitals; shows intense attraction to or love of parent of the opposite sex (Oedipus/Electra complex)	**Preconventional (birth–9 years)** *Stages 1–3* **Stage 3** "Good girl or boy, nice girl or boy"; a conscience emerges; child seeks approval; likes conforming to norms; behavior is based on avoiding punishment or obtaining rewards	**Preconventional** Goal is individual survival with transition to conventional stage involving a change from selfishness to responsibility toward others

(continued)

TABLE 2.1	Developmental Theories (*continued*)				
AGE AND DEVELOPMENTAL STAGE	ERIKSON (PSYCHOSOCIAL DEVELOPMENT)	PIAGET (COGNITIVE DEVELOPMENT)	FREUD (PSYCHOSEXUAL DEVELOPMENT)	KOHLBERG (MORAL DEVELOPMENT)	GILLIGAN (MORAL DEVELOPMENT)
School-aged child (6–12 years)	**Industry versus inferiority** Child wants to produce and achieve; feels inferior when creativity is squelched	**Concrete operations (7–11 years)** Child can classify and organize facts and can consider another's point of view; uses inductive reasoning (particular to general)	**Latency** Energy is directed toward learning and play; sexual impulses are repressed; self-esteem is connected with a sense of industry and accomplishment; parents are no longer viewed as omnipotent	**Preconventional (birth–9 years)** *Stages 4–5* **Stage 4: "Law and order" orientation** Child obeys set rules, respects authority, and abides by rules of society. **Conventional (9–20 years)** **Stage 5: Social contract, utilitarian orientation** Behavior and moral code is based on societal norms as well as needs of society; there is an increased desire to please others and be considered "good"	**Preconventional** Girls (6–18 years) interpret moral dilemmas in the context of human relationships and feelings
Adolescent (12–21 years)	**Identity versus role confusion** Adolescents are concerned with who they are and how they look to others	**Formal operations** They think abstractly; draw logical conclusions; can make and test hypotheses (deductive reasoning)	**Genital** Puberty has been reached; interest in peer relationships and sexual relationships peaks	**Conventional (9–20 years)** **Stage 5: Social contract, utilitarian orientation** Behavior and moral code are based on societal norms	**Conventional** Girls (6–18 years) interpret moral dilemmas in the context of human relationships and feelings; self-sacrifice defines goodness

TABLE 2.2	Temperament Characteristics
TEMPERAMENT CHARACTERISTIC	DESCRIPTION
Activity	Amount of physical energy in child relative to quiet periods
Rhythmicity	Level of predictability regarding child's biologic functions (e.g., eating, elimination, sleeping patterns)
Approach/withdrawal	How child responds when presented with a new person or situation
Adaptability	How long it takes for child to adjust to change
Intensity	Amount of energy released with emotional responses (e.g., crying, laughing, excited)
Mood	Overall demeanor displayed on a day-to-day basis (e.g., happy, sad, positive, negative)
Distractibility	Ease with which child can be distracted by things going on in environment
Attention span and persistence	Child's ability to stay on task and focus
Threshold of responsiveness	How much stimulation child needs to respond to stimuli

Source: Chess and Thomas (1995).

child's and the parents' temperament and personality mesh. These concepts have implications for the assessment of growth and development, particularly when parent and child are not a "good fit," as the risk for abuse or neglect may be increased in such cases.

Developmental Domains

When evaluating a child's growth and development, the assessment categories can be divided into five developmental domains: physical development, neurodevelopmental maturation (gross and fine motor skills; visuomotor skills), cognitive development, language development, and socioemotional development.

Gross motor skills involve the use of large muscles to control the head and shoulders and to sit, stand, balance, walk, and run. *Fine motor skills* involve the use of small muscles to use the pincer grasp to pick up a raisin, turn the pages of a book, stack blocks, and use a crayon to draw or a pencil to write.

Cognitive development encompasses intellectual and adaptive skills. For example, infants first use reflexes but then progress to develop cognitive abilities, such as achieving object permanence. Cognitive development progresses as toddlers learn to match items, preschoolers develop memory, and school-aged children and adolescents develop advanced reasoning abilities.

Language development acquisition begins with receptive abilities, progressing to expressive abilities. A child first recognizes the sound of words, then the meaning of words (semantics), and finally the syntax (rules of grammar). Adult articulation abilities are usually achieved by 7 to 8 years of age. Many factors influence a child's speech and language abilities; these factors are listed in Box 2.1. Bilingual children may reach expressive language milestones later as a result of being exposed to more than one language (American Speech-Language-Hearing Association [ASLHA], 2014).

Socioemotional development encompasses many areas of a child's psychosocial development, including behavior; temperament; parent–child interaction; social interactions with peers, teachers, and other adults; school performance; and psychosexual development.

BOX 2.1 Factors Affecting Speech and Language Acquisition in Young Children

Child abuse and neglect
Autism spectrum disorder
Traumatic brain injury
Cerebral palsy
Fetal drug or alcohol exposure
Hearing impairment
Intellectual ability
Diagnosed language impairment

Source: Prelock, Hutchins, and Glascoe (2008).

EVALUATING CHILD DEVELOPMENT

In 2010, the American Academy of Pediatrics (AAP) (2006) reaffirmed a revised policy statement on identifying developmental delays and disorders in infants and children in the primary care, medical home setting. The AAP uses the term "developmental surveillance" versus "developmental assessment" to connote a continuous process. Developmental assessment includes a thorough history, risk factor identification, physical examination, and developmental screening (AAP, 2010).

History

Before initiating the physical and developmental examination, it is essential to obtain a thorough history to identify causes and risk factors for developmental delays. A complete past medical history is obtained along with a thorough review of systems, family history, and social history. Parents are asked to describe their child's gross and fine motor skills, language abilities, temperament, behavior, and social interactions to guide the provider's assessments.

Medical History

Prenatal History • The provider determines when prenatal care was initiated and if the mother had any illnesses or infections during pregnancy that could cause neurodevelopmental sequelae for the child (see Chapter 22). It is also essential to determine any prenatal exposure to alcohol or drugs, especially cocaine, opiates, methamphetamines, or nicotine.

Prenatal exposure to alcohol can result in low intelligence, impaired memory and judgment, and attention deficits (Vaux & Chambers, 2012). Fetal alcohol spectrum disorder (FASD) and fetal alcohol syndrome (FAS) are direct results of maternal alcohol consumption during pregnancy. FASD is the leading cause of intellectual disability in the Western world and a common cause of developmental delay and behavioral and learning disabilities (Vaux & Chambers, 2012). FAS results in CNS and neurobehavioral abnormalities, including microcephaly, mental retardation, developmental delays, cognitive impairment, and ADHD (Ware et al., 2014).

Some studies have shown that in utero exposure to cocaine adversely affects behavior (Bada et al., 2007) and cognitive, motor, and language skills (Schiller & Allen, 2005). It also causes maternal vasoconstriction and resultant hypertension, decreased uterine blood flow, placental abruption, fetal hypoxemia, and premature uterine contractions (Bhuvaneswar, Chang, Epstein, & Stern, 2008), all of which can contribute to hypoxic-ischemic events or prematurity, resulting in neurodevelopmental complications. Prenatal cocaine exposure also increases the permeability of the fetal blood–brain barrier, leaving the fetus vulnerable to teratogens and infections (Leveno et al., 2007).

Opioid addiction in pregnant women can cause an assortment of negative effects on the developing fetus. Opioid use (i.e., heroin, methadone) during pregnancy has been shown to cause intrauterine growth restriction, decreased birth weight, decreased head circumference, developmental delays, and neonatal seizures (Minnes, Lang, & Singer, 2011).

The effects of methamphetamine use in pregnancy are just beginning to be known. Chang and colleagues (2004) found that some neonates who were exposed to methamphetamine in utero had smaller brains than normal neonates. Neurocognitive assessments conducted on children aged 3 to 16 years whose mothers had ingested methamphetamine during pregnancy found that the children had poor attention spans and slow verbal memory (Chang et al., 2004).

Cigarette smoking during pregnancy exposes the fetus to nicotine, which may cause prematurity, low birth weight, and the associated neurodevelopmental complications (Minnes et al., 2011).

The provider must inquire about any episodes of domestic violence during pregnancy, particularly abdominal trauma. Women who are physically battered during pregnancy are at increased risk for antepartum hemorrhage and preterm labor (Sanchez et al., 2013), which can lead to low birth weight in the infant and the neurodevelopmental comorbidities associated with prematurity (see Chapter 22).

Perinatal History • Information regarding the perinatal history is gleaned with questions about the Apgar score, resuscitation (if needed and for how long), birth trauma, prematurity, low birth weight, or very low birth weight. Neonates who suffer hypoxic-ischemic injury are at high risk for cerebral palsy, hearing and visual impairments, and developmental delays. Premature, low birth weight, and very low birth weight infants are at high risk for cerebral palsy; hearing and visual impairments; and speech, language, and motor delays, which affect the developmental assessment (Blackman, 2007). Preterm infants are also more likely to have learning difficulties, ADHD, and psychological and behavioral problems as they reach childhood (Vanderbilt, Wang, & Parker, 2007).

Neonatal History • The developmental history includes questions about neonatal conditions that may affect a child's developmental status, including episodes of neonatal apnea, bradycardia, or hypoxia; infections; hyperbilirubinemia; hypoglycemia; or hypothyroidism. A history of poor tone or difficulty with sucking and swallowing is also noted, as this can be associated with cerebral palsy (Jones, Morgan, Shelton, & Thorgood, 2007). Genetic syndromes are identified, as some syndromes cause developmental delay or intellectual disability. It is important to document the presence of cyanotic congenital heart defects, as these defects can cause neurodevelopmental sequelae from repeated hypoxic events. A positive phenylketonuria (PKU) screen is necessary because if left untreated, PKU leads to intellectual disability.

Review of Systems • A thorough, detailed review of systems (ROS) involves determining whether the child has been diagnosed with an acute or chronic illness or condition that can affect his or her physical or psychosocial growth and development. For example, acute neurologic infections cause serious neurologic sequelae that permanently affect a child's developmental capabilities (see Chapter 22). Chronic health conditions may also inhibit physical or psychosocial developmental milestones, For example, chronic illnesses that require long-term treatment (e.g., childhood cancers requiring chemotherapy or radiation) can affect a child's physical, psychosocial, and cognitive growth and development in part because of the necessary long absences from school. Some diseases for which children are immunized can cause serious neurologic complications; thus, immunization status must be assessed (see Chapters 9 and 22). The provider should also inquire about past hospitalizations and surgeries to identify potential areas of concern for developmental delays. Any allergies, particularly seasonal allergies, are important to document; some medications used to treat seasonal allergies cause sedation, resulting in poor school performance. The provider also determines if the child has ever had any of the following conditions:

- **General:** alteration in growth patterns, short stature, excess height, or asymmetrical growth
- **Skin:** café-au-lait lesions (neurofibromatosis), hemangiomas, or port-wine stains (Sturge–Weber syndrome)
- **Head/Face/Neck:** microcephaly, macrocephaly, hydrocephaly, or craniosynostosis, plagiocephaly, wide sutures, bulging fontanelles, altered head control, headaches, migraines, or facial dysmorphism (e.g., FAS, FASD)
- **Eyes:** poor vision, blurred vision, diplopia, nystagmus, strabismus, cataracts, or coloboma (associated with CHARGE syndrome)
- **Ears:** low-set ears, pinna deformities, or hearing loss
- **Cardiovascular:** congenital heart disease
- **Respiratory:** asthma or cystic fibrosis
- **Gastrointestinal:** Crohn's disease, celiac disease, or hepatic disease
- **Genitourinary:** Tanner staging, precocious or delayed puberty, ambiguous genitalia, or primary amenorrhea
- **Endocrine/Metabolic:** neonatal hypoglycemia, diabetes mellitus, hypothyroidism, hyperthyroidism, glycogen storage diseases, inborn errors of metabolism, growth hormone deficiency, or congenital adrenal hyperplasia
- **Hematologic/Immunity:** cancers, anemia, or allergies
- **Musculoskeletal:** spasticity of extremities; difficulty with balance, coordination, or muscle strength; cerebral palsy; or paralysis

- **Neurologic:** encephalocele, spina bifida occulta, meningocele, myelomeningocele, hydrocephalus, intraventricular hemorrhage, periventricular leukomalacia, hypoxic-ischemic encephalopathy, seizures (including type), status epilepticus, tremors, spasms, paresthesias, ipsilateral or bilateral weakness, infantile spasms, cerebral palsy, dizziness, history of high fevers, bacterial meningitis, viral meningitis, encephalitis, Reye's syndrome, Duchenne muscular dystrophy, Guillain–Barré syndrome, episodic loss of consciousness, memory loss, changes in concentration, CNS neoplasm, ataxia, aphasia, head trauma, irritability, lethargy, chronic fatigue, sleep disorders, ADHD, dyslexia, learning disabilities, sensory integration disorder, autism, or tics
- **Psychosocial:** drug or alcohol addiction, stress, emotional lability, irritability, breath-holding spells, behavior disorders, eating disorders, anxiety, depression, history of suicidal ideation, schizophrenia, hallucinations, bipolar disorder, mood changes, or aggressive behavior

Injuries

Gathering an accurate history of injuries, particularly head or musculoskeletal injuries, is especially germane to the developmental assessment. Traumatic brain injuries (TBIs), spinal cord injuries, or poisonings often cause permanent damage to the nervous system, affecting the achievement of developmental milestones across all domains. The etiology of some injuries may suggest problems with coordination or impulsive behavior, which require further investigation. The dates of past injuries are obtained and whether the injury was severe enough to require medical intervention. The provider also assesses whether the child has missed school or has experienced any changes in social relationships since the injury; this can affect developmental assessment findings. When inquiring about past injuries, the provider always evaluates whether caregiver abuse or neglect played a role and whether child protective services were or are involved in the family's life. Child abuse and neglect can lead to delays in achieving developmental milestones and poor school performance (Slade & Wissow, 2007). Depending on the type of abuse, a child may suffer from depression, behavior problems, or developmental delays because of neglect or TBI. Any developmental assessment includes questions about discipline practices, specifically corporal punishment. (See Chapter 24 for a discussion of assessing for child abuse and neglect.)

Medications

The provider should inquire about any medications the child is taking on a regular or as-needed basis, including over-the-counter medications and complementary or alternative treatments (see Chapter 6). Questions about medications prescribed for seizures, ADHD, or depression, for example, help to complete the developmental history. The indication, dose, and time of last dose of any medication is noted, as some medications with neurologic or sedating side effects can alter developmental assessment findings. The provider also determines if the child ever received aminoglycosides in the neonatal period, which can result in hearing loss and interferes with language acquisition.

Family History

Genetically transmitted disorders may cause developmental delay or intellectual disability. Inherited disorders that can cause learning problems or intellectual disability include neurofibromatosis, fragile X syndrome, and Duchenne muscular dystrophy, which also causes gross motor muscle weakness and a lack of coordination. Conditions about which the provider should inquire include learning disabilities, speech and language problems, dyslexia, ADHD, intellectual disability, and pervasive developmental disorders (e.g., autism).

Social History

The child's home environment, social situation, and the parenting received have a great impact on a child's world and, consequently, development. The social history assessment is individualized, based largely on the child's age and particular situation.

Primary Caregiver • The health care provider must first identify the child's parent or primary caregiver. This primary relationship greatly influences the child's growth and development. Some specific characteristics of the parent or primary caregiver, such as young parental age, low level of education, high parental stress levels, maternal depression, and parental addiction, increase a child's risk for developmental delay.

A review of the literature spanning the past 30 years reveals that children of adolescent mothers have lower cognitive, vocabulary, and language abilities and are at increased risk for school failure and grade retention (Oxford & Spieker, 2006; Qi, Kaiser, Milan, & Hancock, 2006). These poor language, cognitive, and academic outcomes are also associated with a low level of maternal education, immigrant status, low socioeconomic status, and being from a single-parent family (To et al., 2004). Parental knowledge deficits regarding normal growth and development can also affect attainment of developmental milestones. If parents are unaware of normal developmental expectations, they may not provide the child with age-appropriate activities or opportunities to achieve these milestones. Similarly, if parents do not know what normal developmental milestones are, they will be less likely to recognize deviations and to bring their concerns to the attention of the health care provider.

Maternal depression also negatively influences a child's development and behavior (Wachs, Black, &

Engle, 2009). Depressed mothers of infants respond to their infant's cues more slowly and often with a blunted affect; these mothers are also more easily frustrated and respond less frequently to their infants' needs. Consequently, infants of depressed mothers smile less, are less playful, and show more irritability and fussiness (Johnson & Flake, 2007). Depressed mothers of toddlers and preschoolers have been shown to have a lower tolerance for developmentally normal behaviors, such as crying, tantrums, or the challenges of toilet training; they are more likely to respond in harsh, less nurturing, and negative ways. As a result, this age group is more likely to demonstrate poor social skills, to be more withdrawn and anxious, and to have more temper tantrums (Johnson & Flake, 2007). Preschool-aged children of depressed mothers are also more likely to display such behaviors as attention seeking, aggression, ADHD, and oppositional or defiant behaviors, even when prenatal selective serotonin reuptake inhibitor (SSRI) exposure is controlled (Oberlander et al., 2007). School-aged children of depressed mothers have higher rates of anxiety, depression, and behavior disorders, including conduct disorder and ADHD; they also are at increased risk for poor academic performance and low self-esteem (Schwartz & Schonwald, 2014). Adolescents who have been raised by a mother who is depressed may have strained family relationships and more difficult peer relationships, which may result in decreased school attendance and academic difficulties (Hammen, Shih, & Brennan, 2004).

Home Environment • The provider must determine where the child lives, with whom, and whether the home environment is safe, caring, interactive, and developmentally enriching or one that leaves the child at risk for developmental delays. The home environment should be evaluated for the presence of toxic chemicals (e.g., lead, mercury, environmental tobacco smoke [ETS]) to which the young child may be exposed; these common toxicants have been shown to adversely affect child development (Graff, Murphy, Ekvall, & Gagnon, 2006). For example, a child who lives in an old home with lead pipes or lead-based paint, or who receives lead-based folk remedies, is at risk for lead poisoning, which may result in headaches, irritability, developmental delay (Rumack & Dart, 2012), inattentiveness, distractibility, impulsiveness, and learning problems (Badawy & Conners, 2013). Mercury thermometers, disk button batteries, fluorescent light bulbs, broken thermostats, and the consumption of certain seafoods can lead to mercury poisoning. Prenatal exposure to mercury is neurotoxic (Olson, 2013).

Childhood exposure to high levels of mercury can lead to attention deficits, hearing impairments vision impairments, tremors, ataxia, emotional instability (Olson, 2013), irritability, shyness, memory problems (Agency for Toxic Substances and Disease Registry, 2014), developmental disabilities (Olson, 2013),

intellectual disability, and loss of IQ points (Trasande, Schechter, Haynes, & Landrigan, 2006). Exhaled secondhand smoke or smoke from the burning end of a cigarette, cigar, or pipe emits over 7,000 chemicals, 70 of which are carcinogenic (Centers for Disease Control and Prevention [CDC], 2014). One of these chemicals is nicotine, which is a neurodevelopmental toxicant; children who are exposed to even low levels of ETS have demonstrated deficits in math, reading, and visuospatial reasoning skills (Yolton, Dietrich, Auinger, Lanphear, & Hornung, 2005); they are also more likely to have recurrent middle ear infections (Yolton et al., 2005), which interfere with language acquisition.

A child's home must be safe from other risks for injury and be amenable to safe exploration to enable the child to develop motor skills (see Chapter 7). The provider must identify the family's primary household language; children who hear more than one language as infants and toddlers often develop expressive language skills later than normal because of this exposure (ASLHA, 2014). The amount of screen time (television, Internet, video games) should be noted. Excessive (greater than 2 hours a day in children aged 2 years and older) television screen time is linked to childhood obesity, violent or aggressive behavior, and increased risk-taking behaviors, such as substance abuse, sexual activity, and decreased school performance (AAP, 2001; Christakis & Zimmerman, 2007). Developmentally appropriate assessments should be made regarding the amount and type of free, unstructured play that the child engages in. Play enhances physical and psychosocial development by affording the child opportunities to develop imagination, creativity, problem-solving skills, social skills, and increased physical activity (Milteer & Ginsburg, 2012). The provider should also ask about the child's involvement in other diversional activities, such as reading, sports, hobbies, and other creative outlets.

Parental stress as a result of a recent separation, divorce, family crises, unemployment, poverty, and threats of terrorism or war can adversely affect a child's development and behavior as children readily pick up on parental behavioral cues and become anxious (Laor, Wolmer, & Cohen, 2001; Schechter & Davis, 2007). The primary caregiver's support network must be identified; these persons may also influence the child's growth and development. Disrupted peer relationships, the death of a family member or a pet, or a recent family relocation must be evaluated, especially if the child has been acting out, has become withdrawn or depressed, or if school performance has declined.

Domestic violence causes parental stress and has many adverse effects on children. Mothers in abusive relationships are more likely to abuse their children, both physically and emotionally (Lutenbacher, Cohen, & Conner, 2004). Children, even infants, experience negative behavioral outcomes as a result of being exposed to interpersonal violence between their parents. Examples include impaired bonding, excessive crying, and delayed milestone achievement in infants; anxiety, nightmares, and clinging behaviors in preschoolers; some may even regress with toileting skills and begin to suck their thumb (Hornor, 2005). School-aged children often suffer somatic complaints, such as headaches or stomachaches, and school performance may decline. Adolescents may manifest rebellious behaviors, such as truancy, dropping out of school, running away from home, or drug and alcohol abuse (Hornor, 2005).

Parents who abuse drugs or alcohol are more likely to abuse or neglect their children than parents who are not addicted (U.S. Department of Health and Human Services, 2009). Drug or alcohol intoxication is also associated with a lack of stable housing and an increased risk of interpersonal violence (Bhuvaneswar et al., 2008), including domestic violence. Parents who are intoxicated on a frequent basis are also less likely to provide their children with developmentally enriching experiences (Lambie & Sias, 2005).

Social Environment • Garbarino (1995) identified several social risk factors that create a "socially toxic" environment—that is, one in which a child may not flourish developmentally and is at increased risk for depression, conduct disorders, and other psychosocial problems. These risk factors are violence (including media violence), poverty, breakup of the family, lack of responsible adult supervision and role modeling, and the availability of firearms. Garbarino (1995) also identified protective or mitigating factors to these stressors: resilient temperament and emotional intelligence in the child, spiritual orientation, and a variety of social assets and sources of stability such as a positive, close relationship with at least one adult, and additional emotional support from family, teachers, neighbors, and community. When obtaining the social history, the pediatric provider must assess for the presence of these social mitigating factors.

School Progress • Beginning with preschool-aged children, the provider must determine whether the child goes to school or day care and when the child was enrolled. Some children, for social reasons such as poverty, homelessness, natural disasters, or recent immigration, may have been out of school for extended periods of time; some may never have gone to school. Children who attend preschool will have more advanced developmental capabilities when entering kindergarten than their peers who have had unstructured day care experiences (Magnuson, Ruhm, & Waldfogel, 2007).

The school history for school-aged children and adolescents consists of an assessment of grades and overall school progress, including recent or abrupt declines in school performance, what subjects the child likes and dislikes, whether the child has a best friend, if the child is being bullied, the child's "fit" with the teacher, and whether the child and family feel supported by the teacher, principal, and school. These questions are important because children are more likely to skip school if they feel unsafe. Children with accelerated academic abilities may also want to skip school if they are "bored"; inquiries should be made to the school to determine whether the child is a gifted learner. Inconsistent school attendance affects the child's social, emotional, and cognitive abilities and, consequently, the developmental assessment.

Immigrant and Refugee Status • Children who have recently come to the industrialized world from a developing country have many threats to their physical and psychosocial growth and development. Many of these children have not met their developmental milestones because of malnutrition, disease, war, or natural disasters. Malnutrition, in particular, affects physical growth, cognition, and motor and social development (Neumann, Gewa, & Bwibo, 2004). Poverty also forces families to prioritize, using scant resources for food instead of education (Staton & Harding, 2004); children who do not attend school are unable to meet milestones in the areas of language, reading, writing, and mathematical capabilities.

Institutionalization • Children who have spent time in orphanages, such as internationally adopted children, are at high risk for developmental delays across all domains. Many institutionalized children have been confined to cribs, playpens, highchairs, or walkers for extended periods of time and, therefore, have not had opportunities to develop motor skills. Because institutionalized children have had very little individualized attention or consistent primary caregivers, opportunities for face-to-face contact or adult-to-infant verbalization are limited, causing speech and language delays (Loman, Wiik, Frenn, Pollack, & Gunnar, 2009). This lack of attention, individual interaction, or a consistent caregiver also contributes to delays in social and emotional development in these children, most often demonstrated as poor emotional attachments. Lack of sensory stimulation and age-appropriate toys or play activities also delays social and emotional growth (Loman et al, 2009). When conducting the developmental assessment on a previously institutionalized child, the provider should anticipate these variations and expect delays.

Present History

The provider obtains the present history by asking a parent if he or she has any concerns about the child's behavior or developmental capabilities. The parent or caregiver is then asked about the child's developmental status, including achievement of major age-appropriate motor, language, and cognitive developmental milestones; current memory abilities; ability to adapt to new situations; ability to separate from the primary caregiver; and school performance. One method of obtaining this information is to ask the parent to complete a developmental screening tool while still in the clinic or office waiting room. The provider must be certain that the child does not have a current illness or injury that would have an impact on the assessment findings, such as fever or pain. Likewise, when a child presents with an acute illness or injury, the provider must still include an assessment of any developmental red flags or abnormalities; if any are noted, a follow-up visit is scheduled when the child is well to facilitate assessment of the present concern. Risk factors for developmental delay are listed in Box 2.2. Red flags that may herald an existing developmental problem are listed in Box 2.3. Red flags involving tone and motor control indicate the need to follow up or evaluate the child for cerebral palsy; those involving altered social interaction may indicate child abuse or neglect, autism, pervasive developmental disorder, or visual or cognitive deficits; and any red flags that involve language milestones may indicate hearing loss, autism, or pervasive developmental disorder.

BOX 2.2   Risk Factors for Developmental Delays

Prenatal drug or alcohol exposure
Prematurity
Low birth weight
Hypoxic birth injuries
Perinatal hyperbilirubinemia
Perinatal infection
Head or neurologic injury
Chronic otitis media with effusion
Hearing or vision impairment
Inborn metabolic disorder
Genetic disorder with neurodevelopmental component
Seizure disorders
Chronic health condition affecting mobility or activity
Low level of parental education
More than three children in family
Single parent
Maternal depression
Poor parental social supports
Parental substance abuse
Physical or emotional abuse
Neglect
Institutionalization, international adoptees

Physical Examination

General

Before the developmental assessment is conducted, the health care provider reviews the parental history and physical examination findings from any current or recent health care visits to detect any abnormalities or clues to developmental problems. Next, the provider quietly observes the young child engage in an age-appropriate activity such as stacking blocks, completing a puzzle, coloring, reading, or talking to the parent. The provider then connects with the child verbally in an age-appropriate manner, for example, by cooing to an infant or asking the

school-aged child about his or her friends and activities. This puts the child at ease and garners more accurate results during the developmental assessment. During this time, the examiner notes eye contact, the child's affect, how the child relates to both the provider and parent or caregiver, and how the child age-appropriately separates or does not separate from the parent. The child's overall demeanor is also evaluated. The child's body language may indicate that he or she is angry, depressed, or irritable. The child may talk excessively, interrupt conversation, and constantly move, fidget, or get up from the seat in the exam room; these are possible indicators of ADHD (American Psychiatric Association [APA], 2013). Any repetitive behaviors are noted, and the quality, character, and amount of crying are assessed. A cursory evaluation of receptive and expressive language abilities is also included, with a more detailed evaluation in the complete developmental assessment.

Measurements

As part of the physical examination, a measurement of vital signs is important to detect any physical problems that can interfere with a child's normal growth and development. For example, if the child is febrile, the developmental assessment will not yield accurate results. Tachycardia, tachypnea, or blood pressure abnormalities may indicate cardiac or chronic respiratory conditions that impede a child's growth and opportunities to develop skills. To assess physical growth, the child's weight, height or length, and head circumference (age 3 years and younger) are measured and plotted on age- and gender-appropriate growth charts (see Chapter 8 and Appendix B). Growth measurements are not particularly meaningful in isolation; they should be compared with previous measurements and should follow the same growth percentile curve. It is extremely important to recognize that when a child falls below his or her own previously established growth percentile curve, an investigation is warranted. The physical growth of premature infants must be followed closely, using the growth curves established for premature infants (see Chapter 8). Prolonged periods of poor growth in premature infants are associated with poor neurodevelopmental outcomes, such as cerebral palsy, learning difficulties, and ADHD (Aylward, 2005).

Integument

The skin is inspected for neurocutaneous lesions associated with chromosomal disorders that cause developmental abnormalities or mental retardation. Examples of lesions for which to look include café-au-lait spots (see Chapter 12, Figure 12.3), axillary freckling, port-wine stains (see Chapter 12, Figure 12.5), ash leaf spots, and shagreen patches. The presence of more than six café-au-lait spots 5 mm in greatest diameter and axillary freckling are associated with neurofibromatosis-1 (von Recklinghausen disease), a neurocutaneous disorder that causes cognitive and psychomotor problems, learning

---

BOX 2.3   Developmental Red Flags

3 MONTHS

Rolling before 3 months
Persistent fisting by 3 months
Unable to push up on arms; pushing back with head at 3 months

4–6 MONTHS

Head lag after 4 months
Persistent primitive reflexes after 4 months
Failure to reach for objects by 5 months
No smile by 4–6 months
Poor or no head control at 6 months
Stiff arms; crossed, stiff legs; moves one side of the body more than the other at 6 months

6–12 MONTHS

No cooing after 6 months
Absent stranger anxiety after 7 months
W-sitting at 7 months
Rounded back; poor use of arms; stiff legs, pointed toes; arched back, stiff extremities (8 months)
Cannot bear weight when pulled to stand (8 months)
No reciprocal vocalization by 9 months
Failure to localize sounds by 10 months

12–18 MONTHS

No quadruped crawling; cannot pull to stand; stiff legs, pointed toes; moves one side of the body more than the other at 12 months
No tool use after 12 months
Toe walking; moves one side of the body more than the other; sits with weight bearing to one side; strong hand preference; extremity stiffness at 15 months
No imitative play after 18 months
Hand dominance before 18 months

18–24 MONTHS

No first word (besides "mama"/"dada") by 18 months

Has more than 10–12 episodes of otitis media
No two-word sentences by age 2 years
Very clingy to mother at 24 months

3 YEARS

Speech is less than 75% intelligible; does not speak in full sentences
Incorrect pronoun use
Cannot feed self independently with spoon or fork
Toeing-in; trips when running

4 YEARS

Speech is less than 95% intelligible
Cannot separate from parent
Cannot balance on foot for 2 seconds
Cannot copy a circle or hold a pencil correctly
Cannot name two to three colors
Cannot share with friends
Aggression; acting out

5 YEARS

Excessive fears; night terrors
Unable to identify colors
Speech not 100% understandable

AT ANY TIME

Parental concerns
Slow or excessive physical growth
Child's gait changes
Child stops walking
Cruelty to animals
Fire-setting
Persistent sleep disturbances
Bullying or being bullied
Abusive family or peer relationships
Difficulty with schoolwork
Pervasive sad mood
Any loss of milestones is always abnormal

---

disabilities, and intellectual disability (Bernard et al., 2012). Facial port-wine stains are seen in Sturge–Weber disease; intractable seizures are common with this condition and often cause mental retardation (Bernard et al., 2012). Hypomelanotic, macular, oval-shaped lesions (ash leaf spots) and shagreen patches (firm, yellow-red or pink nodules) are seen with tuberous sclerosis, an inherited disease that causes seizures and intellectual disability in up to 50% of those affected (Bernard et al., 2012). Cutaneous manifestations of trisomy 21 (Down syndrome) include extremely soft skin in early childhood and dry skin in later childhood, with xerosis and atopic dermatitis being the main cause (Chen, 2014).

Palmar creases should also be inspected, especially in newborns. A single transverse palmar crease is associated with Down syndrome (Figure 2.5). Transverse flexion of the palmar crease close to the second and third fingers ("hockey stick" palmar crease) is seen in FASD (Vaux & Chambers, 2012).

The hair is also inspected. A low frontal hairline and thick, markedly arched eyebrows joined at the midline are clinical findings in Brachmann–de Lange syndrome (BDLS), which causes cognitive, speech, behavior, and growth abnormalities (Wilson, 2008). Absent or abnormal *hair whorls* may indicate abnormal brain development (Furdon & Clark, 2003); *alopecia areata* occurs

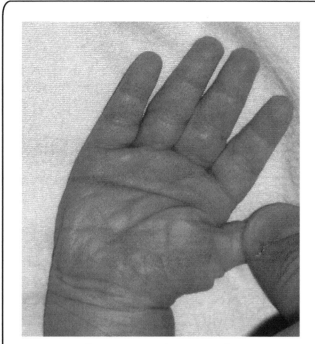

FIGURE 2.5 Palmar crease seen in Down syndrome.

in approximately 6% to 9% of children with Down syndrome (Chen, 2014). Abnormalities of the nails, including hypoplasia, paronychia (lack of a fingernail), micronychia, or polynychia, can indicate ischemic injury or teratogenic exposure in utero (specifically maternal antiepileptic drug use); both of these influences often result in neurodevelopmental injury.

Head, Face, Eyes, and Ears

The head, face, eyes, and ears are inspected for any abnormalities. Abnormal head size or shape and facial dysmorphisms are frequently signs of chromosomal disorders or syndromes that cause developmental delays or intellectual disability. Inspection of the head includes assessment for microcephaly, macrocephaly, or craniosynostosis (see Chapters 13 and 22). Frontal bossing or scalp vein dilation indicates increased intracranial pressure or hydrocephaly, which can also cause developmental abnormalities. Symmetry of the head is another important assessment. Occipital flattening in an infant is a sign of prolonged supine positioning, often indicating neglect and decreased opportunities for the child to attain developmental milestones. The provider also assesses the child for dysmorphic facial features, which are seen in genetic disorders that can cause developmental delays or mental retardation, including a flat midface, short mandible, a long or absent philtrum, and micrognathia. A smooth philtrum, flattened nose bridge, upturned nose, and thin upper lip are characteristics of FASD (Vaux & Chambers, 2012). Upward-slanting palpebral fissures and midface hypoplasia are

seen in Down syndrome (Figure 2.6) (Tsai, Manchester, & Elias, 2012).

The provider also assesses for any abnormalities of the eyes. Cataracts and microphthalmia are seen in congenital rubella syndrome, which causes learning disabilities and developmental delay; epicanthal folds are seen in Down syndrome (see Figure 2.6), and short palpebral fissures in FASD. Hypertelorism (wide-spaced eyes) occurs with Cri du Chat syndrome; both physical growth and mental retardation accompany this syndrome. Hypotelorism (abnormally close eyes) is seen in children with FASD (Tsai et al., 2012).

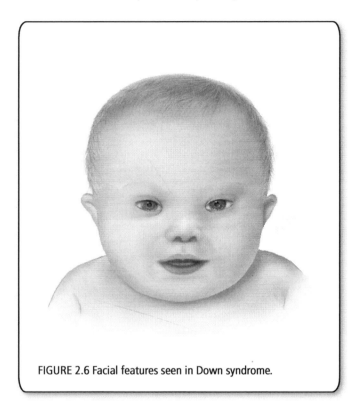

FIGURE 2.6 Facial features seen in Down syndrome.

Pinna abnormalities are associated with some chromosomal anomalies and syndromes. For example, small, dysplastic pinnae are seen in children with Down syndrome. Low-set ears are seen in Noonan syndrome, which causes learning problems and mild developmental delays (Tsai et al., 2012). "Railroad track" ears (outer part of the pinna is undeveloped, folded over, and parallel to the curve beneath it) are seen in FASD (Vaux & Chambers, 2012). Otitis media with effusion often leads to conductive hearing loss, which impedes language acquisition.

Neuromuscular System

The examiner notes whether primitive and postural reflexes are present and whether they are symmetrical or asymmetrical (see Chapters 11 and 22). Primitive reflexes should not persist past age 4 months; if they remain, cerebral palsy is suspected. The examiner also observes the child while sitting, standing, walking, jumping, skipping, hopping, or kicking. In infants and toddlers, specifically, the examiner determines if the child has met normal motor developmental milestones, while noting any motor abnormalities that may indicate cerebral palsy. These motor developmental milestones are achieved at different ages among children; the approximate ages at which these milestones occur are presented in Table 2.3. Other neuromuscular assessments include head control, overall posture and tone, the size and symmetry of

TABLE 2.3	Major Developmental Milestones: Infancy Through Adolescence				
AGE	**GROSS MOTOR**	**FINE MOTOR**	**COGNITIVE**	**LANGUAGE**	**SOCIAL**
0–2 weeks	Head lag; turns head slightly from prone position (2 weeks); moves all extremities; makes crawling movements when prone	Grasps	Primitive reflexes present (e.g., suck, grasp, rooting)	Alerts to sound; may blink, cry, or quiet; startles to loud sounds; undifferentiated crying; reacts to voices	Positive parent–infant interaction; fixes and follows faces; responds to parents' voice
2–4 weeks	Lifts head off bed; turns head from side to side in prone position (4 weeks)	Strong grasp	Primitive reflexes present (e.g., stereotyped repetition of sucking)	Alerts to sound; may blink, cry, quiet, or startle; undifferentiated crying; reacts to voices; cooing begins	Consoled by voices and being held; developing trust in caregiver and environment
2 months	Holds head up to 45 degrees; may have some head control when in upright position	Holds rattle briefly; visually pursues it but will not reach for it; grasp reflex fading	Primitive reflexes present (e.g., stereotyped repetition of sucking); anticipates feedings	Vocalizes (different from crying); enjoys making sounds; locates sounds by turning head; babbles	Social smile; stops crying when parent enters the room; recognizes familiar faces (3 months)
4 months	Rolls from abdomen to back (5 months); no head lag when prone; pushes body up on own hands; can bear weight on legs	Voluntarily grasps objects using raking motion (5 months); plays with hands; bats at objects; brings objects to mouth	Primitive reflexes disappear by age 4 months; attention shifted to objects and environment	Turns head toward sound; responds to own name; recognizes caregivers' voices; babbles, laughs, and squeals; vocalizes consonant sounds	Pulls clothes or blanket over face in play; enjoys social interaction; self-comforts; anticipates feeding; begins to sleep through night
6 months	Good head control established: no head lag when pulled to sit; rolls from back to abdomen; lifts chest and abdomen off flat surface; sits leaning forward (7 months); stands with support	Uses radial-palmar grasp; transfers objects from one hand to the other; mouths objects; eats finger foods; can secure cube on sight and transfer hand-to-hand; can pull to obtain an object	Object permanence beginning; visual search, not reaching; plays peek-a-boo; briefly looks for toy that disappears	Smiles, laughs, and squeals; begins imitating sounds; enjoys hearing own sounds; may begin to use "mama," "dada," and "baba" (nonspecific); lack of vocalization or stopping may indicate deafness	Becomes excited when familiar persons approach; may reach out hands and smile; stranger anxiety begins (peaks at 7–8 months); shows interest in toys; self-comforts by crying, playing, and thumb-sucking; may have a security blanket or favorite toy

(continued)

TABLE 2.3	Major Developmental Milestones: Infancy Through Adolescence (*continued*)				
AGE	**GROSS MOTOR**	**FINE MOTOR**	**COGNITIVE**	**LANGUAGE**	**SOCIAL**
9 months	Sits steadily without support (8–9 months); rolls over completely (8 months); crawls (9 months); pulls self to stand holding onto furniture; creeps with abdomen off floor (11 months)	Radial-digital grasp (grasp with thumb and finger); inferior pincer grasp (10 months); bangs objects; feeds self with fingers; starts to drink from cup; holds crayon with fist and briefly scribbles	Searches for object seen hidden; purposely drops object so it can be picked up (11 months)	Responds to simple verbal commands; stops activity when hears own name or "no-no"; says first words like "dada" and "mama" with meaning	Waves bye-bye; plays pat-a-cake and peek-a-boo; shows wants through gestures and pointing
12 months	Pulls to stand; cruises holding on to furniture or with hands held (10–11 months); walks independently with wide-based gait (11–15 months)	Fine pincer grasp; feeds self; uses a cup but rotates a spoon; attempts to build two-block tower; throws ball overhand; turns several pages at a time	Egocentric thinking; searches for object where it was last seen; interested in cause-and-effect play; associates one event with simultaneous event (transductive reasoning); short attention span; follows one-step commands; names some common objects	Says first word with meaning (12–18 months); imitates vocalizations; says 2–10 words besides "dada," "baba," and "mama"; uses pointing to "ask" for something; understands a new word each week	Becoming ritualistic; wants more autonomy; plays social games; imitates others; shows emotions; temper tantrums may begin
15 months	Walks well independently with wide-based gait; crawls upstairs; stoops; may run	Builds a tower of two cubes; scribbles vigorously; drinks from a cup; feeds self with fingers	Egocentric; will not share toys; sees only own perspective; interested in pictures	Says 3–10 words; understands simple commands; uses pointing or grunting to "ask" for something	Negative; uses "no" even when agreeing to the request; separation anxiety peaks age 15–18 months; imitates during play; imitates housework; plays ball; listens to a short story
18 months	Walks quickly; may run; can walk upstairs with one hand held; can kick ball	Uses spoon and cup; turns pages; builds a tower of three to four cubes	Points to pictures with common objects; knows two or three body parts; begins to distinguish *you* from *me*; follows simple directions; uses push and pull toys	Says 20 or more words; uses two-word phrases; 25% intelligibility; follows directions and understands requests; understands up to 50 words	Temper tantrums increasingly evident; security objects (blanket); transitional object; listens to a short story and looks at pictures; shows affection; can remove own clothing; may show readiness for toilet training (18–24 months)

TABLE 2.3	Major Developmental Milestones: Infancy Through Adolescence (*continued*)				
AGE	**GROSS MOTOR**	**FINE MOTOR**	**COGNITIVE**	**LANGUAGE**	**SOCIAL**
24 months	Gait steadier; goes up and down stairs alone with two feet on each step; kicks ball; jumps crudely	Dresses self in simple clothing; turns book pages one at a time; builds tower of six cubes; imitates vertical or circular strokes; turns single page	Transductive reasoning continues; egocentric; some sense of time (e.g., "Wait a minute"); says "now"; follows two-step commands; can name six body parts	Vocabulary of approximately 300 words; two- to three-word phrases	Ritualistic, has routines; negativistic; imitates adults; puts on own clothing; may name a friend; enjoys rhyming and singing
30 months	Jumps with both feet; can briefly balance on one foot; may pedal a tricycle	Builds tower of eight cubes; holds crayon with fingers rather than fist; imitates horizontal strokes; can copy a cross	Follows two-step commands; states first and last name; knows own sex; begins to ask questions	Uses two-word sentences; uses adjectives and adverbs; knows first and last name; uses pronouns *I, me, you* but may not use them correctly; names a color	Separates more easily from parent; may be toilet trained
3 years	Goes upstairs using alternate feet; rides tricycle; balances 5 seconds; may hop; broad jump	Feeds self completely; pours from bottle or pitcher; begins to use scissors; dresses self almost completely; buttons/ unbuttons easily reached buttons; copies a circle; builds a bridge of blocks; washes own hands	Wants to do things independently; asks "why" constantly; progresses from autonomy to initiative and continues throughout preschool-age; still egocentric but able to share toys; uses "mine"; plays rule games; active imagination; animistic (e.g., gives lifelike qualities to inanimate objects); many fears (e.g., fear of the dark, thunder, monsters); knows several colors	Approximately 900-word vocabulary; uses three- and four-word sentences; 75% intelligibility; uses pronouns and plurals; constantly talks; asks many questions; may stutter; speech understandable to parents	Less negativistic than toddler; separates more easily from parent; may be toilet trained; has beginning self-care skills; interested in gender role functions; development enhanced by regular interaction with same-age peers
4 years	Walks down stairs using alternate footing; rides tricycle or bicycle with training wheels; skips and hops on one foot; balances 3–5 seconds; can heel-to-toe walk; throws overhand; catches bounced ball	Copies a square; draws person with three parts; builds tower of 10 cubes; uses scissors; may tie shoes	Conscience begins to develop; becomes capable of classifying and organizing facts; counts but does not understand quantity; likes to pretend and dramatize; can relate a story sequentially; follows three-step commands; plays rule games; knows opposite; plays doctor or nurse; imaginary	Approximately 1,500-word vocabulary; defines words; uses past tense; tells "tall tales"	Separates from mother easily; selfish, impatient, independent, and boastful; sibling rivalry; very imaginative; imaginary friends common; engages in cooperative play; likes to talk about daily activities; tattles; sings songs;

(*continued*)

TABLE 2.3	Major Developmental Milestones: Infancy Through Adolescence (*continued*)				
AGE	**GROSS MOTOR**	**FINE MOTOR**	**COGNITIVE**	**LANGUAGE**	**SOCIAL**
			playmates are common; believes that thoughts cause events (magical thinking); becoming more able to see others' point of view; names four colors; asks "why" frequently		occasionally needs supervision with dress and hygiene
5 years	Throws and catches a ball well; skips and hops on alternate feet; jumps rope; balances 3–5 seconds; can heel-to-toe walk; may ride two-wheel bicycle	Handedness is established; ties shoelaces; uses scissors and pencil well; prints a few letters, numbers, or words (e.g., first name); can copy a diamond and triangle; can draw person with three to six parts	Still likes to play make-believe; knows name, address, and phone number and days of the week; names coins, four or more colors, and can count to 10; recognizes many letters; fewer fears; asks meanings of words, inquisitive; can tell a story	Approximately 2,100-word vocabulary; good articulation; asks meaning of words; correct use of *me*, *I*, past tense, and plurals	Gets along well with parents; identifies with parent of same sex; plays in group; dresses without help
6 years	Can walk a straight line; rides two-wheel bicycle; may be involved in team sports	Can copy a diamond; dexterity increasing; builds steps with blocks; likes to draw and color; refining ability to print letters	Thinks concretely; reasons inductively; likes to classify and organize facts; beginning pattern recognition; fears from preschool diminish; focuses on here and now; difficulty understanding the hypothetical; new fears may involve school failure, bullies, and so on; likes school; likes chess, checkers, and simple card games; recognizes all colors; shares; more cooperative; continuing to develop a conscience; sees others' point of view	Adult articulation patterns forming; learning to read	Performs bedtime activities without assistance; peers more important; prefers playing with same-sex friends
7–9 years	Increased physical capabilities; during school age, learns to ride a bicycle, roller blade, roller skate, ride a skateboard, run fast, jump, and swim	Writes cursive at 8 years old; increasing dexterity; learning to use keyboard	Curious about the meanings of words; likes to compete; strict adherence to rules; develops principle of conservation and reversibility; understands mass,	Increased ability to articulate and describe thoughts, experiences, and feelings; uses adult sentence structure	Likes school; focus is on sense of industry; strict adherence to rules; feels a sense of inferiority if goals not met

TABLE 2.3	Major Developmental Milestones: Infancy Through Adolescence (*continued*)				
AGE	**GROSS MOTOR**	**FINE MOTOR**	**COGNITIVE**	**LANGUAGE**	**SOCIAL**
			weight, quantities; hierarchies; beginning to learn about how to compute money		
10–12 years	Increased physical capabilities; may become progressively involved in team sports or other athletic activities	Continues to develop fine motor skills through writing, drawing, art, crafts, needle arts, video games, and complex puzzles	Reads for information and enjoyment; begins to be capable of abstraction and deductive reasoning at approximately age 11 years; judges acts by intent rather than consequences	Increased ability to articulate and describe thoughts, experiences, and feelings; uses adult sentence structure	Increasing importance of friends and peers; becoming more independent from parents; starts to feel peer pressure; becoming more aware of own body; household rules still important as part of socialization; chores and responsibilities help to increase child's sense of accomplishment
12–14 years	Rapid physical growth; increasing physical capabilities may not keep pace with each other; may cause clumsiness in teen, especially boys	Continues to refine fine motor skills	Increased ability for complex thought; beginning to formulate and test hypotheses; beginning to develop abstract reasoning	Fully expresses ideas, feelings, and thoughts through oral and written language	Less affectionate toward parents; prefers peers; concerned about body image; mood swings; stronger sense of right and wrong
15–16 years	Increased physical capabilities; may become involved in team sports or other athletic activities	Continues to refine fine motor skills	Abstract reasoning continuing to develop but not fully developed; increasing egocentrism; thinks "it cannot happen to me"	Fully expresses ideas, feelings, and thoughts through oral and written language	Conflicts about independence; parent–child relationships are at low point; peers extremely important; interested in sexual relationships
17–21 years	Increased physical capabilities; increased strength; gross motor abilities have reached adult levels	Fine motor skills have reached adult levels	Thinks abstractly; becomes idealistic; approaches problem solving in systematic manner	Fully expresses ideas, feelings, and thoughts through oral and written language	Importance of peer group is decreased; interpersonal relationships are deeper; planning life goals; refining self-concept

muscles, hypertonia or hypotonia; and the presence of tremors and extremity range of motion. Any polydactyly or syndactyly is noted, as this is often a syndromic feature that could involve developmental delay or mental retardation. Examination of the spinal column determines the presence of cysts, sacral dimples, tufts of hair, or other signs of neural tube defects. (See Chapters 21 and 22 for a discussion of pediatric musculoskeletal and neurologic assessment, respectively.)

Hearing and Vision

Age-appropriate hearing and vision screening are conducted, depending on the child's age and medical history (see Chapter 9). Abnormalities in hearing or vision can cause developmental delays, warranting relevant referrals. (See Chapters 14 and 15 for discussions of children at high risk for hearing or visual impairments, respectively.)

Developmental Examination

The AAP (2010) recommends that all infants and young children receive developmental screening and that this screening be incorporated into each well-child examination within the context of a medical home. Based on the results of the screening, a full developmental evaluation may be necessary. It is vitally important for the pediatric health care provider to conduct periodic screening to detect any developmental disorders that can impede school readiness and lead to behavior and emotional disorders (AAP, 2010). *Bright Futures Guidelines for Health Supervision of Infants, Children and Adolescents* (Hagan, Shaw, & Duncan, 2008) provides an ideal template to guide this screening.

Developmental Surveillance, Screening, and Evaluation

The AAP (2010) distinguishes the terms "developmental surveillance," "developmental screening," and "developmental evaluation" as having separate and distinct meanings. *Developmental surveillance* occurs within the context of the health maintenance visit. This involves the ongoing process of recognizing the child's developmental strengths and weaknesses and social risk factors (see the section on Social History, earlier), as well as readily identifying children at risk for developmental delays. This includes eliciting parental concerns, recording the developmental history, ensuring that observations made on the child are accurate, identifying risk and protective factors, and accurately documenting all findings (AAP, 2010). The AAP recommends that developmental surveillance takes place at all well-child visits and that the timing of these visits accord with the periodicity schedule published by the AAP (2011). (See Chapter 9 for a discussion of the periodicity schedule and relevant assessments during pediatric health supervision visits.)

Developmental screening entails the use of a standardized screening checklist to determine whether the child is achieving expected developmental milestones. This screening can be conducted by the provider or obtained from a report by the parent. The AAP recommendations (2010) suggest developmental screening at the 9-, 18-, and 30-month visits for all infants and toddlers. If the developmental screening reveals that the child is lagging in achievement of age-appropriate developmental milestones, a more thorough developmental evaluation is done.

Developmental evaluation is an in-depth assessment that is performed when a child is suspected of having a developmental delay or disorder; it involves the use of a formal pediatric developmental evaluation tool. Examples of some of these tools are listed in Table 2.4. The pediatric health care provider chooses a tool based on its appropriateness for the population of children with which he or she works, the age of the child, the purpose of the developmental assessment (e.g., concerns about language, behavior, or motor abilities), appropriate psychometric properties, and the provider's familiarity with the tool. To increase the reliability of the findings, it is important that the health care provider be familiar with a particular assessment tool and comfortable in its administration and interpretation.

Most developmental screening and evaluation tools have not been standardized to include premature infants and children born prematurely; for this reason, the provider must be vigilant in assessing growth and development in these populations. When assessing children who were born prematurely, the provider should use the infant's adjusted age as compared with the chronological age until the child is 2 years old and ensure the use of a corrected gestational age up to at least 30 to 36 months for children born earlier than 32 weeks gestation (Vanderbilt et al., 2007).

Preparation

When conducting the developmental examination, the evaluator must keep in mind that the younger the child, the more challenging it is to obtain accurate findings. This may be because of stranger anxiety or a young child's normally short attention span, high-energy level, and easy distractibility. Some children are very shy and may be reluctant to cooperate in an unfamiliar setting. Depending on the individual child's temperament and medical and social histories, these factors may be more or less pronounced.

The setting must be informal and relaxed and, to the extent possible, the evaluation must be done by quiet observation while the child is playing, moving around the room, interacting with the caregiver, or using his or her hands to play, scribble, or draw.

TABLE 2.4	Selected Developmental Assessment Tools			
TOOL	**DOMAINS ASSESSED**	**AGE RANGE**	**NOTES**	**SCORING**
Parent Report				
Ages and Stages Questionnaires (ASQ) http://www.agesandstages .com	Communication, gross motor, fine motor, problem solving, and personal–social	4 months– 5 years	Parent answers simple questions about child's development; takes 10–15 minutes for parent to complete; 2–3 minutes for health care provider; written at 4th–6th grade literacy level; available in other languages besides English; excellent psychometric properties (Prelock, Hutchins, & Glascoe, 2008)	"Yes" answers = 10 points "Sometimes" = 5 points "Not yet" = 0; scores are tabulated and evaluated for each domain
Battelle Developmental Inventory (BDI) http://www .riversidepublishing.com/ products/bdi2/index.html	Motor, communication, personal–social, adaptive, and cognitive	Birth– 7 years, 11 months	Functions as a screening or diagnostic assessment tool; screening test takes 10–30 minutes; complete BDI takes 1–2 hours	Instrument contains 96 items that assess five domains listed at left; raw scores are converted to standard scores of possible values of 0 (normal) 1 (borderline) 1.5 (developmental problem) 2 (serious developmental delay)
Child Development Inventories http://www .pearsonassessments.com	Eight subscales are assessed: social, self-help, gross motor, fine motor, expressive language, language comprehension, letters, numbers; also assesses parental concerns about child's health, growth, hearing, vision, development, and behavior; also useful in determining school readiness	Birth– 6 years	Excellent psychometric properties	Parent report questionnaire consists of 270 items that address the eight subscales; parent answers question with "yes" or "no"; 30 questions address parental concerns, each scale is scored by tallying the number of "yes" answers; scoring 1.5 below the mean is borderline; scoring more than 2 standard deviations below the mean is delayed
Parent's Evaluation of Developmental Status (PEDS) http://www.pedstest.com	Gross and fine motor; self-help; expressive and receptive language; social–emotional development; reading and math (older children)	Birth– 8 years	10 questions answered by parent; available in English, Vietnamese, Somali, Arabic, and Spanish; questions written at 5th grade reading level; excellent psychometric properties (Prelock et al., 2008)	Screening test does not give quantitative results but guide provider via algorithm in identifying areas of concern, when to reassure, refer, screen further, or advise/teach parents

(continued)

TABLE 2.4	Selected Developmental Assessment Tools (*continued*)			
TOOL	**DOMAINS ASSESSED**	**AGE RANGE**	**NOTES**	**SCORING**
Provider Administered				
Bayley Infant Neurodevelopmental Screen (BINS) http://www.pearsonclinical .com/education/products/ 100000163/bayley-infant-neurodevelopmental-screener-bins-bins.html	Neurologic processes (tone; reflexes); neurodevelopmental skills (movement and symmetry); cognitive and language skills (object permanence, imitation, language)	3–24 months	Screens infants at risk for neurodevelopmental delay (e.g., premature or asphyxiated infants); takes 5–10 minutes to administer; available in English and Spanish; moderate sensitivity and specificity	Uses 10–13 provider-elicited items to make assessments; cutoff scores provide three levels of risk classification: low, medium, and high
Brigance Screens http://www .curriculumassociates.com/ products/BRIGANCEoverview .aspx	Fine and gross motor skills; receptive and expressive language; cognitive; academic (quantitative, reading); daily living/self-help; social–emotional	Birth–6 years	Specificity and sensitivity 70%–82%; available in English and Spanish; takes 10–20 minutes to administer	Identifies children who have learning delays, disabilities, or giftedness
Denver II http://denverii.com/denverii	Gross and fine motor/adaptive; personal/social; language	Birth–6 years	Modest sensitivity and specificity, especially in children younger than 3 years; should be used for screening purposes, only	Four domains are divided into 125 items, arranged in chronological order in accordance with the age; ages are listed at the top of the page; through the corresponding age, a vertical line is drawn from top to bottom of the tool; each intersecting item is scored as fail (F); pass (P); refused (R); or no opportunity (NO); if the child fails to pass an item that 25%–90% of children his or her age can perform, the score is "caution"; a "delay" is failure to pass an item to the left of the line; a "normal" exam is one with no delays and a maximum of one caution
Early Language and Milestone (ELM) Scale-2 http://www.proedinc.com/ customer/productView .aspx?ID=784	Auditory receptive, auditory expressive, and visual language function	Birth–36 months	Takes 1–10 minutes to administer, depending on child's age and evaluation technique; available in English, only	Scores are presented as percentiles, standard scores, and age equivalents

TABLE 2.4	Selected Developmental Assessment Tools (*continued*)			
TOOL	**DOMAINS ASSESSED**	**AGE RANGE**	**NOTES**	**SCORING**
Peabody Developmental Motor Scales (PDMS-2) http://www.pearsonclinical.com/therapy/ products/100000249/ peabody-developmental-motor-scales-second-edition-pdms-2.html	Gross and fine motor development	Birth–60 months	Takes approximately 45–60 minutes to administer	Scores are presented as percentiles, standard scores. and age equivalents
Parent Report and Provider Administered				
Capute Scales: Cognitive Adaptive Test/Clinical Linguistic and Auditory Milestone Scale (CAT-CLAMS) http://www .brookespublishing .com/resource-center/ screening-and-assessment/ the-capute-scales	Cognitive, visual, and motor, problem-solving, and language skills; purpose is to screen for autism	3–36 months	Takes 15–20 minutes; some data are obtained from parent report, some assessments are made by provider; high specificity and sensitivity (> 90%); available in English, Spanish, and Russian	A developmental quotient (DQ) is calculated based on child's chronological age and developmental tasks completed; a DQ less than 70 indicates delay and requires referral
Behavioral Scales				
Carey Temperament Scales http://www.pearsonclinical .com/psychology/ products/100000625/carey-temperament-scales-cts .html? pid=015-8040-015&Community=CA_Ed_ AI_OT	Assesses child's temperament and behavioral style	1 month–12 years	Parent report; takes 4–20 minutes to complete, depending on method of scoring; available in English, only; normed on White middle-class children, only	Questionnaires create a temperament profile based on temperament characteristics listed in Table 2.2
Child Behavior Checklist http://www.aseba.org	Assesses social competence and behavior	6–18 years	Parent report or self-administered, depending on child's age; excellent sensitivity and specificity	118 items are scored on a 3-point scale ranging from "not true" to "often true"; there are an additional 20 social competency items; raw scores are interpreted to create behavioral profiles
Eyberg Child Behavior Inventory http://www4.parinc .com/Products/Product .aspx?ProductID=ECBI	Measures conduct problems	2–16 years	Takes 5 minutes to administer, 5 minutes to score; test results provide data for identifying disruptive behavior in children and adolescents	Likert scale questions about disruptive behaviors at home and in school; data can be obtained from parent or teacher
Pediatric Symptom Checklist http://psc.partners.org	Assesses for psychosocial problems	3–18 years	Available in multiple languages; high sensitivity; moderate specificity (Prelock et al., 2008)	Parent completes a 35-item questionnaire; answers are "never," "sometimes," or "often present"; items are summed with a possible total score of 70; for

(*continued*)

TABLE 2.4	Selected Developmental Assessment Tools (*continued*)				
TOOL	**DOMAINS ASSESSED**	**AGE RANGE**	**NOTES**	**SCORING**	
				children ages 3–5 the cutoff score is ≥ 24; for age 6–18, the cutoff score is ≥ 28; exceeding these scores requires mental health referral	
Autism Screening Tools					
Checklist for Autism in Toddlers (CHAT) http://www.helpautismnow.com/CHAT_Checklist_English.pdf	Autism screening tool	18–24 months	Poor sensitivity but excellent specificity; available in English, only	Takes 5 minutes to complete; parent interview (9 items) and child/provider interview (5 items); scored as pass/fail; identifies children at risk for autism	
M-CHAT http://www.schwartzpediatrics.com/images/website322/mchat.pdf	Autism screening tool	16–48 months	Tool available in English, Spanish, Chinese, Japanese, and Turkish	Parent questionnaire (23 items); items are scored as pass/fail	
Pervasive Developmental Disorders Screening Test-II, Primary Care Screener (PDDST-II, PCS) http://www.pearsonclinical.co.uk/Psychology/ChildMentalHealth/ChildAutisticSpectrumDisorders/PervasiveDevelopmentalDisordersScreeningTest-II(PDDST-II)/PervasiveDevelopmentalDisordersScreeningTest-II(PDDST-II).aspx	Autism screening tool	18–48 months	Takes 10–15 minutes to complete, 5 minutes to score; available in English, only; moderate to high sensitivity and specificity	Parent questionnaire (22 items)	
Social Communication Questionnaire (SCQ) http://www.wpspublish.com/store/p/2954/social-communication-questionnaire-scq	Autism screening tool	4+ years	Takes 5–10 minutes to complete; available in English and Spanish; moderate sensitivity and specificity	Parent questionnaire (40 items)	

Sources: American Academy of Pediatrics (2006); Cole (2008).

Procedure for Developmental Surveillance

Using the AAP (2010) policy recommendations as a guide, the provider begins the developmental surveillance by following these steps.

Elicit Parental Concerns • The parents are asked directly about their concerns regarding the child's development, such as: "Do you have any concerns about John's speech, behavior, or ability to play like other children his age?"

Obtain the Developmental History • The provider asks the caregiver to provide an update regarding what new skills the child has acquired since the last visit. An age-specific checklist assists the parent in providing this

information. Using a formal, rather than informal, developmental milestone checklist to complete this assessment is preferred. Informal checklists lack reliability, validity, accuracy, and specific scoring criteria (Glascoe & Robertshaw, 2007). The Ages and Stages Questionnaire (ASQ) and Parents' Evaluation of Developmental Status (PEDS) are examples of formal developmental screening tools that guide the provider regarding when to reassure or teach the parent, additionally screen the child, or refer the child for intervention services (see Table 2.4) (Glascoe, 2007).

Perform Accurate, Objective Assessments • In addition to the physical examination described earlier, the provider must also evaluate neurodevelopment and cognitive and psychosocial development, including gross and fine motor milestones, cognitive growth and development, receptive and expressive language skills, and social–emotional development. Table 2.3 provides an overview of developmental milestones from birth through adolescence. Attention should be paid to developmental milestones that are acquired out of sequence (developmental deviation), or in which one area of development is significantly ahead or behind another area (developmental dissociation); both conditions may indicate cerebral palsy or autism (AAP, 2010).

Identify Risk and Protective Factors • Once the assessments are complete, the provider identifies risk and protective factors for developmental delays and disorders. Risk factors are listed in Box 2.2; protective factors are discussed under assessment of the Social Environment, earlier. In addition, the AAP recommends screening for autism spectrum disorders at the 18-month and 24-month well-child visits (Gupta, Hyman, & Johnson, 2007). This can be done by using one of the autism screening tools listed in Table 2.4 (Cole, 2008).

Document and Process Findings • All portions of the developmental assessment must be accurately documented, with appropriate referrals made as warranted.

LABORATORY AND IMAGING ASSESSMENT

Depending on the child's medical and family history, physical examination, and developmental evaluation, certain imaging or laboratory studies may be needed to complete the assessment. These studies are listed in Table 2.5.

SUMMARY

Developmental surveillance is included as part of every well-child visit. When concerns, risk factors, or red flags are identified through developmental surveillance, a standardized developmental screening tool is used to pinpoint areas of concern. All children at the 9-, 18-, and 30-month visits should also receive developmental screening, even if they are low risk. When developmental screening reveals developmental delays or disorders, prompt referrals must be made to early intervention services to maximize the child's developmental potential and minimize long-term sequelae.

TABLE 2.5	Diagnostic and Laboratory Studies
DIAGNOSTIC STUDY	**INDICATION**
Chromosome analysis	To diagnose chromosomal disorders
Complete blood count	To diagnose anemia (causes fatigue, which may result in delayed milestone acquisition); anemia also occurs concurrently with lead poisoning
Electroencephalogram	To diagnose seizure disorders; also indicated with microcephaly, regression of developmental milestones, and mental retardation
Fragile X karyotype	Known or suspected mental retardation; family history of fragile X syndrome; dysmorphic features (Cole, 2008)
Human immunodeficiency virus (HIV)	Obtained when child shows signs of failure to thrive and shows other signs of HIV/AIDS
Lead levels	To diagnose lead poisoning, which causes developmental delay and cognitive dysfunction
Metabolic testing	Indicated when newborn screen is inconclusive, or child has known or suspected mental retardation, dysmorphic features, or history of lethargy, cyclic vomiting, and early seizures (Cole, 2008)
Muscle biopsy	To diagnose degenerative neuromuscular disorders (e.g., Duchenne muscular dystrophy)
Newborn screening	To diagnose a variety of metabolic disorders that may cause developmental delay or mental retardation
Neuroimaging (computed tomography scan; magnetic resonance imaging; ultrasound)	To diagnose atypical findings on neurologic exam; asymmetric motor exam; microcephaly; traumatic brain injury, space-occupying lesions, spasticity, and ataxia
Wood's lamp evaluation of skin	To screen for hypopigmented macules of tuberous sclerosis (Cole, 2008)

DOCUMENTATION OF FINDINGS

Sample Write-Up: Developmentally Normal Child

Subjective Data

A 12-month-old girl (only child in family) presents for routine well-child care accompanied by her mother. Birth history is unremarkable. Mother denies having any concerns about daughter's developmental abilities, hearing, or vision. Per mother's report, child can pull to stand and cruise, is not yet walking independently, feeds self, says "mama" and "dada," is very attached to security blanket, responds to name, and waves "bye-bye."

Objective Data

Gross motor: per mother's report; child refused to get off mother's lap
Fine motor: picked up Cheerios with fine pincer grasp; drinking from sippy cup
Cognitive: looked for toy that was hidden
Language: per mother's report; did not verbalize during visit
Social–emotional: child and mother interacting responsively; mother comforts child when fretful during visit
Hearing: imitating mother while talking to provider; put toy away when asked
Vision: looked for dropped toy
Assessment: developmentally normal 12-month-old child

Sample Write-Up: Child With Developmental Concerns

Subjective Data

An 18-month-old girl presents to the clinic for the first time, accompanied by her mother. Child is here for a "checkup"; mother denies having any concerns. Birth history is unremarkable per mother. Mother smoked during pregnancy, smokes in the home; mother denies prenatal drug use except for "occasional" marijuana use. Mother is a poor historian; is not certain about answers to questions on developmental screen. Child says "mama" and "baba," only. Mother has not yet introduced the cup. Mother says she is very eager to toilet train but child has no interest. Mother spanks child when she stools in training pants. Mother also states that child has been having temper tantrums, for which mother spanks child.

Objective Data

Weight: 50th percentile
Length: 50th percentile
Head circumference: 50th percentile
General: well-developed female, alert, smiling, and playful; holding security blanket
Skin: no lesions noted
HEENT: tympanic membranes red, dull, and nonmobile bilaterally; landmarks not visible bilaterally; dentition poor, with multiple brown to black spots on maxillary and mandibular incisors; no dysmorphic facial features noted; symmetrical light reflex; red reflex noted bilaterally; extraocular muscles (EOMs) intact bilaterally
Neurologic: normal tone
Gross motor: walks well around exam room; kicked small ball; pushed doll stroller well
Fine motor: did not use spoon well; spilled when drinking from cup; built tower of two cubes; briefly scribbles with crayon
Cognitive: cannot point to any named body part; named three animals in a picture book
Language: says "mama," "baba"; can name one body part
Social–emotional: immediately walks over to provider and puts arms out to be held; mother grunts in response to child pointing to poster on wall
Hearing: turns to name being called
Vision: vision normal per Allen test; named three of seven cards on third attempt
Assessment: bilateral otitis media with effusion; developmental delay; speech and language delay; parental knowledge deficit; abuse and neglect

References

Agency for Toxic Substances and Disease Registry. (2014). Toxic substances portal: Mercury. Retrieved April 18, 2014, from http://www.atsdr.cdc.gov/toxfaqs/TF.asp?id=113&tid=24#bookmark05

American Academy of Pediatrics. (2001). Committee on public education: Children, adolescents, and television. *Pediatrics, 107*(2), 423–426.

American Academy of Pediatrics. (2010). Reaffirmed policy statement: Committee on children with disabilities: Identifying infants and young children with developmental disorders in the medical home: An algorithm for developmental surveillance and screening. *Pediatrics, 125*(2), e444–e445.

American Academy of Pediatrics. (2011). Committee on Practice and Ambulatory Medicine and Bright Futures Steering Committee recommendations for preventive pediatric health care, statement of reaffirmation. *Pediatrics, 127*(3), e857.

American Psychiatric Association. (2013). *Diagnostic and statistical manual of mental disorders* (5th ed.). Arlington, VA: Author.

American Speech-Language-Hearing Association. (2014). *Learning two languages.* Retrieved April 17, 2014, from http://www.asha.org/public/speech/development/BilingualChildren/#problems

Aylward, G. P. (2005). Neurodevelopmental outcomes of infants born prematurely. *Journal of Developmental and Behavioral Pediatrics, 26*(6), 427–440.

Bada, H. S., Das, A., Bauer, C. R., Shankaran, S., Lester, B., LaGasse, L., . . . Higgins R. (2007). Impact of prenatal cocaine exposure on child behavior problems through school age. *Pediatrics, 119*(2), e348–e359.

Badawy, M. K., & Conners, G. P. (2013). *Pediatric lead toxicity.* Retrieved April 18, 2014, from http://emedicine.medscape.com/article/1009587-overview

Bernard, T. J., Knupp, K., Yang, M. L., Kedia, S., Levisohn, P., & Moe, P. G. (2012). Neurologic and muscular disorders. In W. W. Hay, M. J. Levin, R. R. Deterding, M. J. Abzub, & J. M. Sondheimer (Eds.), *Current pediatric diagnosis and treatment* (21st ed., pp. 740–829). New York, NY: McGraw-Hill.

Bhuvaneswar, C. G., Chang, G., Epstein, L., & Stern, T. (2008). Cocaine and opioid use during pregnancy: Prevalence and management. *Primary Care Companion Journal of Clinical Psychiatry, 10*(1), 59–65.

Blackman, J. A. (2007). NICU micropreemies: How do they fare? *Contemporary Pediatrics, 24*(2), 64–73.

Centers for Disease Control and Prevention. (2014). *Smoking and tobacco use: Secondhand smoke facts.* Retrieved April 18, 2014, from http://www.cdc.gov/-tobacco/factsheets/secondhand_smoke_factsheet.htm

Chang, L., Smith, L. M., LoPresti, C., Yonekura, M. L., Kuo, J., Walot, I., & Ernst T. (2004). Smaller subcortical volumes and cognitive deficits in children with prenatal methamphetamine exposure. *Psychiatry Research, 132*(2), 95–106.

Chen, H. (2014). *Down syndrome.* Retrieved April 17, 2014, from http://emedicine.medscape.com/article/943216-overview

Chess, T., & Thomas, A. (1995). *Temperament in clinical practice.* New York, NY: Guilford Press.

Christakis, D. A., & Zimmerman, F. J. (2007). Children and television: A primer for pediatricians. *Contemporary Pediatrics, 24*(3), 31–42.

Cole, L. L. (2008). Autism in school-age children. *Advance for Nurse Practitioners, 16*(3), 38–47.

Erikson, E. (1950). *Childhood and society.* New York, NY: W.W. Norton & Company.

Freud, S. (1938). *An outline of psychoanalysis.* London, UK: Hogarth Press.

Furdon, S. A., & Clark, D. A. (2003). Scalp hair characteristics in the newborn infant: Focus on the physical. *Advances in Neonatal Care, 3*(6), 286–296.

Garbarino, J. (1995). *Raising children in a socially toxic environment.* San Francisco, CA: Jossey-Bass.

Gilligan, C. (1982). *In a different voice.* Cambridge, MA: Harvard University Press.

Glascoe, F. P. (2007). *Parents' evaluations of developmental status: A method for detecting and addressing developmental and behavioral problems in children.* Nashville, TN: Ellsworth & Vandermeer Press Ltd.

Glascoe, F. P., & Robertshaw, N. S. (2007). New AAP policy on detecting and addressing developmental and behavioral problems. *Journal of Pediatric Health Care, 21*(6), 407–412.

Graff, J. C., Murphy, L., Ekvall, S., & Gagnon, M. (2006). In-home toxic chemical exposures and children with intellectual and developmental disabilities. *Pediatric Nursing, 32*(6), 596–603.

Gupta, V. B., Hyman, S. L., & Johnson, C. P. (2007). Identifying children with autism early? *Pediatrics, 119*(10), 152–153.

Hagan, J., Shaw, J., & Duncan, P. (Eds.). (2008). *Bright futures guidelines for health supervision of infants, children and adolescents* (3rd ed.). Elk Grove Village, IL: American Academy of Pediatrics.

Hammen, C., Shih, J. H., & Brennan, P. A. (2004). Intergenerational transmission of depression: Test of an interpersonal stress model in a community sample. *Journal of Consulting and Clinical Psychology, 72*(3), 511–522.

Hornor, G. (2005). Domestic violence and children. *Journal of Pediatric Health Care, 19*(4), 206–212.

Johnson, P. L., & Flake, E. M. (2007). Maternal depression and child outcomes. *Pediatric Annals, 36*(4), 196–202.

Jones, M. W., Morgan, E., Shelton, J. E., & Thorgood, C. (2007). Cerebral palsy: Introduction and diagnosis (Part I). *Journal of Pediatric Health Care, 21*(3), 146–152.

Kelly, Y., Sacker, A., Schoon, I., & Nazroo, J. (2006). Ethnic differences in achievement of developmental milestones by 9 months of age: The Millennium Cohort Study. *Developmental Medicine and Child Neurology, 48,* 825–830.

Kohlberg, L. (1969). Stage and sequence: The cognitive–development approach to socialization. In D. Gastin (Ed.), *Handbook of socialization: Theory and research.* New York, NY: Rand McNally.

Kyle, T. (2008). *Essentials of pediatric nursing.* Philadelphia, PA: Lippincott.

Lambie, G. W., & Sias, S. M. (2005). Children of alcoholics: Implications for professional school counseling. *Professional School Counseling, 8*(3), 266–273.

Laor, N., Wolmer, L., & Cohen, D. J. (2001). Mothers' functioning and children's symptoms 5 years after a SCUD missile attack. *American Journal of Psychiatry, 158*(7), 1020–1026.

Leveno, K. J., Cunningham, F., Alexander, J., Bloom, S., Casey, B., Dashe, J., et al. (2007). Tetralogy, medications and substance abuse. In K. J. Leveno, F. Cunningham, J. Alexander, S. Bloom, B. Casey, J. Dashe, et al. (Eds.) *Williams manual of obstetrics: Pregnancy complications* (22nd ed., pp. 44–52). New York, NY: McGraw-Hill.

Loman, M. M., Wiik, K. L., Frenn, K. A., Pollack, S. D., & Gunnar, M. R. (2009). Postinstitutionalized children's development: Growth, cognitive, and language outcomes. *Journal of Developmental and Behavioral Pediatrics, 30*(5), 426–434.

Lutenbacher, M., Cohen, A., & Conner, N. M. (2004). Breaking the cycle of family violence: Understanding the perceptions of battered women. *Journal of Pediatric Health Care, 18*(5), 236–242.

Magnuson, K. A., Ruhm, C., & Waldfogel, J. (2007). The persistence of preschool effects: Do subsequent classroom experiences matter? *Early Childhood Research Quarterly, 22*(1), 18–38.

Milteer, R. M., Ginsburg, K. R.; the Council on Communications and Media Committee on Psychosocial Aspects of Child and Family Health. (2012). The importance of play in promoting healthy child development and maintaining strong parent-child bond: Focus on children in poverty. *Pediatrics, 129*(1), e204–e213.

Minnes, S., Lang, A., & Singer, L. (2011). Prenatal tobacco, marijuana, stimulant and opiate exposure: Outcomes and practice implications. *Addiction Science and Clinical Practice* (6), 1, 57–70.

Neumann, C. G., Gewa, C., & Bwibo, N. O. (2004). Child nutrition in developing countries. *Pediatric Annals, 33*(10), 658–674.

Oberlander, T. F., Reebye, P., Misri, S., Papsdorf, M., Kim, J., & Grunau, R. E. (2007). Externalizing and attentional behaviors in children of depressed mothers treated with a selective serotonin reuptake inhibitor antidepressant during pregnancy. *Archives of Pediatric and Adolescent Medicine, 161,* 22–29.

Olson, D. A. (2013). *Mercury toxicity.* Retrieved April 18, 2014, from http://emedicine.medscape.com/article/1175560-overview

Oxford, M., & Spieker, S. (2006). Preschool language development among children of adolescent mothers. *Journal of Applied Developmental Psychology, 27*(2), 165–182.

Piaget, J. (1969). *The theory of stages in cognitive development.* New York, NY: McGraw-Hill.

Pillitteri, A. (2003). *Maternal & child health nursing: care of the childbearing & childrearing family* (4th ed.). Philadelphia, PA: Lippincott

Prelock, P. A., Hutchins, T., & Glascoe, F. P. (2008). *Speech–language impairment: How to identify the most common and least diagnosed disability in childhood.* Retrieved April 17, 2014, from http://www.ncbi.nlm.nih.gov/pmc/articles/PMC2491683

Qi, C. H., Kaiser, A. P., Milan, S., & Hancock, T. (2006). Language performance of low-income African American and European American preschool children on the PPVT-III. *Language, Speech, and Hearing in Schools, 37,* 5–16.

Ruben, R. J. (2005). Language and the plastic brain. In T. R. Van De Water & H. Staeker (Ed.), *Otolaryngology: Basic science and clinical review.* New York, NY: Thieme.

Rumack, B. H., & Dart, R. C. (2012). Poisoning. In W. W. Hay, M. J. Levin, R. R. Deterding, M. J. Abzub, & J. M. Sondheimer (Eds.), *Current pediatric diagnosis and treatment* (21st ed., pp. 339– 366). New York, NY: McGraw-Hill.

Sanchez, S. E., Alva, A. V., Chang, G. D., Qiu, C., Yanez, D., Gelaye, B., & Williams, M. A. (2013). Risk of spontaneous preterm birth in relation to maternal exposure to intimate partner violence during pregnancy in Peru. *Maternal and Child Health Journal, 17*(3), 485–492.

Schechter, D. S., & Davis, B. E. (2007). Parenting in times of crisis. *Pediatric Annals, 36*(4), 216–222.

Schiller, C., & Allen. P. J. (2005). Follow-up of infants prenatally exposed to cocaine. *Pediatric Nursing, 31*(5), 427–436.

Schulze, P. A., Harwood, R. L., Schoelmerich, A., & Leyendecker, B. (2002). The cultural structuring of parenting and universal developmental tasks. *Parenting, 2*(2), 151–178.

Schwartz, J., & Schonwald, A. (2014). ADHD in the elementary school years: Dissecting a developmental dilemma. *Consultant for Pediatricians, 13*(1), 25–29.

Slade, E. P., & Wissow, L. S. (2007). The influence of child maltreatment on adolescents' academic performance. *Economics of Education Review, 26*(5), 604–614.

Starr, H. L. (2007). The impact of culture on ADHD. *Contemporary Pediatrics, 24*(12), 38–50.

Staton, D. M., & Harding, M. H. (2004). Protecting child health worldwide. *Pediatric Annals, 33*(10), 647–655.

To, T., Guttmann, A., Dick, P. T., Rosenfield, J. D., Parkin, P. C., Tassoudji, M., ... Harris JK. (2004). Risk markers for poor developmental attainment in young children. *Archives of Pediatric and Adolescent Medicine, 158*(7), 643–649.

Trasande, L., Schechter, C., Haynes, K. A., & Landrigan, P. J. (2006). Mental retardation and prenatal methylmercury toxicity. *American Journal of Industrial Medicine, 49*(3), 153–158.

Tsai, A. C., Manchester, D. K., & Elias, E. R. (2012). Genetics and dysmorphology. In W. W. Hay, M. J. Levin, R. R. Deterding, M. J. Abzub, & J. M. Sondheimer (Eds.), *Current pediatric diagnosis and treatment* (21st ed., pp. 1088–1122). New York, NY: McGraw-Hill.

U.S. Department of Health and Human Services. (2009). *Parental substance use and the child welfare system.* Retrieved April 18, 2014, from https://www.childwelfare.gov/pubs/factsheets/parentalsubabuse.cfm#2

Vanderbilt, D., Wang, C. J., & Parker, S. (2007). The do's in preemie neurodevelopment. *Contemporary Pediatrics, 24*(9), 84–92.

Vaux, K. K., & Chambers, C. (2012). *Fetal alcohol syndrome.* Retrieved April 17, 2014, from http://emedicine.medscape.com/article/974016-overview

Wachs, T. D., Black, M. M., & Engle, P. L. (2009). Maternal depression: A global threat to children's health, development, and behavior and to human rights. *Child Development Perspectives, 3*(1), 51–59.

Ware, A. L., Glass, L., Crocker, N., Deweese, B. N., Coles, C. D., Kable, J. A., ... & the Collaborative Initiative on Fetal Alcohol Spectrum Disorders. (2014). Effects of prenatal alcohol exposure and attention-deficit/hyperactivity disorder on adaptive functioning. *Alcoholism: Clinical and Experimental Research, 38*(5), 1439–1447. doi: 10.1111/acer.12376

Wilson, G. N. (2008). Children with the same congenital malformation pattern. *Consultant for Pediatricians, 7*(4), 155–158.

Yolton, K., Dietrich, K., Auinger, P. Lanphear, B. P., & Hornung, R. (2005). Exposure to environmental tobacco smoke and cognitive abilities among U.S. children and adolescents. *Environmental Health Perspectives, 113*(1), 98–103.

Zeanah, C. H., & Smyke, A. T. (2008). Attachment disorders in family and social context. *Infant Mental Health Journal, 29*(3), 219–233.

Additional Resources

Bright Futures

http://www.brightfutures.org
A set of health supervision guidelines that include child developmental assessment for each well-child visit according to the AAP health supervision guidelines.

Facts for Families

http://www.aacap.org/cs/root/facts_for_families/facts_for_families
A resource for children and adolescents who have behavioral or emotional difficulties; written materials are available in several languages.

Healthy Steps

http://www.healthysteps.org
Healthy Steps for Young Children (Healthy Steps) is a national program that focuses on major behavioral and developmental issues in the first 3 years of life, with a heavy emphasis on involving the whole family.

NCAST

http://www.ncast.org
Provides resources and materials for developmental assessment and help in identifying special needs children.

Reach Out and Read

http://www.reachoutandread.org
A program that seeks to encourage early literacy within the primary care setting by encouraging parents to read to their child each day and by offering free books to children at each primary care visit.

Touchpoints

http://www.touchpoints.org
A program based on the work of Dr. T. Berry Brazelton that is centered on building a provider–parent partnership in learning about the child's growth and development and collaborating when challenges arise.

Zero to Three

http://www.zerotothree.org
A multidisciplinary organization that provides developmental screening, evaluation, and diagnosis for children in the first 3 years of life; also provides information for parents and professionals on general child development, early language and literacy, social and emotional development, temperament, and behavior.

Communicating With Children and Families

PROCESS OF COMMUNICATION

Communication is the exchange of thoughts, ideas, feelings, messages, or information through various means (Ball, Bindler, & Cowen, 2012), including speech but also nonverbal means such as behavior, body language, or eye contact. Developing quality communication skills is essential to success in working as a health care provider because positive communication helps to build trusting relationships with pediatric patients and their families. Understanding the communication process and what leads to good and bad communication will help a health care provider develop positive communication skills.

Communication is a two-way process: it involves sending and receiving messages. The sender transmits information to the receiver with a specific goal and meaning, using verbal and nonverbal communication strategically so that the receiver interprets the message as intended by the sender. The way in which the receiver interprets the message is largely influenced by the verbal and nonverbal delivery used by the sender, as well as the receiver's past experiences, culture, and emotional state (Levetown & American Academy of Pediatrics [AAP] Committee on Bioethics, 2011).

The communication process in the health care setting is complicated because of heightened physical and emotional strain during illness. This process is even more complicated in the pediatric setting because it requires an understanding of the communication techniques needed for each developmental stage (e.g., infant, preschooler, school-aged child, adolescent) when communicating with the child. Communication with the parents and family is also necessary. (Developmental considerations are covered later in this chapter.) The communication process used by the health care provider to work with the pediatric population requires more time and patience than does a typical health care encounter. Taking additional time and using age-specific and family-oriented communication techniques facilitates a smooth communication process in the pediatric setting. It is important to include the child in the communication process of a health care encounter, and care should be taken to ensure that this communication is developmentally appropriate.

UNDERSTANDING FAMILY DYNAMICS AND PARENT–CHILD RELATIONSHIPS

Family dynamics is an important component of the communication process. In pediatrics, important topics to assess include a child's birth order, sibling rivalry, and family composition, as well as the marital status of the parents, stepparents, or foster parents. It is important to consider which communication efforts will be most effective with the particular child and family, based on the family dynamics. Recommendations for improved family communication are based on this assessment. (See Chapter 4 for a discussion of family dynamics.)

Privacy and Confidentiality

Privacy and confidentiality are key components of communication in health care, as many personal topics are discussed. Children and adolescents often feel vulnerable during a time of illness because their privacy is invaded by physical examinations and interviews that necessitate divulging private information. For example, preschoolers are very modest and become embarrassed easily when asked to disrobe. Adolescents often feel uncomfortable disclosing information about sexual activity or risk-taking behaviors. Privacy can be assured by securing an environment that is free from distractions and interruptions. An interview conducted in an environment where conversations can be overheard may be less likely to yield truthful information from a patient or his or her family. With adolescents, it is important to allow time during the interview process without the parent present to encourage communication on sensitive topics such as sexual behavior, drug and alcohol use, smoking, risk-taking behaviors, and nutritional habits (Ball et al., 2012). It is equally important, however, to interview the parents alone so that they are free to discuss their concerns about their child. Ensuring privacy maximizes truthful information obtained from both children and parents during a health care encounter.

Confidentiality in health care means that any information obtained from the patient is not shared with others, with some exceptions. The Health Insurance Portability and Accountability Act (HIPAA) is a federal regulation that includes specific guidelines aimed at protecting the confidentiality of patient health information (Ball et al., 2012). Each health care facility has its own policies for handling confidential records and information. Additionally, most facilities have a HIPAA consent form that patients must sign, outlining the policies of the institution, clarifying patients' rights, and specifying what is considered confidential and what can be shared (e.g., information sent to insurance companies for billing, information sent to other health care providers). Being aware of the facility's policies and upholding these policies are essential to protecting the patients' privacy and confidentiality.

Most patients feel comfortable providing information if they are aware of the facility's policies on confidentiality. Explaining these rights at the beginning of a health care encounter facilitates the communication process. The limitations of confidentiality, insofar as information is shared with the medical team and recorded in the patient's record, should be explained at the beginning of every health care encounter.

Other limitations to confidentiality should also be explained before the start of an encounter, including certain topics such as abuse and suicide. Most states have mandatory reporting laws for patients who verbalize suicidal ideation, the intent to harm others, or suspected or documented abuse (Ball et al., 2012). Health care personnel must be knowledgeable about the laws of the state and the policies of the facility in which they are practicing.

There are slightly different regulations for confidentiality in the pediatric patient population as compared with the adult population. Adult patients generally are the main contact and decision maker in a health care encounter and often indicate with whom their information can be shared. In pediatrics, when children are younger than 18 years (or 21, in some states), the parents or guardians are the main decision makers regarding where and with whom information about the child is obtained and shared, although laws vary from state to state (Ball et al., 2012). For instance, if a pediatric patient's medication is changed, providers are obligated to discuss this with the parents or guardians, not the child alone.

The few circumstances in which the parents' ultimate authority can be overridden include when a child disagrees with the treatment, when the parent decides to withhold lifesaving treatment of a child, when there is a conflict of interest such as in the case of an abusive parent, or when a parent is incapacitated and unable to make decisions (Ball et al., 2012). In these cases, a compromise is sought with the provider, parent, and child; sometimes an ethics committee helps with the decision making. Instances in which a minor may be the primary decision maker include when the minor is the parent of a child patient or when an emancipated minor (i.e., a minor who has been deemed by the court to be self-supporting) makes his or her own decisions (Ball et al., 2012). Most states have laws that allow providers to keep information about sexual behavior, contraception, drug and alcohol use, and sexually transmitted disease confidential for their minor-aged patients, even from parents (Ball et al., 2012).

Establishing Effective Communication Between Children, Caregivers, and Providers

Having a thorough understanding of the complexities of communication is essential for establishing effective communication with pediatric patients and their families. Knowledge of the communication process and communication techniques facilitates the development of communication patterns that are consistent and positive. In pediatrics, being aware of developmental approaches to communicating with the child, having an understanding of family dynamics, and tailoring communication to the specific needs of the child and family are the keys to successful communication.

A study conducted on effective and ineffective communication strategies in the primary care setting focused on physician–patient encounters (Beck, Daughtridge, & Sloane, 2002); however, the principles established in this study are easily extrapolated to encounters between all health care providers and patients. A summary of the findings follows:

- Effective communication techniques include assuming a friendly demeanor, paying attention during the interview, giving positive feedback to patients, and encouraging the patient to talk. Other behaviors that encourage the patient's openness included clarifying and summarizing what the patient said, assuming an age-appropriate level at which to talk to patients, and addressing patients' emotions, problems, and medical reasons for seeking care.
- Behaviors that fall into the category of negative communication include focusing on medical questions, appearing rushed, allowing interruptions, assuming an all-knowing attitude, not making eye contact, and turning away from the patient when recording the history.

Techniques that facilitate effective communication, as well as blocks to communication, are explored in detail in this chapter.

Communication Techniques

Communication techniques are used when obtaining a health history in an outpatient visit or initial admission to the hospital, during follow-up visits, and when relaying important testing and diagnostic information. Each health care encounter requires a combination of communication techniques that will result in effective and positive communication with patients and their families, especially in pediatric encounters.

Building Rapport

Building rapport requires time and the implementation of interventions that help to build a trusting relationship. Rapport with pediatric patients and their families is the base on which good communication is built. It involves being nonjudgmental and demonstrating respectful and honest communication. This is not automatic when first meeting a child and family; a consistent demonstration of honest communication, understanding, and respect forms the foundation for all future communication. Allowing time for questions, answering questions honestly and correctly, respecting patients' beliefs and ideas, and preparing the environment so that it is conducive to positive communication contribute to building rapport with the child and the family.

Establishing rapport with children helps to ease their anxiety about the visit and makes them feel that they are an important part of the process. Recommendations with which to build rapport with children follow (Ball et al., 2012; Rider, 2011):

- Health care providers should place themselves at eye level with the child.
- Young children may be asked about their favorite cartoon character or favorite toy.
- A calm voice and an unhurried manner should always be used with children.
- Adolescents should be included in the conversation about their care.
- Providers should avoid interrupting patients or family members.
- Providers should listen more than they talk.

When working in pediatrics, all of the provider's interactions and conversations should be based on a consideration of the child's feelings and developmental ability so that the child understands what is being communicated (Levetown & AAP Committee on Bioethics, 2011).

Listening

One of the most important components of the communication process is listening. The most effective listening is called *active listening*. Active listening necessitates that the provider observes all aspects, verbal and nonverbal, of the sender's message (Hockenberry, 2011).

It requires that full attention be paid to the person speaking. Distractions should be eliminated and nonverbal cues, such as eye contact, should be used to relay to the sender that the provider is actively listening. Making judgments about what is being said is a natural response, but the health care provider needs to maintain objectivity as much as possible. This allows the provider to obtain the most factual information available and then complete a nonbiased review of the data during the assessment and planning phases. There are several types of listening that are actually blocks to communication. These include attentive listening, selective listening, pretend listening, and ignoring (Covey, 2013; Rider, 2011).

Attentive listening occurs when receivers focus on what the person is saying but actively compare the sender's experience with their own (Rider, 2011). In a health care encounter, comparing personal experience naturally leads to bias and should be avoided.

Selective listening occurs when the receiver hears only what interests him or her; this can cause providers to miss important details. Some providers use selective listening because their time is limited. However, details that seemed unnecessary during the encounter may, once the communication has ended, be found to contribute relevant input to the final review and plan of care.

Pretend listening occurs when providers merely give the appearance of listening. This type of listening is obviously totally ineffective and will not provide enough necessary information with which to work when formulating a plan for the patient.

Ignoring occurs when providers make no attempt to listen and do not even give the appearance of listening. A provider might ignore patients when time is limited, for example, when communicating important test results. Or, providers may relay the information with an adequate explanation but ignore patients' questions. This may leave patients uncertain or confused about what was said. Another example of ignoring occurs when providers finish a progress note while patients are talking. Providers cannot listen adequately and record notes at the same time.

Specific recommendations for listening to children are discussed by Howard (2002) and are summarized here:

- Providers should listen with empathy and good eye contact, responding to the children's attempts at communicating.
- Providers should give children their full attention and not try to accomplish other tasks while the children are communicating.
- Providers should ask the children about any emotions that are being assessed during their encounter.
- Providers should rephrase and summarize what the children have said so the children can confirm that the providers understand what they are trying to communicate.

Empathy

Empathy is the ability to understand and identify with another person's feelings and is often referred to as being able to "put yourself into another person's shoes" (Hockenberry, 2011). Using empathy in pediatrics requires stepping into the shoes of the child and having an understanding of the stages of pediatric development.

Empathizing does not mean that it is necessary to agree with the patient; rather, it means the patient's feelings should not be dismissed. Through words and actions, health care providers must show that they are considering what their patients or their patients' parents are thinking and feeling (Rider, 2011). Empathizing requires that health care providers do not give advice and that they do not share their own thoughts and feelings. Patients and their families can detect if the provider is being empathic through the verbal and nonverbal cues given during the communication. The techniques discussed in this section, such as listening, making eye contact, nodding, and interjecting phrases such as "I understand," rephrasing what was said to clarify, and not judging the patient, demonstrate empathy.

It is important to distinguish empathy from sympathy. Sympathy is sharing similar feelings with another, but empathy is being able to understand another's feelings (Hockenberry, 2011). Empathy is a therapeutic technique whereas sympathy is not. Sympathy might involve the health care provider sharing personal experiences, which decreases the time patients have to express their thoughts. It also does not allow the provider to remain objective and crosses therapeutic boundaries.

Encouraging Conversation

Encouraging parents and children to participate in the health care encounter has been shown to expedite the visit and leave parents feeling satisfied (Hagan, Shaw, & Duncan, 2008). Parents who feel rushed, ignored, or left out of the visit generally feel frustrated, accomplishing less than if open dialogue was encouraged (Hagan et al., 2008). Techniques that help promote communication with children and their parents include using open-ended questions, avoiding questions that elicit a yes-or-no response, including the parent or child in problem solving, using encouraging statements to boost the self-esteem of both parents and children, and being nonjudgmental (Hagan et al., 2008). Table 3.1 illustrates examples of communication that encourage open conversation with parents and children.

When communicating with children, it is important for providers to speak to them at eye level and use language that is understandable for their developmental level, giving them complete attention (Stein, 2006). This demonstrates a willingness to communicate and encourages children to talk. Children should be allowed to complete their thoughts and should not be interrupted (Starr & DeGolier, 2013). Interjecting into the child's attempts to communicate may hinder a full assessment if the child chooses to not complete what he or she expected to relate before the interruption.

Use of open-ended questions is an effective technique to encourage children to talk. Children often feel intimidated when talking to a provider and are often unsure of how to respond to questions (Rider, 2011). Open-ended questions allow for spontaneous answers to questions, and often parents or children answer questions more completely (Rider, 2011). Young children can be offered options, for example: "Some children feel much better after the breathing treatment, but others still feel like they have a hard time catching their breath. Can you tell me how you feel after a breathing treatment?"

TABLE 3.1	Techniques to Foster Provider–Patient Communication
TECHNIQUE	**EXAMPLE**
Open-ended questions	"What brings you and Julia here today?" "So when Brendon does that, how does that make you feel?" "What concerns or questions do you have?"
Encouraging	"Go ahead, continue." "Tell me more." "Is there anything else you want to tell me?"
Including the parent or child in problem solving	"What have you done at home already to alleviate or address the problem?" (This can be any problem that the child is presenting.) "What do you think might help?" "How do you feel about the plan I am proposing for this problem, and do you have any other ideas about what might work?"
Boosting parent and child self-esteem	"That is really great. I think that is a very good idea." "Everything checks out well, I think you are taking really good care of yourself; keep up the good work." "You are raising a great kid; keep up the good work." "I am glad you have these questions, I can tell that you are really concerned and are doing a great job parenting."
Being nonjudgmental	"I see you have a tattoo and a tongue piercing; what was it like to get those?"

Close-ended questions require a focused, simple response. For example, "Has Ella been vomiting?" requires a yes-or-no answer. These questions are appropriate when specific information is being sought for the health history.

Verbal and Nonverbal Communication

Verbal communication refers to the actual words, either spoken or written, that people use to communicate. The words chosen to express thoughts and feelings are powerful and must be chosen carefully. A person's perception of reality can be altered through the sender's spoken word (Hockenberry, 2011). Being direct and honest is always the best approach.

Two examples of verbal communication that may block communication include avoidance language and distancing language. *Avoidance language* occurs when the person speaking uses word choices that avoid describing what they are trying to communicate, such as when a person is avoiding strong emotions and feelings about a subject (Hockenberry, 2011). Examples of this include calling "cancer" a "tumor" or using "passed on" instead of "dead." In a health care encounter, the provider must use very precise language, avoiding ambiguous word choices. The provider can restate what patients say, using precise language, if the children or family members are avoiding direct language to express themselves. Using direct and precise language allows the child and family to discuss the topic about which they have anxiety and promotes therapeutic conversation and effective coping patterns.

Distancing language entails the use of impersonal language such as "it" or "others" to discuss situations pertaining to oneself or one's child (Hockenberry, 2011). Allowing children or family to use impersonal terms may support their denial and prevent them from dealing with pertinent issues. This may, in turn, lead to ineffectual coping. It may also prevent parents from seeking care for a problem if they never deal with a problem directly.

Nonverbal communication is the sending and receiving of wordless messages. Examples include body language, facial expressions, eye contact, clothing, hairstyles, and tone of voice and other qualities of speech. (Stein, 2006). Some studies show that facial expressions of anger, disgust, fear, joy, sadness, and surprise are universal, whereas other nonverbal communication is culture-specific (Ekman & Friesan, 1975; Polhemus, 1978). Cultural variances in communication are addressed in Chapter 5.

Nonverbal communication can be more powerful than verbal communication and usually reveals any emotions felt about the topic being discussed. It has been estimated that nonverbal communication makes up approximately 65% of the substance of a communication encounter (Hall, 1966). When there is a discrepancy between a person's verbal and nonverbal communication,

the receiver usually interprets the nonverbal cue as what the sender really means to communicate over the words that are used (Montague, Chen, Xu, Chenwing, & Barrett, 2013). It is important to note, however, that the meaning of the nonverbal communication is easily misinterpreted.

Understanding the different types of nonverbal communication and assessing one's own nonverbal communication can promote positive nonverbal interactions with patients through self-awareness. Colleagues, too, can provide feedback about nonverbal communication when objectively evaluating a health care encounter.

Assessment of a patient's nonverbal cues and knowledge of when to clarify the nonverbal behavior improve with a thorough understanding of the different nonverbal behaviors and their possible meanings. Examples of how nonverbal communication can add positive or negative connotations to the message are discussed here.

Paralanguage • Paralanguage refers to *vocal elements* that are used to communicate, such as pitch, rate, inflection, volume, quality, enunciation, flatness, and fullness (Eisenberg, 2012). Paralanguage can add enthusiasm or sadness to a conversation; for example, when a specific tone of voice helps to communicate either good news or bad. Paralanguage is an important nonverbal communication cue, particularly when communicating by telephone, as communication cues are limited to the verbal message and paralanguage. There is an increased risk of misinterpretation of messages with these limited cues.

Physical Environment • The environment in which a communication takes place can have an impact on the message. Health care personnel do not always have control over the environment in which they encounter patients, but it is important to be aware of the different environmental factors that affect a health care encounter so that the environment can be adapted to promote positive results. Environmental factors to consider include temperature, size of the room for the number of people involved, seating arrangements, lighting, distractions, noise, and the color of the room (see Chapter 6) (Purvis, 2009).

Distractions and interruptions can cause patients to feel frustrated when revealing sensitive information; too many interruptions may close off communication completely. The health care provider should inform staff to take messages from callers so that every effort can be made to focus on the child and parent. In pediatrics, it might also be difficult for parents to focus on giving information if the child wants their attention. A play area with age-appropriate activities to occupy children's attention while parents are being interviewed helps to alleviate this problem, allowing parents to focus on the questions being asked and communicate more effectively. When relaying important news to patients and families, a conference room may be a more appropriate venue than a patient's shared hospital room. Hospital conference rooms usually maximize environmental aspects that promote communication. In pediatric areas, there are usually activities to keep children occupied.

Physical Appearance • Physical appearance includes clothing, hairstyle, makeup, and hygiene. Physical appearance is the first thing people notice when forming an opinion about a person in a face-to-face encounter. In health care, encounters with patients and families often take place during a vulnerable time. Maintaining a professional appearance relays confidence and trust; patients often feel more comfortable with providers whose outward presentation conveys professionalism. Hospitals and health care facilities often have guidelines on hairstyles, jewelry, and attire to ensure a professional appearance. Being well-groomed and maintaining a clean and pressed uniform or lab coat help convey professionalism.

In a pediatric setting, providers can wear child-friendly lab coats or character pins and use colorful stethoscope covers while still maintaining a professional appearance. These nonverbal cues can have a positive impact on interactions with children who "read" these cues as nonthreatening and friendly.

The physical appearance of patients often gives examiners clues about their health status. Ill patients may present in sleepwear, disheveled and unshowered, which usually indicates that the patient is too ill to dress or shower. This could also indicate a psychiatric illness, especially if the dress or fashion trend is inappropriate (e.g., wearing a woolen cap in the summer). These cues require further questioning before making a judgment.

Body Language • There are two forms of body language: voluntary and involuntary. *Voluntary body language* refers to intentional gestures and movements. The sender is fully aware of the movements and the message they convey to the receiver. *Involuntary body language* refers to movements that are usually provoked by emotion such as facial expressions. Both voluntary and involuntary body language can have positive and negative interpretations, depending on the nonverbal and verbal communication they accompany. Body language that has a positive effect on provider–patient communication includes head nodding, leaning forward, direct body orientation, uncrossed arms and legs, and talking to the patient at eye level (Figure 3.1) (Beck et al., 2002). Cultural differences in body language are addressed in Chapter 5. Examples of body language are discussed here.

■ **Arms or legs crossed or open:** Arms that are crossed may indicate that a person is physically uncomfortable (e.g., too cold) and may be accompanied by shivering. It may indicate a standoff position, meaning that the person is closed to communication. Often closed arms accompany a serious communication encounter and may indicate that a person is in deep thought, which can be either positive or negative. When people

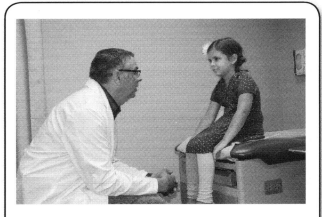

FIGURE 3.1 Positive provider body language includes leaning forward and speaking to the child at eye level.

generally keep their arms open, it may indicate expansiveness and a readiness to communicate. Open arms can also indicate a friendly, relaxed demeanor (Figure 3.2).

■ **Eye contact:** Eye contact can convey friendliness or aggression (Rider, 2011). Making eye contact initially signals a readiness to communicate. Eye contact can also relay honesty and warmth. If eye contact is avoided, it may be interpreted as dishonesty, disinterest, or rudeness, but it could also indicate that the person is not feeling well. Prolonged eye contact may be perceived by the patient as hostile or aggressive, although it may also indicate that the provider is deeply interested in what the parent or child is saying (Hockenberry, 2011). Prolonged eye contact can be frightening to a child younger than 2 years of age if the child is unfamiliar with the provider (Stein, 2006). Cultural variations in the meaning of eye contact are discussed in Chapter 5.

■ **Head tilt:** Tilting the head toward the child or parent indicates interest in what they are saying (Goman, 2008).

■ **Repetitive movement of extremities:** Repetitive movement of the extremities indicates nervousness or stress.

■ **Sitting behind a desk or standing:** Sitting behind a desk may convey distance and may send a message to the child and family that the health care provider is not approachable (Figure 3.3). Standing implies that the provider is in a hurry and may not be fully involved (Stein, 2006).

■ **Gestures:** Gestures can have positive or negative meaning. Head nodding can be affirming to the pediatric patient or parent while they are speaking and relaying their concerns to the provider. Pointing while speaking is considered an aggressive gesture.

Body language is the primary form of communication in children younger than 5 years of age (Hockenberry, 2011). Infants learn to point as an

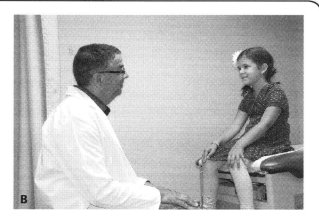

FIGURE 3.2 **A.** Crossed arms may indicate a standoff position. **B.** Open arms, a head tilt, and smile indicate a relaxed, friendly demeanor on the part of the provider.

early form of communication before they are verbal. It is thought that infants are born with inherent body language skills on which they build by watching others (Hockenberry, 2011). Parentese, which is infant-directed speech, includes exaggerated body language such as paralanguage and facial expressions. Infants mimic these sounds and expressions between the ages of 6 and 15 months; by age 3 years, they acquire body language that is similar to that of the adults with whom they have the most contact. A summary of some of the positive effects of body language for infants and young children follows (Faull & Oliver, 2010).

- Body language helps to decrease tension and frustration when the gestures elicit a response.
- Body language leads to deeper communication and improved bonding, which makes the child feel good.
- Body language increases brain connections and contributes to early verbalization.

When communicating with children, it is important for providers to remember that tone of voice and

FIGURE 3.3 Sitting behind a desk may convey distance and may send a message to the child and family that the health care provider is not approachable.

posture should reflect openness to communication. Also, the child's body language should be assessed closely. Providers must maintain nonjudgmental body language when the child is communicating. If emotions or judgment are evident in tone of voice, body movements, and facial expressions, the child may be uncomfortable communicating further (Howard, 2002). Facial expressions should convey sincerity and genuine concern. Facial expressions that convey boredom, disdain, judgment, or distraction destroy patient trust and rapport (Figure 3.4).

Communicating Through an Interpreter

A large population of non-English-speaking people inhabit the United States (Lehna, 2005). Federal and state laws mandate that health care organizations that receive federal funding furnish interpreters for non-English-speaking patients (Lehna, 2005). However, numerous ethical and legal problems can arise if the interpreter is not specially trained in interpreting health care issues.

A number of interpreter services are available. It is important to be aware of these services and the pros and cons of each. It is optimal if providers and other health care personnel speak the language of their patients so that they can speak directly to them during the health care encounter. However, providers should be tested for language and cultural competence to ensure accuracy of interpretation.

Professional interpreters, who are available at the health care facility, usually have been tested for their language skills and trained in the ethics of interpreting health information. They have been trained in ethnic customs and in providing culturally competent interpretations (Lehna, 2005). However, it can be costly to have a variety of interpreters, representing all of the different languages, on site.

Telephone services can provide access to interpreters who speak a wide range of languages. However,

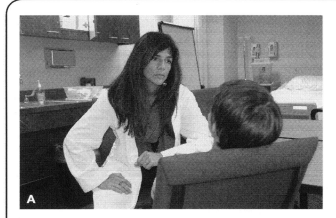 

FIGURE 3.4 Facial expressions can convey nonverbal messages. **A.** The provider's facial expression does not convey openness to communication. **B.** The provider's facial expression conveys warmth and a willingness to listen.

this option can be very costly. It is also potentially impersonal and can be time-consuming. Additionally, because body language is a significant part of communication, when a telephone interpreter is used the information conveyed through nonverbal cues is lost. Finally, one should keep in mind that such services are not regulated; therefore, it is important to be sure the interpreter services test their interpreters for language and cultural competence.

Health care facilities that are mandated by law to have interpreter services often have multilingual providers and use a combination of professional interpreters available on site and telephone interpreter services for patients who speak languages for which they do not have interpreters, or for emergency situations when the on-site interpreters are not available. Many facilities use outside interpreter services and schedule the interpreter before the visit, which offsets the high cost of keeping an interpreter on site at all times.

Use of uncertified bilingual support staff such as secretaries or medical assistants (Lehna, 2005) can be problematic because they are not certified, and there is no way to ensure that they are competent in the required language or culture, which may put the provider and patient at risk for receiving incorrect information. Also, staff may not be available on demand.

Using "chance" interpreters such as friends or family poses many ethical dilemmas and can lead to violations of confidentiality (Lehna, 2005). Use of friends or family also increases the risk that information will be left out. These individuals may not feel comfortable revealing news about a terminal diagnosis or other bad news to a patient who is their friend or relative. The responsibility of having to communicate this information can also cause acute distress to the family member or friend. In addition, they may not understand medical language and thus may interpret the communication incorrectly.

Scenarios that pose ethical dilemmas specifically related to pediatrics include using a child who speaks English to interpret for the non-English-speaking parent. The child may have to interpret information related to his or her own illness or health care. The child often is not able to communicate accurate information because of age and the inability to understand the medical information being discussed. The child may become distressed when given the responsibility to tell his or her parents health-related bad news. Privacy and confidentiality may be breached and, when communicating sensitive subjects, the child or parent may not be truthful or comfortable revealing information if the child interprets.

If a patient speaks limited English, the provider or other health care personnel may try to communicate with the patient directly. Obtaining true informed consent is impossible in this scenario. Also, information that is collected is unlikely to be accurate or complete, and there is no way to ensure that the patient has understood any of the communication, including teaching and follow-up instructions (Lehna, 2005). This is unethical communication, which puts the patient at risk.

Recommendations for facilitating communication with the non-English-speaking child include the following (Levetown & AAP Committee on Bioethics, 2011):

- Providers should assess the patient's language skills and the need for an interpreter; if possible, the same interpreter should be used for each encounter.
- Providers should use a picture board that depicts basic needs, such as bathroom, food, and pain with pictures and words in both English and the child's primary language.
- Providers should learn common words in the child's language to foster trust-building with the child.
- Providers should use a normal tone of voice and pitch when communicating with a child.

Communicating Through Play

Play is considered one of the most important forms of communication to use with children (Hockenberry, 2011). Important assessments can be made through play, and it also provides a safe and familiar environment in which the child can communicate. Using multisensory techniques when talking with children helps both to decrease the time needed to communicate the detailed and complex information that is often exchanged in a health care visit and to ease anxiety about the encounter (Blackstone & Pressman, 2012).

In infant play, mostly nonverbal stimuli such as paralanguage, color, and sound are used to capture the infant's attention. With older infants, making eye contact, playing peek-a-boo, and then moving to touch with pat-a-cake builds trust and allows a smooth transition in which to start the exam (Hockenberry, 2011). Puppets can be used with small children to demonstrate what the provider plans to do in the exam. Dolls can be used to show children how to use an inhaler or demonstrate other procedures that can help to ease a child's anxiety. Allowing older children to touch the provider's instruments (e.g., stethoscope) or have them listen to the provider's heart can make children more comfortable by building familiarity with these objects (Figure 3.5). Periodically using these techniques throughout the examination helps to keep children engaged.

Other play techniques that can be used include storytelling, drawing, and sentence completion. Play techniques are used when trying to obtain information from the child. Children often use stories about imaginary friends or pets to express what they are afraid to reveal (Howard, 2002). If a child spontaneously tells a story during an encounter, providers should pay close attention, document it, and consider what the child's story might mean in the assessment. The child can also be asked to tell a story about a subject that needs to be explored.

Children's drawings can also contain messages that the child is afraid to share or may reveal other information about the child (Rollins, 2005). When interviewing a parent, the provider should make art supplies available to the child so that he or she can draw; the child should then be asked about the drawing. When trying to elicit information about a specific topic, the provider can ask the child to draw something on a related topic; for example, children can be asked to draw their family or their friends at school. Many pediatric hospitals have art therapists on staff who work with children. They specialize in this area and can add important insights to the child's assessment.

Conversational games can also be used to obtain information. In "sentence completion," the provider begins by telling the child that they are going to play a game in which the provider starts a sentence and the child finishes it. It is important to start with statements that will help to supply needed information. For example, the provider might begin with a sentence such as, "The things I like most about my family are (…)," which requires the child to fill in the blank. In "pros and cons," children are asked to relate five things that they like or dislike about certain subjects, such as the hospital, their family, their illness, or being in the fifth grade.

Blocks to Communication

Barriers to communication in pediatrics include the use of medical terminology, provider gender, the child's health status, and the attitude of the health care provider (Ball et al., 2012). Use of medical terminology instead of familiar terms can confuse the child and the parents, who may be embarrassed to ask for clarification (Rider, 2011). Gender may play a role in blocking communication if the child attaches the nurturing role or a negative experience to one or the other gender. A child may then react negatively to a provider with

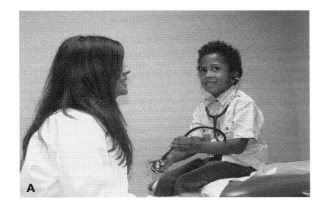
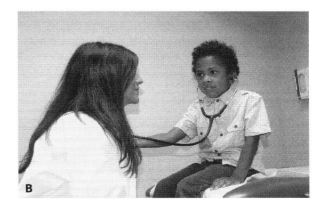

FIGURE 3.5 Allowing children to **A.** touch the stethoscope or **B.** listen to the provider's heart can help make children more comfortable with the physical exam.

the same gender as a person with whom the child had a negative past experience, despite the provider's best efforts at age-appropriate communication (Kolucki & Lemish, 2011). During a child's illness, parents often experience a high level of stress, which may lead to ineffective communication. Parents may be unable to communicate or process even the most basic instructions during a child's illness (Levetown & AAP Committee on Bioethics, 2011). Finally, health care providers who appear apathetic and uncaring instead of caring and empathic can block communication. Patients and families can detect this through verbal and nonverbal cues and will not be open to communication if they feel the provider does not care or is not interested. Other blocks to communication are listed in Table 3.2.

AGE AND DEVELOPMENTAL CONSIDERATIONS

Effective communication with children requires an understanding of age and developmental differences. Communicating with the child so that he or she can relate to the topic allows for a comprehensive and positive visit and limits the time needed in the visit. Developmental considerations and recommendations for communication with each age group are summarized in Table 3.3 and discussed in detail next.

Infants

Infants, newborn to 12 months, communicate with and respond to nonverbal communication. Infants coo, grunt, and cry as well as use facial expressions and body movements to communicate.

Techniques to communicate with infants include smiling, picking them up, cuddling, and using a soft soothing voice, especially when trying to calm an agitated infant (Hockenberry, 2011). Using a high-pitched voice with exaggerated facial expressions and wide eyes can hold an infant's attention during the interview or exam (Faull & Oliver, 2010). When interacting with infants, the provider should hold them close and keep close eye contact while talking or singing to them. Infants like looking at adult faces, and this technique can also keep them engaged during the health care encounter (Faull & Oliver, 2010).

Older infants are generally focused on themselves and their parents and experience anxiety when around strangers. Ensuring infants are in direct sight of their parents or allowing the parent to hold the child during a health care encounter alleviates some of the anxiety and fear the child may be feeling (Hockenberry, 2011).

Toddlers

Toddlers communicate using one- and two-word sentences. They also use nonverbal language, such as pointing or pushing the provider's hand away when being examined, as well as positive and negative facial expressions and body movements (Hockenberry, 2011).

Toddlers are in the age group that is least likely to respond to friendly efforts by providers to interact with them. This is the most challenging age group to approach (Hagan et al., 2008). Toddlers may cry loudly during an examination as a way of expressing fear or displeasure at being examined. They respond to communication directed at them, since they see things only from their own point of view. Effective communication with toddlers includes prompt responses to their efforts to communicate. When toddlers speak in one- or two-word sentences, providers should build on these words to form a complete sentence to acknowledge that they understand and to help them build their vocabulary (Hockenberry, 2011). Toddlers should be given concrete, concise directions and only one direction at a time. Providers must always warn toddlers before making a transition in the health care encounter, especially while examining the child.

Preschoolers

Preschool children can speak in full sentences. Providers can engage them in conversation about favorite colors and toys (Hagan et al., 2008). Preschoolers are concrete thinkers with many fears. Magical thinking plays a major role in how they interpret what is said to them. They interpret words literally; it is important to communicate effectively with this age group and avoid abstractions so these children are not unduly stressed. For example, a phrase such as "coughing your head off"

TABLE 3.2	Blocks to Effective Communication in the Health Care Setting
COMMUNICATION BLOCK	**EXAMPLE**
Providing false reassurance	"I would not worry. I am sure the lymph node biopsy will be normal."
Giving unwanted advice	"If it were my daughter, I would want her to take the medication."
Inappropriate use of authority	"I really think you should to try my suggestion because I am the health care provider, and I know what is best."
Asking leading questions	"You don't drink beer, do you?"
Asking questions that imply blame	"Why did you wait so long to bring her to the clinic?"

TABLE 3.3	**Developmental Considerations When Communicating With Children**
Young infants	Use a quiet, calm voice when interacting initially with infant.
	Smile, use exaggerated facial expressions and an animated high-pitched tone to hold infant's attention and create a positive mood.
	Pick infants up and cuddle them.
	Use a soothing voice to calm infants.
	Hold, rock, and pat infants to comfort them.
	Note a parent's interpretation of infant's nonverbal communication.
Older infants	Establish rapport with parents as well as infants; infants can sense tension and will cry.
	Parents should be in infants' direct line of vision to minimize stranger anxiety, which peaks at 7–8 months.
	Allow parents to hold their children during visit and during exam.
	Make sure older infants have security objects nearby for comfort.
Toddlers	Toddlers like to have their parents or a security object nearby during physical examination.
	Respond promptly to attempts to communicate with you.
	Toddlers are the most difficult age group with which to communicate, so be creative by using dolls, toys, or puppets.
	If possible, allow toddlers to touch medical equipment before beginning physical examination to decrease fear and anxiety.
	Build on their one- or two-word sentences to form a complete sentence so they know you understand them, and help them build their vocabulary.
	Give concise directions and only one direction at a time.
Preschoolers	Preschoolers may also like to have a parent or a security object nearby during physical examination.
	Choose words carefully as preschoolers have many fears.
	Include preschoolers in the encounter by speaking to them and asking them basic questions.
	Answer questions with simple, short, concrete explanations.
	Preschoolers may also want to handle equipment to lessen fear.
School-aged children	Include school-aged children in the health care encounter by asking them basic questions and speaking directly to them.
	Ask about friends, school, and sports.
	Explain procedures and medications in terms school-aged children can understand, and allow them to ask questions.
	Use open-ended questions to encourage them to talk.
Adolescents	Offer choices, when possible.
	Ask about favorite music group, friends, and interests.
	Listen more than you talk.
	Use nonjudgmental listening and responses.
	Do not use popular jargon when speaking with adolescents.
	Allow private time during health care visit, without parent present.
	Explain parts of physical examination and reasons for asking sensitive questions.
	Encourage questions.

could be taken literally, causing the child to be afraid to cough (Hockenberry, 2011). Reassuring phrases such as "you are not sick now" may comfort preschoolers as they begin to understand concrete topics about their health (Hagan et al., 2008). Simple sentences should be used with words that preschoolers will understand. Table 3.4 gives examples of nonthreatening words or phrases to use when working with preschool-aged children.

School-Aged Children

Health information can be retrieved and dispensed more easily with the school-aged child (Hagan et al., 2008). Direct conversation with children related to health promotion allows them to feel a sense of responsibility for their own health (Hagan et al., 2008). School-aged children have a basic understanding of the body and a greater ability to understand hospitalization and illness than younger children (Hockenberry, 2011). They are able to answer direct questions, especially during a sick visit, and take part in the decision-making process (Hagan et al., 2008; Hockenberry, 2011).

Techniques for communicating with school-aged children include the following:

- Providers must build rapport with school-aged children, speaking to them directly and allowing them to answer simple questions about their friends, school, their favorite subject, clothing, or vacations, for example.

TABLE 3.4	Soft Language Choices When Working With Young Children
MEDICAL TERM	**SUBSTITUTION**
Incision; cut	Special opening
Dye (preschooler hears "die")	Special liquid
Worry	Wonder
Shoot an x-ray	Take a picture
Problem	Finding
Stool	Use child's or family's term for stool
Pain	Owie, ouchy, boo-boo, sore, scratchy
Fix	Make it better
Take (as in "take your temperature"; "take your blood pressure")	See how warm you are; hug your arm
Put to sleep (i.e., anesthesia)	Special medicine so you won't feel any ouchie
Catheter	Tube
Electrodes	Stickers
Specimen	Sample
Test	Check to see how your (…) is working

Sources: Brown (2011); Purvis (2009).

- Providers must give school-aged children explanations about procedures, diagnoses, medications, or tests in terms that they can understand. Providers must also encourage these children to ask questions.
- Providers must encourage an open dialogue with the child. For difficult subjects, the following comment and question can be used: "Many children your age have questions about (…); do you have any questions or concerns about this topic?" This allows children to feel comfortable talking about a difficult subject.

Adolescents

The health care provider should always speak directly to adolescents during the health care encounter. Adolescents are generally more aware of and concerned about their bodies. They want to be responsible for their health care needs, and they want to be recognized as adults but at the same time feel misunderstood by adults (Hagan et al., 2008). Providers must prepare parents and adolescents before the visit so that they both know what to expect. Sensitive parts of the health care interview with adolescents should always be conducted without the parent present. Laws vary from state to state regarding topics that can be kept confidential from the parent (Hockenberry, 2011). Adolescents often begin to have sexual encounters and experiment with drugs and alcohol, but they are unlikely to admit to this when their parents are present. Topics about sexual behavior and drug and alcohol use should be discussed in private if state law allows confidentiality from the parent. Providers must clarify with parents and children what topics will be discussed and state the confidentiality limitations before discussing these topics.

Techniques for communicating with adolescents include the following (Hockenberry, 2011):

- Providers must establish trust and rapport.
- Providers must tolerate difference and respect the adolescent's views.
- Providers must be honest, as this enhances trust and increases the likelihood that adolescents will be honest as well.
- Providers must offer choices whenever possible.
- Providers should ask questions about adolescents' interests, such as favorite music groups, to build rapport and demonstrate interest.
- Providers must listen more than they talk.
- Providers must take care not to express disappointment or disapproval when adolescents express themselves.

SUMMARY

Nonjudgmental listening encourages open and honest communication. Communication in the pediatric setting is a dynamic process. Quality communication skills take time to develop as a beginning practitioner, especially in the pediatric setting where there are many special considerations. Being knowledgeable about pediatric-specific communication techniques and developmental considerations leads to successful communication encounters with children and their families. Being aware of family dynamics, encouraging parent involvement, and always including the child in the health care encounter are essential. Having an understanding of these basic elements and regularly using them in practice are keys to successful communication in the pediatric setting.

References

Ball, J. W., Bindler, R. C., & Cowen, K. J. (2012). Pediatric assessment. In *Principles of pediatric nursing: Caring for children* (5th ed., pp. 110–162). Upper Saddle River, NJ: Pearson Education.

Beck, R. S., Daughtridge, R., & Sloane, P. D. (2002). Physician-patient communication in the primary care office: A systematic review. *Journal of the American Board of Family Practice, 15*, 25–38.

Blackstone, S., & Pressman, H. (2012). *Effective communication in children's hospitals: A handbook of resources for parents, patients and practitioners.* Retrieved from http://www.patient-providercommunication.org/pdf/25.pdf

Brown, T. L. (2011). Pediatric variations of nursing interventions. In M. J. Hockenberry & D. Wilson (Eds.), *Wong's nursing care of infants and children* (9th ed., pp. 998–1051). St. Louis, MO: Mosby.

Covey, S. (2013). *The 7 habits of highly effective people.* New York, NY: Simon & Schuster.

Eisenberg, A. M. (2012). Paralanguage. In A. M. Eisenberg (Eds.), *Prescriptive communication for the healthcare provider* (p. 285). British Columbia, Canada: Trafford.

Ekman, P., & Friesan, W. (1975). *Unmasking the face: A guide recognizing emotions from facial clues.* Englewood Cliffs, NJ: Prentice-Hall.

Faull, J., & Oliver, J. M. (2010). Infants' interest in language. In J. Faull, J. M. Oliver (Eds.), *Amazing minds: The science of nurturing your child's developing mind with games, activities and more.* New York, NY: Penguin.

Goman, C. K. (2008). *The nonverbal advantage: Secrets and science of body language at work* (p. 79). San Francisco, CA: Berrett-Koehler.

Hagan, J. F., Shaw, J. S., & Duncan, P. M. (Eds.). (2008). *Bright futures: Guidelines for health supervision of infants, children and adolescents* (3rd ed.). Elk Grove Village, IL: American Academy of Pediatrics.

Hall, E. T. (1966). *The silent language.* New York, NY: Anchor Books.

Hockenberry, M. J. (2011). Communication and physical assessment of the child. In M. J. Hockenberry & D. Wilson (Eds.), *Wong's nursing care of infants and children* (9th ed., pp. 117–178). St. Louis, MO: Mosby.

Howard, B. J. (2002). Communicating with children. In M. Jellinek, B. P. Patel, & M. C. Froehle (Eds.), *Bright futures in practice: Mental health, vol. II: Tool kit* (pp. 84–85). Arlington, VA: National Center for Education in Maternal and Child Health.

Kolucki, B., & Lemish, D. (2011). *Communicating with children: Principles and practices to nurture, inspire, excite, educate and heal.* Retrieved from http://www.unicef.org/cbsc/files/CwC_Web(2).pdf

Lehna, C. (2005). Interpreter services in pediatric nursing. *Pediatric Nursing, 31*(4), 292–296.

Levetown, M., & the American Academy of Pediatrics Committee on Bioethics. (2011). Communicating with children and families: From everyday interactions to skill in conveying distressing information. Statement of Reaffirmation. *Pediatrics, 130*(2), e467.

Montague, E., Chen, P., Xu, J., Chenwing, B., & Barrett, B. (2013). Nonverbal interpersonal interactions in clinical encounters and patient perceptions of empathy. *Journal of Participatory Medicine, 5.* Retrieved from http://www.medscape.com/viewarticle/810476

Polhemus, T. (Ed.). (1978). *The body reader: Social aspects of the human body.* New York, NY: Pantheon Books.

Purvis, M. J. (2009). *The challenges of communicating with pediatric patients.* AAOS Now. Retrieved from http://www.aaos.org/news/aaosnow/feb09/clinical5.asp

Rider, E. A. (2011). Advanced communication strategies for relationship-centered care. *Pediatric Annals, 40*(9), 447–453.

Rollins, J. A. (2005). Tell me about it: Drawings as a communication tool for children with cancer. *Journal of Pediatric Oncology Nursing, 22*(4), 203–221.

Starr N. B., & DeGolier, S. D. (2013). Self-perception issues. In C. E. Burns, A. M. Dunn, M. A, Brady, N. B. Starr, & C. G. Blosser (Eds.), *Pediatric primary care* (5th ed., pp. 304–318). Philadelphia, PA: W. B. Saunders.

Stein. M. T. (2006). Developmentally based office: Setting the stage for enhanced practice. In S. D. Dixon, & M. T. Stein (Eds.), *Encounters with children: Pediatric behavior and development* (4th ed., pp. 72–97). St. Louis, MO: Mosby.

Assessment of the Family

IMPORTANCE OF FAMILY ASSESSMENT

Most children are part of that unique entity called "family." Today, however, if children are asked to draw their family, only some would respond with a traditional two-parent family. Many others would include grandparents and extended family members, stepfamilies, or parents who are either both women or both men. A small number might draw a residential-living setting, because there are no adults to care for them. Regardless of the structure, through birth, adoption, and sometimes less traditional means, children become family members— living, it is to be hoped, among those who are steadfast sources of love, safety, and security. For some children, the family is where they become immersed in the values they will carry into adulthood, and where they learn how to navigate their own complex worlds. For many children, time spent with family is filled with happiness and security; for others, it involves fear, anxiety, and unpredictability, with time away from home offering respite from myriad difficulties.

Health care providers are in a privileged position to be able to assess and evaluate the child within the context of his or her specific family system, however it may be configured. A family assessment gives the provider a unique opportunity to learn about children through the relationships they have with the people they live with. The values, beliefs, and attributes of the family have a significant impact not only on the child's physical health, but also on his or her emotional health, well-being, self-esteem, confidence, future relationships, expectations, and dreams for the future. Health care providers who recognize the value of engaging the family may help identify problems within the family before they escalate into a full-blown crisis.

Most providers who work with families view the family as something broader than simply a grouping of people who are related. According to Thomlison (2007), families are composed of people who live with a shared past, feel a measure of emotional connectedness, and participate together in planning for the future. Members may or may not have biologic and legal ties. Wright and Leahey (2013) suggest that "family" is composed of whomever members consider to be family.

PURPOSE OF FAMILY ASSESSMENT

The overall purpose of family assessment is to examine the family's strengths and weaknesses, to gather information about the family's medical history, to assess family functioning and relationships, to determine the parental knowledge base, and to gain an understanding of the family's concerns and needs. The assessment also influences which interventions are to follow. Traditionally, assessment has focused on problems and symptoms with attention to deficits and difficulties (Tedeschi & Kilmer, 2005). However, using a problem-centered approach disregards family strengths and resources that may support the family through challenging events and times.

STRENGTH-BASED FAMILY ASSESSMENT

An assessment approach that considers family strengths recognizes the family and its members as people with distinct abilities, wherewithal, life skills, and needs that merit consideration (Tedeschi & Kilmer, 2005). Working within a strength-based framework, health care providers may identify needs for family support and resources that are likely to improve the outcomes of planned interventions.

Wells and Stein (2006) identified several family characteristics that are important for children regardless of the family membership and the manner in which the family has come together. Family members require basic life necessities that include food, safe housing, clothing, and access to health care. Children benefit by demonstrated warmth and affection with developmentally appropriate limit setting. An environment that assumes respect for all and prohibits violence assures children that they are safe and secure while teaching them that they, too, are expected to demonstrate respect and cooperation in the family. Family members all benefit from stimulation of cognitive development and recognition of the

---

BOX 4.1   Characteristics of Healthy Families

Safe, Organized, and Nurturing Environment

- Marital or partner relationship is stable.
- Housing is in good repair with sufficient living and sleeping space for family members.
- Sufficient finances are available for family needs.
- Plans to manage emergencies are in place, with family members involved in age- and develop mentally appropriate preparation.
- Predictable routines and expectations are a part of day-to-day family life.
- Secure child care is in place in the absence of parents.

Recognition of Adult and Child Boundaries, Roles, and Responsibilities

- Parents or designated adults actively assume parenting responsibilities.
- A healthy diet is incorporated into family life.
- Parents are able to balance work and home life.
- Parental expectations are appropriate for the child's age and developmental level.
- Television time for children is limited.
- Internet and other isolated activities are monitored by adults.
- Reading is encouraged by all family members.
- Parents serve as positive role models for a healthy lifestyle, communication, and responding to challenges and adversity.

Clarity and Continuity of Communication

- Parents regularly communicate philosophy of childrearing and parenting style.
- Sibling rivalry is addressed in a loving, age-appropriate manner.
- Family members demonstrate effective coping and problem-solving skills.
- Family members have appropriate outlets for frustration.
- Affection is demonstrated among family members.

Utmost Respect for Others

- Family members tolerate and respect differences.
- Discipline is age appropriate, and positive reinforcement is maximized.
- Compromise, family meetings, and other strategies are engaged to address problems that arise.
- Parents spend time together as a couple.
- Parents spend time with each child individually.
- Abusive behaviors are absent.

---

importance of fostering moral reasoning. Children thrive in an environment that encourages meaningful interpersonal relationships, open communication, cooperative problem solving, and motivation to achieve. Socialization among peers and with adults assists children to become cooperative members of their community and society.

CHARACTERISTICS OF HEALTHY FAMILIES

Healthy families can be represented by an assortment of family structures, cultures, ethnicities, or socioeconomic groups. Characteristic of all healthy families are parents or adults in the parenting role who assure (a) a safe, organized, and nurturing environment; (b) recognition of adult and child boundaries, roles, and responsibilities; (c) clarity and continuity of communication; and (d) utmost respect for others. Specific descriptors for each area are listed in Box 4.1.

FAMILY DEMOGRAPHICS

It is useful to consider family demographics before considering specific family structures. In 2009, 87% of American children lived with both biologic parents; an additional 10% lived with one biologic parent and a stepparent, usually the biologic mother and stepfather. Approximately 2% of children living with two parents lived with either two adoptive parents or a combination of an adoptive parent and a biologic parent or an adoptive parent and a stepparent (U.S. Census Bureau, 2011).

For many children, grandparents play a significant role even when a parent is present. In 2009, slightly more than 10% of children who lived with a single mother were grandchildren of the householder. When children lived in households without either of their parents, 59% lived with their grandparents (U.S. Census Bureau, 2011).

In 2009, 77.2% of American children in single-parent homes lived with a single mother, and 8.4% lived in a household with their mother and her unmarried partner. Just over 11% of children lived with a single father, and 1.9% lived with their father and his unmarried partner (U.S. Census Bureau, 2011). Census data also reveal that 16.2% of American households with children age 18 years and younger live below the poverty level (U.S. Census Bureau, 2011).

An important consideration related to the children's well-being involves children's health insurance coverage. For children living in all types of living arrangements in 2009, health insurance coverage increased with family income. However, children who lived in households receiving public assistance were more likely to be covered by health insurance than those who did not. These data, which like all statistics merit careful scrutiny, provide information regarding family organization, economics, and access to health care that is useful to consider when planning a family assessment.

FAMILY STRUCTURE

Current family structure in North America is highly variable. Some families have one adult or child present while others consist of several members of all ages, representing several generations. Parents of young children may be in their 20s or in their 50s. Roles in some families are flexible and shared, while in other families each person assumes a prescribed role that is rarely changed. There are families with minimal resources who dwell in a spirit of wealth and generosity, while other families that enjoy an abundance of material goods are emotionally impoverished.

The capable health care provider, when interacting with families, may need to assume a variety of roles that include resource person, teacher, surrogate, counselor, teacher, mediator, and researcher to help the family move toward health and well-being (Peplau, 1991). This multiplicity of roles provides multifaceted approaches that are the basis of excellence in a provider's practice. Regardless of how a family is structured, it is essential for the health care provider to remember that each family is its own unique entity, with its own culture, traditions, resources, needs, disappointments, and dreams for the future. Every family faces challenges and adversity; the capacity of family members to respond, move forward, learn, and grow from these experiences results ultimately in growth, satisfaction, and contentment.

Two-Parent Families

While historically viewed as "traditional," two-parent families have encountered significant changes in lifestyle and expectations as a result of changes in the workforce and parental roles. Increasingly, both parents are employed outside the home, while occasionally fathers assume the role of the stay-at-home caretaker of young children. Some parents hold multiple jobs, while others commute to jobs in other cities or states.

For two-career families, time together is limited, with many parents attending only to what is absolutely essential during the work week. For all parents of young school-aged children, the need for before- and after-school care is often an added stress. For all parents employed outside the home, employers may not understand the need to be home with sick children, to take children to health care appointments, or to be available for school activities that may conflict with parents' work schedules.

Stepfamilies

Stepfamilies often involve children who may be experiencing their third family unit, following the family unit formed by their biologic parents, then the single-parent family unit, and now the stepfamily unit. Each family member adjusts to the new family structure at his or her own pace, and the joy experienced by the parents in a new relationship may be very different from the feelings experienced by the child who may still be mourning the loss of the original family. Children of all ages tend to react strongly to both divorce and remarriage despite judicious parental planning and preparation for these life-changing events.

Single-Parent Families

Single-parent families occur when individuals choose not to marry or after the divorce or death of a spouse. Families composed of either a mother or father and children may assume a range of family arrangements, and represent various circumstances. A parent who has never married may need to take steps to organize the family in a way that meets members' needs. Parents who have experienced divorce face developmental changes and issues that emerge through that stage of the life cycle, both for themselves and their children. Those who have lost a spouse through death face their own adjustments that may or may not be anticipated while being faced with also caring for children who are responding to the loss of their parent.

Adoptive Families

In 2009, 3.7% of all American families were those that were formed through adoption (U.S. Census Bureau, 2011). Adoptive families differ markedly in both their makeup and history. In some families, adopted children join their parents' biologic children. Some families adopt infants, while others adopt school-aged children. North American families increasingly adopt infants or children from other countries. Many adoptive parents find their anticipation burdened with anxiety related to unexpected alterations in the adoption timeline, changes in government regulations, and other unanticipated delays in the arrival of the infant or child they await. While eagerly awaited, adopted children may bring with them complicated health needs or family histories that challenge even committed, well-prepared parents.

Foster Families

The nature of foster families implies a caregiving role for children who are at risk. Some children who join a foster family require only short-term care; others are delegated to the foster care system for lengthy periods of time. Foster families are presented with the challenge of nurturing a child who may have been moved from home to home—each with its own family culture. At times, the child is returned to a home environment that presents safety or stability concerns to foster parents committed to the overall well-being of the child for whom they are caring.

Grandparent-Led Families

Grandparents may find themselves raising grandchildren or having them in their home at a time when they expected to be free from this kind of responsibility. In 2009, 11.2% of American children were living in households with a grandparent present. Most (59%) lived in situations where the grandparent was the householder. Of children living in housing provided by grandparents, 65% had at least one parent in the household as well (U.S. Census Bureau, 2011). While some grandparents find this arrangement enjoyable or helpful, others find the demands of infant or child care difficult to sustain over time. Some grandparents may have health issues of their own that require significant attention, and occasionally a grandparent may be caring for another family member whose needs are physically, financially, and psychologically demanding.

Gay- and Lesbian-Parent Families

Gates (2013) reported that an estimated 6 million children live with a gay or lesbian parent in the United States. Gay and lesbian parents represent every race, culture, religious or ethnic group, and socioeconomic affiliation in the United States. Several social and contemporary issues challenge gay and lesbian couples who have children. Parenting is stressful under any circumstances, but parenting among gay or lesbian couples typically arouses fears related to heterosexism, homophobia, and general stigma that surround these couples (Goldberg & Smith, 2011; Lobaugh Clements, Averill, & Olguin, 2006). Although all 50 states permit lesbian, gay, bisexual, or transgender (LGBT) people to adopt individually, only 21 states and the District of Columbia have clear laws that permit same-sex couples to adopt (Human Rights Campaign, 2013).

The American Academy of Pediatrics ([AAP], 2013) recognizes that a substantial body of literature offers evidence that gay and lesbian parents can offer their children the same advantages and expectations for health, adjustment, and development as heterosexual parents offer. Despite empirical support that children can thrive and flourish with two parents of the same sex, societal pressures present these families with many challenges.

Homeless Families

Homeless families frequently have multiple health issues in addition to social problems that occur concomitantly with homelessness. Children or adolescents may stay with relatives or friends or may "couch hop" with parents from place to place. Many families cannot access safe shelters, often leaving parents and their children on the streets. Children entering the downward spiral of homelessness are at risk for poor nutrition, disease, violence, substance abuse, sexual abuse, and overall vulnerability. The optimal approach is for community support services to be made aware of families that are at risk of losing safe and secure housing so that actions can be taken to intervene before a perilous situation results.

Families Living With Chronic Illness

Families dealing with chronic illness need to be able to access needed health care, medications, and supplies. These families face insurance difficulties, issues regarding transportation, and other ongoing financial stress. Adults with chronic health conditions may be unable to sustain employment or care for their children or other family members. Parents who are caring for children with chronic health problems may not be able to maintain employment; children may miss school more than is acceptable, and may have developmental or psychological disabilities related to their chronic medical condition. Families dealing with chronic health issues benefit from a strong support network that can be put in place by health care providers to help them with their identified needs.

Teen-Parent Families

Teen parents present with numerous health issues. While teens sometimes exhibit strong parenting skills, their responsibilities related to parenthood are frequently challenged by conflicting issues that may include peer and social pressures, school, financial stress, work-related issues, stressful relationships with parents, and differences of opinion between teen mothers and fathers about their child's care and future. Teen parents benefit from supportive family systems that are able to provide positive role modeling and assistance with child care that allows the teen to continue and complete his or her education.

Older First-Time-Parent Families

Older first-time parents are faced with new responsibilities that may or may not have been expected. As they welcome their first child, these parents may also be faced with other family responsibilities such as the care of an elderly parent. Career responsibilities, established routines, and health issues, including decreased energy, may be issues in these families. Lifestyle changes that may have been discussed in anticipation of this significant change may turn out to be greater than expected. Mature adults who have become accustomed to personal leisure time, spontaneous dinners or other activities, or vacationing with other adults may be stunned by the change in their everyday lives. Those who find themselves in this situation when they had no plan or intention of becoming parents, or perhaps had given up that plan for their lives, may have significant stressors related to their changed lives.

STAGES IN FAMILY DEVELOPMENT

Wright and Leahey (2013) urge health care providers to use the Calgary Family Assessment Model (CFAM) as a framework within which to interact with today's families, which encompass myriad configurations such as two-career families, single-parent households, unmarried couples, gay or lesbian couples, remarried couples (i.e., couples whose members have been either divorced or widowed and then remarried), single-parent adoptions, and other configurations. This model is described in detail later in the chapter. They emphasize the need to avoid language that reinforces stereotypes and critically reflects the influence of culture, gender, ethnicity, race, and sexual orientation on a family's developmental stages. Diverse families and lifestyles may result in developmental stages that differ from those described in this model. The effective engagement of health care providers with families requires an awareness of these differences and shifts.

Stage One: Launching the Single Young Adult

Each person faces the experience of "leaving home." It is a stage that may last for several years, during which young adults confront decisions about which values, traditions, beliefs, and standards they will take from their family of origin and which they will discard, while also deciding which new elements they will incorporate as they move forward in their lives (Wright & Leahey, 2013). Developmental tasks (McGoldrick, Carter, & Garcia-Preto, 2011; Wright & Leahey, 2013) during stage one include:

- Distinguishing the self from the original family (Wright & Leahey, 2013). During this process, the young adult and parents work toward the development of a mutually respectful form of relating. This process varies among ethnic groups, each of which has norms and expectations regarding attachment to family and also issues regarding dependence and independence.
- Developing satisfying and meaningful intimate peer relationships.
- Establishing oneself in the work world by initiating financial goals and career expectations.

Stage Two: Joining Families Through Marriage

When couples marry, each individual brings his or her family of origin to the relationship; thus, at least two but any number of families may come together as a result of this bond. In many situations, stepfamilies may also be present, adding other variables to the dynamics already in play. Increasingly, many couples who are joined in marriage are nonheterosexual, reflecting recent legislation legalizing gay marriages and civil unions, and more frequent formal recognition and celebration of these events by families. Developmental tasks (McGoldrick et al., 2011; Wright & Leahey, 2013) during stage two include:

- Establishing couple identity, which includes negotiation of many issues that were previously defined on an individual basis. Matters to be considered include eating and sleeping patterns, use of space and time, sexual contact, traditions, and rules that will become those of the family, as well as those that will be established in the future.

- Realigning relationships with the extended family to include the spouse, which challenges each family of origin to open itself to new ways of being.
- Making decisions about parenthood; during this time, couples decide whether or not to have children and, if deciding affirmatively, when to conceive. The issue of timing of conception has taken on greater importance given the trend toward later marriages, the changing roles of women in the workforce, and the use of contraceptives.

Stage Three: Families With Young Children

Adults now assume caregiving responsibility for a younger generation. This often occurs at a time when financial resources are stretched and parents are focusing on career development. In two-career families, child responsibilities and household needs can become particularly challenging. Developmental tasks (McGoldrick et al., 2011; Wright & Leahey, 2013) during stage three include:

- Adjusting the marital system to make space for the child, during which time personal space, intimacy, and opportunities for socializing may be significantly challenged. Normal changes during this period include adjustments in relationships with the families of origin, shifts that occur in relation to the child, changes in stress and social support, and changes in the couple (Cowan & Cowan, 2012).
- Sharing of child care, financial responsibilities, and household tasks. The contributions of both mothers and fathers to a child's development are important.
- Realigning relationships with extended families to include parenting and grandparenting roles. During this time the couple develops their parenting roles in addition to their marital roles. Members of each family of origin take on new roles, such as grandmother or uncle. Opportunities for both intergenerational support and conflict are abundant, as expectations regarding childrearing and health practices are expressed within the family.

Stage Four: Families With Adolescents

Wright and Leahey (2013) describe this period as one that can include intense upheaval and transition during which biologic, emotional, and sociocultural changes are rapidly occurring. Developmental tasks (McGoldrick et al., 2011; Wright & Leahey, 2013) during stage four include:

- Shifting the parent–child relationships to permit adolescents to move in and out of the family system at a time when teenagers vigorously question rules. Initially, parents may respond to their adolescent's push for independence by hastily defining rigid rules while recreating an earlier stage of dependency or by allowing premature independence. Wright and Leahey (2013) suggest that parents shift from the parental role to a "protector" role so that adolescents are safe and then to the "preparer" role so that adolescents are prepared for the challenges of adulthood.

■ Refocusing on midlife marital and career issues. During this time, parents are often forced to examine marital and career issues, resulting in what may be a period of positive growth or painful struggle.

■ Beginning a shift toward joint caring for the older generation. During this time, parents often feel they are being besieged by teenagers seeking more freedom and parents seeking more support.

Stage Five: Launching Children and Moving On

Historically, most North American parents have come to believe they will eventually experience an "empty nest." For many, that departure is taking longer as young adults are more often returning home, sometimes repeatedly, after leaving. Some young adults may be reluctant to give up their family's lifestyle, while others have problems finding employment that can support their basic financial needs. Developmental tasks (McGoldrick et al., 2011; Wright & Leahey, 2013) for stage five include:

■ Renegotiating the family as a dyad, allowing the couple to bond once again.

■ Realigning relationships to include in-laws and grown children whereby parents adjust family ties and expectations to include the child's spouse or partner.

■ Dealing with disabilities and death of grandparents, a period frequently requiring time dedicated to illness, loss, or death of an elderly parent.

Stage Six: Families in Later Life

This stage begins with retirement and lasts until the death of both spouses. In North American cultures, this can last 20 to 30 years. The key emotional process during this time is to accept the shift of generational roles. Developmental tasks (McGoldrick et al., 2011; Wright & Leahey) for stage six include:

■ Maintaining functioning and interest in the face of physiologic decline and exploring new familial and social roles. This task can challenge both generations, and adjustments are necessary.

■ Making room in the system for the wisdom and experience of seniors, recognizing that people are living longer. It is not unusual for a person in his or her 70s to be caring for both a parent and grandchild. The lives of older adults no longer match the stereotypes of the past; today's seniors may be employed, actively engaged in volunteerism, and maintain a very active life.

■ Dealing with the loss of a spouse, siblings, and peers and preparing for death. For many this is a period of significant transition and adjustment, and one in which social support contributes to the individual's and family's adaptation over time.

DIVORCE AND THE POSTDIVORCE FAMILY LIFE

People living in the United States increasingly experience changes in marital status and living arrangements over the course of their lives. According to the National Vital Statistics Center (2012), the divorce rate for reporting states was 3.4 per 1,000 in 2009, down from 4.1 per 1,000 in 2000. Families experiencing divorce navigate the same developmental stages as two-parent families, but typically do not have the same resources. Health care providers should be aware that single-parent divorce status alone influences family functioning. It is important for providers to focus on the resilience of family members in the postdivorce period. Resilience typically depends on the ability of parents and their children to establish intimate, meaningful, and reciprocally helpful and caring relationships that will provide support for members when difficulties and challenges appear in their lives (Wright & Leahey, 2013). Furthermore, while most children in divorced families are resilient enough to move on with their lives, some children experience more lasting adjustment problems linked to a range of variables (Lansford, 2009).

Divorce may occur at any time in the family life cycle, irrespective of race, age, or socioeconomic status (Wright & Leahey, 2013). McGoldrick and colleagues (2011) emphasize the emotional process of transition and attitude that are essential for attending to the issues that occur throughout the phases of the divorced family's life cycle. These include:

1. Deciding to divorce, which requires individuals to accept the failure to resolve marital tensions and to accept the part each partner has had in the failure of the marriage.

2. Planning the breakup of the marital system while supporting viable arrangements for all parties, including cooperatively addressing issues related to custody, visitation, and finances.

3. Separating while demonstrating a willingness to continue a cooperative co-parental relationship and joint financial support of children while also working on resolutions of attachment to the spouse, involving the restructuring of marital and parent–child relationships, adapting to living apart, and realigning relationships with the extended family.

4. Finalizing a divorce, which requires more work on overcoming hurt and guilt, while retrieving hopes, dreams, and expectations from the marriage.

5. Defining "postdivorce custodial" or "noncustodial" roles. Parents are faced with maintaining the care of their children while supporting the other parent's

relationship with the children. Parents must maintain visitation arrangements and financial resources, rebuild their social networks, and establish ways to continue effective parenting.

McGoldrick and colleagues (2011) provide a developmental outline for the remarried family that results in children becoming part of yet another family system. The National Stepfamily Resource Center (2014) encourages the use of the term "stepfamily," rather than "blended family" (frequently encountered in the media). The rationale is that "blended family" does not describe family relationships or what occurs when at least one partner in a marriage brings a child or children from a prior relationship. The family involved in a remarriage faces two key tasks (McGoldrick et al., 2011):

- Entering into a new relationship with the desired outcome that adults recommit to marriage and form a new family with preparedness to deal with its inherent complexity

- Conceptualizing and planning the new marriage and family, while acknowledging each member's fears, including those of the new spouse and children, about remarriage and forming a stepfamily

Remarriage and rebuilding the family necessitates accepting a different model of family that, from a developmental perspective, requires realigning relationships and financial arrangements; making room for relationships of all children with biologic parents, grandparents, and other extended family; and sharing memories and histories to enhance stepfamily integration.

The National Stepfamily Resource Center (2014) provides a clear outline of the differences between step- and first-time families (Box 4.2). While these may seem obvious, recognition and acknowledgment of such differences are often helpful.

BOX 4.2   Differences Between Stepfamilies and First-Time Families

Stepfamilies Resulting From a Loss

- Adults grieve the loss of a partner, a marriage relationship, loss of dreams, and losses related to death or divorce.
- Children grieve the loss of a parent (even if visits are regular), loss or lessened availability of remaining parent when courtship and remarriage occur, loss of stability, changes that happen because of divorce or death, and loss of their fantasy of their family the way they want it to be.

Parent–Child Relationship With a Longer History Than the New Couples' Relationship

- Incoming marriage partner may feel like an intruder or outsider.
- New adult partners may have difficulty "being allowed in."
- Stepparents are not a part of the family's history or "memory book," which can only be accomplished as people share time and activities.

Biologic Parent Is in Another Location

- Children need to be allowed to save memories of their other parent.
- Children whose parent is living away must have easy access to them.
- Children need permission from a parent and stepparent to love the other biologic parent.
- Children need permission from both biologic parents to like the stepparents.

- Forcing children to choose among parents places the children in a no-win emotional dilemma.

Children as Members of Two Households

- Parent and stepparent need to discuss household rules for the behavior of children and consequences for broken rules.
- Once rules are clear, they should be communicated to the children by the biologic parent.

Stepparents May Be Asked to Assume a Parental Role Before Emotional Ties With the Stepchild Have Been Established

- Biologic parents grow into their roles; stepparents are often expected to adjust instantly as though parenting were an inborn skill.
- The bonding process typically makes parents more tolerant of their children's personalities and behaviors. The reverse is also true.

There Is No Legal Relationship Between Stepparents and Stepchildren

- Stepparents often have feelings of responsibility with no authority.
- Stepparents may need written authority for certain matters (such as to authorize emergency medical care) through a limited power of attorney.

FAMILY ASSESSMENT

General Guidelines

Wright and Leahey (2013) cite a health care provider's manners, which also have the effect of instilling trust, as a key ingredient to assessment. Suggestions for any encounter with families include the following:

- The health care provider should introduce himself or herself to the patient, family members, or guests who are present, using a full name unless safety concerns deem that disclosure unwise.
- Initially, a formal approach is assumed with patients and family members. Family members should be asked how they want to be addressed.
- All children should be included in introductions and greetings. How children should address the provider should be clarified.
- The provider should position himself or herself so that he or she is at eye level rather than standing above or over patients.
- The provider should explain his or her role and the time period during which he or she will be involved with them.
- The provider should explain things *before* they happen—including procedures or staff changes.
- All commitments should be honored.

It is most beneficial when the provider and family engage in the assessment process with the understanding that optimal outcomes occur when the provider and all family members participate as active partners. The term *process* is essential to acknowledge, as the assessment is more than the completion of a tool or checklist (U.S. Department of Health and Human Services [USDHHS], 2005).

In situations in which angry exchanges occur, it is often useful to step back and view the situation through the eyes of the family. It is likely that each family member will have a different viewpoint, just as each person's experience in a family is different. It is also useful to take the time to find something about the family member or family group that you can affirm. Affirmation that is genuinely offered is both extremely empowering and trust-building.

There are innumerable approaches to creating nurturing and growth in a family, and many parenting styles that produce healthy children who become productive members of society. The path any particular family chooses to provide for the health and development of its members may differ from the one the provider might choose. However, the provider who is for the family is actively aware of ethnic and religious backgrounds, different values, and different beliefs; is open to different ideas; and is likely to partner successfully with families, resulting in satisfactory outcomes that allow families to reach their goals and expectations.

Types of Family Assessment

Many families are never engaged in a formal family assessment process. Yet for all families, it is beneficial when the health care provider practices within the context of a family perspective. Children often appear for well-child appointments or time-limited evaluation of acute conditions, in the course of which the health care provider assesses a problem and intervenes accordingly. It is assumed and expected that providers working in a pediatric setting are competent in assessing growth and development of infants, children, and adolescents, as well as in recognizing developmental issues encountered by families at different stages.

Many capable parents experience a time in their child's development where they find themselves in difficulty; for example, managing bedtime or eating habits. Some families that handle the period from infancy through toddlerhood well find themselves challenged when children enter school. Other families do not particularly enjoy infant care but excel with their preschooler, school-aged child, or adolescent. The important point, once the relationship with the family has been established, is for providers to intervene in helpful ways, preferably before a crisis occurs.

Sensitive Issues

It is helpful for health care providers to consider issues that may be sensitive topics for family members. What has become normalized for the provider through everyday work experiences may not be so for the family. For example, a family may include several young children, each of whom has a different father. Or, a parent may have been reported for abuse or neglect. Families may evince sensitivity about health-related matters if they feel responsible for them. Perhaps a parent is responsible for injuring a child, albeit accidentally. Sometimes families are sensitive about social issues, such as a parent in prison or a family member who has been negatively presented in the media. For others, sensitivity centers on financial strains that limit their ability to purchase essential medications or other necessities. Without genuinely and authentically engaging with the family, it will not be possible to know the diseases, situations, or conditions that families may perceive as carrying a stigma.

Indications for a Comprehensive Family Assessment

Initial interactions with the family may lead the provider to identify the need to further explore an aspect of the family that relates to the presenting health issue; for example, a family's reluctance to attend to a school-aged child's postoperative dressing change. After additional communications with the family, the provider may determine that there is a need for a comprehensive family assessment as described by the U.S. Department of Health and Human Services Administration for Children (USDHHS, 2005). Comprehensive family assessment is always indicated when there is need to involve the child welfare system, with review and updates indicated when there are changes regarding matters such as child placement, reunification decisions, court reviews, and termination of parental rights.

A Brief Family Assessment

Health care providers in all practice settings are challenged by time constraints and patient care issues that necessitate a brief family assessment unless issues or needs emerge indicating that a more in-depth consideration of the family is needed. Within a 10- to 15-minute assessment there is opportunity for purposeful conversation, structural assessment, therapeutic inquiry, and partnership with the family that leads to opportunities to affirm and commend family and individual strengths. Skilled providers are able to integrate the tasks of necessary patient care with engaging, purposeful conversation. In any setting there is opportunity to explore with the family their ideas regarding what is needed to address the presenting problem. Through such conversation, there is also opportunity to recognize the family's skill in managing the health issues they have encountered. All families can be included throughout this type of communication. It is important to note that a critical part of the interview is *listening*! The family is the expert in identifying its needs and in suggesting approaches for addressing them. The provider who is attentive to all methods and levels of communication recognizes important messages family members share.

Structural assessment of the family can be approached through a simple genogram and by identifying external support information. Family members can be asked two or three purposeful questions. Information can be gleaned not just from verbal responses but from all that is perceived as the basis for identifying strengths and affirming the family's dignity and capacity to deal with the circumstance currently confronting it. Providers can clearly state their belief in the family's capacity to embrace the challenges it faces, while also assuring family members that there will be support from health professionals who can best assist them with needs that emerge. The knowledge that a trusted professional believes in the family can be extremely empowering—particularly when that professional also assists as teacher, resource person, coach, or in other capacities that foster the health of the family.

There may be occasions that lead providers to doubt the family members and their abilities. At times, that may be a valid response. Nonetheless, providers must take a moment to suspend assumptions and disbelief and recall the individual patient and family triumphs, both anticipated and unexpected, that have occurred in the health care provider's experience. Perhaps that next triumph is right around the corner, waiting for a provider to facilitate and guide the journey.

The Calgary Family Assessment Model

The CFAM includes three major categories (Wright & Leahey, 2013): (a) structural, (b) developmental, and (c) functional. Each category contains several subcategories, and it is important for the health care provider to decide which subcategories are relevant. The provider may move among categories, synthesizing relevant information into an integrated assessment. The provider who is familiar with CFAM can use it as an organizing framework to help families address problems or issues.

Structural Assessment

The provider considering the family's structure examines who is in the family, the connection among members, and the family context. Internal structure includes family composition, gender, sexual orientation, rank order, subsystems, and boundaries. It is important to note changes in the family's composition, whether transient or permanent. Although it is critical that the provider ask questions for a specific purpose, it is helpful to begin with questions of a less intrusive nature. Box 4.3 suggests questions that may be useful in exploring family structure (Wright & Leahey, 2013).

External structure includes the extended family and larger systems. Ties to extended family members can be highly influential, and it is important to explore how significant the extended family is to this particular family. Larger systems include social service agencies and personnel with whom the family has meaningful contact. Box 4.4 suggests questions that may be helpful in the assessment of external family structures (Wright & Leahey, 2013).

Context is the complete situation that is relevant for the family and includes ethnicity, race, social class,

---

BOX 4.3   Potential Questions Regarding Internal Structure

1. How many people are in your immediate family? Who are they, and how are they related?
2. Which family members live at home? How many of these are children, and what are their ages? Do any nonfamily members live in the home?
3. Has anyone recently moved in or out? If so, how has this move affected the family?
4. Who takes responsibility for administering medication when someone in the household is ill (e.g., flu medicine, antibiotics, diabetes medications)?
5. Does everyone share household tasks equally in your family? Some families have specific roles for certain people. How are the roles divided in your home?
6. Is there any marital discord in the family? What are the issues over which the parents disagree? How are these disagreements handled?
7. How are problems solved in the family? Is one member of the family delegated as the problem solver?
8. If someone in the family was troubled, ill, or depressed, to whom would they be likely to speak? A trusted friend, another relative, or someone from the religious community to which you belong?

spirituality, religion, and environment. Box 4.5 suggests questions that address these areas (Wright & Leahey, 2013).

BOX 4.4 Potential Questions Regarding External Structure

1. Do both parents of the family live at home? If not, where do they live?
2. How often do the children have contact with the parent or parents who do not live at home?
3. How often is there contact with the extended family (e.g., aunts, uncles, grandparents)?
4. Is there any ongoing conflict with the extended family or in-laws?
5. Are there step-relatives in the family?
6. Which relatives are closest emotionally to the immediate family?
7. Who is the most helpful when problems arise? How are these problems solved within the family?
8. Who generally makes all of the important decisions in the family? Does everyone of a certain age have a chance to voice an opinion?
9. Do one or both parents work? If both, who is responsible for child care in their absence? Do older children look after younger children?
10. Have there been any incidents of child abuse or violence in the home?
11. Are there any agencies involved with your family? If so, which ones and why? What has been the most useful help you have received from these agencies?

BOX 4.5 Potential Questions Regarding Context

1. Would you tell me about your Chinese practices regarding illness?
2. How does coming to the United States from Mexico influence your beliefs about when to see a health professional?
3. What does health mean to you?
4. Could you help me to understand what I need to know to be most helpful to you?
5. How many times have you moved in the past 5 years?
6. How many schools have your children attended?
7. How does your insurance situation affect your use of health care?
8. Are you involved with a temple, mosque, church, etc.? Would talking to anyone from this place be a support for you in dealing with your illness?
9. Are your spiritual beliefs a source of stress or support for you?
10. What community services does your family use?
11. On a scale of 1 to 10, with 10 being most comfortable, how comfortable are you in your neighborhood?

Constructing a Genogram

A genogram is a diagram of the family constellation that communicates an abundance of information in a simple format. It provides data about relationships, health, religion, occupation, ethnicity, and migration. Because the genogram focuses on the biologic family, some commentators have criticized its inadequacy in recognizing the importance of the family's interaction with those outside the family. Nevertheless, genograms facilitate an understanding of family constellations and patterns that occur among family members and across generations.

The skeleton of the genogram is a family tree depicting the family structure. It is most helpful to include three generations. Family members are situated in horizontal rows that signify generational lines. Children are denoted by vertical lines and are rank-ordered from left to right, beginning with the eldest child. The person's name and age are noted inside the square or circle, which signify a male or female child, respectively. If a family member has died, the year of death is noted above his or her symbol. Figure 4.1 shows a blank genogram, and Figure 4.2 shows the symbols that are used in a genogram.

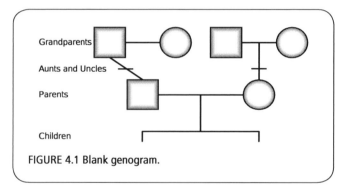

FIGURE 4.1 Blank genogram.

An example of a nuclear and extended family is presented in Figure 4.3, which shows a genogram for the hypothetical Stone family. Alex, age 44, is married to Eva, age 43. They married in 1993 and have three children: Anne, age 13, in grade 7; Marie, age 7, in grade 2; and Joey, age 4, in preschool. Alex's mother Jill has arthritis. Both of Eva's parents are deceased. Her father died in 1990 of a "heart problem" and her mother in 1996 of problems related to diabetes. Alex has an older sister who is depressed. Eva has an older brother and sister.

Family Developmental Assessment

While health care providers who work with children are typically familiar with stages of child development, systematic consideration of family development and family life cycle may not be an active component of provider interventions. However, as the earlier discussion has emphasized, societal changes require a rethinking of traditionally accepted assumptions regarding normality

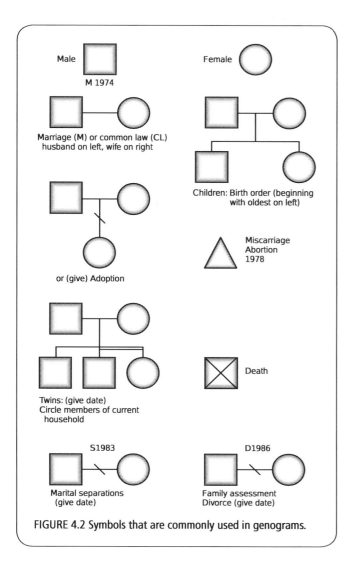

FIGURE 4.2 Symbols that are commonly used in genograms.

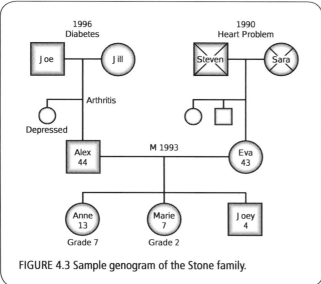

FIGURE 4.3 Sample genogram of the Stone family.

and what family means in the North American culture. All families represent complex systems that experience ongoing growth, transitions, and changes.

Family Functional Assessment

Functional assessment addresses how individuals behave in relation to one another in everyday living. Instrumental functioning refers to activities of daily living, such as meal preparation, caring for a family member's health needs, getting children off to school, doing laundry, and going to work. The expressive aspects of functioning include nine categories (Wright & Leahey, 2013): (a) emotional communication, (b) verbal communication, (c) nonverbal communication, (d) circular communication, (e) problem solving, (f) roles, (g) influence and power, (h) beliefs, and (i) alliances and coalition. Families having difficulty with instrumental issues almost always have challenges in areas of expressive functioning. The primary focus of the functional assessment is on the "here and now." Thus, although past behaviors and future goals are considered, the commitment of the provider is to the present.

SUMMARY

While CFAM may seem detailed, complex, and lengthy, its inclusive and thorough approach need not be overwhelming if the provider uses it as a guide to learn from the family so as to have the information that will optimally guide the care that follows. The provider may elect to use the three main categories to obtain an overview of family strengths and needs. Based on the findings of that overview, the provider may elect to do a more detailed assessment of selected areas prior to considering approaches to address identified needs. Regardless of the approach and depth of inquiry, it is essential that the provider be comfortable with the information obtained, and that the assessment approach then be used to draw all the relevant information together into an integrated body of information.

Although historical data may be important, it should be integrated only insofar as it serves to explain a current situation or the way the family is currently functioning. It is critical to remember that the assessment is not a fixed truth with a guarantee of accuracy. Both the health care provider and family members have individual perspectives that have been gained through mutual inquiry and consideration.

References

American Academy of Pediatrics. (2013). Promoting the well-being of children whose parents are gay or lesbian. *Pediatrics, 131*(4), 827–830.

Cowan, P. A., & Cowan, C. P. (2012). Normal family transitions, couple relationship quality, and healthy child development. In F. Walsh (Ed.), *Normal family processes: Growing diversity and complexity* (4th ed., pp. 428–451). New York, NY: Guilford Press.

Gates, G. J. (2013). *LGBT parenting in the United States*. Retrieved from http://williamsinstitute.law.ucla.edu/wp-content/uploads/LGBT-Parenting.pdf

Goldberg, A. E., & Smith, J. Z. (2011). Stigma, social context, and mental health: Lesbian and gay couples across the transition to adoptive parenthood. *Journal of Counseling Psychology,* 58(1), 139–150.

Human Rights Campaign. (2013). *Parenting laws: Joint adoption.* Retrieved from http://hrc-assets.s3-website-us-east-1.amazonaws .com//files/assets/resources/parenting_joint-adoption_082013.pdf

Lansford, J. E. (2009). Parental divorce and children's adjustment. *Perspectives on Psychological Science, 4,* 140–152.

Lobaugh, E. R., Clements, P. T., Averill, J. B., & Olguin, D. L. (2006). Gay-male couples who adopt: Challenging historical and contemporary social trends toward becoming a family. *Perspectives in Psychiatric Care, 42*(3), 184–195.

McGoldrick, M., Carter, B., & Garcia-Preto, N. (2011). *The expanded family life cycle: Individual, family and social perspectives* (4th ed.). Boston, MA: Allyn & Bacon.

National Stepfamily Resource Center. (2014). *Stepfamily fact sheet.* Retrieved from http://www.stepfamilies.info/faqs/factsheet.php

National Vital Statistics Center. (2012). *Marriages and divorces— number and rate by state.* Retrieved http://www.census.gov/ compendia/statab/cats/births_deaths_marriages_divorces.html

Peplau, H. E. (1991). *Interpersonal relations in nursing: A conceptual framework for psychodynamic nursing.* New York, NY: Springer Publishing.

Tedeschi, R. G., & Kilmer, R. P. (2005). Assessing strengths, resilience, and growth to guide clinical interventions. *Professional Psychology: Research and Practice, 36*(3), 230–237.

Thomlison, B. (2007). *Family assessment handbook: An introductory guide to family assessment and intervention* (2nd ed.). Belmont, CA: Thomson Higher Education.

U.S. Census Bureau. (2011). *Living arrangements of children. June 2011.* Retrieved from http://www.census.gov/prod/2011pubs/ p70-126.pdf

U.S. Department of Health and Human Services. (2005). *Comprehensive family assessment guidelines for child welfare.* Retrieved from http://www.acf.hhs.gov/sites/default/files/cb/ family_assessment.pdf

Wells, R. D., & Stein, M. T. (2006). Special families. In S. D. Dixon & M. T. Stein (Eds.), *Encounters with children: Pediatric behavior and development* (4th ed., pp. 622–647). Philadelphia, PA: Mosby/Elsevier.

Wright, L. M., & Leahey, M. (2013). *Nurses and families: A guide to family assessment and intervention* (6th ed.). Philadelphia, PA: F. A. Davis.

C H A P T E R

Cultural Assessment of Children and Families

According to projections by the U.S. Census Bureau, by 2050, non-Hispanic Whites will comprise less than half (47%) of the American population. The Census Bureau estimates that by that same year, 25% of the population will be of Hispanic descent (U.S. Census Bureau, 2014). The 2010 U.S. Census data revealed that between 2000 and 2010, the Asian American population grew at a faster rate than any other major racial group. During that same period, the American Indian and Alaska Native population grew by 18%, African Americans by 12%, and, Hispanics by 43%. The minority population grew in all 50 states between 2000 and 2010 (U.S. Census Bureau, 2011).

Immigration trends are another factor contributing to the diversity of the American population. In 2010, the countries from which most immigrants arrived to the United States were Mexico, China, the Philippines, India, Vietnam, El Salvador, and Cuba (Center for American Progress, 2014). Pediatric health care providers must be aware of these demographic trends and be culturally

competent to deliver the safest, highest quality care possible to children of widely differing groups.

CULTURE

Definition of Culture

While no universal definition of culture exists, several nurse theorists have defined this concept, which is integral to the practice of nursing. These definitions are presented in Table 5.1. Becoming familiar with a particular child's and family's culture and incorporating this understanding into the health care visit helps to build a trusting, caring, parent–child–provider relationship. A person's culture guides every action he or she makes. Culture determines how each person perceives health and illness, approaches health care, and establishes what he or she is willing to accept as health care treatment. Similarly, health care providers view the world through the lens of their own culture; thus, care must be taken so that providers do not impose their beliefs on others. Several related concepts are defined in Table 5.2.

TABLE 5.1	Definitions of Culture
THEORIST	DEFINITION
Giger (2013); Giger and Davidhizar (2002)	A patterned behavioral response that develops over time through the imprinting of social and religious structures and intellectual and artistic manifestations. It is shaped by values, beliefs, norms, and practices that are shared by the same cultural group
Leininger (2002)	The learned, shared, and transmitted values, beliefs, norms, and lifeways of a particular group
Purnell (2013)	The totality of socially transmitted behavioral patterns, arts, beliefs, values, customs, lifeways, and all other products of human work and thought characteristic of a population or people that guide their worldview and decision making
Spector (2013)	The nonphysical traits such as values, beliefs, practices, habits, attitudes, and customs that are shared by a group of people and passed from one generation to the next

TABLE 5.2	Definitions of Culture-Related Terms
TERM	**DEFINITION**
Acculturation	Changing one's own culture to adapt to the new or dominant culture (Bhugra & Ayonrinde, 2004); values of the original culture are usually retained in some form
Assimilation	Adopting and incorporating traits and aspects of a new culture into one's own cultural practices (Spector, 2013)
Bicultural	Facility in two or more cultures, including the language, norms, and lifeways of each culture (Dunn, 2013)
Cultural bias	A preference for one's own cultural values and beliefs
Cultural competence	A set of congruent behaviors, attitudes, and policies among professionals, agencies, or systems that enables effective work in cross-cultural situations (U.S. Department of Health and Human Services [USDHHS], 2013).
Culture shock	Anxiety, disorientation, confusion, and possible depression felt when one is placed in a new and unfamiliar culture (Ball, Bindler, & Cowen, 2012)
Ethnicity	Identity with a particular group with common characteristics such as language, ancestry, race, national origin, religion, or kin ties (Spector, 2013)
Ethnocentrism	A belief in the inherent superiority of one's own culture over that of other cultures (Ludwick & Silva, 2000); it presents a barrier to delivering culturally sensitive health care
Immigrant	A foreign-born person who is admitted to the United States as a permanent resident to live and work
Lifeways	The way of life, custom, and practices of a cultural group (Srivastava, 2007)
Minority	A group (e.g., ethnic, religious, racial) that makes up a number that is less than the numerical majority of the population (Giger, 2013)
Multiculturalism	The co-existence of diverse cultures (e.g., racial, religious, or cultural groups), as manifested in customary behaviors, cultural assumptions and values, patterns of thinking, and communicative styles (International Federation of Library Associations, 2013)
Norms	Learned behaviors within a cultural group that are determined by the cultural values held by that group
Prejudice	A negative and stereotypical view or opinion applied to all individuals of a certain group
Race	A biologic term classifying people who share the same genetically inherited distinguishing physical characteristics (e.g., skin; hair type, color, or texture; bone structure) (Ball et al., 2012a),
Racism	The belief that one racial group is inherently superior or inferior to another, based on genetically inherited physical characteristics (Ball et al., 2012a).
Refugee	A person who leaves his or her country of birth because of fear of persecution based on race, religion, nationality, social group membership, or political opinion (U.S. Citizenship and Immigration Services, 2013)
Stereotype	The assumption that all people belonging to a particular group share the same characteristics (Ball et al., 2012a)
Subculture	A smaller cultural group within a larger cultural group
Taboo	A strong cultural prohibition against words, actions, or behavior that are considered offensive to the cultural group
Values	Beliefs, attitudes, behaviors, and rules by which peoples' lives are governed (Giger, 2013)
Worldview	The way in which an individual or a group looks out on and understands the world as a value, stance, picture, or perspective about life or the world (Leininger, 2002, p. 83)

Characteristics of Culture, Race, and Ethnicity

The terms *culture*, *race*, and *ethnicity* are sometimes used interchangeably. However, they mean very different things.

Culture

Culture is universal; no people on earth exist without it. Culture is also:

■ **Learned:** A child learns culture through the process of socialization. The first place this occurs is within the family. Parents and extended family members teach a child language, social norms, beliefs, values, and appropriate behavior. This process continues at school and is influenced by peers, the community, subcultural affiliations (e.g., religious or socioeconomic groups), and the media. Recent immigrants also learn the rules of a new culture, but transitioning to a new culture is not always smooth because of language barriers and experiences of grief and loss.

■ **Shared:** Members of a culture share the social norms, beliefs, values, symbols, and language of their cultural group.

■ **Integrated:** Throughout a person's life, culture influences his or her every action, including health beliefs, practices, and behaviors.

■ **Dynamic and ever-changing:** Culture allows people to adapt to changes in society and the environment.

Race

Race is a biologic classification referring to people who share the same genetically inherited distinguishing physical characteristics, such as skin color; hair type, color, or texture; and bone structure. For many years in the United States, race has influenced the development of social systems and social status, which has resulted in the unequal treatment of people belonging to particular groups (Tashiro, 2005). The social systems that have existed based on race have led to disparities in the health status of people of diverse racial and ethnic backgrounds (National Center for Cultural Competence [NCCC], 2014c). The health care provider must work to ensure that care is delivered fairly and equally to all people. Biologic variations also occur among racial groups and can affect the incidence of some diseases and conditions. Examples of some of these conditions are listed in Table 5.3.

Ethnicity

The term *ethnicity* is sometimes used interchangeably with race when describing a person. However, these terms are not equivalent. Whereas race describes biologic identification, ethnicity refers to a cultural group's identification associated with their common geographic origin, language, religion, traditions, values, music, food, and other cultural ties (Spector, 2013).

Poverty as a Culture

Anthropologist Oscar Lewis (1959) coined the phrase "culture of poverty" in his book, *Five Families: Mexican Case Studies in the Culture of Poverty*. He described how the lives of the people he studied were adversely changed by poverty. In his later work, Lewis also found that people living in poverty have strong feelings of dependency, marginality, helplessness, and powerlessness; they lack a sense of belonging and possess strong feelings of inferiority. For people of color, these feelings are exacerbated by racism (Lewis, 1998). Poverty is also a major contributing factor to the health disparities that exist among certain segments of the population. For example, in 2012, approximately 9.7% of non-Hispanic White families lived below the poverty level, contrasted with approximately 27.2% of African Americans and 25.6% of Hispanics (U.S. Census Bureau, 2013).

The importance of recognizing poverty as a culture is driven home by the impact that poverty has on a child's health. Poverty is one of the main reasons that some children and families are unable to access health care. Lack of money, transportation, or insurance; language barriers; racial bias in health care; culturally insensitive care; parental stress; and knowledge deficits about the importance of preventive health care all contribute to high rates of illness and injury in poor children (USDHHS, 2010).

Poor children of any race or ethnicity are also more likely to be developmentally delayed, drop out of school, and give birth during adolescence (Fiscella & Kitzman, 2009). It is important for the provider to be mindful of race, ethnicity, gender, and socioeconomic status as they affect the health of children, and how these factors can influence adult health status (American Academy

TABLE 5.3	**Health Conditions Related to Biologic Variations Among Racial Groups**
RACIAL GROUP	**HEALTH ISSUE**
African/African American	Diabetes mellitus Lactose intolerance Sickle cell disease
Asian/Asian American	Cleft lip and palate Lactose intolerance
Caucasian/European ancestry	Celiac disease Crohn's disease Cystic fibrosis Thalassemia (Mediterranean origin)
Hispanic/Latino	Diabetes mellitus Lactose intolerance
Native American/Alaskan Native	Alcoholism Diabetes mellitus Otitis media

Adapted from Giger (2013).

of Pediatrics [AAP] Committee on Pediatric Research, 2006). A major goal of Healthy People 2020 is to eliminate health disparities among these segments of the population (USDHHS, 2010).

CULTURAL COMPETENCE

Health and Health Care Disparities

Recent reports by the Institute of Medicine (IOM) and USDHHS have highlighted racial and ethnic disparities in health and health care (Mendoza, 2009). Health and health care disparities exist not only among racial and ethnic minorities but also among other vulnerable populations, such as the poor. These disparities are reflected in the higher morbidity and mortality rates in these groups (Centers for Disease Control and Prevention [CDC], 2013). *Health disparities* are defined as increased disease morbidity and mortality rates experienced by minority racial and ethnic groups as compared with the dominant group (USDHHS, 2010). These disparities are primarily a result of decreased access to health care services and other barriers to care. Barriers to health care for minority children include poverty, lack of health insurance, low level of education, language barriers for families that do not speak English, and provider knowledge deficits about culturally appropriate care (USDHHS, 2010). Other reasons include lack of transportation and the geographic location of the health care services. Environmental factors also play a role. For example, families that live in urban areas may be more vulnerable to health or safety hazards such as lead-based paint in old, urban dwellings.

The IOM (Smedley, Stith, & Nelson, 2002, p. 3) defines health care disparities "as racial or ethnic differences in the quality of health care that are not due to access-related factors or clinical needs, preferences, and appropriateness of intervention." Causes of health care disparities include provider racism, bias, and discrimination based on gender, religious affiliation, sexual orientation, or mental or physical disability. Patient factors may include poverty, geographic location, mistrust of the health care system, and refusal of treatment (USDHHS, 2010). Health and health care disparities are inextricably linked; cultural competence on the part of the health care provider is necessary to minimize and ultimately eliminate any differences in quality of health care.

Developing Cultural Competence

To decrease racial and ethnic disparities in health care, health care providers who works with diverse populations must be culturally competent. Such competence begins with the provider ensuring that the health care being provided is culturally appropriate for the specific child and family. Characteristics of culturally competent care include being able to identify and appreciate differences between cultures, having empathy and tolerance

for different views, and having the knowledge of shared human experiences despite varying backgrounds.

Cultural competence is the ability to understand and effectively respond to the cultural needs of the child and family and to demonstrate skill in interacting with those outside one's own culture (Spector, 2013). Subsumed within the concept of cultural competence is "cultural sensitivity"; one cannot be culturally competent without being sensitive to cultural differences (Dunn, 2002). To develop cultural competence, the provider should begin by examining his or her own values, biases, beliefs, prejudices, and stereotypes. The National Center for Cultural Competence (NCCC, 2014b) has developed a self-assessment tool that health care providers can use to determine their cultural competence (see Additional Resources at the end of the chapter). Cultural competence also includes the knowledge that even though the provider's values and beliefs may differ from those of the patient, he or she must accept the child and family as the expert on what is right for them. The development of cultural competence is an ongoing process that is not necessarily sequential. Dunn (2002) discussed six elements that demonstrate cultural competence in the health care provider.

1. **Altering one's worldview:** This can be accomplished by becoming aware of any personal tendencies toward ethnocentrism, bias, or racism and rejecting those tendencies, and at the same time, rejecting any institutional support of racism or discrimination.

2. **Increasing knowledge about the cultural groups with which the provider regularly works:** This can be accomplished by attending cultural events in the ethnic community, traveling to the countries from which patients hail, and reading books about the history of the patients' countries of origin. Learning to speak the language that patients speak is ideal as well, either by taking formal courses or through immersion experiences in a foreign country.

3. **Developing a trusting patient–provider relationship:** This involves making ensuring a welcoming physical environment, one in which the child and family feel comfortable and safe. Ways to achieve this include (a) speaking the child's and family's language or employing a bilingual–bicultural staff, (b) displaying pictures, posters, or artwork that reflect the cultures and ethnic backgrounds of patients with whom the provider works, and (c) ensuring that magazines, brochures, or printed teaching materials in reception areas or the clinic room are of interest to and reflect the different cultures of children and families served in the provider's practice. These materials should also be written in the patients' language and at the appropriate literacy level for the group served.

4. **Becoming familiar with the cultural beliefs about health and illness for a particular group:** The provider could start by asking the child or

parent what he or she thinks causes illness and what he or she believes a person should do to stay well. When asking a child or parent to explain what an illness means, Johnson, Hardt, and Kleinman (1995) suggest asking the following questions:

- What do you call the problem?
- What caused it?
- Why did it start?
- What does the illness do to make one ill?
- How serious is it?
- What do you expect will happen as a result of this illness?
- How should it be treated?
- What are the main problems that this illness has caused?
- About what are you most afraid with this illness?

5. **Developing health care goals that are mutually acceptable to the patient and health care provider:** This is not the same thing as getting the child and family to adhere to the goals and treatment plan set forth by the provider. Cultural beliefs about health and illness may necessitate the use of a "cultural broker" (see Culture Shock, at the end of this chapter) to agree on the plan of care.

6. **Becoming familiar with the core issues of a particular culture:** This includes having knowledge of beliefs about cultural patterns of communication, including eye contact, personal space, touch, and time; family relationships; male and female roles; childrearing practices; who makes the health care decisions in the family; and beliefs about modesty.

Kersey-Matusiak (2012) developed the Cultural Competency Staircase Model for nurses, which embodies the following six steps.

1. **Limited knowledge:** Nurse fails to recognize the importance of culture; may have graduated before this was introduced into the school curriculum.

2. **Growing awareness:** Nurse has a growing awareness but limited self-awareness about cultural groups.

3. **Acquired knowledge:** Nurse has begun to develop cultural awareness about one or two cultures and is attempting to integrate information into the plan of care.

4. **Expanding network:** Nurse has strong cultural awareness and has a network to draw on to get more information about diverse groups; consistently includes this knowledge in the plan of care.

5. **Applied expertise:** Nurse is highly self-aware and not only readily applies knowledge but can also anticipate potential problems.

6. **Problem solvers:** Nurse has attained a high level of self-awareness, a broad knowledge of other cultures, and can problem solve across cultural groups and mentor other nurses with this knowledge. There is still room for growth.

Among the many excellent resources listed at the end of the chapter are several that can help health care providers develop cultural competence.

CROSS-CULTURAL COMMUNICATION

As discussed in Chapter 3, communication is the way in which people share information; this information is transmitted both verbally and nonverbally. Cultural differences in communication can be a major influence on the quality of care. Effective cross-cultural communication involves respect, tolerance, patience, and flexibility. Nonverbal communication, such as eye contact and body language, is important, but spoken language barriers have been shown to have a major effect on health care (American Academy of Pediatrics [AAP] Committee on Pediatric Workforce, 2008). Providers should always strive to ask clear, culturally appropriate questions, involve extended family members in the discussion if requested, and alter nonverbal communication patterns as needed to maintain cultural sensitivity. Accurate, effective communication is essential to elicit an accurate, comprehensive health history, make accurate diagnoses, and develop health care goals that are acceptable to the family and child.

The Office of Minority Health of the USDHHS has developed national standards for effective cross-cultural communication in health care. (See Additional Resources at the end of the chapter.)

Nonverbal Communication

In addition to language differences, cultural differences regarding nonverbal communication can also create communication barriers between a child and family and the health care provider. Nonverbal communication differences include eye contact, perception of time, spatial distance, and touch.

Eye Contact

Providers must be aware of the appropriateness of eye contact when dealing with children and families of various cultures. For some cultures, maintaining eye contact when speaking is a sign of respect and establishes trust. African Americans and Americans of European ancestry use direct eye contact when speaking. For others, direct eye contact is avoided and may even be viewed as disrespectful. Many Native American people are uncomfortable with prolonged eye contact, as are Chinese people and Koreans (University of Washington Medical Center [UWMC], 2014).

Time

The concept of time is viewed in some cultures as something measurable and is defined as past, present, or future. Some people place more emphasis on one type of time orientation. For example, some cultures emphasize the past by stressing the importance of tradition and the influence of ancestors. Afghans (Giger, 2013), Filipinos (Vance, 2013), and Chinese people tend to focus on the past (Giger, 2013). People who focus on the past may pray to ancestors during illness or other times of crisis. Mexicans, Mexican Americans, and Navajo Indians are primarily oriented to the present (Giger, 2013). This may result in the child or parent being less inclined to take preventive measures to treat illness, especially if the child feels well currently or the treatment causes undesired side effects. For those living in poverty, time is also present oriented, and the future is seldom considered; setting goals and planning ahead is rare (Fiscella & Kitzman, 2009). Americans of European ancestry focus more on the future; they are interested in preventive medicine and value new medical procedures and drugs (Giger, 2013).

Another type of time orientation sees past, present, and future as less well defined and more fluid, and the future as less important than the present (Dunn, 2013). For people for whom this time perspective applies, there is no such thing as early or late, so making an appointment for a clinic visit may be difficult. People from Vietnam and some Native American cultures value this time perspective (Giger, 2013).

Spatial Distance

Spatial distance is the amount of physical space between people that is considered an appropriate distance. This distance, often termed *personal space*, varies, depending on the age, gender, social status, social situation, and culture of the people involved (Dunn, 2013). For example, Hispanic/Latino people normally stand close to a person when speaking, whereas Americans of European ancestry prefer to maintain more physical space between themselves and others.

Touch

People use touch as one form of communication. In some instances, touch can convey closeness and help establish trust and rapport. However, health care providers must be cognizant of the cultural norms for touch within the specific group with which they are working. Before touching the child or adolescent, providers should always explain what they will be doing to the child and the reason for touching him or her. In some instances, touch may even be culturally prohibited. For example, when working with an adolescent female Muslim, male providers are prohibited from touching or examining her, particularly for a pelvic examination (Hammoud, White, & Fetters, 2005). Vietnamese people consider the head sacred; thus, the provider should avoid touching a child's head whenever possible. If the head needs to be examined, the provider should also touch the opposite side of

the head or shoulder to make the child feel protected (CDC, 2012).

Verbal Communication

Language

Verbal communication involves both spoken and written language. With spoken language, dialects may differ vastly even among people from the same culture who speak the same language. Some people may speak a language but not read it well, and vice versa. It is vitally important for providers to ascertain whether they can effectively communicate with the parents or child in the same language. In the event that health care providers speak a language that differs from that of the parents or child, providers should make every effort to secure a trained interpreter to be present during the visit (see Chapter 3). Children should not be used to interpret during the health care encounter; in some cultures, this role reversal presents an inappropriate situation in addition to issues of confidentiality (see Chapter 6). The AAP (2008) has also issued a policy statement opposing the use of children and adolescents as medical interpreters for family members. When using an interpreter, the provider should always remember to speak directly to the child and parents and not to the interpreter.

Tone, Pitch, and Cadence

To provide culturally competent care, health care providers should be aware of the cultural differences regarding whom to address during the health care encounter; how to address them in terms of tone, pitch, cadence, vocabulary; and the use of silence (Giger, 2013). A child's parent should always be addressed as "Mr.," "Mrs.," or "Ms."; if they have a title such as "Dr.," that title should be used. In some Asian cultures (e.g., Chinese, Korean, Cambodian, Filipino), the family surname is listed first and then the child's given name. Asian patients may speak in a softer tone of voice and more slowly than health care providers; patients may perceive providers as loud, especially if providers are deliberately speaking loudly because they cannot hear the child or parent, or because a language barrier exists (Giger, 2013). Afghan women may speak loudly; Western health care providers may interpret this as speaking at a high volume. Afghan men speak more softly (Giger, 2013). When speaking to children and families, the provider should always keep the child's and parent's language abilities and level of education in mind; some simple words also have very different meanings and connotations, depending on the culture (Giger, 2013). The meaning of silence differs among cultures as well. Some cultures view silence as very uncomfortable and will try to talk to fill the gap; others, such as American Indians, and traditional Chinese and Japanese, prefer silence and view it as a time to reflect and understand (Giger, 2013).

(See Chapter 3 for further discussion of communication with children and families.)

CROSS-CULTURAL DIFFERENCES

Family Relationships

In the process of providing culturally competent care, health care providers must become familiar with the structure and importance of family for the cultural group with which they are working. This includes identifying the family structure of the particular cultural group, including the presence and influence of the extended family, sex roles, kinship ties (including whether or not this is limited to blood ties), whether the cultural group is patriarchal or matriarchal, and who is the head of the household. The head of the household may be the person to whom the family looks to make important decisions for the family, and this may have an impact on treatment decision making. Providers should also identify behavioral expectations of children for a particular cultural group, determine whether children are respected within the family, and determine whether corporal punishment is considered acceptable. Often, children and families that are new to a country experience great stress because of extra responsibilities, learning a new language, finding new friends, and fitting in at school. For many refugee families from traditional cultures, the power balance can shift because of role reversal when an adolescent must become the breadwinner, interpreter, or cultural liaison. Some children and adolescents must, of necessity, switch back and forth between cultures, adopting American values at school and the values of the family's culture at home. Peers may tease or taunt the immigrant child about his or her cultural background or about speaking with an accent. The child may feel pressure to reject the traditional culture and adopt the values of the new culture. This can cause great stress for children who are less resilient, resulting in somatic complaints such as headaches or stomachaches, difficulties with schoolwork, anxiety, depression, and stress-related illnesses. Chapter 4 discusses family assessment in further detail.

Childrearing Practices

Providers must be mindful during health assessments that childrearing practices differ among cultures. What one cultural or ethnic group considers acceptable in childrearing may not be so in another group. Providers must also avoid making value judgments, while at the same time assessing for any practices that may be harmful or abusive to the child. Specific areas of assessment on which to focus include nutrition, toilet training, discipline practices, sleeping, emphasis on schoolwork, education, reaction to crying, separation anxiety, and interaction with authority figures. Examples of some culturally specific childrearing practices are listed in Table 5.4.

Modesty

In some cultures, people are very modest about being touched or exposing the body without clothing, especially with health care providers of the opposite sex. This can pose challenges for providers who are performing even basic steps of the physical examination. Providers must be aware of populations with specific issues relating to modesty and be sensitive and respectful. For example, Mexican and Mexican American women are very modest, experiencing embarrassment during pelvic or external genitalia examination (Giger, 2013). Amish and Muslim women show modesty by covering their hair and arms. When Muslim girls reach puberty, they can choose to cover their hair with a head scarf and wear long-sleeved clothing and long skirts. For Muslims, this practice of modesty is called *hijab* (Giger, 2013). Adolescent girls who practice *hijab* need a female health care provider to perform breast and pelvic examinations.

HEALTH BELIEFS AND PRACTICES

When working with families from diverse backgrounds, the provider must be familiar with the child and family's perspective on health and illness, and whether they use any traditional healing practices. It is particularly important for the provider to be familiar with various traditional healing practices to ascertain which practices are potentially harmful to children (e.g., lead-based therapies) and to avoid misdiagnosing child abuse (e.g., coining, cupping).

Health Beliefs

Scientific or Biomedical Theory

There are three major belief systems about the causes of illness: scientific, holistic, and magico-religious (Andrews, 2012). The scientific or biomedical theory of health and illness is based on the belief that physiology explains the functioning of the human body. Illness is based on viruses, bacteria, environmental exposures, and bodily trauma. This belief is also referred to as Western medicine. Families who hold this belief expect providers to recommend or prescribe specific interventions, such as medications or surgery. Comfort measures such as rest or heat may not be as readily accepted, as the family or child may believe that nothing concrete is being done to alleviate the problem.

Holistic or Naturalistic Perspective

The holistic or naturalistic health belief posits that a child's illness is a result of the disruption in the balance of nature. Infection or illness can take hold in a child's body when it is not in balance. This belief is common among Native American, First Nation, and some Eastern cultures. Some Asians believe in the yin/yang theory, the belief that during states of good health, balance is maintained in the body. Many Hispanic, Arab, African

TABLE 5.4	Selected Cultural Variations in Childrearing Practices
ETHNIC GROUP	**CHILDREARING PRACTICES**
African American	• There is a strong emphasis on extended family; these family members may be involved in discipline • Scolding and corporal punishment from the matriarch (typical head of household) is often followed by forgiveness and offering of food; behavioral change is not often expected because of a strong belief in fate • Children are expected to show respect to authority figures
Arab American	• Male children are preferred • The father is the disciplinarian • Corporal punishment and shaming are accepted methods of discipline
Asian Indian	• Male children are preferred • Children are controlled and protected more so than American children • Discipline involves threats and occasional spanking • Independence is not encouraged • There is no fixed schedule of activities for young children • Education is highly valued
Cambodian/ Laotian	• Discipline is verbal; corporal punishment is rare • Elders are respected, including older siblings • Infants are carried for a prolonged period of time and thus walk later than Western children • Infants and young children are not allowed to cry
Chinese	• Male children are preferred • Elders are respected • Toilet training begins early • Children are often taught to suppress displays of emotion • Academic excellence and achievement are expected • Displays of open affection are rare
Filipino	• Children are adored • Parenting style is permissive until school age; then children are disciplined through negative feedback • Obedience and politeness are expected; children often seem shy or quiet
Japanese	• The mother views the infant as an extension of herself • Infants co-sleep with adults • Crying is discouraged in infants • Discipline is by example, with occasional light spanking • Elders in the family must be respected • Toilet training begins before 1 year • There is no open expression of emotion • Parenting style is permissive until school age; then the child must learn behavioral control • There is a heavy emphasis on academic achievement • Neatness and good manners are rewarded in children
Korean	• Male children are preferred • Children are highly valued; parents and children have close relationships • Birth order determines the child's status in the family • Elders in the family must be respected
Mexican/Mexican American	• Children are closely protected and highly valued • Children are kept physically close to the mother during first year of life • Children are strongly attached to the mother • Corporal punishment is common • Godparents are involved in childrearing • Overweight children are viewed as healthy
Navajo Indian	• Male children are preferred • A child's name may not be revealed until the first laugh • Infants are kept on cradleboards for protection • Children are taught to respect the elderly, who pass down tradition and wisdom • The grandmother often is the family member who is responsible for toilet training and discipline • Older children are often taught to suppress displays of emotion

TABLE 5.4	Selected Cultural Variations in Childrearing Practices (*continued*)
ETHNIC GROUP	**CHILDREARING PRACTICES**
Puerto Rican	• Children are highly valued; they are seen as gifts from God • Children are expected to be compliant • The mother has the primary role in childcare • Corporal punishment is common
Vietnamese	• Children are highly valued • Discipline may include stern talking, slapping, or occasionally beatings • Children are expected to be quiet and compliant

Sources: Engel (2006); Giger (2013); Spector (2013).

American, and some Asian groups believe the hot/cold theory of health and illness. According to this theory, certain illnesses are classified as hot or cold imbalances in the body and can only be cured by hot or cold remedies, such as consuming a food, beverage, herb, or medicine classified as the opposite of the disease, thereby restoring balance within the body. Examples of some of these illnesses and remedies are listed in Table 5.5.

Magico–Religious Perspective

The third major health belief is the magico–religious perspective. This belief holds that health and illness are determined by supernatural forces such as God, gods, voodoo, witchcraft, spirits, or fate (Andrews, 2012). One health belief that exemplifies this perspective is the "evil eye" (*mal de ojo*) in the Hispanic/Latino community. The evil eye is believed to cause harm or illness to a child, especially a newborn, by looking at the child with envy. A red bracelet made of thread is worn as an amulet or charm to protect the infant from the evil eye.

Folk Illnesses

Folk illnesses or *culture-bound syndromes* are those that are culturally defined. These illnesses often do not have a corresponding illness from a biomedical or scientific perspective and may not be perceived as an illness or affliction by another cultural group. Many folk illnesses have an emotional or spiritual element. Table 5.6 provides examples of selected folk illnesses.

TABLE 5.5	Hot and Cold Conditions and Corresponding Treatment		
HOT CONDITIONS	**COLD REMEDIES USED TO TREAT HOT CONDITIONS**	**COLD CONDITIONS**	**HOT REMEDIES USED TO TREAT COLD CONDITIONS**
Constipation Diarrhea Fever Infection Kidney problems Rashes Sore throat	**Food** • Barley water • Bottled milk • Chicken • Dairy products • Dried fruits • Fish • Fresh fruits • Fresh vegetables • Goat meat • Honey • Raisins **Medicines and Herbs** • Orange flower water • Sage • Milk of magnesia • Bicarbonate of soda	Cancer Headaches Joint pain Malaria Menstrual period Otitis media Pneumonia Stomach pain Teething Tuberculosis Upper respiratory infections	**Food** • Beef • Cheese • Chili peppers • Chocolate • Eggs • Goat's milk • Grains • Liquor • Oils • Onions • Peas **Medicine and Herbs** • Anise • Aspirin • Castor oil • Cinnamon • Cod-liver oil • Garlic • Ginger root • Iron • Tobacco • Penicillin • Vitamins

Sources: Purnell (2013); Wilson and Kneisl (1996).

Health Practices

Traditional Health Practices

Families from various cultural and ethnic groups may seek the care of traditional or folk healers. For some, these healers are consulted first; others use traditional or folk healers when their child is seriously ill or when they have become dissatisfied with scientific or biomedical approaches that have been unable to help their child. The type of healer varies according to the culture; Table 5.7 presents several examples. Traditional or folk healers speak the native language of the cultural group, make house calls, and cost much less than practitioners of Western medicine (Roy, Torrez, & Dale, 2004). Faith healing and religious rituals are often part of many folk healing practices, and items such as food substances,

TABLE 5.6	Selected Folk Illnesses		
ILLNESS	**DESCRIPTION**	**ETHNIC GROUP**	**CLINICAL IMPLICATIONS**
Caudal de la mollera (fallen fontanelle)	Believed to be caused by moving infant too quickly. Symptoms can include irritability and failure to thrive.	Hispanic/Latino	Treatment consists of holding infant upside down by the legs and shaking; may induce head injury similar to shaken baby syndrome.
Empacho (blocked intestines)	Food lodged in digestive tract; may be caused by a hot/cold food imbalance. Symptoms include anorexia, vomiting, diarrhea, abdominal pain, and distention.	Hispanic/Latino	Treatment may include abdominal massage to dislodge food; treatment is often done by *curandero(a)*. Treatment by a folk healer may also include *azarcon* or *greta*, a lead-based powder, which is mixed with water and given to child orally; this can result in lead poisoning in child.
Falling out	Affected person has a sudden collapse and is unable to see or speak, but can hear and understand.	Afro-Caribbean	This is a common response to tragic news such as death of a loved one.
Ceeb or *cheng* (fright illness)	Believed to occur after an intense emotional experience (e.g., fear, anger) but has many causes, including loud sounds, nightmares, falls, and immunizations (Capps, 1999).	Hmong	Signs and symptoms can include fever, crying, cold hands or feet, fear, insomnia, headache, and flailing arms (Moro reflex; Capps, 1999). It is treated by child's mother, grandmother, or in most cases, a traditional Hmong healer. Treatment is healing massage (Capps, 1999).
Mal de ojo (evil eye)	An evil or malevolent look that can cause child to become ill.	Hispanic/Latino	It is believed that children are particularly vulnerable. It can cause fever, rashes, diarrhea, vomiting, insomnia, crying, and irritability.
Susto (soul loss or magical fright)	Fright or shock that causes the soul to leave the body; it may cause anorexia, diarrhea, lethargy, insomnia, despondency, and withdrawal.	Hispanic/Latino	A *curandero(a)* is often used to treat the illness by performing specific rituals. The person suffering from *susto* is allowed to assume the sick role and is relieved from school or work.
Voodoo illness (e.g., hex, fix, witchcraft, spell, black magic)	Belief that illness is caused by a supernatural force.	Afro-Caribbean; Haitian	Symptoms can include nausea, vomiting, diarrhea, seizures, muscle weakness, paralysis, or complaints that animals are living inside the body.

Source: Purnell (2013).

charms, talismans, amulets, medals, or religious items are often worn to protect individuals against disease or evil spirits (Giger, 2013). Some traditional or folk healing practices may be harmful to a child. For example, one practice used by folk healers in the Hispanic/Latino community is *greta*, which is a lead-based powder used to treat abdominal and intestinal complaints;

this treatment can cause lead poisoning. This illustrates why, during the health assessment, health care providers should always ask what, if any, traditional methods of healing are used. Providers must always be nonjudgmental in the approach and help the family to seek alternatives to the traditional healing practice if the one used is harmful to an infant or child.

TABLE 5.7   Selected Types of Folk Healers and Healing Practices

CULTURAL GROUP	TYPE OF HEALING PRACTICE/ HEALER	DESCRIPTION	HEALTH PRACTICES	USE IN CHILDREN	CLINICAL IMPLICATIONS
African African American Haitian Native American	Shamanic Healing/ shaman	A shaman cures illness and conducts soul retrieval; this power is derived from the supernatural; healing powers have been passed down from the shaman's teacher from generation to generation (Giger, 2013)	Divination, soul retrieval, and hypnosis	Treatment of chronic pain	Children must be developmentally capable of cooperating with spiritual healing
Asian Indian Hindu	Ayurveda/ *ayurvedic* physician	This has been practiced in India for centuries; diseases in Ayurvedic medicine are considered to be psychosomatic (Giger, 2013)	Emphasizes diet and herbal remedies; stresses body/mind/spirit connection to disease prevention and treatment; medication not used	Used to cleanse body and restore physical and psychologic balance	Herbs, heavy metals, and minerals used may cause toxicity (e.g., lead poisoning), posing a safety concern for use in children.
African African American Haitian	Voodoo (Vodou)/priest or priestess, shaman (practitioner), "old granny" healers (African American), herbalists	This is folk medicine based on spirituality	Use of home remedies and herbs as suggested by healers or priests (Giger, 2013)	Voodoo healers are used as general caregivers for child and family (Giger, 2013)	Herbs may not be safe for children; those who use voodoo healing system may seek conventional health care for illness and injury only (Giger, 2013)

(continued)

TABLE 5.7	Selected Types of Folk Healers and Healing Practices (*continued*)				
CULTURAL GROUP	**TYPE OF HEALING PRACTICE/ HEALER**	**DESCRIPTION**	**HEALTH PRACTICES**	**USE IN CHILDREN**	**CLINICAL IMPLICATIONS**
African African American Hispanic/Latino	Witchcraft/ *brujos(as)* are witches (Hispanic/ Latino) who treat hexes, evil spells, or bad luck	A hex, evil spell, or bad luck can be placed by one person on another; motive for this is most often hatred or envy (Giger, 2013)	Oils, incense, candles, and amulets are used to repel evil	Used to treat *mal de ojo*	Burning of oils, candles, or incense may exacerbate respiratory problems in children; worn amulets with small pieces may present choking hazards in young children
Chinese Chinese American Vietnamese Vietnamese American	Traditional Chinese medicine/ physician, herbalist, and acupuncturist	Acupressure, acupuncture, coining, cupping, herbal medicine, massage, and moxibustion (heat treatment) restore balance between *yin* and *yang*	Coining entails rubbing the back vigorously with the edge of a coin (Ahn et al., 2006). Cupping entails placing a glass cup on the skin, lighting a candle, and then placing the candle at the base of the cup to create suction. Moxibustion involves igniting moxa plants and placing them near the skin, where small, approximately 1 cm craters will remain. Massage is used to increase circulation, joint flexibility, and increase body's resistance to illness (Giger, 2013; Xu & Chang, 2013).	Coining is used to treat fever, cough, headache, stiffness, and pain; cupping is used to treat pain and respiratory and digestive disorders; moxibustion is used to treat mumps or seizures	Treatment leaves linear (coining) or circular (cupping) bruising; moxibustion leaves small burns; health care providers unfamiliar with these practices may confuse the bruises and burns with physical abuse
Hispanic/Latino	*Curanderismo/* family folk healers • *yerberola* (uses herbs) • *curandero(a)* • *espiritista brujos(as)*	Herbs, massage, ritual cleansing, or religious rituals are used to heal physical and mental illnesses	Use of folk healers, hot and cold foods, herbs, massage, and prayers	Used to treat any illness in children, including folk illnesses listed in Table 4.6; families may combine	Intake of unregulated herbs may interact with other medications and have harmful effects;

TABLE 5.7	Selected Types of Folk Healers and Healing Practices (*continued*)				
CULTURAL GROUP	**TYPE OF HEALING PRACTICE/ HEALER**	**DESCRIPTION**	**HEALTH PRACTICES**	**USE IN CHILDREN**	**CLINICAL IMPLICATIONS**
	are witches and are used after other types of folk healing has failed (Giger, 2013)	Curanderismo and Western medicine. Healing rituals often involve other family members. Healers believe that good health is maintained by achieving a balance of hot and cold (Murray, 2007; Graham, 2010)			relying on curanderismo alone in the event of a serious illness (e.g., cancer, infectious disease) may lead to serious health consequences
Native American	Herbalist, shaman, medicine man or woman	Healing rituals often involve teas, herbs, sweating, and smudging to restore balance and harmony (Giger, 2013)	Ceremonies, herbal therapies, music, smudging, and sweatlodge	Used to treat any illness in children	Certain herbs may be harmful to small children; process of smudging, which involves burning sweet grass or sage, may exacerbate respiratory disorders in children

Complementary and Alternative Medicine

Most health care providers in the United States use modern medical care to treat illness and disease. However, the World Health Organization (WHO) estimates that the majority of people in the developing world use some type of complementary or alternative medicine (CAM) (e.g., herbal medicines, acupuncture, energy healing, spiritual therapies, meditation) or traditional healer for both episodic and primary health care (World Health Organization [WHO], 2014b). It is important for health care providers to be familiar with the types of CAM commonly used by the population with which they most commonly work and to be familiar with the safety and efficacy of these practices, especially when used with infants and young children. In 1998, the National Institutes of Health established the National Center for Complementary and Alternative Medicine (NCCAM). This agency was developed to explore the various types of CAM therapies and study these practices via rigorous, controlled, scientific studies and to disseminate these findings to health care providers and the public (National Center for Complementary and Alternative Medicine [NCCAM], 2012). Table 5.8 lists some examples of CAM therapies and traditional healing practices, and their uses in children.

Religious Practices and Spirituality

Many immigrants originally came to the United States seeking religious freedom. Because of this, a variety of religions are practiced in the United States. Individual differences must be noted, respected, and incorporated into the health assessment and plan of care. For example, Hispanic/Latino families may use prayer for healing, which does not affect the child's health in any adverse way. Alternatively, Jehovah's Witnesses are opposed to blood transfusions under all circumstances, including directed donor blood; this may cause the child's health to deteriorate.

TABLE 5.8	Selected Types of Complementary and Alternative Medicine		
HEALING PRACTICES	**DESCRIPTION**	**USE IN CHILDREN**	**CLINICAL IMPLICATIONS**
Acupuncture	Originated in China and India; the skin is penetrated with needles placed on acupuncture points; the point is massaged to achieve energy balance	To improve immune function, control pain, increase circulation and energy flow, control nausea, and promote relaxation (Murray, 2007); massage can be used for children with a fear of needles	Used mainly for children aged 10 years and older; younger children may not be able to follow instructions and hold still for insertion of needles (Murray, 2007)
Aromatherapy	Use of candles or essential oils from flowers, herbs, or trees to promote healing	To promote a sense of well-being and relaxation	Should not be used for children with asthma as burning of candles or oils may exacerbate respiratory distress
Biofeedback	Use of instrumentation that facilitates patient's awareness of and control over body's autonomic activity to allow voluntary control over certain physiologic processes (Glick & Greco, 2010)	Can be used to treat recurrent headaches and other stress-related disorders, pain associated with sickle cell crisis, juvenile rheumatoid arthritis, recurrent abdominal pain, anxiety, enuresis, encopresis and other chronic disorders (Kemper, Vohra, Walls & the Task Force on Complementary and Alternative Medicine, the Provisional Section on Complementary, Holistic, and Integrative Medicine, 2013)	Most often used as an adjunct to therapy and not as primary mode of treatment
Dietary supplements	Include vitamins, minerals, herbs, botanicals, amino acids, enzymes, organ tissues, and metabolites, which may come in the form of an extract, concentrate, tablet, capsule, gel cap, liquid, or powder	Probiotics to treat atopic dermatitis in children (Schuerman & Vezeau, 2007); echinacea for upper respiratory infections; fish oil for asthma, allergies, hyperlipidemia, bipolar disorder, attention deficit hyperactivity disorder, dyslexia, and rheumatoid arthritis; lactobacillus for gastrointestinal ailments (NCCAM, 2012); and daily multivitamins	Providers should always inquire about dietary supplements when obtaining health history; potential interactions may occur between dietary supplements and prescribed medications; mislabeling, misidentification, and contamination can cause toxicity (Kemper et al., 2013); safe dosages should also be addressed
Distraction techniques	Used to induce relaxation	Can include music, pet, play, and art therapies	Children must be old enough to be able to cooperate with therapy
Massage	Used to treat pain and emotional stress	Can be used for children with musculoskeletal disorders, teething discomfort, sinus pain, and emotional stress; gentle massage also is used in newborns to promote sleep and enhance bonding	Providers should assess for benefits; any fractures contraindicate massage; vigorous massage should be used only in children aged 12 years and older (Murray, 2007)

TABLE 5.8	Selected Types of Complementary and Alternative Medicine (*continued*)		
HEALING PRACTICES	**DESCRIPTION**	**USE IN CHILDREN**	**CLINICAL IMPLICATIONS**
Religious therapies	Include prayer, faith healing, laying on hands, anointing, exorcism, and pilgrimage	Depend on family's faith and severity of child's condition	Religion often strongly influences family's approach to health maintenance and treatment of illness and can give family great comfort when child has a serious illness; can cause harm to child if it *replaces* other therapies (e.g., for infection, oncologic disorders, blood loss)
Therapeutic touch	Uses light touch (no deep palpation) used to balance patient's energy field and restore energy imbalances (Kemper et al., 2013)	Used to treat anxiety, asthma, fatigue, insomnia, pain, and social isolation (Kemper & Kelly, 2004)	Providers should assess for health benefits of therapeutic touch (e.g., increased relaxation, decreased anxiety and pain, increased sense of well-being) (Kemper et al., 2013)

Source: National Institutes of Health, National Center for Complementary and Alternative Medicine (NCCAM; 2012).

ASSESSING IMMIGRANT AND REFUGEE CHILDREN

The children of immigrants present with needs that differ from children whose parents do not have the stressors related to leaving the home of one's birth. People in these groups include not only immigrant families but refugees and those seeking political asylum. Children who are adopted from foreign countries are also considered to be in this group. International adoptees often come from environments that do not meet the child's physical, psychological, or developmental needs, and relevant assessments must be made in these areas.

Assessment of immigrant and refugee children presents several challenges to health care providers. In addition to the likelihood of language and cultural barriers, these children often have unique health care needs. For example, a child may present with written proof of having received immunizations, but it is not known if the vaccines were stored at the appropriate temperature before the child received them; therefore, immunity to certain communicable diseases could be questioned. In particular, the provider should determine whether the child has received the bacillus Calmette-Guérin (BCG) vaccine, a vaccine frequently given in Mexico, the former Soviet Union, and Southeast Asia to prevent certain forms of tuberculosis. Children arriving from developing countries may also have problems that include unusual infectious diseases or nutritional problems with which health care providers in the industrialized world may not be familiar. Sensitivity to culture is also particularly important with respect to modesty, the use of traditional healers, and the presence of extended family members during the health care visit.

History and Physical Examination

When assessing immigrant and refugee children, it is important for the provider to obtain a careful, detailed history. This may take more than one clinic visit, and a trained medical interpreter is often necessary. Questions to ask when eliciting a general pediatric health history can be found in Chapter 6; for immigrant and refugee children, providers should also pay particular attention to the child's and family's social situation, including living arrangements, source of income, how many people are living in the home, and parental occupation. Providers must ask if the child is exposed to secondhand smoke in the home, especially when several adults are living together. The medication history should be obtained in a nonjudgmental manner with the provider asking about use of herbs, alcohol, or animals to treat illness or promote health.

The initial physical examination should be very thorough. In some cases, this may be the first physical examination the child has ever received. In particular, providers should note the child's dentition, any skin rashes, signs of malnutrition, or the presence of any infectious disease. Any signs of trauma or torture should be assessed; the two most common forms of torture are beatings and rape (Green, 2007). Often, these injuries are carried out using various items such as rubber hoses or electrical cables (Green, 2007). Physical evidence of these injuries includes scars, lacerations, burns, electric shocks, and genital trauma.

Providers should assess girls for the presence of female genital mutilation (FGM), which is practiced in some societies for cultural and religious reasons, and involves various degrees of cutting, sometimes removing the clitoris and external genitalia or stitching the vaginal opening closed (infibulation) (WHO, 2014a). Long-term complications of this procedure include cysts, abscesses, and keloid formation; urethral damage that can cause urinary incontinence; sexual dysfunction; prolonged labor and delivery; infertility; anxiety; and depression (WHO, 2014a). Through migration, FGM has spread to Western countries. Most girls who have undergone FGM come from Africa, Asia, and the Middle East. U.S. federal law specifically bans this practice. If a girl has undergone FGM, providers should assess for physical or psychosocial complications and make appropriate referrals as necessary.

The child's physical growth and developmental level should be assessed; significant delays are common among immigrant children. A psychosocial assessment should also be done to assess whether the child is suffering from culture shock, depression, or posttraumatic stress disorder, especially if the child has been witness to or victim of extreme violence or torture. For survivors of torture, further detailed assessments should be made, along with relevant referrals (see Box 5.1 and the Survivors of Torture, International website under Additional Resources). Table 5.9 summarizes some risk factors and medical and social problems that can affect immigrant children.

BOX 5.1   Assessing Immigrant Victims of Violence and Torture

- Has the child or family ever witnessed violence or torture in their country of origin?
- Has anyone in the child's family been a victim of violence or torture?
- Has the child been the victim of violence or torture?
- Would the child or parent like to be referred to a special counselor for help and treatment?

Culture Shock

The process of leaving one's homeland and coming to a new country with different sights, sounds, smells, noises, colors, activities, and with a new and unfamiliar language can cause disorientation and confusion and sometimes even anxiety and depression. People often do not know what behavior is appropriate and what is not. It is very important for providers to assess for signs of culture shock in immigrant or refugee children and families. These signs can include irritability, sadness, depression, powerlessness, disorientation, extreme homesickness, change in appetite and sleep patterns, inability to concentrate, headaches, and stomach pains (Ball, Bindler, & Cowen, 2012; Bhugra & Ayonrinde, 2004). People suffering from culture shock often seek out others who belong to their own culture as a way of finding something familiar and comforting. A *cultural broker* may be helpful to assist the child and family with cultural transition. Cultural brokers are individuals who are bicultural and bilingual and are willing and able to help people new to a country adjust to their new life. The use of a cultural broker also facilitates obtaining access to and helps to ensure the delivery of culturally and linguistically competent health care (NCCC, 2014a).

TABLE 5.9   Assessing Immigrant and Refugee Children

RISK FACTORS LEADING TO POOR CHILD HEALTH IN IMMIGRANT AND REFUGEE CHILDREN	COMMON MEDICAL PROBLEMS	SOCIAL PROBLEMS AFFECTING CHILD HEALTH
• Poor environmental sanitation • Poor hygiene practices • Overcrowded living conditions • Lack of clean water • Poor outdoor air quality • Exposure to indoor smoke and fire from solid fuels • Lack of immunizations • Low level of parental education • Poor or no prenatal care • No access to health care	• Diarrhea • Dehydration • Malnutrition • Acute respiratory infections • Pneumonia • Burns • Malaria • Measles • HIV/AIDS • Perinatal and neonatal morbidity and mortality	• Poverty • Child labor • Sexual exploitation of children • Effects of armed conflict • Child soldiers; psychologic trauma • Homelessness • Lack of formal education (child and parent) • Developmental delays

Sources: Bhuta and Black (2013); Cabral, Soares de Moura, and Berkelhamer (2012); Staton and Harding (2004).

Cultural Assessment

A formal cultural assessment should be included in every initial contact visit with a new child and family; providing culturally competent care to children and their families may mean the difference between health and illness. Box 5.2 presents guidelines for obtaining a cultural assessment.

BOX 5.2   Cultural Assessment

- What is the child or family's race?
- Where was the child born? Was the child born in a developing country? What are the specific physical and psychologic health risks in that country?
- What was the family's immigration experience like (if applicable)?
- Has the child or family spent time as refugees? If so, for how long?
- How long has the family lived in the United States?
- What is the family's current socioeconomic status?
- What is the child's ethnicity, and how strong is the family's ethnic identity?
- Does the family live in a community of people from the same ethnic background?
- What is the child's or family's primary language? Do they speak a secondary language?
- Can the child or family read in the primary language?
- Does the child or family speak and read English?
- What is the child's or family's educational level?
- What are the family's cultural values regarding time, personal space, and touch?
- Is there a specific family member who makes important decisions?
- What is the family's religion and how observant are family members? How do the religious beliefs of family members affect their daily lives and behavior patterns (e.g., modesty, opposite-sex health care providers)?
- What are the health and illness beliefs in the family?
- Does the family visit a traditional healer?
- Does the child or family have any specific food preferences, and are these linked to any cultural or religious rituals?
- Does the adolescent patient have any conflict with the parents concerning cultural norms and customs?
- Does the child, adolescent, or family have any concerns about discrimination or institutional racism?

From Duderstadt and Schapiro (2013).

SUMMARY

The need for the health care provider to be culturally competent is well recognized. Increased globalization contributes to the need for providers to become culturally and linguistically competent when working with children and families of diverse cultures. To convey respect, communicate effectively, make the most accurate assessments, and decrease health disparities, providers must be familiar with the family's cultural background and their spoken language. Becoming familiar with the sociocultural background of the child and family takes the "otherness" out of the health care encounter, decreases the chance of stereotyping, and enriches the experience of health care providers.

References

Ahn, A. C., Ngo-Metzger, Q., Legedza, A. T. R., Massagli, M.P., Clarridge, B.R., & Phillips, R.S. (2006). Complementary and alternative medical therapy use among Chinese and Vietnamese Americans: Prevalence, associated factors, and effects of patient–clinician communication. *American Journal of Public Health*, 96(4), 647–653.

American Academy of Pediatrics Committee on Pediatric Research. (2006). Race/ethnicity, gender, socioeconomic status-research exploring their effects on child health: A subject review. *Pediatrics*, 117(2), 577.

American Academy of Pediatrics Committee on Pediatric Workforce. (2008). Policy statement: Ensuring culturally effective pediatric care: Implications for education and health policy. *Pediatrics*, 114(6), 1677–1685, reaffirmed August 1, 2008.

Andrews, M. M. (2012). *Transcultural concepts in nursing care* (6th ed.). Philadelphia, PA: Lippincott Williams & Wilkins.

Ball, J. W., Bindler, R.C., & Cowen, K. J. (2012). Assessment and management of social and environmental influences. In J. W. Ball, R. C. Bindler, & K. J. Cowen (Eds.), *Principles of pediatric nursing: Caring for children* (5th ed., pp. 431–470). Upper Saddle River, NJ: Pearson Education.

Ball, J. W., Bindler, R.C.,& Cowen, K. J. (2012a). Family-centered care and cultural considerations. In J. W. Ball, R. C. Bindler, & K. J. Cowen (Eds.), *Principles of pediatric nursing: Caring for children* (5th ed., pp. 20–44). Upper Saddle River, NJ: Pearson Education.

Bhugra, D.,& Ayonrinde, O. (2004). Depression in migrants and ethnic minorities. *Advances in Psychiatric Treatment*, 10, 13–17.

Bhuta, Z. A., & Black, R. E. (2013). Global maternal, newborn, and child health—so near and yet so far. *New England Journal of Medicine*, 369, 2226–2235.

Cabral, S. A., Soares de Moura, A. T., & Berkelhamer, J. E. (2012). Overview of the global health issues facing children. *Pediatrics*, 29(1), 1–3.

Capps, L. L. (1999). Fright illness in Hmong children. *Pediatric Nursing*, 25(4), 378–383.

Center for American Progress. (2014). The facts on immigration today. Retrieved from http://www.americanprogress.org/issues/immigration/report/2013/04/03/59040/the-facts-on-immigration-today-3

Centers for Disease Control and Prevention. (2012). Overview of Vietnamese culture. In Centers for Disease Control and Prevention, *Promoting cultural sensitivity: A practical guide for tuberculosis programs that provide services to persons from Vietnam*. Atlanta, GA: Author. Retrieved from http://www.cdc.gov/tb/publications/guidestoolkits/ethnographicguides/Vietnam/chapters/chapter2.pdf

Centers for Disease Control and Prevention. (2013). *CDC health disparities and inequalities report—United States, 2013.* Retrieved from http://www.cdc.gov/mmwr/preview/ind2013_su.html#HealthDisparities2013

Duderstadt, K. G., & Schapiro, N. A. (2013). Comprehensive information gathering. In K. G. Duderstadt (Ed.), *Pediatric physical examination: An illustrated handbook* (2nd ed., pp. 36–54). St. Louis, MO: Mosby/Elsevier.

Dunn, A. M. (2002). Culture competence and the primary care provider. *Journal of Pediatric Health Care, 16*(3), 105–111.

Dunn, A. M. (2013). Cultural perspectives for pediatric primary care. In C. E. Burns, A. M. Dunn, M. A. Brady, N. B. Starr, & C. G. Glosser (Eds.), *Pediatric primary care* (5th ed., pp. 32–43). St. Louis, MO: Saunders.

Engel, J. K. (2006). Beginning the assessment. In J. K. Engel (Ed.), *Mosby's guide to pediatric assessment.* (5th ed., pp. 3–9). St. Louis, MO: Mosby/Elsevier.

Fiscella, K., & Kitzman, H. (2009). Disparities in academic achievement and health: The intersection of child education and health policy. *Pediatrics, 123*(3), 1073–1080.

Giger, J. N. (2013). *Transcultural nursing: Assessment & intervention* (6th ed.). St. Louis, MO: Mosby/Elsevier.

Giger, J.N., & Davidhizar, R. (2002). The Giger and Davidhizar transcultural assessment model. *Journal of Transcultural Nursing, 13,* 185–188.

Glick, R.M., & Greco, C. M. (2010). Biofeedback and primary care. *Primary Care, 37*(1), 91–103.

Graham, J. (2010). *Curanderismo. Handbook of Texas online.* Retrieved from http://www.tshaonline.org/handbook/online/articles/CC/sdc1.html

Green, C. (2007). Politically-motivated torture and child survivors. *Pediatric Nursing, 33*(3), 267–270.

Hammoud, M.M., White, C.B.,& Fetters, M. D. (2005). Opening cultural doors: Providing culturally sensitive healthcare to Arab American and American Muslim patients. *American Journal of Obstetrics and Gynecology 193,* 1307–1311.

International Federation of Library Associations. (2013). *Defining "multiculturalism."* Retrieved from http://www.ifla.org/publications/defining-multiculturalism

Johnson, T., Hardt, E., & Kleinman, A. (1995). Cultural factors in the medical interview. In M. Lipkin, S. Putnam, & A. Lazare (Eds.), *The medical interview* (pp. 153–162). New York, NY: Springer-Verlag.

Kemper, K.J., & Kelly, E. A. (2004). Treating children with therapeutic healing touch. *Pediatric Annals, 33*(4), 248–252.

Kemper, K.J., Vohra, S, Walls, R. & the Task Force on Complementary and Alternative Medicine, the Provisional Section on Complementary, Holistic, and Integrative Medicine. (2013). Statement of re-affirmation: The use of complementary and alternative medicine in pediatrics. *Pediatrics, 131*(5), e1707.

Kersey-Matusiak, G. (2012). *Developing culturally competent nursing care.* New York, NY: Springer Publishing.

Leininger, M. (2002). Theory of culture care and the ethnonursing research method. In M. Leininger, & M. R. McFarland (Eds.), *Transcultural nursing concepts, theories, research and practice* (3rd ed., pp. 71–98). New York, NY: McGraw-Hill.

Leininger, M., & McFarland, M. R. (2006). *Culture care diversity and universality: A worldwide nursing theory* (2nd ed.). Sudbury, MA: Jones and Bartlett.

Lewis, O. (1959). *Five families: Mexican case studies in the culture of poverty.* New York, NY: Basic Books.

Lewis, O. (1998). The culture of poverty. *Society, 35*(2), 7.

Ludwick, R., & Silva, M. C. (2000). Ethics: Nursing around the world: Cultural values and ethical conflicts. *Online Journal of Issues in Nursing, 5*(3). Retrieved from http://www.nursingworld.org/MainMenuCategories/ANAMarketplace/ANAPeriodicals/OJIN/Columns/Ethics/CulturalValuesandEthicalConflicts.html

Mendoza, F. (2009). Health disparities and children in immigrant families: A research agenda. *Pediatrics, 124*(3), S187–S185.

Murray, F. A. (2007). CAM for children. *Advance for Nurses,* 18–21.

National Center for Complementary and Alternative Medicine. (2012). *NCCAM facts-at-a-glance and mission.* Retrieved from http://nccam.nih.gov/about/ ataglance

National Center for Cultural Competence. (2014a). *Bridging the cultural divide in health care settings: The essential role of cultural broker programs.* Retrieved from http://culturalbroker.info/2_role/index.html

National Center for Cultural Competence. (2014b). *Cultural competence health practitioner assessment.* Retrieved from http://nccc.georgetown.edu/resources/assessments.html

National Center for Cultural Competence. (2014c). *Home page.* Retrieved from http://www11.georgetown.edu/research/gucchd/nccc/index.html

Purnell, L. D. (2013). *Transcultural health care: A culturally competent approach* (4th ed.) Philadelphia, PA: F. A. Davis.

Roy, L.C., Torrez, D., & Dale, J. C. (2004). Ethnicity, traditional health beliefs and health-seeking behavior; guardians' attitudes regarding their children's medical treatment. *Journal of Pediatric Health Care, 18*(1), 22–29.

Schuerman, G., & Vezeau, T. (2007). All bugs aren't bad: Probiotics in the treatment of pediatric atopic dermatitis. *American Journal for Nurse Practitioners, 11*(4), 28–36.

Smedley, B.D., Stith, A.Y., & Nelson, A. R. (2002). *Unequal treatment: Confronting racial and ethnic disparities in health care. Institute of Medicine Report.* Washington, DC: National Academies Press.

Spector, R. E. (2013). *Cultural diversity in health and illness* (8th ed.). Upper Saddle River, NJ: Pearson Prentice-Hall.

Srivastava, R. H. (2007). Understanding cultural competence in health care. In R. H. Srivastava (Ed.), *The healthcare profession al's guide to clinical cultural competence* (pp. 3–27). St. Louis, MO: Mosby/Elsevier.

Staton, D.M., & Harding, M. H. (2004). Protecting child health worldwide. *Pediatric Annals, 33*(10), 647–655.

Tashiro, C. (2005). The meaning of race in health care and research-Part I: The impact of history. *Pediatric Nursing, 31*(3), 208–210.

U.S. Census Bureau. (2011). *Overview of race and Hispanic origin: 2010.* Retrieved from http://www.census.gov/prod/cen2010/briefs/c2010br-02.pdf

U.S. Census Bureau. (2013). *Income, poverty and health insurance coverage in the United States: 2012.* Retrieved from https://www.census.gov/newsroom/releases/archives/income_wealth/cb13-165.html

U.S. Census Bureau. (2014). *U.S. Census Bureau projections show a slower growing, older, more diverse nation a half century from now.* Retrieved from http://www.census.gov/newsroom/releases/archives/population/cb12-243.html

U.S. Citizenship and Immigration Services. (2013). *Refugees.* Retrieved from http://www.uscis.gov/humanitarian/refugees-asylum/refugees

U.S. Department of Health and Human Services. (2010). *Healthy people 2020.* Washington, DC: U.S. Government Printing Office.

U.S. Department of Health and Human Services: Office of Minority Health. (2013). *What is cultural competency?* Retrieved from http://minorityhealth.hhs.gov/templates/browse.aspx?lvl=2&lvlID=11

University of Washington Medical Center. (2014). *Culture clues.* Retrieved from http://depts.washington.edu/pfes/CultureClues.htm

Vance, A. R. (2013). Filipino Americans. In J. N. Giger (Ed.), *Transcultural nursing: Assessment & intervention* (6th ed., pp. 403–425). St. Louis, MO: Mosby/Elsevier.

Wilson, H.,& Kneisl, C. (1996). *Psychiatric nursing* (5th ed.). Reading, MA: Addison-Wesley.

World Health Organization. (2014a). *Female genital mutilation.* Retrieved from http://www.who.int/mediacentre/factsheets/fs241/en

World Health Organization. (2014b). *Traditional medicine*. Retrieved from http://www.who.int/topics/traditional_medicine/en

Xu, Y.,& Chang, K. (2013). Chinese Americans. In J. N. Giger (Ed.), *Transcultural nursing: Assessment & intervention* (6th ed., pp. 383–402). St. Louis, MO: Mosby/Elsevier.

Additional Resources

American Public Health Association

http://www.apha.org/programs/additional/mch/programsResource Center.htm

This website provides numerous links for the health care provider regarding children in poverty, minority health, health inequities, multiculturalism, maternal–child health, and health disparities among immigrants.

Amnesty International

http://www.amnesty.org

This is a worldwide organization, the goal of which is to protect human rights for all people.

The Boston Healing Landscape Project

http://www.bmc.org/pediatrics/special/bhlp

This project is affiliated with the Department of Pediatrics at Boston University School of Medicine. It includes a web-based tutorial, focusing on various culturally and religiously based practices of Africans, Haitians, Latin Americans, and Chinese.

Centers for Disease Control and Prevention (CDC): Racial and Ethnic Approaches to Community Health (REACH)

http://www.cdc.gov/reach2010/index.htm

REACH is a national program through the CDC that aims to eliminate racial and ethnic disparities in health.

Complementary and Alternative Medicine

http://www.nccam.nih.gov

National Institutes of Health–National Center for Complementary and Alternative Medicine (NCCAM).

Health Resources and Services Administration (HRSA) Cultural Competence Resources

http://www.hrsa.gov/culturalcompetence

This is a comprehensive listing of cultural competence resources and web links for health care providers, including information about cultural brokers.

National Center for Cultural Competence

http://www11.georgetown.edu/research/gucchd/nccc

The website of the National Center for Cultural Competence (NCCC) at Georgetown University Center for Child and Human Development includes information relating to provider self-assessment of cultural and linguistic competency. Information is also available on the role of cultural brokers in health care delivery and developing cultural broker programs. Web access for the cultural competency self-assessment tool for health care providers is available at: https://www4.georgetown.edu/uis/keybridge/keyform/form.cfm?formID=277

Survivors of Torture, International

http://www.notorture.org/links.html

Survivors of Torture, International is an independent nonprofit organization dedicated to caring for survivors of politically motivated torture. This organization also focuses on educating the professional community and the general public about torture and the needs of torture survivors.

Therapeutic Touch

Healing Touch International: http://healingtouch.net

Nurse Healers–Professionals Associates International, Inc.: http://therapeutic-touch.org

UNHCR: The United Nations Refugee Agency

http://www.unhcr.org/cgi-bin/texis/vtx/home

The UNHCR leads and coordinates international assistance to worldwide refugees, safeguards the rights and well-being of refugees, and helps refugees to seek asylum and find safe refuge, with the option to return home voluntarily, settle locally, or to resettle in a third country.

U.S. Department of Health and Human Services Office of Minority Health

http://www.omhrc.gov

The Office of Minority Health home page offers information on cultural competency and health disparities among minorities.

The Universal Declaration of Human Rights

http://www.unhchr.ch/udhr (translated into hundreds of languages)

This document was developed by several world leaders after World War II and adopted by the United Nations on December 10, 1948. It consists of 30 articles that outline universal human rights according to the General Assembly of the United Nations. The full text can be found at http://www.un.org/Overview/rights.html

University of Michigan Health System Program for Multicultural Health

http://www.med.umich.edu/multicultural/ccp/tools.htm#basic

This is an educational program, the goal of which is to improve the health status of underserved multicultural populations through cultural competency training, cultural health promotion programs, and education for health care systems, academia, and the community.

University of Washington Medical Center

http://depts.washington.edu/pfes/cultureclues.html

This is a series of handouts called "Culture Clues" that briefly summarize the cultural characteristics of a particular group. It is designed to assist the health care provider in learning the basics about a patient's culture quickly and easily.

Medical Interpreters

Languageline.com

http://www.languageline.com

This website provides links to medical interpreters by phone to be used during health encounters; document and video translations are also provided.

Pacific Interpreters

http://www.pacificinterpreters.com
This language services company provides language assistance and interpretation for health care and social service providers by phone.

Suggested Readings

Reading about other cultures and people's experiences can assist providers in achieving the goal of developing cultural competence. The following list of readings is suggested to aid in learning about various cultures. Fiction, nonfiction, and memoirs are included.

Nonfiction

Chang, I. (1998). *The rape of Nanking: The forgotten holocaust of World War Two*. New York, NY: Penguin.

Chang, I. (2003). *The Chinese in America*. New York, NY: Penguin.

Chideya, F. (1999). *The color of our future*. New York, NY: William Morrow.

Fadiman, A. (1997). *The spirit catches you and you fall down*. New York, NY: Farrar, Straus and Giroux.

Gourevitch, P. (1998). *We wish to inform you that tomorrow we will be killed with our families: Stories from Rwanda*. New York, NY: Farrar, Straus and Giroux.

Kotolowitz, A. (1991). *There are no children here*. New York, NY: Doubleday.

Lewis, O. (1959). *Five families: Mexican case studies in the culture of poverty*. New York, NY: Basic Books.

Pipher, M. (2002). *The middle of everywhere: The world's refugees come to our town*. New York, NY: Harcourt Press.

Root, M. P. P., & Kelley, M. (2003). *Multiracial child resource book: Living complex identities*. Seattle, WA: Mavin Foundation.

Thompson, G. (2007). *There's no Jose here: Following the hidden lives of Mexican immigrants*. New York, NY: Nation Books.

Wilson, W. J. (1996). *When work disappears: The world of the new urban poor*. New York, NY: Knopf.

Wu, F. H. (2002). *Yellow: Race in America beyond black and white*. New York, NY: Basic Books.

Memoirs

Chen, D. (1999). *The colors of the mountain*. New York, NY: Anchor Books.

Crow Dog, M. (1990). *Lakota woman*. New York, NY: Grove Weidenfeld.

Him, C. (2000). *When broken glass floats: Growing up under the Khmer Rouge*. New York, NY: W. W. Norton.

Hirsi Ali, A. (2007). *Infidel*. New York, NY: Free Press.

McBride, J. (1996). *The color of water: A black man's tribute to his white mother*. New York, NY: Riverhead.

Trenka, J. J. *The language of blood*. St. Paul, MN: Borealis Books.

Ung, L. (2000). *First they killed my father: A daughter of Cambodia remembers*. New York, NY: HarperCollins.

Ung, L. (2005). *Lucky child*. New York, NY: HarperCollins.

Walls, J. (2005). *The glass castle*. New York, NY: Simon & Schuster.

Children's Books

Fox, M., & Staub, L. (1997). *Whoever you are*. New York, NY: Voyager Books; Harcourt.

Katz, K. (1999). *The colors of us*. New York, NY: Henry Holt.

Krebs, L., & Cairns, J. (2003). *We all went on safari*. New York, NY: Scholastic.

Mayer, G., & Mayer, M. (1998). *Just a little different*. New York, NY: Golden Books.

Miles, M., & Parnall, P. (1971). *Annie and the old one*. New York: Little, Brown and Company.

Moore, S.T., & Futran, E. (1998). *Somewhere today: A book of peace*. Morton Grove, IL: Albert Whitman.

Rappaport, D., & Collier, B. (2001). *Martin's big words*. New York, NY: Scholastic.

Simonds, N., Swartz, L., So, M., & The Children's Museum, Boston. (2002). *Moonbeams, dumplings & dragon boats*. New York, NY: Gulliver Books; Harcourt.

Sister Susan, Nguyen, T. H., & Nguyen, D. (2001). *Each breath a smile: Based on the teachings by Thich Nhat Hanh*. Berkeley, CA: Parallax Press.

THE PEDIATRIC HISTORY AND PHYSICAL EXAMINATION

GATHERING SUBJECTIVE DATA

Obtaining the Pediatric Health History

HOW TO CONDUCT A PEDIATRIC HISTORY INTERVIEW

Obtaining an accurate and complete pediatric health history is essential when providing health care to children. The accuracy of the physical examination and diagnoses depend, in large part, on whether the health history is accurate and complete. In the pediatric population, obtaining a complete health history can be challenging, for example, when the child is preverbal, temperamentally shy, or embarrassed to disclose information about his or her body or life choices. The pediatric health care provider must possess excellent communication skills when working with children and families in order to elicit the most accurate and complete health history while maintaining provider–patient trust.

Communication

Communicating well and establishing rapport with the parent or primary caregiver and the child are the crucial first steps when obtaining the health history interview (see Chapter 3). This not only lays the foundation for a trusting relationship but also conveys to the parent and child that they are important. If trust is established during this interview, the child is likely to be more cooperative during the physical examination, and more accurate data are likely to be obtained. When interviewing the child and parent, the provider must ask questions in a nonjudgmental, unhurried manner, avoiding interruptions whenever possible. The provider should sit down when taking the history, thereby conveying to the child and parent that the provider has time for them and is interested in what they have to say. Maintaining privacy and confidentiality during the interview is also essential and further facilitates the establishment of trust.

Reliability and Accuracy of the History

During the health history interview, it is important for the provider to determine the reliability and accuracy of the historian, in most cases the child's parent or guardian. This involves assessing the quality of the historian's responses to questions with respect to clarity, consistency, or vagueness of the information provided. The provider should also assess the historian's anxiety level. A reliable historian provides clear, consistent information. It is important to assess whether or not the historian fully understands the questions being asked. For this reason, the provider should avoid using medical terminology or jargon, as this may be confusing. If the historian does not speak English, a trained interpreter should be provided. Using the child to translate questions and responses into English should be avoided; in some cultures, when a child assumes such a responsibility, the role reversal is deemed inappropriate and conveys disrespect to the parent (American Academy of Pediatrics [AAP] Committee on Pediatric Workforce, 2008). Also, a young child is unlikely to have the maturity and vocabulary to interpret the interview correctly. This can lead to inaccuracies, which could result in misdiagnoses and potential legal liabilities (Lehna, 2005). This topic is discussed further in Chapter 5.

Developmental Considerations

Whether or not a child participates in providing his or her own history depends on the child's chronologic age, developmental level, and temperament. When developmentally appropriate, all pediatric patients, preschool-aged and older, should participate in the interview process, giving the provider an opportunity to assess the child's language abilities, social skills, and knowledge of health and illness (Instone, 2002). This inclusive approach also allows the provider to note the child's cognitive abilities and intellectual skills and provides a cursory view of the child's or teen's overall behavior and temperament. In addition, it conveys to the child that he or she is important and that the health care provider is interested in hearing about his or her life and concerns. It also prepares the child for being a lifelong, active participant in his or her own health care. The developmental aspects of communicating with children and adolescents are reviewed in Chapter 3.

Infants and Young Children • For infants and preverbal children, the primary source of historical information is the parent or primary caregiver. For older infants and toddlers, it is important that the parent remain within eyesight of the child to minimize stranger anxiety. Parents can then concentrate on answering questions rather than tending to a crying child (Figure 6.1). Some preschoolers can answer questions during the history, depending on their language abilities, developmental level, and temperament. These questions may involve play, toys, likes, dislikes, friends, and school. Young children who are very shy should not be forced to participate in the interview, and children should not be overwhelmed with too many questions. The health care provider should remember to use simple terms and avoid medical jargon.

School-Aged Children and Adolescents • Children who are school-aged and older can provide their own

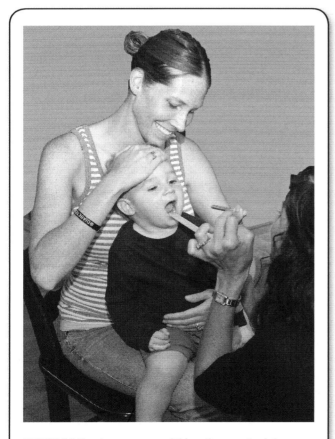

FIGURE 6.1 Keeping a younger child on the caregiver's lap during the interview helps to minimize stranger anxiety and increases the child's sense of security.

health history with verification from the parent or caregiver as needed. Beginning the encounter with the parent in the room is important to make the child feel comfortable and secure. Older school-aged children and adolescents have a heightened need for privacy. For this reason, the parent should be asked to leave the room for certain portions of the history, such as questions that deal with drug or alcohol use, sexual activity, depression, and risk-taking behaviors. The preteen or adolescent is more likely to give accurate answers without the parent present. Before this portion of the health history is obtained, however, it is important for the health care provider to establish a rapport with the child by asking questions about his or her life that are not emotionally charged, such as those concerning school, friends, activities, hobbies, and interests. Then the provider can proceed to more sensitive issues (Instone, 2002). The adolescent should be reassured that what is discussed with the provider is confidential, unless intervention is necessary to avoid harm to the teen or others.

Physical Surroundings

Facilitation of history-taking includes providing an appropriate physical environment. A comfortable and welcoming environment helps the health care provider obtain the most complete health history possible. There should be a place for everyone in the room to sit and an examination table on which the child may lie down. Examination rooms should also be clean, well lit, and child safety-proofed, ensuring that any equipment, needles, or medications are kept out of reach. The room should be kept at a comfortable temperature, and there should be minimal noise that could distract the health care provider, parent, or child. Age-appropriate toys and books in both the waiting and examination rooms provide welcome diversions for children and help to occupy the child so the parent can concentrate on giving a proper history. This also allows the provider an opportunity to assess the child's attention span, ability to play independently, and overall behavior. Additionally, this allows the provider to observe parent–child interactions.

The examination rooms should be decorated in an age-appropriate manner. Pediatric clinics that function as "teen clinics" during off-peak hours should have rooms set aside in which adolescents will feel comfortable and relaxed. Motifs that employ popular cartoon characters are appropriate for very young children but may be off-putting to an adolescent.

TYPES OF PEDIATRIC HEALTH HISTORIES

Before the provider can obtain the health data, the reason for the child's health care visit must be determined; the type of health history that is necessary is dictated by the purpose of the visit. Types of pediatric health histories include:

■ **Initial (comprehensive) health history:** An initial health care visit requires a comprehensive health history, which creates a database of information for the child who is new to the provider's practice.

The data collected in this history focus not just on past or current illnesses, but also on wellness, health patterns, health knowledge, and activities of daily living (ADL). The content of this history creates a baseline against which all future changes in the child's health status are measured.

- **Interval (well-child) health history:** Subsequent well-child visits require an interval history; that is, a history that updates the patient's health status since the last office visit.
- **Focused (episodic) health history:** This history is problem-centered, focusing on the present illness or problem. A focused health history is all that is necessary when the child presents with an acute problem or the exacerbation of a chronic condition.
- **Follow-up health history:** When the child returns to the office after an illness or injury, a follow-up history is taken to assess whether the problem is the same, better, or worse.
- **Emergency health history:** An emergency health history involves the quick collection of data in an acute situation. While this history resembles a focused history, it needs to be obtained rapidly, usually simultaneously with interventions, such as the administration of medications or respiratory treatments.

When obtaining a pediatric health history, it is important to remember that these various histories are not mutually exclusive. For example, if the provider notices that a child appears ill during a yearly well-child visit, a focused history should be obtained regarding the current illness. Similarly, if a child presents for an acute visit but appears to the provider to be underweight and has not reached appropriate developmental milestones, questions must be directed to these problems as well as the presenting illness.

Several components of the health history are common to all types of pediatric health histories. These components include relevant biographical information, such as the child's name, nickname, age, date of birth, gender, race, ethnicity, religion, and the child and family's primary spoken language. The parent or primary caregiver's name, address, and phone numbers (i.e., home, work, cell phone) should also be recorded. An emergency contact, with an address and phone number, should be obtained as well.

The provider should always record the source of historical information and assess the reliability of the informant and that person's relationship to the child. The chief complaint or the reason for seeking health care is recorded no matter what type of health history is obtained. This should be brief and stated in the parent's or child's own words (not paraphrased by the provider). The reason for seeking health care is elicited by asking open-ended questions such as, "What brings you here today?"

The provider should treat all concerns seriously and listen carefully for "hidden agendas." Sometimes the chief complaint of the child is very different from the concerns of the parent or caregiver. Also, adolescents and their parents may differ greatly in what they see as the chief complaint.

For every health care encounter, the child's past medical history (PMH) must be obtained and reviewed as this provides important information about all aspects of the child's general health. The pediatric PMH includes the prenatal and birth histories, the immunization history, and a history of growth and development (see Past Medical History section that follows). This information can be used to make a diagnosis in the child. It may also provide information about the teaching needs of parents. In addition, a pediatric PMH includes a comprehensive review of systems (ROS), the components of which are listed in Table 6.1.

The provider must assess the child's family medical history, as it helps to determine the health status of family members and may help to narrow the differential diagnoses. All pediatric health histories must include an up-to-date allergy history. In addition, a list of current daily and as-needed medications should be elicited, including the dose, the frequency of the drug, and an indication for its use. A list of herbal remedies must also be obtained. The provider should determine if the child's immunizations are up to date or if there have been any reactions to past immunizations.

Initial Health History

The initial health history is a comprehensive health history, one that makes up the child's baseline database. An initial health history is conducted for all pediatric patients when they are seen for the first time. Because taking the initial health history is time-consuming, a full hour should be allotted for the visit, which also includes the physical examination. The initial health history begins by obtaining general biographical information, recording the source of this information, and assessing the reliability of the informant. The reason for seeking health care is documented; it is usually the first visit by the infant, child, or adolescent. A detailed PMH should be obtained, which needs to be updated each time the child is seen.

Past Medical History

Prenatal, Birth, and Neonatal History • The depth of this history-taking depends on the child's age. The younger the child, the more important this information is, as prenatal, birth, and neonatal events are crucial to a child's future physical and psychosocial growth and development and may explain any neurologic or developmental problems. The provider should obtain as much detail as possible in these areas in children 3 years of age and younger and in older children who have ongoing problems because of a birth injury.

TABLE 6.1	Pediatric Review of Systems
General	Overall state of health; recent weight loss or gain (compare to growth charts); obesity; delays in physical, psychosocial, or language development; fatigue; weakness; malaise; difficulty performing activities of daily living; or chronic pain
Integument	General skin texture, birthmarks, or pigmentation; skin color changes (jaundice, cyanosis, mottling, pallor, bruising, or petechiae); rashes or lesions (location and description); excessive skin dryness; pruritus; hives; atopic dermatitis; contact dermatitis; seborrhea; acne; changes in moles; changes in body hair (excessive hair growth or loss or hair color change); nail disorders; or pediculosis
Head	Head size and shape (including fontanelles), microcephaly, macrocephaly, head injuries, headaches, or dizziness
Eyes	Visual problems (blurred vision, double vision, bumping into objects, sitting very close to the television or computer screen, inability to see blackboard, holding book very close to face, squinting, rubbing eyes, photophobia, use of glasses or contact lenses), date of last eye exam and results, strabismus, dizziness, eye drainage or infections, excessive tearing, or eyelid edema
Ears	Ear infections (e.g., otitis media, otitis externa), ear pain, ear drainage, surgery (e.g., myringotomy with tympanostomy tubes), delayed speech, evidence of hearing loss, date of last hearing exam and result, or tinnitus
Nose	Frequent rhinorrhea, upper respiratory infections, sinusitis, allergic rhinitis, stuffy nose, nasal congestion, allergies, mouth breathing, snoring, obstructive sleep apnea, epistaxis, allergic salute, allergic crease, dark circles under eyes, or altered sense of smell
Mouth/throat	Pattern of tooth eruption or loss, number of teeth, teething (infants), dental care, use of fluoride, dental caries, age of first dental visit, date of last visit to dentist, frequency of dental visits, tooth pain, history of dental trauma, sores in mouth or tongue, history of oral candidal infections, gum bleeding, mouth breathing, tonsillar enlargement or infections, history of tonsillectomy, postnasal drip, cleft lip or palate, sore throats, streptococcal infections, difficulty chewing or swallowing, hoarseness, or voice and cry irregularities
Neck	Limitation of movement, pain, stiffness, torticollis, thyroid enlargement, or lymphadenopathy
Chest	Pain, newborn breast enlargement, female thelarche, male gynecomastia, breast lesions, discharge, or enlarged axillary nodes
Lymphatics	Frequent infections, fevers, pain, swelling, tenderness of any lymph nodes, hepatosplenomegaly, chills, night sweats, or pallor
Respiratory	Frequent respiratory infections, dyspnea (shortness of breath), apnea, stridor, croup, pneumonia, cystic fibrosis, asthma, wheezing, chronic cough, sputum production, reduced exercise tolerance, dyspnea at rest or on exertion, cyanosis, or tuberculosis; date of last chest radiograph and skin reaction from tuberculosis skin testing; or history of smoking or secondhand smoke exposure
Cardiovascular	Murmurs, congenital heart defects, poor infant feeding, slow or decreased weight gain, chest pain, cyanosis, tachypnea, tachycardia, hypertension, edema, cold extremities, dizziness, palpitations, fainting spells, exercise intolerance, dyspnea on exertion, fatigue, diaphoresis, rheumatic fever, anemia, or recent blood transfusion
Gastrointestinal	Appetite, food intolerances, dietary history, abdominal pain, ulcers, nausea, vomiting, reflux, recent changes in bowel patterns, gastrointestinal infections, diarrhea, belching, flatulence, constipation, type and frequency of stools, use of laxatives, blood in stools, jaundice, anal itching, fissures, or pinworms
Genitourinary	Dysuria, frequency, urgency, burning, hesitancy, enuresis, urinary tract infections, discharge, pyuria, polyuria, oliguria, hematuria, character of stream, or flank pain; history of epispadias or hypospadias and date of surgery; history of cryptorchidism (include age of child and if orchiopexy performed, include date of surgery); hernia, hydrocele, swelling of scrotum when crying, performance of testicular self-exam in adolescent males, sexually transmitted infections, or sexual activity
Gynecologic	Age of menarche, date of last menstrual period, length of menses, frequency of cycle, dysmenorrhea, history of heavy menstrual bleeding, vaginal discharge, abnormal vaginal bleeding, sexual activity, type of contraception, date of last Pap smear, or obstetric history, if applicable

TABLE 6.1	Pediatric Review of Systems (*continued*)
Musculoskeletal	Usual activity level, history of weakness, clumsiness, ataxia, lack of coordination, unusual movements, joint or muscle pain, cramps or inflammation; swelling, sprains, fractures, mobility problems, back or joint stiffness, abnormal gait, limps, or spinal curvatures
Neurologic	General affect and mood, ataxia, tremors, tics, dizziness, syncope, tingling, sensory changes, paresthesias, unusual movements, seizures, loss of consciousness, memory loss, headaches, aphasia or other speech problems, fears, nightmares, or unusual habits
Endocrine	Disturbances in growth, polyuria, polyphagia, polydipsia, thyroid disease, obesity, type 1 or 2 diabetes, excessive sweating, salty taste to skin, intolerance to temperature changes, signs of early or delayed puberty, or abnormal hair distribution
Hematologic	Anemia, pallor, lymphadenopathy, bleeding disorders, bruising, petechiae, bleeding gums, blood transfusions, toxic drug exposure, radiation, or chemotherapy
Psychosocial development	Developmental delays, behavior changes, tantrums, breath-holding spells, bedwetting, school failure, social withdrawal, irritability, sleep pattern disturbances, depression, substance abuse, eating disorders, or psychiatric disorders

Components of prenatal, birth, and neonatal health histories are summarized in Table 6.2 and discussed in detail in Chapter 11. The prenatal, birth, and neonatal histories are obtained at the child's initial visit and do not need to be updated because the information does not change. In some cases, information may come from the medical records from the hospital or birthing center where the child was born, if the mother or primary caregiver does not know the answers to the medical questions in the histories.

Acute and Chronic Illnesses • This component of the history comprises the child's current health status. The health care provider should inquire about common childhood illnesses such as respiratory infections, ear infections, diarrhea, vomiting, and dehydration. The provider should also ask about chronic illnesses, including congenital anomalies, genetic disorders, cancer, rheumatic fever, heart disease, hypertension, obesity, diabetes, sickle cell disease, cystic fibrosis, asthma, allergies, eczema, seizure disorders, neurologic infections, tuberculosis, renal disease, depression, and anxiety disorders, among others. The age of onset, the treatment, when the treatment was initiated, and any complications should be determined for all illnesses. In addition, the provider should ask about frequent visits to the emergency room for treatment of minor illnesses so that, if necessary, the family can be referred to a primary care provider.

Childhood Infectious Diseases • The provider should determine if the child has had measles, mumps, rubella, varicella, pertussis, streptococcal infections, or has recently been exposed to these illnesses. The age at which the child contracted any childhood infectious diseases and any complications that resulted should be noted.

Allergies • All allergies to medications, food, animals, and insect bites; environmental allergies; and a history of eczema, allergic rhinitis, contact dermatitis, or latex sensitivity should be noted. The type of allergic reaction the child has experienced in the past should be recorded (e.g., rash, hives, itching, respiratory distress), including any anaphylactic reactions. It may be helpful to ask the parent to describe what they believe is an allergic reaction to distinguish it from a side effect of a medication. It is important to have accurate information concerning allergies to any drugs before prescribing medications.

Medications • The provider should ask about all current prescribed or over-the-counter (OTC) medications that the child is taking, for example, antipyretics, topical medications, and cough and cold preparations, especially those containing acetaminophen, to avoid unsafe dosing. The name, dose, and frequency of the drug should be recorded for each medication along with the parent's report of the indication for the drug. Multivitamins, herbal remedies, and the use of complementary and alternative medical (CAM) therapies such as traditional healers, acupuncture, or massage should be included in this assessment.

Hospitalizations • The date, the child's age, and the reason for any hospitalization as well as the name of the hospital and duration of the stay should be recorded. Records of the hospitalization should be obtained as needed. The provider should inquire about the child's psychological reaction to any hospitalizations. It should also be noted whether the child received blood transfusions and if there were any reactions to the transfusions. The provider should evaluate the reasons for and the frequency of hospitalizations to determine whether child neglect is a factor.

Surgeries • The date of any surgical procedure should be recorded, as well as the child's age at the time of surgery, the reason for surgery, the type of surgical procedure, and whether there were any complications. If the

TABLE 6.2	Components of Prenatal, Birth, and Neonatal Histories
Prenatal history	• Maternal age • Month at which prenatal care began • Pregnancy planned? • Methods of contraception • Number of previous pregnancies and outcomes • Mother's health before and during pregnancy (e.g., illnesses such as rubella, varicella, urinary tract infections, hepatitis, sexually transmitted infections; HIV status) • Stresses during pregnancy (e.g., injuries, family problems, crises) • Onset of fetal movement • Medications taken during pregnancy (e.g., prescription or OTC, including vitamins, hormones, and antibiotics) and CAM therapies (e.g., herbal supplements, traditional or folk medicines and healers) • Length of pregnancy • Pregnancy-related conditions (e.g., abnormal vaginal bleeding, placental previa, edema, excessive weight gain, hypertension, preeclampsia, proteinuria) • Radiation exposure • Assessment of mother's diet during pregnancy • Certain fish (e.g., shark, swordfish, king mackerel, tilefish), which should not be consumed during pregnancy, because of high mercury levels • Illegal drug use, including type, frequency, and route • Alcohol use, including amount and frequency • Tobacco use, including type, frequency, and packs per day • Infections transmitted by house pets (e.g., tinea infections) • Family genetic history
Birth history	• Duration of pregnancy • Length of labor • Place of delivery • Amount/type of anesthesia/analgesics used during labor • Type of delivery (e.g., NSVD, induction, forceps, breech, C-section [primary, repeat or emergency C-section for fetal distress], VBAC) • Problems associated with labor and delivery (e.g., nuchal cord, neonatal seizures, intraventricular hemorrhage, fever) • Condition of infant at birth (e.g., onset of cry/Apgar scores) • Respiratory problems after delivery (e.g., oxygen requirements, if any; resuscitation efforts, intubation, ICU admission) • Mother's physical and mental condition postpartum
Neonatal history	• Gestational age • Birth weight, length, head circumference • Problems in the nursery (e.g., hypothermia, fever, hypoglycemia, poor feeder, oxygen requirements, respiratory distress, apnea, cyanosis, seizures, excess sleeping) • Jaundice (physiologic), ABO/Rh incompatibility, sepsis • Congenital anomalies (e.g., cardiac, cleft lip/palate, imperforate anus, diaphragmatic hernia) • Feeding problems/lethargy • Sleep patterns • Number of days in hospital and whether discharged with mother • Discharge weight • Illness (especially fever) within first 2 months of life • Degree of bonding (ask and observe)

C-section, cesarean section; CAM, complementary and alternative medicine; HIV, human immunodeficiency virus; ICU, intensive care unit; NSVD, normal spontaneous vaginal delivery; OTC, over the counter; VBAC, vaginal birth after C-section.

child had a same-day surgical procedure, it should be noted whether the child was able to go home the same day or needed to be admitted to the hospital for complications (e.g., a child who has a tonsillectomy but is unable to be discharged as a result of dehydration secondary to inadequate oral intake or postoperative bleeding). A note on the child's course of recovery of inpatient surgical procedures should be included, and whether the child needs any ongoing treatments after the surgery (e.g., chemotherapy or radiation after surgery for cancer).

Injuries and Ingestions • The date of any injury should be documented in addition to the age of the child when injured, the type and extent of injury, and whether the injury necessitated a visit to an emergency room or other treatment center. Sequelae to any injuries should be noted. Specific inquiries should be made about motor vehicle collisions, falls, head injuries, injuries requiring sutures or surgery, ingestions, choking episodes, burns, or fractures, and whether the child's injuries are fully resolved. An assessment also includes determining whether the injuries were unintentional or intentional and whether any injuries to the child were the result of inadequate parental supervision, abuse, or neglect. These assessments help providers to identify parental teaching needs or to make a decision about reporting intentional injuries to child protective services.

Immunizations • The child's immunization history should include which immunizations were received and at what age. The child's official immunization record should be reviewed rather than relying on the parent's recollections. Parents should also be questioned about any untoward reactions the child may have had after being immunized. If the child's immunization record evidences a delay, the parents should be asked about the circumstances that led to the delay. Lack of insurance, transportation difficulties, or illness are common reasons for parents to postpone immunizations. Religious beliefs and health care neglect may also be factors. Chapter 9 outlines the pediatric immunization schedule recommended by the Centers for Disease Control and Prevention (CDC, 2014a) for current required immunizations.

Screening Procedures • The health care provider should determine if the child has had the recommended age-appropriate routine screening tests such as newborn screening, vision and hearing screening, blood pressure measurement, hemoglobin or hematocrit screening for iron deficiency anemia, lead or tuberculosis screening, or urinalysis. Condition-specific screening tests such as sickle cell anemia, human immunodeficiency virus (HIV), cholesterol, or other metabolic or genetic screenings should also be noted. The dates of each exam and the results should be recorded. (See Chapter 9 for a discussion of recommended screening procedures for children.)

Family Medical History

Obtaining the child's family health history is necessary to determine the health status of immediate family members and to identify and document any inherited disorders that the child may have. The ages and current health status of immediate family members should be recorded in the chart. Any consanguinity should be noted. The provider should ask about common communicable diseases and illnesses related to unhealthy lifestyle behaviors such as smoking or other chemical use.

When working with families from developing countries, it is important to inquire about family travel to areas with poor environmental sanitation so that parasitic illnesses and specific communicable diseases endemic to that particular area of the world are considered. Specific illnesses and conditions about which the provider should inquire include arthritis, asthma, allergies, eczema, heart disease, hypertension, stroke, obesity, hyperlipidemia, diabetes, cancer, blood disorders (e.g., hemophilia and sickle cell disease or trait), tuberculosis, lead poisoning, cystic fibrosis, alcoholism, drug abuse, depression or other mental illnesses, seizure disorders, kidney disease, learning disabilities, intellectual disability, and congenital anomalies. The use of a genogram is helpful to clarify the family history. Chapter 4 provides information about constructing a genogram and questions used in data collection.

Review of Systems

The ROS, described earlier, establishes the past and present health status of each body system. This assessment comprises a history, not current physical findings. The provider must ask questions in terms that the parent or child can understand to be sure that the history is accurate. Positive responses to questions require more thorough questioning about that particular body system. Questions should be general (e.g., "Has Antonio been mostly healthy?" or "Has Lana ever had problems with her ears?"). The order in which these questions are asked is roughly head to toe. It is important to tailor the ROS to the child's age and developmental level because certain health problems are common to certain age groups. For example, questions regarding the timing of menarche would not be appropriate until a girl reaches school age. (See Table 6.2 for the components of a pediatric ROS.)

Pain Assessment

In 2001, the Joint Commission on Accreditation of Healthcare Organizations (JCAHO) established standards requiring that all patients, including infants and children, be assessed for pain (JCAHO, 2001). During the health history, the provider should ask about a history of chronic or current pain. Open-ended questions can be used, such as "Has your child experienced pain in the last few months?" or "Is your child in pain now?" Positive responses require a detailed assessment that is appropriate to the child's age and developmental level. This assessment should include a pain intensity measure. For younger children, the Wong-Baker FACES Pain Rating Scale (www.wongbakerfaces.org) or the Face Legs Activity Cry Consolability (FLACC) scale could be used (Merkel, Voepel-Lewis, Shayevitz, & Malviya, 1997). The FACES scale is a visual analog scale that can be used to rate pain in children as young as 3 years. The child selects the face that best represents his or her pain, with 0 representing no pain and 10 being the worst pain. The FLACC scale can be used to quantify pain in children aged 2 months to 7 years. Each category in this scale is assigned a score of 0, 1, or 2, and the total possible score ranges from 0 to 10 (Box 6.1). For older children and adolescents, a descriptor or general numeric pain rating is appropriate. For more information on the FACES scale please refer to www.wongbakerfaces.org.

Functional Assessment

A thorough assessment of the child's health during the initial health history and in health supervision visits includes asking about specific areas that are important to a child's functioning and ADL. This may entail organizing this assessment around "pattern areas" as described by Gordon (2002), including health beliefs and behavior, nutrition, elimination, activity, sleep, role relationships, coping, self-perception, cognitive/perceptual behavior, sexuality, and values/beliefs. For this discussion, patterns are subsumed in the following assessment categories: nutrition, physical activity, elimination patterns, safety status, sleep patterns, social situation, sexual history, growth and development, and spiritual assessment. All of these areas are assessed as part of the initial health history and then updated with each interval history during subsequent well-child health maintenance visits. Health supervision interview guidelines provide developmentally appropriate interview questions, among them *Bright Futures: Guidelines for Health Supervision of Infants, Children and Adolescents* (Hagan, Shaw, & Duncan, 2008).

Nutrition • This is an important area to assess during both well and illness visits. Pediatric nutritional assessment must be tailored to the child's age.

The information obtained during this assessment helps the provider diagnose any nutritional problems and identify any teaching needs. The best approach to nutritional assessment is to begin with general questions, progressing to questions based on age and developmental level. First, the provider should ask parents to describe the child's appetite and to give a 24-hour dietary recall. The provider should then determine if this recall represents the type of food the family and child typically eat. The provider should inquire about whether the child is on any special diet or if there are any cultural or religious influences affecting the child's diet. The provider must determine if the child has any food intolerances or allergies and, if so, the parents should be asked to describe what reactions, if any, the child has had. Any recent weight loss or gain should be explored. The provider should ask the parent if the television is typically on during meals. It should be pointed out that mealtime television decreases quality time with the family and increases food consumption; caloric intake is difficult to control when there are distractions like television (Horodynski, Stommel, Brophy-Herb, & Weatherspoon, 2010). The provider should ask the parents if they have any overall concerns related to nutrition or diet of their child. Once answers to the general questions are recorded, the provider can proceed to a nutritional assessment that is specific to the child's age and developmental level.

Infants. The younger the child, the more detailed the nutrition history should be. The provider should ask if the infant is breastfed or bottle-fed and how frequently. The provider should note whether breastfed infants are supplemented with formula. For infants who are taking formula, the provider should determine the type of formula and how many ounces of formula the infant

---

BOX 6.1 FLACC Behavioral Pain Assessment Scale

CRITERIA	SCORE 0	SCORE 1	SCORE 2
Face	No particular expression or smile	Occasional grimace or frown; withdrawn, disinterested	Frequent to constant frown, clenched jaw; quivering chin
Legs	Normal position or relaxed	Uneasy, restless, tense	Kicking or legs drawn up
Activity	Lying quietly, normal position, moves easily	Squirming, shifting back and forth, tense	Arched, rigid, or jerking
Cry	No crying (awake or asleep)	Moans or whimpers, occasional complaint	Crying steadily, screams or sobs; frequent complaints
Consolability	Content, relaxed	Reassured by occasional touching, hugging, or being talked to; distractible	Difficult to console or comfort

Interpreting the Behavioral Score
Each category is scored on the 0–2 scale, which results in a total score of 0–10.
0 = Relaxed and comfortable; 1–3 = Mild discomfort; 4–6 = Moderate pain; 7–10 = Severe discomfort or pain or both.

Source: Merkel, Voepel-Lewis, Shayevitz, and Malviya (1997).

consumes per day. The age at which the infant is weaned should be noted. Introduction of the cup in infants older than 6 months should be assessed; the bottle should be discontinued by 1 year of age. The provider should ask the parent if the infant takes the bottle to bed and whether the bottle is propped, a practice that can lead to tooth decay, obesity, choking, and otitis media. It should be determined when the parents introduce solid food, noting the type of solid food that is fed to the child, including whether cereal is added to the bottle. Any allergic reactions to solid foods should be investigated and recorded. Any "spitting up" or vomiting should be noted, including a description of the character and frequency of the vomiting. Periods of prolonged crying should be noted as well. Providers should also ask if parents clean their infant's teeth after meals.

Toddlers. The provider should ask if the toddler drinks cow's milk and, if so, what type (e.g., whole vs. skim) and how many ounces a day. Physiologic anorexia is normal in this age group; parents often report that the toddler is picky, eats small amounts, and eats the same types of foods over and over ("food jags"). The provider should ask the parents about the types of food the toddler likes or dislikes, noting the nutritional value of the food the child usually eats, including a typical meal. Specific inquiries should be made about the number of servings of fruits, vegetables, and protein the child eats each day. The provider should also ask how often the toddler eats fast food and what snacks are provided. It is important to identify any foods that the toddler eats that would present a choking hazard, such as grapes, nuts, hot dogs, popcorn, gum, hard candy, and raw vegetables. The health care provider should ask parents to describe the toddler's mealtime behavior and how they deal with any undesired behaviors that occur at the table.

It should be ascertained whether or not the toddler is still taking a bottle and whether the toddler also takes a bottle to bed. Toddlers should be drinking out of a regular cup and at mealtime only. The use of a no-spill sippy cup should be assessed because these cups have valves in the lids to prevent spillage, which require the toddler to suck on the cup to get the liquid out. This mimics a bottle and as such, is undesirable, especially if a toddler carries a cup around full of a sweetened drink during the day. The provider should assess the amount of juice the child consumes in a day and whether the juice consumption is at mealtime, throughout the day, or both. It is important to ask parents if the toddler drinks soda regularly, and if so, how much. The pattern of tooth eruption in the child should also be noted, as well as what dental hygiene practices are used.

Preschoolers and School-Aged Children. The provider should ask the child and parent to describe a typical meal, the child's favorite food, and a typical snack. Specific inquiries should be made about the number of servings of fruits, vegetables, and protein a day. The provider should inquire about fast food consumption, frequency of junk food snacks, and about the amount of milk, juice, and soda consumed in a day. The provider should note if the child obtains junk food snacks from vending machines at school. Dental hygiene practices should also be assessed; a child should see the dentist for the first semiannual cleaning and dental visit by age 3 years. The pattern of tooth loss in the school-aged child should also be assessed.

Adolescents. Providers should ask adolescents to describe typical meals and snacks and the frequency with which they consume fast food and soda. With the parent out of the room, providers should ask adolescent patients if they are satisfied with their body image or if they view themselves as fat. Providers should inquire about dieting, binging, purging, or taking laxatives or diet pills to control weight. (See Chapter 10 for an in-depth discussion of pediatric nutritional assessment.)

Physical Activity • Once a child is walking well, the provider should ask the parent at each well-child visit how much physical activity the child gets each day, including typical play activities, involvement in sports, and walking to and from school. The provider should ask about the number of hours the child spends each day watching television, playing video games, or using the computer. Any limitations to physical activity should be noted, as well as whether the child requires any special equipment to assist mobility.

Elimination • Assessment of elimination patterns is very specific to the child's age, developmental level, and diet.

Newborns and Infants. For newborns, the provider should ask about number of wet diapers a day (six to eight are normal), and whether the male infant urinates in a straight stream. If the urinary stream aims downward rather than straight, this may indicate hypospadias, which requires surgical repair. The provider should ask the parent about the number and character of daily stools.

In the first few weeks of life, breastfed infants typically stool after each feeding. The stools of breastfed infants are pale yellow, soft, and without much odor. Formula-fed babies pass stools less frequently than breastfed babies, usually two to four stools a day in the first month of life (Dunn, 2013), then one to two stools a day as the infant grows and the gastrocolic reflex becomes less active. The stools of formula-fed babies are also dark in color, firm in texture, and have a distinct odor. The stools of both breastfed and formula-fed infants become firmer, darker, and less frequent as solid foods are introduced (Dunn, 2013). Daily stool patterns vary from infant to infant, with one stool a day to one stool every 2 or 3 days considered within normal limits.

Toddlers and Preschoolers. Renal function is not fully developed until age 2 years, at which time the child's kidneys are able to concentrate and dilute urine. Depending on the child's fluid intake, fluid losses (e.g., diarrhea), body temperature, and the environmental temperature, the number of voids a day varies. Toddlers and preschoolers urinate 8 to 14 times a day (Dunn, 2013). In this age group, the number of stools a day varies, according to the child's diet; one to three stools a day is usual but one stool every 3 to 4 days is within normal limits (Dunn, 2013). When assessing for constipation, it is important for the provider to know how the parent defines constipation. Constipation is defined as hard, painful stool passed infrequently (less than three times a week) with difficulty (Borowitz, 2013). Not having a stool each day does not constitute constipation. Similarly, if the parent reports episodes of diarrhea, the provider should be sure to clarify what the parent means by diarrhea. Diarrhea is stool that is frequent, watery in consistency, and often leaves water rings in the diaper or underclothes. Diarrhea is not the same as loose stools that may be the result of increased dietary fiber or sweetened drink intake. In this age group, the provider should ask about toilet training efforts, which should begin when the child is no younger than 18 to 24 months of age or when the child expresses interest. Providers should ask parents about their attitudes about toilet training. For many people, this is an extremely frustrating task and can lead to harsh or impulsive discipline. It is important to determine if the child has dry naps or sleeps through the night without urinating. The age at which daytime and nighttime bowel and bladder control are achieved should be assessed and recorded.

School-Aged Children. School-aged children should be fully toilet trained. The provider should continue to ask about the number of voids a day (usually five to six, depending on fluid intake) and whether the child remains dry through the night (nocturnal enuresis is within normal limits until the age of 5–6 years). The provider should inquire about urinary frequency or urgency, which may indicate a urinary tract infection, and about polyuria, which may be a sign of type 1 diabetes. The frequency of stools should be assessed (normal ranges from one to three a day, to one stool every 2–3 days), as should the presence of constipation or encopresis.

Adolescents. With adolescents, questions about elimination patterns should continue to focus on the number of voids and stools a day, which varies according to the teen's diet and fluid intake. It is also important to ask about urinary frequency or urgency, which may indicate either urinary tract or sexually transmitted infections. Polyuria in this age group can be a sign of type 1 diabetes. Frequent or chronic diarrhea may indicate laxative use.

Safety • The leading cause of death in American children over 1 year of age is unintentional injuries (CDC, 2014b). Therefore, assessing the safety of the environment of an infant, child, or adolescent is extremely important, and the areas of assessment vary according to age

and developmental level. The type of home environment must be determined before the provider can pose general questions about the child's safety; for example, different risks exist for children living in urban as compared to rural settings. The provider should begin by asking general questions such as:

- Is the hot water heater setting less than 120°F?
- Does the family home have working smoke and carbon monoxide detectors?
- Does the family have a firearm, and if so, is the gun locked and unloaded and is the ammunition kept separately?
- Does the family have a swimming pool?

The provider can then progress to questions that are age-specific, such as:

- Does the child ride in a car seat or wear a seatbelt?
- Are poisons and cleaning supplies stored in a high, locked cabinet?
- Does the child wear a bike helmet?

Chapter 7 explores in-depth assessing the safety of a child's environment, according to age and developmental level.

Sleep • Sleep patterns should be assessed at every well-child visit and as needed when a child is seen for an illness or other complaint. A developmental approach is necessary when obtaining a pediatric sleep assessment. For example, infants should be placed in the supine position for naps and at bedtime because of the association of sudden infant death syndrome (SIDS) with a prone sleep position (AAP, 2011). To avoid upper body gross motor developmental delays, infants should be placed prone while awake ("tummy time") to develop these muscle groups (Figure 6.2). The provider should be sure to emphasize to the parent that the infant must be awake when placed in the prone position. The provider should also be sure to inform the parents that

FIGURE 6.2 Parents should be taught the importance of placing their infants prone while they are awake to facilitate the infant's development of gross motor abilities such as reaching, scooting, and crawling.

co-sleeping during the first year of life is also associated with an increased incidence of SIDS (AAP, 2011).

Sleep patterns vary according to the child's age, with younger children requiring naps during the day to ensure that sleep requirements are met. Sleep problems are common in preschoolers, so it is important for the provider to inquire about nightmares and night terrors in this age group (Frost & Burns, 2013). Table 6.3 outlines the sleep requirements for children, from birth through adolescence, and Table 6.4 summarizes the important questions to ask in a pediatric sleep patterns assessment.

The child's medical history should also be taken into account when evaluating sleep patterns in infants, children, or adolescents. Ear infections, chronic pain, certain respiratory disorders or infections, neurologic problems, obesity, and the side effects of some medications (e.g., bronchodilators), drug or caffeine use, and depression can all affect sleep (Frost & Burns, 2013). Recent parental separation or divorce, maternal depression, a recent move from the family home, or other family stresses can also interfere with the child's quality of sleep.

During the sleep assessment portion of the history, the provider should ask the parent if he or she has any concerns about the child's usual sleep patterns. The provider should assess the child for common pediatric sleep problems such as sleep refusal, nightmares, or trained night feeding. Parents should be taught that infants begin to sleep through the night at 4 to 6 months of age (Frost & Burns, 2013) and that waking at night after that time should not be handled by feeding the infant.

The provider should determine whether or not the parent sees the child's sleep patterns as a problem. For example, some parents find co-sleeping disruptive, while others consider it the norm. A sleep problem is one that interferes with the child's health and well-being and is disruptive to the family (Frost & Burns, 2013). Table 6.5 describes common sleep problems in children.

Social History

Eliciting the social history of a pediatric patient is extremely important because these data tell the health care provider about the child's daily environment. This information explains why a child may have a particular

TABLE 6.3	Sleep Needs of Infants and Children
Birth–6 weeks	Approximately 16.5 hours a day, half of which is daytime sleep; sleeps 2–4 hours at a time
1 month	15.5 hours a day; may sleep 4–6 hours at a time
3 months	15 hours a day; bulk of sleep shifts to nighttime hours
4 months	Begins to nap at regular times during day; may sleep 7–8 hours at a stretch
6 months	14.25 hours a day, including two naps
9 months	14 hours a day, including two naps
12 months	13.75 hours, including one to two naps a day (The morning nap is given up between 12 and 24 months of age. The afternoon nap persists until approximately age 4–5 years.)
18 months	13.5 hours a day, including one nap
2 years	11–12 hours at night, one nap a day lasting 1–2 hours
3 years	12 hours a day total, including one 1-hour nap during the day
4 years	11.5–12 hours of sleep a day; many 4-year-olds stop naps, needing an earlier bedtime to get required sleep
5 years	11 hours, with most children stopping naps at this age
6 years	10.5–11 hours a day
7 years	10.5–11 hours a day
8 years	10.25–10.75 hours a day
9 years	10 hours a day
10–12 years	9.25–10 hours a day
Adolescents	8–9 hours a day

Source: Howard and Wong (2001).

TABLE 6.4	Assessment of Sleep Patterns in Children by Age Group
AGE GROUP	**RELEVANT ASSESSMENTS**
Infant (birth–1 year)	• What is infant's sleep position (should be supine until child is rolling over independently, at approximately age 6 months) • What time does infant go to bed? What are nighttime sleep intervals? What is longest interval? • What is hour of bedtime and hour of rising in the morning? • How many daytime naps? How long do they last? • Where does infant sleep? • Does infant co-sleep with parents? • Does infant sleep through the night (after 4–6 months of age)? • How do parents deal with night waking after age 4 months? Do they feed child? Do they bring child to bed with them? • Is there any soft bedding, quilts, pillows, bumper pads, stuffed animals, or sheepskin in crib? • Are there any bedtime rituals (e.g., bath, story, song)? • How does infant fall asleep? Is infant placed in crib while still awake or rocked to sleep? • Does child self-comfort or are security objects needed? • Is infant placed in bed with a bottle of milk or juice?
Toddler (1–3 years)	• What are bedtime rituals? How is toddler's behavior at bedtime? Is child rocked to sleep? • Where does the toddler sleep? • Does toddler co-sleep with the parent? • Is child placed in bed with a bottle of juice or milk? • How long does toddler sleep at night? Does toddler nap during the day? • Does toddler have a problem falling or staying asleep?
	• Does child sleep through the night? • What is parent's reaction to night waking? • Does child self-comfort or are security objects needed? • What is hour of bedtime and hour of rising in the morning?
Preschooler (3–6 years)	• What are bedtime rituals? How is child's behavior at bedtime? • Where does child sleep? • Does child co-sleep with parent? • How long are sleep intervals? • Does child have difficulty falling or staying asleep? If child awakens, how do parents respond? Can child self-comfort back to sleep? • Does child still nap (most children give up naps by age 5 years)? • Does child experience any sleep problems such as nightmares, night terrors, or bedwetting? • Does child self-comfort or are security objects needed? • What is hour of bedtime and hour of rising in the morning?
School-aged child (6–12 years)	• What are bedtime rituals? How is child's behavior at bedtime? • Where does child sleep? • Does child co-sleep with the parent? • What is hour of bedtime and hour of rising in the morning? • Does child need to be awakened in the morning? • What are sleep intervals overnight? • Does child sleep through the night? • What is parent's reaction to awakenings? • Does child self-comfort or are security objects needed? • Does child experience nightmares/night terrors or bedwetting?
Adolescent (12–18 years)	• What is hour of bedtime and hour of rising in the morning? • Does teen need to be awakened in the morning? • Does adolescent have difficulty falling asleep or staying asleep? • Does adolescent sleep excessively (may indicate depression)?

TABLE 6.5	Common Pediatric Sleep Problems		
SLEEP PROBLEM	**AGE GROUP**	**CLINICAL FINDINGS**	**ASSESSMENTS**
Sleep refusal	Toddler/preschooler	Child refuses to settle once put to bed	Do parents maintain a consistent sleep routine? Are security objects used? Do parents reinforce calling out or crying behaviors?
Night waking	Any age	Child needs help during night to return back to sleep	Do parents put child to bed while he or she is still awake so that child becomes accustomed to falling asleep independently? Do parents rock child to sleep in their arms and then transfer child to bed? Do parents reinforce calling out or crying behaviors? Are security objects used?
Trained night feeder	Infants	Infant older than 4 months awakens, predictably, wanting to be fed	Do parents put child to bed with a bottle? Have parents tried to end this bedtime ritual either by gradually discontinuing night feedings or by discontinuing night feedings completely?
Delayed sleep phase	Any age	Child goes to bed late and awakens late	Have parents tried awakening child 15 minutes earlier each day until appropriate bedtimes and waking times result?
Advanced sleep phase	Any age	Child goes to bed early and awakens early	Have parents tried putting child to bed later so that awakening will occur later?
Unpredictable schedule	Any age	Child goes to bed and awakens at random times	Have parents maintained a predictable family schedule and consistent expectations for bedtime?
Nightmares	Most common in preschoolers; occur from 18 months through adolescence	Child awakens crying and fearful with memory of dream, which usually occurs in the latter half of night; child is slow to return to sleep	Do parents comfort and reassure child? Is a nightlight or closet light used to help child who is afraid of the dark?
Night terrors and sleepwalking	Most common in preschoolers; occur from 18 months through adolescence	Child begins screaming or crying but is not fully awake; child usually has no memory of event; night terrors usually occur in first third of the night; sleepwalkers arise and walk about without being fully awake	Do parents try to protect child from injury? Do parents help child to lie down and return to sleep? Do parents of sleepwalkers use gates at the top of stairs?
Insomnia/hypersomnia	School age and older	Child is unable to sleep or excessive sleeping, which may be related to depression	Do parents ensure that child has no stimulating activities at bedtime that interfere with sleep such as caffeine consumption, rough play, or violent and upsetting television, movies, or other media? Has child been medically evaluated for hypersomnia to rule out medical conditions such as severe anemia, hypothyroidism, or depression?
Obstructive sleep apnea	Preschoolers and older	Child sleeps restlessly, with snoring, periods of respiratory distress, or apnea while sleeping and exhibits daytime fatigue	Has child been referred for sleep studies, allergy consults, or possible adenoidectomy?

Adapted from Frost and Burns (2013).

problem, for example, developmental delay, behavioral issues, obesity, poor school performance, frequent injuries, or depression. These problems can potentially be attributed to the current family situation, parental knowledge deficits, socioeconomic status, or possibly abuse or neglect. With the answers to these questions, the provider is better equipped to address these problems.

Universal Assessments • A pediatric social history is mostly age-dependent, but some questions are universal. The provider should ask the less threatening questions first to establish rapport with the child and family, then progress to the more sensitive, personal questions.

Family. To begin, the child's primary caregiver should be identified. The provider should note if the caregiver is the child's biologic parent. The provider should then ask if the primary caregiver has any concerns about the child's health, welfare, safety, and physical or psychosocial growth and development. The provider should obtain information about the child's family composition, noting which family members live at home (e.g., extended family, siblings, step-siblings, including their ages and sex) and whether the family includes either biologic or adoptive parents. The provider should determine the parents' marital status, noting if they have a stable relationship and if both parents are involved in the child's care. The provider should note whether the child is adopted, and if it is a domestic adoption, whether the child's birth mother or family is involved in the child's life. It should be noted whether the child lives in a single-parent household, and if the parent feels that he or she has adequate child care, finances, and emotional support. It is important for the provider to assess whether the child's primary caregiver is able to provide daily care (e.g., Is the primary caregiver a teenager, homeless, or addicted to drugs or alcohol? Does the caregiver have mental health issues?). Exposure to secondhand cigarette smoke should be assessed. The provider should ask about any episodes of domestic violence in the home, if any guns are kept in the home, and if the child is exposed to violent television or other media.

Home Environment. Assessment of the home environment is another important part of the social history. The type of home in which the family lives should be noted (e.g., single-family home, apartment), and whether the primary caregiver believes that the home is adequate in size, safe, warm, and well lit. The provider should ask the parent about family pets (e.g., what type, how many). Some kinds of animals (e.g., snakes, pit bulls) may be dangerous around small children, and the provider may need to ascertain whether the home with a pet is safe for the child. The provider should ask the parent if the neighborhood is safe (e.g., is there a safe area in which the child can play? Is it safe for the child to walk to school? Is there any gang activity or other type of violence nearby?).

Economic Status. The family's economic status should be assessed, including financial resources or agencies used such as Women, Infants, and Children (WIC), food stamps, or Medicaid. Family stressors should also be noted, including whether the family has recently experienced any major life changes that could affect economic status, such as a divorce or death in the family or parental job loss, and whether the family has recently moved to a new dwelling. Assessment of the child's and family's adjustment to these changes is important because stress may cause alterations in sleep patterns, recurrent abdominal pain, depression, drug or alcohol use in older children, or other physical or psychologic manifestations of stress and grief. The provider should ask what the family does for fun and whether they do things together as a family.

Immigrant Status. The social history includes an assessment of immigrant status, and whether the child has special health care needs as a result. International adoptees also fall into this category. Newly arrived immigrant children often have nutritional deficits, dental decay, developmental and immunization delays. They may suffer from communicable diseases not often seen in the United States. Children in families that come to the United States seeking refuge from persecution because of race, religion, nationality, or politics may not only have physical problems, but may suffer from depression, nightmares, and posttraumatic stress disorder as well. When asking questions on these topics, the provider should be nonjudgmental and culturally sensitive, using an interpreter when necessary. It should be ascertained what language the child and family speaks. Also, it is important to note whether the family and child have any religious beliefs or practices that may have an impact on the child's health (see Chapter 5).

Emergency Room Use. For children of all ages, the provider should also note the frequency of visits to the emergency room or urgent care facilities for frequent illnesses or injuries. This may indicate knowledge deficits, medical neglect, or lack of age-appropriate supervision. Consistent immunization delays should also be noted, as this may also indicate medical neglect.

Age-Specific Assessments • Additional data that comprise the social history should be tailored to the child's age group.

Infants, Toddlers, and Preschoolers. For infants, toddlers, and preschoolers, the provider should ask if the child has a security object, and if so, the age of the child should be noted. The provider should inquire about any habits such as nail biting, thumb sucking, pica, repeated rocking, or head banging, and if the parent expresses any concern over any of the child's habits or overall behavior. It is important to ask about the child's temperament, whether he or she is fussy or easily consoled. Providers should ask parents of toddlers and preschoolers if the child has temper tantrums or breath-holding spells, and how the parent handles these tantrums. The provider should ask about what type of discipline the parent employs, such as "time-outs" or corporal punishment. Parents should be discouraged from spanking and taught about other methods of discipline. Providers should ask parents about any power struggles concerning toilet training and remind parents that toilet training should not be started too soon. The provider should inquire about whether the child is enrolled in day care or preschool and if the parent is satisfied with the arrangement. It is important to ask how the child copes with separation from the primary caregiver when it is time to go to school or day care.

School-Aged Children. Children in this age group can provide some information for the history. A social history for a school-aged child includes information about the child's school progress, interaction with family members, peer relationships, friendships, violent media exposure, and computer/video game or television-watching. The provider should ask the child about particular hobbies or involvement in sports or other types of activities. The provider should ask the parent to describe the child's temperament and to relate any concerns about the child's behavior or habits. It is important to note how much time the school-aged child spends alone after school unsupervised.

Adolescents. Much of the data that comprise the social history of the adolescent patient focus on assessing the teen's school performance; relationships with adults, peers, family members, and teachers; involvement in risk-taking behaviors such as alcohol or drug use, reckless driving, and sexual activity; depression and body image issues; and involvement in violent activities, such as gang membership. The adolescent social history should be obtained without the parent present so that the teen feels comfortable providing truthful answers. The provider should reassure the adolescent that what he or she discusses with the provider will be treated with utmost confidentiality unless the teen reveals information that the provider believes will result in self-harm or harm to others.

A sexual history is an essential part of the adolescent's social history. The provider should approach this subject sensitively and nonjudgmentally. This part of the history is done with the parent out of the room so that the teen feels comfortable giving honest answers to the questions asked. Using open-ended questions, the provider should explore the teen's dating patterns, sexual activity, and use of contraception and condoms. The provider should ascertain the number of sexual partners and the teen's knowledge of safe sex, and screen for sexually transmitted infections and pregnancy. Table 6.6 summarizes the pediatric social history, according to age and developmental level.

Growth and Development

Assessment of growth and development is an essential part of the pediatric health history and should be done at every health care visit, whether the child is well or ill. It is extremely important to determine if the child has achieved age-appropriate physical and developmental milestones and to identify any areas of concern, such as developmental delays, neurologic problems, or neglect. The provider should begin the history by asking the parents if they have any concerns about the child's growth or development. A complete history of a child's growth and development entails determining achievement of developmental milestones in the areas of physical growth, gross and fine motor development, cognitive abilities, language development, social interaction, behavior, and temperament. Past milestones and current abilities should be assessed, which requires knowledge of physical, psychosocial, and language milestones relevant to the child's age group.

- **Gross motor milestones** can be assessed by asking about infant head control, rolling over, sitting and standing without support, crawling, walking, and dressing.
- **Fine motor milestones** can be assessed by exploring areas such as reaching for objects, achievement of a pincer grasp, self-feeding, scribbling, printing, cursive writing and tying shoes.
- **Language milestones** can be assessed by asking about when the child spoke his or her first word with meaning, combined two to three words, and spoke in sentences. It is important to ask about the intelligibility of the child's speech and about any history of otitis media, which can affect hearing and language acquisition. It is also important to note whether the child is exposed to more than one language; bilingual children develop expressive language later than children exposed to only one language.
- **Psychosocial development** can be assessed by asking the parent about the child's temperament, play, attachment to and ability to separate from the primary caregiver, self-care abilities, peer relationships, and school performance.

In some instances, specific developmental screening tools are necessary to assess a child's developmental status thoroughly. These and other aspects of the assessment of pediatric growth and development, from birth through adolescence, are described in depth in Chapter 2.

Spiritual History

Both the family's and the child's religious and spiritual beliefs can affect the child's health. For this reason, it is important for the health care provider to conduct a spiritual assessment as part of the initial health history. The provider should begin by asking about the family's

TABLE 6.6	Age-Specific Pediatric Social History
AGE GROUP	**QUESTIONS TO ASK**
Infant (birth–1 year)	• How is attachment/bonding progressing? • How do parents describe infant's temperament? • How do parents deal with any persistent crying? • What types of toys and developmentally stimulating activities are provided for infant? • Does infant have a security blanket or toy? • How many caregivers or babysitters does child have? • Is infant in day care? • Is home or apartment adequately baby proofed? • Does parent or caregiver report any behaviors such as head-banging or bed-rocking?
Toddler (1–3 years)	• How do parents describe child's temperament? • Does child have temper tantrums or breath-holding spells, or hit or bite others? If so, how do parents handle these behaviors? Do they use corporal punishment? • How do parents feel about child's current toilet training progress? How do parents deal with toileting accidents? • How well does toddler play with other children? Is he or she aggressive? • What type of toys does child have? • In what type of play does child engage? • How much and what type of television does child watch? • Do parents read to child each day? How does toddler separate from parents? • Is toddler showing a desire for independence? • Does child regress developmentally in times of stress?
Preschooler (3–6 years)	• How do parents describe the child's temperament? • Do parents have concerns about child's behavior, such as any instances of lying or stealing? • Does preschooler have any imaginary friends, and does this concern parent? • Does child separate well from parents? • Can child converse with and relate well to those outside the family? • Does preschooler have excessive fears? • Is child enrolled in preschool? If so, how is child doing in school? Does teacher have any concerns about child's behavior? • How well does child play with others? • With what type of toys does child play? • How much and what type of television does child watch? • Does parent read to child each day? • Is child fully toilet trained and, if not, how do parents deal with toileting accidents? Do they use corporal punishment? • Does child know about "good touch/bad touch"?
School-aged child (6–12 years)	• How do parents describe child's temperament? • Is child excessively shy? • Does child have any difficulty separating from parents? • Does child have friends? A best friend? • How does child interact with family members, classmates, and peers? • Is child being bullied? If so, what are the circumstances? • In what type of play activities does child engage? • Is child enrolled in sports, after-school activities? Does child have any particular hobbies or collections? • How many hours of television does child watch a day? • How many hours a day does child spend on a computer or playing video games? • Does child read books for pleasure? • How is child's school performance? Does teacher have any concerns about child's behavior or academic progress? • Is there excessive absenteeism? Is child in special education classes?

TABLE 6.6	Age-Specific Pediatric Social History (*continued*)
AGE GROUP	**QUESTIONS TO ASK**
	• Does child have any nervous habits such as nail biting? • Does child have any problems with bedwetting? • Does parent report excessive sleeping, social withdrawal, or other indicators of possible depression? • Does child know about "good touch/bad touch"? • Do parents use corporal punishment?
Adolescent (12–18 years)	• Does parent have any concerns? • How does parent describe teen's temperament? Does this coincide with how teen sees himself or herself? • With parent absent from the room, ask how teen gets along with his or her parents. • Does teen feel that rules at home are reasonable? • How does teen get along with adults in general, including his or her teachers or other authority figures? • Does teen feel that he or she can confide in the adults in his or her life? • Is teen satisfied with his or her body? Does teen diet, binge, purge, or fast? • How is school going? Has teen been chronically truant or been having academic difficulty? Is teen in special education classes? • How much time does teen spend watching television, using computer, or playing video games a day? • Does teen read for pleasure? • Does teen have a job? • Does teen have a best friend? Several friends? • Is teen being bullied? If so, what are the circumstances? • Is teen involved in any groups, clubs, sports, or after-school activities? • Does teen engage in any aggressive or violent behavior toward himself, herself, or others? • Does teen have easy access to firearms? • Is teen involved with any gang activity? • Ask if teen is involved in a romantic relationship and whether he or she is sexually active. • What are teen's feelings about sex? • Does he or she think there is something wrong with these feelings about sex? • Has teen ever been touched in a manner that made him or her uncomfortable? • Would teen like to ask any questions about contraception? • What is teen's knowledge of safe sex and sexually transmitted infections? • Does teen need LGBT support? • How does teen cope with stress? • Does teen use alcohol or drugs? • Does teen smoke cigarettes? • Teen should be asked if he or she ever feels sad or depressed and if he or she ever feels like killing himself or herself. If the answer is "yes," it should be determined whether he or she has a concrete plan and, if so, teen should be referred immediately for psychiatric care. • An acronym, BIHEADSS, can assist providers in conducting a comprehensive assessment of the teen's social situation: BI = Body image H = Home situation E = Education or school performance A = Activities (e.g., friends, what teen does for fun) D = Drugs or dating patterns S = Sexuality: Does teen know about safe sex? S = Safety (risk-taking), suicidal ideation, or depression

religious beliefs and how these beliefs affect the child's health. It should be noted whether the family is involved in their church and to what extent. Table 6.7 summarizes the components of a complete pediatric health history.

Interval History

Like the initial health history, the interval history is comprehensive and includes the child's past and present health status. The interval history contains information

TABLE 6.7	Components of a Pediatric Health History
Biographical data	Name, age, sex, birth date, ethnicity, religion, child and family's primary spoken language, home address, and telephone number
Source of information	Person providing historical information
Reason for seeking care	Also referred to as chief complaint; the reason for seeking health care is recorded in the child's or parent's own words.
History of present illness	Chronologic narrative of the chief complaint; a summary of the details of the problem
Past medical history	Provides information regarding all aspects of the child's general health • Prenatal, birth, and neonatal history • Previous acute and chronic illnesses • Childhood infectious diseases • Hospitalizations • Surgeries • Injuries, ingestions, or emergency room visits • Immunizations • Screening tests • Family medical history • Allergies • Medications • Pain assessment
Review of systems	Done to establish the past and present health state of each body system • General • Integument • Head • Eyes • Ears • Nose • Mouth or throat • Neck • Chest • Lymphatic • Respiratory • Cardiovascular • Gastrointestinal • Genitourinary • Gynecologic • Musculoskeletal • Neurologic • Endocrine • Hematologic • Psychosocial
Nutritional assessment	Assesses nutritional adequacy and identifies teaching needs
Physical activity	Notes amount of physical and sedentary activities
Elimination patterns	Assessment of stool and urination patterns according to age
Safety	Assesses the safety of the child's environment and identifies teaching needs
Sleep patterns	Hours of sleep per night, naps, or sleep problems
Social history	Varies according to child's age; includes assessment of family situation, child's behavior and temperament, and school performance

TABLE 6.7	**Components of a Pediatric Health History (*continued*)**
Sexual history	Body image, dating patterns, sexual activity, use of contraception, knowledge of safe sex, and screening for sexually transmitted infections
Growth and development	Assessment of physical and psychosocial developmental milestones
Spiritual history	Assessment of family's religious or spiritual beliefs and how they affect health and illness

that updates the history since the child's last visit. The format is the same as the initial health history, except the questions concern the child's current age and developmental level. The reason for the visit is ascertained, usually a health maintenance visit, and it should be determined if the parent (or child, if age-appropriate) has any particular concerns. Questions should be asked regarding any recent illnesses, hospitalizations, surgeries, acute or chronic pain, injuries, or emergency room admissions since the last visit. The allergy history should be updated if applicable, as well as whether the child is currently taking any medications, including the name of the drug, the dose, and frequency of administration. The child's immunization status should be reviewed. An updated ROS should be obtained. The provider should ask age-appropriate questions to update the child's nutritional status, daily physical activity, elimination patterns, the safety of the child's environment, sleep patterns, social situation, including sexual history if applicable, and physical and psychosocial growth and development.

Focused History

A focused (episodic, problem-centered) history is conducted when the child presents with a particular problem such as the onset of an acute illness, injury, psychosocial problem, or the exacerbation of a chronic illness or condition. The focused history addresses only the illness or problem for which the child presents, usually involving only one or two body systems.

Chief Complaint

The chief complaint is the reason for seeking health care. Common illness complaints in the pediatric population include fever, rhinorrhea, sneezing, cough, sore throat, respiratory illnesses, middle ear infections vomiting, abdominal pain, diarrhea, refusal of feedings, lethargy, irritability, and inconsolability. It is important to document the chief complaint in the child or parent's own words while assessing whether or not the informant is a reliable source of information. As with other types of health histories, inquiries should be made about the use of current medications, including both prescription and OTC preparations,

folk remedies, and CAM therapies. Allergies should be noted, along with a current, up-to-date ROS, PMH, inquiries about any recent illnesses, and a review of the child's current immunization status. Data collection focuses only on the illness or problem at hand. If, however, during the course of the visit, the provider notes that a young child is developmentally delayed, is not up to date on immunizations, or has any other problem not stated in the chief complaint, the provider should not ignore the secondary problem, but should treat it as necessary, unless the child's current health status is serious or critical, requiring immediate medical intervention. The provider should assess whether or not the caregiver can safely care for a sick child. This is especially relevant if the parent or primary caregiver is very young, uses drugs or alcohol, is homeless, or is otherwise challenged in providing safe, consistent, reliable care to a young child.

History of Present Illness

An important component of the focused health history is the history of present illness (HPI). The HPI is essentially a chronologic narrative of the chief complaint. The HPI includes questions to ascertain the onset of the symptoms, illness, or problem; the location of symptoms, particularly pain; the timing and duration of the symptoms, illness, or problem; and characteristics of the symptoms, including the severity, quality, quantity, and aggravating or alleviating factors. A helpful mnemonic to remember the elements of the HPI is OPPQRST, which is described in Box 6.2.

Although many providers find this mnemonic useful to guide them in obtaining the HPI, it is limited because it focuses on physical illness. Parents do not always seek care for their children for illness, fever, or pain but may do so for temper tantrums, biting, bedwetting, or other psychosocial problems. A comprehensive approach includes both physical illness and psychosocial concerns. The provider should note how the reason for seeking health care affects the family, and how the child's culture and social situation influence the management plan for any problems identified. A mnemonic that guides this comprehensive assessment is CLIENT OUTCOMES, which is described in Box 6.3 (Rhoads & Petersen, 2014).

BOX 6.2   The OPPQRST Mnemonic: A Guide to the
History of the Present Illness

O = **Onset of symptoms** such as date, time, sudden
versus gradual onset: "When did it start?"
P = **Palliative:** "What makes the problem better
(e.g., medications, positioning)?"
P = **Provoking** factors: "What brings on the
problem?" "What makes the problem worse
(e.g., exercise-induced wheezing)?"
Q = **Quality of symptoms** describes the nature of
the symptoms: "What does it feel like?"
R = **Region/radiation** (with pain as a complaint):
Use a developmentally appropriate pain scale
to quantify pain: "Where is the pain?" "Where
does it radiate?"
S = **Severity of symptoms:** "How bad is it?" Note
aggravating/alleviating/precipitating factors
(e.g., cold air exacerbating wheezing or cold
air improving croup).
T = **Timing** such as frequency and duration of
symptoms: "Are the symptoms continuous or
intermittent?" "How often do they occur?"
"How long do they last?" "Why was help
sought now?" (e.g., "What was the catalyst
that caused you to seek help?" "Was the pain
getting worse?")

Follow-Up History

A follow-up history is necessary when a child returns
to the office or clinic after an illness or injury has
been diagnosed, or some other type of problem has
been identified. Historical questions are generally brief
and focus on ascertaining whether or not the problem
is better, worse, or remains the same. Specific questions are tailored to the child's particular diagnosis.
The provider should ask the parent or child what, if
anything, they have been doing to make the problem
better, such as applying heat or cold, taking prescribed
or OTC medications, ingesting home remedies, or visiting a traditional healer. The provider should determine
whether or not the child has been adhering to the prescribed treatment plan, and if not, why not. Reasons
for not continuing with a provider's recommendations
may include the fact that the child exhibited signs of a
medication allergy or that the prescribed treatment may
have made the problem worse. In some cases, the family may simply not be able to follow the recommended
plan, because of such things as financial or transportation constraints or cultural or language issues. The
provider should also ask the child or parent if they have
any additional problems or concerns. Further follow-
up is necessary if the problem has not fully resolved.

Emergency Health History

The emergency pediatric health history is often conducted in urgent care clinics, emergency rooms, or

pediatric intensive care units. This history involves
the rapid collection of data in emergent, potentially
life-threatening situations. These data are similar to
those obtained in a focused history, except that data
collection must happen quickly (e.g., "What substance
was ingested and how much?") and is often accompanied by a simultaneous physical examination or
intervention.

After the health history is completed, the provider
should ask the parent and child if they would like to
discuss anything else or if they have any other concerns. If there are no further questions or concerns,
objective data are then obtained. Analysis of both subjective and objective data allows the provider to create a problem list, which is a consideration of all the
possible diagnoses based on the information gathered
through interviewing and examining the child. For
each problem enumerated, a corresponding plan must
be formulated.

BOX 6.3   The CLIENT OUTCOMES Mnemonic:
A Guide for a Comprehensive Assessment

C = **Character** of symptoms, including intensity or
severity
L = **Location,** including radiation (if present)
I = **Impact** of the symptoms or illness on child's
ADL or quality of life of child and family
E = **Expectation** (parent and child, if school-aged or
older) of what the health care visit will do for
them
N = **Neglect or abuse,** including signs of physical,
verbal, emotional, or sexual abuse in child,
or evidence of malnutrition, or delayed
immunizations
T = **Timing,** including onset, duration, and
frequency of symptoms
O = **Other symptoms** that are associated with
major presenting symptom
U = **Understanding or beliefs** of child or parent
about possible cause of problem
T = **Treatment** such as medication, elevation, hot or
cold remedies, or any other therapies used to
alleviate symptoms/condition
C = **CAM therapies,** including type of therapies
tried, such as herbs, traditional healing
practices, visits to a traditional healer, message,
and acupuncture
O = **Options for care** that are important to parent
or child (e.g., requesting a second opinion)
M = **Modulating factors** (i.e., factors that
precipitate, aggravate, or alleviate symptoms
or problem)
E = **Exposure** to infection, toxins, chemicals, or
secondhand cigarette smoke
S = **Spirituality,** including beliefs, values, and needs
of child and family that impact health care

<table>
<tr><td>

Notable Clinical Findings

- Unreliable/inaccurate historian
- Language barrier between health care provider and historian
- Inconsistencies between history and clinical findings
- Lack of medical home—incomplete history

</td></tr>
</table>

References

American Academy of Pediatrics. (2011). SIDS and other sleep-related infant deaths: Expansion of recommendations for a safe infant sleeping environment. *Pediatrics, 128*(5), e1341–e1367.

American Academy of Pediatrics Committee on Pediatric Workforce. (2008). Policy statement: Ensuring culturally effective pediatric care: Implications for education and health policy. *Pediatrics, 114*(6), 1677–1685, reaffirmed August 1, 2008.

Borowitz, S. (2013). *Pediatric constipation.* Retrieved from http://emedicine.medscape.com/article/928185-overview

Centers for Disease Control and Prevention. (2014a). *Immunization schedules.* Retrieved from http://www.cdc.gov/vaccines/schedules/index.html

Centers for Disease Control and Prevention. (2014b). *Injury prevention & control: Data & statistics (WISQARSTM).* Retrieved from http://www.cdc.gov/injury/wisqars/leading_causes_death.html

Dunn, A. M. (2013). Elimination patterns. In C. E. Burns, A. M. Dunn, M. A. Brady, N. B. Starr, & C. G. Blosser (Eds.), *Pediatric primary care* (5th ed., pp. 202–217). St. Louis, MO: W. B. Saunders.

Frost, L. A., & Burns, C. E. (2013). Sleep and rest. In C. E. Burns, A. M. Dunn, M. A. Brady, N. B. Starr, & C. G. Blosser (Eds.), *Pediatric primary care* (5th ed., pp. 256–273). St. Louis, MO: W. B. Saunders.

Gordon, M. (2002). *Manual of nursing diagnosis* (10th ed.). St. Louis, MO: Mosby.

Hagan, J. F., Shaw, J. S., & Duncan, P. M. (Eds). (2008). *Bright futures: Guidelines for health supervision of infants, children and adolescents* (3rd ed.). Elk Grove Village, IL: American Academy of Pediatrics.

Horodynski, M. A., Stommel, M., Brophy-Herb, H. E., & Weatherspoon, L. (2010). Mealtime television viewing and dietary quality in low-income African American and Caucasian mother–toddler dyads. *Maternal and Child Health Journal, 14*(4), 548–556.

Howard, B. J., & Wong, J. (2001). Sleep disorders. *Pediatrics in Review, 22*(10), 327–342.

Instone, S. L. (2002). Developmental strategies for interviewing young children. *Journal of Pediatric Health Care, 16*(6), 304–305.

Joint Commission on Accreditation of Healthcare Organizations. (2001). *Pain standards for 2001.* Oakbrook Terrace, IL: Author. Retrieved from http://www.jointcommission.org/pain_management

Lehna, C. (2005). Interpreter services in pediatric nursing. *Pediatric Nursing, 31*(4), 292–296.

Merkel, S. I., Voepel-Lewis, T., Shayevitz, J. R., & Malviya, S. (1997). The FLACC: A behavioral scale for scoring postoperative pain in young children. *Pediatric Nursing, 23*(3), 293–297.

Rhoads, J., & Petersen, S. W. (2014). *Advanced health assessment and diagnostic reasoning* (2nd ed., pp. 2–23). Burlington, MA: Jones & Bartlett Learning.

Assessing Safety and Injury Risk in Children

Ellen M. Chiocca and Claire Sorenson

HEALTH AND SAFETY IN CHILDREN

Unintentional injury is currently the most significant health threat to children living in industrialized nations. It is the number one cause of death and disability in children and adolescents living in the United States, surpassing all diseases combined (Heron, 2013). In 2009, childhood injuries resulted in over 9,000 deaths; almost half of these injury-related fatalities in children involved motor vehicle collisions, the leading cause of death in children in the United States (Heron, 2013). After unintentional injuries, suicide and homicide ranked second and third, respectively, as leading causes of death in children aged 15 to 19 years (Heron, 2013).

The number of childhood deaths each year in the United States resulting from unintentional injuries is unacceptably high, but it does not compare to the number of children who require emergency treatment or hospitalization or who suffer permanent disability because of injuries. Injuries are the second leading cause of hospitalization and the leading cause of emergency room visits among children younger than 18 years of age (Centers for Disease Control and Prevention [CDC], 2012).

The U.S. government formulated objectives to improve the health of American people in the 21st century in a report titled Healthy People 2020 (U.S. Department of Health and Human Services [USDHHS], 2010). The specific goals and objectives in this report that relate to children focus on reducing morbidity and mortality from the major unintentional injuries. Reaching these goals will require regular childhood health supervision that focuses on injury risk assessment according to age and developmental stage.

Infant and Child Mortality

Because of a variety of factors (see Chapter 1), infants and children have different health problems than adults; these vary according to age and developmental level. Throughout

history, infants have had high death rates, particularly in the immediate neonatal period, mainly because of infection. In 2010, the leading causes of death in neonates (birth to 28 days) were congenital anomalies, prematurity and low birth weight, sudden infant death syndrome, and maternal complications of pregnancy (Murphy, Xu, & Kochanek, 2013). Non-Hispanic Black infants have the highest infant mortality rates (MacDorman, Hoyert, and Matthews, 2013). In 2008, the United States ranked 27th for infant mortality, behind many other industrialized nations; at time of publication, preliminary data again placed the United States 27th in the world for infant mortality (MacDorman et al., 2013). In 2010:

- The leading causes of death among children between 1 and 4 years of age were unintentional injuries, congenital anomalies, homicide, malignant neoplasms (cancer), and diseases of the heart (Heron, 2013).
- The five leading causes of death in children between 5 and 9 years of age were unintentional injury, malignant neoplasms, congenital malformations, homicide, and diseases of the heart (Heron, 2013).
- The leading causes of death in children between the ages of 10 and 14 years were unintentional injuries, malignant neoplasms, suicide, homicide, and congenital anomalies (Heron, 2013).
- The leading causes of death in adolescents aged 15 to 19 years of age were unintentional injuries, homicide, suicide, malignant neoplasms, and diseases of the heart (Heron, 2013).
- Of all fatal unintentional injuries in children and adolescents, motor vehicle collisions were the leading cause of mortality (Heron, 2013).

Infant and Child Morbidity

Morbidity describes illness, specifically the ratio of sick to well persons in a population, presented as the number of ill people per 1,000 population. Morbidity refers not only to acute and chronic illness, but disability as well. With the advent of immunizations and antibiotics, communicable diseases have become less threatening as major causes of morbidity and mortality in American children, and pediatric psychosocial illnesses (also known as the "new morbidity") have emerged as concerns to pediatric health care providers. These illnesses are primarily psychosocial in nature and include depression, eating disorders, abuse and neglect, and drug and alcohol abuse. Also included are psychosomatic and stress-related illnesses related to exposure to bullying and peer violence, conflict with friends, academic and extracurricular pressures, parental divorce or domestic violence, media violence, living with poverty or homelessness, and bereavement (Ryan-Wenger, Sharrer, & Campbell, 2005; Skybo, 2005).

PEDIATRIC MORBIDITY AND MORTALITY STATISTICS

Before the provider assesses for injury risk to an infant, child, or adolescent, it is important to be familiar with the facts about injuries in children. This includes the type of injuries that are most prevalent in certain age groups and the related risk factors that are likely to be present. This knowledge helps direct the health assessment in an age-appropriate way so that the provider may design relevant prevention strategies.

Motor Vehicle Injuries

Injuries related to motor vehicle collisions are the leading cause of injury and death in children of all ages from birth through adolescence. In 2010, more than 1,400 children 14 years and younger died in motor vehicle collisions, and approximately 148,000 were injured as occupants in motor vehicles (National Center for Health Statistics [NCHS], 2012a; NCHS, 2013). In 2010, approximately 3,000 15- to 19-year-old drivers were involved in fatal motor vehicle collisions, and 510,000 were injured (NCHS, 2012b; 2013). Of these children who died, 33% were unrestrained at the time of the collision (Sauber-Schatz, West, & Bergen, 2014). Further, between 2001 and 2010, 20% of fatal motor vehicle accidents involved a drinking driver (Quinlan, Shults, & Rudd, 2014). In 2010, 17% of the crashes resulting in fatal injuries in children under the age of 14 years involved an impaired driver; however, of those deaths, more than half were riding in the vehicle with the impaired driver at the time of the crash (National Highway Traffic Safety Administration [NHTSA], 2012b). Most motor vehicle injuries occur when the child is an occupant of the motor vehicle, except for the 5- to 9-year-old age group, when death related to injuries sustained as a pedestrian are more common (NHTSA, 2012a). Use of car seats, booster seats, and seatbelts is the most effective way to prevent motor vehicle injuries to children; in spite of this, in 2011, 41% of children

killed in motor vehicle collisions were unrestrained (NHTSA, 2013b).

Pedestrian Injuries and Deaths

In 2011, 230 children and adolescents 14 years and younger died from pedestrian injuries (NHTSA, 2012b). Most child pedestrian injuries and deaths involve children crossing the street. Children younger than 10 years of age do not have the developmental abilities to interpret traffic signs or judge distance, which puts them at greater risk for pedestrian-related injury or death.

Drowning

Drowning is the second leading cause of unintentional injury death in girls aged 1 to 4 years and has been the leading cause of death in boys aged 1 to 4 years since 2005 (Xu, 2014). Younger children are more likely to drown in the bathtub, backyard swimming pool, or other standing water left unattended at home, whereas adolescents are more likely to drown in natural bodies of water while swimming or boating (Xu, 2014). Parents should be aware of the fact that children are not developmentally ready for swimming lessons until after their fourth birthday (American Academy of Pediatrics [AAP] Committee on Injury, Violence, and Poison Prevention [CIVPP], 2010b). Adult supervision is the most important way to prevent drowning in children.

Fires and Burns

Injuries caused by fires and burns are the third leading cause of unintentional injury deaths in children, mainly in children younger than age 5 years. These injuries include smoke inhalation, flame contact, scalds, sunburn, electrical and chemical burns. Approximately 308 children aged 14 years and younger died due to unintentional fire and burn-related injuries in 2010 (NCHS, 2012b). Nearly 100,000 children 14 years and younger are treated in hospital emergency rooms for burn-related injuries each year (CDC/National Center for Injury Prevention and Control [NCIPC], 2012a). Most of the fires and burns occur in the home, with death resulting from smoke inhalation and asphyxiation rather than from actual burns (CDC, 2012). Younger children are more at risk for dying of fire-related injuries because of their inability to escape from a burning building independently. Young children are also at risk for scald burn injuries from coffee or teapots left on the table, pots on the stove, and when being held on the lap of an adult who is holding hot food or liquid. A working smoke detector and sprinkler system in the home can greatly reduce fire-related deaths in children and families.

Suffocation, Choking, and Strangulation

Injuries related to airway obstruction are the leading causes of unintentional injury deaths in children younger than 1 year of age (NCHS, 2012b). In 2010, 1,118 children aged 14 years and younger died from unintentional airway obstruction; 92% of these children were younger than the age of 4, and approximately 85% of these children were younger than the age of 1 (NCHS, 2012b). Most of these deaths are due to choking on small pieces of food such as hot dogs, gum, hard candy, popcorn, grapes, and raw vegetables. Nonfood items that can cause choking include toys with small, detachable pieces and latex balloons. Airway obstruction injuries can occur as a result of entanglement in window-blind cords, clothing drawstrings, or from strings tied around a child's neck (for example, to secure a pacifier). Infant mortality rates due to accidental suffocation and strangulation in bed have quadrupled since 1984 (Shapiro-Mendoza, Kimball, Tomashek, Anderson, & Blanding, 2009). Children can become entangled between crib slats and between spaces in bunk beds, baby strollers, and high chairs. Young infants can suffocate when placed in the prone or side-lying sleeping position or in soft bedding; these are considered risk factors for sudden infant death syndrome in infants (AAP Task Force on Sudden Infant Death Syndrome, 2011).

Firearm Injuries

The easy availability of firearms to American children contributes to the high number of firearm-related injuries and deaths in children. In 2010, 4,060 children, adolescents, and young adults 21 years of age and younger were killed in gun-related violence; an additional 166 unintentional deaths in children and adolescents were the result of firearms. In 2012, there were 21,837 nonfatal firearm-related injuries in children 21 years of age and younger (CDC/NCHS, 2013). Approximately 34% of American families with children keep at least one gun in the home (State Department of Social and Health Services, 2009). Rural households are less likely to contain a firearm than urban households; neither group consistently follows safe gun storage practices with children in the home, which includes storing guns locked, unloaded, and with the ammunition stored and locked separately (DuRant et al., 2007). The presence of a firearm in the home, especially if kept loaded and unlocked, greatly increases the risk of unintentional firearm fatalities among children (Brady Center to Prevent Gun Violence, 2009). Male children are much more likely to be injured fatally from unintentional firearm injuries than female children, as are urban Black children of lower socioeconomic status (NCHS, 2012c). Not all firearm injuries involve gang activity; most occur between family members and are acts of rage. Also, parents often misjudge a young child's capabilities regarding guns, with many believing that firearms in the home are safe from their children. Few children younger than 8 years of age, can distinguish between real and toy guns or fully understand the consequences of pulling the trigger (Jackman, Farah, Kellermann, & Simon, 2001).

To reduce firearm injuries in children, it is essential for the provider to assess for safe storage of firearms in the home.

Homicide

Homicide is the second leading cause of injury-related death in infants younger than 1 year of age, preceded by unintentional suffocation (NCHS, 2012b), peaking during the first week, and then peaking again in the second month of life, most likely due to the caregiver's reaction to the infant's persistent crying. Shaken baby syndrome (SBS) is an often fatal form of child abuse in infants and toddlers that involves violent shaking and is often committed impulsively as a result of frustration when a young child cries persistently. Approximately 1,300 infants and toddlers are affected by SBS annually, and approximately 300 cases of SBS are fatal (National Center on Shaken Baby Syndrome, 2014).

Homicide is the third leading cause of death in children 1 to 4 years of age, the fourth leading cause of death in teenagers 5 to 14 years of age, and second leading cause of death in teenagers 15 to 19 years of age (NCHS, 2012a). The leading mechanism of injury in these homicides is firearms (NCHS, 2012c). While most homicides of infants and young children are perpetrated by caregivers, 63% by a parent (U.S. Department of Justice, 2011), homicides of adolescents most often are perpetrated by peers or acquaintances (Office of Juvenile Justice and Delinquency Prevention [OJJDP], 2013). Firearms and handguns in the home greatly increase the chance that a child or adolescent will become a homicide victim.

Suicide

Suicide is rare in children younger than 10 years of age, but in 2010, it was the third leading cause of injury death among children aged 10 to 19 (CDC/NCIPC, 2012b). In 2010, a total of 1,933 young people aged 8 to 19 years killed themselves; 749 of them used a gun to take their life (NCHS, 2012b). Native American and Alaskan Native teenagers are at the highest risk for suicide, followed by Hispanic teenagers (CDC/NCIPC, 2014). Although more male than female teenagers complete suicide, attempts at suicide are much more common in female than male teenagers (CDC/NCIPC, 2014).

Poisonings

The incidence of unintentional poisonings in children has decreased dramatically in the past 50 years because of a combination of factors: child-resistant containers, anticipatory guidance, and the establishment of poison control centers, among others (AAP/CIVPP, 2010a). Despite this, young children, especially those less than 6 years of age, are vulnerable to unintentional ingestions of poisons. Adolescents are also at risk for poisonings, both intentional and unintentional. Exposure to lead paint from paint chips in old homes or from toys painted with lead paint can cause lead poisoning, resulting in anemia and damage to the kidneys and central nervous system.

Toy Safety

Unsafe toys pose a variety of hazards, depending on the child's age and developmental level and the type of toy. Most toy-related deaths in children are caused by drowning or choking and subsequent asphyxiation or suffocation on a small toy ball or balloon (U.S. Consumer Product Safety Commission [USCPSC], 2013b). Riding toys (e.g., bicycles, scooters, skateboards, skates) are associated with more injuries than any other category of toys (USCPSC, 2013b). Darts and trampolines are dangerous at any age, and their use should be strongly discouraged. Darts and other projectile or propelled toys can cause cuts or serious eye injuries (Stephenson, 2005). Trampolines are especially hazardous because of the increased risk of neck hyperflexion, hyperextension, and rotation if the child falls from the trampoline. Spinal cord injuries can occur; specifically, cervical disc herniation. Younger or smaller children are at greatest risk for this injury, especially when simultaneously using the trampoline with an older or larger child (Eberl et al., 2009; Windsor et al., 2006). Fatal trampoline injuries are most often due to spinal cord injuries and head trauma (Leonard & Joffe, 2009; Stratbucker & Green, 2006). The AAP Council on Sports Medicine and Fitness advises that trampolines should not be provided for children under any circumstances (2012b). BB guns, pellet guns, air rifles, and paint ball guns can cause serious injury to children and adolescents, including penetration injuries to the eye, skin, internal organs, and bone (AAP/CIVPP, 2012a) and should be thought of as weapons and not toys.

Falls

Falls are common in children and, depending on the child's age and developmental stage, may occur several times a day, especially in toddlers just learning to walk. In 2010, 62 children younger than 14 years of age died as a result of falls (CDC/NCIPC, 2012b). In that same year, nearly 2.4 million children aged 14 years and younger were treated in hospital emergency rooms for falls; 47% of these children were younger than 4 years of age (NCIPC, 2013). In fact, falls are the leading cause of emergency room visits and overnight hospitalizations in children and the most common cause of nonfatal childhood injury, accounting for more than half of nonfatal childhood injuries (NCHS, 2013). African American and Hispanic children are more likely to be injured from falls from heights because of the increased likelihood that they live in urban, high-rise, often deteriorating, low-income apartment houses (AAP, 2010). These kinds of falls tend to be from windows and occur more in spring and summer when windows are more likely to be open. Infants and toddlers often fall in the home by falling off changing tables or beds when crib rails are left down and the child is unattended. In 2010, more than 4,000 children aged 4 years and younger were treated in hospital emergency rooms for baby walker–related injuries (Chowdhury, 2011). Of children who fall while in baby walkers, 75% fall down the stairs at home; these injuries most often cause head injury and hospitalization (AAP/CIVPP, 2012d). Most children who suffer severe injury or die from falls do so because of head injuries (Harborview Injury Prevention and Research Center, 2009).

Bicycle and Tricycle Injuries

In 2011, 66 children younger than age 15 died in bicycle crashes and an additional 9,000 were injured (NHTSA, 2013a). Two thirds of bicycle-related deaths are due to traumatic brain injury (TBI) (NHTSA, 2013a). Most bicycle-related fatalities involve collisions with motor vehicles (NHTSA, 2013c). The most effective way to reduce bicycle-related head injuries and fatalities is through the use of bicycle helmets; however, in 2010, it was estimated that only 48% of children wore a helmet every time they rode a bike, and 29% of children never wore a helmet when riding a bike (Dellinger & Kresnow, 2010). Further, most children who use helmets wear them improperly. Some states and the District of Columbia, as well as some local governments, have passed laws requiring children to wear helmets while bicycling or participating in other wheeled activities (Bicycle Helmet Safety Institute, 2014). The provider should always inquire about helmet use at every health maintenance visit and as needed during episodic visits.

All-Terrain Vehicle Injuries

Children are injured and die both as drivers and as passengers on all-terrain vehicles (ATVs). In 2007 (the most recent year with data considered complete), 135 children younger than 16 years of age died and roughly 40,000 were injured in ATV-related collisions; preliminary data for 2011 report 57 children younger than age 16 were killed in ATV accidents and 29,000 were injured (USCPSC, 2013a). Most fatal ATV-related injuries involve severe head injuries, and death is often instantaneous (Kirkpatrick, Puffinbarger, & Sullivan, 2007). Other injuries to children who ride ATVs include nonfatal head injuries, orthopedic injuries, spinal cord injuries, abdominal injuries, and multiple trauma, including lacerations and fractures (Hagopian, Burkhalter, & Foglia, 2014; USCPSC, 2013a). ATVs are extremely difficult to maneuver, and children younger than 16 years of age do not have the requisite cognitive or physical skills to operate these vehicles safely; also, children younger than 16 years of age should not ride as passengers on ATVs (AAP, 2014b; American Academy of Orthopedic Surgeons [AAOS], 2010; American College of Surgeons [ACOS], 2009). Children must be at least 16 years of age to drive a car; the same standard should apply to the operation of an ATV. The AAP strongly discourages the use of ATVs in the pediatric population; in fact, the AAP has published a policy statement recommending passage of legislation in all 50 states to prohibit the use of two- and four-wheeled off-road vehicles by children younger than 16 years of age and has asked for a ban on the sale of all three-wheeled ATVs, including a recall of all used three-wheeled ATVs (AAP, 2014b).

Playground Injuries

Annually, approximately 210,000 children younger than age 14 years are treated in hospital emergency rooms for playground equipment–related injuries; 75% of these children were aged 5 to 14 years (Figure 7.1) (USCPSC, 2010). Strangulation from entanglement or entrapment is the leading cause of playground equipment–related fatalities, and falls are the most common playground-associated injury (O'Brien, 2009). Falls from slides, swings, playhouses, and monkey bars can cause head injuries, which account for 75% of fall-related deaths involving playground equipment (O'Brien, 2009). Lack of adult supervision is associated with 40% of playground injuries, including playgrounds in schools, parks, and childcare centers, and is also associated with more severe injuries, including

FIGURE 7.1 Young children need a safe area in which to play with adult supervision.

fractures (Lam, Sumanth, & Mahedev, 2013; Petrass, Blitvich, & Finch, 2009).

Sports-Related Injuries

The risk of injury when playing sports depends on the age of the child and the type of sports-related activity in which the child engages. Sports-related injuries in children result in a large number of emergency room visits and hospitalizations. More than 2.6 million children 14 years old and younger are treated each year for sports injuries, mainly resulting from falls, collisions, and overexertion injuries, and approximately 298,000 of these were sports- and recreation-related TBIs in 2009 alone (CDC, 2011b). The sports associated with the most injuries are contact and collision sports: baseball, football, basketball, soccer, and gymnastics; those that predispose children to falls, such as skateboarding and in-line skating; and riding sports such as horseback riding and bicycling (American Academy of Neurological Surgeons, 2011; CDC, 2011b). Numerous injuries can also occur when playing hockey; these injuries primarily involve the upper extremities, particularly fractures, dislocations, sprains, abrasions, lacerations, and contusions (Deits, Yard, Collins, Fields, & Comstock, 2010; Emery et al., 2010). Adolescent males have the greatest number of hockey-related injuries (Deits et al., 2010; Emery et al., 2010). Baseball has the highest fatality rate among all sports played by children aged 5 to 14 years (AAP Council on Sports Medicine and Fitness, 2012a). Most of these deaths are a result of impact injuries to the head (e.g., intracranial bleeding) or to the chest wall (e.g., commotio cordis and subsequent ventricular fibrillation and asystole) from contact with the ball or bat (Harborview Injury Prevention and Research Center, 2006). Many sports-related injuries in children can be prevented if the child wears appropriate protective gear such as knee and elbow pads and, especially, helmets (National Institute of Arthritis and Musculoskeletal and Skin Diseases, 2013).

IDENTIFYING RISK FACTORS FOR CHILDHOOD INJURY DURING A HEALTH ASSESSMENT

The study of epidemiology furnishes the health care provider with an understanding of the nonrandom distribution of risk to certain populations by examining the specific factors that increase the risk (risk factors) or lower the risk (protective factors) for injury. Epidemiological statistics show that injuries are predictable, preventable, and understandable. It is important for the provider to note that the term accident, which implies lack of control over the occurrence, random chance, and lack of responsibility, has been replaced with the term unintentional injury, which implies personal responsibility and control over the cause of the injuries. It is widely thought that if injuries are viewed as avoidable and not random, parents and children can be taught prevention strategies, and injuries will consequently decrease in frequency.

The assessment of injury risk in the pediatric population depends on specific factors. Haddon (1972), in his classic work, developed a conceptual framework to guide the assessment of injuries, which, in turn, has helped health care providers to devise strategies for injury prevention. Haddon's approach considers the interplay of one or more factors that converge to create circumstances that are favorable for injuries to occur (Table 7.1). Haddon's matrix has two axes: one that examines the host (e.g., infant), agent (e.g., toy with small parts), and environment (e.g., crawling on floor unattended near the toy), and another that depicts the environmental circumstances before (pre-event factor), during (event factor), and after (postevent factor) the injury. This approach illustrates, for example, how a child's age and developmental stage, combined with an unsafe toy in an unsupervised environment, can lead to an unintentional injury in the child. The time–interval axis stresses how many childhood injuries are predictable and preventable. With this example, the pre-event factor is whether the infant's environment was childproofed, the event factor is the potential choking episode, and the postevent factor is the availability of emergency services after the injury.

Assessment of injury risk to a child is a critical component of injury prevention in children. When assessing for the risk of injury to a child, it is important to assess for the types of preventive measures that the parent or caregiver already have in place to prevent injury to the child. *Active* strategies to prevent injury are those that require action on the part of the child or parent. An example of an active strategy is the use of a car seat. *Passive* strategies to prevent injury in children are automatic and require no action on the part of the parent or child. An example of a passive strategy is childproof caps on medication bottles. In general, the more effort required on the part of the child or parent, the less effective the safety intervention will be.

Certain children are more at risk for injury than others, depending on their age, developmental stage, socioeconomic status, and other factors. It is important for the provider to be aware of these risk factors, which allow him or her to direct questions properly during the health care encounter. This knowledge can also help the provider design and implement relevant teaching strategies.

Developmental Risk Factors

The causes and types of childhood injuries vary widely according to the child's age and developmental stage. Certain anatomic characteristics predispose young children to injury. For example, young infants are more prone to head injuries in the first few months because of poor head control and large head size. The small, light body of a young child makes the child more prone to injury, especially with motor vehicle or pedestrian injuries, because the child's small body may be thrown more easily. Certain cognitive characteristics place children at higher risk for injury as well. As children become mobile, their natural curiosity and desire to learn, coupled with their lack of ability to assess danger and poor impulse control, can predispose them to numerous safety hazards. Young children are unable to assess their surroundings for danger, and they lack abstract thinking and decision-making skills to protect themselves from injury. Older school-aged children and adolescents may deliberately engage in risky behaviors in an attempt to rebel or express autonomy. Adolescents are prone to injury because they are risk takers, desire

TABLE 7.1	Haddon's Matrix, Choking Injury Example				
	HUMAN FACTORS	**HOST**	**AGENT**	**PHYSICAL ENVIRONMENT**	**SOCIOCULTURAL ENVIRONMENT**
Pre-event	Nonchildproofed environment	Infant; developmentally unaware of choking hazards	Toy with small parts	No safe play area for infant	Unsupervised child
Event	Choking episode	Infant putting small toy parts in mouth and obstructing airway	Size of toy parts	Infant crawling on floor	Product standards
Postevent	Parents' knowledge of foreign body removal in infant; time of arrival of emergency personnel	Degree of choking/aspiration of foreign body in the infant's airway	Ease of removal of foreign body	Distance to hospital	Specialized pediatric facilities

Source: Haddon (1972).

to be accepted by their peers, and as such, often do not consider safety before action. Temperament plays a role as well. Children who are very active, curious, persistent, and defiant are more likely to become injured.

Risk Factors Related to Parenting

Parental knowledge deficits, particularly among very young parents and parents who are unaware of normal growth and developmental patterns in children, can contribute to the incidence of childhood injury. Parents who may not be aware of their infant's or child's capabilities may unwittingly leave them in circumstances in which they can become injured. For example, an older infant or toddler who is given a toy with small detachable parts is at risk for choking. Parenting style also influences a child's risk for injury. Corbett, Morrongiello, Lasenby, Johnston, and McCourt (2006) found that highly permissive parenting styles were more likely to be associated with injuries severe enough to require medical attention. Parents may also ask older children in the home to care for younger siblings, who may not be aware of safety hazards to small children, therefore increasing the risk of unintentional injury (Morrongiello, Schmidt, & Schell, 2010) Lack of age-appropriate adult supervision of young children and parental drug or alcohol use are risk factors for unintentional injury (Morrongiello & McArthur, 2010).

Environmental Risk Factors

Certain environmental risk factors predispose children to injury. The most important risk factor is poverty, the primary predictor of injury risk in children (Hong, Lee, Ha, & Park, 2010). Children living in poverty are more likely to live in substandard or overcrowded living conditions, near busy streets, and near unsafe playground facilities, all factors that increase injury risk (Gielen et al., 2012; Hong et al., 2010). The safety of the home environment is paramount, and how this is evaluated is age dependent. For example, with young children in the house, electrical outlets need to be covered and cleaning solutions stored high and locked. For adolescents, this may mean close monitoring of Internet use. Children living in rural areas are at increased risk for injury-related death because of certain environmental conditions (National Children's Center for Rural and Agricultural Health and Safety, 2014). The safety of the school and neighborhood also play a role in determining a child's safety risk. Thus, assessment should include determining whether the child is being bullied, and whether the child is left home alone for extended periods of time. Having a firearm in the home is another environmental risk factor for injury to children and adolescents.

Nonmodifiable Risk Factors

Risk factors for injury in children that cannot be changed include age, male gender (which is associated with increased risk-taking behaviors and rough play), left-handedness (which presents environmental biases that

---

BOX 7.1 Risk Factors for Unintentional Injuries in American Indian and Alaskan Native Children

- Poverty
- Male gender
- Alcohol abuse
- Alcohol-impaired driving
- Substandard housing
- Rural residences
- Low seatbelt use rates
- Limited access to medical care and emergency services
- Lack of medical insurance
- High rates of depression

Based on data from Murphy et al. (2014).

---

can increase risk for injury), and having a history of a previous injury. Cognitive and developmental disabilities in children may predispose them to injury as well. Race is another nonmodifiable risk factor for injury, although this may have more to do with living in poverty than with race (CDC/NCIPC, 2012a). American Indian and Alaskan Native children suffer the highest mortality rates after unintentional injury, followed by African Americans and Hispanics (CDC/NCIPC, 2012b). The rates of motor vehicle injuries and pedestrian injuries among American Indian and Alaskan Native children is twice as high as Caucasian and three times as African American children in the same age group (CDC/NCIPC, 2012c). Deaths by drowning in American Indian and Alaskan Native children occur at a rate twice that of Caucasian and exceed the rate for African American children by approximately 20% (CDC/NCIPC, 2012b); fire and burn injuries are almost twice as high as in Caucasian children and roughly equal to African American children (CDC/NCIPC, 2012b). Certain risk factors predispose American Indian and Alaskan Native children to unintentional injuries; these risk factors are summarized in Box 7.1. Box 7.2 summarizes specific risk factors that predispose children and adolescents to unintentional injuries.

BOX 7.2 Risk Factors That Predispose Children to Unintentional Injuries

Age

- Younger children are more prone to injuries due to anatomic and cognitive characteristics.

Developmental Characteristics

- Depending on age, child may be unaware of risks or willing to take risks.
- Physical abilities of the child influence injury risk.

(continued)

Environmental Risk Factors

- Poverty
- Crowded, unsafe living conditions
- Living near busy streets
- Living in a rural area
- Non-childproofed environment
- Stress
- Family/social situation

Male Child

- Male children are associated with increased risk taking and rough play.

Parenting

- Permissive parenting style
- Parental knowledge deficits
- Lack of supervision
- Addicted parents

Temperament

- Some children are more aggressive and fearless than others.

Alcohol/Drug Use in Child or Teen

Children With Developmental or Physical Disabilities

Having Firearms in the Home

History of Previous Injuries

Race

INJURY PREVENTION THROUGH HEALTH ASSESSMENT

Assessment for risk of injury and injury prevention in children is an important form of health promotion. Primary care providers can significantly reduce the number of unintentional injuries in children by assessing the safety of the child's environment at each well-child visit and as warranted with episodic care, especially during health care visits to treat injuries or ingestions. These assessments provide concrete, specific data that identify risks to the child and assist greatly in formulating individualized teaching plans to prevent future injuries; their importance cannot be overemphasized. Some children live in unsafe environments because injuries that they sustain are intentional. These injuries may be a result of abuse or self-inflicted harm (see Chapters 23 and 24).

History

An assessment of the health and safety of the child's environment is part of every infant, child, and adolescent health maintenance examination. The provider begins by obtaining the history using a developmentally focused approach. An example would be to start by asking open-ended questions, such as:

- "What type of car seat do you use for Kylie?"
- "Does Jamal take a bottle to bed?"

- "Julie, what is the first thing that you do when you get in the car with Mom?"
- "Does Juanita wear a bicycle helmet each time she rides her bike?"
- "Michael, can you tell me what you would do if a stranger asked you to come with him?"

If possible, questions that require a "yes" or "no" answer should be avoided; this approach limits the amount of information that can be obtained. A checklist is useful when making these assessments as it ensures that all the relevant safety and illness prevention questions are asked for the child's particular age and developmental level. A checklist also helps to expedite the pace of the health care visit. Using *Bright Futures: Guidelines for Health Supervision of Infants, Children, and Adolescents* and the AAP health supervision guidelines as resources to guide these assessments is ideal (Hagan, Shaw, & Duncan, 2008). The AAP has also developed the Injury Prevention Program with the goal of decreasing injuries in children by providing education to parents (AAP/CIVPP, 2007).

Answers to the questions asked during the history determine not only what general and specific injury prevention measures are used for the child, but the parent's knowledge of basic child growth and development as well. For example, what are the parents' expectations of the child? Do they expect a young child to have knowledge of street safety? Is the parent or caregiver aware of choking hazards posed to infants and toddlers? Are the parents aware of the dangers of leaving young children unattended, especially near stairs and water? If children younger than 3 years of age live in the home, is it childproofed? Is there an adolescent in the home who is suffering from depression? The information gleaned from these assessments can be used to develop concrete teaching plans and safety interventions as needed.

Some specific health and safety assessment questions should be asked at every visit, regardless of the child's age. Most involve motor vehicle safety, fire safety, sun and water safety, secondhand smoke exposure, environmental sanitation, living conditions, the family's social situation, whether the family owns any firearms, and the child's exposure to violence in different forms. Box 7.3 summarizes these universal health and safety assessments that should be made regardless of the child's age.

Home Environment

In 2011, approximately 2,700 children 14 years of age and younger died in their homes due to unintentional injuries (National Safety Council, 2011). More than 80% of these deaths were among children aged 4 years and younger (National Safety Council, 2011). Children are at increased risk for death resulting from unintentional injuries occurring in the home largely because this is where they spend most of their time. Most home injury deaths are a result of suffocation and choking, followed by drowning, poisoning, falls, and firearm

---

BOX 7.3   Universal Pediatric Health and Safety Assessments

Safety of Home Environment

- Is home childproofed? Are outlets covered? Are gates and window guards used?
- Are window-blind cords out of reach?
- Is the child exposed to secondhand smoke?
- Are there toys with small parts in the house with children younger than 3?
- Is there age-appropriate adult supervision?
- Is there any lead paint in the older home or apartment?
- Is the child exposed to interpersonal violence among family members or is there evidence of child abuse?
- Are there any drug or alcohol users in the home?

Motor Vehicle Safety

- Are all motor vehicle restraints properly used (see Box 7.6)
- Are children allowed to ride in the cargo area of a pickup truck?

Pedestrian/Traffic/Cyclist Safety

- Do children use helmets when bike riding?
- Is there age-appropriate supervision when crossing streets?

Fire and Burn Safety

- Are there smoke and carbon monoxide detectors in the home?
- Are space heaters used in the winter?
- Are infant bottles warmed in a microwave?
- Are there fire extinguishers in the home? Is there a family plan for escape in case of fire?

Sun Safety

- Are children allowed to play in the sun without protective clothing?
- Are infants younger than 6 months of age kept out of direct sun?
- Do all children older than 6 months of age use sunscreen?
- Do teens use tanning beds?

Water Safety

- Are all young children closely supervised around water?

- Have children 4 years of age and older had swimming lessons (AAP/CIVPP, 2010b)?

Animal Safety

- Have children been taught safe handling of animals; for example, no teasing and no handling of animals when they are eating?
- What kinds of pets are in the house? Are these pets healthy?

Sports/Recreational Safety

- Do children use helmets and other protective gear when playing sports?

School Safety

- Are children bullied by others?
- Is it safe for children to travel to school unsupervised?

Stranger Safety

- Have younger children been taught about never speaking to strangers?
- Have older children been taught about Internet safety?

Media Safety

- Do children see violent media of all types?
- Is Internet use monitored in school-aged children and adolescents?

Firearm Safety

- Are there firearms or other weapons in the home?
- Are guns and ammunition locked and stored separately?

General Health

- What are the household hand-washing practices, especially with a newborn in the house, during cold and flu season, and with other illnesses?
- Are toys ever washed?
- What is the immunization status of everyone in the family, especially members who travel back and forth to developing countries?

---

injuries; with the exception of firearm injuries, most deaths are in children aged 4 years or younger (National Safety Council, 2011).

The home safety assessment begins with general questions about the child's home environment. For children younger than preschool age, the parent should be asked if the home is childproofed. This includes covering outlets, padding table corners, placing gates at the top of stairs, and removing dangling cords, especially those belonging to window blinds, which pose strangulation hazards. The provider should ask parents who live in upper-level dwellings or those with balconies about window guards and railings on balconies. Families with toddlers should be asked whether doors are kept locked to prevent curious toddlers from leaving the home unattended. The provider should determine if parents know first aid as well as how to perform the Heimlich maneuver and cardiopulmonary resuscitation (CPR). The provider should ask preschool-aged and older children if they know how to dial 911. The provider should ask if the Poison Control Center number is clearly posted and readily available. The provider should also ask parents about firearms in the home (i.e., if they are locked and unloaded). It is also important to determine if lawn and garden equipment is kept stored in a locked garage or shed.

The provider should also ask about the parent's role modeling of safety, including safety belt use, drinking and driving, and obeying posted speed limits. Parents should also wear bicycle helmets when riding their bicycles. The provider should ask about the use of tobacco, illegal or prescription drugs, or alcohol in the home environment, and the provider should ask if the child is exposed to interpersonal violence among family members.

Urban Homes • The effects of poverty often have a great impact on the health status and safety of children living in urban settings. Other factors affecting the safety of a child living in an urban area include crowded or unsafe living conditions, traffic-related safety hazards, lead paint exposure in old buildings, exposure to pesticides used in urban schools and homes, noise, crime, air pollution, and gang activity, among others. Homeless children have a higher incidence of trauma-related injuries, and runaway youth and young people living on the streets are at risk for violent injury and victimization (AAP Council on Community Pediatrics, 2013a). Box 7.4 provides a detailed guide that is tailored to the assessment of children living in urban settings.

Rural Homes • Children who live on farms or in rural frontier areas require a different approach to the assessment of a safe environment. This group of children includes not just farm families but children of hired farm workers, the children of migrant farm workers, and children who may just be visiting a farm. These children are exposed to hazards associated with agricultural work and rural environments such as farm machinery, vehicles (ATVs, tractors, and automobiles), livestock, and agricultural chemicals and pesticides (Wright, Marglena, & Lee, 2013). Falls from unstable structures, drowning, animal trauma, horseback riding injuries (Pickett et al., 2005), electrical hazards, fire and explosions, and firearm-related injuries are also safety risks to children living in rural areas (Zaloshjna, Miller, & Lawrence, 2012). Children who live in rural areas with a low population density who live a long distance from health care facilities may also be at increased risk for morbidity and mortality related to injuries sustained while on a farm, as it may take longer to travel to a tertiary facility to receive urgently needed care.

Migrant farm workers' children of all ages are at increased risk for intentional and unintentional injuries and farm-related injuries (AAP Council on Community Pediatrics, 2013b). Factors that may be attributed to this increased risk include language barriers, poverty, mobile lifestyle, overcrowded living conditions, poor environmental sanitation, and unreliable transportation (AAP Council on Community Pediatrics, 2013b). Adolescent migrant farm workers are at risk for these injuries, and they also encounter risks related to traveling without their parents as part of their mobile lifestyle. American Indian and Alaskan Native children are other populations who often live in rural areas. As previously discussed, these children are already at an increased risk

---

BOX 7.4 Safety Assessments for the Child Living in an Urban Setting

- Is the child living in an old, unsafe building? Was it built before 1960?
- Is the child exposed to lead paint or lead paint dust from chipping paint or remodeling of an old home?
- Does the child live in crowded housing conditions? Are there continual loud noise levels?
- Does the child live in a high-rise building? If so, are window guards in place on all windows to prevent falls?
- Is the child exposed to pesticides that may have been applied in their home, school, or day care center to control cockroaches, rats, termites, or other vermin?
- Does the child stay off the grass after lawn chemicals and pesticides have been applied?
- Does the child live in an urban area with high levels of air pollution and poor air quality? (If yes, has the child had episodes of wheezing? Has the child been diagnosed with asthma?)

- Does the child take public transportation alone?
- Does the family live near a busy street or highway? Does the child walk to school alone? If so, is the child developmentally capable of doing so? Is the child competent with traffic safety and street crossing? Is the neighborhood safe enough for the child to walk to school?
- Does the child take a school bus to school? If yes, how does the child get physical activity?
- Has the child ever been the victim of bullying? If so, to what extent? Was physical violence involved?
- Does the child live in a high crime area? Is the child (preschool-aged and older) familiar with the concept of "stranger danger"?
- Is the child involved in or been the victim of any gang-related activity?
- Does the family own any firearms? Are the firearms stored locked with the ammunition kept separately? Has the child been taught about gun safety?

for injury. This underscores the importance of being especially thorough when assessing for injury risk in these children. Box 7.5 summarizes safety assessments for children living in rural areas.

BOX 7.5   Specific Safety Assessments for the Child Living in a Rural Environment

- Does the child regularly visit or live on a farm?
- Is there an enclosed play space for young children away from work areas, animals, and farm machinery?
- Before operating any farm equipment or machinery, is the work area always checked for the presence and location of small children?
- Does the child or adolescent operate farm equipment and, if so, does the child or teen have the requisite knowledge, maturity, and physical abilities to do so? Is the child who operates farm machinery younger than 16 years of age?
- Does the child always use seatbelts when operating a tractor or any other type of farm machinery?
- Are there rollover protection structures on the tractors?
- Is there more than one rider on tractors, mowers, ATVs, or other farm machinery?
- Does the child ever ride in the cargo area of a pickup truck?
- Is the child ever involved in applying toxic pesticides to crops?
- Are farm chemicals and cleaning agents properly stored?
- Is the young child always supervised around standing water or any body of water? Has the child had swimming lessons? Does the child ever swim alone?
- Is the small child kept away from livestock?
- Has the family taught the child safe handling of pets, farm animals, and livestock?
- Does the child wear appropriate safety gear (e.g., helmets) when riding horses?
- Does the child or teen wear hearing-protective equipment when actively involved in farm work?
- Are there any electrical hazards on the farm, especially in barns?
- Does the family have firearms? Are they stored locked and is the ammunition kept separately? Has the child been taught not to handle guns?
- Do the child and family use appropriate hand washing after handling animals or animal manure?

Motor Vehicle Safety

Because motor vehicle collisions are the leading cause of death in American children older than 1 year of age, it is particularly important that the provider ask parents during routine health care visits if their children are properly restrained when riding in a motor vehicle. All children should be secured in a weight- and age-appropriate vehicle restraint that is installed properly. The provider may need to determine whether the car or booster seat has been placed in the vehicle properly and if the child is positioned in the seat correctly. (Figures 7.2 and 7.3). Box 7.6 summarizes the American Academy of Pediatrics 2011 policy statement regarding child passenger safety, and these guidelines should be used when assessing parent and child knowledge of proper car seat safety and vehicle restraint (AAP/CIVPP, 2011; AAP, 2014a). Children with special needs such as premature infants or children with physical disabilities may need some modifications to their vehicle restraints; the provider should determine if these adaptations are in place. When obtaining a health history on adolescents, the

FIGURE 7.2 Infants and toddlers younger than age 2 years must be placed in a rear-facing car seat.

FIGURE 7.3 When a child is 2 years old or has outgrown the rear-facing weight or height limit for his or her car seat, the child may ride in a forward-facing car seat with a harness.

BOX 7.6 Summary of Proper Vehicle Restraint in Children

Premature Infants

■ Should use a car seat without a shield harness
■ Should have an adult ride in back seat if possible

Infants/Toddlers

■ Must ride in rear-facing car seat
■ Must ride in back seat of vehicle
■ Must ride in back seat with side air bags disabled
  ● Should remain in rear-facing car seat until age 2 years, or until car seat manufacturer's weight/height limit has been exceeded (usually 22–40 lb)

Toddlers/Preschoolers

■ After outgrowing rear-facing car seat, must be seated in forward-facing car seat
  ● Must use car seat harness
  ● Must ride in the back seat with side air bags disabled
  ● Should remain in forward-facing car seat as long as they are within manufacturer's height/weight guidelines (usually 40–50 lb)

School-Aged Children

■ Must still ride in rear seat of vehicle
■ Can ride in forward-facing car seat in vehicle
■ Should remain in car seat until they weigh 40 pounds

Older Children

■ Should ride in forward-facing booster seat
■ Should still ride in rear seat of vehicle
  ● Must use belt positioning booster seat
■ Should remain in booster seat until 4 feet, 9 inches in height and 8 to 12 years of age
■ After this age, should wear a seatbelt for all rides, no matter the distance
■ If younger than 13 years, should not sit in the front seat of the vehicle

Source: American Academy of Pediatrics (2014a).

FIGURE 7.4 Assessment of motor vehicle safety is paramount when working with adolescents.

the cargo area of the truck. This practice is exceptionally dangerous; each year, approximately 50 children and adolescents 21 years of age and younger die while riding in the cargo area of a pickup truck (AAP/CIVPP, 2008).

Pedestrian and Traffic Safety

Assessment of motor vehicle safety also includes specifically inquiring about whether the child is always supervised near the street and in driveways, and if the child younger than 8 years of age always holds an adult's hand when crossing the street. The provider should determine if the child rides his or her bicycle, skateboard, or scooter in the street. Children, if school-aged or older, can be asked directly if they know how and where (i.e., crosswalks) to cross the street. Also, the provider should determine if the child walks to school alone. It is important to determine both safe pedestrian practices and safety around strangers.

Bicycle Safety

The provider should ask parents if their child rides a tricycle or bicycle and, if so, if the child wears a helmet that meets bicycle helmet safety standards of the American National Standards Institute or the Snell Memorial Foundation (Figure 7.5). The provider should ask parents to replace helmets that have been damaged or are outgrown. The provider should inquire about children riding as passengers in a rear-mounted seat on an adult bicycle. Infants younger than 1 year should not ride on the back of an adult's bicycle in an infant seat because infants this age cannot support the weight of the helmet and hold their head up during the ride (AAP/CIVPP, 2012b). It should be determined if children older than 1 year who ride in a rear-mounted seat on the back of an adult's bicycle wear an approved helmet for the ride.

provider should ask teens if they wears seatbelts consistently; obey speed limits; drink, use drugs, or text when driving a car; or ride with anyone who does (Figure 7.4). The provider should determine if the parents also consistently wear a seatbelt. Children are more likely to use their seatbelt if they see this behavior consistently in their parents. The provider should ask parents who drive pickup trucks if their children ever ride in

FIGURE 7.5 Children of all ages should wear a helmet when riding bicycles.

Fire Safety and Burn Prevention

The provider should always ask parents if there are working smoke and carbon monoxide detectors on every level of the home and if the batteries are changed at least twice a year. The provider should determine if the family has a fire extinguisher in the home and whether there is an escape plan in the event of a fire. When age-appropriate, children should be taught to feel a door for heat and refrain from opening the door if it is hot; to stay close to the floor if there is smoke; and to stop, drop, and roll if their clothes catch fire. Preschool-aged children and older should be asked if they know how to dial 911 to report a fire. The provider should ask the parent if the home's hot water heater temperature is set at or below 120°F (48.9°C). The provider should ask parents about using a microwave to heat bottled infant formula; this causes uneven heating of the formula, which can burn an infant's mouth. The provider should determine if there are fireworks in the home to which the child or adolescent has access.

Sun Safety

Because young children have a thin, undeveloped epidermis, they develop sunburn more quickly than adults. Assessment of sun safety includes asking parents about keeping their infant or child out of direct sunlight, and about the use of sunscreen, protective clothing, hats, visors, and sunglasses for protection. Sunscreen should not be used on infants younger than 6 months of age, and children of this age should be kept out of direct sunlight at all times. The provider should ask parents whether they apply sunscreen to their children 6 months of age and older when their children are in the sun for prolonged periods.

Water Safety

Because of the prevalence of drowning deaths in children of all ages, the health history should always include information about whether the child is continuously supervised around pools, bathtubs, and natural bodies of water and whether the child wears a life jacket near water. The provider should ask parents of infants and toddlers if they ever leave their child alone in the bathtub or around pools or buckets of standing water. The provider should determine whether a child 4 years of age or older has had swimming lessons. If the family has a backyard pool, the provider should ask if it is properly fenced with self-closing, self-latching gates; the provider should determine if school-aged children or adolescents ever swim alone.

Animal Safety

Having an animal in the home can pose a safety risk to children, particularly children aged 5 to 9 years who are most likely to be bitten (Baddour & Endom, 2013). Children living on farms are also at risk for animal-related injuries. During the health history, the provider should determine the kind of pets kept in the home. The provider should determine if infants and young children are supervised around animals and taught safe handling of pets and farm animals: to avoid touching animals they do not know, not to tease or play roughly with an animal, and never to touch an animal when it is eating. If the parents have recently acquired a pet such as a dog or cat, the provider should ask if the animal has been properly immunized and examined by a veterinarian to minimize the chance of spreading disease to the child.

Sports and Recreational Safety

Children of all ages need toys or age-appropriate activities to enhance their psychosocial development and learning. As part of the well-child visit, the health care provider should determine what toys the child plays with, not just to gauge the child's developmental level, but also to determine whether any safety hazards are present. Although many toys are packaged with labels that state "not intended for children younger than 3 years," this is usually not because the toy is developmentally advanced for a child of that age but because it contains small, detachable pieces on which a child younger than 3 can easily choke. When beginning a sports safety assessment, the provider must first consider the child's age and developmental stage, and formulate questions from that standpoint (see the next section: Assessment of Risk for Injury by Age and Developmental Stage).

For older children who ride skateboards, scooters, or in-line skates or who participate in sports, the provider should inquire about appropriate protective gear, including helmets and mouth guards (AAP, 2014c; AAP/CIVPP, 2102b). The provider should ask about trampoline use in children of all ages and take time to educate parents on the dangers associated with playing on trampolines, and discourage their use. Adolescents should be asked if they ride ATVs and, if so, whether they wear a helmet. The provider should discourage parents from allowing children and teens to ride ATVs, snowmobiles, or jet skis before they are 16 years of age because of the upper body strength and coordination needed to operate these machines (AAOS, 2010; AAP, 2014b; ACOS, 2009). The provider should ask children who ride horses if they always wear a helmet when riding.

Stranger Safety

Beginning in the preschool-aged group, children should be asked what they know about "stranger danger." Children should be able to articulate that they would never go with a stranger, even if bribed or told by the stranger that they knew the child's parents. During the history, the provider could start the assessment by asking the child, "Alyssa, what would you do if a man you did not know came up to you and nicely asked you to come with him to help him find his lost puppy?" Responses resembling, "I would never go with someone I did not know," or "I would scream and run and tell an adult" indicate that the child is aware that going with a stranger is dangerous.

Adolescents are also at risk for being hurt by strangers they may meet through Internet chat rooms, e-mail, or messaging; Internet dating services; or at parties where drugs or alcohol may be used. Because of this, stranger safety must be assessed at health maintenance visits in this age group as well. Special attention should be given to the multiple stranger safety risks that the Internet poses to children and adolescents. These risks include exposure to harassing or threatening e-mails or video posts, being lured into activities that have legal consequences such as revealing personal or financial information, and other safety issues, including sexual assault or other injury as a result of sharing personal information online and then meeting the stranger in person (Federal Bureau of Investigation, Cyber Division 2013). Parents, children, and adolescents should be asked about how much time the child or teen spends online each day, if the time is limited by the parent, whether the computer is kept in a common area of the house, and if parental controls are used. With the parent out of the room, the child or adolescent should be asked about what type of Internet sites they visit, if they have their own e-mail account, or are involved in Internet chat rooms.

Exposure to Media

It is estimated that the average American child spends an average of 3 to 6 hours per day in front of a television, computer, or video screen (MedLinePlus, 2014). When watching television, children are exposed to repeated references to and advertisements for junk food, alcohol, and tobacco (American Academy of Child and Adolescent Psychiatry, 2011; AAP Council of Communications and Media, 2013). Children and adolescents are also exposed to violent and sexual content through television, movies, video, and computer games, the Internet, and through the lyrics of songs. The AAP recommends that children 2 years of age and younger watch no television or videos at all, and children older than age 2 engage in no more than 1 to 2 hours a day of total "screen time," which includes television, movies, hand-held video games, and computer time (AAP Council of Communications and Media, 2013).

During the health maintenance visit, the health care provider has an excellent opportunity to assess a child's exposure to various types of media as part of the health history. This assessment includes asking the parent how many hours a day his or her child watches television and movies, uses the computer and Internet, or plays video games. If the child watches movies each day, the content of the movies should be noted. The provider should also ask if the child has a television or computer in the bedroom, as this makes parental screening of content more difficult; it also makes it next to impossible for the parent to know exactly how much time the child is spending watching television or online. Children and adolescents who view violent media can become desensitized to violence, show increased aggressive behaviors, use violence as a method of conflict resolution, and see the world as an overly violent and scary place. Additionally, over exposure to media may also cause children to engage in risky sexual behavior, substance abuse, or unhealthy eating habits (Strasburger Jordan, & Donnerstein, 2010).

Firearms

Regardless of the child's age, at every visit the provider should ask if firearms are kept in the home and how and where the firearms are stored. Any firearm in the home is dangerous, including BB, pellet, and paint ball guns, which can cause serious injuries to the eye, sometimes leading to blindness. During the safety portion of the health assessment, when the provider asks the parent if any guns are kept in the home, the provider should ask if the firearm is stored unloaded and if it is in a locked container. The provider should determine whether the child or adolescent knows where the gun is kept; only the parent should know where the gun is stored. The provider should determine whether the ammunition is stored separately and in a locked container. Firearm safety assessment and counseling should include the male head of the household to improve knowledge about the presence and storage practices of firearms in homes with children and adolescents (Johnson, Runyan, Coyne-Beasley, Lewis, & Bowling, 2008). Parents of children and adolescents should also be strongly encouraged to eliminate firearms from the home.

General Health Practices

It is important to keep a child safe not just from physical injury but from illness as well. The provider should ask parents if they routinely wash their child's hands, especially before meals, after using the toilet, and when the child returns home from school, day care, or playing outside. The immunization status of all children should also be assessed at every health care visit. Second- and third-hand smoke exposure should be assessed as well. The provider should also ask parents if they know first aid, the Heimlich maneuver, and CPR, especially if the child has a chronic or life-threatening health condition.

Assessment of Risk for Injury by Age and Developmental Stage

In addition to universal safety assessments, pediatric patients must be assessed for risks to safety according to age and developmental stage. All children and adolescents are at risk for injury because of their natural curiosity, impulsiveness, and, depending on developmental level, inability to assess risk (younger children) and desire to take risks (adolescents). With each new developmental achievement, children enjoy exploring their surroundings and are driven to test newly acquired skills. Children and adolescents often attempt activities before they have developed the requisite cognitive and physical skills needed to accomplish the task safely. As children grow, their gross and fine motor abilities develop, but at a faster rate than their cognitive abilities, making them more vulnerable to injuries. In addition, children, especially toddlers and adolescents, in a desire for autonomy and independence, often challenge rules, defy their parents, and become oppositional, making rule enforcement sometimes difficult for parents. School-aged children and adolescents in particular develop a strong desire for peer approval as they grow older, which may lead to risk-taking behavior to impress friends. Personality and temperament of the child also play a large role in influencing injury risk; some children are more aggressive than others and thus are more prone to injury. Tables 7.2 through 7.5 provide detailed guides to age-appropriate safety assessments in the pediatric patients, infancy through adolescence.

Assessment of Infants

Infants younger than 6 months of age have poor head control and until 2 years have a large head in proportion to their body; both factors make them more vulnerable to head and shaking injuries. Older infants become more mobile as they learn to roll over, creep, crawl, and pull to stand. Infants also explore their environment by putting things into their mouths. The developing pincer grasp makes it easier for older infants to place small objects in their mouth, presenting choking hazards and making older infants at risk for poisoning and ingestions (see Table 7.2).

Parents of infants should be asked if their child is placed in an approved car safety seat for all car rides and whether it is rear-facing and installed correctly (see Box 7.6). The provider should ask parents of newborns about sleep position, co-sleeping practices, the space between crib slats, if the crib mattress fits snugly, and if there are stuffed toys and pillows in the crib, which present suffocation hazards. The provider should determine if the parent uses plastic sheets to cover the crib mattress or has plastic bags near the crib, both of which present a suffocation risk. The provider should inquire if parents of infants 2 months of age and younger are aware of the signs of illness in a baby this age, such as fever, refusing feedings, persistent vomiting or diarrhea, inconsolability, lethargy, jaundice, or skin rash. Parents of newborns and infants should also be asked if they attend the baby at all times when he or she is on a bed, a changing table, or in a bath. The provider should also determine if parents ever consume hot liquids while holding their infant, as this increases the risk for unintentional scald burns. The type of toys that are provided for the infant should also be determined, noting if any of these toys present safety hazards such as marbles, latex balloons, or toys with small, removable parts, which can cause choking. Batteries should always be kept away from small children. Toys with sharp edges or points may cause unintentional cuts or lacerations. The provider should ask if the infant plays with toys that have long strings or has a pacifier on a string, both of which are strangulation hazards.

When assessing infants aged 6 to 12 months, the provider should ask if the parents have childproofed the home. Are there gates at the tops of stairs and window guards in upper level rooms? Are outlets covered? Are sharp corners of walls and furniture padded? Are electrical cords concealed to prevent accidental chewing, which

FIGURE 7.6 When infants begin creeping and crawling, the home environment must be childproofed.

TABLE 7.2	Safety Assessment Guidelines for Infants	
DEVELOPMENTAL AND PHYSICAL CHARACTERISTICS	**POTENTIAL INJURIES**	**RELEVANT ASSESSMENTS**
Birth–6 months Poor head control Large head (birth–2 years)	Injury to neck or head	Assess how infant is picked up, held, and moved. Is neck supported? Are older children supervised around infant? Is infant left alone with pets? Is infant ever shaken? What do parents do when baby gets fussy? Is infant placed in a rear-facing car safety seat in rear of vehicle for every car ride?
Primitive reflexes: suck, grasp, rooting, startle	Aspiration of foreign objects, suffocation, strangulation, choking	Is there plastic in or around the infant's bed or changing table? Is infant placed supine for sleeping? Does family co-sleep? Is infant placed on a waterbed or beanbag to sleep? Does infant sleep in a crib or adult bed? Does crib have pillows or stuffed bedding/bumper pads inside? Are there toys, stuffed animals, or crib mobiles with small, detachable parts, strings, or cords? Is crib positioned close to window blinds? Are crib slats ≤ 2³⁄₈ inches apart? Does infant have anything tied around his or her neck such as a bib or pacifier secured with string or shoelace? Does anyone feed infant small finger foods? Is infant's bottle propped? Are latex balloons kept away from infant?
Thin epidermis	Burns	Do parents hold infant while cooking or consuming hot food or beverages? Is infant held while parent is smoking? Is home's hot water heater thermostat set at or below 120°F (48.9°C)? Are there working smoke and carbon monoxide detectors in the home? Are the batteries checked routinely?
	Sunburn	Is infant exposed to direct sun? Do the parents refrain from using sunscreen on infant and keep infant out of direct sunlight instead? Does infant wear a hat in the sun and are all other skin exposed areas covered?
Increasing gross motor abilities correlating with spinal cord myelination: • Rolls, turns, scoots, moves, pushes against objects with feet • May begin to creep or crawl as early as 6 months	Falls	Is infant ever left unattended on a bed or changing table, sofa, or chair? Is infant placed in a bouncy seat while on a table, kitchen counter, or other high surface? Is baby placed in a safe place such as a crib or playpen when not being held? Are there gates at the top of stairs when infant begins to crawl? Are window guards in place on all windows above first floor? Is baby ever in a walker?
	May slide between crib mattress and crib slats	Does infant sleep in a crib with a mattress that fits snugly against crib rails?
	Slip or slide in sink or tub during bath	Is infant ever left unattended during a bath?
	Motor vehicle safety	Is infant placed in an approved rear-facing car seat in back seat for every car ride? Does infant ever ride in the front seat of the car? Does car have a passenger air bag? Does infant ever ride held on an adult's lap?

TABLE 7.2	Safety Assessment Guidelines for Infants (*continued*)	
DEVELOPMENTAL AND PHYSICAL CHARACTERISTICS	**POTENTIAL INJURIES**	**RELEVANT ASSESSMENTS**
Immature body temperature regulation	Hypothermia	Is infant dressed appropriately with head covered in cold weather?
	Hyperthermia	Is infant dressed in light, loose clothing in hot weather? Do parents ever leave infant alone in a parked car?
Immature nonspecific and specific immunity (birth–2 months)	Infection/sepsis	Are parents aware of cord care and circumcision care in the newborn? What are the hand-washing patterns? Can parents recognize early signs of illness: fever > 100.4°F (38°C), irritability, inconsolability, lethargy, poor feeding, red eye or drainage, vomiting, diarrhea, or cyanosis? Do parents know that no antipyretics are given for fever in infants younger than 2 months of age?
6–12 months Increasing gross motor abilities: • Beginning to sit unassisted • Increased mobility with creeping, crawling, and cruising; likes to explore • Begins to push up on hands and knees • Pulls to stand • May stand alone or with support • May walk or climb	Falls	Is infant supervised at all times? Is infant ever left alone on a bed or changing table, or in a high chair? Is crib mattress low enough so older infants cannot climb out of the crib? Are there bumper pads in crib on which infant can climb? Are crib slats ≤ 2 3/8 inches apart? Are gates at the top of all stairs? Are doors closed? Are window guards installed on all windows above first floor? Is sharp-edged furniture padded? Is infant ever placed in a walker? Is infant ever left alone with pets or young siblings?
	Motor vehicle safety	Does infant ride in back seat in a rear-facing car seat for all car rides? (see Birth–6 months, Relevant Assessments)
	Drowning	Is infant ever left unsupervised in a bath? Is bathroom door kept closed and is toilet lid down? Are buckets of water removed? Are there protective enclosures around pools, hot tubs, ponds, or fountains?
	Poisonings, ingestions	Are medications, chemicals, and cleaning agents stored high and locked? Do cabinets have safety latches? Do all medication bottles in house have childproof caps? Are there any poisonous houseplants in the home? Is the Poison Control Center number placed near the phone? Are parents aware that syrup of ipecac is no longer recommended?
Increasing fine motor abilities; pincer grasp developing: • Increasing hand–eye coordination • Infant learning to pick up small objects • Begins to pull and grab at things	Aspiration of foreign objects; choking	Is there a safe place to put baby such as a crib or playpen when parent is unable to hold infant? Are outlets covered and drawers and cabinet doors latched? Are small, sharp objects kept off the floor and out of reach? Are there toys with small, detachable parts? Is the baby ever fed small,

(continued)

TABLE 7.2	Safety Assessment Guidelines for Infants (*continued*)	
DEVELOPMENTAL AND PHYSICAL CHARACTERISTICS	**POTENTIAL INJURIES**	**RELEVANT ASSESSMENTS**
• Transfers objects from one hand to the other • Objects are explored by touching and placing in mouth • Increasing curiosity; does not like to be restrained		hard pieces of food such as popcorn, nuts, hard candy, raw carrots or other vegetables, hot dogs, apples, raisins, grapes, or peanut butter? Is infant's bottle propped? Are topical numbing gels used for teething (may suppress gag reflex and increase chance of aspiration)? Do parents know CPR and Heimlich maneuver?
	Suffocation, strangulation	Are balloons, plastic bags, and plastic wrappers kept out of infant's reach? Does infant have a pacifier tied around neck? Does infant ever sleep on a beanbag chair? Are bibs removed after meals? Are crib toys strung across crib?
	Burns, electrocution	Is bath water checked before infant is placed in tub? Is microwave used to heat formula or baby food? Do parents drink hot beverages, eat hot food, or smoke while holding infant? Are tablecloths removed from tables (can pull down hot liquids)? Are there dangling cords that may be within infant's reach? Are electrical outlets covered with plastic plugs? Are working smoke and carbon monoxide detectors in the home? Are the batteries checked routinely?
	Sunburn	See Birth–6 months, Relevant Assessments. Is sunscreen used? Is prolonged exposure to sun avoided?

Adapted from Dunn (2009).

can result in electrical burns? Parents should be encouraged to keep a gate at the entrance of the kitchen to keep the infant away from knives and the stove. As gross and fine motor skills progress (e.g., crawling on the floor, finding a small piece of a toy), older infants are at high risk for choking and their environment should be assessed for this. The provider should ask about keeping cleaning solutions, poisons, and medications high, locked, and out of reach. The Poison Control Center telephone number should be readily available. The provider should ask parents if the infant is ever placed in a walker, which presents numerous safety risks (see the section on Falls, earlier).

Assessment of Toddlers

Once children are walking, they begin to explore their environment actively, and then walking progresses to running, climbing, and jumping. Once toddlers learn to climb, nothing is out of their reach (Table 7.3). Toddlers have no sense of fear. The fully developed pincer grasp in a toddler increases the risk for aspirations and choking, and this fine motor dexterity allows toddlers to remove bottle caps and to turn doorknobs, placing this

age group at great risk for ingestions, falls, and wandering from the safe confines of home or day care.

Assessment of toddler safety begins by ensuring that the family puts the child in an approved car safety seat (see Box 7.6). The provider should ask parents if the child always rides in the back seat of the vehicle. For newly active and ambulatory toddlers, it should be determined whether there are gates at the tops of stairs and window guards on windows. Parents should be asked if they ever place their child in a walker and if so, this should be discouraged.

It is particularly important to screen this age group for a childproofed environment (see the preceding section, Assessment of Infants). Since this age group is particularly prone to ingestions, the provider should ask whether household cleaning products and medications are stored high and locked, if poisonous plants have been removed, if caustic agents or toxic chemical products are stored in their original container, and if the parents have ready access to the Poison Control Center telephone number. The provider should also inform the parent that it is no longer recommended to keep syrup of ipecac on hand at home, and that this

TABLE 7.3	Safety Assessment Guidelines for Toddlers and Preschoolers	
DEVELOPMENTAL AND PHYSICAL CHARACTERISTICS	**POTENTIAL INJURIES**	**RELEVANT ASSESSMENTS**
Physical Characteristics **Toddlers** Increasing gross motor abilities: • Can walk, run, jump, throw objects • Active climbers • Can move chairs to kitchen counters and climb to cabinets • May be tall enough to reach stove • Can ride tricycle • May ride bicycle by age 5 years	Falls	Is young child supervised at all times during play activities? Do other young children ever supervise younger children? Is outdoor play confined to a fenced in area? Does family have outdoor playground type equipment? Is equipment safe and undamaged, without holes or sharp edges? Is there a soft surface (e.g., wood chips, sand) under play equipment? Until child is at least 3 years of age, are gates placed at tops of all stairs at home? Are doors kept locked and are child-resistant doorknob covers used for doors that lead to stairs or any other elevated area? Is toddler ever placed in a walker? Is play supervised near driveways, sidewalks, or streets? Does child wear a helmet when riding a bicycle or if riding in a seat on an adult bicycle? Does preschooler wear a helmet and other protective gear when skating or using a scooter or skateboard? Are window guards used for windows above the first floor? Are bumper pads removed from crib so toddler cannot climb? Is crib mattress lowered to lowest level to prevent falls? Are crib slats no more than 2 $\frac{3}{8}$ inches apart? If child sleeps in a toddler bed, is mattress close enough to the floor to minimize injury if child falls out of bed? Does child sleep on a bunk bed? Does child play on a trampoline?
	Drowning	At home, is bathroom door kept closed with toilet lid down? Is child ever left alone in bathtub? Do parents know not to leave standing buckets of water around small children? Are all swimming pools fenced? If child is 4 years or age or older, has he or she had swimming lessons? Are parents aware that swimming lessons do not substitute for close supervision in pools, lakes, streams, or oceans? Are child and family near water or on a boat frequently? Does child wear a life vest when boating?
	Contusions, lacerations, abrasions, bites	Is play of small children supervised? Does parent use distraction or time out versus spanking to deal with tantrums or biting? Are small children supervised around pets, especially when animal is eating?
Preschoolers Increasing fine motor abilities: • Turns doorknobs, removes bottle caps, and unscrews lids • Opens doors, windows, gates, drawers, bottles • Pulls on cords, blinds, and tablecloths • May be able to undo seatbelt; may resist car seat • Explores by putting objects in mouth	Poisonings, ingestions	Are cleaning solutions, chemicals, paint, alcohol, and medications stored in a high, locked cabinet? Are childproof caps used on all medication bottles? Do parents refer to medicine as candy? Are "Mr. Yuk" labels placed on bottles of all toxic materials? Is the number to Poison Control Center clearly posted near phone? Are there poisonous plants in house? Are parents aware that syrup of ipecac is no longer recommended? Are pet litter boxes kept away from child's environment?
	Aspiration of foreign objects; suffocation; strangulation	Is the home childproofed? Are cords hidden? For young toddlers, are mobiles or other toys strung across crib rails? Is crib positioned near window blinds? Are door and drawer latches used? Is automatic garage door opener inaccessible? Do toy chests in home have heavy, hinged lids? Are old appliances discarded with doors removed? Are plastic bags kept away from small children? Does child have a pacifier tied on a string around his or her neck?

(continued)

TABLE 7.3	Safety Assessment Guidelines for Toddlers and Preschoolers (*continued*)	
DEVELOPMENTAL AND PHYSICAL CHARACTERISTICS	**POTENTIAL INJURIES**	**RELEVANT ASSESSMENTS**
	Choking	Are mealtimes and snacks supervised? Does child eat foods that could cause choking such as popcorn, grapes, carrots, other raw fruits or vegetables, gum, hard candy, nuts, or peanut butter? Does toddler play with toys with small parts? Is child allowed to run with sharp objects or lollipops in his or her mouth? Are latex balloons kept away from child?
Developmental Characteristics **Toddlers** • Increasing temper tantrums • May hit, bite, or throw things • Do not like to share • Oppositional behavior to be expected in toddlers • Display negativism and desire for autonomy • Easily distracted and unable to assess danger • Reasoning with toddlers is ineffective and impractical • Very curious; like to explore • Want to be more independent • Engage in more active play • Unable to assess danger • Have no sense of fear **Preschoolers** • Active and inquisitive • Still concrete thinkers • Cannot assess danger or problem solve but can understand and heed precautions better than toddlers • Have active imaginations; like to try new things but have many fears • Emergence of magical thinking makes preschoolers think they can attempt dangerous things and escape unharmed • Like to please adults, therefore susceptible to role modeling of good behavior; imitate adults in their lives	Firearms	Does family have a weapon in the home? Is gun safety taught? Are guns kept out of reach, locked, and unloaded?
	Burns	Is hot water heater thermostat set at or below 120°F (48.9°C)? Is bath water checked before placing child in bathtub? When cooking, are pot handles turned toward rear of stove? With especially active toddlers, does parent place gates at entry to kitchen while cooking? Are tablecloths removed so toddler does not pull heavy objects, hot food, or liquids off the table onto himself or herself? Is child kept away from fireplaces, curling irons, electrical tools, and space heaters? Are matches, candles, and lighters kept out of reach? Are unused electrical outlets plugged with plastic outlet covers? Are there working smoke and carbon monoxide detectors in the home? Once child reaches age 4 years old, does family conduct fire drills at home? Can preschooler call 911? Does child live in a smoke-free environment?
	Sunburn	Is sunscreen used? Is prolonged exposure to sun avoided? Does child wear a hat in the sun?
	Motor vehicle trauma (passenger or pedestrian)	Does child ride in a car safety seat according to the AAP's 2011 guidelines? Is child ever left unattended in a parked car? Is child allowed to cross the street unsupervised? Is child supervised when playing near a driveway or street?
	Abuse	Has parent taught preschooler about stranger safety and uncomfortable touches?

Adapted from Dunn (2009).

drug should no longer be used to treat poisonings in the home (AAP/CIVPP, 2010a). Many poisonings in this age group involve ingestion of medications, especially if the child sees an adult take medication or if the parent refers to medication as candy to coax the child into taking the drug. Other common household products that are poisonous if ingested include cosmetics, alcohol, insecticides, pesticides, hydrocarbons (e.g., gasoline, kerosene, lighter fluid, paint thinner), and antifreeze.

Toddlers are still susceptible to choking, so the provider should determine if the child plays with toys with small parts or eats food that may cause choking (e.g., grapes, hot dogs, popcorn, nuts, hard candy, gum, peanut butter). Toys with long strings can present a strangulation risk, as can pacifiers that are tied around the toddler's neck with a string. The provider should ask if the child is continuously supervised and never left alone while in the bath or swimming pool. Since toddlers like to climb, the provider should ask if pot handles are turned to the rear of the stove during cooking and if gates are placed at the entrance of the kitchen for especially active toddlers. The provider should determine if matches and lighters are kept out of reach and if there are any firearms in the home; if so, they should be stored high and unloaded in a locked cabinet with the ammunition stored separately. Electrical hazards persist in this age group; the provider should determine if parents keep appliances unplugged when not in use, especially shredders, lawnmowers, and power tools.

Assessment of Preschoolers

Preschool-aged children are even more physically active than infants and toddlers and like to explore their environment (see Table 7.3). They need supervision around streets, water, and during play. Preschool-aged children are still concrete thinkers with active imaginations and magical thinking. As a result, they cannot assess danger or imagine consequences. Preschoolers also like to imitate parental behavior, and they need role models for safety.

During the safety assessment, the provider should ask the parents of preschoolers about the use of a forward-facing car safety booster seat with harness, and if the child sits in the rear seat of a motor vehicle. Questions should also be included about whether the child's play is supervised, especially near the street and at playgrounds, where injuries frequently happen (see the section on Playground Injuries, earlier). The provider should also determine if the child is supervised while crossing the street; if the child wears a helmet while riding a bicycle, scooter, or skateboard; and if he or she ever bathes or swims unattended. Parents of preschoolers should know that the home should still be childproofed. The provider should inquire about whether matches, lighters, medications, and poisonous substances are stored high and locked. It should also be determined if outlets are covered and electrical cords are out of reach. Parents should be asked if guns are kept out of reach and if the preschooler knows how to use the telephone to call 911.

Assessment of stranger safety depends on the age of the preschooler. For younger children in this age group, the provider should determine if parents have taught their child to avoid contact with strangers. Older preschoolers can be asked directly by the provider if they know to stay away from strangers. The provider should also ask parents if they have introduced the concept of "good touch/bad touch" to their preschooler. The provider can ask older preschool-aged children questions such as: "Are you ever afraid of anyone?," "Does anyone ever hurt you?," and "Does anyone make you keep secrets?"

Assessment of School-Aged Children

Motor skills continue to progress in this age group (Table 7.4). Many school-aged children ride a bicycle, which is dangerous without a helmet and safety gear.

TABLE 7.4	Safety Assessment Guidelines for School-Aged Children	
DEVELOPMENTAL AND PHYSICAL CHARACTERISTICS	**POTENTIAL INJURIES**	**RELEVANT ASSESSMENTS**
Physical Characteristics Increasing motor abilities: • Is more physically coordinated, but new motor abilities increase risk for injuries • Growth in height exceeds muscular growth and coordination • Increased fine motor abilities • Engages in more active play; enjoys physical activity • Rides bicycle by age 5, which takes child away from home • Often involved in organized sports, thus prone to sports-related injuries	Motor vehicle trauma (passenger, pedestrian, or cyclist)	Does child wear a seatbelt for every ride? Does child sit in the rear seat of vehicle? Does child ever ride in the front seat with passenger air bags? If child is below 4 feet, 9 inches in height, is a booster seat used? Does child ever ride in cargo area of a pickup truck? Is child ever left unattended in a parked car? Does parent hold a child's hand while crossing the street if child is younger than 8 years of age? Is child allowed to cross the street unsupervised if younger than 9 years of age? Does child know pedestrian safety rules? Is child supervised when playing near a driveway or street? Does child ride a minibike or an ATV?

(continued)

TABLE 7.4 **Safety Assessment Guidelines for School-Aged Children (*continued*)**

DEVELOPMENTAL AND PHYSICAL CHARACTERISTICS	POTENTIAL INJURIES	RELEVANT ASSESSMENTS
Developmental Characteristics • Wants to produce and achieve; eager to learn new things; a good time to do health and safety teaching • Adventurous; likes to explore • May frequently play in hazardous places or accept dares to do dangerous things • Still a concrete thinker; abstract thinking does not begin until late adolescence • Cognitive skills in school-aged children aid in preventing some types of injuries to which younger children are more susceptible (e.g., can take swimming lessons, learn fire safety, use of seat belts and bicycle safety gear); older school-aged children can cross street safely • Becomes more independent from parents; still needs parents to provide guidance and close supervision • Older school-aged child may begin risk-taking behaviors such as experimentation with alcohol, tobacco, drugs, failure to use seatbelts in cars or helmets or knee and elbow pads when riding a bicycle, roller blades, skateboard, or scooter • Begins to be influenced more by peers than family	Drowning	Are all swimming pools fenced? Has child had swimming lessons? Are parents aware that swimming lessons do not substitute for close supervision in pools, lakes, streams, or oceans? Does child ever swim alone? Are parent and child aware of safe diving practices? Are child and family near water or on a boat frequently? Does child wear a life vest when boating? Do child and family know CPR?
	Fires and burns	Is hot water heater thermostat set at or below 120°F (48.9°C)? Is there a working smoke and carbon monoxide detector in the home? Does family conduct fire drills at home? Does child know how to call 911? Has child been taught to avoid playing with matches and flammable liquids? Does anyone in the home smoke? Has child tried smoking?
	Sunburn	Is sunscreen used? Is prolonged exposure to sun avoided? Does child wear a hat in the sun?
	Firearm safety	Does family have a weapon in home? Is gun safety taught? Are guns kept out of reach, locked and unloaded?
	Falls, contusions, lacerations, abrasions, fractures, bites	Is the younger school-aged child supervised at all times during play activities? Do other young children ever supervise younger children? Is outdoor play confined to a fenced area? Does family have outdoor playground-type equipment? Is equipment safe and undamaged, without holes or sharp edges? Is there a soft surface (e.g., wood chips, sand) under play equipment? Is play supervised near driveways, sidewalks, or streets? Does child engage in sports and strenuous physical activity? Does child wear a helmet when riding a bicycle? Does child wear a helmet and other protective gear when skating or using a scooter or skateboard? Does child play on a trampoline? Does child sleep on bunk beds? Is child aware of safe handling of animals? Is child allowed to operate a power lawn mower or electric tools?
	Suffocation, strangulation, choking	Does child know basic first aid? Is automatic garage door opener inaccessible? Are old appliances discarded with doors removed?
	Poisonings, ingestions	Are cleaning solutions, chemicals, paint, alcohol, or medications stored in a high, locked cabinet in original containers? Do parents refer to medicine as candy? Are safety caps used on medication containers? Is Poison Control number clearly posted near phone? Does child know how to call 911? Are parents aware that syrup of ipecac is no longer recommended?

TABLE 7.4	Safety Assessment Guidelines for School-Aged Children (*continued*)	
DEVELOPMENTAL AND PHYSICAL CHARACTERISTICS	**POTENTIAL INJURIES**	**RELEVANT ASSESSMENTS**
	Abuse	Has parent taught child about stranger safety and uncomfortable touches? Has child been a victim of bullying or excessive peer pressure? Does child spend excessive amounts of time watching television or surfing the Internet?

Adapted from Dunn (2009).

Independence increases in this age group as well (e.g., riding a bicycle takes a child away from home). School-aged children are still concrete thinkers and not adept at fully assessing danger. Older school-aged children begin to look to peers for approval and may begin risk-taking behaviors to win approval or to gain acceptance from a peer group. Some children in this age group have unsupervised time after school ("latchkey kids") while their parents work, which may present safety risks.

School-aged children can be asked directly about their safety habits, with confirmation from the parent as needed. The child should be asked if he or she always wears a seatbelt for every ride in any kind of vehicle. The provider should also ask if the child ever rides in the cargo area of a pickup truck. The provider should determine whether the child wears a helmet for bicycle, skateboard, and scooter use, and protective gear such as helmets and knee and elbow pads for in-line skating. The type of play and whether younger school-aged children are supervised during play, especially near streets and on playgrounds, should be assessed. The child should be asked what he or she knows about crossing the street safely. The provider should ask the child if he or she has had swimming lessons and knows to swim only when an adult is present. Assessment of stranger safety and how to handle unwanted touching is also important in this age group. The provider should ask school-aged children if they know that they should never touch a gun, and if they know how to call for emergency help by dialing 911. The provider should assess school-aged children for cigarette smoking, preferably without the parent present so that an honest response is more likely.

Assessment of Adolescents

Adolescents are at special risk for injury because they are risk takers (Table 7.5). The adolescent's desire for peer approval is a strong motivating factor for experimentation and risk-taking behaviors. In early adolescence, teens are concrete thinkers and because of this, often do not fully understand the consequences of their actions. Adolescents are especially prone to motor vehicle collisions resulting from poor judgment, inexperience, reckless driving, speeding, driving under the influence, failure to use seatbelts, and peer pressure. Peer pressure can also lead to a variety of other injuries related to guns, the use of drugs, and alcohol consumption. Unsafe sex is another manifestation of risk-taking behaviors. Because

of marked physical and emotional changes during this time and underdeveloped coping skills, adolescents are also prone to depression. (See Chapter 23 for screening for suicidal ideation in children and adolescents.)

Injury risk assessment in the adolescent patient is best done with the parent out of the room. The provider is more likely to get honest answers to questions involving risk-taking behaviors than if the teen is worried about the consequences of revealing his or her behavior to the parent. Questions that are asked using a matter-of-fact, respectful, and nonjudgmental tone tend to be answered honestly, as are those that are culturally sensitive. Adolescents should be reassured that whatever they discuss with the provider will not be shared with the parents or caregivers unless the adolescent agrees or the teen discloses information that clearly demonstrates a danger to himself or others (e.g., evidence of an eating disorder, threats of violence or suicide). Asking open-ended questions is especially useful in this context, as is asking the question in the third-person to put the teen at ease; for example, "some teenagers think it's silly to wear a seatbelt. What about you?" This indirect manner may make an adolescent feel more comfortable. For adolescents who are especially reticent about answering sensitive questions, a checklist questionnaire may be a more useful way to gather data.

Assessment of motor vehicle safety is especially important in the adolescent population because of the teen's tendency toward risk taking and desire for peer approval. In every health care encounter with an adolescent, the provider should ask whether the teen wears a seatbelt for every ride, whether driver or passenger, and if he or she ever rides in the cargo area of a pickup truck. The health care provider should check with their state's laws on graduated licensure; some states also have requirements regarding hours of the day that a teen may drive and how many teens 18 and younger may be in the car at one time. The adolescent should also be asked about speeding, drag racing, cell phone use and texting, and driving under the influence of drugs or alcohol. The teen should also be asked if he or she is ever a passenger when someone is intoxicated and driving.

Adolescents should be assessed for alcohol use, including how much, what kind of alcohol, and how often they drink. Drug use should be assessed as well, including the use of marijuana, cocaine, inhalants, amphetamines, and steroids. The provider should assess the quantity and frequency of drug use. The provider

TABLE 7.5	Safety Assessment Guidelines for Adolescents	
DEVELOPMENTAL AND PHYSICAL CHARACTERISTICS	**POTENTIAL INJURIES**	**RELEVANT ASSESSMENTS**
Physical Characteristics Increased body size and abilities: • Rapid growth in height and weight • Maximum increase in height in early adolescence; growth in height ends in females in mid-adolescence (16–17 years of age) and males in late adolescence (18–20 years of age) • Increased physical strength • More physically coordinated but increased motor abilities increase risk for injuries • Often involved in organized sports, thus prone to sports-related injuries	Motor vehicle trauma (passenger, pedestrian, or cyclist)	Does teen wear a seatbelt for every car ride? Has teen taken driver's education classes? Does teen ever drive alone? Does teen drive at night, alone, or with friends? Do teen's friends encourage risk-taking behavior while in the car, such as speeding, drag racing, and taking dares? Does teen ever drive while talking or texting on a cell phone? Is teen aware of pedestrian safety? Does teen ever ride in cargo area of a pickup truck? Does teen ever drive under the influence of alcohol or drugs? Does teen have a reasonable curfew?
Developmental Characteristics • Egocentric • Impulsive • Retains concrete thinking in early adolescence; abstract thinking does not begin until later in adolescence. Under stress, may return to concrete thinking • In late adolescence, teen can think abstractly, can plan, make better choices, is more understanding of consequences of actions • Peer-centered; desires to be part of a group; need for independence from parents; begins to be influenced more by peers than family; may rebel against authority • Risk-takers; may accept dares, particularly to impress peers; often feels invulnerable • Often experiments with alcohol, tobacco, drugs; fails to use seatbelts in cars or helmets and knee and elbow pads when riding a bicycle, roller blades, skateboard, or scooter	Firearm safety	Does family have a weapon in home? Is gun safety taught? Are guns kept locked and unloaded? Does teen carry a weapon? If so, why? Does teen have a non-gunpowder firearm (e.g., BB gun)? Do teen's friends carry weapons or have weapons in the home? Does teen belong to a gang?
	Drowning	Are all swimming pools fenced? Has teen had swimming lessons? Does teen ever combine drugs or alcohol when swimming? Does teen ever swim alone? Is teen aware of safe diving practices? Are teen and family near water or on a boat frequently? Does teen wear a life vest when boating? Do teen and family know CPR?
	Fires and burns	Does teen smoke? Does anyone in home smoke? Are there working smoke and carbon monoxide detectors in home? Does family conduct fire drills at home? Does teen handle firecrackers?
	Sunburn	Is sunscreen used? Is prolonged exposure to sun avoided? Does teen wear a hat in sun?
	Falls, contusions, lacerations, abrasions, fractures	Does teen wear a helmet when riding a bicycle? Does teen wear a helmet and other protective gear when skating or using a scooter, skateboard, or roller blades? Does teen ride a minibike, motorcycle, ATV, or snowmobile? Does teen engage in sports and strenuous physical activity on a regular basis? Does teen jump on a trampoline? Does teen operate a lawn mower, tractor, or any power tools? Does teen know basic first aid and CPR?

TABLE 7.5	Safety Assessment Guidelines for Adolescents (continued)	
DEVELOPMENTAL AND PHYSICAL CHARACTERISTICS	**POTENTIAL INJURIES**	**RELEVANT ASSESSMENTS**
	Abuse	Does teen practice stranger safety? Does teen ever hitchhike? Does teen feel comfortable saying "no" to unwelcome touches? Does teen feel safe at school? Does teen get into fights on a regular basis? Does teen have any self-defense skills? How does teen deal with anger? What does teen know about nonviolent conflict resolution? Has teen been a victim of bullying or excessive peer pressure? Is teen in an abusive intimate relationship?
	Self-injury	Does teen or family have concerns about teen being depressed? How is relationship between teen and his or her parents? Has teen lost pleasure in usual interests? Has teen recently lost or gained a notable amount of weight? Is teen sleeping too much or too little? Does teen seem to be extremely active or overly fatigued? Does teen spend excessive amounts of time watching television or on the Internet? Does teen express feelings of worthlessness or excessive guilt? Has teen's inability to concentrate affected school performance or relationships? Does teen have a distorted body image? Does teen have vague, nonspecific physical complaints for which no cause can be found? Does teen have recurrent thoughts of death or suicide? How does teen handle feelings of anger?
	Poisonings, ingestions, alcohol, drug use	Does teen use alcohol or drugs? How much? How often? What type of drugs? Street drugs? Steroids?
	Sexual activity	Is teen sexually active? Monogamous? Does teen use condoms for each sexual encounter? What type of contraception does teen use? Does teen combine substance abuse with sexual activity?

Adapted from Dunn (2009).

should also determine if the teen smokes cigarettes, and if so, how many packs a day.

Involvement in sports, bicycle, skateboard, ATV, and scooter riding should be assessed along with whether the teen wears relevant protective gear, including helmets. The provider should also assess whether the adolescent knows how to swim and is knowledgeable about water and boating safety, including the dangers of swimming alone and drinking alcohol while swimming or boating. The provider should ask if the teen knows CPR.

Another important area to assess is peer and family relationships, particularly whether these relationships pose any safety threat to the teen. Assessment should include specific questions about gang involvement, peer violence, intimate partner violence, and conflict in the home, including domestic violence between parents. The provider should also ask the teen how he or she is disciplined; physical discipline is never appropriate in this age group. School performance should also be assessed; poor grades often fuel conflict at home and can be a sign of depression in the teen.

Adolescents should be asked if they are sexually active; the provider should ask about the number of partners and whether the teen uses contraception and a condom for each sexual encounter. The teen should also be asked how he or she deals with unwanted sexual advances. At this time, the provider could inquire about the teen's body image, and if he or she ever skips meals or takes laxatives to lose weight to maintain an "ideal" body weight.

Adolescents are not too old to be asked about "stranger danger." The provider should reiterate to the teen that the Internet is especially dangerous, as teens can be stalked or harassed through e-mail, chat rooms, or other messages that threaten or demean. The teen should also be reminded that the Internet can also be used to lure him or her into meeting a stranger in person. The provider should ask adolescents if they ever hitchhike.

Screening for depression in the adolescent is also an important safety assessment. The provider can help prevent suicide in adolescents by becoming familiar with the symptoms of depression and suicidal behavior in this age group and assessing for this during health care encounters (see Chapter 23). This also underscores the importance of asking about the presence of firearms in the home and discouraging people from owning firearms. If the family does own a gun, it is very important to assess the home for safe firearm storage practices, especially if there is a depressed teen in the home (AAP/CIVPP, 2012c).

Assessment of Previous and Current Injuries

Previous Injuries

It is important for the provider to include questions in the history about previous injuries, ingestions, or falls. The provider should inquire about all minor and major injuries, including the nature of the injury, the date the injury occurred, the child's age at the time of the injury, and the injury's cause and severity. The provider should ask if the child needed emergency medical treatment for the injury; for example: Were sutures required for lacerations? Was surgery necessary to correct a fracture? The provider should also determine if the child's injury required hospitalization, and if so, the length of the hospital stay and where the child was hospitalized. It is important for the provider to clarify with the historian the difference between an emergency room visit and an overnight inpatient hospital stay, as this sometimes causes confusion. Knowledge of previous injuries can help the provider identify possible developmental delays in the child, parental/caregiver teaching needs, inadequate parental supervision, and child abuse or neglect.

Current Injury

With minor injuries, the provider should first determine the cause and type of injury, then ask when and how the injury occurred. Intentional injury should be considered if there is a delay in seeking medical care or if there is a discrepancy in the history (see Chapter 24). Parents should be asked if they applied any first aid treatments of their own to the injury, and if so, what type and for how long. A description of symptoms should be sought, including the onset, location, duration, characteristics, and any aggravating and relieving factors. Older children can be asked historical questions directly. (See Chapter 6 for a more detailed discussion of obtaining a focused pediatric health history.)

SUMMARY

Prevention of childhood injuries and injury-related deaths is the responsibility of many who come in contact with children. Providing a safe environment for a child is the responsibility not just of the parent but of the health care provider, nurses, the community, government agencies, and product manufacturers as well. It is important to understand that the health care provider is in a strong position to have a long-term positive impact on the health, safety, and well-being of infants, children, and adolescents. When a thorough and accurate assessment of the risks to the pediatric patient's health and safety is done, and the resulting information is used to formulate an individualized, culturally sensitive teaching plan to address the safety needs of the child and family, it can lead to further health promotion and self-efficacy for the parent and child to guide them in the direction of being full participants in preserving the child's health and safety.

Notable Clinical Findings

- Parent/caregiver denies use of age-appropriate motor vehicle restraint
- History reveals that house/living space is not "baby-proofed" for child/children aged 5 years and younger
- Child aged 3 years and younger plays with toys with small parts or eats small, hard pieces of food
- Parent/caregiver smokes or chews tobacco, or uses alcohol or drugs on a regular basis
- Teen smokes or chews tobacco, or uses alcohol/drugs on a regular basis
- Family is homeless

- Young child (aged 11 years or younger) is left unsupervised
- Family keeps a firearm in the home
- No smoke or carbon monoxide detectors in the home
- Family uses space heater in winter
- Family has a backyard pool
- Child aged 4 years and older does not know how to swim
- Child and family live in a high-crime area
- Child/teen is exposed to domestic violence
- Child/teen does not wear bicycle helmet
- Child/teen does not wear sunscreen
- Child/teen is bullied

References

American Academy of Child and Adolescent Psychiatry. (2011). *Children and watching TV. Facts for Families*, no. 54. Washington, DC: American Academy of Child and Adolescent Psychiatry.

American Academy of Neurological Surgeons. (2011). *Sports related head injury*. Retrieved from http://www.aans.org/Patient%20Information/Conditions%20and%20Treatments/Sports-Related%20Head%20Injury.aspx

American Academy of Orthopedic Surgeons. (2010). *Position statement: All-terrain vehicles*. Retrieved from http://www.aaos.org/about/papers/position/1101.asp

American Academy of Pediatrics. (2010). Policy statement: Falls from heights: Windows, roof and balconies. *Pediatrics, 120*(3), 1438; reaffirmation of policy: (2001) *Pediatrics, 107*(5), 1188–1191.

American Academy of Pediatrics. (2014a). *Car seats: Information for families for 2014*. Elk Grove, IL: Author.

American Academy of Pediatrics. (2014b). Policy statement: All-terrain vehicle injury prevention: Two-, three-, and four-wheeled unlicensed motor vehicles. *Pediatrics, 119*(5), 1031; reaffirmation of policy: (2004) *Pediatrics, 114*(4), 1126.

American Academy of Pediatrics. (2014c). Policy statement: Skateboard and scooter injuries. *Pediatrics, 133*(3), e799; reaffirmation of policy: (1995) *Pediatrics, 95*(4), 611–612.

American Academy of Pediatrics Committee on Injury, Violence, and Poison Prevention. (2007). Office-based counseling for injury prevention. *Pediatrics, 119*(1), 202–206; reaffirmation of policy: (1994). *Pediatrics, 94*(4), 566–567.

American Academy of Pediatrics Committee on Injury, Violence and Poison Prevention. (2008). Children in pickup trucks. *Pediatrics, 119*(5), 1031; reaffirmation of policy: (2004) *Pediatricsv*(4), 857–859.

American Academy of Pediatrics Committee on Injury, Violence and Poison Prevention. (2010a). Policy statement: Poison treatment in the home. *Pediatrics, 126*(2), 404; reaffirmation of policy: (2003) *Pediatrics, 112*(5), 1182–1185.

American Academy of Pediatrics Committee on Injury, Violence and Poison Prevention. (2010b). Policy statement: Prevention of drowning. *Pediatrics, 126*(1), e253–e262.

American Academy of Pediatrics Committee on Injury, Violence and Poison Prevention. (2011). Policy statement: Child passenger safety. *Pediatrics, 127*(4), 788; reaffirmation of policy: (2002). *Pediatrics, 109*(3), 550–553.

American Academy of Pediatrics Committee on Injury, Violence and Poison Prevention. (2012a). Injury risk of non-powder guns. *Pediatrics, 129*(2), e561; reaffirmation of policy: (2004) *Pediatrics, 114*(5), 1357–1361.

American Academy of Pediatrics Committee on Injury, Violence and Poison Prevention. (2012b). Policy statement: Bicycle helmets. *Pediatrics, 129*(2), 450; reaffirmation of policy: (2001) *Pediatrics, 108*(4), 1030–1032.

American Academy of Pediatrics Committee on Injury, Violence, and Poison Prevention Executive Committee. (2012c). Policy statement: Fire-arm related injuries affecting the pediatric population. *Pediatrics, 130*(5), e1416–e1423.

American Academy of Pediatrics Committee on Injury, Violence and Poison Prevention. (2012d). Policy statement: Injuries associated with infant walkers. *Pediatrics, 129*(2), e561; reaffirmation of policy: (2001) *Pediatrics, 108*(3), 790–792.

American Academy of Pediatrics Council on Communications and Media. (2013). Policy statement: Children, adolescents, and the media. *Pediatrics, 132*(5), 958–961.

American Academy of Pediatrics Council on Community Pediatrics. (2013a). Policy statement: Providing care for children and adolescents facing homelessness and housing insecurity. *Pediatrics, 131*(6), 1206–1210.

American Academy of Pediatrics Council on Community Pediatrics. (2013b). Policy statement: Providing care for immigrant, migrant, and border children. *Pediatrics, 131*(6), e2028–e2034.

American Academy of Pediatrics Council on Sports Medicine and Fitness. (2012a). Policy statement: Baseball and softball. *Pediatrics, 129*(3), e842–e856.

American Academy of Pediatrics Council on Sports Medicine and Fitness. (2012b). Policy statement: Trampoline safety in childhood and adolescence. *Pediatrics, 130*(4), 774–779.

American Academy of Pediatrics Task Force on Sudden Infant Death Syndrome. (2011). SIDS and other sleep-related infant deaths: Expansion of recommendations for a safe infant sleeping environment. *Pediatrics, 128*(5), e1341–e1367.

American College of Surgeons. (2009). *Statement on all-terrain vehicle injuries*. Retrieved from http://www.facs.org/fellows_info/statements/st-64.html

Baddour, L. M., & Endom, E. E. (2013). Animal bites (beyond the basics). In M. S. Hirsch (Ed.), *UpToDate*. Retrieved from http://www.uptodate.com/contents/animal-bites-beyond-the-basics

Bicycle Helmet Safety Institute. (2014). *Helmet laws for bicycle riders*. Retrieved from http://www.helmets.org/mandator.htm

Brady Center to Prevent Gun Violence. (2009). *Risks of having a gun in the home*. Retrieved from http://www.bradycampaign.org/risks-of-having-a-gun-in-the-home

Centers for Disease Control and Prevention. (2011a). *Fire deaths and injuries: Fact sheet*. Retrieved from http://www.cdc.gov/homeandrecreationalsafety/fire-prevention/fires-factsheet.html

Centers for Disease Control and Prevention. (2011b). Nonfatal traumatic brain injuries related to sports and recreation activities among persons ≤ 19 years – United States, 2001–2009. *MMWR, 60*(39), 1337–1342.

Centers for Disease Control and Prevention. (2012). *Protect the ones you love: Child injuries are preventable*. Retrieved from http://www.cdc.gov/safechild/NAP/background.html

Centers for Disease Control and Prevention, National Center for Injury Prevention and Control (2012a). *National action plan for child injury prevention*. Retrieved from http://www.cdc.gov/safechild/pdf/National_Action_Plan_for_Child_Injury_Prevention.pdf

Centers for Disease Control and Prevention, National Center for Injury Prevention and Control. (2012b). *WISQARS fatal injury reports, regional and national, 1999–2010*. Retrieved from http://webappa.cdc.gov/sasweb/ncipc/mortrate10_us.html

Centers for Disease Control and Prevention, National Center for Injury Prevention and Control. (2012c). *WISQARS non-fatal injury reports, 1999–2010*. Retrieved from http://webappa.cdc.gov/sasweb/ncipc/nfirates2001.html

Centers for Disease Control and Prevention, National Center for Injury Prevention and Control. (2013). *WISQARS nonfatal injury reports, 2001–2012*. Retrieved from http://webappa.cdc.gov/sasweb/ncipc/nfirates2001.html

Centers for Disease Control and Prevention, National Center for Injury Prevention and Control, Division of Violence Prevention (2014). *Suicide prevention: Youth suicide*. Retrieved from http://www.cdc.gov/violenceprevention/pub/youth_suicide.html

Chowdhury, R. T. (2011). *Nursery product related injuries and deaths among children under age five*. Bethesda, MD: U.S. Consumer Product Safety Commission.

Corbett, M., Morrongiello, B. A., Lasenby, J., Johnston, N., & McCourt, M., (2006). Factors influencing young children's risk of unintentional injury: Parenting style and strategies for teaching about home safety. *Journal of Applied Developmental Psychology, 27*(6), 560–570.

Deits, J., Yard, E. E., Collins, C. L., Fields, S. K., & Comstock, R. D. (2010). Patients with ice hockey injuries presenting to US emergency departments, 1990–2006. *Journal of Athletic Training, 45*(5), 467–474.

Dellinger, A. M., & Kresnow, M., (2010). Bicycle helmet use among children in the United States: The effects of legislation, personal and household factors. *Journal of Safety Research, 41*(4), 375–380.

Dunn, A. M. (2009). Health perception and health management patterns. In C. E. Burns, A. M. Dunn, M. A. Brady, N. B. Starr, & C. G. Blosser (Eds.), *Pediatric primary care: A handbook for nurse practitioners* (4th ed., pp. 182–185). Philadelphia, PA: W. B. Saunders.

DuRant, R. H., Barkin, S., Craig, J. A., Weiley, V. A., Ip, E. H., & Wasserman, R. C. (2007). Firearm ownership and storage patterns among families with children who receive well-child care in pediatric offices. *Pediatrics, 119*(6), e1271–e1279.

Eberl, R., Schalamon, J., Singer, G., Huber, S. S., Spitzer, P., & Hollworth, M. E. (2009). Trampoline-related injuries in childhood. *European Journal of Pediatrics, 168*(10), 1171–1174.

Emery, C. A., Kang, J., Shrier, I., Goulet, C., Hagel, B. E., Benson, B. W., … Meeuwisse, W. H. (2010). Risk of injury associated with body checking among youth ice hockey players. *JAMA, 303*(22), 2265–2272.

Federal Bureau of Investigation, Cyber Division. (2013). *A parent's guide to Internet safety.* Calverton, MD: Author. Retrieved from http://www.fbi.gov/stats-services/publications/parent-guide

Gielen, A. C., Shields, W., McDonald, E., Frattaroli, S., Bishai, D., & Ma, X., (2012). Home safety and low-income urban housing quality. *Pediatrics, 130*(6), 1053–1059.

Haddon, W., (1972). A logical framework for categorizing highway safety phenomena and activity. *Journal of Trauma, 12,* 193–207.

Hagan, J., Shaw, J., & Duncan, P., (Eds.). (2008). *Bright futures: Guidelines for health supervision of infants, children and adolescents* (3rd ed.). Elk Grove Village, IL: American Academy of Pediatrics.

Hagopian, M. M., Burkhalter, L., & Foglia, R. P. (2014). ATV injury experience at a pediatric trauma center: A five year review. *Trauma, 16*(2), 99–102.

Harborview Injury Prevention and Research Center. (2006). *Best practices: Recreational injury interventions: Baseball & softball.* Retrieved from http://depts.washington.edu/hiprc/practices/topic/recreation/baseball.html

Harborview Injury Prevention and Research Center. (2009). *Facts about baby walker injuries.* Retrieved from http://depts.washington.edu/hiprc/about/topics/web/bike_prevmat/wlkfacts.html

Heron, M. P. (2013). National Center for Health Statistics, Centers for Disease Control and Prevention, & National Vital Statistics System, *National Vital Statistics Reports* Deaths: Leading causes for 2004. Retrieved November 2, 2014 from http://www.cdc.gov/nchs/data/nvsr/nvsr62_06.pdf

Hong, J., Lee, B., Ha, E. H., & Park, H., (2010). Parental socioeconomic status and unintentional injury deaths in early childhood: Considerations of injury mechanisms, age at death, and gender. *Accident Analysis & Prevention, 42*(1), 313–319.

Jackman, G., Farah, M., Kellermann, A., & Simon, H., (2001). Seeing is believing: What do boys do when they find a real gun. *Pediatrics, 107*(6), 1247–1250.

Johnson, R. M., Runyan, C. W., Coyne-Beasley, T., Lewis, M. A., & Bowling, J. M. (2008). Storage of household firearms: An examination of the attitudes and beliefs of married women with children. *Health Education Research, 23*(4), 592–602.

Joint Commission on Accreditation of Healthcare Organizations. (2009). Care of the patient: Restraint and seclusion standards. Comprehensive accreditation manual for hospitals: The official handbook, 2009. Oakbrook Terrace, IL: Author.

Kirkpatrick, R., Puffinbarger, W., & Sullivan, J. A. (2007). All-terrain vehicle injuries in children. *Journal of Pediatric Orthopaedics, 27*(7), 725–728.

Lam, K. Y., Sumanth, K. G., & Mahedev, G., (2013). Severity of playground-related fractures: More than just playground factors? *Journal of Pediatric Orthopedics, 33*(3), 221–226.

Leonard, H., & Jofee, A. R. (2009). Children presenting to a Canadian hospital with trampoline-related cervical spine injuries. *Child Health, 14*(2), 84–88. Retrieved from http://www.ncbi.nlm.nih.gov/pmc/articles/PMC2661341

MacDorman, M. F., & Mathews, T. J. (2013). *Recent trends in infant mortality in the United States.* NCHS data brief, no 9. Hyattsville, MD: National Center for Health Statistics.

MedLinePlus [Internet]. (2014). *Screen time and children.* Bethesda, MD: National Library of Medicine (US). Retrieved from http://www.nlm.nih.gov/medlineplus/ency/patientinstructions/000355.htm

Morrongiello, B. A., & McArthur, B. A. (2010). *Parent supervision to prevent injuries. Encyclopedia on early childhood development.* Canada: University of Guelph. Retrieved from http://www.child-encyclopedia.com/documents/Morrongiello-McArthurANGxp-Parents.pdf

Morrongiello, B. A., Schmidt, S., & Schell, S. L. (2010). Sibling supervision and young children's risk of injury: A comparison of mothers' and older siblings' reactions to risk taking by a younger child in the family. *Social Science and Medicine, 71*(5), 958–965.

Murphy, S. L., Xu, J. Q., & Kochanek, K. D. (2013). *Deaths: Final data for 2010. National vital statistics reports, 61*(4). Hyattsville, MD: National Center for Health Statistics.

Murphy, T., Pokhrel, P., Worthington, A., Billie, H., Sewell, M., & Bill, N., (2014). Unintentional injury mortality among American Indians and Alaska natives in the United States, 1990–2009. *American Journal of Public Health, 104*(53), S470–S480.

National Center for Health Statistics, Centers for Disease Control and Prevention, & National Vital Statistics System. (2012a). *Causes of death by age group, 2010.* Hyattsville, MD: NCHS.

National Center for Health Statistics, Centers for Disease Control and Prevention, & National Vital Statistics System. (2012b). *10 leading causes of injury deaths by age group highlighting unintentional injury deaths, United States–2010.* Hyattsville, MD: NCHS.

National Center for Health Statistics, Centers for Disease Control and Prevention, & National Vital Statistics System. (2012c). *10 leading causes of injury deaths by age group highlighting violence-related injury deaths, United States–2010.* Hyattsville, MD: NCHS.

National Center for Health Statistics, Centers for Disease Control and Prevention, & National Vital Statistics System. (2013). *National estimates of the 10 leading causes of nonfatal injuries treated in hospital emergency departments, United States–2011.* Hyattsville, MD: NCHS.

National Center on Shaken Baby Syndrome. (2014). *Home page.* Retrieved from www.dontshake.org

National Children's Center for Rural and Agricultural Health and Safety. (2014). *2014 Fact sheet: Childhood agricultural injuries in the U.S.* Marshfield, WI: Marshfield Clinic Research Foundation.

National Highway Traffic Safety Administration National Center for Statistics and Analysis. (2012a). *Traffic safety facts 2010: Alcohol-impaired driving.* Washington, DC: U.S. Department of Transportation. Retrieved from http://www-nrd.nhtsa.dot.gov/Pubs/811606.PDF

National Highway Traffic Safety Administration National Center for Statistics and Analysis. (2012b). *Traffic safety facts 2010: Pedestrians.* Washington, DC: U.S. Department of Transportation. Retrieved from http://www-nrd.nhtsa.dot.gov/Pubs/811625.PDF

National Highway Traffic Safety Administration, National Center for Statistics and Analysis. (2013a). *Traffic safety facts 2011: Bicyclists and other cyclists.* Washington, DC: U.S. Department of Transportation. Retrieved from http://www-nrd.nhtsa.dot.gov/Pubs/811743.pdf

National Highway Traffic Safety Administration, National Center for Statistics and Analysis. (2013b). *Traffic safety facts: 2011-Children.* Washington, DC: U.S. Department of Transportation. Retrieved from http://www-nrd.nhtsa.dot.gov/Pubs/811767.pdf

National Highway Traffic Safety Administration, National Center for Statistics and Analysis. (2013c). Traffic safety facts 2011: A compilation of motor vehicle crash data from the fatality analysis reporting system and the general estimates system. Washington, DC: U.S. Department of Transportation. Retrieved from http://www-nrd.nhtsa.dot.gov/Pubs/811754AR.pdf

National Institute for Arthritis and Musculoskeletal and Skin Diseases. (2013). *Preventing musculoskeletal sports injuries in youth: A guide for parents.* Bethesda, MD: National Institutes of Health.

National Safety Council. (2011). *Injury facts.* Itasca, IL: Author.

O'Brien, C. W. (2009). *Injuries and investigated deaths associated with playground equipment.* Washington, DC: U.S. Consumer Product Safety Commission.

Office of Juvenile Justice and Delinquency Prevention. (2013). *OJJDP statistical briefing book.* Retrieved from www.ojjdp.gov/ojstatbb/offenders/qa03107.asp?qaDate=2011

Petrass, L., Blitvich, J., & Finch, C., (2009). Parent/caregiver supervision and child injury—A systematic review of critical dimensions for understanding this relationship. *Family and Community Health, 32*(2), 123–135.

Pickett, W., Brison, R. J., Berg, R. L., Zentner, J., Linneman, J., & Marlenga, B., (2005). Pediatric farm injuries involving children injured by a farm work hazard: Five priorities for primary prevention. *Injury Prevention, 11*(1), 6–11.

Quinlan, K., Shults, R. A., & Rudd, R. A. (2014). Child passenger deaths involving alcohol-impaired drivers. *Pediatrics, 133*(6), 1–7.

Ryan-Wenger, N. A., Sharrer, V. W., & Campbell, K. K. (2005). Changes in children's stressors over the past 30 years. *Pediatric Nursing, 31*(4), 282–288, 291.

Sauber-Schatz, E. K., West, B. A., Bergen, G., (2014). Vital signs: Restraint use and motor vehicle occupant death rates among children aged 0–12 years–United States, 2002–2011. *Morbidity and Mortality Weekly Report, 63*(5), 113–118.

Shapiro-Mendoza, C. K., Kimball, M., Tomashek, K. M., Anderson, R.N., & Blanding, S., (2009). US infant mortality trends attributable to accidental suffocation and strangulation in bed from 1984 through 2004: Are rates increasing? *Pediatrics, 123*(2), 533–539.

Skybo, T., (2005). Witnessing violence: Biopsychosocial impact on children. *Pediatric Nursing, 31*(4), 263–270.

State Department of Social and Health Services. (2009). *Gun safety.* Retrieved from http://www.dshs.wa.gov/pdf/ca/gunsafe.pdf

Stephenson, M., (2005). Danger in the toy box. *Journal of Pediatric Health Care, 19*(3), 187–189.

Strasburger, V. C., Jordan, A. B., & Donnerstein, E. (2010). Health effects of media on children and adolescents. *Pediatrics, 125*(4), 756–767. Available at http://pediatrics.aappublications.org/content/125/4/756.full

Stratbucker, W. B., & Green, C. M. (2006). Injury prevention. Retrieved November 11, 2009 from http://emedicine.medscape.com/article/908790-overview

U.S. Consumer Product Safety Commission. (2010). *Public playground safety handbook.* Washington, DC: Author.

U.S. Consumer Product Safety Commission. (2013a). *2011 annual report of all-terrain vehicle deaths and injuries.* Washington, DC: Author.

U.S. Consumer Product Safety Commission (2013b). *Toy related deaths and injuries: Calendar year 2012.* Bethesda, MD: Author.

U.S. Department of Health and Human Services. (2010). *Healthy people 2020.* Retrieved from http://www.healthypeople.gov/2020/

U.S. Department of Justice. (2011). *Homicide trends in the United States,* 1980–2008. Retrieved from http://www.bjs.gov/content/pub/pdf/htus8008.pdf

Windsor, R. E., Nieves, R. A., Sullivan, K. P., Thampi, S. P., King, F. J., & Hiester, E., D. (2006). *Cervical disc injuries.* Retrieved from http://emedicine.medscape.com/article/93635-overview

Wright, S., Marglena, B., & Lee, B. C. (2013). Childhood agricultural injuries: An update for clinicians. *Current Problems in Pediatric and Adolescent Healthcare, 43*(2), 20–44.

Xu, J. Q. (2014). *Unintentional drowning deaths in the United Sates,* 1999–2010. NCHS Data Brief no 149. Hyattsville, MD: NCHS. Retrieved from http://www.cdc.gov/nchs/data/databriefs/db149.pdf

Zaloshjna, E., Miller, T. R., & Lawrence, B., (2012). Incidence and cost of injury among youth in agricultural settings, United States, 2001–2006. *Pediatrics, 129*(4), 728–734.

Additional Resources

American Academy of Pediatrics

http://www.aap.org

American Red Cross—Water Safety Tips

http://www.redcross.org/images/MEDIA_CustomProductCatalog/m11840095_H21309.AquaticsSafetyV3

Brady Center to Prevent Gun Violence

http://www.bradycenter.org; 1-202-289-7319
Educates the public about gun violence and lobbies to enact laws that protect citizens from harm related to guns.

Bright Futures—TIPPS

http://www.brightfutures.org
Focuses on health promotion, teaching, and prevention of illness and injury in children through regular health maintenance visits and anticipatory guidance within a medical home.

Centers for Disease Control and Prevention, National Center for Injury Prevention and Control

http://www.cdc.gov; 1-800-311-3435
Information on health and safety; facts on injuries in children.

Children's Safety Network (funded by U.S. Maternal and Child Health Bureau)

http://www.childrenssafetynetwork.org
Works to educate health care professionals about keeping children safe and to develop injury prevention programs.

Common Sense About Kids and Guns

http://www.kidsandguns.org
Home firearm storage and safety tips to protect young children and teens from firearm injury.

National Highway Traffic Safety Commission

http://www.nhtsa.dot.gov/; 1-888-327-4236
Traffic safety facts; education for safe driving.

Netsmartz.org

http://www.netsmartz.org
A website created by the National Center for Missing and Exploited Children and the Boys and Girls Clubs of America to teach youth how to stay safe on the Internet. Also has resources for parents, guardians, teachers, and law enforcement officials.

Safe Kids Worldwide

http://www.safekids.org; 1-202-662-0600
Statistics on injury and information on preventing unintentional childhood injury.

U.S. Consumer Product Safety Commission

http://www.cpsc.gov; 1-800-638-2772
Information about consumer products that can injure children.

S E C T I O N 2

GATHERING OBJECTIVE DATA

The Pediatric Physical Examination

The physical examination is an essential part of the pediatric health assessment. The health care provider must possess strong physical assessment skills and a knowledge base specific to the developing bodies and minds of children. These assessment skills include inspection, palpation, percussion, and auscultation. Specialized knowledge includes an awareness of the physical and psychosocial developmental stages from infancy through adolescence (see Chapters 1 and 2), which allows the provider to adapt his or her approach to the child's age and developmental level and obtain the most accurate findings while maintaining optimal comfort for the child.

The physical examination is the part of the assessment in which objective data are collected through various examination techniques to validate the subjective data gathered during the history-taking phase of the assessment. A thorough and accurate history is vital because the information obtained from the parents or the pediatric patient guides the physical examination. The pediatric physical examination differs from the adult examination in that the approach to the patient and the sequence of the examination differ according to age and developmental level. Together, the history and physical exam provide information that leads to the child's diagnosis and forms the basis for the provider's management plan.

There are two types of physical examinations: *complete* (head-to-toe) and *focused*. Children who are new to the provider's practice or who are being seen for their annual health maintenance visits, school physicals, or sports physicals require a full head-to-toe physical examination. A focused physical examination complements the focused history (see Chapter 6) and simply concentrates on the area of the chief complaint. This type of physical examination is done when a child presents to the emergency room or clinic with an illness, injury, or other specific complaint.

The physical examination is typically done immediately after the history is completed. For young children, it may be wise to conduct the developmental assessment before the physical examination to take advantage of the child's relatively cooperative state; young children are often agitated after intrusive procedures, such as the otoscopic examination, and may not cooperate for the developmental assessment if it is performed last. Obtaining the history and physical examination on a newborn is discussed in Chapter 11.

PREPARATION OF THE ENVIRONMENT

The examination room should have a comfortable temperature and be well-lit (see Chapter 6). The room should be in a nonthreatening area and decorated in an age-appropriate manner. All instruments should be kept out of the child's view until use, and the examination room should be childproofed (see Chapter 6). Age-appropriate toys and reading material should also be nearby as a distraction and as a means of assessing development. Privacy should be maintained at all times for children of all ages.

Provider Preparation

The health care provider should first determine whether a full head-to-toe examination is required or whether a focused examination will suffice. Knowledge of normal child growth and development is essential so the provider can choose an age-appropriate sequence in which to conduct the physical examination and determine the best place to conduct it (i.e., the exam table, parent's lap, examiner's lap). The provider should always wash his or her hands before the examination, preferably within the parents' or older child's view. The provider should also wear gloves during the physical examination if the child has bloody or exudative lesions. A mask, gown, or eye protection may be necessary if blood spattering is anticipated.

BOX 8.1   Equipment and Supplies Necessary for the Physical Examination of Infants, Children, and Adolescents

For vital sign measurement

- Thermometers (oral, axillary, rectal, tympanic)
- Pediatric stethoscope with bell and diaphragm
- Various infant and pediatric-sized blood pressure cuffs
- Sphygmomanometer
- Doppler device

For anthropometric measurements

- Beam balance scale to measure weight (both infant and adult platform scales)
- Paper to line infant scale
- Measuring board to measure recumbent length in infants (may also measure recumbent length on paper-covered surface)
- Wall-mounted stadiometer (for most accurate measurement of standing height)
- Paper or metal tape measure (to measure head or arm circumference)
- Skinfold calipers (e.g., Lange calipers) to measure skinfold thickness
- Age- and gender-specific Centers for Disease Control growth charts:
  - Weight-for-age (birth–36 months)
  - Length-for-age (birth–36 months)
  - Weight-for-length (birth–36 months)
  - Head circumference-for-age (birth–36 months)
  - Weight-for-age (2–20 years)
  - Stature-for-age (2–20 years)
  - Weight-for-stature (2–20 years)
  - Body mass index-for-age (2–20 years)

For integumentary assessment

- Ruler with centimeter markings
- Wood's lamp
- Magnifying glass

For head and neck

- Small glass of water (for child to swallow during thyroid gland assessment)
- Nasal specula

For ears

- Otoscope with pneumatic bulb
- Ear curettes for cerumen removal
- Tuning fork

For eyes

- Penlight
- Ophthalmoscope
- Snellen eye chart, tumbling E chart, and Allen cards for vision screening
- Cover card

For nose and oral cavity

- Penlight

- Tongue depressors
- Otoscope (to view inside nares)

For lungs, heart, and abdomen

- Stethoscope with appropriately sized bell and diaphragm
- Doppler device to assess peripheral pulses

For musculoskeletal exam

- Measuring tape

For neurologic exam

- Reflex hammer
- Tuning fork
- Tongue depressor
- Sharp and dull testing instruments
- Penlight (to test pupillary reflex)
- Cotton-tipped swabs (to test corneal and blink reflexes)
- Salt and sugar (to test discrimination of sweet and sour taste)
- Coffee, alcohol, or soap (to test smell)

For female genital exam

- Gloves
- Vaginal specula (including pediatric sized)
- Lubricant
- Sterile cotton-tipped swabs or applicators
- Bifid spatula
- Saline
- Slides, fixative, and container
- Specimen containers

For developmental assessment

- Selected developmental assessment tools (e.g., Ages and Stages Questionnaire; see Chapter 2)
- Puppets, small blocks (for assessing pincer grasp), stacking toys, and squeak toys (also for gaining infant's or toddler's attention and for assessing hearing)

Miscellaneous supplies

- Pediatric history and physical forms
- Wristwatch or clock with a second hand
- Calculator (to calculate body mass index; drug doses)
- Various sized paper gowns
- Examination drapes
- Paper to line examination table
- Various sized syringes and needles
- Puncture-resistant sharps disposal container
- Paper towels and tissue
- Cotton balls
- Culture media
- Potassium hydroxide
- Gauze

Equipment for Physical Assessment

When providing health care to children, it is necessary to have appropriately sized equipment for the physical examination, including blood pressure cuffs, otoscope specula, and pediatric resuscitation equipment. All equipment needed for the physical examination should be readily available. Equipment should be clean or sterile as the examination or procedure dictates. It may be necessary to warm some equipment before use to make the examination more comfortable for the infant or child. Any equipment that may be frightening to a young child should be kept out of view. A sharps container should be within easy reach for quick disposal of needles and syringes. To prevent needlestick injuries, needles should not be recapped. Box 8.1 lists the equipment necessary for a pediatric physical examination.

PREPARATION OF THE CHILD

Before examining the pediatric patients, the provider should first consider the child's age and developmental level. Before beginning the examination, he or she should take time to get acquainted with the child in an age-appropriate manner so that the child is as comfortable as possible (see Chapter 3). This may involve using play techniques with infants and young children or talking with a school-aged child or adolescent about his or her interests. When appropriate, toddlers, preschoolers, and school-aged children should be allowed to handle the equipment before the examination begins to demonstrate to the child that the equipment will not be painful; for example, allowing the child to listen to heart sounds of the parents or provider (Figure 8.1) or their own heart sounds is something that most children greatly enjoy, and it often reduces the child's anxiety. During the physical examination, the provider should

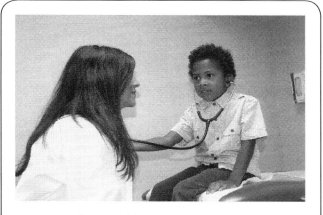

FIGURE 8.1. Allowing children to handle examination instruments may decrease their anxiety and fear.

also explain to the older child what he or she plans to do next; this helps alleviate apprehension and anxiety. If a portion of the examination is going to be painful, the provider should always be honest with the child, informing him or her in a calm, reassuring manner. Lying to the child fosters mistrust and causes the provider to lose credibility.

EXAMINATION TECHNIQUES

Physical assessment involves four major assessment skills: *inspection*, *palpation*, *percussion*, and *auscultation*. These skills are normally performed in this order. However, when assessing the abdomen, the sequence is altered: inspection, auscultation, palpation, and then percussion (see Chapter 19).

When examining a child, providers use their senses to gather objective data. For example, sight is used to assess color, respiratory effort, posture, and gait. Smell assesses hygiene and can help diagnose infections. Touch can help providers find masses or detect skin changes. Hearing allows the provider to assess body sounds.

Inspection

Inspection is always the first step in the physical examination, an assessment skill that involves thoughtful observation of the child from the beginning of the encounter until the end. It begins with inspection of the child's overall appearance (see the next section, General Survey), then continues with a thorough inspection of each individual body system. Inspection is not simply looking at the patient. It involves skilled, purposeful, and systematic observation. The provider uses the technique of inspection to assess behavior and color; it is also used to assess patterns, size, shape, location, and symmetry of lesions and masses, as well as body movement. Inspection allows providers to assess for health concerns or problems so they can then prioritize these problems and develop corresponding management and teaching goals.

The provider should completely expose the body part that he or she is inspecting while covering the rest of the child's body with a disposable paper drape to preserve privacy. Adequate lighting and a comfortable room temperature are essential to obtain accurate inspection findings. Sunlight is the best light in which to obtain inspection findings. Fluorescent lighting can alter the child's actual skin color, and inadequate, dim lighting can cause some abnormalities to be missed. The room should be warm but not hot, which may cause flushing or sweating. A room that is too cool may cause mottling or shivering in the child, confusing assessment findings. Most inspection involves strict observation; some body systems require the use of special equipment to assess them completely (e.g., an otoscope to inspect the tympanic membrane, an ophthalmoscope to inspect the eye).

Although the sequence of the total physical examination in the pediatric patient is altered according to the child's age and developmental level, the technique of inspection should be conducted in the following systematic sequence (King, 1983), regardless of the child's age:

- **General to specific:** The provider should first look at the child as a whole person, then narrow the focus to systems, organs, and then to the sites of any complaints (e.g., first do a general survey, then inspect the mouth, and then focus on the teeth and their overall condition).
- **Head to toe:** The provider should begin inspection at the top of the child's head and end at the feet to be sure that no area of the body is missed.
- **Outside to inside:** When inspecting a body structure with an orifice, the provider should inspect the outside first and then the inside (e.g., when inspecting the ear, first inspect the auricle, then the external auditory canal, and then the tympanic membrane).
- **Medial to lateral:** When performing inspection on a body system or specific structure, the provider should inspect the area from the middle outward (e.g., to examine the breast, first inspect the areolae and nipples, then the breasts, axillae, and then the supraclavicular region).
- **Anterior to posterior:** The provider should always inspect the front of the body first and then the back.
- **Distal to proximal:** This inspection technique applies to the extremities (e.g., the provider should first inspect the toes, and then proceed up the leg to the shin, knee, thigh, and hip).

Palpation

Palpation is an examination technique in which the provider uses touch to gather assessment findings. This technique follows inspection and often confirms what the provider has visualized. Palpation is used to assess skin temperature, moisture, hydration, and texture; peripheral circulation; pulsations; mobility; and shape. It is used to assess organ location and size and to assess for swelling, masses, or lumps. Areas of tenderness or pain are also palpated, but tender or painful areas should be palpated last. If the child experiences tenderness or pain during palpation, the provider should discontinue palpating that area immediately. Watching the child's face during palpation helps the provider ascertain whether or not the child is experiencing any pain, as this will be reflected in the child's facial expressions. Maintaining eye contact with the child is also reassuring to him or her in the event that the child is fearful during this portion of the examination.

Different parts of the provider's hands are used during palpation. To assess temperature, it is best to use the dorsum of the hand. The finger pads should be used to palpate skin texture and consistency, pulses, and organ or mass size. Vibrations are best assessed using the ulnar or palmar surface of the hand. The provider's hands should be warm and fingernails kept short to optimize the child's comfort. Children require a calm and gentle approach when palpation is performed.

Palpation can be light or deep, depending on the amount of pressure applied. Light palpation is used to assess skin temperature, moisture, turgor, and texture; it is also used to assess muscle tone, large masses, edema, and superficial tenderness. Deep palpation is used to palpate the position of organs, large blood vessels, or masses and to note their size, shape, consistency, and mobility. It may also be used to assess for tenderness that was not appreciated with light palpation.

Light palpation is done with the dominant hand and with the fingers together. The fingers are placed on the skin and the area is gently pressed 1 cm (0.4 inches) deep in a circular motion (Figure 8.2). Young children are often ticklish during light palpation of the abdomen; this effect can be lessened if the provider places the child's hand over the provider's palpating hand or by the use of age-appropriate distraction techniques. Light palpation is performed before deep palpation.

Deep palpation involves the use of both hands (Figure 8.3). The provider should place his or her dominant hand on the child's skin and then place the nondominant hand on top of the dominant hand and depress to a depth of approximately 4 to 5 cm (1.5–2 inches). This extra pressure permits the provider to feel structures that are covered by muscle or fat. Deep palpation is most often used during abdominal and gynecologic assessments.

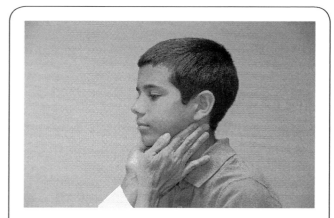

FIGURE 8.2. Light palpation.

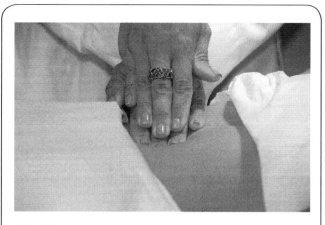

FIGURE 8.3. Deep palpation.

Percussion

Percussion involves the use of tapping to assess underlying organs and structures, either directly or indirectly. This tapping produces sounds that indicate the density of these structures and the borders of internal organs. These sounds are characterized according to pitch, intensity, duration, and quality (Table 8.1). Dense structures produce less sound with percussion. Structures that are filled with air produce loud sounds when percussed. Percussion is also used to assess tenderness or pain, as with blunt percussion, and to elicit reflexes, which requires the use of a reflex hammer (see Chapter 22). Percussion can be *direct*, *indirect*, or *blunt*.

- **Direct percussion** involves tapping an area of the body with one or two fingers directly on the skin (e.g., percussion of the thorax to diagnose pneumothorax).
- **Indirect percussion** requires the use of both hands. This type of percussion is most often used when assessing the chest and abdomen. To perform indirect percussion, the provider should gently place the middle finger (pleximeter) of the nondominant hand on the child's body. Only the pleximeter should be touching the body part that is being percussed. The next step is to use the middle finger (plexor) of the dominant hand (taking care that this fingernail is short) to strike the distal joint of the pleximeter (Figure 8.4). This blow should be quick and sharp, the wrist movement crisp, and the plexor must be perpendicular to the pleximeter. Two taps should be delivered as the provider listens to the tone elicited, percussing from resonance to dullness.
- **Blunt percussion** involves placing one hand flat across the surface of the child's body part to be assessed and using the fist of the other hand to strike the back of the hand while it remains on the body surface. This technique is often used to assess for costovertebral angle tenderness (Figure 8.5).

Auscultation

Auscultation is usually the final step in the four-part physical examination. However, when assessing the abdomen, auscultation should be done *before* palpation and percussion, both of which may alter bowel sounds. Auscultation involves listening to body sounds produced by the airway, lungs, heart, blood vessels, stomach, and intestines. Most of these sounds require the use of a stethoscope to be heard adequately. Some of these sounds can be heard directly by the ear, especially those produced by the upper airway, lungs, gastrointestinal tract, and even speech. For example, a child's inability to speak a complete sentence without respiratory distress tells the provider much about the child's respiratory status.

Sounds heard during auscultation are classified according to intensity (loud or soft), pitch (high or low), duration (length), and quality (musical, crackling). The bell of the stethoscope is used to auscultate low-pitched sounds (e.g., abnormal heart sounds, cardiac murmurs), and the diaphragm is used to auscultate high-pitched

TABLE 8.1	**Percussion Sounds**				
PERCUSSION SOUND	**INTENSITY**	**PITCH**	**DURATION**	**QUALITY**	**WHERE SOUND IS HEARD BEST**
Flatness	Soft	High	Short	Flat	Muscle and bone
Dullness	Soft to medium	High	Medium	Thud-like	Liver, stomach, and diaphragm
Resonance	Medium to loud	Low	Long	Hollow	Normal lung
Tympany	Loud	High	Medium	Drum-like	Gastric air bubble
Hyperresonance	Very loud	Very low	Long	Booming	Lungs of a very young child or lungs with air trapping

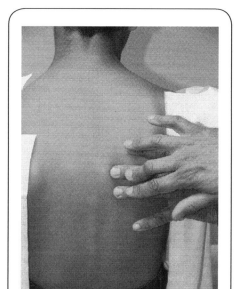

FIGURE 8.4. Indirect percussion.

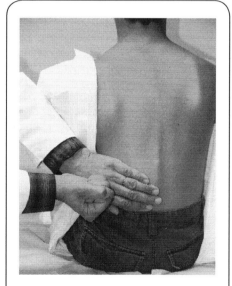

FIGURE 8.5. Blunt percussion to assess the kidneys.

sounds (e.g., normal heart sounds, lung and bowel sounds).

To auscultate body sounds accurately, the provider should ensure that the examination room is as quiet as possible, with little or no environmental noise. It is important for the provider to use a stethoscope with an appropriately sized bell and diaphragm, according to the infant's or child's size. For example, auscultating the chest of a newborn with an adult-sized diaphragm yields heart, lung, and possibly bowel sounds, and the provider is then not able to differentiate the sounds, making it impossible to perform an accurate assessment.

Proper earpiece alignment of the stethoscope is also essential to hear optimally. The slope of the earpieces should point forward toward the examiner's nose, matching the natural slope of the ear canal. Not all ear canals are the same; thus, it is sometimes necessary to adjust the fit. This is important to block out any extraneous noise; this also enhances the acoustic performance of the stethoscope.

The provider should make sure that the stethoscope tubing is not too long, as this increases the distance that the sounds must travel, which can distort the sounds. In addition, it is essential for the provider to avoid placing the diaphragm of the stethoscope too firmly on the surface of the child's skin, as this too can alter the auscultatory findings. Similarly, placing the bell of the stethoscope too firmly against the skin causes the skin to stretch, thus causing the bell to act like a diaphragm. The stethoscope should always be warmed first and then placed directly on the child's skin. Auscultation should not be done through clothing, as this may muffle or alter the sounds. Because of the prevalence of viral respiratory infections in young children, it is wise for the pediatric provider to clean the stethoscope after each patient to avoid the spread of infection among patients.

GENERAL SURVEY

The general survey is the first assessment the provider makes at the beginning of the patient encounter; it begins as soon as the provider enters the examination room. The general survey is a cursory head-to-toe assessment, done before the full, detailed physical assessment. This first impression can tell the provider much about the child's overall state of health by just observing the child's general appearance. The general survey helps the provider to determine assessment and intervention priorities; for example, an immediate intervention is required before a full history is obtained if a child is dusky in color or is in noticeable respiratory distress. Any abnormalities or distress observed during the general survey requires an in-depth assessment of the affected body system. The general survey consists of several elements, all of which are discussed here.

General Appearance

The child's general appearance is the health care provider's assessment of the child's overall physical appearance and includes the child's level of consciousness, facies, posture, position, mobility, hygiene, nutritional state, behavior, demeanor, and interpersonal interactions with parent and provider. A cursory evaluation of the child's developmental level should be made by noting the child's age and comparing that to his or her speech and motor abilities. Assessment of general appearance also includes a brief assessment of the child's color and respiratory status and whether any intervention is required before the visit continues. The child should be pink and in no respiratory distress. Any obvious injuries should be noted, as well as whether the child is in any pain.

Level of Consciousness

The provider should note whether the child looks comfortable or restless, and whether the child is alert and oriented. Chapter 22 discusses in detail the assessment of level of consciousness and neurologic status.

Facies

The child's facial expression can tell the provider a great deal about the child's current physical and mental health. Facial expressions can indicate pain, respiratory distress, fear, anxiety, lethargy, sadness, or depression. The provider should keep in mind that it is normal for many children to be fearful during the health care visit, and these children often cry. Facial features should be symmetrical and move symmetrically with changes in facial expression.

Position, Posture, Gait, and Mobility

The provider should observe the child's position, posture, gait, and mobility. A newborn's arms and legs are normally in a flexed position. A toddler normally has a pot-bellied appearance due to physiologic lordosis, a normal finding in this age group. An older child should have a straight spine and balanced posture. The general survey may allow the provider to assess a lateral curvature of the spine in an older child, which necessitates further assessments and measurements to confirm a diagnosis of scoliosis. In older children, a slumping posture may indicate extreme fatigue or depression.

Upon entering the examination room, the provider should find the infant or young child sitting on the parent's lap, in a chair, or on the examination table in no apparent distress; older children or adolescents should be comfortably seated in no apparent distress. An ill child may assume another body position to alleviate pain or respiratory distress; for example, a child in severe respiratory distress may assume the tripod position (sitting upright, leaning forward with mouth open) to alleviate difficulty breathing, or the provider may find a child with the knees curled up to chest because of severe abdominal pain.

If the child is old enough to walk independently, the child should walk smoothly and with normal balance. A toddler normally appears bow-legged with a wide-based gait when walking. Any limp should be noted during the general survey; this pertains to all age groups. Alterations in range of motion or absence of limb movement can be assessed during the general survey.

Hygiene

As part of the general survey, the child's skin, hair, teeth, and nails should be briefly assessed. Skin and hair should be clean and well groomed. Teeth should be clean without evidence of decay, and nails should be trim and clean. Poor hygiene in a child or infant can be manifested by severe diaper rash or other skin rashes; body odor; lack of overall body cleanliness; dry, dull, unkempt, dirty hair; or dirty clothing. Poor hygiene can be the result of homelessness, poverty, parental knowledge deficits, mental illness, or neglect.

Nutritional Status

The general survey includes an overall impression of the child's nutritional status. The child should appear well nourished with normal body weight, stature, muscle mass, and muscle tone. The child's hair and skin should be lustrous and shiny. Obesity, malnutrition, or evidence of certain eating disorders can be assessed during the general survey. More specific subjective and objective data to gather regarding these disorders are discussed in Chapters 10 and 23.

Behavior

A behavioral assessment is important because an alteration in a child's behavior is often the first clue that a health problem exists. Assessment of behavior includes the child's mood, affect, personality (e.g., shy, slow to warm up, outgoing), level of activity, responsiveness to parents, and the parent's comfort measures. The child should be alert, active, and show age-appropriate reactions to fear, pain, or stress. Older infants and toddlers normally are wary of the provider and cling to the parent. Toddlers are often especially challenging to examine because of the difficulty they have separating from their parents and a desire to express autonomy; this is within normal limits. Children who are preschool aged and older should be able to cooperate with the physical examination, maintain eye contact, and interact with the provider. Lack of eye contact or separation anxiety (when age-appropriate) may indicate child abuse or neglect. In certain cultural groups, however, lack of eye contact is normal and a sign of respect (see Chapter 5). Attention span should be noted in children preschool aged and older. Children in this age group should be able to focus for short periods of time, cooperate with the provider, and follow simple directions. The adolescent's behavior should also be assessed in the areas of eye contact, parent and provider interaction, mood, interest in surroundings and what is going on during the health care visit, reactions to provider or parent requests, distractibility, and cooperation with the history and physical exam.

Development

Developmental assessment must be part of every pediatric health care visit. The provider should begin with a general overview of developmental milestones for age; any initial impressions of developmental delays need to be verified with appropriate screening tests such as the Ages and Stages Questionnaire (see Chapter 2). Areas to assess include gross and fine motor abilities, speech, interaction with the provider, and types of play. During an attempt to engage the child, the provider can conduct a gross assessment of speech, hearing, and vision. The developmental assessment should also include an assessment of whether the child appears to be the stated age, including an evaluation of sexual maturity. Children who appear older than stated age may be living with difficult circumstances such as homelessness, family violence, or addiction. Children who appear younger than stated age may be malnourished or developmentally delayed. Developmental delays can indicate neglect or various medical problems.

GENERAL APPROACH TO THE PEDIATRIC PHYSICAL EXAMINATION

When performing a physical examination on infants, children, and adolescents, the provider should modify his or her approach to the examination according to the patient's age. Providers obviously take a different approach with infants or toddlers than they take with adolescents. Regardless of the child's age, the provider should always remember to perform the least distressing aspect of the physical examination first and the most embarrassing, intrusive, or painful portion last. For example, older infants and toddlers often become uncooperative during the otoscopic examination; thus, this assessment should be done last. Adolescents are cooperative with this portion of the examination; unlike infants and toddlers, they do not perceive it as a body boundary intrusion. However, adolescents may become embarrassed or uncomfortable during the genitourinary portion of the physical examination. Older infants and toddlers, in contrast, have not yet reached the stage when they experience embarrassment when their genitals are examined.

Developmental Approaches to Examining Infants, Children, and Adolescents

Before beginning the physical examination, the provider should be familiar with normal physical and psychosocial developmental milestones in children. For example, infants younger than 4 to 6 months do not have firm head control, so their heads need to be supported during the physical examination. Also, stranger anxiety peaks at 7 to 8 months, so it is important to keep the infant's primary caregiver nearby. If necessary, the physical examination of the infant can even be conducted on

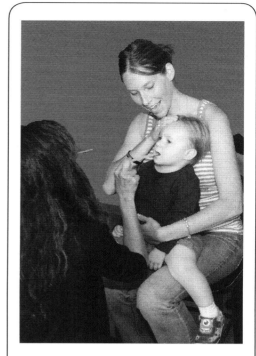

FIGURE 8.6. Allowing the parent to hold the young child during the physical examination makes the child feel safe.

the parent's lap (Figure 8.6). Young children are often slow to warm up and may not be cooperative with the examination. The use of play (e.g., puppets, peek-a-boo, role playing) can assist the provider in enlisting the young child's cooperation. Children preschool-aged and older can be allowed to handle the equipment to see that they will be safe and unharmed. The provider should remember to be kind but firm; canceling the physical examination is not an option. Whenever possible and appropriate, however, school-aged children and adolescents should be allowed to make choices about their care. Adolescents have a strong need for privacy, and this needs to be taken into consideration when conducting the physical examination.

SEQUENCING OF THE PHYSICAL EXAMINATION

Regardless of the child's age, the provider should always gather as much data as possible by inspection first. When determining the sequence of the remaining physical examination, the provider should use a systematic approach; however, flexibility is required to accommodate the child's age, developmental level, and behavior. In children who are late preschool-aged and older, the physical examination should proceed in a head-to-toe fashion. The rationale for this is to have a consistent, systematic approach to be sure that no area of the examination is omitted. When examining infants, toddlers, and young preschoolers, the provider should modify the sequence according to the child's developmental stage while ensuring that all body systems have been assessed. This alteration in the examination sequence takes advantage of the child's quiet state to be ensure that the provider is able to hear heart, lung, and bowel sounds adequately. For example, infants and toddlers dislike having their eyes, ears, and mouth examined. While the infant or toddler is quiet, the provider should conduct a general inspection and heart, lung, and abdominal auscultation. The more intrusive portions of the examination, such as examining the ears and mouth, can be done at the end of the examination, while the infant or toddler is crying. Table 8.2 summarizes approaches to the physical examination, according to age and developmental level.

TABLE 8.2	Sequence of Pediatric Physical Examination According to Age and Developmental Level			
AGE GROUP	POSITION FOR EXAMINATION	PREPARATION	DEVELOPMENTAL CONSIDERATIONS	SEQUENCE
Newborns and young infants (0–6 months)	Place supine on exam table.	Offer breast/bottle/pacifier to quiet newborn for exam. Examine while dressed in a diaper only; remove while examining genitourinary area. When examining neonates, use radiant heat warmer to conserve body heat.	Lack of head control until 4–6 months. Infants respond well to smiling faces and soft voices. May respond well to noisemakers or toys to see or touch. Abrupt, rough movements should be avoided.	Perform least distressing aspects of exam first (i.e., if quiet, auscultate heart and lungs; proceed head-to-toe, then examine ears, nose, and throat last while the child is crying). Elicit Moro reflex last.
Older infants (6–12 months)	May need to examine in parent's lap because of stranger anxiety; if no distress, place on exam table with parent in view.	Keep primary caregiver and security object within eyesight of infant. Ensure that exam room is a comfortable temperature. Offer breast/bottle/pacifier to quiet crying infant. Examine while child is dressed in a diaper only; remove while examining genitourinary area.	Infants prefer smiling faces and soft voices. May respond well to noisemakers or toys to see or hold. Often cry when cold; this may interfere with exam. Abrupt, rough movements should be avoided. Stranger anxiety begins at approximately 7–8 months of age. Gather as much objective data as possible by just observing and not touching (infant will often begin crying vigorously when touched by a stranger). Increased motor abilities cause need for safety measures in exam room; this continues with older pediatric patients, as well.	Perform least distressing aspects of exam first (i.e., if quiet, auscultate heart and lungs; proceed head to toe, then examine ears, nose, and throat last while child is crying).

(continued)

TABLE 8.2	Sequence of Pediatric Physical Examination According to Age and Developmental Level (*continued*)			
AGE GROUP	**POSITION FOR EXAMINATION**	**PREPARATION**	**DEVELOPMENTAL CONSIDERATIONS**	**SEQUENCE**
Toddlers	Examine child on parent's lap or exam table, depending on where child is most cooperative.	Gain toddler's confidence before beginning exam; let toddler see and touch examination instruments; keep parent and security object nearby.	Stranger anxiety decreases by approximately 18 months of age; separation anxiety by approximately 2 years. Toddlers are negativistic; often respond "no" when they mean "yes." Dislike body boundary intrusion and often dislike having clothes removed; therefore have parent remove clothes. Offer simple choices but provider should not give toddler a choice where none exists (e.g., "May I look in your ears?"). Toddlers are often uncooperative with exam; complete exam as quickly but as thoroughly as possible. May need to enlist parents' help in gently restraining child during exam. Use distraction techniques (play, puppets, toys). Praise toddler for cooperation.	Perform least distressing and least intrusive aspects of exam first (i.e., auscultate heart and lungs; examine ears, nose, and throat last). Auscultate, palpate, and percuss whenever quiet. Praise toddler for cooperating with exam.
Preschoolers	Exam table with parent nearby	To allay fears, may use dolls, stuffed animals, or parent to "examine" first before child. Allow preschooler to see and touch equipment. Give preschooler gown; ask child to remove all clothing but underwear.	They like to "help" and are concrete, literal thinkers, and protect their modesty. Magical thinking causes many fears. Provider should take care regarding choice of words (e.g., "take" your blood pressure). Preschooler may think she or he is ill because of bad behavior (magical thinking). Preschoolers need feedback during exam ("Your lungs sound just like they are supposed to.")	Head to toe if cooperative. Otherwise use approach as with toddler. Should be able to examine older preschoolers head to toe.

TABLE 8.2	Sequence of Pediatric Physical Examination According to Age and Developmental Level (*continued*)			
AGE GROUP	**POSITION FOR EXAMINATION**	**PREPARATION**	**DEVELOPMENTAL CONSIDERATIONS**	**SEQUENCE**
			Games, dolls, or toys sometimes helpful when conducting physical exam to gain child's cooperation. Preschoolers should be given choices when possible.	
School-aged children	Exam table	Give child gown and ask child to undress except for underpants. Explain purpose of all equipment. Young school-aged child often prefers parent to be present; older school-aged child may prefer parent to leave room during exam.	Can now address questions more directly to child. Answer child's questions honestly and concretely; diagram and teaching dolls are helpful during explanations. Child often sees physical exam as "fun"; likes to learn about body. Protect privacy and modesty.	Preform head to toe with genitalia last.
Adolescents	Exam table	Provider should explain confidentiality parameters. Offer option for parent to be present or to leave the room during physical exam. Give teen a gown; allow to undress in private; may leave undergarments on.	Elicit active participation from teen when obtaining health history. Confidentiality and privacy are important. Protect modesty. Address teen directly during exam. Discuss issues of sexuality and body development matter-of-factly; emphasize normalcy whenever possible. Include health teaching.	Preform head to toe with genitalia last.

Adapted from Hockenberry (2011).

CHALLENGING PEDIATRIC PATIENTS

Some children may be uncooperative or physically resistant during the physical examination. This is developmentally appropriate in older infants, toddlers, and young children who may resist body boundary intrusions and separation from parents. Some children may even have temper tantrums. Reasons for this may include fear or separation anxiety; some children may have been sexually or physically abused, and some children may just be manipulative (Schmitt, 1984). If a child is uncooperative with the physical examination, the provider should explore possible reasons. One potential reason is that many parents teach their young children not to let strangers touch or undress them; parents should talk to their child before the health care visit so that the child feels safe. A more common reason that children may resist the physical exam is fear. In young children, this is age appropriate and can be minimized by allowing the child to express his or her fears about the examination or health care providers, having the parent or provider explain to the child truthfully and in age-appropriate terms what will happen during the physical examination, and providing reassurance about specific fears. Health care providers should teach parents never to lie to the child about a health care visit (e.g., telling the child that he or she is going to school instead of the clinic, that an injection or blood draw will not be painful, or that they will receive an injection if they misbehave) as this can exacerbate fears related to visiting the health care provider.

Children who have been physically or sexually abused may be very frightened during the physical examination, and the provider must take care to distinguish an abused child from a fearful one, making every effort to gain the child's trust and keeping in mind that suspected or confirmed abuse must be reported to child protective services (see Chapter 24). The techniques for examining fearful children apply to abused children as well, as both require patience and sensitivity during the examination. The provider and parent should remain calm and matter-of-fact during the physical examination, and the parent should stay nearby. Distraction techniques, using toys or games, may be helpful. In addition, the provider may allow the child to see and touch the equipment before the examination begins. It may also be a good idea for the provider to establish brief, nonthreatening physical contact with the child prior to the examination, such as handing the child a toy or even playing with the child briefly. If none of these techniques are effective, the provider should just begin the examination, using a calm, gentle, but firm approach, keeping the parent nearby. If necessary, the child may need to be gently but firmly restrained and protected from injury with the examination performed as quickly but as thoroughly as possible. The provider or parent should not reward tantrums or similar behavior; however, children who are extremely agitated and upset may need to have the examination deferred until they have quieted.

PHYSIOLOGIC AND ANTHROPOMETRIC MEASUREMENTS

Obtaining accurate physiologic and anthropometric measurements in young children is important because these quantify the child's overall health status. The young child's cooperativeness, the provider's technique in obtaining these measurements, and the consistency and accuracy of all measurements are variables to be considered as critical components of child health assessment.

PHYSIOLOGIC MEASUREMENTS

Physiologic measurements, or vital signs, are very important in evaluating a child's physical status. These measurements include body temperature, heart rate, respiratory rate, and blood pressure. At each health supervision and focused visit, a child's vital signs should be measured and compared with normal values for that age group, as well as previous readings for that child. The provider must be familiar with age and gender-specific norms for each of these physiologic measurements (see Appendix A). Techniques for measuring body temperature, pulse, respiratory rate, and blood pressure in infants and children are discussed.

Temperature

Accurate measurement of body temperature is very important in the pediatric population. For example, subnormal body temperature can be a sign of sepsis in the neonate. Fever, or elevated body temperature, one of the most common presenting complaints in children, is a sign of illness in children and helps the provider to make diagnoses. The height of a fever does not necessarily correspond to the severity of illness in a child, and health care providers should remind parents of this. Minor viral illness is the most common cause of fever in children aged 3 months and older (Colvin et al., 2012). Normal variations in body temperature also may occur as a result of several factors, which are summarized in Table 8.3.

The most accurate reflection of a child's true body temperature is the core temperature, which remains relatively constant despite the environmental temperature. In healthy children, the body temperature can be measured orally, axillary, tympanically, rectally, and via the temporal artery. Oral and temporal artery temperatures are the most accurate way of measuring body temperature compared to other noninvasive temperature measures, such as axillary and tympanic membrane (Lawson et al., 2007).

It is important to consider the child's age and developmental level when choosing a site to measure body temperature. The choice of route also depends on several other factors, which are listed in Table 8.4. Appendix A lists normal body temperature ranges based on the method of measurement.

Whenever possible, the site for temperature measurement in children should be the least traumatic for that particular child. The provider should teach parents that diagnosing a fever by touching a child's skin is highly unreliable and that the child's temperature should be measured with a thermometer. Fever strips should not be used to measure body temperature in children, as they are not accurate (Ward, 2013). Likewise, glass mercury thermometers should not be used to measure body temperature, as they are easily broken, and the mercury spillage presents an environmental hazard. Health care providers should advise parents to discard old glass mercury thermometers. The Additional References section at the end of the chapter provides information about the Environmental Protection Agency website that explains how to dispose of old mercury glass thermometers.

Pulse

The measurement of a child's pulse is a very important part of the physical examination and can yield very important assessment data regarding the child's cardiovascular status, effectiveness of drug therapy, or hemodynamic stability after traumatic injury. The pulse, or heart rate, reflects the pressure that is exerted as the heart pumps blood to the peripheral blood vessels. Pulses should be assessed for rate, rhythm, quality, and strength. It is best for the provider to assess an infant

TABLE 8.3   Factors Affecting Body Temperature in Infants and Children

FACTOR	EFFECT
Age	Infants have poor body temperature regulation; they cannot conserve body heat because of neurologic immaturity, greater body surface area, and less adipose tissue than older children and adults Infants younger than 6 months cannot shiver to raise body temperature Marked fluctuations in body temperature often are seen in young infants
Activity, exercise, and vigorous play	Raises body temperature
Autoimmune disorders	Raises body temperature
Circadian variation (varies less than 1 in infants younger than 6 months; approximately 1 in children under 2; as much a 2 diurnal variation may be seen in children 2–6 years of age	Body temperature is lowest in early morning Body temperature is highest in early evening
Dehydration	Raises body temperature
Drug reactions	Raises body temperature
Eating	Raises body temperature
Emotion, stress, and crying	Raise body temperature
Environmental temperature and humidity	Raise body temperature
Immunizations	May raise body temperature
Infection (viral and bacterial)	Raises body temperature
Inflammation	Raises body temperature
Malignancy	Raises body temperature
Medications: • Antipyretics, vasodilators, and anesthetic agents • Prostaglandins	Decrease body temperature Raise body temperature
Neurologic injury and hypothalamic disorders	Raise body temperature
Ovulation	Raises body temperature
Rheumatic fever	Raises body temperature
Swaddling and overdressing	Raise body temperature

Source: Nativio (2005).

or young child's pulse while he or she is quiet or asleep to obtain the most accurate result. All children younger than 2 years of age should have their pulse measured apically because the radial pulse may not be fully palpable in this age group. The pulse should also be measured apically in children with cardiovascular disease or when the radial pulse is irregular or difficult to palpate. Apical pulse assessment is done by placing the diaphragm of the stethoscope over the point of maximal impulse (PMI) of the heart. In children younger than 7 years, this is found at the fourth intercostal space to the left of the midclavicular line; in children older than 7,

the PMI is at the fifth intercostal space *at* the midclavicular line (see Chapter 18). In children older than 2 years without cardiovascular disease, the radial site can be used to measure the pulse. The provider should measure the pulse rate for 1 full minute in infants and children to detect any abnormal rhythms. A normal variation in the pulse rate is a sinus arrhythmia; this is present when the pulse rate increases during respiration and falls to normal during expiration. Several factors that can influence the pulse rate in children are summarized in Table 8.5. Appendix A lists normal heart rates in infants and children.

TABLE 8.4	Temperature Measurement: Routes and Procedures in Infants and Children			
ROUTE	**TYPE OF MEASURING DEVICE**	**AGE**	**PROCEDURE**	**VARIABLES TO CONSIDER**
Oral	Electronic or digital thermometer	Beginning at ages 4–5 years, if cooperative	Thermometer should have probe cover. Place thermometer under tongue in sublingual pouch.	Child must be developmentally capable of holding thermometer under tongue and keeping mouth closed and lips together while temperature is being read. Oral route should not be used if child has moderate to severe nasal congestion, presence of nasal cannula or oxygen mask, recent oral surgery, recent generalized seizures, oral intubation, or is comatose or sedated. Recent ingestion of cold or hot food or liquids requires a delay in measuring temperature via oral route.
Rectal	Electronic or digital thermometer	Birth–3 years if precise temperature reading necessary or no other route is feasible (e.g., child too young or agitated to cooperate with oral or axillary route; child obtunded; infant or child with oral or axillary surgery)	Thermometer should have probe cover, be lubricated, and inserted approximately 0.5 (infants) to 1 inch (children) into rectum; thermometer should not be forced if difficult to insert.	Measures core body temperature and thus most accurate measurement of body temperature; no rectal temperature measurements if child has diarrhea, rectal irritation, or is on chemotherapy. Preschoolers find rectal temperatures a body boundary intrusion.
Axillary	Electronic or digital thermometer	All age groups	Thermometer should have probe cover; probe should be placed fully within axilla, held firmly against body, with infant's or child's arm held close to side of body.	Used most often with newborns. Also used when oral, tympanic, or rectal routes are not possible. Readings are not accurate in infants who have been tightly swaddled, children with altered peripheral circulation, or those in early stages of fever.
Tympanic	Infrared beam sensor tympanic thermometer	3 months and older	Place thermometer tip in external auditory canal. Pinna should be pulled as with otoscopy and measurements should be taken in same ear to get most accurate results.	Using pediatric-sized probes is essential to obtain accurate tympanic temperature reading. Should not be used in infants younger than 6 months because ear probe is too large to fit in external auditory canal. Readings are fast and painless for the child. Readings are not affected by otitis media or presence of cerumen.

TABLE 8.4	Temperature Measurement: Routes and Procedures in Infants and Children (*continued*)			
ROUTE	**TYPE OF MEASURING DEVICE**	**AGE**	**PROCEDURE**	**VARIABLES TO CONSIDER**
Temporal artery	Infrared beam sensor	3–18 years	Roll temperature transducer across child's forehead to collect temperature from arterial blood flow.	Sensitivity in measuring temperature in children is variable, especially in febrile children.

TABLE 8.5	Factors Affecting Pulse Rates in Children
FACTOR	**EFFECT**
Activity	Increased physical activity increases heart rate; after time, regular exercise causes pulse rate to decrease.
Age	Pulse rate decreases with age.
Crying	Crying increases pulse rate.
Disease	Diseases can affect pulse rate; for example, hyperthyroidism increases pulse rate, and hypothyroidism and anorexia nervosa decrease pulse rate.
Fear	Fear increases pulse rate.
Feeding	Infant's pulse rate rises during feeding.
Fever	Fever increases pulse rate.
Hypovolemia	Initially, hypovolemia increases pulse rate; heart rate falls if it is untreated.
Hypoxia	Initially, pulse rate increases with hypoxia, then decreases if the cause of hypoxia is untreated.
Increased intracranial pressure (ICP)	ICP decreases pulse rate.
Medications	Certain medications affect pulse rate, for example, beta$_2$-agonists (e.g., albuterol) increase pulse rate, but digoxin decreases pulse rate.
Pain	Pain increases pulse rate.

Source: Engel (2006).

Peripheral pulses should be assessed to detect any circulatory impairment. These pulses include the radial, femoral, popliteal, and pedal pulses. Pulse strength and quality can also be graded; Table 8.6 summarizes the grading of pulses in children. The radial and femoral pulses should be compared at least once in the newborn period to assess for coarctation of the aorta (see Chapter 18).

Respirations

A child's respiratory status can be affected by many things, making careful assessment of respirations important in the pediatric patients. Assessment of respiration in a child involves observing the respiratory *rate*, *rhythm*, *depth*, and *effort*. The respiratory rate is best measured while the infant or child is quiet

TABLE 8.6	Grading of Pulses
GRADE	
0	Not palpable; absent
+1	Thready, weak, difficult to palpate; obliterates with pressure
+2	Difficult to find; may obliterate with pressure
+3	Easy to palpate; normal; difficult to obliterate
+4	Strong, bounding; does not obliterate with pressure

to obtain the most accurate reading. Respirations are counted by observing a complete respiratory cycle (the rise and fall of the child's chest with each inspiration and expiration). The respirations of infants and young children are mainly diaphragmatic, so the provider should observe abdominal movements while assessing respirations. Respirations should be counted for 1 full minute in newborns and very young infants because of the normal, irregular respiratory movements in this age group. This can be done simultaneously while auscultating the child's breath sounds. Until approximately age 4 months, infants are obligate nose breathers, so it is important for the provider to ensure that the nares are clear of any secretions that could interfere with breathing and affect the respiratory rate or effort. In older children and adolescents, respirations are thoracic and can be counted for 30 seconds and multiplied by two, unless the child is in respiratory distress; then the rate should be counted for 1 full minute. Young children may alter their chest or abdominal movements if they become aware that their respirations are being observed; a child may do this in an effort to "help" the provider. Because this may affect the rate and depth of the respirations, the provider should avoid telling the child when the respirations are being counted. An effective way to accomplish this would be for the provider to keep his or her fingers on the child's radial pulse after the pulse has been counted, then glance at the child's chest to count the respirations.

Respiratory rhythm, depth, and effort are also assessed. Respiratory rhythm should be regular; depth is described as normal, shallow, or deep, and expansion should be symmetrical. Respirations should be effortless and unlabored. Appendix A lists normal respiratory rates in infants and children. Table 8.7 lists factors that affect respirations in children (see Chapter 17 for an in-depth discussion of respiratory assessment).

Blood Pressure

Blood pressure is part of routine vital sign assessment beginning at age 3 years. Infants and children younger than age 3 who have acute or chronic conditions that may affect blood pressure should also have their blood pressure measured. Blood pressure measurements should be taken at birth to screen for coarctation of the aorta, more frequently than annually in children with cardiac or renal disease, and in children who are overweight or obese. With the markedly increased incidence of childhood overweight and obesity, primary hypertension in the pediatric and adolescent population is becoming more common (Assadi, 2012). Because of this trend, it is extremely important for the provider to obtain accurate blood pressure readings in children and adolescents to

TABLE 8.7	Factors Affecting Respirations in Children
FACTOR	**EFFECT**
Activity	Exercise increases respiratory rate and depth during and shortly after physical activity; sleep decreases respiratory rate.
Age	The respiratory rate decreases with age; infants are obligate nose breathers until approximately 4 months; infants and young children are abdominal breathers; older children and adolescents are thoracic breathers. Apnea of 15–20 seconds or less is normal in the neonate. Respiratory rates decrease with age (see Table 1.1).
Fear or anxiety	Respirations increase in rate and depth; crying causes respirations to increase and become irregular.
Fever	Respirations increase in rate and depth.
Hypothermia	Respirations increase in rate with mild hypothermia; moderate hypothermia causes slow and shallow respirations; severe hypothermia causes apnea.
Medical conditions	Respirations can increase in rate, rhythm, and depth with respiratory conditions that decrease oxygenation and increase carbon dioxide levels (e.g., pneumonia, bronchiolitis, asthma, heart failure). Respirations can also be altered with head injuries, increased intracranial pressure, anemia, cardiac conditions, hypovolemia, hyperthyroidism, pain, and cough.
Medications	Opiates, narcotics, anesthetic agents, barbiturates, benzodiazepines, sedatives, large amounts of alcohol, inhalants, anticholinergics, some anticonvulsants, and bicarbonate decrease respirations; amphetamines, salicylates, methamphetamines, caffeine, cocaine, nicotine, and xanthines increase respiratory rate.
Pain	Respiratory rate can increase or decrease.
Position	Sitting up or increasing the angle of the head of the bed can improve ventilation and decrease respiratory rate in patients with respiratory illnesses; slumping forward can interfere with normal respiratory movements.

Source: Engel (2006).

identify and treat hypertensive children, thus minimizing long-term health risks.

In healthy children, blood pressure is measured noninvasively. The preferred method for blood pressure measurement is auscultation (National High Blood Pressure Education Program Working Group on High Blood Pressure in Children and Adolescents, 2005). In newborns and young infants, a Doppler device should be used to measure blood pressure. In older children, the aneroid device is most often used to measure blood pressure, since mercury manometers are less available because of the environmental toxicity of mercury. The provider must ensure that the aneroid manometer is calibrated according to the manufacturer's recommendations so that accurate blood pressure readings are obtained. No matter what the child's age or the type of noninvasive blood pressure measuring device used, it is essential that the appropriate sized blood pressure cuff (i.e., the inner inflatable bladder) be chosen for the reading to obtain an accurate blood pressure measurement. The correct cuff width should be at least 40% to 50% of the arm circumference when measuring at a point midway between the olecranon and the acromion, and the cuff bladder length should cover 80% to 100% of the arm circumference (National High Blood Pressure Education Program Working Group, 2005). A cuff that is too large will cause a low blood pressure reading; a cuff that is too small will result in a blood pressure reading that is falsely high. For obese children and adolescents, an adult-sized or extra-large cuff may need to be used to obtain the most accurate measurement. The blood pressure should be measured on the right arm versus the left arm in the event of undiagnosed coarctation of the aorta (Luma & Spiotta, 2006), which may cause low blood pressure readings in the left arm if accompanied by an interrupted aortic arch (Koutlas, Marziarz, Reade, & Love 2014).

Blood pressure should be measured after the child has been quiet for at least 5 minutes. The child should be seated, feet on the floor with his or her right arm supported, with the cubital fossa at heart level (National High Blood Pressure Education Program Working Group, 2005). Young children may feel most comfortable while sitting in the parent's lap; crying or fear can increase blood pressure readings. Once the blood pressure cuff is secured on the child's arm, the bell of the stethoscope should be placed over the brachial pulse, below the bottom edge of the blood pressure cuff, and the blood pressure should be measured. The child's pulse pressure should be noted as well. Decreased pulse pressure is caused by decreased stroke volume or increased peripheral resistance. Normal blood pressure in children is defined as *systolic* blood pressure (SBP) and *diastolic* blood pressure (DBP) that are less than the 90th percentile for age, gender, and height (National High Blood Pressure Education Program Working Group, 2005). Appendix A lists the normal range of blood pressures in healthy children, according to age, gender, and height.

- **Hypertension** in children is defined as the SBP and DBP being greater than the 95th percentile on three separate occasions (National High Blood Pressure Education Program Working Group, 2005). Box 8.2 lists possible causes of hypertension in children.
- **Hypotension** in children can be caused by hypovolemia, anorexia nervosa, or certain medications.

BOX 8.2   Causes of Hypertension in Children

- Crying
- Poison ingestion
- Substance abuse
- Tobacco use
- Certain medications (e.g., Neo-Synephrine [phenylephrine hydrochloride], prednisone, albuterol, ipratropium bromide)
- Anxiety
- Obesity
- Cardiac disease
- Renal disease
- Increased intracranial pressure
- Thyroid disease
- Pheochromocytoma

Pain

Pain is considered the fifth vital sign. The provider should assess for the presence of pain during each health care encounter. This assessment should be tailored to the child's age and developmental level. See Chapter 6 for a discussion of pain assessment in children.

Anthropometric Measurements

Anthropometric measurements in children include weight, height (or length), and head circumference. In certain circumstances, other measurements may be done, including chest circumference, arm circumference, skinfold thickness, and arm span. In children 2 years and older, body mass index (BMI) is used to assess weight in comparison to height and the child's risk for overweight or obesity. Growth during infancy and childhood is a key indicator of the child's overall health and well-being.

The guidelines set forth by the American Academy of Pediatrics state that children's growth should be measured every 2 months until age 6 months, every 3 months from age 6 to 18 months, and then once a year until age 18 years (Hagan, Shaw, & Duncan, 2008). Assessment of growth is especially important for children who are at risk for growth failure or obesity. Growth failure may be a sign of illness or neglect and must be evaluated promptly. Obesity can lead to serious physical and psychosocial health problems (see Chapter 10).

To avoid unnecessary medical and endocrine referrals, it is vitally important that all growth measurements be done accurately and precisely. This includes using proper equipment, accurate technique, and proper positioning. At each health supervision visit, the provider should measure all growth parameters (i.e., weight, length/height, head circumference if applicable, BMI if applicable) and plot the growth measurements on age- and gender-specific Centers for Disease Control and Prevention (CDC) growth charts (0–36 months, 2–20 years). An important assessment for the provider to make is whether the child's growth is consistent over time, plotting at the same percentile. These growth charts should be kept as part of the child's medical record for comparison at the next health care visit.

Growth Charts

In 2000, the CDC revised the National Center for Health Statistics growth charts that had been in use since 1977. The rationale for this change was that the previous growth charts were not an accurate representation of the various racial, ethnic, and genetic differences among children in the United States (CDC, 2010). The older growth charts also did not reflect the effect that breast or formula feeding has on a young child's growth (CDC, 2010). The revised growth charts also include percentile curves to age 20 years, and they added the 3rd and 97th percentiles (CDC, 2010). Another important addition to the 2000 CDC growth-chart revision was the creation of BMI-for-age charts, which is an essential tool in screening for overweight and obesity in children (see Appendix B for the CDC growth charts for children from birth to 20 years).

Ethnic and Racial Variations in Height and Weight

When measuring height and weight in children, it is important for the provider to be aware of the inherent differences in size that exist among children from various racial and ethnic groups. Native American and Hispanic newborns are shorter at birth than African American or Caucasian neonates (Andrews & Boyle, 2012). Asian children are smaller in weight and length than all other ethnic groups at all ages (Andrews & Boyle, 2012). The CDC growth charts that were revised in 2000 reflect these normal differences.

Breast- and Formula-Fed Infants • The 2000 CDC growth charts can be used for both breastfed and formula-fed infants because these growth charts represent data collected by measuring the growth patterns of both breastfed and formula-fed infants in the U.S. population. In exclusively breastfed infants, growth patterns must be assessed judiciously because these infants have different growth patterns than do infants who are formula-fed only (CDC, 2010).

Premature Infants • The growth of premature infants should be monitored closely, using the corrected gestational age for weight through age 24 months, stature through age 40 months, and head circumference through ages 18 to 30 months. The premature infant's weight, length, and head circumference must be plotted on appropriate growth charts, using the Fenton preterm growth charts until 44 to 48 weeks postmenstrual age, after which the World Health Organization charts can be used (Griffin, 2014). The 2000 CDC growth charts can be used but do not include data from very low birth weight (VLBW) infant measurements (CDC, 2010). The 1999 Infant Health and Developmental Program (IHDP) Growth Percentiles for low birth weight and VLBW infants (less than 1,500 g or 3.3 pounds.) publishes growth charts for preterm infants, but these charts may not accurately represent growth in the current population of preterm infants because the data were collected before premature infants were routinely placed on high-calorie formulas (Carlson, 2005). Carlson (2005) recommends charting a premature infant's growth on both the CDC and IHDP charts.

Children With Chronic Conditions • Certain genetic or chromosomal disorders can cause alterations in growth in children. Some of these conditions include Turner syndrome, Down syndrome, Prader-Willi syndrome, Marfan syndrome, and achondroplasia (CDC, 2010). When caring for children with these conditions, the provider may elect to use condition-specific growth charts to plot the child's growth (see Additional Resources at the end of the chapter).

Weight

Weight is an important indicator of a child's overall health. Because of the expected rapid weight gain during the first year of life, the provider should monitor weight closely to assess normal growth. An infant should double the birth weight by 6 months, triple the birth weight by 12 months, and quadruple the birth weight by 2 years. After age 2 years, the CDC recommends that the BMI be used as a guideline to monitor weight (CDC, 2010). Excessive weight gain should be noted to identify an overweight infant or toddler. Early and excessive weight gain is most often because of overfeeding but can also be caused by lack of physical activity, congenital syndromes (e.g., Prader-Willi syndrome), or medical conditions such as hypothyroidism. Excessive weight gain in the first 6 months of life is associated with overweight and obesity later in life (Young, Johnson, & Krebs, 2012).

Similarly, the provider should also note the child's failure to gain weight. Poor weight gain is most likely a result of malnutrition, malabsorption, neglect, conditions that cause chronic hypoxia (e.g., congenital heart disease, chronic lung disease), renal disease, chronic infections, or psychologic illnesses such as depression or anorexia nervosa (Neumann, Gewa, & Bwibo, 2004).

All infants, children, and adolescents should be weighed at each health maintenance visit, and their weights plotted on the age- and gender-appropriate CDC growth chart. Ill children should also be weighed; this is done so that the provider has a current, accurate weight in the event that medications need to be prescribed. It also quantifies acute weight loss or gain in an ill child, which may be because of dehydration or fluid retention, respectively. Infants until age 12 months should be weighed completely nude on a beam balance scale, which should measure to the nearest 10 g (Figure 8.7). Because the infant is weighed nude, a paper liner is placed on the scale and the scale is zeroed before weighing the infant. Infants in this age group can be weighed lying or sitting, depending on their developmental abilities. The provider should take care to ensure that the infant is never left unattended on the scale to prevent injuries or falls. Weight measurements in this age group should be taken to the nearest 10 g or 0.5 ounces. Once the measurement is obtained, the provider should record it in the infant's chart and plot it on the age- and gender-specific CDC growth chart (birth–36 months).

Until a child can stand well, he or she should continue to be weighed lying down on a beam balance scale. By age 2 to 3 years, an upright scale can be used to measure the child's weight (Figure 8.8). Children who are weighed on an upright scale should be weighed wearing only a dry diaper or underpants and a light paper or cotton gown. The child's shoes should also be removed. The provider should make sure that the child is not holding on to the scale beam, a parent's hand, or the wall, all of which result in inaccurate readings. The weight should be measured to the nearest 100 g or 0.25 pounds, recorded in the child's chart and on the age- and gender-specific CDC growth charts (2–20 years).

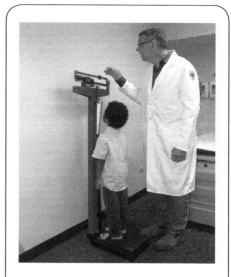

FIGURE 8.8. Weight measurement of an older child.

Body Mass Index

The BMI measurement is considered the standard of care for the early recognition of overweight and obesity in children, a serious and prevalent problem (CDC, 2011). The BMI provides a guideline by which to determine a healthy weight for the child based on height. The provider should calculate and plot the BMI in all children beginning at age 2 years. This calculation is done by dividing the child's weight in kilograms by the height in meters squared. The BMI can also be calculated by dividing the child's weight in pounds by the height in inches squared, then multiplying that result by 703. Table 8.8 lists the BMI interpretation standards for children. The BMI should be plotted for children older than age 2 years, using the current age- and gender-specific growth charts from the CDC. If the child's BMI is above the 85th percentile, further assessment is necessary (see Chapter 10 for a detailed discussion of BMI).

Skinfold Thickness and Mid-Upper Arm Circumference

Two indirect measurements of adiposity in children are skinfold thickness and mid-upper arm circumference (MUAC). Both obesity and chronic undernutrition can be reflected in changes in skinfold thickness and MUAC (CDC, 2007; Jeyakumar, Ghugre, & Gadhave, 2013). Skinfold thickness indirectly measures the amount of adipose tissue and is most often measured at the triceps, subscapular, and abdominal regions. To measure triceps skinfold thickness, the provider should use special calipers, such as Lange calipers. To begin, the provider should ask the child to flex his or her arm 90 degrees.

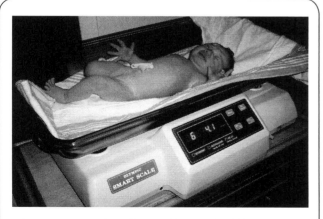

FIGURE 8.7. Measuring infant weight. Care should be taken to ensure the infant's safety while on the scale.

TABLE 8.8	Interpretation of Body Mass Index (BMI) Standards for Children 2 to 20 Years of Age	
CLASSIFICATION	**AGE- AND GENDER-SPECIFIC BMI PERCENTILES**
Underweight	BMI < 5th percentile
Healthy weight	BMI ≥ 5th ≤ 85th percentile
Overweight	BMI ≥ 85th ≤ 95th percentile
Obese	BMI ≥ 95th percentile

Source: Centers for Disease Control and Prevention (2011).

The provider then marks a place on the upper arm that is midway between the olecranon process and the acromion on the posterior aspect of the upper arm. Next, the provider gently grasps the skin away from the underlying muscle and places the caliper jaws onto the skinfold. The provider should wait 2 to 3 seconds and then take a reading. The calipers measure in millimeters (mm); the measurement should be taken to the nearest 0.1 mm (CDC, 2005). Two readings should be done and averaged for a final reading (Hockenberry, 2011).

MUAC is the measurement of the circumference of the upper arm, measured at the midpoint between the tip of the shoulder and the tip of the elbow (olecranon process and the acromion). MUAC is used in children aged 8 years and older (CDC, 2005) to estimate the amount of subcutaneous fat present in the upper arm. Excess fat in the upper arm can indicate overweight or obesity; a decline in subcutaneous fat in the upper arm can indicate malnutrition (Maiti et al., 2012). To measure MUAC, the child should be standing upright, shoulders relaxed, and arms hanging to the side; the arm should not be flexed. The provider should place the tape measure around the MUAC and obtain a reading in centimeters (cm), measured to the nearest 0.1 cm (CDC, 2005). Both skinfold measurements and MUAC values are used to screen children for further evaluation of nutritional status.

Length

To measure linear growth, the recumbent height (i.e., length) in children younger than 2 years of age should be measured rather than a standing height. Most children aged 2 years or younger will not cooperate or be able to stand long enough for the provider to obtain an accurate standing height. Also, children in this age group have physiologic lordosis, which makes a standing height less accurate. For length measurements to be accurate, proper positioning of the child is imperative. It is important to note that the CDC growth charts for birth to 36 months are standardized for recumbent height.

Length is measured with the child on the examination table in the supine position and the body fully extended. The provider should be sure to hold the child's head midline, straighten the child's legs, and dorsiflex the feet. The distance between the top of the child's head and the soles of the feet is then measured. A measuring board is the most accurate way to measure length in an infant or toddler. When using a measuring board (Figure 8.9), the provider places the child's head at the top of the board and the heels firmly at the bottom; the measurement is then taken to the nearest 0.5 cm or 0.25 inch. If a measuring board is unavailable, an alternative is to use the paper that lines the examination table by marking the paper at the top of the child's head and at the bottom of the child's heels and then measuring the distance between the two marks. This measurement technique also requires that the child's body be fully extended. Once the measurement is obtained, the provider should plot it on the age- and gender-specific CDC growth chart.

Height

Height is the measurement of linear growth while the child is standing upright. A standing height should be obtained if the child is older than age 2 years. Height can be measured using a scale with a measuring bar or a wall-mounted unit (stadiometer), which provides the most accurate measurement. To measure a child's standing height, the provider should first ask the child to remove his or her shoes and any hats or hair ornaments that would interfere with the measurement. The child

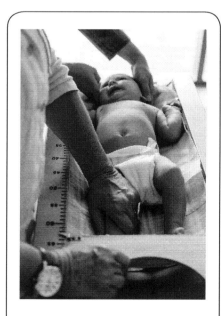

FIGURE 8.9. Measurement of recumbent height (length) of an infant using a measuring board.

should stand straight, look straight ahead, and have his or her head, shoulders, buttocks, and heels touching the wall or stadiometer. The provider should make sure that the child is not slouching. The height measurement should be taken to the nearest 0.1 cm (0.25 inch) and recorded on the age- and gender-specific CDC growth chart for that child. Table 8.9 summarizes normal linear growth patterns in children.

Weight-for-Length

Weight-for-length reflects body weight in comparison to length regardless of the child's age (CDC, 2010). This comparison is used to determine overweight and underweight in infants and young children. Weight-for-length should be plotted for children younger than 2 years of age using the age- and gender-specific CDC growth charts.

Weight-for-Stature

Weight-for-stature is defined as weight compared to height (stature) regardless of a child's age (CDC, 2010). Weight-for-stature is calculated for children aged 2 years and older. Weight-for-stature should be plotted on the CDC growth chart in children from 77 to 121 cm (CDC, 2010) to show the relationship between weight and height (Ariza, Greenberg, & Unger, 2004). Although weight-for-stature is less cumbersome to use than BMI, the BMI is preferred because it measures changes in the weight–height in relationship to age and can be used until age 20 years (Flegal, Wei, & Ogden, 2002). BMI-for-age and weight-for-stature measurements do not yield identical results and are not interchangeable (Flegal et al., 2002).

Arm Span

In some instances, exact height cannot be determined in a child because the child cannot stand or recline completely because of contractures, spinal abnormalities (e.g., scoliosis, myelomeningocele), limb deformities, or amputations. Arm-span measurement, which is nearly equal to height in children, can be used as an alternative to longitudinal measurement; it can also be used as a predictor of height (Nwosu & Lee, 2008). Arm-span measurement is also useful in identifying children with growth abnormalities. Measurement of arm span is done by asking the child or adolescent to extend both arms outward, then measuring the distance from the tip of the middle finger across the chest to the tip of the other middle finger. In children of European ancestry, the arm-span measurement should be 1 cm less than the child's height; in adolescents, the arm-span measurement should equal the height (Kemp & Gungor, 2012). Children and adolescents of Asian ancestry have proportionally shorter arms than those of European and African ancestry; children of African ancestry have significantly longer arms (Kemp & Gungor, 2012). The arm-span measurement exceeds the height with conditions such as Marfan's syndrome, Klinefelter's vertebral abnormalities, and homocystinuria (Nwosu & Lee, 2008). Short arm spans are found in children with skeletal dysplasias (Nwosu & Lee, 2008).

Head Circumference

Measurement of head circumference is a routine part of growth assessment in children aged 3 years and younger and at any time the provider deems necessary (e.g., with noticeable increased head circumference, abnormal growth patterns, provider concern about neurologic functions or developmental milestone achievement). To measure the head circumference, the provider should use a paper or metal measuring tape and place it around the child's head at its greatest circumference; this area is just above the eyebrows and the pinna, and around the occipital prominence (the occipital frontal circumference [OFC]) (Figure 8.10). Cloth measuring tapes should not be used as they stretch and can yield inaccurate results. The tape measure should be placed in the same position in neonates, although this may not reflect the largest measurement because of cranial molding or swelling. Once the measurement is obtained, the provider should plot it on the standardized age- and gender-specific CDC growth chart for head circumference. The head circumference measurement should fall between the 5th and 95th percentiles, be consistent with the child's previous measurements, and be comparable to the child's height and weight percentile measurements. A head circumference measurement that exceeds two standard deviations above the mean for age and sex, exceeds the 95th percentile on the growth charts, or increases too rapidly is defined as *macrocephaly*. A large head could be simply familial (the provider should measure both

TABLE 8.9	Normal Linear Growth Patterns in Children
AGE	**GROWTH VELOCITY PER YEAR**
Birth	50 cm
First year of life	23–27 cm (9–11 in.)
Second year of life	10 cm (4 in.)
Third year growth	8 cm (3 in.)
Fourth year growth	6–7 cm (2.4–2.75 in.)
Seventh year growth	6 cm (2.4 in.)
Annual growth until puberty	5–6 cm (2–2.4 in.)
Pubertal growth spurt	Girls: 8–12 cm (3–5 in.) Boys: 10–14 cm (4–6 in.)

Sources: Nwosu and Lee (2008); Halac and Zimmerman (2004).

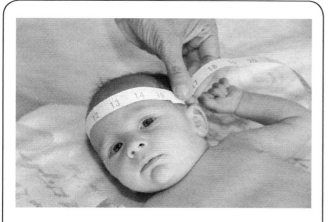

FIGURE 8.10. Measurement of head circumference of an infant. The tape measure should be placed around the point of largest circumference of the head.

parents' head circumferences) or a result of a more serious etiology such as hydrocephaly, subdural hematoma, brain tumors, or other causes of increased intracranial pressure. An increased head circumference in children 2 years of age or older may indicate separation of the cranial sutures, a sign of increased intracranial pressure.

A head circumference that measures less than two standard deviations below the mean for age and sex, measures less than the 5th percentile on the growth charts, or that is increasing too slowly is termed *microcephaly*. A small head in an infant or child may indicate a slowly growing brain, intrauterine growth restriction, or craniosynostosis (premature closure of cranial sutures). Children with microcephaly commonly have neurologic problems and developmental delays. With the success of the American Academy of Pediatrics' Back to Sleep campaign, more infants are presenting with plagiocephaly, specifically occipital flattening that can be helped by placing the infant prone while awake. Plagiocephaly affects OFC measurements and should be noted.

Chest Circumference

Measurement of chest circumference is not routinely done unless the provider suspects abnormal growth in an infant, particularly if the infant's head is of abnormal size. Because of cephalocaudal development (see Chapter 2), the head circumference normally exceeds the infant's chest circumference by 2 cm from birth until age 6 months. Between the ages of 6 and 24 months, the head and chest circumference should be about equal. By age 2 years, the head and chest circumference should be equal, with the chest continuing to grow faster than the head throughout childhood. After age 2, the chest circumference should always be larger than the head circumference. To measure the chest circumference, the provider should place the tape measure around the chest across the nipple line. Measurement of chest circumference is not plotted on any growth chart.

SUMMARY

Accurate measurements are particularly important when dealing with the pediatric population. Obtaining accurate objective data during the pediatric physical examination is essential to developing an accurate problem list and corresponding management plan. It is also very important for the pediatric health care provider to be proficient in performing the four major examination techniques and to be knowledgeable about the physical and psychosocial developmental stages in children.

Notable Clinical Findings

- Vital signs outside of range for age
- Child is febrile
- Child is less than the 5th percentile or greater than the 85th percentile for weight on the NCHS growth charts for age and gender
- Child is less than 5th percentile for length or height on the NCHS growth charts for age and gender
- Child is less than the 5th percentile or greater than the 5th percentile for head circumference on the NCHS growth charts for age and gender
- Child is experiencing pain

References

Andrews, M. M., & Boyle, J. S. (2012). *Transcultural concepts in nursing care* (6th ed.). Philadelphia, PA: Lippincott Williams & Wilkins.

Ariza, A. J., Greenberg, R. S., & Unger, R. (2004). Childhood overweight: Management approaches in young children. *Pediatric Annals, 33*(1), 33–38.

Assadi, F. (2012). The growing epidemic of hypertension among children and adolescents: A challenging road ahead. *Pediatric Cardiology, 33*(7), 1013–1020.

Carlson, S. E. (2005). Feeding after discharge: Growth, development and long-term effects. In R. C. Tsang, R. Uauy, R. Kolezko, & S. H. Zlotkin (Eds.), *Nutrition of the preterm infant: Scientific basis and practical guidelines* (2nd ed., pp. 357–381). Cincinnati, OH: Digital Publishing.

Centers for Disease Control and Prevention. (2005). *National Health and Nutrition Examination Survey. Anthropometry and physical activity monitor procedures manual*. Retrieved from http://www.cdc.gov/nchs/data/nhanes/nhanes_05_06/BM.pdf

Centers for Disease Control and Prevention. (2007). *National Health and Nutrition Examination Survey. Anthropometry procedures manual*. Retrieved from http://www.cdc.gov/nchs/data/nhanes/nhanes_07_08/manual_an.pdf

Centers for Disease Control and Prevention. (2010). *Growth chart home page*. Retrieved from http://www.cdc.gov/growthcharts/cdc_charts.htm

Centers for Disease Control and Prevention. (2011). *About BMI for children and teens*. Retrieved from http://www.cdc.gov/healthy-weight/assessing/bmi/childrens_bmi/about_childrens_bmi.html

Colvin, J. M., Muenzer, J. T., Jaffe, D. M., Smason, A., Deych, E., Shannon, W. D., ... Storch, G. A. (2012). Detection of viruses in young children with fever without an apparent source. *Pediatrics, 130*(6), e1455–e1462.

Engel, J. K. (2006). Body temperature, pulse and respirations. In J. K. Engel (Ed.), *Pediatric assessment* (5th ed., pp. 95–110). St. Louis, MO: C. V. Mosby.

Flegal, K. M., Wei, R., & Ogden, C. (2002). Weight-for-stature compared with body mass index–for-age growth charts for the United States from the Centers for Disease Control and Prevention. *American Journal of Clinical Nutrition, 75*(4), 761–766.

Griffin, I. J. (2014). *Growth management in preterm infants.* Up-to-Date, Topic 5003. Retrieved from http://www.uptodate.com/contents/growth-management-in-preterm-infants

Hagan, J., Shaw, J., & Duncan, P. (Eds.). (2008). *Bright futures: Guidelines for health supervision of infants, children and adolescents* (3rd ed.). Elk Grove Village, IL: American Academy of Pediatrics.

Halac, I., & Zimmerman, D. (2004). Evaluating short stature in children. *Pediatric Annals, 33*(3), 170–176.

Hockenberry, M. J. (2011). Communication and physical assessment of the child. In M. J. Hockenberry & D. Wilson (Eds.), *Nursing care of infants and children* (9th ed., pp. 117–178). St. Louis, MO: Mosby Elsevier.

Jeyakumar, A., Ghugre, P., & Gadhave, S. (2013). Mid-upper-arm circumference (MUAC) as a simple measure to assess the nutritional status of adolescent girls as compared with BMI. *Infant Child and Adolescent Nutrition, 5*(1), 22–25.

Kemp, S., & Gungor, N. (2012). *Growth failure.* Retrieved from http://emedicine.medscape.com/article/920446-overview

King, R. C. (1983). Refining your assessment techniques. *RN, 46*(2), 43–47.

Koutlas, T. C., Marziarz, D. M., Reade, C., & Love, K. (2014). *Coarctation of the aorta and interrupted aortic arch: Surgical perspective.* Retrieved from http://emedicine.medscape.com/article/903965-overview

Lawson, L., Bridges, E. J., Ballou, I., Eraker, R., Greco, S., Shively, J., & Sochulak, V. (2007). Accuracy and precision of noninvasive temperature measurement in adult intensive care patients. *American Journal of Critical Care, 16*(5), 485–496.

Luma, G. B., & Spiotta, R. T. (2006). Hypertension in children and adolescents. *American Family Physician, 73*(9), 1158–1168.

Maiti, S., De, D., Ali, K. M., Ghosh, A., Ghosh, D., & Paul, S. (2012). Evaluation of nutritional status by mid-upper arm circumference amongst affluent children. *Journal of Nepal Paediatric Society, 32*(2), 113.

National High Blood Pressure Education Program Working Group on High Blood Pressure in Children and Adolescents. (2005). *The fourth report on the diagnosis, evaluation, and treatment of high blood pressure in children and adolescents.* May 2005. NIH Publication No. 05–5267. 2014. Retrieved from http://www.nhlbi.nih.gov/health/prof/heart/hbp/hbp_ped.pdf

Nativio, D. G. (2005). Understanding fever in children. *American Journal for Nurse Practitioners, 9*(11/12), 47–48; 51–52.

Neumann, C. G., Gewa, C., & Bwibo, N. O. (2004). Child nutrition in developing countries. *Pediatric Annals, 33*(10), 658–674.

Nwosu, B. U., & Lee, M. M. (2008). Evaluation of short and tall stature in children. *American Family Physician, 78*(5), 597–604.

Schmitt, B. D. (1984). Preschoolers who refuse to be examined. Fearful or spoiled? *American Journal of Diseases in Children, 138*(5), 443–446.

Ward, M. A. (2013). *Patient information: Fever in children (beyond the basics).* Retrieved from http://www.uptodate.com/contents/fever-in-children-beyond-the-basics

Young, B. E., Johnson, S. L., & Krebs, N. F. (2012). Biological determinants linking infant weight gain and child obesity: Current knowledge and future directions. *Advances in Nutrition, 3,* 675–686.

Additional Resources

Auscultation Assistant

http://www.med.ucla.edu/wilkes/intro.html
This site offers audio clips for listening to heart and breath sounds.

Centers for Disease Control and Prevention—Growth Charts

http://www.cdc.gov/nccdphp/dnpao/growthcharts/resources/index.htm
This portion of the Centers for Disease Control website provides the growth charts for children for weight, length, height, weight for length, weight for stature, and BMI. These charts were revised in 2000 to be more representative of the ethnic diversity and current feeding practices in children in the United States. These charts also include percentile curves up to age 20 years and measurements inclusive of the 3rd and 97th percentiles. The CDC website also has self-study materials related to using the CDC growth charts and BMI assessment and interpretation.

Centers for Disease Control and Prevention—Measurement of Skinfold Thickness

http://www.cdc.gov/nchs/data/nhanes/nhanes_07_08/manual_an.pdf

Environmental Protection Agency

http://www.epa.gov/hg/thermometer-main.html
This site provides information on what to do with broken glass mercury thermometers, gives suggestions for alternatives to mercury thermometers, and tells the consumer how to dispose of old mercury glass thermometers.

Growth Charts for Children With Special Health Care Needs

http://depts.washington.edu/growth/cshcn/text/intro.htm

R.A.L.E. Repository

http://www.rale.ca
This website provides digital recordings of normal and abnormal respiratory sounds.

The Health Supervision Visit: Wellness Examinations in Children

A crucial element of pediatric health assessment is health supervision. This involves the determinatin of a child's physical and psychosocial health and wellness, assessment of parent or caregiver knowledge base, and the delivery of clinical preventive services. Wellness care for children lays the foundation for good health as an adult. Many of the health problems that are prevalent in U.S. adults, such as obesity, diabetes, heart disease, and mental health disorders, begin in childhood. The health supervision visit allows the pediatric health care provider to monitor a child's health status within the context of his or her family and community, deliver health promotion and screening; conduct school or sports examinations, prevent disease, and intervene before problems arise.

WELLNESS CARE FOR CHILDREN

With the advent of immunizations and antibiotics, the prevalence of communicable diseases in children has greatly decreased; however, a "new morbidity" has emerged as a cluster of psychosocial health concerns among children. Chief among these are school and learning problems, mood disorders (e.g., anxiety, depression), adolescent suicide and homicide, injury and death related to firearms, school violence, drug and alcohol abuse, human immunodeficiency virus (HIV) and acquired immunodeficiency syndrome (AIDS), the prevalence of sedentary lifestyles and obesity, and the media's influence on sexuality and interpersonal violence (American Academy of Pediatrics [AAP] Committee on Psychosocial Aspects of Child and Family Health, 2001). Other concerns include behavior disorders, family and relationship instabilities, and unsafe communities. Because of this shift in focus, pediatric health

supervision visits are essential to provide physical and psychosocial health screening, teaching, anticipatory guidance, and appropriate referrals.

Influences on Pediatric Well-Child Care

The highest quality preventive health care must be accessible, affordable, comprehensive, and culturally sensitive (Hagan, Shaw, & Duncan, 2008). Pediatric preventive health services must also be delivered by qualified professionals with pediatric expertise, such as pediatricians, pediatric nurse practitioners, advanced practice nurses with expertise in caring for children, and pediatric specialists and subspecialists.

Access to care is defined as having a regular source of comprehensive health care without barriers to services such as high cost, lack of insurance, a scarcity of health care providers (U. S. Department of Health and Human Services [USDHHS], 2013). Socioeconomic factors that affect accessibility to health care, such as poverty, homelessness, and a lack of health insurance or transportation, can adversely affect health outcomes in children (Bethell et al., 2011). For example, children with private health insurance are more likely than children with public health insurance to receive consistent preventive health care services (Bethell et al., 2011).

Access to quality pediatric health care may also be affected by certain *provider factors*. Numerous screening recommendations—coupled with the requisite health teaching, an overwhelming number of patients on a given clinic day, and limited clinic hours—can adversely affect the preventive services that are offered. A scarcity of pediatric health care providers, especially in rural areas (Lindeke & Jukkala, 2005), or providers who are unable to communicate with the child or family because of language barriers also hamper access to adequate health care (Mullin & Ambrosia, 2005). Many African American and Hispanic children in the United States do not have regular access to health care because they are uninsured. Uninsured families or families for whom English is a second language also experience barriers to health care (Mullin & Ambrosia, 2005).

Personal beliefs about what constitutes health care may affect access to health care for children; for example, some parents and caregivers may not view preventive services as valuable. This also includes health beliefs about the importance of oral health. Kelly, Binkley, Neace, and Gale (2005) found that in low-income families, parents' health beliefs about oral health focused on episodic and emergency dental care. These families also face financial constraints, transportation difficulties, and discrimination, which hamper their access to dental care for their children.

Culture plays a role in pediatric preventive health care because of its influence on the beliefs of families about what constitutes health and illness. In addition, families may use traditional healing practices rather than Western preventive health care. Families that rely on traditional healers often seek formal health care only when a person is already ill. (See Chapter 5 for a discussion of the role of culture on health and illness.)

The Medical Home

Ideally, the pediatric health supervision visit is conducted with a consistent pediatric health care provider or group of providers, often referred to as the "medical home." The medical home is defined by the AAP as "a model of delivering primary care that is accessible, continuous, comprehensive, family-centered, coordinated, compassionate, and culturally effective" (AAP, 2008b, p. 184). By providing an ongoing, consistent source of health care for the child, a medical home avoids fragmentation of care and allows for adequate follow-up of all health assessments. It also allows the pediatric health care provider to establish a relationship with the child and family and presents increased opportunities to conduct health supervision, promote breastfeeding, monitor immunization status, conduct developmental surveillance and health screenings, and provide age-appropriate, individualized anticipatory guidance and education regarding nutrition, physical activity, safety, parenting, discipline, and psychosocial issues. An important role for the pediatric health care provider is to encourage all families to establish a medical home.

THE PEDIATRIC HEALTH SUPERVISION VISIT

Various evidence-based, well-child health assessment guidelines exist, including the AAP's *Bright Futures Guidelines for Health Supervision of Infants, Children and Adolescents*, the American Medical Association's *Guidelines for Adolescent Preventive Services* (GAPS), and Healthy People 2020. These guidelines are particularly helpful in assisting the pediatric provider in ensuring that all age-appropriate components of the well-child visit are completed in as much depth as possible.

Timing and Frequency of Visits

Current recommendations by the AAP suggest that the frequency of pediatric health supervision visits be in accord with the Recommendations for Preventive Pediatric Health Care (AAP, 2011). The timing and content of these visits are delineated in the periodicity schedule for well-child visits, published by the AAP, and revised in 2014. Because childhood is a time of rapid growth and change, health supervision well-child visits are more frequent when the child is very young and growth and development are rapid. More or fewer visits may be necessary, depending on the child's health status or the family's circumstances.

Some pediatric health care providers advocate changing the recommended timing of the well-child visits because the periodicity schedule has been traditionally linked to the schedule of childhood immunizations. It is thought that this contributes to the low rate of attendance at well-child health maintenance visits, as many parents view these visits as synonymous with "baby shots" and nothing else (Schor, 2004). Some experts propose identifying priority themes for each visit, according to the child's current developmental stage; for example, the 5-year visit could focus on school readiness and the importance of reading. This approach allows the parent to come prepared for the visit with specific questions for the provider and allows the provider to fine-tune assessments and prioritize the content of the well-child visit (Schor, 2004).

Components

Regardless of the timing and frequency of the pediatric health supervision, each visit contains specific components. These include the health history, identification of parental concerns, physical examination, developmental surveillance, observation of parent–child interactions, health screening, determination of immunization status, anticipatory guidance, and child–family education (Hagan et al., 2008). The health care provider assesses parental knowledge about nutrition, discipline, illness and injury prevention, temperament, and growth and development. In addition, the health care provider assesses the quality of physical care, parental nurturing, and stimulation that the child receives. All assessments are geared to the child's age and developmental stage. Many of these assessment areas overlap with the Bright Futures health-promotion themes, which are listed in Box 9.1.

History

All children new to a pediatric health care provider's practice require a comprehensive and complete

---

BOX 9.1   Bright Futures Health Promotion Themes

- Family support
- Child development
- Mental health
- Healthy weight
- Healthy nutrition
- Physical activity
- Oral health
- Healthy sexual development and sexuality
- Safety and injury prevention
- Community relationships and resources

Source: Hagan, Shaw, and Duncan (2008).

---

initial history. At each subsequent health supervision visit, the provider obtains an interval history, which updates the child's health status since the last visit. (See Chapter 6 for a detailed explanation of these histories.) Part of the history is obtained by using questionnaires that the parent or older child can answer before the clinical interview. Appropriate topics for screening questionnaires include diet, nutrition, exercise, and age-appropriate safety precautions. At each visit, the provider must always remember to elicit any parental–child concerns, inquire about family life, and evaluate the child in the context of the community in which he or she lives.

When providing preventive health care services to children, there are several assessment areas or domains as part of the history that are essential to include. These assessments help formulate interventions and individualize child–parent education and anticipatory guidance. Specific assessment areas include:

- Nutrition (see Chapter 10)
- Risk for overweight and obesity (see Chapter 10)
- Daily physical activity (see Chapters 6 and 10)
- Elimination patterns (see Chapter 6)
- Sleep patterns (see Chapter 6)
- Age-appropriate safety and risk of injury (see Chapters 6 and 7)
- Social and family relationships (see Chapters 4 and 6)
- Behavior (see Chapters 2 and 23)
- Growth and development (see Chapters 2 and 6)

Other areas to assess involve evaluating the parent's discipline practices, including the parent's beliefs about discipline and the discipline practices they employ. Specific questions should be asked about shaking and corporal punishment, both of which can seriously harm an infant or child physically and emotionally (see Chapter 24). Table 9.1 provides some examples of age-specific assessments in these areas.

A mental health assessment is necessary for all children, beginning at age 11 years. This involves screening for depression and substance use (AAP, 2014). Chapter 23 provides details about mental health assessments in children. Pediatric providers must also screen mothers for postpartum depression because of the adverse effects of maternal depression on young children (Earls & Committee on Psychosocial Aspects of Child and Family Health AAP, 2010).

Pediatric health care providers should also assess for spiritual health in the child and family. This may include assessments involving the child and family's connection with a greater power, purpose and meaning in life, or links to any faith-based groups.

The health care encounter presents an excellent opportunity for the provider to evaluate parental knowledge about disease prevention for their child. This includes determining knowledge about simple hand-washing, covering mouths when coughing and sneezing, and the importance of immunizations.

Assessment of oral health begins at the 6-month visit, continuing at the 12-month, 18-month, 2-year, 30-month, and 3-year visits (Hagan et al., 2008). The provider determines if the child has a "dental home," which should be established soon after the first tooth eruption or by 12 months (American Academy of Pediatric Dentistry Council on Clinical Affairs, 2013).

Other assessments include questions about feeding practices, such as bottle-propping (i.e., if the infant is placed in bed with a bottle containing milk or sweetened drinks), if the child has a "companion" bottle or sippy cup that is carried throughout the day, and if the companion bottle contains sweetened drinks. The provider also asks about the child's oral care routine, which should begin in infancy, including questions about whether the older child brushes his or her teeth at least twice a day. The assessments conducted at these visits help the provider determine the level of risk to the child's oral health and the level of parental education that is needed.

The provider should ask parents and children school-aged and older about the use of sunscreen, particularly in the summer and with prolonged exposure to the sun in winter, as with skiing or any other outdoor sport. The provider also asks if the child is kept out of the sun during peak intensity or if the child wears protective clothing or a hat during prolonged sun exposure (see Chapter 7).

During each health supervision visit, the provider asks if the child is exposed to environmental tobacco smoke (ETS) in the form of second- or third-hand cigarette or cigar smoke in the home, car, or homes of extended family, friends, or child care providers. The child's social situation can change between health supervision visits, so this must be reassessed at each visit. When the parent is out of the room, preteens and adolescents are screened for tobacco use.

Adolescents, and in some cases preadolescents, are asked about sexual activity. All adolescent girls who report a late menstrual period, amenorrhea, or sexual activity

TABLE 9.1	Age-Specific Well-Child History Assessments					
	NUTRITION	**ELIMINATION**	**SAFETY**	**SLEEP**	**PSYCHOSOCIAL**	**GROWTH AND DEVELOPMENT**
Infants	Breastfed or formula-fed? Type of formula? Do parents know hunger/satiety cues? Bottle propping? Bottle in bed? Juice? Amount a day? When were solids introduced? Type? Frequency and amount? Has child had first dental visit by 12 months of age?	How many wet diapers a day? Number of stools a day? Character of stools?	Rear-facing car seat use? Any smokers in home? Is infant protected against falls? Is infant fed any foods that are choking hazards? Is infant put to sleep prone? Does parent or caregiver avoid having infant near hot liquids? Are there smoke detectors in home? Is home baby-proofed (e.g., electrical wall socket covers, door latches, etc.)? Do family members employ frequent hand washing with young infant, especially during cold and flu season? Any guns in home?	Does infant sleep supine? Any co-sleeping? Is infant rocked to sleep? Tummy time?	Who is primary caregiver? Who lives in home? Any maternal postpartum depression? Are infant's needs met consistently? How is parent/infant attachment? Is father involved? Any smokers/substance abusers in home? Any domestic violence? Does older infant have security object? Frequency of ER visits? For what reason?	See Chapter 2, Table 2.3.
Toddlers	Does child drink from a cup or bottle? Type or amount of milk a day? Amount of juice a day? Typical meals? Snacks? Do parents brush child's teeth? Does child suck thumb or pacifier? Has child visited dentist? Any rewarding with food? How many hours of TV watched a day?	Has toilet training begun? At what age? Frequency or character of stools?	Is car seat used in rear seat of vehicle? Is house baby-proofed (electrical wall socket covers, door latches, medications out of reach)? Has crib mattress been lowered? Supervised around water? Near streets? Sunscreen used? Smoke detectors in home? Any smokers in home? Any guns in home?	Does child have consistent bedtime? Hours of bedtime and rising? Does child sleep through night? Where does toddler sleep? How many naps?	Does child have security object? Does toddler have tantrums? Any biting, hitting, or other aggressive behavior? Type of rules and discipline? Does caregiver or parent read to child each day? Number of hours of TV watched a day? Type of programs watched? Exposure to media violence or sexuality? Any smokers or substance abusers in home? Any domestic violence?	See Chapter 2, Table 2.3.

TABLE 9.1 Age-Specific Well-Child History Assessments (*continued*)

	NUTRITION	ELIMINATION	SAFETY	SLEEP	PSYCHOSOCIAL	GROWTH AND DEVELOPMENT
Preschool children	Typical meals? Type of snacks? Does child eat breakfast each day? Amount of juice or soda each day? Use food as reward? Does child still use sippy cup? How much time spent a day watching TV? Does child get at least 30 minutes of exercise a day? Does child brush teeth at least twice a day? Visit dentist? Does child suck thumb?	Is toilet training complete or continuing? Problems with urination or defecation? Bedwetting?	Is child still in car seat (until 40 lbs)? Booster seat? Is home child-proofed? Is child aware of "stranger danger"? Does child wear a helmet when riding a bicycle? Is child aware of street safety? Water safety? Animal safety? Has child been taught about "good touch/bad touch"? Any guns in the home?	Does child still nap? Consistent bedtime? Nightmares? Does child sleep through night? Any nightmares or night terrors?	Is child in preschool or day care? Does caregiver or parent read to child each day? Number of hours of TV watched a day? Type of programs watched? Exposure to media violence or sexuality? Type of discipline? Any smokers or substance abusers in home? Any domestic violence?	See Chapter 2, Table 2.3.
School-aged children	Typical meals? Type of snacks? Does child eat breakfast each day? Amount of juice or soda each day? Use food as reward? How much time spent a day watching TV, browsing Internet, or playing video games? Does child get at least 30 minutes of exercise a day? Does child brush teeth at least twice a day? Visit dentist?	Problems with urination or defecation? Bedwetting (WNL until 6 years)? Rushes to bathroom when returns home from school (may indicate bullying at school)? UTIs or constipation (may indicate bullying at school)? (Governo & Siewers, 2008)	Is child in booster seat if < 80 lbs? Does child always wear a seatbelt? Is child aware of "stranger danger"? Does child wear a helmet when riding a bicycle? Is child aware of street safety? Water safety? Animal safety? Has child been taught about "good touch/bad touch"? Any guns in the home?	Consistent bedtime? Nightmares? Does child sleep through night?	Family relationships? Any smokers or substance abusers in home? Any domestic violence? Peer relationships? Does child have a best friend? Type of discipline? Reports of bullying? How does child handle anger? School performance? Homework issues? Learning disabilities? School failure or refusal? School phobia? Involved in extracurricular activities?	See social assessments. See Chapter 2, Table 2.3.

(continued)

TABLE 9.1 Age-Specific Well-Child History Assessments (*continued*)

	NUTRITION	ELIMINATION	SAFETY	SLEEP	PSYCHOSOCIAL	GROWTH AND DEVELOPMENT
Adolescents	Typical meals? Fast food or soda intake a day? Meal skipping, fad diets, or eating disorders? Recent change in appetite? How much time spent a day watching TV, browsing the Internet, texting, or playing video games? Does teen get at least 30 minutes of exercise a day?	Chronic diarrhea, which may indicate laxative intake? Rushes to bathroom when returns home from school, which may indicate bullying at school? UTIs or constipation, which may indicate bullying at school? (Governo & Siewers, 2008) UTIs may also indicate STIs.	Does teen always wear a seatbelt? Does teen smoke, use drugs, drink alcohol, or engage in risk-taking behaviors, such as fast driving? Is teen involved with Internet activities that could be unsafe? Any guns in home?	Bedtime? Hour of waking? Difficulty falling asleep? Difficulty waking up for school? Falling asleep in class? Does teen nap each day? May need evaluation for depression, substance abuse, or sleep cycle disorder if teen naps for > 3 hours each day (Reitman, 2007).	Who lives in home? How are these people related? Recent changes in family? Any smokers or substance abusers in home? Any domestic violence? How is school going? Does teen have friends? What does teen do for fun? How does teen handle anger? Bullying? School phobia? Learning disabilities? ADHD? Recent changes in teen's academic progress? Difficulty with homework? Teen skipping classes? Life plan and goals? Do academic abilities match grades? Reports of interpersonal violence or gang involvement? Is teen sexually active? Does teen use condoms? Evidence of depression or risk-taking behaviors? Changes in relationships with others? Thoughts of hurting himself or herself? Thoughts of hurting others?	See social assessments. See Chapter 2, Table 2.3.

ADHD, attention deficit hyperactivity disorder; ER, emergency room; STIs, sexually transmitted infections; UTIs, urinary tract infections; WNL, within normal limits.

without contraception should be tested for pregnancy. This must be done in a sensitive, private, and confidential manner; Chapter 20 discusses these assessments in detail.

Identifying Parent and Child Concerns

An essential component of the pediatric health supervision visit is soliciting concerns of the parents or child at the beginning of the encounter. This is a vital part of developing a meaningful relationship with the child and family, recognizing that they are the experts on their own health. This enhanced communication fosters a strong provider–child–family relationship, the goal of which is to promote health and prevent illness and injury.

Physical Examination

At each health supervision visit, an essential component is the complete, head-to-toe physical examination. Depending on the child's age, the provider must be certain to focus on specific areas in the physical assessment. These age-specific areas are listed in Table 9.2. (See Chapter 8 for details about the pediatric physical examination.)

TABLE 9.2	Focus of Physical Examination by Age, Health Supervision Visit		
AGE	**ASSESSMENT AREAS**	**AGE**	**ASSESSMENT AREAS**
Newborn	• Length, weight, head circumference • Physical maturity • Cranial molding, birth trauma • Skin lesions, jaundice • Fontanelles • Umbilical cord • Congenital anomalies • Red reflex • Placement of ears • Dysmorphic features • Cardiac murmurs • Femoral pulses • Genitalia; descent of testes • Hips, feet, spine • Grasp, suck, walk, Moro reflexes; muscle tone	2 months	• Length, weight, weight-for-length, head circumference • Congenital anomalies • Skull (positional plagiocephaly) • Skin • Cardiac murmurs • Red reflex; pupils • Reacts to sound • Hips • Genitalia • Grasp, suck, Moro reflexes • Tone
3–5 days	• As newborn visit plus: • Assess for dacryocystitis	4 months	• Length, weight, weight-for-length, head circumference • Skull (positional plagiocephaly) • Skin • Red reflex, pupils • Symmetrical pupillary light reflex • Cardiac murmurs • Femoral pulses • Hip click • Metatarsus adductus • Muscle tone
2–4 weeks	• Length, weight, head circumference • Congenital anomalies • Red reflex • Blink reflex • Reacts to sound • Cardiac murmurs • Assess abdomen for masses • Hips, tibial torsion, metatarsus adductus • Genitalia • Grasp, suck, walk, Moro reflexes	6 months	• Length, weight, weight-for-length, head circumference • Symmetrical pupillary light reflex • Skin • Skull (positional plagiocephaly) • Conjugate gaze • Red reflex • Ocular mobility • Responds to sounds • Cardiac murmurs • Femoral pulses • Muscle tone • Parachute reflex • Grasp, transfer • Hip abduction • Teeth • Genitalia/testes

(continued)

TABLE 9.2	Focus of Physical Examination by Age, Health Supervision Visit (*continued*)		
AGE	**ASSESSMENT AREAS**	**AGE**	**ASSESSMENT AREAS**
9 months	• Same as 6-month visit	4 years	• Height, weight • BMI • Blood pressure • Gait • Fine motor skills • Speech
12 months	• Length, weight, weight-for-length, head circumference • Symmetrical pupillary light reflex • Conjugate gaze • Cover/uncover test • Check teeth for caries • Red reflex • Hips • Gait • Testes	5 years	• Height, weight • BMI • Blood pressure • Funduscopic examination • Teeth • Fine motor skills • Gait • Speech
15 months	• Length, weight, weight-for-length, head circumference • Symmetrical pupillary light reflex • Conjugate gaze • Cover/uncover test • Teeth • Gait • Hips	6 years	• Same as 5-year visit
18 months	• Length, weight, weight-for-length, head circumference • Cover/uncover test • Red reflex • Conjugate gaze • Hips • Gait	7 years	• Height, weight • BMI • Blood pressure • Hips, knees, gait • Teeth • Sexual maturity rating
24 months	• Standing height, weight, weight-for-height, head circumference, BMI • Red reflex • Cover/uncover test • Conjugate gaze • Teeth • Gait • Speech	8 years	• Same as 7-year visit
30 months	• Standing height, weight, weight-for-height, head circumference • BMI • Red reflex • Cover/uncover test • Conjugate gaze • Coordination • Speech	9 years	• Height, weight • BMI • Blood pressure • Skin (abuse, tattoos, piercings) • Forward bending test • Sexual maturity rating
3 years	• Height, weight • BMI • Blood pressure • Funduscopic examination • Speech • Teeth	10 years	• Same as 9-year visit

TABLE 9.2	Focus of Physical Examination by Age, Health Supervision Visit (*continued*)		
AGE	**ASSESSMENT AREAS**	**AGE**	**ASSESSMENT AREAS**
11–14 years	• Height, weight • BMI • Blood pressure • Skin (acanthosis nigricans, acne, tattoos, piercings, abuse, self-injury) • Breasts (female: sexual maturity rating; male: gynecomastia) • Genitalia (female: sexual maturity rating, inspect for evidence of STI; perform pelvic exam based on sexual history [see Chapter 20]; male: sexual maturity rating, inspect for evidence of STI, examine testicles for hydroceles, hernias, varicocele, or masses) • Forward bending test	18–21 years	• Same as 11- –14-year visit; clinical breast exam should be performed on all girls after 20 years of age
15–17 years	• Same as 11- –14-year visit		

BMI, body mass index; STI, sexually transmitted infection.
Source: Hagan, Shaw, and Duncan (2008).

Developmental Surveillance and Behavioral Assessment

Developmental and behavioral assessment encompasses developmental surveillance, psychosocial/behavioral assessment, developmental screening, and autism screening (Hagan et al., 2008). Developmental surveillance and psychosocial/behavioral assessment should occur at every health maintenance visit in partnership with the parent. More frequent assessments may be needed between health maintenance visits if developmental delays are noted or the parent raises a concern. These assessments must be done by an experienced pediatric health care provider, preferably one who sees the child regularly to have an ongoing perspective of the child's development. Formal developmental screening is conducted, using a standardized developmental evaluation tool (see Chapter 2, Table 2.4); this takes place at the 9-month, 18-month, and 30-month health maintenance visits. Autism screening occurs at the 18-month and 24-month well-child visits in all children or when the parent expresses a concern (Centers for Disease Control and Prevention [CDC], 2014). This is done by evaluating behavioral symptoms, using the criteria for autism spectrum disorder outlined in the *Diagnostic and Statistical Manual of Mental Disorders, 5th edition*, (*DSM-5*) or by using one of the autism screening tools listed in Chapter 2, Table 2.4.

Screening for drug and alcohol use is an important part of behavioral assessment in the adolescent. The AAP Committee on Substance abuse recommends that all adolescents be screened for alcohol, tobacco, or other drug use at all health maintenance visits beginning at age 11 years. The recommended screening tool is the CRAFFT Screening Test, a six-item screening tool similar to the CAGE assessment tool used in adults. A positive response to two or more of the six items in this test suggests a problem with drugs or alcohol and requires immediate action (Levy, Kokotailo, & the American Academy of Pediatrics Committee on Substance Abuse, 2011).

Observation of Parent–Child Interaction

The provider should observe the quality of physical care, parental nurturing, and developmental stimulation that the child receives. Observations of parent–child interaction are specific to the child's age and developmental level. Examples include observing whether: (a) the parent recognizes and responds to the infant's needs, (b) the parent talks to the child, (c) the parent and child treat each other respectfully, and (d) the parent has behavioral expectations for the child that are developmentally appropriate.

Health Screening

Bright Futures: Guidelines for Health Supervision of Infants, Children and Adolescents (3rd ed.) has published recommendations for health screening in children, from birth to age 21, which are evidence-based and were extensively reviewed by experts (Hagan et al., 2008). The AAP (2014) recommendations for preventive health care includes updates to these screening recommendations; these updates are summarized in Box 9.2. Conduction of health screening is based on these recommendations and on risk assessment for selective screening.

Newborn Metabolic and Hemoglobinopathy Screening • Newborn screening for metabolic disorders and hemoglobinopathies is critical to diagnosing these conditions in a timely manner and beginning

---

Box 9.2   2014 Updates to American Academy of Pediatrics Periodicity Schedule

- Alcohol and drug use assessment: Screening at age 11 through 21 has been added. Information regarding a recommended screening tool (CRAFFT) was also added.
- Depression: Screening for depression at ages 11 through 21 has been added, along with suggested screening tools
- Dyslipidemia screening: An additional screening between 9 and 11 years of age has been added.
- Hematocrit or hemoglobin: A risk assessment has been added at 15 and 30 months
- STI/HIV screening: A screen for HIV has been added between 16 and 18 years
- Cervical dysplasia: Adolescents should no longer be routinely screened for cervical dysplasia until age 21
- Critical congenital heart disease: Screening for critical congenital heart disease using pulse oximetry should be performed in newborns, after 24 hours of age, before discharge from the hospital

---

referral, disease management, and genetic counseling as needed (CDC, 2013b). The conditions for which newborns are screened vary from state to state; each pediatric health care provider should become familiar with the conditions for which his or her population is screened. There are 29 primary conditions and 25 secondary conditions currently identifiable through newborn screening. Examples of primary conditions include biotinidase deficiency, congenital adrenal hyperplasia, congenital hypothyroidism, cystic fibrosis, galactosemia, homocystinuria, maple syrup urine disease, medium-chain acyl-coenzyme A dehydrogenase deficiency, phenylketonuria, sickle cell disease and other hemoglobinopathies, and tyrosinemia (CDC, 2013b). Newborn screening for metabolic disorders and hemoglobinopathies most often occurs before the neonate is discharged from the hospital after birth, but no later than 1 week of age if the child was born at home or remains hospitalized in the neonatal intensive care unit (NICU).

Measurements • At each health supervision visit, length or height and weight are measured; the head circumference is also obtained on children 2 years and younger (AAP, 2014). Weight-for-length is obtained on children 18 months and younger and, beginning at 2 years, a standing height is obtained. Beginning at 2 years, the standing height and weight are used to calculate the body mass index (BMI). All measurements are then plotted on the age- and sex-appropriate percentile charts (see Appendix B). Blood pressure is measured as part of routine health screening beginning at 3 years. Infants and children younger than 3 years who have acute or chronic conditions that may affect blood pressure should have their blood pressure measured

(National High Blood Pressure Education Program Working Group on High Blood Pressure in Children and Adolescents, 2004). See Chapter 8 for a detailed discussion of blood pressure and anthropometric measurements in children and Chapter 10 for a discussion of calculating the BMI in children.

Hearing • It is important to identify hearing loss in a young child because of the consequences of delayed language acquisition in children with auditory deficits. It is best to identify hearing loss before 3 months; this is achieved through universal newborn screening through auditory brainstem response (ABR) (see Chapter 14). Universal objective hearing screening should take place again at the 4-year, 5-year, 6-year, 8-year, and 10-year visits. At all other health maintenance visits, subjective assessment is conducted by eliciting parental concerns about the child's speech or hearing; conducting developmental surveillance, including speech and auditory skills; and reviewing middle-ear status, according to the AAP periodicity schedule (AAP Joint Committee on Infant Hearing, 2007). If the risk assessment is positive, appropriate referrals are made for diagnostic audiologic assessment.

Vision and Eye Exams • Age-appropriate eye examinations are essential beginning at birth. Various clinical assessments, as well as objective visual acuity measurements detect eye and vision problems so that appropriate referral and treatment are initiated. Evaluation of vision begins with an ocular history, obtained from the parent (see Chapter 15). From birth to 9 months, the provider assesses children for eye problems according to the recommendations in *Bright Futures*, third edition. Beginning at the 12-month visit through the 30-month visit, the provider assesses both pupils for the red reflex, performs the cover/uncover test, and tests for ocular mobility (see Chapter 15). An age-appropriate objective vision examination is added (see Chapter 15), along with ophthalmoscopic examination of the optic nerve and retinal vessels at the 3-year (if the child is cooperative), 4-year, 5-year, 6-year, 8-year, 10-year, 12-year, 15-year, and 18-year health supervision visits. This vision screening is also performed any time the children, parents, or teachers express concern about vision (AAP Committee on Practice and Ambulatory Medicine, 2007).

Hematocrit or Hemoglobin • The purpose of obtaining a hemoglobin or hematocrit level is to screen for anemia, most commonly iron-deficiency anemia (Harper & Conrad, 2013), although hemoglobinopathies, such as sickle cell disease and thalassemia, also cause anemia in children. Premature or low birth weight infants, term infants older than 6 months, infants who consume non-iron-fortified or low-iron formula, infants who are given cow's milk before 12 months of age, children or adolescents who adhere to a strict vegetarian or vegan diet (without iron supplements), menstruating girls, and children living in poverty are at risk for iron-deficiency anemia. The AAP (2014) recommends that infants and children be screened for anemia, depending on these risk factors; however, anemia screening should be done universally at 12 months, with an additional risk assessment done at 15 and 30 months of age. Anemia screening should also be done on all preterm and low birth weight infants and those who are fed non–iron-fortified or low-iron formula at the 4-month visit. At the 18-month, 2-year, 3-year, 4-year, and 5-year visits, and all annual health maintenance visits until 21 years of age, the provider should conducts an anemia risk assessment by investigating whether any of the above risk factors are present and, if so, conduct anemia screening.

Lead Screening • Lead poisoning is one of the most prevalent pediatric health problems in the United States (CDC, 2013a). The most common sources of lead exposure in the United States are lead-based paint in older homes, household dust, contaminated soil and drinking water, lead crystal, and lead-glazed ceramics and pottery (CDC, 2013a). Young children are especially vulnerable to lead poisoning because their bodies absorb lead more readily as a consequence of their greater intake of dietary fat and, in some cases, decreased intake of calcium and iron. Lead damages heme synthesis, causing a decreased number of red blood cells and hemoglobin, resulting in anemia. High lead levels in children can also cause central nervous system toxicity and renal failure. A lead risk assessment is conducted by using a questionnaire; appropriate questions are listed in Box 9.3. Because most children with lead poisoning are asymptomatic, universal blood lead screening is conducted at 12 months and 24 months of age, regardless of risk, but especially for children who meet high-risk criteria or those who are covered by Medicaid. Then screening assessment is conducted at the 6-month, 9-month, 12-month, 18-month, 2-year, 3-year, 4-year, 5-year, and 6-year visits. Some states require that all children receive lead screening regardless of type of insurance.

Tuberculosis Screening • Tuberculosis (TB) has a different presentation in children than in adults, especially in children aged 4 years and younger. These children have a higher incidence of converting from TB infection to TB disease because of their immature immune systems (CDC, 2012). However, children 12 and younger with active pulmonary TB are rarely infectious because they do not produce sputum, have fewer pulmonary tubercle bacilli, and lack the physical force necessary to expel these bacilli through coughing (CDC, 2012). In children, TB screening is selective, based on a risk assessment protocol called "targeted testing," which aims to identify children at high risk for contracting TB (CDC, 2013c). This risk is determined by asking the parent the screening questions listed in Box 9.4; this assessment should occur at the 1-month, 6-month, 12-month, and 24-month visits, then annually from ages 3 to 21 years. Children with a positive screen should be tested for TB using the Mantoux tuberculin skin test. Children infected with HIV and incarcerated adolescents should also receive an annual tuberculin skin test (AAP, 2014).

BOX 9.4 Tuberculosis Risk Assessment Questionnaire

- Has a family member or close contact had tuberculosis (TB)?
- Does the child have signs of TB disease (e.g., fever, night sweats, cough, and weight loss)?
- Does the child have HIV infection or another medical problem that weakens the immune system?
- Has a family member had a positive tuberculin skin test?
- Was your child born in a high-risk country (e.g., most countries in Latin America, the Caribbean, Africa, Asia, Eastern Europe, and Russia)?
- Has your child traveled to or been in contact with any person from a high-risk country for more than 1 week?
- Does the child or adolescent use illegal drugs?
- Does the child live in a homeless shelter, domestic violence shelter, or prison?

Source: Centers for Disease Control and Prevention (2013c).

BOX 9.3 Assessing Risk of Lead Poisoning in Asymptomatic Children

Does your child
- Live in or regularly visit a house or child care facility built before 1950?
- Live in or regularly visit a house or child care facility built before 1978 that has been renovated or remodeled within the past 6 months?
- Have a sibling or playmate who has had lead poisoning?

Source: American Academy of Pediatrics Committee on Environmental Health (2009).

Dyslipidemia • The current epidemic of childhood obesity contributes to the risk for hyperlipidemia in children, an important risk factor for coronary artery disease as they grow into adulthood. In the National Heart, Blood and Lung Institute (2013) published revised guidelines for lipid screening in children; these were endorsed by the APA (2014). The first lipid screening should take place after age 2 years, with an additional screening between 9 and 11 years of age. Overweight and obese children require dyslipidemia screening irrespective of family history or other risk factors.

Sexually Transmitted Infections • According to the CDC guidelines (2010), all sexually active females ages 25 years and younger should be screened annually for

Chlamydia trachomatis and *Neisseria gonorrhoeae.* Adolescent males are screened if they are in settings associated with high chlamydia prevalence (e.g., correctional facilities and sexually transmitted disease [STD] clinics). An HIV screen should be obtained on all adolescents between 16 and 18 years of age, based on a positive risk assessment, using a screening questionnaire (AAP, 2014). Young men who have sex with men, and pregnant adolescent females, may require more thorough evaluation for asymptomatic STDs (e.g., syphilis, trichomoniasis, bacterial vaginosis, herpes simplex virus, human papillomavirus, hepatitis A virus, and hepatitis B virus; CDC, 2010).

Cervical Dysplasia • The AAP (2014) no longer recommends annual screening for cervical cancer until age 21 years. Indications for pelvic examinations are listed in the 2010 AAP statement, "Gynecologic Examination for Adolescents in the Pediatric Office Setting."

Immunization Status • At every pediatric health care encounter, the health care provider reviews the child or adolescent's immunization status and updates any immunizations as necessary. A schedule of recommended immunization is published annually by the CDC Advisory Committee on Immunization Practices (ACIP). A current schedule of immunizations for children can be found on the CDC/ACIP or AAP websites (see Additional Resources).

Anticipatory Guidance • Anticipatory guidance is provided at each well-child, health supervision visit. It educates the parents or caregivers about their child's next stage of physical and psychosocial development so that they know what to expect. Examples include teaching safety related to the mobility of a curious toddler or an adolescent who has just learned to drive, nutrition for the physiologically anorexic toddler, sleep position for the newborn and infant, toilet-training challenges, a school-aged child's adjustment to his or her parent's divorce, or speech and language abilities in the bilingual child. Specific educational topics are based on the assessment findings obtained during the history, physical examination, developmental assessment, and health screening. All teaching must be in the family's language and be culturally appropriate. Written materials must be at an appropriate literacy level for the parent or caregiver.

THE PREPARTICIPATION SPORTS EXAMINATION

The preparticipation sports examination (PPE) is a common reason that school-aged children and adolescents seek primary health care. In some instances, the sports physical may be the child's only contact with a health care provider. For this reason, it is important for the pediatric health care provider to be sure that the child and parent are aware that the PPE is not a substitute for a pediatric health supervision visit, as the focus is on screening the child or adolescent's risk for injury, illness,

or sudden death as a result of the child's participation in a particular sport. The provider should take the opportunity during the PPE to evaluate the child's overall health and to discuss high-risk behaviors (Box 9.5) (American Academy of Family Physicians et al., 2010). The American Academy of Family Physicians AAP, American College of Sports Medicine, American Medical Society for Sports Medicine, American Orthopaedic Society for Sports Medicine, and American Osteopathic Academy of Sports Medicine have endorsed a standardized preparticipation athletic evaluation form that addresses important aspects of the history and examination. These forms can be downloaded from the AAP's website (http://www.aap.org/en-us/about-the-aap/Committees-Councils-Sections/Council-on-sports-medicine-and-fitness/Pages/PPE.aspx).

BOX 9.5 High-Risk Behaviors to Assess With the Preparticipation Sports Examination

- Alcohol use
- Substance abuse
- Driving while intoxicated
- Lack of seatbelt use
- Reckless driving
- Steroid and other performance-enhancing drug use
- Smoking
- Unprotected sexual activity
- Interpersonal violence
- Mental health

History

The PPE begins with a thorough history. Questions should focus on a positive child or family history of certain medical conditions that can affect the child's sports participation, as well as current illnesses, infections, or conditions that would preclude sports participation. Preparticipation cardiovascular screening is especially important to determining the risk for sudden cardiac death. The family history is an essential portion of the cardiac history, as many of these conditions are inherited. When obtaining the PPE history, the provider must gather data on:

- Past medical history, including current medical history
- Surgical history
- Loss of function in one of any paired organs (e.g., eye, testis, kidney)
- History of heat-related illness
- Current prescribed or over-the-counter medications, supplements, or herbal therapy
- Immunization history
- Menstrual history in females
- History of rapid increase or decrease in body weight

Certain medical conditions may limit sports participation, depending on the diagnosis and type of sport in which the child desires to participate. The full list of medical conditions that limit sports participation can be found in the AAP Policy Statement on medical conditions affecting sports participation (AAP, 2008a).

Physical Examination

The physical examination for the PPE focuses on assessing the cardiovascular, respiratory, and musculoskeletal systems and the paired organs. The cardiovascular examination includes auscultation with a focus on provocative maneuvers to screen for hypertrophic cardiomyopathy. Other components of the physical examination include the 2-minute orthopedic screening examination, which involves 12 steps to evaluate musculoskeletal alignment, flexibility, and proprioception, all of which determine musculoskeletal abnormalities

and injury sequelae (Table 9.3). Additional portions of the PPE are listed in Table 9.4.

Laboratory and Diagnostic Examination

In the absence of identified risk factors or positive findings on the history, specific screening tests such as electrocardiography, treadmill stress testing, and urinalysis are not indicated (Hergenroeder, 2013). Menstruating females may need to be screened for iron-deficiency anemia.

SUMMARY

The well-child, health supervision visit presents an excellent opportunity for the pediatric health care provider to improve the health of children through developing meaningful relationships with the child and family while promoting health and wellness, identifying health issues early, and educating children and families in the context of a medical home.

TABLE 9.3	The 2-Minute Musculoskeletal Screening Examination
Instruction to athlete: Stand facing, then away from examiner, with arms at sides (Figure 9.1A, B). **Examination:** Examiner inspects symmetry of trunk and upper extremities. **Area evaluated:** Acromioclavicular joints; general habitus	 
Instruction to athlete: Look at ceiling and then the floor; look to the side and then touch ears to shoulders (Figure 9.2A–D). **Examination:** Examiner observes forward flexion, extension, rotation, and lateral flexion of the neck. **Area evaluated:** Cervical spine motion	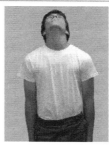 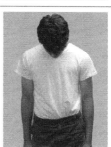  

(continued)

TABLE 9.3	The 2-Minute Musculoskeletal Screening Examination (*continued*)
Instruction to athlete: Shrug shoulders (Figure 9.3). **Examination:** Examiner's hands remain on athlete's shoulders to provide resistance while athlete shrugs shoulders. **Area evaluated:** Trapezius strength	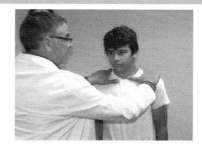
Instruction to athlete: Stretch both arms out at side 90 degrees, then lift arms a few inches (Figure 9.4). **Examination:** Examiner's hands are placed on top of athlete's forearms to resist shoulder abduction. **Area evaluated:** Deltoid strength	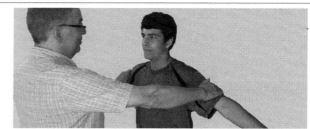
Instruction to athlete: Raise elbows at sides, 90 degrees, and rotate hands backward and forward (Figure 9.5A, B). **Examination:** Examiner observes internal and external rotation of the athlete's shoulders. **Area evaluated:** Range of motion in glenohumeral joint	
Instruction to athlete: Extend and flex elbow (Figure 9.6). **Examination:** Examiner observes elbow motion. **Area evaluated:** Range of motion in elbow	
Instruction to athlete: With arms at sides, flex elbows 90 degrees, and pronate and supinate palms (Figure 9.7A, B). **Examination:** Examiner observes elbow and wrist motion. **Area evaluated:** Range of motion in elbow and wrist	
Instruction to athlete: Clench fists then spread fingers apart (Figure 9.8A, B). **Examination:** Examiner observes hand and finger motion, strength, and deformities. **Area evaluated:** Range of motion in hands and fingers	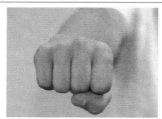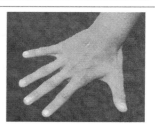

TABLE 9.3	The 2-Minute Musculoskeletal Screening Examination (*continued*)
Instruction to athlete: Stand with back to examiner; with knees straight, and touch toes (Figure 9.9). **Examination:** Examiner observes for thoracic curvature and shoulder and hip asymmetry. **Area evaluated:** Scoliosis, hip motion, and hamstring tightness	
Instruction to athlete: Stand facing examiner and tighten, then relax quadriceps (Figure 9.10). **Examination:** Examiner inspects lower extremities for alignment and symmetry. **Area evaluated:** Symmetry, knee effusions, and ankle effusions	
Instruction to athlete: "Duck walk" four steps away and toward examiner (Figure 9.11). **Examination:** Examiner observes strength and balance. **Area evaluated:** Range of motion in hip, knee, and ankle	
Instruction to athlete: Rise onto toes, then lean back on heels (Figure 9.12A, B). **Examination:** Examiner observes strength and balance. **Area evaluated:** Calf symmetry; leg strength	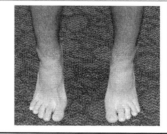 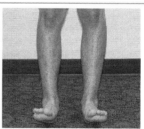

TABLE 9.4	Components of Preparticipation Physical Examination	
AREA OF EXAMINATION	**COMMENTS**	
Abdominal	Examiner palpates for hepatic or splenic enlargement.	
Anthropometry	Height and weight are measured and used to calculate body mass index (BMI). Obesity is a risk factor for heat illness but is not a reason for exclusion from sports. Low body weight may be a reason for restriction from participation, depending upon the degree of malnutrition	
Blood pressure	Results are compared to norm for child's age, height, and sex.	

(*continued*)

TABLE 9.4	Components of Preparticipation Physical Examination (*continued*)
AREA OF EXAMINATION	**COMMENTS**
Cardiovascular	Cardiac exam must include the following: • Measurement of blood pressure and resting pulse • Precordial auscultation in the supine and standing positions • Assessment of femoral pulses in the setting of hypertension or if concerned about coarctation of the aorta • Location of the point of maximal impulse (PMI) • Recognition of the physical stigmata of Marfan syndrome The PMI is palpated for increased intensity, suggesting hypertrophy and failure, respectively. With the patient supine and standing or straining during Valsalva's maneuver, patient is auscultated. A diminished femoral pulse suggests coarctation of the aorta.
Eyes	Vision defects that demonstrate at least one eye with > 20/40 corrected vision are assessed. Lens subluxations, severe myopia, retinal detachments, and strabismus are associated with Marfan syndrome.
General appearance	Excessive height and excessive long-bone growth (i.e., arachnodactyly, arm span more than height, pectus excavatum) suggest Marfan syndrome.
Genitourinary	The 2010 guidelines suggest that the athlete be asked if he or she would prefer to have a chaperone present for the genitourinary examination (AAFP et al., 2010). Examiner assesses for hernias, varicoceles, and testicular masses; these findings do not usually preclude sports participation, but teen should be aware of symptoms of hernia incarceration and complications of injury to testicles. A testicular mass needs a referral.
Musculoskeletal	Examiner conducts 2-minute orthopedic screening examination.
Respiratory	Accessory muscle use or prolonged expiration is inspected, and patient is auscultated for wheezing. Exercise-induced asthma requires exercise testing for diagnosis.
Skin	Examiner inspects for evidence of molluscum contagiosum, herpes simplex infection, impetigo, tinea corporis, or scabies, which would temporarily prohibit participation in sports where direct skin-to-skin contact occurs (e.g., wrestling, martial arts).

Source: Hergenroeder (2013).

Notable Clinical Findings

■ Child has no medical home
■ Child has not had recommended health supervision visits
■ Missing immunizations/immunization delays
■ Existence of risk factor(s) for child behavioral or mental health problems
■ Abnormal anthropometric measurements (see Chapter 8)
■ Abnormal findings on any of the following screenings:
  • Newborn screening
  • Hearing screening
  • Vision screening
  • Anemia screening
  • Lead screening
  • Tuberculosis screening
  • Dyslipidemia screening
  • Critical congenital heart disease screening

Notable clinical findings on preparticipation sports physical examination

■ Atlantoaxial instability
■ Bleeding disorder
■ Cardiovascular disease, including congenital heart disease, dysrhythmia, and murmur
■ Hypertension
■ Vasculitis/vascular disease
■ Cerebral palsy
■ Diabetes mellitus
■ Eating disorder
■ Loss of function of paired organ (eye, kidney, testicle, ovary)
■ Hepatitis C infection
■ HIV infection
■ Hepatomegaly
■ Malignancy
■ Musculoskeletal disorders
■ Neurologic disorders
■ Obesity
■ Pregnancy/postpartum
■ Respiratory conditions
■ Rheumatologic diseases
■ Sickle cell disease/trait
■ Skin infections
■ Splenomegaly (Rice, 2011)

References

American Academy of Family Physicians, American Academy of Pediatrics, American College of Sports Medicine, American Medical Society for Sports Medicine American Orthopaedic Society for Sports Medicine, & American Osteopathic Academy of Sports Medicine; Bernhardt, D., & Roberts, W. (Eds.). (2010). *Preparticipation physical evaluation* (4th ed.). Elk Grove Village, IL: American Academy of Pediatrics.

American Academy of Pediatric Dentistry Council on Clinical Affairs. (2013). *Guideline on periodicity of examination, preventive dental services, anticipatory guidance/counseling and oral treatment for infants, children and adolescents.* Retrieved from http://www.aapd.org/media/Policies_Guidelines/G_Periodicity.pdf

American Academy of Pediatrics. (2008a). Clinical report: Medical conditions affecting sports participation. *Pediatrics, 121*(4), 841–848; reaffirmation of policy: (2011) *Pediatrics, 129*(4), e1103.

American Academy of Pediatrics. (2008b). Statement of reaffirmation: The medical home. *Pediatrics, 122*(2), 450.

American Academy of Pediatrics. (2011). Policy statement: Recommendations for preventive pediatric health care. Reaffirmation of policy: (2011) *Pediatrics, 120*(6), 1376.

American Academy of Pediatrics. (2014). *AAP updates schedule of screening and assessments for well-child visits.* Retrieved from http://www.aap.org/en-us/about-the-aap/aap-press-room/pages/AAP-Updates-Schedule-of-Screening-and-Assessments-for-Well-Child-Visits.aspx#sthash.TrxxnnUR.dpuf

American Academy of Pediatrics Committee on Environmental Health. (2009). Screening for elevated blood lead levels. *Pediatrics, 116*(4), 1036–1046.

American Academy of Pediatrics Committee on Practice and Ambulatory Medicine, Section on Ophthalmology, American Association of Certified Orthoptists, American Association for Pediatric Ophthalmology and Strabismus and American Academy of Ophthalmology. (2007). Statement of reaffirmation: Eye examination in infants, children, and young adults by pediatricians. *Pediatrics, 120*(3), 683–684.

American Academy of Pediatrics Committee on Psychosocial Aspects of Child and Family Health. (2001). The new morbidity revisited: A renewed commitment to the psychosocial aspects of pediatric care. *Pediatrics, 108*(5), 1227–1230.

American Academy of Pediatrics Joint Committee on Infant Hearing. (2007). Year 2007 position statement: Principles and guidelines for early hearing detection and intervention programs. *Pediatrics, 120*(4), 898–921.

Bethell, C. D., Kogan, M. D., Strickland, B. B., Schor, E. L., Robertson, J., & Newacheck, P. W. (2011). A national and state profile of leading health problems and health care quality for US children: Key insurance disparities and across-state variations. *Academic Pediatrics, 11*(3), S22–S33.

Centers for Disease Control and Prevention. (2010). *Sexually transmitted diseases treatment guidelines,* 2010. Retrieved from http://www.cdc.gov/std/treatment/2010/toc.htm

Centers for Disease Control and Prevention. (2012). *Tuberculosis: Children.* Retrieved from http://www.cdc.gov/tb/topic/populations/TBinChildren/default.htm

Centers for Disease Control and Prevention. (2013a). *Lead.* Retrieved from http://www.cdc.gov/nceh/Lead/

Centers for Disease Control and Prevention. (2013b). *Newborn screening.* Retrieved from http://www.cdc.gov/ncbddd/pediatricgenetics/newborn_screening.html

Centers for Disease Control and Prevention. (2013c). *Tuberculosis: Testing.* Retrieved from http://www.cdc.gov/tb/topic/testing/default.htm

Centers for Disease Control and Prevention. (2014). *Autism spectrum disorder: Screening and diagnosis.* Retrieved from http://www.cdc.gov/ncbddd/autism/screening.html

Earls, M. F., & the Committee on Psychosocial Aspects of Child and Family Health American Academy of Pediatrics. (2010). Incorporating recognition and management of perinatal and postpartum depression into pediatric practice. *Pediatrics, 126*(5), 1032–1039.

Governo, M. M., & Siewers, M. H. (2008). Childhood bullying. *Advance for Nurses, 6*(8), 33–36.

Hagan, J. F., Shaw, J. S., & Duncan, P. M. (Eds.). (2008). *Bright futures: Guidelines for health supervision of infants, children and adolescents* (3rd ed.). Elk Grove Village, IL: American Academy of Pediatrics.

Harper, J. L., & Conrad, M. E. (2013). *Iron deficiency anemia.* Retrieved from http://emedicine.medscape.com/article/202333-overview

Hergenroeder, A. C. (2013). *The preparticipation sports examination in children and adolescents.* Retrieved from http://www.uptodate.com/contents/the-preparticipation-sports-examination-in-children-and-adolescents#H12

Kelly, S. E., Binkley, C. J., Neace, W. P., & Gale, B. S. (2005). Barriers to care-seeking for children's oral health among low-income caregivers. *American Journal of Public Health, 95*(8), 1345–1351.

Levy, S. J. L., Kokotailo, P. K., & the American Academy of Pediatrics Committee on Substance Abuse. (2011). Substance use screening, brief intervention, and referral to treatment for pediatricians. *Pediatrics, 128*, e1330–e1340.

Lindeke, L., & Jukkala, A. (2005). Rural NP practice barriers and strategies: One state's story. *American Journal for Nurse Practitioners,* (9), 11–18.

Mullin, K., & Ambrosia, T. (2005). Role of the nurse practitioner in providing health care for the homeless. *American Journal for Nurse Practitioners,* (9), 37–44.

National Heart, Blood and Lung Institute. (2013). *Integrated guidelines for cardiovascular health and risk reduction in children and adolescents.* Retrieved from http://www.nhlbi.nih.gov/guidelines/cvd_ped/index.htm

National High Blood Pressure Education Program Working Group on High Blood Pressure in Children and Adolescents. (2004). The fourth report on the diagnosis, evaluation and treatment of high blood pressure in children and adolescents. *Pediatrics, 114*(2), 555–576.

Reitman, D. S. (2007). "HEADDS" up on talking with teenagers. *Consultant for Pediatricians, 9*(6), 525–526; 529–530.

Schor, E. (2004). Rethinking well-child care. *Pediatrics, 114*(1), 210–216.

U. S. Department of Health and Human Services. (2013). Healthy People 2020. Access to health care services. Retrieved from http://www.healthypeople.gov/2020/topicsobjectives2020/overview.aspx?topicid=1

Additional Resources

The following are suggested resources, some of which include evidence-based health screening guidelines with the goal of prevention, early identification, and health promotion for infants, children, and adolescents.

Agency for Healthcare Research and Quality

http://www.ahcpr.gov
Provides evidence-based clinical practice guidelines for both disease management and preventive services; it includes the *Guide to Clinical Preventive Services* (2012), which is the U.S. Preventive Services Task Force (USPSTF) recommendations on health screening, counseling, and prevention.

American Academy of Pediatrics (AAP)

http://www.aap.org

American Academy of Pediatrics Recommendations for Preventive Pediatric Health Care (Well Child Care Periodicity Schedule)

http://www.aap.org/en-us/professional-resources/practice-support/Periodicity/Periodicity%20Schedule_FINAL.pdf

Bright Futures: Guidelines for Health Supervision of Infants, Children and Adolescents (3rd ed.)

http://www.brightfutures.aap.org

A program of the AAP; the goal is to promote health and wellness in children through theory and evidence-based health supervision guidelines. A comprehensive guide, now in its third edition, outlines the current recommendations for well-child, health supervision standards. Bright Futures also provides educational tools to assist pediatric health care providers in fine-tuning their clinical skills for the health supervision visit.

Centers for Disease Control and Prevention

http://www.cdc.gov

For current immunization schedule: http://http://www.cdc.gov/vaccines. Site also has health statistics on lead poisoning, tuberculosis, and sexually transmitted infections.

Healthy People 2020

http://www.healthypeople.gov

A set of health objectives supported by the U.S. Department of Health and Human Services, the goal of which is to improve the quality and length of life in the United States and to eliminate health disparities.

National Association of Pediatric Nurse Practitioners (NAPNAP)

http://www.napnap.org

Professional membership association for pediatric nurse practitioners; the goal is to provide optimal health care to children through research, scholarship, and practice. Position statements relative to pediatric health supervision and wellness care include (all available online):

- Access to Care
- Age Parameters for Pediatric Nurse Practitioner Practice
- Breastfeeding
- Immunizations
- Integration of Mental Health Care in Pediatric Primary Care Settings
- Pediatric Health Care Home
- Prevention of Tobacco Use in the Pediatric Population
- Prevention of Unintentional Injuries in Children
- School-Based Health Care
- Supporting Infant and Family Well-Being in the First Year of Life
- Supporting Grandparents Raising Grandchildren

National Center of Medical Home Initiatives for Children with Special Needs

http://www.medicalhome.org

Devoted to pediatric medical home principles and resources.

Pediatrics in Practice

http://www.pediatricsinpractice.org

A *Bright Futures*–based health promotion curriculum designed to help pediatric health care providers enhance their health promotion skills in the areas of health, child and family partnership, family-centered communication, health promotion, time management in clinical practice, education, advocacy, and cultural competency.

Pedicases

http://www.pedicases.org

A website affiliated with *Bright Futures* composed of 30 case studies that simulate situations the pediatric health care provider may encounter during health supervision visits. The focus is on health promotion, disease prevention, behavior, growth, and development and adolescent health.

Assessment of Nutritional Status

The assessment of nutrition in children encompasses a wide array of data that can affect their health, self-esteem, academic performance, and long-term health. A thorough assessment of a child's nutritional status helps the provider make accurate diagnoses, deliver appropriate anticipatory guidance, and recommend appropriate nutrition services as necessary.

ASSESSMENT OF PEDIATRIC NUTRITIONAL STATUS

Pediatric nutritional assessment begins with obtaining an age-appropriate history. The nutritional assessment data for each age group varies greatly, according to the child's physical and cognitive capabilities, food preferences, family, culture, and socioeconomic status. Nutritional assessment data are typically obtained from the parent or other primary caregiver. Depending on the age and reliability, the child may also be able to provide information used in nutrition screening.

HISTORY

Prenatal and Birth History

The prenatal and birth history is especially relevant when assessing children aged 3 years and younger. It is important to note the nutritional status of the mother during pregnancy. For example, a mother who is severely anemic will not have enough iron stores, and her infant may be anemic. Any hypoxic events are important to note; these can later affect mobility, predisposing the child to overweight or obesity. A history of prematurity can predispose the child to underweight or failure to thrive. Any chromosomal abnormalities must be noted as well; some of these conditions affect growth adversely.

Past Medical History

The provider should also inquire about past hospitalizations or injuries that may be the cause or result of any nutritional concerns. Examples include any history of overweight or obesity, cardiac problems, diabetes, endocrine or metabolic problems, neurologic diagnoses that impair mobility and thus affect weight, and gastrointestinal or renal problems.

Medications

The provider should inquire about any prescribed, over-the-counter or herbal medications the child is taking, and include the dose and indication. Any weight-loss medications, vitamins, supplements, drugs that cause change in weight (e.g., corticosteroids), stimulants, or other relevant agents should be noted.

Family History

Any family history of obesity, diabetes, hypertension, hyperlipidemia, heart disease, allergies, or stroke should be noted.

Social History

The pediatric nutritional history also includes assessment of the child's social history. Family unemployment, inadequate housing, or lack of health insurance often contribute to nutritional deficits in children (Hagan, Shaw, & Duncan, 2008). Poverty and homelessness also increase a child's risk for poor nutrition due to lack of access to fresh, affordable food. For this reason, these children are often overweight or obese, despite the fact that they may consume *less* food. This is caused by food insecurity and the availability of low-cost, satiating high-calorie prepared foods and snacks, which results in the child consuming more calories than he or she needs for growth. Living in an old building with chipping or peeling paint predisposes a child to lead poisoning, which leads to iron-deficiency anemia.

Review of Systems

A thorough, detailed review of systems involves determining whether the child has been diagnosed with an acute or chronic illness or condition that can have an impact on his or her nutritional status. For example, some medical conditions may interfere with normal food intake. Examples include cancer and its treatment, cerebral palsy, autism, congenital heart diseases, or cleft palate. Any problem that involves the ability to chew and swallow foods properly, and appetite changes, should be examined closely. Cystic fibrosis, inflammatory bowel diseases, celiac disease, or draining abscesses contribute to nutrient losses. Any problems with vomiting, diarrhea, flatulence, and indigestion may interfere with the adequacy of nutrients. Increased nutrient needs can result from fever, infection, burns, cancer, or recent surgical procedures (Haemer, Primak, & Krebs, 2012).

A thorough review of systems should include:

- **General:** Alteration in growth patterns, weight less than the 5th percentile or greater than the 85th percentile on the National Center for Health Statistics (NCHS) growth charts, short stature, increased height, or asymmetrical growth; body temperature
- **Integument:** Poor turgor, poor condition of hair (lack of shine due to poor nutrition, seen in eating disorders), acanthosis nigricans (indicates insulin resistance), pallor (may indicate anemia), petechiae, purpura (related to oncologic etiology), callouses on knuckles from induced vomiting (Russell's sign), dermatitis (micronutrient deficiencies)
- **Head/Face/Neck:** Swollen parotid glands (may be sign of bulimia nervosa), palpable goiter
- **Eyes:** Poor vision, blurred vision, xerosis (vitamin A deficiency)
- **Oral:** Condition of teeth (caries, poor enamel due to induced vomiting), mucosa, lips, tongue; dry mouth
- **Cardiovascular:** Congenital heart disease (results in low weight), murmur (may indicate anemia)
- **Respiratory:** Asthma, allergic rhinitis (may accompany food allergies), cystic fibrosis
- **Gastrointestinal:** Chronic diarrhea, constipation, Crohn's disease, celiac disease, hepatic disease
- **Genitourinary:** Tanner staging, precocious or delayed puberty, amenorrhea
- **Endocrine/Metabolic:** Neonatal hypoglycemia, diabetes, hypothyroidism, hyperthyroidism, glycogen storage diseases, inborn errors of metabolism, growth hormone deficiency, polycystic ovary syndrome, metabolic syndrome, or congenital adrenal hyperplasia
- **Hematologic/Immunity:** Cancers, anemia, or allergies
- **Musculoskeletal:** Spasticity of extremities; difficulty with balance, coordination; poor muscle strength; cerebral palsy, paralysis, or tetany (hypocalcemia)
- **Neurologic:** Disorders that affect mobility, myelomeningocele, cerebral palsy, Duchenne muscular dystrophy, head trauma, chronic fatigue, attention deficit hyperactivity disorder
- **Psychosocial:** Drug or alcohol addiction, stress, emotional lability, irritability, breath-holding spells, behavior disorders, eating disorders, anxiety, depression, history of suicidal ideation

Current Nutritional History

Food and eating provide people not only with nutrients to foster normal growth and protect against some diseases, but also with a pleasurable aspect of life that allows them to express caring, culture, creativity, and personal preferences. Behaviors associated with eating are integral to daily routines, family connections, social interactions, celebrations, and even solace. For these reasons, assessment of nutritional status is incomplete without consideration of dietary patterns. This includes details about types of foods, preparation methods, amounts, and the patterns of meals and snacks. Cultural patterns, religious observations, socioeconomic influences or other lifestyle practices are important factors that influence dietary quality and nutrient intake (Kittler, Sucher, & Nelms, 2012).

Whenever assessing dietary intake, it is important to remember that these data are subjective and prone to error and bias because of memory lapse; lack of knowledge about food composition, preparation methods, or portions; and social desirability. For example, an overweight 14-year-old girl, when asked about the meatloaf that she ate for lunch, may honestly not know whether it was made from beef, pork, turkey, or soy. In addition, she may neglect to mention that she ate it with gravy, although she may have been told to avoid gravies to reduce caloric intake. Perhaps she experienced negative feedback from a previous health care provider as a result of reporting intake of high-calorie foods. However fraught with error, insight into dietary patterns assists in the analysis of suspected nutrient deficits, the need for anticipatory guidelines to prevent nutrition problems, and the response to nutrition interventions.

Assessment of food and nutrient intake is often framed within a "diet history," which combines several components, depending on the health care setting, specific medical conditions, or age of the child. A complete pediatric nutritional history consists of the following:

- Dietary history and eating patterns, appropriate to age
- Typical mealtime
- Child's food preferences and attitude toward food
- Primary caregiver's knowledge of age-appropriate nutrition and daily physical activity requirements
- Food allergies
- Elimination patterns
- Dental health
- Physical activity

Nutritional History by Age

For pediatric populations, the nutrition history must be geared to the age of the child or the medical condition. For all ages, assessment must include questions about food allergies, aversions, or intolerances; a history of dietary restrictions for medical, cultural, or other reasons; a history of weight changes; and vitamin, mineral, or dietary supplement use (Hagan et al., 2008). In addition, general questions should provide some idea about the household dynamics related to food shopping and preparation, family meal times, resources for the household food, and participation in food programs (e.g., Women, Infants, and Children [WIC], National School Lunch program).

Infants

In infants, a feeding history from birth should be completed with quantity, quality, and composition of daily feeding episodes; number of wet diapers; stool patterns; and some description of the feeding relationship with parents or caregivers (Hagan et al., 2008a). As the infant makes the transition to solid foods, dietary intake assessment should include feeding skills such as chewing, hand-to-mouth movement, weaning from bottle to cup, and the incorporation of a broad range of appropriate foods. Patterns of sleep and activity should also be noted.

Whenever possible, observation of parent–infant interaction should be included in the nutritional assessment. This interaction should be affectionate and comfortable (Hagan et al., 2008a). When considering dietary patterns for infants, deviation from the key concepts may indicate the need for further evaluation or intervention.

Breastfeeding is the recommended source of nutrients for infants, unless there is a contraindication. Developmentally, it is usual for breastfed infants to locate the mother's breast, attach to the nipple, and nurse. During the first week, breastfed infants should be eating 8 to 12 times daily with five or more wet diapers and three to four stools daily (Hagan et al., 2008a). Ideally, infants should receive only breast milk for the first 6 months, and breastfeeding should continue until at least 12 months of age, or whenever the mother and infant no longer wish to continue. The mother should be encouraged to seek breastfeeding support if needed. Breastfeeding should occur in a relaxed space with about 20 to 45 minutes devoted to each session. The infant should complete eating at one breast and then be moved to the other. Turning the head from the nipple, closing the mouth, or becoming interested in other activities in the room are signs that the infant is full and finished eating. Infants younger than 4 weeks should not be allowed to sleep for more than 4 hours without feeding (Hagan et al., 2008a).

For formula-fed infants, formula should be prepared according to manufacturer's directions. Formula prepared for more than 24 hours and stored in the refrigerator should be discarded. Ready-to-feed or concentrated formulas that have been in the refrigerator more than 48 hours should be discarded (Hagan et al., 2008a). Formula should not be heated by microwave, as overheating is common, which may burn the infant. A safe water supply is essential for formula feeding.

Infants younger than age 1 year should receive only breast milk or iron-fortified infant formula. Cow, goat, or soy milk should not be used before the first birthday, even mixed in cereals. Reduced-fat milk should not be given until the infant is 2 years or older. Infants can be offered juice in a cup after 6 months with a daily limit of 4 to 6 ounces (Hagan et al., 2008a). Honey, even in processed foods, should not be given to infants because honey can be a source of spores that cause botulism toxicity (Kleinman & Greer, 2013). Care should be taken to prevent choking as more foods are added to the infant's diet. Hard candy, grapes, hot dogs, marshmallows, peanut butter, raw carrots, or raisins should never be given to infants or children younger than 3 years of age (Hagan et al., 2008). Parents and caregivers should always observe infants and children during eating to avoid choking episodes. In addition, infants should not be fed in the car.

It is expected that infants will initially lose about 6% of their birth weight but regain this weight within the first 10 to 14 days. By 6 months of age, infants should double their birth weight, and by 1 year, they should triple it (Hagan et al., 2008a). On average, infants are expected to gain about 5 to 7 ounces a week until they are 4 to 6 months of age (Hagan et al., 2008a). This high-growth velocity slows down to about 3 to 5 ounces a week from 6 to 18 months of age. Length should increase by about 50% in the first year. On average, infants should gain about 1 inch a month in the first 6 months (Hagan et al., 2008a). This growth declines to an average increase of about ½ inch per month from 6 to 12 months. During the first 6 months, when growth velocity is high, energy needs are about 108 kcal/kg/d (Hagan et al., 2008a). With a decline in growth in the second half of the first year, energy needs are decreased to 100 kcal/kg/d on average (Hagan et al., 2008a). Low birth weight and preterm infants younger than 6 months should be evaluated for the need for iron supplements if they are not breastfed or are receiving iron-fortified formula, as they were born with lower iron stores (Garcia-Prats, 2013).

By 4 to 6 months, infants generally show signs of developmental readiness for the introduction of other foods. Parents and caregivers should note which foods are introduced and report this during health care visits. Signs of developmental readiness include coordinated swallowing (more than reflexive sucking), cooperation during feeding, sitting with support, and good control of the head and neck (Hagan et al., 2008a). The infant must be ready to progress with transitional feeding. Choking risk is increased in infants who are not developmentally ready. During this period, infants continue to consume breast milk or formula, in addition to foods with modified consistency that are added to the diet. Initially, an infant cereal without sugar or salt is offered. One single food at a time is added so that tolerance can be monitored to identify any food allergies or intolerances. At 7-day intervals, another food is incorporated into the diet. Generally, infant cereals, vegetables, and fruits are the first food groups included. Pureed or finely chopped meats are added within a couple of months. All foods are modified for consistency as tolerated by the infant. Meal patterns include five or six small meals plus breast milk or formula.

By 6 to 12 months, infants should be chewing in a more coordinated fashion, manipulating food with their fingers, drinking from a cup, starting to use utensils, attempting to feed themselves, and erupting teeth. To ensure an adequate iron supply, any formula and cereals should be iron-fortified. Breastfeeding should continue. Vitamin C food sources should be included to enhance iron absorption (Hagan et al., 2008a).

At 9 months, infants should be offered soft, moist foods such as pasta with sauce, meatloaf, soft cooked vegetables, fruit, and soft cheeses, following the same eating schedule as the rest of the family. In addition, iron deficiency screening should be completed on infants who were preterm or low birth weight; had been fed a non-iron-fortified formula for more than 2 months; had been fed cow's milk before 12 months; consumed more than 24 ounces of cow's milk daily; are from a low income, migrant, or refugee family; or are a participant of the WIC Special Supplement Feeding Program (Janus & Moerschel, 2010). In addition, any infant with medical problems, such as

---

BOX 10.1 Interview Questions for Parents of Infants (Newborn to 4 Months of Age)

How do you think feeding is going?
Do you have any questions about breastfeeding or formula feeding your child?
How does your infant let you know that he or she is hungry?
How do you know when he or she has had enough?
Do you burp the baby?
How often does your infant eat?
Have you noticed any changes in eating?
How do you feel about the way your infant is growing?
Are you concerned about having enough money to buy food or formula?
What is the source of water for drinking or cooking?
What infant formula do you use?

Source: Hagan, Shaw, and Duncan (2008c).

BOX 10.2 Interview Questions for Mothers of Breastfed Infants

Do you need help with breastfeeding?
Do you have any concerns about feeding your infant?
Does your infant attach to your breast and suck well?
Do you hear him or her swallowing when breastfeeding?
Have you had any problems with your breasts or nipples?
Do you restrict any foods in your diet?
Do you drink any wine, beer, or other alcohol?
Do you use any drugs?
Do you know your HIV status?
Are you planning to return to work or school? If so, will you express milk?
How do you plan to store your breast milk after expressing it?

Source: Hagan, Shaw, and Duncan (2008a).

---

chronic infections or inflammatory disorders, should be screened for anemia.

To reduce the risk of dental caries, prolonged and frequent bottle-feeding with high-carbohydrate–containing liquids should be avoided. Infants should not be put to bed with a bottle that contains carbohydrates. After 6 months, the infant should be receiving water from a fluoridated source (at 0.3 ppm), or fluoride supplements should be considered to reduce the risk of dental caries (Hagan et al., 2008). By 12 to 14 months, infants should be weaned from a bottle and drinking from a cup. Boxes 10.1 through 10.4 summarize the pertinent questions to ask when gathering the nutritional history in an infant, from birth to age 1 year.

BOX 10.3 Interview Questions for Parents of Formula-Fed Infants

What type of infant formula do you use?
Is the formula iron-fortified?
How do you prepare the formula?
How do you store the formula after preparation?
How do you clean the nipples, bottles, and other equipment used to mix the formula?
Do you dispose of any formula left in the baby's bottle after a feeding?

Source: Hagan, Shaw, and Duncan (2008a).

> ### BOX 10.4 Interview Questions for Parents of Infants (4–12 Months of Age)
>
> Have you given your baby any food besides breast milk or formula?
>
> If so, what has he or she eaten? Has there ever been a reaction (e.g., rash or hives)?
>
> Does your baby seem interested in food?
>
> Who else feeds the infant besides parents?
>
> Does the infant have teeth yet? How many? Do you clean them? How?
>
> Can the infant feed herself or himself any food? If so, what food?
>
> Does the infant use his or her fingers, spoon, bottle, or cup?
>
> Does the infant put any nonfoods in his or her mouth?
>
> Has your baby tried to drink from a cup? Was she or he successful?
>
> Has your baby ever choked or gagged on food?
>
> How do you prepare any solid food that you give to your baby?
>
> Source: Hagan, Shaw, and Duncan (2008a, 2008b).

Young Children (Ages 2–5 Years)

Parents or caregivers should continue to add new foods to the diet of young children. Developmentally, children from 12 to 18 months of age can grasp and release foods with their fingers, hold a spoon and cup, and want foods that others are eating. Children who are 2 to 3 years old can hold a cup, chew foods better than a 1-year-old child, and express their food likes and dislikes (Hagan et al., 2008b). By age 4 years, children can use a fork, hold a cup by the handle, pour liquids from small containers, request favorite foods, and begin to be influenced by media sources, including television and advertisements (Christakis & Zimmerman, 2007). Between the ages of 4 and 5, children begin to cut their food with a knife and fork, are more adept at drinking from a cup, continue to be influenced by media messages directed at food choices, and may be interested in food preparation (Hagan et al., 2008b).

Fat should not be restricted in the diets of children younger than 2 years old. After 2 years, the diet can be slowly changed to incorporate more whole grains, fruits, vegetables, low-fat dairy products, and lean meats. The dietary pattern should include three meals and three snacks a day. Parents' responsibilities should include purchasing and preparing healthy foods that are developmentally appropriate for meals and snacks, providing appropriate utensils, and establishing regular eating periods during the day (Hagan et al., 2008b). Young children need to eat every 2 to 3 hours during waking periods. Children who are 2 to 3 years old should eat

the same number of servings shown on MyPlate as older children, although the portion is about two-thirds of the suggested portion (U.S. Department of Agriculture [USDA], 2014). By age 4, the serving sizes are similar.

Choking precautions should be maintained for young children, including staying with the child during meals and snacks, making sure the child is seated when eating, and avoiding the foods listed previously. When the child is older than 3, some of this food is modified to make it safer by cutting or chopping. There should be no eating in the car.

Juice should be limited to 4 to 6 ounces a day to prevent dental caries and to discourage children from filling up on juice at the expense of more nutrient-dense foods such as fruits, vegetables, whole grains, and low-fat dairy. Optimal dietary patterns in this age group also include appropriate parental use of food. For example, food should not be used as a reward, bribe, punishment, pacifier, or entertainment. Use of food for these purposes may encourage overeating and rejection of healthy foods (Hagan et al., 2008b). Box 10.5 summarizes the pertinent questions to ask when gathering the nutritional history in a child, aged 2 to 5 years.

School-Aged Children (Ages 5–10 Years)

When conducting a nutritional assessment on a school-aged child, the foods provided by childcare providers and schools need to be considered for children who attend these programs. Young children who are out of the home from early morning through late afternoon are likely to receive two meals and two snacks; thus, more than 60% of their nutrient intake is taken from nonfamily members. Children in these situations are very

> ### BOX 10.5 Interview Questions for Parents of Young Children (2–5 Years of Age)
>
> Do you have any concerns about your child's eating or growth?
>
> What do you do if your child does not like a particular food?
>
> Do you have the appropriate equipment for feeding him or her (e.g., highchair, booster)?
>
> Do you have any concerns about food served away from home?
>
> What is your child's eating pattern or routine?
>
> How much juice does he or she drink each day?
>
> Is your child still using a bottle?
>
> Does your child eat meals with the family?
>
> Has your child ever choked or gagged on food?
>
> How do you prepare any solid food that you give to your child?
>
> What do your child's snacks consist of?
>
> Source: Hagan, Shaw, and Duncan (2008b).

dependent on childcare providers, whether home-based or agency-based, for dietary quality. The same is true for school-aged children who may receive both breakfast and lunch at school. In addition, snacks offered informally from teachers or as part of social events provide sources of energy and nutrients for this group.

School-aged children should eat the minimum number of servings from each food group as outlined in the MyPlate guidelines (USDA, 2014). Regular consumption of nutrient-dense foods should be assessed, and frequent intake of high-sugar and high-fat foods (e.g., sugar-sweetened beverages, butter, salad dressing, candy, cookies, chips) should be discouraged (Hagan et al., 2008c). Breakfast is a good meal at which to begin the intake of high-quality foods and should be a regular habit. In an effort to prevent overweight, parents and caregivers should be role models for optimal dietary patterns. "Screen time" should be limited to 2 hours daily to minimize media suggestions related to unhealthy food choices and to encourage more active use of leisure time (American Academy of Pediatrics [AAP] Committee on Communications, 2001; Christakis & Zimmerman, 2007). Extreme measures, such as weight-loss diets and forbidding certain foods, are not advised for this age group (Hagan et al., 2008c). Box 10.6 summarizes the pertinent questions to ask when gathering the nutritional history on a school-aged child.

BOX 10.6 Interview Questions for School-Aged Children (5–10 Years of Age)

For the Child:

Where did you eat yesterday? At school? At home? At a friend's house?

What do you usually eat or drink in the morning? Around noon? Afternoon? Evening?

Did you drink any milk yesterday?

Do you eat breakfast at home or at school? What do you usually have for breakfast?

How many times did you eat fruits or vegetables yesterday?

What do you usually eat for snacks?

How much juice/soda pop do you drink?

For the Parent:

Do you think your child eats healthy foods?

Does your child eat breakfast every day?

What does your child eat for snacks? Where does she or he eat them?

Do you have any concerns about your child's eating and growing?

How often/how much juice/soda pop does your child drink?

Is there a television in the kitchen or room where you eat meals?

Source: Hagan, Shaw, and Duncan (2008c).

Adolescents (Ages 11–19 Years)

Adolescence is characterized by increasing independence and less reliance on the family; peer influences grow. At the same time, the adolescent experiences growth spurts that require nutrient-dense diets (Hagan et al., 2008d). Adolescent diets have been noted to be lacking in folate, vitamin A, iron, calcium, and zinc, which results from inadequate intake of fruits, vegetables, and dairy products (Hagan et al., 2008d). Adolescent young men and physically active young women require the maximum suggested servings from the MyPlate guideline (Hagan et al., 2008d; USDA, 2014). Low-fat dairy products should be emphasized to maximize bone density, and lean protein sources should be encouraged for adequate iron intake.

The prevalence of overweight adolescents, especially among minority youth, has quadrupled in the United States in the last three decades (Ogden, Carroll, Kit, & Flegal, 2014). In addition, there is a growing concern that lifestyle practices are increasingly contributing to morbidity and mortality. Considering the long latency period between intermediate factors (such as obesity and physical inactivity) with chronic diseases (such as diabetes mellitus and coronary heart disease), the rise in the number of overweight adolescents is an ongoing concern. In addition, when adolescents are overweight, they are likely to engage in unsafe weight-loss strategies (Rosenbaum, 2007). These factors make weight status and related practices important indicators for assessment during adolescence.

Disordered eating patterns are estimated to affect 1% to 2% of adolescent girls (Hagan et al., 2008). Criteria for anorexia nervosa include refusal to maintain a desirable body weight, excessive fear of gaining weight, and a distorted perception of body shape or weight (American Psychiatric Association [APA], 2013). Criteria for bulimia nervosa include recurrent binge eating characterized by the consumption of large amounts of food in private, lack of control when eating, and recurrent inappropriate methods to prevent weight gain from binge episodes (such as vomiting or laxative abuse) (Wilkes & Spratt, 2014). If an eating disorder is suspected, a comprehensive evaluation by an interdisciplinary team with expertise in this area should be completed. Eating disorders are serious conditions that have negative implications for nutritional status and overall health. Box 10.7 summarizes the pertinent questions to ask when gathering the nutritional history on an adolescent patient.

Dental Health

Assessment of the condition of a child's teeth is another essential component of the nutritional history. Numerous dental caries may indicate high sugar intake or bottle propping; changes in the enamel of the front teeth is a sign of frequent vomiting, which occurs with bulimia nervosa. Deciduous teeth that vary in color from pale white to fully white may indicate a

BOX 10.7 Interview Questions for Adolescents (11–20 Years of Age)

For the Adolescent:

What meals do you usually eat each day? How many snacks? What type of snacks?

How often do you skip meals?

What do you usually eat or drink in the morning? Around noon? Afternoon? Evening?

Did you drink any milk yesterday?

How many times did you eat fruits or vegetables yesterday?

Are there any foods you will not eat? If so, which ones?

How much soda do you drink each day? What type?

What changes would you like to make in your eating habits?

How often do you eat at a restaurant? What type of restaurant?

Are you happy with your weight?

For the Parent:

Do you think your child eats healthy foods?

How often does your family eat meals together?

Do you have any concerns about your child's eating and growing?

How often does your child eat fast food?

Is there a television in the kitchen or in the room where you eat meals?

Source: Hagan, Shaw, and Duncan (2008d).

---

lack of full calcification while in utero; these children should be assessed for other nutritional deficiencies. See Chapter 16 for further information on dental assessment in children.

Physical Activity

No pediatric nutritional assessment is complete without evaluating the child's daily physical activity. The AAP recommends that once a child is fully ambulatory, he or she should be physically active for at least 1 hour per day, and TV or computer screen time should be limited to no more than 2 hours per day (AAP Committee on Communications, 2001). This assessment should be included for all children aged 2 years and older

Other Methods of Obtaining the Dietary History

When conducting more specific, in-depth nutrition assessments, other methods may be required that are more detailed than the brief screening questions used in the context of the well-child visit. Some examples of these are the 24-hour dietary recall, food diaries, and food questionnaires.

Twenty-Four-Hour Recall

This retrospective method asks the patient to recall, usually verbally, all foods and beverages consumed in the previous 24-hour period. The child, teen, or parent typically recites the dietary intake in chronologic order while the interviewer records this information either by hand or with the aid of a nutrient analysis software program. Reviewing the food list several times with prompts by the interviewer usually elicits details related to quantity, brand name, cooking methods, or condiments, which are often missed. Strategies to improve completeness of the dietary recall include visual cues, using measuring cups or food models for portion estimates, or mentally rehearsing daily events to improve memory of food intake.

No matter how accurate a 24-hour recall may be, it may not reflect the child's usual intake because of the day-to-day variability of children's meals. A large number of 24-hour recall histories represent the eating patterns of a certain age group when aggregated and nutrient intake is averaged, but for any individual, interpretation of one 24-hour recall should be done with an understanding of the above limitations. In young pediatric patients, a 24-hour recall is often completed with input from the parent or other significant caregiver only, which leads to additional limitations in lack of knowledge about foods served if the child regularly consumes meals away from home.

Food Records or Diaries

An alternative method to the 24-hour dietary recall is to ask the child, parent, or caregiver to write down all foods and beverages consumed over a period of days. This method is has value in that there is less error because of omission and improved representation of food intake if both weekend and weekdays are included. Limitations include the need for a literate child (or parent) who is willing to devote time to this activity, and the possibility that the process of keeping a food diary may itself alter food intake. In theory, food records that are longer (7 compared to 3 days) may be more complete. However, these longer food records often become less complete as the recorder becomes less interested in the task (Samour & King, 2012). Food records provide the health care provider with more insight into food patterns and meal cycles. In addition, this method is often used for self-assessment in monitoring behavioral change over time. The most accurate food records are preceded by a training session with both the child and parents or caregivers so that details about brand name, label descriptors, food preparation, or composition are complete and accurate.

Food Frequency Questionnaires

Food frequency questionnaires (FFQs) can be included in a diet history as a method of evaluating intake by food group. The format of a FFQ is generally similar to a checklist; it includes a listing of food groups, sometimes subdivided, and asks how many servings a day, week, or month are consumed by the patient. This format may reveal the intake of specific food groups that were not identified on the 24-hour recall or recorded in food diaries. For example, yogurt intake may have been absent from a 24-hour recall, but a FFQ may indicate that the child consumes yogurt four times a week, which would increase his or her calcium intake for purposes of the nutritional assessment.

Detailed FFQs have been developed with a focus on certain nutrients, such as calcium or fat. Others provide a general checklist of food-group intake. FFQs do not require as much time to complete as diet records, and they can be completed without an interviewer. However, they may require cognitive restructuring of food groups, and they do not yield a qualitative description of meal patterns; for example, a portion of the questionnaire asks the person to estimate how many times a week or month berries are consumed. This requires the person to think about his or her intake of strawberries, blueberries, blackberries, or raspberries over a 12-month period. Most people consume these more frequently in summer months than winter months, making a value representative of the entire year complex. Comparisons of FFQs to diet records reveal that they overestimate nutrient intakes (Samour & King, 2012).

Evaluation and Interpretation of Dietary Intake Information

Information obtained from the previously described methods can be assessed for both quality and quantity. An optimal quality dietary pattern may be indicated by acceptable responses for the appropriate interview questions included in Boxes 10.1 through 10.7, earlier. Evaluation of information provided should include indications of regular meals and snacks, consumption of nutrient-dense foods with positive family interactions that support anticipated growth and health, which means no battles at mealtime and no force-feeding of undesired foods. Eating disorders may occur in response to demanding parents, or when children are made to feel guilty about eating even small quantities of a high-calorie food. Common concerns include childhood overweight, dependency on bottle-feeding, skipping meals, or the regular omission of any food group.

The Dietary Reference Intakes (DRIs), which encompass six categories, are commonly used reference standards in the United States (National Academy of Sciences, Institute of Medicine, Food and Nutrition Board, 2010). These include eight different categories that cover childhood and adolescence. The Recommended Dietary Allowance (RDA) is the nutrient intake recommended to meet the nutrient needs of healthy individuals within a specific group as defined by age, gender, or other condition. The RDA includes a large "safety net" beyond the minimum amount to prevent deficiency. Intakes that

are estimated to be somewhat below the RDA do not automatically indicate a deficiency, but they may signal a need for further evaluation, especially when considering the subjective nature of dietary data. The Adequate Intake (AI) category is used for nutrients lacking adequate scientific evidence to establish an RDA. Rather, these values are considered to be the goals for intake of that nutrient. The Estimated Average Requirement (EAR) is the estimated nutrient intake necessary to meet 50% of the defined group. The Estimated Energy Requirement (EER) provides a goal for calorie, or energy, intake consistent with normal health, development, and physical activity. Guidelines for carbohydrate, protein, and fat goals are provided by the Acceptable Macronutrient Distribution Range (AMDR) with consideration for disease prevention and nutrient adequacy. Finally, the Tolerable Upper Limit (TUL) nutrient levels are those at which danger of toxicity may result if exceeded consistently. To assess food-group intake, key goals from the ChooseMyPlate.gov dietary guidelines (MyPlate) can be used (USDA, 2014).

PHYSICAL EXAMINATION

Assessment of nutritional status in infants, children, and adolescents must include anthropometric measurements, which are used to measure growth in the child (Centers for Disease Control and Prevention [CDC], 2010; Hagan et al., 2008). Growth and development during childhood depends on optimal nutrition, health, and environmental conditions. Environmental factors that can influence development include the family's economic situation, cultural food practices, work patterns of caregivers, school foods, and physical activity opportunities or challenges (Haemer et al., 2012; Samour & King, 2012). Health conditions that may influences growth include chromosomal abnormalities (e.g., Down syndrome), metabolic disorders (e.g., phenylketonuria), neurologic disorders (especially those resulting in a nonambulatory status [e.g., spina bifida]), or chronic medication use (e.g., corticosteroid use; Kleinman & Greer, 2013). Problems in any of these areas can impair childhood growth and development. In conjunction with other dietary and biochemical data, anthropometric data can help to explain growth patterns, establish nutrition care goals, and evaluate health care services.

Anthropometric Measurements

Fundamental anthropometric measures of children include height and weight. Body weight reflects energy deficits most readily and to a greater extent than stature in times of undernutrition (Hagan et al., 2008). Head circumference should also be used to assess growth from birth to 36 months (CDC, 2010). Accurate measurements are important, as small errors can result in large inaccuracies when calculating body mass index (BMI). The CDC has developed growth charts for various anthropometric indices. These charts and other valuable information appear in Appendix B. The CDC growth charts synthesize age, gender, weight, stature, and other measures and are appropriate for most children. The charts were first developed in 1977 and revised in 2000. There are 16 gender- and age-specific charts that include two broad age categories, birth to 36 months and 2 to 20 years, for each gender. These are summarized in Table 10.1.

Each growth chart is available in either an individual or a clinical format. The individual format is simpler than the clinical format and includes English and metric units. This is the chart that is most appropriate for parents or caregivers. The clinical format includes space for serial assessment data and includes two sets of curves per page except for the body mass index-for-age (BMI-for-age) and weight-for-stature charts. Charts mostly commonly used are those that display the 5th through 95th percentiles. An alternative set, preferred by some health care professionals, displays the 3rd through 97th percentiles. The 10th, 25th, 50th, 75th, and 90th percentiles are noted on each, in addition to the 85th percentile on the BMI-for-age charts. The recent revisions of the CDC growth charts were developed using a larger and more nationally representative sample of the current pediatric population in the United States, including data from several cycles of the National Health and Nutrition Examination Survey.

If a child experiences a deviation from the expected growth pattern, either by falling outside the expected percentile ranges or by experiencing large or abrupt changes in the growth curve, then further evaluation is warranted as this may indicate a nutritional, health, or other psychosocial problem (CDC, 2010). Changes in weight indices usually reflect changes in recent nutrient intake. Inadequate stature measures usually indicate chronic nutrition or health problems.

BMI-for-Age

The gender-specific BMI-for-age measure is currently recommended by the CDC as the most appropriate assessment of weight status, replacing the previously used weight-for-stature measure for children and adolescents (CDC, 2010; Hagan et al., 2008b). This index combines weight and height at various ages in each gender to assess weight status as underweight, overweight, or obese. A child or adolescent whose gender-specific BMI-for-age is equal to the 95th percentile or greater is categorized as obese. Those with a BMI-for-age equal to the 85th percentile or more but less than the 95th percentile for the appropriate gender are considered to be "overweight." Children who are in either of these categories should receive further medical assessment and nutrition counseling for weight management.

Underweight is considered to be a gender-specific BMI-for-age less than the 5th percentile. The adult BMI criteria are not used to assess weight in children and adolescents. Children or adolescents who are underweight should be evaluated for eating disorders, cancer, diabetes, thyroid disease, infections, and gastrointestinal or other health problems (Samour & King, 2012). After the BMI is calculated, it should be plotted on the gender-specific BMI-for-age chart to determine the approximate percentile for weight assessment.

TABLE 10.1	Summary of Centers for Disease Control and Prevention Pediatric Growth Charts	
AGE	**GENDER**	**CHART**
Birth–36 months	Boys	Weight-for-length Weight-for-age Length-for-age Head circumference-for-age
Birth–36 months	Girls	Weight-for-length Weight-for-age Length-for-age Head circumference-for-age
2–20 years of age	Boys	BMI-for-age Weight-for-age Stature-for-age
2–20 years of age	Girls	BMI-for-age Weight-for-age Stature-for-age
2–5 years of age	Boys	Weight-for-stature
2–4 years of age	Girls	Weight-for-stature

An in-depth medical assessment is recommended for overweight or obese children aged 2 to 20 years (Barlow & Dietz, 2007). For children and adolescents who are categorized as overweight, continued screening should include a careful family health history for type 2 diabetes mellitus, obesity, and cardiovascular diseases, as well as the child's blood pressure and lipid levels. If an at-risk child is found to be positive for a family history of elevated blood pressure, lipids, or BMI, then an in-depth medical assessment is indicated.

Weight-for-Stature

Weight-for-stature charts continue to be included as optional tools for children aged 2 to 5 years. The period from 24 to 36 months is considered transitional. Health care providers may measure recumbent length (supine) or stature (standing height). This is noted by the overlap between the two age categories. Depending on which measure is obtained, the corresponding growth chart should be used. For example, if the recumbent length is measured in a girl who is 30 months of age, then the weight-for-length chart for girls, infant to 36 months is used. If that same girl has stature measured, then it is appropriate to use the BMI-for-age growth chart for girls since her standing height is obtained.

Stature-for-Age

The stature-for-age (or length) index is useful to assess linear growth for shortness or tallness. Short stature, or stunting, is defined as stature-for-age less than the 5th percentile. Reasons for short stature should be evaluated. Short stature may result from inadequate intake of key nutrients secondary to food insecurity, highly restrictive diets, or eating disorders (Sinha, 2012). Nonnutritional reasons for short stature include genetic disorders and developmental problems that impair long bone growth (e.g., cerebral palsy, spina bifida, malabsorption syndromes) (Sinha, 2012). In some children, low stature-for-age may be a genetic manifestation and may not reflect abnormal growth (Sinha, 2012).

Weight-for-Age

Weight-for-age is used in early infancy to monitor weight and in older children to monitor weight-for-length. It is not used to assess weight status but rather to monitor changes in health or nutritional status. Infants who are exclusively breastfed experience somewhat different growth patterns. They tend to gain weight more rapidly in the first 3 months and then weigh less than formula-fed infants at the end of the first year (Hagan et al., 2008a).

Weight-for-Length

Weight-for-length (or stature) is not dependent on age and assesses weight status in infants and young children. A child whose weight-for-length exceeds the 95th percentile is considered overweight. Similarly, a child whose weight-for-length is less than the 5th percentile is considered underweight.

Head Circumference-for-Age

Head circumference-for-age is a critical measure for infants younger than 36 months; it reflects brain size and may identify hydrocephalus or microcephaly (which indicates the need for neurologic evaluation). Developmental problems are a concern for children whose head circumference indices are less than the 5th percentile or more than the 95th percentiles (Kleinman & Greer, 2013). Serial data for anthropometric indices are particularly useful in assessing growth and development in children with special conditions.

Special Conditions

When assessing certain groups of infants, children, and adolescents, the CDC growth charts are not appropriate. These include very low birth weight (VLBW) infants, those with genetic disorders, or those with chronic illnesses. Alternative growth charts have been developed for some of these populations (Kleinman & Greer, 2013). For children who cannot stand up straight, linear growth can be approximated using sitting height, arm span, and knee height. However, because these alternative growth charts have often been developed using small reference populations, reliability and validity may be a concern. When assessing a special population, such as those mentioned earlier, it is advisable to use the child as his or her own reference, comparing current to past measures. It is also preferable to use multiple indices such as head circumference, length-for-age, and weight-for-age, rather than a single parameter.

It should be noted that VLBW infants were not included in the reference data used to develop the growth charts because their growth patterns are different from those of infants with birth weights over 2500 mg. To assess growth in VLBW infants, the Infant Health and Development Program (IHDP) charts or the CDC growth charts are appropriate postdischarge (Stewart, 2013). The CDC advises health care providers to make several adjustments when assessing these infants. When assessing the VLBW infant with these charts, postnatal age should be corrected for gestational age from birth to 24 months with either chart. In addition, growth patterns of VLBW infants are similar on either chart except for weight-for-length, which shows a smaller decrease in growth on the IHDP charts than on the CDC charts. When using the CDC charts, VLBW infants will fall in lower percentiles for length and weight-for-age. They will show some catch-up growth in length-for-age and head circumference-for-age but will plot in lower percentiles for weight-for-age and weight-for-length. These infants are often heavier for length until 65 cm in length and then become thinner for length than non-VLBW infants. In general, the IHDP charts reflect growth patterns in VLBW infants when compared to the CDC growth charts except in the weight-for-length category (CDC, 2010).

The CDC growth charts are important tools that health care providers use to assess the growth of infants, children, and adolescents up to 20 years of age in all racial and ethnic groups. Practitioners should use caution when assessing growth patterns of VLBW infants, exclusively breastfed infants, or other specific groups such as children with genetic disorders. One parameter can never provide a complete assessment relative to the health or nutritional status of a child. A combination of objective measures (e.g., anthropometrics, biochemistry) and subjective measures (e.g., diet history) must be included.

Physical Assessments

Nutrition-focused physical assessment includes observation of general appearance and assessment of relevant body systems (Haemer et al., 2012; Samour & King, 2012). A quick, overall assessment allows the provider to assess the child's weight, which must be confirmed on the appropriate growth chart. The skin must be assessed for turgor or any other signs indicating a nutritional problem, such as acanthosis nigricans, which indicates insulin resistance. Subcutaneous fat stores should be assessed for general nutritional status. Four areas commonly observed are the shoulders, triceps, chest, and hands. Loss of fullness or loose skin may indicate wasting. In addition, muscle wasting can be assessed by anthropometric measures or also by observation of the quadriceps femoris (anterior thigh) or deltoid muscle (shoulder) area (Lee & Nieman, 2009). Ascites or edema should be considered when assessing weight status and protein status. Generalized cachexia should alert the practitioner to the need for a more thorough assessment.

Physical findings that would be relevant in a nutritional assessment are summarized in Table 10.2. Many

TABLE 10.2	**Physical Findings Related to Nutritional Problems**			
SYSTEM OR TISSUE	NORMAL APPEARANCE	PHYSICAL FINDING	POSSIBLE NUTRIENT DEFICIENCY	POSSIBLE NUTRIENT EXCESS
Hair	Shiny, not easily pluckable, evenly distributed	Alopecia	Protein-calorie	
		Easily pluckable	Protein, essential fatty acids	
		Dyspigmented	Protein	
		Sparse	Protein, biotin, zinc	Vitamin A
Epithelial	Smooth	Calluses on knuckles		
Skin	Smooth, without rashes, swelling, or scales	Xerosis and scaling	Essential fatty acids, vitamin A, zinc	Vitamin A
		Follicular hyperkeratosis	Vitamins A and C	
		Ecchymoses, petechiae	Vitamins C and K	
		Purpura	Vitamins C and K	
		Desquamation in sun exposed areas	Niacin	
		Yellow pigmentation without sclerae involvement		Carotene

(continued)

TABLE 10.2	Physical Findings Related to Nutritional Problems (*continued*)			
SYSTEM OR TISSUE	**NORMAL APPEARANCE**	**PHYSICAL FINDING**	**POSSIBLE NUTRIENT DEFICIENCY**	**POSSIBLE NUTRIENT EXCESS**
Nails		Koilonychia, spoon shaped	Iron	
Mouth and lips	Pink and moist with intact skin	Angular stomatitis (inflammation at corners of mouth)	Riboflavin, niacin, pyridoxine	
		Cheilosis (inflamed, ulcerated lips)	Riboflavin, niacin, pyridoxine	
Tongue	Pink and moist, with intact skin	Glossitis (inflamed tongue) scarlet, painful, and rough	Riboflavin, pyridoxine, niacin, folate, cobalamin	
		Atrophic lingual papillae (smooth tongue)	Riboflavin, niacin, folate, cobalamin, iron	
		Hypogeusesthesia	Zinc	
Gums	Pink, moist, and smooth	Bleeding, swollen, receding	Ascorbic acid (vitamin C)	
Eyes	Pink membranes	Conjunctival pallor	Iron, folic acid, cobalamin (B_{12})	
	Bright, shiny, and clear	Bitot's spots, xerosis, and night blindness	Vitamin A	
	Intact blood vessels	Corneal vascularization, fissures of eyelid corners	B vitamins	
		Papilledema		Vitamin A
Musculoskeletal	Well developed, some fat stores Normal movement	Costochondral junction enlargement, "beading" on ribs (rachitic rosary), bowed legs, bone pain	Vitamin D	
		Hemorrhages on extremities	Ascorbic acid	
		Muscle wasting, reduced strength	Protein-calorie	
General		Edema	Protein, thiamin	
		Poor skin turgor	Fluid (dehydration)	
		Pallor, anemia	Iron, folic acid, cobalamin (B_{12})	
		Poor wound healing	Protein, vitamin C, zinc	
Neurologic	Psychologically stable Normal reflexes	Mental confusion and dementia; confabulations and disorientation	Niacin, cobalamin, pyridoxine, thiamin	
		Peripheral neuropathy	Niacin, cobalamin, pyridoxine	Pyridoxine
		Tetany	Calcium, magnesium	
		Headache		Vitamin A

TABLE 10.2	Physical Findings Related to Nutritional Problems (*continued*)			
SYSTEM OR TISSUE	**NORMAL APPEARANCE**	**PHYSICAL FINDING**	**POSSIBLE NUTRIENT DEFICIENCY**	**POSSIBLE NUTRIENT EXCESS**
		Drowsiness, lethargy, vomiting		Vitamins A and D
		Cardiomegaly, heart failure, tachycardia	Thiamin, phosphorus	
Gastrointestinal	Symmetrical, flat	Hepatomegaly and distention	Protein-calorie	Vitamin A
		Distention and flatus	Lactose intolerance	

of the abnormal conditions noted in this table are non-specific and may be secondary to causes other than nutrient deficits or excesses, making further biochemical evaluation necessary to substantiate a deficiency (Samour & King, 2012). In addition, suspected nutrient problems should be accompanied by an evaluation of the diet.

LABORATORY AND DIAGNOSTIC TESTS

Some laboratory tests may be needed to compliment the nutritional assessment. Common lab tests include hemoglobin or hematocrit to screen for iron deficiency anemia; iron or ferritin levels (or both) to further evaluate anemia; and lipid screening, serum glucose, serum proteins, or bone radiographs to assess nutrient deficiencies or bone age.

Screening for Iron-Deficiency Anemia

Iron deficiency is the most common nutritional deficiency in children in the United States because of the demands of this nutrient for normal growth from infancy through adolescence (Janus & Moerschel, 2010). Iron deficiency results in cognitive deficits, delays in psychomotor development, behavioral problems, impaired growth, fatigue, increased infections, and an increased risk of lead toxicity (AAP Committee on Environmental Health, 2009; Borgona-Pignatti & Marsella, 2008; Hagan et al., 2008). Certain groups of children are more susceptible to iron deficiency anemia, such as those from low-income households; preterm or low birth weight infants; infants who have been fed non-iron-fortified formula for more than 2 months or who have received cow's milk before 1 year; those who consume large amounts of cow's milk; and those who have suffered blood loss, chronic infection, or inflammatory disorder (Baker, Greer, & Committee on Nutrition, 2010). Children from a migrant, refugee, or low-income

family or a recipient of the WIC Special Supplemental Feeding Program are also at risk for iron deficiency.

The AAP (2014) recommends that infants and children be screened for anemia, depending on these risk factors; however, anemia screening should be done universally at 12 months, with an additional risk assessment done at 15 and 30 months of age. Anemia screening should also be done on all preterm and low birth weight infants and those who are fed non-iron-fortified or low-iron formula at the 4-month visit. At the 18-month, 2-year, 3-year, 4-year, and 5-year visits, and all annual health maintenance visits until 21 years of age, the provider should conducts an anemia risk assessment by investigating whether any of the previously listed risk factors are present and, if so, conduct anemia screening. Any child with iron deficiency should also be assessed for lead toxicity based on the CDC guidelines as the two are often connected (Hagan et al., 2008).

Cholesterol and Triglycerides

In the National Heart, Blood and Lung Institute (2013) published revised guidelines for lipid screening in children; these were endorsed by the APA (2014). The first lipid screening should take place after age 2, with an additional screening between 9 and 11 years of age. Overweight and obese children require dyslipidemia screening irrespective of family history or other risk factors. Elevated lipid levels should be considered in conjunction with weight status, family history of cardiovascular disease or diabetes, and dietary factors to minimize the risk of premature chronic disease risk in the child.

Glucose

Similar to the recommendations for lipid screening in children, the American Diabetes Association recommends glucose screening in children at risk for diabetes based on the overweight status of the child; positive family history for diabetes; symptoms of insulin resistance, such as acanthosis nigricans, polycystic ovarian syndrome, or dyslipidemia; or belonging to an ethnic group with a high prevalence of diabetes, such as Native Americans, African Americans, Hispanic Americans, or Pacific Islanders (CDC, 2012). If a child is found to have a fasting glucose level of 100 mg/dL or more, further evaluation is necessary.

Serum Proteins

Serum albumin is the most commonly measured protein because of its relative availability and reasonable cost. A low serum albumin level may indicate depressed hepatic albumin production as a consequence of low dietary protein intake (Samour & King, 2012). However, albumin is not the most sensitive or specific indicator of protein status. Once nutritional support is started, it may take several weeks to observe a rise in albumin. Nonnutritional factors can also lead to abnormal albumin levels despite adequate protein intake. These include liver or renal disease, fluid retention or deficits, infection, and malabsorption. Health care providers should consider these factors when evaluating albumin and other proteins. Transferrin, retinal-binding protein, and prealbumin are sometimes preferred for the assessment of protein status, as they reflect more recent changes. However, measuring these proteins is more expensive and also subject to the nonnutritional factors mentioned earlier.

Bone Radiographs

Infants and children who have been dependent on parenteral nutrition have been shown to have lower bone mineral content and bone density (Appleman, Kalkwarf, Dwivedi, & Heubi, 2013). Dual-energy x-ray absorptiometry (DXA) is helpful is this population to assess and diagnose bone mass and density. DXA is can also be used in place of radiographs to evaluate bone age in children (Heppe et al., 2012).

SUMMARY

As the growth and development of children are dependent on optimal diet and adequate nutrient intake, health care should include screening of nutritional status. If the screening indicates some risk for nutrition problems, then a complex nutritional assessment should be completed. This includes observation and analysis of anthropometric, biochemical, clinical, and dietary findings. This chapter described common parameters used for these purposes and presented key concepts for interpretation based on age group. Ensuring that both healthy children and those with special needs because of medical conditions receive an optimal diet to foster growth and manage disease is complex and requires a collaborative interdisciplinary approach.

Notable Clinical Findings

- Child is less than the 5th percentile or greater than the 85th percentile for weight on the NCHS growth charts for age and gender
- Child is less than 5th percentile for length or height on the NCHS growth charts for age and gender
- Child is less than the 5th percentile or greater than the 5th percentile for head circumference on the NCHS growth charts for age and gender
- Parent/caregiver knowledge deficits regarding healthful eating
- Child still drinks from bottle after age 12 months
- Child carries "companion" bottle or sippy cup of juice or soft drink
- Infant younger than 1 year old drinks cow's milk
- History of prematurity or complicated neonatal course
- Family history of overweight, obesity, heart disease, diabetes, dyslipidemia

- Presence of endocrine, metabolic, gastrointestinal or renal conditions; any conditions that impair mobility
- Overweight or obese child or adolescent
- Acanthosis nigricans
- Russell's sign
- Child/teen has unrealistic body image
- Food allergies
- Hyperlipidemia
- Iron deficiency anemia
- Excessive juice or soft drink consumption
- Poor dental health
- Less than 1 hour physical activity per day
- Greater than 2 hours TV or computer screen time per day
- Constipation/diarrhea
- Frequent consumption of fast food/junk food snacks/candy

References

American Academy of Pediatrics. (2014). *AAP updates schedule of screening and assessments for well-child visits.* Retrieved from http://www.aap.org/en-us/about-the-aap/aap-press-room/pages/AAP-Updates-Schedule-of-Screening-and-Assessments-for-Well-Child-Visits.aspx#sthash.TrxxnnUR.dpuf

American Academy of Pediatrics Committee on Communications. (2001). Children, adolescents and television. *Pediatrics, 107*(2), 423–426.

American Academy of Pediatrics Committee on Environmental Health. (2009). Screening for elevated blood lead levels. *Pediatrics, 116*(4), 1036–1046.

American Psychiatric Association. (2013). *Diagnostic and statistical manual of mental disorders* (5th ed.). Washington, DC: American Psychiatric Publishing.

Appleman, S. S., Kalkwarf, H. J., Dwivedi, A., & Heubi, J. E. (2013). Bone deficits in parenteral nutrition-dependent infants and children with intestinal failure are attenuated when accounting for slower growth. *Journal of Pediatric Gastroenterology and Nutrition, 57*(1), 124–130.

Baker, R. D., Greer, F. R., & Committee on Nutrition. (2010). Clinical report: Diagnosis and prevention of iron deficiency and iron-deficiency anemia in infants and young children (0–3 years of age). *Pediatrics, 126*(5), 1040–1050.

Barlow, S. E., & Dietz, H. W. (2007). Obesity evaluation and treatment: Expert committee recommendations. *Pediatrics, 119*(2), 405.

Borgona-Pignatti, C., & Marsella, M. (2008). Iron deficiency in infancy and childhood. *Pediatric Annals, 37*(5), 322–338.

Centers for Disease Control and Prevention. (2010). *Growth chart home page.* Retrieved from http://www.cdc.gov/growthcharts/cdc_charts.htm

Centers for Disease Control and Prevention. (2012). *Overweight and obesity.* Retrieved from http://www.cdc.gov/obesity/childhood/basics.html

Christakis, D. A., & Zimmerman, F. J. (2007). Children and television: A primer for pediatricians. *Contemporary Pediatrics, 24*(3), 31–42.

Garcia-Prats, J. (2013). *Anemia of prematurity.* Retrieved from http://www.uptodate.com/contents/anemia-of-prematurity?source=related_link

Haemer, M., Primak, L. E., & Krebs, N. (2012). Normal childhood nutrition and its disorders. In W. W. Hay, M. J. Levin, R. R. Deterding, M. J. Abzug, & J. M. Sondheimer (Eds.), *Current pediatric diagnosis and treatment* (21st ed., pp. 288–315). New York, NY: McGraw-Hill.

Hagan, J., Shaw, J., & Duncan, P. (2008d). Adolescence. In J. F. Hagan, J. S. Shaw, & P. M. Duncan (Eds.), *Bright futures: Guidelines for health supervision of infants, children and adolescents* (3rd ed., pp. 515–575). Elk Grove Village, IL: American Academy of Pediatrics.

Hagan, J. F., Shaw, J. S., & Duncan, P. M. (2008b). Early childhood: 1–4 years. In J. F. Hagan, J. S. Shaw, & P. M. Duncan (Eds.), *Bright futures: Guidelines for health supervision of infants, children and adolescents* (3rd ed., pp. 381–461). Elk Grove Village, IL: American Academy of Pediatrics.

Hagan, J. F., Shaw, J. S., & Duncan, P. (2008a). Infancy. In J. F. Hagan, J. S. Shaw, & P. M. Duncan (Eds.), *Bright futures: Guidelines for health supervision of infants, children and adolescents* (3rd ed., pp. 253–380). Elk Grove Village, IL: American Academy of Pediatrics.

Hagan, J. F., Shaw, J. S., & Duncan, P. M. (2008c). Middle childhood. In J. F. Hagan, J. S. Shaw, & P. M. Duncan (Eds.), *Bright futures: Guidelines for health supervision of infants, children and adolescents* (3rd ed., pp. 463–514). Elk Grove Village, IL: American Academy of Pediatrics.

Hagan, J. F., Shaw, J. S., & Duncan, P. M. (2008). Promoting healthy nutrition. In J. F. Hagan, J. S. Shaw, & P. M. Duncan (Eds.), *Bright futures: Guidelines for health supervision of infants, children and adolescents* (3rd ed., pp. 121–145). Elk Grove Village, IL: American Academy of Pediatrics.

Heppe, D. H. M., Taal, H. R., Ernst, G. D. S., Van Den Akker, E. L. T., Lequin, L. L. H., Hokken-Koelega, A. C.S., . . . Jaddoe, V. W. V. (2012). Bone age assessment by dual-energy X-ray absorptiometry in children: An alternative for X-ray? *British Journal of Radiology, 85*(1010), 114–120.

Janus, J., & Moerschel, S. K. (2010). Evaluation of anemia in children. *American Family Physician, 81*(12), 1462–1471.

Kittler, P. G., Sucher, K. P., & Nelms, M. N. (2012). *Food and culture* (6th ed.). Belmont, CA: Cengage Learning.

Kleinman, R. D., & Greer, F. R. (Eds.). (2013). *Pediatric nutrition handbook* (7th ed). Elk Grove Village, IL: American Academy of Pediatrics.

Lee, R. D., & Nieman, D. C. (2009). *Nutritional assessment* (5th ed.). New York, NY: McGraw-Hill.

National Academy of Sciences, Institute of Medicine, Food and Nutrition Board. (2010). *Dietary reference intakes: Recommended intakes for individuals, vitamins. Dietary reference intakes: Recommended intakes for individuals, elements. Dietary reference intakes: Tolerable upper intake levels, vitamins. Dietary reference intakes: Tolerable upper intake levels, elements. Dietary reference intakes: Acceptable macronutrient distribution ranges. Dietary reference intakes: Recommended intakes for individuals, macronutrients. Dietary reference intakes: Estimated average requirements for groups.* Retrieved from http://www.iom.edu/Object.File/Master/21/372/0.pdf, pp. 1–7.

National Heart, Blood and Lung Institute. (2013). *Integrated guidelines for cardiovascular health and risk reduction in children and adolescents.* Retrieved from http://www.nhlbi.nih.gov/guidelines/cvd_ped/index.htm

Ogden C. L., Carroll, M. D., Kit, B. K., & Flegal, K. M. (2014). Prevalence of childhood and adult obesity in the United States, 2011–2012. *Journal of the American Medical Association, 311*(8), 806–814.

Rosenbaum, M. (2007). Epidemiology of pediatric obesity. *Pediatric Annals, 36*(2), 89–95.

Samour, P. Q., & King, K. (2012). *Pediatric nutrition* (4th ed.). Sudbury, MA: Jones and Bartlett.

Sinha, S. (2012). *Short stature.* Retrieved from http://emedicine.medscape.com/article/924411-overview

Stewart, J. (2013). *Care of the neonatal intensive care unit graduate.* Retrieved from http://www.uptodate.com/contents/care-of-the-neonatal-intensive-care-unit-graduate

U.S. Department of Agriculture. (2014). *MyPlate.* Retrieved from http://fnic.nal.usda.gov/dietary-guidance/myplate-and-historical-food-pyramid-resources

Wilkes, M. A., & Spratt, E. G. (2014). *Pediatric bulimia.* Retrieved from http://emedicine.medscape.com/article/913721-overview#a0156

Assessment of the Neonate

Assessment of the newborn infant requires specialized knowledge and skills. During the transition from intrauterine to extrauterine life, and extending through the neonatal period (first 28 days of life), the infant undergoes numerous physiologic changes. Perinatal and neonatal risk factor assessment and systematic physical assessment by a skilled health care provider are essential to confirm normality and detect abnormalities. Providers require an understanding of neonatal anatomy and physiology as well as the skills to accomplish a comprehensive infant assessment. Newborn assessment, including a comprehensive history and a detailed physical examination, is reviewed in this chapter.

THE HISTORY

Comprehensive History

A comprehensive history is an important aspect of the newborn assessment as it is instrumental in identifying risk factors that may have an impact on the infant's health status. The comprehensive history includes a family history, maternal health history, obstetric history (including pregnancy and labor), and the prenatal, birth and neonatal histories. The history is usually obtained from a parent through an interview and through medical record review. The provider must determine the reliability of the information. For example, the postpartum mother recovering from anesthesia may be unable to provide information, necessitating an interview with the father, a close relative, or a friend. This information should be confirmed at a later time with the mother of the infant. Reviewing medical records may provide valuable information, but these reviews should also be confirmed, when possible, through interviews. Ideally, the provider should interview both parents, either together or individually.

Family History

To assess the family history, providers should inquire about known inherited diseases in the family, such as cystic fibrosis, hemophilia, or muscular dystrophy, and the presence of other genetic disorders, such as intellectual disabilities or heart defects. Previous neonatal or infant deaths must be documented, including the cause of these deaths, if known. The family history must include, at minimum, information about both parents, grandparents, parents' siblings, and siblings of the infant.

A genogram should be constructed if the infant presents with a congenital anomaly or a disease that is known or thought to be genetically transmitted (see Chapter 4).

Maternal Health History

The health status of the mother, including acute and chronic health problems that may affect the neonate's health, should be reviewed (Table 11.1). Chronic conditions such as diabetes, hypertension, and asthma, and acute conditions, such as a current infection or trauma, may have an impact on infant health. Medications taken before and during pregnancy should be documented as some may be teratogenic. The extremes of reproductive age (e.g., adolescents, women older than 35) can be associated with medical conditions that are dangerous for the mother (e.g., preeclampsia, eclampsia, placenta previa).

A social history includes the mother's marital status, living situation, financial and social support systems. Tobacco, alcohol, and illegal substance use by the mother should be noted. These questions should be raised with every mother, without personal bias. A nonjudgmental attitude, conveying a commitment to the infant's health, assists the provider in obtaining accurate information.

Obstetric History

An obstetric history includes maternal data, including age, gravida, and parity. Gravida and parity information is often noted in a shortened form. The gravida number denotes the number of pregnancies, and para is the number of pregnancies resulting in viable births (birth weight of 500 g or more, or gestation of 20 completed weeks

TABLE 11.1	Maternal Health and Fetal Risk Assessment
AREAS OF ASSESSMENT	**COMPONENTS, RISKS, OR PROBLEMS**
Ethnic background	Population risks for genetic disease: • Cystic fibrosis: North American Caucasians of European ancestry and Ashkenazi Jews • Sickle cell disease: African Americans, Africans, Hispanics, Mediterraneans, Middle Easterners, and Caribbean Indians • Tay-Sachs: Ashkenazi Jews, French Canadians, Cajuns • Beta-thalassemia: Chinese, Southeast Asians, Mediterraneans, Pakistanis, Bangladeshis, Middle Easterners, and Africans • Alpha-thalassemia: Chinese, Southeast Asians, and Africans • Bloom's syndrome, Canavan's disease, familial dysautonomia, Fanconi's anemia, Gaucher's disease, Niemann-Pick disease: Ashkenazi Jews
Family history	History of genetic disease that may affect mother or fetus History of previous infant born with genetic disorder or chromosomal anomaly
Maternal age	**Adolescent:** • Preeclampsia and eclampsia • Intrauterine growth restriction • Maternal malnutrition **35 years of age or older:** • Pregnancy-induced hypertension • Diabetes • Obesity • Chromosomal abnormalities • Increased preexisting medical conditions • Increased cesarean section rate • Increased placenta previa
Past maternal medical history	• Inadequate weight gain • Obesity • Anemia • Chronic hypertension • Renal disease • Diabetes mellitus • Heart disease • Endocrine (thyroid) problems • Cancer • Sickle cell disease • Pulmonary disease • Gastrointestinal or liver disease • Blood and clotting disorders • Previous fetal death • Psychiatric conditions
Screening tests	Rubella, rapid plasma reagin, hepatitis B, blood type, antibody status, human immunodeficiency virus, gonorrhea, *Chlamydia*, and Pap smear
Social history	No health insurance Late onset, lack of prenatal care Substance abuse Involvement of child protective services

Sources: Kothari, Wendt, Liggins, Overton, and Sweezy Ldel (2011); Mehta and Sokol (2013).

or more). The parity information may be expanded to four numbers to denote term, preterm, abortions, and living children. For example, the notation of G5 P2-1-1-3 describes a mother who is presenting with her fifth pregnancy, with two term deliveries, one preterm delivery, one abortion (either spontaneous or induced), and who has three living children. Any history of infertility treatments, such as ovarian stimulation or in vitro fertilization; the modality of conception; and the outcome of any previous pregnancies, births, and living children should be noted. The adequacy of prenatal care and compliance with follow-up must also be determined. The obstetric history also includes determination of the woman's estimated date of confinement (EDC), in order to determine the infant's gestational age.

The results of any prenatal testing are also relevant to the neonate's current health. For example, determination of the mother's blood type, Coombs status, hepatitis B status, and rubella immunity is essential. Likewise, syphilis testing (RPR/VDRL), gonorrhea, *Chlamydia*, group B *Streptococcus* and human immunodeficiency virus status, is important when assessing the infant's past medical history. The results of fetal assessment through ultrasound examination findings, amniocentesis, chorionic villus sampling, and percutaneous umbilical blood sampling are also important components of the prenatal history. Complications of pregnancy, such as pregnancy-induced hypertension, gestational diabetes, and maternal illness during pregnancy, are important to assess because these conditions may have an impact on neonatal health. Table 11.2 summarizes the important aspects of the obstetric history and potential risks to the fetus or neonate.

TABLE 11.2 Obstetric History	
CONDITION	**RISK TO THIS PREGNANCY OR INFANT**
Modality of conception	Increased risk for high-risk outcomes with assisted reproductive technologies: • Multiple gestations • Preterm delivery • Low birth weight • Congenital anomalies • Uterine infections
Recurrent abortion	Etiology: • Chromosomal abnormality • Uterine anomalies • Connective tissues disease • Hormonal abnormality • Thrombophilia • Infectious disease of genital tract
Previous stillbirth or neonatal death	Etiology: • Random: low risk • Chromosomal, maternal health, genetic disease, and thrombophilia
Previous preterm delivery	Genital tract infection Uterine or cervical abnormalities
Rh isoimmunization or ABO incompatibility	Positive antibody screen: • Anemia, hydrops fetalis, hyperbilirubinemia, kernicterus, birth asphyxia, and hypoglycemia
Previous infant with genetic disorder or chromosomal anomaly	Risk of recurrence dependent on specific anomaly and genetic history
Teratogen exposure	Drugs (illegal or prescribed) Alcohol and tobacco Infectious agents (e.g., cytomegalovirus, rubella, toxoplasmosis, varicella, listeria)

Sources: Kothari, Wendt, Liggins, Overton, and Sweezy Ldel (2011); Mehta and Sokol (2013).

Birth and Neonatal Histories

The labor and delivery histories include the timing of membrane rupture, the length of labor, maternal fever, and fetal monitoring findings. Prolonged rupture of membranes and maternal fever predispose newborns to infection. The length of labor and fetal monitoring findings are indicators of fetal health.

The birth history includes the mode of delivery and delivery presentation. The need for assistive techniques, such as forceps or vacuum extraction, must be noted. The appearance of the amniotic fluid should be recorded: green fluid indicates meconium passage while yellow or cloudy fluid may indicate infection. Apgar scores and the need for resuscitation should be determined (Table 11.3).

The neonatal history includes the birth history and the infant's status before the health care provider's examination. The provider should determine whether or not the infant has achieved temperature control (*thermoregulation*) and stable vital signs. Thermoregulation is important in the newborn, as cold stress places the infant at risk for hypoglycemia, acidosis, and persistent pulmonary hypertension. A lack of thermoregulation is common in preterm and ill infants. The provider should note whether the infant is breastfed or bottle-fed and whether urine and stool have passed normally.

PHYSICAL EXAMINATION

Immediately After Birth

Physical examination of the neonate first occurs immediately following delivery when the transition to extrauterine life is assessed. The Apgar score provides a convenient shorthand method for reporting the status of the newborn infant and the infant's response to resuscitation (see Table 11.3). Each infant is assigned an Apgar score at 1 and 5 minutes of life, continuing every 5 minutes until the score is greater than 7 (Apgar, 1953, 1966). However, the Apgar score is not used in isolation to establish the diagnosis of birth asphyxia (American Academy of Pediatrics [AAP], Committee on Fetus and Newborn; American College of Obstetricians and Gynecologists [ACOG]; & Committee on Obstetric Practice, 2009, 2006). The 1-minute Apgar score may be low because of prenatal or intrapartum events or medications and is not predictive of outcomes. The 5-minute Apgar score reflects the success of the resuscitation or the severity of the neonatal depression. A 5-minute Apgar score of 0 to 3 is associated with a slightly increased risk of cerebral palsy compared with higher scores. The risk of poor neurologic outcomes increases when the Apgar score is 3 or less beyond 5 minutes (AAP, ACOG, & Committee on Obstetric Practice, 2009).

Along with Apgar scoring, the principles of the American Heart Association and the AAP Neonatal Resuscitation Program are used to assess each newborn's need for resuscitation. The infant's respirations, heart rate, and color are assessed, with subsequent resuscitation efforts based on this assessment. Repeated assessment of these parameters determines the need for continued resuscitation and care (Kattwinkel et al., 2010).

The cursory physical examination of the infant accomplished at delivery determines the infant's gender and the presence or absence of major birth defects. A complete physical examination of the infant is performed later, usually in the first day of life after the infant is stable.

After Stabilization

Behavioral and physiologic changes (e.g., color, respiratory efforts, heart sounds, motor activity, mucus production, bowel sounds) in the normal newborn over the first 10 hours of extrauterine life were first described by Desmond, Rudolph, and Phitaksphraiwan (1966). Behavioral changes are described as periods of reactivity.

- The *first period of reactivity* is described as alertness following birth, lasting around 30 minutes. This is followed by a period of sleep, until the infant is around 3 to 4 hours of age.
- The *second period of reactivity* occurs between 3 and 6 hours after birth, when the infant is awake again. The infant may be alert or have variable motor activity, such as gagging or arching.

TABLE 11.3	Apgar Scoring			
	SCORE OF 0	**SCORE OF 1**	**SCORE OF 2**	**ACRONYM**
Skin color	Blue all over	Blue at extremities	Normal	**A**ppearance
Heart rate	Absent	< 100	> 100	**P**ulse
Reflex irritability	No response to stimulation	Grimace, feeble cry when stimulated	Sneeze, cough, pulls away when stimulated	**G**rimace
Muscle tone	None	Some flexion	Active movement	**A**ctivity
Respiration	Absent	Weak or irregular	Strong	**R**espiration

These periods of reactivity may affect the physical examination of the infant; for example, it may be difficult for the infant to attain and maintain a state of alertness in the sleep period shortly after birth.

Initial Impression

It is important that the parents be present at the initial examination to facilitate a dialogue between the health care provider and the parents. Parents can be informed of the findings, and the infant's strengths can be emphasized. The provider can educate the parents at this time about their infant and infant care.

The health care provider's initial impression of the infant is very important. The experienced provider can quickly evaluate the infant's overall status. Color, transitional state, activity, cry, and respiratory effort are the main components of this initial impression. A pink, active infant, breathing without distress "looks good," while a pale or cyanotic, lethargic, or dyspneic infant "looks bad" and requires physiologic stabilization before physical examination. If the infant "looks bad," assessment for the cause and stabilization should take precedence.

Maintenance of Physiologic Stability

Neonatal assessment should occur in a setting that is conducive to a full examination. The neonate should be kept warm during the assessment; this is difficult in small infants as body heat is lost quickly when they are exposed. Thermal stability is paramount and should not be compromised; a radiant heat source should be used during the examination if needed to prevent cold stress. An infant without an external heat source should not be exposed for long periods of time. A blanket can be used to cover the portions of the infant not being examined. If possible, it is important to observe the undressed infant briefly. The room should be warm and free of drafts, and the provider's hands and stethoscope should be warmed prior to the assessment. The infant should be handled gently and calmed as needed throughout the examination. The infant should be warm and calm at the conclusion of the examination.

Preparation for the Assessment

The health care provider's tools—stethoscope, tape measure, ophthalmoscope and gloves—should be ready for the examination; the stethoscope bell and diaphragm should be cleaned with alcohol, an excellent disinfectant. There should be a plan in place for the assessment so that it can be completed quickly. It is important to develop a system for the comprehensive examination that varies as little as possible, allowing the provider to be efficient and thorough.

Assessment Sequence

Assessment begins with observation, that is, always observation before manipulation. Whether the infant is clothed and wrapped in a blanket or undressed, the health care provider should observe the infant prior to touching. If the infant is sleeping, the provider should observe the general color and body posture, as well as respiratory efforts and sleep activity. If the infant is in a quiet alert state, the provider should observe color, posture, movements, respiratory effort, and the ability to track visually. If the infant is crying, the provider should observe color, posture, movements, and respiratory effort, and then calm the infant for further examination. If the infant is compromised in any way, the examination should be delayed or accomplished with extra care to maintain physiologic stability. An examination can be stressful to a compromised infant. Some portions of the examination must be deferred if the infant is critically ill. Manipulation of the infant on life support cannot be accomplished until the infant is stable and support measures are removed. Responses of the infant who is pharmacologically sedated are altered accordingly.

Many portions of the examination require that the infant be quiet and cooperative; therefore, the provider should start with noninvasive maneuvers before performing the invasive maneuvers; for example, auscultation before palpation. Auscultation of the heart, lungs, and abdomen are completed if the infant is quiet, followed by a head-to-toe examination.

Gestational Age Assessment

Determination of gestational age is accomplished through determination of the maternal EDC, prenatal ultrasound, or physical examination. Determination of the EDC, using the mother's last menstrual period (LMP), is imprecise if the mother's menstrual cycles are irregular or if there is early bleeding that is misinterpreted as menses. In addition, some women are poor historians and do not recall their LMP. Lack of prenatal care increases the uncertainty of gestational age.

The exact gestational ages of infants born as the result of reproductive technologies, such as in vitro fertilization, are easily determined, unless the mother conceived outside of the implantation/fertilization process. Prenatal ultrasound early in gestation is accurate in assessing gestational age (Mongelli & Gardosi, 2014). Ultrasound examinations later in gestation are less accurate because of variations in fetal growth.

Infants born before 37 completed weeks gestation are considered preterm. Infants born between the beginning of week 38 and the completion of week 41 are considered term. Infants born at 42 weeks gestation or later are considered postterm.

Neuromuscular and physical characteristics can be used to estimate gestational age by observing and manipulating the infant in a systematic and standardized exam. In the standardized exam, several indicators of physical and neuromuscular maturity are scored and summed to estimate the infant's gestational age (Figure 11.1).

Score
Neuromuscular — Physical — Total —

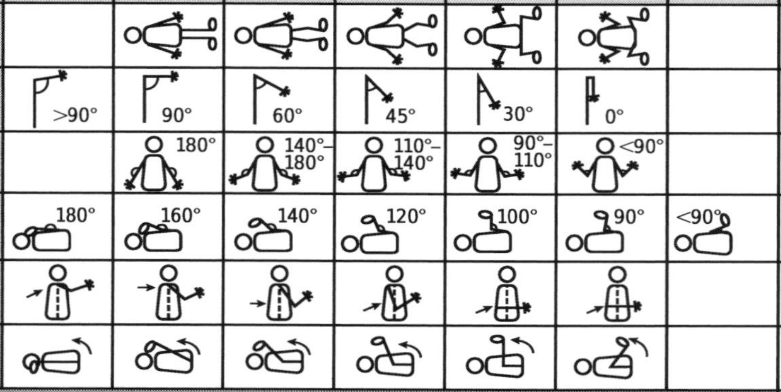

Neuromuscular maturity sign	Score							Record score here
	−1	0	1	2	3	4	5	
Posture								
Square window (wrist)	>90°	90°	60°	45°	30°	0°		
Arm recoil		180°	140°–180°	110°–140°	90°–110°	<90°		
Popliteal angle	180°	160°	140°	120°	100°	90°	<90°	
Scarf sign								
Heel to ear								
Total neuromuscular maturity score								

Maturity rating

Score	Weeks
−10	20
−5	22
0	24
5	26
10	28
15	30
20	32
25	34
30	36
35	38
40	40
45	42
50	44

Physical maturity sign	Score							Record score here
	−1	0	1	2	3	4	5	
Skin	Sticky, friable, transparent	Gelatinous, red, translucent	Smooth, pink, visible veins	Superficial peeling and/or rash, few veins	Cracking pale areas, rare veins	Parchment, deep cracking, no vessels	Leathery, cracked, wrinkled	
Lanugo	None	Sparse	Abundant	Thinning	Bald areas	Mostly bald		
Plantar surface	Heel-toe 40–50 mm: −1 <40 mm: −2	>50 mm no crease	Faint red marks	Anterior transverse crease only	Creases ant. 2/3	Creases over entire sole		
Breast	Imperceptible	Barely perceptible	Flat areola no bud	Stipple areola 1–2 mm bud	Raised areola 3–4 mm bud	Full areola 5–10 mm bud		
Eye-ear	Lids fused loosely: −1 tightly: −2	Lids open pinna flat stays folded	Sl. curved pinna; soft; slow recoil	Well-curved pinna; soft but ready recoil	Formed and firm instant recoil	Thick cartilage, ear stiff		
Genitals (male)	Scrotum flat, smooth	Scrotum empty, faint rugae	Testes in upper canal, rare rugae	Testes descending, few rugae	Testes down, good rugae	Testes pendulous, deep rugae		
Genitals (female)	Clitoris prominent and labia flat	Prominent clitoris and small labia minora	Prominent clitoris and enlarging minora	Majora and minora equally prominent	Majora large, minora small	Majora cover clitoris and minora		
Total physical maturity score								

FIGURE 11.1 New Ballard Score.
Adapted from Ballard, Khoury, Wedig, Wang, Eilers-Walsman, and Lipp (1991).

NEW BALLARD SCORE

Physical examination of the infant's maturity is routinely accomplished in the newborn nursery or neonatal intensive care unit (NICU). Fetal physical and neurologic developmental changes are assessed. The Dubowitz examination (Dubowitz, Dubowitz, & Goldberg, 1970) was created in 1970 but shortened in 1979 by Dr. Jeanne L. Ballard (Ballard, Novak, & Driver, 1979). The full Dubowitz examination includes multiple items, many of which are difficult to accomplish with an infant who is ill, and it does not include criteria for scoring the extremely preterm infant. The New Ballard Score (NBS) developed by Dr. Ballard is a set of procedures to determine gestational age through neuromuscular and physical assessment of a newborn infant (Ballard et al., 1991). The NBS is accurate within 2 weeks in infants born at 26 to 42 weeks gestation if completed within 96 hours of birth; in infants born at less than 26 weeks gestation, the NBS is accurate within 2 weeks if done within 12 hours of birth (see Figure 11.1). The points obtained with the examination are summed; the weeks of gestation are determined by the Ballard maturity rating table (see Figure 11.1).

Assessment of Neuromuscular Maturity

The following information is reproduced with permission from www.ballardscore.com.

Posture

Total body muscle tone is reflected in the infant's preferred posture at rest and resistance to stretch of individual muscle groups. The preterm infant primarily exhibits unopposed passive extensor tone, while the infant approaching term shows progressively less opposed passive flexor tone. To elicit the posture item, the infant is placed supine (if previously prone), and the health care provider waits until the infant settles into a relaxed or preferred posture. If the infant is found supine, gentle manipulation (i.e., flex if extended; extend if flexed) of the extremities allows the infant to seek a baseline position of comfort. Hip flexion without abduction results in the frog-leg position as depicted in Figure 11.1, posture square #3. Hip abduction accompanying flexion is depicted by the acute angle at the hips in Figure 11.1, posture square #4. The figure that most closely depicts the infant's preferred posture is selected.

Angle of Wrist Flexion

Wrist flexibility and resistance to extensor stretching are responsible for the resulting angle of flexion at the wrist. The provider straightens the infant's fingers and applies gentle pressure on the dorsum of the hand, close to the fingers. From extremely preterm to postterm, the resulting angle between the palm of the infant's hand and forearm is estimated.

Arm Recoil

This maneuver focuses on passive flexor tone of the biceps muscle by measuring the angle of recoil following very brief extension of the upper extremity. With the infant lying supine, the provider places one hand beneath the infant's elbow for support. Taking the infant's hand, the provider briefly sets the elbow in flexion, then *momentarily* extends the arm before releasing the hand. The angle of recoil to which the forearm springs back into flexion is noted, and the appropriate square is selected on the score sheet (Table 11.4). The extremely preterm infant does not exhibit any arm recoil (see Figure 11.1, arm recoil score of 0). A score of 4 is selected only if there is contact between the infant's fist and face. This is seen in term and postterm infants.

Popliteal Angle

This maneuver assesses the maturation of passive flexor tone around the knee joint by testing for resistance to extension of the lower extremity. With the infant lying supine and with the diaper removed, the thigh is placed gently on the infant's abdomen with the knee fully flexed. After the infant has relaxed into this position, the provider gently grasps the foot at the sides with one hand while supporting the side of the thigh with the other. Care is taken not to exert pressure on the hamstrings, as this may interfere with their function. The leg is extended until a definite resistance to extension is appreciated. Hamstring contraction may be visualized during this maneuver in some infants. At this point, the angle formed at the knee by the upper and lower leg is measured. It is important that the provider wait until the infant stops kicking actively before extending the leg. The prenatal frank breech position interferes with this maneuver for the first 24 to 48 hours of age as a result of prolonged intrauterine flexor fatigue. The test should be repeated once recovery has occurred; alternately, a score similar to those obtained for other items in the examination may be assigned.

TABLE 11.4	Growth Assessment Terminology	
TERM	**COMMON ETIOLOGIES**	**COMMON RISKS**
SGA = small for gestational age; less than 10th percentile on curve	Placental insufficiency Maternal hypertension Discordant twin Maternal smoking Congenital viral infection Infant factors (genetic syndrome)	Hypoglycemia Thrombocytopenia Hearing loss Poor postnatal growth
AGA = average or appropriate for gestational age; 10th–90th percentile on curve	N/A	N/A
LGA = large for gestational age; greater than 90th percentile on curve	Infant of diabetic mother	Birth trauma Hypoglycemia Hypocalcemia Respiratory distress syndrome

Scarf Sign

This maneuver tests the passive tone of the flexors around the shoulder girdle. With the infant lying supine, the health care provider adjusts the infant's head to the midline and supports the infant's hand across the upper chest with one hand. The thumb of the provider's other hand is placed on the infant's elbow. The provider nudges the elbow across the chest, feeling for passive flexion or resistance to extension of the posterior shoulder girdle flexor muscles, that is, the point on the chest to which the elbow moves easily before significant resistance is noted. Landmarks noted in order of increasing maturity are full scarf at the level of the neck (–1), contralateral axillary line (0), contralateral nipple line (1), xiphoid process (2), ipsilateral nipple line (3), and ipsilateral axillary line (4).

Heel to Ear

This maneuver measures passive flexor tone around the pelvic girdle by testing for passive flexion or resistance to extension of posterior hip flexor muscles. The infant is placed supine, and the flexed lower extremity is brought to rest on the mattress alongside the infant's trunk. The health care provider supports the infant's thigh laterally alongside the body with the palm of one hand. The other hand is used to grasp the infant's foot at the sides and to pull it toward the ipsilateral ear. The provider feels for resistance to extension of the posterior pelvic girdle flexors and notes the location of the heel where significant resistance is appreciated. Landmarks noted in order of increasing maturity include resistance felt when the heel is at or near the ear (–1), nose (0), chin level (1), nipple line (2), umbilical area (3), and femoral crease (4).

Assessment of Physical Maturity

Skin

Maturation of fetal skin involves the development of its intrinsic structures concurrent with the gradual loss of its protective coating, the vernix caseosa. Hence, it thickens, dries, and becomes wrinkled or peels and may develop a rash as the fetus matures. These phenomena may occur at varying paces in individual fetuses, depending in part on the maternal condition and the intrauterine environment. Before the development of the epidermis with its stratum corneum, the skin is transparent and adheres somewhat to the provider's finger. Later it smoothes, thickens, and produces a lubricant, the vernix, that dissipates toward the end of gestation. At term and postterm, the fetus may expel meconium into the amniotic fluid. This may add an accelerating effect to the drying process, causing peeling, cracking, dehydration, and imparting a parchment, then leathery, appearance to the skin. For scoring purposes, the square that describes the infant's skin the most closely should be selected (see Figure 11.1).

Lanugo

Lanugo is the fine hair covering the body of the fetus. In extreme immaturity, the skin lacks any lanugo. Lanugo begins to appear at approximately the 24th to 25th week and is usually abundant, especially across the shoulders and upper back, by the 28th week of gestation. Thinning occurs first over the lower back, wearing away as the fetal body curves forward into its mature, flexed position. Bald areas appear and become larger over the lumbosacral area. At term, most of the fetal back is devoid of lanugo (i.e., the back is mostly bald). Variability in amount and location of lanugo at a given gestational age may be attributed in part to familial or racial differences and to certain hormonal, metabolic, and nutritional influences. For example, infants of diabetic mothers characteristically have abundant lanugo on their pinnae and upper back until close to or beyond full-term gestation. When scoring for lanugo, the provider selects the square that most closely describes the relative amounts of lanugo on the upper and lower areas of the infant's back (see Figure 11.1).

Plantar Surface

This item pertains to the major foot creases on the sole of the foot. The first appearance of a crease is on the anterior sole at the ball of the foot. This may be related to foot flexion in utero, but dehydration of the skin may also be a contributor. Very premature and extremely immature infants have no detectable foot creases. To help define the gestational age of these infants further, measuring the foot length or heel–toe distance is helpful. This is done by placing the infant's foot on a metric tape measure and noting the distance from the back of the heel to the tip of the great toe. For heel–toe distances less than 40 mm, a –2 score is assigned; for those between 40 and 50 mm, a –1 score is assigned (see Figure 11.1).

Breasts

The breast bud consists of breast tissue that is stimulated to grow by maternal estrogens and fatty tissue, which is dependent upon fetal nutritional status. The health care provider notes the size of the areola and the presence or absence of stippling (created by the developing papillae of Montgomery). The provider then palpates the breast tissue beneath the skin by holding it between thumb and forefinger, estimating its diameter in millimeters and selects the appropriate square on the score sheet (see Figure 11.1). Under- and overnutrition of the fetus may affect breast size at a given gestation. Maternal estrogen effects may produce neonatal gynecomastia, on the second to fourth day of extrauterine life, potentially lasting until 2 weeks of age.

Eyes and Ears

The pinna of the fetal ear changes its configuration and increases in cartilage content as maturation progresses. Assessment includes palpation for cartilage thickness, then folding the pinna forward toward the face and releasing it. The provider notes the rapidity with which the folded pinna snaps back away from the face when released, then selects the square that most closely describes the degree of cartilaginous development (see Figure 11.1). In very premature infants, the pinna may remain folded when released. In such infants, the provider notes the state of eyelid development as an additional indicator of maturation. The provider places the thumb and forefinger on the upper and lower lids, gently separating them. The extremely immature infant has tightly fused eyelids (i.e., the provider will not be able to separate either palpebral fissure with gentle traction). These findings allow the provider to select a –2 score. The more mature infant has one or both eyelids fused, but one or both can be separated by the light traction of the provider's fingertips. For loosely or partially fused eyelids, the provider selects a –1 score. The provider should not be surprised by a wide variation in eyelid fusion status in individual infants at a given gestational age, as the rate at which eyelids unfuse may be affected by stress-related intrauterine factors.

Male Genitalia

The fetal testicles begin their descent from the peritoneal cavity into the scrotal sac at approximately 30 weeks gestation. The left testicle precedes the right and usually enters the scrotum during the 32nd week. Both testicles are usually palpable in the upper to lower inguinal canals by the end of the 33rd to 34th weeks of gestation. Concurrently, the scrotal skin thickens and develops deeper and more numerous rugae. Testicles found inside the rugated zone are considered descended. In extreme prematurity, the scrotum is flat, smooth, and appears sexually undifferentiated. At term to postterm, the scrotum may become pendulous and may actually touch the mattress when the infant lies supine. Note that in true cryptorchidism, the scrotum on the affected side appears uninhabited and hypoplastic with underdeveloped rugae compared with the normal side or, for a given gestation, when bilateral. In such cases, the normal side should be scored, or if bilateral, a score similar to that obtained for the other maturational criteria should be assigned (see Figure 11.1).

Female Genitalia

To examine the female genitalia, the provider should only partially abduct the infant's hips (i.e., to approximately 45 degrees from the horizontal with the infant lying supine). Exaggerated abduction may cause the clitoris and labia minora to appear more prominent, whereas adduction may cause the labia majora to cover them. In extreme prematurity, the labia are flat, and the clitoris is very prominent, resembling the male phallus. As maturation progresses, the clitoris becomes less prominent, and the labia minora become more prominent. Nearing term, both the clitoris and labia minora recede and are eventually enveloped by the enlarging labia majora. The labia majora contain fat, and their size is affected by intrauterine nutrition. Overnutrition may result in large labia majora early in gestation, whereas undernutrition, like intrauterine growth retardation or postmaturity, may result in small labia majora with a relatively prominent clitoris and labia minora late in gestation. These findings should be reported as observed, since a lower score on this item in the chronically stressed or growth-retarded infant may be counterbalanced by a high score on certain neuromuscular items.

Growth Assessment

Growth parameters are important aspects of physical assessment. Fetal growth is influenced by many genetic and environmental factors. Normal fetal growth plots are available with the Ballard examination recording sheet (Battaglia & Lubchenco, 1967). It is important to determine if infant growth is normal, allowing close monitoring for risk factors associated with abnormal growth (see Table 11.4).

Measurements of the infant's weight, length, and head circumference (occipital-frontal circumference [OFC]) are obtained following birth. Length is the most difficult measurement to assess reliably; care should be taken to extend the infant fully, using a length board to obtain the most accurate measurement possible (Centers for Disease Control National Health and Nutrition Examination Survey, 2004). Growth parameters are plotted on the growth curve according to the infant's gestational age, determining the appropriateness of growth. The infant's gestational age must be determined as accurately as possible for accurate growth assessment. The infant's weight determines the appropriateness of growth at the determined gestational age.

- **Length:** Normal crown-to-heel length at term is 44 to 55 cm
- **Weight:** Normal weight at term is 2.5 to 3.9 kg
- **Head circumference/Occipital frontal circumference (OFC):** Normal head circumference at term is 33 to 36 cm

■ **Chest circumference:** The chest circumference should be 1 to 2 cm less than the head circumference, thus giving a rough assessment of head size.

Vital Sign Assessment

The infant's axillary temperature is normally 36°C to 37°C. Some health care providers advocate one rectal temperature after birth to rule out imperforate anus. The newborn's pulse is normally 100 to 140 beats per minute (bpm) at rest, but it increases with crying. Some normal newborns have a resting heart rate as low as 80 to 90 bpm at rest. The respiratory rate of a normal newborn is 30 to 60 breaths per minute, but this rate increases with crying. In normal, healthy, full-term infants, the blood pressure is not measured on a routine basis. Blood pressure is difficult to obtain in a newborn because of movement and crying in the newborn, and artifact is common. If a blood pressure measurement is warranted, care must be taken to ensure that the proper cuff size is used to ensure an accurate reading. In neonates, the preferred site to measure blood pressure is the right arm, and the cuff width should be 40% of the circumference of the limb on which the cuff is placed (AAP, 2004). Blood pressure should be monitored closely in ill infants. If congenital heart disease is suspected, blood pressure measurements in all four extremities may be helpful in diagnosing coarctation of the aorta, where the upper extremity (specifically, the right arm) pressure is 15 mmHg or more higher than the lower extremity.

Skin Assessment

Color Variants

Skin color varies according to the racial background of the infant (Thilo & Rosenberg, 2012), but it should be pink at birth. Pallor may indicate anemia or shock. If the infant has dark skin tones, the provider should observe for pink color in the lips, the palms of the hands, and the soles of the feet. Normal variants include the following (Morelli & Prok, 2012; Thilo & Rosenberg, 2012):

■ **Acrocyanosis** is a bluish-purple coloring of the extremities that is worsened by cold stress.
■ **Mottling** (cutis marmorata) is a normal variation unless exaggerated and accompanied by other signs of shock.
■ **Plethora** is a deep red skin color that is normal, especially with crying. If the infant also has a deep red color with purplish extremities, a high hematocrit level (*polycythemia*) may be present. The hematocrit level should be monitored in infants with pallor or plethora.
■ **Harlequin** color change describes an infant who, when lying on one side, is red on the inferior portion and pale on the superior portion. The

cause is unknown, but it is thought to be a temporary imbalance of the autonomic regulatory mechanism of the cutaneous vessels.

■ **Jaundice** is the yellow discoloration of skin because of the subcutaneous accumulation of bilirubin (*hyperbilirubinemia*). Jaundice is pathologic in the first 24 hours and is initially most apparent in the face; however, as the hyperbilirubinemia worsens, jaundice is visible further down the body. Physiologic jaundice is not visible until after 24 hours, depending on the subcutaneous fat composition of the infant. Preterm or thin infants with little subcutaneous fat do not appear jaundiced in proportion to the bilirubin levels. Conversely, infants with generous subcutaneous fat appear jaundiced at lower levels. Jaundice is also less visible in dark-skinned infants. Jaundice color estimation is not a reliable indicator of serum bilirubin levels.
■ **Lanugo** is a fine, soft, downy hair covering of the fetus in utero and some term newborns. It appears at about 20 weeks gestation, peaks at around 28 weeks gestation, and then thins; little is apparent by 40 weeks gestation. Lanugo is more prominent or visible in darker-skinned infants.
■ **Vernix caseosa** is a greasy white or yellow material composed of sebaceous gland secretions and exfoliated skin cells. Vernix caseosa develops during the third trimester and covers the newborn skin, decreasing in amount as the fetus nears 40 weeks gestation.
■ **Meconium-stained skin** is seen if meconium is passed by the fetus and delivery is delayed; the skin takes on a greenish color. This is most pronounced in the umbilical cord and the nails.

Skin Perfusion

Skin perfusion is assessed by inspection and palpation. Poor skin perfusion may be seen with cold stress, hypothermia, or shock. Mottling, a blotchy marbling effect, is common with cold stress, although it is more common in infants with Down syndrome and may be present in infants with low cardiac output. Mottling is less visible in dark-skinned infants.

Capillary refill time is assessed by pressing on the skin, usually over the chest. Blanching of the skin is observed; refill time should be brisk. Abnormal or prolonged capillary refill time is over 3 seconds. Capillary refill time in the extremities is normally more prolonged than over the trunk.

Rashes

Common newborn rashes are listed in Box 11.1. A few examples can be seen in Figure 11.2.

BOX 11.1 Common Skin Variations in the Newborn Infant

- *Erythema toxicum* manifests as small white or yellow papules or vesicles with an erythematous base (see Figure 11.2).
- *Milia* are yellow or white papules about 1 mm size. These are epidermal cysts caused by the accumulation of sebaceous gland secretions (see Figure 11.2).
- *Miliaria* are obstructed sweat ducts: (a) *miliaria crystallina,* 1 to 2 mm vesicles; (b) *miliaria rubra* (prickly heat), which appears as small erythematous papules; and (c) *miliaria pustulosa* (pustular milia), which can lead to a secondary infection of the deeper sweat glands (*miliaria profunda*).
- *Sebaceous gland hyperplasia* manifests as numerous tiny (less than 0.5 mm) white or yellow papules on the nose and upper lip.
- *Neonatal herpes* manifests as vesicles that can appear anywhere. Crusting occurs after opening. This is ominous, as infection can disseminate and be fatal.
- *Petechiae* are pinpoint-sized hemorrhagic spots on the skin. A few are normal over the face following vertex vaginal delivery. Multiple petechiae may indicate thrombocytopenia.
- *Mongolian spots* are commonly seen, especially in dark-skinned infants, over the sacrum/buttocks, but they may be anywhere on the body, indicating melanocytes infiltrating the dermis. Mongolian spots are benign and fade over the first few years of life. These lesions may be mistaken for bruising by those unfamiliar with this common variant (see Figure 11.2).
- *Nevi* are dark brown or black macules. These are generally benign, but malignant changes may occur in up to 10% of larger (greater than 2 cm diameter) nevi. A *spilus* is a nonhairy nevus, while a *pilosus* is a hairy nevus.
- *Accessory nipples* may be seen, usually over an imaginary line drawn from the main nipple to the umbilicus. Breast tissue is usually not present, and the nipple is usually not well formed. Accessory nipples may be similar in appearance to a dark nevus.
- *Café-au-lait patches* are tan or light brown macules or patches with well-defined borders. Larger spots or the presence of more than six lesions may indicate cutaneous neurofibromatosis (von Recklinghausen disease).
- *Cutis aplasia* is the absence of some or all layers of the skin. These are most commonly found on the scalp.
- *Traumatic skin lesions* include forceps marks, which are most common on the cheeks, scalp, or face. The practitioner must examine the child closely for facial palsy, fractured clavicles, and skull fractures (see Figure 11.2).
- *Subcutaneous fat necrosis* is a subcutaneous nodule that is hard and sharply circumscribed; it may be red or purplish. The cause is trauma, cold stress, or asphyxia. These may grow slowly, then resolve over several weeks.
- *Facial bruising* may be present, usually with face presentations or forceps marks at birth.
- *Scalp lesions* can result from scalp electrode placement. A scalp electrode provides monitoring of the fetal heart rate during delivery. The skin is punctured as the spiral electrode is inserted. If the scalp is scratched with electrode placement, the site should be monitored for infection.
- *Edematous skin* and *subcutaneous tissues* under a vacuum cup can result from vacuum extraction, which is used to facilitate delivery as an alternative to forceps. Discoloration and skin abrasions may also be present.
- *Scalp pH sampling* leaves a puncture mark, which should be monitored for infection. Blood is often obtained during labor for pH analysis, indicating the fetal acid-base status, a measure of fetal well-being.
- *Sucking blisters* are vesicles or bullae on the lips, fingers, or hands, resulting from the fetus sucking on the area.
- *Hypoplasia or absence of the nails* is associated with trisomies or Turner syndrome. Abnormal shape of the nails may be a normal variant or associated with anomalies of the hair or skin.
- *Telangiectatic nevi,* or *nevus simplex* are commonly called stork bites. These are found at the nape of the neck and on the upper eyelids, bridge of the nose, and upper lip. They blanch with pressure and fade over the first 1 to 2 years of life (see Figure 11.2).
- *Port-wine stain* or *nevus flammeus* manifests as flat pink or reddish purple lesion consisting of dilated, congested capillaries directly beneath the epidermis. The lesion has sharp borders, does not blanch with pressure, and does not fade over time.
- *Strawberry marks (capillary hemangioma)* are lesions that consist of dilated capillaries. These are usually not present at birth but appear shortly after birth, often as small pinpoint lesions, which grow in size over the first 6 to 12 months of life. They appear as bright red, raised, lobulated tumors. They feel soft when palpated and have sharply demarcated margins. After a year of age, the lesions usually begin to resolve, appearing light in color at the center. Surgical removal is not recommended initially, since cosmetic outcomes are better if the lesion regresses without intervention. Hemangiomas are more common in preterm infants; some have multiple lesions over their body. Intervention is required if the hemangioma is over the eyelid, restricting vision, or if the lesion bleeds excessively.
- *Cavernous hemangiomas* are larger than capillary hemangiomas, purplish, and soft and compressible, with poorly defined borders.

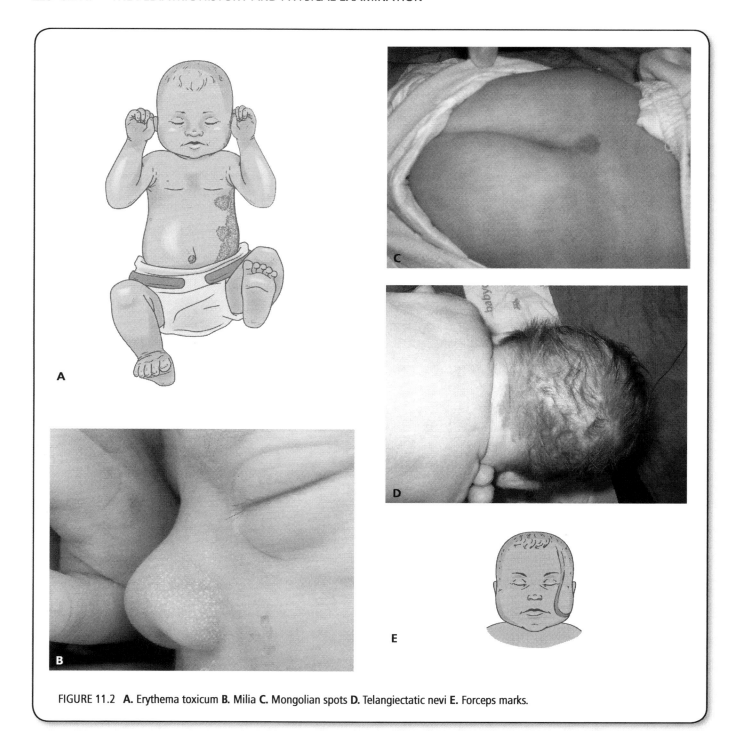

FIGURE 11.2 **A.** Erythema toxicum **B.** Milia **C.** Mongolian spots **D.** Telangiectatic nevi **E.** Forceps marks.

Head and Neck Assessment

Shape and Size

Molding of the head is common with a vaginal delivery, as the head passes through the vaginal canal. Molding may also be seen with a cesarean section delivery if the head descended into the pelvis before the operative delivery. The parietal bones overlap the frontal bones, and the head appears elongated. This resolves very quickly over the first few days of life.

The infant's head has a different appearance following breech delivery, as molding does not occur, and the occiput appears prominent. Other variations in head shape may be seen temporarily, reflecting in utero positioning, and usually resolving over the first few days of life (Figure 11.3).

Occipital-Frontal Circumference

The health care provider should plot the OFC on the Ballard gestational age assessment growth curve

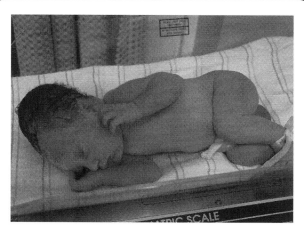

FIGURE 11.3 Molding in the infant's head.

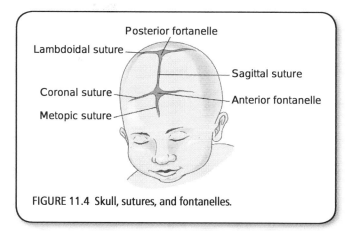

FIGURE 11.4 Skull, sutures, and fontanelles.

(see Figure 11.1). As previously described, normal size is 33 to 36 cm at term (see Figure 11.1). Head circumference that is outside the normal range requires investigation to determine the etiology, guide treatment, and aid in providing an accurate prognosis.

- **Microcephaly** is defined by an OFC less than the 10th percentile. It is associated with congenital viral infections or results from unknown factors. If the microcephaly persists, the developmental prognosis is poor.
- **Macrocephaly** is defined by an OFC greater than the 90th percentile. This may be present with congenital hydrocephalus, or it may be a normal variant that is familial.

Skull

The infant's skull should be examined visually and by palpation. The infant's skull shape, sutures, and bony structure may provide information about congenital malformations or birth trauma. The skull should be assessed when the infant is quiet, as the fontanelles become tense with crying (Figure 11.4). The fontanelles should be soft and flat and measured bone to bone, diagonally. The anterior fontanelle is diamond-shaped. The size varies from less than 1 cm by 1 cm to 4 to 5 cm; it closes by 12 to 18 months of age. The posterior fontanelle is triangle-shaped. Size is usually less than 1 cm, closing by 2 to 3 months of age.

All sutures should be mobile and split less than 1 cm. Sutures may be overlapping because of molding, resolving in the first weeks of life. *Craniosynostosis* describes a condition in which one or more sutures close prematurely, leading to an abnormally shaped head.

Scalp and Hair

The infant's head should be inspected and palpated to detect congenital malformations or birth sequelae.

Caput Succedaneum • This is usually called simply *caput* and indicates edema of the fetal scalp as a result of labor and delivery. It is accentuated by a vacuum-assisted delivery. Edema usually crosses suture lines, and the edges are poorly defined. Caput is noted immediately after birth and resolves in a few days.

Cephalhematoma • A cephalhematoma is a collection of blood between the periosteum and the skull. This is usually not evident immediately after birth because of the slow bleeding process, and it may be masked by an overlying caput. Clearly demarcated edges are visible, not crossing suture lines. A cephalhematoma may take weeks or months to resolve, and may result in jaundice and hyperbilirubinemia (Figure 11.5).

Hair Whorls • One or two hair whorls, where the hair grows in a circular pattern, are normal variants; however, an increased number of hair whorls is associated with abnormal brain development (Painter & Yang, 2008).

Encephalocele • An encephalocele is a herniation of the brain and meninges resulting from a defect in the skull, most commonly in the occipital region. It may be small or large and may or may not include brain matter.

Face

The provider must observe the infant's face when the infant is crying to assess for appropriate movement and for asymmetry. For example, facial palsy might not be apparent unless the infant is crying.

Ears

The ears vary widely in appearance, and the provider must observe the parents' ears for comparison. It is

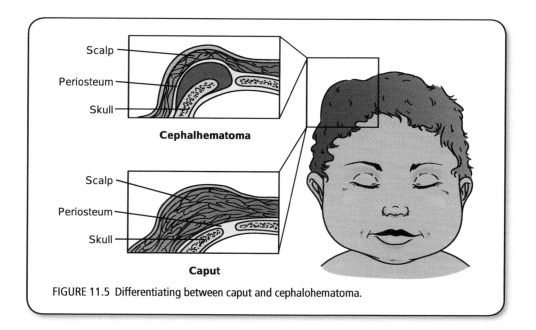

Scalp

Periosteum

Skull

Cephalhematoma

Scalp

Periosteum

Skull

Caput

FIGURE 11.5 Differentiating between caput and cephalohematoma.

important to determine the position or placement of the ears on the infant's head. The provider must extend a line from the inner to the outer canthus of the eye toward the ear. The insertion of the pinna should fall on this line. If the insertion falls below this line, the ears are low-set (see Chapter 14 for ear placement guidelines).

The provider should look for pits and skin tags around the ears; these are commonly found in front of the ear (see Chapter 14). Otoscopic examination is not a part of the newborn examination, as the canals are very small and often filled with vernix.

Eyes

Esotropia (cross-eye) and *exotropia* (walleye) are normal findings until the infant is 4 months of age. The term newborn is able to track visually when in a quiet, alert state. Palpebral fissures describe the elliptical spaces when the eyelids are opened normally. The health care provider should note an abnormal size or shape of the fissures. Edema or bruises of the eyelids are common, as are conjunctival or subconjunctival hemorrhages. The provider should evaluate the placement and size of the eyes. Normal eye spacing is evaluated by measuring the eye width; the eyes are normally one eye width apart. *Hypertelorism* describes eyes that are wide-spaced, and *hypotelorism* describes eyes that are closely spaced (see Chapter 15).

The slant of the eyes should also be evaluated. An upward palpebral slant describes when the outer canthus is higher than inner canthus; a downward palpebral slant describes when the inner canthus is higher than outer canthus. An epicanthal fold is present in Asians, and in infants with Down syndrome.

Other notable abnormalities of the eyes include *ptosis* (drooping of the upper eyelid) and *coloboma* (defect in the closure of a portion of the lid or eye). Tear

formation does not begin until 2 to 3 months of age. Obstruction of the tear duct (*nasolacrimal duct*) is common, resulting in purulent or mucoid eye drainage. This is not usually seen in the first few months. Redness or swelling of the area may indicate an infection.

The eye examination is most easily accomplished when the infant is quiet and alert. The lights should be dimmed, and the ophthalmoscope adjusted to a small round white beam. Assessment should be performed from about 6 inches from the eye to assess pupil size and constriction. The provider should look for a clear red color (red reflex) over the lens. The absence of a red reflex could imply congenital cataracts, retinoblastoma, or glaucoma. The red reflex is pale or pink in dark-skinned infants. The corneal reflex describes blinking in response to blowing into the infant's eye or gently touching the cornea with a cotton swab to elicit a blink.

The iris is dark gray, blue, or brown at birth, differing among racial groups. The provider should examine the iris for Brushfield's spots, which are white specks scattered over the iris; these are associated with Down syndrome. The sclera should be white, light blue, or bluish white. Blue sclera are associated with *osteogenesis imperfecta* (a collagen disorder characterized by brittle bones). Sclera may become yellow with extreme jaundice. Areas of hemorrhage are common following birth. Sunset eyes, where the eyes appear to look downward, may indicate hydrocephalus or other neurologic problems.

Nose

The nose may initially be deviated because of the in utero position and delivery. Patency of the nares must be assessed. Since infants are obligatory nose breathers, it can be assumed that at least one nostril is patent if the infant is quiet and breathing normally. Passing a feeding tube or suction catheter through each nostril confirms patency but is not necessary unless nasal obstruction is suspected.

Choanal atresia, the congenital blockage of nasal passages by membrane or bone, may be an isolated defect or part of a syndrome. The infant with choanal atresia is pink when crying but becomes dyspneic and eventually cyanotic and bradycardic when quiet. An oral airway facilitates respirations. Infants with nasal passages that are partially obstructed by secretions or edema or that are congenitally narrow allow the infant to either inhale normally or inhale with varying amounts of dyspnea, such as nasal flaring or retractions; with exhalation, air may escape through the mouth. *Nasal flaring* is a sign of respiratory distress; the nostrils flare as the infant inhales. Sneezing and stuffiness are common in the newborn infant. Nasal drainage is an abnormal finding and should be evaluated.

A long, smooth philtrum may be present in an infant with fetal alcohol syndrome (FAS). Other features of FAS include short palpebral fissures, short nose, microcephaly, and intellectual disability.

Mouth

The inside of the mouth is examined when the infant is crying, if possible, as opening the infant's mouth is difficult. The infant's cry should be assessed for normalcy; term infants should have a vigorous cry. A tongue blade can be used if necessary, and a bright light, usually the otoscope, can be used to enhance visualization.

A cleft lip is visible immediately. Cleft palate, if complete, is easily visible when the infant cries. The palate is normally intact and highly arched, which can be assessed by placing a gloved finger in the mouth and palpating the palate. A cleft of the soft palate is not easily seen. The health care provider should examine the infant for the presence of the uvula, which should be midline. Absence or clefting of the uvula indicates a soft palate cleft (Tewflik, Kanaan, & Karsan, 2013).

In addition, the tongue size should be assessed; a large tongue (*macroglossia*) is associated with Beckwith syndrome. An infant with Down syndrome appears to have a large tongue, but the infant's mouth is actually small, and the tongue is a normal size. The sublingual frenulum should be observed when the infant cries. A very short frenulum or true tongue-tie (*ankyloglossia*) is rare; providers must look for an indentation at the end of the tongue. The frenulum historically was clipped with a scissors if judged to be short, but this is considered unnecessary as most lengthen over time.

Gums must be inspected; neonatal teeth may be present and should be removed if loose, to avoid aspiration. Sebaceous cysts on the gums (Epstein's pearls) can resemble teeth; however, these are a normal variant and fade over time. The provider assesses the suck and gag reflexes by placing a gloved finger in the mouth.

Excessive oral secretions may indicate the presence of *esophageal atresia*, a congenital malformation where the esophagus ends in a blind pouch, prohibiting swallowing of saliva or feedings. If the esophagus is patent, excessive secretions may indicate a muscular or neurologic problem, resulting in an inability to swallow. Swallowing problems are commonly associated with a history of an abnormally large amount of amniotic fluid (*polyhydramnios*) prenatally. Amniotic fluid is normally swallowed by the fetus; inability to swallow results in excessive amniotic fluid.

A receding chin is common in newborns. A very small chin (*micrognathia*) may be an isolated finding. Infants with the Pierre Robin sequence (a developmental defect)—consisting of micrognathia, glossoptosis (a large tongue), and a cleft palate—may present with severe respiratory distress. The initial event of the Pierre Robin sequence, mandibular hypoplasia, occurs between the 7th and 11th week of gestation. This keeps the tongue high in the oral cavity, preventing the closure of the palatal shelves and causing a cleft in the palate (Cole, Lynch, & Slator, 2008).

Neck

Very little of an infant's neck is visible as it is usually surrounded by skinfolds. Nevertheless, the neck should be palpated for masses. For example:

- **Cystic hygromas** involve lymph channel blockages that dilate into cysts. These may be unilateral or bilateral, occurring over the clavicle. Hygromas range in size from less than 1 cm to several centimeters in diameter.
- **Thyroglossal duct cysts** form from a persistent thyroglossal duct, presenting as a mass high in the neck.
- **Brachial cleft cysts** are congenital epithelial cysts resulting from a failure of the obliteration of the second brachial cleft in embryonic development. Brachial cysts are smooth, nontender, fluctuant masses on the latter part of the neck along the lower anteromediolateral border of the sternocleidomastoid muscle.

Both thyroglossal duct cysts and brachial cysts may be present at birth or manifest later in life and may require surgical removal. A sinus tract from the brachial cyst to the skin may be present (Leung & Robson, 2004). A webbed neck may indicate Turner syndrome or Noonan syndrome. Redundant skin in the back of the neck is a common finding in infants with Down syndrome.

The health care provider should palpate the clavicles, feeling for *crepitus* (crackling feeling) over a fractured clavicle. Callus at the fracture site may be palpated a few days after the fracture. Arm movements bilaterally must be assessed for brachial plexus injury.

The infant's head position must be observed in the supine position at rest and also in a supported sit position. A tilt may indicate congenital muscular torticollis. The head is moved passively, tipping each ear to each shoulder. A decreased ability to touch the ear to the shoulder indicates torticollis. The sternocleidomastoid muscle must be palpated bilaterally for thickening or masses.

Chest and Lung Assessment

Inspection

Respirations • The normal respiratory rate is 30 to 60 breaths per minute. Infants are abdominal breathers so chest movement is low in the chest, with abdominal movement. The abdominal movement with breathing diminishes over the first few months of life. Signs of respiratory distress include nasal flaring, grunting, and retractions. Symmetry in chest movement should be observed (see Chapter 17).

Newborns normally have irregular breathing patterns with short respiratory pauses between periods of breathing, termed periodic breathing. A pause of more than 15 to 20 seconds, accompanied by bradycardia or cyanosis, is termed *apnea* and is pathologic.

Newborn infants have a round-shaped chest. The anterior–posterior (A–P) diameter should equal the transverse diameter. Chest circumference is normally 2 cm less than the OFC. Deviations of the chest include *pectus carinatum*, also called "pigeon chest," with a protruding sternum, *pectus excavatum*, also called "funnel chest" with an indented sternum, and a barrel-shaped chest, with an increased A–P diameter. A barrel chest is seen with air trapping, such as with meconium aspiration.

Nipples and Breasts • The nipples of a full-term infant are raised and stippled with 0.75 to 1 cm of palpable breast tissue. The provider should note wide-spaced nipples, which accompany some syndromes. The space between the nipples should be less than one-quarter of the chest circumference. Engorged breasts may be seen in male or female infants within the first few days of life as a result of maternal hormones. This resolves without intervention over several days. The breasts may secrete milk (i.e., physiologic galactorrhea). Supernumerary (accessory) nipples are raised or pigmented areas below the nipple in a line drawn from the nipple to the umbilicus.

Auscultation

Breath sounds of infants are loud and somewhat coarse. The stethoscope should be warm. The health care provider must use the diaphragm and then the bell, beginning at the top of the chest and moving systematically from side to side. The provider listens to the lower lobes of the lung from the infant's back. Breath sounds are normally vesicular (i.e., soft, short, and low pitched during expiration, and loud, long, and high pitched during inspiration). Breath sounds may be bronchovesicular

over the scapulas. These sounds are louder than vesicular sounds and demonstrate an inspiration and expiration that are equal in quality, intensity, pitch, and duration. Adventitious sounds include the following:

- **Crackles** (rales) may be fine, medium, or coarse. Crackles indicate that airways are popping open or that a liquid film is breaking.
- **Rhonchi** are lower and more musical than crackles and are heard when secretions are loose.
- **Wheezes** are unusual in the newborn. Wheezing indicates narrowing of the airways or bronchospasm.
- **Rubs** are unusual in neonates.
- **Stridor** is a high-pitched hoarse sound on inspiration or expiration at the larynx or upper airways. Stridor indicates partial airway obstruction or malacia of the trachea or larynx and usually requires further evaluation.

Percussion

Percussion is difficult with large hands and a small chest and, therefore, is often not included in the newborn examination.

Palpation

The clavicles should be palpated for fractures or crepitus. The breast tissue should be palpated to evaluate maturity and check for masses. The sternum and ribs should be palpated to evaluate for abnormalities.

Cardiovascular Assessment

Inspection

Inspection of skin and mucous membranes is an important part of the cardiovascular assessment as skin perfusion is an important indicator of cardiac output and function. *Acrocyanosis* (cyanosis of the extremities) is a normal finding but is more apparent in pale-skinned infants and is common when the infant is cold stressed. Plethora is a ruddy red color that may look like cyanosis and may be secondary to polycythemia. The lips and tongue are inspected for central cyanosis. If central cyanosis does not improve with oxygen administration, the infant may have cyanotic heart disease. The provider should note pallor, mottling, and poor perfusion, as these may indicate anemia or shock. Edema is a rare finding in the neonate. Generalized edema at birth is called *hydrops fetalis*.

The health care provider should inspect the precordium for movement. A hyperactive precordium is present with cardiomegaly or cardiac lesions that increase ventricular work. The precordium, which is hyperactive in premature infants as a result of a thin chest wall, should be palpated (using the palm of the hand) for heaves, taps, and thrills.

Palpation

The peripheral pulses—including brachial, radial, femoral, and posterior tibial at a minimum—are palpated, as pulses represent an approximate determination of cardiac output and blood flow to the extremities. Pulse volume and character are graded on a scale of 0 to 4, with 0 indicating absent and 4+ indicating bounding. Normal pulses are designated as 2, or 2/4. Weak pulses are designated as 1 or 1/4, and bounding pulses are designated as 3/4 or 4/4. Bounding pulses are seen with some congenital heart defects such as patent ductus arteriosus, truncus arteriosus, and a systemic arteriovenous fistula. Weak pulses indicate low cardiac output.

The right femoral and right brachial pulses should be palpated simultaneously. A weak or absent femoral pulse indicates coarctation of the aorta until proven otherwise. It could also indicate aortic stenosis or hypoplastic left heart syndrome.

The liver should be palpated, as it becomes engorged and enlarged with congestive heart failure. The liver margin should be felt 2 cm or less below the right costal margin (RCM).

Auscultation

The provider should auscultate for cardiac position (point of maximal impulse, PMI). The PMI should be at the fourth intercostal space (ICS) at the midclavicular line (MCL). The PMI can be displaced with dextrocardia, diaphragmatic hernia, and pneumothoraces. If the heart cannot be heard with a stethoscope or if the heart sounds are muffled but the infant is pink with pulses present, air or gas may be present in the mediastinum (*pneumomediastinum*).

Heart Rate • A normal heart rate in the term infant is 80 to 160 bpm and is higher with crying. A heart rate less than 80 bpm is called *sinus bradycardia*. Sinus tachycardia describes a heart rate that is higher than normal for age. This is usually greater than 160 bpm at rest in a full-term infant.

Supraventricular tachycardia (SVT) is the most common arrhythmia in neonates. A heart rate over 200 bpm is usually SVT. SVT is tolerated well for short periods but leads to heart failure if prolonged.

Sinus arrhythmia is not uncommon. The heart rate increases on inspiration and decreases on expiration.

Bradycardia, a very low heart rate in an infant who is breathing and appears well, is probably congenital heart block. The heart rate may be as low as 40 bpm. If the infant is pink and noncompromised, treatment is not required emergently.

Heart Sounds • Auscultation of heart sounds includes listening over the entire chest and over the back. At minimum, the provider must listen over the following:

- Aortic area, second ICS, right sternal border (RSB)
- Pulmonic area, second ICS, left sternal border (LSB)
- Tricuspid area, fourth ICS, LSB
- Mitral area, fourth ICS, MCL

Also, the provider must auscultate over the clavicles, both sides of the back, the anterior fontanelle (for cerebral arteriovenous fistulas), and the liver (for hepatic arteriovenous fistulas). Heart sounds likely to be heard in the newborn include the following:

- S1 is the closure of the mitral and tricuspid valves, which is loudest at the apex; splitting is very hard to hear and unusual.
- S2 is the closure of the aortic and pulmonic valves, which is loudest at the base; splitting occurs after 16 hours of age. Wide splitting is abnormal.
- S3 and S4 are difficult to hear in neonates as a result of rapid heart rate.
- **Ejection clicks**, high and snappy sounds, are normal in the first 24 hours of life.

Murmurs • Heart murmurs are caused by turbulent blood flow. Pathologic murmurs arise from cardiovascular defects or disease; innocent murmurs are heard with a structurally and functionally normal heart. The presence of a murmur does not indicate congenital heart disease. For example, infants with the most severe defects often present without a murmur. Many heart defects present with a murmur after the first 1 to 2 weeks of life, when pulmonary vascular resistance falls and shunting increases. The provider must distinguish between systolic or diastolic murmurs. Continuous murmurs are heard throughout systole and diastole.

Murmurs are graded according to how loudly they are heard and whether or not there is a thrill present. The murmur must be auscultated, and the hand of the provider must be placed over the precordium to feel a thrill, a rumbling feeling. Murmurs are graded as follows:

- Grade I: barely audible
- Grade II: soft but audible immediately
- Grade III: moderate intensity (no thrill)
- Grade IV: loud (may have thrill)
- Grade V: very loud; can be heard with the stethoscope rim barely on chest (may have thrill)
- Grade VI: extremely loud; can be heard with the stethoscope just slightly removed from the chest (may have thrill)

It is important to discern the location of the murmur and the PMI. By listening to other locations where the murmur is heard, radiation or transmission of the murmur can be determined. The pitch of the murmur is described as high, medium, or low. The quality of the murmur is described as harsh, rumbling, musical, or machinery-like.

Innocent murmurs are usually grade I or II, systolic, and the infant is asymptomatic. Innocent murmurs are common, especially in the first 48 hours of life. Common innocent murmurs include the following:

- **Systolic ejection murmurs** are usually grade I–II/VI and heard over the mid- and upper LSB. These murmurs are vibratory and heard between 1 and 7 days of age. The murmur is a result of increased flow across the pulmonary valve with decreased pulmonary vascular resistance.
- **Continuous systolic or crescendo systolic murmurs** are usually grade I–II/VI and heard over the upper LSB. These murmurs are heard in the infant's first 8 hours of life and are a result of the closure of the ductus arteriosus.
- **Peripheral pulmonic stenosis (PPS)** is an early soft grade I–II/VI midsystolic ejection murmur heard at the upper LSB with radiation to the clavicles and to the back. This murmur is heard at 1 to 2 weeks of age, disappears by 6 months of age, and is the result of turbulence at the bifurcation of pulmonary artery.

Pathologic murmurs may be noted after a few days or weeks of life or be present at birth. Soft murmurs in asymptomatic infants can be observed for 48 hours. Further evaluation is required if the murmur persists beyond 48 hours, is louder than grade II, or the infant is symptomatic.

Blood Pressure • Four extremity blood pressure readings are valuable if coarctation of the aorta is suspected. Upper extremity blood pressure is more than 20 mmHg higher than lower extremity blood pressure if coarctation is present. A wide pulse pressure may be a sign of a patent ductus arteriosus as a result of aortic runoff. Low blood pressure is a late sign of shock. Early signs of shock include poor perfusion, tachycardia, weak pulses, and acidosis (Anderson-Berry, Bellig, & Ohning, 2014).

Abdominal Assessment

Inspection

Providers must inspect the abdomen before auscultation or palpation (see Chapter 19). The abdomen usually moves with the chest during respirations. The shape of the abdomen is observed for symmetry, distention, fullness, or scaphoid appearance. Midline defects are readily apparent and include the following:

- **Omphalocele** is an anterior abdominal wall defect at the base of the umbilical cord that results in herniation of the abdominal contents, covered by the parietal peritoneum, amnion, and Wharton's jelly. Occasionally, the omphalocele is open, indicating a tear or opening in the encapsulating tissue.
- **Gastroschisis** is a herniation of the abdominal contents through an abdominal fusion defect usually to the right of the umbilical cord.

- **Bladder exstrophy** is a malformation of the bladder and urethra in which the bladder is turned "inside out" and exposed outside the body. Cloacal exstrophy involves bladder exstrophy; in addition, the urethra and genitalia are not formed completely, and the anus and vagina appear anteriorly displaced. The pelvic bones are widely separated (*diastasis*). An omphalocele and imperforate anus are usually also present (Heinrich, Huemmer, Reingruber, & Weber, 2008; Islam, 2008; Mac Bird et al., 2009; Mayhew & Mychaskiw, 2009; Stoll, Alembik, Dott, & Roth, 2008).
- **Diastasis recti**, a normal variant, is the gap between the rectus muscles. Visible bulging is apparent over the midline when the infant cries.

The umbilicus is inspected next. Three vessels—two arteries and one vein—should be present. The cord may be thick or thin with Wharton's jelly. The cord should dry quickly and fall off in 1 to 3 weeks. The cord clamp is usually left on for 12 to 24 hours or until the cord is somewhat dry. A green-colored cord at birth results from meconium staining. Clear discharge from the stump suggests a patent urachus or duct, where urine passes from the bladder through the umbilicus.

Umbilical hernias are common in premature infants and African American male infants. They are not present at birth but appear after a few weeks or months postpartum and resolve without intervention in most cases (Figure 11.6).

Health care providers must inspect the anus for patency. An imperforate anus is usually obvious; however, the anus may look normal in the presence of a blind pouch. Female infants commonly pass stool vaginally via a rectovaginal fistula. Male infants may pass meconium from the penis via a rectourethral fistula. Presence of meconium at an anal orifice determines patency. Meconium should be passed within 48 hours of birth. Providers can determine the presence of an anal wink by stroking the perianal area and observing the reflexive contraction of the external anal sphincter. Digital rectal examination is not routine in neonates.

Auscultation

Bowel sounds begin shortly after birth. The provider must listen to all quadrants with the infant at rest.

Palpation

The health care provider must assess tone over the abdomen. Tense, rigid tone suggests peritoneal irritation. Flaccid tone is abnormal and may indicate an absence of musculature. The skin turgor over the abdomen must be noted as well, as it is an indicator of hydration status.

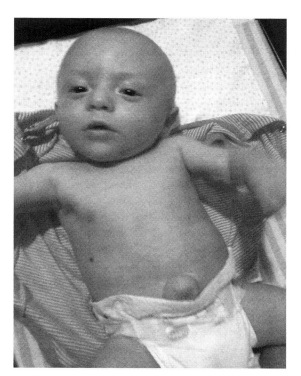

FIGURE 11.6 Umbilical hernia.

The provider palpates the liver by moving the fingers gently up from the groin to the RCM to find the liver's edge. The liver should be palpated at or 1 to 2 cm below the RCM. The spleen is palpated similarly but on the left side. The spleen tip may be palpable, but it is often difficult to palpate unless it is enlarged.

Normal kidneys are difficult to palpate in full-term infants. The provider's fingers are placed under the area adjacent to the umbilicus and pinched gently with the thumbs. Alternatively, the provider places the fingers of one hand under the flank and then presses gently with the other hand. Kidneys are more easily palpated if they are enlarged, if the infant is preterm, or if the infant has decreased abdominal musculature or tone. The bladder lies 1 to 4 cm above the symphysis pubis and is usually not palpable unless it is distended with urine.

A systematic approach should be used for palpation, covering all four quadrants of the abdomen and feeling for masses. At first, palpation should be superficial, then deeper. The descending colon may be palpable in the left lower quadrant.

The groin area must also be inspected and palpated deeply. The inguinal and pubic areas should be flat. Swelling or bulging could indicate an inguinal hernia or undescended testicle. Bulging because of an inguinal hernia may be apparent only with crying, as the intestine descends into the herniated sac.

Providers must palpate femoral pulses bilaterally for they should be equal in intensity. The presence of bilateral femoral pulses virtually eliminates the possibility of coarctation of the aorta unless the ductus arteriosus remains patent.

Genitourinary Assessment

Female Genitalia

The clitoris is prominent in preterm female infants. Hypertrophy of the labia minora is not significant, but hypertrophy of the clitoris requires investigation. The genitalia may be bruised and edematous with breech delivery. The urethral meatus lies just below the clitoris but is difficult to see. The infant should urinate within 24 hours of birth.

A fingertip space should be present between the vagina and the anus in a term infant. Whitish mucoid discharge is normal. Bloody discharge (pseudomenses) may be present for a few days after birth and continues throughout the first month. This indicates withdrawal of maternal estrogen. A *hymenal tag*, consisting of tissue from the hymen and labia minora, is frequently present and visible from the posterior opening of the vagina, usually disappearing by the end of the first month (see Chapter 20).

Male Genitalia

The provider should inspect and palpate the penis. In obese infants, the penis may be almost obscured by a fat pad over the pubic bone. The average penis length from pubic bone to tip of glans is 3.5 cm. Average width is 0.9 to 1.3 cm. The prepuce (foreskin) normally covers the entire glans. This cannot be retracted for a few months. Phimosis, foreskin that is nonretractable, cannot be diagnosed before the infant is 3 months of age. The prepuce can be gently stretched to reveal the urethral opening, but the provider must be careful not to retract the foreskin until the infant is older. The meatus should be at the center of the penile glans. The infant should urinate within 24 hours of birth.

Ventral bowing of the penis is termed *chordee*. A urethral opening on the ventral surface of the penis is termed *hypospadias;* this is a common birth defect. When hypospadias is present, the foreskin is often retracted off the glans. *Epispadias*, an uncommon defect, presents with the urethral opening on the dorsal shaft of penis.

The provider must inspect the scrotum, noting any rugae, the color, size, and symmetry. Rugae can be ridges, wrinkles, or folds appearing on the scrotum at about 34 to 46 weeks gestation. The provider must palpate for testes bilaterally, noting that both testicles can be felt and that one is not moving side to side or back into the inguinal canal. Cryptorchidism, in which one or both testicles are undescended, should be noted. At least one testicle should be palpable below the inguinal canal at term. Stimulation of the scrotum or inner upper thigh activates the cremasteric reflex, which abruptly retracts the testes up the canal (retractile testes). Cold stimulation also causes the testes to retract.

A *hydrocele*, a scrotal mass containing clear fluid, is commonly present. The scrotum can be transilluminated with the otoscope; light transmitted throughout the mass indicates a hydrocele. A *hematocele* is similar to the hydrocele except it is filled with blood instead of clear fluid.

Testicular torsion presents as a hard, painless, scrotal mass. Scrotal skin may be discolored and edematous. This is a surgical emergency, although it may not be possible to salvage the testicle. This may be present at birth or shortly thereafter.

Congenital conditions in which development of the chromosomal, gonadal, or anatomic sex is atypical were previously termed ambiguous genitalia, intersex, hermaphroditism, pseudohermaphroditism, or sex reversal. Disorders of sex development (DSD) is proposed as terminology that is sensitive to parents and patients, as well as encompassing molecular as well as structural variations. Infants with DSD that are apparent at birth should be treated as a genetic emergency. Parents are understandably distressed when they are unable to share the infant's birth with others because the gender has not been determined.

Musculoskeletal System Assessment

Common terms used to describe the musculoskeletal system are listed in Box 11.2 and explained further in Chapter 21.

General Inspection

The neonate's posture reflects the intrauterine position. Legs are externally rotated and bowed with everted feet.

BOX 11.2 Common Terms Used to Describe the Musculoskeletal System

Flexion: bending a limb at a joint
Extension: straightening a limb at a joint
Abduction: moving a limb away from the midline of the body
Adduction: moving a limb toward or past the midline of the body
Pronation: turning face down
Supination: turning face up
Dorsiflexion: flexion toward the back, as in flexion of the foot so that the forefoot is higher than the ankle
Plantarflexion: extension of the foot so that the forefoot is lower than the ankle
Rotation: turning side to side
Valgus: bent outward or twisted away from the midline of the body
Varus: turned inward
Everted: turning out and away from the midline of the body
Inverted: turning inward toward the midline of the body

The intrauterine breech position results in hips that are flexed and abducted with extended knees. Abnormally small amounts of amniotic fluid (*oligohydramnios*) can cause skeletal problems as a result of compression, and the face may have a "smashed" appearance.

The health care provider must observe for symmetry of movement. Asymmetry could be secondary to nerve damage, fractures, or muscular problems. In addition, the provider must inspect the size, shape, general alignment, position, and symmetry of the extremities as well as soft tissues and muscles for swelling, wasting, and symmetry.

Term newborns at rest lie in a symmetrical position with the limbs flexed and the legs partially abducted at the hips. Spontaneous movement is random and uncoordinated, using both flexion and extension. Hands are fisted, often with the thumb under the fingers. A cortical thumb, where the thumb is always tightly under the fingers, is associated with neurologic irritability.

Tremors with movement are common. To differentiate between a tremor and a seizure, the provider must attempt to stop the movement. Tremors can be stopped with restraint but seizures cannot.

The provider must evaluate the upper extremities by performing passive range of motion (ROM) exercises. However, observation of active ROM is more valuable in evaluating for brachial nerve plexus injury. This injury is rarely bilateral. If the arm does not move spontaneously, nerve damage is probably present. Brachial plexus injuries usually resolve spontaneously over the first few days of life. If not resolved within 1 to 2 weeks, further evaluation is required. Brachial plexus injuries for which the provider must be alert include:

- **Erb's palsy:** A traction injury of the upper brachial plexus. The arm is maintained in adduction and internal rotation at the shoulder with the lower arm pronated.
- **Klumpke's paralysis:** Traction injury of the lower brachial plexus. The small muscles of the hand and wrist flexors are affected, causing a "claw hand."

The clavicles are inspected and palpated for size, contour, and crepitus. Fractured clavicles are common and heal in a few days. In addition, the provider must inspect the hands, looking for a simian crease, a normal finding in infants with short, broad hands but also associated with Down syndrome. Overlapping of the second and third fingers is common in trisomy 18. The provider must inspect for *syndactyly* (webbed fingers) and *polydactyly* (extra digits) and assess the nail beds for color and perfusion.

The provider must inspect the spine with the infant prone or side lying, looking for any skin disruption, tufts of hair, masses, hemangiomas, pilonidal cysts, or sinus tracts. The provider must palpate for the presence of normal dorsal spinal processes and for abnormal curvature such as scoliosis, which can be congenital.

Variations of spina bifida, a congenital defect of the vertebral arch through which the meninges and the spinal cord protrude, are obvious. The defect can be open (*spina bifida cystica*) or covered with skin (*spina bifida occulta*). Lower extremity movement is usually decreased, and anal tone may be absent or diminished.

The lower extremities must be inspected as well. The hips are normally flexed and leg movements symmetrical. The provider must inspect the hips for congenital hip dislocation (Figure 11.7) (Tamai & McCarthy, 2014).

Maneuvers

The hips and legs are systematically examined for congenital hip dislocation by inspection and specific maneuvers. Treatment of congenital hip dislocation is facilitated by early detection.

Ortolani Maneuver • The provider first flexes the knee and hip, then grasps the thigh with the third or fourth finger placed over the greater trochanter. Next, the provider abducts the leg with a lifting motion and then adducts the leg. A palpable or audible clunk is noted as the femoral head passes over the acetabulum. High-pitched clicks and snaps can be heard or felt but are usually not associated with hip pathology.

Barlow Maneuver • One hip is stabilized by flexion and held in neutral rotation and abduction. The hip to be tested is held with the provider's thumb over the proximal medial thigh and with the long finger over the greater trochanter. The hip is gently abducted with a posteriorly directed gentle push with the provider's thumb. If the hip is dislocated or subluxatable, a clunk is felt. Gentle pressure anteriorly and medially with the finger over the greater trochanter reduces the femoral head into the acetabulum, giving another clunk.

Galeazzi Maneuver • The Galeazzi maneuver (or Allis sign) can be used to evaluate leg length. With the infant lying supine, the provider places the feet flat on the bed with the femurs aligned and the knees flexed. The height of the knees is then inspected for symmetry.

Leg and Gluteal Folds Evaluation • The provider evaluates the leg and gluteal folds by comparing creases in supine and prone positions. Unequal leg folds or creases may indicate congenital hip dislocation, although minor differences in leg folds or creases may be a normal variant. The health care provider must also inspect the feet and ankles for mobility and abnormalities.

- **Metatarsus adductus** (forefoot varus, metatarsus varus) is caused by intrauterine positioning. The forefoot is abducted. If it is structural, the forefoot does not abduct beyond neutral with manipulation. If it is positional, the forefoot can be abducted beyond midline. Positional deformity corrects without intervention.
- **Clubfoot** (talipes equinovarus) is adduction of the forefoot, varus of the heel, and a downward pointing of the foot and toes. Treatment includes serial casting and possibly surgery.
- **Talipes calcaneovalgus** is excessive dorsiflexion of the ankle and eversion of the foot. This resolves with growth and passive stretching. Severe cases may need surgery.
- **Tibial torsion** is a twisting of the tibiofibular unit around its long axis. This is a normal variant and is the leading cause of in-toeing in toddlers. The cause is probably intrauterine positioning, although prone sleep positioning with the knees and feet tucked under the infant may also contribute; however, this is now a less common cause as a result of recommendations to avoid prone sleep positions.
- **Streeter's dysplasia**, also called amniotic bands, is rare. Fibrous bands from the amnion encircle one or more extremities and occasionally the trunk. These bands may amputate digits or extremities or cause a circumferential narrowing at any point.
- **Syndactyly**, a congenital webbing of fingers and or toes, may be an isolated defect or associated with a congenital syndrome (Figure 11.8).
- **Polydactyly**, a congenital anomaly with one or more extra digits on the hands or feet, is usually familial or associated with a syndrome.

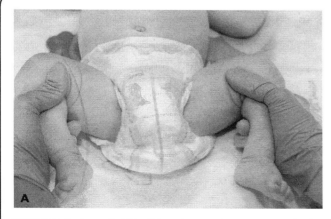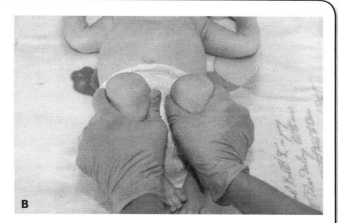

FIGURE 11.7 Congenital hip dislocation examination: **A.** Ortolani's maneuver and **B.** Barlow's maneuver.

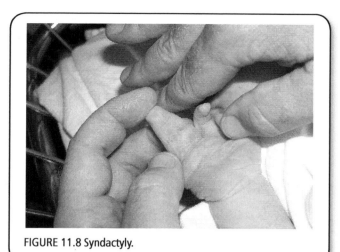

FIGURE 11.8 Syndactyly.

Neurologic Assessment

A general inspection provides important information on the neurologic status of the infant (see Chapter 22). The health care provider must evaluate the cry and observe facial movements when the infant is crying; a shrill or weak cry is abnormal. Stridor is more evident when the infant is crying. The provider must also observe the resting posture as well as the quality of movements, looking for tremors or jitteriness. Resting posture varies according to gestational age; term infants are flexed, and preterm infants are extended at rest. The term infant should be able to lift and turn the head in the prone position. The provider must observe for antigravity movements. The infant's movement and behavior are affected by gestational age, timing of the last feeding, and prior handling and stimulation.

Motor Function

The provider must observe the infant, always looking for symmetry. Resistance to movement can be tested with passive ROM. Minimal resistance is felt at 28 weeks; this increases with maturity, as muscle tone increases. *Hypotonia* can occur as a result of central nervous system, nerve, or muscle pathology. *Hypertonia* is rarely seen in the neonate; this develops over the first year of life and may indicate cerebral palsy. *Transient dystonia* may be seen in preterm infants in the first year of life; hypertonia or hypotonia develops but then tone normalizes (Bonnet et al., 2010). Testing of muscle strength is difficult in the neonate because it is difficult to distinguish tone from strength. Observation of antigravity movement assists in evaluating muscle strength.

Deep Tendon Reflexes • Deep tendon reflexes, usually patellar and biceps, must be tested. The provider should place the infant's head in midline while testing reflexes, since the asymmetrical tonic neck reflex leads to differences between sides if the head is to one side.

- **Patellar reflex:** To elicit the patellar reflex, the provider taps the patellar tendon just below the patella while supporting the knee in a flexed position with his or her hand. Normal response is extension at the knee and visible contraction of quadriceps.
- **Biceps reflex:** To elicit the biceps reflex, the provider holds the infant's arm with the elbow in flexion and the thumb over the insertion of the biceps tendon at the antecubital space. When the provider taps his or her thumb with a hammer, flexion of the biceps occurs.

Hyporeflexia, or weak reflexes, is normal in the preterm infant and is seen in asphyxiated infants, septic infants, and those with dysfunction of the motor unit. *Hyperreflexia*, or exaggerated reflexes, can be seen in asphyxiated infants at a later stage, and in drug withdrawal syndromes. *Clonus* is a rapid movement of a particular joint brought about by sudden stretching of a tendon. This is tested in the ankle by sharply dorsiflexing the foot with the hip and knee in flexion. The clonus response consists of several repetitive jerks (beats) of the foot or no movement. Sustained clonus (greater than six to eight beats) is abnormal.

Postural Tone • Postural tone is tested with the traction response (pull-to-sit maneuver). The provider grasps the infant's hands and pulls the infant slowly from a supine to a sitting position. Full-term infants have significant head lag; complete head lag is abnormal (Figure 11.9). Head lag should not be evident after 3 to 4 months of age and cannot be tested in an ill infant.

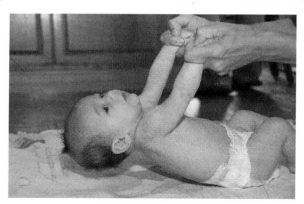

FIGURE 11.9 Head lag.

Ventral suspension, an indicator of overall muscle tone, can be tested in a normal infant but not an ill infant. The provider holds the infant in the palm of the hand prone. The term infant with normal tone can maintain the head in line with the body and attempt to keep the legs in line.

The axillary "slip through" maneuver evaluates shoulder strength and tone. The provider supports the infant in an upright position by placing his or her hands in the axillae. The term infant with normal tone and strength will not "slip through" as the arms stay adducted.

Primitive Reflexes • The primitive reflexes are described in detail in Table 11.5; some of these reflexes are illustrated in Figure 11.10.

TABLE 11.5	Primitive Reflexes			
REFLEX	**AGE OF APPEARANCE**	**AGE OF DISAPPEARANCE**	**ACTION TO ELICIT RESPONSE**	**NORMAL INFANT RESPONSE**
Sucking	26–28 weeks gestation	3–4 months	A gloved finger is placed in infant's mouth to evaluate strength and coordination of suck.	Sucking is normally present, but weaker in preterm than term infants.
Rooting	30–34 weeks gestation	3–4 months	Cheek and corner of infant's mouth are stroked.	Infant's head should turn toward stimulus, and mouth should open.
Palmar grasp	20–26 weeks gestation	3–6 months	Palmar surface of infant's hand is stimulated with a finger.	Infant should grasp provider's finger. Attempts to withdraw finger lead to a tightened grasp. When tested with both hands, term neonate can be lifted off bed for a few seconds.
Plantar grasp	24–30 weeks gestation	8–10 months	Sole of infant's foot and toes are stimulated with a finger.	Toes curl around the finger.
Asymmetrical tonic neck reflex	28–30 weeks gestation	3–4 months	Also called "fencing position"; infant is placed in a supine position, and head is turned to one side.	Extension of infant's arm on side toward which head is turned and flexion of arm on opposite side occurs. Infant's legs mimic arms: extension of leg toward which head is turned and flexion of leg on opposite side.

(*continued*)

TABLE 11.5   **Primitive Reflexes (*continued*)**

REFLEX	AGE OF APPEARANCE	AGE OF DISAPPEARANCE	ACTION TO ELICIT RESPONSE	NORMAL INFANT RESPONSE
Moro reflex	28–32 weeks gestation	4–6 months	Also called "startle reflex" as it is a response to the sensation of loss of support. It can be elicited by a loud noise or bumping the bed. Provider can elicit with neonate supine by grasping neonate's hands and pulling up until shoulders are slightly off bed, then letting go of hands, resulting in shoulders falling onto bed.	Neonates' arms become extended and abducted with hands opened, followed by inward movement and some flexion of arms, with closing of fists. There may also be a cry. Provider should look for symmetry.
Stepping reflex	32–36 weeks gestation	6–8 weeks	Infant is held upright, and feet are allowed to touch a flat surface.	Stepping movements can be observed.
Placing reflex	32–36 weeks gestation	6–8 weeks	Infant is held upright, and top of the foot is gently scraped along underside of a table or counter. Infant flexes leg as if stepping up onto counter and then extends leg.	Infant "steps" up onto table or counter.
Truncal incurvation (Galant) reflex	28–32 weeks gestation	2–4 months	Infant is held in ventral suspension. Firm pressure is applied with provider's thumb or cotton swab to trunk, parallel to spine in thoracic area.	A positive response is flexion of pelvis toward side of stimulus.
Babinski reflex	Birth to 12–18 months; positive response is normal	Should be negative after child is walking	Sole of foot is stimulated from heel to toe with provider's finger.	Toes that extend and fan out are termed a positive response.
Corneal (blink) reflex	32–36 weeks gestation	Never	Provider blows into infant's face or gently touches cornea with a cotton swab to elicit a blink.	Infant blinks.
Extrusion reflex	32–36 weeks gestation	4 months	A tongue blade or spoon is placed on infant's tongue.	Infant's tongue thrusts forward.
Landau reflex/reaction	3 months	15 months–2 years	Infant is placed in a horizontal, prone position to elicit this reaction.	Infant extends neck, head, and arms. Lower extremities are flexed.

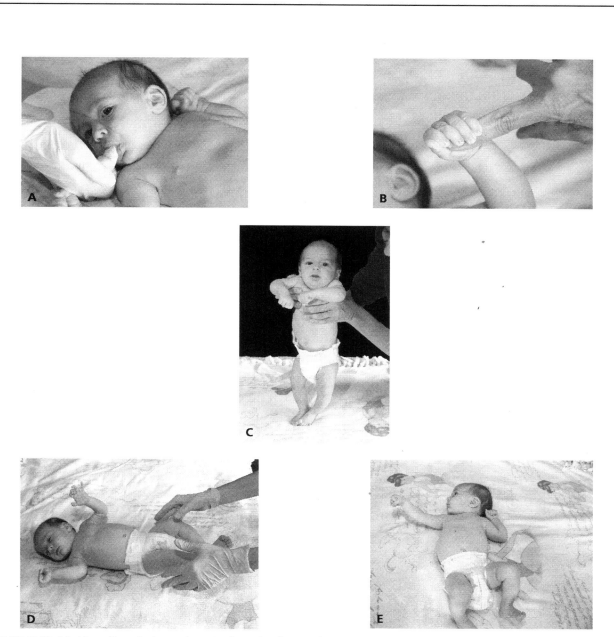

FIGURE 11.10 Primitive reflexes in the newborn: **A.** The suck reflex **B.** Palmar grasp **C.** Stepping reflex **D.** Moro (startle) reflex and **E.** Tonic neck reflex (fencer's position).

Sensory Function

Assessment of sensory function includes an assessment of touch and pain. Pain response is not usually assessed unless the infant has spina bifida or other suspected spinal cord problems. Evaluation of the cranial nerves is difficult to accomplish formally and individually in the newborn infant. Cranial nerves are assumed to be normal if the physical examination is normal. (See Chapter 22 for a detailed discussion of the cranial nerves.)

The autonomic nervous system is not formally assessed. Trends in vital signs and general functioning and response to stress are indicators of autonomic nervous system function.

Behavioral Assessment

Modifications in behavior are influenced by the environment, transitional states, birth phenomenon (i.e., asphyxia, maternal medications), and gestational age.

- **Sleep states:** During a deep sleep, the eyes are closed, there is no eye movement, breathing is regular, and there is no spontaneous activity.

During light sleep, there is low activity, rapid eye movements, and the infant startles easily.

- **Transitional states:** During transitional states such as drowsiness, there is a variable activity level, smooth movements, and occasionally mild startles. The eyes open and close and appear dull and heavy lidded. There is a delayed response to stimuli.
- **Awake states:** If quietly alert, the infant interacts with the environment; the infant has a bright-eyed appearance. If actively alert, there is increased motor activity; however, the infant could also be fussy but consolable. A crying infant is obvious to all.
- **Transitions from state to state:** The provider should note signs of stress or fatigue, when an infant transitions from one state to another; in addition, the provider should note acrocyanosis, mottling, grunting, tachypnea, apnea, vomiting, gaze aversion, jitteriness, hiccups, finger splaying, sneezing, yawning, arching, or stiffening.

Evaluation of behavioral responses includes response to stimuli and habituation. The infant's organizational status is assessed by observing the ability to integrate physiologic and behavioral systems in response to the environment. The organized infant maintains stable vitals, smooth state transitions, and smooth movements.

Neonatal Behavioral Assessment Scale

The Neonatal Behavioral Assessment Scale (NBAS) was developed in 1973 by Brazelton and colleagues (Brazelton & Nugent, 1995). The NBAS can be used on infants from birth through age 2 months to evaluate how the infant responds to environmental stimuli and cues. This assessment of the individual infant's behavior can then be shared with the parents, with the aim of underscoring how each baby is unique in his or her response to stimuli, and similarly, how parental responses to the infant's needs must be individualized.

Assessment of Preterm Infants' Behavior

The Assessment of Preterm Infants' Behavior (APIB) is a neurobehavioral tool that assesses autonomic, motor, state organization, attention, and self-regulation subsystems. It is appropriate for preterm, at-risk, and full-term newborns, from birth to 1 month after the EDC. The APIB is usually used for behavioral intervention and individualized care in the NICU (Als, Butler, Kosta, & McAnulty, 2005).

The March of Dimes offers an excellent educational tool for assessing the behavior of term infants, which is available online (March of Dimes, 2014).

NEWBORN SCREENING

The goal of newborn screening is early identification of infants who are at risk for or diagnosed with selected metabolic or genetic diseases so that medical treatment can begin promptly to prevent irreversible neurologic and developmental sequelae (Centers for Disease Control and Prevention, 2014). Early identification of these conditions is crucial, as timely intervention can lead to a significant reduction of morbidity, mortality, and associated disabilities in affected infants. State laws mandate newborn screening for all newborn infants, but the number and types of diseases screened vary among states.

Hearing

Hearing screening is recommended for all infants before discharge from the newborn nursery, and by 1 month of age at the latest (U.S. Preventive Services Task Force, 2008). Formal screening is accomplished in the nursery by an audiologist or by another trained professional. The preferred methods of screening infants for hearing loss are the evoked otoacoustic emissions (EOAE or OAE) or auditory brainstem response (ABR) tests. The ultimate goal of early audiologic diagnosis of hearing loss is to begin treatment as soon as possible to minimize delay in speech, language, and academic development.

Otoacoustic Emissions

OAE testing measures the presence or absence of sound waves (i.e., OAEs) produced by the cochlear outer hair cells of the inner ear in response to sound stimuli. The OAE test is a rapid, noninvasive, computer-managed, and inexpensive method of assessing cochlear function based on the cochlea's ability to transmit sound to the brain. This test measures the presence or absence of sound waves and also generates low-level sound that is transmitted from the cochlea to the outer ear canal. The OAE is fast and easy to perform but is affected by debris or fluid in the external and middle ear (Doyle, Rodgers, Fujikawa, & Newman, 2000). Newborn infants who fail the OAE should be rescreened using the screening ABR (U.S. Preventive Services Task Force, 2008).

Auditory Brainstem Response

The ABR measures the function of the eight cranial nerve in response to a click stimulus. A diagnostic ABR audiometry is a highly sensitive test for both hearing loss and neural disruption of the auditory pathway that explores threshold loss and activity in the auditory brainstem pathway. If the infant fails the repeat hearing screening, he or she should be referred for audiologic and medical evaluation as soon as possible.

Critical Congenital Heart Disease Screening

Neonates are universally screened via pulse oximetry in the postnatal period to detect critical congenital heart disease (CCHD). This screening is done after the neonate is 24 hours of age, and care must be taken to ensure postductal probe placement. This pulse oximetry screens for seven particular lesions: hypoplastic left heart syndrome, pulmonary atresia with intact ventricular septum, tetralogy of Fallot, total anomalous pulmonary venous return, transposition of the great arteries, tricuspid atresia, and truncus arteriosus (Kemper et al., 2011).

Recommended Uniform Screening Panel

To minimize inconsistencies across states, the U.S. Secretary of Health and Human Services has recommended a uniform screening panel for all newborns (American College of Medical Genetics Newborn Screening Expert Group, 2006). The disorders for which newborns are screened fall into four categories: metabolic, endocrine, hemoglobin, and other. Normal, healthy, full-term infants who are born in a hospital setting will have this screening done prior to discharge. In addition to hearing loss and CCHD, some conditions included in this panel are:

- Primary congenital hypothyroidism
- Congenital adrenal hyperplasia
- Hemoglobinopathies, including sickle cell disease
- Cystic fibrosis
- Classical galactosemia
- Severe combined immunodeficiencies
- Phenylketonuria
- Maple syrup urine disease

ASSESSMENT OF THE PRETERM INFANT AFTER HOSPITAL DISCHARGE

Infants born prematurely may have different appearance and behavior, especially during the first year of life (Kase, Pici, & Visintainer, 2009; Stewart, 2013) (Table 11.6). In addition, these infants may not tolerate examinations as tactile vulnerability and sensory integration problems are common (Weiss & Wilson, 2006). Preterm infants may be less tolerant of bright lights, loud noises, and touch. Growth of the preterm infant over the first 3 years of life should be reviewed, using growth charts specific for preterm infants. Preterm infants often require high-calorie feedings to increase growth and normalize bone calcium accretion (Bozzetti & Tagliabue, 2009).

The infant's head shape may be tall and narrow (*dolichocephalic*) as a result of prolonged side-to-side positioning in the NICU. This may change over time but can be apparent for life (Hummel & Fortado, 2005). The palate may have an exaggerated arch, sometimes with a palatal groove, as a result of head narrowing, or use of an oral endotracheal tube for a prolonged period. The primary teeth may be off-white or gray because of poor enamel, leading to an increased incidence of dental caries. The primary teeth may be a yellow or green color if the infant had cholestatic jaundice (usually because of prolonged total parenteral nutrition) in the NICU. However, secondary teeth are usually not affected (Ferrini, Marba, & Gaviao, 2008).

TABLE 11.6	Preterm Infant Assessment Areas	
AREA OF ASSESSMENT	**ASSESSMENT PEARLS**	**TYPICAL PROBLEMS**
Audiologic	Response to sound is assessed.	Hearing loss: conductive or cortical
Cardiac	Cardiac problems may be the primary disorder (e.g., congenital heart defects), or the complication of a respiratory condition.	Congenital heart defects (see Chapter 18) *Cor pulmonale* Pulmonary hypertension
Dental	Tooth eruption is often delayed in premature infants. Infants who have been intubated for a prolonged period of time may have dental and palate abnormalities.	Dental enamel hypoplasia Dental caries Delayed tooth eruption Tooth discoloration Palatal groove Tooth malalignment Missing teeth
Development	Milestones are attained according to adjusted age.	Delayed milestones Learning and language delays Abnormal muscle tone Motor impairment Cerebral palsy

(continued)

TABLE 11.6	**Preterm Infant Assessment Areas (*continued*)**	
AREA OF ASSESSMENT	**ASSESSMENT PEARLS**	**TYPICAL PROBLEMS**
Genitourinary	Prematurity can predispose infant to structural genitourinary problems that are the result or complication of prematurity.	Cryptorchidism Inguinal hernia
Growth	Preterm infant growth charts are used for 3 years.	Slow growth
Hernia	Infant is assessed for inguinal and umbilical hernias.	Incarceration is rare in inguinal hernias and virtually never seen with umbilical hernias.
Neurologic	Head growth is followed, and infant is observed for seizures.	Hydrocephalus Seizures Microcephaly
Nutrition	Complications and co-morbidities of prematurity can lead to nutritional problems and slow growth.	Gastroesophageal reflux Anemia of prematurity
Ophthalmologic	Premature infants are at high risk for ophthalmologic complications. Corneal light reflex and visual following are assessed.	Retinopathy of prematurity Myopia or hyperopia Anisometropia Strabismus Amblyopia
Respiratory	Breath sounds and work of breathing are assessed.	Apnea of prematurity Reactive airway disease Bronchopulmonary dysplasia Viral illness leading to severe respiratory distress (e.g., respiratory syncytial virus)
Sensory integration	Parents are asked about sensitivities to touch, light, and sound.	Sensory integration disorder
Skin	Scars are inspected for changes, mobility, and joint contractures.	Scarring

The preterm infant requires close ophthalmologic follow-up, particularly in the first few months after discharge. Preterm infants are at risk for abnormal retinal vessel development, retinopathy of prematurity (ROP), which occasionally results in retinal detachment and subsequent blindness. Myopia, amblyopia, and strabismus are common sequelae of ROP (Bashour, Menassa, & Gerontis, 2014). The provider must closely observe the corneal light reflex and visual tracking, as well as verify that the infant is being followed by a pediatric ophthalmologist.

Preterm infants should have hearing testing every 6 to 12 months for the first 3 years of life, as hearing deficits are more common in these infants. Ongoing hearing evaluation is recommended even if the infant passes the discharge screen, as some hearing deficits are progressive (American Academy of Pediatrics Task Force on Newborn and Infant Hearing, 2007).

Preterm infants, especially those with bronchopulmonary dysplasia (BPD), a chronic lung disease, have an increased incidence of reactive airway disease, especially in the first year, and of asthma throughout their life (Dombkowski, Leung, & Gurney, 2008; Kase et al., 2009; Kumar et al., 2008). Breath sounds and respiratory efforts should be closely monitored. Viral infections in the first year may result in severe illness in the preterm infant. Respiratory syncytial virus (RSV) in particular can lead to pneumonia and can be fatal. Prophylaxis during the first and possibly second winter decreases morbidity and mortality associated with RSV infections (American Academy of Pediatrics, 2012).

Hernias, both umbilical and inguinal, are more common in preterm than in term infants. The provider should assess for inguinal hernias with each visit and refer infants for surgical intervention. Incarceration is rare in preterm infants (Hebra, 2012). Umbilical hernias nearly always resolve without intervention and rarely strangulate (Hebra, 2012). Parents may need reassurance regarding hernia management, since most parents are ill-informed concerning surgical treatment. Historic unnecessary measures to reduce umbilical hernias using tape, coins, binders, and other methods continue to be utilized.

The preterm infant's skin is easily damaged by tape or pressure, which may lead to permanent scarring (Sardesai, Kornacka, Walas, & Ramanathan, 2011). Thus, infants hospitalized in the NICU are more likely to have skin scarring. Surgical scars may also be present and should be evaluated. Intravenous infiltration scars may cause joint contraction. Multiple heelstick blood draws may lead to scarring of the heels and sensitivity in the feet. Capillary hemangiomata are more common in preterm infants; some develop multiple small lesions or large cavernous lesions.

Developmental delay is more common in preterm and late preterm infants (Fily, Pierrat, Delporte, Breart, Truffert, & EPIPHAGE Nord-Pas-de-Calais Study Group, 2006; Hack & Costello, 2008; Hoon et al., 2009; Krageloh-Mann & Cans, 2009; Moster, Lie, & Markestad, 2008; Nelson, 2008; Paneth, 2008; Stephens & Vohr, 2009; Woythaler, McCormick, & Smith, 2011). In addition, preterm infants are more likely than full-term infants to develop cerebral palsy. It is important to note muscle tone and record developmental milestones. Milestones should be assessed according to the infant's corrected or adjusted gestational age, not chronologic age. Abnormal tone may normalize over the first year in infants born prematurely (transient dystonia). Therefore, the diagnosis of cerebral palsy is usually not made before 1 to 2 years of age. Low trunk tone and strength are common in preterm infants during the first year of life; these usually improve over the first years of life. Fine motor and speech delays are also common. Attention difficulties and intellectual deficits are more common in preterm infants as compared with term infants but are usually not apparent in infancy. Fifty percent of infants with a birth weight less than 1 kg at birth require special help in school; however, not all of these children show developmental delay in infancy (van Baar, van Wassenaer, Briet, Dekker, & Kok, 2005).

Preterm infants have an increased incidence of intracranial bleeding (usually intraventricular hemorrhage) or cystic brain damage (periventricular leukomalacia) (Kusters, Chen, Follett, & Dammann, 2009). These are detected by screening head ultrasounds. Posthemorrhagic hydrocephalus may be present, usually requiring shunt placement (Brouwer et al., 2008; Miranda, 2010; Willis et al., 2009). Head growth should be closely monitored, as hydrocephalus or microcephaly may develop after discharge. Normal head growth is 0.5 to 2 cm per week. Rapid head growth may indicate hydrocephalus, which requires referral to a neurosurgeon. Slow head growth, indicated by a falling percentile on the growth curve, requires neurologic assessment. Infants with intracranial hemorrhage or cysts are more likely to develop a seizure disorder, also requiring referral to a neurologist (Blackburn, 2009a, 2009b; Kurabe, Sorimachi, Sasaki, Koike, & Fujii, 2009; Petrini et al., 2009).

SUMMARY

Assessment of the newborn infant is a critical component of pediatric care. A complete examination occurs before hospital discharge and in the primary care setting. Although most exams yield normal findings, the provider must maintain a high index of suspicion. Normal variations are extensive, increasing the challenge of detecting abnormalities. Subtle abnormalities are important to detect, as some indicate more extensive pathology. The provider is further challenged because of the infant's nonverbal status, as wellness is assessed through physical and behavioral clues.

This chapter provides the basic techniques of newborn assessment. Proficiency is attained through practice. The provider must be well prepared, using a systematic yet flexible approach. The experienced provider integrates multiple aspects of assessment; for example, behavior is evaluated during the physical assessment, rather than separately. Parents should be included in the exam, providing an excellent opportunity for education.

Notable Clinical Findings

SYSTEM	FINDINGS
Vital signs and measurements	Fever or subnormal temperature
	Tachycardia or bradycardia
	Tachypnea or bradypnea
	Hypertension, hypotension or hypertension in upper extremities only
	Anthropometric measurements < the 5th or > the 95th percentile on the NHCS growth charts
Skin	Lanugo, vernix (help determine gestational age)
	Dry, cracked skin(indicates post-term infant)
	Cyanosis
	Central cyanosis: red flag for congenital heart defect
	Acrocyanosis: within normal limits for the first several hours of life, or when neonate loses body heat
	Pallor
	Nevi
	Jaundice
	Meconium staining
	Rash

(continued)

Notable Clinical Findings (*continued*)

SYSTEM	FINDINGS
Head	Macro-microcephaly Cephalohematoma Caput succedaneum Hair whorls
Face	Wide-spaced eyes Cleft lip Facial deformities Facial asymmetry
Eyes	History of prematurity/perinatal hypoxia Eso- or exotropia Coloboma Dacrostenosis Dacrocystitis Absent red reflex Presence of Brushfield's spots Eye drainage
Ears	Low set ears Skin tags or ear pits Pinna deformities
Nose	Long, smooth or absent philtrum Nasal drainage Sneezing One or both nares not patent
Mouth	Macroglossia Natal teeth Epstein's pearls Cleft palate Excessive saliva Micrognathia
Neck	Cystic hygroma Torticollis Thyroglossal duct cyst Brachial cleft cyst
Thorax chest	Wide-spaced nipples Swollen nipples Drainage from nipples Pectus excavatum/carinatum
Lungs	Tachypnea or bradypnea Cyanosis or duskiness Retractions, flaring, grunting Crackles, wheezes, stridor
Heart	Tachycardia or bradycardia Bounding peripheral pulses Displacement of the point of maximal Impulse Presence of a thrill Weak or absent pulses in the lower extremities Murmur

Notable Clinical Findings

SYSTEM	FINDINGS
Abdomen	Midline defects
	Umbilical or inguinal hernia
	Two-vessel umbilical cord
	Imperforate anus
	Failure to pass meconium after 48 hours of age
	Organomegaly
Genitalia	Chromosomal conditions
	Disorders of sex development
	Female:
	Pseudomenses
	Hymenal tag
	Bruising/edema of external genitalia
	Male:
	Chordee
	Hypospadias
	Epispadias
	Cryptorchidism
	Hydrocele
	Testicular torsion
Musculoskeletal	Erb's palsy
	Klumpke's paralysis
	Metatarsus adductus
	Talipes equinovarus
	Talipes calcaneovalgus
	Polydactyly
	Syndacylty
	Positive Ortolani or Barlow maneuver
	Positive Allis sign
	Spinal cord defects
	Transvere crease on palm of hand
Neurological	History of perinatal hypoxia
	Hypotonia
	Hypertonia
	Hypo- or hyperreflexia
	History of seizures at birth
	Spinal cord defects
Screening	Failure of newborn hearing screening exam
	Positive result on newborn genetic/metabolic screening
	Positive result on screening for critical congenital
	heart defetcts

References

Als, H., Butler, S., Kosta, S., & McAnulty, G. (2005). The Assessment of Preterm Infant's Behavior (APIB): Furthering the understanding and measurement of neurodevelopmental competence in preterm and full-term infants. *Mental Retardation and Developmental Disabilities Research Review, 11*(1), 94–102.

American Academy of Pediatrics. (2004). The fourth report on the diagnosis, evaluation, and treatment of high blood pressure in children and adolescents. *Pediatrics, 114* (suppl 2), 555–576.

American Academy of Pediatrics. (2012). Respiratory syncytial virus. In L. K. Pickering, C. J. Baker, D. W. Kimberlin, & S. S. Long (Eds.), *Red book: 2012 report of the committee on infectious diseases* (29th ed.). Elk Grove Village, IL: American Academy of Pediatrics.

American Academy of Pediatrics Committee on Fetus and Newborn; American College of Obstetricians, & and Gynecologists and Committee on Obstetric Practice. (2009; 2006). Policy statement: The Apgar score. *Pediatrics, 117*(4), 1444–1447. Reaffirmation of policy: (2008) *Pediatrics, 5*(1), 1421–1422.

American Academy of Pediatrics Task Force on Newborn and Infant Hearing. (2007). Policy statement: Newborn and infant hearing loss: Detection and intervention. *Pediatrics, 120*(4), 898–921.

American College of Medical Genetics Newborn Screening Expert Group. (2006). Newborn screening: Toward a uniform screening panel and system—executive summary. *Pediatrics, 117*(5, Pt. 2), S296–S307.

Anderson-Berry, A. L., Bellig, L. L., & Ohning, B. (2014). *Neonatal sepsis*. Retrieved from http://emedicine.medscape.com/article/978352-overview

Apgar, V. (1953). A proposal for a new method of evaluation of the newborn infant. *Current Research in Anesthesia & Analgesia, 32,* 260–267.

Apgar, V. (1966). The newborn (Apgar) scoring system. Reflections and advice. *Pediatric Clinics of North America, 13*(3), 645–650.

Ballard, J. L., Khoury, J. C., Wedig, K., Wang, L., Eilers-Walsman, B. L., & Lipp, R. (1991). New Ballard score, expanded to include extremely premature infants. *Journal of Pediatrics, 119*(3), 417–423.

Ballard, J. L., Novak, K. K., & Driver, M. (1979). A simplified score for assessment of fetal maturation of newly born infants. *Journal of Pediatrics, 95*(5, pt 1), 769–774.

Bashour, M., Menassa, J., & Gerontis, C. C. (2014). *Retinopathy of prematurity*. Retrieved from http://emedicine.medscape.com/article/1225022-overview

Battaglia, F. C., & Lubchenco, L. O. (1967). A practical classification of newborn infants by weight and gestational age. *Journal of Pediatrics, 71*(2), 159–163.

Blackburn, S. (2009a). Central nervous system vulnerabilities in preterm infants, part I. *Journal of Perinatal and Neonatal Nursing, 23*(1), 12–14.

Blackburn, S. (2009b). Central nervous system vulnerabilities in preterm infants, part II. *Journal of Perinatal and Neonatal Nursing, 23*(2), 108–110.

Bonnet, C., Roubertie, A., Doummar, D., Bahi-Buisson, N., Cochon de Cock, V., & Roze, E. (2010). Developmental and benign movement disorders in childhood. *Movement Disorders, 25*(10), 1317–1334.

Bozzetti, V., & Tagliabue, P. (2009). Metabolic bone disease in preterm newborn: An update on nutritional issues. *Italian Journal of Pediatrics, 35*(1), 20.

Brazelton, T. B., & Nugent, J. K. (1995). *The neonatal behavioral assessment scale.* Cambridge, MA: MacKeith Press.

Brouwer, A., Groenendaal, F., van Haastert, I. L., Rademaker, K., Hanlo, P., & de Vries, L. (2008). Neurodevelopmental outcome of preterm infants with severe intraventricular hemorrhage and therapy for post-hemorrhagic ventricular dilatation. *Journal of Pediatrics, 152*(5), 648–654.

Centers for Disease Control and Prevention. (2014). *Newborn screening.* Retrieved from http://www.cdc.gov/newbornscreening

Centers for Disease Control National Health and Nutrition Examination Survey. (2004). *Anthropometry procedures manual.* Retrieved from http://www.cdc.gov/nchs/data/nhanes/nhanes_03_04/BM.pdf

Cole, A., Lynch, P., & Slator, R. (2008). A new grading of Pierre Robin sequence. *Cleft Palate Craniofacial Journal, 45*(6), 603–606.

Desmond, M. M., Rudolph, A. J., & Phitaksphraiwan, P. (1966). The transitional care nursery. A mechanism for preventive medicine in the newborn. *Pediatric Clinics of North America, 13*(3), 651–668.

Dombkowski, K. J., Leung, S. W., & Gurney, J. G. (2008). Prematurity as a predictor of childhood asthma among low-income children. *Annals of Epidemiology, 18*(4), 290–297.

Doyle, K. J., Rodgers, P., Fujikawa, S., & Newman, E. (2000). External and middle ear effects on infant hearing screening test results. *Otolaryngology-Head and Neck Surgery, 122*(4), 477–481.

Dubowitz, L., Dubowitz, V., & Goldberg, C. (1970). Clinical assessment of gestational age in the newborn infant. *Journal of Pediatrics, 77,* 1–10.

Ferrini, F. R., Marba, S. T., & Gaviao, M. B. (2008). Oral conditions in very low and extremely low birth weight children. *Journal of Dentistry for Children, 75*(3), 235–242.

Fily, A., Pierrat, V., Delporte, V., Breart, G., Truffert, P., & EPIPHAGE Nord-Pas-de-Calais Study Group. (2006). Factors associated with neurodevelopmental outcome at 2 years after very preterm birth: The population-based Nord-Pas-de-Calais EPIPAGE cohort. *Pediatrics, 117*(2), 357–366.

Hack, M., & Costello, D. W. (2008). Trends in the rates of cerebral palsy associated with neonatal intensive care of preterm children. *Clinical Obstetrics and Gynecology, 51*(4), 763–774.

Hebra, A. (2012). *Pediatric hernias.* Retrieved from http://emedicine.medscape.com/article/932680-overview

Heinrich, K., Huemmer, H. P., Reingruber, B., & Weber, P. G. (2008). Gastroschisis and omphalocele: Treatments and long-term outcomes. *Pediatric Surgery International, 24*(2), 167–173.

Hoon, A. H., Jr., Stashinko, E. E., Nagae, L. M., Lin, D. D., Keller, J., Bastian, A., . . . Johnston, M. V. (2009). Sensory and motor deficits in children with cerebral palsy born preterm correlate with diffusion tensor imaging abnormalities in thalamocortical pathways. *Developmental Medicine and Child Neurology, 51*(9), 697–704.

Hummel, P., & Fortado, D. (2005). Impacting infant head shapes. *Advances in Neonatal Care, 5*(6), 329–340.

Islam, S. (2008). Clinical care outcomes in abdominal wall defects. *Current Opinions in Pediatrics, 20*(3), 305–310.

Kase, J. S., Pici, M., & Visintainer, P. (2009). Risks for common medical conditions experienced by former preterm infants during toddler years. *Journal of Perinatal Medicine, 37*(2), 103–108.

Kattwinkel, J., Perlman, J. M., Aziz, K., Colby, C., Fairchild, K., Gallagher, J., . . . Zaichkin, J. (2010). Special report: Neonatal resuscitation: 2010 American Heart Association guidelines for cardiopulmonary resuscitation and emergency cardiovascular care. *Pediatrics, 126*(5), e1400–e1413.

Kemper, A. R., Mahle, W. T., Martin, G. R., Cooley, W. C., Kumar, P., Morrow, W. R., Kelm, K., Pearson, G. D., Glidewell, J., Grosse, S. D., & Howell, R. R. (2011). Strategies for implementing screening for critical congenital heart disease. *Pediatrics, 128*(5), e1259–e1267.

Kothari, C. L., Wendt, A., Liggins, O., Overton, J., & Sweezy Ldel, C. (2011). Assessing maternal risk for fetal-infant mortality: A population-based study to prioritize risk reduction in a healthy start community. *Maternal and Child Health Journal, 15*(1), 68–76.

Krageloh-Mann, I., & Cans, C. (2009). Cerebral palsy update. *Brain & Development, 31*(7), 537–544.

Kumar, R., Yu, Y., Story, R. E., Pongracic, J. A., Gupta, R., Pearson, C., . . . Wang X. (2008). Prematurity, chorioamnionitis, and the development of recurrent wheezing: A prospective birth cohort study. *Journal of Allergy and Clinical Immunology, 121*(4), 878–884.e6.

Kurabe, S., Sorimachi, T., Sasaki, O., Koike, T., & Fujii, Y. (2009). Low birth weight as a risk factor for seizure following acute subdural hematoma. *Childs Nervous System, 25*(9), 1101–1104.

Kusters, C. D. J., Chen, M. L. Follett, P. L., & Dammann, O. (2009). "Intraventricular" hemorrhage and cystic periventricular leukomalacia in preterm infants: How are they related? *Journal of Child Neurology, 24*(9), 1158–1170.

Leung, A. K. C., & Robson, W. L. M. (2004). Childhood cervical lymphadenopathy. *Journal of Pediatric Health Care, 18*(1), 3–7.

MacBird, T., Robbins, J. M., Druschel, C., Cleves, M. A., Yang, S., & Hobbs, C. A. (2009). Demographic and environmental risk factors for gastroschisis and omphalocele in the National Birth Defects Prevention Study. *Journal of Pediatric Surgery, 44*(8), 1546–1551.

March of Dimes. (2014). *Understanding the behavior of term infants.* Retrieved from http://www.marchofdimes.com/nursing/index.bm2?uid

Mayhew, J. F., & Mychaskiw, G. (2009). Gastroschisis. *Paediatric Anaesthesia, 19*(1), 54.

Mehta, S. H., & Sokol, R. J. (2013). Assessment of at-risk pregnancy. In A. H. DeCherney, L. Nathan, T. M. Goodwin, N. Laufer, & A. S. Roman (Eds.), *Current diagnosis & treatment in obstetrics & gynecology* (11th ed., pp. 223–233). New York, NY: Lange Medical/McGraw-Hill.

Miranda, P. (2010). Intraventricular hemorrhage and posthemorrhagic hydrocephalus in the preterm infant. *Minerva Pediatrica, 62*(1), 79–89.

Mongelli, M., & Gardosi, J. O. (2014). *Evaluation of gestation.* Retrieved from http://emedicine.medscape.com/article/259269-overview#a30

Morelli, J. G., & Prok, L. D. (2012). Skin. In W. W. Hay, M. J. Levin, R. R. Deterding, M. J. Abzug, & J. M. Sondheimer (Eds.), *Current pediatric diagnosis & treatment* (21st ed., pp. 404–423). New York, NY: Lange Medical/McGraw-Hill.

Moster, D., Lie, R. T., & Markestad, T. (2008). Long-term medical and social consequences of preterm birth. *New England Journal of Medicine, 359*(3), 262–273.

Nelson, K. B. (2008). Causative factors in cerebral palsy. *Clinical Obstetrics & Gynecology, 51*(4), 749–762.

Painter, M. J., & Yang, M. (2008). Neurological examination of the newborn, infant, and child. In A. L. Albright, I. F. Pollack, & P. D. Adelson (Eds.), *Principles and practice of pediatric neurosurgery* (pp. 31–42). New York, NY: Thieme Medical Publishers.

Paneth, N. (2008). Establishing the diagnosis of cerebral palsy. *Clinical Obstetrics & Gynecology, 51*(4), 742–748.

Petrini, J. R., Dias, T., McCormick, M. C., Massolo, M. L., Green, N. S., & Escobar, G. J. (2009). Increased risk of adverse neurological development for late preterm infants. *Journal of Pediatrics, 154*(2), 169–176.

Sardesai, S. M., Kornacka, M. K., Walas, W., & Ramanathan, R. (2011). Iatrogenic skin injury in the neonatal intensive care unit. *Journal of Maternal-Fetal and Neonatal Medicine, 24*(2), 197–203.

Stephens, B. E., & Vohr, B. R. (2009). Neurodevelopmental outcome of the premature infant. *Pediatric Clinics of North America, 56*(3), 631–646.

Stewart, J. (2013). *Care of the neonatal intensive care unit graduate. Up to date.* Retrieved from http://www.uptodate.com/contents/care-of-the-neonatal-intensive-care-unit-graduate

Stoll, C., Alembik, Y., Dott, B., & Roth, M. P. (2008). Omphalocele and gastroschisis and associated malformations. *American Journal of Medical Genetics, 146A*(10), 1280–1285.

Tamai, J., & McCarthy, J. J. (2014). *Developmental dysplasia of the hip.* Retrieved from http://emedicine.medscape.com/article/1248135-overview

Tewflik, T. L., Kanaan, A., & Karsan, N. (2013). *Cleft lip and palate and mouth and pharynx deformities.* Retrieved from http://emedicine.medscape.com/article/837347-overview#a1

Thilo, E. H., & Rosenberg, A. A. (2012). The newborn infant. In W. W. Hay, M. J. Levin, R. R. Deterding, M. J. Abzug, & J. M. Sondheimer (Eds.), *Current pediatric diagnosis & treatment* (21st ed., pp. 9–72). New York, NY: Lange Medical/McGraw-Hill.

U.S. Preventive Services Task Force. (2008). Universal screening for hearing loss in newborns: U.S. Preventive Services Task Force recommendation statement. *Pediatrics, 122*(1), 143–148.

van Baar, A. L., van Wassenaer, A. G., Briet, J. M., Dekker, F. W., & Kok, J. H. (2005). Very preterm birth is associated with disabilities in multiple developmental domains. *Journal of Pediatric Psychology, 30*(3), 247–255.

Weiss, S. J., & Wilson, P. (2006). Origins of tactile vulnerability in high-risk infants. *Advances in Neonatal Care, 6*(1), 25–36.

Willis, B., Javalkar, V., Vannemreddy, P., Caldito, G., Matsuyama, J., Guthikonda, B., . . . Nanda A. (2009). Ventricular reservoirs and ventriculoperitoneal shunts for premature infants with posthemorrhagic hydrocephalus: An institutional experience. *Journal of Neurosurgery Pediatrics, 3*(2), 94–100.

Woythaler, M. A., McCormick, M. A., & Smith, V. C. (2011). Late preterm infants have worse 24-month neurodevelopmental outcomes than term infants. *Pediatrics, 127*(3), e622–e629.

Assessment of the Integumentary System

Assessment of the integumentary system must be a part of every pediatric health assessment, regardless of the reason for the health care visit. The condition of the skin, hair, and nails provides important information about the child's physical and emotional health. Many communicable infectious diseases or infestations common to childhood have characteristic skin rashes as a manifestation of the illness. Assessment of the skin in children also yields crucial information about a child's nutritional, cardiovascular, and hydration status. Alteration in the integrity of the skin can be the result of dehydration, hypothermia, infection, and systemic illness. Poor personal hygiene (e.g., dirty hair or nails) may be an indication of depression or other mental health disorders. Child abuse or neglect may also produce clinical manifestations involving the skin, hair, or nails. For these reasons, the health care provider should be able to recognize dermatologic clues to injury, illness, or systemic disease and to assess and diagnose basic pediatric skin disorders.

ANATOMY AND PHYSIOLOGY

Skin

The skin is the body's largest organ, the major function of which is to keep the body in homeostasis. This is achieved through several distinct functions. One function is to provide a protective barrier against irritants, toxins, microorganisms, trauma, ultraviolet (UV) rays, and loss of body fluids. The skin assists in body temperature regulation through vasoconstriction when the body is cold and vasodilation and sweating when the body is too warm. The skin also helps excrete toxins through sweat glands in a mixture of water, electrolytes, lactic acid, and urea. Vitamin D synthesis occurs in the skin when exposed to sunlight. The skin functions as a

sensory organ when nerve impulses convey sensations of touch, pain, pressure, heat, and cold. The skin also heals itself by replacing cells to repair wounds and by controlling the colonization of pathogens by continual shedding.

The integumentary system allows us to identify with a group through hair and skin color. In addition, the hair or skin may have an effect on self-esteem, particularly in older school-aged children and adolescents, depending on the condition of the hair or skin and society's standards of beauty.

The skin begins to develop during the 11th week of gestation. It consists of three layers; the *epidermis*, the *dermis*, and the *subcutaneous tissue* (Figure 12.1).

Epidermis

The epidermis is the outermost, avascular layer of the skin and is further divided into four or five cell layers, depending on its location on the body (see Figure 12.1).

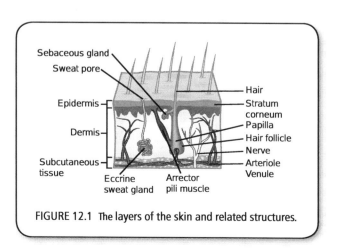

FIGURE 12.1 The layers of the skin and related structures.

In areas where the skin is exposed to chronic friction, such as the palms and soles, the skin has five layers. These layers, from outside inward, are the *stratum corneum* (the horny layer), *stratum lucidum, stratum granulose, stratum spinout,* and *stratum basal.*

■ The stratum corneum, the top layer, functions as a barrier that protects the body's underlying tissues and structures. The thickness of this layer depends on the area of skin in question; skin is thinnest on the face and thickest on the feet. This layer of skin is continually shed and replaced.

■ The stratum lucidum is a translucent layer of the epidermis that lies between the stratum corneum and stratum granulose. This layer is mostly found in the thick skin of the hands and feet.

■ The stratum granulose contains a layer of cells that contain dark-staining granules that are involved in keratin formation.

■ The stratum spinout assists in the continual production of a new epidermis. The stratum basal (basal layer) and stratum spinout are sometimes collectively referred to as the stratum germinativum because this is where the new cells are germinated.

■ The stratum basal houses keratinocytes, which produce waterproof keratin cells whose main function is to protect the skin. This is done when keratinocytes multiply and move upward through the epidermis and form a hard layer of dead keratinocytes, which comprises the stratum corneum. The cells of the stratum corneum are continuously desquamated and replaced with new keratinocytes from below, the process repeating itself every 4 weeks.

The basal layer also contains melanocytes, which synthesize melanin (brown pigment) to protect the skin from damage by UV rays from the sun. Each person possesses a similar number of melanocytes in their skin; the amount of melanin that is made varies from person to person. Melanin production is also stimulated by exposure to sunlight. Skin color depends not only on the amount of melanin, but also on the amount of carotene (yellow pigment), oxyhemoglobin (a bright red pigment), and deoxyhemoglobin (a dark, blue pigment) contained in the skin.

Dermis

The dermis underlies the epidermis and is richly vascular, supplying the epidermis with nutrition (see Figure 12.1). It consists mostly of connective tissue, or collagen, which provides elasticity to the skin, allowing it to stretch and resist tearing. The dermis also contains blood vessels, lymphatic vessels, autonomic nerve fibers, muscles, and hair follicles. The autonomic nerves supply the arrector pili muscles, blood vessels, and sweat glands. Cells in the dermis include fibroblasts, mast cells, and macrophages. Each of these cells has a specific function. Fibroblasts aid in the development of connective tissue, mast cells

release histamine during hypersensitivity reactions manifested by the skin, and macrophages play a role in immunity. Skin appendages are embedded in the dermis and include the nails, hair follicles, sweat glands, and sebaceous glands.

Subcutaneous Tissue

The subcutaneous tissue underlies the dermis and binds it to the underlying body tissue. This layer of skin is composed of adipose and connective tissues and contains blood vessels, nerves, sebaceous glands, sweat glands, and deep hair follicles (see Figure 12.1). The subcutaneous layer cushions the body against trauma and insulates it to maintain body temperature. Subcutaneous tissue is a source of energy for the body and of hormone metabolism and contains the blood supply and nerves of the autonomic nervous system that support the dermis.

Skin Appendages

Hair

Hair consists of a thread of keratinized cells. Hair follicles are found over most of the body except for the lips, palms, knuckles, soles, nipples, labia minora, and penis. Hair consists of a shaft and root. The hair shaft is visible above the skin; the root is surrounded by the hair follicle and a sebaceous gland (see Figure 12.1). Hair on the scalp protects the skin there; nasal hair, ear hair, eyelashes, and eyebrows protect the nearby structures from dust and other airborne debris. Two types of hair can be found on the body. *Vellus hair* is fine, short, pale, and covers much of the body. *Terminal hair* is coarser, longer, and darker than vellus hair and is found on the scalp, eyebrows, pubis, and axillae. Hair color and texture vary and are determined by genetics and the type and amount of pigment produced.

Nails

The purpose of nails is to protect the distal ends of the fingers and toes against trauma. Nails are hard, transparent plates of epidermal cells that are converted to keratin and grow from a root under the skin called the cuticle. Nails (i.e., the *nail plate*) appear pink because of the highly vascular epithelial cells (i.e., the *nail bed*) on which they rest. At the base of the nail is a crescent-shaped, whitish area called the *lunula*, which lies over the *nail matrix* where new keratin cells are formed. The cuticle works to cover and protect the nail matrix, which is the growth region of the nail (Figure 12.2).

Sweat Glands

There are three types of sweat glands: *eccrine, ceruminous,* and *apocrine.* The eccrine glands are widely distributed throughout the body and open directly onto the skin's surface. These glands help maintain fluid and

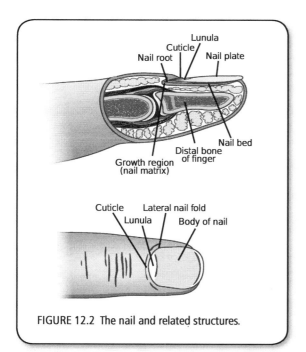

FIGURE 12.2 The nail and related structures.

electrolyte balance, excrete waste (e.g., uric acid and ammonia, both byproducts of protein metabolism) and produce sweat in response to heat and emotional stimuli. These glands are controlled by the sympathetic nervous system. Ceruminous glands are located in the external auditory canal and produce cerumen. Apocrine glands are located primarily in the axillary, genital, and periumbilical regions. They open into hair follicles and require androgens to stimulate their secretions.

Sebaceous Glands

Sebaceous glands are everywhere on the body except the palms and soles (see Figure 12.1). They are most abundant on the scalp and face. The sebaceous glands produce sebum, a lipid substance that is secreted through the hair follicles. Sebum keeps the hair from drying, prevents water evaporation from the skin, moisturizes the skin, and is thought to have some fungicidal and bactericidal effects.

DEVELOPMENTAL CONSIDERATIONS

Skin

Skin development is a dynamic process from the embryonic stage through adulthood. The skin of the neonate continues to change during childhood through late adolescence, at which time the skin achieves adult thickness and characteristics.

The stratum corneum does not develop until 23 to 25 weeks gestation (Telofski, Morello, Correa, & Stamatas, 2012). Therefore, premature infants lack this top layer of skin, which greatly increases the infant's risk for infection, temperature instability, and fluid loss.

When an infant is born, the skin is covered with a thick, white, cheesy substance called *vernix caseosa* (see Chapter 11), which consists of sebum and shed epithelial cells. The earlier the gestation, the more vernix will be covering the infant's skin.

A neonate's skin shares the same structure as mature skin, but the functions are immature. At birth, the epidermis is very thin, with little underlying subcutaneous tissue (Saladin, 2006). These factors result in several consequences for the neonate:

- They lack the ability to shiver to increase body temperature.
- They lose heat rapidly and have difficulty conserving body heat.
- They lose fluid readily, making them susceptible to dehydration.
- Their skin has greater permeability to and increased transcutaneous absorption of potentially harmful chemicals (Ball et al., 2012).
- The thin epidermis allows superficial blood vessels to be visible, causing the newborn skin to appear red to ruddy in color.
- They have a loose attachment between the epidermis and dermis, making them more prone to blister formation. Their skin contains more water than the skin of an older child or adult, making it more susceptible to bacterial infection (Ball et al., 2012).

The pH of the skin in neonates is basic (as opposed to being acidic), which also makes infants prone to skin infections, since an acidic pH creates a hostile environment for bacteria. The epidermis and dermis become more tightly bound by adolescence, increasing resistance to friction injuries and infection.

There is less melanin in the skin at birth, so the skin is lightly pigmented (Ball et al., 2012). Because UV light is required for melanin production, several weeks may pass before the neonate's skin darkens. The skin continues to darken as more pigmented cells rise through the epidermis. This is particularly noticeable in dark-skinned children. Throughout childhood, the hair and skin color changes as the child matures. Melanin reaches adult levels by adolescence. Vascularization of the dermis is well developed by the second year of life.

At the onset of puberty, secondary sex characteristics appear in the skin. In girls, subcutaneous fat deposits increase, especially in the pelvic region. The areola enlarges in diameter and darkens in color, and breast tissue develops. In boys, skin changes include thinning, increased redness, and looseness of the scrotal skin. At puberty, a deceleration of fat mass accumulation occurs, resulting in a higher lean body mass than in girls.

Skin Appendages

Skin appendages are present at birth but, like all other body structures at this age, they are not fully developed.

Hair

Hair follicles develop in the fetus between the third and fourth months of gestation (McPherson, 2009), and by approximately 13 to 16 weeks gestation, the skin of the fetus is covered with fine, downy hair called *lanugo* (see Chapter 11). At approximately 36 weeks of gestation, lanugo begins to disappear and is completely gone by 37 to 40 weeks of gestation, except for the upper arms and shoulders (McPherson, 2009). This lanugo is usually shed by 2 to 3 weeks of age (Ball et al., 2012). In the first few months after birth, lanugo is replaced by fine vellus hair. In a full-term infant, scalp hair is terminal hair, soft in texture, and often patchy. The amount of scalp hair varies, and scalp hair is shed within a few months of birth and replaced, often with hair of a different color and texture (Ball et al., 2012). In children, hair grows approximately 1 cm a month. At the onset of puberty, coarse hair appears in the pubic area and axilla and, in males, on the face.

Nails

Nails are formed in the fifth fetal month. The fetus's fingernails should reach the end of the fingertips by 36 weeks of gestation and extend beyond the fingertips by 37 to 40 weeks of gestation (McPherson, 2009). Nails are spoon-shaped and thin from birth until approximately 2 to 3 years of age. In children, nails grow at a rate of 1 mm or less a day.

Sweat Glands

Eccrine glands begin to function by 2 to 18 days of age but do not fully function until middle childhood. Therefore, infants and very young children sweat minimally and are unable to regulate body temperature as efficiently as older children and adults. This partially explains the high fevers sometimes noted in children this age. Infants do, however, experience palmar sweating in response to heat and emotional stimuli, and this may be helpful when assessing pain in the neonate. Eccrine glands achieve full function at puberty; boys sweat more than girls.

Apocrine glands do not become active until puberty. These glands secrete a fluid in response to heat or emotional stress. Bacteria on the skin react with the fluid produced by apocrine glands to produce body odor.

Sebaceous Glands

Sebum is present for the first few weeks of life, and its presence produces milia (sebaceous cysts seen most often on the nose and chin of the newborn) (see Chapter 11) and seborrhea (e.g., cradle cap in infants and dandruff in adolescents). Sebaceous glands decrease in size and stop producing sebum between 6 and 12 months of age but become active again at puberty when stimulated by testosterone. Decreased sebum production provides less protection against evaporation and drying, interfering with body temperature regulation and skin integrity. Increased sebum production during puberty makes hair and skin oilier, often causing acne.

ASSESSMENT OF THE SKIN, HAIR, AND NAILS

History

Disorders of the skin, hair, and nails can be acute or chronic, localized, or caused by a systemic problem. The reason for the health care visit dictates the type of history to be obtained. When a child is seen for his or her first visit to the practice, the provider should obtain a very inclusive history. This includes questions about nevi (birthmarks), skin changes in the neonatal period, past rashes, a history of injuries involving the skin, past medical history (PMH), family history of skin disorders or allergies, and habits such as nail biting. Children presenting for a health maintenance visit require an updated family and medical history, including recent illnesses, new allergies, and current medications. A focused history is required for children presenting with an integumentary complaint. Regardless of the type of history, the provider should always ask about measures used to protect the child's skin from the sun.

When obtaining the history specific to the integumentary system, it is important for the provider to remember to ask questions in a matter-of-fact, nonjudgmental manner, especially when inquiring about any dermatologic manifestations that may be the result of poor hygiene or unhealthy behaviors. In addition, some dermatologic conditions may be embarrassing to a child or teen, for example, acne and tinea cruris (jock itch), and a sensitive approach when asking questions about these conditions is necessary.

Past Medical History

The purpose of the PMH is to establish a baseline dermatologic assessment against which future assessments can be measured. A history of allergies, illnesses, infections, injuries involving the skin, or sensitivity to UV light may be directly related to rashes the child may have had in the past or may even explain a new rash. A family history is important because certain dermatologic disorders can be inherited (e.g., atopic dermatitis, psoriasis). The PMH also includes the review of systems (ROS) relative to the integumentary system. Included in the PMH are questions about congenital nevi and allergies.

Congenital Nevi • Nevi are a common finding in children. The two most common types of nevi are pigmented (e.g., café-au-lait spots, Mongolian spots) and vascular (e.g., salmon patches, port-wine stains, hemangiomas) (Vernon, Brady, Barber Starr, & Petersen-Smith, 2013). Some nevi should be noted because of their particular characteristics. Two examples of pigmented nevi stand out. Café-au-lait spots are tan to brown macules (Figure 12.3). They are notable because if they measure greater than 0.5 mm in diameter or number six or more, the child should be evaluated for neurofibromatosis type 1 (Pletcher, 2013). Mongolian spots (Figure 12.4) are noteworthy because they must be distinguished from bruises to rule out child abuse.

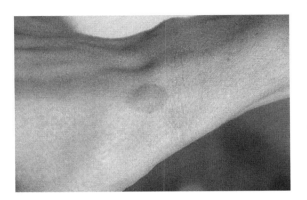

FIGURE 12.3 Café-au-lait spot. Congenital nevus; round to oval light brown macules; if there are six or more and measure over 5 mm in diameter, neurofibromatosis may be present.

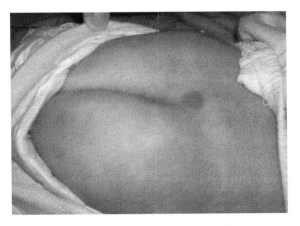

FIGURE 12.4 Mongolian spot. These congenital blue-gray macular lesions are found primarily in the lumbosacral or gluteal area of dark-skinned newborns. The spots usually fade by school age and should be differentiated from bruises.

Vascular nevi are caused by a structural abnormality (vascular malformations) or an overgrowth of blood vessels (hemangiomas). These nevi can be flat, raised, or cavernous. Vascular malformations are present at birth; hemangiomas (Figure 12.5) are not present at birth but emerge by 1 month of age. Vascular malformations (e.g., salmon patches or "stork bites," port-wine stains) grow along with the child (see Figure 12.5); hemangiomas may grow quite rapidly in some cases. Hemangiomas may be superficial, deep, or mixed. Histologically, hemangiomas are benign tumors of capillary endothelial cells. Involution of hemangiomas begins at approximately 12 to 24 months of age, and most are flat by 5 to 7 years of age and the remainder by puberty. Most hemangiomas appear as normal skin after involution, but some leave residual skin changes such as atrophy, telangiectasias, or scarring (Antaya, 2013). Hemangiomas may interfere with body functions, depending on the location of the lesion. Any hemangiomas that obstruct the airway, the eye, or those that cause cardiac complications (e.g., high-output failure) require immediate treatment. The provider should always inquire about any changes in the color, size, or shape of a nevus, or if there is any new onset of tenderness, bleeding, or itching (Table 12.1).

Allergies • The provider should ask the parents if their child has any allergies and should document the type of reaction the child experiences after exposure to the allergen (e.g., itching, rashes, urticaria). The provider should inquire specifically about any history of allergies related to the following: medications, foods, chemicals, insect bites, animals, plants, and environmental allergens. It is also important to determine if the parent has used any treatments for these allergies, and if so, to what effect.

Family History

A family history is important to obtain, focusing on hereditary skin disorders, such as atopic dermatitis, seborrheic dermatitis, psoriasis, or any family history of sensitivities to topical creams or other medications. It is also important to ask about any family history of asthma, allergic rhinitis, environmental or food allergies, persistent rashes, and diabetes. The provider should also ask if any family members have been ill recently, currently have a rash, or if all family members' immunizations are up to date. A family history of skin cancer should be noted.

Review of Systems

The pediatric ROS specific to the integumentary system includes asking the parent or caregiver about the child's usual state of health and any recent illnesses. Many childhood illnesses have cutaneous manifestations, most notably viral exanthems and bacterial illnesses such as streptococcal infections.

The provider should also ask about a history of nutritional deficiencies, many of which alter the condition of the hair, skin, and nails. For example, a lack of vitamins C and K may cause bruising, while a deficit of vitamin A may cause dry hair. Food allergies may also have integumentary manifestations (e.g., rashes,

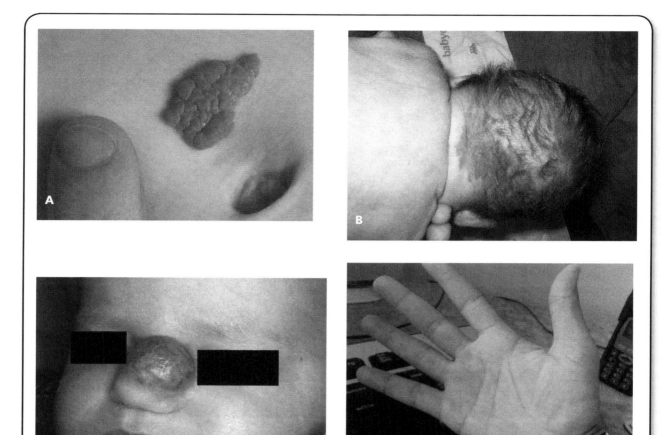

FIGURE 12.5 Types of vascular skin lesions. **A.** A capillary ("strawberry") hemangioma is a soft, bright red, vascular nodule that appears soon after birth and involutes spontaneously, usually by 7 years of age. **B.** Salmon patches, also called "stork bites," are flat, light pink macules that blanch with pressure and fade with time. **C.** A cavernous hemangioma is a raised, soft, compressible lesion, light blue in color that blanches with pressure; it is variable in size. **D.** Port-wine stains are permanent dark red to purple macules; they do not blanch with pressure or fade with time. They can be associated with congenital syndromes.

atopic dermatitis, pruritus, urticaria), and any history of these should be included in the ROS. Other areas to assess include:

- **General health:** Usual state of health; recent illnesses, especially viral or bacterial illnesses; immunization history; a history of immunosuppression; and nutritional disorders or deficiencies
- **Skin, hair, and nails:** Recent or long-term changes in the color, quality, or texture of skin, hair, or nails; history of dry skin, skin disease, or rashes, including acne, atopic dermatitis, contact dermatitis, seborrheic dermatitis, psoriasis; nevi; skin changes in the neonatal period (e.g., jaundice, including day of onset; cyanosis and its cause); diaper rash and what type; burns or bruises and circumstances surrounding injuries; habits such as nail-biting, hair-twisting, hair-pulling (trichotillomania); pressure alopecia (because of persistent positioning on one side, which is mostly seen in infants); traction alopecia (hair loss because of tight hairstyles); hirsutism; history of sunburn or sensitivity to sunlight; fungal infections of the skin, hair, or nails; presence of acanthosis nigricans (Figure 12.6), which may indicate insulin resistance, diabetes, or polycystic ovary syndrome (PCOS); tattoos or piercings; or urticaria

- **Eyes, ears, nose, and throat:** Swelling, itching, drainage, circles around eyes; chronic nasal discharge, mouth breathing, epistaxis; dry mouth, oral lesions, or pain
- **Respiratory:** Asthma, allergic rhinitis, chronic cough, or wheezing
- **Endocrine:** Diabetes; overweight or obesity; PCOS; or current pregnancy (adolescent)

TABLE 12.1	Congenital Skin Lesions
TYPE OF LESION	**CHARACTERISTICS**
Pigmented Skin Lesions	
Café-au-lait spots	Tan to light brown macules with discrete borders
Congenital pigmented nevi	At birth, lesion may be pale pink to tan with soft vellus hairs; during childhood, nevus darkens to light brown to black plaques often with dense hair growth.
Mongolian spots	Dark blue, irregularly shaped macules seen in dark-skinned infants and children, most often seen in the lumbosacral and gluteal areas; may occur on the upper back, shoulders, and extremities. More uniform in color than bruises with well-defined borders; often fade with time; their presence should be documented for medico-legal reasons (see Figure 12.4).
Vascular Malformations	
Port-wine stain or nevus flammeus	Dark red to purple macules that occur unilaterally, usually on face, occiput, or neck. Present at birth and do not enlarge or fade. Can be associated with Sturge-Weber disease (see Figure 12.5D).
Salmon patch ("stork bite") or nevus flammeus	Light pink macules found on forehead, back of neck, glabella, and upper eyelids; present at birth; fade with time, usually by age 1 (see Figure 12.5B).
Hemangiomas	
Capillary hemangioma ("strawberry mark")	May not be present at birth. Begins as gray to white area and then becomes red, raised, and well defined; grows rapidly. Lesions are soft, compressible, and elevated (see Figure 12.5A). Most hemangiomas involute by age 5–7 years.
Cavernous hemangioma	Lesions are beneath the skin and appear bluish; borders are indistinct; lesion fills with blood if patient placed in a dependent position; with blanching, a soft, compressible tumor is felt (see Figure 12.5C).

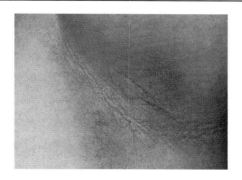

FIGURE 12.6 Acanthosis nigricans. Linear areas of velvety thickening and hyperpigmentation of the skin, most often seen in the skin folds of the neck and axilla; skin tags may also be seen; most common in African American, Native American, and Hispanic children; they are related to obesity and may indicate insulin resistance.

Social History Specific to the Integumentary System

Certain aspects of the child's social situation and lifestyle can influence the condition of his or her skin, hair, and nails. Table 12.2 summarizes what the provider should assess when gathering a social history relative to the integumentary system.

Current Medications

The provider should inquire about any medications the child has taken over the past 3 to 5 days. This includes all prescribed and over-the-counter drugs, topical medications, and any herbal preparations. Side effects or allergic reactions to medications often manifest as skin rashes. The provider should ask the parent what, if any, treatment was used for itching or discomfort, noting the effectiveness of the treatment. The provider should also inquire about the use of anabolic steroids, which have several untoward side effects, especially with chronic

TABLE 12.2	History of Present Illness Specific to the Integumentary System
ASSESSMENT	**RATIONALE**
Emotional disturbance	Depression may interfere with daily hygiene routines such as bathing and hair washing; depression may also lead to self-mutilation behaviors, including self-inflicted scratching, punching, pinching, burning, and cutting (Tumolo, 2005).
Habits	Compulsive nail-biting, hair-pulling, or skin-picking may indicate mental health disorders.
Hobbies	Some hobbies may increase exposure to paint, bleach, glue, chemicals, or the sun, all of which can be drying and irritating to skin.
Hot or humid environment; extreme cold temperature exposure	Chronic sweating can lead to skin rashes, especially in infants and young children; frostbite or burns affect the blood supply and can damage the skin.
Obesity	Rashes in intertriginous areas (i.e., intertrigo) develop from chronic heat, moisture, and friction; acanthosis nigricans may indicate insulin resistance.
Personal hygiene	Inadequate personal hygiene can lead to rashes and skin breakdown as well as dirty hair and nails.
Sun exposure, frequency of sunbathing, and use of sunscreen	Recent or frequent sunburn can lead to dryness of skin or infection and over time increases child's lifetime risk for developing skin cancer.
Use of tobacco (including exposure to secondhand smoke), street drugs, or alcohol	Smoking tobacco interferes with the cell's ability to repair damage (e.g., after intense UV exposure). Street drugs (e.g., amphetamines) can cause dry, itchy skin, and profuse sweating may accompany alcohol use in which case the skin feels cool to the touch but the drinker feels warm.

use. The most obvious integumentary manifestation of steroid use is the development of acne in adolescents who use these drugs.

History of Present Illness

Most pediatric integumentary complaints are related to contagious skin infections, infestations, or communicable diseases. Other complaints include skin dryness, oiliness, bruising, swelling, increased pigmentation, lesions, rashes, changes in birthmarks, hair loss, and a change in the condition of the nails. When a child presents with an integumentary complaint, several key questions are important to formulate a differential diagnosis (Table 12.3). The mnemonic OPPQRST is useful as a guideline when collecting subjective data (see Chapter 6). Table 12.4 lists some common pediatric skin conditions.

Physical Examination

The skin is the most easily examined organ because of its size and accessibility. Assessment of the integumentary system involves inspection and palpation of the skin, hair, scalp, and nails. The integumentary system is unique in that thorough, systematic inspection alone most often provides the most useful data. Palpation is also useful as it enables the examiner to assess the temperature, texture, and turgor of the skin. Palpation also aids in assessing elevated skin lesions. For example, when examining dark-skinned children and adolescents, inspection alone is often inadequate and palpation is an important part of assessment, especially when keloids form or lichenification occurs. The provider should always wear gloves when palpating the skin, especially over areas of lesions and skin breakdown.

Inspection of the skin should take place in a room with good light with neutral-colored walls. Natural daylight is optimal, but if this is not possible, the best alternative is the direct light provided by a gooseneck lamp. The lamp should have at least a 60-watt bulb; fluorescent lighting should not be used because of differences in the spectrum of light emitted, which can distort the natural skin color. The examination room temperature should be comfortable so that acrocyanosis or mottling does not occur as a result of a cool room temperature or flushing or sweating does not occur as a result of a hot room temperature. This environmental response may confuse the clinical picture as such color changes and the diaphoresis can result from cardiac etiologies.

TABLE 12.3	Focused History Related to Skin Assessment
SUBJECTIVE OR OBJECTIVE DATA	**KEY QUESTIONS**
Date of onset of rash or lesions	Sudden or gradual?
Evolution of rash or lesions	Intermittent or continuous? Has rash or lesion changed since its onset (e.g., varicella begins as erythematous macules then progresses to papules, then vesicles, then crusts)?
Location of rash or lesions	Is rash or lesion localized or has it spread? Where is rash located?
Quality of rash or lesions	Are there single or multiple lesions? Is it a primary or secondary lesion (see Tables 12.7 and 12.8)?
Associated symptoms	Is there a history of a recent fever, malaise, systemic illness, or weight loss or gain? All of these can indicate viral or bacterial illness.
Aggravating factors	What makes rash worse?
Alleviating factors	Are any treatments (e.g., prescription or over-the-counter medications, heat, cold, creams, lotions, home remedies) currently being used? If so, what are their effects?
Presence or absence of itching	Is the itching because of dry skin, atopic or contact dermatitis, insect bites, allergies, infection, infestations (e.g., scabies, lice), or systemic illness such as varicella, or is it a prodrome to an asthma attack? Does it awaken child from sleep? Where does it itch?
Prior history of similar rash	Could this be a chronic condition such as atopic dermatitis?
Change in skin or mucous membrane pigmentation	Has child had extensive sun exposure, which can cause skin color changes? Does child have atopic dermatitis, which can cause excessive itching and lead to skin lichenification? Does child have a cardiac condition, which can cause changes in color of skin or mucous membranes? Is child obese? (increased brown pigmentation, especially in the folds of the neck and axillae, can indicate insulin resistance [i.e., acanthosis nigricans; see Figure 12.6]) (Miller & Rapini, 2012)
History of eating large amounts of yellow fruits or vegetables	Is it possible that diet caused yellow skin pigment change (carotenemia)?
Hair loss	Does child have any known nutritional deficiencies? Is there a history of recent weight loss? Does child pull out his or her own hair? Does child have a history of rubbing his or her head against the mattress? Is child receiving chemotherapy?
Change in nails	Does child have any change in nail color or contour?
Immunization status	Is it possible that immunizations for communicable diseases have caused integumentary manifestations?
Current medications	Is it possible that the rash or urticaria is caused by an allergic reaction to medication?
Allergies	Is it possible that child is having an allergic reaction with cutaneous manifestations? Has a new formula or food been recently introduced to child?
Family history	Is the rash a hereditary or contagious problem? Other family members may need to be assessed for the same symptoms (e.g., tinea or pediculosis infections).
Recent travel	Is it possible that recent travel resulted in a communicable disease with cutaneous manifestations?
Recent sun exposure	Is there a recent history of excessive sun exposure, which can cause erythema, vesicles, and burns? Does child wear sunscreen, a hat, and a long-sleeved shirt?

(continued)

TABLE 12.3	Focused History Related to Skin Assessment (*continued*)
SUBJECTIVE OR OBJECTIVE DATA	**KEY QUESTIONS**
Recent exposure to infectious contacts	Has the child been exposed to any contagious skin conditions (e.g., tinea, scabies, impetigo), or communicable (e.g., roseola, varicella, scarlet fever) or infectious (e.g., viral, bacterial, fungal) illnesses? Has the child been exposed to pediculosis or scabies at school or day care?
Plants	Has the child been near plants such as poison ivy, oak, or sumac, which can cause allergic contact dermatitis?

TABLE 12.4	Common Skin Conditions in the Pediatric Patient		
DIAGNOSIS	**PHYSICAL FINDINGS**	**TYPICAL ARRANGEMENT PATTERN**	**LOCATION OF LESIONS**
Allergic and Inflammatory Reactions			
Acne	Closed and open comedones (noninflamed acne); pustules, papules, nodules, and cysts (inflamed acne)	Localized	Face, neck, shoulders, chest, and back
Allergic dermatitis	Erythema, vesicles, and pruritus	Localized or diffuse	Area in which antigen contacted skin
Atopic dermatitis (eczema)	Erythematous, intensely pruritic papules, plaques, and vesicles that ooze and crust. Chronic form has pruritic, dry, scaly rash with lichenification. Secondary lesions often develop because of scratching (e.g., infection, lichenification).	Confluent, localized, or diffuse; symmetrical	*Infantile eczema:* cheeks, forehead, scalp, trunk, and extensor surfaces of extremities. Diaper area spared. *Childhood eczema:* wrists, ankles, and antecubital and popliteal fossae
Contact dermatitis	Pruritic rash that has sharply demarcated borders and often mimics shape of the contact irritant. Papules and bullae may be present.	Confluent, localized, or diffuse; may be linear	Localized to affected area
Diaper dermatitis	Depends on cause: chemical dermatitis causes shiny, peeling, erythematous maculopapular rash, sparing skinfolds; bacterial dermatitis causes erythematous, peeling blisters and pustules.	Localized or confluent	Diaper area
Drug eruptions	Macular or papular, erythematous; intensely pruritic	Confluent or diffuse; symmetrical or morbilliform	Begins on trunk; extends to palms, soles, and face
Insect bites	Erythematous, edematous, and urticarial papules; pruritic. Secondary lesions often emerge as a result of scratching.	Localized to diffuse; grouped	Anywhere on body

TABLE 12.4	Common Skin Conditions in the Pediatric Patient (*continued*)		
DIAGNOSIS	**PHYSICAL FINDINGS**	**TYPICAL ARRANGEMENT PATTERN**	**LOCATION OF LESIONS**
Urticaria ("hives")	Erythematous, pruritic raised wheals with pale, edematous centers that blanch with pressure; accompanied by edema of lips, tongue, eyelids, hands, and feet	Confluent, annular, localized, or diffuse	Face, trunk, and extremities
Infections: Bacterial			
Cellulitis	Erythema, tenderness, and swelling; area warm to touch	Localized	Dermis and subcutaneous tissue of affected area
Folliculitis	Erythematous papule or pustule at hair follicle; pruritic	Localized	Hair follicle
Impetigo	Honey-crusted thin-roofed vesicles on an erythematous base; pruritic	Confluent, localized, or grouped	Superficial layers of skin over affected area
Scarlet fever	Flushed face, perioral pallor, diffuse blanching; sandpapery, pruritic, nontender erythematous papular rash, strawberry tongue; postacute phase desquamation	Confluent; symmetrical	Involves all body surfaces except face; may be more noticeable in joint areas ("Pastia's lines")
Infections: Fungal			
Candidiasis	Erythematous papules and pustules with sharply demarcated borders and surrounding satellite lesions; some loose scales	Localized	Intertriginous regions, especially diaper area; can be associated with oral candida
Tinea corporis	Flat, scaly, erythematous circular patches with central clearing; border of lesions are raised.	Confluent, annular, or localized	Anywhere on body
Tinea cruris	Erythematous to slightly brown, scaly, sharply demarcated lesions with raised border	Arciform; symmetrical	Groin, thighs, and inguinal folds
Tinea pedis	Erythematous, scaly, cracked rash on soles of feet and interdigital spaces; pruritic	Confluent or localized	Feet
Tinea versicolor	Hypopigmented to hyperpigmented scaly macules	Confluent or discrete; annular, localized, or diffuse	Mostly on trunk; can be on neck, shoulders, upper arms, back, and face
Infections: Viral			
Coxsackie virus (hand, foot, and mouth disease)	Mildly painful, shallow ulcers surrounded by red halos; vesicles seen on palate	Diffuse	Face, extremities, and mucous membranes

(continued)

TABLE 12.4	Common Skin Conditions in the Pediatric Patient (*continued*)		
DIAGNOSIS	PHYSICAL FINDINGS	TYPICAL ARRANGEMENT PATTERN	LOCATION OF LESIONS
Erythema infectiosum (Fifth disease)	Patchy facial erythema for 1–4 days, then maculopapular reticular rash appears on extensor surfaces of extremities	Confluent or localized; symmetrical or reticular	Face, scalp, trunk, and extremities
Herpes simplex (canker sores)	Vesicles on an erythematous base; vesicles dry, leaving a crust, then shallow, painful ulcers	Confluent, grouped, or localized	Lips, nose, tongue, genitalia, and buttocks
Herpes zoster (shingles)	Painful, pruritic vesicles	Confluent or localized; zosteriform	Face, scalp, and trunk; lesions cluster along dermatome
Molluscum contagiosum	Sharply circumscribed umbilicated papules that are pearly white in color	Confluent or localized	Face, scalp, trunk, and extremities
Roseola	Erythematous to rose-pink maculopapular rash	Confluent or diffuse	Begins on trunk; spreads to extremities
Rubella (German measles)	Discrete pinkish red maculopapular rash	Diffuse	Begins on face; spreads cephalocaudally
Rubeola (measles)	Pathognomonic exanthema on buccal mucosa (Koplik's spots) evident during prodrome; progresses to erythematous, blanching maculopapular rash; papules enlarge, become confluent, and progress cephalocaudally	Confluent or diffuse; discrete distally	Begins on forehead and behind ears, then spreads to face, neck, and arms, and then back, abdomen, and thighs
Varicella	Erythematous papules evolve into thin-walled vesicles on an erythematous base ("dew drops on a rose petal"); vesicle ruptures, causing crusting; intensely pruritic; lesions appear in crops	Diffuse; symmetrical	Face, palms, soles, trunk, extremities, and mucous membranes
Warts (common warts)	Elevated, flesh-colored papules with scaly surfaces	Confluent, contiguous, or localized	Can be found anywhere on the body; most commonly found on fingers, nails, legs, hands, and feet
West Nile virus	Erythematous, maculopapular rash; painful but not pruritic; blanches with pressure	Morbilliform	Trunk
Infestations			
Pediculosis	Small white nits seen on hair shaft (head lice); excoriated macules or papules (body lice); excoriation over pubic area with small bluish macules and papules (pubic lice); secondary infection commonly because of scratching	Linear	Head, body, or pubic area

TABLE 12.4	Common Skin Conditions in the Pediatric Patient (*continued*)		
DIAGNOSIS	PHYSICAL FINDINGS	TYPICAL ARRANGEMENT PATTERN	LOCATION OF LESIONS
Lyme disease	Distinctive exanthem: *erythema migrans*; appears 4–20 days after tick bite; red macule or papule at bite site; lesion enlarges to form plaque, which clears centrally, becoming annular; lesions warm to touch; mildly pruritic	Annular; localized to diffuse	Groin, axilla, and thigh proximal to tick bite
Scabies	Linear, brownish-gray burrows; intensely pruritic; numerous vesicular lesions in infants; secondary lesions (e.g., crusting, excoriation, infection) often because of scratching	Burrows; linear or diffuse	Trunk; intertriginous areas; webs of fingers and toes; sides of hands, palms, and soles; axillae; belt line; buttocks and extremities
Miscellaneous			
Psoriasis	Thick, dry, well-demarcated, erythematous plaques covered with silvery scales	Guttate	Scalp, ears, forehead, eyebrows, trunk, extensor surfaces of extremities, elbows, knees, and buttocks
Seborrhea	Oily, white to yellow to salmon-colored scaly patches (infants); manifested as dandruff in adolescents.	Confluent, localized, or diffuse	Scalp, eyebrows, eyelashes, and postauricular areas, along hairline; intertriginous areas, neck, axillae, and groin
Sunburn	Erythema, edema, blisters, and desquamation	Localized or diffuse	Sun-exposed areas

Helpful tools that assist the provider during inspection of the skin include a penlight, a magnifying glass to enlarge small areas of the skin for closer inspection, and a centimeter ruler to measure any lesions. It is also helpful to have a glass slide to aid in assessment; the provider could use this to press onto the child's skin gently to assess skin color (e.g., jaundice) and capillary refill time. A Wood's lamp, which provides UV light, is useful to examine fluorescent-positive skin fungal infections. A microscope, potassium hydroxide (KOH), a glass slide, and a cover slip are necessary to diagnose skin fungal infections.

To assess and diagnose any dermatologic conditions accurately in children, the provider must be familiar with the correct terminology used to describe dermatologic lesions (Table 12.5). Before the physical assessment, the provider should prepare the child for the exam. For children of toddler age or younger, an explanation to the parent alone will suffice. However, the provider should alert older children and adolescents about the skin areas that will be examined and touched. To assess the skin accurately, the child should remove all clothes and wear an age-appropriate patient gown. Privacy must be ensured. Infants can remain in a diaper, which can be removed easily when the diaper area is inspected. For the exam, infants can lie on the exam table or be held on the parent's lap. Older children and adolescents should sit on the exam table for the integumentary exam; children of preschool age and younger will likely want their parent nearby.

Skin

Inspection • When examining a child's skin, it is important to examine the child's entire body, not just the exposed areas of skin. The provider should begin by inspecting the scalp, progressing in a head-to-toe fashion to the neck, upper extremities, trunk, and then the lower extremities. The provider should evaluate the skin's color, texture, turgor, and look for edema, rashes, and lesions.

Assessment of the skin should begin by inspecting the child's skin color. Normal skin color varies from

TABLE 12.5	Dermatologic Arrangement Patterns and Descriptive Terms	
ARRANGEMENT PATTERN	**DESCRIPTION**	**EXAMPLE**
Acral	Involving extremities	Infantile acropustulosis
Annular	Ring-shaped	Tinea corporis, erythema migrans, pityriasis rosea
Arciform	Arch-shaped	Tinea cruris
Burrows	Narrow, elevated channel in the skin caused by a parasite	Scabies
Circinate	Circular	Impetigo, tinea capitis
Confluent	Lesions that run together	Smallpox, urticaria
Contiguous	Touching or adjacent	Tuberous sclerosis
Diffuse or generalized	Scattered and widely distributed over the body	Drug eruptions
Discrete	Lesions that are individual and distinct	Nevus
Eczematous	Vesicles with oozing, crusted lesions	Atopic dermatitis
Grouped	Arranged close together	Impetigo, insect bites, contact dermatitis
Guttate	Small, drop-like lesions	Psoriasis
Herpetiform	Grouped lesions that resemble those of herpes	Aphthous ulcers
Iris	Arranged in circles resembling a target	Erythema multiforme
Linear	Arranged in a line	Scratches, poison ivy
Localized	Confined to a local area	Irritant dermatitis
Morbilliform	Looks like measles or other viral exanthems	Drug eruptions
Nummular	Coin-shaped	Nummular eczema
Pedunculated	Having a stalk	Genital warts
Polycyclic	Oval lesions that tend to run together	Psoriasis, contact dermatitis
Punctate	Having tiny spots, points, or depressions	Petechiae
Reticular	Net-like	Erythema infectiosum (Fifth disease)
Scarlatiniform	Small red papules; resembling scarlet fever	Kawasaki disease
Serpiginous	Follows a snake-like, creeping track	Erythema marginatum, tinea corporis
Symmetrical	Balanced on both sides	Gianotti-Crosti syndrome (papular acrodermatitis)
Umbilicated	Lesions with depressed centers	Molluscum contagiosum
Verrucous	Wart-like	Inflammatory verrucous epidermal nevus
Zosteriform	Linear lesions clustered along a nerve root dermatome	Herpes simplex virus

pink, yellow, or olive green, to brown, dark brown, or black, depending on the child's race. It is essential to know the child's normal skin color to assess for color or pigment changes accurately.

Acrocyanosis, a bluish color of the hands and feet in newborns, may persist for 8 to 24 hours after birth. This is a transient, normal variation and reflects the transition to extrauterine life. Acrocyanosis that persists despite warming of the infant may be indicative of congenital heart disease (see Chapter 11 for further discussion of neonatal skin assessment).

Inspection of skin color should be correlated with inspection of the color of the nail beds, earlobes, sclerae, conjunctivae, lips, and mucous membranes. Any variations should be noted. When describing skin color, concrete, specific descriptions are important. Table 12.6 lists the abnormal findings providers may find when inspecting skin color in children.

The provider should also inspect the skin for lesions or rashes. A systematic approach is necessary when assessing and describing these findings.

After reviewing the history, this involves assessing and describing the distribution (i.e., location) and pattern (i.e., anatomic arrangement) of the skin findings (Figure 12.7). Then the provider should identify the morphology of the lesions. Primary lesions (Table 12.7) develop from previously normal skin; secondary lesions (Table 12.8) evolve from primary lesions,

TABLE 12.6	Abnormal Skin Color Findings in Children	
COLOR	**POSSIBLE CAUSES**	**BEST PLACE TO OBSERVE**
Yellow-orange (jaundice)	Hepatitis, hemolytic disease, biliary obstruction, infectious mononucleosis, carotenemia, neonatal sepsis, and chronic renal disease	Sclerae, skin, mucous membranes, fingernails, soles, palms, abdomen; in dark-skinned children, inspect palate, palmar surfaces, sclerae; if renal cause, assess exposed skin only (not sclerae or mucous membranes)
Blue (cyanosis) (Dark-skinned children may not appear blue when cyanotic but gray or pale)	Anxiety, cold temperatures (peripheral cyanosis), and cardiac and respiratory (central cyanosis) problems	Peripheral cyanosis can be observed in nails, soles, and palms; central cyanosis is observed in lips, tongue, and oral mucosa and indicates hypoxemia; the best places to assess are conjunctivae, oral mucosa, and nail beds
White (pallor) (Dark-skinned children appear yellow-brown to gray)	Anemia, shock, syncope, and edema	Face, mouth, conjunctivae, and nail beds
Red (erythema, flushing) (Dark-skinned children may appear purplish)	Fever, blushing, hyperthermia, polycythemia, burns, inflammation, infection, increased vascularity, allergies, and alcohol consumption	Face, localized affected area; inspection may need to be augmented by palpation in dark-skinned children and assessment of skin and body temperature
Absence of color	Vitiligo and albinism	Symmetrical white patches (vitiligo); a generalized absence of pigment involving skin, hair, and eyes (albinism)

usually because of the child scratching or picking the primary lesions. Next, the color and elevation of the lesion should be assessed. The provider should measure the lesion with a centimeter ruler. If the lesions are extremely small, the provider should use a magnifying glass to inspect the lesion's characteristics. During this time, the provider could also teach skin self-examination to a child who is school-aged and older.

The provider should inspect for vascular lesions as well (Table 12.9). There should be no increased vascularity or any evidence of bleeding of the skin.

Petechiae or purpuric lesions (see Figure 12.7) on the skin may indicate systemic disease such as idiopathic thrombocytopenic purpura (ITP), leukemia, or meningococcemia. Bruises, lacerations, abrasions, and other marks on the skin may indicate intentional or unintentional injuries in children, depending on their color, pattern, and location (see Chapter 24) (Hornor, 2012). Any congenital nevi (birthmarks) should be noted; they can be benign or indicate an underlying disorder (see Assessment of the Skin, Hair, and Nails, and Table 12.1, provided earlier). Changes in any birthmarks should be documented in the child's medical record.

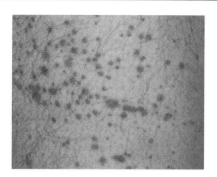

FIGURE 12.7 Petechiae and purpuric lesions. Both lesions indicate bleeding into the skin. Petechiae are small, nonblanching red to purple macules; purpuric lesions are larger macules that are dark red to purple.

The provider should also inspect the skin for piercings and tattoos. These forms of body art may be cultural or a form of self-expression in adolescents (Larzo & Poe, 2006). Areas to assess for body piercing include the ears, eyebrows, nose, tongue, lips, nipples, navel, and genitals (Larzo & Poe, 2006). Tattooed skin can be highly sensitive as a result of pigment additives; in addition, the tattooed area can be itchy and painful several weeks after the tattoo has been placed (Larzo & Poe, 2006). Dermatologic complications for which to look when inspecting pierced or tattooed skin include infection, signs of delayed healing, keloid formation, and allergic and contact dermatitis (Larzo & Poe, 2006).

Inspection of the skin in adolescents should also include looking for unexplained cuts, burns, bruises, and pinch marks on the body, especially on the arms

TABLE 12.7	Primary Skin Lesions		
TYPE	**DESCRIPTION**	**EXAMPLES**	**ILLUSTRATION**
Bulla	> 1 cm vesicle	Pemphigus, herpes gestationis, fixed drug eruption	
Cyst	Raised, circumscribed, encapsulated with a wall and lumen, filled with liquid of semisolid	Digital mucous, epidermal inclusion, pilar	
Macule	< 1 cm in diameter, flat, nonpalpable, circumscribed, abnormal tone	Brown: freckle, junctional nevus, lentigo, melasma Blue: Mongolian spot, ochronosis Red: drug eruption, viral exanthema, secondary syphilis Hypopigmented: vitiligo, idiopathic guttate hypomelanosis	
Nodule	> 1 cm, raised, solid	Wart, xanthoma, prurigo nodularis, neurofibromatosis	

TABLE 12.7	Primary Skin Lesions (*continued*)		
TYPE	**DESCRIPTION**	**EXAMPLES**	**ILLUSTRATION**
Papule	< 1 cm in diameter, raised, palpable, firm	Flesh, white, or yellow: flat wart, milium, sebaceous hyperplasia, skin tag Blue or violaceous: venous lake, lichen planus, melanoma Brown: seborrheic keratosis, melanoma, dermatofibroma, nevi Red: acne, cherry angioma, early folliculitis, psoriasis, urticaria, eczema	
Patch	> 1 cm in diameter, smooth, nonpalpable, irregular shape, discolored	Brown: larger freckle, junctional nevus, lentigo, melasma Blue: Mongolian spot, ochronosis Red: drug-eruption viral exanthema, secondary syphilis Hypopigmented: vitiligo, idiopathic guttate hypomelanosis	
Plaque	> 1 cm, raised, superficial, flat-topped, rough	Psoriasis, discoid lupus, tinea corporis, eczema, seborrheic dermatitis	
Pustule	Raised; superficial; filled with cloudy, purulent fluid	Acne, candidiasis, rosacea, impetigo, folliculitis	
Tumor	Large nodule	Metastatic carcinoma, sporotrichosis	

(*continued*)

TABLE 12.7   **Primary Skin Lesions (*continued*)**

TYPE	DESCRIPTION	EXAMPLES	ILLUSTRATION
Vesicle	< 1 cm, superficially raised, filled with serous fluid	Herpes simplex, herpes zoster, erythema, multiforme, impetigo	
Wheal	Raised, irregular area of edema, solid, transient, variable size	Hives, cholinergic urticaria, angioedema, dermatographism	

Adapted from Rhoads (2006).

TABLE 12.8   **Secondary Skin Lesions**

TYPE	DESCRIPTION	EXAMPLES/CAUSES
Atrophy	Loss of epidermis/dermis; may cause thinning or depression of skin	Striae; consequence of atopic dermatitis or chronic topical steroid use
Crusts	Dried serum, blood, or exudates; slightly elevated; varied color	Impetigo, tinea capitis, atopic dermatitis, varicella, or herpes
Desquamation	Skin peeling in sheets or scales	Poststreptococcal scarlet fever or seborrheic dermatitis
Erosion	Localized loss of epidermis; area often depressed, oozing, and moist; heals without scarring; does not extend into dermis	Herpes simplex, eczema herpeticum, epidermolysis bullosa or aphthous ulcers
Excoriation	Abrasion or hollowed-out area of epidermis, frequently caused by chronic itching	Scratching, atopic dermatitis, intertrigo, or tinea cruris
Fissure	Linear break in the skin extending into the epidermis and dermis	Dry skin, intertrigo, or contact dermatitis
Lichenification	Thickened epidermis with visible furrows caused by chronic rubbing	Chronic itching or irritation; dry skin, atopic dermatitis, or psoriasis
Scales	Thin, exfoliated layers of epidermis	Psoriasis, poststreptococcal scarlet fever, tinea versicolor, pityriasis rosea, or seborrheic dermatitis
Scar	Healed fibrous tissue after a dermal injury; some areas may be hypertrophied	Keloid, burns, or acne
Striae	Pink or silver bands, stripes, or lines on skin where skin has been stretched	Obesity, pregnancy, or chronic topical steroid use
Ulcer	Deeper than erosion; loss of epidermis and dermis; varies in size	Decubitus or stasis ulcer

TABLE 12.9	Vascular Skin Lesions	
TYPE	**DESCRIPTION**	**EXAMPLES/CAUSES**
Ecchymosis (bruise, contusion)	Purple to yellow to green to brown in color, depending on age of injury; irregularly shaped macular or papular lesion > 10 mm in diameter; because of extravasation of blood into skin or mucous membrane; does not blanch with pressure	Injury or trauma
Hematoma	Accumulation of blood from ruptured blood vessel; > 1 cm; bluish-red	Subdural or epidural hematoma from traumatic injury
Petechiae	Pinpoint hemorrhages, < 2 mm in diameter, round and discrete, dark red to purple	Injury, thrombocytopenia, infection, immune suppression, sepsis, meningococcemia, hemophilia, nutritional deficiency, violent vomiting or coughing; anticoagulants, aspirin, and steroids
Purpura	Purple flat, macular lesions 2–10 mm in diameter; dark red to purple	Vitamin C deficiency, Henoch-Schönlein purpura, infection, sepsis, meningococcemia, thrombocytopenia, hemophilia; anticoagulants, aspirin, and steroids
Telangiectasia	Dilated terminal vessels under the skin	Chronic topical steroid use, liver disease
Vascular malformations	Abnormal clusters of blood vessels that occur during fetal development	Port-wine stain, salmon patch, pyogenic granuloma

and legs, which can indicate self-mutilation in teens (Tumolo, 2005). Providers should also assess and document whether or not the teen is wearing long-sleeved shirts and pants during warm weather in an attempt to cover injuries, which is also a warning sign of self-mutilation.

The provider should inspect the skin for needle or "track" marks, which may indicate use of street drugs. Adolescents are the primary age group for which to target this assessment. Areas to inspect include the antecubital fossae, forearms, or any other area of the skin where large veins are noted.

For adolescents who present with weight loss or weight fluctuations; nutritional deficiencies; erosion of dental enamel; dry skin and mucous membranes; dry, dull, and brittle hair and nails, and in some cases lanugo, the provider should inspect the index or middle finger on the dominant hand, noting any abrasion or scarring on these fingers (Russell's sign). This, coupled with the above assessments, may indicate chronic, self-induced vomiting, an indicator of bulimia nervosa.

Any skin odor or taste should also be noted. For example, a salty taste to the skin may indicate cystic fibrosis. Other skin odors may indicate infection, poor hygiene, or neglect. If a child presents with

an illness complaint related to the skin, the provider should start by assessing the child's general appearance. One of the first things that should be determined is whether the child appears ill or is in any type of distress to differentiate a systemic illness from a simple rash. Even when a skin problem is the chief complaint, other body systems should be examined because of the cutaneous manifestations of many childhood diseases. If a systemic illness is suspected, the provider should note the child's age and also assess the child's eyes, nose, mouth, lymph nodes, and lungs to make an accurate diagnosis. Any fever or nuchal rigidity should be noted. The child's nutritional and hydration status should also be assessed. Endocrine, allergic, infectious, and nutritional problems all have possible cutaneous manifestations.

Palpation • The skin should be palpated to assess temperature, texture, turgor, moisture, perfusion, and edema. Any lesions should be palpated as well.

The skin should feel warm when palpated. Skin temperature that is cool to the touch may indicate hypothermia or poor localized circulation. This is a common finding in the neonate who needs to be treated by warming. Hypothyroidism can also cause cool skin temperatures. Skin that feels hot when palpated may be the result of fever, hyperthermia, hyperthyroidism, infection, or recent sunburn.

Normal skin texture in a child is smooth, firm, and even. Skin that feels rough when palpated may indicate overbathing, poor nutrition, or chronic exposure to cold weather or chemicals. The texture of the skin should also be uniform. Older children and adolescents may have rough skin on the palms and soles because of chronic friction. Rough skin may also be the result of prolonged scratching of a specific area. Scratching that is prolonged and intense may lead to lichenification of that area of skin (Figure 12.8). Flaking or scaling of an area of the skin can also be palpated. Scaling or flaking may occur from nutritional deficiencies, fungal infections, contact dermatitis, or atopic dermatitis.

FIGURE 12.8 Lichenification (thickening and roughening of the skin) is caused by prolonged pressure, rubbing, or scratching.

The provider should also assess skin moisture by palpation. The skin is normally slightly dry. Excessive skin dryness may occur in response to overbathing, poor nutrition, sunburn, chronic exposure to cold temperatures, or hypothyroidism. Skin that feels moist in a child could simply be the result of perspiration after physical activity or diaphoreses, which occur in infants and children who have hyperthyroidism or cardiac conditions or who are in shock. Excessively oily skin is associated with acne in adolescents. Mucous membranes should be moist; dry mucous membranes indicate dehydration.

When evaluating perfusion, the provider should palpate the skin for blanching and capillary refill. Pressing a finger against the skin to produce blanching also enables a more accurate assessment of jaundice. Capillary refill greater than 2 to 3 seconds indicates dehydration or hypoperfusion.

Assessment of skin turgor evaluates the elasticity of the skin. With the infant or child lying down, the provider should assess skin turgor by grasping a skinfold on the child's abdomen and quickly releasing it, noting the ease and quickness with which the skin moves (mobility) and returns to place (turgor). Skin that remains folded (i.e., "tenting") indicates dehydration (Figure 12.9). Skin that has decreased mobility indicates edema.

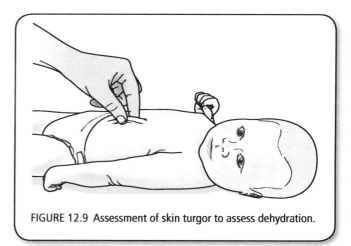

FIGURE 12.9 Assessment of skin turgor to assess dehydration.

Edema is a sign of fluid retention (Figure 12.10). Edema in children can be generalized, dependent, or periorbital. Generalized edema is most serious, likely reflecting a cardiac, hepatic, or renal disorder. Dependent edema is seen in the lower extremities or buttocks and is also likely to have a renal or cardiac etiology. Periorbital edema in children could be the result of recent sleep, crying, allergies, alteration in

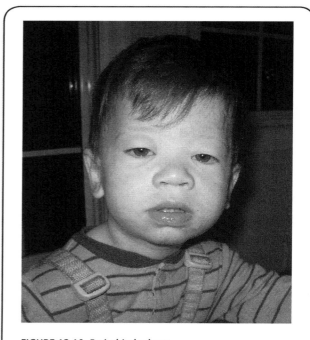

FIGURE 12.10 Periorbital edema.

renal function, or hypothyroidism. Edema can be easily assessed by simple inspection. It should be noted that edema can mask the child's normal skin color, producing a false pallor, because the fluid that causes the edema is between the surface of the skin and the pigmented and vascular areas. The provider should also palpate for edema. This is done by pressing firmly against the skin. If indentations are left after palpation, the edema is positive for pitting, which is associated with cardiac or renal disorders. Pitting is graded on a four-point scale to quantify the extent of the edema (Table 12.10).

With a gloved hand, the provider should gently palpate any rashes, lesions, or nevi. Lesions with scales should also be gently scraped to assess for bleeding (e.g., Auspitz sign in psoriasis) or to note whether the scales are easily removed. The provider can use information gleaned after palpation, coupled with inspection findings, to formulate a diagnosis.

Hair

Inspection • Assessment of the hair begins by inspecting the hair color, quality, cleanliness, and amount. Scalp hair should be shiny, strong, and elastic. Hair that is lusterless, matted, or has an odor may indicate neglect or depression. Hair that is dry and dull can be the result of poor nutrition, hypothyroidism, frequent swimming or shampooing, application of chemicals (i.e., permanents, hair dyes, bleaches), sun damage, heat from curling irons or blow dryers, and genetics. African American hair is naturally drier (see Cultural, Racial, and Ethnic Considerations). Hair that is oily or dirty may be a sign of poor hygiene or neglect.

The provider should also assess the distribution of the child's scalp hair, eyelashes, eyebrows, and body hair. Fine vellus hair should appear on the body. Lanugo is seen in preterm infants and in children or adolescents with extreme weight loss (e.g., anorexia nervosa). Following acute febrile illness or stress, many hairs convert from anagen (growth) to telogen (rest) stage, resulting in noticeably thinner scalp hair that could persist for months. Hair that appears thin may also be the result of the following:

- Poor nutrition
- Abuse or neglect
- Infection of the scalp (e.g., tinea capitis [ringworm], impetigo)
- Hypothyroidism
- Liver disease
- Drug toxicity
- Autoimmune disorders (e.g., alopecia areata)
- Chemotherapy or radiation
- Pressure or traction alopecia
- Trichotillomania (i.e., chronic hair pulling in a child or adolescent may be a clue to anxiety or compulsive disorders)

Hair distribution is also important to note when estimating sexual maturity in a child. Precocious or delayed appearance of body hair may be indicative of hormonal disturbances (see Chapter 20). Increased body hair (hirsutism) could be the result of PCOS (Miller & Rapini, 2012), Cushing's syndrome, endocrine abnormalities, adrenal hyperplasia, testicular or ovarian tumors, hyperinsulinism, and anabolic steroid use. Hair tufts noted over the spine, especially in the sacral area, can indicate spina bifida occulta. Pubic hair in a child younger than age 8 years indicates precocious puberty.

The provider should also inspect the scalp thoroughly. Gray, scaly, well-defined areas with broken hairs may indicate tinea capitis. The provider should separate and lift the hair to inspect it and the scalp for lesions. Seborrhea (oily scales) may be present in an infant or adolescent. Any presence of nits (eggs of head lice) on the hair shaft should be noted. Nits can be differentiated from dandruff by noting whether the nits stick to the hair shaft; dandruff does not. The scalp should also be inspected for ticks, which appear as gray or brown oval bodies.

TABLE 12.10	Grading of Pitting Edema	
SCALE	**DESCRIPTION**	**INDENTATION**
1+	Slight pitting; slight indentation of skin; no perceptible swelling; pitting disappears quickly after being compressed.	2 mm
2+	Slightly deeper pitting; indentation subsides rapidly (~10–15 seconds).	4 mm
3+	Deep pitting; noticeable swelling; indentation remains for a short time; may last for more than 1 minute.	6 mm
4+	Very deep pitting; marked swelling; indentation lasts approximately 2–5 minutes.	8 mm

Palpation • While wearing gloves, the provider should palpate the hair and scalp noting the texture of the hair and assessing for the presence of lesions. Hair should feel soft or silky. Dry, brittle hair can indicate a nutritional deficiency, hypothyroidism, or overuse of chemical hair products. Hair that is very fine can indicate hyperthyroidism. Tinea capitis infection can progress to the development of a kerion, an intense inflammatory response that, when palpated, is a tender, raised, boggy mass (Figure 12.11).

FIGURE 12.11 Tinea capitis with kerion is a raised, boggy, pustular mass that can result in localized scarring.

Nails

Inspection • The provider should inspect the child's nails for color, contour, thickness, texture, cleanliness, and general condition. Nail beds should be pink, smooth, flat, or slightly convex in shape with uniform thickness. Nails that appear white or yellow and thickened can indicate a fungal infection of the nail plate (*onychomycosis*), which is often associated with the application of artificial fingernails.

Nail changes can also be a sign of systemic illness; for example, cyanotic nail beds can indicate hypoxia. Pale nail beds may indicate anemia. In older children, nail polish and artificial nails interfere with an accurate assessment of nail bed color. Artificial nails can also affect the assessment of nail bed contour. Convex or concave nail beds may be hereditary or related to trauma, iron deficiency, or infection. Hypoxia that is chronic affects the shape of the nail bed, causing clubbing (Figure 12.12). A transverse nail furrow may indicate acute infection, anemia, or malnutrition. The provider should note any splinter hemorrhages under the nails, as this may indicate trauma or cardiac conditions such as subacute bacterial endocarditis or mitral stenosis. Nails should also be inspected for signs of biting or picking, which may indicate chronic stress in a child and can also lead to infection.

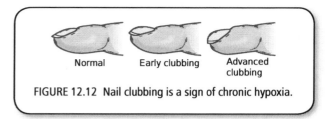

FIGURE 12.12 Nail clubbing is a sign of chronic hypoxia.

The provider should also inspect the tissue surrounding the nail. Inflammation in this area is a sign of *paronychia*, an acute or chronic infection of the epithelium lateral to the nail plate. Thumb-sucking, nail-biting, and the use of artificial nails predispose children or adolescents to this condition. Skin that is macerated at the thumb tip signifies chronic thumb-sucking.

Palpation • The provider should palpate the nail beds and assess time of capillary refill, which should be 2 to 3 seconds or less. Prolonged nail bed capillary refill may indicate poor peripheral circulation. The provider should also palpate the texture of the nail bed, focusing on whether the nail bed is firm, smooth, uniformly thick, and adherent to the nail bed, all of which are normal findings. Dry, brittle nails can be the result of hypothyroidism or poor nutrition (e.g., calcium, vitamin A, protein deficiency). The provider should also palpate the nail beds for tenderness, which indicates inflammation or infection.

CULTURAL, RACIAL, AND ETHNIC CONSIDERATIONS

Assessing Children With Dark Skin

It is important for the pediatric provider to be knowledgeable about normal variations in the hair and skin in children from varying racial and ethnic backgrounds. This includes being knowledgeable about basic skin care, variations that are considered within normal limits, and the natural tendency to show certain cutaneous reaction patterns in the skin. Skin and hair vary in amount, color, texture, and distribution, according to the child's genetic background. The provider should be able to recognize normal variations as well as dermatologic lesions in children with more darkly pigmented skin.

Normal Variations

The skin cells that are shed as part of the normal physiologic process are dark if the cell nuclei have more melanin, as with dark-skinned children (Burrall, 2006). The normal skin exfoliation process in dark-skinned people leaves a fine layer of dry, gray scales. African Americans may refer to their skin as "ashy" when dry and flaky. Also, when the skin of an African American child is cleaned with an alcohol wipe, the wipe looks brownish-gray, not because the skin is dirty but because melanin-rich skin cells have been wiped off the child's skin.

Any alterations in skin color (e.g., pallor, jaundice, cyanosis) in dark-skinned children may be difficult to assess because of increased pigmentation. Mild degrees of erythema may be missed completely, because of the skin's dark color. Some lesions that appear red or brown on a light-skinned child may appear purple or black in darkly pigmented skin. Because of this, assessment of the palms and soles may yield the most useful data.

In children with dark skin, it is normal for the skin to vary in color from one part of the body to another (Burrall, 2006). This is because of the variations of skin thickness over the body; the thicker the skin, the more layers of melanin-rich cells. This is why the elbows and knees of dark-skinned people are darker in color. In persons of all races, the palms and soles produce no melanin, so these areas of the skin are lighter than skin in other areas. This contrast is more noticeable in those with dark skin. Pigmentation of gingival tissue, the hard palate, mucous membranes, tongue, sclerae, and nails correlates with the degree of cutaneous pigmentation (Vernon et al., 2013). Approximately 20% to 30% of dark-skinned people have pigmentary demarcation lines (PDLs), known as Futcher's or Voight's lines, on their upper arms, chest, and abdomen (Galbraith & Esterly, 2006). PDLs are physiologic, sharply demarcated, vertical lines from areas of deeper pigmentation to areas that are more lightly pigmented. This trait is thought to be dominantly inherited (Laude & Russo, 1983).

Cutaneous Reaction Patterns

Children with dark skin from many different racial or ethnic backgrounds may have an exaggerated cutaneous response to common disorders of the skin (Burrall, 2006). These groups include those of African, Latin American, and Asian ancestry. Three identified cutaneous reaction patterns are *pigment changes*, *follicular response changes*, and *mesenchymal reactions*.

Pigment Changes • Inflammatory skin conditions can cause pigmentation lability in dark-skinned children because of alterations in melanin production (Burrall, 2006). If the condition is superficial and involves the epidermis only, normal pigmentation often returns in approximately 6 months (Vernon et al., 2013). Hypopigmentation can occur in dark-skinned children after pityriasis alba, seborrhea, tinea versicolor, or atopic dermatitis (Goodheart, 2009). Hyperpigmentation as a postinflammatory response is more persistent in dark skin. These changes often signify that the changes have gone beyond the epidermis and that the dermis is involved. This can cause permanent skin color changes or changes that last for years (Burrall, 2006). Impetigo, varicella, lupus, infected atopic dermatitis, contact dermatitis, and scars from burns or acne, lacerations, and abrasions can all cause long-lasting or permanent hyperpigmentation (Goodheart, 2009; Vernon et al., 2013).

Follicular Response Changes • Follicular response changes in dark-skinned children are manifested as prominent papules and hair follicles. These changes typically follow injury or inflammation. A papular or follicular response in dark-skinned children often follows atopic dermatitis, nummular eczema, pityriasis rosea, seborrheic dermatitis, tinea versicolor, or pseudofolliculitis barbae (Burrall, 2006; Vernon et al., 2013).

Mesenchymal Reactions • Exaggerated mesenchymal reactions result in hypertrophic scars and keloid formation, primarily in dark-skinned children (Burrall, 2006; Vernon et al., 2013). Keloids are benign overgrowths of skin of variable size that occur after injury (Figure 12.13). Keloid formation often follows infection, ear piercing, surgery, burns, and other skin trauma. Infants are much less likely to form keloids. Although medically benign, keloids may cause the child psychologic distress. Other exaggerated mesenchymal reactions likely to be experienced by dark-skinned children are skin lichenification with chronic pruritus and vesicular or bullous eruptions after bites or staphylococcal infections.

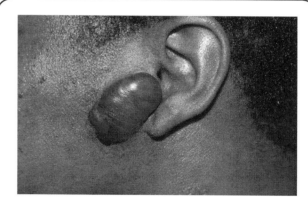

FIGURE 12.13 Keloid is a hypertrophic scar formation beyond original wound area; it is more common in African American children.

Common Problems

Children with dark skin are more prone to certain dermatologic conditions. These conditions occur in dark-skinned children for a variety of reasons, including variations in skin pigment and in grooming practices. The provider should be familiar with these conditions to identify them correctly and plan appropriate management. Table 12.11 summarizes these common dermatologic problems in dark-skinned children.

TABLE 12.11	Common Dermatologic Problems and Cutaneous Reaction Patterns in Children With Dark Skin	
DISORDER OR LESION	**CUTANEOUS REACTION PATTERN**	**CHARACTERISTICS**
Acanthosis nigricans	Hyperpigmentation	Symmetrical brown to black hyperpigmentation with velvety texture in skinfolds and creases in flexural surfaces, most often the neck, knees, elbows, underarms, and groin; considered a cutaneous marker for insulin resistance (Miller & Rapini, 2012)
Atopic dermatitis	Follicular response changes; postinflammatory hypopigmentation	Papules more prominent with follicular accentuation in African Americans; distribution more common on extensor surfaces (Burrall, 2006)
Infantile acropustulosis	Hyperpigmentation	Affects mainly African American boys younger than 2–3 years of age; lesions begin as pinpoint pruritic erythematous macules and papules that evolve into vesicles then pustules; mostly affects hands and feet; lesions heal with macular hyperpigmentation; etiology unknown (Pride, 2012)
Keloids	Mesenchymal reaction	Hypertrophic scarring thought to be related to inflammatory triggers (Burrall, 2006)
Lichenification	Mesenchymal reaction	See Table 12.8
Papulosa nigra	Hyperpigmentation	Most commonly seen among African Americans; multiple firm, dark brown to black flattened papules, most often seen on face; usually begins in adolescence and is rare before 7 years of age (Nowfar-Rad & Fish, 2013)
Pityriasis alba	Hypopigmentation	Scattered patches of poorly defined postinflammatory hypopigmentation, often with a superficial scale, commonly because of atopic dermatitis; takes months or years to resolve
Pityriasis rosea	Exaggerated follicular response	Larger papules occur with the eruption; nodules may even occur (Burrall, 2006)
Pomade acne	Hyperpigmentation (postinflammatory)	Multiple comedones on forehead and along the hairline; seen primarily in African American patients and caused by use of hair oils and pomades
Pseudofolliculitis barbae	Hyperpigmentation; follicular response change	Papules and pustules that form when coarse, curly hair is shaved and the distal end curves, growing back into the skin ("ingrown hair"); occurs predominantly in Blacks; can leave hypertrophic scars
Seborrheic dermatitis	Postinflammatory pigmentary changes; may resolve within 6 months	May appear more annular in African Americans (Burrall, 2006)
Tinea versicolor	Hyperpigmentation, hypopigmentation, or exaggerated follicular response	Postinfection inflammation causes changes in pigmentation and exaggerated follicular response. Hypopigmentation needs to be differentiated from vitiligo.
Transient neonatal pustular melanosis	Hyperpigmentation	Occurs more commonly in Black infants; rash presents at birth with vesicles and pustules that rupture, leaving pigmented macules and scale; a benign disorder; hyperpigmentation fades within 3 weeks to 3 months; etiology unknown (Sorrell & Laumann, 2005); must be differentiated from herpes simplex, staphylococcal infections, and *Candida*
Vitiligo	Hypopigmentation	Hypopigmentation because of loss of melanocytes; cause unknown; can occur after trauma

Assessing the Hair of Children From Diverse Racial and Ethnic Groups

Children from various ethnic groups have different hair shaft patterns with which the provider should be familiar. The hair shaft is described as straight, wavy, spiral, or helical. Children of Asian descent tend to have straight hair, and the hair shaft itself is round. Children of European origin have a wide range of hair shaft shapes, from straight to helical. Children who can trace their ancestry to Africa generally have spiral or helical hair shaft shapes. These children also have hair that is described as kinky or wooly and is tightly curled with a closely knit distribution pattern on the scalp; thus, the hair can get matted or tangled more easily. Also, when the hair shaft is straight, the sebaceous glands are better able to lubricate the hair. This explains why the hair of African American children tends to be drier and why oiling the hair and washing it less often are common practices among this group. African American adolescents may apply chemicals to their hair to change the texture. These chemicals may cause changes in the natural appearance of the hair. The provider needs to keep this in mind when inspecting the hair in this group of children. Also, *pediculosis capitis* (head lice) is less common in African American children (Guenther, Macguiness, & Austin, 2012). This is because of the spiral nature of the hair shaft; in addition, the use of oils or pomades on the hair shaft makes it difficult or impossible for the lice to move or for nits to cling to the hair shaft (Guenther et al., 2012).

Cultural and Ethnic Practices Affecting Pediatric Integumentary Assessment

The grooming, cosmetic, or healing practices of some ethnic groups bear mentioning, as these practices may lead to variations in the hair or skin with which the provider must be familiar. Some of these practices and their possible results include (Vernon et al., 2013):

- The use of hair oils or pomade on African American hair or skin oils for lubrication of Black skin may cause acne.
- Tightly braiding African American hair may cause traction or traumatic alopecia.
- Curling irons or hot combs used to style African American hair may cause burns on the scalp.
- Application of chemical hair straighteners may cause alopecia; broken, dry hair; or scalp contact dermatitis.
- Bleaching creams used on African American skin may cause hypopigmentation and erythematous nodules.
- Tattoos or piercings may leave scars or keloids.
- Henna application to the hair or skin (usually hands and feet) may cause skin discoloration or allergic reactions.
- Coin rubbing (nonabusive, vigorous stroking of the trunk, and back with the edge of a coin) as practiced by Southeast Asian people to treat fever in children leaves linear bruising (see Chapter 24).

- Cupping (a nonabusive Southeast Asian healing practice that involves placing a glass cup of steam against the child's chest, which creates suction) is used to treat pain, gastrointestinal disorders, cough, and wheezing; however, it leaves a circular ecchymosis on the chest where the cup was placed (see Chapter 24).
- Very long hair in girls in some American Indian tribes is common, as the hair is not cut until the coming-of-age ceremony.
- Moxibustion, a traditional Chinese healing practice often done in conjunction with acupuncture, involves burning the skin, which may produce scars after the burn is healed.
- Head-shaving in the first year of life in many Asian cultures, based on the belief that the hair will grow back thicker and longer, may be confused with alopecia.

COMMON DIAGNOSTIC STUDIES

Once the history and physical examination are complete for a child who presents with a dermatologic complaint, the provider can begin to formulate a list of differential diagnoses. A few in-office diagnostic studies can aid in identifying or excluding specific dermatologic disorders during this process. Care must be taken to procure the tissue sample properly; the provider should also wear gloves when doing so. Box 12.1 summarizes these studies.

DOCUMENTATION OF FINDINGS

Sample Write-Up of a Healthy Child

Review of Systems

Skin: denies previous skin lesions, masses, petechiae, bruising, and pruritus; denies temperature or color changes; no birthmarks; reports dry skin ("eczema") with intense itching, especially in winter; applies Eucerin cream after bathing for treatment; parent applies sunscreen when outdoors
Hair: denies recent hair loss, unusual hair growth; no changes in hair texture; no history of scalp infections
Nails: no history of nail infections; has history of chronic nail-biting

Family History

Positive for atopic dermatitis, asthma, and allergic rhinitis; denies history of psoriasis or melanoma

Physical Examination

Skin: color pink without evidence of cyanosis, jaundice, or pallor; pigmentation even; no nevi; skin warm, smooth, and dry with elastic turgor; no evidence of edema; no bruising, rashes, or lesions noted
Hair: hair well distributed; black, fine, silky, straight; hair clean and shiny; no nits or scalp lesions seen
Nails: nails present on all 10 digits, nail beds pink, not brittle; no evidence of clubbing or other deformities; capillary refill < 2 seconds

---

BOX 12.1 Selected Laboratory and Diagnostic Studies Used to Diagnose Dermatologic Conditions

Microscopic Examination of Dermatologic Scrapings

- Identifies presence of bacterial, viral, or fungal infections in skin, hair, or nails.
- Obtain scrapings from edges of skin lesions, hair and its roots, the nail plate, and subungual debris.
- Obtain scrapings of lesions with no. 15 scalpel blade or sterile toothbrush.
- Place scrapings on microscope slide then apply cover slip.
  - Tzanck's smear identifies herpes or varicella; needs application of Giemsa or Wright's stain on scrapings. False-negatives can occur; send viral culture as well.
  - Giemsa or Wright's stain also identifies bacterial infections; use × 40 magnification to examine.
  - Potassium hydroxide (KOH) 20% is used to identify hyphae and spores with suspected fungal infections; gently heat (not boil) slide, use × 10 magnification to view.

Wood's Light (UV) Examination

- Used to examine fluorescent-positive skin infections (e.g., fungi) and depigmenting conditions.
- Apply the light in a dark room; color changes occur according to the type of infection or pigmentary disorder.
- Selected findings related to Wood's lamp examination
  - Tinea versicolor fluoresces a dull golden yellow.
  - *Pseudomonas aeruginosa* fluoresces a yellowish green.
  - Vitiligo (depigmentation disorder) shows no visible pigment; fluoresces white.

Cultures

- Culture infected areas of the skin, hair, or nails to identify the organism and prescribe appropriate treatment.
- Can obtain bacterial, viral, and fungal cultures and grow them in appropriate media.

Skin Testing

- Should be done by dermatologist or allergist.
- Used to diagnose allergic or contact dermatitis.
- For patch testing, apply patches containing common allergens to the skin, then removing after 2 days; a papulovesicular eruption at the site indicates a positive reaction.
- For skin prick or intradermal testing, inject the allergen into the skin, either by scratching (skin prick testing) or intradermally; development of a wheal at the site of injection indicates a positive reaction.

Skin Biopsy

- Should be done by a dermatologist.
- Done to identify accurately the pathology of a skin lesion that has not been definitively diagnosed.
- Done by punch, shave, or excisional method, depending on type of lesion.
- Requires local anesthesia.

Complete Blood Count

- Alterations in white blood cell count indicate infection.

Erythrocyte Sedimentation Rate

- Elevation in erythrocyte sedimentation rate indicates the presence of inflammation.

Sample Write-Up of a Focused Visit

Subjective Data

T. T. is a 7-year-old American Indian male accompanied by his father. T. T. presents with a 1-week history of an itchy rash on his face, which has now spread to his neck. His father denies that the child has had fever, vomiting, diarrhea, loss of appetite, or other constitutional symptoms.

Objective Data

T: 37.2°C (99.0°F); **P:** 88 beats per minute; **RR:** 24 breaths per minute; **BP:** 96/70 mmHg
Skin: numerous vesicles on face and neck; numerous scattered honey-colored crusted lesions on erythematous areas of skin on face and neck; no purulent discharge; no other lesions seen on body; skin elsewhere warm and dry with elastic turgor
ENT: tympanic membranes (TMs) pearly grey with visible landmarks, no nasal discharge, turbinates pink and nonedematous; pharynx pink; no exudates; tonsils 2+
Lymph: pre- and postauricular; posterior cervical lymphadenopathy noted
Heart: S1, S2, RRR (regular rate and rhythm); no murmurs or extra sounds
Lungs: breath sounds clear bilaterally
Assessment: impetigo

Notable Clinical Findings

- ▣ History of extreme prematurity
- ▣ Family/child history
  - Allergies
  - Atopic dermatitis
  - Asthma
  - Allergic rhinitis
- ▣ Nevi
  - Pigmented
  - Vascular
- ▣ Conditions that cause immunosuppression
- ▣ Immunization delays
- ▣ History of sunburn
- ▣ Recent exposures to communicable diseases, contagious skin conditions, infestations, irritants
- ▣ Acne
- ▣ Infections/infestations of hair, skin, or nails
- ▣ Rashes/lesions
  - Primary lesion(s)
  - Secondary lesion(s)
- ▣ Edema
- ▣ Petechiae, purpura
- ▣ Bruises, lacerations, abrasions, other wounds
- ▣ Unexplained cuts, burns, pinch marks
- ▣ Keloids
- ▣ Track marks
- ▣ Alopecia
- ▣ Dry, brittle hair or nails
- ▣ Lanugo
- ▣ Russell's sign
- ▣ Poor turgor
- ▣ Hot/cool skin temperature
- ▣ Capillary refill greater than 2 to 3 seconds

References

Antaya, R. J. (2013). *Infantile hemangioma.* Retrieved from http://emedicine.medscape.com/article/1083849-overview

Ball, J. W., Bindler, R. C., & Cowen, K. J. (2012). *Principles of pediatric nursing: Caring for children* (5th ed.). Upper Saddle River, NJ: Pearson Education, Inc.

Burrall, B. (2006). *Ethnic skin: A spectrum of issues.* Retrieved from http://www.medscape.org/viewarticle/529349

Galbraith, S. S., & Esterly, N. B. (2006). Pigmentary demarcation lines. In J. J. Norlund, R. E. Boissy, V. J. Hearing, R. King, W. Oetting, & J. P. Ortonne (Eds.), *The pigmentary system* (2nd ed., pp. 880–881). Malden, MA: Wiley-Blackwell.

Goodheart, H. P. (2009). *Goodheart's photoguide to common skin disorders: Diagnosis and management.* Philadelphia, PA: Lippincott Williams & Wilkins.

Guenther, L., Macguiness, S., & Austin, T. W. (2012). *Pediculosis (lice).* Retrieved from http://emedicine.medscape.com/article/225013-overview

Hornor, G. (2012). Medical evaluation for child physical abuse: What the PNP needs to know. *Journal of Pediatric Health Care, 26*(3), 163–170.

Larzo, M. R., & Poe, S. G. (2006). Adverse consequences of tattoos and body piercings. *Pediatric Annals, 35*(3), 187–192.

Laude, T., & Russo, R. (1983). *Dermatologic disorders in black children and adolescents.* New Hyde Park, NY: Medical Examination Publishing Co.

McPherson, K. (2009). *Fetal development.* Retrieved from http://www.nlm.nih.gov/medlineplus/ency/article/002398.htm

Miller, J. H., & Rapini, R. P. (2012). *Acanthosis nigricans.* Retrieved from http://emedicine.medscape.com/article/1102488-overview

Nowfar-Rad, M., & Fish, F. (2013). *Dermatosis papulosanigra.* Retrieved from http://emedicine.medscape.com/article/1056854-overview

Pletcher, B. A. (2013). *Neurofibromatosis, type 1.* Retrieved from http://emedicine.medscape.com/article/1177266-overview

Pride, H. (2012). *Acropustulosis of infancy.* Retrieved from http://emedicine.medscape.com/article/1109935-overview

Rhoads, J. (2006). *Advanced health assessment and diagnostic reasoning* (Table 5-2). Philadelphia, PA: Lippincott Williams & Wilkins.

Saladin, K. S. (2006). *Anatomy and physiology: The unity of form and function.* New York, NY: McGraw-Hill.

Sorrell, J., & Laumann, A. (2005). *Transient neonatal pustular melanosis.* Retrieved from http://emedicine.medscape.com/article/1112258-overview

Telofski, L. S., Morello, A. P., Correa, M. C. M., & Stamatas, G. N. (2012). The infant skin barrier: Can we preserve, protect, and enhance the barrier? *Dermatology Research and Practice.* Retrieved from http://dx.doi.org/10.1155/2012/198789

Tumolo, J. (2005). Slice at life: Teens who cut, burn and beat themselves to dull inner pain. *Advance for Nurse Practitioners, 13*(12), 54–56.

Vernon, P., Brady, M. A., Barber Starr, N., & Petersen-Smith, A. (2013). Dermatologic disorders. In C. E. Burns, A. M. Dunn, M. A. Brady, N. B. Starr, & C. G. Blosser (Eds.), *Pediatric primary care* (5th ed., pp. 877–927). St. Louis, MO: W. B. Saunders.

Assessment of the Head, Neck, and Regional Lymphatics

Assessment of the head and neck is an important part of the pediatric health evaluation. Common minor childhood infections often cause symptoms in the head and neck area. For example, upper respiratory infections and acute otitis media often cause ear pain, headaches, and lymphadenopathy. Acute infections or injuries to the head and neck can also lead to long-term developmental delays, disabilities, and even death in infants and children. When obtaining the history and physical examination of the head and neck, the health care provider can also identify parent and child teaching opportunities, such as encouraging repositioning in young infants with positional *plagiocephaly* or the consistent use of bicycle helmets.

ANATOMY AND PHYSIOLOGY

Head

The skull is a hard, bony structure that houses and protects the brain and other structures in the central nervous system; it consists of 22 bones that include the cranium and face. Eight bones comprise the cranium: frontal bone, two parietal bones, two temporal bones, occipital bone, ethmoid bone, and sphenoid bone (Figure 13.1). The face consists of 14 bones; assessment of the face is discussed in Chapter 16.

In neonates, the cranial bones are moveable to accommodate the fetus's head during vaginal delivery. These bones are joined together by soft, fibrous tissue spaces called *sutures* that separate the cranial bones. The sagittal suture line runs from the anterior to the posterior portion of the skull in the midline position; the coronal suture line runs laterally from side to side, beginning at the anterior fontanelle, and the lambdoidal suture runs along both sides of the head, beginning at the posterior fontanelle (Figure 13.2). The sutures intersect at the areas of the skull known as fontanelles. The fontanelles

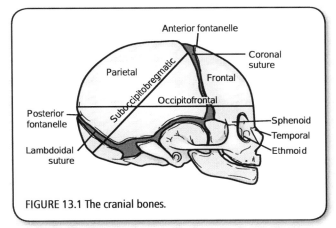

FIGURE 13.1 The cranial bones.

are soft areas of the skull that are formed when two or three cranial bones merge. The fontanelles are named for their anatomic location: anterior, posterior, sagittal (parietal), sphenoidal, and mastoid. The fontanelles that are routinely assessed are the anterior and posterior fontanelles (see Figure 13.2). The anterior fontanelle is diamond-shaped and measures approximately 4 to 5 cm (2 in.) in diameter at its widest part. The posterior fontanelle is triangular and measures approximately 0.5 to 1 cm (0.5 in.) at its widest part.

Neck

The neck is composed of muscles, ligaments, and the cervical vertebrae (Figure 13.3). Nerves, major blood vessels, lymph nodes, the larynx, hyoid bone, trachea, and thyroid gland are also contained within the neck. The cervical vertebrae (C1 though C7) function to support and assist with movement of the head. The major neck muscles are the sternocleidomastoid (sternomastoid) muscle and the trapezius muscle (Figure 13.4). These muscles work together to allow rotation and flexion of the head. The sternocleidomastoid muscle, the largest muscle in the neck, arises from the sternum and clavicle

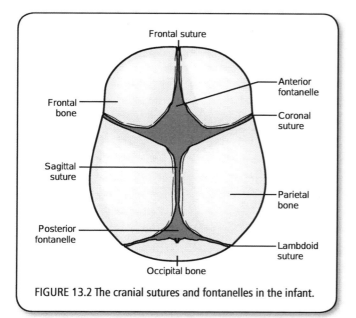

FIGURE 13.2 The cranial sutures and fontanelles in the infant.

and passes diagonally across the neck. The sternocleido-mastoid muscle rotates and flexes the head, as well as acts like an accessory muscle of inspiration by raising the sternum during respiration. The trapezius muscle forms a triangle on the upper back, arising from the occipital bone and 12th thoracic vertebrae, extending and attaching to the scapula and clavicle. This muscle supports, extends, and turns the head and moves the shoulders. The trapezius muscle also rotates the scapula. The sternocleidomastoid and trapezius muscles are innervated by the spinal accessory nerve (cranial nerve XI).

The sternocleidomastoid muscle divides the neck into the anterior and posterior triangles (see Figure 13.4). The boundaries of the anterior triangle are the mandible above, the sternocleidomastoid muscle laterally, the midline of the trachea medially, and the suprasternal notch inferiorly. The sternocleidomastoid muscle to the anterior, the trapezius muscle to the posterior, and the clavicle below demarcate the posterior triangle. These triangles serve as important landmarks for physical assessment. Important structures contained within

the anterior triangle include the larynx and thyroid gland; both triangles contain lymph nodes.

The trachea is located in the middle of the neck (see Figure 13.3). It is a cylinder-shaped structure, composed of smooth muscle and encircled by C-shaped cartilaginous rings. The uppermost ring is termed the cricoid cartilage. The trachea extends from the larynx to the bronchi in the upper thorax to below the sternum. It is the passage through which air enters the lungs and respiratory secretions are expelled.

The thyroid gland also lies within the neck; it is the largest endocrine gland in the body. Butterfly shaped, it consists of two lateral lobes connected by the thyroid isthmus, which lies directly across the fifth or sixth tracheal ring and below the cricoid cartilage (see Figure 13.3). Below the cricoid cartilage lies the thyroid cartilage ("Adam's apple"). Attached to the tongue and at the floor of the mouth is the U-shaped hyoid bone, which lies between the mandible and larynx.

The superior portion of each lateral lobe of the thyroid gland extends upward, toward the thyroid cartilage; the inferior portion of each lobe lies at the portion of the trachea that is partially covered by the sternocleidomastoid muscle. The thyroid gland is highly vascular; it synthesizes and secretes thyroxine (T_4) and triiodothyronine (T_3), hormones that play a large role in normal growth and cellular metabolism. The thyroid gland also produces calcitonin, which regulates calcium ion concentration in the blood by facilitating calcium deposition in the bones. Behind the lateral lobes of the thyroid gland lie four parathyroid glands. These glands are very small and cannot be palpated. The parathyroid glands produce and secrete parathyroid hormone, the function of which is to regulate calcium ion concentration in the blood by increasing calcium absorption by

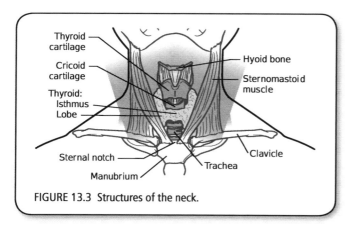

FIGURE 13.3 Structures of the neck.

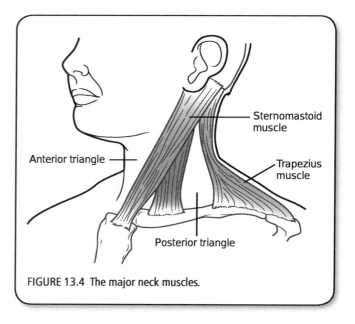

FIGURE 13.4 The major neck muscles.

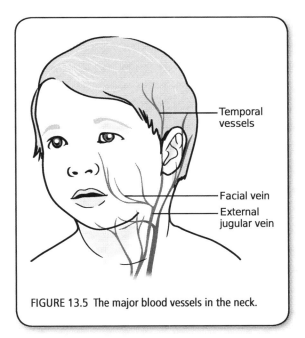

FIGURE 13.5 The major blood vessels in the neck.

- **Tonsillar:** in the angle of the mandible; drain the tongue, floor of the mouth, and oropharynx
- **Submaxillary (submandibular):** on the mandible between the angle and the tip; drain the tongue, teeth, floor of the mouth, and pharynx
- **Submental:** on the mandible under the chin; drain the same areas as the submandibular nodes
- **Superficial cervical:** anterior and superficial to the sternocleidomastoid muscle; include the anterior and posterior groups, which lie along the jugular vein; drain the anterior third of the scalp, face, and thyroid gland
- **Posterior cervical:** in the posterior triangle, along the anterior margin of the trapezius muscle; drain the thyroid gland and posterior two thirds of the scalp
- **Deep cervical:** includes superior and inferior groups; are rarely palpable. The superior deep cervical nodes drain the palatine tonsils and submental nodes; the inferior deep cervical nodes drain the larynx, trachea, thyroid, and esophagus.
- **Supraclavicular:** found deep in the area formed by the clavicle and sternocleidomastoid muscle. Enlargement of a left supraclavicular node often indicates a malignancy in the abdomen or thorax.

The locations of these lymph nodes are illustrated in Figure 13.6.

the intestines and kidneys and releasing calcium from the bones.

Blood vessels in the neck include the common, external, and internal carotid arteries and the internal and external jugular veins (Figure 13.5). The carotid arteries and internal jugular veins are located on either side of the neck, parallel and anterior to the sternocleidomastoid muscle. The external jugular veins lie diagonally over the sternocleidomastoid muscle. The common carotid begins in the thorax and neck and then bifurcates, becoming the external and internal carotid arteries. The external carotid artery circulates blood to the head, face, and neck; the internal carotid artery carries blood to the brain. Deoxygenated blood is drained from the head through the subclavian and jugular veins.

Lymph Nodes of the Head and Neck

Lymph nodes in the head and neck are numerous. These lymph nodes are part of the immune system and play a role in phagocytosis and the production of lymphocytes and antibodies. Lymph nodes consist of an accumulation of lymphatic tissue; they are round and oval structures typically found in chains or clusters. The size and shape of each lymph node varies but should be 1 cm or less in length or diameter. Only the superficial lymph nodes are amenable to physical assessment. Lymph nodes in the head and neck include the following:

- **Preauricular:** anterior to the tragus; drain the eyelids and conjunctivae, temporal region, and pinnae; not usually palpable unless localized infection exists
- **Postauricular:** behind the ear, over the mastoid process; drain the pinnae, external auditory meatus and posterior portion of the scalp
- **Occipital:** found along the occipital ridge of the cranium bilaterally; drain the scalp and head

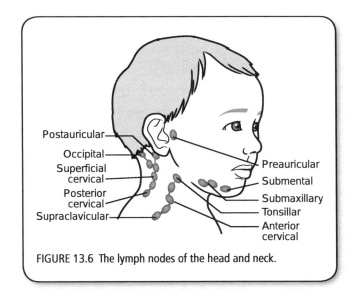

FIGURE 13.6 The lymph nodes of the head and neck.

DEVELOPMENTAL CONSIDERATIONS

Head

During fetal development, the head grows rapidly, accounting for most of the fetus's size. By the eighth week of fetal life, the embryo takes on a human shape, with the head disproportionately large in comparison to the body. At this time in fetal development, the head accounts for approximately one half of the embryo's body size. By the time an infant is born, head size accounts for approximately one fourth of overall body size and one third of the infant's body weight. Normal growth of the cranial bones depends on optimal placental function, adequate nutrition during pregnancy and childhood, as well as hereditary factors. Any alterations in placental function or nutrition can affect skull growth and impede development of the brain. Head circumference averages 32 to 38 cm (12.6 to 14.9 in.) in the full-term newborn, exceeding the infant's chest circumference; these measurements do not become equal until age 2 years. By age 6, the head is approximately 90% of the adult size (Figure 13.7).

The anterior fontanelle closes by 12 to 18 months; the posterior fontanelle normally closes by 2 months. The smaller fontanelles (i.e., sagittal, sphenoidal, mastoid) remain open in the first year of life to allow for rapid brain growth. Ossification of the skull begins in infancy and continues into adulthood.

The cranial sutures are not fully fused at birth to allow for cranial molding during the birthing process and to accommodate brain growth, which is very rapid until school age (see Chapter 1). Cranial sutures begin to fuse by age 6 months, and gradually ossify during early childhood. The cranial sutures can be separated by increased intracranial pressure until approximately age 12. Infants begin to develop head control cephalocaudally, first by turning the head from side to side while prone by 1 month, then by lifting the head while prone by 2 months. By 4 months, the infant should be able to hold the head erect at midline when placed in a vertical position; by 6 months, no head lag should be noted when the infant is pulled to sit.

Neck

Until age 3 to 4 years, infants and children have a proportionately shorter neck. After age 3 to 4, the neck lengthens, becoming more proportionate to body size.

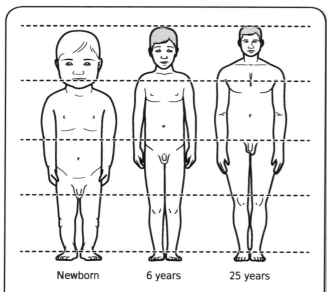

FIGURE 13.7 Proportion of head to body size in an infant, child, and young adult.

In infants and young children, the trachea is short, has a narrow diameter, and is more moveable than that of an adult. In the prepubertal child, the cricoid ring lies between C3 and C4. If tracheal edema occurs, there is no room for expansion, causing further narrowing of the internal diameter of the trachea and consequent potential airway compromise.

The thyroid gland is small but fully functional at birth and is often not palpable in infants and young children because of its small size. The thyroid gland increases slowly in size (by approximately 1 g per year), until age 15, when it reaches adult size.

Lymph Nodes

The lymphatic system begins to develop during the third week of embryonic life. This system continues to change and develop throughout infancy, childhood, and early adolescence. The lymph nodes in infants are difficult to palpate; this lymph tissue gradually increases in size during childhood. Beginning in infancy, the amount of lymphoid tissue increases, and both cervical and occipital lymph nodes enlarge with each respiratory infection. By age 10 years, lymph tissue size is at its largest, approximately two times adult size. Beginning in early adolescence, lymph tissue begins to shrink, becoming adult size by the end of adolescence.

ASSESSMENT OF THE HEAD AND NECK

History

When assessing the head and neck in the pediatric patient, the type of historical data that is gathered depends on the nature of the health care encounter. For a routine health maintenance examination, the focus should be on the child's past medical history, including pre-, peri- and postnatal histories, head or neck injuries or infections, or any genetic or metabolic disorders, all of which can impact the growth and development of the young child. Relevant neck conditions to inquire about include hypothyroidism, and tracheal cysts or masses. When assessing a child with an illness or injury related to the head or neck, the provider should obtain the focused history.

Past Medical History

In addition to the standard information gathered in the pediatric past medical history (PMH) (see Chapter 6), the information described here is important to obtain.

Prenatal, Perinatal, and Neonatal Histories • In children aged 3 years and younger, the provider should review the child's prenatal, perinatal, and neonatal histories. Prenatal exposure to alcohol, drugs, or tobacco smoke can lead to abnormalities involving the head or neck. For example, fetal alcohol syndrome (FAS) can cause microcephaly, and cocaine use can lead to preterm delivery and the complications of prematurity, including asphyxia, intraventricular hemorrhage, hydrocephaly, and cranial molding (dolichocephaly). Maternal cigarette smoking can cause pre- or perinatal asphyxia, and asphyxia can lead to cerebral palsy, which, in turn, affects head control.

The labor and delivery record should be reviewed for any history of prolonged labor, precipitous delivery, or respiratory distress at birth; these conditions can lead to asphyxia, which can cause abnormalities of the head and neck, including hydrocephaly, cerebral palsy, and poor head control. Some neonatal conditions involving severe asphyxia may necessitate extracorporeal membrane oxygenation, which involves cannulation of the jugular vein and carotid artery.

Any history of maternal thyroid disease should be explored, as should any gestational diabetes. Gestational diabetes leads to hypoglycemia and large-for-gestational age neonates, as does congenital hypothyroidism. Feeding difficulties, poor weight gain, constipation, prolonged jaundice, hypothermia, hypotonia, wide anterior and posterior fontanelles, a hoarse cry, an enlarged tongue, and noisy respirations suggest congenital hypothyroidism (Figure 13.8) (Daniel & Postellon, 2014). Congenital hypothyroidism, if untreated, leads to delayed growth and intellectual disability in children (Daniel & Postellon, 2014). The provider should always note any history of congenital hypothyroidism; this condition is detected on newborn screening, which is required in all 50 states (see Chapter 9). Any maternal or neonatal infections should also be noted. Maternal group B streptococcal infection can lead to sepsis; neonatal meningitis and resultant respiratory compromise, and asphyxia can cause intracranial complications that can affect head size and head control (see Chapter 22).

Any history of craniosynostosis (premature closure at birth of one or more cranial sutures) should be noted; this can cause microcephaly and abnormal head shape. Congenital torticollis should also be noted; this condition manifests as a persistent head tilt (Figure 13.9).

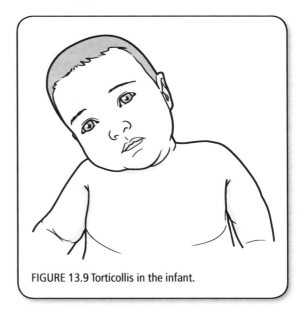

FIGURE 13.9 Torticollis in the infant.

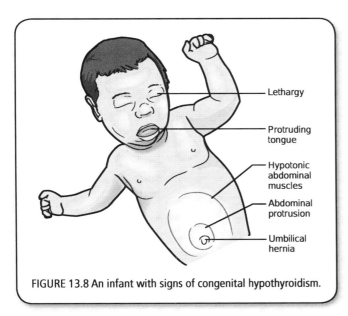

Lethargy

Protruding tongue

Hypotonic abdominal muscles

Abdominal protrusion

Umbilical hernia

FIGURE 13.8 An infant with signs of congenital hypothyroidism.

Review of Systems • In addition to the prenatal and perinatal histories, the pediatric review of systems (ROS), involving the head and neck, includes asking the parent about specific conditions accompanied by signs and symptoms that manifest in the head or neck region. In children school-aged and older, the provider should inquire about any history of headaches, which can have multiple etiologies. A history of fatigue or insomnia may indicate hypothyroidism or hyperthyroidism, respectively. Any dizziness, neck pain, or masses should be investigated. Infections of the head or neck should also be noted, including orbital or periorbital cellulitis or scalp infections, such as impetigo or tinea capitis (see Chapter 12). Other areas of assessment include the following:

- **General health:** Usual state of health, recent and recurrent febrile illnesses, immunization history, sleep position in infants (may lead to plagiocephaly), and history of congenital syndromes (e.g., Turner syndrome can cause neck webbing and extra neck skin folds; Down syndrome can cause extra neck skin folds and enlarged anterior fontanelle)
- **Growth:** Weight gain, short stature (hypothyroidism), and weight loss (hyperthyroidism)
- **Integument:** Dry skin (hypothyroidism); thinning of hair (hyperthyroidism); and coarse, sparse hair (hypothyroidism)
- **Head:** Microcephaly, macrocephaly, craniosynostosis, and craniostenosis
- **Neck:** Pain, injury, stiffness, impaired movement, lumps, masses, torticollis, cystic hygroma, cellulitis, lymphangioma, laryngocele, and opisthotonos
- **Eyes:** Exophthalmia (hyperthyroidism), lid lag, lid retraction, periorbital edema (hyperthyroidism), and vision problems (hypothyroidism)
- **Ears:** Recurrent acute otitis media (causes lymphadenopathy) and vertigo

- **Cardiac:** Jugular venous distention (may be present with some cardiac conditions), Kawasaki disease, congenital heart disease (may affect carotid pulses), palpitations, tachycardia, edema, flushing (hyperthyroidism), and bradycardia (hypothyroidism)
- **Respiratory:** Upper respiratory infections (cause lymphadenopathy in neck)
- **Endocrine:** Hypothyroidism, Hashimoto's thyroiditis, hyperthyroidism, Graves' disease, goiter, thyroglossal duct cyst, amenorrhea (hyperthyroidism), precocious puberty (hypothyroidism [young children]), and delayed puberty (hypothyroidism)
- **Metabolic:** Rickets (may cause craniotabes), dehydration (may cause depressed fontanelle), and lead poisoning
- **Immunity:** Cervical lymphadenitis; lymph node swelling, pain, or erythema; night sweats (suggests lymphoma); infectious mononucleosis; tonsillitis; pharyngitis; mumps, rubella, or roseola; human immunodeficiency virus (HIV); malignancies (cause lymphadenopathy); cat-scratch fever; Epstein-Barr virus, tuberculosis; coxsackievirus; and juvenile rheumatoid arthritis
- **Neurologic:** Meningitis, meningeal irritation (can cause opisthotonos), hydrocephalus, brain tumor, headaches, migraines, neurofibromatosis, intracranial hemorrhage, craniosynostosis, craniostenosis, any conditions that cause increased intracranial pressure, paresthesias, vertigo, syncope, hypotonia (congenital hypothyroidism), tremors (hyperthyroidism), a history of falls, and clumsiness
- **Musculoskeletal:** Osteogenesis imperfecta, facial tics, muscle weakness, fatigue (hyperthyroidism), and character of gait
- **Developmental:** Achievement of developmental milestones (e.g., delayed gross motor control such as head lag may indicate cerebral palsy), developmental delay (congenital hypothyroidism), hyperactivity, and hyperthyroidism

Immunizations • A child's immunization status is particularly relevant to assessment of the head and neck. Several diseases for which children are immunized can cause abnormalities in the head and neck, including infection with *Haemophilus influenzae* type B (Hib) and *Neisseria meningitidis*; *Streptococcus pneumoniae* meningitis (bulging fontanelle in infants, headache, neck pain, stiffness in older children); measles (encephalitis, lymphadenopathy), mumps (parotid gland swelling), rubella, rubeola, and varicella; polio; diphtheria (lymphadenopathy); tetanus (neck muscle rigidity); and pertussis (sunken fontanelle secondary to dehydration). Cervical and occipital lymphadenopathy can also occur as a postimmunization response following the diphtheria-pertussis-tetanus or poliomyelitis vaccine (Leung & Robson, 2004).

Hospitalizations • The provider should inquire about past hospitalizations for infections or injuries involving the head or neck, as well as chronic illnesses that cause lymphadenopathy such as Hodgkin's and non-Hodgkin's lymphoma, tuberculosis, or leukemia. Cervical masses are common in children and can be mistaken for cervical lymphadenopathy; some of these conditions may require hospitalization or surgery. These conditions are listed in Box 13.1.

Injuries • It is important for the provider to obtain any history of falls or other type of head trauma such as blows to the head, gunshot wounds, or shaking injuries. Any of these injuries can cause skull fractures or deformities or intracranial bleeding that can lead to permanent damage to the growing brain, resulting in developmental delays. The provider must also determine past head and neck injuries and ask about the use of car seats, booster seats, seat belts, and bicycle helmets to evaluate risk for head or neck injuries. Trampolines are particularly dangerous and can lead to head and neck injuries (see Chapter 7); providers should inquire if the child plays on a trampoline and specifically if the trampoline is used to jump into a swimming pool.

Surgical History

Providers should ask the parent if the child has had any surgery involving the head or neck, including craniotomy or placement of a ventriculoperitoneal shunt (see Chapter 22), incision and drainage of a lymph node in the head or neck, thyroid surgery, or tracheotomy. The date of the surgery and the condition for which the surgical procedure was done should be ascertained. Providers must also determine whether the condition was resolved with surgery.

BOX 13.1 Causes of Cervical Masses in Children

- Brachial cleft cyst
- Cervical ribs
- Cystic hygroma
- Dermoid cyst
- Hemangioma
- Laryngocele
- Mumps
- Sternomastoid tumor
- Thyroglossal cyst

Source: Leung and Robson (2004).

Family History

It is important for providers to determine the child's family history, focusing on genetic disorders, any reports of recurrent headaches, migraines, or thyroid disease.

Social History

It is important for providers to determine if there are any environmental risks that may cause head or neck complaints. One risk to children is living in housing with peeling, lead-based paint; this can lead to lead poisoning. Lead poisoning can cause headaches, intracranial pressure, and possible encephalopathy. Exposure to secondhand smoke can also cause headaches. Contact with hazardous chemicals or waste, or exposure to radiation can result in head and neck cancers. Children who have declining school performance or headaches may be suffering from hyperthyroidism, which can result in a decreased ability to focus, concentrate, or sit still; hyperactivity; impulsivity; and consequently, poor academic performance (Kaplowitz, 2007). The provider must also inquire about the child's participation in contact sports that increase the risk for head or neck injuries, and whether the child wears a helmet at all times. It is also important for providers to inquire routinely about the presence of firearms in the home (see Chapter 7). Young children may unintentionally cause head or neck injuries when playing with a gun; older children and adolescents who are depressed may harm themselves intentionally.

Developmental History

Evaluation of growth and development is an important element of pediatric head and neck assessment (see Chapters 2 and 8). Measurement of head size as well as length or height helps to identify abnormalities in growth and systemic health problems. Assessment of the child's muscle tone and strength, head control, and the achievement of age-appropriate developmental milestones in both fine and gross motor domains can give providers clues to other abnormalities such as cerebral palsy and developmental delays. Early identification of any developmental delays is critical to maximize the child's potential. Prompt referrals are necessary for children who have difficulty achieving developmental milestones.

Medications

It is important to inquire about any prescribed or over-the-counter medications the child is taking. The indication for the drug may explain an abnormality in the head, neck, or lymph nodes. For example, a child may be taking antibiotics to treat a bacterial infection that has caused neck swelling or cervical lymphadenopathy. Steroids prescribed for a brain neoplasm can cause neck and facial swelling. Also, certain drugs such as isoniazid may cause generalized lymphadenopathy (McClain & Fletcher, 2013).

History of Present Illness

When a pediatric patient presents with a complaint related to the head or neck, the provider must keep in mind the child's age and developmental level, concurrent illness, associated findings, and past health when considering diagnostic possibilities. For example, when children begin to walk, they are more prone to falls, particularly head injuries, due to their proportionately large head size. Similarly, older children who use skateboards or ride bicycles without a helmet are predisposed to more severe head injuries after a fall. Children with a febrile illness who have headache and lymphadenopathy may have a viral or bacterial respiratory infection. When children are school-aged or older, lymphadenopathy is less pronounced during acute infections. Table 13.1 summarizes the data providers need to obtain for the history of present illness (HPI) concerning common pediatric complaints related to the head and neck. Table 13.2 summarizes differential diagnoses relative to head and neck masses in infants and children.

TABLE 13.1	Abnormalities and Complaints Related to the Head and Neck	
CONDITION	**ASSESSMENT**	**EXPLICATION**
Alopecia, dry skin	Onset? Texture of hair? Is skin dry as well?	Thinning of hair occurs with hyperthyroidism. Coarse, sparse hair and dry skin occur with hypothyroidism.
Cough	Recent exposure to respiratory illness? What type? What is child's immunization status? Recent immigrant from a country where tuberculosis infection is widespread?	It may be a viral (e.g., respiratory syncytial virus) or a bacterial (GABHS pharyngitis) respiratory illness that causes cough; lymphadenopathy may be associated with these infections.

(continued)

TABLE 13.1	Abnormalities and Complaints Related to the Head and Neck (*continued*)	
CONDITION	**ASSESSMENT**	**EXPLICATION**
Dizziness	Recent head injury? History of cardiac problems? Any associated loss of consciousness? Vertigo?	Neurologic complaints (see Chapter 22), cardiac problems (see Chapter 18), or inner ear abnormalities (see Chapter 14) may cause dizziness.
Exposure to infection	Recent exposure to infection? What type? What is child's immunization status?	Lymphadenopathy of head and neck can occur with scalp, oral, or respiratory infections.
Fatigue	Onset? Any associated symptoms (e.g., cold intolerance, emotional lability, constipation) or weight loss?	New-onset fatigue can indicate hypothyroidism; fatigue associated with weight loss can indicate malignancy.
Fever	Recent exposure to infection? What type? Is child tugging at his or her ears? Cough or other respiratory complaints? Any infections of scalp? Any oral infections? What is child's immunization status?	Fever is a sign of infection (e.g., lymphadenitis, cellulitis). Unexplained weight loss may be because of malignancy or hyperthyroidism; weight gain may be because of hypothyroidism. Neck swelling may be caused by parotitis (mumps) or other neck masses (see Box 13.1). IV drug use can lead to lymphadenopathy.
Headache	Type of pain, location, intensity, duration?	Detailed description of headaches aids in formulating diagnosis (see Chapter 22).
Head Injury	When did injury occur? Mechanism of injury? Did child fall or was he or she struck? Did child lose consciousness? Was child riding a bicycle or skateboard? Was child wearing a helmet? Was child involved in a motor vehicle collision? Was he or she properly restrained? Does the history align with type and degree of injury?	Head injuries in children can have profound, long-lasting effects on growth and development. The extent to which child is injured must be determined to ensure appropriate assessment and follow up (see Chapters 22 and 24).
Lymphadenopathy of head or neck	Characteristics of lymph tissue: Swelling, pain, mobility, or enlargement of lymph nodes? Fever? Tooth pain? Recent travel?	Lymphadenopathy of head and neck can occur with scalp, oral, or respiratory infections (e.g., tinea capitis, pediculosis capitis, scalp impetigo, acute otitis media, otitis externa, tonsillitis, or pharyngitis (viral or bacterial). Other etiologies include malignancy, Kawasaki disease, collagen vascular diseases, serum sickness, and drug or vaccine side effects (Leung & Robson, 2004), dental infections, or tuberculosis.
Macrocephaly	Occipital-frontal head circumference more than 2 SD above the mean for age and sex or one that is growing too rapidly	May be caused by hydrocephalus, space-occupying lesions (e.g., hematomas, brain tumors), neurofibromatosis, autism, or tuberous sclerosis; may also be familial.
Microcephaly	Occipital-frontal head circumference more than 2 SD below the mean for age and sex, or one that is not growing at the normal rate	May be caused by craniosynostosis, craniostenosis, Down syndrome, fetal alcohol syndrome, or hypopituitarism; it may also be familial.
Neck masses, lumps, or swelling	Intolerant to cold? Heat? When was the onset? Palpitations? Recent fever? Weight loss or weight gain? Immunization status? IV drug use?	A neck mass could be an enlarged thyroid, lymphadenopathy, malignancy, or cervical masses. Cold intolerance is likely due to acquired hypothyroidism; heat intolerance may be caused by hyperthyroidism. Palpitations could be because of hyperthyroidism.
Neck pain	Sleep position? Recent injury? Involved in sports? What type? Recent respiratory or flu-like illness?	Neck pain can be positional after sleep; it can accompany head or neck injury associated with rough play or contact sports; neck pain and stiffness with a history of recent febrile respiratory or flu-like illness may indicate meningeal inflammation.
Neck stiffness	Age of child? Onset of neck stiffness? Recent infection of head or neck? Fever?	Neck stiffness can be due to congenital torticollis; it can also be a sign of meningeal irritation, which occurs with meningitis. Fever with stiff neck can be retropharyngeal or peritonsillar abscess, or bacterial meningitis.

TABLE 13.1	Abnormalities and Complaints Related to the Head and Neck (*continued*)	
CONDITION	**ASSESSMENT**	**EXPLICATION**
Night sweats	Onset? Fever? Lymphadenopathy? Weight loss?	Malignancy or tuberculosis are possibilities that should be investigated.
Plagiocephaly	Sleep position? Was infant born prematurely? Where on skull is the plagiocephaly? Occipital region? Parietal region?	Occipital plagiocephaly is due to prolonged supine positioning, and parietal plagiocephaly is due to prolonged side-lying positioning. Asymmetrical head shape can be caused by craniostenosis or craniosynostosis.
Sore throat	Onset? Fever? Accompanying nasopharyngitis? Tonsillar edema or exudate?	Possible streptococcal pharyngitis or retropharyngeal or peritonsillar abscess.
Weight loss	Fever? Lymphadenopathy? Associated symptoms such as tremors, nervousness, anxiety?	Possible malignancy, hyperthyroidism, or tuberculosis.

GABHS, group A beta-hemolytic *Streptococcus*; IV, intravenous; SD, standard deviation.

TABLE 13.2	Differential Diagnosis of Head and Neck Mass in Infants and Children
TYPE OF MASS	**PHYSICAL FINDINGS**
Congenital	
Hemangioma	Congenital vascular anomaly; red, blue, or purple in color; warm to touch, compressible, then refills with blood; bruit and thrill present
Thyroglossal duct cyst	Midline neck mass
Dermoid cyst	Midline neck mass
Cystic hygroma (lymphangioma)	Posterior to sternocleidomastoid muscle
Brachial cleft abnormalities (e.g., cysts, fistulas)	Anterior to sternocleidomastoid muscle
Cervical rib	Bilateral, hard, immoveable orthopedic anomalies found in neck
Laryngocele	Soft, cystic, compressible neck mass; may cause stridor, dyspnea, and cough; characterized by varying degrees of upper airway obstruction
Sternomastoid tumor	Firm, painless mass in neonate; fusiform in shape; approximately 1–3 cm in length; because of perinatal injury; mass usually grows for roughly 8 weeks, then involutes by age 6 months; usually accompanied by torticollis
Inflammatory/Infections	
Abscesses Retropharyngeal Peritonsillar	Localized infection with inflammation and exudate: Retropharyngeal abscess: sore throat, fever, neck mass, neck stiffness, torticollis, neck swelling in infants; cervical lymphadenopathy Peritonsillar abscess: infection of head and neck region; causes headache and neck pain, also fever, dysphagia, sore throat, malaise, and otalgia; cervical lymphadenitis also seen
Lymphadenitis	Inflamed/enlarged lymph node, most often in response to infection; a single node or group of nodes may be affected; lymph nodes are tender, inflamed, soft, fluctuant, and increase rapidly in size with infection
Lymphadenopathy	See section on Assessment of the Lymph Nodes of the Head and Neck, later in this chapter
Parotitis (mumps)	Inflammation of salivary glands; causes swelling along angle of jaw
Neoplastic	
Benign	
Thyroid nodule	Midline neck mass
Goiter	Located near thyroid
Malignant	
Non-Hodgkin's lymphoma	Lymphadenopathy; mediastinal mass; hepatosplenomegaly
Hodgkin's disease	Asymptomatic lymphadenopathy, unexplained weight loss, fever, and night sweats

Physical Examination

Examination of the head and neck in young children is challenging. Some of the areas to be examined are not easily visualized, and children toddler-aged and younger are often resistant to this portion of the examination. In infants and toddlers, assessment of the head and neck is done near the end of the physical examination, as palpation of the head and neck may cause the infant or young child to become agitated and cry. Purposeful visual inspection of the head and neck is best done when the infant or toddler is quiet and not agitated to yield the most detailed, accurate results. Assessment of the head and neck in older children and adolescents can be done in a head-to-toe sequence. Examination of the head and neck is usually performed with the infant or child sitting upright in front of the examiner, either in the parent's arms or on the examination table.

No specialized equipment is necessary to examine the head or neck. Gloves must be worn during the examination if any lesions are noted. The examiner must have short fingernails when palpating the neck. Good illumination is essential. When assessing the head of a child age 3 years or younger, or if the provider is concerned about head size, a paper or metal tape measure is necessary to measure head circumference (see Chapter 8). This tape measure can also be used to measure lymph node size in the case of lymph node enlargement.

Assessment of the Head

Inspection findings have the potential to vary greatly, depending on the child's age (e.g., head size, open or closed fontanelles, head control). Assessment of the head is critically important in newborns and infants but should not be minimized in older children. Examination of the head and scalp in infants and children can reveal integumentary disorders or infections that should be treated promptly to prevent complications (see Chapter 12).

Inspection • Assessment of the head begins with inspection and can be done informally during initial contact with the child. The provider begins by inspecting the head for size, symmetry, and shape. In infants, head control should be assessed. In infants and toddlers 18 months and younger, the anterior and posterior fontanelles should be assessed; the posterior fontanelle should be assessed in infants aged 2 months and younger.

Brain growth is essential for normal growth and development of the infant and young child. Head size reflects brain growth. Head size is determined by measuring head circumference; this is done at birth (see Chapter 11) and in children 3 years and younger. The head circumference is measured at all health maintenance visits and when the provider has a concern about the child's head size or shape. These measurements should be plotted on age and gender-appropriate growth charts (see Chapter 8). The head circumference reflects estimated brain size. A head that is larger

than normal (macrocephaly) is defined as a head circumference more than two standard deviations (SD) above the mean for age and sex or one that increases too rapidly. Macrocephaly often indicates an enlarged brain, which may be because of hydrocephalus, space-occupying lesions (e.g., hematomas, brain tumors), neurofibromatosis, or tuberous sclerosis (Bernard, et al, 2012). Small head size (microcephaly) is defined as a head circumference two SD below the mean for age and sex or one that is growing more slowly than normal. Microcephaly may be because of premature closure of the cranial sutures (craniosynostosis), craniostenosis, or Down syndrome (Tsai, Manchester, & Elias, 2012). Microcephaly is also a clinical finding in FAS (Vaux & Chambers, 2012) and in newborns who have been exposed to cocaine in utero (Rivkin et al., 2008). The provider must keep in mind that head size may be familial and should compare the child's head size to that of the parents (see Chapter 11). Premature infants also may appear to have large heads because of continuing cephalocaudal development; these infants should have their head circumference measurements plotted, according to conceptual versus chronologic age (Sherman, Lauriello, & Aylward, 2013). Abnormal findings in head circumference measurement necessitate referral to pediatric neurology.

The head should be symmetrical when inspected, without depressions or bulging. Asymmetry of the head such as flattening in one particular area of the skull (i.e., plagiocephaly or brachycephaly) may indicate that the infant or child spends an inordinate amount of time lying in one position. For example, occipital flattening (i.e., brachycephaly) can indicate prolonged supine positioning and is more commonly seen since the inception of the Back to Sleep initiative (Figure 13.10). Plagiocephaly or brachycephaly can also indicate neglect, especially if alopecia is noted over the same area. Asymmetry of the head can also be caused by craniosynostosis, which is caused by premature closure of the coronal sutures; it can have multiple etiologies and must be treated surgically (Table 13.3).

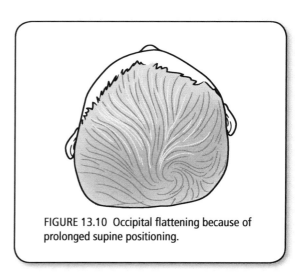

FIGURE 13.10 Occipital flattening because of prolonged supine positioning.

TABLE 13.3	Causes of Craniosynostosis in Children
TYPE OF CRANIOSYNOSTOSIS	**CAUSES**
Primary craniosynostosis	Defect in ossification of cranial bones
Secondary craniosynostosis	Endocrine: hyperthyroidism; vitamin D deficiency; hypercalcemia; and rickets Hematologic: sickle cell disease and thalassemia Inadequate brain growth: microcephaly and shunted hydrocephalus
Syndromic craniosynostosis	Genetic mutations

Source: Sheth, Ranalli, Aldana, Iskandar, and Roy (2013).

Cranial molding refers to an abnormal *shape* of the head that is seen in neonates in the immediate postpartum period. This is caused by pressure exerted on the skull during delivery and is considered normal during the first 7 days of life. The skull shape of infants born prematurely is often *dolichocephalic* (long and narrow), because of positioning of these infants on their side for prolonged periods of time. In most cases, the skull shape normalizes by age 1 to 2 years. Prominence of the frontal area of the cranium ("bossing") is seen with hydrocephalus (see Chapter 22).

Inspection of the head in infants should include assessment of head control. Head control is assessed by determining the infant's ability to hold the head erect when it is unsupported. Infants develop some head control when in the prone position by approximately 2 months. The provider should place infants at this age on the examination table in the prone position and observe whether or not they can lift their head while prone. Older infants can be placed on the examination table in the supine position and then be pulled to a sitting position while the provider assesses head control. Infants 4 months or younger will display some head lag; most infants this age are able to hold their head erect at midline when being held in a vertical position. By age 6 months, no head lag should be noted (Figure 13.11). To assess head control in older infants, the provider can show the infant a colorful object or toy, move it in different directions, and assess whether the child turns his or her head to follow the movement. Head control can be determined in older children by asking them to turn their head from side to side and up and down and assessing whether they are able to follow these simple commands. Head lag is most commonly caused by prematurity, hydrocephalus, and asphyxia injuries, causing alterations in neuromuscular control. Lack of head control after 6 months is abnormal and can be the result of anoxic brain injury and may indicate cerebral palsy.

The fontanelles are best inspected with infants or toddlers in the sitting position. The anterior fontanelle should be flat and open until 12 to 18 months. With vomiting or vigorous crying, the anterior fontanelle may be tense or bulge very slightly; this is a normal finding. Abnormal findings include a sunken or depressed anterior fontanelle; this is a sign of moderate to severe dehydration or malnutrition. A noticeably bulging anterior fontanelle indicates overhydration or increased intracranial pressure. Box 13.2 lists some causes of increased intracranial pressure in infants and children. In some instances, the anterior fontanelle is visibly pulsatile. Pulsations of the anterior fontanelle reflect the peripheral pulse. Marked pulsations can be because of increased intracranial pressure, decreased venous return from the head, or increased pulse pressure.

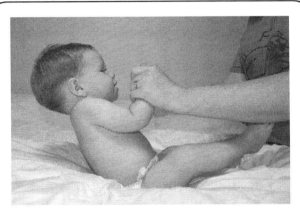

FIGURE 13.11 This infant demonstrates no head lag when pulled to sit.

BOX 13.2 Causes of Increased Intracranial Pressure in Children

- Abscess
- Brain tumor
- Encephalitis
- Head trauma
- Hematomas
- Hepatic failure
- Hydrocephalus
- Hypoxic-ischemic injury
- Intracranial hemorrhage
- Lead poisoning encephalopathy
- Meningitis
- Reye syndrome
- Stroke
- Vitamin A toxicity

The provider should also inspect the fontanelles for size. This is done by measuring the width and length of the open anterior fontanelle. It may be small at birth because of cranial compression during vaginal delivery and then increase in size in the first weeks of life. The open anterior fontanelle should measure approximately 1 to 5 cm (0.4–2 in.) in length and width until 9 to 12 months of age. An anterior fontanelle that measures greater than 4 to 5 cm (2 in.) in diameter may be within normal limits in some children but also may indicate congenital hypothyroidism, rickets, osteogenesis imperfecta, or increased intracranial pressure (Kiesler & Ricer, 2003). The posterior fontanelle may or may not be palpable at birth. If palpable, it should measure 0.5 to 1.5 cm at birth, gradually closing by approximately 2 months. The presence of a sagittal fontanelle (between the anterior and posterior fontanelles) can indicate Down syndrome (see next section for palpation of the fontanelles).

When examining young infants, providers also inspect the scalp veins for dilation, which can indicate chronic intracranial pressure. The scalp should also be inspected for lesions, hair loss, signs of trauma, any areas of discoloration, and overall hygiene (see Chapter 12).

Palpation • Palpation of the head in infants and children involves assessment of the head for symmetry; palpation of the fontanelles (infants and toddlers) and cranial sutures; and assessment for edema, tenderness, masses, depressions, and lesions. (See Chapter 5 regarding cultural considerations involving touching the head in children.)

The provider uses the finger pads of the second or third fingers to palpate the skull in a circular motion, beginning at the frontal area, then moving to the temporal and parietal areas, and working toward the occipital region. The skull should first be palpated for contour and symmetry (see section on Inspection). Asymmetry of the skull can have multiple etiologies (see Inspection).

In infants and toddlers to age 18 months, the provider gently palpates the fontanelles for size, tautness, bulging, and pulsations (see Inspection). Typically, only the anterior and posterior fontanelles can be palpated. In infants 6 months of age or older, it is best to palpate the fontanelles with the infant in the sitting position, ideally when the infant is quiet, as intense crying can cause the anterior fontanelle to bulge. In infants aged 2 months and younger, the anterior and posterior fontanelles are palpated; in infants and toddlers 18 months of age and younger, the anterior fontanelle is palpated. The anterior fontanelle is palpated at the juncture of the sagittal, coronal, and frontal sutures. The posterior fontanelle is palpated at the juncture of the sagittal and lambdoidal sutures. When palpated, the fontanelles should be soft and flat. A fontanelle that is full, bulging, or palpated after the age at which it should be closed often indicates increased intracranial pressure (see Box 13.2). A depressed or sunken anterior fontanelle indicates dehydration.

In infants, the provider palpates the cranial sutures for separation to determine whether they are open, closed, or overriding. Again, using the finger pads, the provider palpates the sagittal, coronal, and lambdoidal suture lines. Normal cranial sutures feel like soft ridges between the cranial bones. Cranial sutures may overlap in the first 6 months of life; this is a normal finding if the head circumference is within normal limits. In some instances, young infants may develop a ridged cranial suture, called *metopic ridge*. This occurs when the two halves of the frontal bone fuse prematurely. This finding is normal if the infant's head shape and circumference are within normal limits. A *metopic suture* (or sagittal suture) occurs when the two halves of the frontal bone remain separated; this is commonly seen in children with Down syndrome (Kiesler & Ricer, 2003). These children should be monitored for increasing head size, particularly in the first year of life. When palpating the suture lines, if extra bone edges are felt, a skull fracture may be present.

Palpation of the cranial bones is done to assess for craniotabes, a softening and thinning of the bones of the skull. Craniotabes is normally found in premature infants and can sometimes be a normal finding in infants of 6 months and younger; the bones become firmer as they ossify with age. Craniotabes can also be caused by hydrocephaly, rickets because of vitamin D deficiency, congenital syphilis, or osteogenesis imperfecta (Graham, 2006). To assess for craniotabes, the provider should palpate the scalp firmly along the cranial suture lines in the temporoparietal area. The presence of craniotabes causes the cranial bones to feel pliable and soft; firm palpation often creates an indentation, similar to pressing on a ping-pong ball.

Palpation of the skull also involves assessing for tenderness, masses, edema, depressions, and lesions. Scalp tenderness can indicate injury or trauma to the head or scalp, tension or migraine headache, scalp infections (e.g., lice, tinea capitis, cellulitis, herpes zoster, osteomyelitis), contact dermatitis, and vasculitis caused by Henoch-Schönlein purpura or Kawasaki disease.

Depending on the location and character of the mass, palpable masses of the scalp may indicate infection, injury, or a benign variation. Palpable masses in the postauricular or occipital region may indicate lymphadenopathy. Palpable, raised, tender boggy masses with scattered pustules on the scalp indicate a kerion, a tinea capitis infection of the scalp (see Chapter 12, Figure 12.11). A palpable, localized, easily moveable, nontender mass may be a lipoma. With a recent history of head trauma, these same findings can indicate an accumulation of subcutaneous blood (i.e., a hematoma).

Normally, the skin covering the scalp should be flush against the scalp, without edema. Edema of the scalp in a newborn often indicates a caput succedaneum (i.e., localized subcutaneous edema over the presenting part of the scalp; edema crosses the suture lines) or a cephalohematoma (i.e., swelling caused by subperiosteal collection of blood; does not cross suture lines) (see

Chapter 11, Figure 11.5). These conditions should resolve by 2 weeks. A depression of the scalp can be felt over the area of the open fontanelles in infants (described earlier in this section) and over the area of a depressed skull fracture. The provider should also palpate the skull for lesions (see Chapter 12).

Percussion • Percussion of the head assesses for resonance, which may indicate hydrocephalus or a brain abscess. Providers tapping the index finger against the surface of the parietal bone create this resonance; such tapping produces a "cracked pot" sound ("Macewen's sign"). In infants whose fontanelles are still open, this is a normal finding. The presence of Macewen's sign in older infants and children whose fontanelles have closed may indicate a separation of the cranial sutures because of increased intracranial pressure.

Assessment of the Neck

Assessment of the neck involves inspection, palpation, and auscultation. In infants and toddlers, the neck is examined with the child lying supine either on the examination table or on the parent's lap. With children 3 to 4 years of age or younger, the provider must extend the head back slightly to expose the shortened neck area. When children are preschool-aged and older, they should sit upright in a position that allows them to rotate and extend their head easily. The neck is examined from medial to lateral and then from front to back.

Inspection • The provider begins inspection of a child's neck for size, symmetry, shape, swelling, cysts, or masses. In infants, the neck is normally short with visible skin folds; the neck lengthens between 3 and 4 years of age. In infants and children, the neck should be symmetrical with the head centered and the trachea midline. Obesity can cause changes in neck size, shape, and symmetry. No swelling should be present. Swelling of the neck may be caused by parotitis (mumps) or infections in the oral cavity. Diphtheria can also cause edema of the soft tissues of the neck (Leung & Robson, 2004). Swelling at midline and immediately above the thyroid cartilage in a young infant can be a dermoid or thyroglossal duct cyst (Connolly & Dillard, 2007). Cystic hygroma is the most common neck mass in neonates; although most are evident at birth, in some cases they may present as late as 2 years (Acevedo, Shah, Neville, & Poole, 2013).

The neck is also inspected for any skin infections, lesions, or scars (see Chapter 12). Young infants may be prone to fungal or bacterial infections of the anterior neck because of their short neck and folds of skin. Scars on the neck may be the result of past injury or surgery on underlying structures such as the thyroid or trachea. The neck must also be examined for webbing and extra skin folds. These variations can be caused by Klippel-Feil, Turner, or Noonan syndrome (Daniel & Postellon, 2013; Tsai et al., 2012). Extra skin folds are also consistent with Down syndrome.

Providers should assess the full range of motion of the neck through inspection. Performing passive range of motion on an infant accomplishes this. To assess neck range of motion in toddlers, a penlight or an engaging toy can be used while the examiner observes the child's range of motion. In older children, the examiner can ask the child to follow simple directions such as to look up, down, to the left, and to the right; then to touch their chin to the chest; and then to look at the ceiling. Normally, the child should not experience any pain or limitations in neck range of motion. Limited range of motion with lateral movement of the neck can indicate torticollis, the result of injury to the sternocleidomastoid muscle. This injury can be congenital (cranial nerve IV palsy) or the result of birth trauma, neck trauma, or spinal cord or cerebellar tumors (Kruer, Reynolds, & Ma, 2012). Cranial nerve XI (accessory) is tested by asking children to shrug their shoulders, while turning their head from side to side. The examiner can assess this either with or without applying resistance to the child's shoulders. The child should be able to resist, using the sternocleidomastoid muscle (see Chapter 22). Pain or resistance to neck flexion may indicate meningeal irritation (positive Kernig or Brudzinski sign) (see Chapter 22). *Opisthotonos*, which is extreme hyperextension of the neck, occurs with significant meningeal irritation, most often because of bacterial meningitis (see Chapter 22). Neck mobility is not assessed in a trauma victim.

Palpation • The mobility of the neck in infants is palpated, as they are not developmentally able to cooperate with the assessment of the range of motion with simple inspection. When palpating to assess neck range of motion in an infant, the provider begins by holding the infant supine and gently holding the infant's head with the dominant hand. Mobility of the infant's neck is then assessed by turning the infant's head from side to side, forward for flexion, and backward for extension. Any resistance to these movements should be noted, especially flexion, which may indicate torticollis. When palpating the neck in older children, it is best to do so with the child in the sitting position. Any pain or resistance to range of motion can indicate head or neck trauma, lymphadenopathy, or injury to the sternocleidomastoid muscle.

The provider also palpates the neck for any masses, cysts, pain, or tenderness. In newborns, cystic hygroma is the most common type of neck mass. Cystic hygromas are typically mobile, nontender, and nonerythematous, with a firm center (Connolly & Dillard, 2007). In newborns, the clavicles are palpated to assess for any fractures that may have occurred during delivery.

The parotid gland must also be palpated, noting any swelling, tenderness, or enlargement. The parotid gland should be nontender and nonedematous. An enlarged parotid gland may result from acute or chronic viral infections such as mumps, paramyxovirus, coxsackieviruses, Epstein-Barr virus, influenza and parainfluenza viruses, herpes simplex virus, cytomegalovirus, HIV, or bacterial infections caused by *Staphylococcus aureus*, *Mycobacterium tuberculosis*, or streptococcal infection (Templer & Leiss, 2013). The noninfectious causes of parotitis include collagen vascular diseases, systemic lupus erythematosus, metabolic disorders, diabetes mellitus, hypothyroidism, and tumors (Templer & Leiss, 2013). Bulimia nervosa can also cause parotid gland swelling (Yager, Scher, Hilty, & Osterhout, 2014).

Auscultation • Auscultation of the neck is done to localize the site of airway obstruction and may reveal a bruit over the thyroid gland if the child has diffuse toxic goiter (see Assessment of the Thyroid Gland).

Assessment of the Trachea

Inspection • It is important for the provider to determine the position of the trachea by inspection. The trachea should be midline; a deviation in tracheal position may indicate the presence of a foreign body, neoplasm, or pneumothorax.

Palpation • The trachea is difficult to palpate in children 3 years of age and younger because of their short, thick necks. The purpose of palpating the trachea is to determine its position and to assess for any masses. To palpate the trachea, the examiner should place the thumb and forefinger on either side of the trachea and then slowly and gently slide the fingers down the trachea. The trachea should be midline with no palpable masses.

Assessment of the Jugular Veins

Using tangential lighting across the neck, the provider inspects the external jugular veins. Inspection of the external jugular veins allows the provider to assess right atrial pressure indirectly. The external jugular vein is not normally distended when the child stands or sits upright. When the child lies down, jugular filling should occur. With the child supine, the jugular veins should appear full but not bulging, and the jugular venous pulse (JVP) should be visible. The JVP should have a normal rate and be gentle, nonbounding, and without bruits. It is not normal to observe jugular venous pulsations when the child is sitting upright. Jugular venous distention or abnormal pulsations should be noted; these findings may be caused by hypervolemia, right-sided heart failure, pericarditis, or mediastinal masses (see Chapter 18).

Assessment of the Carotid Arteries

Inspection • It is important for the provider to inspect the carotid arteries. These blood vessels are located in the groove between the trachea and sternocleidomastoid muscle. The carotid arteries should be inspected for amplitude of the pulsation. Carotid pulsations intensify in children after vigorous exercise but may also be present in children

with anemia, hypertension, hyperthyroidism, patent ductus arteriosus, or aortic insufficiency (see Chapter 18).

Palpation • Palpating the carotid artery in infants and toddlers may be difficult or impossible because of their short, thick necks. When palpating the carotid arteries, the provider must be sure to palpate only one at a time, since these blood vessels supply blood to the brain; occluding them simultaneously can impede all blood flow to the brain. Forceful palpation of the carotid artery can also precipitate a vagal response, causing bradycardia, hypotension, or even asystole. Using the fingerpads of the second and third fingers, the examiner locates the carotid artery, in the groove between the trachea and sternocleidomastoid muscle. Using gentle pressure, the provider palpates the carotid artery to assess the rate, rhythm, and intensity of the carotid pulse. Normally, the carotid pulse is synchronous with the radial pulse, palpable, and regular in rhythm. Both carotid pulses should be equal in intensity.

Auscultation • Using the bell portion of the stethoscope, the provider should auscultate the carotid arteries for bruits (abnormal sounds caused by turbulent blood flow). If children are developmentally capable, it may be helpful to ask them to hold their breath during the auscultation so that the sound of air movement is not confused with a bruit. Bruits may be present in children with hyperthyroidism, anemia or arteriovenous fistula, or other vascular abnormalities (see Chapter 18).

Assessment of the Thyroid Gland

Inspection • In children, the thyroid gland is inspected for size, symmetry, shape, and masses. Tangential lighting may help the provider to locate the thyroid gland in children. To begin inspection of the thyroid, the provider can ask the child to sit upright on the examination table, then tilt the head back. The size of the thyroid gland should be noted. An abnormally large thyroid gland may be evidence of hypothyroidism, hyperthyroidism, or infectious thyroiditis (Daniel & Postellon, 2014; Sinha & Gold, 2013). Next, the provider should ask the child to take a sip of water, then inspect thyroid gland movement when the child swallows; the thyroid should rise as the child swallows.

Palpation • Palpation of the thyroid gland in children can be challenging because young children are often ticklish when the neck area is touched, causing them to move their shoulders upward and squirm. Providers must be creative in devising age-appropriate strategies that facilitate the palpation portion of the thyroid examination.

In newborns, the thyroid cannot normally be palpated. If swelling is noted, the provider first hyperextends the newborn's head slightly to inspect for thyroid enlargement, then palpates with one finger on either side of the gland. If the thyroid gland can be palpated in a newborn, it is enlarged.

In infants and toddlers, the thyroid gland is extremely difficult to palpate because of their short, thick necks. When the provider palpates the thyroid gland in children older than 3 years, size, shape, symmetry, firmness, and the presence of any nodules, tenderness, or masses are noted. The isthmus of the thyroid gland is the only portion of that is normally palpable in children.

The approach for palpating the thyroid gland can be from either an anterior or posterior position. In young children, an anterior position is preferred so the child can see the provider; in the school-aged child and adolescent, a posterior approach is used. To begin with either approach, the provider first locates the cricoid cartilage to use as a landmark. Using the anterior approach, the provider faces the child and then places the pads of the second and third fingers on the thyroid isthmus. This should feel like a band of tissue that crosses over the trachea. Next, the provider places the thumbs on the child's neck. As the provider's right thumb gently displaces in the anterior region of the neck, the left thumb palpates the thyroid isthmus. This is repeated for both sides of the thyroid. From a posterior position, the provider stands behind the child and, with the child's head tilted slightly forward and to the right, uses the pads of his or her second and third fingers to palpate between the trachea and sternocleidomastoid muscle. Again using the cricoid cartilage as a landmark, the provider palpates the thyroid isthmus by displacing it with the left hand and palpating with the right, then repeating on the opposite side (Figure 13.12). The anterior and lateral lobes of the thyroid are not typically palpable in children; if they are, this indicates thyroid enlargement (i.e., goiter). A goiter feels firm and is easily moveable and nontender; the enlargement is symmetrical (Zeitler et al., 2012). The thyroid gland is enlarged in children with congenital hyperthyroidism, Graves' disease, or Hashimoto's thyroiditis (Zeitler et al., 2012). In some children with toxic goiter, the thyroid gland may be mildly enlarged but can also be normal in size, many times normal in size, or difficult to palpate (Corenblum & Adediji, 2013). Enlargement of the thyroid gland or the presence of tenderness or any masses is considered abnormal and warrants referral.

Auscultation • Auscultation of the thyroid gland is done when the provider palpates an enlarged thyroid gland. Using the bell of the stethoscope, the examiner auscultates over the thyroid. Increased blood flow to the thyroid gland may cause a systolic bruit on auscultation if the child has a toxic goiter.

Assessment of the Lymph Nodes of the Head and Neck

The head and neck contain the highest concentration of lymph nodes in the body. Assessment of the lymph node's size, color, location, temperature, mobility, and consistency may yield assessment findings that can signal a benign localized infection or a possible malignancy in the

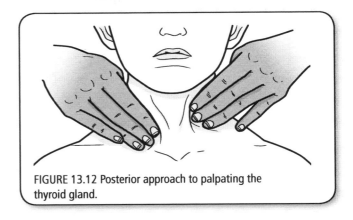

FIGURE 13.12 Posterior approach to palpating the thyroid gland.

area draining into that lymph node. Lymphadenopathy in the head and neck is not uncommon in young children because of frequent upper respiratory infections in this age group. When lymphadenopathy is assessed, it is important to ascertain from which part of the head or neck the lymph node receives drainage; this aids in the diagnosis. For example, cervical lymphadenopathy can indicate infection of the neck or oropharynx, or it can be a sign of generalized infection or illness, such as tuberculosis or lymphoma. A history geared to the child's age (i.e., certain organisms have predilections for specific age groups), assessment of associated signs and symptoms (e.g., fever, weight loss), and a careful physical examination help to determine whether an enlarged lymph node is benign or requires further evaluation (see Table 13.2).

Inspection • Assessment of the lymph nodes in the head and neck begins with inspection. The lymph nodes are inspected for size, swelling, and color; they are inspected in a front-to-back sequence, beginning with the preauricular nodes. In children, the lymph nodes normally range in size from 3 mm in the head to 1 cm in the neck. Lymph nodes that are enlarged and erythematous often indicate a localized infection that is proximal to the affected lymph node. Any nodes that are larger than 2 cm should be palpated carefully (see Palpation). Easily visible swelling of the lymph nodes on inspection requires immediate attention; this often indicates systemic infection. Erythema over a lymph node may reflect inflammation or may not be lymphadenopathy at all but a deep hemangioma.

Palpation • The lymph nodes are palpated for size, mobility, warmth, tenderness, consistency, and degree of fixation. Both superficial and deep palpation should be used. When palpating the lymph nodes, the provider should tilt the child's head slightly upward to have full access to the lymph nodes in that region (Figure 13.13). The provider palpates the lymph nodes, using the distal portion of the fingers and gentle but firm pressure in a circular motion. This circular motion helps to define the characteristics of the lymph node, which is so important when formulating differential diagnoses. The submental and submaxillary nodes are palpated bimanually.

FIGURE 13.13 Palpating the lymph nodes of the head and neck in a child.

The lymph nodes of the head and neck are palpated in the following sequence: preauricular and postauricular, submaxillary and submental, occipital, cervical, and then supraclavicular nodes. Normal lymph nodes are mobile, nontender, and are not warm to the touch. In healthy infants and adolescents, lymph nodes of the head and neck are usually nonpalpable. In young children aged 1 to approximately 10 years, small, nontender, moveable lymph nodes up to 1 cm (0.5 in.) are considered normal (Leung & Robson, 2004).

Lymphadenopathy is defined as lymph node tissue that measures greater than 1 cm in diameter, although anterior cervical lymph nodes as large as 2 cm are considered to be normal (Kanwar & Sills, 2014). Small, firm, rubbery, nontender, mobile lymph nodes ("shotty") are normal and commonly found in children 3 to 10 years of age. When lymph nodes swell (lymphadenopathy) because of infection, the enlargement is painful, and the node is soft and moveable; when lymphadenopathy results from metastasis of malignancy, the swelling is not painful and the lymph node is hard and fixed to the underlying tissue (Leung & Robson, 2004). Lymph nodes that are enlarged, firm, warm, and tender are often indicative of an infection that is proximal to the affected lymph node. The number of lymph nodes affected should be assessed as well; several enlarged lymph nodes are usually a sign of systemic disease (i.e., infection), whereas single nodes are more often caused by malignancy. In young children, the cervical lymph nodes are usually palpable because of the frequency of upper respiratory infections in this age group.

The differential diagnosis of lymphadenopathy in children is broad, but most lymphadenopathy in children is benign, self-limiting, and of viral origin (Kanwar & Sills, 2014). Table 13.4 lists common causes of head and neck lymphadenopathy in children.

COMMON DIAGNOSTIC STUDIES

Various diagnostic tests may be necessary to clarify differential diagnoses of abnormal conditions involving the head and neck. These diagnostic studies and their indications are summarized in Table 13.5.

TABLE 13.4	Causes of Head and Neck Lymphadenopathy in Children
LYMPH NODES	**CAUSES OF ENLARGEMENT**
Cervical	Viral upper respiratory infections, tonsillitis, streptococcal pharyngitis, infectious mononucleosis, cat scratch disease, Kawasaki disease, tuberculosis, rubella, bacterial lymphadenitis, oral or tooth infections; leukemia, lymphoma, or a postimmunization response
Occipital	Scalp infections (e.g., tinea capitis, pediculosis capitis, impetigo), viral infections (e.g., varicella, rubella, roseola), viral respiratory infections (e.g., respiratory syncytial virus, rhinovirus), and postimmunization; also seen in neonates born to mothers with infection during pregnancy
Postauricular	Otitis externa, otitis media, or parotitis
Preauricular	Scalp, local skin, eye, or ear infections
Submandibular	Tonsillitis, pharyngitis, stomatitis, and oral or tooth infections
Submental (submaxillary)	Oral and dental infections and acute lymphadenitis
Supraclavicular	Enlargement of a left supraclavicular node often indicates a malignancy in the abdomen or thorax; supraclavicular lymphadenopathy can also be caused by lymphoma, tuberculosis, histoplasmosis, or coccidioidomycosis.
Tonsillar	Tonsillitis, pharyngitis, stomatitis, and oral or tooth infections

Sources: Kanwar and Sills (2014); Leung and Robson (2004).

TABLE 13.5 Diagnostic Studies Used to Evaluate Conditions of the Head and Neck

TYPE OF TEST	INDICATION	COMMENTS
Biopsy	To establish diagnosis with lymphadenopathy	Biopsy should be obtained on any isolated, nontender, firm mass greater than 2 cm that does not respond to antibiotics (Kanwar & Sills, 2014; Leung & Robson, 2004)
Complete blood count	Helps to diagnose infections of the head and neck (e.g., meningitis, bacterial lymphadenitis, cellulitis)	Leukocytosis with a shift to the left is seen with bacterial lymphadenitis; atypical lymphocytosis is seen with infectious mononucleosis; and pancytopenia points to leukemia (Leung & Robson, 2004)
Computed tomography scan	Assesses head injuries; differentiates cysts from solid neck lesions	Child must remain immobilized during imaging
Culture	To isolate causative organism of infection	Head and neck infections can spread to underlying lymph nodes and blood vessels, potentially spreading to the meninges and causing bacterial meningitis
Erythrocyte sedimentation rate	Localized inflammation of skin or lymph nodes	This is usually markedly elevated with bacterial lymphadenitis (Leung & Robson, 2004)
Magnetic resonance digital subtraction angiography	Evaluates vascular lesions (e.g., hemangiomas, arteriovenous malformations, vascular tumors)	This is a noninvasive test, but it requires injection of contrast
Magnetic resonance imaging (MRI)	Gadolinium-enhanced MRIs are used for circumscribing the invasion of soft tissue by tumor; endocrine tumors are often enhanced on MRI this way; also used to diagnose head injuries and brain lesions	Child must remain immobilized during imaging; thus sedation is required
Newborn screening (for T_4; if low, obtain thyroid-stimulating hormone [TSH]) level	Congenital hypothyroidism	Mandatory screening in all 50 states
Rapid streptococcal antigen test	To diagnose streptococcal infections that cause lymphadenopathy of neck	Findings must be confirmed with culture
Skeletal radiography	To diagnose cranial anomalies	It evaluates cranial abnormalities such as brachycephaly, craniosynostosis, craniostenosis, and micro- or macrocephaly; cervical radiography is done to rule out atlantoaxial instability
Thyroid function testing (TSH; T_4)	To diagnose hypo- or hyperthyroidism	Thyroid tests should be ordered in any child with thyroid enlargement, more than one sign or symptom of hypo- or hyperthyroidism, new-onset fatigue, acquired growth failure, unexplained weight loss, or hyperactivity (Kaplowitz, 2007)
Thyroid imaging (radionuclide thyroid scanning)	To evaluate congenital hypothyroidism	This is done in conjunction with ultrasonography
Ultrasonography	Evaluates intracranial bleeds in neonates; shows cystic versus solid nature of neck masses (Leung & Robson, 2004); can be used to evaluate thyroid masses and diagnose hyper- or hypothyroidism or goiter	It is a noninvasive test, and it requires no sedation

DOCUMENTATION OF FINDINGS

Sample Write-Up: Well Newborn

Subjective Data

Full-term male, 5 days old

> **Prenatal history:** prenatal care begun in first trimester; no history of maternal hypothyroidism
> **Perinatal history:** normal, spontaneous, vaginal delivery
> **Newborn history:** no respiratory distress at birth; Apgar scores 8 and 9

Objective Data

> **Head:** normocephalic, slight molding; anterior and posterior fontanelles open, soft, and flat; overriding sagittal suture; no palpable masses; head circumference 90th percentile
> **Neck:** supple, full range-of-motion, no masses. Clavicles smooth
> **Neonatal screening results:** within normal limits
> **Assessment:** healthy newborn

Sample Write-Up: Well Child

Subjective Data

Healthy 7-year-old girl; PMH noncontributory; no history of injuries

Objective Data

> **Head:** normocephalic; symmetrical, no masses or lesions, hair well-distributed; head circumference 50th percentile
> **Neck:** supple with full range of motion; no swelling, masses; trachea midline; thyroid gland firm without nodules or masses
> **Lymphatics:** no lymphadenopathy in head or neck
> **Assessment:** well child

Sample Write-Up: 1-Year-Old With Neck Mass

Subjective Data

A boy, 13-months-old, is brought to the clinic by his mother for evaluation of a neck mass. The mother noticed the mass the morning of the clinic visit. The child had symptoms of an upper respiratory infection for 3 days, including nasal drainage, snoring, and slight cough. His mother denies any history of shortness of breath, stridor, wheezing, or difficulty breathing. The child has been eating and drinking usual amounts; and has also been playful and alert. He has had one episode of otitis media; no know allergies; he is currently not on medications and his immunications are up to date.

Objective Data

> **T:** 38.2°C (100.8°F); **P:** 160 beats per minute; **RR:** 32 breaths per minute; **oxygen saturation on room air:** 98%; **weight:** 9 kg

> **General:** alert, in no distress
> **Skin:** color pink; no rashes or lesions
> **Nose:** moderate amount of pale green nasal discharge; turbinates pink, slightly edematous
> **Throat:** pharynx pink, no exudate
> **Neck:** mass palpated on left side of neck; mobile, nontender, nonerythematous, no warmth when palpated; center of mass firm to touch
> **Lymphatics:** no nodes palpable
> **Lungs:** vesicular sounds auscultated throughout all lung fields
> **Assessment:** cystic hygroma

Notable Clinical Findings

AREA	NOTABLE FINDING
History	Pre-, neo-, postnatal exposures, hypoxemia, injury
	Genetic or metabolic disorders
	Congenital hypothyroidism
	Fetal alcohol syndrome
	Tracheal cysts or masses
	Head or neck injuries or infections
	Immunization delay
Head	Macro-, microcephaly
	Brachycephaly
	Plagiocephaly
	Dolichocephaly
	Craniosynostosis
	Craniostenosis
	Frontal bossing
	Craniotabes
	Head lag beyond age 4 months
	No head control by age 6 months
	Posterior fontanelle open after age 2 months
	Anterior fontanelle open beyond age 18 months
	Bulging (increased intracranial pressure) or sunken (dehydration) anterior fontanelle
Neck	Neck webbing
	Extra neck skinfolds
	Decreased range of motion
	Torticollis
	Cystic hygroma
	Jugular venous distention
	Neck mass, swelling, pain or stiffness
	Nodules
	Tenderness
Regional lymph nodes	Lymphadenopathy
	Night sweats
	Lymph nodes that are enlarged, firm, warm, and tender
	Single, fixed nodes

References

Acevedo, J. L., Shah, R. K., Neville, H. L., & Poole, M. D. (2013). *Cystic hygroma*. Retrieved from http://emedicine.medscape.com/article/994055-overview

Bernard, T. J., Knupp, K., Yang, M. L., Kedia, S., Levisohn, P., & Moe, P. G. (2012). Neurologic and muscular disorders. In W. W. Hay, M. J. Levin, R. R. Deterding, M. J. Abzub, & J. M. Sondheimer (Eds.), *Current pediatric diagnosis & treatment* (21st ed., pp. 740–829). New York, NY: McGraw-Hill.

Connolly, S., & Dillard, E. (2007). Cystic hygroma. *Consultant for Pediatrics, 6*(8), 479–480.

Corenblum, B., & Adediji, O. S. (2013). *Diffuse toxic goiter*. Retrieved from http://emedicine.medscape.com/article/120140-overview

Daniel, M. S., & Postellon, D. (2013). *Turner syndrome*. Retrieved from http://emedicine.medscape.com/article/949681-overview

Daniel, M. S., & Postellon, D. (2014). *Congenital hypothyroidism*. Retrieved from http://emedicine.medscape.com/article/919758-overview

Graham, J. G. (2006). Skull. In R. E. Stevenson & J. G. Hall (Eds.), *Human malformations and related anomalies* (2nd ed., pp. 249–251). New York, NY: Oxford University Press.

Kanwar, V. S., & Sills, R. H. (2014). *Lymphadenopathy*. Retrieved from http://emedicine.medscape.com/article/956340-overview

Kaplowitz, P. (2007). Thyroid testing: When to worry (not often) and when to reassure. *Contemporary Pediatrics*, p. 2. Retrieved from http://contemporarypediatrics.modernmedicine.com/contemporarypediatrics/news/thyroid-testing-when-to-worry-not-often-and-when-reassure-0?page=full

Kiesler, J., & Ricer, R. (2003). The abnormal fontanelle. *American Family Physician, 67*(12), 2547–2552.

Kruer, M. C., Reynolds, N. C., & Ma, J. (2012). *Torticollis*. Retrieved from http://emedicine.medscape.com/article/1152543-overview#aw2aab6b2b3aa

Kyle, T. (2008). *Essentials of pediatric nursing*. Philadelphia, PA: Lippincott.

Leung, A. K. C., & Robson, W. L. M. (2004). Childhood cervical lymphadenopathy. *Journal of Pediatric Health Care, 18*(1), 3–7.

McClain, K. L., & Fletcher, R. H. (2013). Peripheral lymphadenopathy in children: Etiology. *Up to Date*. Retrieved from http://www.uptodate.com/contents/peripheral-lymphadenopathy-in-children-etiology#H18

Pillitteri, A. (2003). *Maternal & child health nursing: Care of the childbearing & childrearing family* (4th ed., p. 963). Philadelphia, PA: Lippincott.

Rhodes, J. (2006). *Advanced health asseessment and diagnostic reasoning*. Philadelphia, PA: Lippincott.

Rivkin, M. J., Davis, P. E., Lemaster, J. L., Cabral, H. J., Warfield, S. K., Mulkern, R. V., . . . Frank, D. A. (2008). Volumetric MRI study of brain in children with intrauterine exposure to cocaine, alcohol, tobacco, and marijuana. *Pediatrics, 121*(4), 741–750.

Sherman, M. P., Lauriello, N. F., & Aylward, G. P. (2013). *Follow up of the NICU patient*. Retrieved from http://emedicine.medscape.com/article/1833812-overview

Sheth, R. D., Ranalli, N., Aldana, P., Iskandar, B. J., & Roy, S. (2013). *Craniosynostosis*. Retrieved from http://emedicine.medscape.com/article/1175957-overview

Sinha, S., & Gold, J. G. (2013). *Pediatric hyperthyroidism*. Retrieved from http://emedicine.medscape.com/article/921707-overview

Templer, J. W., & Leiss, B. D. (2013). *Parotitis*. Retrieved from http://emedicine.medscape.com/article/882461-overview

Tsai, A. C., Manchester, D. K., & Elias, E. R. (2012). Genetics and dysmorphology. In W. W. Hay, M. J. Levin, R. R. Deterding, M. J. Abzub, & J. M. Sondheimer (Eds.), *Current pediatric diagnosis & treatment* (21st ed., pp. 1088–1122). New York, NY: McGraw-Hill.

Vaux, K., & Chambers, C., (2012). Fetal alcohol syndrome. Retrieved from http://emedicine.medscape.com/article/974016-overview

Weber, J., & Kelley, J. (2007). *Health assessment in nursing* (3rd ed., p. 193). Philadelphia, PA: Lippincott.

Yager, J., Scher, L. M., Hilty, D. M., & Osterhout, C. I. (2014). *Bulimia nervosa*. Retrieved from http://emedicine.medscape.com/article/286485-overview

Zeitler, P. S., Barker, J. M., Travers, S. H., Kelsey, M. M., Nadeau, K., & Kappy, M. S. (2012). Endocrine disorders. In W. W. Hay, M. J. Levin, R. R. Deterding, M. J. Abzub, & J. M. Sondheimer (Eds.), *Current pediatric diagnosis & treatment* (21st ed., pp. 1011–1051). New York, NY: McGraw-Hill.

Assessment of the Ears

The ear is a sensory organ of hearing and vestibular equilibrium, consisting of three parts: the *external, middle*, and *inner* ear. Assessment of the ear begins with the pediatric health care provider obtaining a thorough and accurate history. These historical findings guide the provider in obtaining the physical examination of the external and internal ear, and the assessment of hearing acuity. The complete physical examination involves inspection and palpation of the external ear, the otoscopic examination, and assessment of hearing and speech development. Early screening to identify risk factors for hearing loss and to assess speech and language delays is essential because of the potential impact on a child's psychosocial development, social interaction, and school performance.

ANATOMY AND PHYSIOLOGY

The ear is composed of three major parts: the external, middle, and inner ear. In addition to hearing and interpreting sound, the ears contain the vestibular organs, such as the semicircular canals in the inner ear, which assist with balance and equilibrium. The external ears also contribute to the child's appearance and body image, depending on their size and location on the head.

External Ear

The external ear is structurally designed to collect sound and direct sound waves inward. It is composed of the *pinna* (also called the auricle), the *external auditory canal* (ear canal), and the *tympanic membrane* (eardrum). The pinna consists of elastic cartilage and skin and is covered with very fine hair. The *helix* is the outer cartilaginous rim of the pinna; the *antihelix* is an inner curved rim parallel and anterior to the helix. The *concha* is a hollow, bowl-like structure that leads to the external auditory canal. Anterior to the concha is the *tragus*, a nodular structure that lies at the entrance of the external auditory canal; opposite the tragus is the *antitragus*. Below the antitragus is the *lobule* (earlobe), the fleshy lower portion of the pinna.

The structures of the external, middle, and inner ear are illustrated in Figure 14.1. Figure 14.2 illustrates the landmarks of the pinna.

The external auditory canal, a cartilaginous and bony structure, begins at the concha and terminates

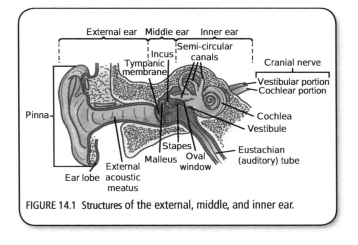

FIGURE 14.1 Structures of the external, middle, and inner ear.

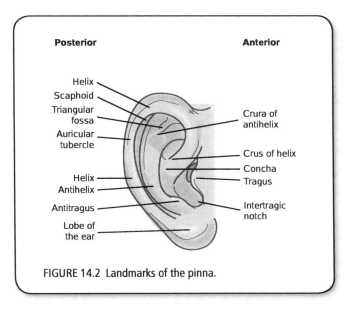

FIGURE 14.2 Landmarks of the pinna.

at the tympanic membrane (see Figure 14.1). This structure further directs sound to the tympanic membrane. Innervation to the medial portion of the external auditory canal is through the trigeminal nerve (cranial nerve V). The inner portion of the canal is innervated by the vagus nerve (cranial nerve X). When the external auditory canal is cleaned or inspected, coughing may occur as a result of stimulating the vagus nerve. The external auditory canal is lined with small hairs, sebaceous glands, and ceruminous glands that secrete cerumen, a sticky or flaky substance, the function of which is to lubricate and clean the ear canal by trapping dirt and other debris and to repel water from the tympanic membrane (Dimmitt, 2005). In addition to keeping the ear canal clean, cerumen also has a somewhat low pH, as well as antibacterial and antifungal properties (Dancer, 2006), which help to protect the external ear from infection.

Cerumen can easily become impacted, especially when cotton-tipped swabs are used to clean the external auditory canal (Dimmitt, 2005). Cerumen impaction complicates its removal and potentially causes conductive hearing loss (CHL). At the end of the external auditory canal lies the tympanic membrane, which separates the external auditory canal from the middle ear.

Middle Ear

The middle ear is an air-filled space inside the temporal bone, which contains three tiny bones known as *ossicles* (see Figure 14.1). Individually, these bones are the *malleus* (*hammer*), *incus* (*anvil*), and *stapes* (*stirrup*). The middle ear begins at the tympanic membrane, an extremely thin, translucent membrane that is pearly gray to pale pink with blood vessels at the periphery. The tympanic membrane can be divided into two major parts: the *pars flaccida* and the *pars tensa*. The pars flaccida is the upper, smaller, triangular portion above the *short process of the malleus*. The pars tensa comprises the remaining portion of the tympanic membrane. The tympanic membrane is surrounded by a fibrous border called the *annulus* that attaches the membrane to the temporal bone. The tympanic membrane is oval and slightly concave because of the presence of the malleus, which holds the membrane slightly inward. This concave shape of the membrane creates a cone of light when the otoscope light is reflected on the tympanic membrane. Because of the translucency of the tympanic membrane, parts of the malleus are easily seen on physical examination: the *umbo* where the tympanic membrane meets the tip of the malleus, the *manubrium* (handle of malleus), which is attached to the tympanic membrane, and the short process of the malleus, an important landmark of the tympanic membrane. Figure 14.3 illustrates these landmarks.

The malleus (hammer), incus (anvil), and stapes (stirrup) transmit sound from the external auditory canal

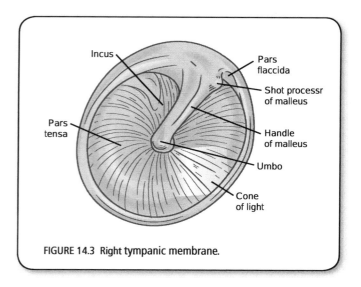

FIGURE 14.3 Right tympanic membrane.

to the inner ear when sound waves touch the tympanic membrane, causing the ossicles to move. The stapes attaches to the *oval window*, a membrane separating the middle and inner ear, which also vibrates with hearing and is in direct contact with the fluids of the inner ear. The *round window* lies inferior to the oval window and also communicates with the inner ear, acting as a pressure valve, bulging outward when fluid pressure increases in the inner ear.

The middle ear is connected by the eustachian tube to the nasopharynx (see Figure 14.1). Normally, the walls of the eustachian tube are collapsed and valve-like, opening only with swallowing, chewing, yawning, or forceful inflation such as nose blowing. The eustachian tube has three main functions: (a) to protect the middle ear from excessively loud sound, pressure fluctuations, and nasopharyngeal secretions; (b) to drain any secretions from the middle ear to the nasopharynx, thus protecting the middle ear from infections; and (c) to equalize pressure on both sides of the tympanic membrane, thus avoiding membrane rupture and allowing the tympanic membrane to vibrate freely.

Inner Ear

Located within the temporal bone, the fluid-filled inner ear contains the structures that are necessary for both hearing and balance (see Figure 14.1). The inner ear contains the *bony labyrinth*, which is filled with a fluid called *perilymph*. Within the bony labyrinth is the *membranous labyrinth*, filled with a fluid called *endolymph*. Sound waves and vibrations are conducted and transmitted through these fluids.

There are three main structures that lie within the bony labyrinth:
- **Vestibule:** The vestibule leads to both the cochlea and semicircular canals; it contains receptors necessary for the maintenance of equilibrium and balance.

- **Cochlea:** The cochlea is a snail-shaped structure that directly communicates with the middle ear via the round window. Within the cochlea is the *organ of Corti,* the sensory organ for hearing, which contains auditory receptor hair cells. These cells transmit impulses to the auditory nerve (cranial nerve VIII, cochlear branch), to the brainstem, and to the brain to be interpreted as sound.
- **Semicircular Canals:** There are three semicircular canals; these structures play a role in maintaining equilibrium by detecting motion and balance. The semicircular canals are attached to the vestibular branch of the auditory nerve and send impulses to the brain to maintain equilibrium. The semicircular canals also keep the eyes still while the head moves.

None of the structures of the inner ear can be directly examined, but inferences can be drawn about their functions from hearing and neurologic assessments.

DEVELOPMENTAL CONSIDERATIONS

The ear begins to develop in utero during the third week of embryonic life and should be fully developed by the end of the third month of gestation. Intrauterine exposure to ototoxic viruses (e.g., rubella), bacteria, and drugs can cause permanent damage to the organ of Corti and impair hearing (Shah & Lotke, 2013).

During embryonic development, differentiation of the ears and renal system occurs at the same time; any disturbances in utero can be the cause of coincidental abnormalities in both systems. Therefore, malformations of the ears should alert the provider to possible renal disorders in the neonate, and vice versa.

External Ear

In the preterm infant, lack of cartilage results in the pinna folding easily and remaining folded; as gestation progresses, resistance to folding allows the pinna to recoil quickly (see Chapter 11). The external auditory canal is short and curves inward and upward in children younger than 3 years; after age 3 the canal points downward and forward. Because the external auditory canal curves, it must be straightened manually before the provider examines the canal or the tympanic membrane. The bony portion of the external auditory canal ossifies by age 2, straightening the canal and allowing better visualization of the tympanic membrane. By school age, the pinna and external auditory canal should be of adult size and configuration. The pinna is approximately 80% of adult size by age 4 to 5 years; the external auditory canal is approximately 1 inch long and 0.25 inches in diameter by about 9 years (Jackson, 2006).

Middle Ear

In newborns, the tympanic membrane lies in a more horizontal plane, making visualization of this structure more difficult. Until approximately age 2 years, the eustachian tube is shorter and wider and lies in a relatively horizontal plane compared to the eustachian tube of an older child or adult (Figure 14.4). Thus, fluid in the middle ear cannot drain easily into the nasopharynx, making infants and toddlers more prone to middle ear infections and effusions. This is especially common in preterm infants, infants and young children with Down syndrome, and those with craniofacial abnormalities such as cleft lip and palate.

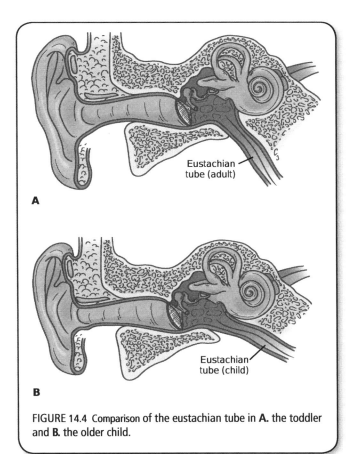

FIGURE 14.4 Comparison of the eustachian tube in **A.** the toddler and **B.** the older child.

Inner Ear

The inner ear begins to develop at the beginning of the fourth week of gestation. The fetus can hear by approximately 20 weeks gestation, and auditory nerve function is mature by approximately 5 months. Any maternal infections (e.g., rubella, cytomegalovirus) or ingestions (e.g., alcohol, drugs) that are potentially ototoxic can damage the developing organ of Corti and impair the developing fetus's hearing. Preterm infants are especially vulnerable to hearing loss because of exposure to noise in the neonatal intensive care unit (NICU), hypoxia, persistent pulmonary hypertension, hyperbilirubinemia, and ototoxic drugs (Shah & Lotke, 2013).

CULTURAL, ETHNIC, AND RACIAL CONSIDERATIONS

Two distinct, genetically determined types of cerumen exist: dry and wet. Dry cerumen is pale brown to gray and flaky and is found in Asians, Inuits, and Native Americans (Petrakis, Pingle, Petrakis, & Petrakis, 2005). Wet cerumen is yellowish-brown and moist and is characteristic of Caucasians and children of African ancestry (Dancer, 2006; Petrakis et al., 2005). The clinical significance of this relates to the difficulty of removing cerumen when it becomes necessary to view the external auditory canal and tympanic membrane. Dry cerumen is more difficult to remove than wet cerumen and is more likely than wet cerumen to become impacted.

ASSESSMENT OF THE EAR

History

The reason for the child's health care visit guides the provider in deciding what type of data to gather for the health history. For children who are being examined for the first time, a complete past medical history (PMH), past surgical history (PSH), family history, and social history are obtained. These histories are updated as needed when the child presents for health maintenance visits, with special attention to additional episodes of otitis media, frequent respiratory illnesses, new allergies, new medications that may have ototoxic side effects, recreational activities (e.g., swimming), and situations (e.g., day care) that may predispose the child to ear infections. The history should also include questions about any parental concerns regarding the child's speech patterns or ability to hear. The provider should always ask how many languages are spoken in the home, as exposure to more than one language may delay language development (Kohnert, 2010). A focused history is required when the child presents with a complaint related to the ear.

Past Medical History

Prenatal and Perinatal History • The PMH specific to the ear begins with an assessment of the child's prenatal and perinatal course. The provider should inquire about prenatal maternal infection with pathogens that can cause congenital sensorineural hearing loss (SNHL) in the infant. These pathogens include cytomegalovirus, herpes simplex, mumps, rubella (congenital rubella syndrome), rubeola, parvovirus B-19, human immunodeficiency virus (HIV), toxoplasmosis, and syphilis (Shah & Lotke, 2013). The provider should also inquire about what prescribed medications were taken by the child's mother during pregnancy. Fetal exposure to ototoxic drugs increases the risk of SNHL (Table 14.1).

TABLE 14.1	Causes of Sensorineural Hearing Loss in Children
CAUSES	**EXAMPLES**
Anatomic	Congenital temporal bone abnormalities, otosclerosis, and osteogenesis imperfecta
Autoimmune/metabolic	Juvenile rheumatoid arthritis, systemic lupus erythematosus, Cogan's syndrome, hypothyroidism, and type 1 diabetes
Genetic/syndromic	Neurofibromatosis type II Syndromes: Alport, CHARGE, DiGeorge sequelae, Jervell Lange-Nielsen, Klippel-Feil sequelae, Noonan, Usher, and Waardenburg
Infectious	Cytomegalovirus; herpes simplex; rubella, mumps, measles; parvovirus B-19; HIV; *Haemophilus influenzae* type B meningitis; *Streptococcus pneumoniae* meningitis; congenital toxoplasmosis; varicella and congenital syphilis
Ototoxic exposures	Drugs: aminoglycosides; loop diuretics; antimalarial agents, especially quinine derivatives; antineoplastic agents; anti-inflammatory agents, including aspirin and naproxen
Pre-, Peri-, Neonatal	Fetal exposure to alcohol, isotretinoin, thalidomide, cisplatin, or mercury; hyperbilirubinemia and kernicterus in the newborn
Traumatic	Temporal bone fractures, head trauma, child abuse, sports injuries, noise, penetrating foreign bodies, and iatrogenic trauma (i.e., radiation therapy, surgery, ototoxic drugs, ECMO)

ECMO, extracorporeal membrane oxygenation; HIV, human immunodeficiency virus.
Sources: Kujawa and Liberman (2009); Shah and Lotke (2013).

Maternal alcohol, tobacco, or illegal drug use that occurred prenatally should also be assessed. Fetal alcohol syndrome (FAS) can cause ear deformities, hearing loss, and language impairment (Vaux & Chambers, 2012). Smoking during pregnancy often leads to low birth weight and prematurity, both of which can lead to SNHL; prenatal maternal smoking can also lead to an increased number of respiratory infections, otitis media, and asthma in children (Cheraghi & Salvi, 2009). The use of cocaine during pregnancy has been associated with renal disorders such as multicystic renal dysplasia, which includes nonrenal malformations such as low-set ears and preauricular pits (Swiatecka-Urban, 2013).

The child's perinatal course is also important to investigate because prematurity, perinatal asphyxia, birth trauma, infection, hyperbilirubinemia, and the use of ototoxic drugs in the nursery can all lead to SNHL (Shah & Lotke, 2013). The provider should note any congenital syndromes, including chromosomal anomalies associated with ear deformities, craniofacial abnormalities, or renal disorders, such as trisomy 18, Down syndrome, Pierre Robin syndrome, cleft lip and palate, Wilms' tumor, or renal agenesis.

Review of Systems • In addition to the prenatal and perinatal histories, the pediatric review of systems (ROS) relative to the ear involves asking the parent or caregiver about the child's usual state of health, focusing on common childhood illnesses that may affect the child's ear or hearing. This includes determining if the child has had frequent upper respiratory illnesses, such as nasopharyngitis, tonsillitis, and pharyngitis. The number of episodes of acute otitis media (AOM) should be determined, including whether otitis media with effusion (OME) has occurred after the acute infections. Chronic OME is associated with CHL in children. The provider should also note whether the child has ever been diagnosed with mastoiditis, meningitis, or encephalitis, all of which can be complicated by hearing loss. In young children, disorders of the ear that disrupt hearing can interfere with speech and language development. The provider should inquire about any episodes of otitis externa, and any oral or dental infections should be noted. Other related assessments include:

- **General health:** Usual state of health; recent and recurrent febrile illnesses, such as respiratory illnesses and AOM; immunization history; history of chemotherapy for cancer treatment; sleep patterns (poor sleep may be because of ear pain or enlarged adenoidal tissue); history of congenital syndromes or chromosomal abnormalities involving the ear; history of head injuries; and seasickness
- **Head:** Microcephaly, facial asymmetry or deformities, depressed nasal bridge, and absent philtrum, which may indicate FAS

- **Skin:** Sunburn of pinnae; pruritus or rashes of the external ear, which may be caused by otitis externa or by middle ear drainage; and café-au-lait spots, which may suggest neurofibromatosis
- **Eyes:** Eye drainage, swelling, itching, excessive tearing (because of sinusitis), and nystagmus (from vertigo)
- **Ears:** Number of episodes of AOM; history of OME; presence of tympanostomy tubes, or tympanic membrane perforation; otitis externa, cholesteatoma, otorrhea, otalgia, and mastoiditis; ear deformities (e.g., microtia), ear pits, and history of a foreign body in the ear; signs of hearing loss such as the need to repeat questions, child speaks loudly, or inattentiveness, especially when the child's back is turned to the person speaking; hearing aids; cochlear implants; and date and results of last objective hearing assessment
- **Nose:** Nasal congestion or discharge; frequent upper respiratory infections, which can lead to AOM; and choanal atresia
- **Mouth/throat:** Tooth decay and dental infections, (which may indicate bottle-propping), can lead to AOM and ear pain; tonsillitis, pharyngitis, and cleft lip or palate can lead to multiple episodes of AOM
- **Respiratory:** Cough, asthma, respiratory illnesses (respiratory infections associated with fever or ear infections), and sinusitis, which can cause otalgia
- **Genitourinary:** History of congenital genitourinary system malformations (associated with congenital ear abnormalities), hematuria, and recurrent urinary tract infections
- **Musculoskeletal:** Temporomandibular joint (TMJ) pain and bruxism, which may cause otalgia
- **Neurologic:** Migraines, nystagmus, vertigo, tinnitus, bacterial meningitis, seizure disorders, and brain tumors
- **Hematologic:** Jaundice, hyperbilirubinemia, ABO incompatibility, and history of exchange transfusion
- **Metabolic:** Hypothyroidism
- **Developmental:** Achievement of language milestones, behavioral problems, school performance, school absences, and school failure, which may be because of hearing loss

Immunizations • The provider should assess the child's immunization status to be certain that all age-appropriate immunizations are up-to-date. This is especially true of immunizations for *Haemophilus influenzae* type B and *Streptococcus pneumoniae*; both of these pathogens can cause bacterial meningitis, which can lead to permanent damage of the auditory nerve and subsequent deafness. Pneumococcal conjugate vaccine also helps prevent some episodes of AOM. Measles, mumps, and rubella infections can also cause hearing loss in children (Shah & Lotke, 2013).

Allergies • The provider should inquire about allergies to medications as well as environmental allergies. Allergic rhinitis can cause nasal symptoms, including swelling of the nasal turbinates and enlarged tonsillar and adenoidal tissue, which can predispose children to AOM, OME, sinusitis, vertigo, and hearing loss. The provider should also inquire about any recent exposures that may have caused contact dermatitis of the ear and surrounding area such as nickel jewelry, soaps, shampoos, hair-styling products, perfumes, or cosmetics.

Hospitalizations • The provider should ask about past hospitalizations, including dates and length of stay, focusing on the reason for the hospitalization and whether it bears any relevance to the health of the child's ear or hearing. For example, a history of hospitalization for bacterial meningitis is important because of the possibility of permanent auditory nerve damage and subsequent SNHL as a consequence of the infection or use of ototoxic drugs such as aminoglycosides.

Injuries • It is important for the provider to determine whether the child has sustained any head, brain, or ear injuries. Injuries to the head or ear may affect the child's hearing secondary to tympanic membrane scarring, inner ear damage, or intracranial edema. Types of injuries to inquire about include any head trauma, such as concussion, skull fractures, temporal bone fractures, or trauma intentionally inflicted on the infant or child (e.g., through forceful shaking or blows to the side of the head). The provider should also inquire about any direct ear trauma that may be the result of the child placing objects in the external auditory canal, causing perforation of the tympanic membrane. It is important for the provider to investigate whether the child has suffered any iatrogenic head trauma (e.g., radiation therapy, surgery,

extracorporeal membrane oxygenation [ECMO]), or chronic exposure to loud noises (Shah & Lotke, 2013).

Past Surgical History

The provider should ask about any previous surgeries the child has had, including the dates of any surgeries and if there were any complications. Special attention should be paid to any ear surgery (e.g., myringotomy with tympanostomy), nose and throat surgery (e.g., tonsillectomy, adenoidectomy), intracranial surgeries, excision of a cholesteatoma, or dental surgery. Any of these surgical procedures, especially if recent, can be the cause of past or current complaints related to the ear, such as otalgia or hearing loss. Complaints related to the ear may also be an indication for the surgical procedure (e.g., chronic otitis media).

Current Medications

The provider should inquire about all medications that the child is currently taking, noting whether any of the drugs have ototoxic or vestibulotoxic side effects. Examples of these drugs include some antibiotics, especially the aminoglycosides; loop diuretics; anti-inflammatory agents, such as salicylates and some nonsteroidal anti-inflammatory drugs (NSAIDs); some chemotherapeutic agents (e.g., vincristine, cisplatin); and antimalarial agents (e.g., quinine) (Shah & Lotke, 2013). Medications that can cause tinnitus include some antibiotics, analgesics, antihistamines, anticonvulsants, diuretics, and chemotherapeutic agents (Bisht & Bist, 2011); specific medications are listed in Table 14.2. Salicylates, aminoglycosides, anticonvulsants, quinine, and loop diuretics can also cause vertigo (Mudd, Edmunds, Glatz, Campbell, & Rybak, 2012).

TABLE 14.2 Medications That Can Cause Tinnitus	
TYPE OF MEDICATION	**EXAMPLES**
Analgesics	Aspirin and ibuprofen
Antibiotics	Clarithromycin, ciprofloxacin, and tetracycline
Anticonvulsants	Carbamazepine, fosphenytoin, and amitriptyline
Antihistamines	Chlorpheniramine
Chemotherapeutic agents	Chemotherapeutic drugs containing platinum compounds (e.g., cisplatin)
Diuretics	Furosemide

Source: Bisht and Bist (2011).

Family History

Any family history of congenital or acquired hearing loss or other problems related to the ear is important for the provider to establish. Many of these conditions are genetic or inherited, such as allergies, which may lead to chronic OME. In addition to inquiring about any family history of allergies, the provider should ask about any family history of congenital syndromes or genetic disorders that are associated with ear conditions or hearing loss such as Down syndrome, FAS, Alport syndrome, neurofibromatosis type II, congenital rubella syndrome, Pierre-Robin syndrome, trisomy 13, and cleft lip or palate. Waardenburg syndrome is the most common inherited cause of hearing loss (Dourmishev & Janniger, 2013; Shah & Lotke, 2013). Characteristics of Waardenburg syndrome include hypertelorism (wide-set eyes), alterations in pigmentation of the hair, skin, and iris (e.g., a forelock of white hair, patches of white pigmentation of the skin, very pale irises, brilliantly blue irises, irises that are two different colors [heterochromia]), lateral displacement of the inner canthus of each eye, and SNHL (Dourmishev & Janniger, 2013). The provider should also assess for any family history of kidney malformations or disorders.

Social History

The social history focuses on aspects of the family's living conditions, lifestyle, and any risk factors that could predispose the child to ear infections or hearing problems. These risk factors include crowded living conditions, secondhand smoke exposure, day-care attendance, and bottle propping, all of which increase the incidence of middle ear and respiratory infections in children. The provider should also ask whether the infant is breastfed or formula-fed. Breastfeeding the infant for at least the first 6 months of life helps protect against middle ear infections because of protective antibodies transferred through the breast milk (Lieberthal et al., 2013) and because of the relatively upright position in which the infant is held during breastfeeding, which helps to prevent milk from draining into the nasopharynx. The provider should ask if the child or adolescent is chronically exposed to loud noise, which can lead to permanent hearing loss (Kujawa & Liberman, 2009).

The provider should determine how many languages the child is exposed to at home, in school, or in day care. If a young child is exposed to more than one language during the normal language-acquisition sequence, this may cause inaccuracies in syntax (Goldstein, Fabiano, & Washington, 2005; Paradis, 2005). It is important for the provider to be sure that the delay in speech development is a result of a bilingual home environment and not a consequence of hearing loss. It is also important for the provider to ask about the child's school progress or any behavior problems reported by either the parent or the teacher. Difficulty in school, inattentiveness, or even school failure may indicate hearing impairment.

The provider should assess the child's sleep patterns. Poor sleep may be the result of otalgia that is often exacerbated when the child is recumbent. Bruxism can also cause temporomandibular joint pain, which can be referred to the ear (Blume & Szperka, 2010). The provider should ask if the child or adolescent is involved in any recreational activities that could potentially affect the ear, such as swimming, scuba diving, or boxing. Prolonged contact with water predisposes the child or adolescent to otitis externa; boxing increases the risk of direct injury to the ear.

The PMH relative to the ear is best tailored to the child's age, as certain assessments are only relevant to that particular age group (e.g., bottle-propping, attendance at day care). Table 14.3 summarizes the history pertinent to the ear, according to age and developmental stage.

History of Present Illness

Common complaints related to the ear that are seen in the pediatric population include otalgia (with or without fever), otorrhea, hearing loss, and less commonly tinnitus, dizziness, and vertigo. If a child presents with an ear-related complaint, the provider should obtain a focused history (i.e., history of the present illness [HPI]) to make an accurate diagnosis. Relevant questions to ask for the HPI can be found in Table 14.4. Questions to ask when the chief complaint is hearing loss are found under Assessment of Hearing Acuity, later in the chapter.

Physical Examination

Physical examination of the ear includes inspection and palpation of the external ear; inspection of the external auditory canal and tympanic membrane, including otoscopic examination; and auditory acuity testing. The necessary equipment includes the following:

- Penlight
- Otoscope with halogen bulb and nickel-cadmium batteries (not alkaline batteries)
- Ear specula (4–6 mm tip diameter for adolescents; 3–4 mm for children; 2 mm for infants)
- Rubber squeeze bulb attachment for the otoscope
- Latex or vinyl gloves (to be worn when blood or drainage from the ear is noted)
- Watch with a second hand for the Romberg test

TABLE 14.3	Past Medical History for Ear Assessment by Age and Developmental Stage
AGE GROUP	**SUBJECTIVE DATA TO GATHER**
Neonate	Is there a history of maternal infection prenatally (e.g., TORCH infections)? Is there a history of maternal smoking, drug, or alcohol use during pregnancy? Is there a history of maternal diabetes, Rh incompatibility, or toxemia? Was neonate born prematurely? What was infant's birth weight? Did neonate spend more than 48 hours in a neonatal intensive care unit? Was neonate treated with aminoglycosides, furosemide, or any other ototoxic drugs? Was neonate born with any craniofacial anomalies such as cleft lip or palate or others with morphologic abnormalities of the pinna and ear canal? Was neonate diagnosed with any renal disorder at birth? Did neonate have hyperbilirubinemia, kernicterus, or an exchange transfusion? Did neonate have a history of asphyxia at birth, ECMO therapy, persistent pulmonary hypertension, sepsis, or bacterial meningitis? What were the results of the newborn hearing screening? Is there a family history of sensorineural hearing loss?
Infant	Has infant ever been diagnosed with AOM with or without effusion? Was he or she treated with antibiotics? Is there a history of otorrhea? Does infant have frequent upper respiratory infections? Does infant attend day care? Do parents use cotton-tipped swabs to clean the ears? Is infant breastfed? If not, is infant's bottle propped during feedings? Is there a history of head trauma in the infant?
Toddler	Has toddler ever been diagnosed with AOM or OME? Have the infections been recurrent? Were the infections treated with antibiotics? Is there a history of otorrhea? Does toddler have frequent upper respiratory infections? Does toddler attend day care? Has toddler been diagnosed with allergies? Does toddler ever pull on his or her ears or put small objects in them? Do parents use cotton-tipped swabs to clean the ears? Does toddler still drink from a bottle or no-spill sippy cup? Is the bottle or cup propped? Is there a history of head trauma in the toddler?
Preschooler	Has child ever been diagnosed with AOM or OME? Was the infection treated with antibiotics? Is there a history of otorrhea? Does child have frequent upper respiratory infections? Has child been diagnosed with allergies? Does child have a history of surgery for tympanostomy, tonsillectomy, or adenoidectomy? Does child attend day care? Does child pull at or put small objects in his or her ears? Do parents use cotton-tipped swabs to clean the ears? Does child drink from a bottle or no-spill sippy cup while lying down? Does child have a history of head trauma?
School-aged child or adolescent	Has child or adolescent had frequent upper respiratory infections or been diagnosed with allergies? Any episodes of AOM? If so, were they treated with antibiotics? Does child or adolescent have a history of surgery for tympanostomy, tonsillectomy, or adenoidectomy? Is there a history of otorrhea? Ear pain? Does child or adolescent swim frequently or been diagnosed with otitis externa? Does child or teen use cotton-tipped swabs to clean the ears? Has child or adolescent ever complained of dizziness or ringing in the ears? Does child or adolescent have a history of head trauma? Does child or adolescent listen to exceptionally loud music on a regular basis with or without headphones? Does adolescent attend rock concerts frequently?

AOM, acute otitis media; ECMO, extracorporeal membrane oxygenation; OME, otitis media with effusion; TORCH, toxoplasmosis, other (congenital syphilis and viruses), rubella, cytomegalovirus, herpes simplex virus.

TABLE 14.4	History of Present Illness: Ear-Related Complaints	
SYMPTOM	**ASSESSMENTS**	**EXPLICATION**
Otalgia or ear pain in children can be primary, arising from the ear itself, or secondary, such as referred pain from areas near the ear (e.g., the mastoid bone, mouth, jaw, neck).	Was onset sudden or gradual?	AOM is associated with a rapid onset of pain. Both AOM and otitis externa are associated with a considerable amount of pain. OME does not cause pain.
	What is the duration and severity of the pain? What is the character of the pain? Is it sharp or dull?	Severe, sharp pain occurs with TM rupture, and then the pain subsides. When age-appropriate, a quantitative pain assessment should be done (see Chapter 6).

TABLE 14.4	History of Present Illness: Ear-Related Complaints (*continued*)	
SYMPTOM	**ASSESSMENTS**	**EXPLICATION**
	What is the location of the pain?	Is the pain on the pinna, in the external auditory canal, inside ear, or in the mastoid area? Pain only on the pinna and in the external auditory canal suggests otitis externa; pain felt inside the ear suggests AOM; postauricular pain or tenderness suggests mastoiditis.
	Does the pain radiate to the ear?	Pain that radiates to the ear can be because of dental disorders, bruxism, mouth infections, TMJ problems, sinusitis, neck problems, tonsillitis, pharyngitis, mastoiditis, and temporal bone fractures (Li & Brunk, 2013). Neck pain from traumatic injury can refer to the ears.
	What is the frequency of the pain?	Continuous pain suggests AOM. Pain with chewing points to otitis externa, dental disorders, or TMJ problems.
	What precipitates the pain or makes it worse?	Lying down can increase the pain of middle or external ear infections, causing an inability to sleep. Pain precipitated by pressure on the tragus suggests otitis externa. Pain with AOM worsens with sucking or swallowing.
	What alleviates the pain?	The provider should ascertain whether over-the-counter pain medications are sufficient to alleviate the pain, and if any nonpharmacologic measures have been used, such as heat application.
	Are there any associated symptoms?	Fever, rhinorrhea, nasal congestion, sneezing, diarrhea, vomiting, loss of appetite, and pulling or tugging at the ear are associated with AOM. A feeling of fullness in the ear points to OME. Otorrhea, fever, and itching can indicate AOM, otitis externa, or chronic suppurative otitis media. Edema, erythema, pain, and itching of the pinna can indicate otitis externa. Fever can also be caused by upper respiratory infections, dental infections, or mastoiditis. Neck pain, swelling, and erythema of the mastoid area, and a displaced pinna are associated with mastoiditis. Neck pain can also be associated with meningitis. Tinnitus and vertigo with otalgia may result from direct trauma to the ear. Hearing loss may be the result of intracranial infection or OME.
	Is there any concurrent illness? Close contacts with similar symptoms?	Upper respiratory infections predispose infants and young children to AOM.
	Has child experienced an injury?	Injuries to the face, head, and neck or directly to the ear can cause otalgia.
Otorrhea or ear drainage in children can be caused by acute or chronic infections of the external or middle ear, injuries to the ear, TM, perforation, or head trauma.	Was onset gradual or sudden?	AOM can cause spontaneous rupture of the TM, resulting in sudden onset of otorrhea. Otitis externa can also cause acute otorrhea. Gradual onset of otorrhea can be because of the presence of a foreign body in the external auditory canal (Heim & Maughan, 2007).
	How long has drainage been present?	Otorrhea that lasts more than 14 days can be because of CSOM, cholesteatoma, or foreign body. Chronic otorrhea can also be a complication of tympanostomy tube placement.
	Location of otorrhea?	Provider should note whether ear drainage is unilateral or bilateral. Unilateral otorrhea is likely a foreign body in the ear; bilateral otorrhea may indicate TM rupture.
	Any recent injury?	Direct trauma to the head can cause ear drainage.

(continued)

TABLE 14.4	History of Present Illness: Ear-Related Complaints (*continued*)	
SYMPTOM	**ASSESSMENTS**	**EXPLICATION**
	What is the color and character of ear drainage?	Clear, mucoid drainage can be because of OME with TM perforation. Clear to purulent otorrhea is associated with granular myringitis (Levi, Ames, Gitman, Morlet, & O'Reilly, 2013). Purulent yellow or green drainage indicates AOM with perforation or otitis externa; basilar skull fracture causes clear, watery (CSF) or bloody ear drainage; bloody ear drainage can also be caused by trauma to the external auditory canal. Brown otorrhea is likely cerumen.
	Does the ear drainage have an odor?	Malodorous ear drainage can be associated with mastoiditis.
	Are there any associated symptoms?	Fever, rhinorrhea, otalgia, fullness in the ear, itching, vertigo, tinnitus, and headache are all associated with ear disorders such as AOM, OME, otitis externa, ear trauma, and mastoiditis (see Otalgia, above). Dizziness, hearing loss, or meningitis can be associated with CSF leaks (Hanson & Kwartler, 2012).
	Is there any concurrent illness or injury?	Upper respiratory infections predispose young children to AOM. Cholesteatoma, granulomas, or polyps of the TM can bleed easily; all potentially cause otorrhea. Basilar skull fractures can cause clear otorrhea, which is CSF.
	Is child complaining of itching?	Itching with otorrhea is associated with otitis externa.
	Does child or adolescent swim frequently?	Frequent swimming can predispose child or adolescent to otitis externa ("swimmer's ear"), which can cause otorrhea.
	How does parent or child clean the ears?	Use of cotton-tipped swabs can injure the external auditory canal, perforate the TM, and cause cerumen impaction.
	Does child place things in his or her ears?	A retained foreign body in the external auditory canal can be the cause of otorrhea; placing sharp objects in the ear can cause trauma to the external auditory canal or TM, also causing infection, bleeding, or otorrhea.
	Are there any alleviating factors?	Provider should ask about any measures used to alleviate the ear drainage, such as use of medications or packing the ear.
	Is there anything that makes the otorrhea worse?	Recumbent position may increase otorrhea.
Tinnitus or ringing in the ears often precedes SNHL in children and adolescents who are chronically exposed to loud noise.	Was onset sudden or gradual?	Sudden onset tinnitus can be caused by AOM, nasopharyngeal infections, environmental allergies, trauma to the ear, barotrauma, vasovagal syncope, head and neck injury, and the current use of ototoxic drugs. Gradual onset tinnitus can be caused by TMJ disorders.
	Location of the tinnitus?	Provider should note whether tinnitus is unilateral or bilateral.
	Is the tinnitus high or low pitched?	High-pitched tinnitus is associated with SNHL; low-pitched tinnitus is associated with CHL.
	Are there any associated symptoms?	Nausea, vomiting, otalgia, otorrhea, fever, itching, hearing loss, dizziness, unsteady gait, seizures, and a feeling of fullness in the ear are all signs and symptoms seen with AOM, OME, or vertigo, all of which can be associated with tinnitus.
	Is there any concurrent illness or injury?	Head trauma, ear infection, ruptured TM, or inner ear disturbances can cause tinnitus.

TABLE 14.4	History of Present Illness: Ear-Related Complaints (*continued*)	
SYMPTOM	**ASSESSMENTS**	**EXPLICATION**
	Is child currently taking any medications?	Some medications cause tinnitus such as NSAIDs, certain antibiotics and antidepressants, and antihistamines.
	What precipitates the tinnitus or makes it worse?	Loud noises can precipitate tinnitus, especially if chronic.
	What makes the tinnitus better?	Certain medications (e.g., sedatives) can improve tinnitus; nonpharmacologic measures such as "white noise" makers can also help tinnitus.
Vertigo is a type of dizziness characterized by a spinning sensation. It is caused by inner ear or auditory nerve (vestibular branch) disturbances.	When was the onset of the vertigo? Is the vertigo constant, or does it come and go?	Long periods of vertigo are associated with vestibular disorders, diabetes, or hypothyroidism.
	What is the severity of the vertigo?	Changes in the activities of daily living and the ability to attend work or school help assess severity.
	Was onset gradual or sudden?	Sudden onset of vertigo may be because of the rupture of the round window in the inner ear.
	Are there associated symptoms (e.g., fever, nausea, vomiting, sweating, nystagmus, tinnitus, otalgia, otorrhea, hearing loss, visual disturbances, aphasia, ataxia, altered LOC, fainting, headache)?	Vertigo in children and adolescents can be because of motion sickness, migraine, vasovagal syncope, brain injury, tumors, or infections.
	Is there any concurrent illness or recent injury?	Head trauma, whiplash, or a severe upper respiratory infection can cause vertigo.
	Is child currently taking any medications?	Certain drugs can cause vertigo (e.g., aminoglycosides, loop diuretics, anticonvulsants, analgesics, hypnotics, antihypertensives).
	What precipitates the vertigo or makes it worse?	Vertigo may occur when the child changes positions, coughs, sneezes, or blows the nose.
	What makes the vertigo better?	Some medications prescribed for motion sickness (e.g., diphenhydramine) may be helpful; nonpharmacologic measures such as position changes may alleviate the vertigo.

AOM, acute otitis media; CSF, cerebrospinal fluid; CSOM, chronic suppurative otitis media; LOC, level of consciousness; NSAID, nonsteroidal anti-inflammatory drug; OME, otitis media with effusion; SNHL, sensorineural hearing loss; TM, tympanic membrane; TMJ, temporomandibular joint.

General Appearance

The provider should begin the physical examination by first inspecting the child's general appearance. This includes observing the child's gait. An unsteady gait or falling may indicate vertigo or a neurologic problem. If the child is verbal, his or her speech should be noted for articulation and intensity. Children who speak too loudly or cannot clearly articulate speech may be suffering from hearing loss. Speech delays may also indicate hearing deficits or hearing loss. The provider should also assess the child's response to verbal instructions. If the child is unable to follow instructions, it may be because of a language barrier, developmental delay, depression, or hearing loss. The provider should note any craniofacial anomalies, which potentially affect hearing (see later section on Assessment of Hearing Acuity).

External Ear

Inspection • The provider should begin inspection of the external ear by examining the pinnae for placement and position. To allow for a proper view of the pinnae, the young infant should be held upright or the child should be seated with the examiner seated or standing at eye level. The provider should measure the height of the pinna by drawing an imaginary horizontal line from the outer canthus of the eye to the occiput. The top of the pinna should meet or cross this line, deviating no more than 10 degrees from a line perpendicular to the horizontal line (Figure 14.5). Low-set ears are associated with renal agenesis, congenital genitourinary disorders, and chromosomal abnormalities such as Turner syndrome, Down syndrome, and trisomy 18 (Gaylord & Yetman, 2013).

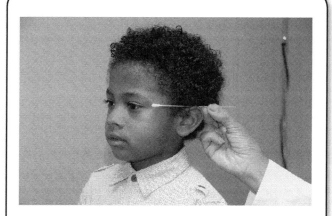

FIGURE 14.5 Ear placement. The outer canthus of the eye should be in alignment with the tip of the pinna.

The pinnae should also be inspected for size, shape, symmetry, and deformity. The pinna should be symmetrical and completely formed, with a patent external auditory canal. Excessively small ears (microtia) may indicate a congenital syndrome or congenital hearing loss. A helix that has an upward or backward slant is within normal limits. Helical-fold abnormalities, asymmetry, or abnormal shape of the pinnae, an absent tragus, or a narrow external auditory canal are associated with renal disease, some congenital syndromes, and chromosomal anomalies (Ostrower, Bent, & Austin, 2013).

The provider should also inspect the external ear for preauricular skin tags or pits. Small skin tags on or anterior to the tragus are most often remnants of embryonic development. Preauricular skin tags are not clinically significant but merely cosmetic, and they can be surgically removed (Ostrower et al., 2013). Ear pits are fistulas that are located anterior to the tragus and arise during embryonic development. They can be unilateral or bilateral. Ear pits may be associated with urinary tract abnormalities (Swiatecka-Urban, 2013) or congenital syndromes (Ostrower et al., 2013). Ear pits are usually of no consequence unless they become infected, which can lead to cellulitis and abscess formation (Ostrower et al., 2013).

The provider should also inspect the ears for flattening or protrusion. The neonate's pinnae are normally flat against the head. In older infants and children, the pinna normally extends slightly outward. Flattened ears in older infants may indicate a prolonged side-lying position; the provider should address infant stimulation needs with the primary caregiver and assess the child for possible neglect. Protruding ears (relative to the size of the concha) may be familial or, depending on the degree of protrusion, may indicate localized swelling because of mastoiditis, mumps, or postauricular abscess. Children with fragile X syndrome have large, protruding ears (Jewell, 2013). The provider should assess the parent's pinnae for comparison. In some children, the lobule is adherent, which is a normal variation.

The provider should also inspect the pinnae for any lesions, inflammation, or signs of infection. Erythema or flaking of the skin may indicate contact or atopic dermatitis. Erythema, swelling, or purulent discharge indicates infection such as the presence of a foreign body or otitis externa. Any ear piercings should be inspected for signs of infection.

Palpation • The provider should palpate each pinna, pulling it up and down or out and back, noting any masses or areas of pain or tenderness. Palpation should also include pushing on the tragus and applying pressure to the mastoid process, noting tenderness. The pinna should be soft, pliable, and nontender. If palpation of the pinna results in pain, the provider should suspect otitis externa, inflammation of the external auditory canal, trauma, or local infection. The provider should palpate the mastoid process as well as the preauricular and postauricular lymph nodes. Auricular lymphadenopathy often accompanies ear infections (see Chapter 13). Pain elicited with palpation of the mastoid process indicates mastoiditis.

External Auditory Canal

Inspection • To begin inspection of the external auditory canal, a penlight can be used to visualize the outer portion of the canal. For optimal visualization of the canal, when examining children aged 3 years and younger, the ear should be pulled downward, backward, and outward. For children older than 3, the pinna should be pulled upward, backward, and outward. The provider should inspect for drainage, edema, erythema, excessive cerumen, foreign bodies, and signs of inflammation or infection. The provider should note the color and consistency of any drainage. Inspection of the outer portion of the ear canal also helps the provider to determine the correct size of the speculum to place over the otoscope tip. Inspection of the internal portion of the external auditory canal and tympanic membrane is performed with an otoscope.

Otoscopic Examination • The otoscope, an instrument used to examine the external auditory canal and tympanic membrane, includes a halogen light, magnifying lens, and an appropriately sized ear speculum. Nickel-cadmium batteries are preferred over alkaline batteries because as alkaline batteries become weak, the light of the otoscope becomes yellowish and dim, which can confuse assessment findings. The light of the otoscope should be bright and white to make the most accurate assessments. A pneumatic bulb attachment is also necessary for insufflation of the tympanic membrane. The provider should wear gloves if any ear drainage is noted.

Older infants and toddlers are normally very resistant to the otoscopic examination. Thus, this procedure is best accomplished at the end of the physical examination for this age group. It may be helpful for the provider to allow young children to inspect and touch the otoscope before the examination so that they become familiar with the equipment in an attempt to decrease their anxiety. Some providers may use puppets or other toys to prepare young children for this examination. Having the toddler sit on the mother's lap can greatly reduce anxiety, ultimately making the child more cooperative. See Chapter 8 for a more in-depth discussion of developmental approaches to examining young children.

Proper positioning of the infant or young child during the otoscopic examination minimizes pain and unintentional injury and maximizes visualization to the external auditory canal and tympanic membrane. Young infants should be placed on the examination table for the otoscopic examination. Older infants and toddlers who can sit independently may be placed in the parent's lap, sitting sideways, with the child's head resting against the parent's chest. The parent can then assist with gentle immobilization of the child during the otoscopic examination. Older children may sit on the examination table.

Cerumen removal is an essential skill for the pediatric health care provider. It is necessary to relieve cerumen impaction and to visualize the tympanic membrane completely when otitis media is suspected. Cerumen should be removed under direct visualization with an otoscope, and the young child must be properly restrained during this procedure to avoid puncture to the tympanic membrane. To facilitate the removal of cerumen, ceruminolytic and softening agents may be used, such as 1% sodium docusate solution, mineral oil, or triethanolamine polypeptide (Cerumenex). Once these agents are instilled, cerumen can be mechanically removed, either with a cerumen spoon or loop or by irrigation. Irrigation of the ear is contraindicated, however, in patients who have a perforated tympanic membrane or a tympanostomy tube in place.

For the otoscopic examination, the provider should choose the largest speculum that comfortably fits into the child's external auditory canal. The speculum should not be too small, as it can then enter too far into the canal and potentially cause injury. To visualize the tympanic membrane fully, the provider should remove any obstructing cerumen; lighting must be adequate. Holding the otoscope in an inverted position, securely braced against the child's head, the provider should insert it gently no more than one quarter to one half inch into the child's external auditory canal (Figure 14.6). To enhance the visualization of the tympanic membrane in children aged 3 years and younger, the provider should grasp the pinna and pull gently downward, outward, and backward, while directing the speculum upward. In children older than 3, the pinna should be pulled upward, backward, and slightly away from the head, and the speculum should be directed downward.

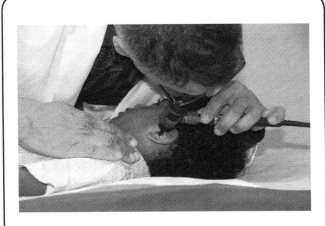

FIGURE 14.6 Secure positioning of a young child for an otoscopic examination.

Inspection of the External Auditory Canal • Using the otoscope, the provider should inspect the external auditory canal, rotating the otoscope as necessary to obtain a complete view. Normally, the external auditory canal is pink, with a small amount of fine hairs and orange to brown cerumen. If the canal is completely free of cerumen, the provider should inquire whether the child or parent uses cotton-tipped swabs to cleanse the canal; the use of these swabs should be discouraged as this can lead to cerumen impaction. There should be no signs of infection or inflammation. Abnormal findings during inspection of the external auditory canal include erythema, abrasions, scratches, lesions, swelling, drainage, scaling, exudate, excessive or impacted cerumen, foreign bodies, or foul odor. Inflammation of the external auditory canal can result from the presence of a foreign body, otitis externa, the use of cotton-tipped swabs to clean the ears, or slapping or hitting the child. Clear or bloody drainage from the ear may be cerebrospinal fluid or blood after a head injury; this finding signifies a basilar skull fracture and requires immediate intervention. Bloody drainage may be secondary to scratching or irritation. Purulent discharge from the ear is most often caused by otitis externa, a foreign body in the ear, or a ruptured tympanic membrane during an AOM infection.

Inspection of the Tympanic Membrane • In the newborn, only patency of the external auditory canal can be determined because of its small size; the tympanic membrane cannot be visualized because the view is obscured by vernix caseosa. In older infants and children, the tympanic membrane is inspected for color, anatomic landmarks, light reflex, contour, and mobility. Normally, the tympanic membrane is pearly gray to light pink. The only blood vessels that are normally visible are those on the periphery of the membrane. Erythema and injection can occur with AOM; injection alone may occur with allergies. An erythematous tympanic membrane can also be seen with fever or crying; this does not necessarily indicate infection. A bluish or purple, bulging tympanic membrane indicates blood in the middle ear, which may be because of trauma or basilar skull fracture.

The landmarks of the tympanic membrane should be easily visible on inspection, including the cone of light reflex. This reflex is seen at the "5 o'clock" position on the right and the "7 o'clock" position on the left. The ossicles should also be visible with the umbo near the middle of the tympanic membrane, the manubrium (handle of the malleus) near the membrane margin, and the short process of the malleus, visible at the "1 o'clock" position (see Figure 14.3).

The contour of the tympanic membrane is normally concave. There should be no bulging, retraction, or evidence of fluid behind the tympanic membrane. The membrane should be intact, without perforations; perforations appear as dark areas or holes in the tympanic membrane and most often occur as a result of a ruptured AOM or trauma. Healed perforations appear as dark patches on an otherwise normal tympanic membrane. If the child has had tympanostomy tubes placed, they will be visible upon inspection.

The presence of a middle ear infection or effusion can cause the contours and landmarks of the tympanic membrane to become distorted or absent as a result of fluid accumulation behind the membrane. For example, an immobile or discolored tympanic membrane indicates OME. With AOM, the light reflex becomes dull or absent, the ossicles may not be visible, and the tympanic membrane may be erythematous, opacified, full, or bulging. Amber-colored bubbles may be visible behind the tympanic membrane as fluid accumulates behind this structure; this indicates OME if accompanied by decreased movement of the tympanic membrane. The tympanic membrane should also be translucent when visualized, without scarring, opacity, or other lesions. Scarring appears as thickened, white areas on a pearly gray tympanic membrane and is most often a consequence of frequent episodes of a ruptured AOM. Bullae on the tympanic membrane, usually accompanied by tympanic membrane color, contour, and landmark changes, indicate bullous myringitis, which can also cause hearing loss (Uliyanov & Schweinfurth, 2012). A small, white cyst-like lesion on or behind the tympanic membrane indicates a cholesteatoma.

Pneumatic Otoscopy • The ability to perform pneumatic otoscopy is an essential skill for the pediatric health care provider to possess, as it is used to confirm the diagnoses of AOM and OME. The purpose of pneumatic otoscopy is to assess the mobility of the tympanic membrane, an important indicator of middle ear pressure. To diagnose AOM accurately, pneumatic otoscopy is necessary, unless the tympanic membrane is bulging.

Pneumatic otoscopy involves the following: (a) attaching a rubber pneumatic squeeze bulb to the otoscopic head (Figure 14.7); (b) squeezing the bulb to create gentle air pressure in the external auditory canal; and (c) assessing movement of the tympanic membrane. Before the insufflation of air, it is essential to have an adequate seal with the speculum and otoscope when it is placed in the external auditory canal. This is achieved by ensuring that the speculum is large enough to fit snugly in the child's external auditory canal. If the seal is adequate, brisk movement of the tympanic membrane is seen when air is injected; reduced or absent mobility suggests a nonpatent eustachian tube, fluid behind the tympanic membrane, or a possible tympanic membrane perforation. Equivocal assessment findings with pneumatic otoscopy can be supplemented with tympanometry or acoustic reflectometry and confirmed with tympanocentesis (see the section on Common Diagnostic Studies). Table 14.5 summarizes normal and abnormal findings of the tympanic membrane.

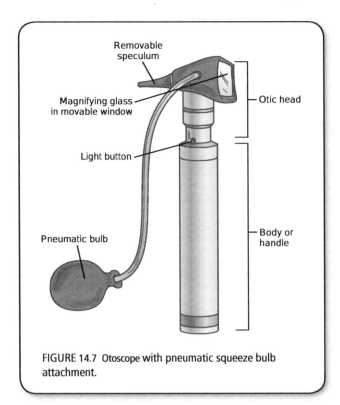

FIGURE 14.7 Otoscope with pneumatic squeeze bulb attachment.

Vestibular Testing • The Romberg test is done to evaluate the function of the vestibular apparatus in the inner ear, which helps to maintain balance and equilibrium. This test also evaluates cerebellar function and proprioception (see Chapter 22). To conduct the Romberg test, the provider should ask the child or adolescent to stand still, feet together, first with the eyes open, then with the eyes closed, and with the arms at the sides. The child or adolescent should be able to maintain this position for 20 seconds with minimal or no swaying. (The provider should stand near the child or adolescent in the event that leaning or falling occurs.) A positive Romberg test occurs when the child or adolescent cannot maintain balance with his or her eyes closed. If he or she leans to one side, moves the feet apart to prevent falling, or falls, this indicates a vestibular or cerebellar dysfunction or loss of proprioception. Vestibular testing to evaluate inner ear function can also be done by rotating the child in a complete circle in each direction, then observing for nystagmus. A normal finding is for the provider to see nystagmus in the same direction in which the child is rotated and in the opposite direction when the movement stops.

ASSESSMENT OF HEARING ACUITY

Assessment of hearing acuity in children is a crucially important component of pediatric health assessment. Children who cannot hear will not be able to acquire age-appropriate language skills, adversely affecting their social and academic abilities. Assessment of hearing involves reviewing the infant's or child's medical history to identify risk factors for hearing loss; listening to parental concerns about their child's hearing, speech, and language skills, or school performance; observing the child for behaviors that may indicate hearing loss; and conducting subjective and objective screening assessments for hearing acuity.

Types of Hearing Loss

There are four types of hearing loss: *conductive, sensorineural, mixed,* and *central.* CHL is caused by blocked

TABLE 14.5	Summary of Normal and Abnormal Findings With Inspection of the Tympanic Membrane	
ASSESSMENT	**NORMAL FINDINGS**	**ABNORMAL FINDINGS**
Color	Pearly gray to pink; injection at the periphery of the TM	Erythema (red) may indicate fever, crying, infection, trauma, or mastoiditis; a blue TM may indicate accumulation of blood, which is associated with trauma such as basilar skull fracture; a yellow TM may indicate AOM; a yellow, amber, or orange color behind TM indicates OME; white patches may indicate scarring or tympanosclerosis; a black spot on TM indicates possible perforation
Contour	Concave	Retracted or bulging TM
Integrity	Intact	Perforated or thickened TM
Landmarks	Light reflex; bony landmarks (ossicles), pars tensa, and pars flaccida easily seen	Decreased visibility of landmarks of TM indicates decreased transparency or altered contour of TM, which can indicate AOM or OME; prominent landmarks may indicate retracted TM
Lesions	None	Scarring; fluid, vesicles (bullae); or cysts (cholesteatoma)
Mobility	Mobile	Immobile; absence of TM movement with injection of a small puff of air via pneumatic otoscopy can indicate AOM or OME; excess mobility can indicate a healed perforation
Transparency	Translucent, shiny	Opacity

AOM, acute otitis media; OME, otitis media with effusion; TM, tympanic membrane.

transmission of sound waves through the external auditory canal to the inner ear, prohibiting sound impulses from reaching the auditory nerve. The most frequent cause of CHL in children is AOM and its sequela, OME (Harlor & Bower, 2009). Other causes include impacted cerumen, allergies, foreign bodies, a perforated tympanic membrane, cholesteatoma, or less frequently, congenital malformations of the pinna or external auditory canal (Harlor & Bower, 2009). CHL is transient, but recurrent episodes of OME during the early childhood stage of language acquisition can cause profound speech delay.

SNHL results from damage to the cochlea or auditory nerve fibers. The etiologies of SNHL are genetic, infectious, autoimmune, anatomic, traumatic, ototoxic, and idiopathic; the most common cause is genetic (see Table 14.1; Shah & Lotke, 2013). Risk factors for SNHL in newborns are summarized in Box 14.1. SNHL may be mild to profound, and the treatment depends on its cause (Shah & Lotke, 2013). Because SNHL is associated with poor school performance and behavioral problems, it is important for it to be promptly identified (Dedhia, Kitsko, Sabo, & Chi, 2013). *Noise-induced hearing loss* (NIHL) is a type of SNHL that is permanent but preventable and is caused by the inner ear's chronic exposure to extremely loud sounds, usually by recreational or occupational noise (Kujawa & Liberman, 2009). Adolescents can be at increased risk for NIHL by listening to excessively loud music (especially with headphones) and attending rock concerts frequently. Other sources of intense noise include firearms (e.g., rifle ranges, target shooting, hunting), recreational vehicles (e.g., motorcycles, snowmobiles) fireworks, and power tools.

Mixed hearing loss refers to a combination of CHL and SNHL; therefore, a problem must exist in both the middle and the inner ear for both types of hearing loss to occur.

Auditory neuropathy spectrum disorder is rare; it involves damage to the inner ear and auditory nerve that affects how the brain interprets sounds (Centers for Disease Control and Prevention, 2013).

History and Physical Examination

Speech and language development occur during the first years of life and depend on adequate hearing in the child. Early screening and identification of hearing loss in a young child are critical to ensure that appropriate treatment referrals are made before the critically sensitive period of time has closed for speech and language development (see Chapter 2).

History

Assessment of hearing in children begins with obtaining a history to determine risk factors for hearing loss. The child's PMH should be reviewed, with special attention to any history of prematurity, low birth weight, hyperbilirubinemia, asphyxia, or intrauterine or neonatal infection. A history of head trauma, bacterial meningitis, cleft lip or palate, mumps, repeated or chronic middle ear infections, exposure to ototoxic drugs, or chronic exposure to loud noise is important to ascertain, as any or all of these conditions may lead to hearing loss (Box 14.2; see also Box 14.1). The provider should also ask about any concerns expressed by the child's parent, day care provider, or teacher regarding the child's developmental, speech, hearing, or language abilities. Examples of these concerns may include the following: (a) the child asking "what" frequently during normal conversation: (b) the child asking for the volume of the television to be increased; (c) the child exhibiting learning difficulties in school; or (d) the child speaking later or less clearly than other children of the same age. The provider should inquire about whether the child uses a hearing aid. Any family history of congenital or permanent childhood hearing loss should be noted. The provider should also review the child's medical record for timing and acquisition of language milestones and determine the date of the child's last hearing assessment.

Physical Examination

The physical examination includes assessment for syndromic features, particularly of the head, face, or neck; craniofacial anomalies; or deformities of the pinna or ear canal. Certain conditions predispose children to CHL, such as cleft palate, which is readily apparent with palpation. Other etiologies of CHL can often be readily identified on physical examination with the visualization of foreign bodies or cerumen impaction or the diagnosis of AOM or middle ear effusion. Children with

---

BOX 14.1 • Risk Factors for Sensorineural Hearing Loss in Newborns

- An illness or condition requiring NICU admission for 48 hours or longer
- Stigmata for syndromes known to include hearing loss (e.g., Usher's syndrome, Waardenburg's syndrome)
- Family history of permanent childhood SNHL
- Perinatal infections (e.g., toxoplasmosis, bacterial meningitis, syphilis, rubella, cytomegalovirus, herpes virus)
- Craniofacial abnormalities (especially morphologic abnormalities of the pinna and ear canal)
- Ototoxic drug exposure
- Birth weight less than 1,500 g
- Hyperbilirubinemia, causing kernicterus or requiring exchange transfusion

NICU, neonatal intensive care unit; SNHL, sensorineural hearing loss.

Sources: Joint Commission on Infant Hearing (2013); Shah and Lotke (2013).

BOX 14.2 Risk Factors and Red Flags for Hearing Loss in Children Aged 29 Days to 2 Years

- Parent, caregiver, or teacher concern regarding hearing, speech, language, or developmental delay
- Family history of permanent childhood hearing loss
- Stigmata associated with syndromes known to include SNHL, CHL, or eustachian tube dysfunction
- Postnatal infections associated with SNHL (e.g., bacterial meningitis)
- In-utero infections such as cytomegalovirus, herpes, rubella, syphilis, or toxoplasmosis
- Neonatal indicators (e.g., hyperbilirubinemia requiring exchange transfusion, persistent pulmonary hypertension of newborn associated with mechanical ventilation, conditions requiring the use of ECMO)
- Neurodegenerative disorders (e.g., Hunter's syndrome) or sensorimotor neuropathies (e.g., Friedreich's ataxia, Charcot-Marie-Tooth syndrome)
- Syndromes associated with progressive hearing loss (e.g., neurofibromatosis, Usher syndrome, osteopetrosis)
- Head trauma
- Recurrent or persistent OME for at least 3 months

CHL, conductive hearing loss; ECMO, extracorporeal membrane oxygenation; OME, otitis media with effusion; SNHL, sensorineural hearing loss.

Source: Joint Commission on Infant Hearing (2013).

---

repeated episodes of AOM or middle ear effusions are at high risk for CHL. Equipment necessary for the assessment of hearing acuity in infants, children, and adolescents includes:

- Noisemakers (e.g., bells, squeeze toys, rattles, tissue paper)
- 512 Hz tuning fork
- Tympanometer
- Audiometer

To assess hearing accurately in infants and children, a developmental approach is necessary (Table 14.6).

Newborns • Newborns react to loud sounds with a startle (Moro) reflex or acoustic blink reflex and react to low-frequency sounds by quieting (see Table 14.6). Fluid or vernix in the external auditory canal of a newborn can affect the newborn's hearing. This subjective hearing screening is not fully reliable; currently, universal newborn hearing screening (UNHS) is required in 36 states and the District of Columbia (National Conference of State Legislators, 2011). UNHS uses objective physiologic methods such as auditory brainstem response or otoacoustic emission testing. States without a policy for newborn screening may do so selectively, especially for infants with specific risk factors (see Box 14.2).

Infants • To assess hearing in the infant, the provider should begin by selecting noisemakers that make sounds of different frequencies. The provider should then ask the parent to hold the infant in his or her lap, with the infant's back to the provider. The parent should engage the infant visually by showing the infant a brightly colored toy or stuffed animal. The provider should then stand approximately 2 feet behind the infant and make a noise with various noisemakers, taking care not to bump the examining table as this can also elicit the Moro reflex. Infants aged 4 months and younger should display the Moro or blink reflex; infants aged 6 months or older should react by turning their head toward the sound. Infants 9 months of age and older should be able to locate sound heard from below and the infant's side. If the infant does not display any of these responses, the provider should consider the possibility of hearing loss and refer the child for audiometric testing.

Toddlers and Preschool-Aged Children • Children aged 12 months and older should be able to localize all sounds they hear above, below, beside, and behind them when they cannot see where the provider stands as he or she makes the noise. Another way to test hearing in children in this age group is for the provider to stand approximately 2 to 3 feet (0.6 to 0.9 m) in front of the child and ask the child to do something, such as point to a body part or show the provider a toy, and then wait for the appropriate response. The provider should always be sure that the child can understand the language in which he or she is being addressed.

School-Aged Children or Adolescents • Children in this age group are developmentally able to cooperate with the whisper test and bone and air conduction tests (Weber and Rinne tests) (see next section, on Screening Tests for Hearing).

Screening Tests for Hearing

The American Academy of Pediatrics Committee on Practice and Ambulatory Medicine (2009) recommends both objective and subjective assessment of hearing in children, from birth through adolescence (Harlor & Bower, 2009). Subjective hearing screening is done at specified intervals during well-child assessments (see Chapter 9). Objective screening tests are done with UNHS, audiometric testing before entering school, parental concern about hearing, or delayed speech development.

TABLE 14.6	Developmental Milestones to Assess Hearing	
AGE	**ASSESSMENTS**	**RED FLAGS FOR HEARING LOSS**
Birth–3 months	Startles to loud noise (Moro reflex); acoustic blink reflex present; cessation of movement in response to low-pitched sounds (newborns); prefers human voice over any other sound; turns head to sound (when sound made at ear level (2–3 months); coos vowel sounds	Diminished or absent Moro reflex; does not awaken to noise
3–6 months	Recognizes and quiets to parent's voice; awakens to loud noises; looks toward sounds (beginning age 3–4 months); babbling, squealing, and giggling begins	Does not turn to sound; responds only to loud noises
6–9 months	Turns toward sound (begins at age 8 months); may respond to own name by age 6–8 months; understands "no" or "bye-bye"; babbles words beginning with a consonant	Does not localize sound after age 6 months; does not babble or babbling stops after age 6 months; responds only to loud noises
9–12 months	May repeat simple words; says "mama" or "dada" with meaning; reacts to music or singing; points to familiar objects	Indifferent to sound; responds only to loud noises
12–18 months	Locates sound by turning head to side and looking up or down; imitates sounds; points to "ask" for things; says 2–10 words, usually, "mama," "dada," "baba," or "bye-bye"	Speech development slower than peers; speaks unintelligibly or not at all; talking decreases; does not respond to name
18–24 months	Rapid language acquisition; should have approximately 20–50 expressive word vocabulary; puts two words together to "ask" question; points to body parts when asked; by age 18 months, begins to recognize noticeably dissimilar words; 50% of speech intelligible to strangers	Speaks unintelligibly or not at all; communicates through gestures, especially after age 15 months; easily frustrated when trying to communicate; may even have tantrums; prefers to play alone; shy and withdrawn; appears to be in his or her "own world"
Preschoolers	Hearing reaches maturity at age 3–4 years; should be speaking in sentences	Speaks unintelligibly or not at all, especially after age 24 months; communicates through gestures; does not hear television, telephone, or doorbell; prefers to play alone; shy and withdrawn Focuses on facial expressions when being spoken to; sits very close to television or turns the volume up very loudly; appears to be in his or her "own world"; often asks for statements to be repeated; hyperactive or inattentive
School-aged children and adolescents	Follows directions at school; auditory acuity reaches peak by age 13 years	Focuses on facial expressions when being spoken to; sits very close to television or turns the volume up very loudly; prefers to play alone; often asks for statements to be repeated; inattentive at school; poor school performance

Whisper Test

The whisper test is used as a gross measurement of hearing acuity in children. This test involves the ability to repeat words correctly that have been spoken in a whisper. The child must be old enough to understand the directions and cooperate with the examination. Children aged 3 years and older are usually developmentally able to cooperate with this assessment. The provider can use his or her judgment regarding whether the test is appropriate for a particular child. To conduct this test, the provider should stand 8 feet behind the child so he or she cannot see the provider's lips. The child should then be instructed to place his or her finger over the tragus of the left ear to obscure any sound. The provider then whispers a word with two distinct syllables toward child's right ear, and the child is asked to repeat the word. Then the process is repeated for the left ear. The child should be able to hear the two-syllable word with each ear and repeat it correctly. An inability to repeat the whispered words may indicate a hearing deficit, and the child should be referred for audiometric testing.

Conduction Tests

A tuning fork is used to evaluate hearing by assessing bone and air conduction of sound. These tests require cooperation of the child and are most useful when conducted on children school-aged and older who understand what is being asked of them during the examination and can follow directions.

Weber Test

The Weber test is done to differentiate conductive from SNHL. To conduct the Weber test, the provider should begin by gently striking the handle of a tuning fork (512 Hz) with one hand to make it vibrate, making sure that his or her hand does not touch the prongs of the tuning fork or the child's or adolescent's head. Next, the provider should place the handle of the tuning fork on the top of the child's or adolescent's head or in the middle of the forehead (Figure 14.8). The provider should then ask the child or adolescent if the sound is heard in the right ear, left ear, or in the middle of the forehead. Hearing the sound in the middle or equally in both ears is the normal response. If the child or adolescent responds that the sound is heard better on one side, the sound is said to be lateralized to that side. Sound is lateralized to the affected ear with CHL. With unilateral SNHL, sound is not heard on the affected side but lateralized to the unaffected ear.

Rinne Test

The Rinne test compares air conduction (AC) to bone conduction (BC) in each ear. To conduct this test, the provider taps the tuning fork softly to create vibration. The tuning fork should then be placed on the child's or adolescent's mastoid process to determine hearing via bone conduction (Figure 14.9). The provider asks if the sound is heard, then asks the child or adolescent to indicate when the sound is no longer audible. The tuning fork is then moved, tines facing forward, 1 to 2 cm in front of the external auditory canal (see Figure 14.9). Sound is transmitted via air conduction, so the provider should then ask the child or adolescent if sound is heard again; it should be. A Rinne test is normal (positive) when air conduction is at least twice as long as bone conduction (AC > BC). With CHL, bone conduction is heard longer than or as long as air conduction (BC > AC or BC = AC). With SNHL, air conduction is heard longer than bone conduction in the affected ear (AC > BC), but with less than a 2:1 ratio. Sound should be heard equally well in both ears.

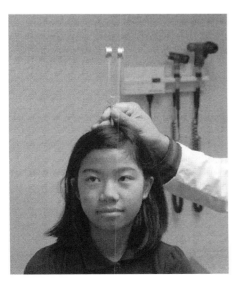

FIGURE 14.8 The Weber test to assess sound conduction via bone.

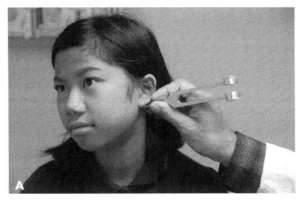

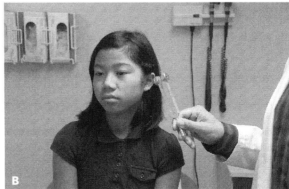

Figure 14.9 The Rinne test. **A.** The stem of the tuning fork is placed on the mastoid process and **B.** the child is asked to signal when the sound stops after the vibrating end of the tuning fork is moved and placed near the external auditory canal.

COMMON DIAGNOSTIC STUDIES

Various diagnostic studies may be used to formulate differential diagnoses related to disorders of the ear. When investigating hearing loss, diagnostic tests should be chosen depending on the type, duration, and progression of hearing loss in the infant or child (Harlor &

Bower, 2009). These studies could include laboratory tests of blood and urine, tympanometry, tympanocentesis, acoustic reflectometry, radiographic studies, and various audiologic tests. These diagnostic studies and their indications are summarized in Tables 14.7 and 14.8 (Harlor & Bower, 2009; Petersen-Smith & Becton McKenzie, 2013).

TABLE 14.7	Diagnostic Studies Associated With the Evaluation of Hearing and Ear Disorders		
TYPE OF TEST	**INDICATION**	**PROCEDURE**	**COMMENTS**
Laboratory studies: • Blood cultures • TORCH titers • Total and direct bilirubin • Thyroid function	Hearing loss (actual or potential)	Simple specimen collection	Infections such as bacterial meningitis may cause permanent hearing loss; TORCH infections, hyperbilirubinemia, and hypothyroidism in the neonate can cause hearing loss and should be treated
Tympanometry	Persistent OME; equivocal inspection findings with otoscopic examination in child for whom chronic AOM has been a problem and antibiotic use needs to be judicious	Assesses mobility of TM and presence of fluid in middle ear by applying air pressure into external auditory canal; pressure is interpreted in a graph called a tympanogram	Test not accurate in infants aged 6 months and younger because of increased flexibility and compliance of external auditory canal; ear canal must be free of cerumen for test to be accurate. Tympanogram results are described as follows: type A reflects a normal TM; type B suggests middle ear effusion; type C reflects negative middle ear pressure and can be associated with eustachian tube dysfunction.
Tympanocentesis	Chronic, persistent otitis media	Needle aspiration of middle ear fluid through TM for culture and identification of pathogen	Usually done by otolaryngologist
Acoustic reflectometry	To assess for presence of middle ear effusion	An acoustic transducer is placed in ear to measure amount of sound reflected back from TM; fluid decreases sound vibrations; presence of OME will cause more sound to bounce back to transducer to be displayed as a gradient	Painless; can be done in primary care office
Radiographic studies: • MRI • Renal ultrasound	May be indicated in the case of chronic ear disease or head trauma	As per radiology	MRI of head and brain can identify anatomic abnormalities or injuries; renal ultrasound is done to identify congenital renal abnormalities that may be associated with pinna deformities

AOM, acute otitis media; MRI, magnetic resonance imaging; OME, otitis media with effusion; TM, tympanic membrane; TORCH, toxoplasmosis, other (congenital syphilis and viruses), rubella, cytomegalovirus, herpes simplex virus.

TABLE 14.8	Screening Tests for Hearing in Children			
SCREENING TOOL	**AGE GROUP**	**DESCRIPTION**	**CLINICAL INDICATION**	**COMMENTS**
Subjective Hearing Assessments				
Moro (startle) reflex	Birth–age 4 months	Infant startles, arms abduct then adduct, and then infant (usually) cries in response to an unexpected loud noise (70 decibels [dB] or more)	Assesses both hearing and neurologic function	Care should be taken not to bump examining table or create air current; this can also elicit startle reflex; abnormal if persists longer than 4 months
Acoustic blink reflex	Birth–12 months	Provider stands approximately 12 in. (30 cm) from infant's head and makes sudden, loud noise (70 dB or more); infant blinks in response to loud noise	Assesses both hearing and neurologic function (cranial nerve VIII)	Low sensitivity; provider should avoid creating air current; this can also cause infant to blink, confusing assessment findings. Repeated attempts to elicit reflex can cause habituation (reflex disappears); no blink response should be followed with objective hearing screening
Language screening	Effective once language has begun to develop; see text regarding bilingual children	Language screening is done to determine whether acquisition of language skills is normal (hearing deficits can affect language skills)	Clinical auditory and developmental screening	Complete developmental assessment may be necessary; child may lag in language milestone achievement because of neglect rather than hearing loss
Whisper test	Age 3 years and older	See text	Clinical auditory screening	Inability to repeat sounds may indicate hearing loss; quiet environment is necessary to conduct test

(*continued*)

TABLE 14.8	Screening Tests for Hearing in Children (*continued*)			
SCREENING TOOL	**AGE GROUP**	**DESCRIPTION**	**CLINICAL INDICATION**	**COMMENTS**
Objective Hearing Assessments				
Audiometry	Children 5 years of age and older; play audiometry can be used for children as young as 24 months by using operant conditioning	Uses bone or air conduction in decibels to assess threshold of hearing. Air conduction audiograms are conducted using earphones; bone conduction audiograms are conducted using a plaque placed over mastoid bone. Pure tone frequencies are measured in hertz (Hz), and loudness is measured in dB. Hearing loss is diagnosed when child needs a higher decibel to hear a tone.	Objective hearing screening in ambulatory pediatrics according to AAP guidelines	Must be developmentally able to cooperate with exam; screening audiogram useful for ambulatory pediatrics; more detailed audiograms must be done by audiologist. Cerumen or the presence of AOM or OME can affect results
Otoacoustic emission (OAE)	Can be done on children of all ages	A rapid series of clicks are delivered to the ears through a probe inserted into the external auditory canal to record sounds generated by the hair cells in the cochlea	Universal newborn screening and children of all ages who are unable to cooperate with audiometry	Most widely used method of screening newborns for SNHL; also can screen for hearing loss because of ototoxicity and NIHL; test takes only 10 minutes; any vernix in ear canal (newborns) or presence of a middle ear effusion can interfere with recording of otoacoustic emissions, causing false-positive results; specialized equipment is necessary; does not detect severity of cochlear damage; should be followed by ABR
Automated auditory brainstem response (ABR)	All ages	Scalp electrodes measure electrical activity in the auditory nerve in response to sound delivered via bone and air conduction	Universal newborn screening	More expensive than OAE but fewer false-positive results; identifies type of hearing loss: CHL, SNHL

AAP, American Academy of Pediatrics; AOM, acute otitis media; CHL, conductive hearing loss; NIHL, noise-induced hearing loss; OME, otitis media with effusion; SNHL, sensorineural hearing loss.

DOCUMENTATION OF FINDINGS

The final write-up should include the assessment of both ears, including assessment of hearing.

Sample Write-Up: Healthy Neonate

Subjective Data

Infant boy born at 38 weeks of gestation. NSVD; no complications at birth; no hyperbilirubinemia; no maternal history of prescription drugs, illegal drugs, alcohol, or tobacco use during pregnancy; no maternal or neonatal infections; maternal history negative for diabetes, TORCH infections, or eclampsia. Mother denies family history of hearing loss.

Objective Data

Skin: no jaundice observed
Ears: pinnae well formed, symmetrical; top of pinnae even with outer canthus of eyes; external auditory canals patent; small amount of vernix seen in canal; unable to visualize tympanic membranes
Mouth: palate intact
Hearing: startle reflex elicited by sudden loud noise; auditory brainstem response audiometry within normal limits
Assessment: normal newborn

Sample Write-Up: Healthy Child

Subjective Data

Healthy 5-year-old boy; PMH: history of AOM × 3 episodes between 12 and 15 months of age, all treated with amoxicillin; mother denies hearing problems. No hospitalizations; ROS: noncontributory except for; AOM and environmental allergies (mold, dust, pollen); PSH: none; allergies: no known drug allergies; history of environmental allergies; medications: on no medications; Immunizations: up to date; family history: no history of hearing problems; positive history of environmental allergies (mother's family); social history: exposed to secondhand smoke in home; attended day care for 5 years; currently in kindergarten, having no difficulties in school; no history of speech delays

Objective Data

Ears: pinnae well formed, symmetrical; top of pinnae even with outer canthus of eyes; left external auditory canal partially blocked with dark orange cerumen; right external auditory canal pink without cerumen; no evidence of masses, erythema, pain, or tenderness of pinnae or mastoid bilaterally
Right ear: TM intact and pearly gray, no scarring or lesions; landmarks clearly visible; good mobility of TM noted
Left ear: TM intact and pearly gray, slightly injected; landmarks and cone of light visible; TM mobile with insufflation; no scarring or lesions noted

Hearing: Weber test (512 Hz): Lateralizes equally to both ears; Rinne test: AC > BC, both ears
Assessment: normal ear examination; normal hearing

Sample Write-Up: Ill Child

Subjective Data

A previously healthy 18-month-old African American girl is brought to clinic with irritability and ear pain. The mother says, "My child is very cranky and keeps pulling at her ears." She has had nasal congestion for the past 5 days; nasal drainage for the past 2 days; thick and green in character. Last night, the child began to "feel hot" and started pulling at her ears. No history of vomiting or diarrhea. Poor appetite for solids for 2 days; drinking "normal" amounts of juice, water, and milk.
PMH: AOM × 4 episodes
PSH: none
Medications: Tylenol 120 mg; last dose 12 hours ago; no other medications;
Allergies: no known allergies; no known drug allergies
Immunizations: up to date
Family history: one brother, aged 3 years, with history of allergies, asthma, AOM × 3 episodes; one brother, aged 6 years, with history of allergies, asthma, AOM × 6 episodes
Social history: both parents smoke in the home and in the car. Attends day care 5 days/week. Speaks in two-word sentences. Still drinks from bottle; takes bottle to bed
ROS: unremarkable except for previous episodes of AOM × 4

Objective Data

T: 103.2° F (39.5° C); **P:** 120 beats per minute; **RR:** 30 breaths per minute; **weight:** 26 lb (11.8 kg) (75th percentile); **height:** 31.5 in. (80 cm) (50th percentile)
General: 18-month-old African American girl, alert, sitting on mother's lap, crying intermittently; occasional cough; responds to name called
Skin: hot, dry, good turgor; no rashes or lesions
Ears: R ear: TM intact, erythematous, bulging; light reflex diffuse, bony landmarks not visible; pneumatic otoscopy deferred; L ear: TM intact, mobile, pearly gray; cone of light and landmarks visible
Nose: thick green mucus both nares; turbinates edematous and bright red
Mouth/throat: pharynx pink, no lesions or exudates, tonsils 2+
Neck: supple, bilateral preauricular lymphadenopathy
Lungs: breath sounds clear to auscultation bilaterally; respirations unlabored
Heart: S1, S2, regular rate and rhythm; no murmur auscultated
Abdomen: soft, nontender, nondistended; bowel sounds present; small umbilical hernia, easily reducible
Diagnosis: AOM, right ear; upper respiratory infection

Notable Clinical Findings

- History of prematurity or birth weight < 1500 g; hyperbilirubinemia, craniofacial anomalies
- History of ototoxic drug exposure
- Second- or third-hand tobacco smoke exposure
- Immunization delay
- History of repeated episodes of acute otitis media
- History of poor school performance (hearing loss)
- Family/Child History
  - Allergies
  - Atopic dermatitis
  - Asthma
  - Allergic rhinitis
  - Hearing loss
  - Pinna deformities
  - Renal disorders
- Erythematous, immobile tympanic membrane
- Bulging tympanic membrane
- Perforated or scarred tympanic membrane
- Clear or yellow fluid, with or without air bubbles visualized behind tympanic membrane
- Otalgia
- Otorrhea
- Tinnitus
- Vertigo
- Skin tags or pits near pinnae, especially if bilateral
- Low-set ears
- Foreign body in external auditory canal
- Impacted cerumen

References

Bisht, M., & Bist, S. S. (2011). Ototoxicity: The hidden menace. *Indian Journal of Otolaryngology and Head & Neck Surgery, 63*(3), 255–259.

Blume, H. K., & Szperka, C. L. (2010). Secondary causes of headaches in children: When it isn't a migraine. *Pediatric Annals, 39*(7), 431–439.

Centers for Disease Control and Prevention. (2013). Hearing loss in children. Retrieved from http://www.cdc.gov/ncbddd/hearingloss/types.html

Cheraghi, M., & Salvi, S. (2009). Environmental tobacco smoke (ETS) and respiratory health in children. *European Journal of Pediatrics, 168*(8), 897–905.

Dancer, J. (2006). *Do you cerumen?* Retrieved from http://nurse-practitioners-and-physician-assistants.advanceweb.com/Article/Do-You-Cerumen.aspx

Dedhia, K., Kitsko, D., Sabo, D., & Chi, D. H. (2013). Children with sensorineural hearing loss after passing the newborn hearing screen. *JAMA Otolaryngology Head and Neck Surgery, 139*(2), 119–123.

Dimmitt, P. (2005). Cerumen removal products. *Journal of Pediatric Health Care, 19*(5), 332–336.

Dourmishev, L. A., & Janniger, C. K. (2013). *Dermatologic manifestations of Waardenburg syndrome.* Retrieved from http://emedicine.medscape.com/article/1113314-overview

Gaylord, N. M., & Yetman, R. J. (2013). Perinatal disorders. In C. E. Burns, A. M. Dunn, M. A. Brady, N. B. Starr, &

C. G. Blosser (Eds.), *Pediatric primary care* (5th ed., pp. 961–999). Philadelphia, PA: W. B. Saunders.

Goldstein, B. A., Fabiano, L., & Washington, P. S. (2005). Phonological skills in predominantly English-speaking, predominantly Spanish-speaking and Spanish-English bilingual children. *Language, Speech and Hearing Services in Schools, 36,* 201–218.

Hanson, M. B., & Kwartler, J. A. (2012). *CSF otorrhea.* Retrieved from http://emedicine.medscape.com/article/883160-overview

Harlor, A. D. B., & Bower, C. (2009). Hearing assessment in infants and children: Recommendations beyond neonatal screening. *Pediatrics, 124*(4), 1252–1263.

Heim, S. W., & Maughan, K. L. (2007). Foreign bodies in the ear, nose, and throat. *American Family Physician, 76*(8), 1185–1189.

Jackson, P. A. (2006). Ears. In K. G. Duderstadt (Ed.), *Pediatric physical examination: An illustrated handbook* (pp. 137–153). St Louis, MO: Mosby Elsevier.

Jewell, J. (2013). *Fragile X syndrome.* Retrieved from http://emedicine.medscape.com/article/943776-overview

Joint Commission on Infant Hearing. (2013). Supplement to the Joint Commission on Infant Hearing position statement: Principles and guidelines for early intervention after conformation that a child is deaf or hard of hearing. *Pediatrics, 131*(4), e1324–e1349.

Kohnert, K. (2010). Bilingual children with primary language impairment: Issues, evidence and implications for clinical actions. *Journal of Communication Disorders, 43*(6), 456–473.

Kujawa, S. G., & Liberman, M. C. (2009). Adding insult to injury: Cochlear nerve degeneration after "temporary" noise-induced hearing loss. *Journal of Neuroscience, 29*(45), 14077–14085.

Levi, J. R., Ames, J. A., Gitman, L., Morlet, T., & O'Reilly, R. C. (2013). Clinical characteristics of pediatric granular myringitis. *Otolaryngology Head and Neck Surgery, 148*(2), 291–296.

Li, J. L., & Brunk, J. (2013). *Otalgia.* Retrieved from http://emedicine.medscape.com/article/845173-overview

Lieberthal, A. S., Carroll, A. E., Chonmaitree, T., Ganiats, T. G., Hoberman, A., Jackson, M. A., . . . Tunkel, D.E. (2013). The diagnosis and management of acute otitis media. *Pediatrics, 131*(3), e964–e999.

Mudd, P. A., Edmunds, A. L., Glatz, F., Campbell, K. C. M., & Rybak, L. P. (2012). *Ototoxicity.* Retrieved from http://emedicine.medscape.com/article/857679-overview

National Conference of State Legislators. (2011). *Newborn hearing screening laws.* Retrieved from http://www.ncsl.org/research/health/newborn-hearing-screening-state-laws.aspx

Ostrower, S. T., Bent, J. P., & Austin, M. (2013). *Preauricular cysts, pits and fissures.* Retrieved from http://emedicine.medscape.com/article/845288-overview

Paradis, J. (2005). Grammatical morphology in children learning English as a second language: Implications of similarities with specific language impairment. *Language, Speech and Hearing Services in Schools, 36,* 172–187.

Petersen-Smith, A., & Becton McKenzie, S. (2013). Ear disorders. In C. E. Burns, A. M. Dunn, M. A. Brady, N. B. Starr, & C. G. Blosser (Eds.), *Pediatric primary care* (5th ed., pp. 652–668). Philadelphia, PA: W. B. Saunders.

Petrakis, N. L., Pingle, U., Petrakis, S. J., & Petrakis, S. L. (2005). Evidence for a genetic cline in earwax types in the Middle East and Southeast Asia. *American Journal of Physical Anthropology, 35*(1), 141–144.

Shah, R. K., & Lotke, M. (2013). *Hearing impairment.* Retrieved from http://emedicine.medscape.com/article/994159-overview

Swiatecka-Urban, A. (2013). *Multicystic renal dysplasia.* Retrieved from http://emedicine.medscape.com/article/982560-overview

Uliyanov, Y. P., & Schweinfurth, J. (2012). *Middle ear, tympanic membrane infections.* Retrieved from http://emedicine.medscape.com/article/858558-overview

Vaux, K. K., & Chambers, C. (2012). *Fetal alcohol syndrome.* Retrieved from http://emedicine.medscape.com/article/974016-overview

Additional Resources

American Academy of Audiology

http://www.audiology.org

American Academy of Pediatrics (AAP), Clinical Practice Guidelines: The Diagnosis and Management of Acute Otitis Media

http://pediatrics.aappublications.org/content/early/2013/02/20/peds.2012-3488

National Center on Birth Defects and Developmental Disabilities

http://www.cdc.gov/ncbddd

National Dissemination Center for Children with Disabilities

http://www.parentcenterhub.org

National Institute on Deafness and Other Communication Disorders

http://www.nidcd.nih.gov/health/hearing

C H A P T E R 15

Assessment of the Eyes

It is vitally important for all infants, children, and adolescents to have a regular eye examination and vision assessment. Early diagnosis, prompt referral, and treatment are essential for all children with ocular abnormalities as some of these conditions may affect a child's vision, impair learning and development, or be a sign of a potentially life-threatening neurologic condition.

ANATOMY AND PHYSIOLOGY

The function of the eye is to perceive near, far, and peripheral visual images and to differentiate colors. Four cranial nerves (CNs) are involved in ocular function: CN II (optic) mediates visual acuity and peripheral vision; CN III (oculomotor) controls pupillary constriction, accommodation, and upper eyelid elevation; and CN III, CN IV (trochlear), and CN VI (abducens) allow extraocular eye movements into the six cardinal fields of gaze. The eye can be divided into two sections: the *external eye* and the *internal eye*.

External Eye

The external eye structures include the *bony orbit*, *eyebrows*, *eyelids*, *eyelashes*, *conjunctiva*, and *lacrimal apparatus*. Along with these structures, the *extraocular muscles* function to protect and support the eye. The external structures of the eye are shown in Figures 15.1, 15.2, and 15.3.

The bony orbit (socket) is an opening in the skull that surrounds and protects the globe (eyeball). Only the anterior portion of the eye is exposed; the remaining portion is housed within the skull. Within the orbit is the *optic foramen*, an opening through which the optic nerve, ophthalmic artery, and ophthalmic vein from each eye pass to the brain.

The eyebrows consist of coarse hairs and grow laterally above the eye in an arch shape. The eyebrow should begin from the inner canthus to just beyond the outer canthus. Their function is to protect the eyes from debris

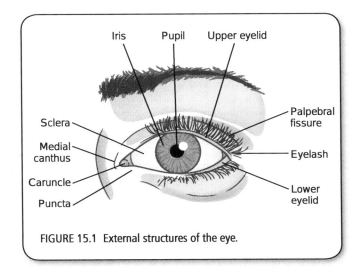

FIGURE 15.1 External structures of the eye.

and foreign objects, prevent perspiration from dripping into the eyes, and to shade the eyes from the sun's rays.

The upper and lower eyelids are two moveable muscular structures that cover the globe; their function is to cover the eyes during sleep, protect the eye from light and injury, and to distribute lubrication over the eye. The upper eyelid is larger and more mobile than the lower eyelid and, when open, normally covers a portion of the top of the iris but not the pupil. When closed, the eyelids normally touch. Contained within the upper eyelids are the *tarsal plates*, small pieces of connective tissue that give the upper eyelid shape. The tarsal plates contain the *meibomian glands*, a type of sebaceous gland that secretes an oily substance to keep the eyes moist and the lids sealed when they are closed. The lower eyelid normally sits on the lower border of the iris. The longitudinal opening between the upper and lower eyelid is the *palpebral fissure* (see Figure 15.1). The points at which the upper and lower eyelids meet at the left and right sides of each eye are the inner (*medial* or *nasal*) *canthus* and outer (*lateral* or *temporal*) *canthus* (see Figure 15.1). The inner canthus contains the puncta, two small openings that permit

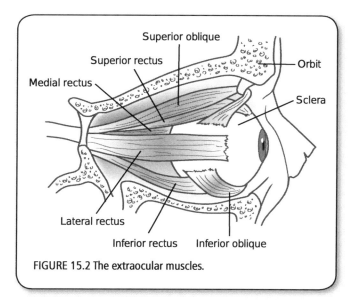

FIGURE 15.2 The extraocular muscles.

The lacrimal apparatus consists of the *lacrimal glands*, *lacrimal ducts*, *nasolacrimal ducts*, *nasolacrimal sacs*, and *lacrimal puncta* (see Figure 15.3). This system produces tears to clean, lubricate, and moisten the conjunctivae and *cornea* and to irrigate foreign substances out of the eye. The almond-shaped lacrimal gland is located in the upper, outer corner of the orbit, slightly below the eyebrow in a small depression within the frontal bone. This gland forms tears that wash over the conjunctiva through two lacrimal ducts in each eye via the lacrimal puncta, which are four tiny openings on the nasal side of the upper and lower lids at the inner canthus. The tears then drain into the lacrimal sac, then into the nasolacrimal duct, then to the inferior meatus of the nose.

There are six extraocular muscles that attach each eye to the bony orbit. These voluntary muscles control movement of the eye in the six cardinal fields of gaze and are innervated by CN III, CN IV, and CN VI. There are four *rectus* muscles and two *oblique* muscles. The rectus muscles (i.e., medial rectus, lateral rectus, superior rectus, inferior rectus) are responsible for straight movement of the eye, that is, top to bottom and side to side (see Figure 15.2). The oblique muscles (i.e., superior oblique, inferior oblique) regulate diagonal eye movement. Coordinated movements of the extraocular muscles allow binocular vision.

Internal Eye

The eyeball is a spherical structure comprised of three layers: the outer layer (the sclera), middle layer (the choroid), and inner layer (the retina) (Figure 15.4).

the drainage of tears into the *nasolacrimal duct*, and the *lacrimal caruncle*, a small, fleshy elevated area that contains sebaceous glands. The eyelashes are stiff hairs that grow out of the eyelid margins; they protect the eyes from dirt, debris, and foreign bodies.

The conjunctiva is a thin, transparent mucous membrane that lines the surface of the inner eyelids and anterior surface of the *sclera*. This delicate membrane acts as a protective covering for the cornea. The conjunctiva has two surfaces: *palpebral* and *bulbar*. The palpebral conjunctiva lines the inner surface of the upper and lower eyelids; it is thin, transparent, and vascular. The bulbar conjunctiva forms the transparent membrane over the sclera up to the *limbus* (the juncture of the sclera and cornea). The bulbar conjunctiva is whitish due to its minimal vascularity and to the white sclera that lies beneath it. Inflammation of the bulbar conjunctivae results in conjunctivitis.

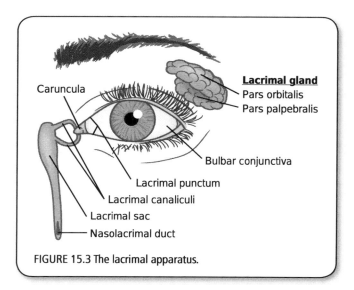

FIGURE 15.3 The lacrimal apparatus.

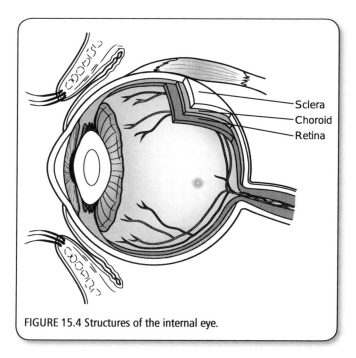

FIGURE 15.4 Structures of the internal eye.

Outer Layer

The outermost layer of the eye consists of the sclera and cornea (see Figure 15.4). The sclera (white of the eye) is an opaque, firm, fibrous tissue that coats the outer eye and is visible just beneath the conjunctiva. It contains nerves and blood vessels and gives the eye its shape. The external ocular muscles insert into the sclera. Contiguous with the sclera is the cornea, the most anterior aspect of the eye. The sclera and cornea meet at the limbus. The cornea is the transparent, avascular, membranous covering of the pupil and iris; this structure allows light to pass through the eye to the lens and retina. The cornea is extremely sensitive to touch and pain and is innervated by the trigeminal nerve (CN V).

Middle Layer

The middle layer of the eye can be divided into two sections: the anterior portion, which contains the iris and ciliary body, and the posterior portion, which contains the choroids. The iris is the pigmented portion of the eye (see Figure 15.1). The color of the iris is inherited and varies from person to person. At the center of the iris is the pupil (see Figure 15.1). The iris contains the sphincter and dilator muscles, which allow the pupil to increase (dilate) and decrease (constrict) in size to control the amount of light entering the eye. Sympathetic stimuli dilate the pupil; parasympathetic stimuli cause it to contract. The lens lies behind the iris; it changes shape to focus light on the retina. This change in shape is controlled by the muscles of the ciliary body. The ciliary body controls accommodation (i.e., near focusing of the eye). The ciliary body also produces aqueous humor in the posterior chamber, which is behind the iris and in front of the lens. This fluid flows from the posterior chamber through the pupil to the anterior chamber through the canal of Schlemm. The amount of aqueous humor in the anterior chamber determines intraocular pressure. The choroid layer lies between the sclera and retina. It has a rich vascular supply that provides necessary blood flow to the retina and prevents uncontrolled light reflection in the eye.

Inner Layer

The innermost layer of the eye is the *fundus*, which is opposite the lens. It includes the retina, *optic disc*, *retinal vessels*, *macula*, and *fovea centralis* (Figure 15.5). These structures can be seen with the ophthalmoscope. The color of the fundus varies, depending on the child's skin color. The retina contains specialized nerve cells, the rods and cones, which transform neuronal impulses to the brain. Rods are quite sensitive to light and function best in dim light; they also control black and white vision. Cones function in bright light and regulate color vision.

The optic disc is where the optic nerve enters the eye. It is a round area located on the nasal (medial) side of the retina that is pale yellow to pink with well-demarcated margins. The physiologic cup is a small, circular, lightly colored area on the optic disc that appears somewhat

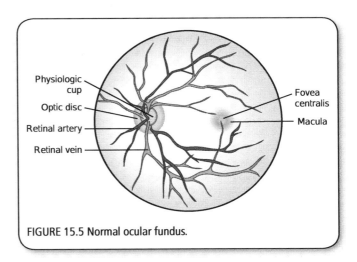

FIGURE 15.5 Normal ocular fundus.

indented. This is the place through which the optic nerve enters the eye.

The retinal vessels are four sets of arteries and veins that emerge from the optic disc and have their greatest diameter there. These vessels extend outward toward the periphery of the fundus, becoming progressively narrower and lighter in color as they extend (see Figure 15.5).

The avascular macula is located temporal to the optic disc. It is slightly darker than the rest of the fundus and is very sensitive to light. The fovea centralis is a pinpoint depression within the macula and is the area of the retina with the greatest visual acuity. Cones are densely concentrated in the fovea centralis. Rods are absent but increase in number toward the periphery of the retina.

Vision

Visual Pathways

The visual pathway begins as light passes through the transparent parts of the eye (i.e., cornea, aqueous humor, lens, vitreous body) and reaches the retina. The retina then transforms the light into neuronal impulses that move through the optic nerve and optic tract to the brain, where the images are interpreted. The retinal image is initially inverted and reversed right to left as it passes through the lens. For example, an image in the upper temporal visual field of the right eye will reflect onto the lower nasal portion of the retina. The point at which the optic nerves from each eye cross over to the opposite side is the *optic chiasm* (Figure 15.6). The right optic tract contains only nerve fibers from the right side of the retina, and the left optic tract has only nerve fibers from the left half of each retina. Therefore, the right side of the brain sees images only from the left side of view and vice versa.

Visual Fields

The visual field or field of vision is the area or range within which objects are visible to the immobile eye. The field of vision of each eye can be divided into four

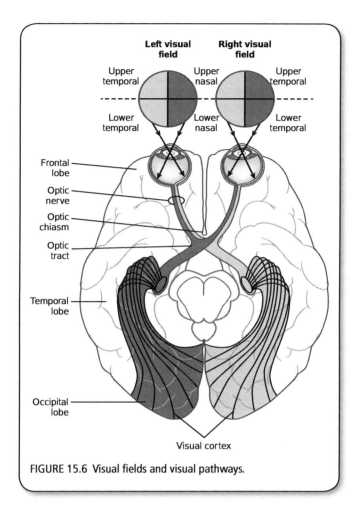

FIGURE 15.6 Visual fields and visual pathways.

quadrants: upper temporal, lower temporal, upper nasal, and lower nasal (see Figure 15.6). The temporal quadrants are slightly larger than the nasal quadrants, and these visual fields overlap, resulting in a slightly different view of the same visual field. This allows for peripheral and binocular vision and depth perception.

Visual Reflexes

The *pupillary light reflex* is the constriction of the pupils in response to light. This reflex can be seen directly when pupillary constriction occurs in the eye upon exposure to light, and indirectly or consensually, when exposure to light in one eye causes the pupil in the contralateral

eye to constrict simultaneously. This is a subcortical reflex mediated by CN III to protect the specialized photoreceptor cells of the retina by preventing excess light exposure.

Accommodation is a reflex that allows the eye to focus on near objects; this occurs when the ciliary muscles, innervated by CN III contract, thereby causing curvature of the lens. This results in the pupils accommodating themselves to objects at close range by constricting and to those farther away by dilating. This reflex cannot be directly observed but can be indirectly assessed when convergence (movement toward) of the eyes and pupillary constriction occur simultaneously.

DEVELOPMENTAL CONSIDERATIONS

Structure and function of the eye are dynamic processes that begin in utero and continue throughout childhood. At 22 days gestation, the eye appears, and by 8 weeks gestation, the eyes are formed. During this time, the developing eye is vulnerable to the effects of intrauterine drug exposure and intrauterine infection. In preterm infants, the eyelids are partially fused. Perinatal hypoxia adversely affects the retina, often causing poor vision or blindness (retinopathy of prematurity [ROP]). In term infants, the eye and visual pathway system are still immature, with most neonates being hyperopic (farsighted). Children are farsighted until about age 7 or 8 years, after which they become increasingly hyperopic (nearsighted) (Ball, Bindler, & Cowen, 2012). Binocularity is established by 3 to 4 months of age. By 4 to 5 months, infants can fixate on an image with both eyes simultaneously with a steady gaze; the ability to distinguish color begins at approximately 5 months of age. Visual acuity in infants ranges from 20/400 to 20/50. The optic nerve is completely myelinated by 2 years, and visual acuity reaches 20/40 by this time. Table 15.1 summarizes the range of visual acuity in infants and children.

The pupils are small with undeveloped reflexes until about 5 months of age. *Transient nystagmus* is common in neonates younger than 6 months (Ball et al., 2012). Extraocular muscle function is poorly coordinated for the first 6 months of life, resulting in intermittent convergent strabismus during this time. Accommodation and convergence should be established by 18 to

TABLE 15.1	Normal Visual Acuity in Infants and Children
AGE	**VISUAL ACUITY**
Newborn–1 month	20/100–20/400
4–6 months	20/200–20/300
1 year	20/40–20/60
2 years	20/40–20/50
3 years	20/40
4 years	20/30
5–6 years	20/20

24 months. There is little pigment in the iris at birth; by 6 to 12 months of age, pigmentation of the eye is complete (Hockenberry, 2011). The lacrimal apparatus is not fully developed at birth. A neonate does not produce tears until approximately 4 to 6 weeks of age, and the lacrimal ducts do not open until approximately age 3 months. The young child's eye occupies a greater portion of the orbit than an adult's, causing it to be more vulnerable to injury. Both the corneal and blink reflexes are present at birth. Eye size reaches that of the adult by about 8 years.

CULTURAL, ETHNIC, AND RACIAL CONSIDERATIONS

Epicanthal folds (folds of excess skin that extend from the nose to the inner canthus) are a normal finding in Asians, Hispanics, and Native American children; they are also observed in children with Down syndrome. The eyelids of Asians may not close completely; this is within normal limits. In dark-skinned children, the sclera may have a yellowish tinge, or brown spots may be seen. The red reflex is also more orange than red in dark-skinned children.

ASSESSMENT OF THE EYE

Assessment of the eye in infants and children must include an ocular history, assessment of vision, and inspection of both the external and internal structures of the eye.

History

To detect vision problems early, a complete past medical history, family history, and social history are important. An ocular history is also essential to identify specific eye and vision problems. A focused history is required when the child presents with an injury or illness related to the eye.

Past Medical History

Prenatal History • The prenatal history is obtained to determine if the child has had any prenatal drug or alcohol exposure or has been exposed to any infections in utero that can cause abnormalities of the eye. Prenatal alcohol exposure has been shown to cause decreased visual acuity in infants (Carter et al., 2005). Infants born with fetal alcohol syndrome (FAS) have facial dysmorphology that includes small, narrow eye openings (see Chapter 16). Valproic acid is a teratogen; maternal ingestion of this drug during pregnancy causes multiple serious complications, including craniofacial anomalies that involve abnormal epicanthal folds. Isotretinoin is also teratogenic; this drug causes hypertelorism (Sladden & Harman, 2007). Some prenatal maternal infections cause serious complications in the eye of the developing fetus. For example,

congenital varicella syndrome causes microphthalmia, cataracts, and chorioretinitis (Speer, 2013). Congenital toxoplasmosis causes chorioretinitis, strabismus, necrotizing retinochoroiditis and blindness (Wu, Evans, & Garcia, 2013). Congenital rubella syndrome (CRS) occurs in infants of women who become infected with rubella during the first trimester of pregnancy. CRS involves ocular abnormalities such as cataracts, infantile glaucoma, and pigmentary retinopathy; in 80% of affected infants, both eyes are involved (Ezike & Ang, 2013).

Perinatal and Neonatal Histories • Detailed perinatal and neonatal histories are essential to obtain a full database when assessing the eye. A history of any episodes of perinatal hypoxia–ischemia, asphyxia, in utero cerebrovascular accidents, developmental brain anomalies, hydrocephalus, or infections of the central nervous system (CNS), such as meningitis and encephalitis, must be determined; these are the major causes of cortical visual impairment (Good & Hou, 2006). Birth asphyxia is also associated with cerebral palsy; some type of visual impairment is a clinical feature in most children with this disorder (Bernard et al., 2012). A history of perinatally acquired infections that affect the eye must be noted, including herpes simplex virus, congenital syphilis, Epstein-Barr virus (EBV), cytomegalovirus (CMV), varicella-zoster virus, gonorrhea, and *Chlamydia*. These infections are transmitted from mother to neonate during passage through an infected birth canal, thus infecting the newborn. Neonatal herpes infections cause chorioretinitis, microphthalmia, cataract, conjunctivitis and keratitis (Anzivino et al., 2009). Glaucoma is seen with congenital syphilis; gonococcal ophthalmitis results in copious purulent discharge and eyelid edema (Thilo & Rosenberg, 2012). Chorioretinitis results from CMV, EBV, varicella-zoster virus, and various fungal infections (Mirza & Guinazu, 2013). Chlamydial conjunctivitis also causes eye drainage, eyelid edema, thickened palpebral conjunctiva, and pseudomembrane formation; this conjunctivitis may be self-limited or severe (McCourt, Enzenauer, Jatla, & Zhou, 2013).

A history of prematurity must be noted, as premature infants have a higher than normal incidence of eye pathology, including ROP, myopia (nearsightedness), anisometropia (refractive imbalance), astigmatism, strabismus, amblyopia, glaucoma, retinal detachment, and blindness (Bashour, Menassa, & Geronitis, 2013). In addition to these pathologies, very low birth weight (≤ 1500 g) infants have a high incidence of poor visual perceptual skills (e.g., visual discrimination, memory; visual–spatial relationships) (Davis, Burns, Wilkerson, & Steichen, 2005). It is also essential to note any history of hyperbilirubinemia; this will cause the sclera to be yellow. The timing of this finding depends on the cause of the hyperbilirubinemia.

Any genetic or hereditary conditions are also an essential component of the history. For example, children with trisomy 21 (Down syndrome) have numerous abnormalities associated with the eye: bilateral epicanthal folds, Brushfield spots (spots on the iris), retinal detachment, strabismus, nystagmus, hyperopia (farsightedness), myopia, astigmatism; excessive tearing from congenital nasolacrimal duct obstruction (dacryostenosis), blepharitis, congenital cataracts, and pseudopapilledema (Chen, 2013). Retinopathy is one of the clinical findings in Alport syndrome. Horner syndrome, either congenital or acquired, causes miosis, ptosis, and heterochromia. Retinoblastoma is an intraocular malignancy that can be inherited.

A history of congenital ocular disorders or defects should also be noted; examples include congenital glaucoma, cataracts, iris coloboma, and dacryostenosis. Congenital glaucoma raises the infant's intraocular pressure, causing myopia, astigmatism, and anisometropia; these refractive imbalances are the cause of reduced visual acuity and, if untreated, blindness (Cibis, Urban, & Dahl, 2013). Congenital cataracts can lead to permanent vision loss. An iris *coloboma* is a defect of the iris in which a portion of the pupil is elongated and keyhole-shaped, causing part of the iris to be black; this may or may not be associated with other anomalies. Dacryostenosis can lead to dacryocystitis or dacryocystocele.

Review of Systems

The pediatric review of systems (ROS) involving the eye includes asking the parent about systemic conditions that can cause ocular abnormalities. Some examples include the following:

- **Skin:** Hemangiomas, facial nevus flammeus, teratoma, and hyperpigmented skin lesions (may indicate tuberous sclerosis)
- **Eyes:** Poor vision, photophobia, ptosis, diplopia, exophthalmos, glaucoma, cataracts, hyphema, pseudostrabismus, strabismus, squinting, conjunctivitis, blepharitis, chalazion, hordeolum, nasolacrimal duct obstruction, orbital or periorbital cellulitis, and ocular tumors (e.g., retinoblastoma)
- **Cardiac:** Subacute bacterial endocarditis (may cause conjunctival hemorrhages)
- **Respiratory:** Upper respiratory tract infections (cause eye drainage) and cystic fibrosis (may cause jaundiced sclera)
- **Endocrine:** Hyperthyroidism (can cause exophthalmos) and type 1 diabetes
- **Metabolic:** Galactosemia and glycogen storage disease (cause jaundiced sclera)
- **Immunity:** Juvenile rheumatoid arthritis (may cause uveitis), allergic rhinitis (causes redness, swelling, itching, tearing), Burkitt's lymphoma, Kawasaki disease (may cause red sclera), and meningococcemia (may cause conjunctival hemorrhages)
- **Renal:** Nephrotic syndrome, acute glomerulonephritis (may cause periorbital edema), and hematuria (may indicate Alport syndrome)

- **Hepatic:** Hepatitis, biliary atresia, and hyperbilirubinemia (causes jaundiced sclera)
- **Hematologic:** Sickle cell disease, leukemia (can cause swelling of optic disc and retinal thickening, retinal hemorrhage or detachment), and bleeding disorders (may predispose to hyphema)
- **Musculoskeletal:** Osteogenesis imperfecta (causes blue sclera)
- **Neurologic:** Bacterial meningitis, encephalitis, hydrocephalus (can cause "sunset eyes"), seizure disorder, traumatic or ischemic brain injury, nystagmus, brain tumor (can affect vision), migraines, Sturge–Weber syndrome, neurofibromatosis, and intracranial hemorrhage
- **Developmental:** Achievement of developmental milestones (e.g., delayed gross motor control such as head lag may indicate poor vision or cerebral palsy). Attention deficit hyperactivity disorder (ADHD) may interfere with the child's ability to cooperate with vision screening. Gross motor abilities (e.g., stumbling or walking into things) may indicate vision problems.

Immunizations

Assessment of the child's immunization status is essential to be certain that all age-appropriate immunizations are up to date. This is especially true of immunizations for *Haemophilus influenzae* type B, *Neisseria meningitidis*, and *Streptococcus pneumoniae*; all of these pathogens can cause bacterial meningitis, which can lead to cortical visual impairment (Bernard et al., 2012).

Allergies

It is important to investigate whether the child has any allergies, particularly environmental allergies or allergic rhinitis. Allergic rhinitis can cause ocular symptoms, including conjunctival injection, itching, tearing, and swelling of the eyes. Anaphylactic reactions can also cause tearing and swelling of the eyes.

Hospitalizations

It is necessary to document past hospitalizations for conditions involving the eye, such as periorbital or orbital cellulitis; bacterial meningitis may occur as a complication of these infections. Bacterial meningitis, as well as encephalitis, traumatic brain injury, and hydrocephalus, can lead to cortical visual impairment in children.

Injuries

It is essential to inquire about a history of any head, brain, or eye injuries. Injuries to the head or brain may affect the child's vision as a result of damage to the optic nerve secondary to increased intracranial pressure. Types of injuries about which to inquire include traumatic brain injuries, skull fractures, blunt trauma, penetrating injury to the eye, orbital fractures, eyelid or conjunctival lacerations, corneal abrasions, chemical burns, cigarette burns of the cornea, and foreign bodies. Sports-related injuries and fractures to the face and orbit may occur, especially if protective gear is not worn.

Injuries to other areas of the body can also cause abnormalities in the eyes. For example, severe shaking injury in infants may result in retinal hemorrhage (Hornor, 2012). Crushing injuries to the chest can raise intrathoracic pressure to the extent that intraocular pressure rises, causing retinal hemorrhages. Ocular injuries may be the result of intentional injuries. Periorbital ecchymosis, subconjunctival hemorrhages, and hyphemas should be considered suspicious if accompanied by an implausible history.

Past Surgical History

Examples of surgical procedures about which to inquire include surgery for strabismus, cataracts, or an injury to the eye. A history of craniotomy should be noted, as well as the reason for the procedure. Traumatic brain injury and some brain tumors may affect a child's vision. The date of the surgery and the condition for which the surgical procedure was done should be noted and recorded, as well as whether the condition was resolved with surgery.

Family History

The family history includes information about any history of genetic or metabolic disorders. Examples include congenital glaucoma, congenital cataracts, congenital retinal dysplasia, congenital ptosis, albinism, and retinoblastoma. Other conditions about which to inquire include a family history of type 1 diabetes, strabismus, amblyopia, refractive errors (e.g., myopia, hyperopia, astigmatism), color blindness, or Marfan syndrome, which can cause myopia, displacement of the lens, and an abnormally flat cornea (Channell & Washington, 2012).

Social History

The social history involves the child's living conditions, specifically, whether any housing safety or sanitation concerns exist that would predispose the child to eye injuries or infections. If the child is involved in sports, the provider must determine if protective eyewear is used. In school-aged children and adolescents, the provider must also screen for street drug abuse; some drugs have systemic effects that can affect the eye examination. These effects include nystagmus, miosis, and mydriasis; or sluggish, delayed, or absent pupil response (Kaul, 2012). Examples of these drugs and their effects are summarized in Table 15.2. School-aged children and adolescents who wear contact lenses may need to be asked about their cleaning routine, especially if eye infections are frequent. This is also true for teens who wear excessive eye makeup without removing it for extended periods of time. Hobbies and occupational hazards are also investigated, with attention paid to chronic exposure to dust, chemicals, or metal fragments.

Developmental History

Because vision plays a vital role in reading and learning, an up-to-date developmental history is essential. Attention must be paid to any concerns voiced by parents, caregivers, or teachers regarding the child's school performance, as this may indicate problems with vision. Developmental milestones must also be assessed, as any delays may be a clue to visual impairment (see Chapter 2 for a guide to developmental assessment).

TABLE 15.2	Effects of Selected Drugs of Abuse on Eye Examination
DRUGS OF ABUSE	**EFFECT ON EYE EXAM**
Benzodiazepines (e.g., alprazolam [Xanax]; flunitrazepam [Rohypnol])	Blurred vision, diplopia, and nystagmus
Cannabis (marijuana)	Conjunctival injection
Club drugs (e.g., stimulants, hallucinogens, dL-3, 4-methylenedioxyamphetamine [MDMA, ecstasy])	Mydriasis (dilation)
Hallucinogens (e.g., D-lysergic acid diethylamide [LSD] and phencyclidine [PCP])	Mydriasis
Heroin and opiates (e.g., morphine, codeine, hydrocodone bitartrate acetaminophen [Vicodin], oxycodone HCl [OxyContin])	Miosis (constriction)
Inhalants (e.g., n-hexane [glue])	Conjunctival injection
Ketamine	Diplopia and nystagmus; also causes an increase in intraocular pressure (Halstead, Deakyne, Bajaj, Enzenauer, & Roosevelt, 2012)
Sedatives/Intoxicants (e.g., alcohol, gamma hydroxybutyrate [GHB])	Nystagmus (alcohol; GHB), delayed or sluggish pupil response (alcohol), and loss of peripheral vision (GHB)
Stimulants (e.g., cocaine, amphetamines, methamphetamines)	Mydriasis

Medications

It is necessary for the provider to obtain a complete list of current medications that the child is taking, including nonprescription over-the counter (OTC) drugs, as well as prescription drugs, such as opiate analgesics, which cause miosis (pupil constriction); or methylphenidate for ADHD, which can cause blurred vision, difficulties with accommodation, cataracts, and glaucoma (Lu, Kuang, & Chou, 2006). Systemic steroids may cause an array of ocular side effects, including cataracts, glaucoma, visual disturbances (Deshmukh, 2007), exacerbation of ocular infection, and secondary ocular infection. Topical ocular steroids can cause transient stinging or burning of the eyes, dry eyes, corneal ulcers, cataracts, and increased intraocular pressure (Janse van Rensburg & Meyer, 2013). Oral contraceptives, diuretics, antiarrhythmics, isotretinoin, and the preservatives in topical eye drops cause a deficit in tear production (Foster, Yuksel, Anzar, & Ekong, 2013). Many OTC cough and cold medications, including decongestants, antitussives, antihistamines, and expectorants, also potentially cause ocular side effects. The anticholinergic effects of antihistamines can cause ocular dryness, mydriasis, and minimally reactive pupils if the antihistamines are ingested in toxic amounts. Blurred vision can also occur with antihistamines. Mydriasis and nystagmus may be observed with dextromethorphan ingestion (Gharahbaghian & Lopez, 2013). Despite the fact that OTC cough and cold medications are no longer recommended for children younger than age 2 years (U.S. Food and Drug Administration, 2007), health care providers should still assess for their use. These OTC medications are still available for older children and adults, and parents or caregivers may unwittingly give them to young children.

Ocular History

When evaluating vision in children, a thorough ocular history is essential. Parents or teachers may observe behaviors in the child that are not seen by the health care provider during the health care visit. Concerns of parents or teachers about the child's ability to see well, including observations of crossed eyes; frequent blinking, tearing or squinting; eye drooping; rubbing the eyes; sitting too close to the television or computer; holding objects close to see better; difficulty seeing the blackboard; reports of headaches caused by reading; or any complaints of stumbling and walking into things require further investigation. Reports by parents that their infant fails to blink when objects approach is a red flag for congenital blindness. Any recent changes in vision or visual disturbances such as blurred or double vision must be noted, as well as whether any visual problems prevent normal daily activities. The provider should note whether the child wears corrective lenses, the date of the child's last vision screening, and the results of the examination.

History of Present Illness

If a child presents with an eye-related complaint, the provider obtains a focused history (i.e., history of the present illness [HPI]) to make an accurate diagnosis. The provider must keep in mind the child's age and developmental level, concurrent illness, any history of recent injury, associated findings, and past health when considering diagnostic possibilities. Common complaints related to the eye that are seen in the pediatric population include eye discharge, pain, burning; eye injuries; and visual complaints. Relevant questions to ask for the HPI can be found in Table 15.3. Other important issues include a recent history of viral infections, fever, headache, nausea, vomiting, dizziness, fatigue, and malaise; recent exposures (ticks, infections), changes in growth, or any neurologic symptoms must also be noted.

TABLE 15.3	History of Present Illness: Abnormalities and Complaints Related to the Eye	
COMPLAINT	**ASSESSMENTS**	**DIFFERENTIAL DIAGNOSES/CAUSES**
Blurred vision	Results of neurologic assessment? Does child take any medications? Recent head injury?	Eye or head injury; refractive eye conditions (myopia, hyperopia, astigmatism), glaucoma, cataracts, migraine, uveitis, keratitis, iritis, or side effect of benzodiazepines
Burning sensation in eyes	Itching of eyes? Foreign body sensation? Family member with diagnosed bacterial conjunctivitis?	Refractive error, blepharitis, conjunctivitis, foreign body, or allergies
Changes in red reflex	Asymmetrical red reflex? White coloration (leukocoria)?	Asymmetrical red reflex is seen in strabismus; leukocoria is seen with retinoblastoma, retinal detachment, or cataracts
Diplopia	Onset? Medical history? Recent head trauma or brain injury?	Congenital cataracts, amblyopia, or blow-out fracture of orbital floor
Discoloration	Erythema of eyelid? Periorbital ecchymosis? Hemorrhage? Recent injury?	Eye trauma; periorbital ecchymosis (Battle's sign) indicates basal skull fracture
Dizziness	Onset? History of head trauma? Associated symptoms? Fever? Vomiting?	Refractive error, vertigo, dehydration, or cerebellar disease

TABLE 15.3	History of Present Illness: Abnormalities and Complaints Related to the Eye (*continued*)	
COMPLAINT	**ASSESSMENTS**	**DIFFERENTIAL DIAGNOSES/CAUSES**
Dry eyes	Does child or teen wear contact lenses? Does child take any medications? Recent illness? Past medical history?	Irritation, exophthalmos, or dehydration; use of isotretinoin or diphenhydramine
Excessive blinking	Itching of eyes? Foreign body sensation? Allergies? Does child wear glasses or contact lenses?	Irritation, foreign body, infection, or tic
Eye drainage	Is conjunctiva red? Tenderness, erythema, or edema over inner canthus? Is discharge purulent? Crusting of discharge? Fever? Current upper respiratory infection? School or day care exposure to bacterial conjunctivitis ("pinkeye")? Does child or teen wear contact lenses?	Allergies (clear), viral (mucoid) or bacterial conjunctivitis (purulent; crusting upon waking), dacryocystitis (purulent); upper respiratory infection, blepharitis (crusting), or keratitis (purulent)
Eye pain	Degree of pain? Location of eye pain? Foreign body sensation? Fever? History of recent injury?	Foreign body; corneal abrasion (pain is exquisite), orbital or periorbital cellulitis, head trauma, eye injury, sinusitis, keratitis, uveitis, or iritis (orbital or periorbital pain)
Eyelid edema	Fever? Eyelid inflammation? Periorbital inflammation? Eye drainage? Eyelashes matted with drainage?	Blepharitis, conjunctivitis, orbital or periorbital cellulitis, nephrosis, nephritis, or SLE
Fever	Recent or current URI? Eye drainage? Type, character, and amount of drainage? Eyelid edema? Conjunctival injection? Immunizations up to date?	Orbital or periorbital cellulitis, uveitis (infectious cause), viral conjunctivitis (occurs with URI); rubeola, rubella, varicella, mumps, and influenza all have ocular manifestations
Foreign body sensation in eye	Type of sensation? Recent injury?	Foreign body; blepharitis, corneal abrasion, or conjunctivitis (especially with sand-like sensation)
Head tilt	Facial turning? Watching television with head turned? Head chronically positioned up or down?	Myopia or strabismus
Headache	Visual changes? Sudden or progressive vision loss? On any medications? Results of funduscopic exam? Recent head injury? Nausea and vomiting? Fever? Respiratory symptoms?	Myopia, hyperopia, migraine, increased intracranial pressure (tumor, cerebral edema, hydrocephalus, idiopathic [pseudotumor cerebri]), viral illness, or sinusitis
Intractable crying	Age of child? Recent injury?	Foreign body (especially in preverbal children)
Inflammation of conjunctivae	Any eye discharge? Type? Is it watery? Purulent? Any blurred vision? Photophobia? Complaints of seeing spots or floaters? Any eye pain? Does child or teen wear contact lenses?	Allergies, corneal abrasion, viral or bacterial conjunctivitis, foreign body, marijuana smoking, iritis, keratitis, or uveitis
Inflammation of eyelid	Any itching? Eye irritation? Do eyes feel dry? Fever?	Allergies, blepharitis, conjunctivitis, dry eyes, or foreign body
Itching	Burning of eyes? Eye discharge? Type of discharge?	Allergies, blepharitis, conjunctivitis, dry eyes, eye fatigue, or foreign body
Lacrimation	Age of child? Conjunctival injection? Emotional state?	Allergic rhinitis; blepharitis, corneal abrasion, nasopharyngitis, dacryostenosis, laughing, or crying
Nasal discharge	Type of discharge? Watery? Purulent? Onset sudden or gradual? Duration? Aggravating factors? Fever? Cough? Sneezing, itching or watery eyes? History of allergies? Does congestion interfere with sleep? What relieves nasal congestion? Is child taking any prescribed or OTC medications for the nasal congestion?	Allergic rhinitis, sinusitis, orbital or periorbital cellulitis

(*continued*)

TABLE 15.3   History of Present Illness: Abnormalities and Complaints Related to the Eye (*continued*)

COMPLAINT	ASSESSMENTS	DIFFERENTIAL DIAGNOSES/CAUSES
Nystagmus	Onset? Results of neurologic examination? Past medical history?	Ocular structural abnormalities, congenital blindness, retinal diseases, optic nerve diseases, cataract, glaucoma, albinism, Down syndrome, or idiopathic nystagmus
Photophobia	Onset? Eye pain? Associated fever or flu-like symptoms?	Corneal abrasion, blepharitis, glaucoma, cataracts, viral or bacterial meningitis, uveitis, keratitis, or iritis
Ptosis	Time of onset? Associated strabismus, amblyopia, refractive errors, astigmatism? Results of neurologic examination?	Congenital ptosis, ocular tumor, or neurologic disorders
Subconjunctival hemorrhages	Onset? Recent injury? Past medical history? Immunization history? Medication history?	Bleeding disorders, eye trauma, ruptured globe, chest trauma, meningococcemia, scarlet fever, measles, shaken baby syndrome, or anticoagulant drugs
Vision changes	Changes in visual acuity? Double vision or blurred vision? Loss of visual field? Does child see flashes or floaters? Eye pain? Tearing or eye drainage? Loss of vision? Results of neurologic examination?	Blepharitis, orbital or periorbital cellulitis, migraine, retinal detachment, retinal hemorrhage, glaucoma, cataracts, CNS disease (e.g., brain tumor, bacterial meningitis), eye trauma, keratitis, or uveitis (spots and floaters)

CNS, central nervous system; OTC, over the counter; SLE, systemic lupus erythematosus; URI, upper respiratory infection.

Physical Examination

To detect any ocular abnormalities, the American Academy of Pediatrics (AAP) recommends eye examinations at every well-child visit, beginning with the newborn visit (AAP Committee on Practice and Ambulatory Medicine, Section on Ophthalmology, American Association of Certified Orthoptists, American Association for Pediatric Ophthalmology and Strabismus, & American Academy of Ophthalmology, 2007). A complete examination of the eye in children includes testing visual acuity and visual fields, extraocular movements, and inspection and palpation of ocular structures. The internal structures of the eye are examined last, using an ophthalmoscope. The following equipment is needed for eye assessment in children:

- Penlight
- Small toy
- Eye occluder
- Visual acuity charts (e.g., Snellen "tumbling E" chart, Snellen letter or number chart, HOTV chart, Allen cards, LEA symbols)
- Color vision charts
- Ishihara color chart (age 4 years and older)
- Random dot E kit
- Ophthalmoscope
- Cotton swab
- Cotton ball
- Disposable latex or vinyl gloves (if eye drainage or exudate present)

age; an infant's or child's ability to see is affected by his or her immature anatomy, which changes and develops as the child grows. The testing method used to evaluate visual acuity in infants and children is dependent on the child's age and developmental level, specifically the ability to cooperate, read, and respond to questions.

Subjective vision screening is recommended at all well-child visits beginning at birth. Objective screening is conducted at 3, 4, 5, and 6 years; again at 8 to 10 years; and once in early adolescence (11–14 years), middle adolescence (15–17 years), and late adolescence (18–21 years). This vision screening should also be performed any time the child, parent, or teacher expresses concern about vision (AAP, 2007). Children who fail the vision assessment or are at high risk for vision problems should be referred to a pediatric optometrist or ophthalmologist. High-risk children include those whose health history is positive for:

- Prematurity or low birth weight
- Developmental delay or neurologic problems such as cerebral palsy
- Systemic disease associated with eye abnormalities or infections
- Congenital infections such as rubella or varicella, toxoplasmosis, syphilis, and gonorrhea
- Family history of vision problems (refractive error, amblyopia, strabismus, blindness, congenital cataract, glaucoma, retinoblastoma)
- Family history of genetic (Down syndrome, fragile X) or metabolic disease

Assessing Visual Acuity (CN II)

The most important assessment of visual function is the evaluation of visual acuity. Visual acuity differs with

Different types of eye charts are available to test visual acuity in children. Listed in order of decreasing difficulty, these are Snellen acuity chart, "tumbling E," HOTV test, Allen cards, and LEA symbols. To maximize the cooperation of a young child during the assessment of visual acuity, the examiner must take developmentally appropriate steps to establish rapport with the child. This includes explaining to the child and parent what will be done, ensuring that the parent is nearby, allowing the child to sit on the parent's lap if necessary, using interesting toys or devices to get the child's attention, and using positive reinforcement to reward cooperation with the exam. To obtain the most accurate findings, the provider must also ensure that the child does not peek, squint, or tilt his or her head during the vision exam.

Birth to 3 Years • Precise measurements of visual acuity are not possible in children under age 3 years. Gross measurement of vision can be accomplished by determining the infant's ability to fix and visually follow an object, first binocularly then monocularly. If the infant can follow the object as it is moved through the six cardinal fields of gaze, extraocular function can be determined. Difficulty with binocular fix and follow after 3 months may indicate eye or CNS abnormalities. Intermittent convergent strabismus is within normal limits until 6 months. Nystagmus may also be noted in the first few weeks of life. The examiner also assesses whether the infant blinks in response to a bright light, puff of air, or rapid approach of an object (i.e., the blink reflex). A strong blink reflex is normal. Absence of the blink reflex suggests impaired light perception (e.g., congenital cataracts) or a CNS abnormality. The red reflex (pupillary light reflex; Bruckner test) and pupil response are also assessed (see Assessment of Internal Eye

Structures and Ophthalmoscopic Examination sections, later in this chapter).

Toddlers with language skills may be able to cooperate with visual acuity testing, using pictures such as Allen cards or LEA symbols. Allen cards use pictures of common items to assess vision in children as young as age 2 years (Figure 15.7A). When these pictures are viewed accurately at a distance of 20 feet, 20/30 vision is present (AAP, 2007). To conduct the Allen card test, the cards are first shown to the child to ensure familiarity with the objects shown on the cards and to be sure that the child can verbally identify the objects. Then testing begins with one eye occluded, using only the cards the child has been able to identify.

Because toddlers may not be able to cooperate with the visual occlusion, the eye occluder is held by the parent, or stick-on occluder patches are used. The testing starts at a near distance. The examiner then walks backward, 2 to 3 feet at a time, showing the cards to the child, two at a time, and continuing to do so until the toddler is unable to identify an object. To calculate the child's visual acuity, the distance (in feet) at which the child could identify the picture accurately is the numerator; 30 is the denominator because a child at this age with normal vision should be able to see the picture at 30 feet (AAP, 2007).

LEA symbols require that the child identify familiar pictures on spiral-bound flash cards. This test is conducted at a distance of 10 feet, and visual acuity is determined by the smallest symbol that the child can see at a distance of 10 feet (AAP, 2007). Four of five symbols must be correctly matched to pass the line.

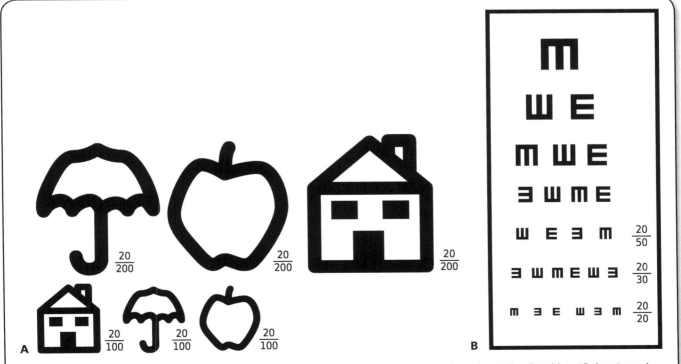

FIGURE 15.7 **A.** Allen cards show pictures of common items that are easy for toddlers to identify. **B.** The Snellen "tumbling E" chart is used for children who cannot read but are able to indicate the direction in which the "E" is pointing.

Age 3 Years and Older • Objective visual acuity testing is recommended for all children starting at age 3 years (AAP, 2007). From ages 3 to 5 years, the Snellen "tumbling E" or HOTV chart can be used to test visual acuity. Using the Snellen tumbling E, the examiner asks the child to indicate in which direction a series of progressively smaller "Es" point (Figure 15.7B). With the HOTV chart, the child matches the letters on a wall chart placed 10 feet away; four of five symbols must be correctly matched before progressing to the next line. Beginning at age 5, the Snellen letter or number charts are the preferred methods of screening for visual acuity (Figure 15.8). If the child wears glasses, he or she should wear them during the screening. To use the Snellen chart, the child stands 10 feet from the chart, covers one eye with an occluder (Figure 15. 9), and then reads the largest line of letters, moving to smaller lines of print until he or she is unable to read a line. To pass the Snellen test, the child must read four of six letters on a line correctly. The results are recorded as a fraction next to the smallest line that the child is able to read; the top number is the distance at which the child could read the line of letters; the bottom number is the distance at which a child with normal vision could read the line. The procedure is repeated for the other eye. Visual acuity norms are listed in Table 15.1.

FIGURE 15.8 The Snellen eye chart, used for children 5 years of age and older.

Accuracy in visual acuity assessment in children is very important. If a 3-year-old child is not able to cooperate with visual acuity testing, the child is retested in 4 to 6 months; a 4-year-old who cannot cooperate is retested in 1 month (AAP, 2007). If the child is still uncooperative, a referral is made to a pediatric ophthalmologist.

Assessing Color Vision

Color blindness is a recessive X-linked disorder or may occur as a result of optic nerve disease.

FIGURE 15.9 For many eye assessments, one eye must be occluded in order for the assessment to be accurate.

Red–green color blindness is the most common type. Inherited color blindness affects only males, and they cannot distinguish shades of red and green. This can affect school performance as well as present safety issues once the child is old enough to drive. Visual acuity is normal. Screening for color blindness is conducted only in boys, once between the ages of 4 and 8 years. This can be done by using Ishihara's test, which is a series of cards that have imbedded colors arranged in a shape, number, or letter on a contrasting colored background. The child is then asked to identify the figure seen in each card. The green and red bars of the Snellen chart could also be used, with the child asked to identify these colors (after ensuring that the child knows his colors); children should be able to differentiate colors by 5 years of age. A child with normal color vision will be able to identify each pattern. A color-blind child will not be able to identify the pattern on the cards or see the red or green color on the Snellen chart.

Assessing Peripheral Visual Fields

Assessment of peripheral visual fields evaluates function of the retina, visual pathways to the brain, and CN II function. Children typically need to be preschool-aged and older to be able to cooperate fully with field of vision assessment. In an infant or toddler, an overall assessment of peripheral vision can be made by watching the child's reaction to the introduction of an interesting object (e.g., bottle, toy, stuffed animal) into the visual fields. To assess field of vision in older children, the examiner conducts the confrontation test. To perform this test, the examiner stands approximately 2 feet in front of the child, face to face, at eye level. Next, the examiner asks the child to look straight ahead, holding the head and eyes steady. The child then covers his or her left eye with an occluder as the examiner covers his or her own right eye. The examiner then slowly moves a small object such as a pencil, penlight, or toy toward the child in an arc, moving clockwise, and beginning at the nose, moving to the temples, then over the top of the head toward the nose, and then from below upward toward the nose (Figure 15.10). The child is asked to say "now" as soon as he or she can see the object each time. This process is repeated for the other eye. The examiner then estimates the angle at which the object first enters the child's peripheral vision. Normal peripheral visual fields are approximately 50 degrees upward, 90 degrees laterally, 70 degrees downward, and 60 degrees medially. Areas of blindness in the peripheral visual field (scotoma) can be caused by migraine, retinal disease, optic neuritis, or amblyopia (Gupta, 2014; Lewis, 2009; Schatz & Carter, 2013).

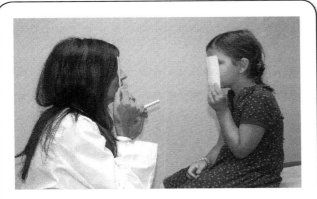

FIGURE 15.10 The confrontation test to assess visual fields.

Assessing Extraocular Muscle Function • The importance of assessing extraocular muscle function and ocular alignment in children cannot be overstated. Untreated ocular misalignment (strabismus) can lead to amblyopia and permanent vision loss. Intermittent strabismus is within normal limits until age 4 to 6 months because of undeveloped neuromuscular control of the eyes. After that time, strabismus may be caused by a variety of amblyogenic conditions involving the structures and pathways of the visual system; by CN III, CN IV, or CN VI damage; or by increased intracranial pressure (Nield, Mangano, & Kamat, 2008). With this assessment, it is important to distinguish strabismus from pseudostrabismus, which is the presence of asymmetrical epicanthal folds that create the illusion of crossed eyes (Figure 15.11).

Extraocular muscle function is evaluated primarily through assessment of ocular alignment. This is achieved via assessment of the corneal light reflex (the Hirschberg test), performance of the cross-cover test, and evaluating

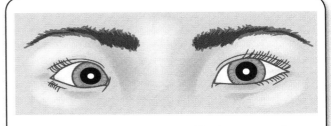

FIGURE 15.11 Pseudostrabismus caused by the presence of epicanthal folds.

the six cardinal fields of gaze. Abnormal findings in any of these examinations necessitate a referral to pediatric ophthalmology.

To perform the corneal light reflex test (Hirschberg test), the examiner stands directly in front of the child at a distance of 18 to 24 inches and then shines a penlight or ophthalmoscope light on the child's cornea as he or she looks straight ahead, gaze fixed on the light. The examiner then determines whether the light shines symmetrically on both corneas. The light reflection appears as a small white dot on the cornea. The light should be reflected in exactly the same place on both corneas; this determines if the child's eyes are in a conjugate position (Figure 15.12). Nasal displacement indicates exotropia; temporal deviation indicates esotropia (Figure 15.13). These conditions can lead to amblyopia, which, left untreated, leads to permanent blindness.

To perform the cross-cover test, the child must focus on an object that is approximately 10 feet straight ahead. In young children, holding up an interesting toy may be helpful. The examiner then covers one of the child's eyes with an occluder for 10 seconds as the child stares ahead at the fixed object.

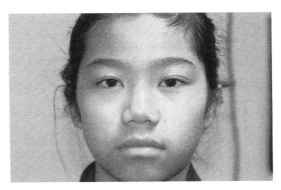

FIGURE 15.12 Symmetrical corneal light reflex (Hirschberg test).

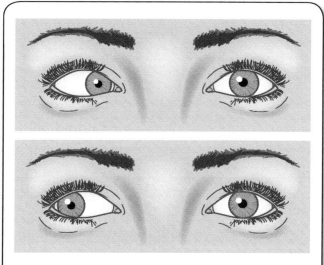

FIGURE 15.13 Esotropia (eye turns nasally); exotropia (eye deviates temporally).

The occluder is then removed as the examiner observes for any movement of the uncovered eye; it should not drift. This test is repeated with the other eye. If the uncovered eye moves as it attempts to refocus on the object, it indicates extraocular muscle weakness (strabismus) (Figure 15.14). Movement of the uncovered eye outward indicates that the eye was deviated inward when covered (esotropia). If the eye moves inward, it was deviated outward when covered (exotropia). Either of these findings warrants referral to a pediatric ophthalmologist.

In older preschool-aged children through adolescence, assessment of extraocular muscle strength is conducted to evaluate the six cardinal fields of gaze. This assessment also tests the functionality of CN III (oculomotor), CN IV (trochlear), and CN VI (abducens), which innervate the ocular muscles. To conduct this assessment, the examiner stands approximately 12 inches in front of the child as he or she looks straight ahead. The child must not move his or her head; with young children, the examiner can hold the child's head still by cupping the child's chin with the free hand or by placing his or her free hand on the child's forehead while keeping the other hand free to conduct the examination. Once positioned, the child is asked to follow the examiner's finger through the six cardinal fields of gaze, as the examiner traces the following path: left and right lateral gaze, left and right lateral inferior gaze, and left and right lateral superior gaze (Figure 15.15). The child's eyes should move in a smooth, even, parallel manner. An inability to move the eye in all directions is likely a result of eye muscle weakness or CN abnormalities. A few beats of nystagmus may be noted during the upward and lateral gaze; this is within normal limits. Marked nystagmus is caused by neurologic abnormalities and must be investigated.

Lastly, convergence is tested. This is the simultaneous movement of the eyes inward to maintain binocular eye alignment as objects move from far to near. This function is mediated by the medial rectus muscle, which is innervated by CN III. Convergence can be tested when the examiner moves his or her finger toward the bridge of the child's nose while asking the child to state when he or she can first see two targets. The child should be able to maintain fixation on the object and both eyes should converge. Lack of convergence indicates some degree of strabismus.

Convergence is necessary for stereopsis (binocular depth perception). Stereopsis can be evaluated using the random dot E stereo test; this test can be used in children as young as age 3 years. If the child wears

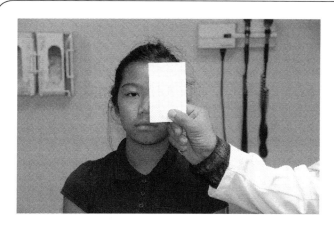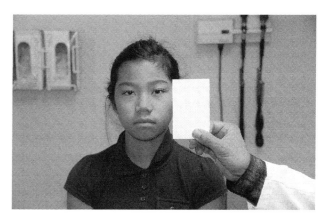

FIGURE 15.14 The cross-cover test. **A.** First the eye is occluded. **B.** Next, the eye is uncovered.

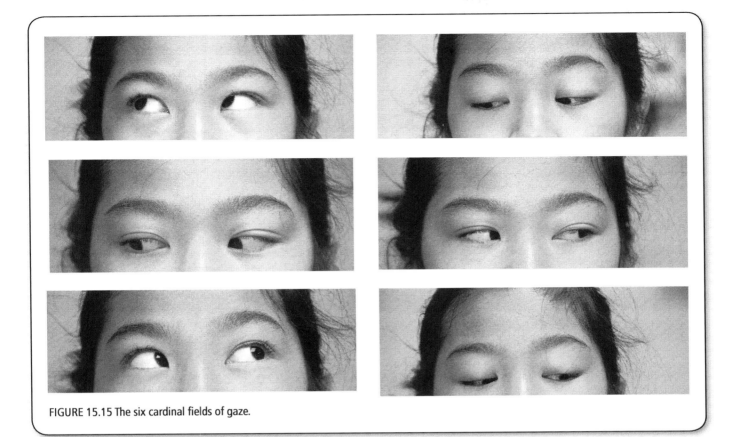

FIGURE 15.15 The six cardinal fields of gaze.

glasses, this test must be done with the corrective lenses in place. To perform this test, the child first places stereo glasses on; if the child wears glasses, the stereo glasses are placed over the child's glasses. With the raised E target and nonstereo target cards held 16 in. from the child's eyes, he or she is asked to look at both cards simultaneously and point to the one with the raised E. This process is repeated up to six times; the child must distinguish the raised E correctly four of six times. Failure to do so indicates a binocular abnormality and defective visual acuity, likely arising from strabismus or amblyopia (Hope & Maslin, 2007).

Inspection

External Eye Structures • The external eye includes the eyebrow, eyelashes, eyelids, eyeballs, conjunctivae, sclera, and lacrimal apparatus. Inspection of the external eye begins with the eyebrow. The examiner inspects the size and shape of the eyebrows, noting placement, the distribution of hair, and whether the eyebrows are symmetrical. The eyebrows should extend just beyond the outer canthus and are normally full with an even distribution of hair. Hair loss in the eyebrows may result from excessive hair plucking for cosmetic reasons, fungal infection, or trichotillomania (hair pulling). The eyebrows are also inspected for the presence of lice or nits. The skin beneath the eyebrow is also inspected; it normally matches the skin of the rest of the face and is free of lesions. If the child is developmentally able to cooperate, function of CN VII can be determined by asking the child to raise and lower the eyebrows; this movement should be symmetrical.

Next, the eyelashes are inspected. The eyelashes are normally full and evenly distributed, extending outward along the entire eyelid margin. No crusts or infestations should be seen. Crusting, scaling, or loss of eyelashes are signs of infection. Bacterial conjunctivitis causes a mucopurulent discharge, which may mat the eyelashes. Tiny, white oval specks on the eyelashes are likely nits (lice eggs).

The eyelids are inspected for symmetry, color, lesions, edema, inflammation, and discharge. The upper and lower eyelids and palpebral fissures are normally symmetrical. In children of African or European ancestry, the palpebral fissure is horizontal; in Asian children or children with Down syndrome, it slants slightly upward. Short palpebral fissures are seen in children with FAS. The upper eyelids should completely cover the superior limbus of the iris (i.e., where the cornea and sclera meet), but not the pupil. The lower eyelid should extend to, or slightly below, the inferior limbus. Inner canthal distance should be approximately 1 inch (2.5 cm); the outer canthus should be aligned with the tips of the pinnae (see Chapter 14, Figure 14.5, and Chapter 16, Table 16.2). The eyelids should fully approximated when closed. Neonates often hold the eyelids tightly shut, especially when crying. The eyelids of children with epicanthal folds may not close completely; this is a normal variation. Incomplete closure of the eyelids can also result from abnormal protrusion of the eye globe (exophthalmos), which is seen with hyperthyroidism. This can also occur when a portion of the sclera is seen above the irises in the case of increased intracranial pressure ("setting sun sign") (see Chapter 22, Figure 22.7); it is also a normal variation in neonates when the infant is moved from a sitting to a supine position. Inversion of the eyelid (entropion) is a normal finding in Asian children. If eyelashes do not cause corneal abrasions, entropion is not a significant finding. Ectropion occurs when the lower eyelid turns outward; this can lead to conjunctivitis. Drooping of the upper eyelid (ptosis) may be the result of birth trauma, damage to CN VII, myasthenia gravis, botulism, encephalitis, and Horner syndrome (Figure 15.16). Unilateral ptosis is concerning because it can result in amblyopia. Children with ptosis require ophthalmic evaluation.

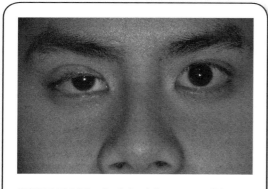

FIGURE 15.16 Ptosis of the right upper eyelid.

There should be no discoloration, swelling, drainage, lesions, or inflammation of the eyelids. The eyelids are normally the same color or slightly darker than the child's surrounding skin. Generalized swelling of the eyelids may be caused by hyperthyroidism or fluid overload. Dehydration results in sunken eyelids. Painless swelling of the margin of the upper eyelid is likely caused by blockage of the meibomian gland, which causes inflammation, erythema (chalazion) (Figure 15.17), or blepharitis (Figure 15.18). Painful redness and swelling of the eyelid margin is a sign of infection of the sebaceous glands at the base of the eyelash (hordeolum or

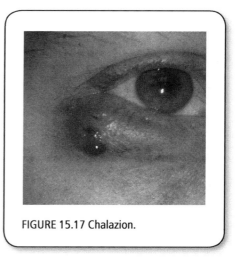

FIGURE 15.17 Chalazion.

"stye") (Figure 15.19) or dacryocystitis. Salmon patches ("stork bites") are commonly seen on the upper eyelids in newborns; these normally disappear by 1 year of age. Capillary hemangiomas of the eyelid may also be seen in newborns (see Chapter 12, Figure 12.5B, C). Amblyopia complicates this condition in 43% to 60%

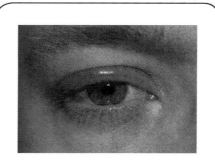

FIGURE 15.18 Blepharitis.

of affected infants (Seiff, Zwick, DeAngelis, & Carter, 2013). Atopic pleats (Dennie-Morgan lines) are folds seen in the lower eyelid (Figure 15.20), which occur with allergic rhinitis. Allergic "shiners" also occur with chronic allergic rhinitis; this is bluish discoloration that causes dark circles under the eyes (see Figure 15.20).

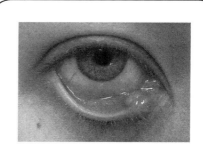

FIGURE 15.19 Hordeolum.

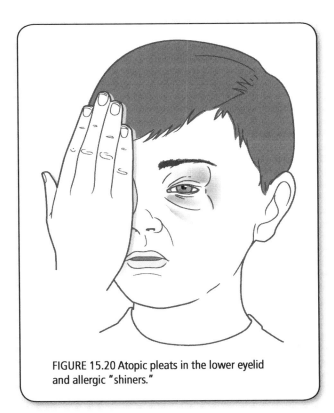

FIGURE 15.20 Atopic pleats in the lower eyelid and allergic "shiners."

dacryostenosis, substance abuse, and hordeolum (stye). Purulent drainage occurs with bacterial conjunctivitis. The sclera is white, smooth, clear, and glistening. In infants, the sclera is thin and may have a slightly blue undertone. A noticeably blue sclera is part of the clinical picture of osteogenesis imperfecta (Elias, Tsai, & Manchester, 2012). The sclera may have a yellowish tinge in children with dark skin; noticeably yellow sclera is due to jaundice.

To inspect the palpebral conjunctivae, the examiner begins with the lower eyelid. The child is asked to look upward while the examiner gently places his or her gloved finger on the skin just below eyelashes of the lower lid of each eye and pushes downward. Healthy palpebral conjunctivae are red because of their rich supply of tiny blood vessels. A pale pink color may indicate anemia. The palpebral conjunctivae should also be moist and free of lesions. The palpebral conjunctiva of the upper eyelid is inspected only when a foreign body or other lesion is suspected because of the discomfort this examination causes. This examination requires skillful maneuvering with a sterile, cotton-tipped swab to evert the eyelid (Figure 15.21).

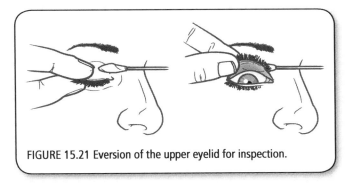

FIGURE 15.21 Eversion of the upper eyelid for inspection.

Position, placement, and a gross assessment of ocular motility and alignment of the eyeballs are assessed next. The examiner begins by first looking at the child's face to note placement of the eyes, comparing one side of the face with the other. In children preschool-aged and older, the examiner stands at the child's eye level, 1 to 2 inches from the child's face, and instructs the child to look straight ahead at the examiner's nose. The child's gaze should be symmetrical and focused directly on the examiner. The eyes should be horizontal, symmetrical, and in line with the top of the pinna; they should not protrude beyond the frontal bone. Shape and spacing are assessed, noting whether the eyes are wide set (hypertelorism) or close set (hypotelorism). Hypertelorism is seen in children with Down syndrome; hypotelorism may be a normal variation, indicate cognitive delay, or may be a dysmorphic feature of a genetic disorder, such as holoprosencephaly (Desai, 2014).

Next, the conjunctivae and sclera are inspected. To inspect the bulbar conjunctivae, the examiner asks the child to look up, down, and side-to-side, while gently pulling the child's lower lids down for easier inspection. The bulbar conjunctivae are normally smooth, clear, moist, and whitish. No drainage should be seen. Generalized redness or inflammation of the conjunctiva may indicate fatigue, eyestrain, conjunctivitis, allergies, foreign body, or marijuana use. Subconjunctival hemorrhages may be seen in the newborn after a precipitous or traumatic vaginal delivery. Watery drainage is associated with allergic rhinitis,

Inspection of the lacrimal apparatus involves assessment of the lacrimal glands and the puncta. Both the area over the lacrimal glands and the puncta should be free of swelling, erythema, or drainage, and the puncta should be clearly visible. Edema of the lacrimal gland or any exudate or erythema around the puncta may be due to nasolacrimal duct obstruction (dacryostenosis) or infection (dacryocystitis). Persistent tearing may be caused by allergies, dacryostenosis, dacryocystitis, or congenital glaucoma.

Internal Eye Structures • The internal eye includes the cornea, lens, pupil, and iris. Assessment of the internal eye begins with inspection of the cornea and lens. To begin, the examiner stands at the child's side and shines a penlight to inspect the cornea; it is normally clear, round, and smooth, without opacities. Any corneal injection, which may result from infection or allergies, must be noted. Irregularities, such as opacities, abrasions, or lacerations, must also be noted. Opacity of the lens occurs with cataracts. Corneal abrasions or lacerations may not be easily visible; thus, a fluorescein stain can be used to highlight any corneal injuries. The corneal reflex can be elicited by gently touching the cornea with a wisp of cotton. CN V carries the afferent sensation to the brain, and the facial nerve (CN VII) carries the efferent message that elicits the blink. The corneal reflex is not routinely tested during examination of the eye but may accompany an assessment of neurologic function.

The pupils are inspected for size, shape, reaction to light, and accommodation. Pupils are normally round and equal in size, with size affected by ambient lighting; age and certain drugs can also affect pupil size (see Table 15.2). Pupil size is measured against a standardized size gauge; the normal range in infants and children is 2 to 6 mm (Figure 15.22). Infants normally have miotic (constricted) pupils. Children normally have larger pupils than infants or adults (Braverman, 2012). If the examiner notes asymmetrical pupils, the size should be noted. Anisocoria, or asymmetry of pupil size, is within normal limits if less than 1 mm; in this case, it must be documented to establish a baseline assessment for the child in the event of a future neurologic injury. If the asymmetry is greater than 1 mm, this may be a sign of neurologic disease and requires a referral.

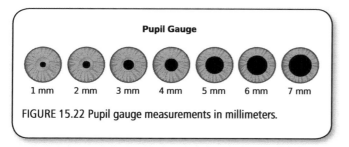

FIGURE 15.22 Pupil gauge measurements in millimeters.

Using a penlight and in a darkened room, the pupils are assessed for reaction to light and accommodation. First, both pupils are observed for direct response to light when the examiner shines the light directly on each pupil and then quickly removes it. The pupils should react briskly to light. Pupils that display a sluggish reaction to light may indicate a neurologic abnormality. Unilateral pupillary dilation and lack of responsiveness to light is an ominous sign, often indicative of eye trauma or severe neurologic injury.

Next, the examiner assesses the pupils for direct (same side) and consensual (opposite side) response by blocking the light from the eye not being examined, either by holding a hand down the midline of the eye or by asking the child (if developmentally able to

cooperate) to hold an occluder between his eyes and parallel to his nose. Next, the examiner shines the light on the right eye, observing both the right and left pupils for prompt constriction. The procedure is then repeated for the left eye. If CN III is intact, both pupils should respond by constricting. Constriction of the pupil into which the light is shone is a direct response to light; in the other pupil, it is considered a consensual response to light.

Pupils are also assessed for accommodation. Pupils accommodate to objects at close range by constricting and to those at long range by dilating. The pupils also converge (move together) as an object is moved toward the face. The examiner can test for pupillary accommodation and convergence by holding a pen approximately 12 inches from the child's face and asking the child to follow it with his or her eyes. As the examiner slowly moves the pen toward the child's nose, the pupils should constrict and converge. It is customary to document pupils that are equal, round, and react to light and accommodation as "PERRLA."

The iris is inspected for color and shape. For the first 6 months of life, the iris is blue to grayish in light-skinned infants and muddy brown in dark-skinned infants. The iris transitions to its permanent color by 12 months; the colors include variations of blue, green, and brown. Occasionally the irises are different colors (heterochromia); this can occur with Horner syndrome or may be a normal finding. Mild-to-complete absence of pigment of the iris occurs in albinism; the degree of pigmentation depends on the type of albinism (Bashour, Hasanee, & Ahmed, 2012; Braverman, 2012). The iris should be circular. Any coloboma should be noted. Brushfield spots are tiny white spots on the iris, usually arranged in a concentric circle around the pupil. These spots are seen in Down syndrome and tuberous sclerosis (Chen, 2013; Franz & Thomas, 2013). Pale brown nodules (Lisch nodules) may be seen on the iris; these occur with type I neurofibromatosis and appear during late school age. Aniridia (absence of the iris) may occur with autosomal dominant transmission or with Wilms' tumor (Braverman, 2012). Aniridia causes poor vision and is associated with corneal opacities, cataracts, and glaucoma (Braverman, 2012).

Palpation of External Eye Structures

The bony orbit, eyebrows, lacrimal apparatus, and preauricular lymph nodes are gently palpated for tenderness, swelling, or masses. Gloves are worn when palpating the nasolacrimal duct. The eye itself should feel firm and nontender. There should be no tenderness, masses, or movement of the bone. The lacrimal glands should be nonpalpable and nontender. No drainage should be expressed from the puncta when palpating the nasolacrimal duct; this may indicate dacryostenosis. Tenderness, erythema, and exudate occur with dacryostenosis and dacryocystitis.

Ophthalmoscopic Examination

The ophthalmoscopic examination enables the examiner to inspect the ocular fundus. It involves inspection of the red reflex, optic disc, retinal vasculature, and macula. This assessment requires cooperation from the child, who must be still and keep his or her eyes open during the examination. In preterm infants, this examination is done by a pediatric ophthalmologist and requires the use of a dilating agent and lid speculum for adequate view of the fundus. In healthy, full-term infants, only the red reflex is elicited, and full ophthalmoscopy is deferred. Symptomatic older infants and toddlers should be examined while supine with the parent holding the child securely. The ophthalmoscopic examination should be part of the routine assessment beginning at age 3 years.

The ophthalmoscope provides illumination and magnification to view the inner eye anatomy. Details on the technique for using an ophthalmoscope in children are given in Box 15.1. The first step of the ophthalmoscopic examination is assessment of the red reflex. From about 12 to 15 inches away, the beam of the ophthalmoscope light is shined on the pupil. This elicits a reflection of the retinal background, the red reflex (Figure 15.23). The red reflex should be seen in both eyes. Each pupil should be reddish orange in light-skinned children, and brownish red in dark-skinned children. An absent red reflex suggests cataracts, glaucoma, or ROP. An absent or white reflex (leukocoria) may indicate retinoblastoma or retinal detachment. Absence of the red reflex requires an immediate referral to a pediatric ophthalmologist.

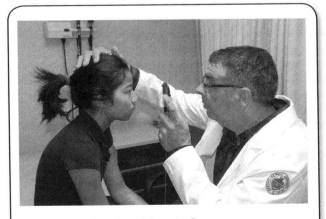

FIGURE 15.23 Elicitation of the red reflex.

BOX 15.1 Pediatric Ophthalmoscopic Examination

- Have the parents remain nearby to hold and comfort the child.
- Position infants and toddlers in the supine position, held securely by a parent.
- Children preschool-aged and older can sit on the examination table, facing the examiner.
- With children preschool-aged and older, explain the procedure to the child, providing reassurance that ophthalmoscopy is not painful.
- If the child wears glasses, ask him or her to remove them.
- Do not open the child's eyes forcibly; this will exacerbate the child's fear, discomfort, and agitation, thus inhibiting or precluding the examination.
- Ask the child to remain as still as possible.
- Darken the room so the pupils dilate, exposing more of the retina for examination. Explain to the child why the room is darkened to alleviate fears.
- Start by using the smallest round light beam on the ophthalmoscope, and then adjust the beam to the maximum brightness that the child can tolerate.
- Ask the child to look at something at eye level on a far wall.
- Set the lens of the ophthalmoscope to 0 diopters.
- Approach the child from about 12 inches away, gradually moving closer, adjusting the focus on the ophthalmoscope as needed.
- To magnify the structures of the eye, adjust the lens of the aperture as needed.
- The examiner uses his or her right hand and right eye to examine the child's right eye, and left hand and left eye to examine the child's left eye.
- The procedure is done on both eyes.

The red reflex is then assessed *simultaneously* in both pupils (Bruckner test). In a darkened room, from a distance of approximately 2 to 3 feet, the examiner views both pupils simultaneously through the ophthalmoscope as the child fixates on the light. The red reflex in each eye should be equal in color, brightness, and size. An asymmetrical red reflex may be caused by cataracts, retinoblastoma, refractive errors (e.g., myopia, hyperopia, astigmatism), or strabismus; an asymmetrical red reflex also requires a referral.

The next step is to examine the fundus. To facilitate this, the examiner asks the child to focus on a distant focal point, such as a picture on the wall, while keeping his or her eyes as still as possible. Approaching the child from a distance of about 12 inches and at a

15-degree angle, the provider centers the light from the ophthalmoscope on the child's eye. The lens setting on the ophthalmoscope should be adjusted as necessary to focus properly. The first structure that is located is the optic disc, which is normally light yellow to pink and is round and flat with distinct edges. The physiologic cup is a small depression just lateral to the center of the optic disc, slightly lighter in color than the disc. The shape, size, and color of the cup are noted. A pale white optic disc is seen in meningitis, optic neuritis, or encephalitis. Swelling of the optic disc is evident when the disc margins are blurry or obliterated and the physiologic cup cannot be seen (papilledema). This is caused by increased intracranial pressure, which, if untreated, may lead to optic nerve atrophy and blindness. Papilledema is rarely seen in children younger than 2 years of age because their cranial sutures are not fully fused. The optic disc and physiologic cup are compared for size; the cup should be no greater than one third the size of the disc, and the cup-to-disc ratio should be compared in both eyes for symmetry. Increased intraocular pressure (e.g., glaucoma) causes the size of the physiologic cup to increase.

The four sets of arteries and veins that emerge from the optic disc are inspected next. The arteries are thinner and a brighter red than the veins, which are larger and darker. The arteries reflect light; the veins do not. The normal retinal arterial-to-venous ratio is approximately 2:3 in children. A change in this ratio may signal a vasoconstricting disease. The retinal background is also inspected; it is normally red-orange or dark brownish red, depending on the child's skin color. A lighter area is normally seen near the optic disc. Any areas of hemorrhage or exudate are noted. Retinal hemorrhages, which may result from head trauma, including shaking injuries, appear as red lesions. Retinal telangiectasis can

cause dilation of the retinal vessels and exudation (white lesions), giving the retina a pale yellow appearance, and in some instances, leukocoria. Exudate can be either hard (made of protein or fat) or soft (tiny retinal infarctions, often termed "cotton wool exudates") (Orient, 2005). If the exudate accumulates near the macula, blindness results. Inflammation and exudate in the retina can also be caused by toxoplasmosis, CMV, herpes simplex virus, varicella, measles, leukemia, diabetes, congenital syphilis, or rubella infections (Orient, 2005). Retinopathy is also seen in premature infants and in children with diabetes or sickle cell disease (Braverman, 2012; Phillpotts, Duong, Shapiro, Castro, & Fiscella, 2012).

The avascular macula is then located. It should be the same size as the optic disc, located approximately 3 mm from the temporal edge of the disc, and have a bright spot in the center, the fovea centralis. The macula is very sensitive to light; blinking and tearing result when light from the ophthalmoscope is directed onto the macula, causing pupillary constriction and making further assessment difficult. Therefore, the macula is examined last. Figure 15.24 shows a normal fundus. A summary of the components of the eye examination for well children is given in Table 15.4.

COMMON DIAGNOSTIC STUDIES

Laboratory and radiologic studies are not a routine component of the evaluation of the eye and vision in a child. For children with dysmorphic features, chromosomal studies are indicated. A finding of exophthalmos may necessitate thyroid function tests to evaluate the child for hyperthyroidism. Screening for Lyme disease is necessary for children who present with CN VI or CN VII palsy and who live in or have a recent history of travel to

TABLE 15.4	Summary of Well-Child Eye Examination Screening
AGE	**ASSESSMENTS**
Neonate	External (penlight) examination for lesions, edema, and discharge Red reflex (pupillary light reflex; Bruckner test) Pupillary examination Ocular alignment (corneal light reflex) Congenital cataracts
6 months–3 years	As for neonate, plus: Ability to fix and follow light, face, or small toy Ocular alignment (corneal light reflex, Hirschberg test, cover-uncover test)
3–5 years	As for neonate through age 3 years, plus: Visual acuity (Allen cards, HOTV, Snellen tumbling E) Ophthalmoscopic examination (red reflex, funduscopic exam)
6 years and older	As for neonate through age 5 years, plus: Visual acuity (Snellen letters or numbers)

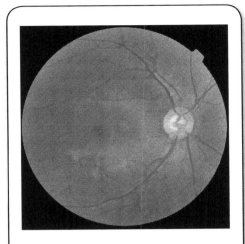

FIGURE 15.24 Normal ocular fundus.

Sclera: white; **conjunctiva:** clear and not injected
Cornea: clear, smooth; no opacities
EOMs (extraocular movements): intact
Pupils: PERRLA (pupils equal, round, reactive to light and accommodation)
Corneal light reflex: symmetrical bilaterally
Peripheral vision: visual fields intact bilaterally
Accommodation and convergence: present bilaterally
Direct and consensual light: present bilaterally
Cover/uncover: negative
Funduscopy: red reflex present bilaterally; no opacities
Discs: well marginated, pale yellow; vessels present in all quadrants; arteries/veins ratio 2:3; no papilledema; retinal background light red; no hemorrhage or exudate; macula avascular without scarring
Assessment: eye exam normal; visual acuity 20/20

an area where Lyme disease is endemic. In children who may be exhibiting signs of bacterial meningitis, a complete blood count, blood culture, and cerebrospinal fluid culture are necessary. Imaging studies are indicated for children with a suspected brain mass, with magnetic resonance imaging being the preferred study to detect intracranial abnormalities that may be the cause of acutely acquired strabismus. A computed tomography (CT) scan of the head, with and without contrast, is useful in emergency situations to diagnose intracranial masses, infections, fractures, or vascular injuries. An orbital CT scan can reveal orbital fractures, infections, and abnormalities of the extraocular muscles (Nield et al., 2008).

DOCUMENTATION OF FINDINGS

Sample Write-Up: Well Child

Subjective Data

A 15-year-old boy denies difficulty with vision; does not wear corrective lenses; denies eye pain, swelling, or discharge. Last vision exam was 1 year ago.

Objective Data

Visual acuity: 20/20 OD (right eye), 20/20 OS (left eye), 20/20 OU (both eyes) (Snellen), without corrective lenses

Sample Write-Up: Injured Adolescent

Subjective Data

A 16-year-old boy presents to the emergency room with a history of being struck in the right eye with a baseball 1 hour prior. Reports double vision and marked eye pain; denies blurry vision. Denies headache, bleeding, or clear fluid leaking from nose. Past medical history is noncontributory.

Objective Data

T: 98.2°F (36.8°C); **P:** 96 beats per minute; **RR:** 20 breaths per minute; **BP:** 130/80 mmHg
General: right eyelid markedly edematous; periorbital edema with marked ecchymosis; slight enophthalmos; no eyelid laceration; conjunctival injection and hyphema noted; no active bleeding from eye, nose, or mouth; no clear drainage from nose
Eye: cornea and iris intact; sclera white; conjunctiva clear; pupils equal, round, and reactive; pupils OD (right eye) 3/3 = 3/1 OS (left eye); EOMs restricted with downward gaze
Ear: tympanic membranes intact without hemotympanum bilaterally
Assessment: maxillofacial CT scan shows right inferior orbital blow-out fracture without facial fracture

---

Notable Clinical Findings

- History of prematurity or birth weight < 1500 g/perinatal hypoxia
- Immunization delay
- Taking medications that can cause change in pupil size
- Strabismus beyond age 6 months
- Eso- or exotropia

- Coloboma
- Dacrostenosis
- Dacrocystitis
- Changes in red reflex
- Presence of Brushfield's spots
- Complaints of blurred or double vision
- Burning/itching/dry eyes

(continued)

Notable Clinical Findings (*continued*)

- Excessive lacrimation with or without rhinorrhea
- Eye drainage
- Conjunctival injection
- Eye pain
- Foreign body sensation in eye
- Burning/itching/painful or edematous eyelid

- Reports of head tilt, especially when looking ahead
- Nystagmus
- Photophobia
- Ptosis
- Subconjunctival hemorrhage
- Changes in vision

References

American Academy of Pediatrics Committee on Practice and Ambulatory Medicine, Section on Ophthalmology, American Association of Certified Orthoptists, American Association for Pediatric Ophthalmology and Strabismus, & American Academy of Ophthalmology. (2007). Statement of reaffirmation: Eye examination in infants, children, and young adults by pediatricians. *Pediatrics, 120*(3), 683–684. *Pediatrics, 111,* 902–907.

Anzivino, E., Fioriti, D., Mischitelli, M., Bellizzi, A., Barucca, V., Chiarini, F., & Pietropaolo, V. (2009). Herpes simplex virus infection in pregnancy and in neonate: Status of art of epidemiology, diagnosis, therapy and prevention. *Virology Journal, 6,* 40.

Ball, J. W., Bindler, R. C., & Cowen, K. J. (2012). Eyes, ears, nose, and throat. In J. W. Ball, R. C. Bindler, & K. J. Cowen (Eds.), *Principles of pediatric nursing: Caring for children* (5th ed., pp. 514–550). Upper Saddle River, NJ: Pearson Education, Inc.

Bashour, M., Hasanee, K. & Ahmed, I. I. K. (2012). *Albinism.* Retrieved from http://emedicine.medscape.com/article/1200472-overview

Bashour, M., Menassa, J., & Geronitis, C. (2013). *Retinopathy of prematurity.* Retrieved from http://emedicine.medscape.com/article/1225022-overview

Bernard, T. J., Knupp, K., Yang, M. L., Kedia, S., Levisohn, P. M., & Moe, P. G. (2012). Neurologic and muscular disorders. In W. W. Hay, M. J. Levin, R. R. Deterding, M. J. Abzug, & J. M. Sondheimer (Eds.), *Current pediatric diagnosis & treatment* (21st ed., pp. 740–829). New York, NY: McGraw-Hill.

Braverman, R. S. (2012). Eye. In W. W. Hay, M. J. Levin, R. R. Deterding, M. J. Abzug, & J. M. Sondheimer (Eds.), *Current pediatric diagnosis & treatment* (21st ed., pp. 424–464). New York, NY: McGraw-Hill.

Carter, R. C., Jacobson, S. W., Molteno, C. D., Chiodo, L. M., Viljoen, D., & Jacobson, J. L. (2005). Effects of prenatal alcohol exposure on infant visual acuity. *Journal of Pediatrics, 147*(4), 473–479.

Channell, K., & Washington, E. R. (2012). *Marfan syndrome.* Retrieved from http://emedicine.medscape.com/article/1258926-overview#a0112

Chen, H. (2013). *Down syndrome.* Retrieved from http://emedicine.medscape.com/article/943216-overview

Cibis, G. W., Urban, R. C., & Dahl, A. A. (2013). *Primary congenital glaucoma.* Retrieved from http://emedicine.medscape.com/article/1206081-overview

Davis, D. W., Burns, B. M., Wilkerson, S. A., & Steichen, J. J. (2005). Visual perceptual skills in children born with very low birth weights. *Journal of Pediatric Health Care, 19*(6), 363–368.

Desai, J. (2014). *Holoprosencephaly.* Retrieved from http://emedicine.medscape.com/article/2060996-overview

Deshmukh, C. T. (2007). Minimizing side effects of systemic corticosteroids in children. *Indian Journal of Dermatology, Venerology and Leprology, 73*(4), 218–221.

Elias, E. R., Tsai, A. C., & Manchester, D. K. (2012). Genetics and dysmorphology. In W. W. Hay, M. J. Levin, R. R. Deterding, M. J. Abzug, & J. M. Sondheimer (Eds.), *Current pediatric*

diagnosis & treatment. (21st ed., pp.1088–1122). New York, NY: McGraw-Hill.

Ezike, E., & Ang, J. Y. (2013). *Rubella.* Retrieved from http://emedicine.medscape.com/article/968523-overview

Foster, C. S., Yuksel, E., Anzar, F., & Ekong, A. S. (2013). *Dry eye syndrome.* Retrieved from http://emedicine.medscape.com/article/1210417-overview

Franz, D. N., & Thomas, C. W. (2013). *Tuberous sclerosis.* Retrieved from http://emedicine.medscape.com/article/1177711-overview

Gharahbaghian, L., & Lopez, N., (2013). *Cough, cold, and allergy preparation toxicity.* Retrieved from http://emedicine.medscape.com/article/1010513-overview

Good, W. V., & Hou, C. (2006). Sweep visual evoked potential grating acuity thresholds paradoxically improve in low-luminance conditions in children with cortical vision impairments. *Investigative Ophthalmology and Visual Science, 47,* 3220–3224.

Gupta, B. K. (2014). *Monofixation syndrome.* Retrieved from http://emedicine.medscape.com/article/1199953-overview

Halstead, S. M., Deakyne, S. J., Bajaj, L., Enzenauer, R., & Roosevelt, G. E. (2012). The effect of ketamine on intraocular pressure in pediatric patients during procedural sedation. *Academic Emergency Medicine, 19*(10), 1145–1150.

Hockenberry, M. J. (2011). Communication and physical assessment of the child. In M. J. Hockenberry & D. Wilson (Eds.), *Wong's nursing care of infants and children* (9th ed., pp. 117–178). St. Louis, MO: Mosby.

Hope, C., & Maslin, K. (2007). Random dot stereogram E in vision screening of children. *Clinical and Experimental Ophthalmology, 18*(3), 319–324.

Hornor, G. (2012). Medical evaluation for child physical abuse: What the PNP needs to know. *Journal of Pediatric Health Care, 26*(3), 163–170.

Janse van Rensburg, E., & Meyer, D. (2013). *Astute and safe use of topical ocular corticosteroids in general practice: Practical guidelines.* Retrieved from http://www.ajol.info/index.php/cme/article/viewFile/88007/77645

Kaul, P. (2012). Adolescent substance abuse. In W. W. Hay, M. J. Levin, R. R. Deterding, M. J. Abzug, & J. M. Sondheimer (Eds.), *Current pediatric diagnosis & treatment* (21st ed., pp. 153–166). New York, NY: McGraw-Hill.

Lewis, D. W. (2009). Pediatric migraine. *Neurologic clinics, 27*(2), 481–501.

Lu, C., Kuang, T., & Chou, J. C. (2006). Methylphenidate (Ritalin)-associated cataract and glaucoma. *Journal of the Chinese Medical Association, 69*(12), 589–590.

McCourt, E. A., Enzenauer, R. W., Jatla, K. K., & Zhou, F. (2013). *Neonatal conjunctivitis.* Retrieved from http://emedicine.medscape.com/article/1192190-overview

Mirza, A., & Guinazu, D. E. (2013). *Chorioretinitis.* Retrieved from http://emedicine.medscape.com/article/962761-overview

Nield, L. S., Mangano, L. M., & Kamat, D. (2008). Strabismus: A close-up look. *Consultant for Pediatricians, 7*(1), 17–20, 22–25.

Orient, J. M. (2005). The eye. In J. M. Orient (Ed.), *Sapira's art and science of bedside diagnosis* (3rd ed., pp. 183–240). Philadelphia, PA: Lippincott Williams & Wilkins.

Phillpotts, B. A., Duong, H. Q., Shapiro, M. J., Castro, O., & Fiscella, R. G. (2012). *Hemoglobin retinopathy*. Retrieved from http://emedicine.medscape.com/article/1225300-overview

Schatz, M. P., & Carter, J. E. (2013). *Childhood optic neuritis*. Retrieved from http://emedicine.medscape.com/article/1217290-overview

Seiff, S. R., Zwick, O. M., DeAngelis, D. D., & Carter, S. (2013). *Capillary hemangioma*. Retrieved from http://emedicine.medscape.com/article/1218805-overview

Sladden, M. J., & Harman, K. E. (2007). What is the chance of a normal pregnancy in a woman whose fetus has been exposed to isotretinoin? *JAMA Dermatology, 143*(9), 1187–1188.

Speer, M. E. (2013). *Varicella-zoster infection in the newborn*. Retrieved from http://www.uptodate.com/contents/varicella-zoster-infection-in-the-newborn

Thilo, E. H., & Rosenberg, A. A. (2012). The newborn infant. In W. W. Hay, M. J. Levin, R. R. Deterding, M. J. Abzug, & J. M. Sondheimer (Eds.), *Current pediatric diagnosis & treatment* (21st ed., pp. 9–72). New York, NY: McGraw-Hill.

U.S. Food and Drug Administration. (2007). *Public health advisory: Nonprescription cough and cold medication use in children*. Retrieved from http://www.fda.gov/Drugs/DrugSafety/DrugSafetyPodcasts/ucm078927.htm

Wu, L., Evans, T., & Garcia, R. A. (2013). *Ophthalmologic manifestations of toxoplasmosis*. Retrieved from http://emedicine.medscape.com/article/2044905-overview#a1

Assessment of the Face, Nose, and Oral Cavity

Assessment of the face, nose, and throat is an essential skill for the pediatric health care provider. Upper respiratory infections, allergies, oral or facial trauma, dental caries, and pharyngitis are common diagnoses in children. When obtaining the history and physical examination of the face, nose, and throat in children, the health care provider can also identify parent and child teaching opportunities, for example, encouraging regular dental care, compliance with antibiotic therapy for streptococcal pharyngitis, and the consistent use of sports safety gear to avoid oral and facial injuries.

ANATOMY AND PHYSIOLOGY

The Face

The face is composed of 14 bones, which are illustrated in Figure 16.1. Each of these bones articulates at sutures except for the mandible, which is able to move up and down and side to side at the temporomandibular joint. The bones of the face include the two nasal bones, which form the bridge of the nose, the two inferior conchae, two palatine, two lacrimal, and one vomer bones. The

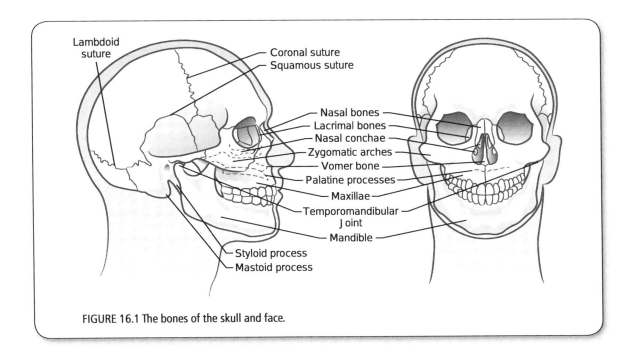

FIGURE 16.1 The bones of the skull and face.

zygomatic arch (two bones) creates the cheek prominence; the *maxilla* (two bones) forms the upper jaw on either side of the face. The upper surface of the maxilla comprises the floor of the orbit; the lower portion forms most of the hard palate. The unpaired *mandible* (one bone) forms the lower jaw.

The Nose

The nose is the entry point for the respiratory system. It has four main functions: (a) to act as the main site for air entry, inspiration, and expiration; (b) to warm, moisten, and filter inhaled air; (c) to allow for sound resonation with speech, and (d) to act as the sensory organ for smell. The upper third of the external portion of the nose is composed of bone, and the lower two thirds is composed of cartilage. The nose can be divided into four areas: the superior bony portion or nasal bridge; the cartilaginous middle of the nose or vault; the inferior corner or "tip" with two oval openings called the *nares* (nostrils); and immediately inside each naris, the interior *vestibule*.

The internal nose, or *nasal vestibule*, is composed of two cavities separated by the bony and cartilaginous nasal *septum*. It extends from the opening of the nares to the *nasopharynx*. Commonly, the nasal septum is not perfectly straight and may deviate toward one side. The anterior portion of the nasal septum contains *Kiesselbach's plexus*, a highly vascular area that is a common site of nosebleeds. The lateral wall of each nasal cavity has three bony projections known as the *superior*, *middle*, and *inferior turbinates*, which are highly vascular and lined with cilia and mucous membranes. The structure of the turbinates serves to increase surface area to warm and humidify inhaled air. Secreted mucus and cilia function to filter inhaled air by trapping small particles. Under each turbinate is a cleft, or *meatus*. The *middle meatus* drains the sinuses and the

inferior meatus drains tears from the nasolacrimal duct. The *olfactory receptors* are found on the mucosa along the *superior turbinate* and upper third of the nasal septum. These smell receptors trigger cranial nerve (CN)I (olfactory) to transmit impulses to the temporal lobe of the brain for interpretation. Figure 16.2 illustrates the structures of the internal nose.

The Nasopharynx

The nasopharynx forms the superior portion of the pharynx (throat) and is continuous with the *oropharynx*. It is located above and posterior to the nasal cavity and extends inferiorly to the uvula. The *pharyngeal tonsils* (adenoids) are located on the superior posterior wall of the nasopharynx and the openings to the *eustachian tubes* are located along the lateral walls. The inferior portion of the nasopharynx is formed by the soft palate; the remaining portion of the nasopharynx is surrounded by bone.

The Paranasal Sinuses

The paranasal sinuses are air pockets on either side of the nasal cavity. They are named according to the cranial bones within which the sinuses lie (Figure 16.3):

- The *frontal* sinuses are located in the frontal bone superior and medial to the orbits, just above the eyebrows.
- The *maxillary* sinuses, the largest of the sinuses, lie in the maxillae along the side walls of the nasal cavity, under the eyes.
- The *ethmoid* sinuses are located between the nose and orbits.
- The *sphenoid* sinuses lie in the sphenoid bone, behind the eyes and nose and under the pituitary gland deep within the skull.

The sinuses communicate with and are lined with the same ciliated mucous membrane as the nasal cavity.

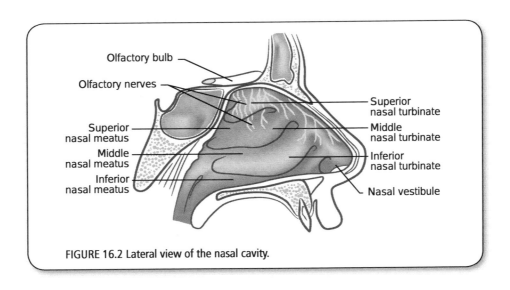

FIGURE 16.2 Lateral view of the nasal cavity.

Olfactory bulb

Olfactory nerves

Superior nasal meatus

Middle nasal meatus

Inferior nasal meatus

Superior nasal turbinate

Middle nasal turbinate

Inferior nasal turbinate

Nasal vestibule

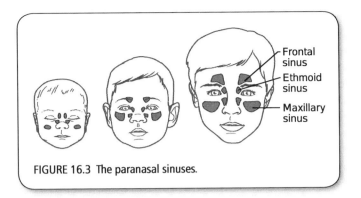

FIGURE 16.3 The paranasal sinuses.

Sinuses lighten the weight of the skull, serve as resonators for sound production, and produce mucus that drains into the nasal cavity. The sinus openings are narrow and occlude easily, often leading to inflammation or sinusitis.

The Mouth

The mouth, or oral cavity, has several functions: to act as an additional airway for the respiratory system; to function as a starting point for the digestive system, encompassing taste, mastication, salivary secretion, and swallowing; and to form sounds for normal speech articulation. The oral cavity is composed of the *lips*, *cheeks*, *hard* and *soft palates*, *tongue*, *teeth*, *salivary glands*, and *pharynx* (Figure 16.4). The mandible and maxilla comprise the bony structure that supports the oral cavity.

The lips act as an entranceway into the mouth, lying on the anterior border of the oral cavity. The lips are quite vascular and are sensitive to temperature. The cheeks form the lateral border of the oral cavity and are lined inside with *buccal mucosa*. The lips and cheeks are innervated by CNs V (trigeminal) and VII (facial). These CNs control sucking, swallowing, chewing, biting, and talking.

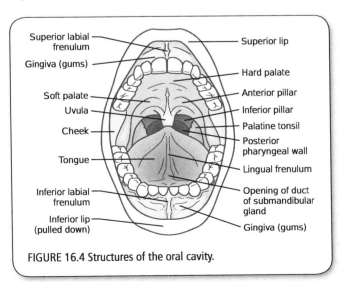

FIGURE 16.4 Structures of the oral cavity.

The palate separates the nasal and oral cavities and forms the roof of the mouth. The palate is divided into two parts: the hard palate and soft palate. The hard palate comprises the anterior two thirds of the palate and is made of bone. The posterior third of the palate is the soft palate, which is composed of muscle and is part of the lateral pharyngeal wall. Extending from the soft palate is the *uvula*, a vertical muscular structure that hangs from the middle of the soft palate. The soft palate and uvula receive motor innervation from CN IX (glossopharyngeal); this motor ability is essential for the creation of the palatal sounds that are necessary for normal speech articulation. The uvula also functions by closing the nasopharynx during swallowing.

The tongue is a muscle that lies at the floor of the oral cavity and is attached to the hyoid bone and mandible. The dorsal surface and sides of the tongue are covered with papillae, which contain taste buds. The ventral surface of the tongue is covered by a thin mucous membrane with multiple visible blood vessels. The tongue is attached to the floor of the mouth by mucosal tissue, the *lingual frenulum*. The muscular movement of the tongue allows for mastication, swallowing, and the formation of speech. The tongue is innervated by CNs IX (glossopharyngeal) and X (vagus) for sensation and taste, and CN XII (hypoglossal) for motor function.

There are three paired salivary glands in the mouth, all of which secrete enzymes that begin the first step in digestion. Saliva also aids in mobilizing and destroying oral bacteria that can lead to dental caries and tooth decay. The largest pair of salivary glands, the *parotid glands*, lies on the side of the face anterior to the ear. These glands become inflamed with *parotitis* (mumps). The parotid glands secrete saliva into the *Stensen's ducts*, which open into the buccal mucosa opposite the upper second molar. The *submandibular glands* are the second largest and lie on the floor of the mouth, secreting saliva through the *Wharton's ducts*, which are found on either side of the frenulum. The smallest salivary glands, the *sublingual glands*, are located on the floor of the mouth beneath the tongue. In addition to these three pairs of major salivary glands, there are hundreds of very small salivary glands scattered throughout the oral cavity, lining the mucous membranes and oropharynx.

Between the ages of 6 and 8 months, the first *deciduous* or *primary* teeth begin to erupt. Each tooth consists of a *root*, which is embedded in gingival tissue and encased in bone, and the *crown*, the visible part of the tooth that is white and covered in enamel, the most calcified tissue in the body. The first teeth to erupt are the central mandibular incisors, followed by the maxillary central incisors, then the mandibular and maxillary lateral incisors. Figure 16.5 illustrates the normal sequence of primary tooth eruption. By 30 months, all 20 deciduous teeth should have erupted except the second molars; these should be in place by 3 years. Nutritional, genetic,

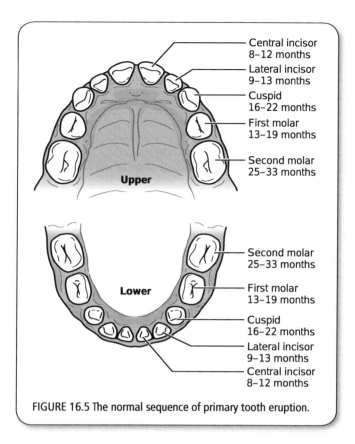

Central incisor
8–12 months

Lateral incisor
9–13 months

Cuspid
16–22 months

First molar
13–19 months

Second molar
25–33 months

Upper

Second molar
25–33 months

First molar
13–19 months

Lower

Cuspid
16–22 months

Lateral incisor
9–13 months

Central incisor
8–12 months

FIGURE 16.5 The normal sequence of primary tooth eruption.

and environmental factors can affect the timing and sequence of tooth eruption in children.

The deciduous teeth exfoliate between 6 and 12 years of age, and the mandible and maxilla grow in size. By 12 years of age, the child should have all 32 permanent teeth. Figure 16.6 depicts the normal sequence of the eruption of permanent teeth.

The Pharynx

The pharynx, or throat, located behind the mouth and nose, is divided into three parts according to the anatomic area: the nasopharynx, oropharynx, and hypopharynx. The upper part is the nasopharynx, which is posterior to the nasal cavity; below the soft palate lays the oropharynx, and below the oropharynx lays the hypopharynx. Masses of *lymphoid tissue*, the *palatine tonsils*, are located on either side of the oropharynx, just behind the arches of the soft palate. The palatine tonsils form the anterior and posterior tonsillar pillars. The lingual tonsils are found at the base of the tongue and the pharyngeal tonsils, or adenoids, are located in the roof of the nasopharynx. Only the palatine tonsils are visible on inspection.

DEVELOPMENTAL CONSIDERATIONS

The facial structures begin to develop between the fourth and eighth weeks of gestation. From the eighth week

of development until birth, facial development occurs slowly and primarily involves changes in position and proportion of the facial structures.

The nose begins to develop in utero during the foruth week of gestation, and is completed by the 12th week of gestation. In the newborn, the nose is composed mainly of cartilage, making the nose soft and malleable; the position of the fetus in the uterus can result in temporary deformities of the nose that resolve spontaneously after birth. Infants have a flat narrow nasal bridge and are obligate nose breathers until they are 4 months of age. Because of this, young infants with nasal congestion can develop respiratory distress quite rapidly, and their ability to breathe is impeded during feedings. Until approximately 6 years of age, the inferior meatus does not function except for draining the nasolacrimal duct; this explains the increased nasal drainage in children when crying or with ocular inflammation. The nasal septum ossifies by 3 years; by adolescence, the nose becomes triangular and develops a bony structure. Sense of smell is poor at birth but develops with age.

Adenoids (nasopharyngeal tonsils) begin forming in the third month of fetal development and are fully formed by the seventh fetal month. The adenoidal tissue begins to shrink in late childhood. The function of adenoids decreases with the decrease in size.

The ethmoid and maxillary sinuses form during gestational months 3 to 4 and, thus, are present at birth. The ethmoid sinuses develop rapidly between 6 and 8 years of age, and again during adolescence. The sphenoid sinuses are fully formed by age 5; the frontal sinuses develop at approximately 7 to 8 years of age but are not fully developed until late adolescence (Singh, 2013). Generally, full development of the paranasal sinuses occurs from ages 8 to 14 years as the cranial bones enlarge at that time, roughly attaining adult size (Singh, 2013).

During the seventh and eighth weeks of gestation, the palate begins to form and is completed by the 12th week of gestation, with fusion of the primary and secondary palates. Failure of fusion during this process is known as *cleft palate*. The mouth of a young infant is short and smooth with a longer soft palate. This proportionately larger soft palate in the young infant increases the risk of airway obstruction. By 6 months of age, the mouth is proportioned like that of an adult. Salivary secretions increase at approximately 3 to 4 months of age. This, coupled with an underdeveloped swallowing reflex, explains the increased drooling noted in infants in this age group (Hockenberry & Wilson, 2011).

Both sets of teeth, temporary and permanent, begin developing in utero between the sixth and eighth weeks of gestation. Calcification of the primary teeth takes place during the fourth month of gestation and is complete by 1 year of age. Permanent molars calcify between ages 18 months and 3 years. Teething is

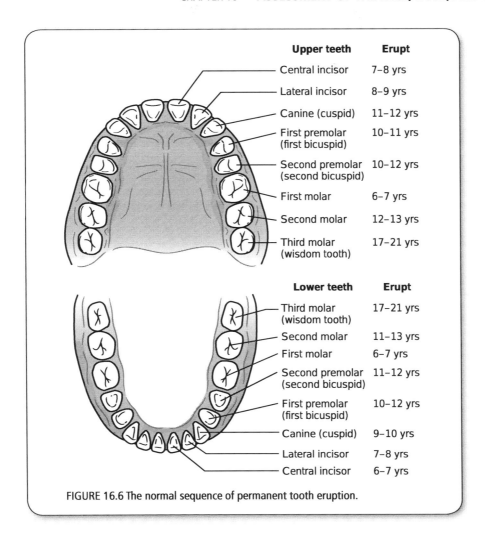

Upper teeth	Erupt
Central incisor	7–8 yrs
Lateral incisor	8–9 yrs
Canine (cuspid)	11–12 yrs
First premolar (first bicuspid)	10–11 yrs
Second premolar (second bicuspid)	10–12 yrs
First molar	6–7 yrs
Second molar	12–13 yrs
Third molar (wisdom tooth)	17–21 yrs

Lower teeth	Erupt
Third molar (wisdom tooth)	17–21 yrs
Second molar	11–13 yrs
First molar	6–7 yrs
Second premolar (second bicuspid)	11–12 yrs
First premolar (first bicuspid)	10–12 yrs
Canine (cuspid)	9–10 yrs
Lateral incisor	7–8 yrs
Central incisor	6–7 yrs

FIGURE 16.6 The normal sequence of permanent tooth eruption.

normally preceded by a period of increased drooling, local gingival inflammation, and irritability. Teething itself is not associated with fever or diarrhea.

Infants normally have a large tongue in proportion to the size of their mouth; this persists until age 8 to 12 years, when the mandible has a growth peak (Swamy Chidananda & Mallikarjun, 2004). The rooting, gag, suck, and extrusion reflexes persist until age 4 months. The sense of taste is immature at birth but quickly develops around age 2 to 3 months as the taste buds mature. The sense of taste is not fully developed until approximately 2 years of age.

The palatine tonsils are normally large in young children (size 2+ to 3+) and continue to enlarge gradually over the first 8 to 10 years of life, at which time the tonsils begin to shrink.

CULTURAL, ETHNIC, AND RACIAL CONSIDERATIONS

Certain conditions occur more frequently in various racial or ethnic groups, depending on cultural practices, environmental and socioeconomic factors, or in some instances, genetics. *Cleft lip* and cleft palate, for example, occur most commonly in Asians and Native Americans and least commonly in Blacks (Tinanoff, 2011). A *bifid uvula*, a condition in which the uvula is partially or completely split, is more common in Native Americans and Asians (Heathcote, 2005). Cultural factors may influence the health of a child's teeth. Lack of knowledge regarding the importance of primary teeth, fear of the dentist, health beliefs about disease causation and prevention, and multiple extended family caregivers, especially elders, affect access to preventive dental care (Hilton, Stephen, Barker, & Weintraub, 2007). Hispanic children have the highest rate of dental caries in the United States; this is because of multiple factors, including parental health beliefs and knowledge deficits, delays in seeking dental care, and economic and social factors. African American children also have a higher incidence of dental caries and gingivitis than Caucasian children (Centers for Disease Control and Prevention [CDC], 2013a). Dental caries in young children that occurs as a result of being put to bed with sweetened drinks in a bottle or sippy cup (early childhood caries) are more prevalent in Hispanic, Native American, and Alaskan Native children and among children of recent immigrants (CDC, 2013a).

ASSESSMENT OF THE FACE, NOSE, AND MOUTH

History

When obtaining the history of the face, nose, and mouth, the focus is on the presence of any congenital syndrome involving craniofacial abnormalities, a history of trauma to the face or mouth, or a history of frequent upper respiratory infections, particularly group A streptococcal infections and sinusitis.

Past Medical History

In addition to the standard information gathered in the pediatric past medical history (see Chapter 6), it is important to ascertain the following information.

Prenatal History • The provider should determine if the child has a history of any prenatal exposures that can cause abnormalities of the face, nose, or mouth. This requires inquiries about maternal prenatal use of anticonvulsants, specifically phenytoin, which may cause cleft lip and palate in the fetus (Hill, Wlodarczyk, Palacios, & Finnell, 2010). Prenatal maternal smoking and alcohol consumption also increase the risk for cleft lip or palate, while folic acid may have a protective effect (Boyles et al., 2010; CDC, 2013b). Consanguinity has also been found to be a risk factor for orofacial clefts (Ravichandran et al., 2012). Prenatal alcohol exposure causes distinctive facial abnormalities in the fetus, including midface hypoplasia, a long philtrum, and a short nose with anteverted nares (fetal alcohol syndrome [FAS]) (see Chapter 13). Maternal use of inhalants such as glue has a similar effect on the developing fetus (Tsai, Manchester, & Elias, 2012).

Neonatal History • The neonatal history involves reviewing the child's past medical history for congenital disorders that cause abnormalities of the face, nose, and mouth. The provider must pay particular attention to any conditions that cause difficulty sucking, feeding, or breathing through the nose. Examples of conditions about which to inquire include:

- **Face:** Encephalocele and FAS
- **Nose:** Choanal atresia, choanal stenosis, and nasal dermoid cysts
- **Mouth:** Cleft lip, cleft palate, adontia (congenital absence of teeth), oligodontia (partial absence of teeth), neonatal teeth, Epstein's pearls, and ankyloglossia (tongue tie)

Some congenital syndromes include clinical findings that involve the face, nose, or mouth. For example, Marfan syndrome involves a high-arched palate with crowded dentition; cleft lip or palate may occur as part of trisomies 13 and 18; and cleft palate occurs alone with Pierre-Robin sequence (Tsai et al., 2012).

Nasal polyps are seen with cystic fibrosis. It is also important to inquire about prolonged oral or nasal intubation in the neonatal period, as this can cause tissue trauma to the alveolar ridge.

Review of Systems

The pediatric review of systems, involving the face, nose, and mouth, includes asking the parent about specific conditions with signs and symptoms that manifest in these anatomic regions. Some examples include the following:

- **General health:** Usual state of health; recent and recurrent febrile illnesses; and a history of any congenital syndromes that are associated with oral or facial anomalies
- **Skin:** Atopic dermatitis (comorbid condition with allergic rhinitis)
- **Head and Face:** Facial asymmetry or deformities, depressed nasal bridge, or absent philtrum, which may indicate FAS
- **Nose:** Frequent upper respiratory infections, nasal congestion or discharge (including characteristics); allergic rhinitis, nasal stuffiness, recurrent epistaxis (nosebleeds), sinusitis, foreign body in the nose, snoring, trauma to the nose, or regular use of nasal sprays
- **Mouth and Throat:** Cleft lip or palate, frequent sore throats, pharyngitis, stomatitis, tonsillitis, retropharyngeal abscess, peritonsillar abscess, toothaches, difficulty chewing, dental caries, dental infections, gingivitis, dental malocclusion, dental injuries, eruption cysts, chronic mouth breathing, difficulty swallowing, hoarse or nasal voice quality, benign migratory glossitis (geographic tongue), herpes stomatitis, coxsackievirus, recurrent aphthous ulcers, or oral candidiasis
- **Respiratory:** Upper and lower respiratory infections; cystic fibrosis, which is associated with nasal polyps; or asthma (comorbid condition with allergic rhinitis)
- **Immunity:** Allergies, tonsillitis, pharyngitis, or facial cellulitis

Immunizations

A child's immunization status is particularly relevant to assessment of the face, nose, sinuses, or oral cavity. Several diseases for which children are immunized can cause medical conditions involving these structures. In diphtheria a membranous covering forms over the upper airway, causing obstruction and respiratory distress, and tetanus can cause contraction of the facial muscles. Poliomyelitis causes muscle weakness or paralysis, resulting from altered function of the CNs, which causes an asymmetric soft palate that, in turn, leads to difficulty swallowing and speech disorders (Kedlaya, 2013). *Haemophilus influenzae* type b (Hib) can cause epiglottitis; children with this condition experience acute respiratory distress, including nasal flaring and mouth breathing as a result of severe air hunger (see Chapter 17). *Streptococcus pneumoniae* can lead to sinusitis.

Hospitalizations

It is important to inquire about past hospitalizations for acute or chronic illnesses or infections involving the face, nose, or oral cavity. Examples include facial trauma, cellulitis, and conditions that cause difficulty swallowing and consequent dehydration, such as tonsillitis, retropharyngeal or tonsillar abscess, stomatitis, or infectious mononucleosis. Any condition requiring endotracheal intubation is also noteworthy; oral intubation can result in injury to the teeth.

Injuries

Injuries to the face and mouth in children are not uncommon and occur in the course of the child's play activity or as a result of a lack of developmentally appropriate supervision. Some injuries to the face and mouth in children result from intentional injury or child abuse (see Chapter 24). Injuries about which to inquire include burns, falls, motor vehicle collisions, or intentional trauma that affects the face, nose, or mouth. It is important to ascertain if there is a history of animal or insect bites to the face, as these injuries can result in cellulitis. Providers must ask the parents of older infants and toddlers about a history of foreign bodies placed in the nose, which can cause bleeding, chronic irritation, and nasal drainage.

Surgical History

Examples of surgical procedures about which to inquire include tonsillectomy, adenoidectomy, nasal septum reconstruction, nasal polyp removal, or cleft lip or palate repair. It is also important to inquire about dental extractions. The date of the surgery and the condition for which the surgical procedure was done should be noted. The provider must also ask the parent (or child if age appropriate) if the condition was resolved with surgery.

Family History

The family history is elicited by asking about congenital syndromes, cleft lip or cleft palate, nasal polyps, snoring, mouth breathing, allergic rhinitis, atopic dermatitis, asthma, or frequent upper respiratory infections in other family members.

Social History

As part of the social history, the provider must determine the type of housing, how many people are living in the home with the child, and whether they practice good hygiene (e.g., frequent hand washing). These are particularly important assessments to make if a child presents with frequent respiratory infections and nasal discharge. Because pet dander is an allergen, the presence of any pets in the home must be noted. Children with cystic fibrosis or asthma are especially vulnerable to recurrent respiratory infections. Infants can also present with oral infections if household hygiene is inadequate. Another important assessment is to determine if the child is exposed to environmental tobacco smoke, which can cause inflammation of the nasal passages and frequent respiratory infections in children, especially those who live with "indoor smokers" (U.S. Department of Health and Human Services, 2006). With the parent out of the room, adolescents can be asked in a nonjudgmental manner about their use of cigarettes, marijuana, or inhaled cocaine or methamphetamine, all of which are respiratory tract irritants. The provider must also ask the teen about the use of chewing tobacco; this can cause gums to recede, leukoplakia (white patches on the buccal mucosa), and oral malignancy (Muscari, 2010). Inhaled cocaine use is associated with nasal perforation and epistaxis (Silvestre, Perez-Herbera, Puente-Sandoval, & Bagan, 2010). Methamphetamine use is associated with bruxism and severe tooth decay (McGrath & Chan, 2005). It is important to inquire about whether the child or teen is involved in any type of sports, during which injuries and fractures to the face, teeth, and mouth may occur, especially if protective gear is not worn.

Medications

Knowledge of current prescribed and over-the-counter (OTC) medications or home remedies the child is taking is essential; the indication for the drug or remedy may explain an abnormality in the face, nose, or mouth. For example, antibiotics, which may have been prescribed to treat acute or chronic sinusitis, may cause yeast overgrowth in the oral cavity (e.g., thrush, oral candidiasis); this manifests as adherent white plaques on the buccal mucosa. Certain anticonvulsants (e.g., phenytoin) may cause gingival hyperplasia. Antihistamines, decongestants, intranasal corticosteroids, and nasal cromolyn are often prescribed to treat seasonal, perennial, or episodic allergic rhinitis. It is important for the provider to ask the parents of teething infants if they have been applying OTC topical lidocaine to treat teething pain. The provider must advise parents to apply this medication sparingly, especially with older infants who frequently place objects in their mouths as local anesthesia that extends to the posterior pharynx may lessen the gag reflex, thus increasing the infant's risk for choking.

Allergies

It is important to investigate whether the child has any allergies, particularly environmental allergies or allergic rhinitis. Allergic rhinitis causes nasal symptoms, including rhinorrhea, swelling of the nasal turbinates, "cobblestoning" of the posterior pharynx (see later discussion), and enlarged tonsillar and adenoidal tissue.

Allergies can also lead to chronic mouth breathing, which can cause discoloration of the frontal incisors and a high-arched palate (Beck, 2013).

Dental and Oral History

The oral and dental history is a particularly important portion of the pediatric oral examination. Essential elements include:

■ **Determining if the child has a dental home.** It is important to determine the child's source of regular dental care; a "dental home" should be established soon after the first tooth eruption or by 12 months. The provider must determine the frequency of dental visits as well as the date of the last dental visit. Children should be seen by a dentist every 6 months or more frequently if needed (American Academy of Pediatric Dentistry, 2013).

■ **Determining the timing of eruption and shedding of primary teeth and the eruption of permanent teeth.** The presence of mixed dentition should be noted; this may cause complications such as plaque accumulation, gingival irritation, and malocclusion. A history of natal teeth, dental fractures, or tooth avulsions is also important.

■ **Determining oral hygiene habits.** The teeth should be brushed and flossed at least twice a day. Providers must ask parents of infants if they clean the baby's teeth after feeding and what they use to clean the teeth. Providers must ask adolescents who wear braces about oral hygiene practices; diligent cleaning is essential to avoid decay.

■ **Assessing feeding practices.** The frequency of bottle and breastfeeding is determined; frequent breastfeeding of infants who have begun teething can lead to tooth decay. The provider must ask if the infant is held for all feedings; a bottle should never be propped in the infant's mouth, as this leads to tooth decay and otitis media and can cause the aspiration of liquids. Parents of toddlers older than 12 months must be asked whether the child still drinks from a bottle or no-spill sippy cup, how often, what type of liquid is in the bottle or cup (i.e., juice, milk, soda pop), and if the child goes to sleep with the bottle or cup. This is an important question, as prolonged use of a bottle or sleeping with a bottle or sippy cup is associated with an increased risk of tooth decay (early childhood caries) and middle ear infection (Fung, Wong, Lo, & Chu, 2013).

■ **Assessing dietary habits.** The provider should inquire about the consumption of cariogenic food, snacks, and treats such as crackers, bread, presweetened cereals, dried fruits, cookies, chewing gum, and candy. Beginning at 6 months, infants should receive fluoride supplements if exclusively breastfed or if the water used to mix the formula is not fluoridated (American Dental Association, 2005). In older children, the provider should note whether the child drinks fluoridated water. The parents of young children should be asked if they share utensils, cups, spoons, or toothbrushes with the infant or young child or if the parents put the pacifier in their own mouths before giving it to the infant. These practices can lead to the infectious process of dental decay by transmitting *Streptococcus mutans* from the caretaker to the child's mouth (Marrs, Trumbley, & Malik, 2011).

■ **Assessing harmful oral habits.** The provider must also inquire about any harmful oral habits such as sucking the thumb or finger after 5 years of age or pacifier use beyond 18 months, which can affect dental arch development, resulting in malocclusion (Hagan, Shaw, & Duncan, 2008). Dipping the pacifier in sugar, honey, or other sugary substances can cause dental decay; this practice must be assessed and discouraged. Preteens and adolescents should also be asked about smoking and the use of smokeless tobacco, both of which increase the risk or periodontal disease and oral cancer.

■ **Determining if there is a history of eating disorders.** The repetitive self-induced vomiting associated with bulimia nervosa can cause wearing of tooth enamel, resulting in tooth decalcification, erosion, and decay; the self-induced starvation that characterizes anorexia nervosa leads to vitamin deficiencies, causing potential injury to the teeth (Bernstein, 2012).

■ **Determining if there is a history of oral injury, infection, or other dental problems.** Orofacial trauma can occur when the child or adolescent is involved in contact sports; the provider asks about the child's or teen's participation in such sports and asks if mouth guards are worn. Adolescents may have their tongues pierced; any history of hemorrhage or infection as a result of the piercing is noted. Oral sexual activity can lead to infections in the mouth. Any history of bruxism or malocclusion is also noted.

■ **Determining a family history of dental caries,** noting the rate of dental caries or other dental problems.

In 2003, the American Academy of Pediatrics recommended that the primary health care provider conduct an oral health risk assessment. The criteria for this assessment are listed in Box 16.1 (Hale, 2003).

History of Present Illness

When a child presents with a complaint related to the face, nose, or mouth, the provider should obtain a focused history (i.e., history of present illness [HPI]). It is important to gather details of all presenting symptoms, including information about onset (sudden or gradual), duration, and progression (see Chapter 6). Common problems related to the face, nose, and throat in children include general complaints such as nasal drainage or congestion, sore throat, sneezing (with or without fever), pain (facial, throat, and tooth), and epistaxis (nosebleeds). Conditions include nasopharyngitis, sinusitis, pharyngitis, streptococcal pharyngitis, and stomatitis.

Injuries to the face, nose, or mouth are considered closed head injuries, and relevant precautions must be taken, including stabilization of the cervical spine if the child has a history of loss of consciousness. The mechanism of injury must be ascertained and determination of airway patency is essential. Injuries to the nose and mouth often cause profuse bleeding with possible bone or tooth fractures, all of which may obstruct the child's airway. Relevant questions to ask for the HPI can be found in Table 16.1.

TABLE 16.1	History of Present Illness: Abnormalities and Complaints Related to the Face, Nose, and Mouth	
COMPLAINT	ASSESSMENTS	DIFFERENTIAL DIAGNOSES/CAUSES
Cough	Onset sudden or gradual? Productive? Paroxysmal cough? Color of sputum? Associated fever? Sick contacts? Nasal discharge? Aggravating and alleviating factors?	Upper or lower respiratory tract infection, viral pharyngitis, sinusitis, tuberculosis (paroxysmal cough), or asthma
Dry mouth (xerostomia)	Onset sudden or gradual? History of prolonged mouth breathing or allergies? Refusal to swallow liquids? On any medications? What type? Any illicit drug use?	Thirst, mouth breathing, allergic rhinitis, adenoiditis, dehydration, diabetes, or mumps; may be associated with drug use
Dysphagia	Onset sudden or gradual? Past medical history? Child's immunization status? Severity of dysphagia? Precipitating and alleviating factors?	Viral or bacterial pharyngitis, peritonsillar or retropharyngeal abscess, epiglottitis, GERD, cleft palate, or cerebral palsy
Dyspnea	Onset sudden or gradual? Child's immunization status? Fever? Precipitating and alleviating factors? Associated symptoms? Nasal flaring? Neck or throat pain? Any swelling of the face or neck?	Peritonsillar or retropharyngeal abscess, epiglottitis, trauma, upper or lower respiratory tract disorders, or infections
Epistaxis	Onset sudden or gradual? Unilateral or bilateral bleeding? Frequency? How long do nosebleeds last? Is bleeding prolonged or profuse? Precipitating factors? Alleviating factors? Is child on any medications?	Trauma (intentional or unintentional), bleeding disorders, nose-picking, nasopharyngitis, foreign body in the nose, allergic rhinitis, or illicit drug use
Facial pain	Onset? Duration? Location? Degree of pain? Any pressure? Fever? Sneezing or nasal drainage? Characteristics of nasal drainage? Recent upper respiratory infection? History of allergies? What alleviates the pain or pressure?	Trauma (intentional or unintentional), sinusitis (acute or chronic), headaches, or migraines
Gingival hyperplasia	Past medical history? Onset? On any medications?	Phenytoin- or cyclosporine-induced gingival hyperplasia or idiopathic or familial gingival hyperplasia

(continued)

TABLE 16.1	History of Present Illness: Abnormalities and Complaints Related to the Face, Nose, and Mouth (*continued*)	
COMPLAINT	**ASSESSMENTS**	**DIFFERENTIAL DIAGNOSES/CAUSES**
Gum recession	On any medications? What type? Dental hygiene habits? Halitosis? Toothaches? Bleeding gums? Gums red, tender, and swollen?	Vigorous tooth brushing; poor oral hygiene, or tooth decay; may be caused by chewing tobacco
Halitosis	Medical history (e.g., chemotherapy, diabetes)? Type of odor? Associated symptoms? Any harmful oral habits? Dental hygiene habits? On any medications?	Poor oral hygiene, tooth decay, gingivitis, oral candidiasis, postnasal drip, sinusitis, tobacco use, xerostomia, or fecal impaction
Lesions on buccal or labial mucosa	Type of lesions (i.e., ulcers, vesicles, Koplik's spots, thick, white deposits on buccal mucosa)? Onset sudden or gradual? Color, location, or lesions? Are sores painful? Immunization status? Sick contacts? Fever? Poor appetite? Precipitating and alleviating factors? Signs of dehydration? Sore throat? Malaise? Lesions or rash elsewhere on body? Does child attend day care? Recent antibiotics? Is child on any medications? Any oral piercings? Sexual practices?	Herpangina, coxsackievirus, enterovirus (hand, foot, and mouth disease), aphthous ulcers, oral candidiasis, herpesvirus 1 or 2, measles
Nasal congestion	Onset sudden or gradual? Duration? Aggravating factors? Fever? Cough? Sneezing, itching, or watery eyes? History of allergies? Does congestion interfere with sleep? What relieves nasal congestion? Is child taking any prescribed or OTC medications for the nasal congestion?	Allergic rhinitis, nasopharyngitis, sinusitis, or foreign body in the nose
Postnasal drip	Onset? Associated cough? Fever? Aggravating and alleviating factors? Painful or erythematous throat? History of allergies?	Allergic rhinitis, nasopharyngitis, sinusitis, or foreign body in the nose
Rhinorrhea	Onset? Acute or chronic? Bilateral? Unilateral? Continuous or intermittent? Precipitating factors? Character of nasal drainage? Associated symptoms (e.g., fever, facial pain; sneezing, itchy, or watery eyes)? Is child on any medications? History of allergies?	Foreign body in the nose (unilateral), allergic rhinitis (clear, watery discharge from both nares), nasopharyngitis (green-to-yellow drainage, both nares), or sinusitis; chronic rhinorrhea may be caused by inhalant use
Sore throat	Onset? Duration? Frequency? Severity of sore throat? Fever? Hoarseness? Rash? Pharyngeal, or tonsillar exudate? Palate petechiae? Difficulty swallowing? Sick contacts? What alleviates the throat pain? What makes it worse? On any medications?	Viral or bacterial pharyngitis, tonsillitis, or seasonal allergies
Tonsillar enlargement	Onset? Any fever? Difficulty swallowing or breathing? Nasal symptoms? Tonsillar erythema or exudate? Palate petechiae?	Viral or bacterial pharyngitis, tonsillitis, or infectious mononucleosis
Tooth decay	Last dental visit? Visible caries? Tooth pain? Difficulty chewing? Associated sore throat? Any mixed dentition? Does child drink from bottle or sippy cup?	Tooth decay associated with sore throat may be caused by self-induced vomiting, poor oral hygiene, or early childhood caries
Tooth pain	Onset sudden or gradual? Location of pain? Last dental visit? Visible caries or tooth discoloration? Does child drink from bottle or sippy cup? Gingival exudate or hyperplasia? Halitosis? History of oral injury?	Tooth avulsion or fracture or tooth decay
Trauma	Mechanism of injury? Areas of active bleeding? Lacerations? Abrasions? Bruising? Evidence of fractures? Visible hematomas? Nasal obstruction caused by swelling or bleeding? Nasal discharge? Type? Does nasal discharge test positive for glucose? Is child able to open mouth? Move mandible? Any malocclusion? Fractured or missing teeth? Results of eye (vision, extraocular movements) and neurologic examinations?	Sports-related injury, intentional or unintentional injury due to falls or play, or child abuse and neglect

GERD, gastroesophageal reflux disease; OTC, over the counter.

Physical Examination

Examination of the nose and mouth in infants and young children can be challenging. The oral and nasal cavities are not easily visualized and young infants and toddlers are frequently resistant to the internal examination of the nose and mouth, making this examination difficult. In infants and toddlers, examination of the oral and nasal cavities should be deferred until after the heart, lungs, and abdomen are auscultated and after the ear has been inspected. If the child is crying, the health care provider should take the opportunity to inspect the oral cavity at that time. Proper positioning of the child is essential to ensure comfort and avoid accidental injury. The best choice for securing the young child is to place the child on the examination table while the parent or caregiver secures the child's arms by his or her sides and supports the head. Preschool-aged children are less resistant to this portion of the physical examination and may even find it fun to open their mouth and stick out their tongue. If the child is indeed cooperative, he or she can be examined while sitting on the examination table, facing the provider. If the child is not cooperative, he or she can be placed on the parent or caregiver's lap with the head held at the forehead and arms secured at the sides (Figure 16.7).

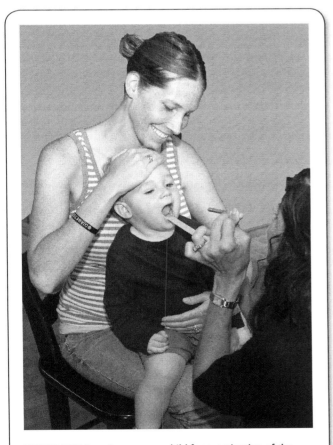

FIGURE 16.7 Securing a young child for examination of the oral cavity.

If the child is quite uncooperative, the parent or caregiver may need to secure the child's legs between their own legs. Another option is for the parent or caregiver and the provider to sit knee-to-knee and place the child on the lap that this position creates. The parent or caregiver can secure the child's head while providing reassurance to the child and the provider can then lean forward and directly inspect the child's nose and mouth. Assessment of the face, nose, and mouth in children school-aged and older can be done in a head-to-toe sequence with the child sitting upright on the examination table in front of the examiner.

The following equipment is necessary to examine the face, nose, and oral cavity in children:
- Penlight
- Tongue blades
- Gloves
- Otoscope with halogen light and short wide-tipped nasal speculum attachment

Assessment of General Appearance

Examination of the face, nose, and mouth begins with an overall assessment of the infant's, child's, or adolescent's general appearance. This helps the provider focus on areas of assessment that require more thorough investigation. For example, when the provider enters the examination room, facial symmetry, mouth breathing, nasal flaring, and nasal discharge are often readily apparent and assist in directing the focus of any detailed examination.

Examination of the Face

Assessment of the face involves primarily inspection and palpation.

Inspection • Inspection of the face includes assessment of the skin, facies, and facial features; facial expression; symmetry of facial movements (CN VII); and any involuntary movements.

Assessment of the face begins with inspection of the skin for color, lesions, and signs of trauma or edema. The skin should be pink and free of lesions (see Chapter 12). In the neonate, the examiner should note any bruising from birth trauma, especially with a face presentation delivery; forceps marks should also be noted. Facial edema can be marked with face presentation deliveries and associated soft tissue swelling can distort the facial features. With marked facial edema, the newborn should be reexamined in 24 to 48 hours to assess for resolution of the swelling and to assess the facial features without the edema. Swelling of the face in older infants and children may be caused by chronic use of corticosteroids (Cushing's syndrome) or by acute injury. Swelling of the face due to injury is most often accompanied by injuries to the skin, such as burns, bruises, lacerations, abrasions, or puncture wounds. All injuries to the face must be evaluated to determine whether the injuries were accidental or intentional (see Chapter 24). In older children and adolescents, facial puffiness or swelling around one or both eyes or eyebrows may indicate sinusitis (Wald et al., 2013). Allergic shiners (dark, bluish circles under the eyes) are a result of vasodilation or nasal congestion and are often seen in children with allergic rhinitis (Figure 16.8). The parotid gland may be swollen as a consequence of viral infection (e.g., parotitis or "mumps," human immunodeficiency virus [HIV]), or bacterial infection (e.g., dental infections). An infected parotid gland also causes facial erythema and produces purulent saliva if infected with bacteria (Templer & Leiss, 2013). With bulimia nervosa, bilateral parotid gland swelling is seen (Yager, Scher, Hilty, & Osterhout, 2014).

The facies are also inspected, including the overall facial proportions, while noting the size, shape, symmetry, and spacing of facial features. Abnormal facial proportions (e.g., high or low forehead, receding chin) may be indicative of a syndrome or may be familial. Forehead size can also result from neonatal conditions. For example, premature infants often have small, narrow foreheads, but neonates with hydrocephalus present with an enlarged forehead. Table 16.2 lists the normal physical measurements for facial features in term infants. Some congenital and genetic disorders present with distinctive dysmorphic features or abnormal proportions; some examples of these syndromes are given in Table 16.3. The child's facial expression must also be noted. A lack of emotional expression (e.g., blunted or flat affect) may indicate depression, schizophrenia, or child abuse.

The provider should observe the newborn and older infant or child while the child is crying or smiling to assess for symmetry of facial movements. Any facial asymmetry may indicate facial nerve (CN VII) paralysis or facial fracture. In children who are developmentally able to cooperate, the provider should ask the child to raise his or her eyebrows, smile, frown, and open his or her eyes against resistance, noting strength and symmetry of the facial muscles. These maneuvers assess function of CNs V (trigeminal) and VII. Any involuntary movements of the face may be caused by tics, seizures, or athetoid cerebral palsy. Involuntary tremors may be a result of mercury poisoning (Olson et al., 2013). Involuntary contraction of the facial muscles can also occur in children with hypocalcemia or tetany. Facial grimacing and twitching are also seen in children with chronic nasal itching from allergic rhinitis.

Palpation • Gentle palpation of the face is necessary if any swelling is noted upon inspection or if there is a history of facial injury, prolonged upper respiratory infection, sinusitis, or parotitis. With a history of injury to the face, the examiner should systematically palpate the

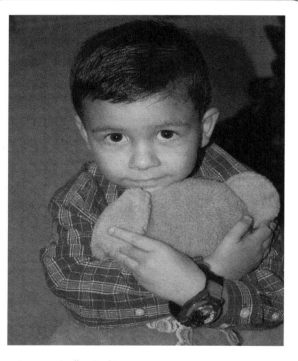

FIGURE 16.8 Allergic shiners.

TABLE 16.2	Physical Measurements of Facial Features in Term (38–40 weeks) Infants
MEASUREMENT	RANGE (CM)
Interpupillary distance	3.3–4.5
Palpebral fissure	1.5–2.1
Inner canthal distance	1.5–2.5
Outer canthal distance	5.3–7.3
Philtrum	0.6–1.2

Source: Tsai, Manchester, and Elias (2012).

TABLE 16.3	Genetic and Congenital Abnormalities Associated With Dysmorphology of the Face, Nose, or Oral Cavity	
DISORDER	**FACIAL ABNORMALITY/DYSMORPHOLOGY**	
Beckwith-Wiedemann syndrome	Macroglossia (enlarged tongue), facial dysmorphism (hypertelorism), and cleft palate	
Cleft lip and cleft palate	Cleft lip may be unilateral or bilateral; it may occur alone or with cleft palate. Palate cleft may involve just anterior and gingival ridge or extend into the posterior palate.	
Congenital hypothyroidism	Low hairline, coarse facial features, and macroglossia	
Fetal alcohol syndrome	Flat midface, thin upper lip, absent philtrum, and micrognathia	
Fragile X syndrome	Oblong facies and prominent jaw	
Marfan syndrome	Long, thin facies; slanting palpebral fissures; high, arched palate; and crowded dentition	
Pierre-Robin sequence	Micrognathia, glossoptosis (tongue falls to back of throat), and cleft palate; macroglossia and ankyloglossia occur more rarely.	
Sturge–Weber disease	Facial nevus; can involve upper part of face or include lower part of face, mouth, lip, neck, and torso (Bernard et al., 2012).	
Trisomy 13 syndrome	Anophthalmia, colobomas, and cleft lip and palate. The abnormal facies associated with trisomy 13 can be viewed at http://medgen.genetics.utah.edu/photographs/pages/trisomy_13.htm	
Trisomy 18 syndrome	Dysmorphic features including a characteristic face. The abnormal facies associated with trisomy 18 can be viewed at http://medgen.genetics.utah.edu/photographs/pages/trisomy_18.htm	
Trisomy 21 (Down syndrome)	Up-slanting palpebral fissures; epicanthal folds; midface hypoplasia; short, flat nose; protruding tongue; and macroglossia	
Williams syndrome	Coarse, elfin-like features, prominent lips	

Source: Tsai, Manchester, and Elias (2012).

facial bones, specifically the orbital rims, nasal bones, and temporomandibular joints to assess for tenderness, crepitus, or irregularities in bone contour. Reduced sensation below the eye with palpation suggests damage to the infraorbital nerve, which can occur with a blowout fracture of the orbit (Rupp & Karageanes, 2013). Crepitus or midface instability may be appreciated by stabilizing the child's forehead with one hand, while gently pulling on the maxillary incisors with the other gloved hand. Bimanual palpation of the mandible and maxilla with a gloved hand reveals instability or tenderness of these bones. Mobility of the hard palate during this maneuver indicates a maxillary fracture (Rupp & Karageanes, 2013). With a history of repeated or prolonged upper respiratory infections or sinusitis, facial tenderness upon palpation suggests acute sinusitis (see later section on examination of the paranasal sinuses). An acutely inflamed parotid gland feels exquisitely tender on palpation (Templer & Leiss, 2013).

Examination of the Nose

Although it is a brief portion of the assessment, physical examination of the nose in children yields important findings that provide clues to genetic or congenital disorders, respiratory distress, allergies, and other common pediatric respiratory problems. In children, examination of the nose includes inspection and palpation.

Inspection • Inspection of the nose involves observing both the external and internal nose. Examination of the external nose begins by the provider assessing the quiet child for flaring of the nares. Nasal flaring occurs with vigorous crying, when one naris is not patent, or with respiratory distress (see Chapter 17). The external nose is also inspected for shape, symmetry, and midline placement on the face. Normal placement of the nose can be determined by drawing an imaginary line down the center of the child's face, between the eyes, to the top of the child's upper lip. The nose should be symmetrical and in the center of the child's face. A flattened nasal bridge is a normal finding in African American and Asian children; a flattened nose may also indicate a congenital syndrome. A cleft lip or palate may extend through the alveolar ridge, through the upper lip and into the nose; this may be unilateral or bilateral. Nasolabial folds are also inspected. When the child smiles or cries, the nasolabial folds should be symmetrical; asymmetry can be due to injury to the facial nerve (CN VII).

The examiner should also note any lesions, swelling, inflammation, excoriation, or bleeding of the external nose. In the newborn, small, white cysts (milia) are normal findings and resolve spontaneously. Inflammation and swelling are abnormal findings of the external nose. These findings are often seen with nose piercing or can result from an insect bite or local infection, such as impetigo. Excoriation of the external nose is seen with frequent nasal drainage and nose wiping. A horizontal crease (allergic crease) across the lower third of the nose may be present in children with allergic rhinitis; it is caused by the frequent upward rubbing of the nose (allergic salute) to alleviate itching and to wipe nasal drainage (Figure 16.9). Bleeding of the external nose can occur as a result of the child simply picking at a sore or from physical trauma.

FIGURE 16.9 The allergic salute.

To inspect the internal nose, an external light source is used, such as a penlight or otoscope with a nasal speculum attachment. When examining infants and young children, the provider should use a penlight because it is less invasive and requires less cooperation from the child. When an otoscope is used to inspect the internal nose, the child must be still and breathe out of his or her mouth during the nasal inspection; for this reason, an otoscope with a nasal speculum is only used for older, cooperative children. However, the nasal speculum with an otoscope attachment provides better light and magnification during inspection. When using a penlight, the examiner should gently push the tip of the infant or young child's nose to inspect the internal nose. When using a nasal speculum, the older child should first tilt his or her head back slightly. Using the thumb of the nondominant hand, the examiner then lifts the tip of the child's nose while the remaining portion of the examiner's hand rests on the child's forehead to keep it steady. The speculum is then inserted gently about 1 cm into each naris, while avoiding the sensitive nasal septum.

Inspection of the internal nose begins by inspecting the nares for patency. The nares are normally patent and free of any blockage or obstruction. This is particularly important for infants 4 months of age or younger, who are obligate nose breathers and do not instinctively open their mouths to breathe (see Chapter 11). Patency of the nares in older children can be determined by occluding one nostril and observing how the child breathes out of the other nostril, repeating on both sides. Breathing should be smooth, effortless, and without noise. Another way to assess for nasal patency is for the examiner to hold a small mirror under both nares and then observe the circles of condensation that form as the child exhales. Condensation circles that vary in size may indicate a partial nasal obstruction; absent condensation demonstrates complete obstruction of that naris. Lack of patency of either naris in older infants and children may indicate a deviated septum, swelling of the nasal turbinates, or discharge caused by upper respiratory infection or allergic rhinitis, polyps, nasal trauma, or the presence of a foreign body. Unilateral nasal flaring occurs when one naris is not patent; this is frequently a sign of foreign body obstruction in a young child or choanal atresia in the neonate.

The provider then inspects the inferior and middle nasal turbinates, beginning with determination of color and the presence of swelling. The nasal mucosa is normally pink and without edema; the nasal turbinates should be firm, pink, and moist. A small amount of thin, clear, watery nasal discharge is normal. Boggy (chronically edematous), pale, or bluish nasal mucosa or turbinates indicate allergic rhinitis. Bright red, edematous nasal mucosa indicates inflammation, which accompanies upper respiratory infections. The color, character, and amount of any nasal drainage should be noted and described. A small amount of clear, thin, watery nasal discharge (rhinorrhea) may be normal, especially if the child was recently crying; it can also be a result of cold ambient air temperatures. Rhinorrhea in large amounts can be attributed to allergic rhinitis. If the child has recently suffered head trauma, any rhinorrhea must be tested for the presence of glucose, which confirms that the drainage is cerebrospinal fluid. Nasal drainage from an upper respiratory infection is often a yellow-to-green color, thick in consistency, and draining from both nares. Thick, yellow-to-green nasal drainage accompanied by erythematous nasal mucosa may indicate bacterial sinusitis; purulent drainage from the middle meatus is diagnostic for acute sinusitis (Wald et al., 2013). Purulent nasal drainage from only one naris indicates the presence of a foreign body, especially when the drainage has a foul odor.

The examiner also inspects the internal nose for any signs of bleeding. Often, dried blood may be present in the nares as a result of chronic irritation from the child "picking." More noticeable bleeding may be caused by the presence of a foreign body, allergies, or conditions that affect blood clotting such as leukemia or other blood dyscrasias. Frank blood draining from the nose is caused by head or facial trauma. Epistaxis (nosebleed) can be caused by facial or nasal trauma, foreign bodies, allergic rhinitis, forceful nose blowing, sneezing, infection, the use of nonsteroidal anti-inflammatory drugs, chronic use of nasal steroids, or coagulation disorders. Epistaxis is common in children school-aged and younger; this is because of the anterior location of Kiesselbach's plexus, which is easily irritated during nose-picking or low humidity (Nguyen, 2013). Cocaine use may cause epistaxis in adolescents (Silvestre et al., 2010).

The examiner also inspects the nasal septum for alignment, perforation, bleeding, or lesions. The nasal septum should be straight and midline. Deviation of the nasal septum can be congenital or result from facial trauma; significant deviation can interfere with breathing. Perforation of the nasal septum is apparent if light shines through the perforation into the opposite naris. This is an abnormal finding and can result from intranasal steroid, amphetamine, or cocaine use; digital trauma; or the insertion of a foreign body into the nasal vestibule (Mocella et al., 2013). Septal erythema, friability, excoriation, or bleeding is often a consequence of low humidity, chronic nose-picking, or cocaine use.

Children with chronic respiratory conditions (e.g., allergy, cystic fibrosis) often develop nasal polyps, which are moist, shiny, grape-like sacs that are a gray-to-green color and protrude into the nasal vestibule. Polyps can cause nasal obstruction, in which case surgical removal is warranted (McClay, 2012).

Palpation • The external nose is palpated for pain or tenderness. The bridge of the nose normally feels firm; the remaining area of the external nose should feel soft. The child or adolescent should not feel any pain or tenderness upon palpation. Painful or tender nasal tissue may result from sinusitis, infection, inflammation, or injury.

Assessment of Smell

Assessment of smell (CN I) is usually tested in children as part of the neurologic assessment. See Chapter 22 for a discussion of testing olfaction in children.

Examination of the Paranasal Sinuses

The paranasal sinuses are assessed in children aged 2 years and older. Only the frontal and maxillary sinuses are accessible for physical examination. Assessment of the paranasal sinuses involves inspection, palpation, percussion and, in some instances, transillumination.

Inspection • The sinuses cannot be directly inspected, but the facial area over the sinuses is evaluated for periorbital edema or erythema; these findings may indicate sinusitis (Wald et al., 2013).

Palpation • Palpation of the paranasal sinuses is done in children school-aged and older. This assessment includes evaluation of the frontal and maxillary sinuses. Palpation of the frontal sinuses is done by placing the thumbs on the child's forehead at the orbital ridge, then pressing gently upward to assess for tenderness. The maxillary sinuses are then palpated by pressing up under both zygomatic arches with the thumbs (Figure 16.10).

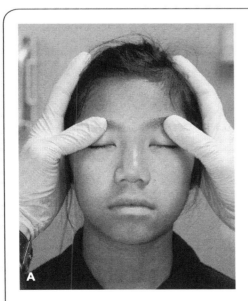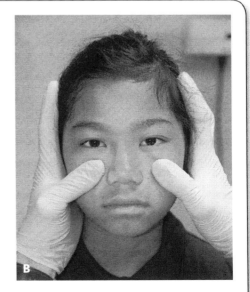

FIGURE 16.10 Palpating the sinuses. **A.** Frontal. **B.** Maxillary.

When palpated, the sinuses are normally nontender and nonedematous bilaterally. Tenderness or swelling is present in acute sinusitis; tenderness alone may occur with chronic headaches (Radojicic, 2012).

Percussion • Percussion of the sinuses is not usually performed in children, as it does not yield any useful findings.

Transillumination • Transillumination of the sinuses does not yield useful data in children younger than 10 years because of their undeveloped sinuses and is not conducted on the pediatric client for this reason (Wald et al., 2013).

Examination of the Oral Cavity

Examination of the oral cavity includes assessment of the lips, buccal mucosa, gums, teeth, tongue, palate, uvula, pharynx, and tonsils.

Inspection • Lips and perioral area inspection of the oral cavity begins with inspecting the exterior of the mouth, specifically the lips and perioral area. The lips should be inspected for color, moisture, texture, fissures, swelling, symmetry, lesions, or clefts. The perioral area is inspected for color, lesions, rashes, or excoriation.

The lips are normally a darker pink color than the surrounding skin. Lips are pink to red in light-skinned children and pale bluish gray in dark-skinned children. Lips that are pale pink can be indicative of anemia. Lips that are a blue-to-purple color may simply be an indication of temporary vasoconstriction resulting from cold ambient temperature or be a sign of cyanosis. Blue or purple lips also indicate cyanosis in fair-skinned children; in dark-skinned children, the lips become a more ashen color with cyanosis. A dark, cherry red color to the lips is seen with acidosis or carbon monoxide poisoning.

The child's lips should be moist and smooth. Dry, cracked lips may be the result of living in a dry climate, chronic mouth breathing, habitual lip-licking or biting, dehydration, or fever. Fissures of the lips most often appear at the corners of the mouth; these may indicate deficiencies of riboflavin or niacin. Swelling of the lips may occur with injury to the mouth, allergic reactions, insect bites, local infection, or generalized edema.

The lips are normally symmetrical when relaxed or crying or when the child speaks. Asymmetry of the lips or excessive drooling may indicate facial nerve impairment. A thin upper lip accompanied by a long philtrum suggests FAS (Figure 16.11). A cleft in the upper lip is easily visible on inspection in newborn infants and older children when not yet surgically repaired; surgical scars are seen once the cleft lip has been surgically closed (Figure 16.12). A cleft lip may be unilateral or bilateral and may extend past the upper border of the lip and into the naris (Figure 16.13). Lesions on the lips should be inspected closely. Young infants will often have a small callus or blister on the upper lip due to vigorous sucking. Other lesions may indicate oral infections, such as

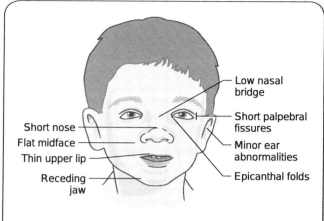

FIGURE 16.11 Typical facies noted with fetal alcohol syndrome. Note the thin upper lip and long philtrum.

Low nasal bridge
Short palpebral fissures
Minor ear abnormalities
Epicanthal folds
Short nose
Flat midface
Thin upper lip
Receding jaw

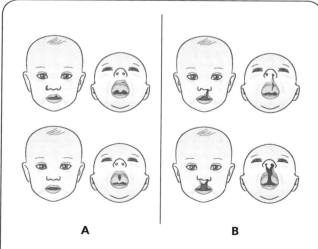

FIGURE 16.12 Cleft lip.

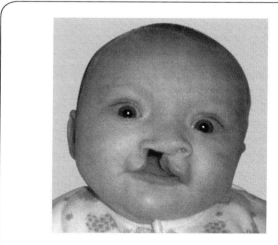

FIGURE 16.13 **A.** A cleft lip may be minimal or extend past the upper border of the lip or **B.** may be unilateral or bilateral and extend into the nares.

impetigo; vesicles on or around the lips may indicate herpes simplex infection (herpetic gingivostomatitis).

The skin around the lips (perioral area) is also inspected; it should be pink, clean, and clear, without rashes, lesions, or excoriation. Circumoral pallor in children can result from streptococcal pharyngitis, scarlet fever, erythema infectiosum (Fifth disease) (Zellman et al., 2013), anemia, or shock. Circumoral cyanosis can occur in infants after feeding; this is transient and considered normal. Circumoral cyanosis can also indicate hypoxemia. Oral infections may spread from the mouth to the perioral area, as with herpetic gingivostomatitis, which causes visible lesions. The perioral skin may also become inflamed, scaly, and excoriated with repetitive licking of the lips ("lip lickers' dermatitis").

Breath • Next, the child's breath is assessed; it should smell clean; breath odor often indicates pathology. Foul breath odor (halitosis) may be due to bacterial accumulation between the teeth and on the tongue with infrequent tooth brushing, lack of flossing, or with tooth decay. Other causes of halitosis in children and adolescents include prolonged mouth breathing, tobacco use, sinusitis, nasal polyps, nasal foreign body, tooth decay, dental abscesses, chronic constipation, diabetic ketoacidosis, and streptococcal pharyngitis.

Buccal Mucosa • Using a penlight and tongue depressor, the provider inspects the buccal mucosa for color, moisture, lesions, and ulcers. The Stensen's ducts are also inspected. In light-skinned children, the buccal mucosa should be pink; in dark-skinned children, the buccal mucosa is bluish. Erythema of the buccal mucosa results from infection or inflammation.

Pallor of the buccal mucosa may be the result of anemia, shock, or vasoconstriction; cyanosis results from hypoxemia, though cyanosis may not be visible in an anemic child. The buccal mucosa should also be moist and free of lesions. Dry oral mucosa can result from prolonged mouth breathing, prolonged nasal congestion, or from moderate-to-severe dehydration. White, curd-like patches on the buccal mucosa that cannot be scraped off with a tongue depressor and that leave the mucosa erythematous and bleeding indicate oral candidiasis, which may occur in infants and young children after oral antibiotic therapy or in children with HIV/AIDS (Figure 16.14). Tiny bluish white dots surrounded by red halos on the buccal mucosa are *Koplik's spots*; these spots are considered pathognomonic for the onset of measles (Figure 16.15). Petechiae on the buccal mucosa may be a result of biting or can indicate blood dyscrasias or infection. Vesicles on the buccal mucosa or tongue may be caused by coxsackievirus, especially if the lesions also occur on the hands and feet. Vesicles that rupture quickly, leaving shallow ulcers surrounded by an erythematous halo, are caused by herpes simplex type 1. Similar ulcers on the buccal or labial mucosa that were not preceded by vesicle formation are aphthous ulcers (canker sores), painful lesions that take

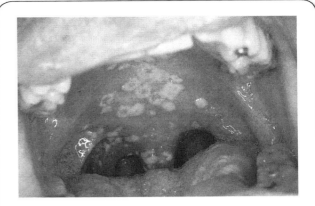

FIGURE 16.14 Oral candidiasis.

approximately 1 to 2 weeks to heal. Aphthous ulcers can be caused by stress, mild trauma, or food allergies (Plewa, 2013). The openings to the parotid glands, or Stensen's ducts, should be visible upon inspection. These ducts are located opposite the upper second molar and appear as a small indentation. Normally, the Stensen's ducts are not erythematous or edematous, and saliva should be visible in the oral cavity. The opening to the Stensen's ducts is erythematous with parotitis (mumps).

The Gums • The gums are inspected for color, swelling, and lesions. The gums are normally pink in light-skinned children and bluish or pale in dark-skinned children, with areas of concentrated melanin along the gingival margin. *Erythematous*, bleeding gums, can indicate poor oral hygiene, gingivitis, malnutrition, or oral infection. *Gingival hyperplasia* can occur as the side effect of certain drugs such as phenytoin, cyclosporine, nifedipine, and certain calcium antagonists (Mejia & Lozada-Nur, 2012). Gingival hyperplasia can also occur during puberty and in pregnancy (Markou, Eleana, Lazaros, & Antonios, 2009). An *eruption cyst* may be noted; this is a soft, clear fluid-filled cyst that occurs on the gums in children who are teething. Eruption cysts are caused

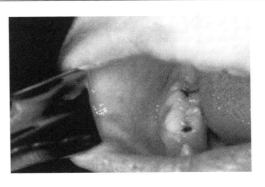

FIGURE 16.15 Koplik's spots.

by an accumulation of fluid between the tooth and overlying gum tissue and are most commonly seen in the mandibular molar area. An *eruption hematoma* differs from an eruption cyst in that it is filled with blood rather than clear fluid. An eruption hematoma appears as a bluish vesicle-like swelling on the alveolar ridge, especially with the first and second molars. Because the tooth erupts through these lesions, they resolve without treatment. If the lesion shows signs of infection, an immediate dental referral is warranted.

The Teeth • The teeth should be inspected for number, type, and condition. Occasionally, an infant will be born with teeth; these are termed *natal teeth*; teeth that erupt in the first 30 days of life are called *neonatal teeth*. It is important to assess these teeth for mobility because loose teeth present the risk of aspiration; tooth mobility greater than 1 mm is an indication for extraction. Gingival inflammation may also be present with natal or neonatal teeth. Natal or neonatal teeth occur in normal n ewborns or may occur with cleft palate (Mhaske et al., 2013).

Beginning at 4 months, the alveolar ridge should be inspected for the eruption of teeth. Once the teeth have erupted, they should be inspected systematically and in good light, beginning with the upper teeth, then moving to the lower teeth. The number of primary and permanent teeth should be determined; the child should have all 20 primary teeth by age 3. A child with complete permanent dentition has 32 teeth. Exfoliation of primary teeth and eruption of permanent dentition begin at about 6 years and occur in the same sequence as eruption of primary teeth. Variations in the number of expected teeth should be assessed, noting any deviations in patterns of tooth eruption, such as permanent teeth erupting before primary teeth have exfoliated; this requires a dental referral. The color and condition of the teeth are assessed; teeth should be uniformly white without variations in the surface. Dental plaque is sticky areas of accumulated clear-to-white film seen on the teeth; large amounts indicate poor dental hygiene. Brown or black teeth indicate dental caries; tobacco use may result in brown or yellow teeth. Brown or black spots seen primarily on the maxillary central incisors suggest early childhood caries (Figure 16.16). Erosion of tooth enamel is seen with bulimia nervosa. Loose teeth may be normal as a result of exfoliation or be caused by trauma, dental infection, or gingivitis. Any *malocclusion* is also noted. This is assessed by asking the child to bite down while the examiner notes any marked misalignment or protrusion of the teeth. Malocclusion can occur as a result of thumb-sucking, cleft palate, or micrognathia. Worn areas on the chewing surfaces of the teeth can be due to bruxism or misaligned teeth.

The Tongue • The tongue is inspected for movement, color, texture, moistness, size, and lesions. If the child is developmentally capable, the examiner asks the child to stick out his or her tongue for inspection. The tongue

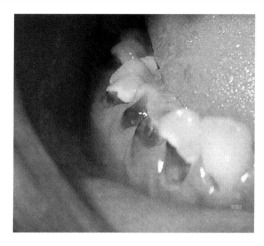

FIGURE 16.16 Early childhood caries.

should be midline. The ability to stick out the tongue verifies intact CN XII (hypoglossal) function. In infants and young children who are not able to stick out the tongue on command, an ability to suck or speak allows the examiner to assess adequate tongue movement; tongue movement can also be visualized when the infant or young child cries vigorously. *Ankyloglossia* (tongue-tie) is the complete or partial fusion of the lingual frenulum to the floor of the mouth, thus restricting movement of the tongue. This condition occurs in newborns and makes breastfeeding difficult or impossible because of the inability of the tongue to reach the palate. Signs of complete ankyloglossia are evident when the tongue does not protrude past the alveolar ridge, cannot rise to touch the hard palate, cannot move laterally, and appears heart-shaped when extended (Tewflik, Kanaan, & Karsan, 2013).

The dorsal portion of the tongue is normally pink to pale pink, moist, and without lesions. Changes in the color of the tongue can result from recent consumption of colored food, drinks, or medications. An erythematous tongue can result from glossitis, an acute or chronic inflammation of the tongue that can be caused by viral infections (herpes simplex); trauma; injury (bites or burns); exposure to irritants such as tobacco, alcohol, or hot food; or by a localized allergic reaction. Aphthous ulcers or erythema multiforme (Stevens-Johnson syndrome) can also cause glossitis. Streptococcal scarlet fever and Kawasaki disease are associated with a "strawberry tongue" in which the tongue first has a white coating through which erythematous papillae project, then the white coating peels, leaving an inflamed tongue with erythematous papillae, mimicking the appearance of a strawberry (Figure 16.17). A yellow color to the tongue, particularly the ventral surface, indicates jaundice; this is often the first area where jaundice is identified in a dark-skinned child. A dry tongue can indicate mouth

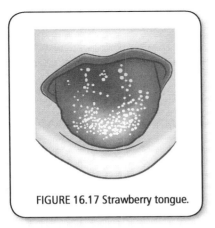

FIGURE 16.17 Strawberry tongue.

breathing or may result from dehydration. The dorsal surface of the tongue will appear rough from papillae. In some children, painless, inflamed, irregularly shaped furrows and grooves may be noted, often extending to the lateral areas of the tongue. These lesions are red, with whitish borders and absent papillae in the center. This is a benign condition known as *geographic tongue* (benign migratory glossitis) (Figure 16.18). The etiology is unknown, but it is thought to be inherited; it also occurs with increased frequency in persons with allergies or psoriasis (Kelsch, 2012). An enlarged tongue (macroglossia) is seen in Down syndrome, hypothyroidism, and Pierre-Robin syndrome (Tsai et al., 2012). The ventral surface of the tongue is a thinner layer of skin than the dorsum, with easily visible blood vessels. This surface should be pink and moist.

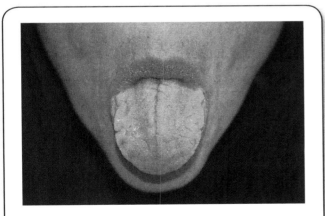

FIGURE 16.18 Geographic tongue.

Hard and Soft Palates • In infants and toddlers, a tongue blade is needed to open the mouth and examine the palate unless the child is vigorously crying. Children preschool-aged and older are able to cooperate by opening their mouth and saying "ah." If the child shows any signs of epiglottitis, such as absence of spontaneous cough, drooling, or agitation, neither the palate nor throat should be examined in

any way; this may stimulate the gag reflex, thereby precipitating complete obstruction by inducing a reflex laryngospasm.

Once the oral cavity is open, the examiner can use a penlight to shine a light on the palate to obtain a full view. The hard and soft palates should be inspected for color, shape, intactness, and lesions; the soft palate is also evaluated for movement. The hard palate is normally pale pink, smooth, dome-shaped, and contiguous with the soft palate. A high-arched palate may be caused by chronic mouth-breathing and is also seen with Marfan syndrome. The soft palate is pinker than the hard palate, moist, and soft. The soft palate and uvula normally rise symmetrically and at midline when the child says "ah." Both palates and the uvula should be intact without clefts (bifid uvula). Both the hard and soft palates may be cleft and the openings may be small or may involve the entire palate (see Figure 16.13). Symmetrical movement of the soft palate and uvula indicates intact function of CN X (vagus). Deviation of the uvula may indicate damage to CN X, poliomyelitis, diphtheria, or peritonsillar abscess. Touching the uvula elicits the gag reflex; this also tests the function of CNs IX (glossopharyngeal) and X. In a jaundiced child, the hard palate is yellowish. White patches that bleed when scraped with a tongue depressor indicate oral candidiasis. In the newborn, small (1 to 3 mm), white cystic nodules or papules noted along the juncture of the hard and soft palates are *Epstein's pearls*; these are not significant and resolve spontaneously through exfoliation within the first few weeks of life (Goldman, 2013). Petechiae on the palate are seen in bleeding disorders, streptococcal infections, and with infectious mononucleosis, where palatal petechiae are typically seen at the juncture of the hard and soft palates (Bennett & Domachowske, 2012).

The Pharynx • The pharynx, or throat, is inspected for color, swelling, and lesions. The tonsils are also inspected. In young or uncooperative children, it may be necessary to depress the tongue with a tongue blade to view the pharynx and tonsils fully, while avoiding the posterior pharynx and uvula to prevent eliciting the gag reflex.

Normally, the pharynx is pink, moist, and without exudate or lesions. Pharyngeal erythema is seen with upper respiratory infections. "Cobblestoning" may be seen on the posterior pharynx; this is a term used to describe streaks of lymphoid tissue on the posterior pharynx, which is often seen with allergic rhinitis. Erythematous macules that evolve into vesicles that ulcerate, leaving an erythematous halo, are caused by herpangina. These lesions are usually less than 5 mm in diameter and are found on the posterior pharynx, soft palate, tonsils, and occasionally the tongue and posterior buccal mucosa. Herpangina also causes mild to severe pharyngeal erythema (Gompf, Casanas, Carrington, & Cunha, 2012). Pharyngeal edema may result from streptococcal pharyngitis, diphtheria, peritonsillar or retropharyngeal abscess, cervical adenitis, food allergy, foreign body in the throat, or chemical ingestion.

The Tonsils • The tonsils are inspected for size, color, exudate, pitting, enlarged crypts, or membranous coverings. The tonsils should be equal in size; tonsillar size should be quantified, according to the scale presented in Table 16.4. and illustrated in Figure 16.19. This quantitative guideline is especially helpful when examining children with chronic tonsillar enlargement. Tonsils that are unequal in size usually indicate the presence of a *peritonsillar abscess*. The tonsils are normally the same color as the buccal mucosa. Tonsils that are erythematous and enlarged are seen with humoral changes, allergies, and infection. Tonsillar hypertrophy can cause obstructive sleep apnea in adolescents, particularly in teens who are obese. Enlarged, erythematous tonsils with or without exudate indicate infection. White or yellowish-white exudate on an erythematous posterior pharynx and on the tonsillar crypts suggests streptococcal pharyngitis or infectious mononucleosis (Figure 16.20). Pitting or enlarged tonsillar crypts occur in children who have had recurrent respiratory infections or chronic allergies. Thick, gray exudate may signify diphtheria. A thin, gray membranous covering over the tonsils that does not bleed when removed is likely a result of infectious mononucleosis.

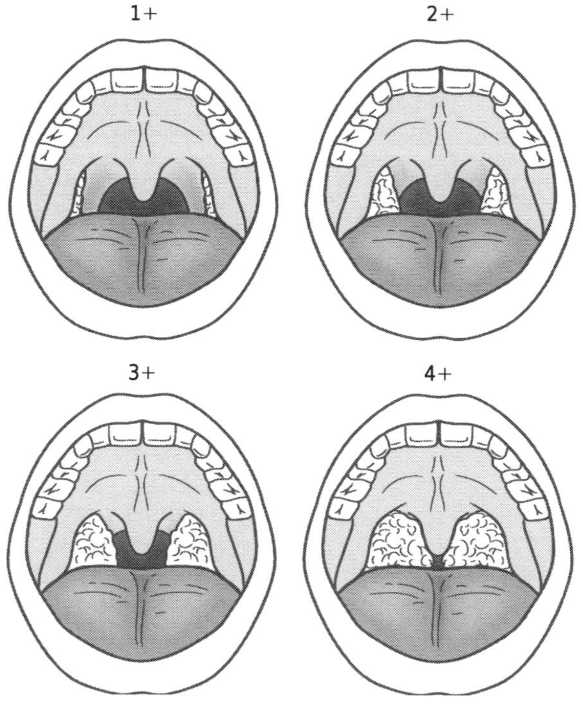

FIGURE 16.19 Grading of tonsillar size in children.

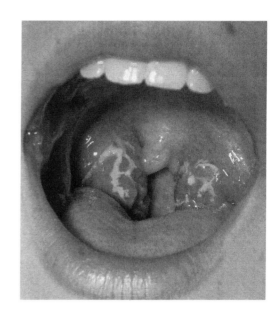

FIGURE 16.20 Tonsillar exudate and enlargement, as seen with streptococcal pharyngitis and infectious mononucleosis.

Palpation • Structures in the oral cavity that are palpated include the gums and palate. Gloves should be worn when palpating the inside of the mouth. The gums are palpated for tenderness and bleeding. Normal, healthy gum tissue is not tender and does not bleed with palpation. Findings of gum tenderness, pain, or friability with palpation suggest infection and require a dental referral. In the neonate, the hard and soft palates are palpated to assess for a cleft that is not easily visible on inspection (see Chapter 11). A submucosal cleft palate can be palpated and may be

TABLE 16.4	Grading Tonsillar Size in Children
GRADE	**DESCRIPTION**
0	Atrophic tonsils
1+	Tonsils slightly visible
2+	Tonsils enlarged; meet halfway between tonsillar pillars and uvula
3+	Tonsils almost touching the uvula
4+	Tonsils touching each other at midline

thin and slightly arched; this occurs when a cleft is in the hard or soft palate but is covered by mucous membrane and is not easily visible on inspection. A submucosal cleft palate is often associated with a bifid uvula. The strength of the neonate's suck reflex is also evaluated at this time. Once the intactness of the palate is established, it is not routinely palpated in subsequent physical examinations unless lesions, edema, or erythema are noted.

EVALUATION OF SPEECH

As part of the assessment of the face, nose, and mouth, the quality of the child's speech is also evaluated. For example, a nasal quality to the voice often indicates allergic rhinitis or a submucosal cleft palate. Transitional dentition (when both primary and permanent teeth are present), cleft lip and palate, dental injuries, neurologic injury (i.e., CN X), and tooth decay can lead to speech articulation difficulties. Some of these problems may also lead to difficulties with feeding and swallowing and may cause recurrent middle ear infections. Appropriate referrals to a speech pathologist, otolaryngologist, and pediatric dentist may be necessary.

COMMON DIAGNOSTIC STUDIES

Various diagnostic tests may be necessary to clarify differential diagnoses of abnormal conditions involving the face, nose, and mouth. Some examples of these diagnostic studies and their indications are summarized in Table 16.5.

DOCUMENTATION OF FINDINGS

Sample Write-Up: Well Child

Subjective Data

A 10-year-old boy is seen in the clinic for a health maintenance visit.

Objective Data

Face: symmetrical features; no periorbital edema; paranasal sinuses nontender on palpation
Nose: nose smooth, symmetrical alignment; no deviation or lesions; septum midline without deviation; nares patent bilaterally; turbinates pink, nonedematous; no polyps, lesions, or drainage seen; CN I intact
Oral cavity: lips pink; no lesions. Buccal mucosa pink without lesions; has four upper and four lower permanent teeth (lateral and central incisors); first mandibular premolar loose; teeth without plaque or visible caries; no malocclusion; gingival tissue pink without bleeding; tongue midline, pink, free of lesions, protrudes strongly at midline (CN XII); soft palate rises symmetrically; tonsils 2+ bilaterally without injection or exudate; uvula midline; pharynx pink; no injection, exudates, or drainage; gag reflex (CN IX and CN X) intact; CN VII and CN IX intact for taste
Assessment: healthy 10-year-old boy

Sample Write-Up: 8-Year-Old With Sore Throat

Subjective Data

An 8-year-old girl is brought to the clinic by her mother with complaints of a severe sore throat and fever. Her mother states the child has been complaining of severe sore throat with pain on swallowing for 2 days. The girl is also complaining of generalized weakness and fatigue, headache, loss of appetite, and stomach pain. She has been febrile for 2 days with fever as high as 102°F (38.9°C); her mother is giving her acetaminophen. The mother states that a note was sent home by the school nurse that two cases of streptococcal pharyngitis have been confirmed in her child's classroom. The girl has had three episodes of otitis media. She has no allergies, is on meds, and her immunizations are up to date.

TABLE 16.5	Diagnostic Studies Used to Evaluate Conditions of the Face, Nose, and Mouth	
DIAGNOSTIC STUDY	**INDICATION**	**COMMENTS**
Computed tomography (CT) scan	Injuries to face that involve loss of consciousness (> 1 minutes), amnesia, lethargy, focal neurologic deficits, skull fracture, seizures, or persistent vomiting (Rupp & Karageanes, 2013); acute or chronic sinusitis	CT scanning is necessary to obtain accurate diagnosis in maxillofacial fractures; radiographs are difficult to interpret in children (Alcala-Galiano et al., 2008); also used as an adjunct in diagnosing sinusitis in children older than 6 years (Wald et al., 2013).
Throat culture	To isolate causative organism of infection	Streptococcal infections must be treated with antibiotics to avoid long-term complications.
Radiographs	Chronic or recurrent sinusitis	Waters' view needed to demonstrate sinusitis on radiograph.
Rapid streptococcal antigen test	To diagnose pharyngeal streptococcal infections	Findings must be confirmed with culture.

Objective Data

T: 103.3°F (39.6°C); **P:** 160 beats per minute; **RR:** 20 breaths per minute; **BP:** 98/60 mmHg; **weight:** 27 kg

General: alert, mouth breathing, in no acute distress

Skin: no rashes noted

Nose: no nasal drainage

Throat: pharynx beefy red; tonsillar exudate; petechiae noted on soft palate

Neck: supple; no masses

Lymph nodes: bilateral painful cervical lymphadenopathy

Lungs: vesicular sounds auscultated throughout all lung fields

Labs: rapid strep test: positive; throat culture sent to lab

Assessment: streptococcal pharyngitis

Notable Clinical Findings

AREA	NOTABLE FINDING
History	Pre-, neo-, postnatal exposures, hypoxemia
	Craniofacial anomalies
	Oro-facial trauma
	Genetic or metabolic disorders
	Congenital hypothyroidism
	Fetal alcohol syndrome
	Cleft lip/palate
	Allergies
	Sinusitis
	Frequent respiratory infections
	Strep pharyngitis
	Immunization delay
	Tonsillitis
	Tonsillectomy/adenoidectomy
	Eating disorders
	Excessive consumption of sweetened drinks/cariogenic foods
	Bottle propping/companion bottle
	Bruxism
	Malocclusion
	Use of any type of tobacco products
	Use of alcohol
	Use of methamphetamine
Face	Facial pain
	Facial deformities
	Cleft lip
Nose	Nasal congestion
	Edematous/injected or pale nasal turbinates
	Rhinorrhea
	Recurrent epistaxis
Oral cavity	Dental caries
	Visible plaque
	Evidence of oral injuries
	Gingival hyperplasia
	Gum recession
	Lesions on buccal mucosa or tongue
	Halitosis
	Tooth pain
	Post-nasal drip
	Tonsillar enlargement
	Pharyngeal pain/injection/exudate
	"Cobblestoning" of posterior pharynx
	Cleft palate
	Bifid uvula

References

Alcala-Galiano, A., Aribas-Garcia, I. J., Martin-Perez, M. A., Romance, A., Montalvo-Moreno, J. J., & Juncos, J. M. (2008). Pediatric facial fractures: children are not just small adults. *Radiographics, 28*, 441–461.

American Academy of Pediatric Dentistry. (2013). *Guideline on periodicity of examination, preventive dental services, anticipatory guidance/counseling, and oral treatment for infants, children, and adolescents.* Retrieved from http://www.aapd.org/media/Policies_Guidelines/G_Periodicity.pdf

American Dental Association. (2005). *Fluoridation facts.* Chicago, IL: Author.

Beck, J. M. (2013). *Pediatric allergic rhinitis.* Retrieved from http://emedicine.medscape.com/article/889259-overview

Bennett, N. J., & Domachowske, J. (2012). *Pediatric mononucleosis and Epstein-Barr virus.* Retrieved from http://emedicine.medscape.com/article/963894-overview

Bernard, T. J., Knupp, K., Yang, M. L., Kedia, S., Levisohn, P., & Moe, P. G. (2012). Neurologic and muscular disorders. In W. W. Hay, M. J. Levin, R. R. Deterding, M. J. Abzug, & J. M. Sondheimer (Eds.), *Current pediatric diagnosis & treatment* (21st ed., pp. 740–829). New York, NY: McGraw-Hill.

Bernstein, B. E. (2012). *Pediatric anorexia nervosa.* Retrieved from http://emedicine.medscape.com/article/912187-overview

Boyles, A. L., DeRoo, L. A., Rolv, T. L., Taylor, J. A., Jugessur, A., Murray, J. C., & Wilcox, A. J. (2010). Maternal alcohol consumption, alcohol metabolism genes, and the risk of oral clefts: A population-based case-control study in Norway, 1996–2001. *American Journal of Epidemiology, 172*(8), 924–931.

Centers for Disease Control and Prevention. (2013a). *Disparities in oral health.* Retrieved from http://www.cdc.gov/OralHealth/oral_health_disparities/

Centers for Disease Control and Prevention. (2013b). *Facts about cleft lip and* cleft palate. Retrieved from http://www.cdc.gov/ncbddd/birthdefects/cleftlip.html

Fung, M. H. T., Wong, M. C. M., Lo, E. C. M., & Chu, C. H. (2013). Early childhood caries: A literature review. *Oral Hygiene & Health, 1*(1), 1–7.

Goldman, K. E. (2013). *Mandibular cysts and odontogenic tumors.* Retrieved from http://emedicine.medscape.com/article/852734-overview#a1

Gompf, S. G., Casanas, B. C., Carrington, M., & Cunha, B. A. (2012). *Herpangina.* Retrieved from http://emedicine.medscape.com/article/218502-overview

Hagan, J. F., Shaw, J. S., & Duncan, P. M. (2008). Promoting oral health. In J. F. Hagan, J. S. Shaw, & P. M. Duncan (Eds.); American Academy of Pediatrics. *Bright futures: Guidelines for health supervision of infants, children and adolescents* (3rd ed., pp. 155–168). Elk Grove Village, IL: American Academy of Pediatrics.

Hale, K. J. (2003). American Academy of Pediatrics Section on Pediatric Dentistry. Oral health risk assessment timing and establishment of the dental home. *Pediatrics, 111*(5), 1113–1116.

Heathcote, G. M. (2005). The prevalence of cleft uvula in an Inuit population. *American Journal of Physical Anthropology, 41*(3), 433–437.

Hill, D. S., Wlodarczyk, B. J., Palacios, A. M., & Finnell, R. H. (2010). Teratogenic effects of antiepileptic drugs. *Expert Review of Neurotherapeutics, 10*(6), 943–959.

Hilton, I. V., Stephen, S., Barker, J. C., & Weintraub, J. A. (2007). Cultural factors and children's oral health care: A qualitative study of carers of young children. *Community Dentistry and Oral Epidemiology, 35*(6), 429–438.

Hockenberry, M. J., & Wilson, D. (2011). *Wong's nursing care of infants and children* (9th ed.). St. Louis, MO: Mosby.

Kedlaya, D. (2013). *Postpolio syndrome.* Retrieved from http://emedicine.medscape.com/article/306920-overview

Kelsch, R. (2012). *Geographic tongue.* Retrieved from http://emedicine.medscape.com/article/1078465-overview

Kyle, T. (2008). *Essentials of pediatric nursing.* Philadelphia, PA: Lippincott.

Markou, E., Eleana, B., Lazaros, T., & Antonios, K. (2009). The influence of sex steroid hormones on gingival of women. *Open Dentistry Journal, 3*, 114–119.

Marrs, J., Trumbley, S., & Malik, G. (2011). Early childhood caries: Determining the risk factors and assessing the prevention strategies for nursing intervention. *Pediatric Nursing, 37*(1), 9–15.

McClay, J. (2012). *Nasal polyps.* Retrieved from http://emedicine.medscape.com/article/994274-overview

McGrath, C., & Chan, B. (2005). Oral health sensations associated with illicit drug abuse. *British Dental Journal, 198*(3), 159–162.

Mejia, L. M., & Lozada-Nur, F. (2012). *Drug-induced gingival hyperplasia.* Retrieved from http://emedicine.medscape.com/article/1076264-overview.

Mhaske, S., Yuwanti, M. B., Mhaske, A., Ragavendra, R., Kamath, K., & Saawarn, S. (2013). Natal and neonatal teeth: An overview of the literature. *ISRN Pediatrics, 2013.* doi:10.1155/2013/956269.

Mocella, S., Muia, F., Giacomini, P. G., Bertossi, D, Residori, E., & Sgroi, S. (2013). Innovative technique for large septal perforation repair and radiological evaluation. *Acta Otorhinolaryngologica Italica, 33*(3), 202–214.

Muscari, M. E. (2010). A tough one to chew on: Smokeless tobacco and teens. *Medscape.* Retrieved from http://www.medscape.com/viewarticle/724317

Nguyen, Q. A. (2013). *Epistaxis.* Retrieved from http://emedicine.medscape.com/article/863220-overview#aw2aab6b2b2aa

Olson, D. A., Brenner, B. E., Corden, T. E., Diner, B. M., Harchelroad, F., Mullins, M.E., . . . Windle, M. L. (2013). Mercury toxicity. Retrieved from http://emedicine.medscape.com/article/1175560-overview

Pillitteri, A. (2003). *Maternal & Child health nursing: Care of the childbearing & childrearing family* (4th ed.), Philadelphia, PA: Lippincott.

Plewa, M. C. (2013). *Aphthous ulcers.* Retrieved from http://emedicine.medscape.com/article/909213-overview

Radojicic, C. (2012). *Sinusitis. Cleveland Clinic Center for Continuing Education.* Retrieved from: http://www.clevelandclinicmeded.com/medicalpubs/diseasemanagement/allergy/rhino-sinusitis

Ravichandran, K., Shoukri, M., Aljohar, A., Shazia, N. S., Al-Twaijri, Y., & Al Jarba, I. (2012). Consanguinity and occurrence of cleft lip/palate: A hospital-based registry study in Riyadh. *American Journal of Medical Genetics, 158A*(3), 541–546.

Rhodes, J. (2006). *Advanced health assessment and diagnostic reasoning.* Philadelphia, PA: Lippincott.

Rupp, T. J., & Karageanes, S. (2013). *Facial fractures.* Retrieved from http://emedicine.medscape.com/article/84613-overview

Silvestre, F. J., Perez-Herbera, A., Puente-Sandoval, A., & Bagan, J. V. (2010). Hard palate perforation in cocaine abusers: A systematic review. *Clinical Oral Investigations, 14*(6), 621–628.

Singh, A. (2013). Paranasal sinus anatomy. Retrieved March 31, 2014 from http://emedicine.medscape.com/article/1899145-overview

Swamy Chidananda, M. N., & Mallikarjun, D. (2004). Applied aspects of anatomy and physiology of relevance to pediatric anesthesia. *Indian Journal of Anesthesia, 48*(5), 333–339.

Templer, J. W., & Leiss, B. D. (2013). *Parotitis.* Retrieved from http://emedicine.medscape.com/article/882461-overview

Tewflik, T. L., Kanaan, A., & Karsan, N. (2013). Cleft lip and palate and mouth and pharynx deformities. Retrieved from http://emedicine.medscape.com/article/837347-overview#a1

Tinanoff, N. (2011). Cleft lip and palate. In R. M. Kliegman, B. M. D. Stanton, J. St. Geme, N. F. Schor & R. E. Behrman (Eds.), *Nelson textbook of pediatrics* (19th ed., pp. 1252–1253). Philadelphia, PA: Saunders Elsevier.

Tsai, A. C., Manchester, D. K., & Elias, E. R. (2012). Genetics and dysmorphology. In W. W. Hay, M. J. Levin, R. R. Deterding, M. J. Abzug & J. M. Sondheimer (Eds.), *Current pediatric diagnosis & treatment* (21st ed., pp. 1088–1122). New York, NY: McGraw-Hill.

U.S. Department of Health and Human Services. (2006). *The health consequences of involuntary exposure to tobacco smoke: A report of the Surgeon General.* Atlanta, GA: Author, Centers for Disease Control and Prevention, Coordinating Center for Health Promotion, National Center for Chronic Disease Prevention and Health Promotion, Office on Smoking and Health. Retrieved from http://www.ncbi.nlm.nih.gov/books/NBK44324/

Wald, E. R., Applegate, K. E., Bordley, C., Darrow, D. H., Glode, M. P., Marcy, S. M., . . . Weinberg, S. T. (2013). Clinical practice guideline for the diagnosis and management of acute bacterial sinusitis in children aged 1 to 18 years. *Pediatrics, 132*(1), e262–e280.

Weber, J., & Kelley, J. (2007). *Health assessment in nursing* (3rd ed.). Philadelphia, PA: Lippincott.

Yager, J., Scher, L. M., Hilty, D. M., & Osterhout, C. I. (2014). *Bulimia nervosa.* Retrieved from http://emedicine.medscape.com/article/286485-overview

Zellman, G. L., Elston, D. M., Boysen, M., Kwon, K. T., Perry, V., Slapper, D., . . . Wolfram, W. (2013). *Erythema infectiosum.* Retrieved from http://emedicine.medscape.com/article/1132078-overview

Assessment of the Thorax, Lungs, and Regional Lymphatics

Respiratory infections and disorders are common in infants and children. Contributing factors include anatomic and physiologic immaturity of the respiratory and immune systems, as well as frequent exposure to respiratory viruses in school or day care. Because of the potential severity of respiratory disorders in infants and children, it is essential that the health care provider possess excellent pediatric respiratory assessment skills.

ANATOMY AND PHYSIOLOGY

Thorax

Thoracic Cage

The thoracic cage includes the *sternum*, 12 *thoracic vertebrae*, 12 pairs of *ribs*, and *costal cartilage intercostal*

and *thoracic muscles* (Figure 17.1). The purpose of the thoracic cage is to support and protect the structures within the thoracic cavity. For simplification, the thoracic cage can be divided into three main sections: the sternum anteriorly, the ribs laterally, and the vertebrae posteriorly. The sternum, which lies in the center of the chest, can be divided into three parts: the *manubrium* (top portion), *gladiolus* (body), and the *xiphoid process* (the tip) (see Figure 17.1). The manubrium, a triangular bone, attaches to the *clavicles* and the first and second ribs on either side (see Figure 17.1). The manubrium also is the point at which the *sternocleidomastoid* and *pectoralis* major muscles attach; both of these muscles are accessory muscles of *inspiration*.

Two important anatomic landmarks are located on the manubrium. The *suprasternal notch* is located at the

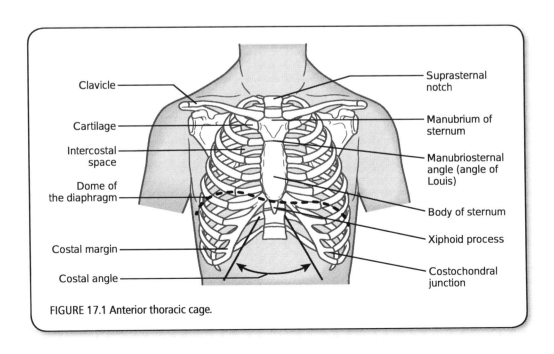

FIGURE 17.1 Anterior thoracic cage.

Clavicle

Cartilage

Intercostal space

Dome of the diaphragm

Costal margin

Costal angle

Suprasternal notch

Manubrium of sternum

Manubriosternal angle (angle of Louis)

Body of sternum

Xiphoid process

Costochondral junction

superior border of the manubrium (see Figure 17.1). Just below the suprasternal notch is the sternal angle, or *angle of Louis*, a palpable bony prominence where the manubrium meets the body of the sternum. The angle of Louis also marks the place at which the second pair of ribs articulates with the sternum; this is a clinical reference point for counting ribs and intercostal spaces.

Twelve pairs of ribs comprise the thoracic cage, articulating with the thoracic vertebrae posteriorly. Only the top seven pairs of ribs articulate directly with the sternum. Costal cartilage, which connects these seven ribs to the sternum, allows for expansion and contraction of the thoracic cage with respiration. Beneath the sternum, ribs 7 through 10 connect to the costal cartilage of the pair of ribs lying superior to them, forming the *costal angle*, a frequently used assessment landmark (see Figure 17.1). The remaining two pairs of ribs are connected only to the vertebrae.

There are 11 pairs of intercostal and 8 pairs of thoracic muscles that work with the diaphragm to move the thoracic cage during inspiration and expiration. During periods of respiratory distress, intercostal muscles become more visible as infants and young children use these muscles to assist respiration. When assessing the chest, imaginary vertical reference lines are used to describe the location of physical findings. These lines are illustrated in Figure 17.2 and are summarized in Table 17.1.

Thoracic Cavity

The thoracic cavity is the chamber that contains multiple structures and organs of the cardiovascular, respiratory, gastrointestinal, and endocrine systems. The thoracic cage protects these structures. The *mediastinum*, or center portion of the thoracic cavity, contains the *trachea*, *esophagus*, *heart* and *great vessels*, *thymus gland*, and *lymph nodes* of the chest. The *lungs* are positioned on either side of the mediastinum. The diaphragm, the main muscle of respiration, separates the thoracic cavity from the abdominal cavity.

Pleural Cavity

The thoracic cavity is surrounded by a thin, serous membrane called the *pleura* that is divided into two layers: the *parietal pleura*, which lines the chest wall, and the *visceral pleura*, which lines the lungs, blood vessels, and *bronchi*. The *pleural space* is the thin space between these two layers. Within the pleural space is *pleural fluid*, which lubricates the pleural membranes and permits the pleural layers to move smoothly against each other during respiration.

Lungs

The lungs are two paired, conical structures within the thoracic cavity that serve as a medium for the exchange

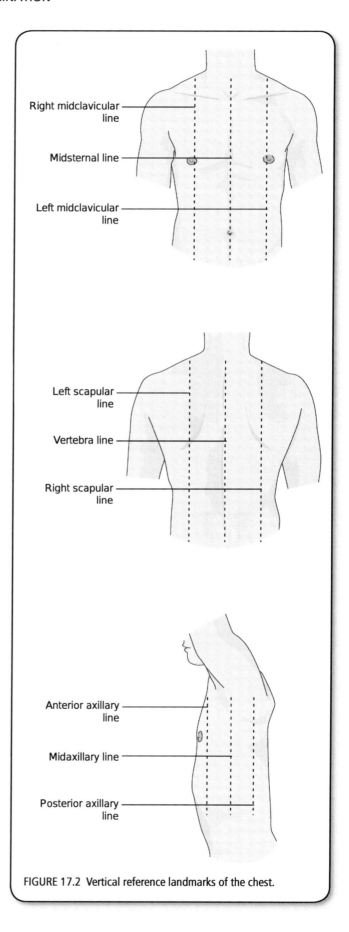

FIGURE 17.2 Vertical reference landmarks of the chest.

TABLE 17.1	Vertical Reference Landmarks of the Chest		
ANTERIOR CHEST	**POSTERIOR CHEST**	**LATERAL CHEST**
Right midclavicular line	Left scapular line	Anterior axillary line
Midsternal line	Vertebral line	Midaxillary line
Left midclavicular line	Right scapular line	Posterior axillary line

of gases (Figure 17.3). The *apex* is the pointed portion that reaches slightly above the clavicle. The *base* is the wide portion at the bottom that extends to the diaphragm. The right lung consists of three lobes; the left lung has two lobes. Within the lungs are the *trachea* and *bronchi* (see Figure 17.3). The trachea bridges the upper and lower respiratory tracts; it extends from the larynx to the bronchi in the upper thorax to below the sternum. The lower portion of the trachea bifurcates into the left and right mainstem bronchi (see Figure 17.3). Both of these structures function as passageways for air moving to the lower respiratory tract for gas exchange.

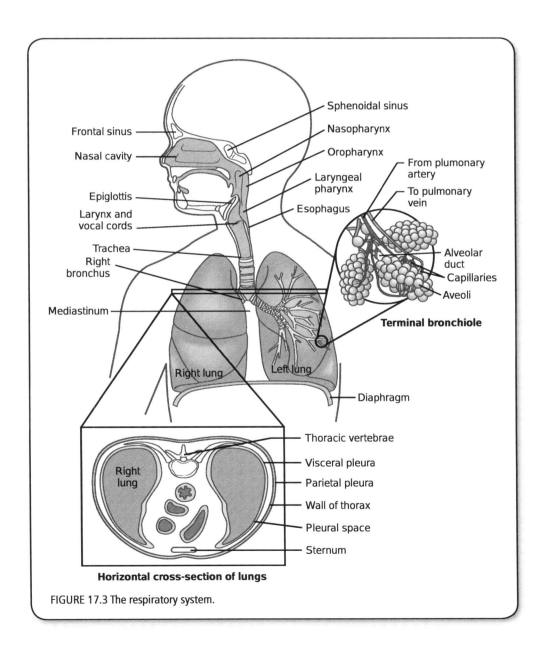

FIGURE 17.3 The respiratory system.

The right main bronchus is shorter and lies in a more vertical plane than the left bronchus; this explains why aspirated objects are more likely to enter the right bronchus. The bronchi then further branch into the *bronchioles*, which become even smaller and terminate into the *alveolar ducts*, *alveolar sacs*, and *alveoli*, where gas exchange occurs (see Figure 17.3).

Respiratory Mechanics

During the respiratory cycle, the lungs transport oxygen from the atmosphere to the tissues and cells, and return carbon dioxide from the tissues and cells to the atmosphere. One respiratory cycle involves an inspiratory and an expiratory phase. During inspiration, the diaphragm contracts and flattens to enlarge the thoracic cavity, and the intercostal muscles lift the sternum and elevate the rib cage. This creates negative pressure, which draws air into the lungs, enhancing venous blood return to the heart. During expiration, the diaphragm and intercostal muscles relax and the lungs compress, creating positive pressure within the alveoli, which forces air out of the lungs. At the end of each expiration, some air remains in the alveoli because of *surfactant*, a lipoprotein that is secreted by type II alveolar cells to reduce the surface tension of pulmonary fluids and to prevent alveolar collapse. Respiration is involuntary, and the rate of respiration is controlled by age, metabolic rate, fever, and cardiovascular and neurologic function.

DEVELOPMENTAL CONSIDERATIONS

Embryonic Development

In the early embryonic period (weeks 1–5), lung buds appear, and the pulmonary vein develops to join the lung bud. By the end of week 5, the trachea begins to develop. Between weeks 5 and 17, the major lobes of the lungs begin to develop, and the main bronchi are formed.

The pulmonary capillary bed also develops, which connects the bronchial blood supply. Between weeks 13 and 25, type II alveolar epithelial cells appear and eventually become responsible for the production of surfactant. During this time, the airway begins to increase in size and in diameter and become more tubular in shape (John & Brady, 2013). At 25 weeks, alveolar sacs are formed, but the ability for gas exchange is limited by the immaturity of type II cells and their inability to release adequate amounts of surfactant. After week 26, type II cells gradually become more numerous and mature, and more alveoli form. Near the end of the sixth gestational month, the alveoli are capable of gas exchange. Lung size increases rapidly until week 36 of gestation, and more surfactant is secreted. At birth, the lungs are filled with fluid, which is expelled as the infant moves through the birth canal and as the lungs fill with air after the umbilical cord is cut.

Structure

An infant's chest is round and barrel shaped, and the anterior–posterior (A–P) diameter equals the transverse diameter (Figure 17.4A). The chest circumference should closely match the head circumference from age 6 months to 2 years; chest circumference should then exceed head circumference at age 2 years (Hockenberry & Wilson, 2011). By the age of 5 to 6, the thorax approximates the adult shape; by adulthood, the A–P diameter is twice the transverse diameter (Figure 17.4B). From birth to age 3 years, the ribs lie in a horizontal plane; this restricts the infant's ability to expand his or her chest fully and limits tidal volume (Bissonnette et al., 2011). The ribs are also flexible and provide very little support for the lungs; negative intrathoracic pressure is poorly maintained, and the work of breathing is thus increased. This explains why children use accessory muscles during times of respiratory distress.

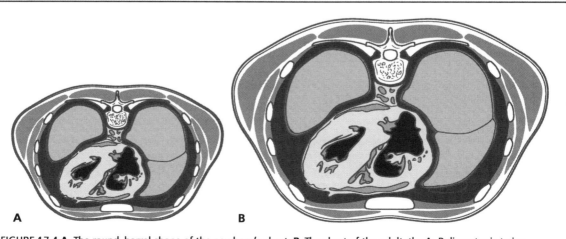

FIGURE 17.4 **A.** The round, barrel shape of the newborn's chest. **B.** The chest of the adult; the A–P diameter is twice the transverse diameter.

The airway and nasal passages of the infant and child are small and narrow, and the larynx is narrowest at the level of the cricoid cartilage (Bissonnette et al., 2011). One millimeter of airway edema can narrow an infant's airway by 60% (Bissonnette et al., 2011). Newborns produce little respiratory mucus, increasing their susceptibility to respiratory infections (Bissonnette et al., 2011). The oropharynx is proportionately smaller and narrower and the trachea is proportionately shorter and has a smaller diameter than that of an older child or an adult; this increases the potential for obstruction (Ball, Bindler, & Cowen, 2012). From birth until approximately 8 to 10 years, the larynx is located two to three cervical vertebrae higher at the level of C3–C4, which makes the young child more vulnerable to aspiration (Bissonnette et al., 2011). Until age 5 years, the tracheal cartilage is elastic and collapses easily, leaving the child vulnerable to airway obstruction and resistance to airflow. The trachea continues to grow in diameter and triples in size between birth and puberty (Ball et al., 2012).

In infants and toddlers, the mucous membranes lining the respiratory tract are more loosely attached and very vascular, making the potential for airway edema greater and increasing the potential for airway obstruction. In infants and young children, the right bronchus is significantly shorter, wider, and more vertical than the left bronchus. In this age group, the trachea bifurcates at the level of T3, a higher level than the older child or adult, where bifurcation occurs at T4 or T5 (Ball et al., 2012). Both of these factors increase an infant's or young child's susceptibility to aspiration of foreign bodies into the right bronchus. Also, this causes breath sounds to be louder and higher in pitch in infants and young children than in adolescents or adults.

Function

In neonates and infants until age 3 months, the hypoxic and hypercapnic drives are not fully developed (Bissonnette et al., 2011). Because of the neurologic immaturity of the respiratory drive, *periodic breathing* (i.e., apnea ≤ 10 seconds) without cyanosis or bradycardia is within normal limits in the neonate. Apnea that lasts longer than 20 seconds (*central apnea*) is outside normal limits.

Oxygen consumption in the neonate is almost twice that of the adult (Bissonnette et al., 2011); however, the alveoli are thick walled at birth, and infants have only roughly 10% of the total number of alveoli found in the adult lung, which affects total gas exchange. Over the first 8 years of life, alveoli increase in number, and existing alveoli grow in size (Bissonnette et al., 2011); a full-term newborn has 25 million immature alveoli, compared with 300 million fully developed alveoli in the adult (Brashers, 2010). Respiratory failure is also common in premature infants because of surfactant deficiency, causing alveolar collapse (Bissonnette et al., 2011). From birth through school age, there is a large amount of anatomic dead space in the tracheobronchial tree where gas exchange does not take place (Sarniak & Heidemann, 2011). These factors explain why the respiratory rates in infants and children are more rapid than those of the adult.

From birth until age 6 years, infants and children breathe by using the diaphragm and abdominal muscles (Ball et al., 2012). From birth until approximately age 2, the intercostal, scaleni, sternocleidomastoid, and diaphragmatic muscles have few type I muscle fibers, which are used in sustained respiratory activity (Bissonnette et al., 2011). Thus, immature respiratory muscles must work hard to assist in respiratory effort; nasal flaring may occur, and poorly developed respiratory muscles hinder the expulsion of thick respiratory secretions. Respiratory muscles that are easily fatigued can result in retention of carbon dioxide, apnea, and respiratory failure. Respiration may be inefficient when the infant or young child is crying or with anything that restricts breathing, such as abdominal distention (Bissonnette et al., 2011). Breathing becomes thoracic between 8 and 10 years, and the respiratory rate lowers to near-adult levels.

CULTURAL, RACIAL, AND ETHNIC CONSIDERATIONS

Cystic fibrosis is a genetic disease that occurs primarily in Caucasians of northern European ancestry. Asthma occurs in all races, but the highest prevalence occurs among African American boys (Bloom, Cohen, & Freeman, 2012). Pectus deformities, which may affect respiration, are more common in Caucasian children (Cataletto, 2013; Hebra, 2012).

ASSESSMENT OF THE THORAX, LUNGS, AND REGIONAL LYMPHATICS

History

Prenatal, Perinatal, and Neonatal Histories

The prenatal, perinatal, and neonatal histories are crucial elements of the respiratory assessment in children. Maternal prenatal substance abuse can result in respiratory complications in the infant. For example, prenatal cocaine use causes placental vasoconstriction, resulting in fetal hypoxia, and third-trimester cocaine use can result in uterine contractions, causing premature delivery and consequent respiratory complications of prematurity (Kim & Koren, 2012). Maternal tobacco and cocaine use can also lead to meconium aspiration during delivery (Clark & Clark, 2014); infants exposed to cigarette smoke in utero are also at risk for lower birth weight and intrauterine growth restriction (U.S. Department of Health and Human Services, 2007).

In children from birth to age 3 years, it is important to obtain the child's Apgar scores, noting any score below 7; a score this low suggests respiratory distress at birth with possible perinatal asphyxia. A history of meconium aspiration is another important assessment notation, as are histories of endotracheal intubation or prolonged positive pressure ventilation (PPV) with supplemental oxygen; these interventions predispose the infant to barotrauma, a factor in the development of bronchopulmonary dysplasia (BPD) (Ambalavanan, 2013). Any history of congenital heart defects is also important to consider, especially defects that increase pulmonary blood flow. For example, patent ductus arteriosus (PDA) has been associated with the development of BPD, especially in very low birth weight (VLBW) infants (Chock et al., 2013).

It is important to note a history of prematurity, making sure to include the gestational age at which the child was born, birth weight, and the nature and degree of postnatal respiratory complications, such as asphyxia, mechanical ventilation, apnea, and any oxygen requirements. Preterm infants, particularly VLBW and extremely low birth weight (ELBW) infants who have been diagnosed with respiratory distress syndrome, are especially vulnerable to the development of BPD (Ambalavanan, 2013).

Review of Systems

The past medical history is thoroughly reviewed for any conditions that have respiratory manifestations or atopic components. The provider should also pay special attention to a history of more than six to ten upper respiratory infections a year, frequent lower respiratory tract infections, the number of acute otitis media episodes, chronic cough, wheezing episodes, or any chronic respiratory conditions, such as asthma, BPD, or cystic fibrosis. Children who have respiratory symptoms coupled with a failure to gain weight should be referred to a pediatric pulmonologist; these findings may indicate cystic fibrosis.

A typical review of systems in an assessment of the thorax, lungs, and regional lymphatics includes the following:

- **Skin:** Atopic dermatitis
- **Ear:** Acute otitis media or otitis media with effusion
- **Cardiovascular:** Congenital heart defects that increase pulmonary blood flow
- **Respiratory:** Upper respiratory infections (also note frequency), viral croup, epiglottitis, viral or bacterial pharyngitis, tonsillitis, peritonsillar abscess, retropharyngeal abscess, foreign body aspiration, bacterial tracheitis, asthma, chronic cough, pertussis, laryngomalacia, tracheomalacia, cystic fibrosis, pneumonia, bronchiolitis, tuberculosis, or pneumothorax
- **Immunity:** Allergic rhinitis or allergic angioedema

Immunizations

Many of the communicable diseases against which children are immunized affect the respiratory tract. When considering diagnostic possibilities in children with respiratory complaints, it is essential to review a child's immunization status. This is particularly true for infants and very young children and for children from developing countries who may not only lack immunizations but also be malnourished and are thus more vulnerable to respiratory infections.

Allergies

All allergies must be noted in children undergoing a respiratory assessment. Examples of allergies about which to inquire include those to ragweed, grass, trees, pet dander, feathers, dust mites, mold spores, and food. Depending on the individual, allergic rhinitis can have numerous triggers, but the end result will be some degree of inflammation of the nasal turbinates, eustachian tubes, middle ear, sinuses, and pharynx. Because both allergic rhinitis and atopic dermatitis are immunoglobulin E–mediated reactions, the provider should assess the child for both conditions.

Hospitalizations

Any past hospitalizations for respiratory conditions, such as bronchiolitis, reactive airway disease, asthma, croup syndromes (e.g., epiglottitis, laryngotracheobronchitis), pneumonia, foreign body aspiration, gastroesophageal reflux, and cystic fibrosis, are noted. The date, child's age, underlying medical conditions, and length of stay are also noted. The provider should pay particular attention to repeated hospitalizations for respiratory conditions, which indicate a poorly controlled condition for which medical management may need to be adjusted, a sign of difficulty accessing care, or even neglect.

Injuries

Certain injuries can potentially affect the child's respiratory status and function. Smoke inhalation may accompany burns the child has sustained in a fire. Aspiration of a caustic substance, such as acids (e.g., drain cleaners, battery fluid) or alkalis (e.g., oven cleaners, lye), can cause severe respiratory distress; for example, alkali aspiration causes tissue liquefaction necrosis. Respiratory complications of caustic substance aspiration include upper airway obstruction, laryngeal edema, bronchospasm, severe respiratory distress, and respiratory failure (Kardon, 2012). Blunt chest trauma can cause injury to underlying abdominal organs or lead to a pneumothorax.

Surgical History

It is important to note all past surgeries, with particular attention paid to procedures such as tracheostomy, tonsillectomy or adenoidectomy, Nissen fundoplication for reflux, or chest tube placement. The dates, reasons, and outcomes of the surgeries are important data for the pediatric history.

Current Medications

A complete medication history is essential, focusing on any medications that the child uses for treatment of asthma or allergies. The dose and frequency of bronchodilators, inhaled or oral corticosteroids, mast cell stabilizers, leukotriene receptor agonists, or methylxanthines are assessed and recorded. If the child is currently taking antibiotics prescribed by another health care provider, it should be determined if the indication relates to a respiratory condition, such as acute otitis media or bacterial pneumonia. Use of any over-the-counter decongestants, expectorants, or antihistamines is also noted; this assessment is especially important in children younger than 2 years for whom these medications are dangerous and not recommended (U.S. Food and Drug Administration, 2013). The provider should also inquire about the use of complementary and alternative medicine (CAM). In some instances, the use of CAM may displace the use of biomedical therapies. For example, Adams, Murdock, and McQuaid (2007) found that for some children, CAM use displaced the use of biomedical therapies for the treatment of asthma, thus decreasing the level of asthma control.

Family History

The family history includes any history of atopy. Examples include eczema, seasonal and environmental allergies, asthma, snoring, mouth breathing, frequent upper respiratory infections, nasal polyps, or cystic fibrosis among family members. It is important to note the family member's relationship to the child.

Social History

Multiple aspects of a child's day-to-day life and living conditions can affect his or her respiratory status and frequency of respiratory symptoms. For example, it is important to ask about the child's living conditions, assessing whether the child is exposed to high levels of air pollution, dust mites, mold spores, or secondhand smoke. School-aged children and adolescents should also be asked if they smoke tobacco or marijuana. Any exercise intolerance is noted. It is also important to note whether an infant or young child attends day care as these children have more frequent respiratory infections. The provider should also inquire about any occupation or hobbies the child or family members may have that necessitates the use of paint, paint thinner, or other chemicals that can trigger an exacerbation of asthma. In addition, the child's social situation is assessed to determine if tuberculosis screening is necessary (see Chapter 9).

History of Present Illness

Because of the immaturity of the respiratory and immune systems in infants and young children, respiratory diagnoses are very common. The immaturity of the respiratory system also poses concerns related to quick respiratory deterioration in very young children. Common respiratory complaints in children include nasal congestion, cough, throat or ear pain (with and without fever), difficulty breathing, and wheezing. Associated complaints may include headache, vomiting, abdominal pain, poor feeding, or lethargy. When evaluating these complaints, the provider must consider the child's past medical history for any chronic respiratory conditions, such as asthma, cystic fibrosis, or repeated episodes of acute otitis media or streptococcal pharyngitis.

When obtaining the history, important data to gather include the onset of the respiratory symptoms and the presence of any fever or cough. When did the child get sick? For example, did the child have an upper respiratory infection before wheezing began? Are the respiratory symptoms worsening? If the child has a cough, when did it start? How would the child or parent describe the cough? Is it worse at night?

It is also important to evaluate the child's immunization status, assess for any sick contacts, and determine if the child is exposed to secondhand smoke at home, in the car, or in the day care setting. Children exposed to secondhand smoke have a higher incidence of upper respiratory infections, reactive airway disease, asthma, bronchitis, and pneumonia (Oberg, Jaakola, Woodward, Peruga, & Pruss-Ustun, 2011). Table 17.2 lists some respiratory conditions commonly seen in infants and children.

TABLE 17.2	History of Present Illness: Respiratory Complaints		
CONDITION	**AGE**	**CAUSE(S)**	**SIGNS AND SYMPTOMS**
Allergic rhinitis	6 months and older	Indoor and outdoor allergens (pollen, mold spores); cigarette smoke, dust mites, pet dander, wood smoke, and pollution	Sneezing, itching, tearing, and rhinorrhea; allergic "shiners," lateral nasal crease, boggy nasal turbinates, and injection and swelling of palpebral conjunctivae; Dennie-Morgan lines (creases below inferior eyelid); "cobblestoning" of pharynx
Asthma	2 years and older	Numerous triggers (e.g., exercise, cigarette smoke, mold spores, dust mites, pet dander, wood smoke, pollution); other indoor and outdoor allergens; respiratory infections, fear, cold air, and food (e.g., nuts, dairy products); food additives or reflux disease	Cough, shortness of breath, wheezing (characteristic breath sound), retractions, and nasal flaring

(continued)

TABLE 17.2	History of Present Illness: Respiratory Complaints (*continued*)		
CONDITION	**AGE**	**CAUSE(S)**	**SIGNS AND SYMPTOMS**
Bacterial tracheitis (membranous croup)	1 month–13 years (peak 3–10 years)	*Staphylococcus aureus* (most common)	Begins as URI, then progresses to high fever, hoarseness, stridor, and copious purulent secretions; child "looks toxic," and rapid deterioration is common
Bronchiolitis	Birth–2 years	Viral (e.g., RSV [50%], adenovirus, parainfluenza virus, influenza virus, rhinovirus)	Begins as URI, then progresses to wheezing, fever, decreased appetite, tachypnea, and varying degrees of respiratory distress; paroxysmal cough that may be followed by vomiting; very young infants become very ill and experience the most respiratory distress
Bronchopulmonary dysplasia	Premature infants treated with oxygen	Positive pressure ventilation, oxygen therapy, inflammation, and persistent hypoxia	Tachypnea, wheezing, crackles, nasal flaring, retractions, grunting, irritability, pulmonary edema, failure to thrive; barrel-chest because of air trapping. Severity depends on gestational age at birth, length of time of positive pressure ventilation, and postnatal respiratory complications.
Chest pain	School age–adolescent	*Respiratory:* RAD, bronchitis, pneumonia, pleurisy, and pneumothorax *Cardiac:* hypertrophic cardiomyopathy, anomalous coronary artery, pericarditis, myocarditis, and arrhythmia *Gastrointestinal:* esophagitis and gastric ulcer disease *Musculoskeletal:* injury, rib fracture, and costochondritis *Psychogenic* (Reddy & Singh, 2010)	Possible pain, dyspnea, dizziness, stridor, and anxiety (Reddy & Singh, 2010)
Croup (laryngotracheo-bronchitis)	6 months–6 years	Viral (parainfluenza viruses, adenoviruses, RSV)	Usually preceded by URI; slight dyspnea, fever, tachypnea, and retractions; harsh, barking cough and inspiratory stridor
Cystic fibrosis	Birth throughout life	*S. aureus, Haemophilus influenzae, Pseudomonas aeruginosa* are organisms responsible for causing pulmonary infections.	Clinical manifestations in respiratory system include chronic, frequent, dry cough; repeated episodes of bronchitis, bronchiectasis, and pneumonia; bronchospasm often follows paroxysms of coughing; recurrent sinusitis, nasal polyps, and digital clubbing also seen; respiratory problems are chronic, progressive, and can lead to respiratory failure and death
Epiglottitis	1–5 years	*H. influenzae* type b	Rapid onset, high fever, severe sore throat, dysphagia, drooling, muffled voice, tripod breathing, no spontaneous cough, and agitation
Foreign body aspiration	1–3 years (peak age)	Object becomes lodged in some portion of the respiratory tract	Depends on nature of object aspirated (e.g., size and material of object), age, size of child, and location of airway where object is lodged; sudden episodes of coughing, chronic cough with fever and unilateral wheeze, hemoptysis, and recurrent pneumonia are all possible clinical findings

TABLE 17.2	History of Present Illness: Respiratory Complaints (*continued*)		
CONDITION	**AGE**	**CAUSE(S)**	**SIGNS AND SYMPTOMS**
Nasopharyngitis	All ages	Viral	Nasal congestion, nasal drainage, and cough; may have fever and decreased appetite; may have sore throat
Pertussis	All ages	*Bordetella pertussis*	URI precedes illness; fever and high-pitched cough, which occurs on inspiration and makes a "whoop" sound; cyanosis, diaphoresis, and fatigue after paroxysms of cough; infants aged 6 months and younger become very ill; possible pneumonia and apnea
Pharyngitis	Viral pharyngitis seen in all ages; streptococcal pharyngitis less common in children aged 2 years and younger; most common in children aged 5–15 years	Viral (e.g., adenoviruses, parainfluenza viruses, enteroviruses, herpesvirus, Epstein-Barr virus); bacterial (*Mycoplasma pneumoniae*, GABHS, *Neisseria gonorrhoeae*, *Corynebacterium diphtheriae* [rare])	**Viral:** gradual onset, nasal symptoms, sore throat, mild cough, and low-grade fever **Bacterial:** abrupt onset, no nasal symptoms, marked sore throat with exudate, moderate-to-high fever, petechiae on soft palate, tender cervical lymphadenopathy, and abdominal pain with nausea and vomiting in some cases
Pneumonia	All ages	Viral, bacterial	Fever, cough, crackles or decreased breath sounds; dyspnea, and varying degrees of respiratory distress, depending on child's age and amount of lobar infiltration or consolidation
Reactive airway disease	Birth–2 years	Airway inflammation that occurs without a viral trigger	Same as asthma
Sinusitis	1 year and older (Wald et al., 2013)	Bacterial (e.g., *Streptococcus pneumoniae, H. influenzae, Moraxella catarrhalis*, nontypeable *H. influenzae, S. aureus*)	Frequent complication of URI; facial pain or pressure; headache, dental pain, eye pain, purulent rhinorrhea, and postnasal drip on oral examination
Tonsillitis	Same as pharyngitis	Same as pharyngitis	Tonsillar enlargement, throat pain, difficulty swallowing, and difficulty breathing because of tonsillar enlargement ("kissing tonsils"); mouth breathing when adenoids enlarge with dry mouth and throat; nasal voice; otitis media is a frequent complication
Tuberculosis (TB)	Birth throughout life	*Mycobacterium tuberculosis*	Infants, children, and adolescents with latent TB (exposed and infected but not infectious) are asymptomatic. Children aged 4 years and younger are more likely to convert from TB infection to TB disease because of their immature immune system. Young children do not produce sputum and cannot usually generate enough force when coughing to expel infected sputum. Symptomatic children present later in the course of the disease with persistent cough, weight loss, failure to gain weight, fever, fatigue, night sweats, chills, wheezing, crackles, and decreased breath sounds.

GABHS, group A beta-hemolytic strep; RAD, reactive airway disease; RSV, respiratory syncytial virus; TB, tuberculosis; URI, upper respiratory infection.

Physical Examination

Physical assessment of the respiratory system in children involves inspection, auscultation, palpation, and percussion. Inspection and auscultation are essential components of the pediatric respiratory assessment. Palpation and percussion may be difficult to perform on infants and toddlers and may not yield useful information. A stethoscope is the only necessary piece of equipment for respiratory assessment; however, the following equipment may be useful:

■ A pulse oximeter to measure oxygen saturation if a child presents in acute respiratory distress
■ An otoscope, if the child is febrile, has nasal symptoms and a sore throat, and is complaining of ear pain (see Chapter 14)
■ A tongue blade to examine the throat (see Chapter 16)
■ A marking pencil to measure diaphragmatic excursion

In quiet infants and toddlers, the chest is auscultated first to maximize the accuracy of assessment findings. Children preschool-aged and older can be examined in the customary head-to-toe fashion (see Chapter 8). Inspection is also done with the infant or young child quiet or asleep, as crying can mimic or exacerbate retractions.

Vital Signs

Vital sign measurements in a child reflect the child's respiratory status and vice versa. For example, a febrile child will become tachypneic to decrease body temperature. With conditions that cause hypoxia, the heart rate increases as the body's demands for oxygen increase. The respiratory rate also increases with conditions that cause hypercarbia, in the body's effort to rid itself of excess carbon dioxide. Therefore, a rapid respiratory rate suggests lower respiratory tract disease. Normal vital signs, according to age, are provided in Appendix A.

Current Growth Parameters

As part of the respiratory assessment, it is important for the health care provider to assess physical growth in the child; lack of physical growth may indicate chronic hypoxia. A new-onset drop in weight or height measurements on the growth curve indicates an acute problem (see Chapter 8).

Inspection

General Appearance • The first step in pediatric respiratory assessment is inspection of the child's general appearance. This begins with observing respiratory effort, noting any signs of dyspnea or respiratory distress. These signs include nasal flaring (especially in infants), grunting, and a prolonged respiratory phase

(indicates carbon dioxide retention). Mouth breathing may be a sign of respiratory distress or may indicate simple nasal congestion or enlarged adenoids due to chronic allergies. Drooling that is accompanied by sitting in the tripod position (i.e., upright, leaning forward, chin thrust forward, mouth open) is an especially ominous sign that points to epiglottitis, a medical emergency (Figure 17.5). The child may also appear acutely ill or "toxic" in the case of septicemia that accompanies the respiratory condition. In infants, fatigue and head bobbing is a sign of dyspnea. The position of the trachea is also inspected; it should be midline. With tension pneumothorax or a large pleural effusion, the trachea shifts *away* from the affected side. In the case of atelectasis, the trachea shifts *toward* the affected side.

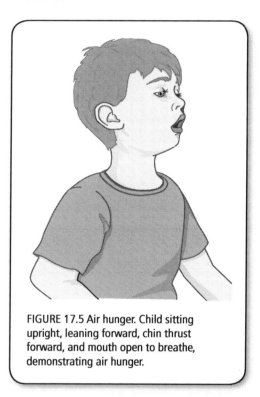

FIGURE 17.5 Air hunger. Child sitting upright, leaning forward, chin thrust forward, and mouth open to breathe, demonstrating air hunger.

Skin color is also inspected, noting any pallor, mottling, or cyanosis. When assessing skin color in dark-skinned children, the mucous membranes, palms of the hands, and soles of the feet are inspected. Pallor may indicate anemia or hypotension. Mottling and peripheral cyanosis (cyanosis seen on the hands and feet or around the mouth) can occur with cool ambient room temperatures; mottling can also occur with severe hypoxemia. Acrocyanosis (cyanosis of the hands and feet only) is a normal finding in the newborn (see Chapter 11). Central cyanosis (cyanosis along the midline) is a late sign of respiratory distress and can also indicate cardiopulmonary disease. Children who are anemic may not become cyanotic as early as children with normal hemoglobin levels because of less deoxygenated hemoglobin near the skin surface.

Chest • The chest should be examined with the child's head in the midline position. Chest size, shape, symmetry, and movement are inspected. Scars on the chest are noted, with inquiries about the etiology (e.g., past medical and surgical procedures). The diameter of the child's chest changes from birth to young adulthood (see Developmental Considerations). Infants normally have a round thorax, with the A–P and transverse diameters being equal. By age 6 years, the thorax reaches the adult ratio of 1:2 (A–P to transverse diameter). Alterations in chest shape are assessed, noting any chest wall deformities such as *pectus excavatum* ("funnel chest"), a depression of the chest wall (Figure 17.6), or *pectus carinatum* ("pigeon chest"), a protuberance of the chest wall (Figure 17.7). Of all congenital anterior chest wall deformities, pectus excavatum occurs much more commonly (90%) than pectus carinatum (5% to 7%) (Hebra, 2012). Pectus excavatum becomes more pronounced as the child grows, with the onset of symptoms occurring by about age 10. Depending on the degree of concavity in the anterior chest wall, the child's symptoms may range from chest and back pain to cardiac and pulmonary compression, shortness of breath, diminished breath sounds at the bases, and poor posture (Hebra, 2012). In adolescents, body image is also a concern. Pectus carinatum can be present at birth but becomes more evident between ages 11 and 15 years (Cataletto, 2013). This condition primarily causes cosmetic concerns and does not cause respiratory complications. Spinal deformities (e.g., scoliosis, kyphosis, lordosis) can also interfere with respiration, depending on the degree of spinal curvature.

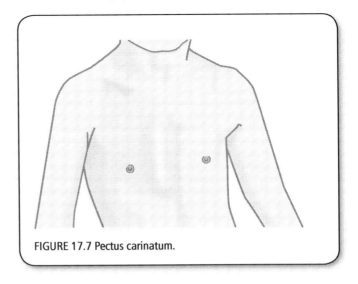

FIGURE 17.7 Pectus carinatum.

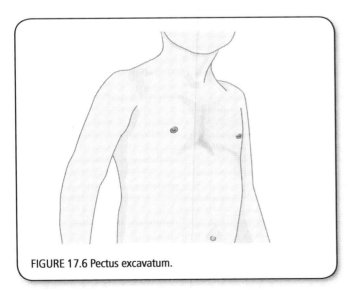

FIGURE 17.6 Pectus excavatum.

The examiner inspects the child's thorax for movement during the respiratory cycle, noting respiratory effort. Respirations should be smooth, symmetrical, easy, and without the use of accessory muscles (retractions). Retractions occur when heightened respiratory effort is necessary to inhale extra oxygen. This use of accessory muscles of breathing is seen in infants and young children; older children and adolescents use the diaphragm for increased work of breathing. Any condition that leads to hypoxia can cause retractions. Retractions may be suprasternal, supraclavicular, intercostal, substernal, or subcostal (Figure 17.8). The location and severity of the retractions can provide clues to the diagnosis; for example, the use of sternocleidomastoid muscles (suprasternal or supraclavicular retractions) suggests upper airway obstruction, such as croup or epiglottitis, and the use of intercostal and abdominal muscles in children younger than 6 years of age suggests lower airway disease, such as pneumonia or bronchiolitis.

The child's respiratory rate and type of breathing are also observed. *Tachypnea* is seen with fever, severe anemia, anxiety, pain, cardiac disorders, lower respiratory tract disorders (e.g., pneumonia), and metabolic acidosis.

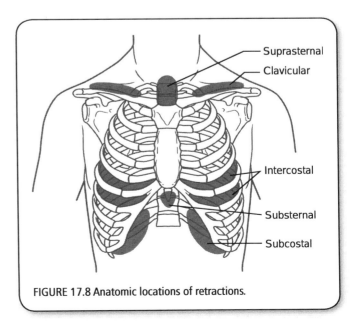

FIGURE 17.8 Anatomic locations of retractions.

Periodic breathing (up to 20 seconds of apnea) is within normal limits in neonates. Diaphragmatic breathing (i.e., the abdomen rises with inspiration) is normal in infants and children until age 7; in older children, breathing should be thoracic. Any paradoxical breathing should be noted (i.e., the diaphragm falls, rather than rises, during inspiration), which is associated with upper airway obstruction, rib fracture, pneumonia, asthma, bronchiolitis, BPD, and neuromuscular diseases (Newth & Hammer, 2005). Asymmetrical chest movements may be seen with pneumonia. A prolonged expiratory phase occurs in conditions that cause carbon dioxide retention, such as transient tachypnea of the newborn, or obstructive respiratory conditions such as asthma or cystic fibrosis. Deep and labored breathing (Kussmaul breathing) is a form of hyperventilation that occurs with metabolic acidosis.

Signs of Chronic Respiratory Disease • Overall inspection continues for any signs of chronic respiratory disease. One sign is a barrel-shaped chest (Figure 17.9); this may result from chronic hyperinflation, as with

A Normal chest **B** Barrel chest

Cross section
of thorax

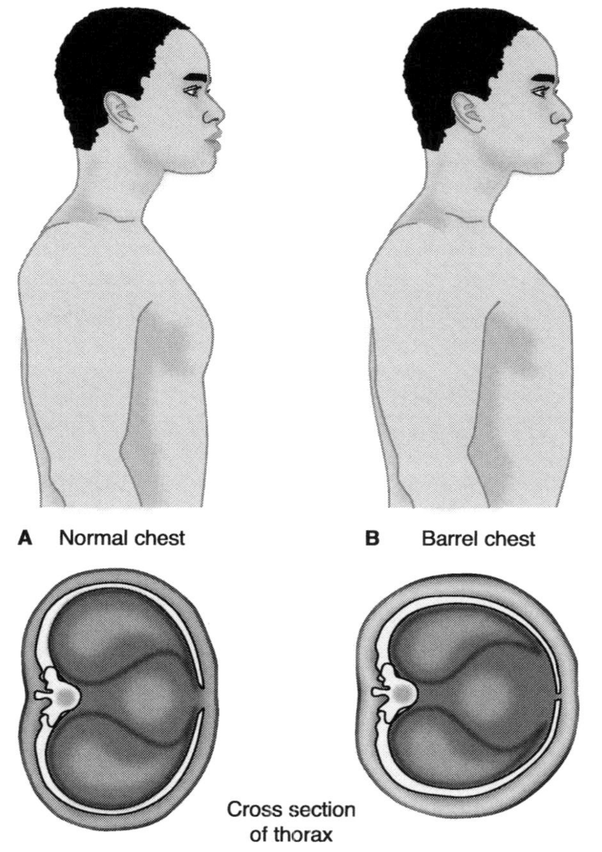

FIGURE 17.9 Comparison of **A.** normal chest shape and **B.** barrel-shaped chest. Note that in the normal chest, the A–P diameter is less than the transverse diameter; in the barrel chest, the transverse and A–P diameters are equal.

cystic fibrosis or asthma. Finger clubbing is associated with conditions that cause chronic hypoxia, such as cystic fibrosis. This occurs when the angle between the nail and nail bed is flattened as capillary growth increases in an attempt to supply the peripheral tissues with oxygen. Finger clubbing occurs in three stages: normal, early, and late. These stages are illustrated in Figure 12.12.

Poor weight gain and decreased adipose tissue are other signs of chronic respiratory disease, namely cystic fibrosis. Other signs of chronic respiratory disease include nasal polyps, which occur with cystic fibrosis and may interfere with respirations. Any signs of atopy are investigated, such as persistent clear nasal discharge or signs of atopic dermatitis (see Chapter 12); these findings are associated with asthma.

Associated Findings • Any stridor is noted; this is a loud, coarse, high-pitched sound that occurs as a result of upper airway narrowing caused by inflammation, edema, or the presence of a foreign body. Stridor most often occurs with inspiration and is commonly associated with viral croup or foreign body aspiration. Stridor can be heard without a stethoscope.

Cough is frequently present with respiratory conditions but may also be associated with nonrespiratory etiologies. In very young children, cough is usually nonproductive because children usually swallow expectorated respiratory secretions. To narrow the list of differential diagnoses, it is important to determine the onset and type of cough, noting whether it is "wet" or "dry," productive or associated with fever, and what the aggravating and alleviating factors are (Nield & Kamat, 2012). Care must be taken to quickly determine if the cough is associated with any life-threatening condition that requires immediate action. Table 17.3 lists common causes of cough in children. Rhinorrhea, sore throat, ear pain, tonsillar enlargement, and tonsillar exudate are other clinical findings associated with the respiratory assessment; these complaints are discussed in detail in Chapters 14 and 16.

Auscultation

Auscultation of the infant or toddler's chest requires some alteration of assessment techniques. Children this age have their chest auscultated *first*, before palpation or percussion, which can elicit crying in the young child and cause alterations in auscultation assessment findings. Optimally, the examination room should be as quiet as possible. To maximize the child's comfort and decrease fear and stranger anxiety as much as possible, it is best to have the infant or toddler remain in the parent's lap, facing the parent so the child feels safe and secure. Older children should sit upright on the examination table. Preschoolers and school-aged children are curious about their bodies and will often ask if they can listen to what the provider hears. This is developmentally appropriate and helps the examiner gain the child's cooperation, maximizing the accuracy and thoroughness of the assessment findings.

TABLE 17.3	Differential Diagnosis of Cough in Children
TYPE OF COUGH	**DIFFERENTIAL DIAGNOSES**
Acute, paroxysmal	Pertussis (followed by "whoop" sound) and RSV
Acute, harsh, barky	Viral croup (LTB), foreign body, and tracheitis (with purulent sputum)
Acute, loose, productive	URI, pneumonia, and asthma
Acute, dry, hacking	Viral pneumonia, bronchiolitis, and pertussis
Chronic dry, hacking	Bronchitis, smoking, conditions causing pulmonary edema, and CHF
Chronic, dry, irritated	Allergies
Chronic, productive	Asthma, cystic fibrosis, and TB
Chronic, nonspecific	Chronic URI, environmental toxin exposure, allergies, postnasal drip, and psychogenic (tic)
Disappears with sleep	Psychogenic (tic)
Honking	Psychogenic
Loose, productive	URI, bronchitis, and cystic fibrosis
Post-tussive emesis	RSV and pertussis
Staccato	Neonatal chlamydial pneumonia
Tight, productive	Bronchiolitis and pneumonia
Tight, nonproductive	Asthma
Wheezing cough	Asthma, bronchiolitis, GER, and RAD

CHF, congestive heart failure; GER, gastroesophageal reflux; LTB, laryngo-tracheobronchitis; RAD, reactive airway disease; RSV, respiratory syncytial virus; TB, tuberculosis; URI, upper respiratory infection.

Sources: Shields and Thavagnanam (2013); Nield and Kamat (2012).

For the most accurate auscultation findings, it is essential to use a stethoscope with an infant or pediatric diaphragm. An adult-sized stethoscope with a diaphragm that is too large yields confusing and inconclusive findings. For older and overweight children, a stethoscope diaphragm that is too small will not be sensitive enough to transmit subtle auscultatory findings. For maximum comfort, the stethoscope should be warmed before use.

Auscultation is performed in a routine, systematic fashion, with the diaphragm placed firmly against the skin of the child's chest, never over the clothes or examination gown; this changes the auscultatory findings. Moving from side to side, the examiner auscultates the chest over all lung fields, noting air movement anteriorly, posteriorly, and laterally, following the sequence

depicted in Figure 17.10. The examiner auscultates for one full respiratory cycle at each location. Both sides of the chest are compared. In infants and toddlers, the sounds may seem louder and harsher and be difficult to localize because of the thinness of the chest wall. In this age group, crying may be transmitted throughout all lung fields as well. Children who are old enough to cooperate developmentally are asked to breathe in and out, slowly and deeply through the mouth. During this process, the examiner evaluates the timing, pitch, amplitude, and quality of breath sounds and compares the ratio of inspiration to expiration (duration).

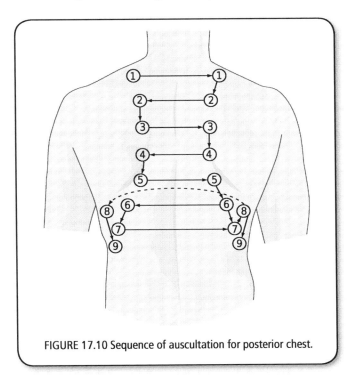

FIGURE 17.10 Sequence of auscultation for posterior chest.

Based on these assessments, breath sounds are classified as *vesicular*, *bronchovesicular*, or *bronchial*. Normal breath sounds are clear throughout all lung fields. The inspiratory and expiratory phases should be equal. A prolonged expiratory phase indicates carbon dioxide retention, as with asthma or bronchiolitis. Table 17.4 explains the classification of normal breath sounds.

During auscultation, any abnormal or adventitious ("extra") breath sounds, such as consolidated or diminished breath sounds, are also noted. Adventitious breath sounds, such as crackles or rales, rhonchi, wheezes, and pleural rub, can be heard over normal breath sounds. Table 17.5 explains the classification of abnormal and adventitious breath sounds.

In an uncooperative infant or crying child, assessing voice transmission can help clarify auscultatory assessment findings. These assessment techniques are used when areas of fluid or consolidation in the lung are suspected. Normally, voice sounds are muffled on auscultation. If the infant's cry is loud and clear or if the child is

TABLE 17.4	Classification of Normal Breath Sounds				
TYPE	PITCH	QUALITY	DURATION	LOCATION	ILLUSTRATION
Bronchial	High	Harsh or hollow	Shorter inspiration time; longer expiration time	Heard over trachea	
Bronchovesicular	Moderate	Mixed	Inspiratory and expiratory time are equal	Heard between first and second intercostal space; at point of bifurcation of trachea, and between scapulae	
Vesicular	Low	Blowing sound	Inspiration time is longer than expiration time	Heard throughout peripheral lung fields	

Adapted from Engel (2006).

TABLE 17.5	Abnormal and Adventitious Breath Sounds in Children	
BREATH SOUND	DESCRIPTION	ASSOCIATED CONDITION
Crackles or rales	High-pitched, soft, cracking, popping sound (fine crackles) or low-pitched, gurgling (coarse crackles); may be localized or diffuse, heard mainly at end of inspiration; do not clear with cough	Pneumonia, bronchiolitis, and atelectasis
Diminished breath sounds	Breath sounds that are less audible over an area of lung field	Pneumonia, pleural effusion, and pneumothorax
Pleural friction rub	Low-pitched, grating, or creaking sound; loudest on inspiration; occurs when inflamed pleurae rub together	Pneumonia, tuberculosis, and pleural effusion
Rhonchi	Low-pitched, loud, often rattling, bubbling, or gurgling; heard mainly at the beginning of inspiration; caused by secretions in large airways; often clears with coughing; low-pitched, snoring sounds during expiration result from narrowing of large airways, swelling, or obstruction	Asthma, pneumonia, bronchitis, and bronchiolitis
Stridor	Loud, coarse, high-pitched sound; occurs as a result of upper airway narrowing due to inflammation, edema or the presence of a foreign body; stridor mainly occurs with inspiration and can be heard without a stethoscope	Viral croup or foreign body aspiration
Wheezes	High-pitched, musical, whistling or squeaky; may be inspiratory or expiratory (predominantly expiratory); caused by airway narrowing	Reactive airway disease, bronchiolitis, asthma, foreign body aspiration, and bronchospasm

able to say "99" several times in a normal voice, and it is loud and clear and not muffled, the finding is termed *bronchophony*. The older child is then asked to whisper "99" several times while the examiner auscultates several areas over each lung. If the child's words are heard loudly and are not muffled, this is *whispered pectoriloquy*. With young children who can cooperate, the presence of *egophony* is assessed by asking the child to say "ee" continuously while auscultating the child's lungs.

The sound heard should be a muffled "ee" sound; if it sounds like "ay," consolidation is likely present. All of the findings that raise the suspicion for lung consolidation should be confirmed with a chest radiograph.

Palpation

Palpation of the chest is done to evaluate *respiratory excursion* and to assess for *tactile fremitus*.

These assessments are typically done in children aged 3 years and older who are able to cooperate with the examination. Palpation of the chest is also done to identify any tenderness, lumps, masses, or crepitus (crackling sensation or "popping" sound with palpation). Lymph nodes in the chest are also palpated.

Assessment of respiratory excursion is an evaluation of symmetrical chest expansion. In the neonate, chest expansion can be observed without palpation; asymmetry of chest expansion in this age group can be caused by diaphragmatic hernia or pneumothorax. In older children, both anterior and posterior expansion is assessed while the child is sitting upright. Beginning with the posterior chest, the examiner places his or her palms on the lateral chest and the thumbs on the child's back at approximately the level of the 10th rib, moving the thumbs together on the chest to create a small skinfold (Figure 17.11). The child is asked to inhale deeply and then exhale as the examiner observes his or her thumbs on the child's chest for symmetry of movement. With normal chest expansion, the examiner's thumbs are equidistant from the starting point when the child fully inhales. Respiratory excursion is decreased with chest pain and pneumothorax. Asymmetrical chest expansion occurs with acute pneumothorax or the presence of a foreign body.

This process is repeated on the anterior chest, with the examiner placing both hands pointing upward, on the costal margins at the xiphoid process. The child is again asked to inhale deeply, as the examiner observes for asymmetry of chest movement. Chest movement should be symmetrical and easy as the child breathes.

Tactile fremitus is also assessed. This is the presence of vibrations in the chest when the child speaks or an infant cries. Using the fingertips or palmar surface of the hands, the examiner moves along the child's chest in a systematic pattern, while asking the child to say "99" or "blue moon." Tactile fremitus is normal in the upper chest near the bronchi and clavicles and posteriorly between the scapulae; fremitus should be equal bilaterally. There should be little to no tactile fremitus in the lower chest. Decreased fremitus in the upper portion of the chest indicates obstruction (e.g., asthma, foreign body) or pneumothorax; increased fremitus indicates consolidation of lung tissue, as with pneumonia, atelectasis, or pleural effusion.

The chest and neck areas are also palpated for *crepitus*. In the newborn, the clavicle is palpated for crepitus, which is heard with a fractured clavicle. Crepitus is also present when air is between the lungs and subcutaneous tissue, which occurs in chest trauma or alveolar rupture.

The supraclavicular and axillary lymph nodes are palpated for size; mobility, warmth, tenderness, consistency, and degree of fixation, using both superficial and deep palpation techniques while the child holds his or her arms at the side in a relaxed position (see Chapter 13 for details on lymph node assessment).

Percussion

Percussion of the chest is done to locate any air, fluid, or masses in a child's lungs and to locate organ boundaries. This examination technique is typically done in children aged 2 years and older who are able to cooperate. Also, in younger children, percussion of the chest may not be accurate because of the size of the examiner's fingers. Percussion can be done directly or indirectly (see Chapter 8 for a description of these techniques). Indirect percussion is most often used when assessing the chest. Figure 17.12 depicts the correct hand position necessary for indirect percussion. For best results, the child should be sitting upright. The examiner should always percuss between the child's ribs rather than directly over them.

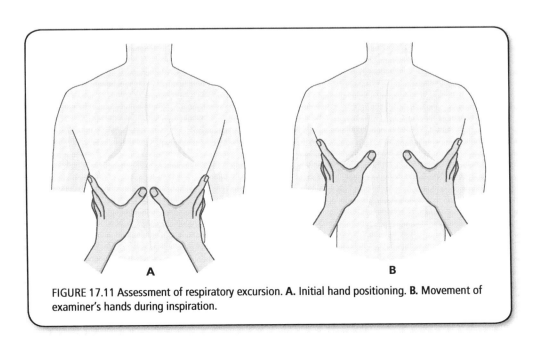

FIGURE 17.11 Assessment of respiratory excursion. **A.** Initial hand positioning. **B.** Movement of examiner's hands during inspiration.

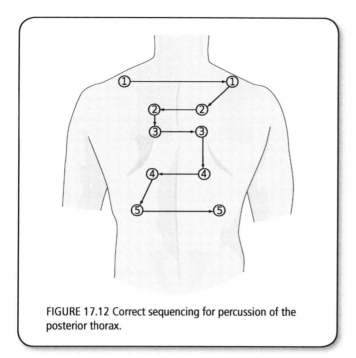

FIGURE 17.12 Correct sequencing for percussion of the posterior thorax.

The examiner begins with light percussion of the child's anterior chest, then moves to the posterior chest. In a healthy child, the entire anterior chest is resonant (hollow sounding), except the cardiac region where the percussion note is dull (thud-like). Continuing downward, resonance should continue until the area over the liver is percussed; this sounds dull, and the percussion note over the stomach should be tympanic (musical; drum-like). Next, the posterior chest is percussed, following the sequence shown in Figure 17.12. When percussing the posterior chest, resonance should be heard throughout. *Hyperresonance* (a booming sound) may be normal in small children and in children or adolescents who have thin chest walls; on the left side of the child's chest, hyperresonance may result from air in the stomach. Hyperresonance also occurs over areas of hyperinflation, as with asthma, bronchiolitis, pneumothorax, or foreign body obstruction. Dullness is heard over fluid-filled areas or solid tissue and is present in pneumonia, pleural effusion, and pneumothorax. Extreme dullness is described as flat when percussed; this percussion note is heard over the sternum and atelectatic lung.

Percussion is also used to assess diaphragmatic excursion. This assessment technique is done when the provider observes shallow respirations or the child reports painful breathing. To perform diaphragmatic excursion, the posterior chest is percussed along the scapular line, beginning at the apex to the lower edge of the right lung. The percussion note should start as resonant over the apex and end as dull over the diaphragm. Once these percussion notes are identified, the examiner then marks the spots on the child's chest where the sounds changed from resonant to dull, both on deep inspiration and expiration. The distance between these marks constitutes the diaphragmatic excursion. This measurement is normally 3 to 5 cm in children, with the diaphragm on the right side slightly higher because of the presence of the liver. Diaphragmatic excursion is limited in children with surgical conditions such as abdominal trauma or repaired diaphragmatic hernia. Auscultation may need to be repeated to confirm findings obtained during percussion and palpation.

COMMON DIAGNOSTIC STUDIES

Various diagnostic tests may be necessary to clarify differential diagnoses of respiratory complaints in children. Some examples of these diagnostic studies and their indications are summarized in Table 17.6.

TABLE 17.6	Diagnostic Studies Used to Evaluate Respiratory Conditions	
DIAGNOSTIC STUDY	**INDICATION**	**COMMENTS**
Allergy skin testing	To identify allergies in children with allergic rhinitis or asthma	Child must be observed for anaphylaxis after test.
Arterial blood gases (ABGs)	Acute respiratory distress	ABGs can be very painful and are most commonly obtained in acute care setting.
Chest radiograph	Complaints of chronic cough (Nield & Kamat, 2012); evidence of lower respiratory tract infection—child appears acutely ill, febrile, tachypneic, crackles auscultated; also used when tachypneic after injury and with suspected foreign body aspiration	Radiographs confirm a diagnosis of pneumonia, pneumothorax, tuberculosis, or foreign body.
Complete blood count	Persistent fever with respiratory symptoms	Leukocytosis may occur with tracheitis, pertussis, or pneumonia; leukopenia occurs with pneumonia.
Computed tomography (CT) scan	Persistent respiratory symptoms after normal chest radiograph (Nield & Kamat, 2012); the use of CT scans to diagnose sinusitis in children and adolescents is not routine (Wald et al., 2013)	CT scans are more sensitive than radiographs and can demonstrate pneumonia, tuberculosis, bronchiectasis, or the presence of an aspirated foreign body (Nield & Kamat, 2012).

TABLE 17.6	Diagnostic Studies Used to Evaluate Respiratory Conditions (*continued*)	
DIAGNOSTIC STUDY	**INDICATION**	**COMMENTS**
Pulmonary function test	To measure lung function and diagnose lung conditions associated with dyspnea	Child needs to be developmentally able to cooperate with testing.
Pulse oximetry	To monitor oxygen saturation of hemoglobin during respiratory distress	This is noninvasive; false readings may occur with movement or hypoperfusion, and it is not a substitute for ABGs.
Radioallergosorbent test (RAST)	To detect allergies by assessing for the presence of immunoglobulin E antibodies in the blood	RAST is often done on children with atopic dermatitis, psoriasis, or food allergies; blood sample may need to be sent to referral lab.
Rapid streptococcal antigen test	To diagnose pharyngeal streptococcal infections	Findings must be confirmed with culture.
Sputum culture	To identify specific pathogens in the respiratory tract	This is cultured from sputum, not saliva, so it is difficult to obtain in young children who may not be developmentally able to cooperate.
Sweat chloride test	Family history of cystic fibrosis; frequent respiratory infection in first 6 months of life	It diagnoses cystic fibrosis.
Throat culture	To isolate causative organism of infection of pharyngitis or tonsillitis	Streptococcal infections must be treated with antibiotics to avoid long-term complications.
Tuberculin (Mantoux) skin test	Chronic/productive cough and fever	This is used for screening for tuberculosis; it must be administered correctly to be accurate; an intradermal injection is necessary.

DOCUMENTATION OF FINDINGS

Sample Write-Up: Normal Respiratory Examination

Subjective Data

A 2-day-old female; prenatal, perinatal history unremarkable; NSVD, 38 weeks; Apgar scores 8 and 9.

Objective Data

T: 97.9°F (36.6° C); **P:** 130 beats per minute
RR: 36 breaths per minute
General: regular; no retractions, nasal flaring, or grunting; chest symmetrical; trachea midline; lungs clear bilaterally
Assessment: normal respiratory status in newborn

Sample Write-Up: Child With Respiratory Complaint

Subjective Data

An 8-year-old male presents with a history of asthma, upper respiratory infection for past 3 days; no fever; began frequent coughing the previous night. Recent exposure to wood smoke at camp (known trigger). Has albuterol 2 puffs ordered as rescue med; denies taking med before coming to clinic.

Objective Data

T: 99.7°F (37.6°C); **P:** 84 beats per minute; **RR:** 32 breaths per minute; oxygen saturation reading 92% in room air

General: slight shortness of breath; audible wheeze present; mild nasal flaring, and intercostal retractions; breath sounds equal bilaterally with expiratory wheezing all lung fields; no crackles
Assessment: asthma exacerbation

Notable Clinical Findings

- History of prematurity or prolonged ventilation in neonatal period
- Second- or third-hand tobacco smoke exposure
- Immunization delay
- Allergies
- Diagnosis of respiratory condition (e.g., asthma, cystic fibrosis)
- Poorly controlled asthma
- Duskiness or cyanosis
- Tachypnea, tachycardia
- Retractions, nasal flaring, grunting
- Sitting in tripod position
- Stridor
- Cough (acute or chronic)
- Abnormal auscultatory findings (wheezes, crackles, diminished breath sounds)
- Finger clubbing
- Pectus excavatum
- Lymphadenopathy in thorax

References

Adams, S. K., Murdock, K. K., & McQuaid, E. L. (2007). Complementary and alternative medication (CAM) use and asthma outcomes in children: An urban perspective. *Journal of Asthma, 44*(9), 775–782.

Ambalavanan, N. (2013). *Bronchopulmonary dysplasia.* Retrieved from http://reference.medscape.com/article/973717-overview#aw2aab6b2b2aa

Ball, J. W., Bindler, R. C., & Cowen, K. J. (2012). *Principles of pediatric nursing: Caring for children* (5th ed.). Upper Saddle River, NJ: Pearson Education, Inc.

Bissonnette, B., Anderson, B. J., Bosenberg, A., Engelhardt, T., Mason, L. J., & Tobias, J. D. (2011). *Pediatric anesthesia: Basic principles-state of the art-future.* Shelton, CT: People's Medical Publishing House.

Bloom, B., Cohen, R. A., & Freeman, G. (2012). *Summary health statistics for U.S. children: National health interview survey, 2011. Vital and Health Statistics (10),* 254. Hyattsville, MD: Summary Health Statistics for U.S. Children: National Health Interview Survey, 2011: U.S. Department of Health and Human Services. Centers for Disease Control and Prevention National Center for Health Statistics.

Brashers, V. L. (2010). Structure and function of the respiratory system. In K. L. McCance, S. E. Huether, V. L Brashers, & N. R. Rote (Eds.), *Pathophysiology: The biologic basis for disease in adults and children* (6th ed., pp. 1242–1265). St Louis, MO: Elsevier.

Cataletto, M. (2013). *Pectus carinatum.* Retrieved from http://emedicine.medscape.com/article/1003047-overview

Chock, V. Y., Punn, R., Oza, A., Benitz, W. E., Van Meurs, K. P., Whittemore, A. S., ... Silverman, N. H. (2013). Predictors of bronchopulmonary dysplasia or death in premature infants with a patent ductus arteriosus. *Pediatric Research, 75,* 570–575. doi:10.1038/pr.2014.1.

Clark, M. B., & Clark, D. A. (2014). *Meconium aspiration syndrome.* Retrieved January 17, 2014, from http://emedicine.medscape.com/article/974110-overview

Engel, J. (2006). *Pediatric assessment* (5th ed., p. 217). St. Louis, MO: Mosby.

Hockenberry, M. J., & Wilson, D. (2011). *Wong's nursing care of infants and children* (9th ed.). St. Louis, MO: Mosby.

Hebra, A. (2012). *Pectus excavatum.* Retrieved from http://emedicine.medscape.com/article/1004953-overview

John, R. M., & Brady, M. A. (2013). Respiratory disorders. In C. Burns, A. M. Dunn, M. A. Brady, N. B. Starr, & C. G. Blosser (Eds.), *Pediatric primary care* (5th ed., pp. 708–738). St. Louis, MO: W. B. Saunders.

Kim, E., & Koren, G. (2012). Infants of drug-addicted mothers. In G. Buonocore, R. Bracci, & M. Weindling (Eds.), *Neonatology: A practical approach to neonatal management* (pp. 369–374). New York, NY: Springer.

Kardon, E. M. (2012). *Caustic ingestions treatment & management.* Retrieved from http://emedicine.medscape.com/article/813772-treatment

Newth, C. J. L., & Hammer, J. (2005). Measurements of thoraco-abdominal asynchrony and work of breathing in children. In J. Hammer & E. Eber (Eds.), *Pediatric pulmonary function testing (progress in respiratory research)* (pp. 148–156). Unionville, CT: Karger.

Nield, L. S., & Kamat, D. M. (2012). Chronic cough in children and teens: A simplified approach to the evaluation. *Consultant for Pediatricians, 44*(7), 189–193.

Oberg, M., Jaakola, M. S., Woodward, A., Peruga, A., & Pruss-Ustun, A. (2011). Worldwide burden of disease from exposure to second-hand smoke: A retrospective analysis of data from 192 countries. *Lancet, 44*(9760), 139–146.

Reddy, S. R. V., & Singh, H. R. (2010). Chest pain in children and adolescents. *Pediatrics in Review, 44*(1), e1–e9.

Sarniak, A. P., & Heidemann, S. M. (2011). Gas exchange in health and disease. In R. M. Kliegman, B. M. D. Stanton, J. St. Geme, N. F. Schor, & R. E. Behrman (Eds.), *Nelson textbook of pediatrics* (19th ed., p. 1420). Philadelphia, PA: Saunders Elsevier.

Shields, M. D., & Thavagnanam, S. (2013). The difficult coughing child: prolonged acute cough in children. *Cough, 44*(11), 1–5.

U.S. Department of Health and Human Services. (2007). *Children and secondhand smoke exposure. Excerpts from the health consequences of involuntary exposure to tobacco smoke: A report of the Surgeon General.* Atlanta, GA: U.S. Department of Health and Human Services, Centers for Disease Control and Prevention, Coordinating Center for Health Promotion, National Center for Chronic Disease Prevention and Health Promotion, Office on Smoking and Health. Retrieved from www.surgeongeneral.gov/library/reports/smokeexposure/fullreport.pdf

U.S. Food and Drug Administration. (2013). *Public health advisory: FDA recommends that over-the-counter (OTC) cough and cold products not be used for infants and children under 2 years of age.* Retrieved from http://www.fda.gov/Drugs/DrugSafety/PostmarketDrugSafetyInformationforPatientsandProviders/DrugSafetyInformationforHeathcareProfessionals/PublicHealthAdvisories/ucm051137.htm

Wald, E. R., Applegate, K. E., Bordley, C., Darrow, D. H., Glode, M. P., Marcy, S. M., ... Weinberg, S. T. (2013). Clinical practice guideline for the diagnosis and management of acute bacterial sinusitis in children aged 1 to 18 years. *Pediatrics, 132*(1), e262–e280.

Assessment of the Cardiovascular System

It is estimated that 50% to 80% of children have a heart murmur detected during childhood, especially during a febrile illness (Frank & Jacobe, 2011). In most instances, the murmur is innocent. In contrast, structural heart disease affects 10,000 to 12,000 per million live births (Hoffman, 2013). A murmur can be identified as either pathologic or innocent by conducting a comprehensive cardiac assessment. The cardiovascular evaluation of a child includes taking a detailed history and conducting a comprehensive physical examination that includes inspection, palpation, and auscultation. Further evaluation is recommended if the physical examination findings and medical history are suggestive of heart disease.

ANATOMY AND PHYSIOLOGY

The heart is cone shaped and located behind the sternum in the mediastinum just to left of the midline of the thorax. It lies just above the diaphragm between the medial and lower borders of the lungs. The upper portion is called the base, and the narrow lower tip is called the apex. The position of the heart can vary slightly, depending on the patient's size, body type, and chest cavity. Compared to adults, the heart in infants and children lies more horizontally, with the apex reaching the fourth left intercostal space. By approximately 7 years, the position of the heart is similar to that of an adult (Hockenberry, 2011). In certain situations, the heart position may be located on the right side or more toward the middle of the chest; this condition is known as *dextrocardia*. With dextrocardia, the heart may be rotated or be the mirror image of a normally positioned heart. Dextrocardia can be associated with asplenia, polysplenia, and situs inversus, a condition in which the stomach is located on the right and liver is on the left. *Mesocardia* is a condition in which the heart is located in the midline of the chest.

The heart is encased in a fibrous, double-walled sac called the *pericardium*, which acts as a protective covering. Serous fluid is contained between the two layers of the pericardium, allowing for frictionless movement of the heart. The thin, outer, muscular layer covering the heart is called the *epicardium*; the thick, muscular, middle layer, which is responsible for contraction of the heart, is called the *myocardium*; and the innermost layer that lines the four heart chambers and the valves is called the *endocardium*.

Normal Cardiac Anatomy and Circulation

There are four chambers of the heart. The upper chambers (atria) are separated from the lower chambers (ventricles) by the atrioventricular valves. The *right atrioventricular valve* or *tricuspid valve* has three leaflets and lies between the right atrium and the right ventricle. The *left atrioventricular valve* or *mitral valve* has two leaflets and lies between the left atrium and the left ventricle. When the atria contract, the tricuspid and mitral valves open, allowing blood to enter the ventricles. When the ventricles contract, the atrioventricular valves snap shut, preventing blood from re-entering the atria.

The semilunar valves have three leaflets each and separate the great arteries from the ventricles. The pulmonary valve regulates communication between the right ventricle and the pulmonary artery. Likewise, the aortic valve acts as a gate between the left ventricle and the aorta. *Ventricular contraction* (*systole*) opens the semilunar valves, allowing blood to enter the great arteries. *Ventricular relaxation* (*diastole*) causes the semilunar valves to close, preventing blood from flowing back into the ventricles.

Normal circulation consists of desaturated blood flow returning to the right atrium by way of the *superior vena cava* and *inferior vena cava*. It then flows through the tricuspid valve into the right ventricle and then through the pulmonary valve into the main pulmonary artery, left and right branch pulmonary arteries, and into the lungs. The lungs allow oxygenated blood flow to return to the heart by way of the four pulmonary veins, which drain into the left atrium. Blood flow then travels through the mitral valve into the left ventricle and then through the aortic valve and into the aorta. The *ascending aorta* supplies the head and upper trunk with oxygen-rich blood, while the *descending aorta* supplies the liver, kidney, and lower trunk with oxygen-rich blood (Figure 18.1).

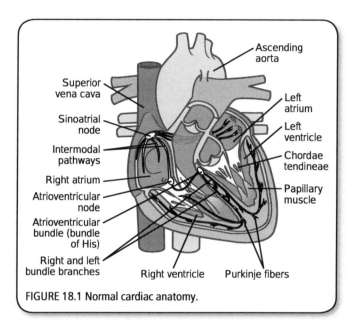

FIGURE 18.1 Normal cardiac anatomy.

Cardiac Cycle

The cardiac cycle consists of two phases; systole and diastole. At the beginning of systole, the atrioventricular valves close because of increased ventricular pressure. This produces the first heart sound (S1), which is typically described as a "lub" sound on auscultation. During systole, blood is ejected from the right ventricle into the pulmonary artery and from the left ventricle into the aorta. The pressure within the ventricles continues to rise until it is higher than the pressure in the corresponding great artery. This forces the semilunar valves to open, ejecting blood into the great arteries. As the ventricles eject blood, the pressure in the ventricles drops below the pressure in the great arteries, allowing the semilunar valves to close. This produces the second heart sound (S2), which is typically described as a "dub" sound on auscultation. The S2 has two components: A2, reflecting closure of the aortic valve, and P2, reflecting closure of the pulmonary valve. As the ventricular pressure continues to drop below the atrial pressure, the atrioventricular valves open, allowing blood that has collected in the right atrium from the superior and inferior vena cavae

and in the left atrium from the pulmonary veins to fill the relaxed ventricles.

During diastole, atrial contraction occurs, causing blood to enter the ventricles. It is during diastole that the coronary arteries are perfused. When ventricular filling is altered, additional heart sounds may be detected. The third heart sound (S3), which sounds like "Kentucky" on auscultation, is heard in conditions in which there is ventricular dilation or decreased ventricular compliance. A fourth heart sound (S4), which sounds like "Tennessee," can occasionally be heard when the atria are forcing blood into ventricles with decreased compliance or when congestive heart failure is present. Auscultation of S4 in children is always abnormal (Park, 2014).

The two phases of the cardiac cycle are then repeated, with ventricular contraction and atrial filling occurring at approximately the same time. The amount of blood returning to the heart (preload) and the amount of force the ventricles must overcome to eject blood from the heart (afterload) affect the timing of the components of the cardiac cycle. Pressure differences caused by stenosis or valve regurgitation can lead to premature or delayed right- or left-sided atrioventricular or semilunar valve closure. This may be heard on auscultation as a split S1 or S2, indicating that the atrioventricular or semilunar valves do not close simultaneously. Conditions contributing to altered cardiac output can alter the timing of the two phases of the cardiac cycle and ultimately cardiacoutput (Park, 2014).

Electrical Conduction Pathway

The electrical system of the heart coordinates the series of muscular contractions that occur during the cardiac cycle. The electrical impulse starts at the sinoatrial node located at the superior vena cava and right atrial junction. Here *cellular depolarization* begins, activating adjacent atrial muscles, beginning high in the atrial septum and traveling downward and laterally to activate the left atrium. Sinus node depolarization is too small to be recorded from body surface leads. However, atrial muscle cell depolarization is reflected as the P wave on the electrocardiogram (ECG). After the electrical impulse travels through the atrium, depolarization of the atrioventricular node begins. The atrioventricular node is located within the *triangle of Koch*; the perimeter of the triangle consists of the membranous septum, the tricuspid valve, and the coronary sinus, which is located in the right atrium. Typically, conduction through the atrioventricular node is slow and varies according to the timing of the atrial impulses. Electrical activity of the atrioventricular node is not directly transmitted onto the ECG recording; the P-R interval provides the best estimate of atrioventricular node conduction. Once the electrical impulse passes through the atrioventricular node, it travels down the *bundle of His*, splits into right and left bundle branches, and then onto the *Purkinje fibers* located in the ventricular myocardium before activating the ventricular myocytes. Ventricular contraction begins at the apex and travels toward the base of the heart. The QRS complex reflects depolarization of the ventricle (Delaney, Schroeder, & Baker, 2011).

DEVELOPMENTAL CONSIDERATIONS

Embryologic Development of the Heart

Knowledge of cardiac embryology can assist clinicians in understanding the time association between teratogenic exposures in utero and abnormal fetal heart development. The heart is the first functioning organ in the embryo. Cardiogenesis starts on the 18th day of gestation, beginning with the formation of the cardiogenic crescent derived from the precardiac mesoderm (Delaney et al., 2011). During the third week of gestation, the endocardial tube is present, and it is at this time that the heartbeat is believed to begin. By day 21 of gestation, the endocardial tube loops either to the right, forming normally related ventricles (D-loop), or to the left, creating inverted ventricles (L-loop). Embryologic ventricular formation occurs on days 22 to 35 of gestation. By this time, cardiac loop formation is complete. The endocardial cushion forms, right ventricular trabeculations develop, and the truncoconal portion of the heart moves to lie over the atria. Circulation also commences, and there is evolution of the aortic arches. From days 27 to 45 of gestation, the endocardial cushion divides the atrioventricular canal into the mitral and tricuspid valves. There is further expansion of the endocardial tissue, forming the septum primum followed by the septum secundum. The conotruncal cushions divide the main trunk or truncus arteriosus into the aorta and pulmonary artery. The pulmonary veins are incorporated into the left atrial wall. During the fifth week of gestation, the right ventricle enlarges in comparison to the left ventricle. During the sixth and seventh weeks of gestation, closure of the interventricular and membranous part of the ventricular septum occurs, and aortic arch evolution is complete. By this time, the inferior and superior vena cavae have formed, and the semilunar valves are created by the truncal cushions and the aorticopulmonary septum. Cardiogenesis is complete by the 45th day of gestation and continues beyond the postnatal period (Delaney et al., 2011).

Fetal Circulation

Comprehending the role of the fetal shunts in utero provides a foundation for understanding the pathophysiology as well as the presenting time frame of cyanotic and acyanotic congenital heart lesions. In fetal circulation, the placenta is primarily responsible for oxygenating and filtering the blood. Oxygenated blood is carried from the placenta to the fetus by the umbilical vein. The fetal lungs are collapsed and receive approximately 15% of the cardiac output (Park, 2014). Thus, *pulmonary vascular resistance* (i.e., the amount of opposition to blood flow caused by the pulmonary vasculature or the force against which the right heart pumps) is nearly equal to *systemic vascular resistance* (i.e., the amount of opposition to blood flow caused by the systemic vasculature or the force against which the left ventricle has to pump). The collapsed fetal lungs result in alveolar hypoxia, which further contributes to increased pulmonary vascular resistance. Since blood flow follows the path of least resistance and—in the fetus—pulmonary pressures are elevated, the majority of blood flow bypasses the lungs through the *fetal shunts*, preferentially shunting oxygen-rich blood to the brain and myocardium. There are four fetal shunts, including the placenta, which has the lowest impedance to blood flow and receives 55% of the total (right and left) ventricular output. The other three fetal shunts include the ductus venosus, the foramen ovale, and the ductus arteriosus (Park, 2014).

In fetal circulation, oxygen-rich blood bypasses the liver through the ductus venosus. Oxygenated blood travels from the placenta to the umbilical vein and then through the ductus venosus to the inferior vena cava, which then drains into the right atrium. The foramen ovale is an opening between the right and left atria that allows blood to shunt from the right to left side of the heart, bypassing the lungs. The ductus arteriosus is a muscular communication between the pulmonary artery and the aorta. It allows blood to bypass the lungs by shunting blood directly from the pulmonary artery to the aorta, brain, and other vital organs (Figure 18.2).

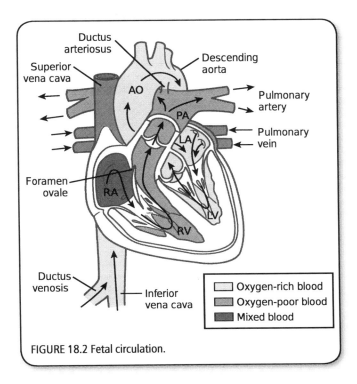

FIGURE 18.2 Fetal circulation.

Closure of Fetal Shunts

Clamping of the umbilical cord at birth stimulates closure of the fetal shunts either because of lack of blood return from the placenta (as in the case of the ductus venosus) or pressure changes. Interruption of the placental blood flow results in the lungs assuming the role of oxygenation of the blood. Lung expansion occurs because of a decrease in pulmonary vascular resistance and an increase in pulmonary blood flow. With the first breath of life, the lungs fill, and pulmonary vascular resistance drops. Right-sided pressures fall, and the left atrial pressure increases as a result of an increase in blood return from the pulmonary veins. Thus, there is functional closure of the foramen ovale as a result of the increase in left-sided pressure or *systemic vascular resistance* as compared with the right-sided pressure or *pulmonary vascular resistance*. Lower right-sided pressures, along with increased arterial saturations and decreased levels of prostaglandin E_1 in the body, cause the medial smooth muscle of the vessels of the ductus arteriosus to constrict, resulting in functional closure of the ductus arteriosus within 10 to 15 hours after birth. Anatomic closure typically occurs by 2 to 3 weeks; however, prolonged patency of the ductus arteriosus can be seen in premature infants and in infants with ductal-dependent congenital heart disease (CHD) with the use of an intravenous infusion of prostaglandin E_1 (Park, 2014).

Neonates have right ventricular dominance as a result of elevated right-sided pressures. Once the pulmonary circulation is established and the fetal shunts close, the left ventricle becomes responsible for pumping blood to the systemic circulation, which has a higher pressure than the pulmonary circulation. This results in a relative increase in left ventricle mass, which continues to develop throughout infancy. By 1 year of age, the relative size of the left ventricle compared with the right ventricle reaches a ratio approximating 2:1, which is comparable to the adult heart (Delaney et al., 2011).

ASSESSMENT OF THE CARDIOVASCULAR SYSTEM

History

Taking a comprehensive health history is one of the most important steps in evaluating whether a child is at risk for or already has heart disease. Components of the history should include the maternal health history, family health history, and the child's medical history, including birth and postnatal events.

Maternal Health History and Prenatal History

The maternal health history may help identify infants at risk for heart disease because of the strong association between maternal conditions and CHD. Infants of diabetic mothers, for example, have a higher incidence

of cardiomyopathy and congenital heart defects, such as transposition of the great arteries, ventricular septal defects, and patent ductus arteriosus (Jenkins et al., 2007). Likewise, infants born to mothers with systemic lupus erythematosus or connective tissue disorders have a higher incidence of congenital heart block. Infections during the first trimester of pregnancy can also result in congenital anomalies. Maternal rubella during the first trimester has been associated with peripheral pulmonary stenosis and patent ductus arteriosus, and maternal infections such as cytomegalovirus, herpesvirus, and coxsackievirus B have been associated with the development of myocarditis. Maternal use of some medications during pregnancy has been identified as being teratogenic to the fetus, resulting in myriad congenital defects, such as tetralogy of Fallot (warfarin [Coumadin]), tricuspid valve anomalies (lithium), patent ductus arteriosus (phenytoin [Dilantin]), persistent pulmonary hypertension of the newborn (nonsteroidal anti-inflammatory agents or aspirin), and ventricular septal defect (amphetamines). Fetal exposure to alcohol also results in congenital heart defects, including atrial and ventricular septal defects, patent ductus arteriosus, and tetralogy of Fallot (Park, 2014). While many medications can cause congenital heart defects, the amount of exposure is an important variable.

Perinatal History

Gestational age and Apgar scores may be predictive of CHD (Altman, 2014; Park, 2014). Details of the delivery and conditions immediately preceding and following the birth should be elicited. Questions that should be asked include the following:

- Were there concerns about fetal distress at birth?
- Was the infant cyanotic at birth?
- Was oxygen required *at* birth?
- Was oxygen required *after* birth?
- How soon was the infant discharged after birth?

If the infant's discharge was delayed, the details surrounding the delay should be elicited. Red flags for CHD include prematurity, low Apgar scores, a history of fetal distress, and cyanosis or oxygen requirement at birth. Delayed discharge because of poor feeding, lethargy, or color change should also raise concern about the presence of heart disease, especially if other findings on physical examination or from the maternal history are suspicious for CHD.

Postnatal History

Neonates are universally screened using pulse oximetry in the postnatal period to detect critical congenital heart disease (CCHD). This pulse oximetry screening identifies seven lesions: hypoplastic left heart syndrome, pulmonary atresia with intact ventricular septum, tetralogy of Fallot, total anomalous pulmonary venous return, transposition of the great arteries, tricuspid atresia, and truncus arteriosus (Kemper et al., 2011). At 6 to 8 weeks of life, when the pulmonary pressures drop, lesions that cause left-to-right shunts are likely to be noted. These include large ventricular septal defects, atrioventricular canal defects, double-outlet right ventricle, and patent ductus arteriosus. The toddler may present with an atrioventricular septal defect, ventricular septal defect, or acquired heart disease such as Kawasaki or cardiomyopathy. Since children are living longer with CHD, those with a staged palliation may be cyanotic if they have narrowing of a shunt that provides pulmonary blood flow or if complications from the palliation arise. School-aged children are more likely to present with acquired heart disease such as cardiomyopathy. However, they may be found to have coarctation of the aorta. Adolescents are more likely to present with acquired heart disease, such as cardiomyopathy, hyperlipidemia, and hypertension. They may also present with coarctation of the aorta that was identified on a sports physical examination. Syncope is reported most often in older children, and although rare, may be associated with long QT syndrome or idiopathic cardiomyopathy. In both age groups, children with known CHD should be monitored for the long-term sequelae of their disease. Primary care practitioners should collaborate with the child's cardiologist in screening for complications and progression of their disease.

Review of Systems

A thorough review of systems is conducted to identify whether the child has any cardiac abnormalities or conditions that could lead to cardiovascular complications. The date and length of any hospitalizations for any of these conditions are also noted.

- **General health:** Dysmorphic in appearance, presence of other anomalies or syndromes
- **Growth:** Obesity, poor weight gain, or poor linear growth
- **Integumentary:** Cyanosis, pallor, impetigo (can lead to rheumatic heart disease), erythema marginatum, erythema chronicum migrans (Lyme disease), previously undiagnosed maculopapular rash (streptococcal infection; Kawasaki disease), subcutaneous nodules, clubbing, edema, ascites; petechiae, or splinter hemorrhages (indicates rheumatic heart disease)
- **Cardiovascular:** Congenital or acquired heart disease, vasovagal syncope, subacute bacterial endocarditis, tachycardia, bradycardia, cardiomegaly, murmurs, clicks, S3, S4, splits, gallops, hypertension, decreased lower extremity pulses, chest pain, palpitations, or jugular venous distention
- **Respiratory:** Cough, tachypnea, shortness of breath, pulmonary edema, or frequent respiratory infections
- **Neurologic:** Dizziness or syncope

- **Hematologic:** Sickle cell disease (can lead to congestive heart failure)
- **Endocrine:** Hyperthyroidism or hypothyroidism
- **Infectious disease:** Lyme disease, history of untreated streptococcal infection
- **Immunologic:** Persistent low-grade fever with or without rash, streptococcal infection, Kawasaki disease, or atopic dermatitis (itching can lead to impetigo)
- **Rheumatologic:** Connective tissue disorders (Marfan, Ehlers-Danlos), autoimmune disorders (systemic lupus erythematosus or Sjögren syndrome)
- **Gastrointestinal:** Hepatomegaly, poor feeding (infant), diaphoresis with feeding (infant), vomiting, or takes frequent breaks during feeds
- **Genitourinary:** Renal disorders (cause hypertension)

Immunization Status

It is important to review the child's immunization status to determine children at risk for infections that can be associated with acquired heart disease such as pneumococcus. Children with congenital or acquired heart disease who develop respiratory infections may experience a more severe form of the illness requiring hospitalization. Therefore, immunization education should be provided to the parent or guardian. An immunization plan should be discussed with the cardiologist for children who have undergone heart transplantation, those with asplenia, or children with DiGeorge syndrome since they may be immunocompromised. It is also essential to determine the rubella status of the pregnant teenager; exposure during the first trimester is associated with congenital rubella syndrome of the fetus.

Surgical History

The child's past surgical history is an important part of the cardiovascular assessment. Any history of cardiovascular surgeries should be noted, with a record made of the type of cardiac lesion, the reason for the surgery, the timing of the surgery, and the child's postoperative course. The provider should also inquire if the child with a cardiac lesion has received prophylaxis for subacute bacterial endocarditis before any surgery.

Medications

The health care provider must note any medications that the child is taking for cardiovascular conditions or medications that can affect the heart. Examples include digoxin, diuretics, angiotensin-converting enzyme inhibitors, beta blockers, antihypertensives, or antibiotics for rheumatic heart disease. The child may also be taking medications prescribed for conditions that are not cardiac in nature but have cardiac side effects. One example is albuterol, which can cause tachycardia.

Family History

Family history is an important risk factor for both acquired heart disease and CHD. It incorporates genetic susceptibilities as well as shared environmental, behavioral, and cultural factors (Green, 2007). In the clinical setting, it is used predominantly for diagnostic purposes. Obtaining a detailed family history aids in determining the risk of disease and in promoting prevention. Family history can also be cost-saving by providing guidance for referrals and diagnostic testing. Red flags for acquired heart disease include a family history of the sudden, unexplained, or premature death of a first-degree relative, arrhythmias, early myocardial infarction, hyperlipidemia, hypertension, or obesity.

Approximately 9 in 1,000 infants are born with CHD each year (American Heart Association, 2013). More adults and children are living with CHD because of advances in neuroprotection, surgical techniques, and medical management (Marelli, Mackie, Ionescu-Ittu, Rahme, & Pilote, 2007). The cause of CHD is not clear; most cases seem to occur randomly. However, for some defects, there is a genetic link. In recent years, characterization of mutations affecting cardiovascular development have been linked to mendelian, multifactorial, or complex (combination) traits (Mitchell, Sander, Klinkner, & Tomita-Mitchell, 2007; Sharma, Peters, Moorhouse, van der Spek, & Bogers, 2006; Weismann & Gelb, 2007). Further, there is a roughly threefold increased risk for CHD when a relative has CHD, and this risk is even higher for certain defects, suggesting an even stronger genetic influence (Øyen, Poulsen, Boyd, Wohlfahrt, Jensen, & Melbye, 2009). Some major syndromes are also associated with cardiovascular disease; examples include the following: cri du chat syndrome (ventricular septal defect, patent ductus arteriosus, atrial septal defect), DiGeorge syndrome (interrupted aortic arch and other aortic arch anomalies, truncus arteriosus, tetralogy of Fallot, ventricular septal defect, patent ductus arteriosus, coarctation of the aorta), glycogen storage disease (cardiomyopathy), Marfan syndrome (aortic aneurysm, aortic or mitral regurgitation), Noonan syndrome (valvular pulmonic stenosis, hypertrophic cardiomyopathy), Turner syndrome (bicuspid aortic valve, coarctation of the aorta), and Down syndrome (atrioventricular canal defect, ventricular septal defect) (Park, 2014). Red flags for CHD include parental consanguinity or a family history notable for any first-degree relative with a structural heart abnormality or any relative with a hereditary disease. In addition to CHD and genetic syndromes, other red flags for a family history of cardiovascular disease include sudden cardiac death before age 50, hypertension, rheumatic fever, and hypercholesterolemia.

Social History

It is important to ask if the child or adolescent is involved in any type of sports; regular physical activity can be the cause of a slow resting heart rate. Likewise, any family history of syncope, sudden death, or arrhythmias while playing sports can be a clue to a family history of long QT syndrome or hypertrophic cardiomyopathy, which may preclude the child from playing certain sports.

The use of recreational drugs should be assessed; for example, cocaine raises the heart rate and can lead to arrhythmias, myocarditis, and myocardial infarction (Weekes & Lee, 2013). The consumption of cola, coffee, tea, energy drinks, or other caffeinated drinks is also determined; excessive caffeine intake is also associated with fluid loss, tachycardia, increased sympathetic activity, and decreased parasympathetic activity. Children are more susceptible to the effects of caffeine than adults (Seifert, Schaechter, Hershorin, & Lipshultz, 2011).

History of Present Illness

When an infant, child, or adolescent presents with a cardiovascular or respiratory complaint, a careful, detailed, focused history is essential to narrow the list of differential diagnoses. Common complaints in these areas include growth failure, exercise intolerance, respiratory complaints, palpitations, chest pain, syncope, joint pain, neurologic signs, cyanosis, and congestive heart failure.

Growth Failure • Growth failure and developmental delay may suggest heart disease. Poor feeding, dyspnea during feedings, or the need to take frequent rest periods during feedings are exhibited by children with congestive heart failure. Plotting the child's growth on the appropriate growth chart is mandatory. If possible, the child's growth should be compared with that of siblings and parents. Weight and height percentiles should be proportionate. Children with heart disease often show growth delay resulting from increased calorie expenditure without much effect on height or head circumference. Red flags for CHD include infants over 36 weeks gestation who are unable to gain at least 30 grams a day, infants who plot under the 16% percentile for weight, or children who have fallen off their own growth curve (da Silva, de Oliveira Lopes, & de Araujo, 2007).

Exercise Intolerance • Limited exercise tolerance may also be a sign of heart failure. Activity levels should be elicited from the parents in measurements that are appropriate for the child's age. When evaluating the exercise tolerance of an infant, for example, parents should be asked how long the infant takes to feed, whether the infant requires rest periods during the feedings, and if the infant displays dyspnea when feeding. For older children, soliciting the child's normal exercise capacity is important. Questions should be posed to the parent and child to determine the child's activity level. In what after-school activities does the child participate? Does the child participate in sports? Is the child able to keep up with peers? If the child leads a sedentary lifestyle, does this mimic the parents' involvement in exercise or is it a result of other limitations? Is this a recent change in the child's activity level or is this normal?

What is the child's exercise capacity? It is important to determine the child's ability in measurable terms such as the number of blocks the child can run or the number of stairs the child can climb without stopping or becoming fatigued. Additional questions should determine whether the child experiences any symptoms during exercise such as shortness of breath or palpitations. Red flags for congenital or acquired heart disease in infants include a history of prolonged feeding time (greater than 30 minutes) that requires several "rest" periods because of the increased work of breathing or exhaustion. For the child and adolescent, concerns about heart disease should be raised if the child reports an inability to keep up with peers, chest pain during exercise, or limited or no exercise tolerance (inability to climb stairs or walk multiple street blocks without experiencing shortness of breath and stopping because of fatigue).

Respiratory Complaints • A history of frequent lower respiratory infections may be associated with congestive heart failure. This is caused by large left-to-right shunts, resulting in increased pulmonary blood flow, which, in turn, can predispose the child to lower respiratory infections. Children with unrepaired CHD are more likely to require a hospital admission because of a respiratory syncytial virus (RSV) lower respiratory infection. Infants with moderate-to-severe pulmonary hypertension, cyanosis, or congestive heart failure are at the highest risk for suffering RSV-induced morbidity and mortality. A history of frequent upper respiratory infections is not related to the presence of CHD but may indicate the presence of a vascular ring that should be evaluated.

Palpitations • Evaluating complaints of palpitations poses a challenge for practitioners. Children as young as preschoolers may complain of palpitations caused by irregular heartbeats. Children who chronically experience tachycardia may not identify palpitations as a symptom in contrast to children who notice a change in their heart rate for the first time. When soliciting a history from the older child, attempts should be made to differentiate between tachycardia and irregularity. Investigation into the etiology of the complaint should focus on identifying the precipitating event, frequency, duration, accompanying symptoms, and a detailed medical history, including a history of structural heart disease, arrhythmias, or metabolic disorders. In addition, school-aged children and adolescents should be questioned about over-the-counter and prescription medication use, recreational drug use, and the quantity of caffeine ingested each day (e.g., soda, power drinks, coffee). If tachycardia is suspected, attempts should be made to capture it on a 12-lead ECG, but the highest probability of documenting the tachycardia is by a 24-hour Holter monitor. Red flags for heart disease or arrhythmias include complaints of sudden-onset palpitations associated with pallor, diaphoresis, dizziness, chest pain, or syncopal events (Delaney et al., 2011; Park, 2014).

Chest Pain • Chest pain is a frequent complaint of children seen by pediatricians. In most instances, the chest pain does not have a cardiac etiology (Geggel & Endom, 2013). The most common causes of chest pain in children are idiopathic factors, musculoskeletal, psychiatric, breast-related, respiratory, gastrointestinal and, finally, cardiac, which accounts for 1% to 6% of cases (Geggel & Endom, 2013).

To differentiate between pathologic and nonpathologic causes of chest pain, the clinician should obtain a detailed description of the precipitating events from the child and parent. Questions to ask about chest pain include:

- Is it related to exercise?
- Is it associated with syncope or palpitations?
- Does it occur at rest or when watching television?
- Does it wake the child up at night?
- Does it occur at the same time each day?

In addition, the duration of the pain should be established (seconds, minutes, hours). The child should be asked to point to the location of the pain and to indicate whether it always occurs at the same location or radiates, and what, if anything, relieves it. The child should also be asked to describe the pain (sharp or dull, stabbing, squeezing, or pressure) and to rate the intensity on a scale of 1 to 10. If the child specifically states that the chest pain is related to his or her heart, the practitioner should attempt to find out why. Determine if there is a family history of angina or sudden death in the family. Red flags for a cardiac origin of chest pain are a family history of sudden death at a young age; chest pain described as a deep, heavy pressure; or a squeezing sensation that is triggered by exercise and associated with symptoms of pallor, dizziness, diaphoresis, or syncope.

Syncope • Syncope is a transient loss of consciousness and muscle tone. It occurs in up to 15% of children by the age of 21 years (Salerno & Coleman, 2013). In contrast to adults, most syncopal cases in children are benign and result from a vasovagal episode, orthostatic hypotension, hyperventilation, or breath-holding. However, any episode of syncope warrants careful investigation because of the risk of structural heart disease or arrhythmias (Park, 2014; Salerno & Coleman, 2013). Cardiac causes of syncope are typically triggered by exercise; however, cardiac syncope can occur in the recumbent position and is often associated with chest pain. Information that should be elicited includes a description of the preceding events, the timing of onset (gradual or sudden), and the progression and duration of the syncopal event and recovery period. The frequency with which the events happen and any prodromes should also be identified. Signs and symptoms accompanying the event should be determined, such as the presence and duration of loss of consciousness, pallor, cyanosis, diaphoresis, palpitations, nausea, incontinence, seizure activity, and chest pain. Details regarding the child's past and current medical history should include use of over-the-counter and prescription medications, recreational drug use, and the presence of metabolic or neurologic disease. Patients who describe a history of syncope associated with swimming should be evaluated for long QT syndrome (Sovari, Kocheril, Assadi, R., & Baas, 2014). Red flags for a cardiac cause of syncope include a past medical history of structural heart disease or a family history of CHD or sudden death. Syncopal events that are triggered by exercise and associated with symptoms of chest pain, pallor, and diaphoresis are also suspicious for a cardiac origin.

Joint Symptoms • Acute rheumatic fever is rare in the United States. Rheumatic arthritis should be considered when the primary complaint is pain in a large joint. To determine whether the child has acute rheumatic fever, information about the number of joints involved, how long the symptoms have been present, and whether the pain is stationary (in one joint) or migratory must be gathered. A history of streptococcal pharyngitis 1 to 5 weeks before the onset of symptoms is common. Therefore, parents should be asked if the child had a throat culture done at the time of the pharyngitis. Other symptoms associated with rheumatic fever include pallor, malaise, fatigue, abdominal pain, and epistaxis. Information about whether the child had a rash, has difficulty walking, and what actions or medications relieve the symptoms should be collected. Massaging the affected joint does not relieve the pain in rheumatic fever, but salicylates may suppress the symptoms of rheumatic fever; therefore, it is important to inquire about a medication history. A family history of rheumatic disease and crowded living conditions along with joint symptoms should also raise suspicion for the disease.

Neurologic Symptoms • Cyanotic heart disease or infective endocarditis should be considered in a patient presenting with a history of stroke. Polycythemia in the cyanotic child and thrombus on an infected valve can place the child at high risk for stroke. Complaints of chronic headaches can be a manifestation of cyanotic heart disease, cerebral hypoxia, polycythemia, or brain abscess. Children with coarctation of the aorta may present with complaints of headaches resulting from hypertension proximal to the coarctation site. A history of syncope or choreic type movements may also have a cardiac cause. Small children with hypertension may be described as irritable by parents and exhibit head banging or head rubbing. Older children with hypertension may complain of visual disturbances, dizziness, or headache.

Cyanosis • A history of cyanosis warrants further investigation into the etiology of symptoms. A detailed history should include age at onset of symptoms; frequency, severity, and duration of episodes; and precipitating events (e.g., feedings, exercise). Attempts should be made to differentiate between a true cyanotic spell and a breath-holding spell. A history of squatting or

assuming a knee-chest position when tired in association with cyanosis is suspicious for tetralogy of Fallot and requires immediate evaluation.

Congestive Heart Failure • Tachycardia, dyspnea on exertion, and swelling, especially around the eyes, can all be signs of congestive heart failure. A history of irritability, poor feeding, tachypnea that worsens with feedings, and poor weight gain are all consistent with congestive heart failure. Reports of diaphoresis, a mottled appearance of the skin, and cool extremities are also associated with decreased cardiac function and congestive heart failure. Parents of older children with congestive heart failure may report a history of shortness of breath with exercise, easy fatigability, and discomfort when lying flat, thus the use of multiple pillows for sleep (Table 18.1).

Physical Examination

The biggest challenge for the practitioner is trying to examine a frightened or crying child. To optimize the yield from the examination, infants and toddlers can be assessed while sitting in their parent's lap to decrease separation anxiety. Methods of distraction (e.g., playing age-appropriate movies) can be used during the examination. Privacy for the adolescent must be maintained by pulling the shades down, closing the doors, and providing gowns to wear during the examination. The provider should speak to the child individually to obtain his or her perspective on the chief complaint when developmentally appropriate. However, both the parent and the child should be included when taking the history. Warming the hands and stethoscope before the examination increases the child's comfort and decreases anxiety. Lastly, a systematic approach that is routinely followed should be used for the examination so that no cardiovascular components are missed. A suggested format includes first listening to the heart sounds and then the lung sounds. Cardiac auscultation should include identifying S1, S2, and the splitting of S2, and describing any murmurs, noting the timing, intensity, quality, location, and transmission. Palpation of femoral pulses, liver, and spleen should be the last part of the examination because it may cause discomfort. School-aged children and adolescents should be placed in a comfortable position during the physical examination. The child may be most comfortable in a supine position with the knees bent and feet flat on the examination table. For the school-aged child who is ticklish, the child's hand can be placed on top of the practitioner's hand when palpating the liver and spleen. This may decrease any anxiety or discomfort.

Vital signs, including the heart rate, respiratory rate, upper and lower extremity blood pressure, and oxygen saturation as well as height, weight, and head circumference, should be measured on all children. Measurements outside the normal range for the child's sex and age should be investigated. Blood pressure measurements

TABLE 18.1	Signs and Symptoms of Congestive Heart Failure
SYSTEM	**SIGNS AND SYMPTOMS**
Cardiac	Tachycardia Gallop rhythm Diaphoresis Cool extremities Delayed capillary refill Cardiomegaly on chest film
Pulmonary	Tachypnea Increased work of breathing Congestion Pulsus alternans Increased pulmonary vascular markings on chest film Pleural effusion on chest film (chronic congestive heart failure or severe form)
Gastrointestinal	Prolonged feeding time (greater than 30 minutes) Requires rest periods or tires during feedings Poor weight gain (infant) or excessive weight gain (older child) Vomiting Hepatomegaly or hepatosplenomegaly
Neurologic	Irritability Lethargy (decreased exercise tolerance) Complaints of discomfort unless sitting forward or upright at a 30-degree angle or more (older child)

should be part of the cardiac physical examination, and the preferred method for blood pressure measurement is auscultation. To ensure accurate measurements, an appropriate-sized cuff should be used. The width of the cuff should be 40% to 50% of the circumference of the limb on which the blood pressure is measured. The same rules apply for lower extremity blood pressure measurements. The bladder should be long enough to encircle the limb completely. For optimal readings, the child should sit upright with the arm that has the blood pressure cuff positioned at heart level. Current recommendations are to repeat the blood pressure measurement if the reading is greater than the 90th percentile for age (Luma & Spiotta, 2006).

Inspection

General Appearance • The physical examination should begin by inspecting the child for abnormalities. The child's overall health status should be determined. Does the child appear ill or in distress? Infants in distress appear diaphoretic, pale, and fretful. What is the child's affect? Is the child irritable or happy? Is the child consolable? Is the older child talkative or lethargic? What is the child's nutritional status? Is the child well nourished or obese? If the child appears dysmorphic, he or she may have a chromosomal, hereditary, or nonhereditary syndrome that could be associated with heart disease. The parents must be asked if the child has ever been tested or seen by a geneticist. Approximately 50% of children with Down syndrome have a congenital heart defect, primarily atrioventricular canal defect, or ventricular septal

defect. Sixty-five percent of newborns with CHARGE association (a syndrome of coloboma, heart disease, choanal atresia, retarded growth, and genital and eye abnormalities) have a conotruncal abnormality or aortic arch abnormality (Park, 2014). Abnormal findings warrant further investigation for a possible cardiac origin.

Growth Pattern • Evidence of the child falling off his or her own growth curve or a trend of poor weight gain may be indicative of CHD that causes a left-to-right shunt, leading to congestive heart failure or lesions that decrease pulmonary blood flow, resulting in cyanosis. Approximately 45% of children with congestive heart failure and up to 80% of children with cyanotic heart disease plot below the 16th percentile for weight (da Silva et al., 2007). Therefore, it is important to plot height, weight, and head circumference on the appropriate growth chart for comparative norms. Length and head circumference are minimally affected by the presence of structural heart disease. Children with severe cyanotic lesions may have overall growth retardation (Vogt et al., 2007). The combination of CHD and associated syndromes or extracardiac anomalies may place these children at additional risk for growth delay.

Respirations • Children with left-to-right shunts that result in increased pulmonary blood flow may exhibit signs of congestive heart failure. Tachypnea, retractions, nasal flaring, and grunting are indicative of right-sided heart failure. A resting respiratory rate of greater than 60 beats a minute is abnormal at any age and should be evaluated. Tachypnea accompanied by tachycardia may be an early sign of left-sided heart failure.

Determining the type of respirations (i.e., shallow and rapid or deep and rapid), and how the child tolerates the type of breathing pattern may assist in differentiating between a cardiac and a pulmonary cause of the tachypnea (Park, 2014).

Cyanosis • As part of the overall assessment, infants and children should be inspected for cyanosis and pallor. If cyanosis is noted, the degree and distribution of the cyanosis should be documented, noting that mild cyanosis is difficult to detect in patients with normal hemoglobin levels. To optimize detection, the patient should be examined in a well-lighted room. The lips and mucous membranes as well as the tongue, nail beds, and conjunctiva should be examined, especially in children with deep pigmentation. Pulse oximetry should be used when available to confirm suspicions of arterial desaturation.

In addition to measuring oxygen saturation, it may be helpful to obtain a hematocrit in determining why a child looks cyanotic. Children who are polycythemic may appear cyanotic but have a normal arterial saturation. Evaluating the location and extent of cyanosis can provide clues as to the etiology. Circumoral cyanosis can be a normal finding in fair-skinned children or a symptom of cyanotic heart disease. Peripheral cyanosis may be caused by sluggish peripheral blood flow or polycythemia. Acrocyanosis, a bluish discoloration of the fingers and toes, is a normal finding in the newborn.

Clubbing • Clubbing develops when chronic arterial desaturation (of greater than 6 months' duration) is present. Typically, in the early stages of clubbing, the phalanges begin to turn red. This is first noted in the thumb. As clubbing becomes more severe, the ends of the fingers and toes become wider and thicker, the shape of the fingernails changes to become more convex, and angle between the nail and the thumb becomes blunted (see Figure 12.12). Clubbing is seen in both pulmonary and cardiac disease states that cause arterial desaturation, cirrhosis of the liver, and subacute bacterial endocarditis. Familial clubbing is a rare condition in which clubbing is noted in patients without a chronic health condition.

Edema • Eyelid swelling and a rounded face are often seen in children with congestive heart failure. Unlike the adult patient with congestive heart failure, lower extremity pitting edema is rare in children. Similarly, it is difficult to assess jugular vein distention in infants because of their short necks, and thus it is not typically found. Abdominal ascites is a manifestation of longstanding disease and requires immediate evaluation.

Diaphoresis • Infants with CHD often experience diaphoresis, especially during feedings. Diaphoresis is a manifestation of decreased cardiac output caused by an increased sympathetic response to the demands placed on the heart in the setting of decreased ventricular function or an increased volume or pressure load on

the heart. Parents also report the infant to be sweaty when they fall asleep in their arms. Parents of preschool children often note that the child's pillow is wet upon his or her awakening from sleep.

Chest Deformity • Left-sided chest prominence is a manifestation of CHD. The deformity is the result of a significantly enlarged and active left or right ventricle during chest wall development. It is commonly seen in children with left-to-right shunts. The presence of a precordial bulge is a hallmark of chronic cardiac enlargement. *Pectus carinatum*, a condition in which the sternum protrudes on the midline, is not typically associated with cardiac disease. *Pectus excavatum*, a condition in which the sternum is concave, rarely causes cardiac compromise. It may cause a pulmonary ejection murmur or the appearance of cardiomegaly on the posteroanterior view of the chest radiography. The presence of pectus excavatum should prompt the practitioner to look for signs of Marfan syndrome (Hebra, 2012).

Extracardiac Anomalies • The overall incidence of extracardiac anomalies among children with congenital heart defects is approximately 22%, with the incidence varying according to the type of CHD (Øyen et al., 2009). For example, the incidence of associated anomalies with transposition of the great arteries is quite low, but anomalies are seen in up to 50% of patients with truncus arteriosus (Park, 2014). A good rule of thumb is to investigate for other defects if the infant is found to have other anomalies in addition to a congenital heart lesion. This is especially true for midline defects. Certainly if the child is diagnosed with a syndrome, a full evaluation for associated health problems is necessary. For example, Gonzalez and colleagues (2009) found that at least 50% of neonates with a congenital heart lesion had an extracardiac comorbidity.

Palpation

Precordial Activity • The cardiac examination should begin with inspection and palpation of the chest. To determine precordial activity, apical impulse, point of maximal impulse, and the presence of thrills and heaves, the clinician should palpate the supraclavicular region and four areas on the chest while the patient is in the supine position. These include the left ventricular area located at the apex of the heart (fourth or fifth intercostal space along the midclavicular line), the right ventricular area located in the region of the third to fifth intercostal space along the left sternal border, the pulmonic area located at the second intercostal space along the left sternal border, and the aortic area. A hyperactive precordium characterized by the presence of a lift, heave, or thrill, is indicative of CHD, which results in a volume overload on the heart. Lesions causing right ventricular volume overload include defects with large left-to-right shunts (e.g., ventricular septal defect, patent ductus arteriosus) (Park, 2014). Lesions that cause left ventricular volume overload include defects with severe left-sided valvular regurgitation such as mitral regurgitation and aortic regurgitation. The presence of increased precordial activity should heighten concerns about a pathologic finding when abnormal heart sounds are detected on auscultatory examination. However, a hyperactive precordium may also be associated with fever, anemia, stress, and anxiety.

Apical Impulse • The provider should use the fingertips to palpate for the apical impulse to identify the location, duration, and amplitude. This can be challenging in young children. For optimal assessment, older children can be instructed to exhale or hold their breath for a few seconds during palpation. The location of the apical impulse varies according to the child's age; for instance, in children 7 years of age or younger, the apical impulse is normally palpated at the fourth intercostal space just left of the midclavicular line, and in older children, at the fifth intercostal space along the midclavicular line. If the apical impulse is palpated either laterally or inferiorly to the fourth or fifth intercostal space, the provider should suspect cardiomegaly. If the duration of the apical impulse lasts longer than half of systole or if the amplitude is increased, a hyperkinetic state may be present.

Point of Maximal Impulse • The point of maximal impulse (PMI) is the farthest point from the sternum where the cardiac impulse can be palpated. The PMI in an adult is normally located at the intersection of the fifth intercostal space and the left midclavicular line. In children, it is located at the fourth intercostal space just medial to the left nipple (Figure 18.3). Determining the location of the PMI can differentiate ventricular dominance. The correct technique for determining right ventricular activity is to apply firm pressure over the parasternal region. The PMI can be felt at the lower

left sternal border or over the xiphoid process when right-ventricular dominance is present and at the apex when left-ventricular dominance is present. Right-ventricular dominance is normal in newborns and infants, but right-ventricular activity is typically nondetectable in normal adults; if found, it may suggest pulmonary hypertension. Displacement of the PMI suggests abnormal left-ventricular size, function, or compliance. With volume overload, the PMI rises slowly and is diffuse (known as a *heave*), but with pressure overload, the PMI is well localized and sharp (known as a *tap*).

Thrills • Thrills are vibratory sensations felt on the chest when turbulent blood flow moves rapidly from a high-pressure area to a low-pressure area within the heart or blood vessels. They are best palpated with the palm of the hand to maximize detection. The palmar surface of the metacarpals is more apt to pick up low-frequency vibrations, whereas the fingertips are best able to localize a thrill or a tap (Park, 2014). Findings of a thrill are always pathologic.

The location of the thrill can provide clues as to the origin of the pressure gradient. Thrills in the upper right sternal border indicate aortic stenosis, but those in the upper left sternal border indicate pulmonary stenosis, pulmonary atresia, or patent ductus arteriosus (rarely). Thrills in the lower left sternal border indicate ventricular septal defect, while thrills located in the suprasternal notch indicate atrial stenosis, pulmonary stenosis, patent ductus arteriosus, or coarctation of the aorta. Thrills over the carotid arteries represent a carotid bruit, but a bruit felt along with a thrill in the suprasternal notch indicates aortic valve disease, such as atrial stenosis or coarctation of the aorta; thrills associated with coarctation of the aorta are found in the intercostal spaces in older children as a result of the presence of extensive intercostal collaterals.

Auscultation

Cardiac auscultation provides valuable information about structural abnormalities and cardiac function. Both the bell and the diaphragm of the stethoscope are used during auscultation; using one or the other may cause the examiner to miss a significant auscultatory finding. The bell of the stethoscope is used to detect low-frequency sounds, while the diaphragm is used to pick up high-frequency events. To ensure a comprehensive cardiac examination, the entire precordium as well as the supraclavicular region, sides, and back are included in the examination (Menashe, 2007). A systematic approach, including assessment of the heart rate and regularity, heart sounds (S1 to S4), and murmurs, should be used during auscultation to avoid missing important components of the examination.

First Heart Sound • The S1 occurs with ventricular systole, is generated by closure of the atrioventricular valves, and is synchronous with the apical pulse. It is

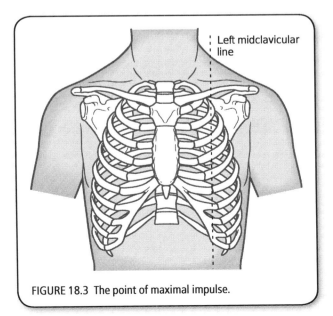

FIGURE 18.3 The point of maximal impulse.

Left midclavicular line

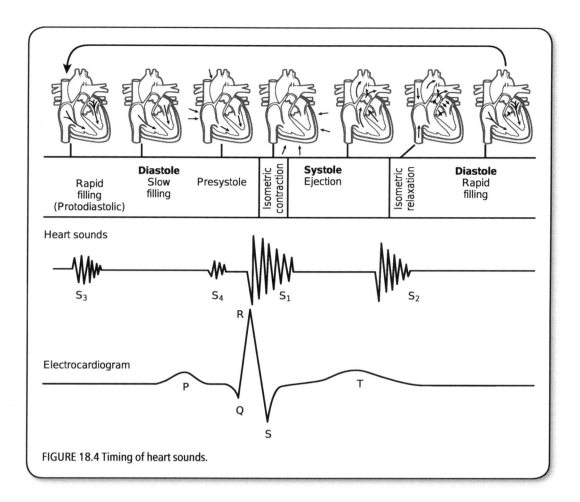

FIGURE 18.4 Timing of heart sounds.

best heard at the apex or lower left sternal border and marks the beginning of systole (Figure 18.4). Rarely, splitting of S1 may be detected on examination, but it can be a normal finding in children. A widely split S1 may be associated with right bundle branch block or Ebstein's anomaly, which is an anomaly of the tricuspid valve, resulting in atrialization of a portion of the right ventricle and tricuspid regurgitation. A split S1 may be confused with a systolic ejection click, which is best heard at the upper left sternal border, or an S4.

Second Heart Sound • The S2 is associated with closure of the semilunar valves. It is best heard at the upper left sternal border using the diaphragm of the stethoscope. The S2 marks the beginning of diastole. It has two components, A2, which reflects closure of the aortic valve, and P2, which reflects closure of the pulmonary valve. Determining the normal intensity for each of the S2 components is challenging, especially in younger children with faster heart rates. However, it is essential to identify all components during the cardiac examination, and this requires practice in listening to normal children. The intensity of A2 is usually louder than P2 in the upper left sternal border. A P2 that is loud in comparison to A2 may indicate a pathologic condition, such as pulmonary hypertension. A P2 that is soft in comparison to

A2 is heard in patients with severe pulmonary stenosis, tetralogy of Fallot, and tricuspid atresia. Timing of aortic valve closure in relation to pulmonary valve closure as well as the intensity of each of the S2 components should be evaluated during auscultation.

Physiologic splitting of S2 can occur with respiration and is normal (Figure 18.5). The degree of splitting varies, increasing with inspiration and decreasing with expiration. This variation in S2 splitting is related to the vascular resistance in the systemic and pulmonary circuits. It has also been attributed to the increased negative thoracic pressure during inspiration, resulting in an increase in systemic venous blood

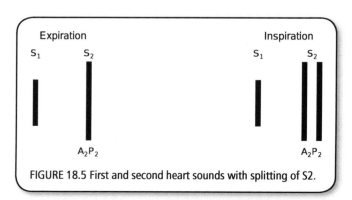

FIGURE 18.5 First and second heart sounds with splitting of S2.

return to the right atrium, which, in turn, lengthens right ventricular ejection time and delays closure of the pulmonary valve.

Findings of a widely split and fixed S2, narrowly split S2, single S2, or paradoxically split S2 are abnormal and indicate the presence of a pathologic condition. Findings of a *widely split and fixed* S2 indicates pathologic conditions that alter ventricular ejection time. Right ventricular ejection time is prolonged in the presence of increased right ventricular volume load or afterload, resulting in delayed closure of the pulmonary valve in relation to the aortic valve. Right ventricular volume overload can be caused by an atrial septal defect (a hole between the upper chambers of the heart), resulting in left-to-right shunting and anomalous pulmonary venous return; at least one or more of the four pulmonary veins drain abnormally to the right side of the heart, resulting in an increase in blood return to the right atrium. Another condition that causes right ventricular pressure overload is pulmonary stenosis, which causes prolonged right ventricular ejection time because of the increased pressure against which the right ventricle must pump to force blood out the small pulmonary valve. A conduction abnormality that results in a prolonged right ventricular ejection time is right bundle branch block, which causes delayed electrical activation of the right ventricle. Mitral regurgitation can shorten left ventricle ejection time, resulting in early closure of the aortic valve, which results in the backflow of blood into the left atrium through the mitral valve during ventricular contraction. Subsequently, left ventricular ejection time is shortened, resulting in early closure of the aortic valve. Occasionally, a fixed, split S2 is detected, and the patient is referred for an echocardiogram, but the findings are normal. The etiology of the widely split and fixed S2 in an otherwise healthy child is the result of idiopathic dilation of the pulmonary arteries (Park, 2014).

A *narrowly split* S2 reflects altered closure time of the semilunar valves. It may be a normal finding in children; however, it can be associated with pathologic conditions such as pulmonary hypertension, resulting in early closure of the pulmonary valve, or aortic stenosis, resulting in delayed closure of the aortic valve. A *single* S2 is found in aortic atresia or pulmonary atresia where only one semilunar valve is present. A single S2 is also detected in conditions where the P2 is not audible, such as in transposition of the great arteries, tetralogy of Fallot, or severe pulmonary stenosis. Findings of a single S2 may also indicate the presence of pulmonary hypertension resulting from an early P2 component or delayed aortic valve closure caused by aortic stenosis. A *paradoxically split* S2 is heard when aortic valve closure occurs after pulmonary valve closure. This occurs in conditions such as severe aortic stenosis and left bundle branch block where the electrical activation of the left ventricle is delayed. Occasionally, it is also found in patients who have Wolff–Parkinson–White syndrome.

Third Heart Sound • The S3 is associated with rapid filling of the ventricle. The timing of S3 occurs in early diastole and is best heard at the apex or lower left sternal border. It is a low-frequency sound and may normally be heard in thin school-aged children and adolescents. In adults and children, a loud S3 is abnormal and indicates pathologic conditions that cause ventricular dilation with decreased compliance, such as congestive heart failure. It sounds like "Ken-tuck-y" when tachycardia is present (see Figure 18.4).

Fourth Heart Sound • The S4 is heard immediately preceding the first heart sound. It is associated with atrial contraction and excessive flow across the atrioventricular valves. It is rare in children, always pathologic, and suggests decreased ventricular compliance or congestive heart failure. The S4 is best heard at the apex but transmits widely. It can be accentuated by placing the patient in a left lateral recumbent position, having the patient hold his or her breath, or having him or her exercise. It sounds like "Ten-nes-see" when tachycardia is present (see Figure 18.4).

Gallop Rhythm • Tachycardia in combination with a normal S1, S2, and audible S3 with or without an S4 is called a gallop rhythm. The presence of a gallop is typically pathologic and caused by conditions of volume overload such as congestive heart failure.

Pericardial Friction Rub • A pericardial friction rub is commonly found in the initial postoperative period following open-heart surgery and is caused by the heart rubbing against the pericardium. Auscultatory findings reveal a harsh, to-and-fro sound often heard best at the lower left sternal border. Pericardial friction rubs may be biphasic or triphasic and the intensity of the sound may vary in systole and diastole. The presence of a pericardial friction rub in an otherwise healthy child or in a child being seen in clinic following cardiac surgery is always pathologic and indicates pericarditis. The rub may disappear with increased accumulation of fluid in the pericardial space. To differentiate a pericardial rub from other extracardiac sounds, the patient should be asked to lean forward; if the sound is caused by a pericardial rub, it will become louder.

Clicks • A systolic ejection click occurs in early systole, immediately following S1, and is heard in children with lesions involving the semilunar valves. It is best heard at the right or left upper sternal border. The ejection click associated with pulmonary stenosis is heard best at the second and third intercostal spaces and becomes louder on expiration. The ejection click associated with aortic stenosis is best heard at the second right intercostal space but may be louder at the apex or mid-left sternal border. In addition, an ejection click may also be heard in children with pulmonary hypertension. A midsystolic click is typically associated with mitral valve prolapse and is heard at the apex (Figure 18.6).

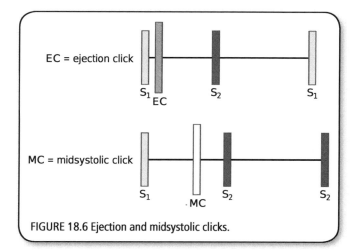

FIGURE 18.6 Ejection and midsystolic clicks.

as diamond-shaped, with the apex of the diamond occurring in the early part of systole when only mild stenosis is present (Figure 18.7). With increasing severity of the stenosis, the diamond shape elongates horizontally, and the apex shifts toward S2 to mimic the murmur becoming longer in duration.

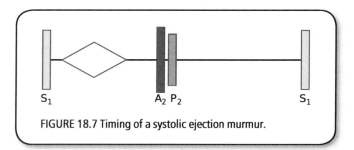

FIGURE 18.7 Timing of a systolic ejection murmur.

Systolic Murmurs

Systolic Murmurs • Systolic murmurs occur between S1 and S2 and represent the majority of heart murmurs heard in children. A comprehensive examination should include auscultation of the four classic locations (i.e., right upper sternal border, left upper sternal border, left lower sternal border, apex), as well as the axilla, back, carotid, and supraclavicular area. Murmurs should be described according to intensity, timing, location, transmission, and quality, which can provide clues to the etiology. Both the bell and the diaphragm of the stethoscope should be used to assess heart sounds.

Types • Systolic murmurs occur between S1 and S2 and can be classified into two subtypes according to onset using the Aubrey Leatham classification, or they can be classified into four subtypes according to onset and termination using the Joseph Perloff classification. The Leatham classification identifies systolic murmurs as either ejection type or regurgitant type. The Perloff classification identifies systolic murmurs as either midsystolic, holosystolic, early systolic, or late systolic. Perloff's classification of midsystolic murmurs is synonymous with Leatham's classification of ejection-type murmurs and Perloff's classification of holosystolic-type and early systolic-type murmurs is the same as Leatham's classification of regurgitant-type murmurs. Late systolic murmurs are classified separately based on their timing during systole. Late systolic murmurs begin in middle to late systole and end at S2. Late systolic murmurs are audible when mitral valve prolapse is present (Park, 2014).

Ejection murmurs (midsystolic murmurs) are associated with normal blood flow through stenotic or malformed semilunar valves, or result from increased blood flow through normal semilunar valves as occurs in pregnancy, fever, anemia, or thyrotoxicosis. However, an ejection or midsystolic murmur may also be reflective of an innocent murmur. Ejection murmurs have variable duration and are best heard at the second right or left intercostal space. Ejection murmurs are depicted

Regurgitant murmurs (holosystolic and early systolic murmurs) begin with S1 and typically last throughout systole. When differentiating between ejection-type murmurs and regurgitant-type murmurs, it is important to note the timing of the onset of the murmur in relation to S1. In regurgitant murmurs, no gap exists between S1 and the onset of the murmur (Figure 18.8). In holosystolic murmurs, the intensity of the regurgitant murmur plateaus from S1 to S2 and is depicted as rectangular, extending from S1 to S2. Early systolic murmurs begin with S1 and end well before S2, decreasing in decrescendo typically at or before midsystole. Regurgitant murmurs are always pathologic and result from blood flowing from a high-pressure system to a low-pressure system, usually when the semilunar valves are closed. The three conditions that cause regurgitant murmurs (holosystolic murmurs) are ventricular septal defects, mitral regurgitation, and tricuspid regurgitation. When tricuspid regurgitation

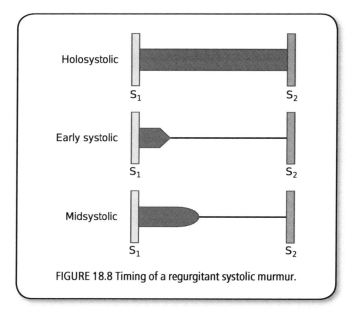

FIGURE 18.8 Timing of a regurgitant systolic murmur.

is present and right ventricular systolic pressure is elevated, a holosystolic murmur is heard. However, when tricuspid regurgitation is present but right ventricular pressure is normal, an early systolic murmur is heard. An early systolic murmur is also detected in neonates with a large ventricular septal defect, children and adults with a very small ventricular septal defect, or children with a large ventricular septal defect and pulmonary hypertension.

Intensity • Each murmur should be evaluated in terms of intensity from grade I to grade VI. The difference between grades III and IV is the presence of a thrill. Differentiating between grades V and VI may be subjective (Table 18.2). An increase in the intensity of the murmur reflects an increase in the amount of turbulent flow through a valve or vessel because of progressive stenosis or blockage. Conditions that increase cardiac output, such as fever, anemia, or exercise, may produce

TABLE 18.2	Intensity of Systolic Murmurs (Grades I–VI)
GRADE	**SOUND QUALITY**
I	Barely audible
II	Soft, but easily heard
III	Moderately loud, no thrill
IV	Loud, accompanied by a thrill
V	Louder (heard with a stethoscope barely on the chest)
VI	Heard with a stethoscope off the chest

a new murmur not audible at baseline or may intensify a preexisting murmur.

Location • In addition to differentiating between ejection and regurgitant murmurs, the PMI where the murmur is heard the loudest should be identified (Figure 18.9). There are four key locations where murmurs are generally detected: (a) the upper left sternal border, (b) the upper right sternal border, (c) the lower left sternal border, and (d) the apex. Determining the timing and location of the murmur in combination with other findings from the physical examination, ECG, and radiologic studies can help determine the diagnosis.

Systolic murmurs, which are best heard at the upper left sternal border or pulmonary area, are typically an ejection type (midsystolic) and include innocent murmurs (e.g., pulmonary flow murmur of the newborn, pulmonary flow murmur of older children) and pathologic murmurs (e.g., pulmonary stenosis, atrial septal defect, atrial stenosis, tetralogy of Fallot, coarctation of the aorta, patent ductus arteriosus with pulmonary hypertension, total anomalous pulmonary venous return, partial anomalous pulmonary venous return) (Table 18.3).

Systolic murmurs best heard at the upper right sternal border or aortic area are ejection type (midsystolic) caused by stenosis of the aortic valve (e.g., aortic stenosis, subvalvar aortic stenosis, supravalvar aortic stenosis). The murmur is heard equally well in the upper left sternal border and apex, transmits to the neck region, and often is associated with a thrill over the carotid arteries (see Table 18.3).

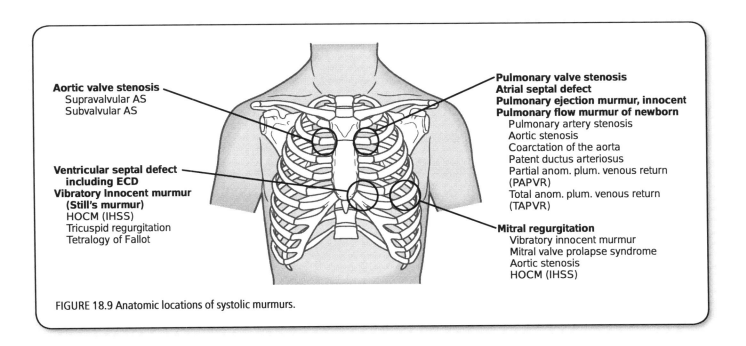

Aortic valve stenosis
Supravalvular AS
Subvalvular AS

Ventricular septal defect including ECD
Vibratory Innocent murmur (Still's murmur)
HOCM (IHSS)
Tricuspid regurgitation
Tetralogy of Fallot

Pulmonary valve stenosis
Atrial septal defect
Pulmonary ejection murmur, innocent
Pulmonary flow murmur of newborn
Pulmonary artery stenosis
Aortic stenosis
Coarctation of the aorta
Patent ductus arteriosus
Partial anom. plum. venous return (PAPVR)
Total anom. plum. venous return (TAPVR)

Mitral regurgitation
Vibratory innocent murmur
Mitral valve prolapse syndrome
Aortic stenosis
HOCM (IHSS)

FIGURE 18.9 Anatomic locations of systolic murmurs.

TABLE 18.3	Systolic Murmurs	
CARDIAC DEFECT	**QUALITIES**	**LOCATION**
Aortic stenosis	• Grade II–V/VI systolic ejection murmur • +/– thrill (at second right intercostal space and supraspinal notch) • Ejection click (at apex, second left intercostal space, and third right intercostal space)	Upper left sternal border
Aortic valve stenosis	• Grade II–IV/VI systolic ejection murmur (at second right intercostal space but louder at third left intercostal space) • +/– thrill at upper right sternal border, suprasternal notch, and carotid arteries • Ejection click • S2 may be single	Upper right sternal border; transmits to neck
Atrial septal defect	• Grade II–III/VI systolic ejection murmur • Widely split • Fixed S3	Upper left sternal border
Atrioventricular canal defect	• Grade II–IV/VI regurgitant murmur • Diastolic rumble • + thrill • Gallop rhythm (in infants)	Lower left sternal border
Coarctation of the aorta	• Grade I–III/VI systolic ejection murmur • Weak or absent femoral pulses • Hypertension in arms	Upper left sternal border; heard in back
Hypertrophic obstructive cardiomyopathy	• Grade II–IV/VI regurgitant murmur with a medium pitch • +/– thrill • May have mitral regurgitation murmur	Lower left sternal border or apex
Mitral regurgitation	• Grade II–III/VI regurgitant murmur • May be holosystolic • May be loud in mid-precordium	Apex; transmits to left axilla in infants
Mitral valve prolapse	• Midsystolic click • +/– late systolic murmur • Thoracic anomalies common	Apex
Partial anomalous pulmonary venous return	• Grade II–III/VI systolic ejection murmur • Widely split • Fixed S3	Upper left sternal border
Patent ductus arteriosus	• Grade II–III/VI continuous murmur • +/– thrill • Bounding pulses	Upper left sternal border; left infraclavicular area
Pulmonary valve stenosis	• Grade II–IV/VI • +/– thrill • Ejection click at second left intercostal space	Upper left sternal border; transmits to back
Subaortic stenosis	• Grade II–IV/VI systolic ejection murmur • High-pitched diastolic murmur of aortic regurgitation at third left intercostal space may be present	Upper right sternal border
Supravalvular stenosis	• Grade II–III/VI systolic ejection murmur • +/– thrill	Upper right sternal border; transmits to back
Tetralogy of Fallot	• Grade II–IV/VI systolic ejection murmur • +/– thrill • Loud single S2 (no P component) • Cyanosis with severe pulmonary stenosis	Mid-left sternal border

TABLE 18.3	Systolic Murmurs (*continued*)	
CARDIAC DEFECT	QUALITIES	LOCATION
Total anomalous pulmonary venous return	• Grade II–III/VI systolic ejection murmur • Widely split • Fixed S2 • Gallop rhythm • Diastolic rumble at lower left sternal border	Upper left sternal border
Tricuspid regurgitation	• Grade II–III/VI regurgitant murmur • Gallop rhythm • If severe, may have enlarged liver	Lower left sternal border
Ventricular septal defect	• Grade II–IV/VI regurgitant murmur • May be holosystolic • + thrill • P2 may be loud	Lower left sternal border

Systolic murmurs best heard at the lower left sternal border may be either ejection type (midsystolic) or regurgitant (holosystolic or early systolic). Conditions that result in this type of murmur include innocent murmurs (e.g., Still's murmur) and pathologic murmurs (e.g., small muscular ventricular septal defect, hypertrophic obstructive cardiomyopathy, tricuspid regurgitation, tetralogy of Fallot) (see Table 18.3).

Systolic murmurs best heard at the apex include ejection (midsystolic), regurgitant (holosystolic), and late systolic murmurs. Systolic murmurs located at the apex can be either nonpathologic (e.g., Still's murmur) or pathologic murmurs (e.g., mitral regurgitation, mitral valve prolapse, aortic stenosis, hypertrophic obstructive cardiomyopathy) (see Table 18.3).

Transmission • Determining whether a systolic murmur transmits to another location can assist with the identification of the murmur's etiology. Transmission to the neck region is typically aortic in origin, and transmission to the back is typically pulmonary in origin. A systolic murmur that is best heard at the apex is caused by mitral regurgitation if it transmits to the left axilla and lower back and is aortic in origin if it transmits to the upper right sternal border and neck.

Quality • The ability to accurately describe the quality or pitch of the murmur takes practice. Many cardiac lesions are associated with a classic pitch or tone. For example, the murmur of mitral regurgitation or a ventricular septal defect possesses a blowing-type quality. Thus, differentiating the quality or pitch of the murmur can help with the diagnosis.

Diastolic Murmurs

Types • Diastolic murmurs are always pathologic, and patients with these murmurs should be referred for evaluation. Diastolic murmurs occur between S2 and S1, are best heard with the diaphragm of the stethoscope at the left sternal border, and are classified into three different types: early diastolic, mid-diastolic, and late diastolic or presystolic murmurs.

Early diastolic murmurs begin immediately after the S2 and are depicted as decrescendo-type murmurs (Figure 18.10). They are associated with regurgitation through the semilunar valves. The murmurs of aortic and pulmonary regurgitation are best heard at the third left intercostal space; however, the aortic regurgitation murmur is high pitched and radiates to the apex, while the murmur of pulmonary regurgitation is medium pitched and radiates along the left sternal border (Table 18.4; Park, 2014).

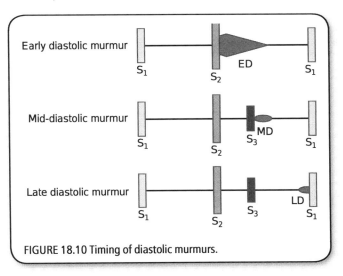

FIGURE 18.10 Timing of diastolic murmurs.

Mid-diastolic murmurs start with a loud S3 and are heard in early or mid-diastole. They are low pitched, best heard with the bell of the stethoscope, and are caused by turbulent blood flow through stenotic atrioventricular valves. Mid-diastolic murmurs

TABLE 18.4	Diastolic Murmurs	
CARDIAC DEFECT	**QUALITIES**	**LOCATION**
Aortic regurgitation	• Grade II–III/IV high-pitched diastolic murmur • If severe, bounding pulses are present	Third left intercostal space; transmits to apex
Mitral stenosis	• Grade II–III/IV low-pitched diastolic murmur • Loud S1 at apex with short opening snap	Left lower sternal border
Pulmonary regurgitation	• Grade II–III/IV diastolic murmur • Occurs early in diastole	Third left intercostal space; radiates along left sternal border
Tricuspid stenosis	• Grade II–III/IV low-pitched diastolic murmur • Heard in mid-diastole • Starts with loud S3	Audible along the left sternal border or at the xiphoid; increases with inspiration

associated with mitral stenosis are heard best at the apex of the heart, while mid-diastolic murmurs associated with tricuspid stenosis are heard best along the left sternal border. *Late diastolic* or *presystolic murmurs* are low frequency in pitch and are associated with the atria contracting against anatomically small or stenotic mitral or tricuspid valves (Park, 2014).

Intensity • Each murmur should be evaluated in terms of intensity from grades I to IV. An increase in grade reflects an increase in the audibility of the murmur, with grade IV being heard with the stethoscope barely on the chest (Table 18.5).

TABLE 18.5	Intensity of Diastolic Murmurs (Grades I–IV)
GRADE	**PITCH**
I	Barely audible
II	Easily audible
III	Loud
IV	Audible with a stethoscope barely on the chest

Continuous Murmurs • Continuous murmurs may be innocent (functional) or indicate the presence of a pathologic condition; they begin in systole and continue into diastole. Causes include aortopulmonary or arteriovenous connections as well as disturbed venous and arterial flow (Figure 18.11).

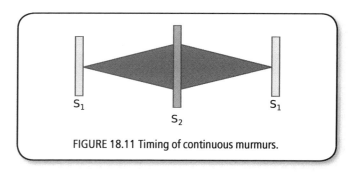

FIGURE 18.11 Timing of continuous murmurs.

Continuous murmurs must not be confused with to-and-fro murmurs, which are heard when a systolic murmur (e.g., aortic or pulmonic stenosis) coexists with a diastolic murmur (e.g., aortic or pulmonic regurgitation).

Pathologic continuous murmurs include the crescendo–decrescendo murmur of patent ductus arteriosus. Described as a machinery murmur, it increases in systole until reaching a peak at S2 before decreasing in diastole. However, if pulmonary hypertension is present, the diastolic component may be absent. Regardless, this murmur is best auscultated in the left precordium in either the infraclavicular or upper left sternal regions.

A second pathologic continuous murmur arises from severe coarctation of the aorta. Collateral flow allows this to be heard over the intercostals. Finally, a third murmur in the class, resulting from pulmonary artery stenosis, can be heard bilaterally over both the anterior and posterior chest.

Continuous murmurs that occur in the absence of any structural heart disease are called innocent murmurs. They are generally high frequency in tone, and the location varies, depending on the cause of murmur.

Innocent Murmurs • It has been reported that up to 80% of children have innocent (or functional) murmurs during childhood (Menashe, 2007). Many are the result of transient high-output states such as fever and anemia. Therefore, the challenge is to differentiate these murmurs from those that result from more serious disease (Box 18.1). There are five common innocent heart murmurs, including the classic vibratory murmur or Still's murmur, pulmonary ejection murmur, pulmonary flow murmur of the newborn, venous hum, and the carotid bruit.

Still's Murmur • A Still's murmur is the most common innocent murmur in children. It is generally detected in children between ages 3 and 6 years, but it may be detected at any age. The cause of the murmur is thought to be low-frequency vibrations generated by normal pulmonary valve leaflets during systole or periodic vibrations generated by a left ventricular false tendon. This low-frequency murmur is midsystolic, grade II–III/VI in intensity, and best auscultated between the lower left sternal border and the apex. It may sound like a twanging string or have a musical quality, but it is not associated with a thrill. Providers should use the stethoscope bell when the child is supine. The murmur may dissipate with the Valsalva maneuver or fade when the child is in the upright position.

Pulmonary Ejection Murmur • The pulmonary ejection murmur is a grade I–III/VI systolic ejection murmur best heard at the upper left sternal border in children 8 to 14 years of age. The origin of the murmur is an exaggeration of normal ejection vibrations within the pulmonary trunk (Park, 2014). It occurs in early to midsystole with a normal S2 and is described as grating in quality. The murmur may be increased when thoracic deformities (e.g., pectus excavatum, kyphoscoliosis) are present. Compared with the pulmonary stenosis murmur, there is no ejection click, no widely split and fixed S2 (atrial septal defect), nor any ECG evidence of right ventricular hypertrophy.

Pulmonary Flow Murmur of the Newborn • The pulmonary flow murmur of the newborn can be detected in infancy and is commonly present in low birth weight newborns. The etiology is turbulence created at the bifurcation of the relatively small branch pulmonary arteries of the newborn. The small size of the branch pulmonary arteries occurs because of decreased use in the fetal circulation, with most blood (85%) bypassing the lungs through the patent ductus arteriosus and going directly out the aorta. The pulmonary flow murmur is a grade I–II/VI systolic ejection murmur that occurs in early to midsystole. Although it is best auscultated at the upper left parasternal area, it can also be heard bilaterally in the chest, both anteriorly and posteriorly. If the child has features that are characteristic of rubella or Williams's syndrome or if the murmur persists beyond 6 months of age, structural narrowing of the pulmonary artery should be suspected, and the infant should be referred to a cardiologist (Park, 2014).

Venous Hum • A venous hum is a grade I–II/VI continuous murmur in which the diastolic component may be louder than the systolic component. It is heard bilaterally or on either side in the infraclavicular or supraclavicular region because of turbulent flow in the jugular veins. It can be heard in preschool children up to 6 years of age. The venous hum is heard only when the child is sitting upright; it disappears when the child is lying down or when the head is turned to the left and the neck veins are compressed. The murmur of a venous hum may be confused with that of a patent ductus arteriosus; however, the murmur of patent ductus arteriosus is best heard in the upper left sternal border or left infraclavicular space, it has a louder systolic component, and it may

be associated with bounding peripheral pulses and wide pulse pressure.

Carotid Bruit • A carotid bruit is a grade II–III/VI early systolic ejection murmur, resulting from turbulent flow in the brachiocephalic or carotid arteries that can be heard at any age. It is best heard in the supraclavicular space or over the carotid arteries where a thrill may be palpable. A carotid bruit should be differentiated from the murmur of aortic stenosis, which is louder in the upper right parasternal area, where it may be associated with a thrill, and which often includes an ejection click.

HELPFUL MANEUVERS: ASSESSMENT OF PERIPHERAL PULSES, LUNGS, AND LIVER

The characteristics of pathologic murmurs are listed in Box 18.1. Occasionally, it may be difficult to differentiate between a pathologic murmur and an innocent murmur. Various maneuvers can aid in identifying the cause of the murmur. Inspiration intensifies right-sided lesions because it increases venous return, such as the murmur of pulmonary stenosis. Inspiration also accentuates the S3 component of tricuspid regurgitation. Expiration decreases venous blood return and can make the ejection click of pulmonary stenosis louder. Postural changes from a squatting position for 30 seconds to a standing position decrease venous blood return to the heart and the systemic blood pressure. Therefore, this maneuver can be used to intensify murmurs of left-sided obstructive lesions and mitral valve prolapse. The murmur of hypertrophic obstructive cardiomyopathy is increased as a result of this position change because of decreased venous return to the left ventricle, which is already structurally narrow. The Valsalva maneuver, which decreases venous blood return, may also increase and prolong the murmur of hypertrophic obstructive cardiomyopathy. To perform this maneuver, patients must be old enough to hold their breath midway through the respiratory cycle. The Valsalva maneuver can also cause the mid- to late systolic ejection click, associated with mitral valve prolapse, to occur earlier in systole. This happens when the mitral valve leaflets reach their maximal distention prematurely because the left ventricle receives less blood return. To increase the murmur of aortic regurgitation, the child should squat or sit, lean forward, and hold his or her breath. The murmur of aortic regurgitation can be heard in the midchest using the diaphragm of the

---

BOX 18.1 Characteristics of Pathologic Murmurs

- Presence of a systolic murmur more than III/IV
- Presence of a thrill
- Presence of a loud systolic murmur, which is loud in duration
- Presence of a diastolic murmur
- Presence of a pansystolic murmur

stethoscope. The supine position can decrease the intensity of innocent murmurs. Still's murmur is the exception; it is heard best with the child lying down. During the Valsalva maneuver, the murmur may disappear. Supination can help to differentiate between the murmur of a patent ductus arteriosus and a venous hum. The venous hum disappears when the child lies down and turns his or her head to the left or when neck veins are compressed. The murmur of a patent ductus arteriosus becomes more readily heard on supination. The left lateral decubitus position intensifies the murmur of mitral valve prolapse. It is heard best with the diaphragm of the stethoscope at the apex of the heart (Evangelista, 2007).

Peripheral Pulses

The strength of the peripheral pulses and the pulse rate should be evaluated to determine if abnormalities are present. The pulse rate should be counted for a full minute and noted for any irregularities. The normal pulse rate varies with age and physical condition. Pulse rate should be compared with age-appropriate norms. Nonpathologic causes of tachycardia (stress) and bradycardia (a physically active teen) should be differentiated from a cardiac etiology such as congestive heart failure or heart block.

A comprehensive cardiac examination should include an assessment of the carotid (in older children), brachial, radial, femoral, and *dorsalis pedis* or *tibialis posterior* pulses for equality in strength. Abnormal findings of strong upper extremity pulses compared with diminished or absent lower extremity pulses are strongly suggestive of coarctation of the aorta. A unilateral weak brachial pulse in an infant with single ventricular anatomy is associated with a Blalock-Taussig shunt or a subclavian flap angioplasty for repair of coarctation of the aorta. If the left brachial pulse is found to be weaker than the right, the etiology may be either a coarctation of the aorta proximal to or near the takeoff of the left subclavian artery or supravalvar aortic stenosis. When both upper and lower peripheral and central pulses are weak, heart failure or shock is present. Bounding peripheral pulses may indicate the presence of systemic hypertension or aortic run-off lesions, such as patent ductus arteriosus, aortic regurgitation, large systemic arteriovenous fistula, or neonatal truncus arteriosus. Weak lower extremity or femoral pulses may also be attributable to vessel injury sustained as the result of repetitive, same-site cardiac catheterizations. *Pulsus paradoxus*, a marked variation of the arterial pulses with the respiratory cycle, may be associated with a large pericardial effusion with tamponade physiology, constrictive pericarditis, or respiratory distress resulting from asthma or pneumonia. Pulsus paradoxus is confirmed by the use of a sphygmomanometer by first inflating the blood pressure cuff 20 points higher than the patient's baseline systolic pressure. The cuff pressure is slowly lowered

until Korotkoff sound (A) is heard for some but not all cardiac cycles. The cuff pressure is lowered again until the systolic sounds are heard for all cardiac cycles (B). If the difference between A and B is greater than 10 mmHg, then pulsus paradoxus is present.

Lungs and Liver

The lungs and liver should be evaluated for signs of congestion. Tachypnea and the presence of rales or wheezes may indicate pulmonary congestion. The presence of hepatomegaly is a sign of elevated central venous pressure. A liver edge measuring more than 2 cm below the right costal margin is abnormal in children and may be consistent with congestive heart failure. Monitoring the size of the liver can assist in determining the progression of the disease and effectiveness of therapy. A palpable spleen is highly suspicious of bacterial endocarditis. Splenomegaly as an isolated finding is rarely caused by congestive heart failure. The presence of abdominal situs inversus with or without thoracic situs inversus warrants further investigation for the presence of CHD.

COMMON DIAGNOSTIC STUDIES

Laboratory tests, ECG, and chest films are generally abnormal only when the CHD or acquired heart disease is significant enough to cause hemodynamic changes. However, these diagnostic tests (see Table 18.6) can provide useful information about the progression of the disease as well as the health status of children living with heart disease, especially those who have undergone a palliative procedure, surgical correction, or cardiac transplant.

Routine laboratory tests such as a complete blood cell count and blood chemistries can assist in diagnosing and monitoring the progression of cardiovascular disease. Polycythemia is found in patients with cyanotic heart disease; however, the degree of polycythemia is dependent on the patient's arterial saturation. Severe anemia can cause a murmur or congestive heart failure; polycythemia can cause a murmur. *Leukocytosis* may be present in congestive heart failure, bacterial endocarditis, and acute rheumatic fever. Thrombocytopenia is commonly found in adolescents with longstanding cyanotic heart disease. Electrolytes and liver function studies can provide information about the perfusion and functional status of the liver and kidneys in the presence of either a ductal-dependent lesion with longstanding congestive heart failure or cyanotic heart disease. It can also provide clues to the impact of medical therapies used to manage these patients. Newer screening tools have recently become available, such as the brain natriuretic peptide (an active amino acid peptide released from the cardiac ventricles in response to stretching of the chambers), that have utility as a marker for the progression of congestive heart failure.

TABLE 18.6	Diagnostic Studies Used to Evaluate Cardiac Conditions	
DIAGNOSTIC STUDY	**INDICATION**	**COMMENTS**
12-Lead electrocardiogram (ECG)	Can aid in diagnosis of CHD, acquired heart disease, and arrhythmias	ECGs of infants and children differ from those of adults in that there is right ventricular dominance in infants. ECG findings should be correlated with patient's history and physical examination to determine diagnosis, hemodynamic impact, and need for a cardiology consult.
Blood chemistries	To monitor fluid status, assess for side effects of cardiac medications and complications of longstanding congestive heart failure or cyanotic heart disease	Electrolytes and liver function studies can provide information about perfusion and functional status of the liver and kidneys in the presence of either a ductal-dependent lesion with longstanding congestive heart failure or cyanotic heart disease
Cardiac catheterization	To diagnose or treat congenital heart defects	Measures oxygen saturations and pressures in the heart, great arteries, and lungs. With the aid of radiopaque dye injected into the heart vessels, cardiac anatomy and stenotic vessels can be identified. Cardiac catheterization can also be used for intervention purposes, for example, to close septal defects, dilate vessels, or create communications between chambers.
Chest radiograph	To diagnose or monitor congenital or acquired heart disease	Can provide information about heart size, cardiac silhouette, enlargement of specific cardiac chambers, pulmonary vascular markings, blood flow patterns, lung parenchyma, and thorax.
Complete blood count	Used to monitor status and progression of heart disease	Polycythemia is found in patients with cyanotic heart disease; the degree of polycythemia is dependent on arterial saturation. Severe anemia can cause a murmur or congestive heart failure; polycythemia can cause a murmur. Leukocytosis may be present in congestive heart failure, bacterial endocarditis, and acute rheumatic fever. Thrombocytopenia is commonly found in adolescents with longstanding cyanotic heart disease.
Echocardiogram	Used to diagnose and evaluate congenital heart disease.	Uses ultrasound to evaluate cardiac structures and their movement through a cardiac cycle; depending on the type of echocardiogram, the rate of blood flow through the heart can also be assessed.
Pulse oximetry	To screen for critical congenital heart disease (CCHD); to monitor oxygen saturation of hemoglobin in children with diagnosed congenital heart disease	Used as a method of universal screening for CCHD

DOCUMENTATION OF FINDINGS

Sample Write-Up: Healthy Child

Subjective Data

A 15-year-old male presents for a sports physical. Family history is negative for cardiac disease, hypertension, syncope, and hypercholesterolemia.

Objective Data

T: 99.6°F (37.6°C); **P:** 76 beats per minute; **RR:** 24 breaths per minute; **BP:** 96/72 mmHg
General: well-nourished male in no distress; height and weight in 75th percentile; color pink, normal precordial activity; no thrill or heaves; strong, equal peripheral pulses; capillary refill less than 2 seconds in upper and lower extremities, S1, S2, regular rate; no murmurs auscultated; breath sounds clear and equal bilaterally
Assessment: normal cardiac assessment

Sample Write-Up: Ill Child

Subjective Data

An 8-month-old girl presents with history of frequent upper respiratory infections. Mother says child has difficulty finishing bottle and falls asleep after about 4 ounces, "all sweaty and tired looking." Sweat chloride test negative. The child does not attend day care and has no sick contacts.

Objective Data

T: 98.42°F (36.9°C); **apical pulse:** 110; **RR:** 36 beats per minute; **BP:** 88/60 mmHg; **weight:** 10th percentile; **height:** 25th percentile

General: color pink centrally and peripherally; equal peripheral pulses; capillary refill less than 2 seconds in upper and lower extremities; palpable thrill along left sternal border; low-pitched, grade III holosystolic murmur at LLSB; no hepatosplenomegaly; EEG normal; chest radiography reveals slight right ventricular enlargement, echocardiogram shows ventricular septal defect

Assessment: ventricular septal defect

Notable Clinical Findings

- History of prematurity or prolonged ventilation in neonatal period
- Second- or third-hand tobacco smoke exposure
- Immunization delay
- Diagnosis of congenital heart disease
- Vital signs outside the normal range
- Cyanosis or duskiness
- Exercise intolerance
- Palpitations
- Growth failure
- Chest pain
- Respiratory complaints
- Edema
- Diaphoresis
- Chest deformity
- Bounding peripheral pulses
- Displacement of the point of maximal impulse
- Presence of a thrill
- Presence of S_3 or S_4
- Systolic murmur more than III/IV in intensity
- Pansystolic murmur
- Diastolic murmur
- Gallop rhythm
- Presence of a click
- Syncope
- Joint symptoms
- Neurological symptoms
- Finger clubbing
- Hepatosplenomegaly

References

Altman, C. A. (2014). *Congenital heart disease (CHD) in the newborn: Presentation and screening for critical CHD. Up to Date.* Retrieved from http://www.uptodate.com/contents/congenital-heart-disease-chd-in-the-newborn-presentation-and-screening-for-critical-chd

American Heart Association. (2013). *Understand your risk for congenital heart defects.* Retrieved from http://www.heart.org/HEARTORG/Conditions/CongenitalHeartDefects/UnderstandYourRiskforCongenitalHeartDefects/Understand-Your-Risk-for-Congenital-Heart-Defects_UCM_001219_Article.jsp

da Silva, V. M., de Oliveira Lopes, M. V., & de Araujo, T. L. (2007). Growth and nutritional status of children with congenital heart disease. *Journal of Cardiovascular Nursing, 22*(5), 390–396.

Delaney, A., Schroeder, M. L., & Baker, A. (2011). The child with cardiovascular dysfunction. In M. J. Hockenberry & D. Wilson (Eds.), *Nursing care of infants and children* (9th ed., pp. 1340–1408). St. Louis. MO: Mosby Elsevier.

Evangelista, J. K. (2007). Assessment of pediatric heart sounds. *American Journal for Nurse Practitioners, 11*(3), 15–28.

Frank, J. E., & Jacobe, K. M. (2011). Evaluation and management of heart murmurs in children. *American Family Physician, 84*(7), 793–800.

Geggel, R. L., & Endom, E. E. (2013). *Approach to chest pain in children. Up to Date.* Retrieved from http://www.uptodate.com/contents/approach-to-chest-pain-in-children

Gonzalez, J. H., Shirali, G. S., Atz, A. M., Taylor, S. N., Forbes, G. A., Zyblewski, S. C., & Hlavacek, A. M. (2009). Universal screening for extracardiac abnormalities in neonates with congenital heart disease. *Pediatric Cardiology, 30*(3), 269–273.

Green, R. (2007). Summary of workgroup meeting on use of family history information in pediatric primary care and public health. *Pediatrics, 120,* S87–S100.

Hebra, A. (2012). *Pectus excavatum.* Retrieved from http://emedicine.medscape.com/article/1004953-overview

Hockenberry, M. J. (2011). Communication and physical assessment of the child. In M. J. Hockenberry & D. Wilson (Eds.), *Nursing care of infants and children* (9th ed., pp. 117–178). St. Louis, MO: Mosby Elsevier.

Hoffman, J. I. E. (2013). The global burden of congenital heart disease. *Cardiovascular Journal of Africa, 24*(4), 141–145.

Jenkins, K. J., Correa, A., Feinstein, J. A., Botto, L., Britt, A. E., Daniels, S. R., & Webb, C. L. (2007). Noninherited risk factors and congenital cardiovascular defects: Current knowledge: A scientific statement from the American Heart Association Council on Cardiovascular Disease in the Young: Endorsed by the American Academy of Pediatrics. *Circulation, 115*(23), 2995–3014.

Kemper, A. R., Mahle, W. T., Martin, G. R., Cooley, W. C., Kumar, P., Morrow, W. R., . . . Howell, R. R. (2011). Strategies for implementing screening for critical congenital heart disease. *Pediatrics, 128*(5), e1259–1267.

Luma, G. B., & Spiotta, R. T. (2006). Hypertension in children and adolescents. *American Family Physician, 73*(9), 1558–1568.

Marelli, A. J., Mackie, A. S., Ionescu-Ittu, R., Rahme, E., & Pilote, L. (2007). Congenital heart disease in the general population: Changing prevalence and age distribution. *Circulation, 115*(2), 163–172.

Menashe, V. (2007). Heart murmurs. *Pediatrics in Review, 28,* 19–22.

Mitchell, M. E., Sander, T. L., Klinkner, D. B., & Tomita-Mitchell, A. (2007). The molecular basis of congenital heart disease. *Seminars in Thoracic & Cardiovascular Surgery, 19*(3), 228–237.

Øyen, N., Poulsen, G., Boyd, H. A., Wohlfahrt, J., Jensen, P. K., & Melbye, M. (2009). Recurrence of congenital heart defects in families. *Circulation, 120*(4), 295–301.

Park, M. (2014). *Pediatric cardiology for practitioners* (6th ed.). Philadelphia, PA: Mosby Elsevier.

Salerno, J. C., & Coleman, B. (2013). *Causes of syncope in children and adolescents. Up to Date.* Retrieved from http://www.uptodate.com/contents/causes-of-syncope-in-children-and-adolescents

Seifert, S. M., Schaechter, J. L., Hershorin, E. R., & Lipshultz, S. E. (2011). Health effects of energy drinks on children, adolescents, and young adults. *Pediatrics, 127*(3), 511–528.

Sharma, H. S., Peters, T. H., Moorhouse, M. J., van der Spek, P. J., & Bogers, A. J. (2006). DNA microarray analysis for human congenital heart disease. *Cell Biochemistry & Biophysics, 44*(1), 1–9.

Sovari, A., Kocheril, A. G., Assadi, R., & Baas, A. S. (2014). *Long QT syndrome*. Retrieved from http://emedicine.medscape.com/article/157826-overview

Vogt, K. N., Manlhiot, C., Van Arsdell, G., Russell, J. L., Mital, S., & McCrindle, B. W. (2007). Somatic growth in children with single ventricle physiology impact of physiologic state. *Journal of the American College of Cardiology, 50*(19), 1876–1883.

Weekes, A. J., & Lee, D. S. (2013). *Pediatric cocaine abuse*. Retrieved from http://emedicine.medscape.com/article/917385-overview

Weismann, C. G., & Gelb, B. D. (2007). The genetics of congenital heart disease: A review of recent developments. *Current Opinion in Cardiology, 22*(3), 200–206.

Assessment of the Abdomen and Regional Lymphatics

The abdomen contains numerous organs that are responsible for a broad range of vital functions. The pediatric health care provider must have a thorough knowledge of anatomy and physiology of the gastrointestinal and urinary systems in order to perform accurate physical examinations, particularly on younger children who are often developmentally unable to cooperate with the exam. The ability to gather historical data relevant to these body systems is also important, especially in the event that the historian is the older child or adolescent.

ANATOMY AND PHYSIOLOGY

The abdomen is a large hollow cavity that lies between the thorax and the pelvis and contains both solid and hollow organs, which are surrounded by muscles, the peritoneum, and the vertebral column. The *solid organs* are the *liver, spleen, pancreas, kidneys, adrenal glands,* and *ovaries.* The *hollow organs* are the *stomach, gallbladder, small intestines, large intestines, urinary bladder,* and *uterus.* The primary functions of the abdominal organs are digestion and absorption of nutrients, transportation and excretion of wastes, filtration of blood and lymph, and reproduction. The spleen, located above the stomach, is a highly vascular organ comprising mainly lymphoid tissue that stores blood, filters blood and blood cells, and plays a role in immunity Dividing the abdomen into four quadrants—right upper and lower quadrants (RUQ, RLQ) and left upper and lower quadrants (LUQ, LLQ)—permits the examiner to assess the numerous abdominal organs systematically and to identify organomegaly or abnormal masses. The four abdominal quadrants are illustrated in Figure 19.1; Box 19.1 lists the contents of each quadrant.

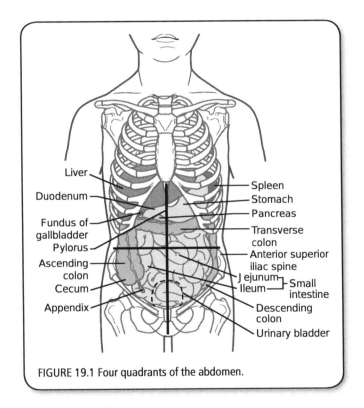

FIGURE 19.1 Four quadrants of the abdomen.

Gastrointestinal System

The gastrointestinal system encompasses the *mouth, oropharynx, esophagus,* and the *organs of the abdominal cavity.* The function of the gastrointestinal tract is threefold: (a) digest and absorb nutrients, (b) maintain fluid and electrolyte balance, and (c) protect the body from toxins and pathogens.

The gastrointestinal tract begins at the mouth. The mouth, oropharynx, teeth, salivary glands, and tongue are discussed in Chapter 16. The esophagus is a tube-like structure located behind the trachea and in front

BOX 19.1 Abdominal Organs Within Quadrants

RUQ	LUQ
Liver (right lobe)	Stomach
Gallbladder	Liver (left lobe)
Duodenum	Spleen
Pancreas (head)	Pancreas (body)
Right kidney (upper pole)	Left adrenal gland
Right adrenal gland	Left kidney (upper pole)
Hepatic flexure of colon	Splenic flexure of colon
Ascending colon (part)	Transverse colon (part)
Transverse colon (part)	Descending colon (part)
Stomach (pylorus)	

RLQ	LLQ
Right kidney (lower pole)	Left kidney (lower pole)
Cecum	Descending colon (part)
Appendix	Sigmoid colon
Ascending colon (part)	Left ovary
Right ovary	Left fallopian tube
Right fallopian tube Right ureter	Uterus, if enlarged (otherwise, the uterus is midline LLQ and RLQ)
Right spermatic cord	Left ureter Left spermatic cord

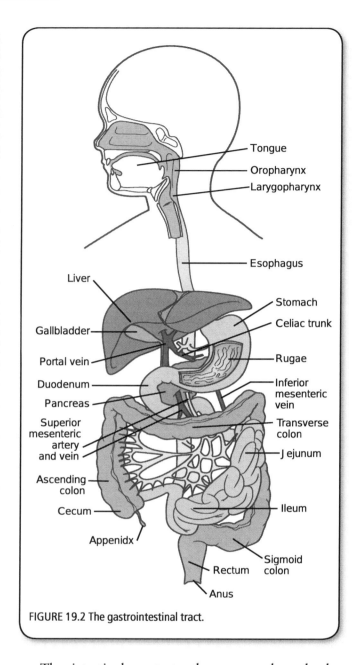

FIGURE 19.2 The gastrointestinal tract.

of the vertebral column (Figure 19.2) that connects the mouth to the stomach. It secretes mucus to facilitate swallowing and to prevent gastric acid from eroding the esophageal wall. Peristalsis and gravity move food toward the stomach.

The stomach is an elongated, hollow, pouch-like structure located below the diaphragm in the upper abdomen, lying primarily left of the midline (see Figure 19.2). The stomach is involved in the second stage of digestion after mastication (chewing). It secretes hydrochloric acid and digestive enzymes that, when mixed with food, form a liquid substance known as *chyme*. Chyme stimulates the release of hormones, which activate enzymes from the liver, gallbladder, pancreas, and duodenal mucosa that break down fat, protein, and carbohydrates. Once this process occurs, chyme passes through the pyloric valve into the *duodenum*, the first of three parts of the small intestine (see Figure 19.2). The small intestine is a tube-like structure that extends from the pyloric sphincter to the *ileocecal valve*, filling most of the lower abdominal cavity. The second part, the *jejunum*, which follows the duodenum, absorbs water, protein, carbohydrates, and vitamins from chyme. The *ileum*, the third and final part of the small intestine, absorbs bile salts, chloride, and vitamins C and B$_{12}$.

The intestinal contents then move through the ileocecal valve into the *cecum*, the first part of the large intestine (see Figure 19.2). The large intestine completes digestion by further absorbing vitamins and water and forming feces for elimination as solid waste.

The cecum is located in the RLQ. At the bottom of the cecum is the *appendix*, a vestigial structure that is only clinically significant if it becomes inflamed or infected (see Figure 19.2). The *colon*, the next portion of the large intestine, is divided into the *ascending colon*, *transverse colon*, and *descending colon*. Beginning at the iliac crest and located on the anterior surface of the sacrum, the colon becomes the S-shaped *sigmoid colon*. This portion of the colon ends in the rectum, where fecal matter is stored until peristalsis moves it through the *anal canal* and *anus* during the process of defecation. Figure 19.2 illustrates these structures.

Other abdominal organs also play a role in digestion and metabolism. The liver, the largest organ in the body, is located under the diaphragm in the RUQ of the abdomen (see Figure 19.2). It has two lobes and is an extremely vascular organ, receiving its blood supply from the abdominal aorta and portal vein. The liver has numerous functions: (a) it metabolizes carbohydrates, fats, and proteins; (b) it stores iron, glycogen, fat-soluble vitamins, and some water-soluble vitamins; (c) it metabolizes drugs and toxins; (d) it excretes waste products; (e) it produces antibodies and prothrombin and fibrinogen, which are essential for coagulation; and (f) it continuously produces bile, which is stored in the gallbladder.

The gallbladder is a pear-shaped structure located under the surface of the liver (see Figure 19.2). It is connected to the upper portion of the duodenum by the common bile duct. The gallbladder concentrates and stores bile then secretes it into the duodenum to aid in the digestion of fats.

The pancreas is a lobulated structure, located behind the stomach in the LUQ (see Figure 19.2). The wide end connects to the duodenum, and the narrow end touches the spleen. The *pancreatic duct* opens into the duodenum and secrets digestive enzymes that help break down carbohydrates, fats, and protein. The pancreas also produces insulin and glucagon directly into the bloodstream to control blood glucose levels.

The spleen is also located in the LUQ above the stomach; it is a highly vascular organ comprising mainly lymphoid tissue (see Figure 19.1). The spleen stores blood, filters blood and blood cells, and plays a role in immunity.

Genitourinary System

The genitourinary system comprises both the genital and urinary systems. The male and female genital systems are discussed in Chapter 20. The urinary system includes two kidneys, two ureters, the urinary bladder, and the urethra (Figure 19.3). The kidneys lie between the thoracic and lumbar regions in the RUQ and LUQ of the abdomen and are surrounded by two layers of fat, the renal fascia, and the eleventh and twelfth ribs, which help to cushion and protect them. Each kidney receives its blood supply through the renal arteries, which arise from the abdominal aorta. The right kidney sits slightly lower than the left, owing to the presence of the liver in the abdominal cavity (see Figure 19.3). On top of each kidney lies an adrenal gland, which secretes epinephrine and norepinephrine in response to stress, and corticosteroids that control the body's metabolism of fat, protein, and carbohydrates. These glands also help regulate sodium and potassium levels and affect body growth and male secondary sex characteristics.

The kidneys are composed of three layers: the *cortex*, *medulla*, and *renal sinus* and *pelvis*. The cortex is the outermost portion of the kidney that contains

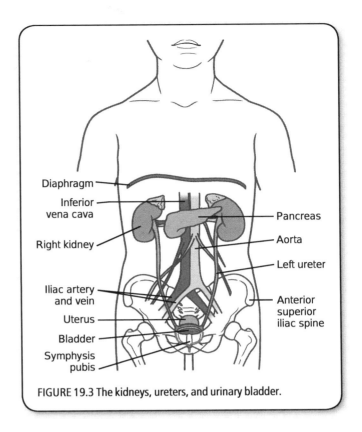

FIGURE 19.3 The kidneys, ureters, and urinary bladder.

the *glomeruli*, *proximal* and *distal convoluted tubules*, and collecting ducts of the *nephron*. The medulla is the middle portion of the kidney that contains the *renal pyramids*, straight portions of the *tubules*, *loops of Henle*, *vasa recta*, and terminal collecting ducts. The renal sinus and pelvis make up the innermost part of the kidney.

The structural and functional unit of the kidney is the nephron. Each kidney contains approximately 1 million nephrons, which are located in both the renal cortex and medulla. The functional component of the nephron is the *glomerulus* and *glomerular (Bowman's) capsule*. The nephrons play several vital functions, including:

- **Maintenance of homeostasis**, which occurs through the regulation of electrolyte concentrations, and maintenance of blood volume by maintaining osmolality of extracellular fluid within a narrow range necessary for optimal cellular function
- **Regulation of acid–base balance**, which is controlled through renal reabsorption of bicarbonate and renal secretion of hydrogen ions
- **Regulation of blood pressure** through the renin-angiotensin-aldosterone system
- **Secretion of hormones**, such as erythropoietin, which stimulates red blood cell production, and vitamin D, which regulates blood levels of calcium and phosphorus
- **Excretion of excess water and nitrogenous waste**, particularly urea, uric acid, and creatinine along with water, a process that leads to the production of urine

Ureters are long, narrow, muscular tubes that carry urine from the kidneys to the urinary bladder through peristalsis. The left ureter is longer than the right ureter because the left kidney sits higher in the abdominal cavity than the right kidney. The urinary bladder is an ovoid, hollow, muscular organ that collects urine (see Figure 19.3). When it is empty, it is located underneath the symphysis pubis, but when it is full, it can be readily palpated above the symphysis pubis. Urine flows from the bladder through the urethra outside the body. In females, the urethra is distinct and separate from the reproductive tract; in males, the urethra also functions as a passage for semen (see Chapter 20).

DEVELOPMENTAL CONSIDERATIONS

Gastrointestinal System

The gastrointestinal system begins to form during the third week of embryonic life. At this time, a liver bud is present, and the mesentery begins to form. By week 4, the intestines are present, and the esophagus and stomach are distinct. By the seventh week of gestation, the intestines herniate into the umbilical cord to begin the process of rotation and elongation. Between weeks 9 and 10, the intestines re-enter the abdominal cavity and continue rotation. Disruption in this process results in abdominal wall defects, such as omphalocele and gastroschisis (Figure 19.4). Both conditions involve herniation of the abdominal wall contents, usually the small bowel. With omphalocele, the abdominal contents are covered with a membrane or sac, but with gastroschisis, there is no membrane or sac covering the abdominal contents. By week 12, the muscular layers of the intestines are present, and active transport of amino acids begins. The pancreatic islet cells and bile also appear at this time. Between weeks 13 and 14, peristalsis can be detected, and by week 16, meconium is present. By 20 weeks, secretion of insulin begins. By 24 weeks, ganglion cells are present in the rectum. By week 34, sucking and swallowing become coordinated, and by 36 to 38 weeks, the development of the gastrointestinal system is complete.

Although the gastrointestinal system is physically developed at birth, it is functionally undeveloped until age 2 years. Neonates have lower esophageal sphincter tone, which increases the incidence of gastroesophageal reflux in this age group (Ball, Bindler, & Cowen, 2013a). The stomach capacity is approximately 60 mL for a neonate, approximately 500 mL for a toddler, and approximately 1,000 to 1,500 mL for an adolescent (Ball et al., 2013a). Gastric pH is alkalotic at birth, and gastric acid production slowly increases to adult levels by 2 years of age (Swamy Chidananda & Mallikarjun, 2004).

Infants and toddlers have weak abdominal muscle tone, which causes a protuberant abdomen in neonates and a prominent abdomen in toddlers. This weak abdominal musculature poorly protects the liver and spleen. Infants also have a cylindrical abdomen; thus, a distended

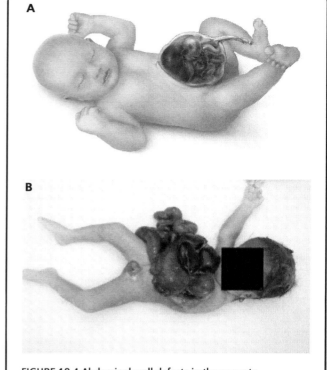

FIGURE 19.4 Abdominal wall defects in the neonate. **A.** Omphalocele includes a membranous sac covering the abdominal organs. **B.** In gastroschisis, the abdominal contents are not covered by a membrane or sac.

or scaphoid abdomen indicates pathology. The abdomen is larger than the chest in children from birth until age 4, creating a "pot-bellied" appearance (Figure 19.5).

Pancreatic enzyme activity is decreased from birth until 4 to 6 months (Ball et al., 2013a). This results in varied bioavailability of drugs that may depend on specific enzymes to aid in drug absorption. The liver is functionally immature from birth until age 1 (Macfarlane, 2006; Swamy Chidananda & Mallikarjun, 2004). The liver has decreased hepatic enzyme function in the child until it reaches adult size at adolescence (Swamy Chidananda & Mallikarjun, 2004). In the neonate, liver conjugation reactions are impaired, which explains why physiologic jaundice is so common. Decreased hepatic enzyme function also results in long drug half-lives in children from birth until age 3 to 4 years (Swamy Chidananda & Mallikarjun, 2004). From birth until age 1, the liver synthesizes and stores glycogen less effectively than it does in older children, so these children are prone to hypoglycemia (Swamy Chidananda & Mallikarjun, 2004).

The length of the infant's small intestine is proportionately longer relative to body size, which provides a greater surface area for absorption until toddlerhood (Potts, 2012). Until 6 to 8 months of age, infants have

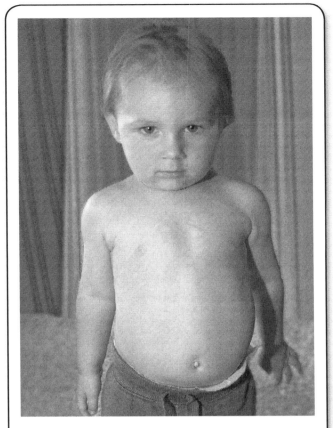

FIGURE 19.5 The typical "pot-bellied" appearance of the toddler.

prolonged gastric emptying and transit time through the small intestine, which may affect the absorption of nutrients and medications, increasing the chance of adverse side effects and toxicities (Guthrie, 2005). The gastrocolic reflex is rapid in infants, explaining the frequency of stools. As the spinal cord myelinates and the musculature of the anus develops, the child is able to control the bowel voluntarily.

Genitourinary System

Embryologic development of the genitourinary system begins within the first weeks after conception and progresses through three stages. The first stage is the *pronephros*, also called "fore kidneys," which appear at 3 to 4 weeks gestation and play a role in normal organogenesis. The pronephroi degenerate by the fifth week and become the *mesonephros*, or "midkidneys," which are fully developed by 37 days. The mesonephros consists of 30 to 40 glomerulotubular units, which regress by the end of the second month of gestation. At 8 weeks, the mesonephros then becomes the *metanephros*, or "hind kidneys." At this stage, nephrons and permanent kidneys begin to form. The kidneys produce urine by approximately 3 months of gestation. The urinary bladder develops at approximately 6 weeks of gestation, and formation of the urethra is completed by the end of the first trimester.

The kidneys are immature at birth with increased renal vascular resistance and incomplete glomerular and tubular development, which results in decreased renal blood flow, glomerular filtration rate, and tubular function. This developmental variation continues until age 2 (Swamy Chidananda & Mallikarjun, 2004). This renal immaturity puts children in this age group at risk for dehydration or hypovolemia.

Until children reach preschool age, the kidneys are proportionately larger than those of the adult and are surrounded by less fat (Ball et al., 2013b). This variation permits the tip of the right kidney to be palpated because of the thin abdominal wall, especially during the inspiratory phase of respiration. This also makes the child's kidneys more susceptible to trauma because more of the kidney is exposed. From birth until age 3 years, the urinary bladder lies between the symphysis and the umbilicus, and the ureters are relatively short. The urinary bladder then descends into the pelvis shortly before puberty, which affects the approach to the physical examination (Montagnino & Ring, 2011). The urinary bladder capacity varies, according to the child's age. The newborn bladder has a predicted capacity of approximately 20 to 30 mL. A formula can be used to calculate an older infant or child's bladder capacity: age in years + 2 = number of ounces × 30 = number of milliliters (Kitchens, Herndon, & Joseph, 2007).

CULTURAL, ETHNIC, AND RACIAL CONSIDERATIONS

An umbilical hernia is an abdominal wall defect that is eight times more common among African American children than among Caucasian children (Erickson & Golladay, 2014). The incidence of lactose intolerance, the inability to digest lactose (milk sugar), is highest in children of Hispanic, African, Asian, and Mediterranean ancestry, and lowest in people of northern European ancestry (Roy, Komanapalli, Shojamanesh, Bashir, & Choudhary, 2013). Cystic fibrosis is a multisystem disease among Caucasian children and has several gastrointestinal effects (Tsai, Manchester, & Elias, 2012). Meconium ileus and fibrocystic disease of the pancreas are associated with cystic fibrosis.

ASSESSMENT

History

Prenatal, Perinatal, and Neonatal Histories

It is important for the pediatric health care provider to review the past medical history for any conditions diagnosed in the prenatal, perinatal, or neonatal period that involve the gastrointestinal or genitourinary tracts. The prenatal history can reveal maternal polyhydramnios, which is associated with intestinal atresias and tracheal esophageal fistula. Maternal oligohydramnios can cause urinary obstructive lesions, polycystic kidneys, renal agenesis, and gastrointestinal atresias (Carter & Boyd, 2012). In the preterm infant, perinatal asphyxia and immature immune function may play a role in developing necrotizing enterocolitis (Springer & Annibale, 2014). Neonatal conditions about which to inquire include abdominal wall defects such as omphalocele, gastroschisis, diaphragmatic hernia, or prune belly syndrome; intestinal obstruction, such as pyloric stenosis, imperforate anus, and biliary, jejunal, ileal, or duodenal atresia; or malrotation. The timing of the first meconium stool is also important; delayed passage of meconium (meconium ileus) may indicate Hirschsprung disease or cystic fibrosis. A history of hyperbilirubinemia should be noted, and physiologic and nonphysiologic hyperbilirubinemia should be differentiated. Myelomeningocele causes lifelong alterations in bowel and bladder control. A history of cleft lip or palate is important, as these structural defects can affect feeding and weight gain.

Any history of congenital anomalies of the genitourinary tract is also investigated. Conditions about which to inquire include exstrophy of the bladder, hydronephrosis, ambiguous genitalia, hypospadias, epispadias, hydrocele, cryptorchidism, inguinal hernia, chordee, or polycystic kidney disease. A history of low-set or abnormally formed pinnae should be noted, as this can be associated with renal disease.

Review of Systems

The pediatric review of systems (ROS) includes any history of conditions involving the gastrointestinal or genitourinary tracts. Some examples follow.

- **General health:** Growth history or unusual weight gain or loss
- **Skin:** Jaundice or diaper rash (dermatitis due to frequent loose stools)
- **Cardiac:** Congenital heart disease or congestive heart failure (may cause hepatomegaly)
- **Respiratory:** Cystic fibrosis or streptococcal pharyngitis (may cause abdominal pain)
- **Gastrointestinal:** Recurrent abdominal pain (RAP), inflammatory bowel disease, ulcerative colitis, Crohn's disease, celiac disease, gastroesophageal reflux disease (GERD), pyloric stenosis, anal fissure, skin tags or polyps, intussusception, Hirschsprung disease, umbilical hernia, gastroenteritis, peritonitis, hepatitis, or peptic ulcer disease
- **Genitourinary:** Urolithiasis, urinary tract infections, nocturnal enuresis, pyelonephritis, diabetes insipidus, nephrotic syndrome, acute glomerulonephritis, inguinal hernia, appendicitis, patent urachus, exstrophy of the bladder, or cryptorchidism
- **Endocrine:** Diabetes mellitus
- **Gynecologic:** Menstrual history, dysmenorrhea, endometriosis, pelvic inflammatory disease, or ectopic pregnancy
- **Hematologic:** Sickle cell disease or blood dyscrasias (may cause hepatomegaly or splenomegaly)
- **Neurologic:** Cerebral palsy or myelomeningocele
- **Psychosocial:** Anorexia nervosa, bulimia nervosa, RAP, alcoholism (vomiting), anxiety, or depression

Immunizations

Immunization status is an essential component of the pediatric health history. Some diseases for which children are immunized can cause medical conditions involving the gastrointestinal or genitourinary tracts. For example, both hepatitis A and B can cause anorexia, jaundice, and hepatomegaly. Rotavirus causes anorexia, vomiting, abdominal pain, diarrhea, and dehydration.

Allergies

Food allergies and their myriad manifestations, which include oral, gastrointestinal, cutaneous, and respiratory symptoms, occur in 5% to 6% of children aged 3 years and younger (Sicherer & Sampson, 2010). Thus, this is an important part of the history. Children with oral allergy syndrome develop signs later in infancy and into childhood. Gastrointestinal manifestations that indicate a food allergy include nausea, vomiting, and abdominal pain within minutes to 2 hours of ingesting the allergenic food, then diarrhea 2 to 6 hours after the ingestion. Typical foods implicated in these reactions are milk, eggs, peanuts, soy, wheat, fish, tree nuts, and shellfish (Sicherer, 2014). Anaphylaxis may also occur, underscoring the importance of this assessment. A history of atopic dermatitis should be noted, as children with this condition have a higher risk of developing food allergies, particularly infants and toddlers with atopic dermatitis that is resistant to therapy (Sicherer, 2014).

Hospitalizations

It is important to inquire about past hospitalizations for acute or chronic illnesses or infections involving the gastrointestinal or genitourinary tracts. For example, it is important to note hospitalizations for dehydration secondary to gastroenteritis or vomiting, management of abdominal pain, encopresis, or surgical problems, such as pyloric stenosis.

Injuries

The provider should ask about any history of abdominal injury. Blunt or penetrating abdominal trauma can lead to severe splenic, hepatic, or renal injuries. The circumstances leading to the injury may provide clues as to neglect; reveal knowledge deficits about motor vehicle, bicycle, or street safety; or indicate abuse.

Surgical History

Surgical procedures involving the gastrointestinal or genitourinary tract are noted along with the date of surgery and the condition for which the surgical procedure was done. The provider should also note if the condition was resolved with surgery. Examples of surgical procedures about which to inquire include appendectomy, hernia repair, surgery for ulcerative colitis or Crohn's disease, nephrectomy, or orchiopexy for testicular torsion.

Current Medications

The provider must note any medications the child is taking that have an impact on the gastrointestinal or genitourinary tract, such as diuretics, which affect urine output. Anemic menstruating females may be taking iron supplements, which may cause constipation. Adolescent girls may be taking diuretics or laxatives to control their weight (Yager, Scher, Hilty, & Osterhout, 2014).

Family History

Any family history of gastrointestinal disorders, such as irritable bowel disease, Crohn's disease, lactose intolerance, or sickle cell disease, is important to note. Assessment of genitourinary conditions likely to be seen in pediatric patients, such as congenital anomalies involving the renal or genitourinary system, polycystic kidney disease, testicular or renal cancer, and renal infections, is important. A family history of cystic fibrosis or diabetes must also be investigated because cystic fibrosis has gastrointestinal manifestations, such as meconium ileus, steatorrhea, and poor weight gain, and poorly controlled diabetes can lead to renal failure. Wilms' tumor (nephroblastoma) may be associated with some genetic syndromes and can run in families (Paulino & Coppes, 2013).

Social History

Multiple aspects of a child's social history can affect abdominal assessment findings. For example, lead poisoning, which can be caused by living in an old dwelling with peeling, lead-based paint, causes nausea, vomiting, poor appetite, weight loss, abdominal pain, constipation, or diarrhea. The child's family situation must be assessed because exposure to parental strife and domestic violence is associated with RAP in children (Berkowitz, 2005). Poor school performance or refusal to go to school should be noted as this may be caused by bullying, another cause of RAP (Rosati et al., 2011). Drug use and alcohol use are assessed in older school-aged children and adolescents; drug and alcohol withdrawal can cause nausea, vomiting, and acute abdominal pain; acute alcohol intoxication can cause nausea and vomiting. It is important to note if the child attends day care, because these children have more episodes of gastroenteritis (Sacri et al., 2014). The type of pets in the home is another important assessment, as certain pets (e.g., reptiles, birds, cats, dogs, horses, farm animals) carry salmonellosis, a bacterial disease that causes acute diarrhea and abdominal pain (Centers for Disease Control and Prevention, 2014). Children who travel with their families to Mexico, Central America, or Asia are at risk for infection with waterborne bacteria or parasites, which is also assessed as part of the social history.

Nutritional History

The nutritional history is an essential component of the abdominal assessment. Diet plays a role in weight, hydration status, and urine and stool output, and can be related to complaints of abdominal pain. A typical nutritional history is obtained (see Chapters 6 and 10), focusing on usual appetite, intake of fiber-rich foods such as fruits and vegetables, grains, and beans; and the amount and type of fluid intake each day. Excessive amounts of cow's milk can lead to constipation and iron-deficiency anemia. Children who drink excessive amounts of juice may have delayed toilet training and often have chronic diarrhea (American Academy of Pediatrics Committee on Nutrition, 2013). Excessive caffeine intake associated with coffee, tea, or energy drinks causes diuresis, nausea, and indigestion (Seifert, Schaechter, Hershorin, & Lipshultz, 2011). A history of lactose intolerance is also assessed; this condition causes bloating; abdominal pain; loose, watery stool; excessive flatus; and fecal urgency when milk products are consumed (Guandalini, Frye, Rivera, & Borowitz, 2013).

Elimination Patterns

Assessment of normal elimination patterns is an important part of an abdominal assessment. The details of an age-specific elimination history are given in Chapter 6. For children who present with RAP, assessment of stool elimination patterns includes determining the frequency and consistency of bowel movements and the level of pain, if any, with bowel movements. A history of constipation is noted, including treatments, especially over-the-counter laxatives. The provider must be sure to determine the parent's definition of constipation; for example, it is considered normal to have a bowel movement once every 3 days, depending on the child's age and diet (Dunn, 2012). Reports of blood in the stool or rectal bleeding must also be investigated; the color and presentation of the blood can provide clues to the etiology. For example, streaks of bright red blood on the outside of a hard, formed stool suggest an anal fissure. Currant jelly stools accompanied by intense abdominal pain in an infant suggest intussusception. A history of diarrhea, including the onset, frequency of loose stools, and the parent or child's definition of diarrhea, must be noted; in some instances, soft stools that occur as a result of increased dietary fiber are mistaken for diarrhea. In infants and toddlers, a history of frequent diaper rash, which may result from frequent or chronic diarrhea, is also noted.

Any urinary frequency, dribbling, or incontinence must be assessed; these findings suggest enuresis or a urinary tract infection. Frequent urination may suggest diabetes. Inquiring about toilet training is also important; some toddlers are fearful during this process, especially with defecation, which may lead to withholding stool. Dysuria may be a sign of a urinary tract or sexually transmitted infection; an age-appropriate sexual history must also be obtained (see Chapter 20).

History of Present Illness

When an infant, child, or adolescent presents with an abdominal complaint, a careful, detailed, focused history is essential to narrow the list of differential diagnoses. Common abdominal complaints in children include pain, vomiting, diarrhea, constipation, and change in appetite. Less common complaints include rectal bleeding, dysphagia, and jaundice. Because abdominal complaints are so common in children, differential diagnoses can be formulated based on age or presenting complaint, depending on the historical data obtained. Table 19.1 categorizes these differential diagnoses according to age. Table 19.2 presents differential diagnoses according to symptom complex, and Table 19.3, according to location. Common urinary complaints in children are presented in Table 19.4.

Physical Examination

Preparation for the Examination

Examination of the abdomen in children may be difficult, especially in the toddler or young child who may be crying or ticklish. In the young child, the abdomen is typically examined after the heart and lungs in the event that the abdominal examination elicits crying. When a child is experiencing abdominal pain, the abdominal assessment is best left until the end of the physical examination. Efforts to put the child at ease include playful examination techniques, performing first on a stuffed animal or a doll, and eliciting the caregiver's support and encouragement for the examination. Inspection is most accurate when the child is relaxed and not crying, and in a supine position. For the toddler, older child, and adolescent, a comfortable position on the examination table is preferred. Infants may be laid supine in the caregiver's lap. Older children may perceive the abdominal assessment as invasive. The overweight older child or adolescent may be uncomfortable, and efforts to respect modesty are an important component of the examination. The caregiver is asked to refrain from feeding the infant immediately before the abdominal examination to avoid vomiting precipitated by palpation of the full abdomen.

Preparation for the examination includes a warm, nonthreatening environment. The child should be

TABLE 19.1	Differential Diagnosis of Abdominal Pain Based on Age
AGE GROUP	**COMMON CAUSES OF ABDOMINAL PAIN**
Birth–2 years	Gastroenteritis Trauma Intussusception Incarcerated hernia Urinary tract infection Intestinal malrotation
2–5 years	Gastroenteritis Constipation Trauma Incarcerated hernia Urinary tract infection Sickle cell disease Right lower lobe pneumonia Lead poisoning Celiac disease
5–10 years	Gastroenteritis Constipation Trauma Urinary tract infection Sickle cell disease Irritable bowel disease Appendicitis Abdominal migraine **Less common:** Henoch-Schönlein purpura Postsurgical adhesions Malrotation
10–18 years	Gastroenteritis Constipation Trauma Urinary tract infection Sickle cell disease Irritable bowel disease Abdominal migraine Appendicitis Testicular torsion Ovarian cyst Dysmenorrhea Mittelschmerz (ovulatory pain) Pelvic inflammatory disease **Less common:** Pancreatitis Cholecystitis Urolithiasis Peptic ulcer disease Postsurgical adhesions Ectopic pregnancy Peritonitis Intestinal obstruction

TABLE 19.2	Differential Diagnosis of Abdominal Pain in Children Based on History
SYMPTOM COMPLEX	**DIFFERENTIAL DIAGNOSES**
Abdominal pain with fever	Infectious gastroenteritis Appendicitis Pelvic inflammatory disease Pneumonia Urinary tract infection
Abdominal pain with change in bowel habits	**With diarrhea:** Infectious gastroenteritis Irritable bowel syndrome Inflammatory bowel disease (ulcerative colitis, Crohn's disease) Lactose intolerance Drug-induced diarrhea Intussusception Henoch-Schönlein purpura **With constipation:** Encopresis Hirschsprung disease Henoch-Schönlein purpura
Abdominal pain associated with midline or epigastric pain	Gastroesophageal reflux disease Peptic ulcer disease Chronic hepatitis B or C Pancreatitis Hydronephrosis Intestinal obstruction Trauma
Abdominal pain with vomiting	**Structural or surgical:** Intussusception Volvulus or small bowel obstruction Appendicitis Incarcerated inguinal hernia Testicular torsion Fecal impaction Peritonitis **Infectious:** Gastroenteritis Pneumonia Meningitis **Inflammatory:** Gastritis Reflux esophagitis Henoch-Schönlein purpura **Endocrine:** Diabetic ketoacidosis Thyrotoxicosis **Toxins:** Alcohol intoxication Drug withdrawal Lead poisoning Mercury poisoning **Malignancy:** Neuroblastoma (Lacayo & Davis, 2012)

TABLE 19.3	Differential Diagnosis of Abdominal Pain in Children Based on Location
URINARY COMPLAINT	**DIFFERENTIAL DIAGNOSES**
Cloudy urine	UTI, STI, urolithiasis, or glomerulonephritis
Dysuria	UTI, STI, urolithiasis, or pyelonephritis
Dysfunctional voiding (urinary frequency, urgency, hesitancy, straining)	UTI, constipation, neurogenic bladder, or vesicoureteral reflux (Cooper et al., 2013)
Enuresis	UTI, neurogenic bladder, constipation, or psychosocial causes
Foul-smelling urine	UTI or STI
Hematuria	Idiopathic hematuria, UTI, glomerulonephritis, trauma, congenital urologic anomaly, or vesicoureteral reflux (Gulati & Pena, 2013)

STI, sexually transmitted infection; UTI, urinary tract infection.

undressed to allow full evaluation of the entire abdomen. Appropriate draping to ensure modesty is essential in the older child or adolescent. Adequate lighting is essential. The order for the abdominal assessment is inspection, auscultation, percussion, and palpation. Auscultation follows inspection because palpation may alter bowel sounds.

Equipment Needed

Equipment for the abdominal examination includes a stethoscope, a metric measuring tool, and gloves if lesions are present. Lubricant may be needed if a rectal examination is required. Appropriate supplies for point-of-care testing and specimen collection may be necessary.

Vital Signs

A complete set of vital signs is obtained prior to beginning the examination. Particular attention should be focused on abnormalities that may be important for the abdominal assessment (Box 19.2).

Current Growth Parameters

Provision of adequate nutrition in infancy is most important for growth and development. Nutrition plays a greater role during infancy than growth hormone.

TABLE 19.4	Urinary Tract Problems in Children
LOCATION	**DIFFERENTIAL DIAGNOSES**
RLQ pain	Acute appendicitis Constipation Irritable bowel disease Inflammatory bowel disease Inguinal hernia Mesenteric adenitis Ischemic bowel disease Urolithiasis Mittelschmerz Pelvic inflammatory disease Ectopic pregnancy Ovarian cyst or torsion Salpingitis
RUQ pain	Hepatitis Right lower lobe pneumonia
LLQ pain	Constipation Irritable bowel disease Inflammatory bowel disease Inguinal hernia Ischemic bowel disease Urolithiasis Pyelonephritis Mittelschmerz Pelvic inflammatory disease Ectopic pregnancy Ovarian cyst or torsion Salpingitis
LUQ pain	Gastritis Splenomegaly Left lower lobe pneumonia
Epigastric pain	Abdominal aortic aneurysm Peptic ulcer disease
Diffuse abdominal pain	Sickle cell crisis Gastroenteritis Peritonitis Diabetic ketoacidosis Intestinal obstruction
Flank pain	Pyelonephritis Ovarian torsion Urolithiasis Musculoskeletal pain
Periumbilical pain	Acute appendicitis Gastroenteritis Colitis Bowel obstruction Urinary tract infection

Children with chronic gastrointestinal or renal disease may require gastric tube feedings during infancy.

Almost all gastrointestinal conditions are associated with anorexia as a result of chronic inflammation of the

---

BOX 19.2 Findings That May Indicate Abnormalities in the Abdominal Assessment

Fever
- Primary abdominal infectious or inflammatory processes
- Secondary to systemic infectious or inflammatory process

Tachycardia
- Secondary to fever, fear, anxiety, crying, or pain
- Consider blood loss in the peritoneal or retroperitoneal or pelvic compartments
- Consider infection from disruption of hollow abdominal organs
- Consider inflammation from diseased abdominal organs

Tachypnea
- Secondary to fever, fear, anxiety, crying, or pain
- Consider blood loss in the peritoneal or retroperitoneal or pelvic compartments
- Consider infection from disruption of hollow abdominal organs
- Consider inflammation from diseased abdominal organs
- Consider diaphragmatic irritation from inflamed abdominal organs
- Consider causes such as basilar pneumonia, which will result in abdominal pain; however, the primary etiology is pulmonary

Hypertension
- Primary hypertension due to renal disease
- Secondary hypertension due to fear, anxiety, or pain

Hypotension
- Most often due to shock

Hypovolemia
- Consider blood loss in abdominal compartments, dehydration from fluid losses, or inadequate fluid intake

Septic
- Consider abdominal infectious process
- Consider cardiogenic causes
- Consider anaphylactic causes

gastrointestinal tract. It is essential to assess the child's energy intake through dietary sources. The child's body generally slows or halts growth in response to decreased energy and nutrition intake. If the problem is resolved quickly, the systemic slowdown of growth can be reversed. However, with chronic disease and long-term inadequate nutritional intake, the downregulation of growth may not be easily reversed.

Many therapies (e.g., potent corticosteroids) necessary for the treatment of chronic, life-threatening diseases are unfortunately often also associated with delayed or retarded growth. An emphasis on nutrition in these chronic diseases is sometimes able to counteract this serious side effect in some children.

Growth in chronic renal failure (CRF) is adversely affected by nausea, vomiting, and acidosis, which are responsible for inadequate intake and utilization of nutrients. Children who receive transplants exhibit additional delays in growth as a result of corticosteroid therapy, which follows transplantation. The earlier the child is diagnosed with CRF, the more severe are apt to be the consequences: skeletal growth delays and delay of secondary sex characteristic development. The growth spurt normally seen in puberty is also retarded. Despite dialysis and therapies, these children rarely catch up.

Inspection

Assessment of the abdomen begins with inspection. Ideally, this is performed when the child is at rest, supine, and not crying, either on the examination table or in the caregiver's lap. The abdomen is observed from above and tangentially. The abdominal contour is assessed. Normally, the protuberant abdomen in the infant or toddler, which results from weak abdominal muscles, becomes flat when lying supine. The protuberant abdomen, which remains convex, should be evaluated for abdominal distention. The scaphoid abdomen in a newborn may indicate a diaphragmatic hernia. In the older child, a scaphoid abdomen may indicate malnourishment.

Skin turgor of the abdomen is also assessed. Normal abdominal skin turgor is elastic. If tenting is present, dehydration is a distinct possibility.

Generally, the abdomen is assessed for symmetry and any visible masses, pulsations, or protrusions. Umbilical hernias are common, especially among African American children (Figure 19.6). An umbilical hernia may indicate hypothyroidism in a Caucasian infant. Midline pulsations of the abdominal aorta may be seen in very thin children.

The newborn may also exhibit other defects in the abdominal wall, such as omphalocele, an extreme umbilical hernia in which some abdominal contents are located outside of the body; however, these are relatively uncommon. An omphalocele is always midline, in reference to the location of the umbilicus. An omphalocele may be an isolated finding or associated with other defects. The second abdominal wall defect seen in newborns is gastroschisis. This is similar to an omphalocele; however, the herniation of abdominal contents is not midline in the abdomen and is not covered with a membrane. Gastroschisis is caused by an embryonic vascular deficiency.

A separation of the rectus muscles may be easily visualized when the child is crying or struggling. A bulge between the rectus muscles indicates a diastasis recti, or herniation. This is most commonly found in African American children and usually disappears by early childhood (see Figure 19.6). Incarceration of an umbilical hernia is rare. Most umbilical hernias may be reduced by gentle pressure from the examiner's fingers. Also, the inguinal area is examined for any bulges, indicating an inguinal hernia (Figure 19.7). Any other visible abdominal masses must be noted.

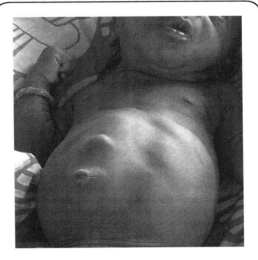

FIGURE 19.6 Umbilical hernia with diastasis recti.

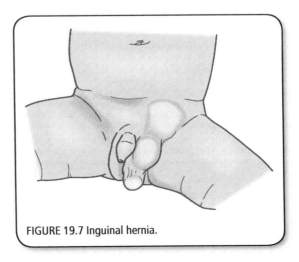

FIGURE 19.7 Inguinal hernia.

The abdomen from the area inferior to the xiphoid process to the area above the symphysis pubis is inspected for the presence of a peristaltic wave, which is not normally visible. Pyloric stenosis should be considered if a peristaltic wave is observed moving from left to right across the abdomen.

The abdominal surface is inspected for lesions, rashes, bruising, and signs of injury, particularly pattern injuries, which may indicate abuse (see Chapter 24).

The umbilicus is routinely examined in the delivery room for the presence of two arteries and one vein. If there is only a single artery, further evaluation for congenital defects is necessary. During the newborn period, the umbilical stump is inspected for signs of infection, including redness, odor, and purulent drainage on the underlying skin at the base of the stump, which indicates omphalitis. A spot of blood from the umbilical stump is not unusual. Umbilical granulomas at the base of the umbilical stump may drain serous fluid or occasionally bleed. Most umbilical cords detach spontaneously within 10 days, but it is not abnormal for it to take several weeks.

A rectal exam on children is rarely performed; however, inspection of the diaper area, including the anus, is necessary. In newborns, the anus is inspected for patency. An imperforate anus may have a blind dimple where the anus would normally be. Female newborns may have a rectovaginal fistula, which allows the passage of stool through the vagina. The provider should note when the newborn passed meconium which should occur within the first 24 to 48 hours of life.

During the health maintenance examination, the provider should inspect the child's genitalia for signs of injury, such as bruising, abrasions, or teeth marks. Incongruences between the history and physical assessment are red flags for intentional injury. The undergarments of preschool and school-aged children must also be inspected for discharge or bleeding. These findings may indicate injury or sexually transmitted infections if the child or teen has been sexually abused or assaulted.

Auscultation

Auscultation follows the inspection of the abdomen. However, providers may follow the respiratory auscultation with the abdominal auscultation, if the child is quiet and cooperative at that time.

Positioning is the same as for inspection, and eliciting cooperation from the child aids in the differentiation of audible sounds. The abdomen is auscultated for bowel and vascular sounds. The diaphragm of the stethoscope is used for bowel sounds, and the bell is used for vascular sounds.

Bowel sounds are normally audible in all children. It is customary to begin at the RLQ, in proximity to the ileocecal valve, which often allows hypoactive bowel sounds to be heard. Bowel sounds are systematically auscultated in each of the four abdominal quadrants. If a child presents with abdominal pain, the area of pain is auscultated last, as placement of the stethoscope over an area of tenderness may elicit pain, after which the child may not cooperate. Adequate time must be allowed for the assessment. Bowel sounds are not considered absent until the provider has listened for 2 full minutes without audible sounds.

In the newborn, bowel sounds are audible within the first few hours after birth. Metallic tinkling can be heard every 15 to 20 seconds. In older children, bowel sounds are audible every 10 to 20 seconds. Hypoactive bowel sounds represent decreased peristalsis or intestinal activity. This may indicate a paralytic ileus, often from diffuse peritoneal irritation. Hyperactive bowel sounds indicate rapid movement of contents through the intestine, often associated with diarrhea or an obstruction.

Auscultation of abdominal vascular sounds in the child is done with the diaphragm or the bell of the stethoscope. Vascular bruits in children are uncommon. However, the presence of a vascular bruit over the renal arteries may be associated with renovascular hypertension, and further diagnostic studies are indicated. Auscultation of the renal arteries is performed approximately 2 cm above the umbilicus and 1 to 2 cm to the right and left of this position. The exact position depends on the size of the child's abdomen.

Percussion

Percussion helps to determine the presence of air, fluid, or a mass and to delineate the size of abdominal organs or masses. Abdominal tympany is generally present in young children, as they swallow air with feedings and crying. Tympany is the most common percussion note throughout the abdomen in all children because of gas in the stomach, small bowel, and colon. A dull sound over the suprapubic area may indicate a full bladder. Percussion of the abdomen follows a systematic assessment of all four quadrants.

Percussion is also used to determine the dimensions of the liver. Providers must percuss from the right midthoracic area in the midclavicular line. Percussion proceeds downward until a change in tone is noted from resonance to dullness. This is the upper border of the liver, usually at the fifth intercostal space. This point is marked on the child's skin. Next, the provider percusses from the RLQ upward until a change in tone is noted from tympany to dullness, in the midclavicular line. This is the inferior border of the liver. This point is marked, and the distance between the two marks is measured. The resulting measurement is the liver span. The normal liver span is dependent on the child's age. At 2 months of age, the liver span ranges from 3.5 to 7.2 cm, averaging 5.5 cm. By age 5, the normal liver span ranges from 6.5 to 10 cm, with an average of 8.2 cm (Elridge & Newton, 2007).

Percussion is also used to assess for splenic enlargement in the older child and adolescent (Figure 19.8).

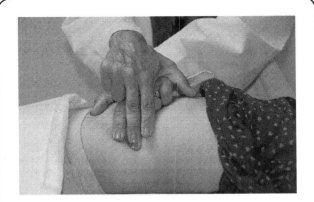

FIGURE 19.8 Percussion of the spleen.

Normally in this age group, the spleen is under the thoracic cage and lies posteriorly in the abdominal compartment. Splenic enlargement may be percussed as the spleen moves downward and toward the midline. Percussion for splenic enlargement is performed with the child lying supine. The provider must percuss from the posterior axillary line anteriorly to the anterior axillary line at the lowest intercostal space. A dull percussion note at or beyond the anterior axillary line indicates splenic enlargement.

Assessment for renal tenderness is performed with the child sitting upright. The technique used is fist percussion. This may be direct or indirect. Direct fist percussion is done with the examiner standing behind the child. The provider gently strikes the child with a closed fist in each of the costovertebral areas overlying the kidneys. Indirect fist percussion is also performed from behind the seated child; however, the examiner places an open hand against the costovertebral area and then gently strikes his or her own hand on each side. In the presence of renal inflammation, infection, or pyelonephritis, the child will have extreme pain even with gentle fist percussion. This technique is used judiciously, usually toward the end of the assessment, especially if the provider suspects pyelonephritis.

Palpation

Palpation is considered the most important technique in the assessment of the abdomen. Various methods of gaining the child's cooperation may be used. Distractions, allowing the infant to remain in the caregiver's lap, or sucking on a pacifier are a few examples. The newborn may be assessed while supporting the hips and legs in a flexed position, facilitating relaxation of the abdominal wall. The older child may be instructed to lie supine with knees flexed. Palpation is used to identify areas of tenderness or rigidity, to identify masses, and to identify enlarged organs, specifically the liver and the spleen. Two levels of palpation are used, *light* and *deep* palpation.

Light palpation is used to find areas of tenderness or rigidity; deep palpation is used to evaluate the underlying structures. Light palpation requires the pads of the fingers to be used, not the fingertips (Figure 19.9). Jabbing motions must be avoided. The fingers are lifted when moving from one area to another. Involuntary rigidity of the abdominal muscles indicates localized or diffuse peritoneal irritation. The provider must observe the child during light palpation for indications of discomfort or pain. When a tender area is identified during light palpation, that area is examined last with deep palpation.

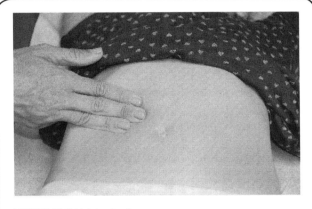

FIGURE 19.9 Light palpation.

Palpation follows a systematic sequence in all four quadrants, allowing for palpation of the area of discomfort last. The groin is palpated for inguinal lymph nodes, noting the number, size, and tenderness of the nodes. Each femoral pulse is palpated, noting the characteristics of each pulse. Deep palpation is performed with one hand for a younger child or bimanually for an older child or adolescent with the underlying abdominal structure in mind. Enlargement of the abdominal organs or masses may be identified. Gentle but firm and steady pressure is applied to the abdomen (Figure 19.10).

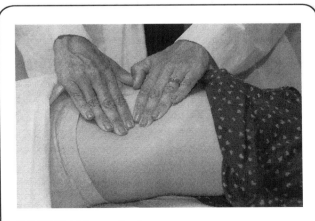

FIGURE 19.10 Deep palpation.

Infants with pyloric stenosis may have a firm, olive-like mass palpable in the RUQ. Children with constipation may have stool, resembling a firm sausage-like mass, palpable in the LLQ.

When an area of tenderness is identified in an older child, the provider must determine if *rebound tenderness*, a sign of peritoneal irritation, is present. The abdomen is palpated slowly and deeply away from the area of tenderness, quickly removing the palpating hand. If the child experiences pain in the area of inflammation when the palpating hand is removed quickly, rebound tenderness exists. Rebound tenderness may also be diffuse, as in peritonitis.

Palpation of the liver in infants and toddlers may be performed with one hand by grasping the child's RUQ and placing the thumb anteriorly and the rest of the hand posteriorly. An alternative technique for this age group is similar to that for older children and adolescents. The examiner's fingertips are placed below the costal margin in the right midclavicular line, palpating toward the liver until the firm edge of the inferior liver border is palpable upon inspiration (Figure 19.11). This may resemble a bump or a nudge by the liver as it is displaced downward during the child's inspiration. It is important to note the distance between the palpable liver border and the inferior costal margin. Infants and children may have a palpable liver border 1 to 2 cm below the costal margin. Palpation of the inferior border of the liver 3 cm or more below the costal margin indicates hepatomegaly.

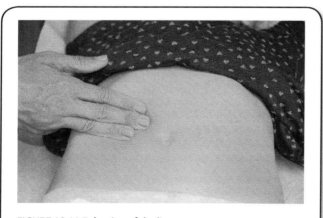

FIGURE 19.11 Palpation of the liver.

Palpation of the spleen is similar to palpation of the liver, though more difficult. A spleen must be enlarged to at least two times its normal size to be palpable. The examiner's dominant hand is placed flat beneath the left upper quadrant and below the posterior costal margin. This hand presses inward and upward while the other hand palpates anteriorly for the tip of the spleen during inspiration (Figure 19.12). Splenomegaly, an enlarged spleen, will be palpable by the examiner's hand on the anterior abdomen. Gentle palpation of the spleen is

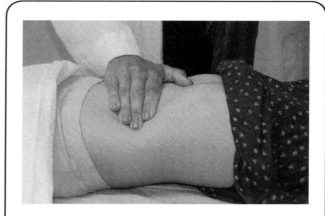

FIGURE 19.12 Palpation of the spleen.

necessary because of the high vascularity of this organ. In the presence of possible splenic trauma, caution is advised during any splenic palpation because it is possible to dislodge a clot and precipitate a hemorrhage.

Palpation of the kidneys is most easily achieved in the infant. Kidneys are palpable as round and smooth. The right kidney is more inferior to the left, and thus often easier to palpate. One hand is placed in the child's flank area, and the other is on the anterior abdomen. While pushing upward with the posterior hand, the provider palpates the corresponding upper abdominal quadrant with fingertips. In this manner, the kidney may be trapped, and thus palpable between the examiner's hands. This is repeated on the other side.

Special Techniques

The following techniques are best performed with an older and cooperative child when possible.

Iliopsoas Test

The iliopsoas test is used to identify intra-abdominal inflammation. This is most commonly used in the evaluation of possible appendicitis. The child is positioned on the unaffected side and is asked to extend the other leg at the hip, against resistance from the examiner. Irritation of the psoas muscle from abdominal inflammation produces pain with this maneuver. Pain of the right psoas muscle is a sign often seen with appendicitis.

Obturator Test

The obturator test is similar to the iliopsoas test to identify intra-abdominal inflammation. The child is positioned supine while the examiner flexes each leg at the hip and rotates the hip internally and externally. Inflammation adjacent to the obturator muscle elicits pain during this maneuver. Appendicitis often presents with a positive right obturator test.

Rectal Exam

A rectal examination in children is not often required, but if it is necessary to perform this exam, it is best to reserve this invasive procedure until the end of the physical examination. Indications for a rectal exam include evaluation of sphincter tone, constipation, rectal bleeding, or suspicion of sexual abuse. An informed discussion with the parent or older child helps to gain their assent. Positioning for an infant is supine with both hips and legs flexed. The older child or adolescent is positioned on the left side with the right hip and leg flexed or both hips and legs flexed. Even young children should be positioned and draped to maintain modesty. A lubricated finger, usually the examiner's smallest finger, is gently inserted at the rectal verge. As the sphincter relaxes, the finger is moved toward the child's umbilicus. Sphincter tone, constrictions, or masses are assessed. Stool may be present. It should be noted if the stool is soft or hard. Often in the constipated child, the rectal exam facilitates passage of stool. Digital pressure toward the child's RLQ that elicits pain may be a sign of appendicitis. Any stool obtained must be tested for the presence of occult blood.

Pelvic Exam

A pelvic examination is often helpful to evaluate the older child or adolescent presenting with abdominal complaints (see Chapter 20 for a discussion of pelvic examination in adolescents).

COMMON DIAGNOSTIC STUDIES

Various laboratory and imaging studies may be used to evaluate abdominal conditions. These diagnostic studies and their indications are summarized in Tables 19.5 and 19.6.

TABLE 19.5	**Laboratory Studies Used to Evaluate Abdominal Conditions**		
DIAGNOSTIC STUDY	**NORMAL VALUES**	**INDICATION**	**COMMENTS**
Albumin	1–16 years: 3.6–5.2 g/dL Older than or equal to 16 years: 3.9–5.1 g/dL	Useful in diagnosing liver disease	Albumin is the main protein in human blood; made by liver. Liver disease results in decreased albumin production.
Alkaline phosphatase (ALP)	Infant: 150–420 U/L Child 2–10 years: 100–320 U/L Adolescent female: 100–320 U/L Adolescent male: 100–390 U/L	Useful in diagnosing liver disease	ALP is an enzyme in cells that line biliary ducts of liver; it is also found in other organs, including bone, placenta, and intestine. When ALP is elevated, gamma-glutamyl transferase (GGT) can be ordered to confirm that elevated ALP is derived from liver or biliary tract.
Amylase	0–3 months: 0–30 U/L 3–6 months: 0–50 U/L 6–12 months: 0–80 U/L Older than 1 year: 30–100 U/L	Indicative of pancreatic injury or disease when lipase is also elevated	Amylase is produced mainly by pancreas and salivary glands, and is metabolized in part by kidneys and liver.
Bilirubin	**Total bilirubin:** Term newborn: < 2 mg/dL 0–1 days: < 8 mg/dL, 1–2 days: < 11.5 mg/dL 3–5 days: < 12 mg/dL Older infant: < 1.2 mg/dL	Useful in diagnosing liver disease	Bilirubin is produced from breakdown of hemoglobin. Liver clears bilirubin from the body by excreting it through bile into intestine. Elevated bilirubin levels can indicate liver disorders or blockage of bile ducts. *Total bilirubin* is a measurement of all bilirubin in the blood. *Direct bilirubin* is a measurement of a form of bilirubin made in liver.

(continued)

TABLE 19.5	Laboratory Studies Used to Evaluate Abdominal Conditions (*continued*)		
DIAGNOSTIC STUDY	**NORMAL VALUES**	**INDICATION**	**COMMENTS**
Blood urea nitrogen (BUN)	Newborn: 2–19 mg/dL Infant/Child: 5–18 mg/dL	Used to evaluate kidney function and monitor kidney disease	BUN concentrations may be elevated when there is excessive protein catabolism, significantly increased protein in diet, or gastrointestinal bleeding.
Complete blood count (CBC)	**Hematocrit:** Infant: • 1–6 months: 36%–44% • 6–24 months: 33%–36% Child: • 2–6 years: 34%–37% • 6–12 years: 35%–40% Male adolescent: 36%–43% Female adolescent: 37%–41% **Hemoglobin:** Infant: • 1–2 months: 9.4–13.9 g/dL • 6–24 months: 10.5–12 g/dL Child 6–12 years: 11.5–13.5 g/dL Male adolescent: 13–14.5 g/dL Female adolescent: 12–14 g/dL **Platelet count:** Newborn: 84,000–478,000 μL Others: 150,000–400,000 μL **RBCs:** 6 months–2 years: 3.7–5.3 million/mm^3 2–6 years: 3.9–5.3 million/mm^3 6–12 years: 4–5.2 million/mm^3 Adolescent: 4.1–5.3 million/mm^3	Helps to diagnose infections and anemia or blood loss	CBC is most often correlated with differential of white blood cells.
Creatinine (serum)	Newborn: 0.3–1.0 mg/dL Infant: 0.2–0.4 mg/dL Child: 0.3–0.7 mg/dL Adolescent: 0.5–1 mg/dL	Used to detect diseases or conditions that affect kidney function, including glomerulonephritis, pyelonephritis, acute tubular necrosis, urinary tract obstruction, or conditions that decrease blood flow to the kidney (shock, dehydration)	A combination of blood and urine creatinine levels may be used to calculate creatinine clearance to determine how effectively kidneys are filtering small molecules like creatinine. Creatinine can also increase temporarily as a result of muscle injury.

TABLE 19.5	Laboratory Studies Used to Evaluate Abdominal Conditions (*continued*)		
DIAGNOSTIC STUDY	**NORMAL VALUES**	**INDICATION**	**COMMENTS**
Erythrocyte sedimentation rate (ESR)	Child: 0–10 mm/hr	Assists with diagnosis of inflammatory conditions (e.g., mesenteric adenitis)	ESR is a nonspecific test for conditions associated with acute and chronic inflammation, including infections, cancers, and autoimmune diseases.
Electrolytes, serum	**Sodium:** Younger than 1 year: 130–145 mEq/L Older than 1 year: 135–147 mEq/L **Potassium:** Newborn: 3.7–5.9 mEq/L Infant: 4.1–5.3 mEq/L Child: 3.4–4.7 mEq/L Adolescent: 3.5–5.1 mEq/L **Chloride:** 0–6 months: 97–108 mEq/L 6–12 months: 97–106 mEq/L Child/Adolescent: 97–107 mEq/L	Ions are measured to assess renal, endocrine, and acid–base function	Potassium is the electrolyte used as a hallmark of renal failure. Frequent causes of hypokalemia include alkalosis, and diarrhea and vomiting. Hyponatremia may result from diarrhea, vomiting, and cystic fibrosis. Hypernatremia may also be seen with dehydration.
GGT	0–1 months: 13–147 U/L 1–2 months: 12–123 U/L 2–4 months: 8–90 U/L 4 months–10 years: 5–32 U/L 10–15 years: 5–24 U/L Male adolescent: 11–49 U/L Female adolescent: 7–32 U/L	Useful in diagnosing liver disease	GGT is an enzyme that is useful clinically when compared with ALP. By comparing the two, it can be determined if patient has bone or liver disease.
Hemoccult	Negative	Used to determine the presence of occult blood in stool	
Hepatitis testing	HAV IgM anti-HAV HBsAg IgM anti-HBc anti-HCV (see comments)	Used to diagnosis acute or chronic hepatitis	**Hepatitis A (HAV) infection:** A positive antigen test (HAV test) and positive antibody test (IgM anti-HAV antibody test) indicate acute HAV infection. Previous HAV infections produce a negative antigen test, but antibody test will be positive. **Hepatitis B (HBV) infection:** A positive antigen test (HBsAg or HBV surface antigen test) and positive antibody test (IgM anti-HBc or IgM HBV core antibody test) indicate acute HBV infection. In chronic hepatitis (6 months or more of infection), antigen test will be positive, but antibody test will be negative. If child

(*continued*)

TABLE 19.5	Laboratory Studies Used to Evaluate Abdominal Conditions (*continued*)		
DIAGNOSTIC STUDY	**NORMAL VALUES**	**INDICATION**	**COMMENTS**
			has had a full series of HB immunizations, antigen test will be negative, and antibody test will be positive. **Hepatitis C (HCV) infection:** A positive antibody test (anti-HCV or antibody to HCV test) indicates current acute HCV infection. To determine if infection is chronic, tests are done to measure amounts of specific HCV viral proteins (antigens) present in blood. If these tests remain positive for several months, disease is said to be chronic. If newborn is tested for antibodies to HCV, test may return a positive result because of detection of maternal anti-HCV antibodies present in infant.
Lipase	1–6 months: 4–29 U/L 6–12 months: 4–23 U/L Older than 1 year: 3–32 U/L	Useful in diagnosing pancreatitis	Lipase is more specific than serum amylase for pancreatitis; it is also used in diagnosis of peritonitis, strangulated or infarcted bowel, and pancreatic cyst.
Liver function tests: (Alanine aminotransferase [ALT]) (Aspartate aminotransferase [AST])	**ALT:** Infant younger than 12 months: 13–45 U/L 1–3 years: 5–45 U/L 4–6 years: 10–25 U/L 7–9 years: 10–35 U/L 10–11 years: • Female : 10–30 U/L • Male: 10–35 U/L 14–15 years: • Female : 5–30 U/L • Male: 10–45 U/L Older than 16 years: • Female : 5–35 U/L • Male: 10–40 U/L **AST:** 0–10 days: 47–150 U/L 10 days–24 months: 9–80 U/L		**ALT (SGPT):** ALT is primarily found in liver, skeletal muscle and myocardium; it is a more specific test for detecting liver abnormalities. **AST (SGOT):** AST is not only found in liver. It is also normally found in heart, skeletal muscle, brain, erythrocytes and kidney tissue. Injury to any of these tissues can cause an elevated blood level.

TABLE 19.5	Laboratory Studies Used to Evaluate Abdominal Conditions (*continued*)		
DIAGNOSTIC STUDY	**NORMAL VALUES**	**INDICATION**	**COMMENTS**
	Older than 24 months: • Female: 13–35 U/L • Male: 15–40 U/L		
Prothrombin time (PT)	11–15 seconds	Useful in diagnosing liver disease	PT is used to evaluate blood clotting. Prothrombin is a clotting factor from the liver. If liver is injured or damaged, clotting factors are not produced normally, and PT is elevated.
Sweat chloride test	Less than 60 mEq/L	Used to diagnose cystic fibrosis	Cystic fibrosis includes gastrointestinal manifestations such as steatorrhea and poor growth.
Urine human chorionic gonadotropin (HCG)	Negative	Used to determine pregnancy	HCG is found in blood and urine during pregnancy.
Urinalysis	**Specific gravity:** 1.003–1.035 **pH:** Infant younger than or equal to 12 months: 5–7 Older than 1 year: 4.8–7.8 **Protein:** negative **Blood:** negative **Glucose:** negative **Ketones:** negative **Leukocyte esterase:** negative **Nitrites:** negative	Most commonly used to identify urinary tract infection; also used to detect kidney disease, hyperglycosuria, and evaluate dehydration	Microscopic analysis provides specific number of WBCs and RBCs seen. Microscopic evaluation may also identify abnormal findings, such as casts, trichomonads, yeast, or sperm.
Urine culture and sensitivity	No growth of pathogen	To identify specific bacteria and susceptible antibiotics	It is often difficult for young children to obtain a clean-catch, midstream specimen.
24-hour urine volume	Infant: 350–550 mL/d Child: 500–1000 mL/d Adolescent: 700–1400 mL/d	Useful in diagnosing renal disease	Urine must be kept refrigerated.
WBC differential	**Neutrophils:** Bands: 3%–5% Segments: 54%–62% **Eosinophils:** 2%–4% **Basophils:** 0%–75% **Monocytes:** 4%–9% **Lymphocytes:** 25%–61%; peaks at age 1 year	Assists in differentiating if condition may be viral or bacterial; may be helpful in identification of allergic conditions.	Leukocytosis with a shift to the left is seen with acute bacterial infections.

RBCs, red blood cells; SGOT, serum glutamic oxaloacetic transaminase; SGPT, serum glutamic pyruvic transaminase; WBCs, white blood cells.
Sources: Arcara (2012); Ashan and Noether (2012).

TABLE 19.6	Imaging Studies Used To Evaluate Abdominal Conditions		
DIAGNOSTIC TEST	**NORMAL FINDINGS**	**INDICATION**	**COMMENTS**
Computed tomography scan	Negative for abnormalities	Evaluates abdominal organs and can localize the presence of intra- or retroperitoneal air or fluid	Child must remain immobilized during imaging. Oral, intravenous, or rectal contrast may be used. Consult with radiologist for specific recommendations.
Ultrasonography	Negative for abnormalities	Most commonly used to evaluate liver and gallbladder; also used to evaluate pelvic organs in female children. May include transvaginal ultrasound in older adolescent	It is noninvasive, so child requires no sedation.

DOCUMENTATION OF FINDINGS

Sample Write-Up: Well Child

Subjective Data

Healthy 8-year-old female, PMH noncontributory, no history of injuries, FH noncontributory; immunizations up to date; no medications; no allergies.

Objective Data

Abdomen: abdomen symmetrical, nondistended; no visible scars, abnormal lesions, or skin discoloration; no visible peristalsis; bowel sounds normoactive in four quadrants; abdomen tympanic to percussion; liver span 5 cm in midclavicular line; abdomen soft, nontender to palpation; liver edge smooth, palpable at 1 cm below right costal margin; spleen not palpable; no masses or abnormal pulsations; kidneys not palpable; no CVA tenderness; no inguinal lymphadenopathy; bilateral femoral pulses 2+
Assessment: healthy school-aged child

Sample Write-Up: Child With Abdominal Pain

Subjective Data

Ten-year-old female accompanied by parents complaining of abdominal pain for 2 days. Denies abdominal injury; pain began in periumbilical area; has now localized to RLQ. She describes pain as "bad hurt" and rates pain as 10 on FACES Pain Scale. She has decreased appetite and nausea but no vomiting. Fever (T_{max} 100.8°F) noted today; loose stool last night; no blood in stool and light brown in color.

PMH: noncontributory; previously healthy
PSH: none
Allergies: none known
Current medications: ibuprofen, last dose 1 hour ago
Immunizations: up to date
ROS:
GU: denies dysuria, frequency, or change in color of urine
Other ROS: noncontributory

Objective Data

T: 101.8°F (38.8°C); **P:** 128 beats per minute; **RR:** 26 breaths per minute; **oxygen saturation on room air:** 98%; **weight:** 38 kg
General: appears frightened, lying on her side; behavior appropriate for age and condition
Skin: color pale; no rashes or lesions; warm and dry; capillary refill < 2 seconds; turgor elastic
Abdomen: symmetrical, nondistended; no visible scars, abnormal lesions, or skin discoloration; no visible peristalsis; bowel sounds hyperactive in all quadrants; abdomen tympanic to percussion, although percussion reproduces pain in RLQ; liver span 5.4 cm in right midclavicular line; tender to palpation RLQ and LLQ; involuntary guarding in RLQ; localized tenderness at McBurney's point; minimal rebound tenderness; obturator and psoas sign positive; rovsing's sign positive; no masses; kidneys nontender to palpation; no inguinal lymphadenopathy; femoral pulses 2+ bilaterally
Assessment: acute abdominal pain, R/O acute appendicitis

Sample Write-Up: Child With Dysuria

Subjective Data

A 22-month-old toddler accompanied by mother. The mother states that the child has been crying and not wanting to try the potty chair. The child cries that it hurts to go potty. Mother states this is second day of crying associated with urination; severity increasing. Mother states child is urinating frequently as she can tell by her crying. Denies hematuria or malodorous urine. Takes bubble bath each night, appearing more comfortable during the bath. Child not cooperative with pain rating at this time.

PMH: previously healthy, normal spontaneous vaginal delivery at 39 weeks, denies history of urinary tract infections or genitourinary concerns previously; no additional PMH

PSH: none

Allergies: none known

Current medications: none

Immunizations: up to date

ROS:

General: denies fever, chills, or rash; denies recent abdominal or pelvic injury

GI: denies vomiting or diarrhea; denies constipation; last bowel movement this morning and seemed "normal" to mother; somewhat decreased appetite noted by mother

Other ROS: noncontributory

Objective Data

T: 100.8°F (38.2°C); **P:** 118 beats per minute; **RR:** 26 breaths per minute; **oxygen saturation on room air:** 98%; **weight:** 13 kg

General: alert, behavior appropriate for age, reluctant to leave mother's arm

Skin: color pink; no rashes or lesions; warm and dry, capillary refill 1 second; turgor elastic

Abdomen: symmetrical, nondistended; no visible scars, abnormal lesions, or skin discoloration; no visible peristalsis; bowel sounds normoactive in four quadrants; abdomen tympanic to percussion; liver span 3.5 cm in midclavicular line; abdomen soft with suprapubic tenderness; child crying; however, no involuntary guarding noted; no rebound tenderness; liver edge smooth, palpable at 2 cm below right costal margin; spleen not palpable; no masses or abnormal pulsations; kidneys not palpable; no inguinal lymphadenopathy, bilateral femoral pulses, 2+

Urinalysis: specific gravity = 1.016; pH = 6.0; protein = negative; blood = trace; glucose = negative; ketones = negative; nitrites = small; leukocyte esterase = large; microscopy: 0 to 5 RBCs, 25 to 50 WBCs

Assessment: acute cystitis (UTI)

Notable Clinical Findings

- History of prematurity or prolonged ventilation in neonatal period
- Immunization delay
- History or diagnosis of lead poisoning
- History of gastrointestinal or genitourinary condition
- History of urinary tract infections
- History of recurrent abdominal pain
- Vital signs outside the normal range
- Hypertension
- Complaints of current abdominal pain
- Overweight or obesity
- Underweight
- Eating disorders
- Altered nutrition patterns for age
  - Dysuria
  - Urinary frequency
  - Foul-smelling or cloudy urine
  - Enuresis
  - Hematuria
- Altered elimination patterns for age
  - Diarrhea (chronic or acute)
  - Constipation
- Abdominal distention
- Umbilical hernia
- Inguinal hernia
- Decreased bowel sounds
- Hepatosplenomegaly
- Palpable abdominal mass
- Positive iliopsoas or obturator test
- Blood in stool

References

American Academy of Pediatrics Committee on Nutrition. (2013). The use and misuse of fruit juice in pediatrics. Statement of reaffirmation. *Pediatrics*, 132(3), e1715–e1716; 1210–1213.

Arcara, K. M. (2012). Blood chemistries and body fluids. In M. M. Tschudy, & K. M. Arcara (Eds.), *The Harriet Lane handbook* (pp. 639–650). Philadelphia, PA: Elsevier.

Ashan, S., & Noether, J. (2012). Hematology. In M. M. Tschudy, & K. M. Arcara (Eds.), *The Harriet Lane handbook* (pp. 322–353). Philadelphia, PA: Elsevier.

Ball, J. W., Bindler, R. C., & Cowen, K. J. (Eds.). (2013a). Alterations in gastrointestinal function. In *Child health nursing: Partnering with children & families* (3rd ed., pp. 754–802). Upper Saddle River, NJ: Pearson Education.

Ball, J. W., Bindler, R. C., & Cowen, K. J. (Eds.). (2013b). Alterations in genitourinary function. In *Child health nursing: Partnering with children & families* (3rd ed., pp. 804–846). Upper Saddle River, NJ: Pearson Education.

Berkowitz, C. (2005). Recognizing and responding to domestic violence. *Pediatric Annals, 34*(5), 395–401.

Carter, B. S., & Boyd, R. L. (2012). *Polyhydramnios and oligohydramnios*. Retrieved from http://reference.medscape.com/article/975821-overview

Centers for Disease Control and Prevention. (2014). *Salmonella*. Retrieved from http://www.cdc.gov/salmonella

Cooper, C. S., Arlen, A. M., Cilento, B. G., Hellerstein, S., Koo, H. P., Nepple, K. G., & Windle, M. L. (2013). *Voiding dysfunction*. Retrieved from http://emedicine.medscape.com/article/1016198-overview

Dunn, A. M. (2012). Elimination patterns. In C. E. Burns, A. M. Dunn, M. A. Brady, N. B. Starr, & C. G. Blosser (Eds.), *Pediatric primary care* (5th ed., pp. 202–217). St. Louis, MO: Saunders.

Elridge, D. L., & Newton, D. A. (2007). Organomegaly. In R. M. Perkin, J. D. Swift, D. A. Newton, & N. G. Anas (Eds.), *Pediatric hospital medicine* (2nd ed., pp. 114–116). Philadelphia, PA: Wolters Kluwer/Lippincott Williams & Wilkins.

Erickson, K. M., & Golladay, E. S. (2014). *Abdominal hernias*. Retrieved from http://emedicine.medscape.com/article/189563-overview

Guandalini, S., Frye, R. E., Rivera, D. M., & Borowitz, S. M. (2013). *Pediatric lactose intolerance*. Retrieved from http://emedicine.medscape.com/article/930971-overview

Gulati, S., & Pena, D. (2013). *Hematuria*. Retrieved from http://emedicine.medscape.com/article/981898-overview

Guthrie, E. W. (2005). Pediatric dosing considerations. *U.S. Pharmacist*, *30*(12), 5–10.

Kitchens, D. M., Herndon, A., & Joseph, D. B. (2007). Pediatric urodynamics: Basic concepts for the neurosurgeon. *Neurosurgical Focus*, *23*(2), E8.

Lacayo, N. L., & Davis, K. L. (2012). *Pediatric neuroblastoma*. Retrieved from http://emedicine.medscape.com/article/988284-overview

Macfarlane, F. (2006). *Pediatric anatomy, physiology and the basics of pediatric anesthesia*. Retrieved from http://www.frca.co.uk/article.aspx?articleid=100544

Montagnino, B., & Ring, P. A. (2011). The child with renal dysfunction. In M. J. Hockenberry & D. Wilson (Eds.), *Wong's nursing care of infants and children* (9th ed., pp. 1135–1180). St. Louis, MO: Elsevier Mosby.

Paulino, A. C., & Coppes, M. J. (2013). *Wilms' tumor*. Reprinted from http://emedicine.medscape.com/article/989398-overview

Potts, N. (2012). Gastrointestinal alterations. In N. L. Potts, & B. L. Mandleco (Eds.), *Pediatric nursing: Caring for children and their families* (3rd ed., pp. 739–787). Stamford, CT: Cengage Learning.

Rosati, P., Jenkner, A., DeVito, R., Boldrini, R., Chiodi, P., Celesti, L., & Giampolo, R. (2011). "Tell me about your pain": Abdominal pain and a history of bullying. *BMJ Case Reports*, March 24. pii: bcr1220103611. doi:10.1136/bcr.12.2010.3611.

Roy, P. K., Komanapalli, S. D., Shojamanesh, H., Bashir, S., & Choudhary, A. (2013). *Lactose intolerance*. Retrieved from http://emedicine.medscape.com/article/187249-overview

Sacri, A. S., De Serres, G., Quach, C., Boulianne, N., Valiquette, L., & Skowronski, D. M. (2014). Transmission of acute gastroenteritis and respiratory illness from children to parents. *Pediatric Infectious Disease Journal*, *33*(6), 573–588.

Seifert, S. M., Schaechter, J. L., Hershorin, E. R., & Lipshultz, S. E. (2011). Health effects of energy drinks on children, adolescents, and young adults. *Pediatrics*, *127*(3), 511–528.

Sicherer, S. H. (2014). *Food allergies*. Retrieved from http://emedicine.medscape.com/article/135959-overview

Sicherer, S. H., & Sampson, H. A. (2010). Food allergy. *Journal of Allergy and Clinical Immunology*, *125*(2, suppl 2):S116–S125.

Springer, S. C., & Annibale, D. J. (2014). *Necrotizing enterocolitis*. Retrieved from http://emedicine.medscape.com/article/977956-overview

Swamy Chidananda, M. N., & Mallikarjun, D. (2004). Applied aspects of anatomy and physiology of relevance to pediatric anesthesia. *Indian Journal of Anesthesia*, *48*(5), 333–339.

Tsai, A. C., Manchester, D. K., & Elias, E. R. (2012). Genetics & dysmorphology. In W. W. Hay, M. J. Levin, R. R. Deterding, M. J. Abzug, & J. M. Sondheimer (Eds.), *Current pediatric diagnosis & treatment* (21st ed., pp. 1088–1122). New York, NY: McGraw-Hill.

Yager, J., Scher, L. M., Hilty, D. M., & Osterhout, C. I. (2014). *Bulimia nervosa*. Retrieved from http://emedicine.medscape.com/article/286485-overview

Assessment of the Reproductive and Genitourinary Systems

Assessment of the reproductive system can provoke a great deal of anxiety for the child or adolescent, the parent, and the provider. Because of discomfort or embarrassment on the part of the child, parent, or provider, it is tempting to omit this portion of the assessment. However, this is an essential portion of the history and physical examination during health maintenance visits and when formulating differential diagnoses during focused visits. This can lead to critical assessments and diagnoses that can identify infections or surgical emergencies, preserve a child's future fertility, or diagnose sexual abuse.

ANATOMY AND PHYSIOLOGY

Female Genitalia

The external structures of the female genitalia include the *mons pubis*, *labia majora*, *labia minora*, *urethral* and *vaginal orifices*, and *clitoris*. The internal structures include the *ovaries*, *fallopian tubes*, *uterus*, *cervix*, and *vagina*. The female urinary tract is separate and distinct from the female reproductive tract.

External Genitalia

The female external genitalia are collectively known as the *vulva*. The most visible part is the mons pubis, an area of adipose tissue covered with skin. After a girl reaches puberty, the mons pubis is covered with coarse, curly *pubic hair*. The mons pubis also acts as a protective covering for the pubic bone. The labia majora are two small folds of fatty tissue located on either side of the vaginal opening. These folds of tissue are joined at the mons pubis, just above the *perineum*. Once a girl has reached puberty, the labia majora also become hair-covered. The labia minora are two hairless folds of tissue that lie between the labia majora and the urethral

and vaginal orifices. The labia minora are smaller than the labia majora and are joined anteriorly at the edge of the clitoris, forming a hood, and posteriorly, just below the vaginal opening. This latter area is known as the *fourchette*.

Located just below the mons pubis is the clitoris, a small structure composed of erectile tissue. Like the penis, the clitoris is very vascular and sensitive to touch and becomes engorged with blood and enlarged during sexual arousal.

The area covered by the labia minora is known as the *vestibule*. The vestibule contains the *urethral meatus* and vaginal orifice. The urethral meatus is the urinary tract's external opening and leads into the urethra and urinary bladder. This structure is located approximately 2.5 cm posterior to the clitoris and is a small, irregularly oval-shaped structure. The *Skene's glands*, located on either side of the urethral meatus, produce mucus that is secreted through ducts that are not visible to inspection but can easily become infected. This mucus protects the surrounding tissue against irritation from urine.

The vaginal orifice, or *introitus*, is the entrance to the vagina, located posterior to the urethral meatus. The shape of the vaginal orifice depends on the condition of the *hymen*. The hymen is a fold of mucous membrane that partially covers the vaginal orifice. The size and shape of the hymen varies greatly among girls and women, depending on their age, whether they are pre- or postpubertal, or whether they have given birth. It is important for the pediatric health care provider to be familiar with common, normal hymenal configurations to be able to identify signs of trauma or evidence of sexually transmitted infections (STIs). Examples of normal hymenal configurations include annular, crescentic, fimbriated, cribriform, or septate, the most common being annular and crescentic (Hornor, 2010).

On either side of the vaginal orifice are the *Bartholin's glands*, which produce a clear lubricating mucus during intercourse. This mucus is secreted through Bartholin's glands ducts, located on either side of the vaginal orifice. Like the Skene's glands, the Bartholin's glands can become blocked, leading to infection. The external female genitalia are illustrated in Figure 20.1.

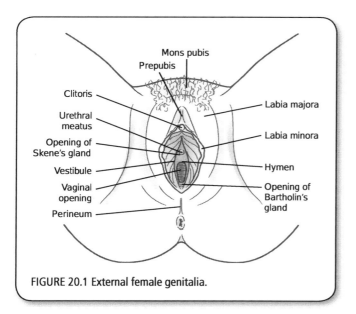

FIGURE 20.1 External female genitalia.

Internal Genitalia

The ovaries are two almond-shaped organs located on either side of the uterus. Each ovary is held in place by ligaments that connect them to the abdominal and pelvic walls. Beginning at puberty, the ovaries develop ova (eggs), normally releasing one mature ovum a month. The ovaries also produce the female hormones, estrogen and progesterone, which perform many functions during menstruation and reproduction.

The fallopian tubes are two long, muscular tubes that have a funnel-shaped opening at one end that extends close to or over the ovaries; this end is termed the *fimbriated* end. Projections at the fimbriated end pull the ovum into the fallopian tube after it is released from the ovary. The remainder of the tube curves around the top of the ovary and attaches to the uterus. Fertilization of the egg usually occurs inside the fallopian tube. If fertilization does not occur, menstruation occurs.

The uterus is located deep within the pelvis between the urinary bladder and rectum. Shaped like an inverted pear, the uterus is a hollow, muscular organ, the size of a closed fist. When a girl or woman is standing, the top of the uterus points forward and slightly upward. A group of eight ligaments support the uterus. The uterus is lined with a soft, spongy layer, known as the *endometrium*. Under the influence of estrogen and progesterone, this lining becomes thick and vascular each month during the menstrual cycle, in preparation to nourish a fertilized ovum. If the ovum is not fertilized, the lining sheds, resulting in menstruation.

The uterus is divided into three parts: the *fundus*, the *corpus*, and the *cervix*. The fundus is the top section of the uterus into which the fallopian tubes connect. The corpus, or the body of the uterus, is the largest section and houses the fertilized ovum, which becomes the embryo and then the fetus. The cervix lies at the end of the uterus and connects to the vagina. It is a long, narrow canal with openings at either end. The opening that extends into the corpus is the *internal os*; the external os opens into the *vagina*. In the nulliparous female, the cervix's opening, the external os, appears as a doughnut-shaped area with a small, circular hole at the center.

The vagina is a tubular structure comprising three layers: a muscular layer, a loose connective tissue layer, and a layer of mucous membrane. In the prepubertal girl, the vagina is rigid, thin-walled, and nonelastic. After puberty, the vagina becomes very elastic to accommodate a newborn's head. The lower one third of the vagina is very sensitive to touch; the upper two thirds have little sensation. The internal female genitalia are illustrated in Figure 20.2.

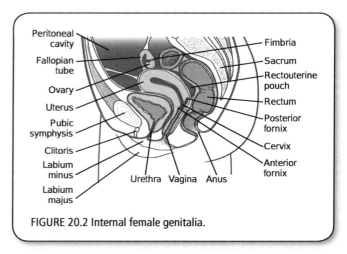

FIGURE 20.2 Internal female genitalia.

Male Genitalia

The male genital structures consist of the *penis, scrotum, testis, epididymis, vas deferens, seminal vesicles,* and *prostate gland* (Figure 20.3). The *urethra* is located within the male reproductive tract.

Penis

The penis consists of the shaft, *glans, corona,* and *prepuce.* The shaft of the penis is composed of three columns of erectile tissue: the *corpora cavernosa* and the *corpus spongiosum.* The corpus spongiosum expands into an area of erectile tissue called the glans. The *corona* is the prominence formed where the glans joins the shaft. The urethra is contained within the corpus spongiosum, with the *external meatus* extending to the tip, forming an opening at the glans. Over the glans, the skinfolds form a flap; this is the *foreskin* or prepuce. The foreskin is surgically removed during circumcision.

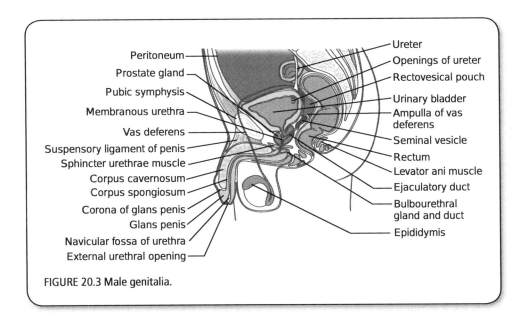

Peritoneum
Prostate gland
Pubic symphysis
Membranous urethra
Vas deferens
Suspensory ligament of penis
Sphincter urethrae muscle
Corpus cavernosum
Corpus spongiosum
Corona of glans penis
Glans penis
Navicular fossa of urethra
External urethral opening

Ureter
Openings of ureter
Rectovesical pouch
Urinary bladder
Ampulla of vas deferens
Seminal vesicle
Rectum
Levator ani muscle
Ejaculatory duct
Bulbourethral gland and duct
Epididymis

FIGURE 20.3 Male genitalia.

Scrotum and Testicles

The scrotum is a loose cutaneous pouch that hangs beneath the base of the penis and contains the testicles (see Figure 20.3). The main function of the scrotum is temperature regulation of the testicles; the testicles must be 2° to 3°C cooler than the peritoneal cavity for spermatogenesis to take place. The scrotal wall is formed by an outer layer of thin skinfolds, or *rugae*, and an underlying *cremaster muscle* layer. The cremaster muscle allows contraction of the scrotum in response to ambient temperature. When the ambient temperature is cold, the muscle contracts, bringing the testes closer to the body to absorb heat, thereby preserving sperm viability. The resultant skin then appears wrinkled with furrows and ridges. When the ambient temperature is warm, the scrotal muscles relax, the scrotum lowers, and the skin appears smooth.

Inside the scrotum, a wall separates the sac into two halves; each half contains a *testicle*, its epididymis, and part of the *spermatic cord* (see Figure 20.3). The testicles, which produce sperm and testosterone, are ovoid and held by the spermatic cord. The left testicle hangs lower than the right because the left spermatic cord is longer. The epididymis is a crescent-shaped structure that is curved over the top of the testicle. Sperm matures and is stored in the lower portion, or tail of the epididymis, near the vas deferens. The *vas deferens* begins at the tail of the epididymis and joins other structures (i.e., arteries, veins, lymphatics, nerves, and cremaster muscle) to form the spermatic cord. The spermatic cord moves upward through the inguinal canal into the abdomen behind the bladder where it merges with the duct of the seminal vesicle. The seminal vesicles are paired glands that lie behind the urinary bladder and in front of the rectum. Secretions produced by the seminal vesicles play a role in producing seminal fluid.

These secretions flow through the *ejaculatory duct*, which empties into the urethra.

The walnut-shaped prostate gland lies below and behind the urinary bladder, surrounding the urethra. The prostate gland secretes a thin, white, milky, alkaline ejaculation fluid that helps with sperm viability.

Inguinal Area

The *inguinal area*, or *groin*, is the area in which the lower abdominal wall and the thigh meet (Figure 20.4). The *inguinal canal* lies between two layers of abdominal muscle and superior to the inguinal ligament. The femoral canal lies inferior to the inguinal ligament. Incomplete closure of the process vaginalis, a dimple-like structure in the peritoneum, allows abdominal contents to move through the inguinal canal or scrotum, resulting in an inguinal hernia.

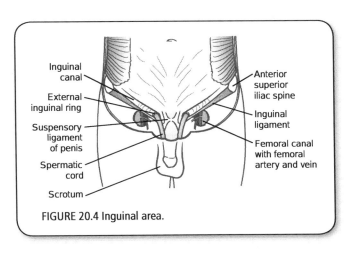

Inguinal canal
External inguinal ring
Suspensory ligament of penis
Spermatic cord
Scrotum

Anterior superior iliac spine
Inguinal ligament
Femoral canal with femoral artery and vein

FIGURE 20.4 Inguinal area.

The Breast

The breasts are specialized mammary glands that are located on either side of the anterior chest between the second and sixth ribs. They are separated from underlying muscles and ribs by connective tissue. The *nipple* is located at the center of the breast. It is composed of round, protuberant tissue with tiny milk duct openings. The *areola* is a circular area of tissue surrounding the nipple. Small sebaceous glands, called *Montgomery's glands*, give the areola a bumpy appearance. These glands secrete a fatty substance that lubricates and protects the nipple during breastfeeding. The nipple and areola are more darkly pigmented than the rest of the breast, with the color varying from pink to brown, according to skin color. The external landmarks of the female breast are illustrated in Figure 20.5.

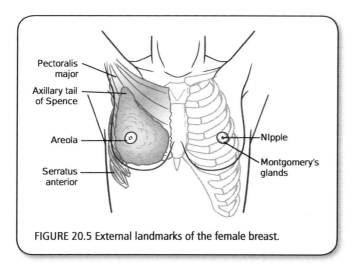

FIGURE 20.5 External landmarks of the female breast.

The breast is composed of three types of tissue: (a) glandular tissue, (b) fibrous tissue, and (c) adipose tissue. The glandular tissue contains approximately 15 to 20 lobes radiating from the nipple; each lobe is further divided into lobules; these lobules contain

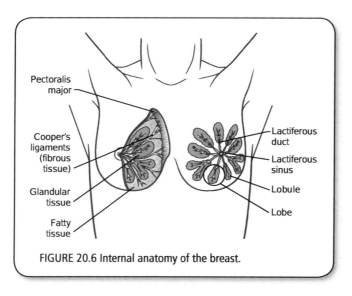

FIGURE 20.6 Internal anatomy of the breast.

milk-producing cells that empty into the lactiferous duct. Strong, fibrous tissue and suspensory ligaments (*Cooper's ligaments*) support the breast and attach the breast tissue to the chest wall muscles. The internal anatomy of the breast is illustrated in Figure 20.6.

The male breast is similar to the female breast until puberty, at which time the female breast develops under the influence of estrogen.

DEVELOPMENTAL CONSIDERATIONS

At 5 to 6 weeks gestation, the fetal gonads have not yet differentiated into a testicle or ovary; during week 6, this process begins. Differentiation of the external genitalia occurs between 8 and 12 weeks gestation. In the female, approximately 400,000 immature ova are present in the ovaries at birth. Beginning at puberty, the ovaries normally alternate releasing one mature ovum a month; this is a part of the menstrual cycle. Between 17 and 20 weeks gestation, the testicles develop in the abdominal cavity. In the later months of gestation, the testicles descend through the inguinal canal into the scrotum, completing this process before birth. Because of this timing, cryptorchidism and inguinal hernia are more common in preterm boys. Testicles enlarge between 9 and 13 years.

The preterm female neonate's labia majora may not cover the labia minora, resulting in a protuberant clitoris that is easily visualized. Term neonates have enlarged labia majora due to the effects of maternal estrogen. The swelling soon recedes, and the external genitalia remain small until puberty. Until approximately 2 to 4 years, the hymen is comprised of redundant folds of epithelial tissue and is pale pink.

During the fourth week of embryonic life, breast development begins with the formation of the mammary ridge ("milk lines"), which extend from the axilla to the groin bilaterally. Between 12 and 16 weeks gestation, the nipple and areola form. Breast development continues in utero under the influence of maternal estrogen. From 32 to 40 weeks gestation, milk ducts form within the nipple. At birth, only the lactiferous ducts within the nipple are present. Additionally, both the male and female breasts may be swollen at birth and the neonate may secrete colostrum ("witch's milk") as a result of the exposure to maternal estrogen. Few changes in the breast occur before puberty.

PHYSIOLOGIC CHANGES AT PUBERTY

Puberty involves several physical and psychosocial changes in the adolescent caused by the increased secretion of sex hormones. These changes occur at different rates among adolescents, but all include a growth spurt, establishment of fertility, and the development of secondary sex characteristics.

Females

Pubertal changes in girls take place as estrogen stimulates the development of secondary sex characteristics; this process takes an average of 3 years. The first signs of puberty in girls are breast development and the growth of pubic hair. This usually occurs between ages 8 to 13.5 years. The stages of pubic hair development in girls are depicted in Figure 20.7. Menarche usually occurs approximately 2 years after the appearance of breast buds. Axillary hair appears approximately 2 years after the onset of pubic hair. Menarche occurs in breast development stage 3 or 4, usually around age 12 years.

Before a girl reaches puberty, her breasts will appear as only areolae and nipples. At *thelarche* (the beginning of breast development at puberty, approximately age 11), the presence of the hormone estrogen stimulates the development of breast tissue. The milk ducts then develop inward from the nipple, and adipose tissue accumulates around the ducts, causing the breasts to become larger. Breast development is usually completed by age 16. Although the age of thelarche varies, the five stages of breast development follow Marshall and Tanner's (1969) classic sexual maturity rating, or Tanner staging (Marshall & Tanner, 1969).

Tanner stage 1 is the preadolescent breast, which has only a small elevated nipple and no underlying breast tissue. Stage 2 is the breast bud stage in which the breast and nipple elevate as a small mound, and the areola widens. In stage 3, there is further enlargement of the breast and areola, and the areola becomes darker. In stage 4, the areola and nipple form a secondary mound over the breast tissue. Stage 5 is the mature breast. Only the nipple protrudes; in some healthy women, the areola continues to form a secondary mound. The stages of breast development in girls are shown in Figure 20.8.

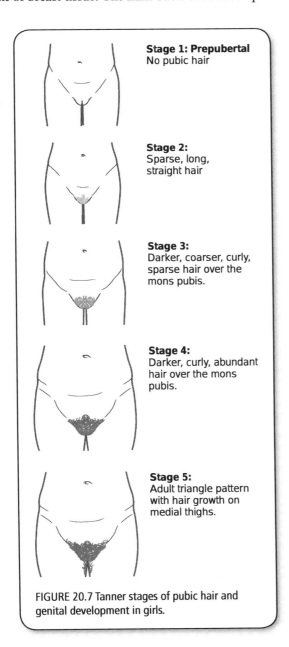

Stage 1: Prepubertal
No pubic hair

Stage 2:
Sparse, long, straight hair

Stage 3:
Darker, coarser, curly, sparse hair over the mons pubis.

Stage 4:
Darker, curly, abundant hair over the mons pubis.

Stage 5:
Adult triangle pattern with hair growth on medial thighs.

FIGURE 20.7 Tanner stages of pubic hair and genital development in girls.

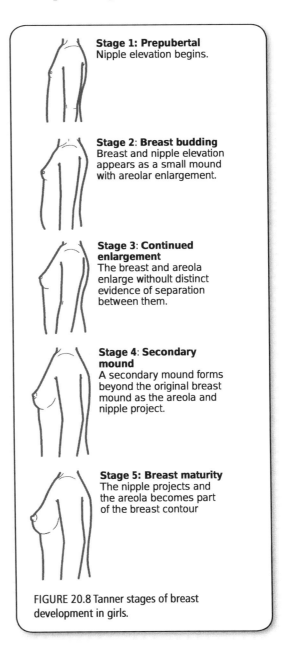

Stage 1: Prepubertal
Nipple elevation begins.

Stage 2: Breast budding
Breast and nipple elevation appears as a small mound with areolar enlargement.

Stage 3: Continued enlargement
The breast and areola enlarge withoult distinct evidence of separation between them.

Stage 4: Secondary mound
A secondary mound forms beyond the original breast mound as the areola and nipple project.

Stage 5: Breast maturity
The nipple projects and the areola becomes part of the breast contour

FIGURE 20.8 Tanner stages of breast development in girls.

Males

In boys, puberty typically begins between ages 9.3 and 13.5 years, at which time the testicles begin to enlarge. Next, pubic hair begins to grow, and lastly penis size increases. Maturation from preadolescent boy to adult man usually lasts approximately 2 to 5 years. The stages of pubic hair and genital development in boys are illustrated in Figure 20.9.

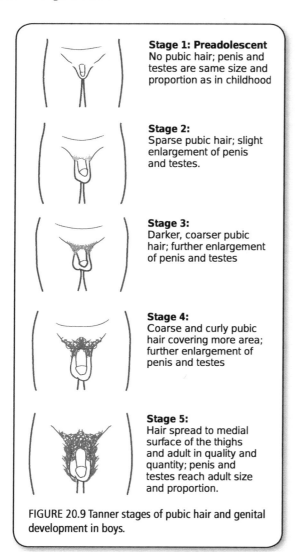

Stage 1: Preadolescent
No pubic hair; penis and testes are same size and proportion as in childhood

Stage 2:
Sparse pubic hair; slight enlargement of penis and testes.

Stage 3:
Darker, coarser pubic hair; further enlargement of penis and testes

Stage 4:
Coarse and curly pubic hair covering more area; further enlargement of penis and testes

Stage 5:
Hair spread to medial surface of the thighs and adult in quality and quantity; penis and testes reach adult size and proportion.

FIGURE 20.9 Tanner stages of pubic hair and genital development in boys.

CULTURAL, RACIAL, AND RELIGIOUS CONSIDERATIONS

When assessing the genitalia of a child or adolescent, the health care provider must consider the child and family's cultural and religious beliefs to ensure sensitivity and respect. For example, an adolescent girl may not have had a pelvic examination because of modesty. An adolescent boy may have genitourinary complaints that remain untreated because of his reluctance to call attention to the problem due to embarrassment. Depending on the child or adolescent's beliefs, he or she must be examined by a provider of the same gender, with great care taken to preserve modesty. This is especially true of Mennonite, Amish (Carteret, 2011), Orthodox Jews (Berkowitz, 2008), Arabic, and Muslim girls (Hammoud, White, & Fetters, 2005). Questions about specific sexual practices and beliefs about monogamy, abstinence, and sexual orientation must be handled with respect and sensitivity.

Some racial differences are important to consider during assessment of the reproductive system in children and adolescents. Black and Mexican American girls reach thelarche, pubarche, and menarche earlier than White girls of the same age (Rosenfield, Lipton, & Drum, 2009).

Genital circumcision is a specific example of a religious and cultural practice involving the genitourinary tract. Circumcision of newborn males is practiced as part of a ritual ceremony by the followers of Islam and Judaism (Berkowitz, 2008). Female genital mutilation (FGM) or infibulation is practiced in some parts of the Middle East and Asia. FGM involves the partial or total removal of the clitoris or labia. Infibulation involves cutting the labia, with or without the removal of the clitoris, then stitching the remaining tissue together, leaving a small opening through which urine and menstrual blood can pass (World Health Organization, 2014). It is culturally accepted among participating groups that FGM makes a girl's genitalia aesthetically pleasing and means that she is "clean" (World Health Organization, 2014). FGM causes many complications such as cysts, abscesses, keloid formation, urinary incontinence, sexual dysfunction, prolonged labor and delivery, anxiety, and depression (World Health Organization, 2014).

ASSESSMENT OF THE GENITOURINARY SYSTEM

History

Any genitourinary evaluation should begin with a thorough history. Although in the pediatric setting, a history is usually obtained from both a primary caregiver and the child, it is extremely important that the provider interview an adolescent alone for at least a brief period of time to obtain a sexual history. The provider must make it clear to the adolescent patient that any sexual history information is private and confidential.

Past Medical History

The genitourinary history gives the provider important information about known and potential problem areas, for example, recurrent urinary tract infections (UTIs). The reasons for any past hospitalizations are ascertained, noting whether the reason for the hospitalization involved the genitourinary or reproductive tracts. Some examples include vesicoureteral reflux, acute pyelonephritis, and pregnancy.

Prenatal, Perinatal, and Neonatal Histories • The prenatal, perinatal, and neonatal histories are important elements of the assessment of the genitourinary and reproductive systems in children. Some chromosomal defects involve the genitourinary tract, such as trisomy 13 and trisomy 18, which are both associated with hydronephrosis. Girls with Turner syndrome have abnormally formed ovaries and associated ovarian failure (Daniel & Postellon, 2013). Certain congenital anomalies affect the function of these systems and may cause chronic genitourinary difficulties. Examples of some of these conditions are listed in Box 20.1.

BOX 20.1 Congenital Anomalies Affecting the Genitourinary Tract

- Hypospadias
- Epispadias
- Chordee
- Cryptorchidism
- Inguinal hernia
- Ambiguous genitalia
- Labial fusion
- Urogenital sinus
- Exstrophy of the bladder
- Hydrocele
- Vesicoureteral reflux

Immunizations • In all children and adolescents, immunization status is reviewed, with special attention paid to whether the hepatitis B and human papillomavirus (HPV) vaccines have been given. A possible route of transmission for hepatitis B includes unprotected sexual contact; this virus is transmitted through blood, semen, vaginal secretions, and wounds. It is important to determine if preadolescents or adolescents have received the HPV vaccine, which protects against HPV infection that can lead to genital warts and cancers of the cervix, anus, vagina, and vulva (Centers for Disease Control and Prevention, 2013).

Injuries • It is important to obtain any history of abdominal, perineal, or groin injuries. Blunt or penetrating abdominal trauma can lead to severe renal injuries. Injuries to the perineum or groin may be due to falls that cause straddling injuries to the external genitalia in girls or testicular injuries in boys. It is essential to determine the circumstances leading to the injury; this may provide clues as to neglect; may reveal knowledge deficits about motor vehicle, bicycle, or street safety; or may indicate abuse.

Review of Systems • The pediatric review of systems (ROS) that is specific to the reproductive system focuses on the endocrine and genitourinary systems, male and female genitalia, and the breasts. Specific conditions about which to inquire include:

- **Genitourinary:** Dysuria, urinary frequency, or urgency; UTI, hematuria, enuresis, vesicoureteral reflux, cryptorchidism, testicular torsion, hydrocele, varicocele, spermatocele, chordee, hypospadias, epispadias, balanitis, epididymitis, urethritis, STI, genital or penile lesions, or rashes
- **Gastrointestinal:** Constipation, pinworms, anal fissure, anal skin tag, or inguinal hernia
- **Hematologic:** Sickle cell disease (can cause priapism in males)
- **Endocrine:** Polycystic ovary syndrome (PCOS), diabetes, hypothyroidism, or hyperthyroidism
- **Neurologic:** Myelomeningocele (causes neurogenic bladder)
- **Reproductive:** Gynecomastia (males), dysmenorrhea, menorrhagia, amenorrhea, pelvic inflammatory disease, or pregnancy
- **Integumentary:** Acne, frontal or temporal hair loss, hirsutism or acanthosis nigricans in girls (may indicate PCOS); alopecia may indicate hypothyroidism
- **Growth:** Obesity may be sign of PCOS in girls (Lucidi et al., 2013) and is also associated with early puberty (Rosenfield et al., 2009); it may also cause gynecomastia in boys
- **Psychosocial:** Anorexia nervosa, bulimia nervosa, or morbid obesity; all can result in amenorrhea; obesity can also cause gynecomastia in males

Medications • A medication history must include any medication the child is taking or has taken in the past. Both prescription and over-the-counter medications are included, paying close attention to medications that can affect the reproductive or genitourinary system. The indication for the medication is also determined. Examples of medications about which to inquire include antibiotics, which may have been prescribed for a UTI or an STI; oral contraceptives; and steroids. It is also important to ask about the use of any topical creams or medications applied to the child's genital or anal area.

Surgical History

It is important to determine if there have been any surgeries of the reproductive tract. If so, there should be documentation of what type and at what age the procedures were performed. It is also important to ascertain the reason for reproductive tract surgery. In girls, any gynecologic surgery must be noted, such as surgery for dysfunctional uterine bleeding, ectopic pregnancy, removal of an ovarian cyst or adnexal mass, or dilation and curettage for spontaneous abortion. In boys, repair of hypospadias, epispadias, cryptorchidism, varicocele, hydrocele, testicular torsion, and hernias are some examples of genitourinary surgeries.

Family History

Some conditions that affect the genitourinary and reproductive systems may be genetic. During the initial patient encounter, the provider should inquire about any family history of these conditions. Box 20.2 lists topics about which to ask when gathering this family history.

BOX 20.2   Family History

Girls

- Maternal age at menarche
- Family history of dysmenorrhea, dysfunctional uterine bleeding, or endometriosis
- Hypo- or hyperthyroidism
- Wilms' tumor
- Female reproductive tract cancers
- Polycystic ovary syndrome

Boys

- Wilms' tumor
- Cryptorchidism
- Hypospadias
- Epispadias
- Testicular malignancy

BOX 20.3   Genitourinary and Reproductive Social History for Preadolescents and Adolescents

- Family members
- Who lives in home and relationship to child/adolescent
- Family problems
- History of running away from home
- School progress, likes and dislikes, grades, extracurricular activities
- Feelings about self
- Stressors
- Drug or alcohol use
- Sleep patterns
- Insomnia
- Depression
- Support system
- Thoughts of self-harm or harm to others
- Relationship with parents
- Friends, relationships, peer group
- Dating history
- Typical free-time activities
- Amount of exercise each day
- Involvement in sports
- Employment
- Episodes of nocturnal enuresis
- Age of toilet training
- Ask preschool and school-aged child directly if anyone has touched his or her genitalia and then told them not to tell

---

Social History

The social history is an important component of the genitourinary and reproductive assessment in children. For example, family strife or sexual abuse may be the etiology of secondary nocturnal enuresis (von Gontard, Baeyens, Van Hoecke, Warzak, & Bachmann, 2011). A history of depression can lead to alcohol or drug use, which can, in turn, result in impulsive or nonconsensual sexual encounters. Any history of eating disorders in girls must be noted; excessive or low body fat can affect the menstrual cycle. Excessive stress can affect school performance, relationships, and, in girls, menstrual cycles. Involvement in contact sports may increase the risk of injury to the genital area. Box 20.3 lists other components of the social history as it relates to the genitourinary and reproductive systems.

Menstrual History

Starting at approximately age 8 or 9 years, girls should be sensitively questioned about whether or not they have begun menstruating. Adolescent girls often have irregular cycles; a full menstrual history must be obtained. Areas of questioning that should be explored in a menstrual history are listed in Box 20.4.

BOX 20.4   Menstrual History

- Age of menarche
- Last menstrual period
- Regularity of periods
- Duration of a normal period
- Any skipped periods
- Irregularity, dysmenorrhea, metrorrhagia, or amenorrhea longer than 3 months
- Presence of premenstrual syndrome
- Presence of other symptoms with menses, such as headaches, migraines, cramps, bloating, tender breasts, or mood changes

---

Sexual History

The adolescent sexual history must be obtained with the teen fully clothed in a comfortable, nonthreatening environment. The environs must be age appropriate and oriented toward the developmental level of the adolescent. To ensure privacy and confidentiality, the interview should take place with the parent, friend, or significant other out of the room. A matter-of-fact, nonjudgmental tone must be maintained so that the adolescent feels comfortable giving honest and accurate answers. It may be helpful to begin with a statement such as, "Often boys and girls your age experience…," to convey that what the adolescent is experiencing is normal and expected. It is important

BOX 20.5 Adolescent Sexual History

- Current sexual activity
- Age at first intercourse
- Number of sexual partners (current and lifetime)
- Frequency of sexual intercourse
- Type of sexual activity (oral, anal, vaginal)
- Encounters with same sex, opposite sex, or both
- Characteristics of partners (e.g., monogamous, intravenous drug user)
- Alcohol and drug use
- Exchange of sex for food, shelter, money, or drugs
- Method of contraception use
- History of unprotected intercourse
- Use of condoms
- History of sexually transmitted infection
- Use of douches, powders, or sprays in vaginal area
- History of pregnancy
- History of miscarriage or abortion
- History of sexual abuse or rape

to use open-ended questions such as, "When did you...?" rather than "Did you...?" This is less threatening because it implies that the topic is normal and expected. The provider should convey that questions are welcome as well. Examples include: "Many times adolescents have questions about sexual activity. Do you have any questions about birth control, pregnancy, or STIs such as herpes, gonorrhea, or *Chlamydia*?" Box 20.5 lists the components of an adolescent sexual history.

History of Present Illness

A detailed, focused history of a patient's current problem is a critical piece of the provider's assessment. As with all history of present illness (HPI) assessments, it is important to note the onset, duration, and severity of the problem as well as aggravating and alleviating factors. Any treatment of the problem, including both prescriptions and home remedies, must be documented. Questions relating to HPI of the reproductive system in boys and girls can be found in Tables 20.1 and 20.2.

TABLE 20.1	History of Present Illness: Abnormalities and Complaints Related to the Reproductive System in Boys	
COMPLAINT	**ASSESSMENTS**	**DIFFERENTIAL DIAGNOSES/CAUSES**
Dysuria	Is urine cloudy, discolored, or foul smelling? Hematuria? Burning or discomfort with urination? Does urine stream look straight?	Cystitis, urethritis, UTI, or STI
Deflected urinary stream	Placement of urethral meatus? Is urinary stream downward or to the side? Chordee present?	Hypospadias, epispadias, or ambiguous genitalia
Penile pain, lesions, or discharge	Past medical history? Type of lesions? Dysuria? Is child or adolescent circumcised?	Priapism (can occur during vaso-occlusive crisis in sickle cell disease), STI, balanitis, or nonspecific urethritis
Testicular swelling or mass	Associated pain? Is mass mobile?	A painless mobile mass suggests spermatocele; painless firm nodule on testicle suggests testicular malignancy
Testicular pain	Acute onset? Intensity of pain? Testis enlarged or tender? Is child or teen anxious? Is scrotum on involved side warm to touch, edematous, or tender? Does moving the testis increase pain? Is cremasteric reflex present?	Acute onset of excruciating testicular pain suggests testicular torsion, a surgical emergency. Scrotal edema, warmth, and erythema are associated with testicular torsion. Cremasteric reflex is absent with testicular torsion. Testicular trauma, orchitis, or epididymitis also cause acute pain. Dull pain with a sensation of pulling may be a varicocele.
Scrotal bulging or swelling	Pain associated with scrotal swelling? Does swelling increase as the day progresses? Is swelling symmetrical? Does swelling transilluminate? Are both testis descended?	Inguinal hernia, inguinal lymphadenopathy, epididymitis, orchitis, hydrocele, spermatocele, varicocele, Henoch-Schönlein purpura, testicular tumor, or torsion; painless swelling occurs with hydrocele
Scrotum feels empty	On palpation, one or both testes cannot be palpated	Retractile testes, cryptorchidism, or anorchia

STI, sexually transmitted infection; UTI, urinary tract infection.

TABLE 20.2	History of Present Illness: Abnormalities and Complaints Related to the Reproductive System in Girls	
COMPLAINT	**ASSESSMENTS**	**DIFFERENTIAL DIAGNOSES/CAUSES**
Breast tenderness or pain	When does it occur, and where is it? Is there any relation to menstrual cycle?	Cyclic pain or fibrocystic breast conditions
Dysuria	Is urine cloudy, discolored, or foul smelling? Hematuria? Burning or discomfort with urination?	Cystitis or urethritis, UTI, vulvovaginitis, vaginal foreign body, urethral prolapse, injury, trauma, or STI
Hematuria	Is urine cloudy, discolored, or foul smelling? History of renal or genitourinary conditions?	UTI, urethral injury, trauma, or renal or genitourinary condition
Pelvic pain	Lower abdominal pain? Cervical motion tenderness? Adnexal tenderness? Right upper quadrant tenderness? Fever? Vaginal discharge? Menorrhagia?	Dysmenorrhea, PID, disseminated gonococcal infection, or gastrointestinal causes (see Chapter 19)
Vaginal bleeding	Type? Amount? Frequency? Clots?	Vulvovaginitis, hemangioma, trauma, menorrhagia, menometrorrhagia, pregnancy, or spontaneous abortion
Vaginal discharge	Type of discharge? Odor? Color? Cervix friable?	Physiologic leukorrhea, vulvovaginitis, urethral prolapse, bacterial vaginosis, STI, or vaginal foreign body
Vulvar itching, pain, or rash	Frequency of perineal hygiene? Any discharge? Type of discharge? Vulvar edema or rash? Bleeding? Visible lesions?	Vulvovaginitis, chemical urethritis, pinworm infestation, foreign body, labial adhesions, lichen sclerosis, urethral prolapse (Adams, 2014), herpes, or HPV

HPV, human papillomavirus; PID, pelvic inflammatory disease; STI, sexually transmitted infection; UTI, urinary tract infection.

Physical Examination

Physical examination of the genital area in children and adolescents can cause stress and anxiety; this is normal. Many children have been told that it is not appropriate for strangers to touch their private parts, and they may feel that the provider fits into this category. They may also be afraid that the exam will cause pain. Once children are preschool aged and older, they are often embarrassed when their genital area is examined. The health care provider must be sensitive to this concern, maintaining privacy and a matter-of-fact demeanor. The examination should be explained to the child in a developmentally appropriate way. To build on an already established rapport, it is best to examine the genitalia and adolescent female breasts last.

To enhance cooperation, young children can be examined while lying supine on the parent's lap. Young children should be allowed to keep their underpants on until the genital exam. Older girls are positioned supine on the examination table; knees slightly bent, feet flat on the table, and legs slightly apart. The girl's legs should be covered with a sheet or drape.

Equipment for the genitourinary examination in the prepubertal child includes gloves, lubricant, and a penlight. To conduct the pelvic examination in adolescent females, additional equipment is necessary (see Adolescent Pelvic Examination).

Inspection of the Female Genitalia

The external female genitalia are inspected for color, swelling, symmetry, lesions, and discharge. Tanner staging is also evaluated. To begin, the mons pubis is inspected for skin discoloration or lesions. The area is also inspected for pubic hair, and the stage of sexual maturity is evaluated (see Developmental Considerations). In the adolescent, pubic hair appears as an inverted triangle, extending along the labia majora, and onto the medial surface of the thighs in Tanner stage V. The pubic hair is inspected for distribution and infestations. Irregular or sparse pubic hair suggests hormonal abnormalities. Precocious development of pubic hair is the presence of pubic hair before age 8 years; this is more common in females (10:1) and is often caused by premature adrenarche (Rosenfeld, 2013). Dark, coarse, and curly pubic hair on the labia major in girls (and base of the penis in boys) is the first observable sign. Girls with premature adrenarche have a higher incidence of PCOS and syndrome X (i.e., obesity, hypertension, insulin resistance, type 2 diabetes, dyslipidemia) (Rosenfeld, 2013). Any infestations in the pubic hair should be noted; tiny white nits attached to the pubic hair shaft indicate lice infestation. With pubic lice, the mons pubis area is also further inspected for lesions secondary to bites and scratching, which can become secondarily infected.

The labia are then inspected. In the newborn, the labia are prominent. There may also be some mucoid or bloody discharge. This is a transient condition and is considered a normal finding that results from maternal estrogen, which influences a female infant for the first 8 weeks of life (Carlo, 2011). In prepubertal girls, the labia majora are pale pink and free of hair or lesions, such as warts or ulcers, signs of STIs, and sexual abuse. The presence of *condyloma acuminatum* in children may or may not be a result of sexual abuse, depending on the child's age and mode of transmission. Vertical transmission can occur from mother to infant during delivery. Autoinoculation can occur in children younger than 2 years of age after contact with HPV fomites. HPV is also transmitted through sexual contact, which must be considered when evaluating genital lesions (Hornor, 2011). Edema, tenderness, or erythema of the labia majora suggests vulvovaginitis, which is often seen in young girls secondary to poor perineal hygiene. In adolescent girls, the labia majora are pink and free of lesions with an even hair distribution.

To visualize the labia minora, the provider must gently separate the labia with gloved fingers. The labia minora in prepubertal girls are normally thin; moist; without discharge, redness or lesions; and pale pink, becoming darker after puberty. Accumulation of a sticky, white substance is smegma, which indicates poor hygiene. In prepubertal girls, the tissue between the labia minora may be fused as a result of being in a hypoestrogenized state, a condition known as *labial adhesions* (Figure 20.10). This tissue needs to be separated, as it can lead to dysuria, rash, and vulvovaginitis.

The clitoris is inspected for size and position. Because of its sensitivity, it is not palpated. An enlarged clitoris may indicate precocious puberty, congenital adrenal hyperplasia, or the use of anabolic steroids. In a newborn, an enlarged clitoris may be mistaken for a penis in a child with ambiguous genitalia. A smaller than normal clitoris may be a sign of *hypopituitarism*.

The urethral meatus is inspected next. There should be no erythema, discharge, or swelling. Signs of inflammation indicate irritation which may be caused by soaps, laundry detergent, or pinworms. Vulvovaginitis or urethritis may occur secondary to poor hygiene or STI. Marked urethral erythema may be caused by prolapsed urethral mucosa, especially in patients with a history of hematuria or dysuria.

The vaginal orifice is also inspected; it is normally pink, moist, and free of discharge. Erythema or excoriation in the vulvar area can indicate pediculosis pubis, vulvovaginitis, STI, or enterobiasis (pinworm infestation), especially if these signs are found in the perianal area as well. A small amount of whitish odorless, mucoid discharge in the prepubertal girl is normal; this is physiologic leukorrhea. Girls begin to menstruate approximately 2 years after the appearance of breast buds; at that time, the amount and type of vaginal discharge varies, according to the menstrual cycle. A thick, white discharge in an adolescent girl taking oral contraceptives is likely vaginal candidiasis. Any discharge that is green, yellow, or foul smelling may be caused by a foreign body in the vagina or an STI. Vaginal discharge suggests an infection and warrants a pelvic exam if persistent (Braverman, Breech & the American Academy of Pediatrics Committee on Adolescence, 2013). While continuing to separate the labia with a gloved hand, the provider visualizes the hymen. The hymen is just inside the vaginal orifice. There are several variations of the hymenal configuration; these variations are listed in Box 20.6. In prepubertal girls, the intact hymen is thin, reddish, and sensitive to touch. After puberty, the hymen becomes pinker, thicker, and more compliant, owing to

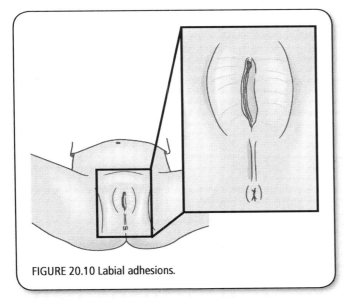

FIGURE 20.10 Labial adhesions.

BOX 20.6 Types of Hymenal Configurations

TYPE	DESCRIPTION
Annular	Round, circumferential hymenal tissue; most common at birth
Crescentic	Hymenal tissue that forms a crescent shape; this is common in girls after 3 years of age
Cribriform	Hymenal tissue that has numerous small openings
Fimbriated	Hymenal tissue that has an irregular edge
Imperforate	The hymen is not open; minor surgery is necessary to allow menstrual blood to flow
Redundant	Hymenal tissue that protrudes and folds in on itself
Septate	A hymen that has a band of tissue running vertically, creating two openings to the vaginal orifice

the effects of estrogen. In sexually active adolescents, the hymen is not visible. Visible lacerations, bruising, or healed hymenal tissue indicate penetrating vaginal trauma, which must be differentiated from sexual abuse (see Chapter 24).

Palpation of the Female Genitalia

With a gloved hand, the provider palpates the labia majora and minora for edema, tenderness, or lesions. The labia are normally soft, nontender, and without edema or lesions. Palpable masses may indicate papilloma, condyloma, or abscess. The Bartholin's and Skene's glands are not normally palpable. In prepubertal girls, edema of the labia occurs with an infection of these glands. Enlarged, palpable glands may indicate gonorrhea or cysts.

Adolescent Pelvic Examination

The first gynecologic exam for an adolescent girl can be an important factor in the development of a healthy sexual identity. The skill and sensitivity of the provider can teach the adolescent that sexuality is a healthy, normal aspect of human existence and can encourage responsible sexual behavior. To help normalize the experience for the adolescent, the provider can inform her that the gynecologic exam, the questions the provider will ask, and the procedures that will be performed are those that are important for all women.

The pelvic exam is not done on a routine basis in adolescence. Indications for a pelvic examination are as follows (Braverman et al., 2013):
- Persistent vaginal discharge
- Dysuria or urinary tract symptoms in a sexually active female
- Dysmenorrhea unresponsive to nonsteroidal anti-inflammatory drugs
- Amenorrhea
- Abnormal vaginal bleeding
- Lower abdominal pain
- Contraceptive counseling for an intrauterine device or diaphragm
- Pap test
- Suspected or reported rape, or sexual abuse
- Pregnancy

For cervical cancer screening purposes, the American Academy of Pediatrics (AAP) (2014) no longer recommends annual screening for cervical cancer until age 21 years. The American College of Obstetricians and Gynecologists (ACOG) recommends that the first gynecologic visit take place between the ages of 13 and 15 to establish a provider–patient relationship, to answer questions, to assess sexual development, to take menstrual and sexual histories, and to determine the need for contraception or testing for STIs. This visit does not typically include an internal pelvic examination (ACOG, 2010).

Preparation for the Exam • The provider must have a thorough knowledge of the anatomy and physiology of the female reproductive system and of appropriate teaching techniques for adolescents. If the adolescent girl is more comfortable with a female provider, every effort should be made to schedule one for the exam. Ideally, the provider already has an established relationship with the adolescent as a result of taking care of her other health care needs.

Staff who schedule appointments for gynecologic exams should be sure to explain to patients that the pelvic exam should not be scheduled during menstruation and that the patient should refrain from intercourse, douching, and the application of any intravaginal medications for at least 24, and preferably 48, hours before the appointment. If at all possible, extra time should be scheduled for a first pelvic exam. At the beginning of the visit, objectives for the visit should be verbalized by the provider. If the adolescent girl is accompanied by her mother, she should be asked privately if she wants her mother to be present during the exam; her wishes should be honored.

Preparation of the adolescent, particularly for the first pelvic exam, is essential to the success of the exam. Using charts and models, the provider must first review the relevant pelvic anatomy, showing the patient the speculum and reassuring her that only the blades are inserted into the vagina. If a Pap test is appropriate, the patient should be shown the spatula and cytobrush that will be used and where the specimen will be obtained. If a mirror and flashlight are available, the patient can be encouraged to look at the external genitalia during the provider's inspection and at the cervix during the speculum exam. Even if this is not the first pelvic exam, the provider must not assume that the patient has all the information she needs about the exam. Previous experiences may not have been informative. Relaxation techniques, such as abdominal breathing (breathe in through the nose and out through the mouth, with both hands on the diaphragm, focusing on making the hands go up and down), can be useful during the exam; the provider should explain that the more relaxed the patient is, the more comfortable the exam is. The provider should also inform the patient at every step of the exam about what is happening. All of the interactions with the patient up to this point should be done with her fully clothed, making sure the bladder is empty and securing any urine specimens that are warranted by the history. Blood should be drawn for serologic testing for syphilis as necessary.

Preparation of the environment includes putting a paper barrier on a stand or table placed on the non-dominant side of the examiner. On this stand, the provider should place any equipment needed for the Pap test, such as one or two slides labeled in pencil, fixative, wooden or plastic Ayre's spatula, cytobrush for conventional Pap, tube with solution, and cytobrush for liquid-based Pap; equipment needed for STI testing (e.g., for such diseases as gonorrhea, Chlamydia) and herpes cultures or PCR testing; and equipment needed for a wet mount, such as dropper bottles of normal saline and 10% potassium hydroxide (KOH), slides, cover slips, and cotton swabs.

It is important to choose the appropriately sized speculum based on the patient's history (e.g., parity); two different sizes can be put on the tray so that the most appropriate size can be chosen after an initial assessment of the vagina. All plastic specula must be inspected for cracks or rough edges, and metal specula must be inspected to be sure they are working properly.

Large swabs for clearing any excessive discharge from the cervix should be available, as well as a container of warm water for lubricating the speculum. Only water is used as a lubricant during the speculum exam. In addition, water-soluble lubricant (single-use packets are preferable to multi-use tubes to maintain asepsis); two pairs of clean gloves (one pair to put on before starting the exam, and an extra pair in case of contamination), and pH paper are also necessary. It is also important to have a good light source, a gown and sheet for the patient, lab requisitions as necessary, and a wastebasket for contaminated materials.

Pelvic Exam Procedure • There are certain principles that should be observed when doing a pelvic examination, such as using an aseptic technique, doing the exam as efficiently and quickly as possible while still obtaining the necessary specimens and information, explaining to the patient at every step what is happening, and minimizing the patient's discomfort. At the beginning of the exam, the provider should elevate the head of the exam table 45 degrees and cover the patient from the waist down with the drape. The patient may need the provider's help to position herself on the table with her feet in stirrups and her buttocks just off the bottom edge. The patient should be told to feel along the sides of the table until she reaches the bottom and move herself into position while covered by the drape. When the patient is in position, the drape should be moved slightly between the legs so that the provider can see the patient's face during the exam.

When the exam begins, the provider can review the relaxation techniques and remind the patient that the exam will proceed slowly and that an explanation will be given for each step. The light should be positioned before beginning, and then the provider should put gloves on both hands. (Some providers will glove only their dominant hand, which means that they can only use that hand when palpating the external genitalia.) Lubricant is not used for the first part of the exam.

The external genitalia are examined using inspection and palpation. The inguinal lymph nodes are palpated first, using one or both hands. (Some beginning examiners find it easier to use just one hand palpating each side separately, so they can better focus on what they are feeling.) The provider should touch the inside

of the patient's thigh with the back of the dominant hand before touching the pubic area. First touching the patient in a less sensitive area prepares her for having her genitalia touched. The provider first inspects the pubic hair, looking for hair distribution, lice, nits, and lesions, using both hands to separate hair and palpate the area. Some lesions (e.g., suspected herpes) may require a culture. Having a magnifying glass may be useful during this exam. The Tanner stage of pubertal development, according to pubic hair type, amount, and distribution, is noted.

The examination moves posteriorly beginning with inspection and palpation of the labia majora. The labia are separated and the provider retracts the hood of the clitoris; inspects the clitoris, urethral meatus, introitus, and perineum; and looks for lesions, discharge, edema, erythema, or tenderness. Using the back of the hands, the provider separates the buttocks for inspection of the anal region for lesions or hemorrhoids. The provider can offer the patient a mirror at this point of the examination so that she can visualize the external anatomy. The provider may want to say, "Everything looks healthy on the outside," or relate specific findings if that is not the case. The provider's index finger is then inserted about 2 cm into the vagina and pressed down on the perineal muscles. The provider can then explain that these are strong muscles that the patient needs to keep relaxed to make the exam as comfortable as possible; however, pressing firmly with downward pressure on the perineum should not be painful. The provider then advances the index finger further into the vagina to locate the cervix, noting whether it is anterior, posterior, or deviated to one side; and noting the length of the vagina to determine how to aim the speculum when it is inserted. The muscle tone of the vagina is evaluated to estimate the appropriate speculum size to use. Experienced providers may skip this step of locating the cervix prior to speculum insertion, but beginners may find it very helpful.

When the index finger is withdrawn, it should be pressing on the anterior vaginal wall to "milk" the Skene's glands; the provider should look for a discharge from the urethra, which should be cultured if present. The index finger can also be left just inside the vagina with the thumb on the outside to be used to palpate the posterior labia majora on both sides, evaluating for swelling or tenderness in the Bartholin's glands. At this time, the glove from the nondominant hand is removed and thrown away. From now on, the ungloved hand is used only to manipulate equipment and not to touch the patient.

Speculum Exam • To begin the speculum examination, the provider should touch the inside of the thigh with the back of the gloved dominant hand and place the index finger into the vagina about 2 cm, pressing down and reminding the patient to keep her muscles relaxed. The provider then inserts his or her middle finger while asking the patient to squeeze the examiner's fingers with the perineal muscles. To assess muscle tone, the provider spreads his or her fingers apart and asks the patient to bear down. The provider looks anteriorly for a bulge, which could indicate cystocele, and looks posteriorly for a bulge, which could indicate rectocele. (These findings are not likely in an adolescent, but might be found in a parous teenager.)

The provider should then pick up the speculum with the nondominant, clean hand, dip it in warm water, and hold the blades together between the index and middle fingers. The provider presses down with the two fingers of the gloved hand that are in the vagina; they are then spread apart slightly to create a small space into which the speculum is inserted at a slight angle; the fingers are withdrawn slowly as the speculum is inserted (Figure 20.11). At this point, the provider should check to be sure the labia or pubic hairs are not caught in the speculum. The handle of the speculum is then transferred to the dominant hand and inserted the rest of the way, while the provider rotates it to a horizontal position, pointing slightly downward (Figure 20.12).

Next, the provider inserts the closed blades of the speculum into the posterior fornix, withdrawing slightly and then opening the blades (Figure 20.13). The speculum is not locked at this point, but the cervix should be visible. If not, the blades are closed, partially withdrawn, and then reinserted at a different

angle, before they are opened again (Figure 20.14). Before locking the blades of a plastic speculum, the provider should warn the patient about the loud click that will be heard. The blades are then locked into position, and the light is adjusted to allow good visualization of the cervix.

When inspecting the cervix, the provider assesses for color, lesions, ectropion, discharge, scars, nodules, bleeding, and the shape of the os (Figure 20.15). Specimens are obtained for lab tests as needed. If doing both gonorrhea and Chlamydia testing and a Pap test, the provider performs the Pap test first so that potentially malignant cells are not removed during other tests. Excessive discharge that obscures the cervix may need to be removed gently with large cotton swabs

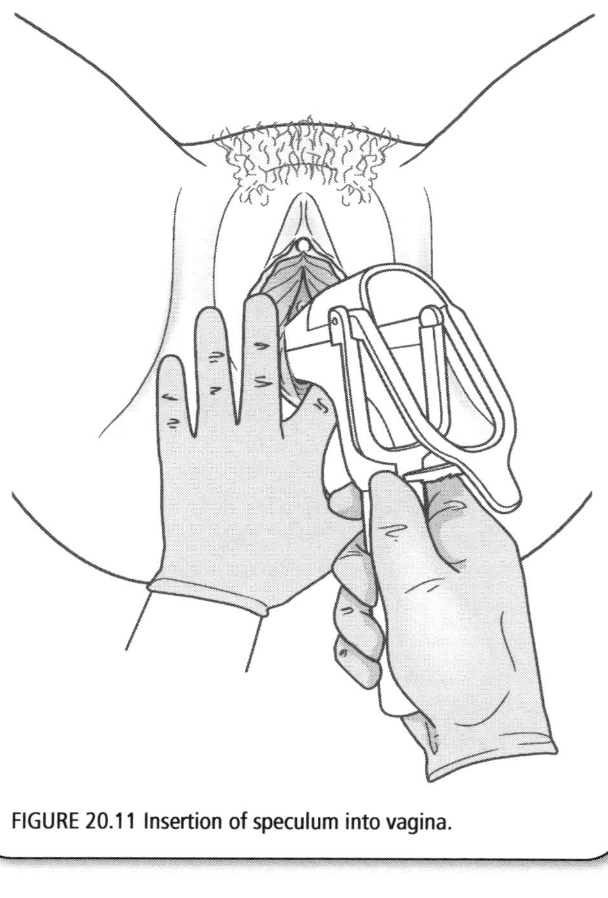

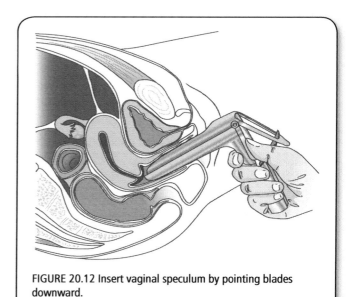

FIGURE 20.12 Insert vaginal speculum by pointing blades downward.

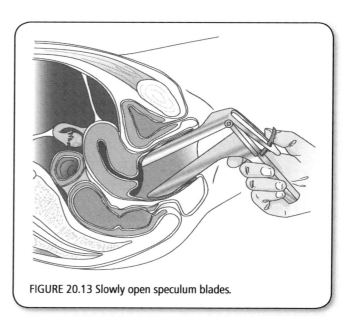

FIGURE 20.13 Slowly open speculum blades.

FIGURE 20.11 Insertion of speculum into vagina.

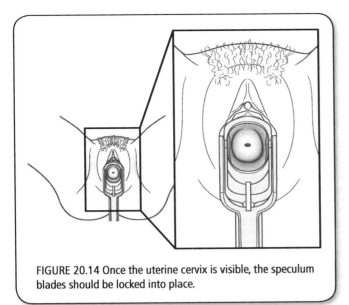

FIGURE 20.14 Once the uterine cervix is visible, the speculum blades should be locked into place.

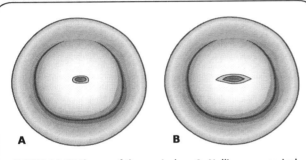

FIGURE 20.15 Shapes of the cervical os. **A.** Nulliparous cervical os. **B.** Parous cervical os.

prior to obtaining specimens. Any purulent discharge from the cervix should be cultured. If the history or findings during the exam are suspicious for vaginitis, a wet mount is obtained, and the pH of the vaginal secretions is tested to make sure it is a vaginal secretion and not a cervical discharge.

Before unlocking the speculum, the provider should warn the patient about the click that will be heard. Keeping a downward pressure, the provider rotates the speculum when it is withdrawn; the provider then inspects the vaginal walls, gradually closing the blades so that they are completely closed by the time the end of the blades reach the introitus.

The discharge on the lower blades of the speculum is assessed for unusual odors, particularly fishy odors, which result from amines released by bacteria that cause bacterial vaginosis; if present, this would be considered a positive "whiff" test. Then two to three drops of 10% KOH are inserted into the discharge. (Note: only the provider's clean hand is used to touch the dropper

bottle.) The patient should then be informed about what was found.

Bimanual Exam • For the bimanual exam, the provider should turn off the light and move it out of the way. Gloves are changed as necessary, for example, if KOH contaminated a glove. The provider should explain to the patient what will be done in the bimanual exam. First, the provider lubricates the index and middle fingers of the gloved hand. Next, the provider touches the inside of the thigh with the back of the hand and inserts the index finger and then the middle finger into the vagina, keeping the pressure downward to avoid the anterior periurethral structures. The vaginal walls are felt for nodularity or tenderness. The provider then locates the cervix and feels for lesions, keeping in mind what was seen during the speculum exam. The length, position, and patency of the os are noted. The provider then puts a finger on each side of the cervix and moves it from side to side, while asking the patient if this movement is painful. ("I am moving your cervix; this may be a little uncomfortable, but is it really painful?") Severe pain is a sign of pelvic inflammatory disease.

The examiner leaves the fingers in place on the cervix and places the other hand on the lower abdomen to palpate for the location of the body of the uterus, trapping the uterus between the inside and outside hands. Starting about halfway between the symphysis and the umbilicus, the provider palpates the uterine outline, noting the shape, consistency, and any irregularity and estimates the width and length. Then the provider moves the inside fingers into the anterior fornix, using the inside hand to palpate as much of the anterior surface as possible and using the abdominal hand to palpate as much of the posterior surface as possible. If the provider does not feel the uterus anteriorly, the inside fingers are moved up the cervix, following the cervical outline as it merges into the body of the uterus. The provider's fingers will likely end up in the posterior fornix; the provider should push up to determine if there is a firm bulge there, which would indicate a retroverted uterus. This can be confirmed later on a rectovaginal exam, if indicated.

If the provider has trouble reaching as far as the posterior fornix, he or she can rest an elbow on the patient's knee for leverage to push harder while keeping the pressure downward as much as possible to avoid the sensitive periurethral areas. The abdominal hand can also be used to push the uterus down toward the inside fingers.

The provider next examines the adnexa by placing the fingers in the right lateral fornix with the palmar surface of the fingers facing anterolaterally and pointing almost straight up. The back of the fingers should be against the cervix. The outside hand is placed just above the inguinal area and swept down toward the inside hand. If nothing is felt, the fingers of both hands are moved medially and then another sweep is attempted to bring the structures in the adnexa (fallopian tube, ovary, and any masses in the area) between the provider's two hands. The fallopian tubes will not be palpable unless there is a mass there. The ovary may be felt as a firm, oval, 2 cm by 3 cm mass. If the ovary is palpated, the size and contour are noted. Any tenderness or pain on palpation of the adnexa is noted.

The provider then moves the fingers to the left lateral fornix, with the palmar surface facing anterolaterally. This is awkward to do if the right hand is the examining hand. Repeat the maneuvers to palpate the left adnexa. The bimanual examination is illustrated in Figure 20.16. The provider should inform the patient of any findings.

Rectovaginal Exam • It is usually not necessary to perform a rectovaginal exam on an adolescent girl.

Conclusion of the Exam • When the pelvic exam is completed, the provider can help the patient to sit up and step down from the exam table. The patient should be given tissues with which to remove any lubricant from the perineum. If a Pap test has been done, the provider should explain that spotting may occur after the exam. If the cervix was friable, there may be enough bleeding to warrant giving the patient a sanitary pad. The patient should be given privacy to get dressed and afterward should sit down with the provider to answer any questions she may have.

A skilled and sensitive provider, with enough time and teaching, usually will be able to perform a satisfactory pelvic exam, even on a reluctant and nervous adolescent. Occasionally, an adolescent, despite a provider's best efforts, will not allow the examination. In such cases, sexual abuse should be suspected, which will require further assessment by a provider who specializes in these examinations (see Chapter 24).

Inspection of the Male Genitalia

Both the penis and scrotum are inspected. Tanner staging is also evaluated. The penis is inspected for size, position of the urethral meatus, foreskin, hygiene, and lesions. The glans and shaft are also examined. The newborn infant's penis normally measures approximately 2 to 3 cm (1 in) in length. The penis grows in length and width during puberty. An enlarged penis in the prepubertal child can indicate precocious puberty or anabolic steroid use. An abnormally small penis in the infant may in fact be a clitoris in a genetically female infant. In obese boys, the penis appears to be smaller due to the large amount of adipose tissue obscuring the base of the penis. An abnormally small penis also occurs in boys with Prader-Willi syndrome, Klinefelter syndrome, and hypopituitarism.

The penis is normally straight. Ventral curvature may be caused by a *chordee*, a band of connective tissue between the urethral meatus and the glans that causes the penis to curve. This condition is associated with hypospadias.

The glans is then inspected; it is normally pink, smooth, and cone-shaped. Any lesions, swelling, discharge, or inflammation are noted. In the circumcised child, the glans should be smooth, pink, and free of edema. The child in diapers may have an irritated meatus owing to ammonia irritation. This is more common in circumcised infants. In the uncircumcised newborn, the foreskin is usually not retracted to examine the glans (see Chapter 11). Erythema and edema of the glans indicate balanitis, which is often caused by poor hygiene. Urethral discharge, redness, lesions, or edema suggest urethritis. In the prepubertal child, sexual abuse must be considered with these findings. The glans is then inspected for placement of the urethral meatus, a slit-like opening normally in the center of the glans. In hypospadias, the urethral meatus is located on the ventral surface of the penis; in epispadias, the urethral meatus is located on the dorsal surface of the penis (Figure 20.17). In both instances, it is important to note this; the infant should not be circumcised, because the foreskin tissue may be used for the surgical repair. If possible, the examiner should observe the urine stream of the infant boy. The urine stream should be straight, strong, and form a slight arc. A weak urinary stream can indicate a neurogenic bladder.

Next, the shaft of the penis is inspected in the circumcised child or adolescent. The skin covering the penis is normally smooth and pink, and the dorsal vein may be visible. There should be no swelling, inflammation, discoloration, lesions, vesicles, ulcers, or papules. In the uncircumcised male, the foreskin of the child older than 3 years should be gently retracted; it should

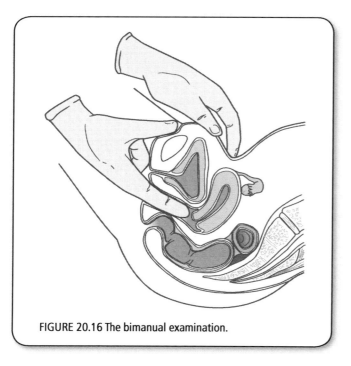

FIGURE 20.16 The bimanual examination.

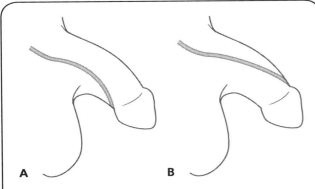

FIGURE 20.17 **A.** Hypospadias in which the urethral meatus is located on the ventral surface of the penis. **B.** Epispadias in which the urethral meatus is on the dorsal surface of the penis.

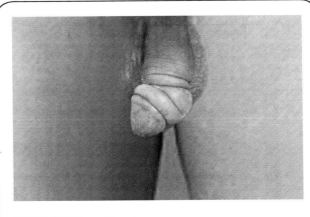

FIGURE 20.18 Paraphimosis.

retract easily. Some foreskin adhesions are normal until approximately 4 years of age in most boys. The foreskin must not be forcibly retracted. If the foreskin cannot be retracted, the child has *phimosis*. If the foreskin remains constricted and cannot be returned to the original position, the child has *paraphimosis*. Paraphimosis is considered a urologic emergency to avoid ischemia or infarction of the glans (Donohoe, Burnette, & Brown, 2012) (Figure 20.18). Some smegma under the foreskin is a normal finding.

Pubic hair development should be consistent with age, and Tanner staging is evaluated (see Figure 20.9). Pubic hair should be in a diamond-shaped pattern at puberty, coarse, and without infestations, such as lice. Premature pubarche (the presence of pubic hair in boys younger than 9 years of age) may be a sign of premature adrenarche, which includes other signs of early puberty, such as axillary hair, increased body odor, oily skin, and acne (Rosenfeld, 2013).

The scrotum is inspected for color, size, symmetry, lesions, inflammation, and the presence of the testicles. In Caucasian infants, the scrotum appears pink. In dark-skinned infants, the scrotum appears dark brown. After puberty, the scrotal skin is a deeper color than surrounding skin. The scrotum should hang loosely from the perineum behind the penis. The left side of the scrotum normally hangs lower than the right side. Scrotal rugae should be prominent on inspection; well-developed scrotal rugae indicate that the testicles have descended even if they cannot currently be palpated in the scrotum. Although scrotal size varies with ambient temperature, bulges or masses are abnormal findings. Lesions on the scrotum may be sebaceous cysts or caused by folliculitis in adolescent males. Scrotal skin that is red and shiny suggests orchitis (mumps). Scrotal bulges or masses in children and adolescents may be caused by an inguinal hernia, epididymitis, orchitis, spermatocele, hydrocele, varicocele, Henoch-Schönlein purpura, testicular tumor, or testicular torsion. One inspection technique to help differentiate hydrocele from incarcerated inguinal hernia

is to transilluminate the scrotum with a transilluminator or bright penlight. The fluid in the hydrocele will cause the scrotum to transilluminate; a hernia will not.

Palpation of the Male Genitalia

Palpation of the male genitalia includes palpating the penis, scrotum, testes, and spermatic cord. When palpating the male genitalia, the examiner must remember to warm his or her hands and make the child or adolescent as comfortable as possible; this is done to minimize the possibility of eliciting the cremasteric reflex. This normal reflex is evident when the cremaster muscle draws descended testicles back into the abdomen; anxiety or the touch of cold hands can elicit this reflex when the inner thigh is stroked. If the child has an erection at any time, the provider should react matter-of-factly, reassuring him that this is a normal reaction to touch.

The shaft of the penis is palpated for masses or nodules; they are normally absent. Next, the glans is gently compressed between the examiner's thumb and forefinger. There should be no discharge; a discharge suggests an STI. The scrotum is palpated for the presence of the testicles, which are palpated for size, shape, symmetry, consistency, and masses. Helpful maneuvers may be necessary to facilitate the stretching of the cremaster muscle to prevent it from contracting and thus moving the testicles upward. Positioning the child in a squatting position, asking him to sit with his legs crossed in front of him, or placing the infant supine with his legs raised and spread are maneuvers that help to move the testicles into the scrotum. Blocking the inguinal canals by gently pressing upward from behind the scrotum with the thumb and forefinger of the opposite hand also help to minimize the cremasteric reflex (Figure 20.19).

When palpated, the testicles should feel smooth, firm, almond-shaped, and of equal size bilaterally (approximately 1.5 to 2 cm until puberty), without palpable masses. Each epididymis should be soft and nontender.

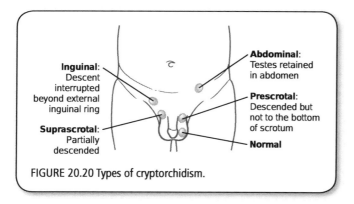

FIGURE 20.19 Technique to minimize the cremasteric reflex.

The testicles should also be easily moveable and fully within the scrotum. Retractile testicles are those that move between the scrotum and external ring; this is within normal limits until puberty. Testicles that are fully undescended or those that cannot be palpated (cryptorchidism) are associated with sterility and testicular cancer. Therefore, documentation of palpated testes is very important because once palpated, they are considered descended, even if they are retracted at the next visit. If the scrotal sac feels empty, the provider should search for the testicles along the inguinal canal and try to milk them down. If the scrotal sac remains empty beyond 6 to 12 months, a referral to a urologist should be made since almost all boys who experience spontaneous descent do so by age 6 months (Sumfest, Kolon, & Rukstalis, 2012). Figure 20.20 illustrates the types of cryptorchidism.

If the provider has difficulty palpating the testicles, the toddler or child can be asked to squat in the "catcher's" position, which may force the testes down. Alternatively, the child can be asked to sit cross-legged to relax the cremasteric reflex. Beginning at age 15, the health care provider should teach the adolescent male how to perform the testicular self-examination. Masses in the scrotum are abnormal and require investigation.

Inspection and Palpation of the Inguinal Area

The inguinal area is inspected and palpated for masses, lymphadenopathy, and hernias. The inguinal area is normally free of visible bulges, which may indicate inguinal lymphadenopathy or hernia (Figure 20.21). In the adolescent, the provider should also palpate the inguinal canal bilaterally. For the right side, the provider places his or her index finger on the lower portion of the right scrotal half and palpates up to the external inguinal ring, invaginating the scrotum (Figure 20.22). Providers may or may not be able to insert their finger. If the provider's finger easily inserts, the finger is gently advanced, and the patient is asked to bear down. If there is a hernia, a mass will be felt either at the tip of the finger or against the side of the finger medially as the patient bears down. In the absence of a hernia, nothing should be felt as the patient bears down. Hernias in children always require surgical correction.

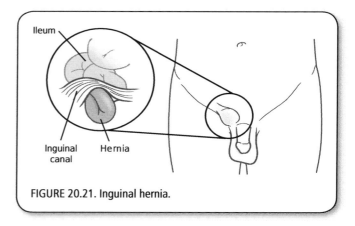

FIGURE 20.21. Inguinal hernia.

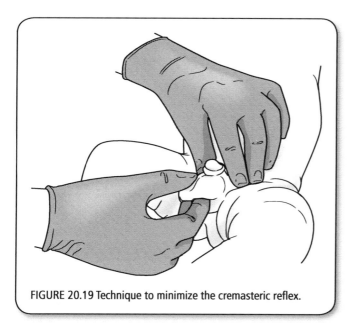

FIGURE 20.20 Types of cryptorchidism.

Inguinal: Descent interrupted beyond external inguinal ring

Suprascrotal: Partially descended

Abdominal: Testes retained in abdomen

Prescrotal: Descended but not to the bottom of scrotum

Normal

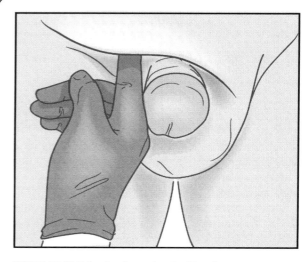

FIGURE 20.22 Palpating for an inguinal hernia.

The horizontal chain of inguinal lymph nodes is palpated next. Occasionally, a soft, small (< 1 cm) node may be palpated. Enlarged, tender, hard, or fixed lymph nodes are abnormal findings and may indicate infection or malignancy.

Examination of the Anus

The anus and rectum are not routinely examined in children and adolescents. Children who present with a history of constipation or anal itching may have an anal fissure, pinworms, or dermatitis caused by detergents or poor toilet hygiene. In these instances, inspection of the anus is necessary to make an accurate diagnosis. Anal discharge or proctitis can also occur with *Chlamydia trachomatis*, *Neisseria gonorrhoeae*, *Treponema pallidum*, and herpes simplex viruses (Fortenberry, 2005). If any visible lesions suggest child abuse or STIs, a detailed history is essential, accompanied by a thorough inspection of the anal region (see Chapter 24). In the young child, examination of the anus is best performed with the child supine, in the frog-leg position, or in the knee–chest position, whichever is most comfortable. In older children and adolescents, the left lateral position is preferred. The anus should appear moist with dark, folded skin. The opening should be tightly closed, and there should be no lesions. Scratch marks around the anus may indicate pinworms. Any fresh or healed injuries are noted, including secretions, bruising, tears, lacerations, rashes, or STI lesions. Papular anal lesions may be caused by HPV (Hornor, 2011). Poor anal sphincter tone or anal laxity may be caused by the passage of large, hard bowel movements, unintentional injury to the anus after impalement, or sexual abuse (Giardino & Finkel, 2005). See Chapter 24 for a complete discussion of the assessment of child abuse.

Examination of the Breasts

In the young adolescent girl, the provider can assess pubertal development by inspection of the breasts, using the Tanner stages of development (see Figure 20.8). For the teen with mature breast development and no reports of changes or symptoms involving the breasts, there is no good evidence to support performing a routine clinical breast examination or for teaching breast self-examination (BSE). The American Cancer Society (ACS) recommends that beginning in their 20s, women should be informed of the benefits and limitations of BSE and be taught the procedure if desired (ACS, 2013). In spite of the evidence that, for populations as a whole, clinical breast exams and BSE are not effective in reducing breast cancer mortality, many breast changes that prove to be malignant are discovered by BSE. Therefore, it may be beneficial for the older teen to receive a clinical breast exam and be taught BSE. All females should become familiar with the normal state of their breasts and changes that may occur with the menstrual cycle. One way to accomplish this is by teaching BSE during the course of a physical examination.

History Related to the Breasts • As part of a complete health history, obtaining data about the breasts is appropriate by using the following questions:

- When did breast development begin?
- How do you feel about your developing breasts?
- What do you know about breast anatomy and physiology?
- Have you had any pain or swelling of the breasts; if so, what is the relationship to the menstrual cycle?
- Have you had any nipple discharge?
- Have you noticed any lumps or bumps?
- What is the breastfeeding history (for parous teens)?
- Have you had breast augmentation surgery (not unknown in teens)?
- What was the date of the last menstrual period (LMP)?

Clinical Breast Examination • The provider should first explain the purpose of the clinical breast examination. If the patient wants to do a self-examination at home, the provider should explain that it should be done each month about a week after menstruation begins, as any premenstrual swelling or tenderness should have resolved by then.

To begin the exam, the provider should position the patient on the end of the exam table and then ask the patient to drop her gown to her waist. The provider then inspects the breasts, observing shape, contour, and size, looking for dimpling, redness, scaliness, areas of skin that resemble an orange peel (a sign of underlying edema), or anything that looks different from one breast to the other. This inspection is repeated with the patient's arms raised over her head and again with her hands pushing in on her hips. Any areas of retraction or deviation of the nipple during these maneuvers should be noted. While performing the inspection, the provider should explain to the patient what findings are expected. The provider should also explain that the patient can do the same kind of inspection by standing in front of a mirror at home.

The patient is then instructed to lie down and put one arm behind her head, keeping the breast that is not being palpated covered. The provider then uses the pads of the fingers, not the fingertips, and begins palpating in little circles about the size of a quarter, starting in a line even with the middle of the axilla and moving in an up and down pattern as far up as the clavicle and down to the ribs (Figure 20.23). This pattern is continued over the entire breast, including the nipple, until the middle of the sternum is reached.

At each location where the pads of the fingers are placed, three quarter-size circles are made, the first with light pressure, the second with medium pressure, and the third with firm pressure, thus enabling the

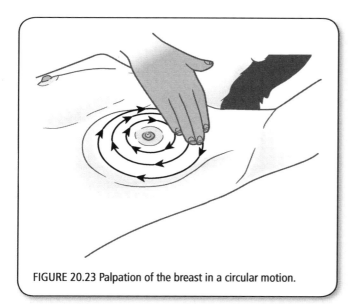

FIGURE 20.23 Palpation of the breast in a circular motion.

examination of the various levels of breast tissue. If any masses are palpated, the size, shape, location, consistency, mobility, and tenderness are noted. The patient can be asked to feel a particular area and whether she has noticed this lump before. If there is any question about whether this is normal breast tissue, the same area on the other breast should be palpated. It is unlikely that an abnormal lesion would occur at the same location in both breasts. It is normal to find a firm ridge of tissue at the lower edge of each breast (inframammary ridge).

Expression of the nipples is optional. If this is done, two fingers are placed on either side of the areola, exerting first downward, then inward pressure to bring the fingers together, and looking for any nipple discharge. If found, the amount and characteristics (e.g., bloody, serous, purulent) are noted. The fingers are then moved to the top and bottom of the areola, and the maneuver is repeated.

To examine the axilla, the patient's arm is supported with the nonexamining hand of the provider and angled slightly away from her side. The axilla should be viewed as an upside-down cup, and the entire inside of the cup is palpated, pressing against the humerus laterally and the ribs medially. Any palpable lymph nodes in the axilla are noted. If this breast exam is not part of a general physical exam, it may be appropriate to palpate the supra- and subclavicular lymph nodes as part of the breast exam. The procedure is then repeated on the other side.

As each part of the exam is performed, the provider explains how this can be done at home during a BSE. Some providers also advise that the breasts can be examined during a shower, where the soap and water may increase the sensitivity of the palpating hand. Patients should be reassured that most breast masses are not cancer but that any changes should be reported promptly to the health care provider.

Although this explanation of the breast exam is focused on females, any complaints about the breasts by adolescent boys should also be assessed. Gynecomastia is common even in nonobese pubertal boys but usually resolves on its own as the sex hormones achieve a testosterone-dominant state. Breast development is usually distressing for a boy, and he and his parents may require reassurance that this is usually normal and will likely resolve spontaneously.

COMMON DIAGNOSTIC STUDIES

Various diagnostic tests may be necessary to clarify differential diagnoses and abnormal conditions involving the genitourinary and reproductive tracts. Some examples of these diagnostic studies and their indications are summarized in Box 20.7.

DOCUMENTATION OF FINDINGS

Sample Write-Up: Healthy Adolescent
Subjective Data

A 16-year-old girl presents for her first pelvic exam. Menarche began at age 13. Menstrual cycle occurs every month and lasts for 8 days. Flow is heavy for first 2 days and then moderate to light for the rest

---

BOX 20.7 Common Diagnostic Tests Used in Genitourinary Assessment

Urine dip: A urine dip usually includes specific gravity, pH, glucose, ketones, protein, red blood cells, and leukocyte esterase. This is often the preliminary test performed in the office to assess for urinary tract infection (UTI).

Urinalysis: The urinalysis is same as the urine dip test, but this test is sent to the laboratory.

Urine culture: Urine culture is the gold standard for diagnosing a UTI. Positive results delineate the infectious organism.

Ultrasonography: Used to evaluate testicular and scrotal masses and edema

CT scan: Used to evaluate metastasis with testicular cancer

Gonorrhea/*Chlamydia* swab: A specimen is obtained, using a laboratory-provided swab. Secretions are sampled from endocervical swabs on girls and urethral swabs on boys to check for the presence of *Neisseria gonorrhoeae* and *Chlamydia trachomatis*.

Pap smear: This test evaluates endocervical cells to screen for cervical cancer. It is normally performed annually on girls and women, beginning 3 years after intercourse or at the age of 21 years, whichever comes first (ACOG, 2010).

of the menses. She has dysmenorrhea that is relieved by over-the-counter nonsteroidal anti-inflammatory drugs. LMP February 22. Sexually active; reports oral and vaginal intercourse. Last vaginal intercourse 2 days ago. Does not use any barrier method of contraception. Denies abnormal vaginal discharge or urinary symptoms. No sores or lesions in vaginal area.

Objective Data

External genitalia: no swelling, lesions, or discharge; Tanner stage 5 breast development
Internal genitalia: vaginal walls without lesions; cervix pink and without lesions; scant, clear mucoid discharge present
Bimanual exam: no cervical motion tenderness, and no enlargement of uterus; adnexa nontender, and ovaries not enlarged
Assessment: normal pelvic examination

Sample Write-Up: Symptomatic Child

Subjective Data

A 4-year-old Caucasian girl comes to the clinic complaining of burning with urination. She has a 3-day history of burning with urination and itching in vaginal area. Today, the patient has been crying with urination. Babysitter gave the patient a bubble bath this weekend.

Objective Data

T: 98.9°F (37.2°C); **BP:** 102/68 mmHg
Abdominal exam: bowel sounds noted in all four quadrants; soft, nondistended, no suprapubic tenderness; no masses or organomegaly
External genitalia: marked erythema of labia; no vaginal discharge noted; urine dip: negative for protein, nitrites, leukocytes
Assessment: vulvovaginitis

Sample Write-Up: Symptomatic Adolescent

Subjective Data

A 16-year-old boy presents to emergency room (ER) with 2-hour history of severe unilateral scrotal and flank pain. Began vomiting in the car on the way to the ER. Denies fever, chills, or blood in urine. No sick contacts. Had appendix removed at age 12 years.

Objective Data

Oral temperature: 98.4°F (37.8°C)
Genitourinary exam (male): scrotum edematous, erythematous; unable to palpate testicles; cremasteric reflex absent; pain increases with elevation of scrotum; transillumination of the scrotum reveals solid mass
Assessment: testicular torsion

Notable Clinical Findings	
AREA	**NOTABLE FINDING**
History	Genetic or metabolic disorders
	Disorders of sex development
	Immunization delay
	Eating disorders
	Use of any type of tobacco products
	Use of alcohol or illegal drugs
	Sexually transmitted infections
	Urinary tract infections
	Multiple sexual partners
	Sexual abuse or assault
Females	Pseudomenses
	Hymenal tag
	Bruising/edema of external genitalia
	Tanner stage
	Breast pain/tenderness
	Abnormalities on clinical breast examination
	Poor hygiene
	Cervical discharge or lesions
	Cervical tenderness
	Vaginal discharge or lesions
	Primary or secondary amenorrhea
	Severe dysmenorrhea
	Pregnancy
	Hematuria
	Dysuria
Males	Tanner stage
	Chordee
	Hypospadias
	Epispadias
	Retractile testes
	Cryptorchidism
	Scrotal bulging/swelling
	Inguinal hernia
	Hydrocele
	Groin/testicular pain
	Testicular torsion
	Phimosis/paraphimosis
	Balanitis
	Dysuria
	Poor hygiene
	Lesions on penis or foreskin

References

Adams, J. (2014). *Genital complaints in pre-pubertal girls.* Retrieved from http://emedicine.medscape.com/article/954024-overview

American Academy of Pediatrics. (2014). *AAP updates schedule of screening and assessments for well-child visits.* Retrieved from http://www.aap.org/en-us/about-the-aap/aap-press-room/pages/AAP-Updates-Schedule-of-Screening-and-Assessments-for-Well-Child-Visits.aspx#sthash.TrxxnnUR.dpuf

American Cancer Society. (2013). *Breast awareness and self-exam.* Retrieved from http://www.cancer.org/cancer/breastcancer/moreinformation/breastcancerearlydetection/breast-cancer-early-detection-acs-recs-bse

American College of Obstetricians and Gynecologists. (2010). *The initial reproductive health visit.* Retrieved from http://www.acog.org/Resources_And_Publications/Committee_Opinions/Committee_on_Adolescent_Health_Care/The_Initial_Reproductive_Health_Visit

Berkowitz, B. (2008). Cultural aspects in the care of the Orthodox Jewish woman. *Journal of Midwifery and Women's Health, 53*(1), 62–67.

Braverman, P. K., Breech, L. & the American Academy of Pediatrics Committee on Adolescence. (2013). Statement of reaffirmation: Gynecologic examination for adolescents in the pediatric office setting. *Pediatrics, 126*(3), 583–590.

Carlo, W. A. (2011). Nursery care. In R. M. Kliegman, R. E. Behrman, H. B. Jenson, & B. F. Stanton (Eds.), *Nelson textbook of pediatrics* (19th ed., p. 538). Philadelphia, PA: Saunders Elsevier.

Carteret, M. (2011). *Modesty in healthcare: A cross-cultural perspective.* Retrieved from http://www.dimensionsofculture.com/2010/11/modesty-in-health-care-a-cross-cultural-perspective/

Centers for Disease Control and Prevention. (2013). *Human papillomavirus (HPV).* Retrieved from http://www.cdc.gov/hpv/vaccine.html

Daniel, M. S., & Postellon, D. C. (2013). *Turner syndrome.* Retrieved from: http://emedicine.medscape.com/article/949681-overview

Donohoe, J. M., Burnette, J. O., & Brown, J. A. (2012). *Paraphimosis.* Retrieved from http://emedicine.medscape.com/article/442883-overview

Fortenberry, J. D. (2005). Sexually transmitted infections (STIs): Screening and diagnosis guidelines for primary care pediatricians. *Pediatric Annals, 34*(10), 803–810.

Giardino, A. P., & Finkel, M. A. (2005). Evaluating child sexual abuse. *Pediatric Annals, 34*(5), 382–394.

Hammoud, M. M., White, C. B., & Fetters, M. D. (2005). Opening cultural doors: Providing culturally sensitive healthcare to Arab American and American Muslim patients. *American Journal of Obstetrics and Gynecology, 193*(4), 1307–1311.

Hornor, G. (2010). A normal ano-genital exam: Sexual abuse or not? *Journal of Pediatric Health Care, 24*(3), 145–151.

Hornor, G. (2011). Medical evaluation for child sexual abuse: What the PNP needs to know. *Journal of Pediatric Health Care, 25*(4), 250–256.

Lucidi, R. S., Alderman, E., Barnes, A. D., Ferry, R. J., Levitsky, L. L., Pritzker, J. G., … Zaenglein, A. L. (2013). *Polycystic ovary syndrome.* Retrieved from http://emedicine.medscape.com/article/256806-overview

Marshall, W. A., & Tanner, J. M. (1969). Variations in patterns of pubertal changes in girls. *Archives of Disease in Childhood, 44,* 291–303.

Rosenfeld, R. L. (2013). *Premature adrenarche.* Up to date. Retrieved from http://www.uptodate.com/contents/premature-adrenarche#H7

Rosenfield, R. L., Lipton, R. B., & Drum, M. L. (2009). Thelarche, pubarche, and menarche attainment in children with normal and elevated body mass index. *Pediatrics, 123*(1), 84–88.

Sumfest, J. M., Kolon, T. F., & Rukstalis, D. B. (2012). *Cryptorchidism.* Retrieved from http://emedicine.medscape.com/article/438378-overview

von Gontard, A., Baeyens, D., Van Hoecke, E., Warzak, W. J., & Bachmann, C. (2011). Psychological and Psychiatric issues in urinary and fecal incontinence. *Journal of Urology, 185*(4), 1432–1437.

World Health Organization. (2014). *Female genital cutting.* Retrieved from http://www.who.int/mediacentre/factsheets/fs241/en/index.html

Assessment of the Musculoskeletal System

A healthy musculoskeletal system is essential for normal growth and development of the child. Strong, healthy bones and muscles allow for normal linear growth, gross and fine motor physical activity, body movement and play. Assessment of the musculoskeletal system requires strong knowledge of gross and fine motor developmental milestones and the impact that physical growth has on a child's body image and self-esteem. Excellent pediatric musculoskeletal assessment skills are essential, particularly when musculoskeletal injury has occurred. Repetitive-use injuries, epiphyseal plate fractures, and intentional injuries to children require immediate recognition and appropriate referrals.

ANATOMY AND PHYSIOLOGY

There are 206 bones (207 in an infant), three types of joints, and more than 600 muscles in the human body. The primary functions of the musculoskeletal system are to support and protect the inner structures of the body and to allow mobility. The musculoskeletal system includes the *bones, joints, ligaments, cartilage, muscles,* and *tendons.* These structures allow for various movements that are described in Table 21.1.

Skeletal System

Individual bones complete the skeleton, which serves as the body's framework. It can be broken down into three parts: the *axial* skeleton, the *appendicular* skeleton, and the *joints.* Eighty bones make up the axial skeleton, which consists of the *vertebral column, sternum, ribs,* and *skull.* The appendicular skeleton is composed of 126 bones, which include the *arms, legs,* and *hips* (Figure 21.1). In addition to providing structure and support to the body, the bones also produce red and

white blood cells, store calcium and phosphorus, and release these minerals into the bloodstream as needed. The skeletal system includes five major bone types; their names reflect their shape: *long* bones (e.g., the humerus, femur); *short* bones (e.g., the carpals); *flat* bones (e.g., the skull, sternum, scapulae); *irregular* bones (e.g., the vertebrae), and *sesamoid* bones or bones embedded by tendons (e.g., the patellae). The long bones are especially important in children because of their structure and makeup. Long bones are composed of a rounded end termed the *epiphysis* and a long shaft, or *diaphysis.* Between these two portions is the *metaphysis,* the part of the bone that grows during childhood. Between the epiphysis and metaphysis is the *physis* or *growth plate* (Figure 21.2). This growth plate is structurally weak because it is made of cartilage and does not fully ossify until early adulthood. Thus, traumatic or shearing forces or any epiphyseal fracture can result in early or incomplete closure of the growth plate, causing numerous complications, including limb deformity, shortening of the bone, and arrest of growth (Mehlman & Koepplinger, 2012).

Bone tissue formation, or *osteogenesis,* is a continuous process that occurs as active cells (*osteoblasts*) build new bone tissue, while tissue destruction (reabsorption) is driven by *osteoclasts.* In childhood and adolescence, bone growth exceeds reabsorption, but in early adulthood, these processes are balanced; beginning in middle age, bone tissue reabsorption outpaces bone growth. Because osteogenesis occurs more rapidly in children, fractured bones in children heal more rapidly than those in adults (Poduval, 2013).

Joints are the places at which adjoining bones meet. The joints are held together by ligaments and are cushioned by cartilage. Ligaments are strong, fibrous cords

TABLE 21.1	Skeletal Positions
TERM	**DEFINITION**
Abduction	Movement away from the midline
Adduction	Movement toward the midline
Circumduction	Rotation or circular movements of the limbs
Dorsiflexion	Movement of hands or feet upward
Eversion	Movement of an extremity or part of an extremity away from the body
Extension	Increase in the angle of a joint; opposite of flexion
External rotation	Turning anterior surface of a limb outward or away from midline
Flexion	Decrease in the angle of a joint; opposite of extension
Hyperextension	Increase in the angle of a joint beyond the normal angle
Internal rotation	Turning anterior surface of a limb inward or toward midline
Inversion	Movement of an extremity or part of an extremity toward the body
Luxation	Dislocation
Plantarflexion	Movement of hands or feet downward
Pronation	Palmar surface turned downward or toward posterior surface of body
Rotation	Movement around a central axis
Subluxation	Partial dislocation
Supination	Palmar surface turned upward or toward anterior surface of body
Valgus	Deviation away from the midline
Varus	Deviation toward the midline

of connective tissue that bind the joints firmly together. All synovial joints include ligaments. Cartilage is an avascular tissue that receives its nutrients from synovial fluid through diffusion. Cartilage is a firm but flexible tissue that cushions joints and helps soften any impact.

There are three types of joints: *synovial*, *cartilaginous*, and *fibrous*. Synovial joints are the most common joint type and also the most mobile. Components of these joints include a *joint capsule*, synovial *membrane*, *articular cartilage*, and synovial *cavity*. This cavity is filled with synovial fluid to lubricate the joint and enhance movement. There are six types of synovial joints in the body; examples include the carpals of the wrist, the elbow (between the humerus and ulna and between the radius and the ulna), the wrist, the thumb, the shoulder, the knee, and hip joints. Figure 21.3 illustrates the components of a synovial joint of the hip. In synovial joints, cartilage covers the surface of bones where they meet. Cartilaginous joints connect two bones with cartilage, allowing only slight movement. The pubic bone juncture and the joint between the manubrium and

sternum are examples of cartilaginous joints. Fibrous joints are the least mobile of the three types of joints. These joints tightly connect the articular surfaces of two bones with dense connective tissue. An example of a fibrous joint is the cranial suture in the infant skull. Examples of major joints and types of motion are listed in Table 21.2.

The Spine

The vertebral column (spine) consists of 33 individual bones (*vertebrae*) that connect to form a flexible column. The *spine* can be divided into four curves: *cervical*, *thoracic*, *lumbar*, and *sacral* vertebrae (Figure 21.4). Individual vertebrae can be further divided according to anatomic region: 7 cervical, 12 thoracic, 5 lumbar, and 5 (fused) sacral vertebrae, and the *coccyx* ("tailbone"), which comprises 3 to 4 fused vertebrae. The spinous processes of the vertebrae begin at the seventh cervical vertebra and continue to the sacrum. The thoracic vertebrae articulate with the ribs and form the thoracic cage (see Chapter 17). The lumbar vertebrae are the largest of the vertebral column because they are the

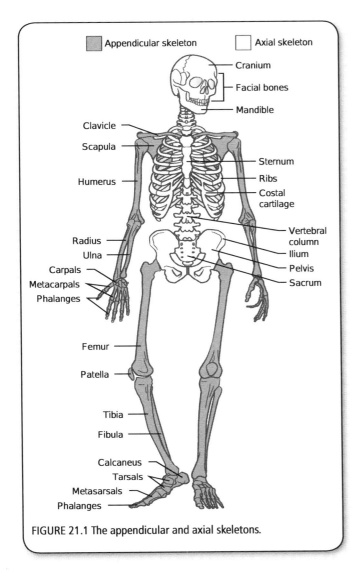

FIGURE 21.1 The appendicular and axial skeletons.

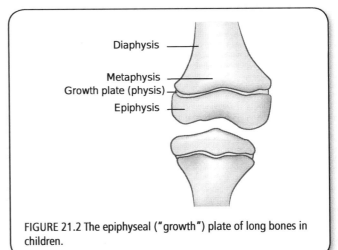

FIGURE 21.2 The epiphyseal ("growth") plate of long bones in children.

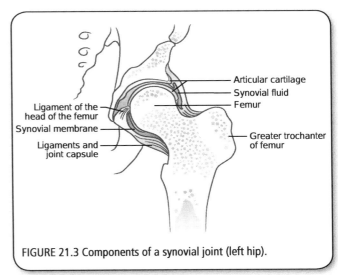

FIGURE 21.3 Components of a synovial joint (left hip).

TABLE 21.2	**Major Joints and Joint Movements**				
JOINT	**MOTION**	**JOINT**	**MOTION**	**JOINT**	**MOTION**
Scapulothoracic	Forward rotation Backward rotation Adduction	Wrists	Supination Pronation Palmar flexion Extension Dorsiflexion	Knee	Flexion Extension Minimal rotation
Acromioclavicular	Flexion Extension Circumduction Internal and external rotation	Fingers	Flexion Extension Hyperextension Limited abduction Limited adduction Circumduction	Ankle	Extension Dorsiflexion Plantarflexion
Vertebral column	Flexion Hyperextension Lateral deviation Rotation	Thumb	Flexion Extension Circumduction Abduction Adduction Opposition (thumb moves toward fingers)	Foot	Flexion Extension Inversion Eversion

(continued)

TABLE 21.2	Major Joints and Joint Movements (continued)				
JOINT	MOTION	JOINT	MOTION	JOINT	MOTION
Elbow	Flexion Extension Supination Pronation	Hip and femur	Extension Hyperextension Abduction Adduction Internal rotation External rotation Circumduction	Toes	Flexion Extension Abduction Adduction

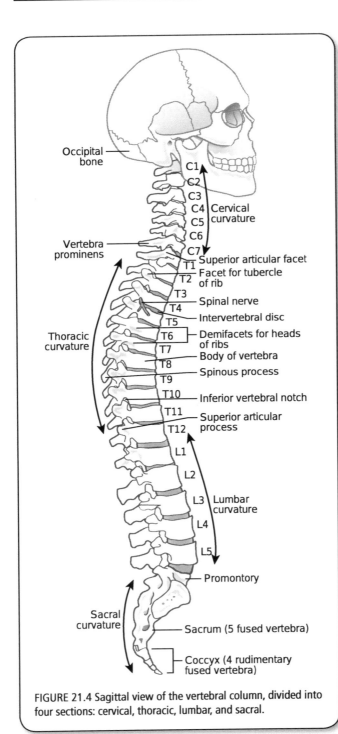

FIGURE 21.4 Sagittal view of the vertebral column, divided into four sections: cervical, thoracic, lumbar, and sacral.

main weight-bearing portion of the spine and allow for flexion and extension. The *sacrum*, a fusion of five vertebrae, articulates with the *ilium* at the sacroiliac joint. This is a strong joint, joined by ligaments, that allows for the movements necessary for standing, walking, turning, and sitting. The three or four lowest vertebrae are fused to form the coccyx, which articulates with the sacrum. The vertebral column houses the spinal cord (see Chapter 22).

Clavicle and Upper Extremities

There are two *clavicles*, each articulating with the sternum proximally and scapula distally. The scapulae and upper extremities are supported by two strong ligaments: the *trapezoid* and *conoid*. The scapula is attached by muscles to the thoracic cage. Movement is possible between the scapula and thorax and between the scapula and humerus. The humerus extends from the shoulder to the elbow. The structures of the shoulder are illustrated in Figure 21.5.

The elbow is composed of the humerus, radius, and ulna. The ulna is larger than the radius and runs from the elbow to the wrist on the lateral side; the radius is on the medial side. The bony prominence of the elbow is the *medial epicondyle*, which with the *lateral condyle* form an area where the humerus and the proximal surface of the ulna articulate. The structures of the elbow are illustrated in Figure 21.6.

The distal end of the radius articulates with the distal end of the ulna to create the proximal portion of the wrist. Eight *carpal bones* bound by ligaments make up the wrist. The hand and fingers include the 8 carpals of the wrist, 5 metacarpals of the palm, and 12 phalanges of the fingers. Each finger contains three phalanges. The thumb is composed of one metacarpal bone and two phalanges (Figure 21.7).

Pelvis and Lower Extremities

The pelvic girdle consists of two *innominate* (hip) bones, the sacrum, and the *coccyx*. Each innominate bone is divided into the ilium, *ischium*, and *symphysis pubis*. The *femur*, the longest and strongest bone in the body, extends from the hip to the knee. The strongest ligament

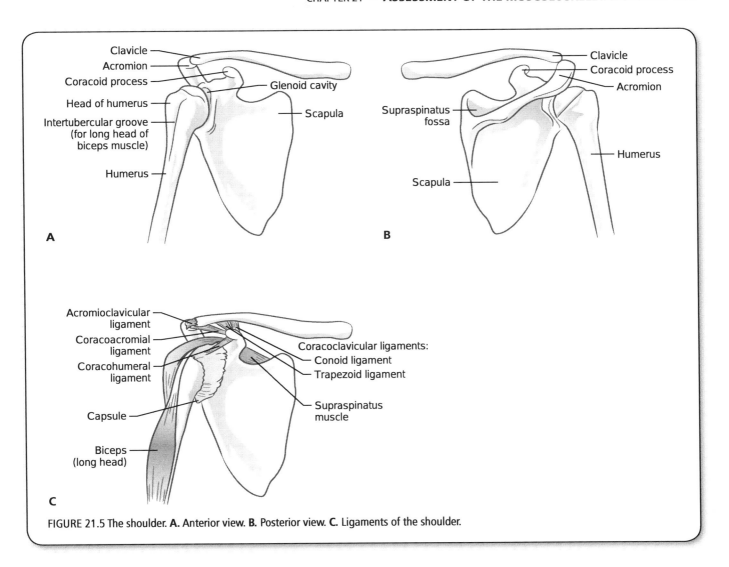

FIGURE 21.5 The shoulder. **A.** Anterior view. **B.** Posterior view. **C.** Ligaments of the shoulder.

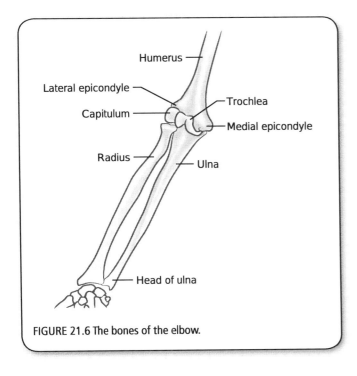

FIGURE 21.6 The bones of the elbow.

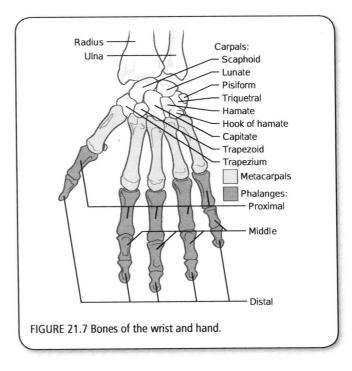

FIGURE 21.7 Bones of the wrist and hand.

in the body, the iliofemoral ligament, connects the femur to the ilium (see Figure 21.3).

The articulation of the femur, tibia, and patella forms the knee joint, which connects the distal end of the femur to the proximal end of the tibia (Figure 21.8). The tibia and fibula are the two bones below the knee; the tibia, the larger of the two, begins at the knee and extends to the ankle on the medial side. The fibula begins below the knee and extends to the ankle on the lateral side. Proximally, the fibula articulates with the tibia but not with the femur. The patella also articulates with the femur and forms the "knee cap." The knee joint is composed of and stabilized by cartilage, ligaments, tendon, and muscles.

At the distal ends of the tibia and fibula, the *talus* (ankle bone) articulates with the *calcaneus* (heel). Five *tarsals* and three *metatarsals* form the medial longitudinal arch; two tarsals and metatarsals form the lateral longitudinal arch. The metatarsals and distal row of tarsals make up the transverse arch. Two phalanges comprise the great toe; three phalanges make up each of the small toes. The bones of the foot are illustrated in Figure 21.9.

Muscles and Tendons

Muscles are tissues composed of fibers or bundles of cells. They vary in size, shape, and arrangement. The muscles contract to move bones, while the joints allow the movement to occur. There are three types of muscles in the body: skeletal, smooth, and cardiac. Skeletal muscles are voluntary, striated, and arranged in bundles, such as the triceps, biceps, and quadriceps muscles. Smooth muscles are nonstriated and perform involuntary movements, such as those in the respiratory, urinary, and gastrointestinal systems. Cardiac muscle is the striated, involuntary muscle in the heart. Tendons are firm, strong cords of fibrous tissue that connect the muscle to the periosteum of the bone.

DEVELOPMENTAL CONSIDERATIONS

Embryologic Development

The axial and appendicular skeletons begin to form in the fourth week of gestation. Limb formation also begins in the fourth gestational week when limb buds develop from outpouchings of the embryonic wall and proceed in a proximal–distal fashion. The limb buds evolve into paddles, then plates, and finally into digits. Limb abnormalities (e.g., *polydactyly*, *syndactyly*) originate during the crucial embryonic period of days 22 to 24. The critical period for lower limb development occurs between days 26 and 44; the type of limb abnormality depends on the timing and cause of the defect. The joints develop from intra-embryonic mesoderm. Continued differentiation of the mesoderm results in the formation of the three specialized muscle groups.

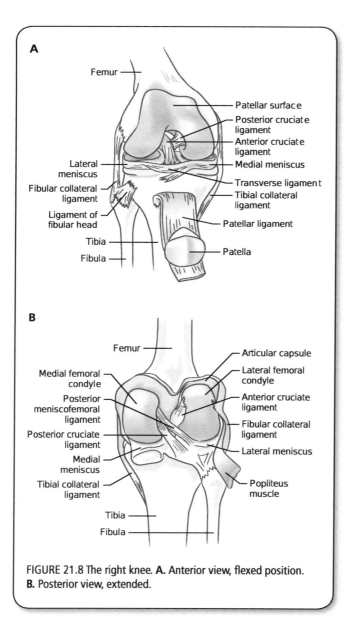

FIGURE 21.8 The right knee. **A.** Anterior view, flexed position. **B.** Posterior view, extended.

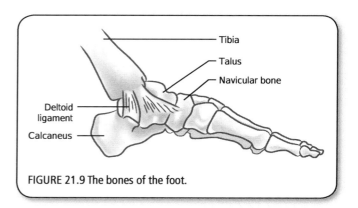

FIGURE 21.9 The bones of the foot.

Skeletal Development

Numerous differences exist between the skeletal system of a child and that of an adult. The skeleton grows continuously but at varying rates among children over a period of 19 to 20 years. The bones are not fully ossified until adulthood, making them more pliable, soft, and easily bent (Poduval, 2013). This is clinically significant because in very young children, bones most often bend rather than break. Therefore, the type and location of any fracture must be fully evaluated in reference to the child's age and developmental level to distinguish between intentional and unintentional injuries (see Chapter 24).

Until puberty, the percentage of cartilage in the ribs is high, making the ribs flexible and pliant (Ball, Bindler, & Cowen, 2012). Because of this, rib fractures are uncommon in young children, and the ribs provide minimal protection to underlying organs and blood vessels.

From birth until approximately 3 to 4 months, the spine is C-shaped. This affects the infant's ability to control his or her head. *Lordosis*, or convex curvature of the spine, is a normal variation in infants and toddlers, which causes the appearance of abdominal distention in this age group (see Chapter 19, Figure 19.5) (Wilson & Curry, 2011). Infants and toddlers have normal physiologic bowing of the legs (*genu varum*) because the leg muscles bear the weight of a relatively large trunk (Figure 21.10A). *Genu valgum* (knock-knees) is a normal variation, beginning at 2 to 3 years and resolving by approximately 7 to 8 years (Figure 21.10B). *Pes planus* (flat feet) is a normal variation in infants as they first begin to walk; this slowly resolves as they grow, at which point the muscles in the foot strengthen, and the arch develops.

A growth spurt occurs in adolescence, peaking at age 12 for girls and age 14 for boys. The skeleton also grows faster than muscles during this time, causing the hands and feet to grow faster than the body.

Muscle Development

During infancy, muscles comprise 25% of an infant's weight, compared with 40% in adults (Ball et al., 2012). Infants also have less muscle tone and coordination during infancy, increasing their risk for injury. As myelination proceeds, voluntary muscle control progresses. Muscle growth contributes greatly to weight gain during childhood, and walking and weight bearing stimulate the growth of bone and muscle. Muscle growth continues into adolescence, with growth occurring more rapidly during this time because of the presence of sex hormones, particularly testosterone. Rapid muscle growth during this time can cause clumsiness, increasing the adolescent's risk for injury.

CULTURAL, ETHNIC, AND RACIAL CONSIDERATIONS

Some musculoskeletal conditions occur more frequently in certain racial or ethnic groups, depending on cultural practices, environmental and socioeconomic factors, or in some instances, genetics. For example, Blount's disease (tibia vara) occurs most commonly in Scandinavian and African American children (Lamont, Fragomen, & Rozbruch, 2013). Caucasian children have a high incidence of developmental dysplasia of the hip (DDH), as do indigenous North American people who keep their newborns tightly swaddled because of the cold, thereby keeping the hips in adduction. Developmental dysplasia of the hip may also have a genetic component (Tamai & McCarthy, 2014). *Talipes equinovarus* (true clubfoot) is most common in Polynesian groups, particularly in Tongan people (Patel & Herzenberg, 2013).

ASSESSMENT

History

Musculoskeletal problems in children can be acute or chronic. The reason for the child's health care visit guides the provider in deciding what data to gather for the health history. For children who are being examined for the first time, a complete past medical history (PMH), family history, and social history are obtained (see Chapter 6). These histories are updated as needed when the child presents for health maintenance visits, with special attention to assessment of developmental milestones and any history of musculoskeletal injury or infection. The onset of puberty is noted in adolescents (see Chapter 20) to estimate the amount of remaining musculoskeletal growth for the child. A developmental history is especially important, as delays in achieving

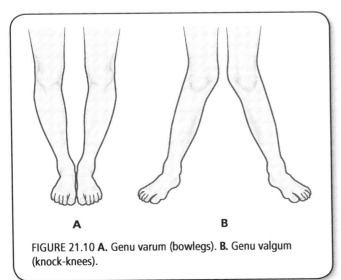

FIGURE 21.10 **A.** Genu varum (bowlegs). **B.** Genu valgum (knock-knees).

developmental milestones can result from congenital musculoskeletal and spinal deformities, indicate a musculoskeletal injury or infection, or be the result of neglect. A focused history is required when the child presents with a pain, musculoskeletal injury, infection, or developmental delay.

Past Medical History

Prenatal History • The stage of pregnancy at which prenatal care began should be noted, as well as whether the child has had any prenatal exposure to drugs, alcohol, or intrauterine infections that can cause musculoskeletal abnormalities. Intrauterine position can influence developmental dysplasia of the hip, torticollis, and *metatarsus adductus* (positional clubfoot). Oligohydramnios is a risk factor for developmental dysplasia of the hip (Tamai & McCarthy, 2014).

Perinatal and Neonatal History • The child's birth history is reviewed; special attention is paid to whether any perinatal or neonatal asphyxia occurred, which could increase the child's chances of developing cerebral palsy. Any history of congenital musculoskeletal deformities should be explored; some examples of these conditions are listed in Table 21.3. A history of breech or shoulder presentation is noted; a fractured clavicle can result from a shoulder presentation. Breech presentation increases the likelihood of DDH (Tamai & McCarthy, 2014). It is essential to assess for any history of prematurity; very low birth weight premature infants are prone to osteopenia (Abrams, 2014) and often have gastrointestinal conditions that impede absorption of nutrients essential for bone growth and ossification (Blackman, 2007).

Review of Systems

The pediatric review of systems (ROS) includes asking not only about specific musculoskeletal conditions, but chronic conditions involving other body systems. These conditions may involve signs and symptoms that manifest in the bones, tendons, joint, or muscles; affect physical growth and stature; and interfere with participation in sports. Some examples include the following:

- **Integumentary:** Café-au-lait marks (more than five marks suggest neurofibromatosis), nevi (tuberous sclerosis), or hemangioma (Klippel-Trénaunay syndrome)
- **Cardiovascular:** Congenital heart defects (cause poor growth)
- **Respiratory:** Poorly controlled asthma or cystic fibrosis (cause poor growth)
- **Gastrointestinal:** Celiac disease, cystic fibrosis, inflammatory bowel disease, or short bowel syndrome
- **Hematologic:** Hemophilia (can cause bleeding in bones and joints) or sickle cell disease (can cause bone and joint pain)
- **Infectious:** Tuberculosis (can infect spine and joints), osteomyelitis, Lyme disease (can cause arthritis, which affects large joints, especially the knee), or septic arthritis
- **Metabolic:** Obesity (can cause slipped capital femoral epiphysis [SCFE] and Blount's disease)
- **Musculoskeletal:** Torticollis, metatarsus adductus (positional clubfoot), talipes equinovarus (clubfoot), fractures, genu varum (bowlegs), genu valgum (knock-knees), pes planus (flat feet), DDH, scoliosis, spinal deformities, juvenile rheumatoid arthritis (JRA), limited range of motion, polydactyly, syndactyly, achondroplasia, amniotic bands;

TABLE 21.3	Congenital Musculoskeletal Deformities
DEFORMITY	**DESCRIPTION**
Neck Torticollis ("wry neck")	Involuntary muscle contractions of neck caused by birth trauma or intrauterine positioning that leads to fibrosis and shortening of sternocleidomastoid muscle
Wrist and Hand Polydactyly	Extra digits on hand or foot formed by abnormal soft tissue and bone; may be associated with a syndrome; abnormal hand function possible.
Syndactyly	Occurs when digits of hands or feet fail to separate; may also be associated with syndrome complexes.
Talipomanus (clubhand)	Congenital absence of radial or ulna causes marked inward deviation of hand and extremely short forearm.
Hip Developmental dysplasia	Involves a range of disorders affecting the proximal femur and acetabulum from preluxation to complete dislocation of the femoral head
Foot and Ankle Pes planus (flatfoot)	Laxity of ligaments supporting foot's longitudinal arch
Metatarsus adductus	Medial deviation of forefoot occurring as a result of intrauterine positioning; does not involve muscles, tendons, and bone
Talipes equinovarus (clubfoot)	Internal rotation of foot with forefoot adduction; involves muscles, tendons, and bone

sacral sinus or dimple, SCFE, Legg-Calvé-Perthes disease, Osgood-Schlatter disease, toxic synovitis of the hip, osteogenesis imperfecta, or Marfan syndrome
- **Renal:** Polycystic kidney disease, renal tubular acidosis, chronic glomerulonephritis, nephritic syndrome, or Fanconi syndrome
- **Endocrine:** Growth hormone deficiency, hypothyroidism, premature epiphyseal closure (androgen or estrogen excess), or primary or secondary amenorrhea
- **Neoplastic:** Acute lymphocytic leukemia (can cause bone and joint pain), Ewing's sarcoma, multiple myeloma, or osteosarcoma
- **Neurologic:** Hydrocephalus, spina bifida occulta, meningocele, myelomeningocele, or Erb's palsy
- **Neuromuscular:** Cerebral palsy or muscular dystrophy
- **Psychosocial:** Anorexia nervosa or bulimia nervosa
- **Syndromes:** Turner syndrome, Noonan syndrome, Prader-Willi syndrome, or Down syndrome

Hospitalizations

It is necessary to note any past hospitalizations for conditions involving the musculoskeletal system, such as traction, including the indication for the traction; fractures; treatment for osteomyelitis; hospitalizations for osteogenesis imperfecta; and chronic problems related to cerebral palsy, muscular dystrophy, or the complications of immobility after spinal cord injury.

Any complications of casting or traction must also be noted, such as neurovascular compromise, skin breakdown, compartment syndrome, and osteomyelitis resulting from pin site infection with skeletal traction.

Injuries

An essential part of the musculoskeletal history is to determine any past history of injuries. This includes fractures, dislocations, subluxations, sprains, or strains. Fractured clavicles are very common in neonates and young children. Specific sports-related injuries are noted, including whether repeated injuries have taken place. The type and location of any fracture is especially important to note, along with the history of the mechanism of injury. This information, coupled with the child's age and developmental level, assists the provider in discerning intentional from unintentional injuries (see Chapter 24). Frequent minor injuries may indicate neglect or poor adult supervision in young children or risk-taking behavior in the adolescent.

Surgical History

The provider must determine what surgeries related to the musculoskeletal system the child has undergone. Some examples include open reduction with internal fixation of fractures or musculoskeletal deformities, tendon-lengthening procedures for cerebral palsy, surgical intervention for clubfoot, DDH, SCFE or scoliosis, the placement of skeletal traction, or surgical debridement for osteomyelitis.

Current Medications

The provider should inquire about any medications the child is taking on a regular or as-needed basis, including over-the-counter and complementary or alternative treatments (see Chapter 6). In particular, the provider should note if the child is taking any steroids, nonsteroidal anti-inflammatory drugs, aspirin, acetaminophen, muscle relaxants, sedatives, narcotics, anticonvulsants, or any neuromuscular agents. The indication for the drug as well as the dose must be obtained. Youth who are involved in sports should be asked about vitamins, iron, or herbal supplements. Use of anabolic steroids, stimulants, or laxatives is assessed in a nonjudgmental manner, preferably with the parent out of the room.

Family History

Certain portions of the family history are relevant to the musculoskeletal assessment. For example, the provider should inquire about any family history of genetic or idiopathic short stature, or genetic disorders such as achondroplasia (dwarfism), muscular dystrophy, arthritis, DDH, scoliosis, or osteogenesis imperfecta. When obtaining the preparticipation sports history and physical, particular attention should be paid to any family history of asthma; cerebrovascular accident; myocardial infarction before age 50; sudden, unexplained death in an adolescent or young adult relative; prolonged QT syndrome; Marfan syndrome; hypertrophic cardiomyopathy, or any other cardiac abnormalities (Hoang, Coel, Vidal, Wilson, & Pengel, 2012). A family history of hemophilia or sickle cell disease is relevant in children with bone or joint pain or with a limp (Leung & Lemay, 2004).

Social History

The social history focuses on the family's living situation; persons living in the home; and any risk factors that could predispose the child to falls, musculoskeletal injuries, or infections. An essential part of this history includes determining the quality of the caregiver–child relationship, particularly with children 3 years of age and younger. This assessment can assist in determining whether neglect is taking place, which affects the attainment of gross and fine motor developmental milestones and can result in musculoskeletal injuries. Children in this age group are also vulnerable to injuries inflicted by the parent or caregiver (see Chapter 24). If the child is involved in sports, the child's age and type of sport is noted, as well as whether appropriate protective gear is used at all times. The amount, type, and frequency of exercise is also noted, including weight-lifting regimens and warm-up exercises.

Developmental History

A comprehensive developmental history is essential when evaluating the musculoskeletal system. The timing of the child's acquisition of gross and fine motor milestones should be reviewed, noting any developmental delays (see Chapter 2). Delays in achieving developmental milestones may be the result of hearing, vision, language, or learning abnormalities, which may accompany spinal deformities. The child's growth charts are evaluated, with special attention to slow growth or the child falling off his or her own growth curve. The child's growth must also be compared with that of the parents and siblings if possible.

Nutritional History

A nutritional history is often necessary when conducting a musculoskeletal assessment. Children who are obese often suffer musculoskeletal complications, including SCFE, which results when excess weight places a shear force on the growth plate in the hip (Walter, Lin, & Schwartz, 2013), and Blount's disease (tibia vara), which results from excess body weight compressing the medial knee, resulting in varus deformities of both tibia (see Figure 21.10A) (Lamont et al., 2013).

For children involved in sports, particular attention is paid to calcium and iron intake, as well as adequate hydration while participating in exercise or sports. Adequate calcium intake is essential to normal bone growth; iron is vital to oxygen transport and metabolism, and all child athletes must be assessed for anemia. Body image and weight are especially important to gymnasts, runners, and wrestlers; these children and adolescents must be assessed for eating disorders (Lilly & McCambridge, 2008).

Rickets, a condition caused by deficiency of vitamin D, calcium, or both, is reemerging as a problem in developing countries. This condition causes softening of the bones and is more prevalent in winter months in temperate climates when exposure to sunlight is limited, in dark-skinned children, in children who are vegetarians, and in breastfed infants who do not receive vitamin D supplements (Schwarz, Greer, & Finberg, 2013). It is particularly important to review the child's growth charts, noting trends toward overweight, obesity, or underweight, which may signal a need for vitamin supplements.

History of Present Illness

In an evaluation of musculoskeletal complaints, the child's age and developmental level, concurrent illness, history of recent injury, associated findings, and past health are relevant when considering differential diagnoses. For example, fever associated with joint pain, stiffness, and swelling may present different diagnostic possibilities than joint pain and swelling alone. Examples of musculoskeletal complaints in children include pain, limp, fractures, and sports injuries. Relevant questions to ask for the focused history can be found in Table 21.4.

Physical Examination

Physical examination of the musculoskeletal system in children is achieved through inspection and palpation, focusing on general configuration, symmetry and length of extremities, deformities, masses, crepitus, and point tenderness. A developmental approach to the physical examination is necessary because of the child's motor

TABLE 21.4	**History of Present Illness: Musculoskeletal Complaints**	
COMPLAINT	**ASSESSMENTS**	**DIFFERENTIAL DIAGNOSES/CAUSES**
Back pain	Onset? Recent injury? Involved in sports? Strenuous exercise? Does child carry heavy school backpack? Severity of pain? Aggravating and relieving factors? Response to pain medication? Does pain wake child at night? Any fever?	Contusion, sprain, strain, spondylolysis, kyphosis, acute disc herniation, degenerative disc disease, sacroiliac inflammation, diskitis, osteomyelitis, spinal tumor (MacDonald & D'Hemecourt, 2007), or apophyseal injury (Lilly & McCambridge, 2008)
Hip pain	Onset? Recent injury? Recent URI? Any fever? Limited range of motion? Limb shortening? Swelling? Involved in sports? Is child obese? Severity of pain? Aggravating and relieving factors? Response to pain medication? Does pain wake child at night?	Apophyseal avulsion injury in adolescent athlete, slipped capital femoral epiphysis (obese child or adolescent), acetabular labral tear, femoral neck stress fracture (Heyworth, Voos, & Metzl, 2007), toxic synovitis of the hip, septic arthritis, osteoarthritis, Legg-Calvé-Perthes disease, or fracture
Knee pain	Onset? Recent injury? Swelling? Limited range of motion? Involved in sports? Is child obese? Severity of pain? Aggravating and relieving factors? Response to pain medication? Does pain wake child at night? Any fever?	Cerebral palsy (Senaran, Holden, Dabney, & Miller, 2007), anterior cruciate ligament injury, meniscus tear, Osgood-Schlatter disease, osteochondritis, fracture, septic arthritis, JRA, or osteogenic sarcoma

TABLE 21.4   History of Present Illness: Musculoskeletal Complaints (*continued*)

COMPLAINT	ASSESSMENTS	DIFFERENTIAL DIAGNOSES/CAUSES
Leg pain	Onset? Recent injury? Swelling? Limited range of motion? Involved in sports? Is child obese? Severity of pain? Aggravating and relieving factors? Response to pain medication? Does pain wake child at night? Any fever?	Shin splints, stress fracture, iliotibial band syndrome, patellar femoral pain syndrome, muscle strain (Lilly & McCambridge, 2008), osteoarthritis, leukemia, tumor, or sickle cell disease
Ankle pain	Onset? Recent injury? Swelling? Limited range of motion? Involved in sports? Is child obese? Severity of pain? Aggravating and relieving factors? Response to pain medication? Does pain wake child at night? Any fever?	Sprain, fracture, septic arthritis, JRA, pes planus, metatarsus adductus, ingrown toenail, or poorly fitting shoes
Limp	Age of child? Onset of limp? Recent injury? Involved in sports? Strenuous exercise? Associated pain? Aggravating and relieving factors for limp? Past medical history? Family history? (Rush, 2013)	Trauma, fractures, sprains, overuse injuries, developmental dysplasia of the hip, septic arthritis, osteomyelitis, toxic synovitis, Legg-Calvé-Perthes disease, JRA, leukemia, or tumors (Rush, 2013)

JRA, juvenile rheumatoid arthritis; URI, upper respiratory infection.

development and the normal physiologic variations in musculoskeletal development. Equipment necessary for the musculoskeletal examination in children includes a reflex hammer, tape measure, and scoliometer.

Preparation

For a thorough, accurate, and comprehensive musculoskeletal examination, the neonate or infant must be fully undressed and supine. Children toddler aged and older who are walking must also be undressed except for underwear. Shoes and socks must be removed to evaluate standing posture and limb symmetry accurately. In older children, particularly adolescent girls, modesty must be preserved as much as possible; a gown may be worn when inspecting the posterior thorax and spine.

Developmental Approach to the Examination

The child's age and developmental level are major considerations when conducting the examination of the musculoskeletal system. These factors influence the manner in which the examination is conducted, as well as how the assessment findings are interpreted. Because infants are not able to cooperate with commands, joint movement must be assessed through spontaneous movement and through passive range of motion. Toddlers can be asked to play games such as "Simon says" or "follow the leader." Children preschool aged and older are able to follow the provider's commands during the physical examination.

Assessment of General Appearance

The musculoskeletal examination begins with simple observation of the child. When the provider enters the examination room and while gathering the history, much can be learned about the child's musculoskeletal status by observing any spontaneous motor activity. Examples include observing the child's body position, limb symmetry, and tone, noting range of motion, posture, and obvious deformities; observing an infant or child sit; and watching a child walk or play. In neonates and infants, head control, the ability to sit, and overall tone are noted, as well as the position and spontaneous movement of all four extremities. In older children, normal posture is upright with good alignment of the head, shoulders, and hips.

Skin • In each age group, the skin is inspected for any nevi, café-au-lait marks, or hemangiomas (see Chapter 12), which may indicate syndromes associated with musculoskeletal complications, such as neurofibromatosis or Klippel-Trénaunay syndrome. Bruising, erythema, swelling, or any scars from past injuries are noted. As needed, the skin is also palpated for laxity of ligaments (Ganel, Dudkiewicz, & Grogan, 2003).

Head, Neck, and Clavicles • In all age groups, the full musculoskeletal examination begins with inspection and palpation of the head, neck, and clavicles and continues in a head-to-toe sequence. Assessment of the head and neck is discussed in Chapter 13.

Gait • By 12 to 15 months, a child should progress beyond cruising to walking. The provider must add the assessment of gait to simple observation of the child's spontaneous activity and play. The normal gait cycle consists of the stance phase and swing phase. The stance phase begins when one foot is placed on the ground, heel first, and the opposite foot is lifted off the ground. Next is the mid-stance, when the center of gravity is directly on the foot that is on the ground. The terminal stance occurs last when the center of gravity is over the supporting foot, and the opposite foot is placed on the ground. The swing phase begins with the toe off the ground until the knee is maximally flexed, which causes the tibia to be perpendicular to the ground. The tibia is then moved down until it becomes vertical, touching the ground (Bogey, 2012). The health of the child's joints and muscles affects the child's gait; conditions such as JRA, muscular dystrophy, and cerebral palsy affect gait.

The child's age and developmental level influence how gait is assessed. Toddlers can just be observed; children preschool aged and older are asked to walk across the room barefoot, wearing only a patient gown (Rush, 2013). Additionally, the provider may ask the child to stoop, climb onto the parent's lap, or take large steps. The examiner observes the child's gait for balance, noting the child's ability to bear weight, toe-walking, genu valgus, genu varum, toeing-in, or toeing-out. Toddlers are normally bow-legged, have a wide-based gait, and walk in short, quick steps to keep their balance. Until approximately age 7 to 8 years, slight genu valgum (knock-knee) is within normal limits. Intoeing can be caused by metatarsus adductus, internal tibial torsion, or femoral anteversion (McKee-Garrett, 2013). If the child is developmentally able to cooperate, instructing the child to toe-walk across the room and heel-walk back helps to assess motor strength of the S1 and L4 nerve roots (MacDonald & D'Hemecourt, 2007).

Any abnormalities in the child's gait are noted. Examples include limp, antalgic gait (gait to avoid pain), toe-walking, and scissoring. A limp is a symmetrical gait abnormality that can be caused by shortening of a limb, muscle weakness, paralysis, or pain. A limp can also result from Legg-Calvé-Perthes disease, SCFE, toxic synovitis, septic arthritis, previously undetected DDH, or JRA (Rush, 2013). A marked limp or refusal to walk accompanied by fever, point tenderness, or limited range of motion in the hip suggests acute hematogenous osteomyelitis of the proximal femur (hip) or lateral distal tibia (ankle) (Kalyoussef & Tolan, 2014). In the adolescent, an antalgic gait (shortened time standing on affected side), accompanied by an externally rotated hip, out-toeing, and thigh or knee pain, points to SCFE (Walter et al., 2013).

Older children with previously undetected DDH have a characteristic limp and often toe-walk. To test for undiagnosed DDH in an older child, the child is asked to hold a chair or the parent or provider's hands and bear weight on each foot, one at a time. When bearing weight on the affected hip, the pelvis will drop on the affected side. This is a positive Trendelenburg sign, an indication of DDH (Figure 21.11). Toe-walking may be idiopathic; it may also be caused by congenital short Achilles tendon, muscle spasticity, Duchenne muscular dystrophy, cerebral palsy, and autism (Cole, 2008; Schwentker, 2012). A scissoring gait suggests cerebral palsy.

Upper Extremities and Shoulders • Assessment of the upper extremities includes inspection and palpation for equal length, symmetry, strength, spontaneous movement, swelling, pain, tenderness, and range of motion. Muscles are also assessed for size, strength, and tone. Any limb contractures are noted.

In the newborn, lack of spontaneous movement of an upper extremity may result from a fractured clavicle or Erb's palsy, a birth injury to cranial nerves V and VI. There may be a palpable, bony prominence in the area

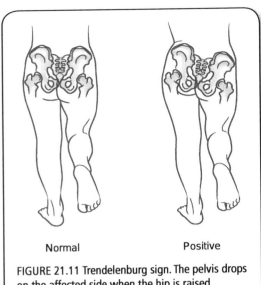

Normal   Positive

FIGURE 21.11 Trendelenburg sign. The pelvis drops on the affected side when the hip is raised.

of a healed clavicle fracture. Short, bowed extremities with possible fractures are seen in osteogenesis imperfecta (Erickson, Polousky, & Merritt, 2012). The neonate's hands are inspected for shape, size, and number of digits. Polydactyly (multiple digits) can occur in the upper or lower extremities, a condition that may be inherited (Figure 21.12). Syndactyly (fused digits) is often

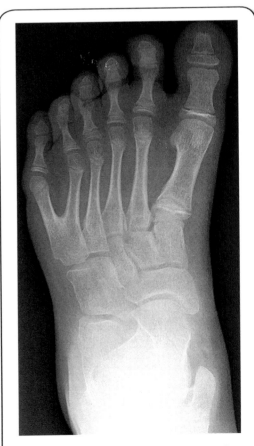

FIGURE 21.12 Polydactyly of the lower extremity.

associated with congenital syndromes (Deune, 2013) (Figure 21.13). The palms are also inspected for palmar creases, whorls, finger loops, or ridges. A transverse or "simian" crease occurs in children with Down syndrome (Figure 21.14).

After the neonatal period, the hands and wrists are inspected for any swelling, warmth, tenderness, erythema, deformity, strength, and range of motion. No nodules, redness, or swelling should be seen. There should be no warmth or tenderness with palpation. Warm, tender joints indicate JRA or Kawasaki disease (Scheinfeld, Jones, Ogershok, & Parrillo, 2014). Tender joints may also be present with trauma, infection, tumors, hemoglobinopathies, systemic lupus erythematosus, Lyme disease, or Henoch-Schönlein purpura (Kimura & Southwood, 2014). Symmetrical, painful swelling of the hands can be caused by sickle cell crisis. Joint deformities occur with some congenital conditions or syndromes or with JRA. Long, slender fingers with hyperextensible joints are seen with Marfan syndrome (Erickson et al., 2012).

In children preschool aged and older, upper extremity strength is evaluated by asking the child to squeeze the provider's fingers. The strength of both upper extremities should be equal; asymmetry may be caused by pain, hemiparesis, or muscle weakness resulting from cerebral palsy or muscular dystrophy (Jones, Morgan, & Shelton, 2007a).

If the child is developmentally able to cooperate, range of motion is evaluated in the shoulders, elbows, fingers, and wrists. Range of motion is assessed by asking the child to move the shoulders up and down. Range of motion of the elbow is evaluated by asking the child to bend and straighten the elbow and pronate and supinate the hands. Full range of motion should be noted. Decreased range of motion in the shoulder or elbow may be caused by pain related to repetitive-motion injuries, particularly if the child is involved in sports, such as tennis, baseball, or swimming. Unilateral limitation of range of motion in one arm, with resistance of supination or pronation of forearm or an inability to flex or extend the elbow, suggests subluxation of the radial head ("nursemaid's elbow"). Because ligaments are normally weak in young children, this condition is more prevalent in toddlers and is caused by pulling firmly on the child's arm (Wolfram & Boss, 2014). Range of motion in the hands and wrists is evaluated by asking the child to abduct and adduct fingers; make a fist; and flex, extend, abduct, and adduct the wrists. Limited range of motion may be caused by pain, inflammatory disorders, or fracture.

Spine • The spine is assessed for range of motion, congenital abnormalities, and curvatures. In the newborn and infant, the spine is inspected and palpated for pigmented areas, tufts of hair, dimples, sinuses, or sacs in the lumbar region. Areas of pigmentation, tufts of hair, or sacral dimpling can indicate spina bifida occulta. Obvious sacs in the lumbosacral region indicate meningocele or myelomeningocele. These abnormalities are illustrated in Figure 21.15.

Once a child is walking, the spine is inspected with the child standing and undressed from the waist up, preserving modesty. The child's posture is evaluated first. When standing, the child's head should be in direct alignment with the midline of the sacrum (Rosenberg, 2011). Range of motion of the spine is assessed by asking the child or adolescent to bend forward, side to side, and backward; no pain or limitation of movement should be evident. With the child standing straight, the provider inspects the child's spine from an anterior, lateral, and posterior view. Any spinal curvatures are noted. Lumbar lordosis (convex curvature) is normal in toddlers. Kyphosis, or concave curvature of the thoracic spine (Figure 21.16), can be caused by myelomeningocele, tumors of the spinal cord, or simply poor posture.

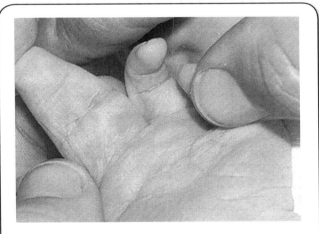

FIGURE 21.13 Syndactyly.

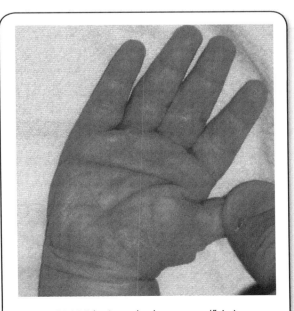

FIGURE 21.14 A horizontal palmar crease ("simian crease") seen with Down syndrome.

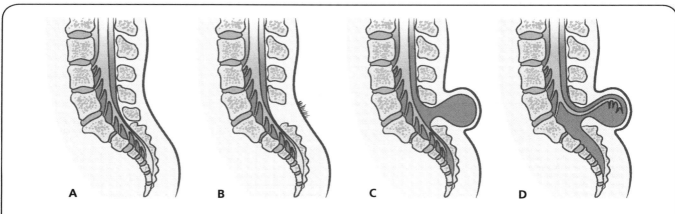

FIGURE 21.15 Spinal cord abnormalities. **A.** Normal spinal cord. **B.** Spina bifid occulta. **C.** Meningocele. **D.** Myelomeningocele.

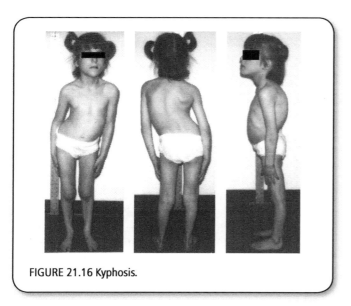

FIGURE 21.16 Kyphosis.

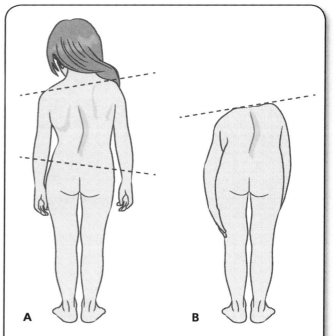

FIGURE 21.17 **A.** Visible lateral curvature of the spine. Note the right shoulder elevation. **B.** Prominent scapula when bending forward indicates scoliosis.

Unequal shoulder height, an uneven waistline, or any rib humps can indicate scoliosis (lateral curvature of the spine). Further assessment of scoliosis includes the Adam's forward-bending test. This test is performed with the child or adolescent standing straight, facing away from the examiner, feet together, and knees straight. The examiner then asks the child to bend forward at the waist, arms dangling, and touch his or her toes. With the child bending forward, the examiner inspects the child's back for spinal alignment, deformity, curvature, or visible hump. A visible lateral curvature of the spine when the child is standing or a prominent scapula on the affected side when bending indicates scoliosis (Figure 21.17). A scoliometer can also be used to measure the degree of curvature. Children with a lateral curvature of 25 degrees or more require treatment (Rosenberg, 2011).

Hips • In the first year of life, evaluation of the hips is a critical assessment to detect DDH as early as possible so that treatment can be initiated to prevent hip

dislocation. When evaluating the hips for DDH, the newborn or infant must be warm, comfortable, and relaxed. The infant must also be supine with the diaper off. One hip is evaluated at a time. The important examination assessments are the Ortolani and Barlow maneuvers. To perform the Ortolani maneuver, the provider places his or her thumb over the infant's inner thigh and the index finger over the greater trochanter. The leg is then abducted and the knees flexed 90 degrees with gentle pressure placed over the greater trochanter. With DDH, a palpable, but not audible, "clunk" is felt when the hip dislocation is reduced. This is a positive Ortolani sign, signifying a dislocated hip (Tamai & McCarthy,

2014). Continuing with the hips adducted, slight, gentle pressure is applied to the posterior hip. If the hip is dislocated, a "clunk" is palpable, but not audible, as the hip dislocates out of the acetabulum. This is a positive Barlow sign, which occurs with DDH (Figure 21.18). With the infant remaining supine, the provider inspects thigh lengths. To do this, the infant's hips and knees are flexed with the soles of the feet placed on the examination table, near the infant's buttocks. Knee height is compared. Uneven knees indicate that one leg is shorter than the other, a sign of unilateral hip dislocation, with shortening of the limb on the affected side (Figure 21.19). This finding is a positive Galeazzi sign

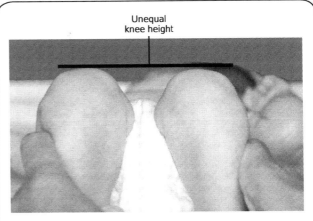

FIGURE 21.19 Uneven knee height noted with developmental dysplasia of the hip (DDH).

(Tamai & McCarthy, 2014). With the infant prone, the provider assesses symmetry of thigh folds. Asymmetric thigh and gluteal folds also indicate hip dislocation, with an extra skinfold on the affected side (Figure 21.20).

In older children, the hips are evaluated for pain, swelling, redness, position, and limited range of motion. The hips should have full range of motion without pain. Hip pain in an older child is always a concern that requires immediate evaluation. Older children may be unable to bear weight and experience pain or resistance to movement with passive range of motion. Redness, swelling, or point tenderness of the hip suggests infection. Limited range of motion with decreased internal rotation suggests SCFE, particularly in preadolescent and adolescent males (Walter et al., 2013). Table 21.4 reviews possible differential diagnoses for hip pain in children.

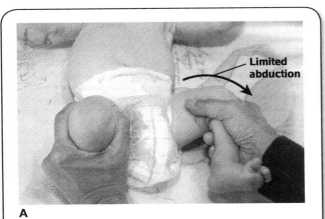

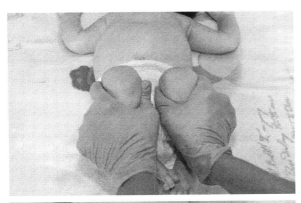

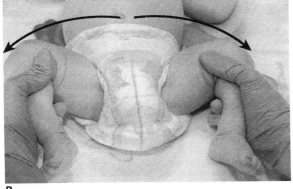

FIGURE 21.18 Assessing for hip "clunk" with **A.** the Ortolani maneuver and **B.** Barlow maneuver

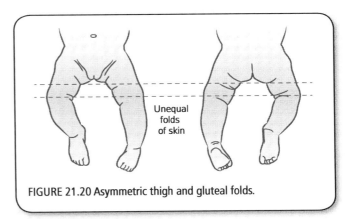

FIGURE 21.20 Asymmetric thigh and gluteal folds.

Lower Extremities, Feet, and Ankles • The lower extremities are inspected and palpated for equal length, symmetry, spontaneous movement, strength, swelling, pain, tenderness, and range of motion. Muscles are assessed for size, strength, and tone. Any limb contractures are noted. There should be no obvious swelling, deformity, or erythema. The lower limbs should be symmetrical and equal in length. In the neonate, lower extremity deformities and contractures are often seen in children with myelomeningocele and osteogenesis imperfecta (Erickson et al., 2012). In older children, limb length is evaluated with the child supine, legs extended, and legs aligned. Limb length discrepancies can be caused by DDH, SCFE, cerebral palsy, scoliosis, or after a femoral fracture (Rosenberg, 2011; Rush, 2013; Walter et al., 2013). Lack of spontaneous movement can indicate pain or an underlying condition that causes muscle paralysis.

The examiner tests for limb strength by asking the child to push firmly with the soles of the feet against the palms of the examiner's hands. Lower extremity strength should be firm and equal. Unequal lower limb strength can be caused by pain, hemiparesis, or paralysis. Pain, swelling, or tenderness in the lower extremities can be caused by trauma, infection, or tumor, leukemia, sickle cell disease, hemophilia, or Henoch-Schönlein purpura (Kalyoussef & Tolan, 2014). Pain with plantarflexion can indicate Achilles tendonitis; pain in the arch or heel is caused by plantar fasciitis; both conditions are seen in adolescent runners (Gottschlich, Eerkes, Lin, & Schwartz, 2013; Young, 2014).

With the child standing straight facing the examiner with the ankles together, the knees are inspected for contour, deformity, tenderness, warmth, redness, swelling, alignment, and range of motion. Genu varum (bowlegs) is normal until age 3 to 4 years (see Figure 21.10A). Genu valgum (knock-knees) is normal until age 7 to 8 years, after which time it can be caused by rickets (see Figure 21.10B). If genu varum persists beyond that time, it is termed tibial torsion, which can be caused by rickets, JRA, osteomyelitis, neoplasia, or trauma (Erickson et al., 2012). Blount's disease also causes a varus deformity of both tibias (see Figure 21.10A). Genu varum differs from Blount's disease in that both the femur and tibia are involved with genu varum, while Blount's disease affects only the tibia.

There should be full range of motion of the knee with normal alignment; limited knee flexion may be caused by abnormalities of the quadriceps. Laxity of the knee joint points to a tear in the anterior or posterior cruciate ligament. The knees are palpated on either side of the patella to assess for tenderness, swelling, or bogginess. The patella should not move when palpated. Tenderness, warmth, and bogginess over the knee can indicate synovitis, sprain, or a torn meniscus. Tenderness and swelling over the tibial tubercle may indicate Osgood-Schlatter disease. If swelling is seen or felt in the knee, further examination is required. Elicitation of the ballottement sign is useful in this instance. The examiner asks the child to extend the knee. The examiner then grasps the patella with the thumb and index finger of the dominant hand, pushing the patella down while applying pressure. If fluid is present in the knee, this moves the patella down toward the femur. Pressure is then released quickly. If the examiner can feel a "tap," this is the patella striking the femur; this is a positive ballottement sign and indicates joint effusion.

Knee joint laxity can be assessed by performing the McMurray test. With the child lying supine, the provider has the child flex the affected knee and hip. With one hand, the examiner holds the child's knee and flexes it to 90 degrees while holding the child's foot with the other hand. The examiner then externally rotates the lower leg while extending the knee to 90 degrees. Pain or clicking during this maneuver indicates a sprain or other damage to the meniscus.

The feet and ankles are inspected and palpated for position, alignment, range of motion, and any visible swelling or deformities. In newborns and infants, foot position and alignment are inspected. Forefoot adduction may be due to metatarsus adductus, the positional incurving of one or both feet caused by intrauterine positioning (Figure 21.21). Physical findings reveal the heel in varus position, with a flexible forefoot that can be abducted beyond the midline. This condition usually resolves spontaneously, particularly with weight-bearing.

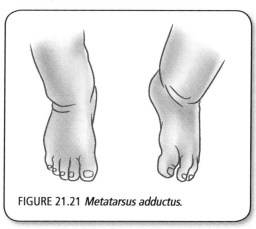

FIGURE 21.21 *Metatarsus adductus.*

Talipes equinovarus, or true clubfoot, is a rigid deformity involving muscles, tendons, and bone. Three clinical findings are evident on inspection: (a) forefoot adduction, (b) forefoot supination, and (c) equinus of the ankle (plantarflexion of the foot at the ankle) (Figure 21.22). Internal torsion of the tibia may also

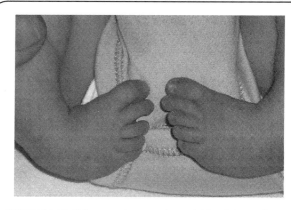

FIGURE 21.22 *Talipes equinovarus* (true clubfoot). Note the forefoot adduction, forefoot supination, and plantarflexion at the ankle.

be seen. *Talipes equinovarus* may be idiopathic, neurogenic, or occur as a feature of a syndrome. Children with talipes equinovarus must be assessed for associated syndromes or spinal deformities (Erickson et al., 2012). Unlike metatarsus adductus, talipes equinovarus requires serial casting and possible surgery to correct the deformity.

Pes planus (flat foot) is a congenital condition of the foot involving laxity of the ligaments supporting the foot's longitudinal arch, causing flattening of the foot arch. Physical findings reveal a convex medial border of the foot. This condition may be permanent or occur only when the child bears weight. The ankle is palpated for swelling, tenderness, and range of motion. Full range of motion should be noted. Limited range of motion accompanied by swelling, redness, or tenderness can be caused by JRA or more serious conditions such as osteomyelitis. Symmetrical, painful swelling of the ankles and feet can be caused by sickle cell crisis.

Ninety-Second Musculoskeletal Screening Examination

The goal of the 90-second preparticipation sports musculoskeletal examination is to find previously undetected musculoskeletal conditions and to prevent injury. The requisite health history is outlined in Chapter 9. The standardized preparticipation musculoskeletal examination includes the components listed in Table 21.5.

Assessment of Motor Function

Assessment of motor function, an essential portion of the pediatric musculoskeletal examination, includes evaluation of muscle tone, strength, and size and assessment of involuntary movements. Muscle tone, movement, and posture are routinely evaluated in newborns and young infants through assessment of the primitive reflexes and gestational age (see Chapter 11).

Muscle Tone • Muscle tone, the state of partial contraction of a muscle while at rest, is assessed by passive range of motion in infants and children. Muscle tone changes in accordance with myelination and development of the cerebral cortex. Normal muscle tone shows a mild degree of tension while at rest and is evaluated by looking at resting posture, upper and lower extremity tone, and head control. Tone is assessed for flaccidity (hypotonia), rigidity, or spasticity (hypertonia) and can vary between the upper and lower extremities. Assessment of general muscle tone is done by first observing the infant or child in a resting state to evaluate overall posture. In term newborns, normal tone is demonstrated by the arms and legs in a semiflexed position with the hips slightly abducted (Figure 21.23). Hypotonic infants will be positioned with the legs in external rotation or in a frog-leg position. Lack of flexion is also seen in premature infants and as a result of central nervous system (CNS) trauma before or during delivery (see Chapter 11). When the

TABLE 21.5	The 90-Second Musculoskeletal Screening Examination
INSTRUCTION TO CHILD	**AREA OF ASSESSMENT**
Stand facing examiner.	Acromioclavicular joints; extremity symmetry, general posture, and ease of mobility
Look up, down, left, and right; touch ears to shoulders.	Cervical spine range of motion
Shrug shoulders as examiner applies resistance.	Trapezius strength
Hold arms outstretched at side, and lift them as examiner applies resistance.	Shoulder range of motion
Raise elbows at side 90 degrees, and rotate hands backward.	Deltoid strength; shoulder motion
Hold arms at sides with palms upward; flex and extend elbows.	Elbow range of motion
Hold arms down in front of body; flex elbows so that hands are straight out. Rotate hands face up and face down.	Wrist range of motion
Spread fingers, then make a fist.	Hand and finger strength; range of motion or deformities
Stand on one leg, bent at the knee; repeat with other leg.	Symmetry of legs; knee or ankle effusion
"Walk like a duck" by squatting and walking four steps away.	Hip, knee, and ankle range of motion
Stand with back to examiner and with knees straight, and bend over to touch toes.	Shoulder symmetry, scoliosis, hip range of motion, and hamstring tightness
Stand on tiptoes and then heels.	Calf symmetry and leg strength

Sources: Hoang et al., (2012; Garrich (1977).

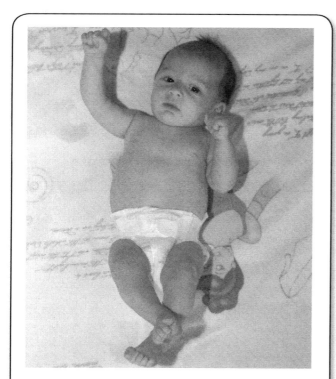

FIGURE 21.23 Normal flexed tone of newborn infant

CNS infections, including encephalitis and meningitis and as a complication of kernicterus and traumatic brain injury (e.g., abusive head trauma). Hypertonia (i.e., increased muscle tone, spasticity, rigidity, persistent primitive reflexes, delay of normal motor skill acquisition) is seen in children with upper motor neuron lesions, such as cerebral palsy and genetic or metabolic diseases that damage the child's developing CNS (Mandingo & Anderson, 2006). Abusive head trauma can also lead to motor dysfunction, spasticity, cerebral palsy, and quadriparesis (Christian, Block & the Committee on Child Abuse and Neglect, 2009).

Muscle Strength and Size • Both upper and lower extremity muscle strength and size are evaluated with assessment of motor function. Muscle weakness is the most common presenting symptom of neuromuscular disease. Muscle strength is graded on a scale of 0 to 5 (Table 21.6); muscle symmetry is also assessed.

In infants, upper extremity strength can be evaluated by rotating each arm at the shoulder, elbow, and wrist while noting muscle strength. Upper extremity strength can be assessed in children by assessing pronation, grip, and fine motor abilities. To assess pronation, the examiner asks the child to stand, eyes closed, with arms extended, palms facing upward; this position is maintained for 30 seconds. The examiner then notes any tendency the child has to turn the palms down (pronation), lower the arms, or bend them at the elbows; any tremors are also noted. If these responses occur, upper motor neuron disease must be considered. Muscle strength can be determined by testing the child's elbow flexion and extension. This is done by holding the child's upper arm with one hand and grasping the wrist with the other, then asking the child to pull his or her arm toward the body as the examiner pulls the child's arm away from the body. This is done on both arms, and the results are compared. To test wrist dorsiflexion, the examiner asks the child to hold his or her right arm at the side of the body, elbow flexed, and the forearm extended forward. While the child makes a fist, the examiner places his or her left hand on the child's forearm, just behind the wrist, and the right hand over the child's fist. The examiner then exerts downward pressure on the child's fist while asking the child to resist. Normally, the child should be able to resist the pressure. This assessment is done on both arms, and the results are compared for symmetry. Continued

term infant is horizontally suspended with the thorax firmly supported, the extremities should maintain flexion tone. In hypotonic infants, the extremities dangle limply. Abnormal muscle tone in an infant indicates neurologic injury or dysfunction, likely because of prenatal or perinatal or hypoxic-ischemic injury. In children toddler aged and older, muscle tone and posture are evaluated by observing the child playing or walking.

Muscle tone in the head and extremities of the infant is assessed by gently pulling the infant from a sitting to a standing position; no head lag should be evident by age 6 months (see Chapter 13, Figure 13.11), and the extremities should have normal, symmetrical tone. Abnormal positioning of the head, neck, or extremities indicates neurologic dysfunction. Decreased muscle tone (hypotonia) is seen in genetic disorders, such as Down syndrome, trisomy 13, Werdnig-Hoffman disease, and developmental disabilities, such as cerebral palsy and congenital hypothyroidism. Hypotonia is also seen after

TABLE 21.6	Motor Strength Grading
0/5	No muscle movement
1/5	Visible muscle movement, but no movement at joint
2/5	Movement without gravity
3/5	Movement against gravity
4/5	Movement against gravity resistance
5/5	Normal strength

assessment of upper extremity muscle strength includes testing the child's grip. This is done by asking the child to grasp the examiner's extended middle and index fingers firmly. Both hands should be tested simultaneously. As the child grasps the examiner's fingers, the examiner attempts to extract his or her fingers from the grip; it should be difficult to do so. When noting upper extremity strength, the examiner also notes any marked preference for one hand displayed by the child. Marked handedness in children younger than early school age can indicate cerebral palsy or paresis on the affected side.

Muscle strength in the lower extremities can be assessed in the infant, beginning at 4 to 6 months, by pulling the infant from the sitting to the standing position. With children toddler aged and older, lower extremity muscle strength can be evaluated by observing the child's gait and balance or by asking the child to press the soles of his or her feet against the examiner's hands while the examiner pushes back; the child should be able to resist. When evaluating muscle strength in ambulatory children, the provider assesses for the Gower sign, which is seen in children with myopathies. This occurs when a child with muscle weakness of the extensors of the hips attempts to stand up from the floor. The child first sits up, then shifts his or her body weight to the hands and knees, and then uses the hands and arms to climb up his or her own legs to stand (Figure 21.24).

When assessing muscle size, the provider begins by inspecting the muscles for enlargement, contractures, or atrophy, and then measures the circumference of both upper and lower extremities, comparing sides. For example, enlargement of the calf muscles occurs with Duchenne muscular dystrophy (Wilson, 2011).

The manner of assessment to evaluate fine motor abilities depends on the child's age (see Chapter 2). Fine motor coordination does not begin until approximately 5 months with raking, progressing to a fine pincer grasp by 12 months. Depending on the child's age, fine motor abilities can be assessed by asking the child to pick up small pieces, turn the pages in a book, stack blocks, complete a puzzle, draw a picture, or cut with scissors.

Involuntary Movements • During assessment of motor function, the examiner notes any involuntary movements, including tremors, seizures, clonus, myoclonus, dystonia, tics, chorea, and athetosis. Tremors, or coarse, repetitive shaking movements, are considered normal in the neonate in the first few days of life but must be distinguished from seizures. Neonatal seizures may manifest as ocular movements, lip-smacking, chewing, or pedaling (Sheth, 2013). Seizures in older children are characterized by simple twitching, tonic–clonic movements (jerking with stiffness), or automatisms (lip-smacking, gesturing, repeating words), depending on the type of seizure (Wilfong, 2012). *Clonus* is a rapid and rhythmic, jerking movement of the foot caused by the sudden stretching of a tendon. Clonus is normal in the newborn (see Chapter 11). Sustained clonus beyond six to eight beats or clonus that continues past the neonatal period may indicate an upper motor neuron abnormality, such as cerebral palsy (Jones, Morgan, Shelton, & Thorgood, 2007b). *Myoclonus* is a brief, rapid (less than 0.25 seconds) muscle jerk that can occur in isolation or be associated with seizures. *Dystonia* is a muscle contraction that lasts longer than myoclonus and can result in a muscle spasm that can cause hyperextension of the joint. Tics are involuntary muscle contractions or vocalizations that result in stereotyped movements. Tics may herald the onset of Tourette syndrome (Robertson, 2014b). *Chorea* is characterized by brief, irregular, purposeless, nonrepetitive jerking and writhing movements that move from one muscle to the next in an unpredictable way (Robertson, 2014a). Chorea in children is associated with inborn errors of metabolism, hyperthyroidism, hypoparathyroidism, pertussis, diphtheria, varicella, bacterial endocarditis, viral encephalitis, Lyme disease, cerebral palsy, metabolic and glycemic abnormalities, and the side effects of several classes of drugs (Robertson, 2014a). Chorea often occurs with athetosis, which is characterized by slow, writhing movements, often in the hands and feet. Athetosis is seen in children with certain types of cerebral palsy.

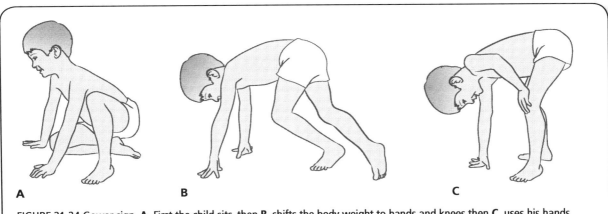

FIGURE 21.24 Gower sign. **A.** First the child sits, then **B.** shifts the body weight to hands and knees then **C.** uses his hands to "climb up" to stand.

COMMON DIAGNOSTIC STUDIES

Various diagnostic tests may be necessary to clarify differential diagnoses of abnormal conditions involving the musculoskeletal system. Some examples of these diagnostic studies and their indications are summarized in Table 21.7.

DOCUMENTATION OF FINDINGS

Sample Write-Up: Normal Musculoskeletal Examination

Subjective Data

Newborn assessment of a 3-day-old male.

> **Prenatal history:** prenatal care was begun in first trimester; no prenatal exposure to drugs, alcohol; no history of maternal infection

Perinatal history: normal, spontaneous, vaginal delivery; no distress at birth; Apgar scores 8 and 9

Objective Data

General: alert, good muscle tone
Musculoskeletal: chest is symmetrical, no obvious bony deformities; no swelling or tenderness at clavicles; upper limbs present, equal length and size; moves upper extremities freely; five digits on each extremity; no fusion of digits noted; no palmar creases; lower limbs present, equal length and size; spontaneous movement of both lower extremities, five digits on each extremity; no fusion of digits noted; symmetrical gluteal thigh folds, knee heights equal; negative Ortolani

TABLE 21.7	Diagnostic Studies to Evaluate Musculoskeletal Conditions in Children	
DIAGNOSTIC STUDY	**INDICATION**	**COMMENTS**
Arthrocentesis	Joint effusion	To evaluate for septic arthritis
Blood cultures	Fever or joint inflammation	Aids in diagnosis of osteomyelitis or septic arthritis
Complete blood count	Fever, joint pain, limp, and fracture	Can diagnose or rule out bone infection (osteomyelitis, septic arthritis, toxic synovitis), and hemorrhage after traumatic bone injury; also aids in diagnosing hemoglobinopathies, chronic infections, and malignancy (Rush, 2013)
C-reactive protein	Joint inflammation or infection	Aids in diagnosis of osteomyelitis or septic arthritis
Computed tomography scan	To evaluate severity of osteomyelitis, Legg-Calvé-Perthes disease, or slipped capital femoral epiphysis	Especially useful in diagnosing pelvic and spinal problems (Rush, 2013)
Erythrocyte sedimentation rate	Joint inflammation or infection	Aids in diagnosis of osteomyelitis or septic arthritis
Magnetic resonance imaging	Helpful in diagnosing diskitis and spinal cord tumor; also useful for diagnosing fractures in the presence of marked edema, stress fractures, osteomyelitis, malignancy, and early Legg-Calvé-Perthes disease (Rush, 2013)	Requires the child to be completely still during examination; young children require sedation but adolescents may be able to remain still
Radiographs	To diagnose fracture, joint effusion, or avascular necrosis	Differentiates between metatarsus adductus and talipes equinovarus
Radionuclide bone scintigraphy	Used when history and physical examination and other imaging studies do not identify source of injury or pathology; aids in diagnosis of occult fracture, osteomyelitis, diskitis, avascular necrosis, bone infarct, and tumor (Rush, 2013)	More sensitive than plain radiographs (Rush, 2013)
Ultrasound	To diagnose developmental dysplasia of the hip	Preferred diagnostic study for evaluating the hips for developmental dysplasia of infants age 6 months and younger (Tamai & McCarthy, 2014); also helps diagnose joint effusion or abscess

and Barlow maneuvers; feet in normal anatomic position; no equinovarus deformity

Assessment: normal newborn

Sample Write-Up: Child With Musculoskeletal Complaint

Subjective Data

A 15-year-old obese male presents with complaints of right hip pain for approximately 3 weeks; pain now beginning in knee. States that it has been difficult to walk because of pain. Mother denies recent illness or fever.

Objective Data

Weight: 190 lb (86 kg) (> 97th percentile); **height:** 66 inches (25th percentile); **BMI** (body mass index): 30 (> 97th percentile).

General: sitting on exam table, holding right hip in passive external rotation; antalgic gait and out-toeing noted when walking across exam room

Musculoskeletal: internal rotation of right hip decreased and painful; child denies pain in left hip

Assessment: slipped capital femoral epiphysis

Notable Clinical Findings

- Child is less than the 5th percentile or greater than the 85th percentile for weight on the NCHS growth charts for age and gender
- Child is less than 5th percentile or greater than the 85th percentile for length or height on the NCHS growth charts for age and gender
- Child is less than the 5th percentile or greater than the 5th percentile for head circumference on the NCHS growth charts for age and gender
- History of traumatic brain injury
- Head lag after age 4 months
- No head control after age 6 months
- Immunization delay
- History/diagnosis of:
  - Torticollis
  - Metatarsus adductus
  - Talipes equinovarus
  - Talipes calcaneovalgus
  - Genu varum
  - Genu valgum
  - Polydactyly
  - Syndacylty
  - Developmental dysplasia of the hip
  - Pes planus
  - Juvenile rheumatoid arthritis
  - Slipped capital femoral epiphysis

- Cerebral palsy
- Fractures
- Toxic synovitis
- Sports injuries
- Osteogenesis imperfect
- Positive Ortolani or Barlow maneuver
- Positive Allis sign
- Alterations in range of motion
- Joint or muscle pain
- Joint swelling or tenderness
- Antalgic gait
- Limp
- Toe-walking/scissor gait
- Obesity
- Spinal abnormalities
  - Lordosis after age 3 years
  - Kyphosis
  - Scoliosis
  - Tufts of hair
  - Dimples, sinuses
- Hypo- or hypertonia
- Clonus
- Myoclonus
- Dystonia
- Chorea
- Seizure disorder

References

Abrams, S. S. (2014). *Management of neonatal bone health. Up to Date.* Retrieved from http://www.uptodate.com/contents/management-of-neonatal-bone-health

Ball, J. W., Bindler, R. C., & Cowen, K. J. (2012). Alterations in musculoskeletal function. In J. W. Ball, R. C. Bindler, & K. J. Cowen (Eds), *Principles of pediatric nursing: Caring for children* (5th ed., pp. 943–986). Upper Saddle River, NJ: Pearson Education.

Blackman, J. A. (2007). NICU micropreemies: How do they fare? *Contemporary Pediatrics, 24*(2), 64–73.

Bogey, R. (2012). *Gait analysis.* Retrieved from http://emedicine.medscape.com/article/320160-overview

Christian, C. W., Block, R. B., & the Committee on Child Abuse and Neglect. (2009). Abusive head trauma in infants and children. *Pediatrics, 123,* 1409–1411.

Cole, L. L. (2008). Autism in school age children: A complex collage of development, behavior and communication. *Advance for Nurse Practitioners, 16*(3), 38–48.

Deune, E. G. (2013). *Syndactyly.* Retrieved from http://emedicine.medscape.com/article/1244420-overview

Erickson, M. A., Polousky, J. D., & Merritt, J. D. (2012). Orthopedics. In W. W. Hay, M. J. Levin, R. R. Deterding, M. J. Abzub, & J. M. Sondheimer (Eds.), *Current pediatric diagnosis & treatment* (21st ed., pp. 830–848). New York, NY: McGraw-Hill.

Ganel, A., Dudkiewicz, I., & Grogan, D. P. (2003). Pediatric orthopedic physical examination of the infant: A 5-minute assessment. *Journal of Pediatric Health Care, 17*(1), 39–41.

Garrich, J. G. (1977). Sports medicine. *Pediatric Clinics of North America, 24,* 737–747.

Gottschlich, L. M., Eerkes, K. J., Lin, D. Y., & Schwartz, E. (2013). *Achilles tendonitis.* Retrieved from http://emedicine.medscape.com/article/85115-overview

Heyworth, B. E., Voos, J. E., & Metzl, J. D. (2007). Hip injuries in the adolescent athlete. *Pediatric Annals, 36*(11), 713–718.

Hoang, Q. B., Coel, R. A., Vidal, A., Wilson, P. E., & Pengel, K. B. (2012). Sports medicine. In W. W. Hay, M. J. Levin, R. R. Deterding, M. J. Abzub, & J. M. Sondheimer (Eds.), *Current pediatric diagnosis & treatment* (21st ed., pp. 849–880). New York, NY: McGraw-Hill.

Jones, M. W., Morgan, E., & Shelton, J. E. (2007a). Primary care of the child with cerebral palsy: A review of systems (Part II). *Journal of Pediatric Health Care, 21*(4), 226–237.

Jones, M. W., Morgan, E., Shelton, J. E., & Thorgood, C. (2007b). Cerebral palsy: Introduction and diagnosis (Part I). *Journal of Pediatric Health Care, 21*(3), 146–152.

Kalyoussef, S., & Tolan, R. W. (2014). *Pediatric osteomyelitis.* Retrieved from http://emedicine.medscape.com/article/967095-overview

Kimura, Y., & Southwood, T. R. (2014). *Evaluation of the child with joint pain or swelling. Up to Date.* Retrieved from http://www.uptodate.com/contents/evaluation-of-the-child-with-joint-pain-or-swelling

Lamont, L., Fragomen, A. T., & Rozbruch, S. R. (2013). *Blount disease.* Retrieved from http://emedicine.medscape.com/article/1250420-overview#a0199

Leung, A. K. C., & Lemay, J. F. (2004). The limping child. *Journal of Pediatric Health Care, 18*(5), 219–223.

Lilly, K., & McCambridge, T. M. (2008). Running injuries. *Contemporary Pediatrics, 25*(7), 46–66.

MacDonald, J., & D'Hemecourt, P. (2007). Back pain in the adolescent athlete. *Pediatric Annals, 36*(11), 703–712.

Mandingo, C. E., & Anderson, R. C. E. (2006). Management of childhood spasticity: A neurosurgical perspective. *Pediatric Annals, 35*(5), 354–362.

McKee-Garrett, T. (2013). *Lower extremity positional deformations. Up to date.* Retrieved from http://www.uptodate.com/contents/lower-extremity-positional-deformations

Mehlman, C. T., & Koepplinger, M. E. (2012). *Growth plate (physeal) fractures.* Retrieved from http://emedicine.medscape.com/article/1260663-

Patel, M., & Herzenberg, J. (2007). *Clubfoot.* Retrieved from http://emedicine.medscape.com/article/1237077-overview

Poduval, M. (2013). *Skeletal system anatomy in children and toddlers.* Retrieved from http://emedicine.medscape.com/article/1899256-overview#a1

Robertson, W. C. (2014a). *Chorea in children.* Retrieved from http://emedicine.medscape.com/article/1181993-overview

Robertson, W. C. (2014b). *Tourette syndrome and other tic disorders. Chorea in children.* Retrieved from http://emedicine.medscape.com/article/1182258-overview

Rosenberg, J. J. (2011). Scoliosis. *Pediatrics in Review, 32*(9), 397–398.

Rush, J. K. (2013). *Limping child.* Retrieved from http://emedicine.medscape.com/article/1258835-overview#a1

Scheinfeld, N. S., Jones, E. L., Ogershok, P. R., & Parrillo, S. J. (2014). *Kawasaki disease.* Retrieved from http://emedicine.medscape.com/article/965367-overview

Schwarz, S. M., Greer, F. R., & Finberg, L. (2013). *Rickets.* Retrieved from http://emedicine.medscape.com/article/985510-overview

Schwentker, E. P. (2012). *Toe walking.* Retrieved from http://emedicine.medscape.com/article/1235248-overview

Senaran, H., Holden, C., Dabney, K. W., & Miller, F. (2007). Anterior knee pain in children with cerebral palsy. *Journal of Pediatric Orthopedics, 27*(1), 12–16.

Sheth, R. (2013). *Neonatal seizures.* Retrieved from http://emedicine.medscape.com/article/1177069-overview

Tamai, J., & McCarthy, J. J. (2014). *Developmental dysplasia of the hip.* Retrieved from http://emedicine.medscape.com/article/1248135-overview

Walter, K. D., Lin, D. Y., & Schwartz, A. J. (2013). *Slipped capital femoral epiphysis.* Retrieved from http://emedicine.medscape.com/article/91596-overview

Wilfong, A. (2012). *Overview of the classification, etiology, and clinical features of pediatric seizures and epilepsy. Up to Date.* Retrieved from http://www.uptodate.com/contents/overview-of-the-classification-etiology-and-clinical-features-of-pediatric-seizures-and-epilepsy

Wilson, D. (2011). The child with neuromuscular or muscular dysfunction. In M. L. Hockenberry & D. Wilson (Eds.), *Wong's nursing care of infants and children* (9th ed., pp. 1689–1731). St. Louis, MO: Mosby Elsevier.

Wilson, D., & Curry, M. (2011). The child with musculoskeletal or articular dysfunction. In M. J. Hockenberry & D. Wilson (Eds.), *Wong's nursing care of infants and children* (9th ed., pp. 1619–1688). St. Louis, MO: Mosby.

Wolfram, W., & Boss, D. N. (2014). *Nursemaid elbow.* Retrieved from http://emedicine.medscape.com/article/803026-overview

Young, C. C. (2014). *Plantar fasciitis.* Retrieved from http://emedicine.medscape.com/article/86143-overview

Assessment of the Neurologic System

From birth through late adolescence, the brain continues to grow physically and functionally. Depending on age and other developmental factors, children are can be very vulnerable to neurologic injury or infection. The pediatric health care provider must be adept at neurologic assessment to ensure early diagnosis and treatment of any neurologic disorders or developmental delays that can have an impact on the child's physical or psychosocial growth and development.

ANATOMY AND PHYSIOLOGY

The neurologic or nervous system is the most complex, intricately balanced system in the body, controlling all body functions. It is composed of two parts: the *central nervous system* (CNS) and the *peripheral nervous system* (PNS). The CNS consists of the *brain* and *spinal cord*. The PNS is divided into the *somatic* nervous system (SNS) and the *autonomic* nervous system (ANS). The SNS includes all of the neurons associated with voluntary skeletal muscles, skin, and sense organs. The ANS divides into the *parasympathetic* and *sympathetic* systems and controls the involuntary functions in the body. The PNS includes 12 pairs of *cranial nerves* (CNs) and 31 pairs of *spinal nerves*. The *cell* is the basic unit of the nervous system.

Nerve Cells

Two major cell types make up the nervous system: *neurons* and *glial cells*. Neurons, the basic brain units, conduct impulses to and from the CNS and transmit impulses between nerve centers within the CNS. Glial cells (neuroglia) are nonexcitable cells that support and protect the neurons; most of the cells in the nervous system are glial cells.

Neurons have three components: the *dendrite, cell body*, and *axon* (Figure 22.1). Dendrites are short, twig-like projections that receive impulses from adjacent cells and relay them to the cell body. A nucleus within the cell body maintains complex metabolic functions to keep the cell functioning. The axon is a long projection that transmits impulses away from the cell body. Most neurons are insulated by *myelin*, a white, fatty substance that allows nerve impulses to travel quickly and smoothly. Both spinal nerves and CNs are myelinated; myelinated neurons are also located in the white matter of the brain and spinal cord. Support of the neuron by glial cells is accomplished by holding the neuron in place and forming myelin, thereby creating myelin sheaths; insulating the conduction of nerve impulses; and supplying oxygen and nutrients to the neurons.

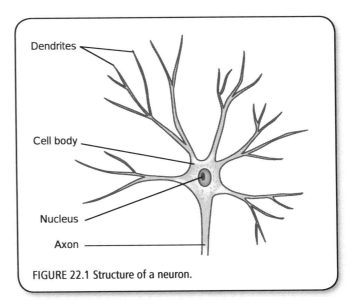

FIGURE 22.1 Structure of a neuron.

Central Nervous System

Brain Structures

The brain is divided into the *cerebrum, cerebellum,* and *brainstem* (Figure 22.2). The brain is housed by the skull, or *cranium;* the major cranial bones are labeled according to the lobe of the brain they cover: frontal, parietal, temporal, and occipital. These bones are connected by immoveable joints (sutures) (see Chapter 13).

The brain is covered by three protective layers of meninges: the *dura mater, arachnoid,* and *pia mater.* A narrow groove called the *subdural space* separates the dura mater from the arachnoid; a second groove, the *subarachnoid space,* lies between the arachnoid and pia mater (Figure 22.3).

Each of the brain's four ventricles contains a bundle of capillaries, the *choroid plexus.* This is where *cerebrospinal fluid* (CSF), a clear, colorless, odorless fluid, is produced; its functions are to lubricate the brain and spinal cord, protect these structures from injury, and to transport waste and nutrients. CSF flows from the ventricles and circulates through the brain and spinal cord. The spinal cord exits the cranium via the foramen magnum, an opening located at the base of the skull.

Cerebrum • The cerebrum is the largest part of the brain. Its outer surface or cerebral cortex is covered by a thin layer of unmyelinated neurons, called the *gray matter.* The inner core of the cerebrum, called the *white matter,* contains myelinated axons. The cerebral cortex (gray matter) consists of a complex network of neurons that control most of the brain's high-level functions, including memory, behavior, and reasoning. The *basal ganglia* are located deep within the white matter; they affect motor function by regulating voluntary body movements, inhibiting excessive body movement, controlling fine motor movements, and maintaining muscle tone. Alterations to the basal ganglia can result in motor tremors and rigid muscle tone.

The cerebrum is divided into two hemispheres, left and right. A band of tissue, the *corpus callosum,* located at the base of the fissure that divides the two hemispheres, allows communication between them. The right hemisphere controls the left side of the body, and the left hemisphere controls the right side of the body. Thus, a lesion in one cerebral hemisphere causes signs and symptoms on the opposite side of the body. The outer layer of the cerebrum contains furrows termed *sulci.* These sulci separate the cerebral hemispheres into four lobes: *frontal, temporal, parietal,* and *occipital* (see Figure 22.2). Each lobe has distinct functions:

■ **Frontal lobe.** The frontal lobe contains the *precentral gyrus,* which controls voluntary musculoskeletal movement. The prefrontal area controls high-level functions such as personality, thought processes, intellectual functions, and the ability to concentrate; in addition, this area partially controls respirations, gastrointestinal activity, circulation, pupillary reactions, and emotions. Broca's area in the frontal lobe controls the ability to articulate speech. Damage to this area causes expressive aphasia. The written speech area of the frontal lobe controls the ability to write words.

■ **Parietal lobe.** The parietal lobe controls sensory function. The *postcentral gyrus* receives impulses from the spinal cord and interprets the sensations, such as temperature, pressure, pain, vision, hearing, taste, and smell; in addition, the parietal lobe allows intact proprioception.

■ **Occipital lobe.** The occipital lobe is the visual sensory area of the brain. It interprets and integrates visual images, and it associates visual images with past experiences.

■ **Temporal lobe.** The temporal lobe perceives and interprets sounds. It integrates sound stimuli into

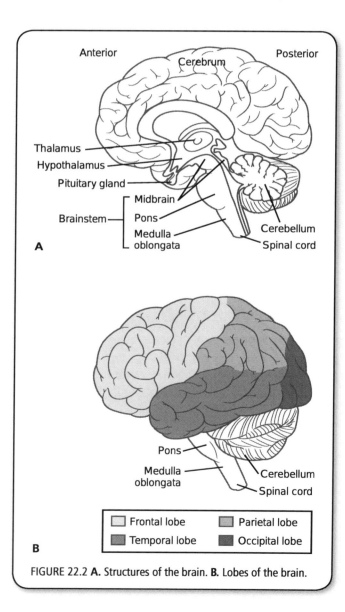

FIGURE 22.2 **A.** Structures of the brain. **B.** Lobes of the brain.

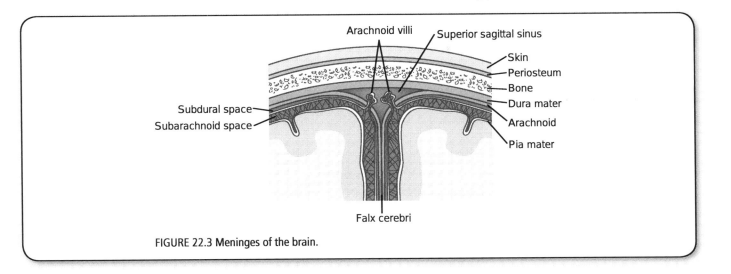

FIGURE 22.3 Meninges of the brain.

pitch, quality, and loudness, and also plays a role in controlling behavior and emotion.

■ **Wernicke's area.** This area is where the parietal and temporal lobes meet. It works in conjunction with the temporal lobe in interpreting spoken and written language. Injury to this area of the brain causes receptive aphasia.

Embedded deep within the cerebrum is the *diencephalon*, which contains the *thalamus, hypothalamus,* and *epithalamus* (see Figure 22.2). The thalamus relays sensory input, assists in motor function, and regulates consciousness and alertness. The hypothalamus, which is part of the ANS, regulates appetite, thirst, body temperature, heart rate, and blood pressure, sleep and wake cycles, and emotions, such as anger and fear. It also contains neurons that regulate adrenocorticotropic hormone, follicle-stimulating hormone, luteinizing hormone, prolactin, and growth hormone. The epithalamus contains the *pineal body,* an endocrine gland that produces melatonin, a hormone that regulates the sleep–wake cycle.

The *limbic system* is also contained within the diencephalon; it includes the *hippocampus* and the *amygdala.* The hippocampus is responsible for long-term memory and olfaction (smell). The amygdala controls emotions, such as fear, aggression, and affection; it also is involved in memory formation and behavior patterns related to mating.

Cerebellum • The next largest part of the brain, the cerebellum, is located posterior and inferior to the cerebrum between the occipital lobes and brainstem (see Figure 22.2). The cerebellum is also divided into two hemispheres, each of which is composed of gray and white matter. The cerebellum does not initiate movement; it coordinates voluntary movements, such as walking, balance, coordination, and maintenance of muscle tone. The cerebellum is integrated with the vestibular system, which also influences the maintenance of balance and equilibrium. Lesions in a cerebellar hemisphere produce signs and symptoms on the same side of the body.

Brainstem • The brainstem lies between the cerebral cortex and the spinal cord; it is primarily composed of nerve fibers. It contains three structures: the *midbrain, pons,* and *medulla oblongata* that control primarily involuntary functions (see Figure 22.2). CNs III through XII also arise from the brainstem.

The midbrain conducts and relays impulses between the higher cerebral centers (the cerebrum) and the lower cerebral centers (the pons, medulla, cerebellum, and spinal cord). A tubular structure, the *aqueduct of Sylvius,* runs through the center of the midbrain to transport CSF between the third and fourth ventricles. The midbrain also houses nuclei for CNs III and IV (Table 22.1).

The pons, located between the midbrain and medulla oblongata, connects the cerebellum to the cerebrum and the midbrain to the medulla. It contains ascending and descending fiber tracts. The pons also contains nuclei for CNs V (motor and sensory nuclei), VI, VII, and VIII (see Table 22.1). Neurons within the pons allow humans to recognize and remember other human faces, which is essential for maternal–infant bonding (Wilson, 2008).

The medulla oblongata, a continuation of the spinal cord, lies between the pons and cerebellum; it contains all ascending and descending fiber tracts that connect the brain to the spinal cord. Motor nerve fibers cross to the opposite side (*pyramidal decussation*) in the medulla. The medulla controls the body's respiratory function, heart rate, blood pressure, and other life-supporting reflexes such as gagging, coughing, and swallowing. This structure also contains nuclei and motor components for CNs VIII through XII (see Table 22.1). Together with the thalamus and hypothalamus, this structure comprises the reticular activating system, which is essential for maintaining arousal, wakefulness, and consciousness.

TABLE 22.1	Summary of Cranial Nerve Function and Location			
NUMBER	NERVE	TYPE	FUNCTION	ANATOMIC LOCATION
I	Olfactory	Sensory	Smell	Olfactory bulb and tract
II	Optic	Sensory	Visual acuity and peripheral vision	Optic nerve, chiasm, and tract
III	Oculomotor	Motor Sensory	Extraocular movement, pupil constriction, and accommodation of upper eyelid elevation	Midbrain
IV	Trochlear	Motor	Extraocular eye movement	Midbrain
V	Trigeminal	Motor	Mastication, lateral mandibular movements	Pons
		Sensory	Facial sensation; corneal reflex	
VI	Abducens	Motor	Extraocular eye movement (i.e., lateral gaze)	Pons
VII	Facial	Sensory	Taste (on anterior two thirds of tongue); stimulates submaxillary and sublingual gland secretions; stimulates tears from lacrimal glands	Pons
		Motor	Facial muscle movement	
VIII	Acoustic (vestibulocochlear)	Sensory	Hearing and balance	Pons
IX	Glossopharyngeal	Sensory	Taste (on posterior one third of tongue)	Pharynx
		Motor	Swallowing, gag reflex, and cough	
X	Vagus	Motor	Controls swallowing, gag reflex, movement of palate and larynx, and speaking; controls heart rate, diaphragm, abdomen, and production of gastric acid	Medulla
		Sensory	Sensation from throat, larynx, heart, lungs, bronchi, gastrointestinal tract, and abdominal viscera	
XI	Spinal accessory	Motor	Provides motor function for sternocleidomastoid and trapezius muscles (i.e., head and shoulder movement; head rotation)	Cervical
XII	Hypoglossal	Motor	Provides motor function to tongue	Medulla

Cerebral Blood Supply

The brain is supplied with blood through four arteries: two *vertebral arteries* and two *carotid arteries*, which arise from the aortic arch or its branches. The vertebral arteries supply blood to the posterior portion of the brain. The point where the two vertebral arteries meet is the *basilar artery*, which supplies blood to the pons, cerebellum, and posterior cerebrum. The internal carotid arteries supply blood to the anterior and middle brain. The vertebral and carotid arteries are connected at the base of the brain by an arterial anastomosis, the *circle of Willis*. This connection ensures continued blood flow to the brain if one of the arteries becomes occluded. Venous drainage from the brain occurs through sinuses in the dura mater, which connect to the cerebral veins, and continues to the superior vena cava, and ultimately to the right atrium. Cerebral blood flow is maintained through cerebral autoregulation or a steady state of blood flow irrespective of systemic blood pressure changes.

Blood–Brain Barrier

The blood–brain barrier is a semipermeable membrane composed of tightly packed endothelial cells. It protects the brain from harmful substances (e.g., drugs, toxins, chemicals), while allowing essential metabolic functions to occur (e.g., the passage of water, waste, nutrients, oxygen, carbon dioxide, glucose). To pass through the blood–brain barrier, molecules must be small, lipid-soluble, and have low ionic permeability. For example, water-soluble substances, such as sodium and potassium, have difficulty reaching the brain, whereas lipid-soluble substances, such as alcohol, narcotics, anticonvulsants, or drugs easily pass through. Hypertension, increased intracranial pressure (ICP), hyperosmolality of a substance, radiation, infection, inflammation, trauma, ischemia, or injury to the brain can result in a break-down of the blood–brain barrier.

Spinal Cord

The spinal cord is a long, cylindrical structure that is an extension of the medulla oblongata. It begins at the fora-men magnum and extends to the lumbar region (L1–L2). Like the brain, the spinal cord is covered with the dura mater, arachnoid, and pia mater. The spinal cord is housed and protected by the vertebral column (Figure 22.4).

The spinal cord itself is composed of white and gray matter. The white matter contains thousands of myelin-ated nerve fibers, which form the ascending (sensory) and descending (motor) tracts. The ascending tract conveys impulses from the spinal cord to the brain; the descending tract transmits impulses from the brain to the motor neurons of the spinal cord. Within the white matter is the H-shaped gray matter, with anterior and posterior horns (Figure 22.5). Cell bodies in the anterior horn relay motor impulses from the CNS to the skeletal muscles. The posterior portion relays sensory impulses from the body to the CNS.

Pathways of the Central Nervous System

There are two major neural pathways of the CNS: sensory and motor. Knowledge of these neural pathways helps the health care provider interpret clinical findings and formulate differential diagnoses.

The sensory pathways can be divided into the *spinothalamic tract* and *posterior (dorsal) columns*, two ascending neural pathways. In the sensory path-ways, sensory impulses travel to the brain by means of afferent fibers in a peripheral nerve, through the posterior (dorsal) root, and then into the spinal cord. The spinothalamic tract relays sensations of pain, temperature, and crude or light touch; the posterior columns transmit sensations of position, vibration, and fine touch.

The motor pathways are two descending neural pathways, the *corticospinal (pyramidal) tract* and *extra-pyramidal tract*. The corticospinal tract transmits motor impulses to the muscles from the medulla, where they

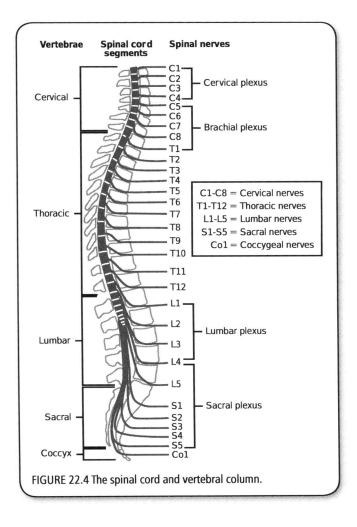

FIGURE 22.4 The spinal cord and vertebral column.

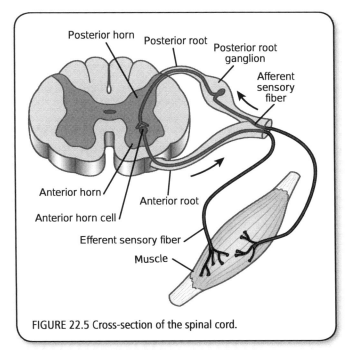

FIGURE 22.5 Cross-section of the spinal cord.

cross to the opposite side of the body. These impulses produce voluntary movements that involve skill. The extrapyramidal tracts contain motor neurons, arising from the motor cortex, basal ganglia, brainstem, and spinal cord that are outside the corticospinal tract. These neurons conduct impulses that help to maintain muscle tone and control of gross body movements, such as walking.

Peripheral Nervous System

The PNS includes the SNS, and the ANS, the spinal nerves, and the cranial nerves. The peripheral nerves contain a sensory (dorsal) and a motor (ventral) root, which transmit impulses to the CNS by means of sensory (afferent) fibers and send messages from the CNS through the efferent fibers. The PNS, which is not protected by bone like the CNS, is vulnerable to injury.

Somatic Nervous System

The SNS controls all voluntary muscle function in the body with the exception of the reflex arc. The *reflex arc* is an involuntary process that functions at an unconscious level. Reflexes allow the body to respond quickly to potentially harmful or painful situations and help to maintain normal muscle tone. Spinal nerves transmit impulses to the spinal cord and back to the muscle to create the reflexes, such as deep tendon and superficial reflexes.

Autonomic Nervous System

The ANS controls all unconscious, automatic body functions and is involved in emotional responses to stress and situations requiring increased energy. Impulses from the ANS are carried by both cranial and spinal nerves; these nerves carry both somatic and autonomic nerve fibers. Somatic fibers innervate the skeletal (voluntary) muscles; the autonomic fibers innervate the smooth (involuntary) muscles, cardiac muscle, and glands.

The ANS is divided into the sympathetic and parasympathetic nervous systems, which function together to maintain homeostasis. Impulses from the sympathetic and parasympathetic nervous systems have antagonistic effects to accomplish this; for example, the sympathetic nervous system regulates the body's energy in times of stress and evokes such responses as pupillary dilation, bronchodilation, increased heart rate, and decreased peristalsis. The parasympathetic nervous system restores balance in the body after stress by decreasing heart rate, and by controlling the body's normal, daily activities, such as digestion and elimination.

Spinal Nerves

There are 31 pairs of spinal nerves that originate in the spinal cord and exit the vertebral column, each having a motor and sensory root. These spinal nerves are named according to their exit point on the spinal cord (see Figure 22.4). There are:

- Eight pairs of cervical spinal nerves (C1–C8)
- Twelve pairs of thoracic spinal nerves (T1–T12)
- Five pairs of lumbar spinal nerves (L1–L5)
- Five pairs of sacral spinal nerves (S1–S5)
- One pair of coccygeal spinal nerves

These nerves innervate the torso and extremities to carry touch, temperature, pain sensations, and motor impulses that control the skeletal muscles and involuntary muscles of the viscera. The area of the body that is innervated by the plexus (nerve network) of a spinal nerve is called a *dermatome* (Figure 22.6). In the event of a spinal cord injury or lesion, the spinal nerves no longer function above the injury level.

Cranial Nerves

There are 12 pairs of CNs that arise from the brainstem, innervating the same side of the body from which they originate. These nerves transmit sensory and motor impulses. Table 22.1 summarizes the number, name, and functions of the cranial nerves.

Upper and Lower Motor Neurons

Upper motor neurons are located completely within the CNS. They originate in the motor area of the cerebral cortex or the brainstem and convey impulses to the lower motor neurons in the spinal cord. Cerebral palsy is an upper motor neuron disease. Lower motor neurons are located mainly in the PNS. They connect the brainstem and spinal cord to muscle fibers, permitting the nerve impulses to travel from the upper motor neurons to the muscles. Spinal cord lesions, muscular dystrophy, and poliomyelitis are lower motor neuron diseases.

DEVELOPMENTAL CONSIDERATIONS

Central Nervous System

Brain and Spinal Cord Development

The development of the brain and spinal cord begin with the formation of the *neural tube*, which is completed and closed by 28 days gestation, which allows the CNS and cranial nerves to form. The growth of the neural tube eventually leads to the appearance of the skull and vertebrae. Failure of the neural tube to close dorsally results in defects such as myelomeningocele, encephalocele, and anencephaly. Failure of the anterior neural tube to close results in facial and forebrain defects, such as cleft lip or palate or holoprosencephaly.

The full-term neonate's brain weighs approximately 325 grams (g). Brain growth is very rapid in the first year of life; the cranial sutures are not fully fused at birth through age 1 year to accommodate the rapid brain growth. Cranial sutures begin to fuse by 6 months and gradually ossify during childhood

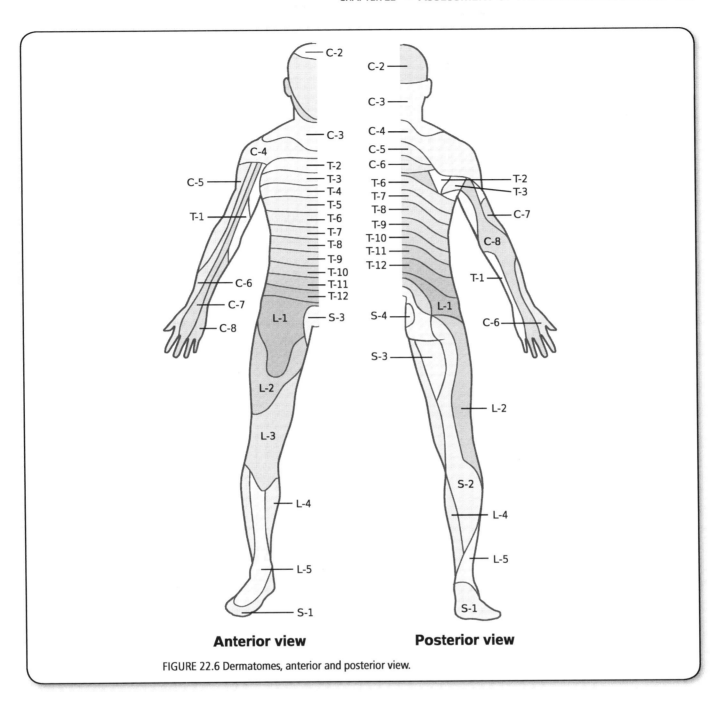

FIGURE 22.6 Dermatomes, anterior and posterior view.

(see Chapter 13, Figure 13.2). The cranial sutures can be separated by increased ICP until approximately age 12 years. *Fontanelles* are areas of connective tissue between the sutures, which gradually close and ossify; the posterior fontanelle closes by 2 months, and the anterior fontanelle by 12 to 18 months (see Chapter 13, Figure 13.2). Cranial bones that are not fully ossified leave the infant more vulnerable to skull fracture and subsequent brain injury after falls or other trauma.

By 1 year of age, the infant's brain weighs approximately 1000 g; by 12 years of age, the brain reaches approximately 75% of its adult size. In the term infant, the head size increases approximately sixfold in the first

year of life, during which time the infant is very vulnerable to head and spinal cord injuries, particularly shaking injuries. Any neurologic injuries, infections, or diseases occurring at this time can permanently affect the growth of the brain.

The young child depends on continuous blood flow to the brain to meet its high demands for oxygen, which occur through autoregulation. However, premature infants have limited cerebral autoregulation; in addition, their cerebral vessels are thin walled and fragile, predisposing these infants to intraventricular hemorrhage (Macfarlane, 2006). The blood–brain barrier is underdeveloped at birth and, therefore, more permeable, not fully developing until the middle of the first year of life (Swamy Chidananda & Mallikarjun, 2004).

Neuronal Development and Myelination

Neuronal proliferation, migration, organization, and myelination are processes that are essential to the developing brain and that occur during the embryonic period; toxic exposures or maternal nutritional deficiencies can adversely affect these processes.

Neuronal Proliferation • Neuronal proliferation occurs between 2 and 4 months gestation; any exposure in utero to toxins or particular genetic diseases can affect the number of neurons. For example, prenatal exposure to tobacco, marijuana, opiates, cocaine, and other stimulants can result in neurobehavioral teratology. Conduct disorder has been associated with tobacco exposure. Prenatal exposure to cocaine is associated with numerous adverse physiologic and psychosocial effects, including developmental delays, difficulties with self-regulation, increased impulsivity, and lower IQ (Minnes, Lang, & Singer, 2011).

Inadequate maternal folic acid intake can also result in CNS malformation. By 36 weeks gestation, neuronal proliferation is almost complete; this contributes in large part to the process of brain growth and the development of brain function.

Neuronal Migration • Neuronal migration peaks between 3 and 5 months gestation. By 6 months, neurons migrate to their permanent neural circuit in the cortex. This process is essential for the development of the cerebral cortex. Failure of this process to occur correctly results in structural abnormalities in the brain, which can lead to agenesis of the corpus callosum or cranial nerves; seizures in the neonate may be the first clinical manifestation of these disorders.

Neuronal Organization • Neuronal organization, including cell differentiation, development of cell synapses, neurotransmitters, and myelination, occurs at approximately 27 to 28 days gestation and provides the underpinning for brain function. Neuronal organization and myelination play a large role in brain growth and maturation.

Myelination • Myelination begins early in the third trimester, occurs rapidly in the first 2 years of life, and is completed by approximately age 7 years of age (Swamy Chidananda & Mallikarjun, 2004). The neurologic system is anatomically complete at birth, but since it is not fully myelinated, it is functionally immature until myelination is complete. The first areas of the nervous system to become myelinated are the motor–sensory roots, special senses, and brainstem, all of which are necessary for intact reflex function and survival. Myelination otherwise occurs in a cephalocaudal and proximodistal pattern that correlates with the head-to-toe acquisition of motor developmental milestones. For example, with

cephalocaudal development, head control develops first, then trunk control (sitting), followed by control of the lower extremities (walking). Proximodistal development begins with shoulder control, then control of the upper extremities, followed by fine motor control (e.g., pincer grasp).

Peripheral Nervous System

At birth, the neonate has little voluntary motor control; primitive reflexes (e.g., Moro, rooting, palmar) control most movement. These reflexes are present in the normal term infant at birth and diminish as the infant's CNS matures over the next 4 to 6 months. As the infant's neurologic system develops, advanced cortical functions and voluntary motor control prevail, and the primitive reflexes diminish. As this occurs, postural reflexes (e.g., the Landau, parachute) replace the primitive reflexes; this occurs cephalocaudally and proximodistally. The postural reflexes emerge at 3 to 8 months of age. Persistence of primitive reflexes or a failure of the postural reflexes to develop indicates an upper motor neuron abnormality (e.g., cerebral palsy).

Autonomic Nervous System

Parasympathetic and sympathetic functions in neonates and infants are undeveloped; these functions are less able to control blood pressure and may respond to pain with tachycardia or increased blood pressure (Swamy Chidananda & Mallikarjun, 2004). Cerebral vessels are thin-walled and fragile in premature infants, predisposing them to intraventricular hemorrhage (Macfarlane, 2006).

ASSESSMENT OF THE NEUROLOGIC SYSTEM

History

Neurologic problems in children can be acute or chronic. The reason for the child's health care visit guides the provider in deciding what type of data are relevant for the health history. For children who are examined for the first time, a complete past medical history, surgical history, family history, and social history are obtained. These histories are updated as needed when the child presents for health maintenance visits, with special attention to assessment of developmental milestones and any history of neurologic injury or infection. A developmental history is especially important, as delays in achieving developmental milestones can indicate a neurologic injury or illness. A focused history is required when the child presents with a neurologic complaint or developmental delay.

Past Medical History

Prenatal History • The prenatal history is essential when completing a pediatric neurologic assessment; any prenatal insult (e.g., intrauterine hypoxia, infection, toxic exposure) can cause long-term neurodevelopmental sequelae. The provider should determine when prenatal care was initiated and whether the mother took prenatal vitamins, specifically folic acid. Any maternal illnesses during pregnancy are noted, particularly infectious diseases (e.g., hepatitis) and infections (e.g., toxoplasmosis, syphilis, rubella, cytomegalovirus, herpes, tuberculosis, chorioamnionitis, sexually transmitted infections, human immunodeficiency virus). Episodes of bleeding during pregnancy, gestational diabetes, preeclampsia, or toxemia are also important components of an assessment. It is important to determine the mother's age as well as her alcohol consumption, drug ingestion (e.g., methamphetamine, cocaine, heroin), prescribed and over-the-counter (OTC) medications, cigarette smoking, and exposure to radiation during pregnancy. A history of previous spontaneous abortions or stillbirths is relevant, including the etiology, if known (e.g., genetic disease).

Perinatal History • The provider must determine if the child was diagnosed with any perinatal conditions that could lead to a hypoxic-ischemic insult, which can cause permanent neurodevelopmental deficits in the child. For example, infants who experience asphyxia during the perinatal or neonatal period are at increased risk for various disabling neurologic conditions (e.g., cerebral palsy, periventricular leukomalacia, hearing and visual impairments, developmental delay). Additionally, it is important to ask about meconium aspiration, abruptio placentae, or nuchal cord.

The provider notes if the child was born by normal, spontaneous vaginal delivery or by cesarean section, including the reason for the surgical birth (e.g., abruptio placentae, fetal distress, nuchal cord). The child's Apgar scores should be reviewed, noting if the mother received pain medications during labor; if there was any fetal distress, birth trauma, or use of forceps; or if the infant required any resuscitation and for how long. Complications of birth trauma, such as cephalohematoma, should be noted, as it may lead to hyperbilirubinemia or kernicterus.

It is particularly important to note any history of prematurity and low birth weight. These infants are at high risk for neurodevelopmental complications, such as cerebral palsy; hearing and visual impairment; and speech, language, and motor delays, which result in an abnormal neurologic examination (Blackman, 2007). Preterm infants are also more likely to have other neurologic complications, such as seizures, learning difficulties, attention deficit hyperactivity disorder (ADHD), periventricular leukomalacia, intraventricular hemorrhage (IVH), as well as psychologic and behavioral problems as they reach childhood (Vanderbilt, Wang, & Parker, 2007).

Neonatal History • The provider must inquire about any conditions that may have occurred during the neonatal period, such as severe respiratory distress, extreme hypoxia, or extreme acidosis, which lead to permanent neurologic complications. These conditions may necessitate the use of extracorporeal membrane oxygenation, which predisposes the neonate to stroke. The provider must determine if hyperbilirubinemia or bilirubin encephalopathy (kernicterus) occurred in the neonatal period; both of these conditions can lead to intellectual disability and deafness. Box 22.1 lists some causes of hyperbilirubinemia in the neonate. Meningitis, sepsis, hypoxia, seizures, IVH, periventricular hemorrhage, and episodes of apnea/bradycardia in the neonatal period can lead to neurologic complications such as cerebral palsy (Jones, Morgan, Shelton, & Thorgood, 2007), as can hypoglycemia and hypothyroidism. A history of poor tone and difficulty with sucking and swallowing in the neonatal period can be associated with cerebral palsy and must be noted (Jones et al., 2007). The examiner notes the presence of congenital heart defects, focusing on the type of defect; defects that cause decreased pulmonary blood flow can lead to repeated hypoxic events and resultant neurologic sequelae. A phenylketonuria (PKU) screen is necessary because if PKU is not treated, intellectual disability and seizures may result.

Review of Systems • Obtaining the review of systems as it relates to the neurologic system involves determining if the child has ever had any of the following conditions:

- **General health:** Alteration in growth patterns (i.e., height, length, weight, body mass index, head circumference), history of high fevers, changes in appetite or weight, and fatigue
- **Skin:** Café-au-lait lesions (e.g., neurofibromatosis), hemangiomas, port-wine stains (e.g., Sturge–Weber syndrome), or pigmentation changes
- **Head, face, and neck:** Microcephaly, macrocephaly, hydrocephaly, craniosynostosis, plagiocephaly, wide sutures, bulging fontanelles, altered head control, facial pain, nuchal rigidity or pain,

---

BOX 22.1 Causes of Hyperbilirubinemia in Neonates

- Biliary atresia
- Cephalohematoma
- Cystic fibrosis
- Galactosemia
- Hepatitis
- Sepsis
- Syphilis
- TORCH infections

TORCH, toxoplasmosis, other (e.g., coxsackievirus, *Listeria*, human parvovirus), rubella, cytomegalovirus/*Chlamydia*, herpes simplex/hepatitis B/human immunodeficiency virus.

headaches, migraines, or facial dysmorphism (e.g., fetal alcohol syndrome)

- **Eyes:** Blurred vision, diplopia, nystagmus, strabismus, sunset eyes (indicates increased ICP), pupillary changes, or photophobia
- **Ears:** Low-set ears (can indicate a syndromic feature), hearing loss, vertigo, or tinnitus
- **Cardiovascular:** Hypertension, widened pulse pressure, orthostatic hypotension, bradycardia, vasovagal syncope, fainting spells, arrhythmia, stroke, congenital heart disease, or rheumatic heart disease
- **Respiratory:** Irregular respirations, conditions that cause hypoxia, or acid–base imbalance
- **Genitourinary:** Tanner staging or urinary tract disease
- **Musculoskeletal:** Spasticity of extremities; difficulty with balance, coordination, or muscle strength; cerebral palsy, paralysis, or muscular dystrophy
- **Neurologic:** Encephalocele, spina bifida occulta, meningocele, myelomeningocele, Chiari II malformation, aneurysm, infantile spasms, IVH, hypoxic-ischemic encephalopathy, seizures (including type), status epilepticus, tremors, spasms, paresthesias, ipsilateral or bilateral weakness, dizziness, bacterial meningitis, viral meningitis, encephalitis, Reye's syndrome, Guillain-Barré syndrome, episodes of loss of consciousness, memory loss, changes in concentration, CNS neoplasm, ataxia, aphasia, head trauma, irritability, lethargy, chronic fatigue, sleep disorders, ADHD, or tics.
- **Metabolic:** Diabetes mellitus (hyperglycemia causes lethargy, confusion, coma; hypoglycemia causes confusion, lethargy, loss of consciousness, seizures), thyroid disorders (hyperthyroidism causes tremors, irritability, restlessness, fatigue, difficulty sleeping, muscle weakness, and possible mental status changes; hypothyroidism causes enlarged posterior fontanelle, lethargy, and coma), or hyper- or hypokalemia, which can cause seizures
- **Hematologic:** Sickle cell disease (predisposes child to stroke), polycythemia, or coagulopathies
- **Immunologic:** Leukemia, lymphoma, history of radiation, or chemotherapy
- **Psychosocial:** Drug or alcohol addiction, stress, emotional lability, irritability, breath-holding spells, behavioral disorders, eating disorders, anxiety, depression, history of suicidal ideation, schizophrenia, hallucinations, bipolar disorder, or mood changes
- **Developmental:** Age of achievement of major developmental milestones, intelligence, memory, ability to adapt to new environments or tasks, or speech and language disorders

Immunizations • The provider must determine whether the child's immunizations are up to date for age. Certain diseases for which children are immunized can cause serious neurologic complications. For example, *Haemophilus influenzae* type B, *Streptococcus pneumoniae*, and *Neisseria meningitidis* can cause bacterial meningitis. Varicella can cause acute postinfectious cerebellar ataxia, encephalitis, Reye's syndrome, aseptic meningitis, Guillain-Barré syndrome, and polyradiculitis, although these complications are rare (Papadopoulous, Janninger, & Schwartz, 2013).

Hospitalizations • The provider must ask about past hospitalizations, including dates and length of stay, focusing on the reason for the hospitalization and whether it bears any relevance to the child's neurologic status. Examples of specific conditions about which to inquire include bacterial meningitis, head trauma, shock, brain tumor, seizures, hydrocephalus, and myelomeningocele.

Injuries • The provider should inquire about any history of injuries that could have an impact on the child's neurodevelopmental status, including traumatic brain injuries, spinal cord injuries, poisoning, ingestions, dehydration, and near drowning (Table 22.2). Musculoskeletal injuries may suggest problems with coordination (e.g., posterior fossa brain tumors) or impulsive behavior (e.g., ADHD). The provider should obtain the date and time of the injury, the details of the injury (i.e., how and why the injury occurred), whether anyone witnessed the injury, what the child's symptoms have been since the injury, and if the child has any physical or neurodevelopmental deficits as a result of the injury. The provider should also assess whether the child has had to miss school or has experienced any changes in social relationships since the injury. When obtaining the history, the provider should continually evaluate whether abuse or neglect played a role in the child's injuries (see Chapter 24).

Surgical History

The provider must determine what surgeries the child has undergone that are related to his or her neurologic status or diagnoses. The dates and any complications of all surgeries should be included. Examples of the kinds of surgical procedures that are important to include are:

- Surgery after head trauma to evacuate a hematoma
- Surgery to remove a brain tumor
- Shunt placement, including the reason for placement (e.g., obstructive or nonobstructive hydrocephalus), type of shunt (ventriculoperitoneal, atrioventricular), number of revisions, any shunt infections
- Surgery to treat epilepsy
- Surgical repair of meningocele, myelomeningocele, or encephalocele

Family History

The provider must obtain a family medical history to assess the prevalence of neurologic conditions or genetic

TABLE 22.2 **Types of Traumatic Brain Injuries in Children**

CATEGORY AND DESCRIPTION OF BRAIN INJURY	CAUSES	ASSESSMENTS
Concussion (Mild Traumatic Brain Injury): "A complex pathophysiologic process affecting the brain, induced by traumatic biomechanical forces secondary to direct or indirect forces to the head" (Centers for Disease Control and Prevention [CDC], 2011)	Motor vehicle collision Sports injuries Violence Falls Bicycle-related injuries	A thorough history and physical examination are conducted related to: • Head • Eye • Ear • Face • Neurologic system • Vision The provider should inquire about the circumstances surrounding injury and about the following (Mason, 2013): • Headache • Visual disturbances • Nausea/vomiting • Fatigue • Sleep disturbances • Impaired memory • Mood/personality changes Later complaints include: • School difficulties • Behavior problems • Memory problems • Attention/concentration problems (Mason, 2013). The Acute Concussion Evaluation (ACE) tool, published in the CDC's "Heads UP: Concussion in Your Practice," is also an excellent resource to assess acute concussion and postconcussion symptoms (www.cdc.gov/concussion) The use of bicycle helmets and other protective sports equipment, booster seats, and seatbelts in motor vehicles should be noted, as well as any history of abuse or neglect.
Diffuse Axonal Injury (DAI): Shearing type of brain injury causing disruption in axons and nerve fiber tracts, usually caused by violent motion such as motor vehicle collision; loss of consciousness lasts ≥ 6 hours in the absence of any focal deficits	Motor vehicle injuries Shaking injuries	Thorough neurologic history and physical are necessary; DAI is typically the underlying injury in AHT (see Chapter 24).
Skull Fracture: Break in one or more of the cranial bones caused by injury to the head *Linear skull fracture:* • Basilar skull fracture *Depressed skull fracture:* • Simple • Compound • Closed • Open	As with concussion *plus:* • Neglect • Abuse	As with concussion *plus:* Type of skull fracture is noted; any history of rib or long bone fractures and injuries to nose or mouth should be noted; history of seizures, including type and onset, and history of repeated injuries are noted (may point to abuse; see Chapter 24). Basilar skull fractures cause leakage of CSF from the nose or ear, blood behind the TM, and ecchymosis behind the ear (Battle's sign) or under the eyes (raccoon eyes).

(continued)

TABLE 22.2	Types of Traumatic Brain Injuries in Children (*continued*)	
CATEGORY AND DESCRIPTION OF BRAIN INJURY	**CAUSES**	**ASSESSMENTS**
Epidural Hematoma: Bleeding between the skull and dura mater in the epidural space; often caused by linear skull fractures; without rapid intervention, patients with arterial epidural hematomas quickly deteriorate and die.	Blow to head Skull fracture Falls Motor vehicle collisions	As with concussion and fractures *plus:* Examiner assesses for history of seizures, headaches, nausea and vomiting; weakness, hemiplegia, or personality changes; aphasia, ataxia, and visual field deficits (Liebeskind, 2014).
Subdural Hematoma: Bleeding between the dura mater and the arachnoid into the subdural space; signs and symptoms include gradual onset of headache, drowsiness, confusion, occasional focal deficits, and seizures.	As above *plus:* • AHT • Arachnoid cyst • Use of anticoagulants	As with concussion and fractures *plus:* Examiner assesses for decreased level of consciousness, history of seizures, headaches, weakness, hemiplegia; personality changes, memory loss, alterations in cognitive function, speech, ataxia, and blurred vision (Meagher & Young, 2013).
Subarachnoid Hemorrhage: Bleeding in the subarachnoid space; neurologic function may be normal but may cause acute neurologic abnormalities.	*Traumatic:* • Acute head injury • Birth trauma • AHT • *Nontraumatic:* • Sickle cell disease • Polycythemia • Coarctation of the aorta • Intracranial aneurysm • AVM • Brain tumor	Examiner assesses for any long-term neurologic sequelae.

AHT, abusive head trauma; AVM, atriovenous malformation; CSF, cerebrospinal fluid; TM, tympanic membrane.

disorders, such as Tay-Sachs disease, congenital hypothyroidism, galactosemia, maple syrup urine disease, PKU, or primary adrenal hypoplasia. Any consanguinity should be determined, as this increases the child's risk for genetic disorders (Yunnis, El Rafei, & Mumtaz, 2008). The provider also determines if there is a family history of seizures, migraines, learning disorders, or ADHD.

Social History

The social history focuses on aspects of the family's living conditions, lifestyle, and any risk factors that could predispose the child to neurologic infections, injuries, or developmental delays. For example, the provider must assess the child's home environment for lead exposure, especially in homes built before 1960, which may have old, chipping paint; children living in these homes are at risk for lead poisoning. The provider must ask about the safety of the home or apartment (e.g., whether there are balconies or high windows from which the child could easily fall). It is very important to inquire about the caregiver–child relationship to determine whether neglect is a factor; neglect can affect the shape and symmetry of an infant's skull (e.g., flattened occiput if the infant is consistently placed in a supine position and left in this position for long periods of time), the child's neurodevelopmental status, and the achievement of developmental milestones.

It is important to identify who lives in the home and each person's relationship to the child. More detailed assessments include determining whether the child's caregivers have social supports, consistent employment, or a history of substance abuse or domestic violence, all of which are risk factors for abuse or neglect of a child (CDC, 2014). Questions about family discipline practices that involve corporal punishment are vitally important because shaking injuries are associated with long-term neurologic consequences, such as mental and cognitive impairments, hearing and visual impairments, seizure disorders, developmental delays, motor deficits, spasticity, cerebral palsy, quadriparesis, hydrocephalus, and microcephaly (Christian & Block, 2009). Inflicted head trauma in children can result in all of the aforementioned consequences in the long term; the short-term neurologic clinical presentation can include unexplained loss of consciousness, respiratory distress, apnea, irritability, hypotonia, seizures, coma, recurrent vomiting, or poor feeding in an infant or young child (Christian & Block, 2009).

The provider should ask the child's primary caregiver if there are any prescription medications or illegal drugs in the home. Children of all ages may ingest these drugs inadvertently or intentionally, resulting in mild to severe neurologic impairment, depending on the child's age, weight, and the quantity ingested. The older school-aged child and adolescent should be asked (with the parent out of the room) about their drug use. Cocaine use and glue sniffing predispose the child to stroke; alcohol toxicity can lead to brain damage. Traumatic brain injury can occur with alcohol use if it is associated with a motor vehicle collision.

Providers must ask about the child's school progress or any behavior problems reported by either the parent or the teacher. Difficulty in school, inattentiveness, and even school failure may indicate hearing impairment, developmental delay, intellectual disability, ADHD, or depression.

Developmental History

It is imperative to obtain an accurate developmental history, particularly for children 6 years of age and younger. This includes ascertaining when the child attained age-appropriate language, gross and fine motor milestones, and social and cognitive milestones, all of which reflect the child's neurodevelopmental status. If a child has lost a skill or has regressed, referral to a pediatric neurologist is needed (see Chapter 2 for a full discussion of the developmental history).

Medications

The provider should inquire about any medications the child is taking on a regular or as needed basis, including OTC medications and complementary or alternative treatments (see Chapter 6). Some medications have neurologic, vestibulotoxic, or sedating side effects that must be noted. Examples of these include medications prescribed for migraines, muscle relaxants, anticonvulsants, antidepressants, antihistamines, narcotic or opioid analgesics, antipsychotics, anxiolytics, CNS stimulants (e.g., methylphenidate or pemoline for ADHD), or aminoglycosides, as neurotoxicity can occur with high doses and prolonged therapy of these drugs. The examiner must determine whether adolescent girls are using oral contraceptives, as these may predispose them to stroke. The indication, ordered dose, and time of last dose of any medications should also be noted, as the side effects of some of these medications may affect the neurologic examination.

Allergies

Assessment of allergies, including the type of reaction, should be included as part of a pediatric neurologic assessment. For example, chronic environmental allergies may cause nasal congestion, affecting smell; allergies may cause headaches as well. A history of severe allergies or anaphylaxis should be considered when an atopic child presents for care and has an altered level of consciousness (LOC).

History of Present Illness

When a child presents with a neurologic complaint (e.g., head or spinal injuries, recurrent headaches, persistent fever, developmental delays, identified neurologic disorder), the provider must obtain a focused history (i.e., history of the present illness [HPI]), including information about onset (sudden or gradual), duration, and progression. For infants and young children, the parent provides the information. Older children may have difficulty with memory or speech after a head injury, and the parent may need to provide the historical information. With adolescents, the history may need to be obtained with the parent out of the room to glean the most accurate information, especially concerning drug and alcohol use or a possible pregnancy, which can be associated with fainting. Assessment of acute neurologic injury is discussed at the end of this chapter. Some examples of neurologic problems seen in the pediatric population are listed in Box 22.2. Relevant questions to ask for the HPI can be found in Table 22.3.

Physical Examination

The pediatric neurologic examination can be completed by general observation integrated within the overall physical assessment or by a more purposeful, specific neurologic assessment, which is generally performed when a child presents with a developmental delay or neurologic complaint. Both approaches require that the examination be tailored to the child's age and developmental level. Physical assessment of the neurologic system includes a general physical examination of relevant body systems (see Developmental Approach to Neurologic Assessment), a developmental assessment, and a focused neurologic examination. The focused pediatric neurologic examination includes an assessment of mental status, speech, language, CN function, sensation, motor function, muscle strength, gait, balance, coordination, deep tendon reflexes (DTR), and

---

BOX 22.2 Selected Pediatric Neurologic Problems

- Ataxia
- Cerebral palsy
- Developmental delay
- Headaches
- Head injuries
- Lead poisoning
- Meningitis
- Myelomeningocele
- Seizures
- Spinal cord injuries
- Status epilepticus

TABLE 22.3	History of Present Illness: Neurologic Complaints	
SYMPTOM	**ASSESSMENTS**	**EXPLICATION**
Ataxia	Neonatal and birth history? Social history? Child's age? Fever? Is child on medications? Type? Dose? Time of last dose? Associated headache? History of migraines? Onset? Recent alcohol ingestion? Nystagmus? Results of sensory examination?	Acute onset often caused by toxic ingestion (unintentional in young children or intentional in older child) of drugs or alcohol; infectious etiologies (e.g., meningitis; encephalitis); hemorrhage or brain tumor that cause increased ICP. Chronic ataxia may be caused by neurodegenerative disorders, migraine, cerebral palsy, or sequelae of head trauma or lead poisoning (Bernard et al., 2012).
Behavioral changes	Irritability? Change in appetite, attention span, school performance? Emotional lability? History of drug or alcohol use?	Behavioral changes may be clues to ADHD, drug use, depression, or other mental health problems.
Changes in cry (infants < 6 months)	Prenatal, perinatal, and neonatal history? Focal neurologic findings? Duration of cry? Character of cry? Pain assessment? Social history?	High-pitched cry is a sign of increased ICP in young infants. Intractable crying in an infant may be due to injury.
Developmental delay	Prenatal, perinatal, and neonatal history? Home environment (e.g., lead exposures)? Vision or hearing impairments? Current developmental milestone assessment? Loss of milestones or chronic developmental delay? Past medical history (metabolic disorders, seizures, cerebral palsy, sleep disorders)? Any neurologic soft signs present? Social history? School progress? Behavior issues? Family history? Medication history? Acute or chronic illness? History of injury? What are parental concerns (see Chapter 2)?	Premature infants and those who suffer intraventricular hemorrhages or hypoxic-ischemic insults are likely to have developmental delay; FAS, injury, lead poisoning, lack of stimulating environment; abuse or neglect can also cause developmental delay (see Chapter 2).
Dizziness	Associated tinnitus, vertigo? Current medications, including OTC medications and herbal remedies? Eating disorders? History of hypoglycemia or diabetes? Has child ever fallen as a result of dizziness? Any significant cardiac or neurologic history? Nystagmus? History of drug or alcohol use?	Thorough neurologic exam is needed. Dizziness can be caused by migraine, demyelinating disease, acoustic tumors, or cerebellar lesions.
Fever	Height of fever? Child's age? Concomitant infection? Nuchal rigidity? Immunization status? History of febrile seizures?	Generalized seizure may accompany fever, especially in children with a previous history or family history of febrile seizures. Fever with seizure often indicates bacterial meningitis.
Headaches	Onset? Location? Character of headache? Duration? Intensity of pain (use pain scale)? History of previous headaches or migraines? Aura? Associated vomiting? Visual changes? Vertigo or dizziness? Any triggers (e.g., menses, certain foods, stress)? Photophobia? Phonophobia? Speech disturbances? Sleep problems? Seizures? Current illness (e.g., viral upper respiratory infection; sinusitis)? Teeth pain? Chronic ear infections? Does child wear glasses? Pain on palpation of sinuses? Temporomandibular joint pain? Caffeine, tobacco, or drug use? Current medications (e.g., OTC medications; herbal remedies)? Medications used to treat headache and time of last dose? What makes headache worse or better?	Different types of headaches have different characteristics (e.g., nausea and vomiting, photophobia, or phonophobia occur with common migraine; chronic tension headaches are mild to moderate in intensity without nausea or vomiting (Lewis & Koch, 2010). Headaches in children can be caused by idiopathic intracranial hypertension, acute viral illness, sinus, ear or intracranial infections, brain abscess, systemic infection, tumor, Chiari I malformation, intracranial hemorrhage, trauma, ocular abnormalities, bruxism, drug or alcohol withdrawal, epilepsy, allergies, hypertension, sickle cell disease or cervical spine abnormalities (Blume & Szperka, 2010).

TABLE 22.3	**History of Present Illness: Neurologic Complaints (*continued*)**

SYMPTOM	ASSESSMENTS	EXPLICATION
Head injury	Mechanism of injury? Time of occurrence? Events surrounding injury? Did injury involve a fall? From what height did child fall and onto what surface? Motor vehicle collision? Sports-related injury? Area of head injured? Loss of consciousness at time of injury? Since injury? Any evidence of abuse or neglect? Any vomiting, ataxia, seizures, or visual disturbances? Any associated injuries (e.g., lacerations, fractures)? Drainage from nose or ear?	It is very important to get a detailed neurologic history and physical examination regarding type of head injury. Symptoms of different types of TBIs overlap; some are mild and transient, others are serious and life-threatening and can lead to prolonged disability.
Hearing loss	Onset? Associated injury or infection? Other neurologic signs or symptoms? Current medications? Past medical history?	Hearing loss may indicate cranial nerve damage.
Hypotonia ("floppy infant")	Onset? Duration? History of prenatal or perinatal asphyxia? Delay in reaching developmental milestones? Family history? Social history?	Hypotonia can be caused by asphyxia before or during birth, CP, CNS infections, myopathies, or neglect.
Incoordination	Onset? Recent injury? Current medications? Medical history? Diagnosis of CP? History of drug or alcohol abuse? Developmental delay?	Motor incoordination in children may result from CP, autism, exposure to toxins, side effects of medications, or intoxication.
Irritability	Age of child? Onset? Associated vomiting or headache? Fever? Ataxia? Recent injury? Current medications? Past medical history? History of mental health disorders or addiction? Is infant or child easily consoled?	Irritability, vomiting, headache (particularly upon awakening), and ataxia in children aged 6 years and younger points to medulloblastoma (Jallo & Marcovicci, 2012). Cause in infant may be benign or simple (e.g., fatigue, hunger, thirst, colic, hair tourniquet) or result of an inflicted injury. Irritability occurs with acute otitis media, headache, head trauma, hypoglycemia, sleep disorders, and chronic pain. Irritability may be a side effect of some medications (e.g., albuterol, some antiepileptic drugs). Irritability is also associated with alcohol and drug withdrawal, anxiety, and depression.
Memory loss	Recent head injury? Traumatic emotional event? History of drug or alcohol use?	Memory loss is associated with TBI; it can also be related to stressful or traumatic events.
Muscle wasting	Prenatal, perinatal, and neonatal history? Past medical history (e.g., musculoskeletal or neurologic disorders; chronic endocrine or metabolic illnesses)? History of trauma? Weakness? Pain? Weight loss? Loss of sensation? Alcohol or drug use? Steroid use?	Muscle atrophy in children likely caused by muscular dystrophy, Werdnig-Hoffmann disease (spinal muscular atrophy), CP, paralysis associated with myelomeningocele, hypothyroidism, protein deficiency, rheumatoid arthritis, spinal cord injury, or prolonged bedrest.
Nuchal rigidity	Onset? Associated fever?	Nuchal rigidity is caused by meningeal irritation and points to CNS infection.
Paresthesia	Location? Associated symptoms? Fainting? History of seizures? Past medical history? History of breath-holding spells? Current medications, including OTC medications and herbal remedies? Cardiac history?	Numbness and tingling in children may be due to hypothyroidism, diabetes, as a complication of trauma, lead poisoning, drug overdose (e.g., some antibiotics, chemotherapy), or breath-holding spells. Direct nerve compression can be caused by carrying heavy objects, such as a heavy school backpack.

(*continued*)

TABLE 22.3	History of Present Illness: Neurologic Complaints (*continued*)	
SYMPTOM	**ASSESSMENTS**	**EXPLICATION**
Seizures	Age of child? Onset (sudden or gradual)? Cyanotic during seizure? Did child report an aura? Loss of consciousness? Has child regained consciousness? Type of motor movements (e.g., bilateral? Tonic–clonic?) Child febrile? Height of fever? Associated head injury? Duration of seizure? Loss of bowel or bladder control? Visual, auditory, or olfactory disturbance? Behavioral change? Previous known seizures? Compliance with anticonvulsant regimen? Medication history? Drug and alcohol use? Recent ingestions (e.g., poisons, medications)? Focal neurologic findings (abnormal deep tendon reflexes)? Bulging fontanelle or nuchal rigidity with fever suggests bacterial meningitis? Current blood sugar, electrolytes, and oxygen saturation?	Type of seizure needs to be differentiated to define etiology of seizure and treat appropriately; partial seizures may progress to generalized seizures. CNS injury or infection needs to be treated; CNS imaging studies may need to be obtained to diagnose space-occupying lesion.
Slurred speech	Onset? Medical history? Recent head injury or an intracranial or craniofacial infection?	Cardiac and hematologic disorders; coagulopathies, vascular anomalies and trauma can cause stroke in children. Head injuries or infections can cause cranial nerve damage, causing difficulty speaking.
Syncope	Paresthesia? Menstruating female? History of seizures? Past medical history (e.g., diabetes, vertigo, breath-holding spells, orthostatic hypotension)? Family history? Cardiac history (e.g., prolonged QTC)? Fainting related to athletic activity? History of eating disorders?	A detailed and complete history is important to identify cardiac etiology of syncope during physical activity and to differentiate syncope from seizures.
Pain	Onset? Acute or chronic pain? Recent injury or illness? Location of pain? Associated symptoms?	It is important to identify source of pain to make an accurate diagnosis and develop an appropriate treatment plan.
Photophobia	Onset? Associated with fever? Headache? Immunization status?	Photophobia can indicate meningeal irritation or migraine.
Vertigo	Onset? Gradual or acute onset? Associated head injury? Aggravating or alleviating factors? Child taking any medications? Has child ever fallen because of vertigo? Any problems with hearing? Nystagmus?	Vertigo indicates inner ear abnormality; may also be caused by cranial nerve VII abnormality or occur as a side effect of medication; vertigo is also associated with migraines.
Visual changes	Type of visual change? Diplopia? Loss of vision? Onset? Associated head injury or infection? Other neurologic signs or symptoms?	Visual changes can indicate increased intracranial pressure or cranial nerve abnormalities.
Vomiting	Onset? Associated head injury or infection? Other neurologic signs or symptoms? Fever?	Vomiting can be a sign of increased ICP, migraines, or viral illness.

ADHD, attention deficit hyperactivity disorder; CNS, central nervous system; CP, cerebral palsy; FAS, fetal alcohol syndrome; ICP, intracranial pressure; OTC, over the counter; TBI, traumatic brain injury.

primitive reflexes. The necessary equipment includes the following:

- Tape measure for measuring head circumference
- Penlight
- Ophthalmoscope
- Tongue blades
- Reflex hammer
- Tuning fork
- Familiar small objects (e.g., coins, paperclips, pencil)
- Aromatic substances familiar to children (e.g., bubble gum, mint, chocolate, soap, isopropyl alcohol)
- Sweet and sour items for tasting (glucose, salt, lemon juice)
- Two small tubes: one containing hot water and the other containing cold water
- Safety pin
- Cotton balls
- Cotton-tipped applicators
- Snellen chart

■ Toys, such as stuffed animals, finger puppets, or hand-held windmill to engage young children

■ Small ball

■ Developmental Screening Test (e.g., Ages and Stages Questionnaire, Parents' Evaluation of Developmental Status)

Developmental Approach to the Neurologic Examination

When performing the pediatric neurologic examination, the provider must consider the child's age, developmental level, and temperament; children preschool aged and younger may not be able to cooperate developmentally with parts of the examination. The first step is to just observe the child's spontaneous activity (e.g., feeding, talking, playing, walking), followed by a more purposeful examination. Abnormal findings in any assessment area may indicate a developmental delay or underlying neurologic abnormality. Young children respond well to a playful approach to the examination; the use of finger puppets or stuffed animals, for example, is helpful in engaging a young child. School-aged children and adolescents can be examined in an organized and systematic way. With all ages, the least pleasant aspect of the examination should be done last (e.g., eliciting the gag reflex, inspecting the fundus), as these maneuvers often result in crying, particularly in young children; this may alter examination findings.

General Physical Examination

When conducting the pediatric neurologic examination, a general physical examination is included. The essential parts of this examination that should be noted include the following.

Vital Signs • When vital signs are assessed, the following measurements are recorded: temperature (i.e., fever), heart rate, respiratory rate, blood pressure (e.g., wide pulse pressure indicates increased ICP). Fluctuations in heart rate, blood pressure, and body temperature accompanied by sweating may indicate autonomic instability.

Somatic Growth • Height and weight are measured and plotted on growth charts (see Appendix B) and compared with previous measurements (see Chapter 8); these percentiles should also be compared with head circumference measurements.

Head • Measurement of head circumference, which is the most accurate reflection of brain growth, is measured and plotted on the appropriate growth chart for age and sex. A small head (microcephaly) or a large head (macrocephaly or hydrocephalus) reflect neurologic abnormalities in infants and children. Hydrocephaly is often accompanied by an enlarged frontal area, tense anterior fontanelle, and in some cases, sunset eyes. The head is also inspected for symmetry and shape. In neonates, positional molding and craniosynostosis need

to be differentiated. Some genetic conditions and chromosomal anomalies are known to be associated with craniosynostosis (e.g., Apert, Crouzon, and Pfeiffer syndromes) (Cole & Hollier, 2012). In infants and toddlers, the fontanelles are inspected and palpated until age 2; a bulging fontanelle indicates increased ICP. Signs of increased ICP are delayed in children with open fontanelles.

Head control is assessed in young infants; lack of head control beyond age 6 months is likely a result of cerebral palsy. Auscultation over the skull above the eyes can reveal a cranial bruit, which may indicate an intracranial vascular malformation. The skull should be percussed for any split cranial sutures (Macewen's sign) (see Chapter 13).

Integument • The skin is inspected for dermatologic manifestations of neurocutaneous syndromes. Some examples are given in Table 22.4.

Dysmorphic Features • Facial dysmorphism should be noted; this often accompanies syndromes or genetic conditions that include macrocephaly, microcephaly, and intellectual disability.

Neck • The neck is assessed for nuchal rigidity, which indicates meningeal irritation. Muscle tone of the neck is also assessed.

Eyes • The eyes are inspected for the presence of the "sunset sign," which suggests increased ICP (Figure 22.7). Nystagmus and strabismus are noted, which may be signs of periventricular leukomalacia. The pupils are examined, noting if they are equal in their reaction to light, if they are round, and if accommodation is normal. Extraocular eye movements are assessed (CNs III, IV, VI), and any ptosis is noted. A red reflex and blink are elicited. A funduscopic eye examination is performed as part of a complete pediatric neurologic examination. Any retinal hemorrhages in the lethargic neonate may indicate abusive head trauma (Levin, 2010). Papilledema on funduscopic exam indicates increased ICP. Assessment of the child's vision is included in the neurologic assessment (see Chapter 15).

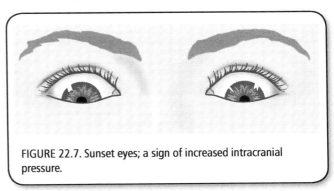

FIGURE 22.7. Sunset eyes; a sign of increased intracranial pressure.

Ears • The ears are inspected for any deformities. Low-set ears may be seen in children with chromosomal

TABLE 22.4	Dermatologic Abnormalities and Associated Neurocutaneous Syndromes
DERMATOLOGIC ABNORMALITY	**NEUROCUTANEOUS SYNDROME**
Oculocutaneous telangiectasia (Bernard et al., 2012).	Ataxia telangiectasia (Louis-Bar syndrome)
Linear, yellowish, hairless nevi found in craniofacial area (Schwartz & Jozwiak, 2014).	Linear sebaceous nevus
Six or more café-au-lait macules over 5 mm in greatest diameter (prepubertal children); over 15 mm in greatest diameter in postpubertal children; axillary or inguinal freckling (Bernard et al., 2012).	Neurofibromatosis 1
Port-wine stain over the face that covers the forehead and upper eyelid (i.e., the ophthalmic division of the trigeminal nerve) (Bernard et al., 2012).	Sturge-Weber syndrome
Hypopigmented macules ("ash-leaf spots") that follow dermatomes, facial hamartomas (Bernard et al., 2012).	Tuberous sclerosis

abnormalities and other syndromes. The child's hearing is assessed, which evaluates CN VIII (see Chapter 14).

Cardiovascular System • The blood pressure is measured in more than one reading. Abnormally high readings can predispose the child to hemorrhagic stroke. A child who presents with headaches, hemiplegia, aphasia, dystonia, seizures, and sensory motor deficits may be experiencing an ischemic stroke. Any congenital or acquired cardiac abnormalities predispose the child to ischemic stroke (Fullerton, Wu, Sidney, & Johnston, 2007).

Abdomen • The abdomen is palpated for organomegaly, which can indicate the presence of any of the storage diseases (e.g., Tay-Sachs disease, Niemann-Pick disease) that involve CNS degeneration.

Tanner Staging • Sexual maturity rating is done in children of all ages (see Chapter 20). Precocious puberty can be caused by brain tumors, CNS injury (e.g., head trauma, surgery, inflammation, radiation therapy, abscess), and congenital anomalies (e.g., hydrocephalus, arachnoid cysts) (Kaplowitz, 2013).

Spine • The lumbosacral area of the spinal column should be inspected for abnormalities, including tufts of hair, sinuses, or dimples (or sacs). A dimple or small sac with a tuft of hair in the lumbosacral area indicates spina bifida occulta. The spine is assessed for scoliosis in children school aged and older.

Developmental Assessment

The pediatric neurologic examination must include an assessment of the child's neurodevelopmental milestones. Achieving these milestones is an important indicator of CNS maturation and development; any delays or abnormal patterns in achieving developmental milestones may signal underlying neurologic disease. The

health care provider must be familiar with the timing of major age-appropriate developmental milestones (e.g., head control, walking, talking, playing) to conduct a developmental assessment competently (see Chapter 2).

Neurologic Examination

The pediatric neurologic examination is conducted in the following sequence, beginning at the highest level of neurologic functioning and concluding with the lowest: cerebral functioning (behavior and mental status), CNs, motor function, sensory function, and reflexes.

Mental Status Evaluation

The mental status evaluation is an essential portion of the pediatric neurologic examination. It begins with initial contact with the child and continues until the end of the encounter. This examination is conducted according to the child's age and developmental level. Much of this portion of the neurologic examination can be integrated throughout the complete history and physical examination. Abnormal findings in pediatric mental status evaluation may indicate anxiety, depression, neurologic illness or injury, or a metabolic disturbance.

The pediatric mental status examination includes the assessment areas described here.

Appearance • The provider assesses the child's overall appearance, including whether the child appears to be the stated age, is clean and well groomed, and is dressed appropriately for age and weather. Appearing younger or older than stated age may indicate neglect. In adolescents, lack of grooming or cleanliness may indicate depression; in young children, it often indicates neglect. Thus, an assessment of the family's socioeconomic status is important, as poverty and homelessness can have a major impact on the child's dress and hygiene.

Level of Consciousness • The LOC, which is assessed according to age and can be quantified by the pediatric Glasgow Coma Scale (GCS) score (Table 22.5), is the most sensitive indicator of a child's neurologic status. The GCS assesses three major areas: eye opening, motor response, and verbal response. Decreased responsiveness to commands or decreased pinprick or pain response in any age group indicates a deteriorating LOC.

Thought Processes • A thorough evaluation of thought organization and appropriateness of responses is an important assessment, keeping in mind the child's age and developmental level. This is assessed in toddlers by asking the child to point to pictures or body parts; preschoolers can be asked to identify colors. In children older than 4 to 5 years, the provider can ask the child questions about his or her life, family, friends, and pets, and then judge the appropriateness of the answers, at the same time assessing the child's demonstration of logic and ability to stay focused. Abnormal thought processes occur with intellectual disability, schizophrenia, and depression.

TABLE 22.5   **Adapted Glasgow Coma Scale for Infants and Children**

EYE OPENING

SCORE	INFANTS AND CHILDREN YOUNGER THAN 1 YEAR	INFANTS OLDER THAN 1 YEAR
4	Open spontaneously	Open spontaneously
3	To loud noise	To verbal command
2	To pain only	To pain only
1	No response	No response

MOTOR RESPONSE

SCORE	INFANTS AND CHILDREN YOUNGER THAN 1 YEAR	INFANTS OLDER THAN 1 YEAR
6	Movements purposeful and spontaneous	Obeys commands
5	Localizes pain	Localizes pain
4	Flexion withdrawal to pain	Flexion withdrawal to pain
3	Flexion involuntary and abnormal (decorticate rigidity)	Flexion involuntary and abnormal (decorticate rigidity)
2	Involuntary extension (decerebrate rigidity)	Involuntary extension (decerebrate rigidity)
1	No response	No response

VERBAL RESPONSE

SCORE	BIRTH–23 MONTHS	CHILDREN AGED 2–5 YEARS	CHILDREN OLDER THAN 5 YEARS
5	Smiles, coos, cries, vocalizes	Appropriate words and phrases	Oriented and converses
4	Cries	Inappropriate words; confused	Disoriented and converses
3	Inappropriate crying and/or screaming	Cries and/or screams	Inappropriate words
2	Grunts	Grunts	Incomprehensible, nonspecific sounds
1	No response	No response	No response

Note: Score is obtained by determining the score for each of the three criteria (eye-opening, best motor response, best verbal response) and adding them. 13–15 = mild head injury; 9–12 = moderate head injury; and < 8 = severe head injury.
Source: Barkin and Rosen (2003).

Mood and Affect • Mood is how the child feels, and affect is the observable emotion that manifests the mood. Children who are preschool aged and older can be asked directly how they are feeling (e.g., happy, sad, worried). The child's affect should match the stated mood and be appropriate to the child and family's current circumstances (e.g., it is normal for children to have a sad or depressed mood after a loss of a family member or pet). An affect that is flat, blunted, euphoric, or labile may indicate depression or drug use; a flat, euphoric, or labile affect may indicate bipolar disorder. Poor eye contact may indicate depression or may be the cultural norm for that child (see Chapter 5).

Language and Speech • In children of all ages, receptive and expressive language skills are assessed. In children aged 6 years and older, the provider assesses the volume, rate, and tone of the child's speech, noting any speech impediments or stuttering. Children younger than 6 years of age may still have articulation difficulties that are within normal limits for age. Slow speech may indicate depression or intellectual disability; rapid speech may indicate a manic episode of bipolar disorder. In children who are preschool aged or older, written speech is also assessed, keeping in mind whether the child has attended preschool.

Judgment and Impulse Control • Evaluation of judgment and impulse control is based on the child's developmental level. Examiners can ask preschool-aged and school-aged children what they would do if confronted by a stranger; adolescents can be asked what they would do if they found a gun. Past history of patterns of behavior can also be assessed. An inability to use judgment or control impulses in a developmentally appropriate manner may indicate intellectual disability, ADHD, brain tumor, bipolar disorder, schizophrenia, substance abuse, or long-term inhalant use.

Insight • This assessment determines whether children are able to articulate their perceptions of themselves. A child must be school aged or older to complete this assessment. The provider may ask the child why he or she is seeking care or to explain certain likes and dislikes. Children and adolescents with mental illness such as bipolar disorder, intellectual disability, or severe anxiety are likely to have poor insight.

Memory • Both short- and long-term memory are assessed. Short-term memory is evaluated by asking the child to recall something that happened very recently (e.g., ask the child what he or she had for dinner the night before). Long-term memory is assessed by asking the child about something that occurred in the past, such as the name of a former babysitter or teacher. The provider should validate this information with the parent. Memory impairment occurs in children who have suffered anoxic brain injuries, brain tumor, or TBI or who have ADHD.

Attention Span • Older infants and toddlers normally have very brief attention spans. Preschool-aged children can be expected to have an attention span long enough to be able to complete a simple task, such as drawing a person with three to six parts or following simple directions (e.g., to copy a square). In children who are school aged and older, attention can be assessed through rote memory (e.g., asking the child to repeat a series of words or letters 5 minutes after he or she heard them). Attention span is shortened in children with ADHD or intellectual disability, and after a neurologic infection or TBI.

Abstract Reasoning • Abstract reasoning is assessed in children aged 11 years and older. It can be done by asking the child to explain the plot of a story or to explain a common proverb. The provider must be certain that the child is developmentally able to think abstractly and that the child has the linguistic and cultural abilities to interpret the story or proverb. Abstract reasoning is impaired with intellectual disability, severe anxiety, or mental illness.

Cranial Nerve Assessment

As part of a complete pediatric neurologic examination, CN function is assessed. Some of the assessments can be made during observations of spontaneous activity during the health care encounter. For example, ptosis (CN III), facial asymmetry (CN VII), hoarse voice (CN X), expressive language difficulties (CNs V, VII, X, and XII), abnormal eye position (CNs III, IV, and VI), and abnormal pupillary reactions (CNs II and III) can easily be evaluated by observation. CNs IV, VI, IX, XI, and XII can only be assessed in children who are developmentally able to cooperate with the assessment. CN I is not typically assessed in neonates and young infants unless an olfactory abnormality is suspected. Preschool-aged and school-aged children often enjoy this portion of the examination, especially when the assessments involve the use of toys or games to elicit the cranial nerve responses. Table 22.6 summarizes cranial nerve testing in the neonate and infant. Table 22.7 lists cranial nerve testing for toddlers and older children.

Assessment of Cerebellar Function

Normal cerebellar function is determined by assessment of balance and coordination. A child must be developmentally able to cooperate with these assessments; typically, children preschool aged and older are able to do so, depending on the assessment.

Cerebellar function can be assessed by evaluation of gait, the Romberg test, hopping in place, heel-to-toe walking (tandem walking), the heel-to-shin test, and the finger-to-nose test. When making these assessments, the examiner notes symmetry and smoothness of movements. Impairment in the ability to perform these tests (e.g., nystagmus, ataxia, weakness, or inability to complete the test) indicates a cerebellar dysfunction.

TABLE 22.6	Assessment of Cranial Nerve Function in Neonates and Infants		
CRANIAL NERVE	**ASSESSMENT METHOD**	**NORMAL FINDINGS**	**ABNORMAL FINDINGS**
CN I, olfactory	CN I is rarely tested in neonates and infants; when tested, place a strong smelling substance (e.g., isopropyl alcohol) under infant's nose.	Neonate or infant startles, grimaces, sniffs, or cries in response to strong odor.	Congenital anosmia may indicate Kallman's syndrome, which runs in families (Tritos, 2013); it also occurs in albino children (Lalwani, 2008).
CN II, optic	Assess infant's response to bright light; test pupillary reaction with ophthalmoscope (see Chapter 15).	Neonate and infant blink, and pupils constrict equally in response to light; able to fix and follow for 60 to 90 degrees.	No response to light may indicate congenital blindness or retinoblastoma.
CN III, oculomotor; CN IV, trochlear; CN VI, abducens	**Sensory function:** Pupillary response to light and blink reflex are assessed. **Motor function:** Infant's spontaneous ability to gaze in all directions is noted; "doll's eye" maneuver is performed (gently rotate infant's head side to side; eyes should move in opposite direction of rotation); blink reflex is assessed.	**Sensory:** Pupils round, equal in size, and reactive directly and consensually in response to light and accommodation; infant blinks in response to bright light. **Motor:** Disconjugate gaze within normal limits through 6 months; doll's eye maneuver normal, which indicates brainstem is intact.	**Sensory:** Absent blink reflex may indicate congenital blindness. **Motor:** Disconjugate gaze or asymmetrical light reflex after 6 months of age requires referral to avoid neurologic blindness (see Chapter 15). When doll's eye maneuver is performed and eyes remain fixed in original gaze, brainstem injury should be suspected.
CN V, trigeminal	**Sensory function:** Infant's cheek is touched with a wisp of cotton; corneal reflex is assessed. **Motor function:** Infant's ability to suck and swallow is assessed by placing gloved finger into infant's mouth.	**Sensory:** Infant should turn cheek toward stimulus; corneal reflex elicits blinking or tearing. **Motor:** Infant should suck vigorously on gloved finger.	**Sensory:** Absent corneal reflex in neonate is associated with severe brain damage. **Motor:** There is difficulty sucking or swallowing.
CN VII, facial	**Sensory function:** Taste is not usually tested in infants. **Motor function:** Symmetrical facial movement is assessed when the child cries or smiles; ability to suck and swallow is assessed.	**Sensory:** Taste is not usually tested in infants; infants prefer sweet tastes. **Motor:** Symmetrical facial movement is noted when child is crying or smiling; there is no difficulty sucking or swallowing.	**Motor:** Facial asymmetry is noted; difficulty with sucking or swallowing.
CN VIII, acoustic (vestibulocochlear)	Response to startle (up to 4 months) and acoustic blink reflex (up to 12 months) is assessed; objective hearing assessment (i.e., ABR) is performed (see Chapter 14).	Infant responds to sound by quieting to voice or blinking to hand clap; objective hearing assessments (i.e., ABR) are within normal limits).	No response to sound may be because of conductive or sensorineural hearing loss, depending on age of infant and past medical history (see Chapter 14).
CN IX, glossopharyngeal; CN X, vagus	**Sensory function:** Gag reflex and ability to suck and swallow are assessed. **Motor function:** Infant's cry is evaluated for pitch and strength, stridor, or hoarseness.	**Sensory:** Gag reflex intact; infant is able to suck and swallow. **Motor:** Normal cry is loud and lusty and not hoarse.	**Sensory:** Inability to suck or swallow. **Motor:** Shrill, high-pitched cry indicates increased ICP; high-pitched cat-like cry indicates cri du chat syndrome.

(continued)

TABLE 22.6	Assessment of Cranial Nerve Function in Neonates and Infants (*continued*)		
CRANIAL NERVE	**ASSESSMENT METHOD**	**NORMAL FINDINGS**	**ABNORMAL FINDINGS**
CN XI, spinal accessory	With infant lying supine, examiner turns infant's head to one side.	Infant should bring head to midline.	Inability to bring head to midline may indicate CN XI dysfunction or torticollis.
CN XII, hypoglossal	Infant's ability to suck and swallow is evaluated when feeding; infant's tongue is inspected for lateral deviation when crying or cooing.	Sucking and swallowing should be coordinated, and there should be no tongue deviation.	Difficulty sucking or swallowing is evident.

ABR, automated auditory brainstem response; CN, cranial nerve; ICP, intracranial pressure.

TABLE 22.7	Assessment of Cranial Nerve Function in Toddlers and Older Children		
CRANIAL NERVE	**ASSESSMENT METHOD**	**NORMAL FINDINGS**	**ABNORMAL FINDINGS**
CN I, olfactory	Testing is started at preschool age: nares are checked to be sure they are not occluded by mucus. With one nostril occluded and eyes closed, the examiner asks the child to smell something familiar such as soap, bubble gum, chocolate, or mint. This is repeated on untested nostril, using a different odor.	Child can identify familiar smell.	Anosmia (lack of olfaction) in children may be temporary or permanent; upper respiratory infections, allergies, sinusitis, nasal polyps, or a deviated septum may cause temporary anosmia; permanent anosmia may be due to Kallman's syndrome, head injury, brain tumor, or CHARGE syndrome (Chalouhi et al., 2005; Tritos, 2013).
CN II, optic	Each eye is tested for visual acuity; funduscopy is performed; visual fields and pupillary response on both eyes are assessed (see Chapter 15).	Visual acuity normal; no papilledema visualized; peripheral vision intact; child able to fix on object and follow for 60 to 90 degrees; pupils constrict in response to light.	Abnormalities in vision may be caused by cataracts, conditions that cause increased ICP (e.g., brain tumors), or uncorrected strabismus.
CN III, oculomotor; CN IV, trochlear; CN VI, abducens	**Sensory function:** Direct and consensual pupillary response to light; pupil size and accommodation are assessed (see Chapter 15). **Motor function:** Extraocular eye movements are tested through the six cardinal fields of gaze; upper eyelid elevation and convergence of eyes are assessed; "doll's eye" maneuver (see Chapter 15) is performed; child is asked to clench teeth.	**Sensory:** Pupils are round, equal in size, and constrict directly and consensually in response to light and accommodation. **Motor:** Extraocular movements are normal; no lid lag, ptosis, or nystagmus seen.	**Sensory:** Absence of pupillary constriction in response to light or accommodation indicates abnormality in sensory portion of CN III; physiologic anisocoria (difference in pupillary size by up to 20%) is within normal limits. **Motor:** Inability to look upward, downward, or inward is noted; any ptosis or lid lag indicates abnormality in CN III; inability to gaze downward or inward is also caused by abnormality in CN IV; inability to move eyes laterally is caused by abnormality in CN VI; these abnormalities may result from head trauma or space-occupying lesions. Diplopia is an abnormal finding attributable to CN III abnormality. An abnormal doll's eye test indicates vestibular abnormality and often results from brainstem lesions.

TABLE 22.7   Assessment of Cranial Nerve Function in Toddlers and Older Children (*continued*)

CRANIAL NERVE	ASSESSMENT METHOD	NORMAL FINDINGS	ABNORMAL FINDINGS
CN V, trigeminal	**Sensory function:** This is tested by touching child's forehead, cheek, and chin with a cotton ball while child's eyes are closed; reaction to stimulus is observed. This is repeated with both a safety pin and a cotton ball, and child is asked to distinguish sharp and dull. Tubes of hot and cold water are placed on the cheek to assess temperature perception. Corneal reflex is assessed by *gently* touching a cotton ball to the child's cornea. (This test is often avoided because of discomfort involved.) **Motor function:** This is tested by observing child chewing and swallowing; if a young child does not cooperate, examiner asks the child to make a "mean" face to assess jaw muscles. Masseter and temporal muscles are palpated (at temple and jaw areas) as child bites down.	**Sensory:** Child moves away from stimulus; assessment of corneal reflex elicits blinking and tearing. **Motor:** Function of the jaw should be strong and symmetrical.	**Sensory:** Diminished or absent corneal reflex may be caused by a sensory (CN V) or motor (CN VII) abnormality. Loss of sensation over either cheek indicates compression of CN V. **Motor:** Deviation of mandible to one side when mouth is opened or inability to chew, bite down, or swallow indicates paralysis of CN V.
CN VII, facial	**Sensory function:** This is tested by asking child to identify a familiar taste by placing a familiar flavor on anterior two thirds of tongue. **Motor function:** This is tested by inspecting child's face at rest, noting any facial asymmetry or drooping; examiner asks child to smile, raise eyebrows, make a funny face, puff out cheeks, or show his or her teeth.	**Sensory:** Child is able to identify familiar flavors. **Motor:** Movement of facial muscles is symmetrical; there are no facial drooping, tics, or eyelid sagging noted.	**Sensory:** Ageusia (loss of taste) on anterior two thirds of tongue indicates CN VII dysfunction, which can be caused by space-occupying lesions proximal to CN VII. **Motor:** Paralysis of facial muscles (Bell's palsy), facial asymmetry, or impairment of eye closure indicates abnormality in CN VII.
CN VIII, acoustic (vestibulocochlear)	**Sensory function:** Hearing is assessed to differentiate conductive and sensorineural hearing loss; whisper test is performed; Weber and Rinne tests and audiometric testing are performed as needed. **Vestibular function:** Vertigo is assessed by performing Romberg test (see Chapter 14).	Hearing is normal and correlates with language development. No vertigo or dizziness reported.	Sensorineural hearing loss is caused by disorders of CN VIII; lateralization to unaffected ear occurs; vertigo can be caused by abnormalities in vestibular branch of CN VI, such as tumors or ear infections (i.e., blocked eustachian tube) (see Chapter 14).
CN IX, glossopharyngeal; CN X, vagus	**Sensory function:** Taste receptors are assessed by placing a familiar flavor on posterior one third of tongue and also by eliciting gag reflex with tongue blade.	**Sensory:** Child is able to identify familiar tastes; child can feel touch on palate and gag reflex being elicited (CN IX).	**Sensory:** Ageusia (loss of taste) on posterior one third of tongue is evident; loss of sensation to soft palate or pharynx indicates CN IX dysfunction, which can be caused by intracranial lesions proximal to CN IX.

(*continued*)

TABLE 22.7	Assessment of Cranial Nerve Function in Toddlers and Older Children (*continued*)		
CRANIAL NERVE	**ASSESSMENT METHOD**	**NORMAL FINDINGS**	**ABNORMAL FINDINGS**
	Motor function: This is tested by assessing tongue strength and swallowing movements; examiner asks child to say "ah" and inspects palate; voice quality, hoarseness, or stridor are noted.	**Motor:** Gag reflex is intact (CN X); tongue is strong; uvula and palate should rise promptly and symmetrically with ipsilateral deviation of uvula when soft palate is touched ("palatal reflex") (CN X); child is able to swallow without difficulty and controls oral secretions (CN IX and CN X); voice quality and ability to articulate palatal sounds are intact; there is no hoarseness.	**Motor:** Lesions to CN X result in absence of gag and palatal reflexes; unilateral CN IX and CN X paralysis result in deviation of uvula to unaffected side when soft palate is touched; mild difficulty swallowing is noted; bilateral paralysis of CN X results in severe dysphagia; there is no palate elevation with stimulation and hoarseness of voice.
CN XI, spinal accessory	Examiner tests function of SCM by asking child to lower his or her chin against resistance; examiner asks child to shrug shoulders upward with and without resistance against examiner's hand; child is asked to nod head and turn head from side to side against resistance to assess trapezius function.	Child able to apply resistance using SCM; normal strength of SCM and trapezius muscles is seen.	Head or neck trauma, CNS tumors, or infections can cause paralysis of SCM or trapezius muscles.
CN XII, hypoglossal	Examiner asks child to stick out his or her tongue and move it from side to side; examiner listens to child speak and notes articulations; tongue strength is assessed by asking child to press tongue against a tongue blade; child's ability to pronounce the letter "r" is evaluated.	Tongue thrust should be smooth and symmetrical; child should be able to move tongue blade with tongue. Fasciculations are noted; examiner notes if tongue deviates toward one side.	Lesions of CN XII cause tongue deviation or paralysis, resulting in difficulty articulating lingual sounds (dysarthria).

CHARGE syndrome, coloboma, congenital heart disease, choanal atresia, mental and growth retardation, genital anomalies, ear malformations and hearing loss; CN, cranial nerve; CNS, central nervous system; SCM, sternocleidomastoid.

Gait and Balance • The child's gait can be assessed by observing as the child walks across the room, turns, and walks back. Uncooperative or fearful toddlers can be asked to walk toward their parent instead of the examiner. The examiner can evaluate the child's coordination and stance while also noting any limp or ataxia; the child's gait should be smooth and symmetrical with an easy alternate arm swing. The toddler normally has a wide-based gait as a result of physiologic lordosis; a wide-based gait is abnormal beyond toddler age. It is normal for preschool-aged children to be knock-kneed when ambulating. Some abnormalities in gait include cerebellar ataxia, scissors gait, and toe-walking. Cerebellar ataxia can occur with a brain tumor, cerebral

palsy, cerebellar dysfunction, alcohol intoxication, or as a side effect of some medications (e.g., anticonvulsants, antihistamines). A scissors gait is described as a gait with short steps in which the thighs overlap with each step; this is often seen in children with cerebral palsy. Toe-walking is considered normal until age 3; after this age, it is likely a result of muscle spasticity, most commonly caused by spastic cerebral palsy (Schwentker, 2012).

Romberg Test • This test assesses proprioception and is primarily performed in children who are preschool aged and older; young children may not be able to cooperate fully. To conduct this test, the provider asks the child to stand upright with the feet together, eyes closed, and arms at his or her sides while the provider observes the child's balance for several seconds. The provider always stands behind the child in case the child loses balance. Only mild swaying should occur. If the child leans to one side or loses his or her balance, this indicates a problem with proprioception.

Hopping in Place • By age 4, the child should be able to hop in place. The examiner asks the child to stand straight, bend one knee, and then hop in place, first on one leg and then on the other. The child with intact cerebellar function should be able to maintain balance on one leg.

Heel-to-toe Walking (Tandem Walking) • The child is asked to walk heel-to-toe in a straight line; children are typically able to do this by age 6 (Figure 22.8). If a child has a hemispheric lesion, walking in this manner decreases support for the upper body; some side-to-side swaying is normal. Ataxia, lack of coordinated movement, or impaired judgment of distance indicates cerebellar dysfunction.

Rapid Alternating Movements (Children 8–9 Years or Older) • To assess rapid alternating movements, the examiner instructs the child to place his or her hands face down on the thighs and then rapidly turn his or her hands over with palms up, then lift them off the thighs in quick alternating movements. The child is then asked to repeat the process as rapidly as possible for 10 seconds; movements should be quick and rhythmic. Inability to perform rapid alternating movements is likely a result of cerebellar tumor.

Finger-to-Nose Test (Children 8–9 Years or Older) • This examination tests fine motor movements in the child. It involves having the child close his or her eyes and hold the arms out in front of the body. The examiner asks the child to touch the tip of his or her nose with the right index finger, then the left index finger, repeating this process several times, with gradually increasing speed. Movements should be smooth and accurate (Figure 22.9).

Heel-to-Shin Test (Children 8–9 Years or Older) • This test assesses coordination of the lower extremities. The provider asks the supine child to place the right heel on the left shin, just below the knee, and then slide the heel down the shin to the top of the foot. This maneuver should be repeated as quickly as possible and then repeated with the opposite foot. The child should be able to perform this maneuver without difficulty. If not, the provider should suspect an alteration in motor strength, proprioception, or a cerebellar lesion. An asymmetrical finding suggests an ipsilateral cerebellar lesion.

Sensory Examination

The sensory examination evaluates the child's ability to perceive and discriminate sensation. This includes assessment of light touch, deep pressure, pain, proprioception, temperature, and vibration. Evaluating response to a painful stimulus can determine sensory function in the neonate. This examination is limited in infants and young children because of their inability to cooperate; most children older than 3 years of age can cooperate. For each portion of the sensory examination, the child's eyes should be closed and the provider should compare both sides of the body. If sensory discrimination is absent, the examiner should describe boundaries. The sensory examination includes the following assessments.

Light Touch • The examiner lightly touches the child's skin in various areas with a stretched cotton ball. The

FIGURE 22.8 Assessment of heel-to-toe walking.

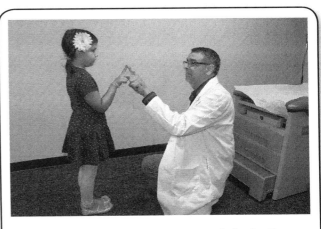

FIGURE 22.9 Finger-to-nose test to assess cerebellar function.

child should be able to identify the area of the body that is being touched. The provider asks the child to describe any difference in sensation in different areas tested.

Proprioceptive Sensation • The examiner assesses motion and position sense of the limbs by grasping the child's toe and moving it up and down and then asking the child what direction the toe is being moved and what position it is in; this process is repeated on the other foot. The child should correctly identify the direction of movements.

Pain • Using the sharp and dull ends of a reflex hammer, the examiner checks for mild pain sensation by asking the child to identify sharp or dull sensations verbally (see Chapter 6 for a detailed discussion of pain assessment). The child should be able to differentiate between sharp and dull sensations.

Temperature • Assessment of the child's ability to identify hot and cold temperature is only done when the child's perception of pain is abnormal. When tested, the examiner uses two tubes, one filled with hot water and the other with cold water, and then touches the skin in different areas, asking the child if the sensation felt is hot or cold. The child should be able to distinguish between hot and cold temperatures over various areas of the skin.

Vibration • Vibration perception is assessed by using a low-pitched tuning fork placed on a bony prominence (e.g., on the wrists, elbows, medial malleoli, patella). The examiner strikes the tuning fork and then holds the base of the tuning fork on the bony prominence. The child is asked to state when the vibration stops; this is then repeated on the opposite side of the body for comparison. The child should correctly identify the sensation.

Tactile Discrimination • Children 5 years of age and older are usually able to cooperate with tests to evaluate tactile and spatial discrimination through assessment of graphesthesia, stereognosis, and two-point discrimination. Loss of sensation often signals an alteration in the PNS, spinal cord, brainstem, or cerebral cortex. Some examples of conditions that illustrate these alterations include brain or spinal cord tumors, spinal cord injuries, myelomeningocele, CNS infections, and inherited demyelinating neuropathies. The child's eyes must be closed with each of these examinations.

Graphesthesia. The ability to identify shapes traced on the palm of the hand is tested by asking the child to close his or her eyes, at which point the examiner draws a large number or letter on the palm of the child's hand with a blunt end of a pencil. The test should be done on both palms to ensure accuracy. The child should be able to identify the number or letter; an inability to do so may indicate a sensory, spatial, or proprioceptive deficit. Sensory impairments in children, including

impaired proprioception, can be caused by cerebral palsy (Bleyenheuft & Gordon, 2013).

Stereognosis. The ability to recognize objects by touch is tested by placing a familiar object in the child's hand, such as a coin, paperclip, or pencil, and asking the child to name the object; this is repeated in the opposite hand. Impaired stereognosis in children can be caused by cerebral palsy (Bleyenheuft & Gordon, 2013).

Two-Point Discrimination. This tests spatial discrimination by asking the child to discriminate touch. At different spots on the skin, first with two points in proximity and then with one point, the examiner asks the child to identify if one or two pinpricks were felt. The child should be able to correctly identify the points touched.

Reflex Testing

Reflex testing is a particularly useful portion of the neurologic examination. Because the results are quantified, reflex testing provides concrete, objective data about the level of functioning of the nervous system. Reflex testing is especially useful with children because it requires minimal cooperation. Both deep tendon and superficial reflexes are assessed, with attention paid to symmetry and strength of reflexes tested. Assessment of neonatal reflexes is discussed in Chapter 11.

Deep Tendon Reflexes • DTRs, are elicited by tapping a tendon briskly with a reflex hammer, which causes the tendon to suddenly stretch and contract. These reflexes are assessed to evaluate the function of the reflex arcs and the spinal cord segments. When assessing DTRs, they should be tested bilaterally, and the response is graded as follows:

- 0 Absent
- +1 Hypoactive
- +2 Normal
- +3 Hyperactive without clonus
- +4 Hyperactive with clonus

Hyperactivity of DTRs indicates upper motor neuron lesions, hypocalcemia, or hyperthyroidism. The following DTRs are assessed as part of the pediatric neurologic examination.

Biceps Reflex (C5–C6). The examiner flexes the child's arm at the elbow with the palm slightly lower than the elbow. The examiner then places his or her thumb on the child's biceps tendon in the antecubital space, then strikes the thumb with the reflex hammer. The normal response is a slight flexion of the arm at the elbow and a contraction of the biceps (Figure 22.10).

Triceps Reflex (C7–C8). This reflex appears at approximately 6 months. With the child's arm flexed at the elbow (see procedure for biceps reflex), the examiner strikes the child's triceps tendon slightly proximal to the olecranon between the epicondyles. A normal response is triceps contraction and elbow extension (see Figure 22.10).

Brachioradialis Reflex (C5–C6). The examiner begins by asking the child to rest his or her forearm on the abdomen so that the palm is slightly lower than the elbow. The examiner then strikes the brachioradialis tendon (approximately 1 to 2 inches above the wrist), over the radius. The forearm should rotate laterally with the palm supinated (see Figure 22.10).

Patellar Reflex (L2–C4). This reflex is present at birth. For older children, the examiner asks the child to sit on the examination table, knees bent, and legs hanging freely. The examiner then strikes the child's distal patellar tendon with the reflex hammer. The knee should extend, and the quadriceps muscle should contract (see Figure 22.10).

Achilles Tendon Reflex (S1–C2). The child is asked to dorsiflex his or her foot slightly at the ankle; the examiner then strikes the Achilles tendon. Plantarflexion is the normal response (see Figure 22.10).

Superficial Reflexes • Superficial reflexes are motor responses to stimulation of the skin. These include the abdominal, plantar, cremasteric, and anal wink reflexes. Superficial reflexes are evaluated as present or absent; symmetry is also evaluated. Superficial reflexes are

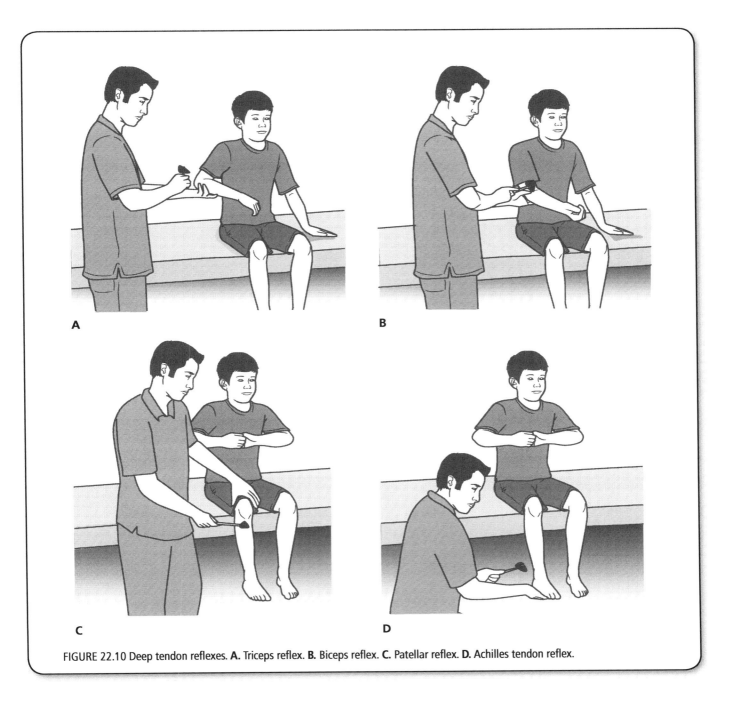

FIGURE 22.10 Deep tendon reflexes. **A.** Triceps reflex. **B.** Biceps reflex. **C.** Patellar reflex. **D.** Achilles tendon reflex.

absent in the presence of motor neuron lesions or spinal cord damage.

Abdominal Reflex (T8, T9, and T10 Innervation in Upper Quadrants; T10, T11, and T12 Innervation in Lower Quadrants). With the handle of the reflex hammer, the examiner gently strokes the abdomen toward the umbilicus. The abdominal muscles should contract, and the umbilicus should move toward the stimulus in all four quadrants. This reflex may be difficult to elicit in obese children, and it may be absent after a child has abdominal surgery; neither are abnormal findings.

Plantar Reflex (L4–L5, S1–S2). This is tested by stroking the lateral aspect of the sole of each foot with the end of the reflex hammer. The examiner observes for flexion of the toes, which is normal (Figure 22.11). An abnormal finding is extension of the big toe and fanning of the other toes (Babinski sign) (Figure 22.12). For children who are not yet walking, a positive Babinski sign is normal for the age group, because of the immaturity of the nervous system. If the child has a positive test, it may indicate lesions of the pyramidal tract or motor nerves.

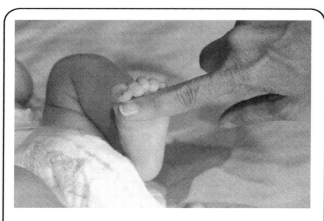

FIGURE 22.11 Plantar reflex.

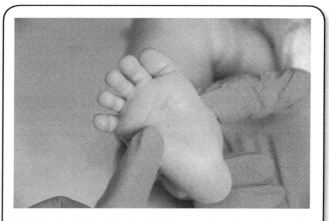

FIGURE 22.12 Babinski reflex. This is normal until age 12 months.

Cremasteric Reflex (T12, L1). This is tested in the male patient. To elicit this reflex, the provider lightly strokes the child's inner thigh with the end of a cotton applicator. A normal response is elevation of the scrotum on the same side; the cremasteric muscle contracts as the ipsilateral testis rises in the scrotum.

Anal Wink Reflex (L4–S1). This is tested by stimulating the perianal area with a cotton tip applicator. A normal response is quick contraction of the anal sphincter.

Primitive and Postural Reflexes • The primitive reflexes are involuntary reflexes found in the infant. These reflexes (Box 22.3) are present at birth, and most disappear by 4 to 6 months. Asymmetrical, absent, or persistent primitive reflexes indicate a neurologic abnormality (see Chapter 11, Table 11.5). Primitive reflexes should be tested in children aged 1 year and younger (see Chapter 11, Table 11.5). Postural reflexes replace primitive reflexes at 5 to 6 months, and assessment of these reflexes should begin at this time. Some of these reflexes are described in Table 22.8 and illustrated in Figures 22.13 and 22.14.

BOX 22.3 Primitive Reflexes
■ Moro reflex
■ Rooting
■ Sucking
■ Stepping (placing)
■ Palmar grasp
■ Ankle clonus
■ Galant (truncal incurvation) reflex
■ Asymmetrical tonic neck reflex

Neurologic Soft Signs

Neurologic soft signs (NSS) in children are minor abnormalities found in the neurologic examination in the absence of any diagnosed neurologic disorder. NSS are normal in infants but are often present in children with cognitive or behavioral dysfunction. Children with a history of perinatal trauma or infection, ADHD, autism, or those who have been neglected are more likely to have NSS on examination. Typically, NSS resolve by late school age to adolescence (Ianetti, Mastrangelo, & Di Netta, 2005). Box 22.4 lists the NSS seen in children (Ianetti et al., 2005).

Neurologic Assessment of the Acutely Ill or Injured Child

A focused neurologic assessment is required if an infant, child, or adolescent presents with an acute neurologic injury or illness. Some pediatric neurologic emergencies include altered LOC, acute ataxia, head trauma, increased ICP, meningitis, acute onset of seizures, and status epilepticus. If the child was injured, types of injuries about which to inquire include trauma to the head

TABLE 22.8	Postural Reflexes				
REFLEX	AGE APPEARS	AGE DISAPPEARS	HOW TO ELICIT	RESPONSE	COMMENTS
Positive support	3–4 months	Persists throughout life	Infant is held upright, firmly supported under arms with feet touching a flat surface.	Infant should extend legs in an attempt to bear weight. By 5–6 months, infant is able to fully support own weight; by 7 months, infant is able to bounce.	Reflex absent in infant with corticospinal tract disease.
Landau	4–5 months	12 months–2 years	Infant is placed prone on flat surface or suspended firmly supporting abdomen.	Infant should raise head and legs and arch back (see Figure 22.13).	Absence of Landau reflex suggests problem with motor development, (e.g., cerebral palsy).
Parachute	8 months	Persists throughout life	Infant is suspended prone and firmly supported, then quickly lowered toward flat surface.	Infant should extend arms and legs in "protective" manner (see Figure 22.14).	Response should be symmetrical.
Protective extension-sitting position	5–7 months	Persists throughout life	Infant is placed in a sitting position, then gentle force is applied to displace infant's center of gravity.	Arms should abduct, and infant should extend his or her arm outward on side of the fall, palm open, to stop the fall.	Asymmetrical response is often an early sign of hemiparesis.

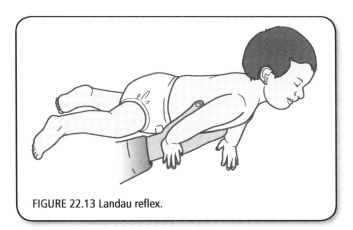

FIGURE 22.13 Landau reflex.

or face, including skull fractures sustained in falls or motor vehicle collisions. If the injury involved a bicycle or scooter, it is important to ask if the child was wearing a helmet. If the injury involved a motor vehicle collision, the provider should ask if the child was in an approved vehicle restraint. In cases of head trauma or skull fractures, the provider must consider whether the trauma was intentionally inflicted on the infant or child in the form of forceful shaking or blows to the side of the head. The provider must always ascertain whether the history is compatible with the type and degree of injury that the child has sustained to rule out intentional injury (see Chapter 24).

History • A focused neurologic assessment begins by asking the following questions:

- When did the neurologic symptoms begin?
- Was the onset sudden or gradual?
- Has the child had a fever?
- Has the child ingested anything?
- Is the child currently taking any medications, including OTC medications and herbal remedies?
- Were the symptoms associated with any injury or trauma?
- How, when, and where and did the injury take place? What was the mechanism of injury?
- Did the child lose consciousness?
- Does the child have a headache? Nausea or vomiting? Visual changes? Photophobia? Tinnitus or vertigo? Memory loss? Lacerations?
- Has there been any follow-up since the event? Any diagnostic imaging studies?
- Any pain? What is the location of the pain? How does the child rate the pain (see Chapter 6)?
- Any numbness or tingling?

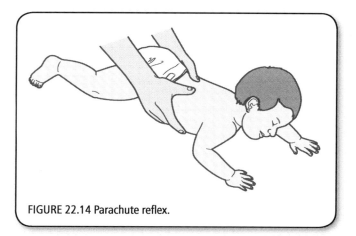

FIGURE 22.14 Parachute reflex.

BOX 22.4 Neurologic Soft Signs

- **Astereogenesis:** Inability to recognize familiar object through tactile recognition
- **Dysgraphesthesia:** Inability to recognize numbers or letters written on the skin
- **Apraxia:** Inability to perform purposeful movement in the absence of any other neurologic disturbance
- **Dysdiadochokinesis:** Inability to perform rapid alternating movements
- **Hypotonia:** Decreased resistance to passive movement
- **Incoordination:** Low level of competence in motor skills in the absence of neurologic disease
- **Choreiform movements:** Rapid, purposeless, asymmetrical movements of the extremities, with an inability to stand still for 30 to 40 seconds, eyes closed, feet together, and supinated arms outstretched
- **Mirror movements:** Simultaneous, contralateral, involuntary, identical movement that accompanies intentional movement

- Are there changes in behavior? Changes in the quality of the cry? Any somnolence?
- Does the child have a fever?
- What is the child's past medical history? Does the child have a ventriculoperitoneal shunt? Brain tumor? Learning or behavior disorder? Seizures?
- Does the child or teen abuse drugs or alcohol?
- Any history of depression or ADHD?
- Has the child ingested any toxic substance?

BOX 22.5 Assessment of Responsiveness

Alert, fully awake, responsive, smiles
Verbal, reactive to voice; cooing, babbling, vocalizing
Pain, responsive to pain only
Unresponsive to painful stimulation

Physical Examination • In acute neurologic illness or injury, the physical examination begins with an assessment of physiologic status. Airway, breathing, circulation, and color are assessed along with vital signs. The provider should note fever or temperature instability, bradycardia, difficulty breathing, or wide pulse pressure, all of which may indicate increased ICP. Next, a thorough neurologic examination should be done, including assessment of the child's LOC, orientation, memory, eyes, pupils, cranial nerves, reflexes, and motor and sensory function. Using the acronym AVPU (alert, verbal, pain, unresponsive), LOC can be assessed quickly in the infant (Box 22.5), or it can be quantified, using the adapted GCS for infants and children and adolescents (see Table 22.5). Orientation and memory can be tested in children preschool aged and older by asking simple questions such as what his or her name is, what day it is, or to remember three numbers in sequence and repeat them after 5 minutes. Pupil size, reactivity, and equality are also assessed along with extraocular movements. The provider also performs a funduscopic examination to assess for retinal hemorrhages or papilledema, which may indicate abusive head trauma or increased ICP, respectively. In acute injury, the provider assesses motor response as spontaneous, spastic, or flaccid, or in the comatose child, decorticate (abnormal flexion of arms with legs flexed; seen with lesions of corticospinal tract) (Figure 22.15) or decerebrate posturing (rigid extension of arms and legs seen with brainstem lesions) (Figure 22.16). To evaluate sensory function, the examiner tests the child's responses to touch, pain, and temperature in all four extremities, the trunk, and the face. DTR and the Babinski reflex (in children younger than age 1 year) are also assessed.

The provider looks for any signs of increased ICP, such as headache, nausea, vomiting, visual changes, seizure activity, sunset eyes, a bulging anterior

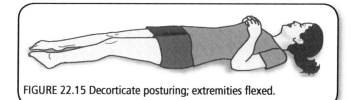

FIGURE 22.15 Decorticate posturing; extremities flexed.

FIGURE 22.16 Decerebrate posturing; extremities extended and pronated.

fontanelle in infants, papilledema, or altered pupillary reactions. The presence of Cushing's triad is a late sign of increased ICP. Cushing's triad includes bradycardia, hypertension with widened pulse pressure, and irregular respirations.

Assessment of cranial nerve function is routinely done with acute head injury or any type of neurologic impairment (see Tables 22.6 and 22.7). Included in the neurologic assessment is an assessment of the total body for other injuries that may have been sustained in the incident. Inspection of the skin includes observation for bruises, hematomas, or lacerations, which may indicate serious injury. Specifically, the examiner looks for conjunctival hemorrhages, ecchymosis around the mastoid region (Battle's sign), or periorbital ecchymosis (raccoon eyes); these signs likely indicate basal skull fracture. The nose, mouth, ears, and hypopharynx are inspected for any injuries; clear drainage from the nose or ear may be CSF. The examiner should also palpate the skull for tenderness, swelling, deformity, or crepitus and the fontanelles in infants and assesses for rib or long-bone fractures.

Assessment of Meningeal Irritation

Assessment of meningeal irritation should be done in cases of CNS irritation, infection, or with intracranial hemorrhage. If the provider suspects any of these conditions, he or she should begin by assessing for general signs of meningeal irritation, such as irritability, lethargy, severe headache, or photophobia. With bacterial meningitis, fever, nausea, and vomiting may also accompany these signs. Neonates and infants 2 months of age and younger are not able to localize infection, so meningeal irritation may not be recognized until late stages, for example, when a bulging anterior fontanelle is visible.

To assess for meningeal irritation in older children, the provider begins by assessing for nuchal rigidity. To begin, the provider first ensures that the child has no injury to the neck. The child is placed supine, and then the neck is flexed forward until the child's chin touches the chest. The child should be able to flex the neck forward easily. Pain, stiffness, or resistance upon flexion may be a sign of meningeal inflammation, irritation, or neck injury. *Opisthotonos* (Figure 22.17), or severe arching of the back, is a sign of meningeal irritation but can also occur with tetanus, subarachnoid hemorrhage, brain tumor, and severe head injury. Opisthotonos is more common in infants and children than in adults because of their immature neurologic systems. Children with opisthotonos require immediate intervention. Signs of meningeal irritation also include Kernig's sign and Brudzinski's sign.

Kernig's Sign • With the child lying supine, the provider lifts the child's leg, flexes the hip at a right angle, then flexes the knee 90 degrees (Figure 22.18). The provider then attempts to extend the child's knee. Pain and resistance

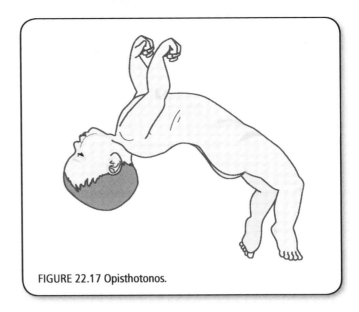

FIGURE 22.17 Opisthotonos.

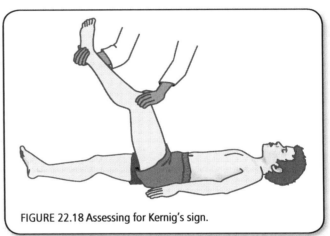

FIGURE 22.18 Assessing for Kernig's sign.

with knee extension and hip flexion and an inability to straighten the leg indicates a positive Kernig's sign.

Brudzinski's Sign • With the child lying supine, the examiner places one hand under the child's neck and the other on the child's chest to prevent movement of the torso. The provider then flexes the child's neck toward the sternum (Figure 22.19). A positive Brudzinski's sign is spontaneous hip and knee flexion upon flexion of the neck.

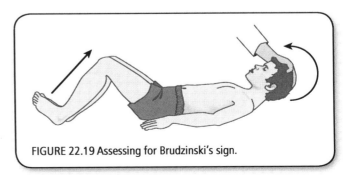

FIGURE 22.19 Assessing for Brudzinski's sign.

COMMON DIAGNOSTIC STUDIES

Several diagnostic imaging studies can be done to evaluate neurologic conditions. Because the etiology of a neurologic impairment may include metabolic disorders, drug reactions or overdoses, syncope or stroke, and neonatal hyperbilirubinemia, other diagnostic tests may be ordered in addition to imaging studies, based on historical and clinical findings. These diagnostic studies are summarized in Table 22.9.

DOCUMENTATION OF FINDINGS

Sample Write-Up: Normal Newborn

Subjective Data

A 48-hour, term male, born via normal spontaneous vaginal delivery; no significant prenatal or perinatal history; no hyperbilirubinemia or birth injury.

Objective Data

Posture: quiet-alert state; lying supine in flexed position, no jitteriness or tremors noted
Skin: no lesions or birthmarks
Head: normocephalic; mild cranial molding; head symmetrical; fontanelles soft and flat; sutures open; no hair whorls
Neck: no extra skinfolds; neck supple
Face: symmetrical features; no dysmorphism
Eyes: symmetrical light reflex, conjugate gaze, corneal and blink reflexes intact
Ears: helix of ear in line with outer canthus of eyes
Chest: no respiratory distress or apnea

Spine: intact, no dimples, sinuses, or tufts of hair; no masses
Movements: symmetrical, spontaneous body movements
Muscle tone: no flaccidity, normal ventral suspension; mild head lag
Reflexes: strong grasp and Babinski (bilaterally), suck, Moro, and gag
Cranial nerves: PERRLA; EOM (extraocular movements) full and conjugate; strong suck and swallow; lusty cry
Assessment: normal newborn

Sample Write-Up: Well Child

Subjective Data

A 3-year-old girl presents for annual health maintenance visit accompanied by her grandmother, who is the primary caregiver. According to the grandmother's report, the child has been in preschool for the past 3 months; the child is able to wash and dry her own hands; pedals a tricycle; speaks in sentences.

Objective Data

General: alert, cooperative with exam; follows simple directions two of three instances
Musculoskeletal: gait steady, hops on one foot; threw ball overhead
Neurologic: DTRs 2+ bilaterally; muscle strength equal bilaterally; CN II–XII intact
Developmental: copied a circle; language 90% intelligible (4 to 5 word sentences); Denver II not indicated
Assessment: well child; neurologically intact; no developmental delay

TABLE 22.9	Diagnostic Studies Used to Evaluate Neurologic Conditions in Children
TYPE OF TEST	**INDICATION**
Computed tomography (CT); CT angiography	To diagnose intracranial tumors and hemorrhage, hydrocephalus, and inflammatory disorders; CT angiography used to diagnose aneurysms or arteriovenous malformations
Electroencephalography (EEG), sleep-deprived	To diagnose and categorize seizure disorders
Electromyography	To diagnose neuropathies and myopathies
Magnetic resonance imaging, magnetic resonance angiography (MRA)	To detect neurologic injury such as hemorrhage; useful in identifying demyelinating disease and cerebral infarction; more specific than CT scan; MRA used to diagnose suspected intracranial vascular abnormality or neurologic problems with accompanying visual changes
Positron emission tomography scan	To evaluate blood flow, oxygen use, and glucose metabolism in the brain
Ultrasound	To diagnose hydrocephalus and intraventricular hemorrhages, particularly in neonates
Video EEG	To diagnose seizures after equivocal results from sleep deprived EEG or capture nocturnal episodes

Sample Write-Up: Acutely Ill Child

Subjective Data

A 9-year-old boy is brought to urgent care center accompanied by his mother. Approximately 3 hours ago, child was hit in head with a baseball while batting during a baseball game. Mother says child was struck on forehead above left eye and was briefly "stunned." Child left game and then became sleepy but did not fall asleep. Now feels nauseated but denies vomiting, syncope, memory loss, or diplopia. Complains of "bad headache" not relieved by acetaminophen given 1 hour ago.

Objective Data

General: vital signs stable; alert, responsive, responding appropriately to questions; GCS = 15

Skin: small contusion noted on forehead over left eyebrow, no ecchymosis noted under eyes or behind ears

Head/Face: no evidence of fracture or hematoma on palpation

Eyes: PERRLA, EOM full and conjugate, visual acuity 20/40 bilaterally; optic disk visualized; margins clear; vessels within normal limits bilaterally

Ears: no drainage

Nose: no drainage

Neurologic: CNs II–XII intact; pinprick, vibration, and light touch present bilaterally; stereognosis intact; DTRs 2+ bilaterally, abdominal and cremasteric reflexes present; gait steady, heel-to-toe, Romberg, finger-to-nose, and rapid alternating movements intact

Assessment: mild head injury

Notable Clinical Findings

- History of prematurity or prolonged ventilation in neonatal period
- History of ventriculoperitoneal shunt placement
- Head lag after age 4 months
- No head control after age 6 months
- History of traumatic brain injury
- History of lead poisoning
- Immunization delay
- Seizure disorder
- History of spinal cord injury
- History of bacterial meningitis
- Altered mental status
- Complaints of chronic headache
- Nuchal rigidity with fever
- Slurred speech/speech delay
- Syncope
- Vertigo
- Paresthesia
- Photophobia
- Hearing changes
- Visual changes
- Vomiting with headache
- Fever with headache
- Signs of meningeal irritation (opisthotonos, positive Kernig's sign. Positive Brudzinski's sign)
- Persistence of primitive reflexes beyond age 4 months
- Persistence of Babinski reflex beyond age 12 months
- Presence of neurological soft signs
- Signs of precocious puberty
- Developmental delay (fine and gross motor, speech, cognitive, social)
- Hypotonia
- Hypertonia
- Hyper- or hypoactive deep tendon reflexes
- Complaints of ataxia
- Glasgow Coma Scale Score < 13

References

Barkin, R. M., & Rosen, P. E. (2003). *Emergency Pediatrics: A guide to ambulatory care* (6th ed.). St. Louis, MO: Mosby.

Bernard, T. J., Knupp, K., Yang, M. L., Kedia, S., Levisohn, P., & Moe, P. G. (2012). Neurologic and muscular disorders. In W. W. Hay, M. J. Levin, R. R. Deterding, M. J. Abzub, & J. M. Sondheimer (Eds.), *Current pediatric diagnosis & treatment* (21st ed., pp. 740–829). New York, NY: McGraw-Hill.

Blackman, J. A. (2007). NICU micropreemies: How do they fare? *Contemporary Pediatrics, 24*(2), 64–73.

Bleyenheuft, Y., & Gordon, A. M. (2013). Precision grip control, sensory impairments and their interactions in children with hemiplegic cerebral palsy: A systematic review. *Research in Developmental Disabilities, 34*(9), 3014–3028.

Blume, H. K., & Szperka, C. L. (2010). Secondary causes of headaches in children: When it isn't a migraine. *Pediatric Annals, 39*(7), 431–439.

Centers for Disease Control and Prevention. (2011). *Heads up: Brain injury in your practice*. Atlanta, GA: Author.

Centers for Disease Control and Prevention. (2014). *Child maltreatment prevention scientific information: Risk and protective factors*. Retrieved from http://www.cdc.gov/violenceprevention/childmaltreatment/riskprotectivefactors.html

Chalouhi, C., Faulcon, P., Le Bihan, C., Hertz-Pannier, L., Bonfils, P., & Abadie, V. (2005). Olfactory evaluation in children: Application to the CHARGE syndrome. *Pediatrics, 116*(10), e81–e88.

Christian, C. W., & Block, R. (2009). Abusive head trauma in infants and children. *Pediatrics, 123*(5), 1409–1411.

Cole, P., & Hollier, L. H. (2012). *Craniosynostosis syndromes. Up to Date*. Retrieved from http://www.uptodate.com/contents/craniosynostosis-syndromes

Fullerton, H. J., Wu, Y. W., Sidney, S., & Johnston, S. C. (2007). Risk of recurrent childhood arterial ischemic stroke in a population-based cohort: The importance of cerebrovascular imaging. *Pediatrics, 119*, 495–501.

Ianetti, P., Mastrangelo, M., & Di Netta, S. (2005). Neurological "soft signs" in children and adolescents. *Journal of Pediatric Neurology, 3*(3), 123–125.

Jallo, G. I., & Marcovicci, A. (2012). *Medulloblastoma*. Retrieved from http://emedicine.medscape.com/article/1181219-overview

Jones, M. W., Morgan, E., Shelton, J. E., & Thorgood, C. (2007). Cerebral palsy: Introduction and diagnosis (Part I). *Journal of Pediatric Health Care, 21*(3), 146–152.

Kaplowitz, P. B. (2013). *Precocious puberty*. Retrieved from http://emedicine.medscape.com/article/924002-overview

Lalwani, A. K. (2008). Olfactory dysfunction. In A. K. Lalwani (Ed.), *Current diagnosis & treatment in otolaryngology: Head and neck surgery* (2nd ed., pp. 232–237). New York, NY: McGraw-Hill.

Levin, A. V. (2010). Retinal hemorrhage in abusive head trauma. *Pediatrics, 126*(5), 961–970.

Lewis, D. W., & Koch, T. (2010). Headache evaluation in children and adolescents: When to worry? When to scan? *Pediatric Annals, 39* (7), 399–406.

Liebeskind, D. S. (2014). *Epidural hematoma*. Retrieved from http://emedicine.medscape.com/article/1137065-overview

Macfarlane, F. (2006). *Pediatric anatomy, physiology and the basics of pediatric anesthesia*. Retrieved from http://www.frca.co.uk/article.aspx?articleid=100544

Mason, C. N. (2013). Mild traumatic brain injury in children. *Pediatric Nursing, 39*(6), 267–272.

Meagher, R. J., & Young, W. F. (2013). *Subdural hematoma*. Retrieved from http://emedicine.medscape.com/article/1137207-overview

Minnes, S., Lang, A., & Singer, L. (2011). Prenatal tobacco, marijuana, stimulant and opiate exposure: Outcomes and practice implications. *Addiction Science and Clinical Practice, 6*(1), 57–70.

Papadopoulous, A. J., Janninger, C. K., & Schwartz, R. A. (2013). *Chickenpox*. Retrieved from http://emedicine.medscape.com/article/1131785-overview

Schwartz, R. A., & Jozwiak, S. (2014). *Epidermal nevus syndrome*. Retrieved from http://emedicine.medscape.com/article/1117506-overview

Schwentker, E. P. (2012). *Toe walking*. Retrieved from http://emedicine.medscape.com/article/1235248-overview

Swamy Chidananda, M. N., & Mallikarjun, D. (2004). Applied aspects of anatomy and physiology of relevance to pediatric anesthesia. *Indian Journal of Anesthesia, 48*(5), 333–339.

Tritos, N. A. (2013). *Kallmann syndrome and idiopathic hypogonadotropic hypogonadism*. Retrieved from http://emedicine.medscape.com/article/122824-overview

Vanderbilt, D., Wang, C. J., & Parker, S. (2007). The do's in preemie neurodevelopment. *Contemporary Pediatrics, 24*(9), 84–92.

Wilson, G. N. (2008). Children with the same congenital malformation pattern. *Consultant for Pediatricians, 7*(4), 155–158.

Yunnis, K., El Rafei, R., & Mumtaz, G. (2008). Consanguinity: Perinatal outcomes and prevention—a view from the Middle East. *NeoReviews, 9*(2), 59–65.

UNIT

ASSESSMENT OF CHILD MENTAL HEALTH AND WELFARE

Assessment of Mental Disorders in Children and Adolescents

Mental disorders affect an estimated 13% to 20% of American children, and the prevalence of these conditions is increasing (Perou et al., 2013). Mental disorders in children and adolescents can cause significant emotional distress and interfere with their abilities to study, work, or interact with family and peers. It is vitally important for the pediatric health care provider to incorporate mental health assessment into every health maintenance visit, and into episodic visits as warranted.

RISK FACTORS FOR MENTAL DISORDERS

The World Health Organization (WHO) (2012) and Chartier, Walker, and Naimark (2011) described risk factors for children and adolescents developing a mental disorder or experiencing difficulties in psychosocial development. The following risk factors were identified:
- Chronic medical illness
- Obesity
- Poverty
- Homelessness
- Exposure to domestic violence
- Maternal depression
- Parental separation or divorce
- Prenatal exposure to alcohol, illegal drugs, and tobacco
- Substance abuse in child or teen
- Substance abuse in family member
- Chronic physical or mental illness in family member
- Children of military families
- Children of parents who are incarcerated
- Parental knowledge deficits
- Child social skills deficits
- School failure
- Learning disability
- Low self-esteem
- Bereavement

- Exposure to war, community violence, natural disaster
- Discrimination; social, racial or gender inequalities
- Child abuse and neglect

Knowledge of these risk factors, as well as careful screening and a comprehensive assessment, can help a health care provider identify mental disorders, allowing effective treatment for affected children and adolescents.

ASSESSMENT OF CHILDREN WITH KNOWN OR SUSPECTED MENTAL DISORDERS

The American Academy of Pediatrics (AAP) 2014 recommendations for preventive health care include updates to the screening protocol for child behavioral and developmental assessment. At all well-child visits, children and adolescents, aged 11 through 21 years, are to be screened for depression and alcohol or drug use (AAP, 2014). Any child mental health assessment also includes interviews with the child or adolescent, parents or caregivers, teachers, as well as the collection of information about the child's behavior, peer and family relationships, school performance, and data from standardized tests and screening tool checklists or questionnaires. Excellent age- and developmentally appropriate communication skills are necessary to ensure that the child feels safe sharing information.

Communication

Attentive listening, directing conversation, establishing rapport, and following up on important cues are the general guidelines to a successful interview. The provider must observe interactions between the child or adolescent, and the parent or caregiver. Young children often express themselves through play activities (e.g., drawings, puppets, storytelling, therapeutic games), while older children and adolescents are able to respond directly. The provider should exhibit a warm, calm, and pleasant demeanor. If possible, the setting should reflect the age group being served (e.g., bright, colorful, small furniture for young children). Mental health brochures and teaching materials should also represent the patient population (Cottrell, Nield, & Perkins, 2006).

When interviewing the child, adolescent, or parents, the provider should begin with less sensitive topics, progressing to emotionally intense subjects once trust and rapport have been established (Cottrell et al., 2006). Confidentiality and safety are also discussed. The child or adolescent should be told what kind of information must be shared with the parents. Any information regarding situations that are potentially harmful to the child's or adolescent's health or safety, or to the safety of others, cannot be kept confidential (Cottrell et al., 2006). See Chapter 3 for an in-depth discussion regarding communicating with children.

History

The mental health assessment begins with a thorough medical and psychosocial history. Children with mental disorders may have physical co-morbidities that are either the cause or result of their mental health problem. For example, chronic headaches, recurrent abdominal pain, or episodes of shortness of breath may have a psychological etiology, or be due to a physical problem. Likewise, poor school performance may be indicative of chronic hearing loss in a child, rather than a manifestation of behavioral problems. A detailed history can also help reveal a child's loss, grief, separation, or trauma, which may be the cause of psychological illness.

Past Medical History

A child's past medical history (PMH) is relevant to his or her current mental health status. The PMH also includes an assessment of prenatal, birth, and neonatal histories, determining if the child has had any acute and chronic illnesses or injuries that affect the central nervous system, trauma, hospitalizations, and surgeries.

Prenatal, Birth, and Neonatal Histories • Prenatal exposure to drugs or maternal infections; prematurity; perinatal hypoxia; congenital defects or chromosomal abnormalities; and central nervous system infections or injuries are some examples of problems that can affect the child's behavior or mental health.

Allergies • The provider must inquire about any allergies that the child has, especially allergic rhinitis. To treat the allergy symptoms, the parent or caregiver may administer over-the-counter antihistamines such as diphenhydramine. This drug causes drowsiness and sedation, but in some children it may have a paradoxical effect and result in hyperactivity.

Hospitalizations • The date, length, and reason for each hospitalization should be determined, with notation of any hospitalizations for abdominal pain, mental or emotional disorders, substance abuse, depression, suicide attempts, seizures, head injuries, or other neurologic problems.

Surgeries • The provider should also note the date and reason for all surgeries, assessing whether the surgery was related to a mental health disorder.

Current Medications

The provider should conduct a thorough, detailed inventory of all medications the child or adolescent is currently taking or has taken within the last week. This includes medications that were prescribed for mental disorders, and over-the-counter preparations aimed at treating mental disorders (e.g., St. John's wort for depression). The provider should inquire about whether the child takes any medications that cause central nervous system or behavioral side effects. The provider should also inquire about the use of anabolic steroids in the adolescent client. Side effects of anabolic steroids may include aggression, paranoia, confusion, sleeping disorders, anxiety, hallucinations, euphoria, depression, suicidal ideation, and severe psychosis (Nanda & Konnur, 2006).

Family History

The provider should inquire about any family history of anxiety, depression, addiction, eating disorders, or hospitalization for mental illness. Any family history of attention deficit hyperactivity disorder, suicidal behavior or completed suicide, or adjustment, conduct, somatoform, or any other mental disorders must also be noted.

Social History

The family life and social situation contribute greatly to the child's or adolescent's mental health. A thorough family and cultural assessment should be completed (see Chapters 4 and 5). Any history of separation from the parent or family should be noted. Marital strife or domestic violence, parental stress, or unemployment can adversely affect a child's mental health. Traumatic events such as a death in the family, loss of a friend, family relocation or significant household changes, school changes, hospitalizations, death of a pet, natural disasters, or any other type of stressful life experience, grief, or loss are important assessments. The mental health of the parents or any other adults living in the home is also a crucial part of the social history. Parental addiction, mental illness, grief and loss, or parental incarceration affects the mental health of all children in the family. It is also important to ask about parental attitudes regarding discipline, and how the child is disciplined. The provider should ask whether or not corporal punishment is used and to what extent. It is also important to note any verbal discipline that could be characterized as verbal abuse (see Chapter 24).

Developmental History

The developmental history should include an assessment of the child's attainment of developmental milestones; temperament; and description of eating, sleeping, elimination habits, and routines. Age-appropriate attachment behaviors must also be assessed. For example, an older infant or toddler who does not exhibit stranger anxiety is displaying signs of an insecure or poor attachment to a primary caregiver. The parent or caregiver should be asked about the child's types of play, noting any indicators of developmental delay or themes of aggression in the play. Social skills and friendships should also be assessed for any signs of extreme shyness or introversion. An age-appropriate school assessment should also be done. This includes current or most recent grade, scholastic problems, reports of bullying, school refusal, behavioral problems, truancy, and suspensions or expulsions.

Sexual History

The sexual history should include the child's age at puberty, and an assessment of the child's knowledge of sexuality. In the adolescent, dating patterns and sexual activity should be assessed. This information should be obtained in a matter-of-fact, nonjudgmental manner, with the parent out of the room. A full sexual history should be obtained as needed (see Chapter 20), to assess for multiple partners, promiscuity, or sexually transmitted diseases. Any signs of sexual abuse must be investigated (see Chapter 24).

Review of Systems

The pediatric review of systems specific to mental health assessment in children focuses on determining if there is a history of any past acute illnesses or current chronic illnesses that may have behavioral manifestations. This assessment also illuminates whether any mental illnesses are causing physical manifestations such as substance abuse, eating disorders, or vague, nonspecific somatic complaints. Some examples include the following:

- **General health:** Congenital defects (e.g., fetal alcohol syndrome), prematurity, overall state of health, chronic fatigue, mood, recent significant weight gain or loss, exercise tolerance, increased or decreased need for sleep, poor or absent attachment to primary caregiver (young children), drug or alcohol use; human immunodeficiency virus infection (needle sharing, sexual practices), chromosomal abnormalities.
- **Integument:** Changes in skin; dry, yellowish skin (seen in anorexia nervosa); acanthosis nigricans (obesity); scars on knuckles ("Russell's sign"), which indicates repeated self-induced vomiting; cuts, burns, or bruises (self-injury); burns or picking at the skin (methamphetamine use); severe acne (anabolic steroid use); dry, thin, brittle hair, or lanugo (anorexia nervosa); hirsutism (anabolic steroid use); habits such as hair-twisting or hair-pulling (trichotillomania) or nail biting; premature balding (anabolic steroid use)
- **Head:** Chronic headaches; microcephaly (fetal alcohol syndrome); macrocephaly (hydrocephalus); history of traumatic brain injury
- **Eyes:** Conjunctival injection (marijuana use); watery eyes (narcotic use); dilated pupils (cocaine or hallucinogens)
- **Nose:** Chronic rhinorrhea (inhalant use), snoring, or obstructive sleep apnea (obesity)
- **Mouth and throat:** Tooth decay and sore throat (chronic vomiting); gum recession (chewing tobacco); dry mouth (drug use)
- **Chest:** Chest pain (cocaine use); gynecomastia in boys, small breast size in girls (steroid use)
- **Respiratory:** Chronic cough (nicotine, inhalant use); dyspnea (obesity, cigarette smoking); shortness of breath (anxiety, respiratory disorders)
- **Cardiac:** Hypotension, bradycardia, cardiac arrhythmia (eating disorders, inhalant or amphetamine use); hypertension (obesity); tachycardia (stimulant use)
- **Gastrointestinal:** Diarrhea (laxative use), constipation (opioid use), vomiting (purging, alcohol or drug overdose, nicotine toxicity); gastritis, peptic ulcer disease, and heartburn (chronic alcohol use, purging); liver disorders (drug or alcohol use; anabolic steroids); recurrent abdominal pain
- **Endocrine:** Obesity; intolerance to cold (anorexia nervosa, hypothyroidism), excessive sweating (drug use); precocious puberty (anabolic steroid use)
- **Genitourinary:** Testicular atrophy (anabolic steroid use)
- **Gynecologic:** Pregnancy; irregular menses (abnormally low body weight due to eating disorders; anabolic steroid use)
- **Musculoskeletal:** Stunted growth, increased muscle mass (anabolic steroid use)
- **Neurologic:** Impaired coordination, tremors, seizures, nystagmus, memory loss (drug or alcohol use)
- **Lymphatic:** History of frequent infections (chronic malnutrition secondary to eating disorders, infection after intravenous drug use)
- **Developmental:** Developmental delays, impaired cognition, speech or language delays, slurred speech, impaired gross or fine motor development, reduced attention span
- **Behavior:** School truancy, poor school performance, poor school attendance, difficulty with concentration, dropping out of school, apathy, change in attention span, mood swings, mania, emotional lability, paranoia, aggressiveness,

cruelty to animals, violent behavior, difficult relationships at home and school (depression, drug or alcohol abuse)

■ **Psychosocial:** Family history of mental health disorders; current parental psychopathology, parent–child relationship quality, parental supervision, type of discipline used by parents; peer relationships, community violence, socioeconomic risk factors, attention deficit hyperactivity disorder, conduct disorder, bipolar disorder, eating disorders, anxiety disorders, panic attacks, hallucinations, flashbacks, depression, suicidal ideation, and suicide attempts

History of Present Illness

When a child or adolescent presents with a mental health complaint, the provider should inquire about the onset of symptoms, the development and duration of problems, the severity and impact of the problem,

and what, if any, help has been sought and tried (e.g., medication, counseling, hospitalization). The provider should also determine if the problem has had an effect on life at home or school or on the family or siblings. Certain significant events that occur before or concurrently with the problem (e.g., illness, hospitalization, separation, divorce, death) may have an effect on the child's behavior.

Physical Examination

A complete, head-to-toe physical examination should be conducted, focusing on hearing, vision, neurologic assessments, and neurologic soft signs (see Chapter 22). A mental status exam should also be done, as well as an assessment of the child or adolescent's general appearance, behavior, and manner of relating. A developmental assessment should also be included in the examination (see Chapter 2). Table 23.1 summarizes the important mental health assessments.

TABLE 23.1	Categories of Assessment Data	
ASSESSMENT	**DATA TO COLLECT**	**POSSIBLE FINDINGS**
Neurologic assessment	Cerebral functions Cerebellar functions Sensory functions Reflexes Cranial nerves Functions can be observed in developmental assessment and while playing games involving a specific ability (e.g., "Simon says, touch your nose")	Neurologic or developmental problems Evidence of head injury
Coordination or motor function	Posture Gait Balance Gross motor movement Fine motor movement Writing and drawing skills Unusual characteristics (e.g., bizarre postures, tiptoe walking, hand flapping, head banging, hand biting)	Cerebral palsy
Child or adolescent mental status assessment	**General Appearance:** Size (height and weight) General health and nutrition Dress and grooming Distinguishing characteristics Gestures and mannerisms Looks or acts younger or older than chronologic age **Speech:** Rate, rhythm, and intonation Pitch and modulation Vocabulary and grammar appropriate to age Mute, hesitant, or talkative Articulation problems Other expressive problems Unusual characteristics (e.g., pronoun reversal, echolalia, gender confusion, neologisms)	Neurologic problems causing disorientation Hallucinations Evidence of eating disorders Depression Autism spectrum disorder Developmental delay

TABLE 23.1	Categories of Assessment Data (*continued*)	
ASSESSMENT	**DATA TO COLLECT**	**POSSIBLE FINDINGS**
	Intellectual Functions: Fund of general information Ability to communicate (e.g., follow directions, answer questions) Memory Creativity Sense of humor Social awareness Learning and problem solving Conscience (e.g., sense of right and wrong, accepts guilt and limits)	
Development assessment	Psychomotor Language Cognitive Interpersonal and social Behavior (e.g., response to stress, changes in the environment) Problem-solving and coping skills (e.g., impulse control, delay of gratification) Energy level and motivation	Developmental delay Neglect Abuse
Characteristics of child's play	Age-appropriate use of toys Themes of play Imagination and pretend play Role and gender play Age-appropriate play with peers Relationship with peers (e.g., empathy, sharing, waiting for turns, best friends)	Depression Grief Loss Anxiety Abuse
Activity level	Hyperactivity/hypoactivity Tics, other body movements Autoerotic and self-comforting movements (e.g., thumb sucking, ear or hair-pulling, masturbation)	ADHD, Tourette's syndrome, trichotillomania, and autism spectrum disorders
Thought processes and content	Orientation Attention span Self-concept and body image Sex role, gender identity Ego-defense mechanisms Perceptual distortions (e.g., hallucinations, illusions) Preoccupations, concerns, and unusual ideas Fantasies and dreams	Drug or alcohol abuse, neurologic problems, ADHD, loss, and grief
Manner of relating	Eye contact Ability to separate from caregiver and be independent Attitude toward interviewer Behavior during interview (e.g., ability to have fun or play; low frustration tolerance, impulsive, aggressive)	Shy temperament PTSD Separation anxiety
Sensitive subjects	Substance use by adolescent: type of substance, duration of use, quantity, effects, and consequences (i.e., medical, personal or interpersonal, school or job, legal, financial) Suicide ideas/attempts: seriousness, methods, and drug- or alcohol-associated, consequences Violence/delinquency: nature or history; legal system involvement (e.g., arrests, incarcerations), illegal behaviors for which adolescent was apprehended Physical or sexual abuse: exact nature of events, perpetrator, and legal system involvement, and effects on adolescent and family	Drug or alcohol use Depression Eating disorders Conduct disorder

ADHD, attention deficit hyperactivity disorder; PTSD, posttraumatic stress disorder.

Mental Health Screening Tools

Because the pediatric primary care provider is often first to identify a child's mental health problem, selected screening tools may be helpful to use during the primary care visit. The AAP (2014) recommends selected mental health screening and assessment tools for primary care. Examples of some of these screening tools are listed in in the next section, under each selected disorder; the complete list can be found on the AAP's website (www.aap.org/en-us/advocacy-and-policy/aap-health-initiatives/Mental-Health/Documents/MH_ScreeningChart.pdf).

ASSESSMENT OF SELECTED MENTAL HEALTH DISORDERS IN CHILDREN

Autism Spectrum Disorder

Autistic spectrum disorder is characterized by severe and pervasive impairment in several areas of development, such as reciprocal social interaction skills, maintaining relationships, and difficulties with nonverbal communication, such as poor eye contact, abnormal facial expressions, tone of voice or gestures, or the presence of stereotypical behavior and speech, interests, and activities (American Psychiatric Association [APA], 2013). These disorders affect many areas of development, are exhibited early in life, and cause significant impairments in functioning. The onset of autism spectrum disorder is before 3 years of age. The parents or caregivers are often the first to notice the atypical behavior, when the infant often does not appear to be interested in others or socially responsive through facial gestures and eye contact. Common behavior problems include head banging, biting, aggression, and hair pulling.

According to the criteria in the *Diagnostic and Statistical Manual* (5th ed., *DSM-5*; APA, 2013), to make a diagnosis of autism spectrum disorder at least two of four major areas must be met: (a) stereotypical patterns of speech, motor movements or use of an object; (b) repeated adherence to specific routines or rituals involving patterns of verbal or nonverbal behavior, or excessive resistance to change; (c) extremely specialized interests that are abnormal in intensity or focus; and (d) extreme under- or overreaction to sensory input or intense interest in sensory aspects of the environment. In many cases, intellectual disability, or speech and language delays are associated diagnoses. Box 23.1 summarizes the data to gather when assessing children for autism spectrum disorder.

Attention Deficit Hyperactivity Disorder

Attention deficit hyperactivity disorder (ADHD) is characterized by a persistent and marked pattern of inattention or hyperactive and impulsive behavior, present in multiple settings (e.g., social, academic, and extracurricular functioning) (APA, 2013). Symptoms involve inattention, hyperactivity, and impulsivity that involve failure to pay attention to details, problems with organizational skills, and difficulty staying still or seated for any length of time. It is difficult to diagnose in children younger than 5 years of age because of developmental variations. When assessing a child or teen, a screening tool should be used to quantify the behavioral signs. One such tool is the Vanderbilt ADHD Assessment Scale. Using this checklist, to make a diagnosis of ADHD, a child must have at least six symptoms from either (or both) the inattention group of criteria and the hyperactivity and impulsivity criteria, while older adolescents and adults (older than age 17 years) must present with at least five symptoms (Box 23.2).

Disruptive Behavior Disorders

Oppositional Defiant Disorder

Children with oppositional defiant disorder exhibit a recurrent pattern of negativistic, defiant, disobedient,

---

BOX 23.1 Pertinent Assessment Data: Autism Spectrum Disorder

- Assess the quality of attachment (bonding) between the child and parents or caregivers.
- Observe the child's quality of eye contact, facial gestures, and body movements.
- Assess developmental levels. Note developmental lags in cognition, language, behavior, and social skills.
- Assess the child's behavior and style of play.
- Observe for uneven development and loss of acquired skills.

The AAP recommends screening for autism spectrum disorder at both the 18- and 24-month well-child care visits, using the Modified Checklist for Autism in Toddlers (M-CHAT) screening tool (Johnson, Meyers, & the American Academy of Pediatrics Council on Children with Disabilities, 2010).

BOX 23.2 Pertinent Assessment Data: Attention Deficit Hyperactivity Disorder

- Assess the attention span, verbal activity, and physical activity of the child.
- Observe the child's ability to follow directions.
- Assess the impact of the child's behavior on relationships at school and home.
- Determine the parent's or caregiver's responses to the child's behavior.
- Assess parental skills and their abilities to cope with the child's behavior.
- Administer an ADHD checklist to parents, teachers, or caregivers, such as the Vanderbilt ADHD Assessment Scale.

and hostile behavior toward authority figures. Symptoms are categorized as being of three types: angry/irritable mood, argumentative/defiant behavior, and vindictiveness. These children generally do not exhibit serious physical aggression against others (APA, 2013).

Conduct Disorder

Conduct disorder is one of the most common mental disorders diagnosed in children. This disorder is characterized by aggressive behavior toward others and the serious violation of societal norms or rules (APA, 2004). Children or adolescents with this disorder may exhibit threatening, bullying, or intimidating behaviors toward others. The *DSM-5* categorizes conduct disorder into four areas: (a) aggression to people and animals, (b) destruction of property, (c) deceitfulness or theft, and (d) serious violations of rules (APA, 2013). Box 23.3 lists data to gather when assessing children for disruptive behavior disorders.

BOX 23.3 Pertinent Assessment Data: Disruptive Behavior Disorders

- Assess the seriousness of the aggressive behavior toward others.
- Assess the impact of the child's aggressive behavior on family life, school performance, and social life.
- Assess the degree of empathy for others and the ability to learn from mistakes.
- Determine the child's willingness to take responsibility for his or her own behavior.
- Explore the child's image of self and others.
- Assess for psychological co-morbidities.

Eating Disorders

Eating disorders are characterized by a marked disturbance in eating patterns. They are chronic, serious, life-threatening conditions (Wilkes & Spratt, 2014). The onset of eating disorders can be seen in children as young as 10 years of age. Unlike most mental disorders, eating disorders can cause severe physical problems. Anorexia nervosa, bulimia nervosa, and obesity are briefly discussed.

Anorexia Nervosa

Anorexia nervosa is characterized by a severe restriction of caloric intake relative to body requirements, distorted perception of body shape or weight, and an intense fear of weight gain (APA, 2013). The *DSM-5* describes two types of anorexia nervosa: restricting types and binge-eating/purging types. The APA has revised the diagnostic criteria for anorexia nervosa to place more emphasis on the behavioral aspects of the disorder, such as severe

caloric restriction, and has removed the diagnostic criteria of low body weight (85% of expected weight), and amenorrhea (APA, 2013). The mortality rate for anorexia nervosa hovers around 10%, with death most often occurring as a result of suicide, starvation, or electrolyte imbalance (Bernstein, 2014). Box 23.4 lists assessment data for anorexia nervosa.

Bulimia Nervosa

Bulimia nervosa is characterized by periods of binge eating (2,000 to 10,000 calories) followed by self-induced vomiting, purging, and exercise to prevent weight gain. *DSM-5* criteria include (a) recurrent episodes of binge eating, (b) recurrent compensatory behaviors to rectify the binge eating (e.g., self-induced vomiting; misuse of laxatives, diuretics, or other medications; fasting; or excessive exercise), (c) the binge eating/compensatory behaviors must be present for at least once a week for 3 months, (d) the client cannot realistically evaluate own behavior due to distorted body image, and (e) the disturbance does not occur exclusively during episodes of anorexia nervosa (APA, 2013).

The incidence of bulimia nervosa in adolescence is approximately 1%; the average age of onset is usually

---

BOX 23.4 Pertinent Assessment Data: Anorexia Nervosa

- Assess body mass index, height, weight, vital signs, and average daily calorie intake.
- Perform a physical examination, and order blood work (complete blood count, chemistry panel, pregnancy test, urinalysis).
- Determine whether the child or adolescent requires hospitalization (i.e., medical or psychiatric).
- Assess for suicidal ideation and other self-destructive behaviors.
- Determine eating patterns and activity level.
- Assess perception of body image and self-esteem.
- Explore fears and concerns about weight.
- Record last normal menstrual period.
- Assess family functioning and the child's or adolescent's perception of autonomy and independence.

Significant findings on physical examination include the following:

- Thin physical appearance
- Lanugo (fine body hair over body)
- Delayed puberty
- Dull, thin, brittle hair
- Dry, yellowish skin
- Hypotension
- Bradycardia
- Use of laxatives and diuretics

---

19 years, and the condition is more common in girls. These adolescents report feeling "out of control" and are often reluctant to discuss their eating patterns. Shame and secrets often prevent these adolescents from getting treatment (Yager, Scher, Hilty, & Osterhout, 2014).

Physical complications are a result of diuretic and laxative abuse and purging behaviors. Adolescents may also experience other mental disorders, such as substance abuse, depression, and anxiety (Box 23.5).

BOX 23.5 Pertinent Assessment Data: Bulimia Nervosa

- Perform a physical examination and order blood work (e.g., complete blood count, chemistry panel, urinalysis, and urine toxicology screen; pregnancy test; amylase level) (Yager et al., 2014).
- Assess eating patterns, body mass index, height, weight, vital signs, and menstrual history.
- Complete the mental status examination by assessing mood, suicidal potential, and other self-destructive behaviors (e.g., cutting).
- Determine whether the adolescent requires hospitalization (i.e., medical or psychiatric).
- Assess the adolescent and parent's or caregiver's perceptions of family functioning.
- Refer the adolescent for a psychiatric or psychologic evaluation.
- Assess perception of body image and self-esteem.

Significant findings on physical examination include the following:

- Puffy cheeks (enlarged parotid glands)
- Scars on the knuckles from self-induced vomiting (Russell's sign)
- Decay of the front teeth
- Irregular menses
- Dehydration or fluid retention
- Hypotension, decreased heart rate, or irregular heart rate
- Sores around cheeks and mouth
- Sore throat or hoarseness
- Low energy
- Alteration in elimination patterns (e.g., diarrhea, constipation, indigestion, heartburn)

Typical laboratory or other tests include the following:

- Complete blood count, which may show anemia; blood chemistries may reveal abnormalities in serum electrolytes, magnesium, and increased blood urea nitrogen
- Electrocardiogram, which may show cardiac arrhythmias
- Thyroid function tests, which may show abnormal triiodothyronine (T_3) levels

---

Childhood Obesity

In 2012, more than one third of children and adolescents were overweight or obese. This prevalence has more than doubled in children and quadrupled for adolescents in the past three decades (Ogden, Carroll, Kit, & Flegal, 2014). Body mass index (BMI) is used to identify overweight and obesity in children and adolescents. The Centers for Disease Control and Prevention (CDC) defines obesity as weight at the 95th percentile or greater on the growth chart (CDC, 2012).

Compared with children of a healthy weight, overweight children and adolescents have risk factors for heart disease such as high cholesterol and high blood pressure. These children are also at risk for type 2 diabetes and metabolic syndrome (CDC, 2014a). Obese children or adolescents are often ridiculed and teased, which can cause depression, anxiety, and low self-esteem. Childhood obesity can lead to long-term physical, emotional, and social consequences, which can persist through adulthood (Box 23.6).

BOX 23.6 Pertinent Assessment Data: Childhood Obesity

- Assess body mass index, height, weight, average daily calorie intake, and vital signs.
- Determine eating patterns and activity level.
- Perform a physical examination and order blood work (fasting glucose, lipid profile, thyroid function tests, serum leptin) (Schwartz, 2013).
- Ask parents or caregivers about the child or adolescent's sleeping pattern, specifically noting snoring, irregular breathing episodes, or difficulty breathing.
- Assess perception of body image and self-esteem.
- Assess family, social, and school functioning.

Significant findings on physical examination include the following:

- BMI of 25 or greater
- Elevated blood pressure
- Signs of insulin resistance (acanthosis nigricans)
- Dyspnea, snoring, or stridor

Typical results of laboratory tests may include high cholesterol levels.

Anxiety Disorders

Anxiety disorders are the most common mental disorders of childhood and adolescence, affecting one in eight children (Anxiety and Depression Association of America, 2014). These children and adolescents may also exhibit signs of depression. Parents of children or adolescents with anxiety disorders often report depressive episodes and anxiety as well. Social anxiety disorder, separation anxiety disorder, and posttraumatic stress disorder (PTSD) are discussed.

Social Anxiety Disorder

Social anxiety disorder (formerly social phobia) is the most common childhood mental disorder, affecting 5% to 12% of youth at some time in their life (Schneier, 2013). In the past, social anxiety disorder was often dismissed as "childhood shyness," and the disorder was therefore under-identified and undertreated. The average age of onset is 11 to 12 years of age. However, the disorder has been reported in children as young as 6 years of age (Bothe & Olness, 2007; Ginsburg & Grover, 2005). According to Ginsburg and Grover (2005), social anxiety disorder is chronic and often continues into young adulthood.

According to the *DSM-5* criteria, this disorder affects several domains of functioning: personal, academic, social, and familial (APA, 2013). Children with social phobia have low self-esteem. They often feel as though people are viewing them negatively and often use avoidance behaviors as coping mechanisms. They generally avoid school and social activities and, in adolescence, dating. Ginsburg and Grover (2005) reported that social withdrawal impedes the development of appropriate social skills.

Academically, children with social phobia have problems in the classroom. For example, speaking in class or working in a group activity can cause severe anxiety or emotional distress. At home, the children are reluctant to attend family gatherings and often prefer solitary activities (e.g., computer games, reading a book). These children may also exhibit physical symptoms, such as stomachaches, headaches, and panic attack symptoms (Ginsburg & Grover, 2005; Schneier, 2013). Assessment of social phobia in children and adolescents (Box 23.7) should include data from teachers, parents, clinical interviews, as well as

rating scales (e.g., Multidimensional Anxiety Scale for Children [MASC], Social Phobia and Anxiety Inventory for Children [SPAI-C], Social Anxiety Scales for Children and Adolescents [SAS], or the Kutcher Generalized Social Anxiety Scale for Adolescents [KGSADS]).

Separation Anxiety Disorder

According to the *DSM-5*, separation anxiety disorder is fairly common. This disorder is characterized by persistent and excessive anxiety beyond that expected for the child's developmental level related to separation or impending separation from the home or primary attachment figure, as evidenced by at least five of the following (APA, 2013; Bernstein, 2013):

- Recurrent significant distress when anticipating or experiencing separation from home or from major attachment figures
- Persistent and excessive worry about losing major attachment figures or about possible harm to them, such as illness, injury, disasters, or death
- Persistent and excessive worry about experiencing an event that causes separation from a major attachment figure (e.g., getting lost, being kidnapped, having an accident, becoming ill, dying)
- Persistent reluctance or refusal to leave home to go to school, work, or elsewhere because of fear of separation from primary attachment figure
- Persistent and excessive fear about being alone or without major attachment figures at home or in other settings (e.g., school, friend's or relative's home)
- Persistent reluctance or refusal to sleep away from home or to go to sleep without being near a primary attachment figure
- Repeated nightmares involving the theme of separation or loss
- Repeated complaints of physical symptoms (e.g., headaches, stomachaches, nausea, vomiting) when separation from major attachment figures occurs or is anticipated

In separation anxiety disorder, physical symptoms are generally worse on evenings and mornings before school and are absent on weekends and holidays, except the night before school starts. School absences can affect a child's academic performance (Bernstein, 2013). These children also are often preoccupied with death, dying, and illnesses (APA, 2013) Box 23.8 lists relevant assessment data.

Posttraumatic Stress Disorder

PTSD is characterized by the development of emotional and behavioral symptoms following a traumatic, unexpected event that is outside the range of usual human experience and during which the individual feels intense

---

BOX 23.7   Pertinent Assessment Data: Social Anxiety Disorder

- Assess the level of the child's anxiety and the child's ability to function at school and at home.
- Determine the level of involvement in social activities at home and school.
- Administer standardized assessment tools (e.g., rating scales) to the child or adolescent, and obtain assessment data from parents or caregivers, and teachers.
- Assess academic performance and school attendance.
- Recommend supportive counseling for the child or adolescent and for the parents or caregivers.

BOX 23.8 Pertinent Assessment Data: Separation Anxiety Disorder

- Assess the level of the child's anxiety and the child's ability to function at school (e.g., absenteeism).
- Collect data about school attendance. If the child missed more than a week of school, immediate referral for a psychiatric evaluation is recommended. The longer the child is out of school, the more difficult it is to reenter school.
- Determine the child's current and past ability to separate from the parent or caregiver.
- Remember normal separation anxiety is often seen in toddlers.
- Gather data about the family life (e.g., death of a pet, parent, sibling; illness of a parent; recent moves).

BOX 23.9 Pertinent Assessment Data: Posttraumatic Stress Disorder

- Determine the traumatic event.
- Assess the child's or adolescent's emotional, social, physical, and cognitive responses to the traumatic event.
- Assess the social supports and the family's responses to the traumatic event.
- Note any physical co-morbidities if the traumatic event was injury.

Selected screening tools may be helpful in assessing PTSD, as follows:

- Child and Adolescent Psychiatric Assessment: Life Events Section and PTSD Module (CAPA-PTSD)
- Children's PTSD Inventory (CPTSDI)
- Child PTSD Symptom Scale (CPSS)
- Abbreviated UCLA PTSD Reaction Index
- Trauma Symptom Checklist for Children (TSCC)
- Impact of Events Scale
- Screen for Child Anxiety Related Disorders (SCARED)
- Beck Depression Inventory

---

fear and hopelessness. Children may respond with agitated or disorganized behavior (APA, 2013). For children and adolescents, the traumatic events are the same as for adults: rape, kidnapping, violence, and disruption caused by environmental disasters (e.g., fires, floods, hurricanes, tornadoes), among others. The child or adolescent may experience the event directly or indirectly (Lubit & Giardino, 2014).

According to the *DSM-5*, symptoms of PTSD in young children differ from those exhibited by adults, adolescents, and children older than 6 years. These symptoms must occur for 30 days or longer to meet the criteria for PTSD. Initial effects include fear of death and fear of separation from parents, especially in young children. Affected children withdraw from new experiences. Reexperiencing the event may occur in the form of nightmares, daydreams, or repetitive, potentially dangerous reenactments in symbolic play or in actual behavior (APA, 2013). Children may develop physical symptoms, such as stomach problems and headaches. Sleep disturbances may interfere with activities of daily living. Children frequently exhibit regressive behaviors (i.e., show behaviors characteristic of a previous developmental stage). Box 23.9 lists relevant assessment data.

Substance Use Disorders

The diagnosis of substance use disorder in the *DSM-5* combines the *DSM-IV* categories of substance abuse and substance dependence into a single disorder measured on a continuum from mild to severe (APA, 2013). Substance abuse is characterized by a maladaptive pattern of substance use manifested by significant and recurrent consequences related to the persistent use of substances (APA, 2013). Adolescent substance use can have deleterious effects on family and peer relationships, cognitive processes, school functioning, and physical and mental health. Adolescent violence (e.g., assaults, rapes) and adolescent substance use are also correlated.

The substance most commonly abused by adolescents is alcohol (U.S. Department of Health and Human Services [USDHHS], 2014). The updated periodicity schedule for well-child visits (AAP, 2014), recommends screening adolescents for alcohol and drug use, beginning at age 11 years, using the CRAFFT screening tool. Box 23.10 lists relevant assessment data.

BOX 23.10 Pertinent Assessment Data: Substance Use Disorders

- Assess family, social, and school functioning.
- Perform a physical examination, and order urine and blood tests (e.g., toxicology screens).
- Complete the mental status examination by assessing mood, suicidal potential, and other self-destructive behaviors.
- Determine if the adolescent requires hospitalization (i.e., medical, psychiatric).
- Administer drug screening tests (e.g., CRAFFT screening tool).
- Assess substance use (i.e., type of substances used; frequency and amount of use; methods of use such as oral, inhalation, or injection; contexts of use; and history of use).
- Assess the adolescent's self-esteem.
- Use multiple assessment methods from a variety of sources (i.e., adolescent, parent or caregiver, siblings).
- Refer adolescent or family for a psychiatric or psychologic evaluation.

Mood Disorders

The symptoms of mood disorders in children and adolescents are similar to those in adults; however, the developmental stage of a child or adolescent may modify the expression of these symptoms. Children and adolescents sometimes have trouble talking about their emotions and so may resort to acting out behaviors. The AAP (2014) recommends screening children and adolescents for depression at all well-child visits, beginning at age 11 years. Examples of recommended screening tools include the Beck Depression Inventory and the Kutcher Adolescent Depression Scale (KADS). Mood disorders are briefly discussed.

Major Depressive Disorder

Depression affects approximately 11% of American teens, aged 13 to 18 years; roughly 3% of these adolescents will suffer depression that is serious and debilitating (Merikangas et al., 2010). Major depressive disorder is characterized by the following symptoms: sadness, irritability, hopelessness, feelings of worthlessness, changes in weight and sleep patterns, loss of interest in activities, low energy level, fatigue, low self-esteem, poor concentration, restlessness, and thoughts of death or suicide. Children and adolescents often have school problems, including school refusal, reluctance to attend school, or poor academic performance (APA, 2013). Depressed children and adolescents generally have at least one other mental disorder, such as anxiety disorder, substance abuse disorder, disruptive disorder, or an eating disorder. Somatic symptoms, such as stomachaches and headaches, are also common in children and adolescents (Giardino & Benton, 2014).

Persistent Depressive Disorder (Dysthymia)

Persistent depressive disorder is characterized by depressed mood for at least 1 year (APA, 2013). The symptoms are less severe and debilitating than major depressive disorder, but may persist for several years. According to Rogers and Spalding (2014), the average duration of a dysthymic period in children and adolescents is about 4 years.

Prevalence rates for dysthymic disorder have been reported that range from 0.6% to 1.7% in children and 1.6% to 8.0% in adolescents (Rogers & Spalding, 2014). Major depressive disorder and dysthymic disorder are equally common in boys and girls before puberty (Rogers & Spalding, 2014). However, after age 15, depression is twice as common in girls as in boys (Rogers & Spalding, 2014).

Bipolar Disorder

According to the *DSM-5*, the diagnostic criteria in children and adolescents are the same as for adults. Symptoms include extreme mood swings, intermittent aggressive behavior, impulsivity, high levels of distractibility, periods of irritability, and sleep disturbances. These adolescents may have difficulty with normal day-to-day functioning and may require hospitalization. Other mental disorders or conditions may be present such as ADHD, disruptive disorders, substance abuse disorders, or psychotic features (e.g., hallucinations, delusions) (Schapiro, 2005).

Adolescents are also at risk for sexually transmitted diseases because of unsafe sex practices and promiscuous behavior. The prevalence rate of bipolar disorder increases with age. Bipolar disorder is rare in children. The disorder generally begins in adolescence. Box 23.11 lists relevant assessment data.

BOX 23.11 Pertinent Assessment Data: Mood Disorders

- Perform a mental status examination.
- Assess sleeping and eating patterns.
- Assess social, school, and family functioning.
- Inquire about recent losses (e.g., death, relationship difficulties; recent move).
- Administer self-report mood disorder checklists.
- Assess suicidal potential using a screening tool.
- Establish a "no harm or no suicide" contract if needed.
- Determine whether the child or adolescent requires hospitalization.

Suicide

Suicide is not considered a mental disorder; however, the presence of a mood disorder increases the likelihood of suicide. The incidence of suicide attempts reaches a peak during the mid-adolescent years, and mortality from suicide increases steadily through the teen years. In 2010, suicide was the second leading cause of death among children aged 12 to 17 years (CDC, 2013) and the third leading cause of death among youth and teens between the ages of 10 and 24 years (CDC, 2014b).

Boys are more likely to commit suicide than girls, whereas girls are more likely to *attempt* suicide (CDC, 2014b). Minorities are at higher risk for suicide, with Native American/Alaskan Native youth having the highest rates of completed suicide (CDC, 2014b). The availability of firearms in the United States is a factor in the suicide rate. Suicide by firearm is the most common method used by adolescents, accounting for 45% of completed suicides in this age group (CDC, 2014b).

Suicidal gestures should always be taken seriously by parents, teachers, and health care providers. A thorough suicide assessment should be done. Any child or adolescent who is expressing suicidal ideation needs emergent referral and psychiatric follow-up. Box 23.12 lists initial assessment data that should be gathered. Several suicide screening tools are available; these are listed in Table 23.2.

Nonsuicidal Self-Injury

Nonsuicidal self-injury (NSSI) is the "direct, deliberate destruction of one's own body tissue in the absence of

---

BOX 23.12 Pertinent Assessment Data: Suicide

- Determine the presence of mental disorders (e.g., depression, anxiety, conduct disorder, or substance abuse).
- Include a history of previous suicidal attempts.
- Identify all stressful life events (school and legal problems, relationship problems).
- Address the lack of supportive family members (chaotic, unpredictable, home environment, marital conflict).
- Identify parents with mental disorders (substance abuse, affective disorders).
- Identify parents, relatives, friends, or role models who have attempted suicide or completed suicide
- Assess access to highly lethal methods (e.g., guns).

Source: Stafford, Talmi, and Burstein (2012).

---

intent to die" (Butler & Malone, 2013, p. 324). The most common forms of self-injury are cutting, burning, banging, scratching, biting, self-hitting, and excessive rubbing (Butler & Malone, 2013). The incidence of self-injury among adolescents is increasing.

Adolescents who engage in NSSI generally have low self-esteem, a history of physical or sexual abuse, and difficulty expressing their emotions. The act of mutilation becomes a way for the adolescent to show or express psychological pain. Self-injury behaviors may be present with other mental disorders such as affective disorders, anxiety disorders, eating disorders, and substance abuse disorders. The self-injurious behavior is more common in girls than boys. These adolescents often stir up emotions in health care providers, which is called countertransference. D'Onofrio (2007) defined countertransference as the projection of a health care provider's experiences, values, and emotions onto the patient. Strong emotions either positive or negative may indicate countertransference in the provider. Education about the dynamics of self-injury decreases negative emotions toward these adolescents and ensures an accurate assessment and proper treatment. Box 23.13 lists relevant assessment data to be gathered.

BOX 23.13 Pertinent Assessment Data: Self-Injury

- Address self-esteem issues (e.g., low self-esteem).
- Identify school, social, and family problems.
- Discuss relationship difficulties.
- Assess physical or sexual abuse.
- Identify any mental disorder (e.g., depression, substance abuse, eating disorder, anxiety disorder).
- Assess the difficulty expressing or managing emotions.
- Assess for suicidality.

Source: Aguirre and Smith (2007).

COMMON DIAGNOSTIC STUDIES

Physical health problems can produce behavioral manifestations in children similar to those resulting from mental health disorders. In such cases, specific laboratory or radiology studies can be helpful in determining whether a physical problem is causing the behavioral changes observed in the child or adolescent (Table 23.3).

SUMMARY

Thorough, sensitive physical and psychological assessment plays an important role in the accurate diagnosis and treatment of mental disorders in children and adolescents. Many of the mental disorders diagnosed in children are treatable if detected early. The pediatric primary care provider plays a vital role in this process.

TABLE 23.2	Screening Tools to Identify Suicide Risk in Children and Adolescents
SCREENING TOOL	**SOURCE**
Adapted SAD PERSONS	www.cscwv.org/pdf/SuicideAssessment.pdf
Global Appraisal of Individual Needs – Short Screener (GAIN-SS)	www.gaincc.org/gainss
Massachusetts Youth Screening Instrument–Second Version (MAYSI-2)	www.nysap.us/MAYSI2.html
Patient Health Questionnaire (PHQ-9)	www.uacap.org/uploads/3/2/5/0/3250432/phq-a.pdf
Suicidal Behaviors Questionnaire-Revised (SBQ-R)	www.glaje.com/Scales/Suicidal_Beh_Quest_pre_assessment.pdf
Suicidal Ideation Questionnaire (SIQ)	www4.parinc.com/Products/Product.aspx?ProductID=SIQ

Source: National Action Alliance for Suicide Prevention: Youth in Contact with the Juvenile Justice System Task Force (2013).

TABLE 23.3	Laboratory and Radiology Studies That May Aid in Identifying Physical Problems That Cause Behavioral Changes	
STUDY	**POSSIBLE DIAGNOSES**	**POSSIBLE BEHAVIORAL MANIFESTATIONS**
Complete blood count (CBC)	Anemia	Lethargy, irritability, restlessness, anorexia, developmental delays, or pica
Thyroid function tests	Hypothyroidism or hyperthyroidism	*Hypothyroidism:* delayed mental responsiveness in neonates, lethargy, poor school performance *Hyperthyroidism:* emotional instability, weight loss, insomnia, behavioral problems, difficulty concentrating, or poor school performance
Lead level	Lead poisoning	Learning disabilities, hearing impairment, developmental delays, hyperactivity, behavioral problems, chronic headache, or pica
Urine toxicology screen	Substance abuse	Behavior changes, personality disorders, depression, paranoia, hallucinations, mood swings, aggression, insomnia, anxiety, loss of concentration, memory loss, personality changes, flashbacks, decreased motivation, or antisocial behavior to support habit
Electroencephalogram	Seizures	Partial seizures, resulting in staring spells and alteration in behavior
CT scan or MRI of the brain	Intracranial mass	Behavior changes, irritability, lethargy, staring, or automatisms (partial seizures)
Chromosomal analysis	Fragile X syndrome	Intellectual disability, developmental and language delays, short attention span, hyperactivity, intolerance to change in routine, autistic-like behaviors, aggressive behavior, comorbidities of depression, obsessive-compulsive disorder, and sensory integration disorder (Jewell, 2014)

CT, computed tomography; MRI, magnetic resonance imaging.

Notable Clinical Findings

- History of mental illness (including hospitalization for mental illness)
- History of developmental delays
- Depression
- Parent reports that child/teen has extreme mood swings
- Child or adolescent is taking medication for mental health
- History of traumatic brain injury
- History of psychological trauma
- Refugee status
- Poor school performance
- Few friends
- Parent/teacher reports of "hyperactivity"
- Short attention span
- Few social supports
- Family poverty; stressful life circumstances
- Family has made frequent relocations
- History of school suspension/expulsion
- Child/teen avoids eye contact
- Child/teen is aggressive or uncooperative during interview
- History of problems with the law
- Child/teen uses alcohol, recreational or illegal drugs
- Child/teen appears intoxicated
- History of eating disorder
- History of sexual abuse
- Evidence of self-injury
- History of conduct disorder
- Recent loss of significant other
- Morbid obesity
- Child expresses suicidal or homicidal thoughts

References

Aguirre, B., & Smith, B. D. (2007). Handling young patients who cut themselves. *The Clinical Advisor, 10*(8), 64–69.

American Academy of Pediatrics. (2014). *AAP updates schedule of screening and assessments for well-child visits.* Retrieved from http://www.aap.org/en-us/about-the-aap/aap-press-room/pages/AAP-Updates-Schedule-of-Screening-and-Assessments-for-Well-Child-Visits.aspx#sthash.TrxxnnUR.dpuf

American Psychiatric Association. (2013). *Diagnostic and statistical manual of mental disorders* (5th ed.). Washington, DC: American Psychiatric Publishing, Inc.

Anxiety and Depression Association of America. (2014). *Facts and statistics.* Retrieved from http://www.adaa.org/about-adaa/press-room/facts-statistics

Bernstein, B. E. (2013). *Separation anxiety and school refusal.* Retrieved from http://emedicine.medscape.com/article/916737-overview

Bernstein, B. E. (2014). *Anorexia nervosa.* Retrieved from http://emedicine.medscape.com/article/912187-overview

Bothe, D., & Olness, K. (2007). Worried sick: Anxiety among youth. Part I. *Contemporary Pediatrics, 24*(7), 58–63.

Butler, A. M., & Malone, K. (2013). Attempted suicide v. non-suicidal self-injury: Behaviour, syndrome or diagnosis? *British Journal of Psychiatry, 202,* 324–325.

Centers for Disease Control and Prevention. (2012). *Overweight and obesity.* Retrieved from http://www.cdc.gov/obesity/childhood/basics.html

Centers for Disease Control and Prevention. (2013). *Injury center: Violence prevention. Youth violence: National statistics. Five leading causes of deaths among persons ages 10–24 years, 2010.* Retrieved from http://www.cdc.gov/violenceprevention/youthviolence/stats_at-a_glance/lcd_10-24.html

Centers for Disease Control and Prevention. (2014a). *Adolescent and school health: Childhood obesity facts.* Retrieved from http://www.cdc.gov/healthyyouth/obesity/facts.htm

Centers for Disease Control and Prevention. (2014b). *Injury center: Suicide prevention.* Retrieved from http://www.cdc.gov/violenceprevention/pub/youth_suicide.html

Chartier, M., Walker, J. R., & Naimark B. (2011). Health risk behaviors and mental health problems as mediators of the relationship between childhood abuse and adult health. *American Journal of Public Health, 99*(5), 847–854.

Cottrell, L., Nield, L., & Perkins, K. C. (2006). Effective interviewing and counseling of the adolescent patient. *Pediatric Annals, 35*(3), 164–172.

D'Onofrio, A. A. (2007). Introduction: Self-injury on the front lines. In A. A. D'Onofrio (Ed.), *Adolescent self-injury: A comprehensive guide for counselors and health professionals* (pp. 3–18). New York, NY: Springer.

Giardino, A. P., & Benton, T. D. (2014). *Pediatric depression.* Retrieved from http://emedicine.medscape.com/article/914192-overview

Ginsburg, G., & Grover, R. (2005). Assessing and treating social phobia in children and adolescents. *Pediatric Annals, 34*(2), 119–127.

Jewell, J. A. (2014). *Fragile X syndrome.* Retrieved from http://emedicine.medscape.com/article/943776-overview

Johnson, C. P., Meyers, S. M., & the American Academy of Pediatrics Council on Children with Disabilities. (2010). Statement of reaffirmation: Identification and evaluation of children with autism spectrum disorders. *Pediatrics, 120*(5), 1183–1215.

Lubit, R. H., & Giardino, E. R. (2014). *Posttraumatic stress disorder in children.* Retrieved from http://emedicine.medscape.com/article/918844-overview

Merikangas, K. R., He, J., Burstein, M., Swanson, S. A., Avenevoli, S., Cui, L., . . . Swendsen, J. (2010). Lifetime prevalence of mental disorders in U.S. adolescents: Results from the National Comorbidity Survey Replication–Adolescent Supplement (NCS-A). *Journal of the American Academy of Child & Adolescent Psychiatry, 49*(10), 980–989.

Nanda, S., & Konnur, N. (2006). Adolescent drug & alcohol use in the 21st century. *Pediatric Annals, 35*(3), 193–199.

National Action Alliance for Suicide Prevention: Youth in Contact with the Juvenile Justice System Task Force. (2013). *Screening and assessment for suicide prevention: Tools and procedures for risk identification among juvenile justice youth.* Washington, DC: Author.

Ogden C. L., Carroll, M. D., Kit, B. K., & Flegal, K. M. (2014). Prevalence of childhood and adult obesity in the United States, 2011–2012. *Journal of the American Medical Association, 311*(8), 806–814.

Perou, R., Bitsko, R. H., Blumberg, S. J., Pastor, P., Ghandour, R. M., Gfroerer J. C., . . . Huang, L. N. (2013). Mental health surveillance among children—United States, 2005–2011. *Morbidity and Mortality Weekly Report (MMWR), 62*(2), 1–35.

Rogers, E. S., & Spalding, S. L. (2014). *Dysthymic disorder.* Retrieved from http://emedicine.medscape.com/article/913941-overview

Schapiro, N. A. (2005). Bipolar disorders in children and adolescents. *Journal of Pediatric Health Care, 19*(3), 131–141.

Schneier, F. (2013). *Social anxiety disorder: Epidemiology, clinical manifestations, and diagnosis.* Retrieved from http://www.uptodate.com/contents/social-anxiety-disorder-epidemiology-clinical-manifestations-and-diagnosis?source=search_result&search=social+anxiety&selectedTitle=2~150

Schwartz, S. M. (2013). *Obesity in children.* Retrieved from http://emedicine.medscape.com/article/985333-overview

Stafford, B., Talmi, A., & Burstein, A. (2012). Child and adolescent psychiatric disorders & psychosocial aspects of pediatrics. In W. W. Hay, M. J. Levin, R. R. Deterding, M. J. Abzug, & J. M. Sondheimer (Eds.), *Current pediatric diagnosis & treatment* (21st ed., pp. 179–222). New York, NY: McGraw-Hill.

U.S. Department of Health and Human Services. (2014). *Substance abuse.* Retrieved from http://www.hhs.gov/ash/oah/adolescent-health-topics/substance-abuse

Wilkes, M. A., & Spratt, E. G. (2014). *Pediatric bulimia.* Retrieved from http://emedicine.medscape.com/article/913721-overview#a0156

World Health Organization. (2012). *Risks to mental health: An overview of vulnerabilities and risk factors.* Retrieved from http://www.who.int/mental_health/mhgap/risks_to_mental_health_EN_27_08_12.pdf

Yager, J., Scher, L. M., Hilty, D. M., & Osterhout, C. I. (2014). *Bulimia nervosa.* Retrieved from http://emedicine.medscape.com/article/286485-overview

Assessment of Child Abuse and Neglect

One of the most critical assessments the pediatric health care provider can make is to determine whether a child is being emotionally, verbally, physically, or sexually victimized. In 2011, nearly 3.7 million children in the United States underwent a child protective services (CPS) investigation; approximately 681,000 children were confirmed victims of maltreatment. There were 1,750 child deaths from abuse in 2011; 81.6% of these children were younger than age 4 years (U.S. Department of Health and Human Services Administration on Children, Youth and Families [USDHHS/ACF], 2012).

At each health maintenance health visit, the pediatric provider must screen for risk factors for child abuse and neglect, assess for abusive discipline practices, and teach families about age-appropriate behavior, normal developmental milestones, and alternatives to corporal punishment. Pediatric health care providers must also be able to recognize signs of neglect, and emotional and verbal mistreatment; differentiate intentional from unintentional injuries; and recognize signs of sexual abuse. This screening is vital as children who are victims of abuse or neglect are at high risk for developing both serious physical and psychosocial complications.

TYPES OF CHILD MALTREATMENT

There are five types of child maltreatment: neglect, physical abuse, verbal abuse, emotional abuse, and sexual abuse. It is important to note that emotional abuse is a component of all types of child maltreatment.

Neglect

Child neglect involves *acts of omission*, such as deprivation of basic necessities, including clean and safe housing and the provision of adequate amounts of nutritional food, basic hygiene, weather-appropriate clothing, education, and emotional support. Neglect also includes poor or inadequate supervision. Frequently, family poverty and parental knowledge deficits are factors that lead to child neglect (Block, Krebs, & the Committee on Child Abuse and Neglect, & the Committee on Nutrition, 2009). For example, while a severe diaper rash may result from parental negligence, it may also result from poverty (e.g., families cannot afford disposable diapers or a washing machine).

Various subtypes of neglect exist. *Emotional neglect* results from the parent or caregiver failing to meet the child's emotional needs in age-appropriate ways, such as ignoring the child, failing to provide emotional support, or being emotionally unavailable. *Medical neglect* is failure to obtain necessary health maintenance or episodic care for the child (e.g., immunization delays, failure to follow prescribed health recommendations). *Educational neglect* is the failure to ensure that a child attends school each day or to adhere to any special education needs set forth by the teacher or school district. *Supervisory neglect* often results from parental substance abuse, mental illness, or depression; for example, a young child is left with a person who is unable to care for small children. Supervisory neglect also involves failure to provide age-appropriate supervision to infants or young children (e.g., letting the child play alone near the street or a swimming pool; leaving a young child unattended in a bathtub, in the home, or in a vehicle). In older children, supervisory neglect may entail leaving a child alone with guns, allowing underage alcohol or drug use, and allowing long periods of unsupervised time on the Internet or at the mall (Hymel et al., 2006).

Another form of neglect is *exposure to known hazards*. Examples include in utero drug exposure; exposure to hazards in the home, such a lead or other poisons; smoking around children; allowing children to ride in a vehicle without a car seat or seatbelt; allowing children to ride a bicycle without a helmet; and exposure to domestic violence (Dubowitz, 2004).

The most extreme form of child neglect is *child abandonment*. This occurs when a parent does not retrieve a child who has been left in the care of friends or relatives or abandons a child outside the parameters of safe relinquishment provided by law. In the past decade, safe-haven relinquishment procedures have been developed in all 50 states to prevent unsafe infant abandonment and infanticide. The specific laws vary state to state regarding who may relinquish the child and where. In general, under these laws, new mothers can anonymously relinquish their newborn without fear of prosecution. Infant relinquishment must take place at locations to which the safe-haven laws apply, such as police stations, hospitals, or firehouses (USDHHS/ACF, 2013).

Physical Abuse

Physical abuse is the *nonaccidental* injury of a child by an older child (e.g., sibling) or an adult (e.g., a parent, relative, babysitter). Physical injuries include, but are not limited to, punching, beating, kicking, biting, hair-pulling, burning, shaking, throwing, stabbing, choking, and hitting (e.g., with a hand, belt, or stick). Any injury to a child is considered abuse whether or not there was an intent to harm before the injury occurred (Paulk, 2004).

In some families, *corporal punishment* is used to discipline children, raising questions for the health care provider about what constitutes physical abuse as defined by societal and cultural norms. Straus (2001, p. 4) defines corporal punishment as "the use of physical force with the intention of causing a child to experience pain, but not injury, for the purpose of correction or control of the child's behavior." The most common types of corporal punishment used are spanking, slapping, roughly shoving, and hitting, often with objects (i.e., hair brush, belt, paddle) (Straus, 2001).

Munchausen syndrome by proxy (MSP) is a form of physical abuse in which one person, most often the child's mother, purposely causes the child to be ill; this is also a form of emotional abuse (Abdulhamid, 2013). The average age of a child victim of MSP is 48.6 months (Abdulhamid, 2013). Often, the perpetrator has a medical background, which facilitates making the false history sound credible. The signs and symptoms demonstrated by the child are only witnessed by the perpetrator, who appears quite concerned about the child's illness. Signs and symptoms disappear when the child is separated from the perpetrator. Children who are made intentionally ill by their mothers may be subjected to needless laboratory and diagnostic studies, hospitalizations, and even surgery. Historical and physical findings of MSP are listed in Table 24.1.

Verbal Abuse

Verbal abuse involves a deliberate attempt on the part of the perpetrator to belittle a child or destroy his or her self-esteem. This can include aggressive scolding, screaming, swearing, blaming, criticizing, threatening, name-calling, insulting, mocking, excessive teasing, ridiculing, shaming, humiliation, or harassment (Teicher, Samson, Polcari, & McGreenery, 2006). It is important for the pediatric health care provider to watch for clues that a child is being verbally abused, even though this abuse may be difficult to quantify. Children and adolescent who are verbally abused are more likely to suffer from anxiety and depression as adults (Sachs-Ericsson, Verona, Joiner, & Preacher, 2006; Wang & Kenny, 2013). Verbal and emotional abuse are similar, and overlap is common.

Emotional Abuse

Emotional abuse can be even more harmful to a child than other forms of abuse because of the way in which it damages self-esteem. This type of abuse involves a pattern of behavior, usually perpetrated by a parent, caregiver, or peer, that aims to belittle, berate, humiliate, or criticize. Exposing a child to domestic violence can also be considered emotional abuse (Hornor, 2012a). While emotional abuse always accompanies other forms of abuse, it can occur alone. Examples of emotional abuse are listed in Box 24.1.

TABLE 24.1	Findings in Munchausen Syndrome by Proxy
HISTORICAL FINDINGS	**EXAMPLES OF POSSIBLE PHYSICAL FINDINGS**
• Symptoms are unusual, rare, or inconsistent with clinical, laboratory, and diagnostic study findings • Symptoms disappear when caretaker is absent • Parent has medical knowledge or background • Parent requests many diagnostic tests to be done • Child does not tolerate tests or treatments well • Child is unresponsive to treatment • Child has numerous past hospitalizations • Parents are extremely concerned for child	• Inconsistencies between history and physical findings • Seizures witnessed only by parent • Poisonings with medication, salt, or hydrocarbons • Recurrent apparent life-threatening events or apnea (because of suffocations) • Vomiting (caused by poisonings) • Recurrent diarrhea (induced by laxatives) • Multiple infections with unusual pathogens in unusual sites • Hypoglycemia (from receiving insulin or oral hypoglycemics) • Hematuria or guaiac-positive stools without renal or gastrointestinal abnormality • CNS depression produced by drugs

CNS, central nervous system.
Source: Abdulhamid (2013).

BOX 24.1 Examples of Emotional Abuse

- Isolating
- Ignoring
- Use of the silent treatment
- Threatening
- Rejecting
- Excessive criticism
- Betraying
- Belittling
- Taunting
- Having developmentally inappropriate expectations
- Excessive control
- Withholding love, friendship, support, or affection
- Corrupting
- Terrorizing
- Pressuring
- Exposure to domestic violence

Bullying, another form of emotional abuse, is seen when a child or adolescent is targeted by another person and teased, tormented, criticized, humiliated, or even physically bullied (e.g., tripped, hit, pushed) (Governo & Siewers, 2008). This can be perpetrated by a parent, stepparent, sibling, extended family member, teacher, or peer. Bullying can also be perpetrated by more than one person, as for example, when a child is shunned from a friendship or clique. Children and adolescents can also be harassed, bullied, threatened, and demeaned using the Internet through chat room talk, blogs, and e-mail messages (Governo & Siewers, 2008; McColgan & Giardino, 2005). All types of emotional abuse impair a child's self-esteem and often have lifelong negative consequences (Hornor, 2012a).

Sexual Abuse

Sexual abuse occurs when a child is forced to engage in sexual activity by someone who *knows* the child, such as a parent, stepparent, sibling, or other relative. Because the offender is known, the child is coerced into secrecy. Sexual abuse of a child typically occurs over a period of time and can include exhibitionism, fondling a child's genitals, penetration, rape, incest, sodomy, sexual innuendo, exposure to pornography in print or via the Internet, or prostitution (Paulk, 2004).

EPIDEMIOLOGY OF CHILD ABUSE AND NEGLECT

Child abuse and neglect occur in all races and socioeconomic groups, with African American, American Indian, Alaska Native, and multiracial children having the highest rates of victimization, at 14.3, 11.4, and 10.1 victims, respectively, per 1,000 children in the population of the same race or ethnicity (USDHHS/

ACF, 2012). Neglect is the most common form of child maltreatment (USDHHS/ACF, 2012). The highest rates of child maltreatment occur in girls (51.1%) and children younger than age 2 years (USDHHS/ACF, 2012). Of these confirmed cases, 61% involved child neglect, and 15.1% involved more than one type of child maltreatment (USDHHS/ACF, 2012). Risk factors for child abuse involve the interaction of the parent, child, and their social environment.

Parental Characteristics

Certain characteristics of the parent increase the risk for abuse or neglect of a child. In 2011, data from the U.S. Department of Health and Human Services revealed that of the parents who neglected or abused their children, 53.6% were women, 45.1% were men, and 1.3% were gender unknown (USDHHS/ACF, 2012). In addition, parental characteristics such as youth and inexperience, poor parenting skills, low level of education, knowledge deficits regarding normal child development milestones, single parenthood and lack of support system all increase the child's risk for abuse or neglect (Centers for Disease Control and Prevention [CDC], 2014).

Parents who abuse their children were also likely abused themselves as children, never having observed a positive parenting role model (CDC, 2014; Lutenbacher, Cohen, & Conner, 2004). Parental substance abuse is another major risk factor strongly associated with child maltreatment and neglect (CDC, 2014; USDHHS/ACF, 2012). In addition, parents at risk for abusing their children may look to the child to fill their emotional needs, a type of role-reversal that constitutes emotional abuse of the child. Maternal depression is another risk factor of great concern, particularly postpartum depression. Women who are depressed are more likely to abuse or neglect their children; in the first year of a child's life, its mother may still be suffering from postpartum depression (Johnson & Flake, 2007). This is significant because physical injuries to neonates or infants, especially shaking injuries, are more likely to be fatal (Ashton, 2010). During the health care encounter, the provider is able to observe and assess the degree of emotional availability on the part of the parent. A poor parent–child relationship can lead to negative effects on the child's socioemotional development. A summary of risk factors that increase the potential for the parent to abuse the child are listed in Box 24.2.

Characteristics of the Child

Certain characteristics of the child may place him or her at risk for maltreatment or neglect. Infants and toddlers, for example, are at high risk for serious physical abuse because of their complete dependence on the parent, communication through crying, the challenges of toilet training, and temper tantrums. Physical or mental disability, such as intellectual disability, mental illness, vision or hearing impairment, learning or

---

BOX 24.2 Parent/Caregiver Risk Factors for Abuse or Neglect

- Substance abuse
- Poverty
- Poor parenting skills
- Lack of knowledge of normal growth and development; unrealistic expectations
- Low level of education
- Low intelligence
- Parental/caregiver developmental delay
- Single parent
- Adolescent mother
- Parent of many children
- Parent of premature or sick infant with history of prolonged hospitalization
- Domestic violence
- Depression
- Mental illness
- Anger management issues; poor impulse control
- Low self-esteem
- Social isolation; poor social supports
- Unemployment
- Homelessness
- History of child abuse or neglect as a child
- Previous involvement with child protective services

Sources: Block, Krebs, and the Committee on Child Abuse and Neglect and the Committee on Nutrition (2009); Moore and Florsheim (2008); Paulk (2004).

---

physical disability, behavior problems, or chronic medical problems also predispose a child to abuse or neglect (USDHHS/ACF, 2012). In addition, children who have a history of prematurity or perinatal illness requiring a prolonged hospital stay have a higher risk for abuse and neglect because of impaired parent–infant bonding (Block et al., 2009).

Environmental Stressors

Adverse living conditions can predispose a child to abuse or neglect. Households in which domestic violence takes place put the children at risk for physical and emotional abuse or injury (Berkowitz, 2005; CDC, 2014; Hornor, 2005a). The chronic stress related to unemployment or poverty, including substandard housing, crowded living conditions, a large number of dependent children, and hunger, can lead parents to lash out at their children impulsively. The presence of a nonbiologically related father figure living in the home (e.g., the mother's male partner) also increases the child's risk for abuse or neglect (CDC, 2014).

Cultural and Religious Considerations

When evaluating a child for suspected child abuse, it is imperative to consider the family's cultural and religious beliefs. Certain folk remedies, for example, *coin rubbing* ("cao gio") and *cupping*, may mimic physical abuse. Coin rubbing, a traditional Southeast Asian nonabusive healing practice, involves the vigorous rubbing of the edge of a coin on the child's anterior and posterior chest to treat fever, fatigue, or cough. This leaves a pattern of linear bruises in the shape of a fir tree. Cupping, which is primarily used to treat respiratory complaints, involves placing a glass cup on the skin on the child's forehead or trunk; a candle is then lit, creating suction that leaves an area of ecchymosis and petechiae in the shape of a circle. *Moxibustion* is a traditional Chinese healing practice often performed with acupuncture; it involves burning the skin, which may produce scars after the burn is healed. *Azarcon*, or *greta*, both Mexican folk remedies, contain lead and may lead to unintentional lead poisoning of the child. Religious traditions regarding fasting during religious holidays may be the cause of temporary dehydration, a factor to consider when examining the child.

Cultural beliefs about corporal punishment are diverse. Corporal punishment is a common practice in African American (Ibanez, Borrego, Pemberton, & Terao, 2006) and Caribbean cultures (Westby, 2007). Religious beliefs may also influence the practice of corporal punishment, as parents who believe in biblical inerrancy or literalism are more likely to use corporal punishment and physically abuse their children (Socolar, Cabinum-Foeller, & Sinal, 2008). Health care providers must respect a family's religious beliefs but must always remember that the child's physical and psychological well-being are paramount in all circumstances.

ASSESSMENT OF CHILD MALTREATMENT AND NEGLECT

The pediatric health care provider may incidentally find signs of abuse or neglect when children come for health maintenance or episodic visits. The child may present with an acute physical injury or psychosocial complaints that result from longstanding verbal or emotional abuse. To ensure that an accurate diagnosis is made and to avoid false allegations, some of the child's past and current history must be reviewed. When obtaining any part of the history with suspected child abuse or neglect, it is essential for the health care provider to do so in a sensitive, nonjudgmental manner. This approach enhances provider–caregiver trust and conveys to the child and parent that the health care provider is there to help.

Obtaining a History

General History

Numerous portions of the child's medical and social history are extremely important when determining if a child has been neglected or abused. These factors include the child's past medical history including any history of past injuries; the social history, the family's discipline practices, and an assessment of the child's behavior.

Past Medical History

The child's past medical history is a necessary component of the assessment to identify risk factors and red flags for abuse and neglect and to diagnose diseases that may mimic abusive injuries. The child's birth and neonatal histories are reviewed, noting any history of prenatal drug exposure, prematurity or perinatal asphyxia. Children with special needs, such as those who have postnatal complications or chronic illnesses, are at high risk for abuse or neglect (USDHHS/ACF, 2012). Chronic respiratory illnesses such as asthma, allergies, ear infections, and sinusitis must be noted, especially if the parents or anyone else smoke in the home. Secondhand smoke exposure exacerbates chronic respiratory conditions in children (Best & the American Academy of Pediatrics Committee on Environmental Health, Committee on Native American Child Health, Committee on Adolescence, 2009). In some states, exposing a child to secondhand smoke constitutes child neglect (Jarvie & Malone, 2008).

Any medical conditions associated with clinical manifestations that could be mistaken for child maltreatment are noted, such as hemophilia A (factor VII deficiency) or hemophilia B (factor IX deficiency), both of which can lead to spontaneous bruising, pain, bleeding, pain and stiffness of the joints, intracranial bleeding, hemorrhage, spontaneous hematuria, and intramuscular hemorrhage (Zaiden et al., 2013a; Zaiden, Furlong, Crouch, & Besa, 2013b). Von Willebrand disease is another inherited bleeding disorder that can cause easy bruising, prolonged bleeding from wounds, and recurrent epistaxis (Geil, 2012). Osteogenesis imperfecta, also known as "brittle bone disease," is an autosomal recessive condition of abnormal collagen formation that results in fractures after minor trauma (Ramachandran, Achan, Jones, & Panchbhavi, 2012).

A history of past injuries should focus on the child's age at the time of injury, the mechanism of injury, and whether medical care was sought. A history of repeated injuries is a red flag for abuse. The dates and reasons for any hospitalizations are also assessed, with attention to whether the hospitalization was a result of injury or neglect. A history of any psychosocial illnesses is assessed, such as depression, anxiety disorders, phobias, or substance abuse, which may or may not be the result of child maltreatment. The child's immunization status is evaluated, noting any delays and determining if the delays are a result of medical neglect. The provider must note the reasons for any frequent emergency room use, as this may indicate injuries resulting from lack of supervision, intentional injuries, or medical neglect. The child's medications are reviewed, with the indications and side effects for each drug considered. Medications ordered for hyperactivity, anxiety, depression, or other psychosocial illnesses may be the cause or result of abuse. Side effects of certain drugs can cause irritability, hyperactivity, or restlessness, which may precipitate physical abuse in parents or caregivers with poor coping skills.

Social History

Many aspects of the child's family life and interactions at school are important when evaluating a child for emotional or physical abuse. The child's living situation is assessed for any predisposing factors for abuse (see section on Epidemiology of Child Abuse and Neglect), such as parental mental illness or depression, social isolation, economic difficulties, and lack of social supports. It is important to determine who lives in the home and each person's relationship to the child.

Parental substance abuse is a crucial assessment to make as this often results in child maltreatment or neglect. Children of parents who use drugs or alcohol to the extent that daily functioning is impaired may assume many parental responsibilities ("parentalized child"), a form of emotional abuse. School-aged and adolescent children are assessed for mental illness and substance abuse as well. Parental stress is an important risk factor for abuse; Box 24.3 provides a list of questions the provider can ask to determine the level of parental stress. Children who live in families where domestic violence takes place are at risk for being physically injured (Berkowitz, 2005) and also suffer emotional abuse as they witness the interpersonal violence between adults. Children who witness domestic violence are also at risk for posttraumatic stress disorder (PTSD) (Hornor, 2005a; Teicher et al., 2006). Mothers who are victims of domestic violence are also more likely than their counterparts to abuse their children physically or emotionally, even when they are in nonabusive relationships (Lutenbacher et al., 2004).

The presence of a gun in the home greatly increases a child's risk for harm, especially in homes where domestic violence takes place (Hemenway, Barber, &

BOX 24.3 Assessment of Parental Stress

- Does the parent have a steady source of income?
- Does the family have a stable place to live?
- Does the parent have a support system? Who or where?
- Does the parent engage in self-care activities, including getting enough rest and having a healthy diet as well as soothing, restful outlets for frustration?
- Does the parent take breaks (e.g., leave the child in the care of a trusted family member or friend) for an afternoon to de-stress?
- Does the parent cope with the stresses of parenting by using tobacco, drugs, or alcohol?
- Is the mother depressed? Has she seen a health care provider who has diagnosed her with postpartum depression? Is she being treated for it?
- Is there community support for the parents, such as parent support groups or parenting classes?

Miller, 2010). A child's school performance and relationships with friends at school are evaluated; difficulties in these areas can be a result of abuse or neglect.

Children who have lacked a consistent primary caregiver, such as those in foster care or orphanages, those who have been abandoned, or have a primary caregiver who is incarcerated or otherwise absent are at risk for attachment disorders. These social circumstances result in developmentally inappropriate attachments caused by either a lack of a primary caregiver or one disrupted attachment after the other. Previously considered one diagnosis, these psychological disorders are now divided into two separate diagnoses: reactive attachment disorder (RAD), and disinhibited social engagement disorder (DSED). Infants and children who display signs of RAD are often apathetic during interpersonal exchanges and disinterested in their surroundings, whereas those with DSED are indiscriminate with their affection, display no stranger anxiety, and readily interact with unknown persons (American Psychiatric Association [APA], 2013).

Caregiver Discipline Practices

The provider must elicit parental discipline practices to get a full picture of the family dynamic to assess risk for potential physical and psychological injury. It is imperative to ask about the parents' beliefs about corporal punishment and to gain a full understanding of what the parent's definition of corporal punishment is; this may range from minor spanking to severe beating with or without weapons. Reasons for and the frequency of corporal punishment must be determined. Questions should also be asked about shaking in children younger than 2 years of age. Parental triggers for the use of corporal punishment or shaking should be determined. For example, inconsolable crying, toileting accidents, messy or curious toddlers, temper tantrums, sibling fights, running into the street, and poor school performance are examples of parental triggers that may elicit the use of harsh discipline or corporal punishment. Hunger and fatigue are common reasons that young children cry or have a tantrum, which is normal, age-appropriate behavior. Any parental knowledge deficits regarding this behavior should be noted and appropriate education delivered. Likewise, spanking a 1-year-old child for soiling his or her pants reveals lack of knowledge about a toddler's ability to control the bowel and bladder. Parents should be asked what they do when their child cries inconsolably or has a temper tantrum and whether there is a "safe area" in the home in which the toddler can play, away from the stove, stairs, or electrical outlets; this obviates the need to "spank" to teach the child a "lesson." Safe outside play areas are also necessary, away from streets or alleys. The use of verbal reprimands and scolding are explored, as needed, to assess whether these practices

cross the line to harsh criticism, emotional isolation, or rejection, all of which constitute emotional abuse.

Behavioral History

The behavioral history provides critical information in the assessment of child maltreatment. At all developmental levels, deviations in developmentally normal behavior can be a sign of abuse or neglect. For example, infants who do not display stranger anxiety at the expected age demonstrate a lack of secure attachment to a primary caregiver, which is a sign of neglect. Similarly, curiosity about the genitals is developmentally normal for preschoolers, but knowledge of adult sexual behavior in this age group suggests sexual abuse. Any history of anger-based behaviors is noted, such as repeated fights at school, destruction of property, difficulty with relationships, and bullying. Nonsuicidal self-injury in adolescents can be associated with anger, depression, or loss, the origins of which should be investigated (Peterson, Freedenthal, Sheldon, & Anderson, 2008). Assessments of past episodes of suicide attempts are critical to the behavioral history, including the precipitating factors.

A history of cruelty to animals is very concerning because it shows a lack of empathy regarding pain and suffering, and is a red flag that the child has been mistreated. Juvenile animal abuse can result when children have been exposed to violence; this can later lead to violence toward human beings (Flynn, 2011; Muscari, 2004). Reports of deliberate fire setting are also an important part of the behavioral history; this can be symptomatic of extreme stress, rage, and revenge-seeking or be a sign of delinquent behavior, resulting from extreme family stress (Dadds & Fraser, 2006).

Interval History

When obtaining the interval history during a routine health maintenance visit, much information can be gleaned about the child's and family's life that may raise reds flags for abuse or neglect. Routine areas of health assessment, such as nutrition, elimination patterns, safety, sleep patterns, and the child's social and developmental history, may present red flags for abuse (Table 24.2). Developmental delays, such as lags in achieving age-appropriate motor, language, and social abilities, may result from neglect. Again, any parental knowledge deficits regarding age-appropriate behavior must be noted.

Assessing Neglect
History

Intentional neglect may be difficult to identify when obtaining the history because its causes are so closely related to poverty. The provider must focus on historical factors that overlap with risk factors for neglect and abuse. For example, it is important to determine

TABLE 24.2	Red Flags for Possible Abuse or Neglect Seen During Routine Assessment	
ASSESSMENT DOMAIN	**RED FLAGS FOR POSSIBLE ABUSE OR NEGLECT**
Elimination patterns	Chronic constipation or encopresis Nocturnal enuresis past age 5–6 years
Growth and development	Physical growth less than fifth percentile of NCHS growth charts Overweight or obesity Delay in achieving motor, language, and psychosocial developmental milestones Sexual precocity; knowledge of sexual matters inappropriate for age
Nutrition	Obesity Malnourishment Eating disorders Poor weight gain or growth failure Numerous, untreated dental caries or severe dental decay Bottle propping
Safety	Frequent injuries resulting from lack of age-appropriate supervision Frequent visits to emergency room or urgent care center for treatment of injuries Incidental finding of injuries during routine health care examination Finding of injuries in various stages of healing
Sleep	Sleep refusal Difficulty falling asleep Difficulty staying asleep Nightmares
Social	No stranger anxiety in an infant after age 7 months until preschool age Alcohol or drug abuse in child, teen, or parent or anyone else living in the home Poor school performance Depression in child or teen Maternal depression Suicide attempts by child, teen, or parent Child or teen runs away from home Cruelty to animals Homelessness Use of corporal punishment Domestic violence

NCHS, National Center for Health Statistics.

whether the child's primary caregiver suffers from mental illness or substance abuse, which increases a child's risk for neglect. The child's growth charts are reviewed, looking for evidence of poor growth. It is important to ask about bottle propping in infants, as well as any history of inconsistent or sporadic feeding of the child. Any history of repeated injuries is also important, as this may be the result of a lack of age-appropriate supervision. Assessment of any delays in seeking necessary medical or dental care, untreated medical or dental problems, a lack of necessary immunizations, or smoking around a child, particularly one with respiratory problems, must be included in the history. In older children, poor school performance may signal chronic truancy, a sign of neglect. Prolonged amounts of unsupervised screen time can also constitute neglect, particularly if the television programming is inappropriate for young children. Media violence has been shown to have numerous negative effects on children, including desensitization to violence, seeing violence as justified, viewing violence as a way of solving problems, perceiving the world as a violent and scary place, increasing aggressive behaviors, and seeing violence as something entertaining and funny (Christakis & Zimmerman, 2007). Prolonged screen time can also lead to overweight and obesity, a negative health consequence for the child that constitutes neglect (Christakis & Zimmerman, 2007; Dubowitz, 2004).

Behavioral Indicators

When assessing children who have been neglected, certain parent–child interactions are important to note. Impaired child–parent bonding as evidenced by poor eye contact between parent and child, lack or warmth or attentiveness to the child, and reacting minimally or ignoring a child's cries for hunger, thirst, or pain during the visit all are red flags for poor attachment or bonding.

During the health care visit, the health care provider may also note deficits in parenting skills and knowledge of age-appropriate behavior (Hornor, 2013). Neglected infants may appear listless and respond minimally to stimulation. Children who have poor attachment to a primary caregiver will not display stranger anxiety and may demonstrate affection indiscriminately (APA, 2013). This is particularly concerning in older infants when stranger anxiety is normally at its peak, because it shows that the child has no secure primary attachment.

Physical Examination

The physical examination of a neglected child often reveals poor hygiene, diaper rash, soiled diapers, dirty or inappropriate clothing (e.g., long-sleeved shirt in hot weather), indications of malnutrition, dental decay, or developmental delays. Infants and toddlers may appear excessively passive. Fatigue or listlessness may be noted. Children who have been in orphanages may also have positional plagiocephaly with accompanying hair loss in that area of the scalp as a result of lying in one spot in a crib or bed for prolonged periods of time.

Failure to Thrive

Failure to thrive (FTT) is demonstrated as poor weight gain or severe weight loss, developmental delays, and abnormal behaviors, all of which can be caused by neglect. These behaviors may be accompanied by a lack of eye contact, smiling, or vocalization; no stranger anxiety; a disinterest in social interactions; or an aversion to being touched. Physical findings may include loss of subcutaneous tissue, loose skinfolds, dull eyes, or oral lesions secondary to malnutrition. FTT is defined as decreased growth or a cessation of growth over time (e.g., weight-for-age falling two major percentile lines on the National Center for Health Statistics [NCHS] growth charts from previously established growth patterns) or weight less than 80% of ideal body weight for age (Block et al., 2009). The cause of FTT is multifactorial, involving poor nutrition, most often resulting from poverty and some level of altered parenting and neglect (see Box 24.1). FTT can be fatal if it is not recognized and treated.

Differential Diagnoses

Developmental delays, malnutrition, and a failure to gain weight can result from organic causes, such as those that cause chronic hypoxia or malabsorption. Examples include congenital heart disease, cleft lip or palate, cystic fibrosis, sickle cell disease, gastroesophageal reflux, celiac disease, lead poisoning, or human immunodeficiency virus (HIV)/acquired immunodeficiency syndrome.

Assessing Physical Abuse

History

When a child presents with a suspicious injury, a complete history must be obtained from the person bringing the child for medical attention. A complete description of the injury is necessary, along with an inquiry regarding who was present to witness the injury. Several critical questions must be asked to determine if the injury is unintentional or inflicted:

- Is the historian the child's primary caregiver?
- Does the history match the type and degree of injury? Inconsistencies between the history and type and degree of injury are the most important factor to consider when making the decision to notify CPS.
- Is the child developmentally capable of injuring himself or herself in the manner described? Suspicion for abuse is raised when the parent or caregiver states that an injury occurred during motor activity of which the child is not yet capable (e.g., falling after climbing in a preambulatory infant).
- Is the parent unable to explain fully how the injury happened? An absent history raises a red flag for abuse.
- Do the parents give conflicting accounts of what happened?
- Does the history change when told more than once or told to different health care providers?
- Does the child, when interviewed with the parent out of the room, plainly state that he or she was hit or injured in some way?
- Was there any delay is seeking medical attention for the injury? This is a red flag for abuse, presenting the possibility that the abusive parent or caregiver hoped that the problem would resolve on its own.
- Does the child have a history of multiple injuries or ingestions, necessitating visits to the emergency room or urgent care center? At minimum, this is a red flag for neglect.
- Was the reason for seeking health care something other than the injury? For example, was the chief complaint an upper respiratory infection, and a fractured radius was found incidentally?
- Is the parent uncomfortable, irritable, or defensive when questioned about the injury?
- Does the parent show concern, attention, and love to the child, or is the parent preoccupied, withdrawn, or annoyed?
- How is the child behaving toward the parent? Clinging? Submissive? Afraid? Is the child trying to make eye contact?

When the child is developmentally capable, beginning approximately at age 3 years, he or she should be interviewed separately from the parent to allow the child to speak without any fear of intimidation and to assess the compatibility of the histories. Open-ended questions are used such as, "What happened to your arm?" These types of questions do not lead the child to any specific answer. Leading questions such as, "Did your mom's boyfriend burn your arm?" are biased, and a young child may then answer in the affirmative in an effort to please the provider, even if the answer is not yes. Examples of less direct questions that may provide clues that a child is being abused include: "Are you afraid of anyone?" "Does anyone ever hurt you?" "Does anyone make you keep secrets?" Affirmative answers to any of these questions require further investigation regarding the details of the abuse (Hornor, 2013).

Behavioral Indicators

While gathering the history and conducting the physical examination of suspected physical abuse, the behavioral demeanor of both the child and parents is assessed. The child may display excessive fearfulness of the parent, apathy, or withdrawal, or may cry or cling to the parent. The parent may minimize the child's injuries or blame a sibling for the injury. Some parents may be overly attentive to the child, particularly in the case of MSP.

Physical Examination

It is common for young children to be injured accidentally during play or as part of their activities of daily life. It is therefore essential for the pediatric health care provider to be able to discern unintentional from intentional injuries in children. To do this, the provider must be thoroughly familiar with child growth and development so that a determination can be made as to whether the history provided is compatible with the injury observed. In addition to examining any obvious injuries, a thorough, head-to-toe physical examination must be conducted on all children in whom physical abuse is suspected. Some injuries are readily apparent, such as burns or bruises; others are not visible during a quick overall inspection, such as intraocular hemorrhages. While conducting the physical assessment, the examiner must compare the history to the physical findings, and evaluate the behavior and demeanor of the parent and child, watching for behavioral signs of abuse. The provider must also be able to recognize conditions that can mimic physical abuse, such as osteogenesis imperfecta, bleeding disorders, birthmarks, or folk remedies or cultural practices that may leave marks on the skin.

General Assessments • A current weight, length or height, weight for stature, and body mass index (BMI) are obtained to evaluate whether the child's growth is within normal limits. Overweight and obesity are prevalent in children but may also signal neglect (Dubowitz, 2004) or depression related to abuse, including sexual abuse (Irish, Kobayashi, & Delahanty, 2010). Physical growth below the third to fifth percentile on the NCHS growth charts may be within normal limits for a particular child, or may result from organic causes, such as malabsorption disorders, congenital hyperthyroidism, or FTT.

Bruises • When evaluating bruises in children, it is important to consider the location, size, shape, color, and pattern of the bruise (Hornor, 2005b). The child's age must also be considered. In healthy, ambulatory children, bruises normally occur in the course of play and activities of daily living and tend to be small. Bruises over bony prominences such as the extensor surfaces of the lower leg, knees, elbows, and forehead are the most common sites of *accidental* bruising in childhood (Thompson, 2005). Bruises that occur on a child who is not yet cruising or walking should raise a red flag for abuse unless the child has an underlying bleeding disorder (Mudd & Findlay, 2004).

Inflicted bruises often occur on the chest, abdomen, back of the body, or soft tissue areas of the face, ears, neck, upper arm, inner thigh, genital area, or buttocks (Figure 24.1) (Hornor, 2012b; Thompson, 2005). Bruises on the genital area or buttocks are always suspicious because the child's diaper or pants should afford some protection to the skin over this area (Figure 24.2). Bruises to the pinna or earlobe may occur with firm pinching or twisting. Bruising to the entire ear area may result from punching the child in the ears ("boxing" the ears); this can also cause bleeding behind the tympanic membrane (hemotympanum).

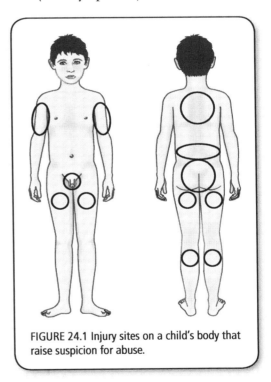

FIGURE 24.1 Injury sites on a child's body that raise suspicion for abuse.

Previously, it was thought that the age of bruises could be estimated based on their color, but research has shown that this practice is not fully reliable (Thompson, 2005). The color of a bruise is affected by the location of the bruise, the child's skin pigmentation, the intensity of force that caused the bruise, whether the child is on any anticoagulants, and whether the child has an underlying bleeding disorder (Mudd & Findlay, 2004; Thompson, 2005). Multiple bruises in different places usually indicate repeated intentional injury. The shape and pattern of the bruise are also an essential part of the assessment, as these can provide clues to the type of weapon used to inflict

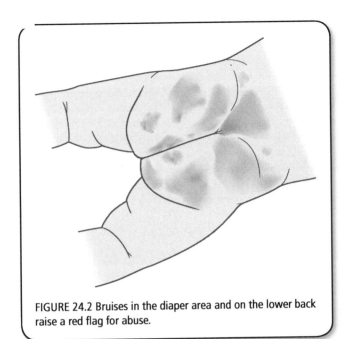

FIGURE 24.2 Bruises in the diaper area and on the lower back raise a red flag for abuse.

the injury (see Pattern Injuries, later). If a child presents with one or more suspicious bruises or accompanying lacerations, the child's entire body must be examined for any further injuries.

Burns • When assessing burns in children, a review of the history is essential to distinguish intentional from accidental burns. Important information includes the child's age, the consistency of the history, the pattern and location of the burn, and whether there was any delay in seeking medical attention (Hornor, 2012b). Several factors must be considered when evaluating burns in children: (a) the age of the child, to determine developmental capabilities and estimate the thickness of the skin; (b) the length of contact with the heat source; (c) the temperature of the heat source; and (d) the blood supply to the affected tissue (Reece & Christian, 2008). Most cases of inflicted burns involve children younger than 3 years because of the child's complete dependence on the caregiver, potential inconsolable crying, or toilet training challenges.

Accidental burns tend to be asymmetrical, irregular (e.g., occur in a splash pattern), partial thickness, and reflect the child's motor capabilities; thus, accidental burns most often occur on the face, neck, trunk, or upper extremities (Thompson, 2005). Accidental burns are worse at the top of the body and form an inverted triangle, as the liquid flows downward, for example, as when a toddler pulls a pot of boiling water down from the stove (Hornor, 2012b).

Intentional burns are often symmetrical, full-thickness with uniform depth, and may be older than the historian indicates, dirty, or infected. Immersion burns are those that occur when a child is forcibly placed in scalding hot water; these are the most common type of

inflicted burns in children (Thompson, 2005). These burns have a clear line of demarcation in a "stocking" or "glove" pattern. Another type of immersion burn occurs when a child is submerged into a bathtub of scalding water. When the child is placed in the water, he or she instinctively draws up his or her hands and feet while the perpetrator forcibly holds the child down, causing a distinctive burn pattern known as the "doughnut"; the outer buttocks, upper thighs, and genital area are burned with the central area of the buttocks less burned as a result of being held against the comparatively cooler bottom of the tub (Figure 24.3).

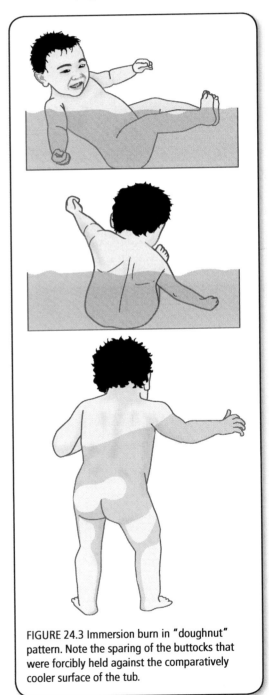

FIGURE 24.3 Immersion burn in "doughnut" pattern. Note the sparing of the buttocks that were forcibly held against the comparatively cooler surface of the tub.

Contact burns are the second most common type of inflicted burns in children (Thompson, 2005). These burns include cigarette or cigar burns that characteristically result in small, crater-like, deep, indurated, circular burns (Figure 24.4). These burns are approximately 8 to 10 mm in diameter and are typically found on areas of the body that are concealed by clothing, the palms of the hands, soles of the feet, torso, and buttocks.

Branding injuries from a hot object often reflect the shape of the item used to burn the child, such as a lighter, an iron, or the hot grill of a hair dryer (Figure 24.5) (Thompson, 2005).

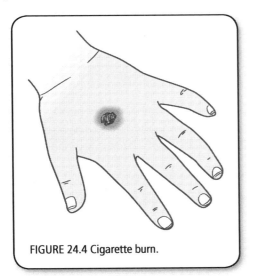

FIGURE 24.4 Cigarette burn.

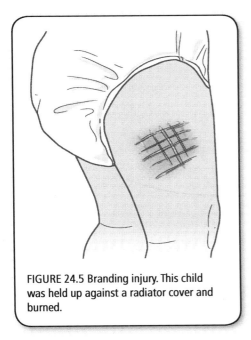

FIGURE 24.5 Branding injury. This child was held up against a radiator cover and burned.

Oral Injuries • Injuries to the mouth can manifest as oral bruises, lacerations, or a torn frenulum. Lacerations and bruising to the lips can occur with a firm blow to the mouth. Bruising around the mouth or lips can result when an adult places a hand firmly over an infant or child's mouth to silence crying. Oral lacerations occur when sharp objects are firmly pushed into the child's mouth. For example, a torn frenulum can also be caused by vigorously pushing a child's mouth closed or by forcibly placing a pacifier or bottle in an infant's mouth.

Pattern Injuries • Pattern injuries are bruises, lacerations, abrasions, or other soft tissue injuries that form recognizable marks on the child's body in the shape of the weapon used to inflict the injury. For example, small, oval-shaped bruises on the upper arms of infants may be the result of the perpetrator's firm grip during shaking or forcible restraint. Facial bruises may reflect a pattern of the perpetrator's fingers after a forceful slapping. Bruises in the shape of a loop or parallel lines, most often on the child's back or buttocks, may have been inflicted by a coat hanger, rope, or looped electrical cord (Figure 24.6). Other pattern injuries include bruises in the shape of the heel of a shoe, spoon handles, paddles, belts, or chains. Strangulation or restraint marks may manifest as circular abrasions around the neck, ankles, or wrists if a child has been choked or tied down (Figure 24.7). In some instances, the item used to restrain the child may be tied so tightly that circulation may be compromised to the distal portion of the extremity.

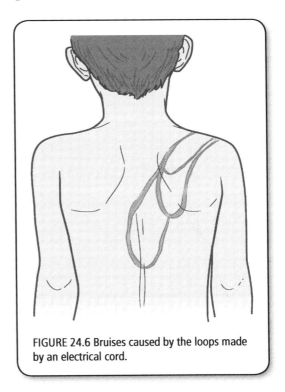

FIGURE 24.6 Bruises caused by the loops made by an electrical cord.

Bite Marks • The ability to recognize human bites is essential for all pediatric health care providers. Some parents or caregivers, in an attempt to cover the abuse, will state during the history that the child was bitten by an animal. However, humans have four incisors and short canines while dogs have six incisors and long canines (Fischer & Hammel, 2003). Human bite

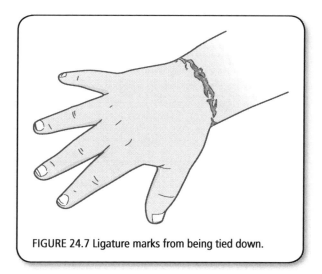

FIGURE 24.7 Ligature marks from being tied down.

marks occur in a circular, oval, or crescent-shaped pattern with visible teeth marks within these areas. The severity of a human bite depends on the location of the bite and the amount of force used to bite the child. It is important to distinguish a child's bite from that of an adult. Bites by children who still have their deciduous teeth are more superficial and have a distance of less than 3 cm between the canines. Adult bites tend to be deeper and have a space of more than 3 cm between the canines (Shah & Lucchesi, 2006). Preverbal toddlers often bite as a way of expressing frustration. There is never a plausible reason for a child to present with an adult bite. Once an injury is determined to be an adult human bite, the wound is swabbed for DNA; this assists forensic and law enforcement personnel in identifying the perpetrator. The bite is then measured and photographed for analysis by a forensic dentist for identification of the perpetrator. The bite should then be cleaned and dressed to prevent infection.

Eye Injuries • Intentional injuries to the eye can present with or without external evidence of injury. For this reason, all children with signs of physical abuse should have a funduscopic examination. Possible external injuries of the eye include corneal abrasions, bruises beneath one or both eyes ("black eye"), orbital fracture, subconjunctival hemorrhage, or hyphema. These injuries can occur when a child is struck with a closed fist or weapon. Internal injuries of the eye include retinal hemorrhages, which occur with severe shaking or head injuries. Retinal detachment can also occur after trauma to the eye.

Abdominal Trauma • Blunt abdominal trauma is the second-leading cause of death from abusive injury in children (National Center for Child Death Review Policy and Practice, 2013). Most victims of intentional abdominal trauma are children are aged 6 months to 3 years (Hudson & Kaplan, 2006). These children are often more seriously injured than older children because the weapon used or the adult hand or foot causing the injury covers such a large portion of the abdomen. Young children also have less fat and weaker abdominal muscles, which fail to absorb the force of the blow to the abdomen, transmitting the force to the internal organs, causing intra-abdominal hemorrhage and hypovolemic shock (Thompson, 2005). Young children may have very few objective signs of injury, so a delay in seeking medical attention is common. Presenting signs of acute abdominal injury can include abdominal guarding, rigidity, vomiting, lethargy, abdominal distention, decreased bowel sounds, anemia, or shock and fever caused by peritonitis. Bruising around the umbilicus may be present (Cullen's sign) roughly 24 to 48 hours after the infliction of blunt abdominal trauma. Older children may complain of abdominal pain. There may be associated findings, including fractures, head trauma, or soft tissue injury, such as bruising to the abdominal wall. To determine the extent and severity of the abdominal trauma, a computed tomography (CT) scan of the abdomen, liver enzymes, and urinalysis must be obtained. A CT scan of the head and a skeletal survey are ordered to assess for other injuries (Hornor, 2012b).

Skeletal Trauma • Skeletal injuries may occur in children during the course of active play or as the result of sports injuries. The key in evaluating skeletal injuries in children is to consider the child's age, developmental capabilities, and the mechanism of injury as stated in the history. For example, subluxation of the radial head can occur as the result of suddenly pulling or yanking a young child's arm to protect him or her from running in the street, or it can occur when swinging a child during play. This injury can also be the result of the caregiver deliberately pulling the child roughly.

Any fractures that occur in the preambulatory infant, fractures in multiple stages of healing, old fractures that are incidental findings, and fractures in children younger than age 2 years are suspicious for abuse. In children who do not yet walk, a spiral fracture of the long bone is also suspect, as a strong, twisting motion is necessary to create the injury (Figure 24.8). Fractured ribs are highly suspect because the percentage of cartilage in the ribs is high, making the ribs more flexible and pliant, thus more difficult to break. "Bucket handle" or "metaphyseal chip" fractures are considered pathognomonic for abuse. This type of fracture involves fragmentation of the distal end of the metaphysis, often in the leg, close to the knee. The mechanism of injury is violent yanking or shaking, or using the child's limb as a handle (Dwek, 2011). Radiographic skeletal surveys should be done on any child younger than 2 years of age who presents with a femur fracture and on older children based on the history compared with the child's age, developmental level, and physical findings (Thompson, 2005).

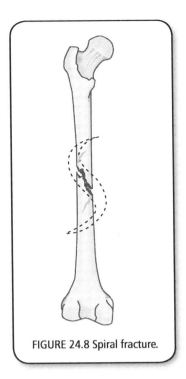

FIGURE 24.8 Spiral fracture.

Head Trauma • Central nervous system injuries, such as asphyxia, direct blows to the head, or shaking, are the leading cause of death resulting from inflicted injury (National Center for Child Death Review Policy and Practice, 2013). Depending on the type and extent of injury, children with neurologic injuries may present with nonspecific signs, such as irritability, sleepiness, and poor appetite, or more specific signs of altered neurologic status, such as vomiting, lethargy, seizures, or coma. Children who have been choked or asphyxiated may have strangulation marks or bruising on the neck. Any tenderness, deformity, or swelling of the head or scalp may indicate inflicted head trauma. Any soft tissue injuries of the scalp, skull fractures in preambulatory infants, injuries to the head that are over soft tissue, fractures or soft tissue injuries in multiple stages of healing, pattern injuries, or any head injuries associated with mouth or eye injuries raise suspicion for abuse (Hornor, 2012b).

Abusive Head Trauma • AHT (formerly referred to as shaken baby syndrome) is a severe form of whiplash in which the infant or toddler is held by the upper body and shaken violently. Retinal hemorrhages, subdural hematomas, and damage to the spinal cord and neck often occur as the result of violent shaking. Children younger than age 5 years are more susceptible to this type of injury because of their large heads, friable intracranial vasculature, and weak neck muscles (Parks, Annest, Hill, & Karch, 2012). If the infant is thrown after shaking, skull fracture may occur. These infants may also sustain rib fractures if the perpetrator squeezes the child's rib cage with significant force (Dwek, 2011). Clinical manifestations of AHT may include poor feeding, vomiting, listlessness, and irritability. Signs of injury are not usually visible. Intracranial edema causes an infant to have a full anterior fontanelle. In some instances, the infant is so severely shaken that significant alterations in level of consciousness, changes in muscle tone, seizures, bradycardia, or apnea occur. This degree of shaking injury often results in death or long-term neurologic impairment (Christian, Block, & the Committee on Child Abuse and Neglect, 2009).

Differential Diagnoses

The pediatric health care provider must be aware of any medical conditions that the child may have that may be confused with physical abuse. Most of these conditions are readily diagnosed by conducting a thorough history and physical examination and by using relevant diagnostic studies. Examples include hemophilia, von Willebrand disease, idiopathic thrombocytopenic purpura, leukemia, erythema multiforme, or Henoch-Schönlein purpura, all of which can be mistaken for intentional bruising. Bullous impetigo (Figure 24.9), allergic reactions, staphylococcal scalded skin syndrome, or moxibustion may mimic burns. Mongolian spots (see Chapter 12), which typically appear over the sacral area, may be confused with bruises inflicted during spanking; however, bruises fade in about a week, whereas Mongolian spots take years to fade (Mudd & Findlay, 2004). Coining and cupping may also be confused with bruising. Allergic shiners and raccoon eyes that occur with allergies and accidental head trauma, respectively, are also included in the differential diagnosis with bruising. Fractures may occur with osteogenesis imperfecta, Ehlers-Danlos syndrome, rickets, osteomyelitis, or malignancy that has metastasized to the bone and may be confused with intentional fracture injury.

FIGURE 24.9 The impetigo lesion on the child's nose may be mistaken for a burn.

Assessing Emotional and Verbal Abuse

Both verbal and emotional abuse are difficult to substantiate, especially as there are no visible manifestations. Although physical signs are lacking, several possible behavioral, emotional, and even cognitive signs may indicate that a child is being emotionally or verbally abused.

History

If emotional or verbal abuse is suspected, the provider should review the child's past medical history, social history, and behavioral history, focusing on any previously diagnosed mental health disorders, a history of poor school performance, bullying, violent behavior, or regression to make accurate assessments.

Behavioral Indicators

Children often demonstrate a change in behavior as a result of emotional or verbal abuse. Some children may become excessively shy, fearful, or clingy. They may have difficulty forming relationships, have an inability to relate to other children, and lack self-confidence. Teachers may report that the child is intensely afraid of making any mistakes or that their school performance is poor (Berkowitz, 2005). Some children may become "parentalized"; that is, they become overly responsible as they may be expected to assume an adult role at home. Other children have sleep problems, developmentally regress in response to the stress of emotional abuse, or demonstrate attention-seeking behaviors. More serious behavioral indicators of emotional or verbal abuse are substance abuse, depression, suicide attempts (Teicher et al., 2006), running away from home, self-mutilation, and problems with the law (Hutchinson & Mueller, 2008). Bullying may begin, which may be the cause or result of being emotionally abused. Depending on a child's temperament, children who are emotionally abused at home may become hostile and aggressive and cruelly bully other children or animals. Conduct disorders may develop (Finch, Nelson, & Hart, 2006). Other children may react to the emotional abuse at home by becoming shy, helpless, and hopeless, thus becoming easy targets for bullies (Hutchinson & Mueller, 2008). Children who have been traumatized may also experience developmental delays and difficulties with reading, comprehension, and abstract thinking. PTSD may occur as a result of chronic emotional or verbal abuse, sexual abuse, or exposure to domestic violence (Lubit & Giardino, 2014). Behavioral indicators are also evident in the parent when a child is being emotionally or verbally abused. These include the parent having unreasonable age-inappropriate behavioral expectations or being harsh or critical of the child in front of the health care provider. Conversely, the parent or caregiver may be completely behaviorally appropriate.

Physical Examination

Children who are emotionally or verbally abused should be evaluated for signs of FTT, developmental delays, enuresis, sleep disorders, self-injury, eating disorders, depression, and suicidal ideation.

Differential Diagnoses

Previously diagnosed emotional or mental health illnesses must be considered when evaluating emotional abuse in a child. PTSD can occur in the child, resulting from causes other than emotional abuse or exposure to domestic violence, such as witnessing traumatic events, including natural disasters, suffering the chronic stress of living in high-crime areas, or experiencing war and terrorism (Lubit & Giardino, 2014). Depression, bipolar disorder, generalized anxiety disorder, separation anxiety disorder, social phobias, obsessive-compulsive disorder, and oppositional defiant disorder are all diagnoses to consider when a child has been verbally or emotionally abused.

Assessing Sexual Abuse

Child sexual abuse may present in a variety of ways. The child may be in the provider's care for a routine health maintenance visit, and because of certain historical or physical findings, sexual abuse may become evident. The child may be brought to the health care provider by the parent specifically for suspected sexual abuse, or the child may be brought to the health care provider by social service or law enforcement personnel for evaluation of sexual abuse. In instances of acute sexual abuse, the child may be brought to the emergency department for evaluation, collection of evidence, and crisis management (Kellogg & the Committee on Child Abuse and Neglect, 2005).

History

When child sexual abuse is suspected, the parent and child should be interviewed separately (Jenny & Crawford-Jakubiak, 2013). Beginning at age 3 years, the child can be interviewed alone (Kellogg & the Committee on Child Abuse and Neglect, 2005). Before beginning the assessment, the pediatric health care provider must remember that sexual abuse of a child involves a range of sexually inappropriate activities, such as exposure to pornography, being photographed for pornography, being exposed to adult sexual activity, and sexual contact with an adult (Giardino, Isaac, & Giardino, 2013). First, the provider must elicit certain information from the adult who accompanies the child. This information includes determining (Giardino & Finkel, 2005):

- Why the adult suspects sexual abuse
- To whom the child made any disclosures and what the child said

- What, if anything, the adult witnessed or heard
- Any changes in the child's behavior and what these changes are
- Specific chief complaints for the visit (e.g., genital discharge or bleeding; pelvic or genital pain)
- Who lives in the home with the child and the child's relationship to each person
- If the adult accompanying the child is not the parent, where the parents are and what role, if any, they play in the child's life

It is also important to obtain the child's past medical history in the event the child has any conditions that may mimic sexual abuse (see Differential Diagnoses). Children who have been sexually abused may present with nonspecific anogenital complaints such as pain, itching, erythema, or burning on urination. More specific complaints may include rectal or genital bleeding, difficulty walking or sitting, the development of sexually inappropriate behavior for the child's age, genital discharge, or genital lesions (Kellogg & the Committee on Child Abuse and Neglect, 2005; Paulk, 2004). When evaluating the presence of genital discharge or lesions in children, the provider must keep in mind that not all sexually transmitted infections (STIs) require oral-to-genital or genital-to-genital contact to infect the child. Some STIs can be transmitted through fondling if the perpetrator has infected secretions on his or her hand (Giardino & Finkel, 2005). Transmission of anogenital warts, for example, can occur through sexual contact but also by autoinoculation, direct contact with an infected caregiver who is shedding the virus, and direct contact with nonporous surfaces contaminated with human papillomavirus fomites (Horner, 2004). Vertical transmission of STIs must be considered in children younger than age 1 year (Giardino & Finkel, 2005). STIs that are considered diagnostic for sexual abuse in children are gonorrhea, syphilis, and *Chlamydia* (if not perinatally acquired), and HIV (if not perinatally or transfusion acquired) (Giardino et al., 2013).

Obtaining the history from the child must be done in the most nonthreatening, nonjudgmental, caring manner possible. Trust must first be established between the child and health care provider; this involves a slow pace, a developmentally appropriate approach, and allowance for the child or adolescent to have as much control over the process as possible (Giardino et al., 2013). In young children, it is necessary for the examiner to determine what terminology the child uses when referring to his or her genitals and to avoid using medical terminology. Simple, open-ended questions are necessary (e.g., "What happened?") versus leading questions (e.g., "What did your mom's boyfriend do to you?"), which may influence the child's answer. Brief answers should be followed with encouraging statements, such as, "Tell me more" or "then what happened," until the provider is satisfied that the child has completed his or her story

(Giardino et al., 2013). Approaches to interviewing the young child may include the use of anatomically correct dolls, the use of puppets, or encouraging the child to draw a picture about what happened.

In adolescent girls, a gynecologic history must be obtained, including the date of the last menstrual period, number of pregnancies, past surgery, or trauma to the anogenital region, STI history, date of last consensual intercourse, and contraception use (Botash, 2013).

Behavioral Indicators

A child who is sexually abused may demonstrate certain nonspecific behaviors as a result of the abuse, some of which may immediately raise the suspicions of the provider. Some nonspecific behaviors include sleep disturbances, abdominal pain, enuresis, encopresis, or phobias (Kellogg & the Committee on Child Abuse and Neglect, 2005); poor school performance, acting out, or regression; and the development of eating disorders, anxiety, depression, or suicidal ideation. Behaviors that should raise a red flag include knowledge of and preoccupation with any type of sexual act (e.g., intercourse, oral sex, inserting objects into the vagina or anus, masturbation), sexualized behaviors, use of sexually explicit language, sexually explicit drawings made by the child, acting out sexually with siblings or peers, or compulsive cleanliness of the perineal area (Botash, 2013). Some children may deny the sexual abuse while others make outright statements that they are being sexually abused. All children who are suspected of having been sexually abused must have an overall assessment of behavioral, mental, and emotional status to identify any urgent psychosocial needs. PTSD is common in children who have been sexually abused (Botash, 2013; Jenny & Crawford-Jakubiak, 2013).

Physical Examination

Physical indicators of sexual abuse vary, according to the type and nature of abuse and when the last incident occurred. The physical examination alone is not specific enough to confirm sexual abuse in a child; corroborating statements and laboratory findings are necessary to complete the picture. If the alleged incident occurred within 72 hours or less or if there is acute injury or visible bleeding, a full examination of the anogenital region is required. The health care provider must take care to collect any evidence of the abuse according to "chain of evidence" protocols (see Collection of Evidence, later). If more than 72 hours have passed since the alleged abuse occurred or there are no acute injuries, the physical examination can be deferred if circumstances warrant a delay (Jenny & Crawford-Jakubiak, 2013).

When conducting the physical examination to determine if any sexual abuse has taken place, the utmost care and sensitivity is required. The child must have a caring adult with them at all times (one not involved in the abuse) and, if age-appropriate, the examination should be explained to the child. The child must be reassured that he or she has done nothing wrong.

With recent anogenital trauma, instruments may need to be used to illuminate and magnify the relevant structures; this may include colposcopy, a noninvasive method to light and magnify anogenital structures for examination. Still and video photography of anogenital injuries may also be necessary (Giardino et al., 2013). Digital and speculum examinations are not performed on a prepubertal child (Giardino et al., 2013).

If a child who is unable to cooperate with the physical examination presents with blunt force penetrating trauma or if the examiner senses that the child will suffer psychologically because of the nature of the examination, conscious sedation may be used for the examination with the child's vital signs closely monitored according to protocol (Giardino & Finkel, 2005; Kellogg & the Committee on Child Abuse and Neglect, 2005). Older children may be allowed to participate in the examination to give them a sense of control over the situation (Giardino & Finkel, 2005).

In children of both sexes, the focus of the physical examination is on areas involved in sexual activity: the mouth, genitals, perineal region, buttocks, and anus; however, there may also be bruises on the face, neck, breasts, or buttocks.

In female children, the genital examination includes inspection of the inner thighs, labia majora and minora, clitoris, urethra and surrounding area, hymen, hymenal opening, fossa navicularis, and posterior fourchette (Giardino et al., 2013). Certain factors affect the examiner's ability to inspect the child's inner anatomic structures: (a) the child's degree of relaxation, (b) the amount of traction that the examiner places on the labia majora, and (c) the position the child is in for the examination (i.e., supine, lateral, knee to chest). Concerning (not diagnostic) findings include bruising of the inner thighs or genitals, tearing or scarring of the labia minora, or enlargement of the hymenal opening.

Physical findings in female children may vary, depending on whether the sexual trauma is acute or chronic. In many children, the examination findings will be within normal limits (Giardino et al., 2013). Signs of acute sexual trauma may include loss of integrity of the hymen, vaginal abrasions, tears, or bleeding; the presence of ejaculate or vaginal discharge; or lesions that may indicate a STI. Findings that are suggestive of chronic sexual abuse include scarring of the fossa navicularis, remodeling of the hymenal tissue from repeated trauma, and tears or scarring of the posterior fourchette (Giardino et al., 2013). Any objective signs of pregnancy must be noted.

In male children, the thighs, penis, and scrotum are examined for acute injury such as bruising, bleeding, burns, bite marks, abrasions, or other soft tissue injuries (Kellogg & the Committee on Child Abuse and Neglect, 2005). Any penile discharge or lesions, suggesting STIs, must be noted. Evidence of past injuries, such as scarring or ligature marks, must also be noted.

In both sexes, the anus is examined, using the supine or left side-lying position. The knee–chest position should not be used as this is likely the position in which the abuse took place. If the abuse was recent, the examiner notes any pain, signs of injury such as bruising, bleeding, laceration, or soft tissue tears around the anogenital region. Any evidence of STIs is noted, such as discharge or anal lesions. If the injury was not recent, laxity of the anal sphincter should be noted, keeping in mind that this is a nonspecific finding and may be caused by the passage of large bowel movements. Also, if the perpetrator used lubrication or penetration without force, anal laxity will not be present (Giardino et al., 2013).

Differential Diagnoses

Some conditions or injuries involving the anogenital area may mimic sexual abuse. It is vitally important for the health care provider to be familiar with these conditions to avoid any false allegations, which can have catastrophic sequelae for the child, family, and the accused. Common conditions in this category include diaper dermatitis, hymenal tags, labial adhesions, vulvovaginitis, anal fissures, and perianal skin tags that can result from chronic constipation. Less common conditions are congenital malformations, poor hygiehne, physical abuse, accidental straddle or impaling injuries of the anogenital region (Kellogg & the Committee on Child Abuse and Neglect, 2005), foreign bodies in the vagina or anus, pinworm infestation, and anal or rectal skin tags associated with Crohn's disease or cystic fibrosis.

Collection of Evidence

A board-certified pediatric sexual assault nurse examiner (SANE-P) should be used for the collection of evidence of sexual abuse. The SANE-P is a registered nurse who is specially trained to conduct forensic examinations, provide emotional support to the child and family, ensure a chain of evidence, and provide expertise for effective courtroom testimony if needed (Bechtel, Ryan, & Gallagher, 2008). If the sexual abuse took place within the last 72 hours or if there is evidence of acute injury, collection of biologic evidence (e.g., hair, blood, semen) should proceed (Kellogg & the Committee on Child Abuse and Neglect, 2005). Before obtaining cultures to determine the presence of STIs, the provider must consider the type of sexual contact. If the history indicates oral, genital, or rectal contact or the child is symptomatic, cultures are obtained to diagnose STIs (Kellogg & the Committee on Child Abuse and Neglect, 2005). If the child presents with acute genital or anal trauma attributed to accidental straddle or impaling injuries, it is necessary for law enforcement to conduct an investigation of the scene where the injury took place and to interview any witnesses to determine the veracity of the history (Giardino & Finkel, 2005).

COMMON DIAGNOSTIC STUDIES

The type of diagnostic study required to clarify the type and severity of physical, sexual, or psychological injury to a child depends on the history, location, and type of injury. The goal of obtaining these diagnostic studies is to diagnose or exclude inflicted injury. Conditions that may ensue as a result of prolonged neglect also need to be defined and treated. Table 24.3 lists some of these diagnostic studies and their indications.

DOCUMENTATION AND REPORTING OF ABUSE AND NEGLECT

All pediatric nurse practitioners, nurses, physicians, and physician assistants are mandated by law to report any suspected or confirmed child abuse or neglect to the CPS agency in the state in which they practice. The provider must also determine if the child needs to be hospitalized because of the severity of his or her injuries or for protection.

It is extremely important for the health care provider to document all historical and physical findings in a clear, objective manner, as these notes will likely be used to assist law enforcement personnel in prosecuting any crime. Any statements made by the child must be documented verbatim in the medical record, in quotations (Jenny & Crawford-Jakubiak, 2013). Body diagrams and color photographs may be necessary to augment written documentation of physical findings. All physical injuries must be described in terms of location, distribution, size, depth, color, and pattern (Hornor, 2012b). The child's emotional and physical demeanor, overall hygiene, and the nature of the interaction with the parent are also documented. With sexual abuse, it is important to document who was present when the child disclosed the abuse and what prompted the disclosure, and to document the child's words in direct quotes (Botash, 2013).

Sample Write-Up: Neglect

Subjective Data

A 12-month-old girl is seen for annual health maintenance visit accompanied by her mother. Mother and child are currently living in a homeless shelter. Child has had one set of immunizations that her mother "knows of." Child drinks 8 to 10 bottles of milk and approximately

TABLE 24.3	Diagnostic Studies to Evaluate Child Abuse	
CONDITION	**TYPE OF STUDY**	**COMMENTS**
Abdominal trauma	CBC with platelet count; serum chemistry, urinalysis, liver function tests, serum amylase; CT of abdomen	Anemia points to hemorrhage; hematuria suggests renal injury; elevated amylase can indicate pancreatic trauma; liver trauma causes elevated hepatic transaminases; CT of abdomen will show major organ trauma
Ano-genital injury, lesions or discharge	Culture for gonorrhea, syphilis, *Chlamydia*, condyloma acuminata, *Trichomonas vaginalis*, bacterial vaginosis; obtain HIV and serum pregnancy test	To confirm sexual abuse
Altered neurologic status; signs of acute head trauma	Radiographic skull series; CT and MRI studies	Determines presence of skull fractures, intracranial bleeding
Bruising	PT, PTT, CBC with platelet count	Coagulation studies obtained to confirm or exclude bleeding disorders
Skeletal trauma	Radiographic skeletal survey	To determine type and extent of fracture; also determines if child has clinically undetected fractures, or multiple fractures in various stages of healing

CBC, complete blood count; CT, computed tomography; MRI, magnetic resonance imaging; PT, prothrombin time; PTT, partial thromboplastin time.
Sources: Christian, Block, and the Committee on Child Abuse and Neglect (2009); Kellogg, and the Committee on Child Abuse and Neglect (2005).

16 to 24 ounces of apple juice a day. Mother reports that she is eager to toilet train the child who has no interest. Mother smokes in presence of the child.

Objective Data

    Measurements: weight: 95th percentile; **height:** 25th percentile; **head circumference:** 25th percetile **BMI:** > 95th percentile

    General: alert, obese female walks over to provider and puts arms up to be held

    Integument: poor hygiene, extensive excoriation noted in diaper area

    Oral: poor dentition, multiple brown and black areas over maxillary and mandibular central incisors

    Neurologic: hearing, vision grossly normal

    Developmental: walks well, does not use spoon well, does not drink from cup, cannot build tower of two cubes, briefly scribbles with crayon; says, "mama," "baba," and "dada"; cannot point to any named body part

    Assessment: neglect

Sample Write-Up: Physical Abuse

Subjective Data

A 2-year-old boy presents to urgent care clinic accompanied by his mother. Mother states that, 2 days ago, she was holding child while drinking hot coffee, and child reached for the cup, spilling coffee on his hand and arm. Mother immediately immersed arm in cold water. PMH noncontributory.

Objective Data

Left hand noted to have full-thickness burn in a glove pattern, with a clear line of demarcation at the wrist. No splash burn marks noted on arm. Hand edematous with skin peeling. Child crying during examination.

    Assessment: inflicted burn

Sample Write-Up: Sexual Abuse

Subjective Data

A 4-year-old girl is being seen for her annual health maintenance visit. Mother mentions that child frequently complains of "itching on her privates." Mother appears tentative and fearful about mentioning this complaint.

Objective Data

Child became combative during examination and refused inspection of perineal area, stating that "He puts his finger there, and it hurts." Refuses to say who "he" is while mother is in the room. SANE-P called to continue examination.

    Assessment: presumptive sexual abuse

Notable Clinical Findings

Presence of Risk Factors for Neglect or Abuse

- Inexperienced, isolated, stressed mother
- Inadequate support
- Mental illness
- Poverty
- Family stress
- History of prolonged hospitalization in neonatal period

Neglect

- Weight < 5th percentile
- Both height and weight below 5th percentile with long-standing neglect
- Poor hygiene
- Severe diaper rash
- Multiple dental caries
- Immunization delays
- Lack of well-child medical care
- Developmental delays
- **Infants with severe neglect**
  - Global developmental delays
  - Poor eye contact
  - Dislike being touched/held
  - Apathetic when left alone
  - Intense interest in inanimate objects/very little interest in social interaction
  - Delayed growth
  - No stranger anxiety

Physical Abuse

- The history is incompatible with the type/degree of injury: story doesn't "fit" (**most important criterion used to report to DCFS**).
- The history of the mechanism of injury is vague
- The history changes during the course of the health care encounter
- The parents or caregivers, when interviewed separately, give contradictory histories
- The history is not credible (e.g., the history is incompatible with the child's developmental level)
- History of repeated "accidents," ingestions,
- Injuries in various stages of healing seen
- There is often a significant delay between the time of injury and time when medical care sought
- The parent/caregiver may not show an appropriate degree of concern or may be overly concerned/solicitous
- Inappropriate parent–child interaction may be observed (e.g., ignoring child, anger, etc.)

- Child withdrawn/submissive/clings to parents
- Child lies to cover for parents
- **Physical Findings**
  - Burns, bruises, welts, scars; bite, restraint marks
  - Oral injuries due to force feeding
  - Restraint, tourniquet marks, descriptive marks, pattern marks
  - Fractures in multiple stages of healing
  - Physical complaints that only occur in the presence of one specific caregiver

Sexual Abuse

- Redness, bruising around genitalia
- Genital discharge
- Genital lesions
- Frequent urinary tract infections (girls)
- Vaginal/rectal tears
- Parental report of change in behavior/acting out
- Fear of being around alleged perpetrator
- Outright statements made by child
- Poor school performance
- Phobias
- Eating disorders
- Evidence of depression
- Evidence of self-mutilation
- Suicide attempts

References

Abdulhamid, I. (2013). *Pediatric Munchausen syndrome by proxy.* Retrieved from http://emedicine.medscape.com/article/917525-overview

American Psychiatric Association. (2013). *Diagnostic and statistical manual of mental disorders* (5th ed., pp. 265–270). Arlington, VA: Author.

Ashton, R. (2010). Practitioner review: Beyond shaken baby syndrome: what influences the outcomes for infants following traumatic brain injury? *Journal of Child Psychology and Psychiatry, 51*(9), 967–980.

Bechtel, K., Ryan, E., & Gallagher, D. (2008). Impact of sexual assault nurse examiners on the evaluation of sexual assault in a pediatric emergency department. *Pediatric Emergency Care, 24*(7), 442–447.

Berkowitz, C. (2005). Recognizing and responding to domestic violence. *Pediatric Annals, 34*(5), 395–401.

Best, D., & the American Academy of Pediatrics Committee on Environmental Health, Committee on Native American Child Health, Committee on Adolescence. (2009). Secondhand and prenatal tobacco smoke exposure. *Pediatrics, 124*(5), e1017–e1045.

Block, R. W., Krebs, N. F., the Committee on Child Abuse and Neglect, & the Committee on Nutrition. (2009). Failure to thrive as a manifestation of child neglect. *Pediatrics, 116*(5), 1234–1237; Statement of reaffirmation: *Pediatrics, 123*(5), 1421–1422.

Botash, A. (2013). *Child sexual abuse in emergency medicine.* Retrieved from http://emedicine.medscape.com/article/800770-overview

Centers for Disease Control and Prevention, National Center for Injury Prevention and Control. (2014). *Child maltreatment: Risk and protective factors.* Retrieved from http://www.cdc.gov/violenceprevention/childmaltreatment/riskprotectivefactors.html

Christakis, D. A., & Zimmerman, F. J. (2007). Children and television: A primer for pediatricians. *Contemporary Pediatrics, 24*(3), 31–45.

Christian, C. W., Block, R., & the Committee on Child Abuse and Neglect. (2009). Abusive head trauma in infants and children. *Pediatrics, 123*, 1409–1411.

Dadds, M. R., & Fraser, J. A. (2006). Fire interest, fire setting, and psychopathology in Australian children: A normative study. *Australian and New Zealand Journal of Psychiatry, 40*(6–7), 581–586.

Dubowitz, H. (2004). Neglect. In S. J. Parker, B. S. Zuckerman, & M. C. Augustyn (Eds.), *Developmental and behavioral pediatrics: A handbook for primary care* (pp. 248–250). Philadelphia, PA: Lippincott Williams & Wilkins.

Dwek, J. R. (2011). The radiographic approach to child abuse. *Clinical Orthopaedics and Related Research, 469*(3), 776–789.

Finch, A. J., Nelson, W. M., & Hart, K. J. (2006). Conduct disorder: Description, prevalence and etiology. In W. M. Nelson, A. J. Finch, & K. J. Hart (Eds.), *Conduct disorders: A practitioner's guide to comparative treatments* (pp. 1–13). New York, NY: Springer.

Fischer, H., & Hammel, P. W. (2003). Human bites versus dog bites. *Images in Clinical Medicine, 349*(11), e11.

Flynn, C. P. (2011). Examining the links between animal abuse and human violence. *Crime, Law and Social Change, 55*(5), 453–468.

Geil, J. D. (2012). *Pediatric Von Willebrand disease.* Retrieved from http://emedicine.medscape.com/article/959825-overview

Giardino, A. P., & Finkel, M. A. (2005). Evaluating child sexual abuse. *Pediatric Annals, 34*(5), 382–394.

Giardino, A. P., Isaac, R., & Giardino, E. R. (2013). *Child sexual abuse.* Retrieved from http://reference.medscape.com/article/915841-overview

Governo, M. M., & Siewers, M. H. (2008). Childhood bullying. *Advance for Nurses, 6*(8), 33–36.

Hemenway, D., Barber, C., & Miller, M. (2010). Unintentional firearm deaths: A comparison of other-inflicted and self-inflicted shootings. *Accident Analysis sand Prevention, 42*, 1184–1188.

Horner, G. (2004). Ano-genital warts in children: Sexual abuse or not? *Journal of Pediatric Health Care, 18*(4), 165–170.

Hornor, G. (2005a). Domestic violence and children. *Journal of Pediatric Health Care, 19*(4), 4–11.

Hornor, G. (2005b). Physical abuse: Recognition and reporting. *Journal of Pediatric Health Care, 19*(1), 206–212.

Hornor, G. (2012a). Emotional maltreatment. *Journal of Pediatric Health Care, 26*(6), 436–442.

Hornor, G. (2012b). Medical evaluation for child physical abuse: What the PNP needs to know. *Journal of Pediatric Health Care, 26*(3), 163–170.

Hornor, G. (2013). Child maltreatment: Screening and anticipatory guidance. *Journal of Pediatric Health Care, 27*(4), 242–250.

Hudson, M., & Kaplan, R. (2006). Clinical response to child abuse. *Pediatric Clinics of North America, 53*, 27–39.

Hutchinson, L., & Mueller, D. (2008). Sticks and stones and broken bones: The influence of parental verbal abuse on peer related victimization. *Western Criminology Review, 9*(1), 17–30.

Hymel, K. P., Block, R. W., Hibbard, R. A., Jenny, C. J., Kellogg, N. D., Spivak, B. S., & Stirling, J. (2006). When is lack of supervision neglect? *Pediatrics, 118*(3), 1296–1298.

Ibanez, E. S., Borrego, J., Pemberton, J. R., & Terao, S. (2006). Cultural factors in decision-making about child physical abuse: Identifying reporter characteristics influencing reporting tendencies. *Child Abuse and Neglect, 30*(12), 1365–1379.

Irish, L., Kobayashi, I., & Delahanty, D. L. (2010). Long-term physical health consequences of childhood sexual abuse: A meta-analytic review. *Journal of Pediatric Psychology, 35*(5), 450–461.

Jarvie, J. A., & Malone, R. E. (2008). Children's secondhand smoke exposure in private homes and cars: An ethical analysis. *American Journal of Public Health, 98*(12), 2140–2145.

Jenny C., & Crawford-Jakubiak, J. E. (2013). The evaluation of children in the primary care setting when sexual abuse is suspected. *Pediatrics, 132*(2), e558–567.

Johnson, P. L., & Flake, E. M. (2007). Maternal depression and child outcomes. *Pediatric Annals, 36*(4), 196–202.

Kellogg, N., & the Committee on Child Abuse and Neglect. (2005). The evaluation of sexual abuse in children. *Pediatrics, 116*(2), 506–512.

Lubit, R. H., & Giardino, E. R. (2014). *Posttraumatic stress disorder in children.* Retrieved from http://emedicine.medscape.com/article/918844-overview#aw2aab6b2b3

Lutenbacher, M., Cohen, A., & Conner, N. M. (2004). Breaking the cycle of family violence: Understanding the perceptions of battered women. *Journal of Pediatric Health Care, 18*(5), 236–242.

McColgan, M. D., & Giardino, A. P. (2005). Internet poses multiple risks to children and adolescents. *Pediatric Annals, 34*(5), 405–414.

Moore, D. R., & Florsheim, P. (2008). Interpartner conflict and child abuse risk among African American and Latino adolescent parenting couples. *Child Abuse and Neglect, 32*(4), 463–475.

Mudd, S. S., & Findlay, J. S. (2004). The cutaneous manifestations and mimickers of physical child abuse. *Journal of Pediatric Health Care, 18*(3), 123–129.

Muscari, M. (2004). Juvenile animal abuse: Practice and policy implications for PNPs. *Journal of Pediatric Health Care, 18*(1), 15–21.

National Center for Child Death Review Policy and Practice. (2013). *Types of child deaths: Child abuse and neglect.* Retrieved from http://www.childdeathreview.org/causesCAN.htm

Parks, S. E., Annest, J. L, Hill, H. A., & Karch, D. L. (2012). *Pediatric abusive head trauma: Recommended definitions for public health surveillance and research.* Atlanta, GA: Centers for Disease Control and Prevention.

Paulk, D. (2004). How to recognize child abuse and neglect. *The Clinical Advisor, 10*, 43–49.

Peterson, J., Freedenthal, S., Sheldon, C., & Anderson, R. (2008). Nonsuicidal self-injury in adolescents. *Psychiatry, 5*(11), 20–26.

Ramachandran, M., Achan, P., Jones, D. H. A., & Panchbhavi, V. K. (2012). *Osteogenesis imperfecta.* Retrieved from http://emedicine.medscape.com/article/1256726-overview

Reece, R. M., & Christian, C. (2008). *Child abuse: Medical diagnosis and management* (3rd ed.). Elk Grove Village, IL: American Academy of Pediatrics.

Sachs-Ericsson, N., Verona, E., Joiner, T., & Preacher, K. (2006). Parental verbal abuse and the mediating role of self-criticism in adult internalizing disorders. *Journal of Affective Disorders, 93*(1–3), 71–78.

Shah, B. R., & Lucchesi, M. (2006). Child maltreatment. In B. R. Shah, & M. Lucchesi (Eds), *Atlas of pediatric emergency medicine* (pp. 1–32). New York, NY: McGraw-Hill.

Socolar, R., Cabinum-Foeller, E., & Sinal, S. H. (2008). Is religiosity associated with corporal punishment or child abuse? *Southern Medical Journal, 101*(7), 707–710.

Straus, M. A. (2001). *Beating the devil out of them: Corporal punishment in American families.* San Francisco, CA: Jossey-Bass Publishers Inc.

Teicher, M. H., Samson, J. A., Polcari, A., & McGreenery, C. E. (2006). Sticks, stones, and hurtful words: relative effects of various forms of childhood maltreatment. *American Journal of Psychiatry, 163*(9), 993–1000.

Thompson, S. (2005). Accidental or inflicted? Evaluating cutaneous, skeletal, and abdominal trauma in children. *Pediatric Annals, 34*(5), 373–381.

U.S. Department of Health and Human Services, Administration for Children and Families, Administration on Children, Youth and Families, Children's Bureau. (2012). *Child maltreatment 2011.* Retrieved from https://www.acf.hhs.gov/sites/default/files/cb/cm11.pdf

U.S. Department of Health and Human Services, Administration for Children and Families, Administration on Children, Youth and Families, Children's Bureau. (2013). *Child welfare information gateway: Infant safe haven laws.* Retrieved from https://www.childwelfare.gov/systemwide/laws_policies/statutes/safehaven.cfm

Wang, M., & Kenny, S. (2013). Longitudinal links between fathers' and mothers' harsh verbal discipline and adolescents' conduct problems and depressive symptoms. *Child Development, 85*(3), 908–923.

Westby, C. E. (2007). Child maltreatment—a global issue. *Language, Speech, and Hearing Services in Schools, 38*(20), 140–148.

Zaiden, R. A., Besa, E. C., Crouch, G. D. ,Furlong, M. A., Jardine, L. F., Lorenzana, A., … Seiter, K. (2013a). Hemophilia B. Retrieved from http://emedicine.medscape.com/article/779434-overview

Zaiden, R. A., Furlong, M. A., Crouch, G. D., & Besa, E. C. (2013b). *Hemophilia A.* Retrieved from http://emedicine.medscape.com/article/779322-overview

Resources

Edinburgh Postnatal Depression Scale (EPDS)

http://www.dbpeds.org/media/edinburghscale.pdf
A scale designed for use in the outpatient area to screen women for postpartum depression.

Parent Support Groups
Parents Anonymous

http://www.parentsanonymous.org
A nationwide support group for parents to find help with parenting challenges in the safety of a confidential peer support group.

Postpartum Depression

PSI: Postpartum Support International
http://postpartum.net
1-800-994-4PPD
Provides information and support to mothers suffering from postpartum depression. Website has directory for local support groups, resources, and events.

Position Statements Opposing Corporal Punishment in Children

American Academy of Pediatrics (AAP)—Committee on Psychosocial Aspects of Child and Family Health
Guidance for Effective Discipline
http://aappolicy.aappublications.org/cgi/content/full/pediatrics;101/4/723
American College of Emergency Physicians
http://www.acep.org/practres.aspx?id=29154 PolicyStatements/peds/CorporalPunishmentChildren.htm
National Association of Pediatric Nurse Practitioners (NAPNAP)
http://download.journals.elsevierhealth.com/pdfs/journals/0891=5245/PIIS089152450600410X.pdf
The United Nations Committee on the Rights of the Child (CRC)
The U.N. Committee recommends that states that are parties to the Convention on the Rights of the Child (1989) prohibit corporal punishment in institutions, in schools, and in the home.
http://www2.ohchr.org/english/bodies/crc/

SYNTHESIZING THE COMPONENTS OF THE PEDIATRIC HEALTH ASSESSMENT

The Complete History and Physical Examination: From Start to Finish

The pediatric physical examination differs from the adult examination in that the approach to the patient and the sequence of the examination differ according to age and developmental level. Together, the history and physical exam provide information that leads to the child's diagnosis and forms the basis for the provider's management plan. This chapter summarizes the complete, head-to-toe pediatric physical examination for each age group.

THE NEONATE AND INFANT

History

When conducting the history and physical examination on a neonate or infant, it is essential to review the prenatal, neonatal, and postnatal histories. It is especially important to note the maternal health history, including any intrauterine exposures. The gestational age assessment should also be noted, and performed if not already completed.

Physical Examination

It is recommended that the physical examination of the neonate or infant be conducted in the following sequence: vital signs, anthropometric measurements, general appearance, chest and heart, abdomen, head and face, neck, upper then lower extremities, spine and rectum, genitalia, neuromuscular, ears, nose, mouth, throat, and finally eyes.

Vital Signs

- Assess body temperature, heart rate, respiratory rate, and blood pressure and compare to norms

Anthropometric Measurements

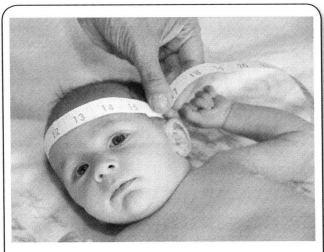

FIGURE 25.1 Assess body weight, length, and head circumference and plot growth charts.

General Appearance

- Color, perfusion, respiratory effort
- Level of consciousness, alertness
- Body posture, symmetry, muscle tone, movement
- Character of cry
- Sleep state

Chest and Heart

- Inspect skin over chest and thorax for rashes or lesions
- Inspect chest for respiratory effort, abdominal breathing (normal)

- Inspect chest for shape (normally round), symmetry, retractions
- Note any precordial hyperactivity
- Inspect nipples and breast tissue for size and location; note presence of physiologic galactorrhea
- Palpate apical pulse to assess for thrill and precordial hyperactivity
- Auscultate heart and lung sounds in all locations

Abdomen

- Inspect skin over abdomen for rashes or lesions
- Inspect abdomen for distention or scaphoid appearance
- Inspect umbilicus—count number of vessels, note umbilical hernia; inspect cord stump for signs of infection
- Auscultate bowel sounds in all four quadrants
- Palpate skin turgor
- Palpate for organomegaly
- Palpate femoral pulses, inguinal lymph nodes
- Percuss all four quadrants

Head and Face

- Inspect for size, molding, caput succedaneum, cephalohematoma
- Inspect fontanels; note sinking or bulging
- Inspect scalp for lesions or infections
- Palpate fontanels
- Inspect face for abnormalities or asymmetry of facial features
- Inspect spacing of eyes
- Inspect eyelids for edema

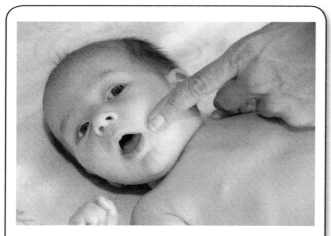

FIGURE 25.2 Elicit rooting reflex.

Neck

- Inspect neck for extra skinfolds, masses, webbing, neck contractions
- Inspect neck for midline trachea
- Palpate thyroid, lymph nodes; note any neck masses

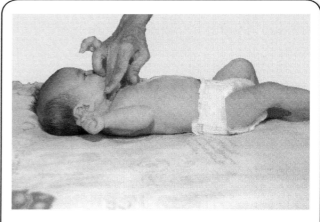

FIGURE 25.3 When infant is supine, elicit tonic neck reflex.

Upper Extremities

- Inspect skin for color, rashes, lesions
- Inspect muscle tone, range of motion
- Inspect digits for number, movement, color of nail beds
- Inspect palms for palmar crease

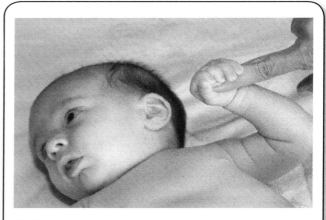

FIGURE 25.4 Elicit palmar reflex.

Lower Extremities

- Inspect skin for color, rashes, lesions
- Inspect muscle tone, range of motion
- Inspect legs for symmetry of gluteal folds
- Perform Ortolani and Barlow maneuvers
- Inspect digits for number, movement, color of nail beds
- Inspect feet for alignment
- Palpate pedal pulse
- Elicit Babinski reflex

Spine and Rectum

- Inspect spine for lesions, tufts of hair, sacral dimple
- Elicit trunk incurvation reflex
- Assess for patency of anus

Genitalia

- Assess diaper area for general hygiene, rash, or any other lesions
- Females
  - Inspect labia for swelling or pseudomenses in neonatal period
  - Inspect external genitalia for signs of infection
- Males
  - Note position of urethral meatus
  - Note direction of urine stream, if able
  - Inspect scrotum for swelling
  - Palpate testes and document if in scrotum

Neuromuscular

- Note level of activity
- Inspect muscle tone and movement
- Elicit Moro reflex
- Turn infant over and place supine or in parent's lap for final part of exam

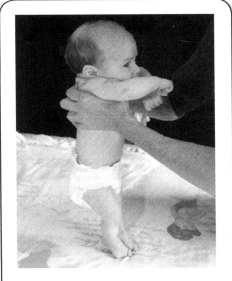

FIGURE 25.7 Elicit stepping and placing reflex.

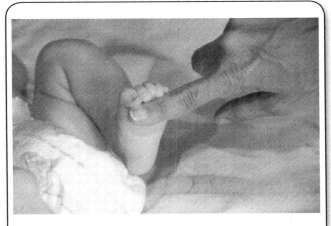

FIGURE 25.5 Elicit plantar reflex.

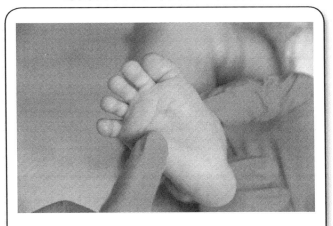

FIGURE 25.8 Elicit Babinski reflex.

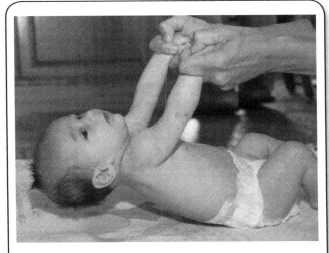

FIGURE 25.6 Inspect head lag and head control.

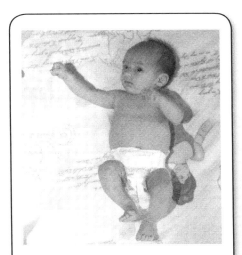

FIGURE 25.9 Assess presence of primitive reflexes according to age.

Eyes

- Inspect for nystagmus
- Note any eye drainage
- With ophthalmoscope: elicit red reflex in both eyes

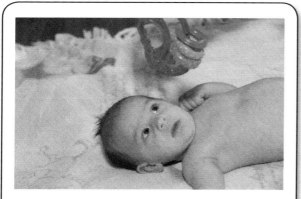

FIGURE 25.10 With penlight: assess corneal light reflex in both eyes, elicit blink reflex, assess tracking.

Ears

- Inspect pinnae for placement
- Inspect for skin tags, ear pits
- Inspect auditory canal and tympanic membrane (with otoscope)

Nose

- Assess patency of nares by occluding one naris at a time and assessing respirations; note any respiratory distress
- Inspect for nasal drainage, or nasal flaring
- Inspect for deformities of nose

Mouth and Throat

- Inspect lips, gums
- Note clefts in lip
- Note natal teeth, Epstein's pearls
- Note any oral lesions
- Note rooting reflex
- Inspect palate

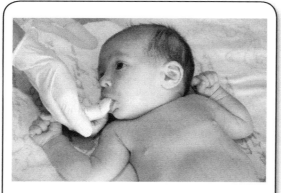

FIGURE 25.11 Palpate palate with gloved finger; note sucking reflex.

Concluding the Assessment

When the examination is complete, discuss the findings with the parents and record all findings.

THE TODDLER

The toddler can be very challenging to examine. It is within normal developmental limits for these children to be negativistic, dislike body boundary intrusion, and dislike having their clothes removed. Younger toddlers, in particular, dislike being restrained, and prefer to have the parent nearby during the examination. In order to make the physical examination flow as smoothly as possible, it is best for the examiner to conduct as much of the exam as possible without touching the child (i.e., by observation only), and to save the intrusive portions of the exam for last.

History

- Fully review past medical, surgical, family, and social histories
- Collect the relevant health history (e.g., initial, interval, focused, follow-up; see Chapter 6)
- Obtain an interval developmental history

Vital Signs

- Assess body temperature, heart rate, and respiratory rate and compare to norms
- Blood pressure reading is not needed until age 3 years

Anthropometric Measurements

- Assess body weight, length, weight for length, and head circumference and plot growth charts
- Calculate and plot body mass index on growth chart beginning at age 2 years
- Toddlers are weighed on a standing scale beginning at age 2 years
- Toddlers should be weighed in diaper and gown, only; no clothes, shoes, and so on
- Toddlers have a recumbent length measured until age 2 years, then a standing height
- Head circumference is measured until age 3 years

Physical Examination

The parent is asked to undress the toddler. The examination can be performed on the parent's lap or an examination table, wherever the child is most cooperative. If the child is more cooperative on the parent's lap, the provider should sit directly facing the parent, with both the provider's and the parent's knees touching to create a "table." The child should be supine on the parent's lap, facing the provider, to begin the exam.

General Appearance

When obtaining the history and while preparing to begin the physical assessment, assess the following:

- Alertness, facies
- Child's posture, gait, muscle tone, and mobility

- Child's speech, type of interaction with toys or security object
- Hearing
- Color, perfusion, respiratory effort
- Hygiene
- Nutritional status
- Behavior, tantrums
- Parent–child interaction
- Parent's reaction to child's crying or fear

Chest and Heart

- Inspect skin over chest and thorax for rashes or lesions
- Inspect chest for respiratory effort
- Inspect chest for shape, symmetry, retractions
- Note any precordial hyperactivity
- Palpate apical pulse to assess for thrill and precordial hyperactivity
- Auscultate heart sounds with bell of stethoscope in all locations; note murmurs, abnormal heart sounds
- Auscultate lung sounds with diaphragm of stethoscope; note adventitious breath sounds

Abdomen

- Inspect skin over abdomen for rashes or lesions
- Inspect abdomen for distention
- Inspect periumbilical area for signs of infection
- Auscultate bowel sounds in all four quadrants
- Palpate skin turgor
- Palpate for organomegaly
- Palpate femoral pulses, inguinal lymph nodes
- Percuss all four quadrants

Genitalia

- Assess diaper area for rash or any other lesions
- Females
  - Inspect external genitalia for signs of infection
  - Assess Tanner stage
- Males
  - Assess Tanner stage
  - Inspect uncircumcised males for retractability of foreskin and hygiene
  - Palpate testes

Upper Extremities

- Inspect skin for color, rashes, lesions
- Inspect muscle tone, range of motion
- Inspect digits for number, movement, color of nail beds
- Palpate radial pulse
- Elicit biceps and triceps reflexes with reflex hammer

Lower Extremities

- Inspect skin for color, rashes, lesions
- Inspect muscle tone, range of motion
- Inspect legs for symmetry of gluteal folds
- Inspect digits for number, movement, color of nail beds

- Palpate pedal pulse
- Inspect feet for alignment
- Elicit plantar, Achilles, and patellar reflexes
- Note gait

Head, Face, and Neck

- Inspect fontanelles; note sinking or bulging
- Inspect scalp for lesions, infestations, or infections
- Palpate fontanelles
- Inspect face for abnormalities or asymmetry of facial features
- Inspect spacing of eyes
- Inspect eyelids for edema
- Inspect neck for midline trachea

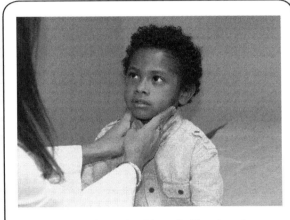

FIGURE 25.12 Palpate thyroid, cervical lymph nodes; note any neck masses.

Eyes

- Inspect conjunctivae and sclerae
- Note any eye drainage
- With penlight, assess corneal and pupillary light reflexes in both eyes
- Perform cover test as needed
- Assess cardinal fields of gaze
- With ophthalmoscope, elicit red reflex in both eyes
- Perform funduscopic exam, if toddler is cooperative

Nose

- Inspect for nasal drainage, or nasal flaring
- Inspect for deformities of the nose
- Inspect nasal turbinates (with otoscope) for edema, bogginess, erythema

Ears

Toddlers are normally very resistant to inspection of the auditory canal and tympanic membrane. It may be helpful to have the parent assist by holding the child securely in his or her lap, with the child facing sideways, legs tucked between the parent's legs, and one arm held close to the parent's body, between the parent's arm and torso. The parent can use one hand to secure the child's forehead and hold the other arm with his or her remaining free hand.

- Inspect pinnae for placement
- Inspect for skin tags, ear pits
- Inspect both auditory canals and tympanic membranes (with otoscope)

Mouth and Throat

Toddlers are often very uncooperative with this portion of the physical examination. If the child is crying after the ears have been inspected, it may be easier to inspect the oral cavity; if not, a tongue blade may be used (Figure 25.13).

- Inspect lips, gums
- Note any oral lesions on tongue or buccal mucosa
- Inspect teeth for caries, visible plaque
- Inspect palate
- Inspect pharynx for erythema, tonsillar edema, exudate

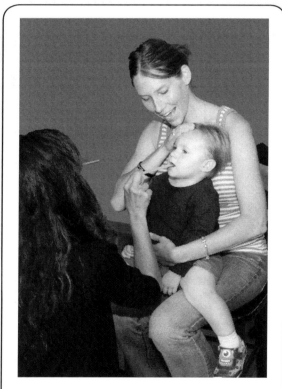

FIGURE 25.13 Examine the mouth and throat of a toddler with help from the parent.

Concluding the Assessment

Praise the toddler for cooperating with the exam and discuss the assessment findings with the parent or caregiver. Record all findings.

THE PRESCHOOL- AND SCHOOL-AGED CHILD, AND ADOLESCENT

Beginning with the preschool age group, the physical examination can be conducted in a head-to-toe manner while the child is on the examination table, lying supine, dressed in a gown. As with all health assessments, relevant subjective data are collected first (i.e., the history), then objective data are obtained (i.e., the physical examination). Younger preschool-aged children may still be fearful when interacting with the health care provider. For this reason, it is important that the parent remain nearby. The child should be given a child-sized gown and asked to undress except for underpants. Young school-aged children often prefer the parent to be present; older school-aged children may prefer the parent to leave the room during the exam.

History

- Collect the relevant health history (e.g., initial, interval, focused, follow-up; see Chapter 6)
- Obtain an interval developmental history

General Appearance

When obtaining the history and while preparing to begin the physical assessment, assess the following: (Figure 25.14).

- Alertness, facies
- Child's posture, gait, muscle tone, and mobility
- Child's speech; type of interaction with toys, book, electronics
- Hearing
- Color, perfusion, respiratory effort
- Hygiene
- Nutritional status
- Behavior, tantrums
- Parent–child interaction
- Parent's reaction to child or teen's crying or fear
- If not previously measured when child was placed in exam room by staff, obtain vital signs and anthropometric measurements

FIGURE 25.14 Assess a child's general appearance.

Vital Signs

- Assess body temperature, heart rate, respiratory rate, and blood pressure and compare to norms

Anthropometric Measurements

- Calculate body mass index
- Plot on growth charts

FIGURE 25.16 Perform cover test as needed.

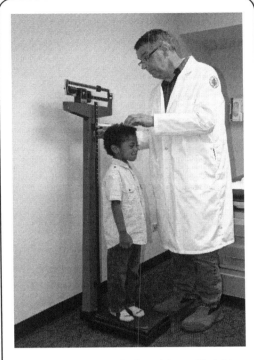

FIGURE 25.15 Measure body weight, and height.

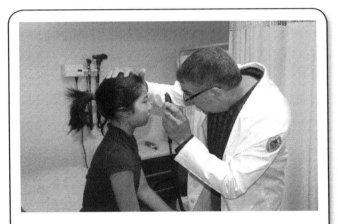

FIGURE 25.17 Perform funduscopic exam.

Ears

- Inspect pinnae for placement
- Inspect for skin tags, ear pits
- Palpate auricle and tragus; note tenderness

Head and Face

- Inspect scalp for lesions, infestations, or infections
- Inspect face for abnormalities or asymmetry of facial features
- Inspect neck for midline trachea
- Palpate frontal and maxillary sinuses
- Palpate thyroid, cervical lymph nodes; note any neck masses

Eyes

- Inspect eyelids for edema
- Inspect conjunctivae and sclerae
- Note any eye drainage
- With penlight, assess corneal and pupillary light reflexes in both eyes
- Assess six cardinal fields of gaze
- Darken room
- With ophthalmoscope, elicit red reflex in both eyes

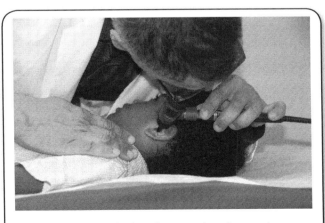

FIGURE 25.18 Inspect both auditory canals and tympanic membranes (with otoscope).

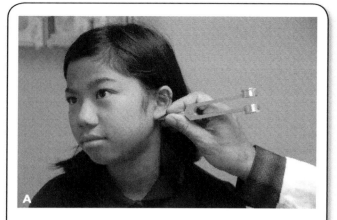

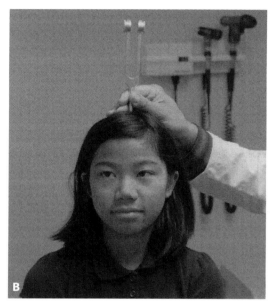

FIGURES 25.18 Assess hearing with **A.** Weber and **B.** Rinne tests.

Nose

- Inspect for nasal drainage, or nasal flaring
- Inspect for deformities of nose
- Inspect nasal turbinates (with otoscope) for edema, bogginess, erythema

Mouth and Throat

- Inspect lips, gums
- Ask child to stick out tongue
- Note any oral lesions on tongue or buccal mucosa
- Inspect teeth for caries, visible plaque
- Inspect pharynx for erythema, exudate, cobblestoning
- Inspect tonsils; grade size

Neck

- Inspect and palpate neck for midline trachea
- Assess range-of-motion of head and neck

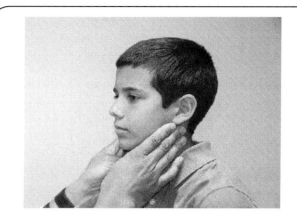

FIGURE 25.19 Palpate thyroid, cervical lymph nodes; note any neck masses.

Chest, Thorax, and Lungs

- Inspect skin over chest and thorax for rashes or lesions
- Inspect chest for respiratory effort
- Inspect chest for shape, symmetry, retractions
- Percuss chest over lung fields
- Auscultate lung sounds with diaphragm of stethoscope; note adventitious breath sounds
- Perform forward bending test to assess for lateral curvature of spine

Heart

- Inspect for visible precordial hyperactivity
- Palpate apical pulse to assess for thrill and precordial hyperactivity
- Auscultate heart sounds with bell and diaphragm of stethoscope in all locations; note murmurs, abnormal heart sounds

Upper Extremities

- Inspect skin for color, rashes, lesions
- Inspect muscle tone, range of motion
- Inspect digits for number, movement, color of nail beds
- Palpate radial pulse
- Assess range-of-motion and muscle strength of shoulders, arms, hands
- Elicit biceps and triceps reflexes with reflex hammer

Abdomen

- Inspect skin over abdomen for rashes or lesions
- Inspect abdomen for distention

- Inspect periumbilical area for signs of infection
- Auscultate bowel sounds in all four quadrants
- Palpate skin turgor
- Palpate femoral pulses, inguinal lymph nodes
- Percuss all four quadrants

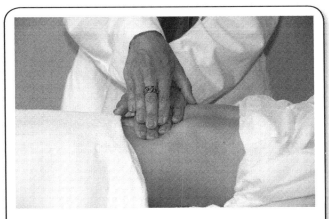

FIGURE 25.20 Palpate for organomegaly (light, then deep palpation).

Lower Extremities

- Inspect skin for color, rashes, lesions
- Inspect muscle tone, range of motion
- Inspect digits for number, movement, color of nail beds
- Palpate popliteal, posterior tibial, pedal pulses
- Inspect feet for alignment
- Assess child's gait while toe-walking
- Assess gait with child's shoes off

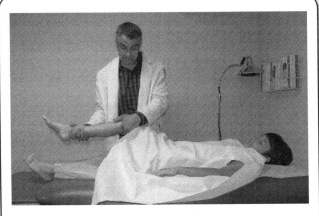

FIGURE 25.21 Assess range of motion of hips, knees, ankles, and feet.

Neurologic

- Assess sensation, superficial pain, light touch, vibration
- Test stereognosis
- Perform finger-to-nose test
- Ask child to run each heel down opposite shin
- Assess Romberg's sign
- Elicit plantar, Achilles, and patellar reflexes
- Elicit Babinski reflex

FIGURE 25.22 Assess heel-to-toe walking.

Genitalia

- Females
  - Inspect external genitalia for signs of infection or infestation
  - Assess Tanner stage
  - Perform pelvic examination, if indicated
- Males
  - Assess Tanner stage
  - Inspect uncircumcised males for retractability of foreskin and hygiene
  - Palpate testes
  - Assess for inguinal hernia

Concluding the Assessment

Discuss the assessment findings with the child, parent, or both, and document all findings. Consider sensitive issues when working with older school-aged children and adolescents, and maintain privacy and confidentiality as appropriate.

Normal Vital Signs in Infants, Children, and Adolescents

Normal Heart Rate and Respiratory Rate Ranges

AGE	HEART RATE, NORMAL RANGE (BEATS PER MINUTE)	RESPIRATORY RATE, NORMAL RANGE (BREATHS PER MINUTE)
Preterm	141–171, depending on chronologic age	40–70, depending on chronologic age
Neonate	95–170	30–50
1–11 months	90–170	30–45
1–2 years	90–150	20–30
3–4 years	70–130	20–30
5–7 years	65–130	20–25
8–11 years	70–110	14–22
12–15 years	Female: 70–110 Male: 65–105	12–20
>15 years	Female: 55–95 Male: 50–90	12–20

Normal Temperature Ranges

AGE	FAHRENHEIT	CELSIUS
Preterm infant	97.7–98.6	36.5–37
Term infant	97.2–99.9	36.2–37.7
0–6 months	97.2–99.4	36.2–37.4
6–12 months	96–99.7	35.6–37.6
1–13 years	95.9–99	35.5–37.2
>13 years	96.4–99.6	35.8–37.6

Note: Measurement method and circadian rhythm must be considered in evaluating normal.

Blood Pressure Levels for Boys by Age and Height Percentile

AGE (YEAR)	BP PERCENTILE ↓	SYSTOLIC BP (mm Hg) ← PERCENTILE OF HEIGHT →							DIASTOLIC BP (mm Hg) ← PERCENTILE OF HEIGHT →						
		5th	10th	25th	50th	75th	90th	95th	5th	10th	25th	50th	75th	90th	95th
1	50th	80	81	83	85	87	88	89	34	35	36	37	38	39	39
	90th	94	95	97	99	100	102	103	49	50	51	52	53	53	54
	95th	98	99	101	103	104	106	106	54	54	55	56	57	58	58
	99th	105	106	108	110	112	113	114	61	62	63	64	65	66	66
2	50th	84	85	87	88	90	92	92	39	40	41	42	43	44	44
	90th	97	99	100	102	104	105	106	54	55	56	57	58	58	59
	95th	101	102	104	106	108	109	110	59	59	60	61	62	63	63
	99th	109	110	111	113	115	117	117	66	67	68	69	70	71	71
3	50th	86	87	89	91	93	94	95	44	44	45	46	47	48	48
	90th	100	101	103	105	107	108	109	59	59	60	61	62	63	63
	95th	104	105	107	109	110	112	113	63	63	64	65	66	67	67
	99th	111	112	114	116	118	119	120	71	71	72	73	74	75	75
4	50th	88	89	91	93	95	96	97	47	48	49	50	51	51	52
	90th	102	103	105	107	109	110	111	62	63	64	65	66	66	67
	95th	106	107	109	111	112	114	115	66	67	68	69	70	71	71
	99th	113	114	116	118	120	121	122	74	75	76	77	78	78	79
5	50th	90	91	93	95	96	98	98	50	51	52	53	54	55	55
	90th	104	105	106	108	110	111	112	65	66	67	68	69	69	70
	95th	108	109	110	112	114	115	116	69	70	71	72	73	74	74
	99th	115	116	118	120	121	123	123	77	78	79	80	81	81	82
6	50th	91	92	94	96	98	99	100	53	53	54	55	56	57	57
	90th	105	106	108	110	111	113	113	68	68	69	70	71	72	72
	95th	109	110	112	114	115	117	117	72	72	73	74	75	76	76
	99th	116	117	119	121	123	124	125	80	80	81	82	83	84	84
7	50th	92	94	95	97	99	100	101	55	55	56	57	58	59	59
	90th	106	107	109	111	113	114	115	70	70	71	72	73	74	74
	95th	110	111	113	115	117	118	119	74	74	75	76	77	78	78
	99th	117	118	120	122	124	125	126	82	82	83	84	85	86	86
8	50th	94	95	97	99	100	102	102	56	57	58	59	60	60	61
	90th	107	109	110	112	114	115	116	71	72	72	73	74	75	76
	95th	111	112	114	116	118	119	120	75	76	77	78	79	79	80
	99th	119	120	122	123	125	127	127	83	84	85	86	87	87	88

Blood Pressure Levels for Boys by Age and Height Percentile (*continued*)

AGE (YEAR)	BP PERCENTILE ↓	SYSTOLIC BP (mm Hg) ← PERCENTILE OF HEIGHT →							DIASTOLIC BP (mm Hg) ← PERCENTILE OF HEIGHT →						
		5th	10th	25th	50th	75th	90th	95th	5th	10th	25th	50th	75th	90th	95th
9	50th	95	96	98	100	102	103	104	57	58	59	60	61	61	62
	90th	109	110	112	114	115	117	118	72	73	74	75	76	76	77
	95th	113	114	116	118	119	121	121	76	77	78	79	80	81	81
	99th	120	121	123	125	127	128	129	84	85	86	87	88	88	89
10	50th	97	98	100	102	103	105	106	58	59	60	61	61	62	63
	90th	111	112	114	115	117	119	119	73	73	74	75	76	77	78
	95th	115	116	117	119	121	122	123	77	78	79	80	81	81	82
	99th	122	123	125	127	128	130	130	85	86	86	88	88	89	90
11	50th	99	100	102	104	105	107	107	59	59	60	61	62	63	63
	90th	113	114	115	117	119	120	121	74	74	75	76	77	78	78
	95th	117	118	119	121	123	124	125	78	78	79	80	81	82	82
	99th	124	125	127	129	130	132	132	86	86	87	88	89	90	90
12	50th	101	102	104	106	108	109	110	59	60	61	62	63	63	64
	90th	115	116	118	120	121	123	123	74	75	75	76	77	78	79
	95th	119	120	122	123	125	127	127	78	79	80	81	82	82	83
	99th	126	127	129	131	133	134	135	86	87	88	89	90	90	91
13	50th	104	105	106	108	110	111	112	60	60	61	62	63	64	64
	90th	117	118	120	122	124	125	126	75	75	76	77	78	79	79
	95th	121	122	124	126	128	129	130	79	79	80	81	82	83	83
	99th	128	130	131	133	135	136	137	87	87	88	89	90	91	91
14	50th	106	107	109	111	113	114	115	60	61	62	63	64	65	65
	90th	120	121	123	125	126	128	128	75	76	77	78	79	79	80
	95th	124	125	127	128	130	132	132	80	80	81	82	83	84	84
	99th	131	132	134	136	138	139	140	87	88	89	90	91	92	92
15	50th	109	110	112	113	115	117	117	61	62	63	64	65	66	66
	90th	122	124	125	127	129	130	131	76	77	78	79	80	80	81
	95th	126	127	129	131	133	134	135	81	81	82	83	84	85	85
	99th	134	135	136	138	140	142	142	88	89	90	91	92	93	93
16	50th	111	112	114	116	118	119	120	63	63	64	65	66	67	67
	90th	125	126	128	130	131	133	134	78	78	79	80	81	82	82
	95th	129	130	132	134	135	137	137	82	83	83	84	85	86	87
	99th	136	137	139	141	143	144	145	90	90	91	92	93	94	94

(continued)

Blood Pressure Levels for Boys by Age and Height Percentile (*continued*)

AGE (YEAR)	BP PERCENTILE ↓	SYSTOLIC BP (mm Hg) ← PERCENTILE OF HEIGHT →							DIASTOLIC BP (mm Hg) ← PERCENTILE OF HEIGHT →						
		5th	10th	25th	50th	75th	90th	95th	5th	10th	25th	50th	75th	90th	95th
17	50th	114	115	116	118	120	121	122	65	66	66	67	68	69	70
	90th	127	128	130	132	134	135	136	80	80	81	82	83	84	84
	95th	131	132	134	136	138	139	140	84	85	86	87	87	88	89
	99th	139	140	141	143	145	146	147	92	93	93	94	95	96	97

BP, blood pressure

Notes: The 90th percentile is 1.28 SD, 95th percentile is 1.645 SD, and the 99th percentile is 2.326 SD over the mean.

For research purposes, the standard deviations in Appendix Table B–1 allow one to compute BP Z-scores and percentiles for boys with height percentiles given in Table 3 (i.e., the 5th, 10th, 25th, 50th, 75th, 90th, and 95th percentiles). These height percentiles must be converted to height Z-scores given by (5% = −1.645; 10% = −1.28; 25% = −0.68; 50% = 0; 75% = 0.68; 90% = 1.28%; 95% = 1.645) and then computed according to the methodology in steps 2–4 described in Appendix B. For children with height percentiles other than these, follow steps 1–4 as described in Appendix B.

Blood Pressure Levels for Girls by Age and Height Percentile

AGE (YEAR)	BP PERCENTILE ↓	SYSTOLIC BP (mm Hg) ← PERCENTILE OF HEIGHT →							DIASTOLIC BP (mm Hg) ← PERCENTILE OF HEIGHT →						
		5th	10th	25th	50th	75th	90th	95th	5th	10th	25th	50th	75th	90th	95th
1	50th	83	84	85	86	88	89	90	38	39	39	40	41	41	42
	90th	97	97	98	100	101	102	103	52	53	53	54	55	55	56
	95th	100	101	102	104	105	106	107	56	57	57	58	59	59	60
	99th	108	108	109	111	112	113	114	64	64	65	65	66	67	67
2	50th	85	85	87	88	89	91	91	43	44	44	45	46	46	47
	90th	98	99	100	101	103	104	105	57	58	58	59	60	61	61
	95th	102	103	104	105	107	108	109	61	62	62	63	64	65	65
	99th	109	110	111	112	114	115	116	69	69	70	70	71	72	72
3	50th	86	87	88	89	91	92	93	47	48	48	49	50	50	51
	90th	100	100	102	103	104	106	106	61	62	62	63	64	64	65
	95th	104	104	105	107	108	109	110	65	66	66	67	68	68	69
	99th	111	111	113	114	115	116	117	73	73	74	74	75	76	76
4	50th	88	88	90	91	92	94	94	50	50	51	52	52	53	54
	90th	101	102	103	104	106	107	108	64	64	65	66	67	67	68
	95th	105	106	107	108	110	111	112	68	68	69	70	71	71	72
	99th	112	113	114	115	117	118	119	76	76	76	77	78	79	79
5	50th	89	90	91	93	94	95	96	52	53	53	54	55	55	56
	90th	103	103	105	106	107	109	109	66	67	67	68	69	69	70
	95th	107	107	108	110	111	112	113	70	71	71	72	73	73	74
	99th	114	114	116	117	118	120	120	78	78	79	79	80	81	81

Blood Pressure Levels for Girls by Age and Height Percentile (*continued*)

AGE (YEAR)	BP PERCENTILE ↓	SYSTOLIC BP (mm Hg)							DIASTOLIC BP (mm Hg)						
		← PERCENTILE OF HEIGHT →							← PERCENTILE OF HEIGHT →						
		5th	10th	25th	50th	75th	90th	95th	5th	10th	25th	50th	75th	90th	95th
6	50th	91	92	93	94	96	97	98	54	54	55	56	56	57	58
	90th	104	105	106	108	109	110	111	68	68	69	70	70	71	72
	95th	108	109	110	111	113	114	115	72	72	73	74	74	75	76
	99th	115	116	117	119	120	121	122	80	80	80	81	82	83	83
7	50th	93	93	95	96	97	99	99	55	56	56	57	58	58	59
	90th	106	107	108	109	111	112	113	69	70	70	71	72	72	73
	95th	110	111	112	113	115	116	116	73	74	74	75	76	76	77
	99th	117	118	119	120	122	123	124	81	81	82	82	83	84	84
8	50th	95	95	96	98	99	100	101	57	57	57	58	59	60	60
	90th	108	109	110	111	113	114	114	71	71	71	72	73	74	74
	95th	112	112	114	115	116	118	118	75	75	75	76	77	78	78
	99th	119	120	121	122	123	125	125	82	82	83	83	84	85	86
9	50th	96	97	98	100	101	102	103	58	58	58	59	60	61	61
	90th	110	110	112	113	114	116	116	72	72	72	73	74	75	75
	95th	114	114	115	117	118	119	120	76	76	76	77	78	79	79
	99th	121	121	123	124	125	127	127	83	83	84	84	85	86	87
10	50th	98	99	100	102	103	104	105	59	59	59	60	61	62	62
	90th	112	112	114	115	116	118	118	73	73	73	74	75	76	76
	95th	116	116	117	119	120	121	122	77	77	77	78	79	80	80
	99th	123	123	125	126	127	129	129	84	84	85	86	86	87	88
11	50th	100	101	102	103	105	106	107	60	60	60	61	62	63	63
	90th	114	114	116	117	118	119	120	74	74	74	75	76	77	77
	95th	118	118	119	121	122	123	124	78	78	78	79	80	81	81
	99th	125	125	126	128	129	130	131	85	85	86	87	87	88	89
12	50th	102	103	104	105	107	108	109	61	61	61	62	63	64	64
	90th	116	116	117	119	120	121	122	75	75	75	76	77	78	78
	95th	119	120	121	123	124	125	126	79	79	79	80	81	82	82
	99th	127	127	128	130	131	132	133	86	86	87	88	88	89	90
13	50th	104	105	106	107	109	110	110	62	62	62	63	64	65	65
	90th	117	118	119	121	122	123	124	76	76	76	77	78	79	79
	95th	121	122	123	124	126	127	128	80	80	80	81	82	83	83
	99th	128	129	130	132	133	134	135	87	87	88	89	89	90	91

(continued)

Blood Pressure Levels for Girls by Age and Height Percentile (*continued*)

AGE (YEAR)	BP PERCENTILE ↓	SYSTOLIC BP (mm Hg) ← PERCENTILE OF HEIGHT →							DIASTOLIC BP (mm Hg) ← PERCENTILE OF HEIGHT →						
		5th	10th	25th	50th	75th	90th	95th	5th	10th	25th	50th	75th	90th	95th
14	50th	106	106	107	109	110	111	112	63	63	63	64	65	66	66
	90th	119	120	121	122	124	125	125	77	77	77	78	79	80	80
	95th	123	123	125	126	127	129	129	81	81	81	82	83	84	84
	99th	130	131	132	133	135	136	136	88	88	89	90	90	91	92
15	50th	107	108	109	110	111	113	113	64	64	64	65	66	67	67
	90th	120	121	122	123	125	126	127	78	78	78	79	80	81	81
	95th	124	125	126	127	129	130	131	82	82	82	83	84	85	85
	99th	131	132	133	134	136	137	138	89	89	90	91	91	92	93
16	50th	108	108	110	111	112	114	114	64	64	65	66	66	67	68
	90th	121	122	123	124	126	127	128	78	78	79	80	81	81	82
	95th	125	126	127	128	130	131	132	82	82	83	84	85	85	86
	99th	132	133	134	135	137	138	139	90	90	90	91	92	93	93
17	50th	108	109	110	111	113	114	115	64	65	65	66	67	67	68
	90th	122	122	123	125	126	127	128	78	79	79	80	81	81	82
	95th	125	126	127	129	130	131	132	82	83	83	84	85	85	86
	99th	133	133	134	136	137	138	139	90	90	91	91	92	93	93

BP, blood pressure

Notes: The 90th percentile is 1.28 SD, 95th percentile is 1.645 SD, and the 99th percentile is 2.326 SD over the mean.

For research purposes, the standard deviations in Appendix Table B–1 allow one to compute BP Z-scores and percentiles for girls with height percentiles given in Table 4 (i.e., the 5th, 10th, 25th, 50th, 75th, 90th, and 95th percentiles). These height percentiles must be converted to height Z-scores given by (5% = −1.645; 10% = −1.28; 25% = −0.68; 50% = 0; 75% = 0.68; 90% = 1.28%; 95% = 1.645) and then computed according to the methodology in steps 2–4 described in Appendix B. For children with height percentiles other than these, follow steps 1–4 as described in Appendix B.

CDC Growth Charts

Birth to 36 Months: Boys
Length-for-Age and Weight-for-Age Percentiles

NAME _____

RECORD # _____

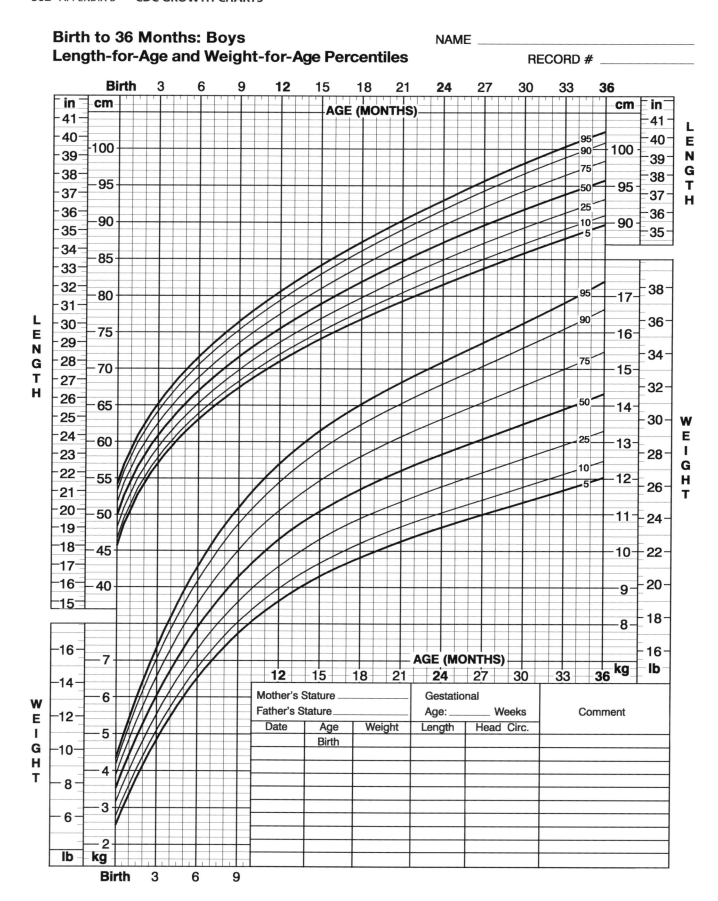

Birth to 36 Months: Girls
Length-for-Age and Weight-for-Age Percentiles

NAME _____

RECORD # _____

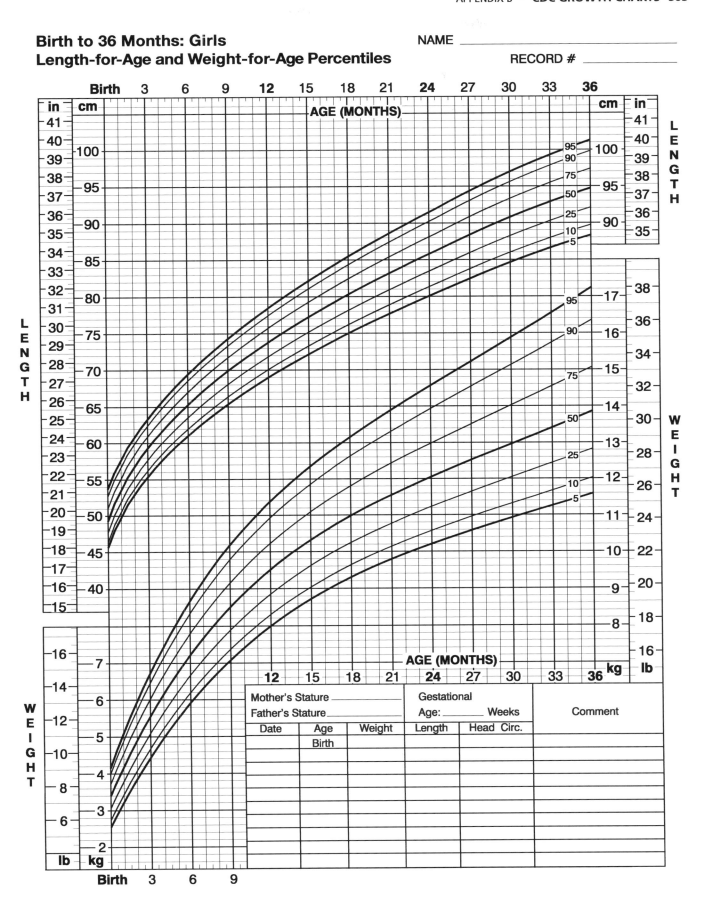

Birth to 36 Months: Boys
Head Circumference-for-Age and
Weight-for-Length Percentiles

NAME _____

RECORD # _____

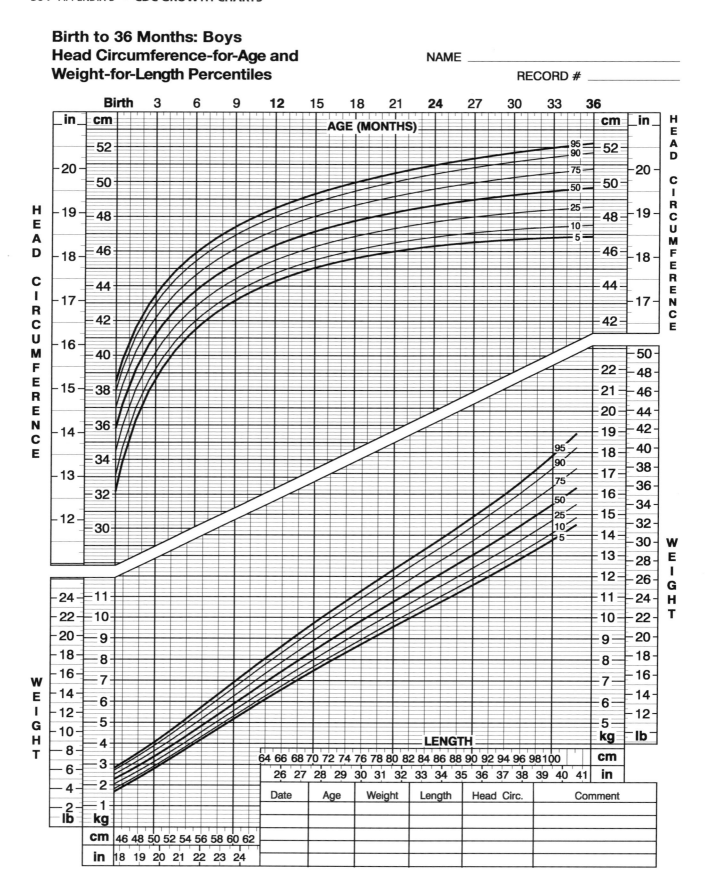

Birth to 36 Months: Girls
Head Circumference-for-Age and
Weight-for-Length Percentiles

NAME _____

RECORD # _____

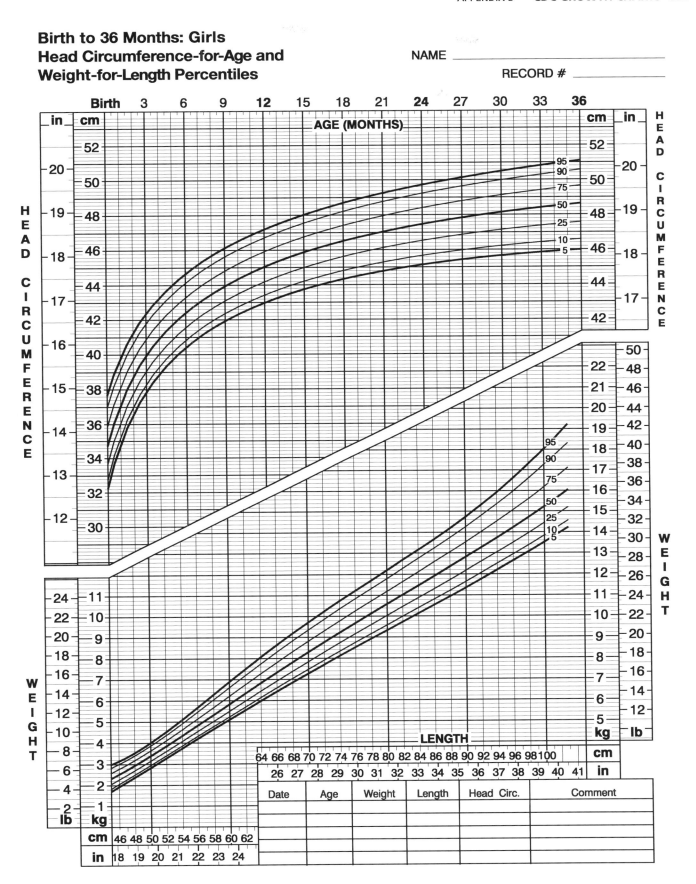

Date	Age	Weight	Length	Head Circ.	Comment

2 to 20 Years: Boys
Stature-for-Age and Weight-for-Age Percentiles

NAME _____

RECORD # _____

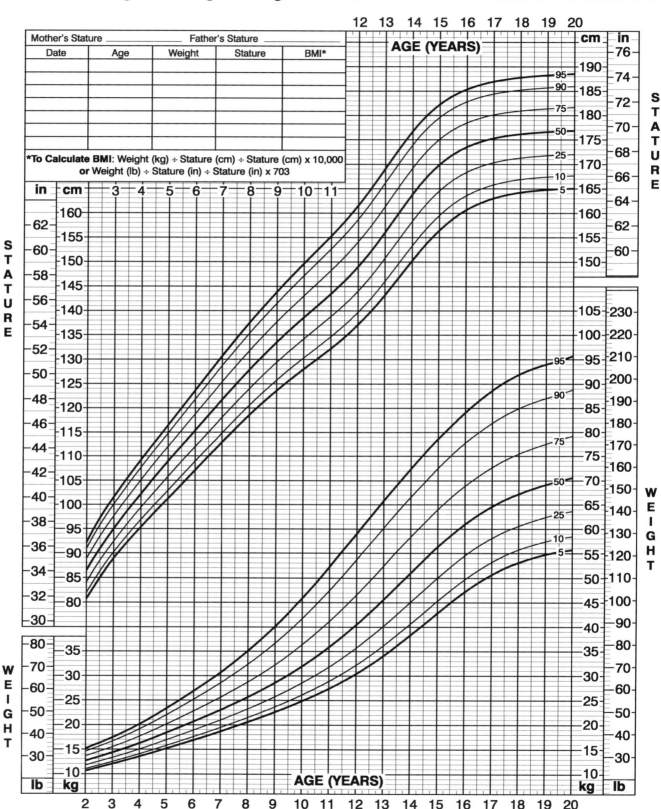

Mother's Stature _____ Father's Stature _____

Date	Age	Weight	Stature	BMI*

*To Calculate BMI: Weight (kg) ÷ Stature (cm) ÷ Stature (cm) x 10,000
or Weight (lb) ÷ Stature (in) ÷ Stature (in) x 703

2 to 20 Years: Girls
Stature-for-Age and Weight-for-Age Percentiles

NAME _____

RECORD # _____

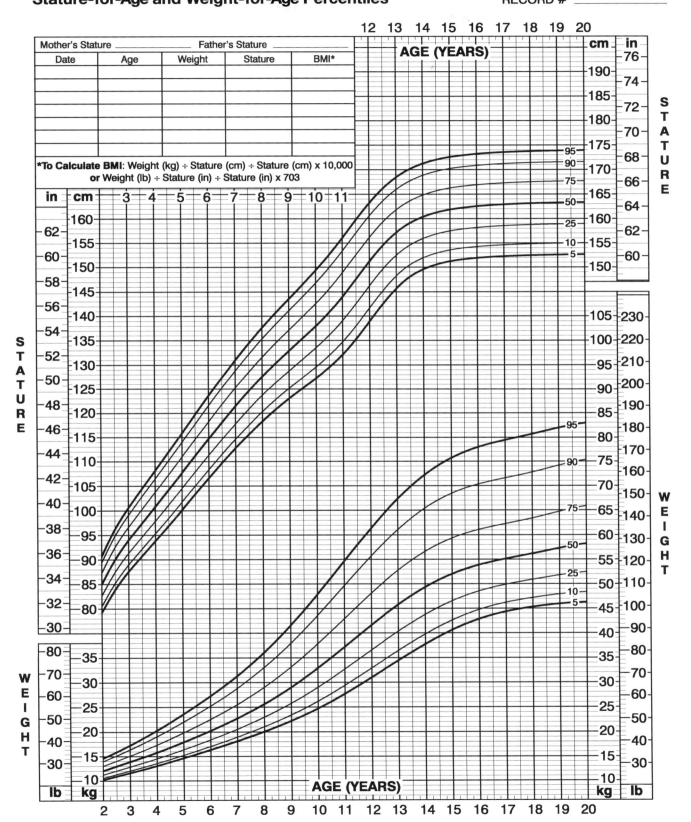

*To Calculate BMI: Weight (kg) ÷ Stature (cm) ÷ Stature (cm) x 10,000
or Weight (lb) ÷ Stature (in) ÷ Stature (in) x 703

2 to 20 Years: Boys
Body Mass Index-for-Age Percentiles

NAME _____

RECORD # _____

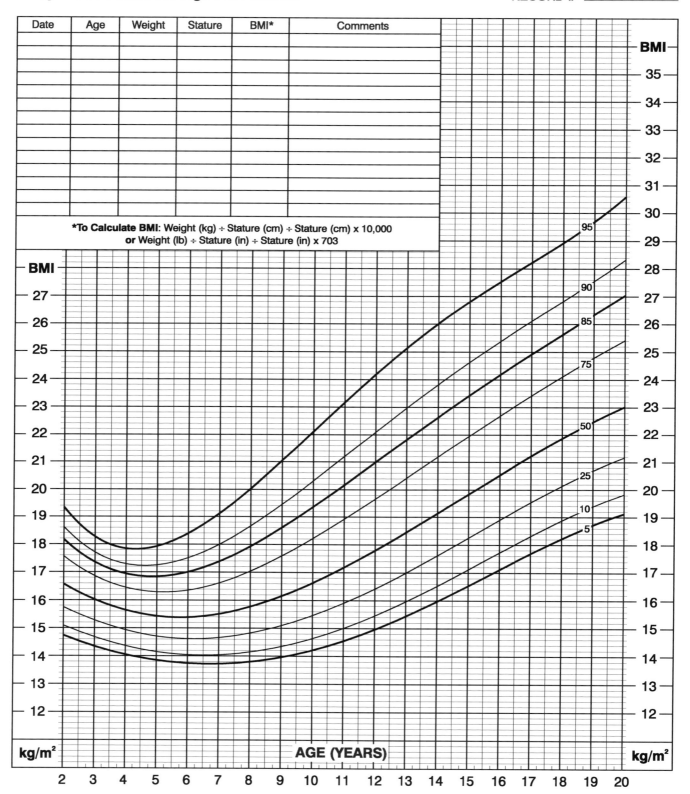

Date	Age	Weight	Stature	BMI*	Comments

*To Calculate BMI:** Weight (kg) ÷ Stature (cm) ÷ Stature (cm) x 10,000
or Weight (lb) ÷ Stature (in) ÷ Stature (in) x 703

BMI

- 27
- 26
- 25
- 24
- 23
- 22
- 21
- 20
- 19
- 18
- 17
- 16
- 15
- 14
- 13
- 12

kg/m²

AGE (YEARS)

2 3 4 5 6 7 8 9 10 11 12 13 14 15 16 17 18 19 20

BMI

- 35
- 34
- 33
- 32
- 31
- 30
- 29
- 28
- 27
- 26
- 25
- 24
- 23
- 22
- 21
- 20
- 19
- 18
- 17
- 16
- 15
- 14
- 13
- 12

kg/m²

95
90
85
75
50
25
10
5

2 to 20 Years: Girls
Body Mass Index-for-Age Percentiles

NAME _____

RECORD # _____

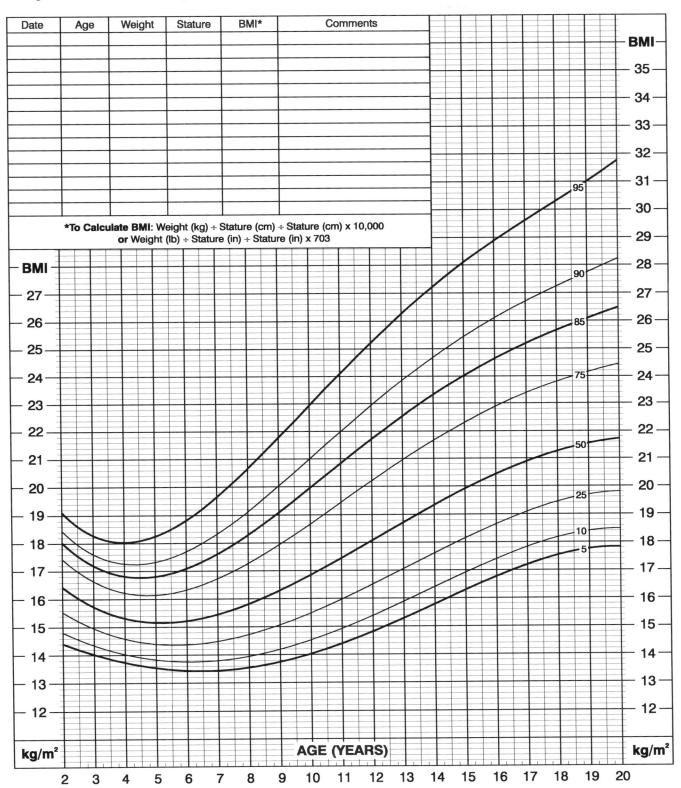

*To Calculate BMI: Weight (kg) ÷ Stature (cm) ÷ Stature (cm) x 10,000
or Weight (lb) ÷ Stature (in) ÷ Stature (in) x 703

Weight-for-Stature Percentiles: Boys

NAME _____

RECORD # _____

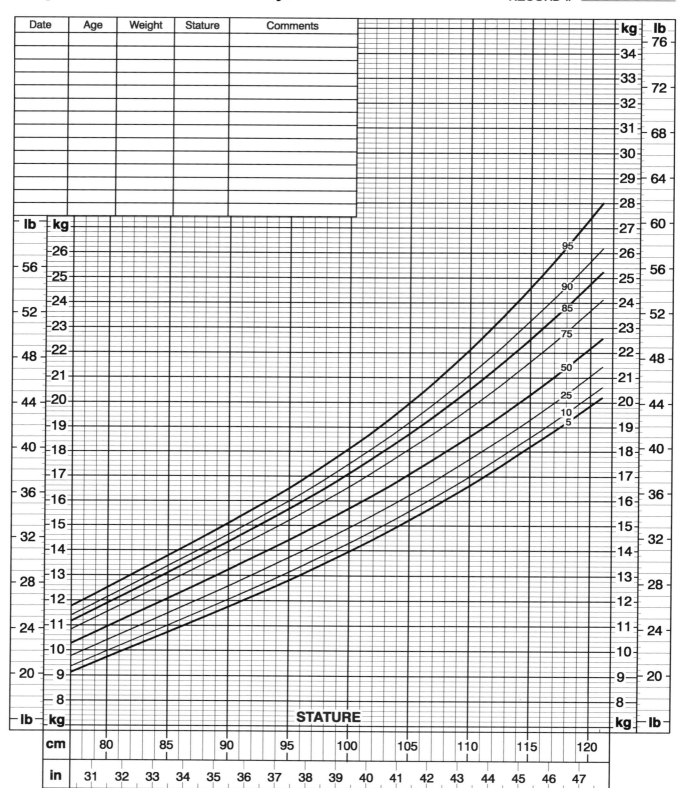

Date	Age	Weight	Stature	Comments

Weight-for-Stature Percentiles: Girls

NAME

RECORD #

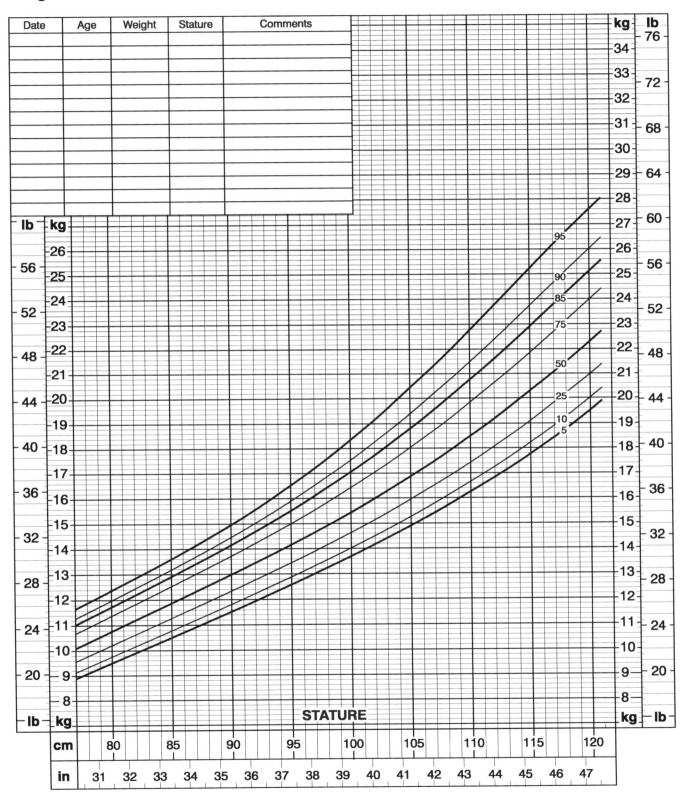

Index

Note: Page numbers followed by *b, f,* or *t* indicates material in boxes, figures, or tables respectively.